The Miracle of Mata Ortiz

Juan Quezada
and
the Potters
of Northern Chihuahua

by

Walter P. Parks

THE COULTER PRESS

ACKNOWLEDGEMENTS

Several people helped with this book and deserve special thanks. Spencer MacCallum was especially generous, opening all of his files to me and reviewing the text. Elizabeth Parks and Katy Parks Wilson also spent many hours editing. Dr. Ben Brown corrected the historical sections and Tom Fresh the technical section. José (Pino) Molina supplied much information about the village.

Meeting Juan Quezada, his family, and the other potters was a unique experience, and I have tried to tell the story as accurately as possible. My apologies to any I have neglected. The only intent was to honor the potters for their artistry and courage.

Finally, many thanks to Tom, John Wingate and all the other *viajeros* for all the trips and all the miles.

W.P.P.

The Coulter Press
6154 Hawarden Dr., Riverside, CA 92506

Cover: *Pottery by Juan Quezada.* Photograph © 1993, Michael J. Elderman

THE MIRACLE OF MATA ORTIZ

Juan Quezada
and
the Potters of Northern Chihuahua

by
Walter P. Parks

Table of Contents

PREFACE

Fifteen years ago a beautiful ceramic ware appeared in shops in El Paso, Tucson and Los Angeles. Each handmade piece was light, perfectly symmetrical and covered with intricate painted designs in red and black. In the years since, these skillfully executed bowls, jars and effigy figures have become famous as "Modern Casas Grandes" or "Mata Ortiz" ware. They now appear in the permanent collections and gift shops of the great museums of the West, including the Heard in Phoenix, the Southwest Museum in Los Angeles and the Museum of Man in San Diego.

All of this pottery comes from one tiny village on the remote high plains of northern Chihuahua, Mexico. The story of the originator of this unique ware, Juan Quezada, his discovery by an anthropologist, and the economic effect on the village is the "Miracle of Mata Ortiz."

Palanganas River and El Indio peak.

Mata Ortiz, Chihuahua.

INTRODUCTION

On the high plains of northern Chihuahua, Mexico, a crumbling village lies at the base of a notched peak called El Indio. The village, much longer than it is wide, stretches between the Palanganas, a branch of the Casas Grandes River, and the Chihuahua Al Pacifico Railroad. The plaster peels from low rectangular buildings across from the old railroad station. Adobe bricks show through, disfiguring the painted advertising of former stores and cabarets. No trace is left of the huge lumber mill which once made the village a boom town. The railroad repair yard which serviced the rolling stock for a vast network of northern Chihuahuan trains is also gone. Cattle graze beyond the single line of tracks, sometimes wandering across into the dusty streets of the village. A first glance suggests a place with a past but no future.

However, a second look reveals signs of something else. A few of the houses have new plaster covering the old adobe. Walls have been repaired and additions made. A new house stands along the back street next to the river. The interior of this house has plasterboard walls, acoustical ceiling, and a kitchen that looks like it was ordered from a Sears catalog. The young man who lives here with his wife and their baby makes a living creating thin-walled bowls and jars, decorating them with delicately painted red and black designs.

Mauro Quezada, barely twenty years old, is a second generation potter who has never had any other occupation. He and his work are examples of a ceramic art movement which burst forth in recent years in the half-forgotten village of Mata Ortiz on the remote plains of what the Mexicans call *El Norte*.

Mauro was a tiny baby when his uncle, Juan Quezada, began to make his pottery. Since his own childhood, Juan had been experimenting with clay and colors. His only teachers were the prehistoric pottery shards he found on the ground while gathering firewood. He stuffed these beautifully-painted little pieces in his pockets and wondered about the ancient people who made them. If these long-vanished artists could make such beautiful objects, there must be clay somewhere nearby in the mountains, plains, or arroyos. Eventually, he found it in all those places. He brought the clay home, mixed it with water, and tried to make little pots. But he failed. He tried again and failed. The bottoms were not right; the clay cracked; the paint would not stick; and there was no one who could help him. The shards were his only guide. So he studied them some more and continued trying. Finally, a step at a time, he learned until he mastered the process.

By the time his nephew Mauro was born, Juan had taught himself to make bowls and jars, decorated with detailed designs like his shards. Without any instruction, without ever seeing a pot being made, he recreated the entire technology and art of ceramics from processing and forming the clay through decorating and firing.

When Juan began to sell a few of his pieces, Consolación, his oldest sister and Mauro's mother, recognized right away the importance of this to the family. It could be a means to break out of the poverty and dead-end occupations available in the village and surrounding countryside. Most of the men worked seasonally in the orchards of Colonia Juárez, a Mormon town a few miles to the north. Others worked at back-breaking jobs on the railroad, jobs with no future except premature age and infirmity. Many, including Juan, had gone to the border at one time or another to wade across the river and look for work. At best, some in the village had a few cattle grazing on the plains.

Consolación and other Quezada family members asked Juan to teach them his hard-won skills, and he did. They worked diligently to master each step, and eventually several became experts (although none ever matched Juan). Consolación also made sure her five children learned, and by the time Mauro was ten he was making his own pots.

The family members taught others, beginning a ceramic art movement that has swept through the entire village. In the short span of Mauro's life as many as 300 potters have learned to make a distinctive ware that rivals any hand-built ceramic art in the world.

The origins of this art, its discovery, its effect on the village, and the emergence of Juan Quezada as a major ceramic artist are the pieces of the story that make up the Miracle of Mata Ortiz.

I met Juan in 1984, while he was teaching his ceramic techniques to a summer art class in the San Jacinto Mountains above Palm Springs, California. The Director of the art program needed help in transporting Juan and his family back to Mata Ortiz, and I volunteered. This became the first of many long trips to this little village on the high plains of northern Chihuahua. There I found wide open spaces, listened to old stories of Pancho Villa, and met the potters. Their pottery fascinated me. Eventually, I worked almost five years with Juan and other potters selling their ware in the United States.

Walter P. Parks

Olla, *Juan Quezada.*

Olla, *Juan Quezada.*

CHAPTER 1
DISCOVERY

Spencer's Odyssey

Seventeen years ago, a man wandered into a junk shop in southern New Mexico and made a discovery that changed his life and the lives of the inhabitants of a small decaying village in northern Mexico. In addition, his discovery was to make a major impact on the world of ceramics.

The man was Spencer Heath MacCallum, an anthropologist by training and an inveterate junk store habitue. In 1976, he was in Deming, New Mexico, helping an 88-year-old friend reopen a gold mine that had been flooded for sixty years — ultimately an unsuccessful venture.

With time on his hands, he wandered into Bob's Swap Shop at the east end of town to look around. There, among the battered pans and chipped china, three handmade ceramic pots caught his eye. Each was perfectly symmetrical with red and black painted geometric designs covering the extremely thin clay walls. They sat among the used debris of the store like three orbs from another planet. Spencer was fascinated. He thought they must be prehistoric, although at the time he did not know of the great ceramic tradition of the Casas Grandes culture farther south in what is now Chihuahua, Mexico. However, the lady who owned the store assured him the pots were not old. Some poor people had traded them to the store for used clothing. Spencer studied the three pieces for several minutes, turning them in his hands, and it dawned on him that it did not matter whether they were old or new; they had integrity as works of art. Spencer purchased the pots and took them back to his home in San Pedro, California.

As he pursued his other interests over the next month, Spencer could not get the three pots or their unknown maker out of his mind. Somewhere there was an extraordinary artist who was completely unknown if his or her work was being marketed in junk stores.

On his next trip to visit the mine, one month later, Spencer visited Bob's Swap Shop again and asked the owner if she had any idea where the pots came from. She did not, but suggested that "Mexico would be a good place to start." Spencer made up his mind to look. His mother was visiting an old friend in Deming and he invited the two older ladies to go along for the adventure. Early on a Saturday morning, they crossed the border at Columbus into the tiny town of Palomas, Chihuahua. Spencer carried photographs of the pots. He showed them "to any likely or unlikely person," asking where

Opposite: Olla, *white clay, Juan Quezada.*

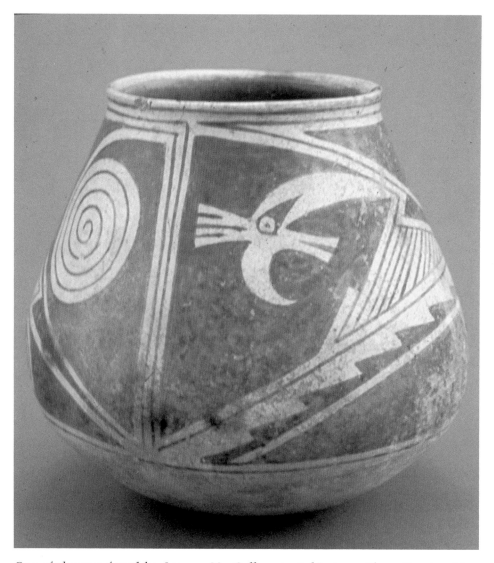

One of the pots found by Spencer MacCallum in Bob's Swap Shop, Deming, New Mexico in 1976.
Photo: N. Prasad

he might find the "woman" potter. Traditionally, the great potters of the American Indian Southwest have been women: Nampeyo, who revived the Hopi pottery tradition; María Martínez of San Ildefonso Pueblo; and Lucy Lewis of Acoma Pueblo being three of the most famous.

As they traveled south on the only paved road, Spencer talked with everyone he came in contact with at each settlement, including the little boy who shined his shoes and the policeman who gave him a speeding ticket. Northern Chihuahua is wide open country with few villages or towns, and by the end of the first day, the three travelers found themselves 150 miles south in Nuevo Casas Grandes, the only town of any size between Chihuahua City and the border. In this prosperous agricultural town, Spencer was directed to a man named Manuel Olivas, reported to know something about pottery. However, they were very tired and turned in at the local hotel.

The next morning, they talked with Olivas and found out that he made pots for a living, having learned his trade from his grandfather. In his workshop, he and his family made (and still make) crude ware on hand-turned wheels fashioned from automobile water pumps. Manuel, a friendly man, was anxious to help Spencer. He stated immediately that he had not made the pots in the photos, but if Spencer would like, he could make some just like them. Well, thanks no, Spencer had said, pointing to the pictures again, he really wanted to find the maker of those.

Manuel then told him of a village called Mata Ortiz about twenty miles away, down very bad dirt roads, where the villagers might know something about the potter. Others in Nuevo Casas Grandes the previous day had tentatively mentioned Mata Ortiz. Spencer said goodbye to Manuel, who offered again to duplicate the pots, and continued southwest toward Colonia Juárez, a farming village established by Mormons from Utah in the late 19th century. The pavement ended in this strange little town with its mixture of Utah-style brick houses and Mexican adobes scattered among the apple orchards.

The road south to Mata Ortiz was rutted as it left Colonia Juárez, and the car jolted against rocks sticking through the thin soil. Soon it began to meander across a high plain, where it became nothing more than ambiguous tracks through the mesquite. To the west rose the main ridges of the Sierra Madre Occidental. To the east sat a lower range with one dominant crag, "El Indio," so named because of its resemblance to an Indian head tilted toward the sky.

Beneath El Indio, between a little river, the Palanganas, and the Chihuahua Al Pacifico railroad line, Spencer found Mata Ortiz. He asked a few questions, and a boy on a burro led him along a dusty street to a small adobe house that backed up to the river. A woman answered the door and invited Spencer and the two ladies inside. As Spencer was explaining himself and bringing out the pictures, Juan Quezada came in the back door from the river side of the house.

Juan was a compactly-built man of medium height in his mid-thirties with long wavy black hair, sideburns, and a ready smile. His right forearm and hand displayed a series of tattoos. He had no idea who this *norteamericano* was in his tiny living room, but he cordially invited Spencer and the ladies to sit down. Spencer showed him the photographs, and after studying them a moment, Juan acknowledged that he had made the pots about six months before. Spencer must have looked dubious, because he still thought he was looking for a woman potter. So Juan went to a shelf and took down two pots. Spencer recognized immediately the perfect symmetrical shapes and intricate designs. All doubts were eliminated. He had found his man.

This ended the first phase of Spencer's odyssey. The full impact of Juan's brilliance would not register until later, but as he held those pots in his hands in that tiny adobe room, Spencer knew he was on the edge of a special experience.

The Second Trip

Initially, Spencer completely surprised Juan. He never dreamed that any-one would be interested enough in his pots to photograph them let alone trav-el hundreds of miles looking for him. Therefore, he became a bit defensive. What did this American want? He told Spencer he could do better work but no one was willing to pay him for the time it would take. Spencer said he was only interested in Juan's best work. He would return in two months. In the meantime, he asked Juan to make examples of his best work.

In March, 1976 Spencer returned to Mata Ortiz accompanied by photogra-pher Bobby Furst. Juan had made ten pots, all similar to those Spencer had already seen. Although they were nice pieces, Spencer was a bit disappointed. He had expected something different. Maybe Juan had not believed he would really come back.

But he had come back, and he had a professional photographer with him. Juan readily agreed to be photographed the next day while making a pot. Bobby prepared for an early shoot, but the day dawned foul and windy. Strong gusts picked up the sun-dried dusty soil and blew into the equipment; snow began to fall. So Bobby set up his lights and cameras inside the house. The entire family, a few neighbors, and many curious children crowded into the little three-room house to watch. Juan assembled his clay and tools on the kitchen table and went to work.

First, he placed a small tortilla of well-kneaded clay into a small concave mold made of plaster-of-Paris. After pushing the clay into place, he added a large doughnut-shaped coil of clay to the top of the mold. He carefully worked the bottom of this coil into the top edge of the clay tortilla, then began to shape the pot by pinching around and around the fat coil of clay with his sensitive fingers. Spencer watched astonished as the pot grew in front of him. He knew the pots were not thrown on a wheel in the European/Japanese style, but he had assumed that they would be made up of a series of thin coils in the manner of American Indian pots. Juan's technique, what came to be called the "single coil" method, was completely new to Spencer.

As Bobby clicked away over the next two hours, the pot took shape. Working with complete concentration, Juan evened the surface with a broken hacksaw blade, the only tool he used in the entire process. He added a lip by placing a tiny coil on top of the opening of the formed pot and shaping it. Finally he smoothed the entire surface with the straight side of the blade. At midday, Guille, Juan's wife, interrupted to serve everyone a hot *caldito de papas*, delicious thin potato soup, for lunch.

Juan began the afternoon's work by brushing a cream-colored liquid clay or slip over the outside of the pot. After this dried for a few minutes, he began to paint. People moved in and out of the tiny room while children played on the floor. Bobby moved the camera equipment here and there. Juan responded to questions, but nothing distracted his eyes from the pot. He dipped his brush, made of a few human hairs about two inches long tied to a sucker-sized stick, into a tiny jar of jet-black paint, touched the tip to the pot, and pulled the length of the fine hairs across the surface, to leave behind a thin

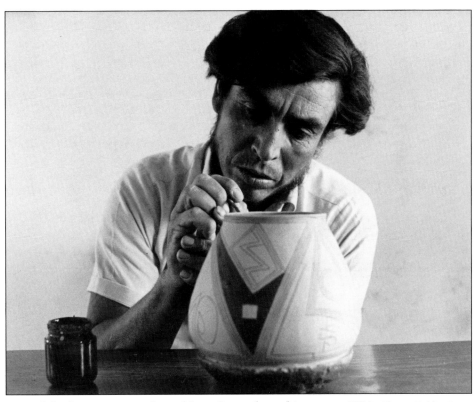

One of the first pictures taken of Juan Quezada making a pot, 1976. Photo: Bobby Furst

uniform line. A series of these lines formed a maze of curves, triangles, diamonds, and squares. When he was satisfied with the lines, he cleaned the little brush in water, set it aside, and picked up a fatter, shorter brush. He spent the next two hours filling in certain sections of the maze with red and black paint. Then he carefully outlined the red areas again with the first brush. Finally, he looked up at Spencer and Bobby and nodded that he was finished. The pot, a kaleidoscope of black, red, and cream, was clearly his "best work."

Though the pot still had to dry and be fired, Bobby had his pictures, the first of Juan at work and the first of many more by hundreds of photographers. Juan would give many demonstrations in Mata Ortiz and in the United States, and it would always be the same — a fascinated group with cameras crowding around, asking the same questions and receiving courteous answers without distracting the artist from his task. With this as the beginning, Spencer and Juan would work together for the next eight years gradually bringing this special pottery, unique to Mata Ortiz, to the attention of the art world.

Spencer Heath MacCallum

Spencer's chance encounter with Juan's pots in the Deming junk store would cause him to live out a destiny his mother had planned for him thirty-six years before.

Lucile Heath MacCallum reacted differently than most to the disruption and patriotic fervor generated by World War II. Her husband, an architect, went into the service and spent the war in England, leaving her with two teen-age boys, Crawford and Spencer. She was not content with the typical role of the wife left behind on the home front packing Bundles for Britain. She poured her energies into preparing her sons for after the war, reasoning that there would be a new order of things with Europe less important, and relationships with Latin America more critical. Therefore, she wanted Crawford and Spencer to understand Latin cultures.

So, as her contribution to the war effort, Lucile packed her boys and a nephew off to Mexico (this freed her sister to join the WACS.) For two and one half years, right in the middle of the war, they moved from place to place, studying and visiting the sights. Young Spencer became fascinated with archaeology, and many of their stops were in towns famed for their ruins. The boys enrolled in the local schools where, according to Spencer, his brother studied and he read comic books. Nevertheless, all three boys learned Spanish and learned to love Mexico.

After the war, the family moved to Virginia. Spencer completed high school at Phillips Academy in Massachusetts and was accepted at Princeton University, graduating in 1955 with a BA in art history. In typical MacCallum fashion, he explored new ground even as an undergraduate. His senior thesis was on Northwest Coast Indian art, the first thesis ever permitted by the Princeton Art Department on a New World subject. It brought to light a major collection of pre-twentieth century Indian art of the Alaskan Haida and Tlingit that had been moldering in Princeton's Geology Department for over 50 years unknown even to scholars working in the field.

It was during this period of study and research that he began his own collection of Northwest Coast Indian art. The sale of this collection, together with the cultural legacy of his sojourn in Mexico during the War, would later enable Spencer to devote virtually full time to Juan Quezada and the potters of Mata Ortiz.

After Princeton, he received a master's degree in social anthropology in 1961 from the University of Washington. This special interest in anthropology stemmed in part from his experiences as a boy in Mexico, and in part from the influence of his grandfather and namesake, Spencer Heath, a noted social philosopher and writer. Spencer, the grandson, devoted much of his life to discovering and promoting a new understanding relating to human freedom, based on his grandfather's ideas of social organization. In 1967 he created the Heather Foundation as a vehicle for promoting and publishing these and related ideas. His work with the Mata Ortiz potters was done in the name of this foundation. A fine writer, he has written extensively on a variety of subjects including Northwest Coast Indian art, urban land use, Libertarian philosophy, and the economics of outer space. This was no ordinary man who

6

stumbled upon an emerging ceramic art form in Bob's Swap Shop that fateful day in 1976.

The Quezada Family

Though Spencer realized he had discovered a completely unknown ceramic artist of incredible ability, he knew nothing about him or how he had learned his art. Spencer had been accepted into Juan's home as a guest, and he had purchased Juan's pots. And he burned with questions, but he knew not to push too hard. Also his Spanish was extremely shaky after 30 years of disuse. As time passed, he became close to members of the Quezada family, particularly Juan's parents, Don José and Doña Paulita. As he gained their confidence, bits and pieces of family history emerged.

José Quezada, Juan's father, was born in Santa Bárbara Tutuaca, a town several hours south of Mata Ortiz. He had been raised by his uncle and aunt, Don Savino Hernández and Doña Lupe. José worked his uncle's cattle and raised horses, performing the work of a Chihuahua cowboy. When he was 28, he met Paulita, who had come from nearby San Lorenzo to work in a kitchen in Tutuaca. When she returned to San Lorenzo, José rode over to court her and they soon married.

José and Paulita had ten children. The first six, Consolación, Reynalda, Genoveva, Jesús, Hilario, and Juan were born in Santa Bárbara Tutuaca. Four more, Nicolás, Rosa, Lydia, and Reynaldo were born in Mata Ortiz. Juan was born on May 6, 1940, one year before the entire family, including Don Savino and Doña Lupe, moved north to Mata Ortiz.

Long before the move, their new home had particular significance to the Quezada family because of an old story told and retold by Don Savino about his trek there during the Revolution. Desperate to save the family's possessions from marauding soldiers, he loaded everything on six burros and escaped north. He could get through some of the rugged mountains only by driving his burros through long railroad tunnels with no idea when a train might enter from the other end. He survived a series of these tunnels, plodding along with his six loaded burros in the dark, fearing for a sudden bright light ahead.

When he reached the high plains of Mata Ortiz, he found extraordinarily tall grass. Moving his burros into this grass, he hid from renegade soldiers passing by. Eventually he returned to Lupe in Tutuaca with their possessions and animals intact. But he never forgot that tall grass.

One day years later, Don Savino decided to go back. When he was ready to make the move, there was no question but that José would leave his birthplace with Paulita and the children and move to the new community with his now elderly aunt and uncle.

In 1941, northern Chihuahua was a remote and rugged place still suffering from the ravages of the Revolution. Much had been destroyed and the ground soaked in blood during the convoluted struggles between the forces of Pancho Villa and his various adversaries. Communication remained primitive and travel by horse and wagon common. The railroad line, running southwest from Ciudad Juárez on the Texas border through Mata Ortiz, provided the only communication and, for many in the village, the only employment. However, Savino and José chose to ignore the railroad and stayed with the land, raising cotton and later cattle.

In Mata Ortiz, even with five new children José and Paulita faithfully cared for aging Don Savino and Doña Lupe until these two passed away. Time passed. José and Paulita witnessed many changes as the trappings of the twentieth century — trucks, electricity, television — found their way to them. But nothing seemed so remarkable as the development of their home into a major ceramic center, led by their third son Juan, and involving all of their sons, daughters, grandchildren, and neighbors.

Juan

Juan grew up as a shy boy content to spend long hours alone. He revered his father, José, and still shows great respect for the lean, white-bearded old man. From him Juan learned the skills of a Chihuahua cowboy. Entering school late at age nine, he only attended for three years. Juan says he spent most of that time looking out the window. His family says he spent his school time drawing pictures. He did love to draw — designs, doodles, and imaginary animals — with a pencil or with paints he made himself. Sometimes he closed himself in his room for hours, asking his parents to tell his friends that he was not home. Inside alone, he drew and painted on the walls. When every surface was covered floor to ceiling, he cleaned the walls with newspaper soaked in kerosene and started over.

He constantly experimented with natural substances to make his paint colors — rocks, plants, insects, anything he could find. He ground them on the old grinding stones he found in the ruins and mixed them in various ways. He logged each experiment into his memory. Walking over the countryside, he found the minerals which later became the basis for his pottery decoration, iron oxide deposits which make beautiful reds and manganese which makes a solid black.

Times were hard, and to help his family Juan began leaving school to hike into the mountains with the family burro, gathering firewood to sell for fuel. Back in the village, he always turned the wood over to his brothers to sell door-to-door, being too shy himself for this part of the transaction.

He also gathered wild honey (learning to extract it from the bee tree without being stung,) edible cactus, acorns, and maguey shoots, baking the shoots Indian fashion in a shallow, stone-lined pit before packing them back to the village. When he encountered rattlesnakes, he killed them with a long, sharp stick and added the meat to his inventory. Dried rattlesnake meat was considered beneficial for certain ailments. On a few occasions, Juan has killed and skinned rattlesnakes in front of his pottery students from the United States. None were interested in the health benefits of the meat.

At twelve, Juan left school to gather mountain products full time. Later he worked picking fruit for the Mormon farmers around Colonia Juárez or in the fields to the north across the border. In those days the "Bracero" program allowed Mexican workers to cross legally for short periods. Juan and his companions went to Chihuahua City where they were loaded into cattle cars for the trip to Ciudad Juárez across the border from El Paso, Texas. Farm representatives met the train, selected workers by a raffle system and sent the fortunate ones on buses all over the U.S. When Juan was not picked, he waded across the Rio Grande and found work on his own. Once, he and his brother, Nicolás, walked 170 miles to Douglas, Arizona to look for work. Years later they both would be driven over the same route to be the honored guests at gala gallery exhibitions.

Recreation in the village centered around *vaquero* or cowboy skills such as roping and bull riding. Fiesta days usually featured a *jaripeo*, a version of the rodeo where the young men of the village showed off their skills in front of family, neighbors, and an enthusiastic local band. Few other sports existed except boxing. Baseball had not yet come to the village, as it would later for Juan's sons.

The boxing coach was Señor José Molina, a long-time friend of the Quezada family. Known to everyone as "Pino," he had worked for the railroad since he was 15, first as a telegraph operator and later in sales and customer service. He eventually retired after 40 years. Always involved in sports, he was still entering distance races in his sixties.

Pino taught Juan the rudiments of boxing and entered him in three local fights when Juan was fourteen. Juan won all three, earning the equivalent of about $17. A promoter saw him and wanted to take him to Mexico City and the big time. However, his mother, Doña Paulita, found out about it, and his boxing career was over. Juan retired undefeated.

He did not have much time for such things anyway because he needed to support himself and help his family. Trekking back and forth across the plains into the mountains to gather wild products, he found more and more evidence of the prehistoric people who had lived and worked there. In nearly every mountain gully and wash he found *trincheras,* which were apparently used to divert water for farming and to prevent erosion. He explored mounds where the remains of walls of houses could be traced, and where summer rain washed away the soil exposing stone axes, grinders, mortars, turquoise, bones, and pottery shards.

Juan carefully picked through the broken pottery pieces, looking for elaborate red and black designs on a yellow or pure white clay. At home he spread his collection on the kitchen table and studied them. He thought about the shards as he hiked across the plains with his burro. He reasoned that if the ancient people could make pots, then the clay and other materials had to be nearby. He began to look for clay; he wanted to find the purest. When he thought he had it, he soaked the chunks in water and strained it through cloths. When it was dry enough to form, he attempted to make simple bowl shapes, but he could not get the bottoms right. After much frustration, he took a small dish from his mother's cupboard and pushed the clay in and smoothed it. This formed a round bottom from which he was able to build an acceptable pot. This little dish mold was a rediscovery of the Indian "puka" mold, used continuously since prehistoric times.

Still most of his pots cracked as they dried. He tried purer and purer clays

Juan and the clay, 1976.　　　　　Photo: Bobby Furst

and they still cracked. Then, looking at the broken edges of his shards collection, he realized that the old clay contained rough material. He went the other way and began experimenting with mixtures — sand, volcanic ash — in the clays. This "temper" helped the formed clay dry evenly without cracking, another breakthrough.

Now he could work on forming pots, smoothing them, and preparing them for painting. He did not attempt to copy his shard models exactly, but he did make sure each step of the process could be done with materials and tools available to the ancient people. Minerals that he played with as a child made the best paints, and he learned to mix and apply them with long thin brushes made from children's hair. For the paint not to smear when polishing the pot before firing, it needed to be set flush into the surface of the wet clay by gently burnishing the painted designs with a smooth object. Juan tried the back of a spoon, but it was too soft. After a number of tries, he found a very smooth little stone which worked well to set the paint and to burnish the entire surface to a high sheen. The final step was firing. It was common knowledge in the village that clay hardened when it was heated in a fire, but the breakthrough for Juan was finding a fuel that provided an even hot temperature. After much experimenting with various woods and charcoal, Juan learned to fire with dried cow chips.

Through years of work, trial and error, experimentation and observation, Juan rediscovered the entire sequence of ceramic technology. This is the miracle. Juan had no instruction nor had he ever seen a pot being made. His only teachers were the shards. Many of his techniques had been used for centuries in the American Indian Southwest and other cultures, like firing with dried cow chips. Other traditional techniques he never used even though the materials were at hand. Sometimes his substitution was better. The human hair brush was his own device. He never used the yucca brush that Acoma Indians and other pueblo potters made from this common desert plant for their fine-line painting.

By this time, Juan was married with children. In 1964, Guillermina Olivas Reyes, 19, had come to Mata Ortiz to visit friends and to look for work. She was from Namiquipa, a farming community to the southeast, famous in the chronicles of Pancho Villa. Juan, who was 24, had just returned from working across the border, and he looked very elegant in his brand-new clothes. Guille thought he must be very rich. She stayed in Mata Ortiz, they became acquainted and soon married. Their first three children, daughters María Elena ("Nena") and Mireya, and son Noe were all to become accomplished potters, particularly Noe. Eventually they had eight children.

Juan worked hard at whatever jobs he could find to support this growing family. For a year he and Guille moved to Namiquipa, where he tried sharecropping beans. They loved living alone in their tiny adobe away from everyone, but the results were not enough to live on. So they returned to Mata Ortiz and Juan went to work for the railroad, the traditional occupation of the men of Mata Ortiz. They made their home in a converted box car, moving from work site to work site over the entire rail system of northern Chihuahua. The work was hard; the men worked in gangs with picks and sledge hammers to replace rails and rotted ties. However, the young couple enjoyed moving from place to place. Juan extended his knowledge of the country, and on his off hours, found more shards.

He sometimes found ways to escape the brutal labor. His boss loved a dish prepared from prickly pear cactus or *nopal.* From his years in the mountains, Juan knew exactly where to get the best *nopal* and how to prepare it. Often when his co-workers were laboring on the tracks, Juan was off in the hills gathering cactus for the boss.

Soon after Juan and Guille returned from Namiquipa, Juan fired the first pots that satisfied him. After years of trying, he could consistently reproduce sound, well-formed pieces. He gave away his first successful pieces to friends. Some of these ended up in the hands of small-time traders in Nuevo Casas Grandes and Palomas. The traders found out about Juan and came to Mata Ortiz to buy. Many of these early buyers used various tricks to make the pots look old. These were sold across the border as genuine prehistoric Casas Grandes ware. A friend told Juan of a famous American Indian potter who signed her pots on the bottom. Juan thought this was a good idea and began to paint his name on the bottoms of his pots. Sales immediately slumped.

Photo: Bobby Furst

Shortly, however, sales picked up again. Juan was bewildered, but soon found out that the clever traders were grinding off the painted name in sand. Artifact sales were better than ever. At Spencer's suggestion, Juan now etches his name in the clay and this practice has become standard in the village.

Pottery sales evolved into an important supplement to Juan's family income. Others members of the family became interested, and Juan showed them what to do. His brother Nicolás learned first. Nicolás began working with clay seriously in 1972. Juan's older sisters, Consolación and Reynalda, understood clearly the economic implications of their younger brother's skills and began in 1973-74. Soon they were teaching their children as well.

By the time Spencer arrived in 1976, about twelve villagers were making pottery. Juan's youngest brother, Reynaldo, and youngest sister, Lydia, were Spencer's favorites. Lydia's friend Taurina Baca, Juan's first non-family pupil also stood out. Others of the early group included: Oscar Gonzáles Quezada, Consolación's oldest son; Chela López Hernandez; Yolanda López Quezada, Reynalda's daughter; Jesús Quezada, another brother of Juan; Rosalia Rojo Quidera; Lupita Cota Delgado; Neli Cota Duran; and Felix Ortiz. All were related to Juan or had close ties to the family except Felix Ortiz.

Felix lived at the far end of the long narrow village in a section called "Barrio Porvenir." He, like every potter in Mata Ortiz, was influenced by Juan, but very early he developed his own technique and style which had a great influence in his own neighborhood. Usually, his pieces were large coiled vessels with big geometric or animal designs painted over a slip (liquid clay)

Juan's pottery in the late 1970's.   Photo: Warren Bowen

applied to the surface. His success inspired others in Porvenir to take up pottery. For a long time it was easy to identify shapes and designs of the ware from this barrio, and to distinguish it from the work more directly influenced by Juan. Many of these earlier distinctions are becoming blurred as the potters become more sophisticated and develop their own styles. However there is still much work produced in Barrio Porvenir that reflects the old Felix Ortiz style.

By 1975, Juan was selling enough of his pots to take a year's leave of absence from the railroad. He never returned. He became the first in Mata Ortiz to quit his job and support his family by making pottery. Dozens, hundreds, would follow him as the artistic and economic miracle unfolded. The catalyst was the arrival of Spencer MacCallum.

CHAPTER 2
SPENCER AND JUAN, 1976–1983

The Commitment

At first Spencer had no clear idea of what to do with his discovery. He wanted to encourage and help Juan to develop his full potential, but it was hard to know how to do this. How were the needs of the pure artist to be balanced against the need of that artist to feed a large family? And there was the cultural gap. Experienced and compassionate as he was, Spencer was never able to completely bridge that gap.

On the first two trips he bought everything Juan had made, even the less successful and cracked pieces because he was so intrigued by the designs.

On his third trip, he asked Juan which of the several new pots on the table he had most liked making. When Juan looked thoughtful, then replied that he had been too busy working on them to look at them, Spencer knew his arrangement was wrong. Buying everything without question did not encourage high quality. He proposed giving Juan a regular stipend with no strings attached. Juan could work with complete freedom, experimenting and trying new ideas. He could reach for whatever he wanted artistically and even fail without the pressure to put tortillas on the table. Spencer paid Juan about $300 per month, and received all of the successful and unsuccessful pieces. For three years this system worked very well. Later, they tried other arrangements, none as satisfactory, as outside pressures began to work on the relationship. For the first two years they worked together, stimulated only by the challenge of the art and what they could do with it. Spencer said those years were "magical."

"I Am Not A Salesman"

As Spencer began to spread the word about the artist he had discovered, he always said, "I am not a salesman." He described himself as a student, researcher, or anything but a salesman. Of course, he was a master salesman, almost evangelical in his approach. Lean and ascetic in appearance and well spoken, he could hold an audience and make believers of the most casual passersby.

He contacted museums, curators, galleries, colleges, and universities from San Francisco to Rhode Island to organize exhibitions, workshops, and demonstrations. Juan and various others from Mata Ortiz were transported all over the country in Spencer's little Datsun pickup, towing a trailer full of pots.

First, in May, 1977 Patrick Houlihan, director of the Heard Museum in Phoenix, showed 34 pieces of Juan's work in conjunction with their exhibition, "The Other Southwest, Indian Arts and Crafts of Northwest Mexico."

Opposite: *Anne MacCallum, Spencer MacCallum and Juan.* Photo: Bobby Furst

Arizona State Museum Winter Show, December, 1977.

Photo: Helga Teiwes
Arizona State Museum

"The Other Southwest" is a simple but meaningful term that goes a long way in explaining the impact of artificial modern borders on traditional cultures and art forms. Nevertheless, it offended some Mexicans who asked how Americans would feel if they mounted an exhibition of the American Southwest entitled, "The Other North."

The Winter Show at the Arizona State Museum opened seven months later in December, 1977. To Spencer the formal reception for the opening was a special experience. It was Juan's first major opening, their relationship was new and fresh, and each detail stood out in vivid detail. Spencer and his wife Anne drove Juan and Guille from Mata Ortiz for the event. Anne took Guille to a beauty shop for the first time in her life, and she was enthralled. She and Juan rode an elevator for the first time in the museum building, and when they arrived at the reception, press photographers, university officials, the Mexican consul, and other dignitaries swarmed around them. Yet Spencer thought they displayed the poise and dignity of Parisian artists.

The exhibit, created by Ernest E. Leavitt and executed by Arthur G. Brownlee, showed off the pots well. Behind the glass cases on the walls hung Bobby Furst's photo murals of Juan working. The show was extended twice, eventually closing in early May, 1978 after five successful months.

In the meantime articles began to appear in various publications. The *Los Angeles Times* sent a staffwriter, Chuck Hillinger, and a photographer with Spencer in his Datsun truck to Mata Ortiz to do a story which appeared July 31, 1977. The Winter, 1977 issue of *American Indian Art* magazine featured an article written by Spencer with many color photographs of Juan's early pieces. That issue has now become a collectors' item. The opening line of the article reads:

"A rare happening, a truly indigenous art revival, is underway in a remote village in northern Chihuahua, Mexico."

Spencer sold Juan's pots individually during this period to keep the process going. They cost between $100 and $400. Such sales were a necessary part of promotion and building a market. However, they did not cover costs. Spencer's main emphasis was to promote Juan and the other Mata Ortiz potters. He wanted them to receive the recognition in the art world that their skills and art form deserved. In this he was completely unselfish. In hearing the tale of the trader buying from the indigenous craftsman and reselling at a higher price, eyebrows are raised and exploitation suspected. But in this instance, any such suspicion is unfounded. Spencer devoted eight years to Juan and the other potters. Among other things, he sold his fine collection of Northwest Coast Indian art to provide capital, and in 1983 ended his adventure in debt.

In fact after Juan's first flush of fame, his pots became difficult to obtain. Fourteen pieces were available and sold at the Winter Show, but then a combination of factors diminished the supply relative to demand. Spencer needed to hold back enough representative pieces to form a collection with which to respond to museum requests for exhibitions. In addition, he carefully cataloged each piece chronologically with five black-and-white photographs and one color slide which took a great deal of time and clogged the supply line. Also, Juan became ill and did not work during the late winter and early spring of 1978. Spencer thinks that first trip, in which they traveled on from Tucson to California and were feted on every side, was too long. Perhaps Juan found it more difficult to cope with the cultural gap than his calm demeanor suggested. He always called himself a man of the mountains and said it made him a little ill just to go into Nuevo Casas Grandes.

Spencer made some pots available in late 1978, but retained the best work for a still larger traveling show which, after a few changes and false starts, would open in the spring of 1979.

Juan's New House

When summer came, Juan finally recovered from his illness. By this time the steady income from his arrangement with Spencer enabled him to improve his situation. He moved his family to a new, larger house on the northern outskirts of the village. This adobe house, near an old stand of cottonwoods along the river, had five rooms: kitchen, living room, two bedrooms, and workshop. When Juan and his helpers were digging material for

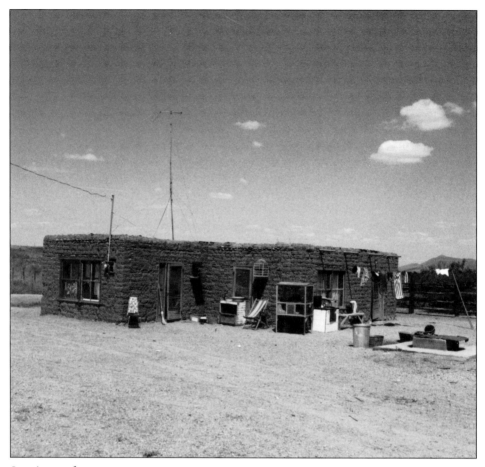

Juan's new home.

the adobe bricks on the house site, they uncovered the remains of a prehistoric Casas Grandes dwelling. An ancient family also had liked this location near the river. This seemed a sign that good things would happen to the new dwellers.

This house served Juan and his family for ten years. Here in 1980, Guille and Juan brought their eighth child, Laura, who was born in the hospital in Nuevo Casas Grandes. Laura grew up making many trips with her parents for classes and exhibitions.

In back of the house was a well from which water was at first drawn up by a bucket on a rope and hauled to the kitchen. Juan later installed an electric pump which should have been easier for Guille, except that the pressure was so great that it blew the water out the back side of a wash basin without filling it.

Despite its distance from the center of the village, the new house soon became a gathering place. All sorts — relatives, hunters, pottery buyers, old friends — stopped by. On the warm evenings after work, the folks sat outside on the kitchen stools before supper while children played at their feet. As the moon rose, conversation would touch on all subjects, frequently cattle and the lack of rain. Juan once asked Spencer if he really believed what people were saying, that men had walked on the moon. He himself was clearly skeptical. Then supper would be ready. Guille often cooked for a crowd, sometimes serving fifteen to twenty in relays from her tiny kitchen. In place of the kitchen table, Juan had a workshop with a large worktable, where materials and work-in-process could be spread out and left when the day ended. By the time Juan and his family moved again, the product from this table would be featured in galleries and museums throughout the United States.

The Competition

Spencer made many close contacts with members of the museum and art world including Bill Miles, Ceramics Professor at New Mexico State University, Las Cruces; Dr. Patrick T. Houlihan, Director of the Heard Museum in Phoenix (and later of the Southwest Museum in Los Angeles); and Dr. Charles DiPeso, Director of the Amerind Foundation in Dragoon, Arizona. These and many other professionals were interested in his discovery. They served as mentors to Spencer, and watched Juan's progress carefully.

Dr. DiPeso is famous for the excavation in the late fifties of the southern half of the great central city of the Casas Grandes culture, Paquimé, a dozen or so miles north of Mata Ortiz. There is a story that while he was on the dig, he saw some of Juan's pots which had been "aged" to appear prehistoric. He is supposed to have said that the pots did not need to be made to look like something they were not; they were good enough to stand on their own merit. He did make this statement to Spencer years later, but at that time Juan was too young to be making pottery. Dr. DiPeso first saw Juan's pots years later when Spencer stopped by the Amerind. He became very enthusiastic about them, and when Spencer suggested a competition in the village, DiPeso immediately offered to sponsor the event through the Amerind. The idea was to create an expert panel of judges to review the pottery entered into the competition and to award cash prizes.

Spencer took this idea to Mata Ortiz where it was received with enthusiasm. A date was set for November 20, 1978, the festival day honoring the beginning of the 1910 Revolution. All could enter except those who had achieved "Master Potter" status. This was defined as a potter who had exhibited in the United States and had sold a pot for $200 or more. Of course at the time, those criteria applied only to Juan, which was the intent. Three categories were established: Effigy, Innovative, and Standard. A cash award would be made for first, second, and third in each category. An overall grand prize of 1000 pesos, then about eighty dollars, would be awarded for the single piece judged "Best in Show." Three non-cash honorable mentions would also be made for each category. Gloria Fenner, chief editor of the massive archaeolog-

Winners of the pottery competition and their parents, November 20, 1978. From left: Felix Ortiz, Don José, Lydia, Doña Paulita, Doña Jesusita Ortiz, Nicolás, Reynaldo.

ical report on DiPeso's work at Paquimé, donated some of the prize money.

With this all settled, a very learned panel of judges traveled to the Amerind Foundation facility in the Sonoran desert outside of the tiny town of Dragoon, Arizona on November 10, 1978. They were: Dr. Patrick T. Houlihan, Director of the Heard Museum; Professor Clara Lee Tanner, anthropologist, University of Arizona and well-known writer of Southwest Indian art; Dr. William Longacre, archaeologist, University of Arizona; John Tanner, trader in Southwest Indian art and chairman of the Gallup Indian Ceremonial; and host Dr. Charles C. Dipeso. That such a group could be attracted to the competition was a measure of the excitement the phenomenon in Mata Ortiz was generating. The panel reviewed the pots, determined the winners, and the results were announced in Mata Ortiz during the fiesta ten days later. Spencer described the event:

> "November 20 was a day brilliant with sunshine. The first event was to be a parade which would end at the plaza late in the morning. The afternoon would be devoted to rodeo events. A villager had lent us an enormous baker's table, and by mid-morning, four volunteers had moved it into place near the bandstand. We draped it with russet-colored velvet and set up a display of all the winning pottery against a backdrop of black velvet flags hung with the brightly colored ribbons and rosettes that Anne had spent all week making by hand. The parade arrived, and the plaza filled with people. Anne and I

found ourselves on the bandstand with all the flags and the music for the ceremony of awarding prizes. Lydia made a beautiful acceptance speech for the Grand prize, and the mothers of the potters were honored with arrangements of red rosebuds. Afterwards, Doña Paulita invited the dozen American visitors into her home, where she and the other women of the family had prepared a traditional chicken mole dinner."

Lydia, with her fine technical mastery, took six of the ten cash prizes including Best in Show. Felix Ortiz took two cash prizes and seven of the nine honorable mentions. The judges liked his bold designs and imagination, but they felt his technical level did not do justice to his concepts. Reynaldo and Nicolás each won one cash prize. They both had just begun concentrating on high-quality work, and they only entered a few pieces. As it was, Nicolás barely missed a first place and a chance for "Best in Show."

On the surface this competition had the aspects of a small-town country fair. But it was much more. Experts in the field, as represented by the panel, recognized the ceramic movement in Mata Ortiz as a significant cultural and artistic event. To the potters, the competition revealed that high quality should be their objective. Juan had always stressed quality and encouraged it for others, but here was a dollar-and-cents lesson. Spencer has suggested that it was this competition that stimulated Nicolás to perfect his skills. Nicolás is now one of the most technically proficient potters, especially with paints and colorants. Very soon afterwards, all who won cash prizes — Lydia, Felix, Nicolás, and Reynaldo — were exhibiting their work in the U.S. and selling pieces for more than $200. They had become "Master Potters."

Lydia's Wedding

In February, 1978, a few months after the competition, Lydia married Rito Talavera, a handsome young man from the nearby village of Anchondo. Spencer and his wife Anne were among the 300 guests. Don José and Doña Paulita asked Spencer to be a a *padrino*, a kind of god-parent relationship which is an important kinship bond in northern Mexico. His duties at the wedding included getting the bride to the church Saturday afternoon and helping with the cost of the musicians at the wedding party afterward. Most important, this firmly established Spencer's already close relationship with Don José, and particularly Doña Paulita. They now addressed each other as *Comadre* or *Compadre.* Spencer has always considered this a great privilege.

Lydia, though young, was considered to be one of the best potters in the village. Rito helped prepare her clays for a long time after they were married, but as he learned the techniques, he began to produce a distinctive black ware of his own.

Juan provided a cow for the wedding party which was barbecued in a large pit. Musicians played for twelve straight hours, and the wedding party danced all night. Just before dawn, the bride, still in her bridal dress and veil, cut the wedding cake. Then all had a breakfast of *menudo* which had been cooking in a copper cauldron over an open fire since the day before.

As the sun came up, the exhausted guests and family began to straggle off to their homes to sleep. To Spencer and Anne's surprise, Rito left with his family for Anchondo, and Lydia stayed home and went to bed. When the Quezada family awoke refreshed after a few hours, they gathered around Lydia and all went together for a last family picnic outing and bath at a nearby natural warm spring. After this last outing with her, the family delivered the bride, rested and radiant, to her new home where Rito waited.

The Traveling Exhibition,
"Juan Quezada and the New Tradition"

The most important of the many exhibitions that would feature Juan's work opened April 20, 1979, at the art gallery of California State University, Fullerton. This was the first of five locations for a show which would continue for more than a year and a half. The opening capped two years of hard work, frustration, and setbacks, but the show was an enormous success. The October 13, 1979 issue of *Art Week* described the exhibit, designed by J.R. "Skip" Pahl, gallery director of the Rex Wignall Museum at Chaffey College, the second location, as "mounted as a gallery would display precious jewels." Pahl placed each pot on a plexiglass ring with lighting which made it appear to float in space. Bobby Furst's large photomurals of Juan and his family hung on the walls as a counterpoint to the floating "jewels" in the cases.

Dextra Frankel, the gallery director at California State University, Fullerton, directed the project. This involved funding applications, scheduling, publicity, plus detailed logistics and personnel management. Much of the funding came from the National Endowment for the Arts, supplemented by the Mexican National Tourist Council and the five institutions involved.

Nicolás and Lydia attended the opening at Fullerton with Juan. All three demonstrated their pot-making techniques for the fascinated guests. The exhibition featured mainly Juan's work, but Nicolás, Lydia, Reynaldo, Felix Ortiz, and Taurina Baca had all been asked to show pieces, tangible evidence of their artistic progress.

After Chaffey, the third stop for the exhibition was the prestigious Maxwell Museum of Anthropology in Albuquerque in December, 1979. There were some different aspects to this version of the show, not the least of which was the presence at the opening of thirteen Quezadas including Don José and Doña Paulita. Spencer, with help from artist/rancher Ellen Ellinwood from Deming, performed this feat of personnel logistics, transporting the group, entertaining them, and finding them accommodations at a Presbyterian church school in Albuquerque. The group that made this trip north included six of the then eight Quezada family potters: Juan, Nicolás, Reynaldo, Lydia, Consolación, and Oscar. Only Reynalda and her daughter Yolanda did not come. Spencer commented that the highlight of this opening for him was seeing the great pleasure illuminating the faces of Don José and Doña Paulita as the dignitaries and the great crowds of guests admired their children's work.

Another feature at the Maxwell, an idea of museum director J.J. Brody, was a small introductory exhibit using examples from the four major pueblo ceramic revivals—Acoma, San Ildefonso, Zuni, and Casas Grandes. He placed four large prehistoric shards beside the corresponding modern-day pot, comparing and contrasting the prehistoric inspiration and the modern result.

Juan's first experience with modern Indian potters came after the Maxwell opening. Until then he had only heard of María Martínez of San Ildefonso, the famous creator of burnished black ware, and probably the inspiration through a visitor for Juan's initial attempt in 1975 to sign his pots — the attempt that so frustrated the antiquity traders.

Anita Dā, María Martínez's daughter-in-law, who had visited Mata Ortiz that year with Spencer and Ellen Ellinwood, wrote to Spencer and invited him to bring Juan to San Ildefonso when they came to New Mexico. Spencer accepted this invitation and brought Juan and twelve other Quezadas. With Mrs. Dā as hostess, María, then 92, and her family, talked with the Quezadas for over an hour in Spanish. Spencer, Anne, and Ellen discreetly withdrew. Mrs. Dā later entertained the group in Albuquerque.

The same week, Juan and Guille were invited to the Acoma Pueblo to visit the family of Lucy Lewis, the famous Acoma potter. Mary Lewis Garcia, Lucy's daughter, had attended Juan's demonstration at the Maxwell. In her home at Acomita, she showed Juan her paints and clay and how she used them. With Spencer interpreting, they discussed their techniques — what worked, what did not — and exchanged paint and clay samples. Afterwards, Mary Lewis Garcia served a luncheon of blue-cornmeal mush and red chile. Spencer described their leave taking:

> "As we were ready to leave, Mary Lewis' daughter, about 14 years old and learning to make pottery, asked Juan if she might take his hands — so that she could become a great potter too. She took and held them tightly for a moment, then quickly brought them to her mouth. Mary then took Juan's hands, and after a moment of holding them much as her daughter had done, she spoke in her own tongue what I took to be a blessing. I noticed that there were tears in her eyes."

Juan eventually met Lucy Lewis herself when they both were teaching at the Idyllwild School of Music and the Arts. As she watched Juan work with the clay, she is reported to have said to her daughters (in Keresan, the Acoma language) that Juan must be Acoma. Her people tell an old story of the church in their sacred village of Sky City high on a mesa above the New Mexican desert. The Spaniards made the Indians build a Catholic church with a bell tower in this village, but there was no money for the bell. So the Spaniards kidnapped Acoma children, took them down into Mexico and traded them for a bell. With such talent, Lucy thought Juan must be descended from one of those lost children.

In Idyllwild where this took place, Juan met and worked beside many

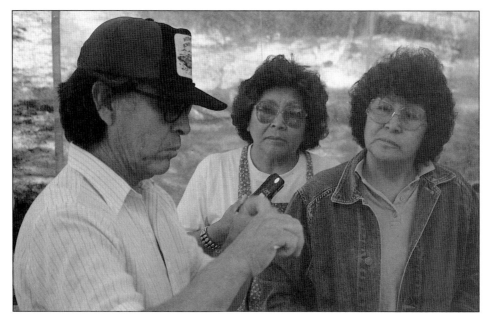

Juan shows Dolores Lewis Garcia and Emma Lewis Mitchell, famous Acoma Indian potters, how he makes a human hair brush, 1988.

other prominent Indian potters including Blue Corn of San Ildefonso, Priscilla Nampeyo of Hopi, Jody Falwell of San Ildefonso, and Lucy's daughters Dolores and Emma.

The exhibition continued its travels, stopping at the Lowie Museum in Berkeley between April 4 and June 15, and the Heard Museum in Phoenix between September 22 and November 15, 1980. The Berkeley curators added a series of twenty mounted photographs by Bobby Furst, showing Juan performing all of the steps of making a pot. At the Heard, Pat Neary, Exhibit Designer, and Jon Erickson, Curator of Collections, did a particularly fine job of exhibiting the pieces. Spencer said their presentation rivaled the "precious jewels" of the Cal State Fullerton show.

Nicolás and Lydia flew to Berkeley to do the demonstrations there, as Juan had to stay home with Guille, who was expecting a baby. They were guests of the Richard Riemanns, friends of Spencer, in a palatial stone Gothic home overlooking San Francisco Bay. They were entertained each night, once at a traditional Japanese dinner complete with chopsticks.

The Berkeley demonstration was filmed by the local Spanish-language stations. Lydia said she and Nicolás had been unprepared for the world away from Mata Ortiz. It was so different, she said, so beautiful, and with such good people.

Nicolás and Lydia joined Juan at the next show at the Heard Museum in Phoenix for the demonstrations there. Guille brought her new baby, Laura, the first of many such trips for this little girl.

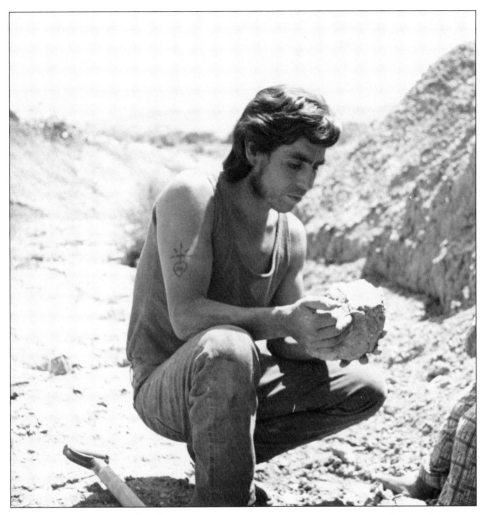

Juan examines a new clay deposit, 1976.   Photo: Bobby Furst

Experiments and Breakthroughs

When not traveling during the period from late 1978 through the middle of 1980, Juan continued his experiments with new clays and pigments. Juan had always been intrigued with clay that would fire pure white, *blanco blanco*. He had found many white shards and knew that it was possible. In September, 1979 he blended three clays which worked well for small pieces but was too brittle for anything large. This was a breakthrough, and Juan kept the source of these clays to himself. Others potters gradually found their own sources, but working the white clay still bedevils experienced potters and students alike. In Mata Ortiz a great deal of time and skilled effort has been put into white pots that often, at some stage of the process, crack. Still, these pots are greatly admired in the village, and the sources of white clay are jealously guarded.

Black-on-black pot, Juan Quezada, 1980.   Photo: N. Prasad

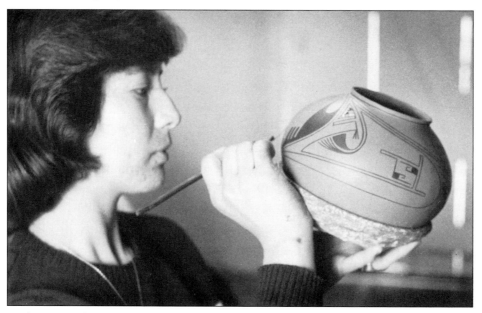

Lydia Quezada, Juan's youngest sister, 1979.   Photo: Diana Hubbs

In 1981, Juan found a superior deposit of white clay. He showed the result of his first test of this special clay to Spencer. Instead of just a test slab, he had fashioned a small conch shell. The opening of the shell formed a cave with a tiny cave dwelling inside. This miniature and subsequent pieces were a lovely off-white color which provided a beautiful base for Juan's red and black designs. He later used this clay to blend with others to get a variety of colors, particularly a delicate yellow.

Overall, Juan's pots continued to change. A collection from late 1980 looked quite different from those made two years before for the traveling exhibition. New shapes and designs evolved with more departure from the basic Casas Grandes inspiration. Among other things, he developed a distinctive light sand-yellow color, something like Jeddito ware (one of the precursors to modern Hopi pottery), by firing twice a clay that normally fired orange. He also discovered a pigment that fires a lustrous black under normal oxidizing conditions. This style of black pot later became the staple product of several journeymen potters in the village.

Juan progressed so fast during this period that Bill Miles, the professor of ceramics at New Mexico State University, said that he had never seen or heard of an artist who had advanced his art so rapidly in a comparable period, an achievement even more remarkable having been self-directed.

Lydia was also experimenting, and had developed an independent version of the black-on-black technique María Martínez had made so famous. She fires the pot twice. The first results in a plain shiny black surface. She paints designs on this, then fires the piece again. The final result is a matte black design on the shiny surface. Lydia discovered this when she became dissatisfied with a polychrome piece she had painted and fired it black. Some of her painted lines showed through so she retouched them, noticing the contrasting black-on-black effect. Intrigued, she experimented even more and eventually mastered the technique. This style is popular with customers and now is probably the most common in the village.

The Relationship

Spencer has described his first three years working with Juan as "magical." However strains began to develop in the relationship, exacerbated by cultural and language differences and the great distance between San Pedro, California, and Mata Ortiz. Spencer could only manage a trip about every two months, not enough to keep on top of the changing situation in the village. The long trips to the United States for exhibitions and demonstrations were hard on Juan in spite of his stolid demeanor. Others with their own agendas added doubt and mistrust. Traders told Juan that Spencer was becoming wealthy. "Spencer has all of the pots and you have nothing," they said. Militant Mexican-American students publicly heckled Spencer at some of his slide presentations, and privately told Juan and Guille that Spencer was exploiting them.

At first, Spencer purchased all of Juan's work, the intention being to allow Juan complete freedom of artistic expression. He kept most of the pieces for exhibition until 1979 when he began to concentrate more on selling. In the meantime, the two tried other financial arrangements which would work for a while and then break down. The lack of emphasis on sales and an otherwise restricted budget put limits on what Spencer could pay. Because of the publicity generated by Spencer, more and more traders, tourists, and collectors began to find their way to the village, and when they arrived, they wanted to buy. So, by the middle of 1980, Juan began selling to anyone.

Spencer continued as a major buyer, but often when he arrived after a prolonged absence, he found the situation with Juan and the other potters different from his previous understanding. Pots might not be ready while others might already have been sold. Juan, on the other hand was unsure of the value of the long, arduous trips to the U.S. In short, the expectations about what the other could or should do were not always met.

This still can happen. For example, a buyer sees a pot in progress. He gives the potter an advance for the pot and expects to pick it up on his next trip. In the meantime another buyer sees the completed pot on the shelf, and falls in love with it. He offers a higher price. This presents a real dilemma to the potter who a short time ago never dreamed of receiving such amounts and, at the moment, is a little short of cash. Some potters hold to their original bargains; others break down and sell to the second buyer, probably thinking they can make another piece acceptable to the first buyer. Sometimes this works, but other times the first buyer is very upset when he returns and finds "his" piece gone.

In spite of the pressures on their relationship, Juan and Spencer worked hard together over the next two years, and 1980 and 1981 remain banner years for the exhibition of Mata Ortiz pottery.

Publications and Appearances

Before the big opening of the traveling exhibition at the Heard Museum in Phoenix, Spencer took Juan, Nicolás, Lydia, and Reynaldo to Indian Market weekend in Santa Fe, driving them up from Mexico in the Datsun truck. They were to give a demonstration at "The Santa Fe Store at the Inn at Loretto." The owner of this new sales gallery, Sudye Kirkpatrick, had purchased over 200 pieces of Mata Ortiz pottery, and she and Spencer were worried that the potters might receive a cool reception in Santa Fe because they were not American Indians. The demonstration was originally scheduled for Friday and Sunday, but after a surprisingly warm reception the first night, they decided to add a third on Saturday. Word got around and the gallery was packed. Sales went well, and Kirkpatrick was so enthusiastic that she gave special ribbon shirts to all the potters and Spencer, which they immediately put on and wore.

The *Santa Fe Reporter* published a special supplement for Indian Market which included a well-written article on the Mata Ortiz potters entitled, "How to Start a Pottery Revival," a strangely fitting and at the same time misleading title. The article told Juan's story, relating his art to the prehistoric pueblo cultures of the American Southwest and northern Chihuahua. It also promoted the demonstrations and show at the Santa Fe Store, noting a unique service that Juan and Spencer offered. Collectors were invited to bring to the Store old and new "Casas Grandes" pieces to be authenticated if old or identified if new and unsigned. Some of the supposedly old pots turned out to be new but "distressed" pieces which had been sold as genuine prehistoric Casas Grandes. With the exception of a few pieces by Manuel Olivas, the independent potter Spencer met first in Nuevo Casas Grandes, all of those were from Mata Ortiz, and usually the maker could be identified.

A second important article appeared just before the Heard opening in the September, 1980, issue of *Ceramics Monthly.* Entitled "Juan Quezada, Potter in a New Tradition," it was an eight-page in-depth article by Elaine Levin, a California ceramic arts writer, with photographs by Bobby Furst. The article is particularly interesting today since the detailed description of the process includes steps that Juan has long since changed. The writer states that "before the pot dries, a cream or light beige slip is applied." It has been years since Juan has painted slip (liquid clay) over the pot as a base for the design. Though this is a common technique in the Indian Southwest, and several Mata Ortiz potters still use it, particularly in the Porvenir barrio, Juan never cared much for slipping. When he found finer clays that were still strong enough to form vessel walls, he began to paint directly on the clay body of the pot.

The article also described Juan painting and polishing his pots while they were wet. Today he usually lets them dry completely, then sands them with ordinary sandpaper and rubs in a light coating of vegetable oil before he decorates. This method permits him to paint a very fine line without bleeding. Juan says that the ancient people probably painted and polished wet pots because the stone polishing compressed the clay and made the walls stronger and less porous. Here he sacrifices some strength for better design, and it does not matter about the porosity since these pots are not for use anyway.

The NCECA Conference

The big news of 1981 was the invitation to do a demonstration at the annual conference of the National Council on Education for the Ceramic Arts (NCECA), the professional society of potters for the United States and Canada. This invitation came about through the efforts of Bill Miles, then ceramics professor at New Mexico State University, Las Cruces. The annual conference is a major event in the world of ceramics, drawing over a thousand potters. Each year an important potter is asked to demonstrate. María Martínez was invited one year. Now Juan, Nicolás, Reynaldo, and Lydia received invitations to the 1981 conference to be held at the Wichita Convention Center. Wichita's new Indian Center Museum would host a full exhibition of their work, timed to coincide with the conference. The men all accepted this major honor, but Lydia had to decline because she was expecting a baby.

Spencer rented a U-Haul trailer in San Pedro, filled it with the exhibition collection, and pulled it with his truck to Deming, New Mexico. He left the trailer there, crossed the border and continued to Mata Ortiz to pick up the potters and their entourage. Guille accompanied Juan, and sixteen-year old Rosa Lucero came in Lydia's place. After recrossing the border and retrieving the trailer, they stopped at a cattle-watering tank by a windmill to pick up dried cow chips for firing. Since the trailer was already full of exhibition pottery, baggage, and food, the cow chips went into the truck with the passengers.

Bill Price, an anthropology professor and film maker at New Mexico State University, put them up for the night at his home in Alamagordo. Price was very interested in the happenings in Mata Ortiz, and had done considerable filming on site there in preparation for a documentary, which he later produced on video in 1992. He and his wife Stephanie had become friends of Juan and Guille and had been asked to be the godparents, or *padrinos,* of Laura.

This miniature caravan with its potters, pots, and cow chips left early the next morning and finally arrived in Wichita, where it stayed a week. The exhibition opened on a Sunday, and the family spent the first few days making pots to use in the demonstrations and firings. Spencer lectured both at Wichita State University and at a Conference meeting. After each event, the conferees crowded around, thanking the Quezadas and Spencer and giving them gifts of their own work. Years later, students turned up in Juan's and Nicolás' classes who had first heard of Mata Ortiz pottery at this NCECA conference.

Spencer described the dramatic firing which finished the last demonstration:

> "As it turned out, the high point of our demonstration at the Conference was Saturday afternoon. The firing was scheduled for three. By two o'clock it had begun to rain, and a wind was rising. Juan was preheating his jar in a food-warming oven and preparing for firing. The walls of the Museum were glass; surely, I thought, he couldn't be so unobservant as not to notice it was raining! I tried tactfully several times to draw his attention to the fact by asking if we shouldn't cancel. I couldn't imagine his risking the superb jar he had made a few days earlier. Whatever the exact words of his reply when it finally came, the sense of it was, 'Look, I'm busy...'

> As three o'clock approached, it was raining in earnest, the drops driven aslant by the wind. The spectators, protected by the glass walls of the Museum, were dry. Reynaldo and I, one on either side, each held up a bulletin board over Juan in an effort to keep him dry while he prepared the firing. Rainwater ran across and down the boards onto our shoes. Water was everywhere. Juan was undaunted. Minutes later the dung fire was burning, and Juan said we could take away the boards; cow chips burn so hot that no amount of rain could affect it now. When it had been burning for approximately seventeen minutes, he scattered the embers and removed the pot. I held

my breath, but Juan was self-possessed. He quickly carried the pot, glowing red on the end of a poker, into the Museum and set it down to cool on three brick fragments he had prepared ahead. The firing was perfect.

I wondered afterwards what the experience must have been for the spectators, most of them potters well schooled in the complexities of cone temperatures and kiln types, as they watched a self-taught rustic from Chihuahua fire to perfection in the rain and the wind, in a pile of cow chips!"

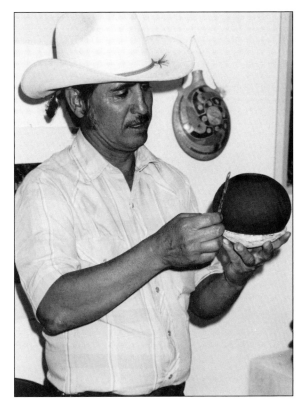

Reynaldo Quezada at the Center Gallery of Indigenous Arts, Idyllwild, California, May, 1993.

Sales and Promotion

By 1981, Spencer's promotional efforts were in full swing. Besides lecturing and promoting exhibitions, he had opened a gallery at Fort MacArthur in San Pedro; where he had a permanent gallery display and regularly held functions to show off the work from Mata Ortiz. Reynaldo lived for a time at the gallery and frequently demonstrated at the functions. Spencer was invited for the second time to exhibit at the Native American Arts Festival in Exposition Park, Los Angeles, and in August, he returned to Indian Market in Santa Fe, this time with Consolación, Nicolás, and Reynaldo.

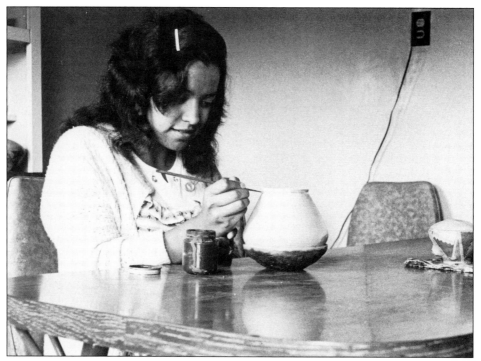

Taurina Baca, Juan's first non-family student, 1977. Photo: Bobby Furst

Unfortunately, in June before Indian Market, he had to close the San Pedro gallery because the Lower Bluff area of Fort MacArthur was to be removed for the new Cabrillo Marina complex. To celebrate the closing, he put on a "Farewell Fiesta." Reynaldo came to demonstrate and to help with the cooking. He outdid himself, forming and painting pots and firing twice — the first an oxidation firing and the second a reduction firing to show how blackware is made. Over 130 guests enjoyed Reynaldo's twin performances, first the pots and second the Mata Ortiz-style meal.

One of the guests, Rick Petterson, Director of the Fine Arts Program of the Los Angeles County Fair at Pomona, was so impressed with Reynaldo that, on the spot, he asked him to demonstrate at the fair in September. After further conversation with Spencer, Petterson decided to install the entire traveling exhibition including the photomurals in the fairground's Fine Arts Building. This benchmark collection would enjoy one more outing at the fair.

Therefore, a week after he had returned the family members from the Santa Fe Indian Market, the indefatigable Spencer picked up Reynaldo, Taurina Baca, and Taurina's mother Socorro Tena de Baca in Mata Ortiz and drove them to Pomona in his now somewhat tired pickup. This was its thirty-seventh trip to Mata Ortiz.

Taurina Baca, a lovely young woman of 20, had grown up across the street from Juan's family. A good friend of Lydia's, she became interested in the pottery early, and Juan took her as his first non-family student. She learned quickly and by now was doing excellent work.

For eighteen days at the fair, Reynaldo, Taurina, and Spencer, were "on" from 10:00 AM to 10:00 PM, making pots, painting pots, firing pots, selling pots, and talking pots to the crowds that came by their booth. They advertised a firing every evening at seven o'clock. Reynaldo handled the firing and proved to be an excellent showman. Taking an unfired pot decorated with painted polychrome designs, he set it up for firing under a "beehive" of cow chips in advance of the firing so that the spectators did not see it. Shortly after seven, he ignited the chips and fired the pot in a reduction atmosphere (absence of oxygen). It emerged 20 or so minutes later, to everyone's admiration, as a lustrous black "jewel." Then he told the spectators he would refire it in the regular way (allowing oxygen to circulate) and to watch what happens. He stacked fresh cow chips around the cover over the pot, ignited them, and after another 20 minutes, scattered the burned chips and removed the cover to reveal the pot the crowd had seen before as shiny black. Only now it was transformed into a polychrome painted pot on yellow clay. The crowd loved it, and as a result, there was always great activity around the booth throughout the fair.

The only hitch for the performance was finding cow chips to fire pots every evening. There was plenty of manure in Southern California, but the only kind that works for firing is from grass-fed cows, which is not so common. Major John R. DeMill of JRD Polled Herefords in Chino came to the rescue and generously provided a steady supply.

It was during one of the firings at the fair that Spencer first obtained a pyrometer and measured the dung firings at just over 1600 degrees, higher than most suspected. He corroborated this measurement at subsequent firings.

As American Southwest Indians were also demonstrating and exhibiting at the fair, there were plenty of opportunities to become acquainted and to compare materials and techniques. The most dramatic difference was in firing. Both used cow chips, but the Indian potters fired six or more pots together for two to three hours. The technique Juan Quezada developed required only 20 to 30 minutes. Juan Tafoya of San Ildefonso, with whom the Mata Ortiz potters became particularly well acquainted, doubted that the short firing time would give him the lustrous black color he sought. He thought perhaps the clays were different. However, he was convinced when Reynaldo first fired a thin-walled, Mata Ortiz-style pot made with Tafoya's clay, and then a thick-walled San Ildefonso pot made with Mata Ortiz clay, and both came out a deep, lustrous black.

Also, the Mata Ortiz potters generally fire only one pot at a time. This innocuous difference has important economic and artistic ramifications. Firing one at a time makes each piece special as it reduces output and the volume available for sale. On the other hand, the impetus to take an artistic chance is much less when a large number of pots is at risk in the firing. Losing one pot is a minor matter. Losing many in one bad firing can be a disaster. Anthropologist Michael Williams, in his masters thesis study of Mata

Ortiz, *La Lucha del Barro*, suggests that the single-pot firing has much to do with the rapid creative flowering in Mata Ortiz. Fledgling and experienced potters alike will reach out and take chances when only risking a single piece.

One of the visitors to the fair took more than a casual interest in the pottery demonstrations and made a point of getting acquainted with Spencer, and because of his fluent Spanish, Taurina and Reynaldo. His name was Tom Fresh, and he worked for the Idyllwild School of Music and the Arts (ISOMATA) in Idyllwild, California. This was a fortuitous meeting. Tom, also a potter, was interested personally in studying with Juan, and he liked the idea of involving Juan and the potters with the Native Arts program at ISOMATA. Fate had stepped in at the right moment because Spencer's relationship with the potters was moving toward a close.

New England, Spring 1982

In April, 1982, an invitation came to visit Rhode Island College. Spencer, Juan, Guille, Lydia, and Lydia's seven-month-old Paulita made the trip, expanding it into an extraordinary tour through the Northeast. They arrived at Boston Airport in a snowstorm to claim their luggage and six large bags of cow chips checked through from El Paso. The next two weeks they watched spring come to New England while they lectured, demonstrated, and worked with college students at Rhode Island College; Salve Regina College, a Catholic college in Newport; Roger Williams Museum in Providence; Princeton University; and Montgomery College in Rockville, Maryland.

At Princeton they stayed in the museum-like home of Spencer's old friend Gillett G. Griffen, curator of Precolumbian art at the Princeton Art Museum, who lives surrounded by ancient art. When the Quezadas arrived, he served them wine in 2500-year-old Grecian cups. At the university they met the head of the ceramics program, Toshiko Takaezu, one of America's most famous and highly regarded potters. She invited them to lunch at her home and studio in Quakertown, New Jersey. Later they spent one day in New York City seeing the skyscrapers, Wall Street, the Staten Island Ferry, and the Statue of Liberty — amazing sights for villagers from northern Chihuahua. Juan, however, was most taken with the Greek marble statues in the Metropolitan Museum of Art.

The *El Paso Times* wrote up the story of this trip in the April 21 edition. There was almost more to report. On the return flight to El Paso, one landing gear of the airliner collapsed on the runway. The airplane fell to one side dragging one wing along the runway and showering sparks. The pilot finally got the airplane stopped, and all passengers were evacuated safely through the tail-door escape slide, a grand finale to the tour. That night while they watched the accident on television, Juan said thoughtfully, "I thought in the United States everything worked."

After such a trip, what happened to Juan's style and technology, now that he had seen Greek art, Chinese art, and modern art? Did the jolt of exposure to the world's great artistic traditions knock him off his path or cause him to

34

imitate some imagined superior style? While Juan seemed to enjoy these experiences, the answer is they had little effect on the growth of his work. That seemed to come solely from within. No outside influences had affected his basic artistic integrity since he first picked up a prehistoric shard.

The following summer the pottery troupe went west to Idyllwild in the Southern California mountains. Juan's first class at the Idyllwild School of Music and the Arts is described in Chapter 3. Suffice to say it was a success. The *Los Angeles Times* covered the session with a detailed story with pictures headed "Professionals Study Under Mexican Master."

Spencer and Juan made an excellent team — Spencer organizing, lecturing, and translating and Juan teaching and performing his magic with the clay. However, behind the scenes of their beautiful presentations, misunderstandings grew. There had been no exclusive arrangement between the two since 1980, but Spencer remained Juan's principal buyer, agent, and promoter. After ISOMATA, they attempted to find firmer ground for their relationship through another exclusive agreement. Spencer brought in an experienced gallery owner from Switzerland, Peter Tellini, and they proposed to buy all of Juan's work for a set amount per month. Juan seemed amenable to this, and on this basis they began 1983.

Ghost Ranch and Goodbye

The New Mexico Potters Association announced in its March, 1983, newsletter an "intensive participatory workshop" at its annual meeting in June at Ghost Ranch. It would be a "primitive" style pottery workshop conducted by one of the world's outstanding potters, Juan Quezada. Participants were expected to get their hands dirty. The workshop would be at the Conference Center of the 21,000 acre Ghost Ranch near Abiquiu (Georgia O'Keefe's home), New Mexico.

At the same time, the famous Southwest artist, Amado Peña, proposed a show for Juan at his new gallery, "El Taller," in Santa Fe. A huge, impressive man with a good understanding of the Indian pueblo scene, Peña produced paintings and prints for his own galleries in New Mexico and Texas as well as for other galleries throughout the country. He liked Juan's work and in recent months had purchased and displayed pieces from Spencer and others. Juan brought some large, spectacular pots for this show which sold for high prices, some well over $1,000. During their stay, Peña lavishly entertained Juan, Guille and the other members of the entourage.

The workshop itself was another success. The Conference Center sits at the base of a great mass of cliffs facing west, catching and reflecting the sunset colors. Beyond is an unending panoramic view of mountains and desert. Forty-five students attended, mostly experienced potters. Working in this setting, they established a warm rapport with each other and with Juan as Spencer translated. However something was in the wind. It turned out that, after eight years, Juan and Spencer's work together was almost over.

It is hard to know what makes a seemingly sound relationship fall apart. No one will ever really know about this one. Some blame Spencer, some

Olla, *Juan Quezada, 1991.*

blame Juan, some blame Guille, some blame Amado Peña and some blame others who put pressure on Juan and Guille. Obviously, there were strains as Juan emerged from obscurity to fame. At the same time, Spencer struggled financially to keep the project going. This was one of the reasons he brought in Peter Tellini. Certainly the financial success of Amado Peña's show and Peña's entertaining and impressive style appealed to Juan and Guille. However, the signs of stress were evident long before Ghost Ranch. Looking back, there was probably not one person or event responsible; the relationship had simply run its course.

So when Juan and Guille made ready to leave on the bus, Juan told Spencer that he did not want to work with him any more. Peña would be his principal buyer. Although initially shocked, Spencer accepted the situation and went on to other things. He renewed old contacts and soon was working as a land analyst with a real estate consulting firm in Los Angeles. Gradually he worked himself out of debt, and began writing and speaking extensively on social anthropology. He felt secure in what he had done in the little village. In a sense he had fulfilled the destiny his mother had prepared him for many years ago. A prosperous Mata Ortiz is his monument.

In 1986, Spencer returned to the village for the first time in three years. The long drive was uneventful except that he forgot his passport and had to convince a reluctant Automobile Club manager in Tucson to give him an affidavit to enable him to cross the border. (Not bad for one who claims he is not a salesman.)

When he arrived, everyone, including Juan, greeted him warmly. Doña Paulita, his *comadre*, cried and insisted that he stay with her and Don José. Before Spencer left for their house, he and Juan talked cordially. In the workshop, Juan took out each of his new pieces and displayed them on the table. Spencer examined each one carefully with obvious pleasure. These two men had traveled a long way together over the years, not always smoothly. However they did not talk of these things. As before, Juan showed Spencer his best work, and Spencer questioned, commented, and approved.

During the next day, Spencer visited other old friends and distributed small gifts. On his rounds, he noted several changes. Noe, just a boy when Spencer had last seen him, now made very sophisticated animal and fish effigies. There were many new potters, and most gratifying, the overall quality was high.

Spencer is proud of his association with Juan and the potters of Mata Ortiz, and he still lectures about his experiences to anthropology classes and other groups.

Juan and Spencer, 1989.   Photo: Topi Arvi

ISOMATA class at the Cave of the Olla in the Sierra Madre above Mata Ortiz, 1990.
From top left: José (Pino) Molina, Judith Anderson, Kathleen Koopman, Walter Parks,
Tony Soares, Trudy Adler, Peter Slavish, Susana de Falla. Bottom: Tom Fresh, Nancy
Reid, Nicolás Quezada. Photo: Trudy Adler

CHAPTER 3
ISOMATA 1982-1990

Nena Quezada

Idyllwild School of Music and the Arts

In 1982, Juan was invited to teach at the Idyllwild School of Music and the Arts (ISOMATA) in the San Jacinto Mountains of Southern California. Spencer worked out the details with the staff, and that summer brought Juan, Guille, Reynaldo, Taurina Baca, and little Laura to the beautiful campus above Palm Springs. No one knew it at the time, but this was the beginning of an entirely new phase of Juan's story and the Mata Ortiz miracle.

ISOMATA existed as the fulfilled dream of Max Krone, a charismatic professor of music from the University of Southern California (USC), and his wife Beatrice. They had vacationed in Idyllwild in 1941, and on impulse bought a summer cabin. There, on the porch overlooking a creek, they dreamed of creating a school that emphasized music, art, nature, and the human spirit — an offset to a world dehumanized by war. Their particular concept revolved around participation. They wanted people to become involved — making music, painting, throwing pots, dancing — not just continue to be spectators of art and life.

So after the war, Krone acquired 350 acres of a sheep ranch along Strawberry Creek, called Domenigoni Flats. Since he had no money, he subdivided about 100 acres of the land, sold lots to friends, and ended up with enough for the down payment. What came to be the renowned ISOMATA began as 250 rugged acres of meadow and forest land with three ramshackle cabins and an old jeep.

Not only was Max Krone the Dean of Fine Arts at USC, his wife Bea conducted music workshops and wrote books on classroom music instruction. So between them, they were familiar with all levels of music — from children's lessons to the most advanced orchestral and choral work. They saw a need for elementary school teachers to be trained in music to fulfill aspects of their multiple roles which included being song leaders and music teachers. Their school began as a series of two-week music classes for teachers in the summer of 1950. Classes have continued every succeeding summer.

As the couple was well-connected in the music world of Hollywood and Southern California, many stars became regular instructors in their program, including songwriter Meredith Wilson, and folk singers Marais and Miranda. As popularity increased, more classes were added including visual arts, painting, ceramics, sculpture, and dance. The expanding catalog of summer offerings contained such well known names as painters Francoise Gilot and Harry Sternberg, writer Norman Corwin, sculptor Lorna Steere, dancer Bella Lewitsky, ceramist Susan Peterson, and Indian potter María Martínez.

The last two names bear directly on Juan's story. Susan Peterson is one of the best known writers and teachers of ceramic art in America. In 1974 she

39

obtained an NEA grant to present an Indian pottery workshop at ISOMATA. That summer María, in her late eighties, and her family came to the campus to demonstrate and teach, the first time ever for them in a non-Indian environment. This workshop and earlier presentations at ISOMATA by the Chickasaw/Choctaw lecturer Ataloa set a precedent for traditional arts on a campus that had been devoted primarily to the classic arts.

María and her family returned to ISOMATA each summer through 1977. Other Indian artists were invited to teach, and by the mid 1980s, the full-fledged *Mother Earth Father Sky* Native Arts program had evolved under the direction of Tom Fresh. The classes offered eventually included all phases of American Indian art: pottery, baskets and jewelry, as well as native art from Mexico and New Zealand. In addition to María and her family, the artist/instructors have included Lucy Lewis, Blue Corn, Priscilla Nampeyo, Jody Falwell, and Michael Kabotie.

None made quite the stir that Juan Quezada did when he arrived in Idyllwild the summer of 1982. His uniqueness was part of the attraction — an obscure Mexican recreating a complete ceramic art form. The *Los Angeles Times* ran a feature story in September that brought many to the mountains to see Juan.

The pottery itself was the other part of the attraction. With its thin walls and delicate fine-line decoration, it clearly was in a class of its own. Even the great Indian potters were impressed and openly admired the work.

Juan taught at ISOMATA for eight summers with additional classes held in Mata Ortiz under the *Mother Earth Father Sky* "on-site" program. Each class at the campus was accompanied by an exhibition and sale of Juan's pottery. The classes and exhibitions were so successful that Juan's name became identified with ISOMATA in Southern California.

The first summer, Juan's young assistants, brother Reynaldo and Taurina Baca, were very popular with the students. Several young women made a special effort to befriend Taurina, helping her bridge the cultural gap in spite of the language difference. Others became quite enamored with Reynaldo which he did not seem to mind.

After Juan and the others returned to Mexico, Reynaldo stayed living for awhile with Spencer in San Pedro and later with a potter in Santa Monica. He conducted several workshops with the group of students that had built up around the original ISOMATA nucleus.

Tom Fresh

In 1974, Tom Fresh, a former teacher in the Children's Art Center at ISOMATA was experimenting with solar kilns when he heard that María Martínez was coming to ISOMATA. He drove up the mountain to see if he could learn more about traditional firing techniques. He brought in his truck a big bag of clay he had dug in the desert and processed. Trading the bag of clay for a place in the class, Tom then helped María and her family to fire their pots, and he continued helping for the next four summers. He met other Indian artists, and worked with them on the campus and in their homes on the various reservations throughout the Southwest.

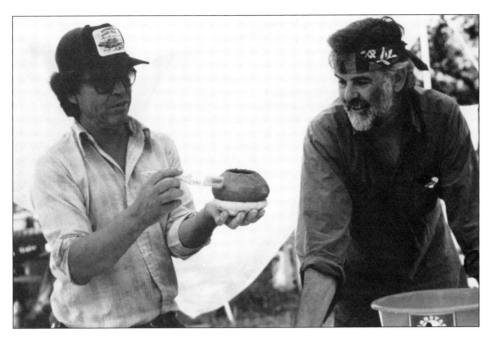

Tom Fresh and Juan Quezada conducting class in Mata Ortiz, 1988.

Gradually he gained a working knowledge of the divergent cultures of the Southwest and became an expert in traditional ceramic techniques. Working across the cultures, he learned the strengths and weaknesses of each. This unique knowledge, combined with his understanding of the chemical and physical properties of the clays, enabled him not only to make his own pottery but to work with experienced native artists on their technical problems.

In 1983, Tom took over the Indian arts at ISOMATA which he expanded into the *Mother Earth Father Sky* program, covering a spectrum of native cultures. He followed Max and Bea Krone's "hands on" principle, whereby all the students worked side by side with the Indian artists, learning skills while developing insights into another culture.

Tom saw Reynaldo and Taurina demonstrate at the Pomona Fair the summer of 1981. He suggested to the Director of ISOMATA that they invite the Mata Ortiz potters to the campus the following summer. When Juan arrived and met Tom, there was an instant rapport. Both appreciated clay and a good joke. Besides, Tom was fluent in Spanish. He had spent several years in Cuba, Spain, and Mexico working as an artist, and he was able to translate for Juan's students. After the class Juan invited Tom to his home in Mata Ortiz. Tom accepted and made his first trip the following year. On the way, he got lost in a rainstorm and scraped off part of his car's tailpipe on a particularly rough stretch of dirt road. Eventually, he found his way to the village and to Juan's house. He stayed for several days, digging clay, making pots, and meeting other Quezada family potters: Nicolás, Reynaldo, Lydia,

Consolación, and Reynalda. It was the first of many trips over the next seven years teaching, making, selling, buying, and talking pottery.

Established Style, Changing Markets

Juan came back to ISOMATA in 1983 and every summer thereafter through 1989. Since his working relationship with Spencer MacCallum was over, he began shipping pots to Amado Peña via a man from El Paso, Conrad Pussman. For some reason, this arrangement did not work out. Pussman then bought a few pieces on his own, but an associate of his, Bobby Rodríguez, also from El Paso, soon became the principal buyer. Bobby Rodríguez sold Quezada family pottery and Indian art successfully all over the Southwest and eventually opened his own art gallery, "Galería De Las Americas," in Socorro, Texas, outside of El Paso.

Fluent in Spanish and much closer to Mata Ortiz than Spencer, Bobby was able to maintain better control of his pottery sources by making more quick trips to the village. He took Juan's class in Idyllwild, relieving Tom as interpreter, and provided pots for the ISOMATA sales gallery. However, even with his experience across the border, Bobby eventually became frustrated with the cultural differences which interfered with the business relationships. He began to concentrate on other aspects of Southwest art, and his purchases in Mata Ortiz declined.

Juan's work had been well received in the marketplace. Promoted by Spencer, Bobby, and others, the prices for his work were at a relatively high level. However when Bobby began to purchase less, this left Juan with no regular buyer and no promoter for his work. More and more traders were coming to the village, but most were buying lower-priced pottery which could be sold easily. It was at this point, the fall of 1985, that I became directly involved with Juan.

By this time, Juan's basic style and technique were established even though he would always continue to experiment with clays and designs. His earliest designs had followed closely the prehistoric examples from the shards. Only the sides of the pots were painted, so that his design field was a horizontal band around the pot. He left the curved bottoms plain as is the style in much of the Indian Southwest. The band he divided into panels which he filled with geometric shapes. Shortly before his discovery by Spencer MacCallum in 1976, Juan realized there was an unfinished "canvas" on the bottom of each vessel. He turned the pots over and began painting circular and curved patterns that fit the circular surface. He left the traditional line around the pot that now separated the two related but different designs. This was the style Juan was moving toward when Spencer found him in 1976, and many of these pots were featured in the traveling show of 1979-80. Spencer called them "transitional" pots. See the picture on page 13.

Gradually Juan did away with the separation between the sides and the bottom until he painted the entire surface as one. His designs now became more curvilinear than geometric, and utilized more open space. Elements of the prehistoric Casas Grandes designs could always be found, but interpreted in new ways and used as building blocks for other original designs. While some pieces still had a traditional look, others were strikingly contemporary. No longer could Juan be described only as a traditional potter. He was a modern contemporary artist whose work far surpassed its traditional origins. Nicolás, Reynaldo, Lydia and others followed his example. Likewise the design elements of Noe, Juan's oldest son and the best of the second generation, frequently bear little resemblance to the prehistoric.

The First Trip

When I made my first trip to Mata Ortiz in September, 1984, these were the kind of pots I saw. I had become friends with Tom Fresh while I was consulting in ISOMATA's finance office. Tom introduced me to Juan on campus that summer, and I became fascinated with his story. I urged Tom to take me to Mata Ortiz. He did not take me seriously because everyone around the campus wanted to join Tom on his trips. However, one day toward the end of the summer session, he suddenly asked me what kind of car I drove. I reminded him he had been in my Honda several times, but that would not do. The classes were over, and he needed a large vehicle to take Juan, Guille, daughter Laura, and Taurina Baca back to Mata Ortiz. After a few telephone calls, I managed to borrow my father's big black 1977 Chrysler New Yorker. The Chrysler only made one trip, but Tom and I would make many similar ones over the next six years.

We were supposed to leave Wednesday, September 12, but Tom had to take Juan to Bluestone Editions in Anaheim to sign his first set of etchings, *Mis Animales,* a project initiated by Tom which is elaborated on later. They did not get back to the campus until after four, too late to go to the bank. So we rescheduled for nine-thirty the next morning, time enough to pack and get to the bank by ten for traveling money. Tom arrived covered with wasp stings. In trying to fix the water system at his ranch he had unearthed a nest of wasps. Finally ready, we filled every square inch of the Chrysler with gear and people. Try as we might, there was no room for Juan's great-grandmother's pot, a large *olla* for making *tesgüino.* Spencer had found this years before in San Lorenzo, Juan's mother's village, and taken it to San Pedro. However, the large *olla* had to wait for another trip to return to Mexico.

The route was via Interstate 10, east through Palm Springs to Blythe, across the Colorado River into Arizona where the giant Saguaro cacti begin. Juan was fascinated by the date gardens in Indio, but we could not find dates for sale. It took three hours to cross the desert of western Arizona from the Colorado River to Phoenix. From Phoenix Interstate 10 turns south to Tucson. The prehistoric ruin of Casa Grande (singular — not to be confused with Casas Grandes) is to the east of the highway near the town of Coolidge. This is a national monument with an interpretive center on a site of the Hohokam, the major farming culture which covered much of southern Arizona in ancient times. The interesting point is that its rammed-earth construction is remarkably similar to that of Paquimé and the other ruins of the Casas Grandes (plural) culture far to the south in Chihuahua.

After Tucson, the 10 turns east again. Shortly at Benson, we turned south on Highway 80, passing through Tombstone over Mule Pass to the old mining town of Bisbee perched on the hills above a gigantic open pit. We stayed at the Copper Queen Hotel, a restored relic of the heyday of the great Phelps Dodge mine. Tom disappeared the next morning so for the first time I was alone with Juan and his family in the dining room with nothing but mostly-forgotten high school Spanish. The Mexican people are very polite and helpful in these situations, and together we got through the menu and ordered breakfast. However, I was very nervous and vowed to study the language.

Douglas, Arizona, on the border is about 30 minutes from Bisbee. Approaching the town, we could see the huge twin stacks of the smelter with their mile-long plumes of smoke trailing downwind. (Later after a long environmental battle the smelter was closed down, and in 1991 the stacks and smelter were removed.) On the main street of Douglas is the Gadsden Hotel, another faded monument to the mining era. Inside we took a few minutes to look at the gilded pillars and the genuine Tiffany windows depicting plants of the Sonoran Desert. I bought Mexican travel insurance at a nearby agency and was warned that I might have trouble at the border because I did not own the car. Sure enough, the Mexican official at the border rejected my hastily contrived "permission" letter because it was not notarized. We would have to talk to a higher official.

After much discussion, Tom suggested *veinte dolares.* The official suggested *cuarenta.* We settled on *treinta* and drove the big Chrysler into Agua Prieta, Douglas' sister town across the border.

Sprawling along the border next to Douglas in the state of Sonora, Agua Prieta was the scene of Pancho Villa's last great battle in the fall of 1915. From their camps in the hills south of town, his troops and cavalry charged the Federal forces at night. But huge searchlights fed by electricity from Douglas exposed them to machine gun fire; men and horses went down in a bloody tangle, and Villa suffered a decisive defeat. Looking across the town straggling south from the border into the dusty plains, it was hard to imagine this was the field of battle that reduced the great Villa from a commander of armies to essentially a guerrilla fighter.

A few miles south of the border the highway entered the first of three small mountain ranges, beyond which is more of the Sonoran desert. Beyond the second range are wide-open high plains with nothing in sight in any direction but the distant mountains. At the top of the third range, after climbing narrow switchbacks is a 40-50 foot pass cut through the rock which divides the state of Sonora from Chihuahua. After Agua Prieta, there are no towns until Janos, in Chihuahua, an old colonial town with an eighteenth-century church, now a truck stop at the intersection of the highways to Douglas, El Paso, and Nuevo Casas Grandes. Before climbing into the forest of oaks at the base of the last range, we stopped at a tumble-down adobe truckers' restaurant for cokes, flour tortillas and beans.

Between Janos and Nuevo Casas Grandes, the plains gradually change to lush farmland. The first community is Dublan, originally a Mormon village, now grown together with Nuevo Casas Grandes. The latter is the only town of any size in northern Chihuahua except Ciudad Juárez on the border adjacent to El Paso. Nuevo Casas Grandes was formed along the railroad in the late nineteenth century and, due in part to Mormon enterprise, has grown into the agricultural center of northern Chihuahua.

In the 1880s when Utah was trying to become a state, thousands of Mormons fled to this area to escape the censure on polygamy. They started growing apples, and their farms and packing sheds soon expanded into a major industry. Many returned to the United States after the 1910 Revolution when Villa's men roamed the area. Enough stayed, however, to maintain an Anglo-style enclave with excellent schools. One well-known local name is Romney, the family of George Romney, the former American Motors Company president and Michigan politician. Many Mexicans who can afford it send their children to the Mormon schools. Classes are taught in English and Spanish, and American-style football is played. Graduates often go on to college in Chihuahua City or the United States.

Also many Mennonites live near Nuevo Casas Grandes, moving there from Canada and the United States in their perpetual search for a peaceful place to practice their religion. The white cheeses from their dairies are sold in roadside stands along the highway. They can be readily seen walking the streets of Nuevo Casas Grandes among the Mexican shoppers, cowboys, and Tarahumara Indians — the men and boys in bib overalls and straw hats and the women and girls in long dresses and bonnets.

After buying groceries and picking up Juan's truck, we delivered Taurina to her parent's house at the south end of Nuevo Casas Grandes. She was very anxious to get home after a few weeks in the United States. The house was a small yellow block building facing a dirt street where we were greeted warmly by her parents and invited to sit on the plastic covered sofa. The Baca family is from Mata Ortiz and still maintains a house and cattle there. The living room where we sat was decorated with a print of the "Last Supper," a large wedding photo of Taurina's parents, and highly-glazed ceramic animals, a decorative style typical of the homes in Mata Ortiz. Taurina's mother served us apples, and Tom gave Señor Baca some medicine he had requested. He had hurt his head in an accident in the hills looking for cattle. Taurina showed us some of her very large pots that had cracked, a perennial problem for her. Tom and Juan talked with her at length about the firing problems of such large pieces.

We followed Juan in his truck out of town passing through orchards and pasture land until we could see above the trees the steeples of the church of Casas Grandes. This is Casas Grandes *Viejo*, the old village near the great ruined city of Paquimé. It too was the site of at least two battles in the Revolution. After one, Villa was supposed to have lined up his prisoners in a column and shot them with one bullet to save ammunition. A few miles farther is Colonia Juárez, the other principal Mormon settlement along the way. The many brick houses and the two-story brick school with cupola and wrought iron gate trace their style directly to nineteenth-century Utah. Above the town are ranch-style houses owned by prosperous Mormon farmers which would not be out of place in a Southern California suburb.

The paved road crosses the Piedras Verdes River on a very narrow single-

San Diego, a former hacienda of Luis Terrazas, three miles from Mata Ortiz.

lane bridge. Past the bridge, the route turns left, leaving the pavement for 12 jolting miles of rocky dirt roads. Beyond the orchards, fields, and scattered adobe houses south of Colonia Juárez, the road enters the *llano*, the high plains (over 6,000 feet) between the Sierra Madre to the west and a smaller range, the Cerro Rejado, to the east. The prominent notched peak in the Cerro Rejado, El Indio, looks like a great Indian head turned up at the sky. It is the backdrop to Mata Ortiz and our landmark. The dirt roads tend to change from trip to trip, but we are on course as long as we head toward El Indio and as long as it stays light.

One dark night, rather than stay in Nuevo Casas Grandes, we headed out across the *llano* in two vehicles with Tom in the lead. We could not see anything at all, let alone El Indio, except for Tom's tail lights. I commented to my passengers that it seemed we had been on this road a long time. Suddenly, Tom stopped, turned around and roared past us in the opposite direction shouting, *"Encinos,* there are no damned *encinos* in Mata Ortiz!"* I explained to my startled riders as I turned around and tried to catch up, that Tom had seen oak trees, *encinos,* along the road and had realized that we were heading into the mountains away from Mata Ortiz toward Zaragoza. Located high in the Sierra, this little lumber town was originally called "Willy" after a gringo who ran a whiskey still there. After the Revolution, all such towns with anglo names were renamed after Mexican heroes. However, locals still refer to Zaragoza as "Weelee." The road to Willy through the oaks was not where we were supposed to be.

The road we wanted runs to the southeast through the *Ejido* of San Diego. Prior to the Revolution, this was one of the haciendas of the powerful Luis Terraza. The largest land owner in Chihuahua with over one million acres, he was reputed to have ninety-nine haciendas over his feudal domain. The road passes in front of a great house with initials L T carved in the stone lintel. This crumbling edifice and the huge store house and stables nearby are reminders of the feudal system that concentrated the wealth of the country into a few families like the Terrazas prior to 1910. A mile or two farther is the fence line between *Ejidos* San Diego and Mata Ortiz. The road goes up a rise, and suddenly Mata Ortiz is laid out below, stretching along the river with El Indio in the background. The first row of houses faces west, fronting the railroad station. Along the tracks, box cars are parked, some old and dilapidated and others newly painted bright orange, matching the railroad bridge crossing the river in the distance.

This first trip, Juan and his family still lived on the outskirts of town. Their house of adobe brick stood near the road on a slight rise which sloped to the river. From the flat roof poked a TV aerial and the electrical power lines which came to Mata Ortiz in 1975. The well in back had a low cement curb to keep out dirt. A plastic bucket with a rope sat nearby. It had been a wet summer, and the land was very green and thick with yellow and purple flowers. Horses, horse-drawn wagons, and pickups passed the house up and down the road.

We arrived in the early evening. A large group of adults and children waited along the road. They surrounded us talking and laughing. Juan and Guille were obviously glad to be home. Juan has a warm relationship with his children, particularly with Juan Junior, the cowboy of the family. Junior took everyone to see the big corral he and Noe had made while their father was gone. They had split railroad ties to make the posts and rails. It was very large and impressed me. Then Junior brought out something else to show his father, a beautiful pot made by Noe. Juan looked over the piece carefully and smiled with pleasure.

Dusk fell and Guille went to the kitchen while the men strolled down to the river. There were jokes and laughter as they brought Juan up to date on recent events. When dinner was called, the men gathered in the kitchen around a round table made by a local *carpintero*. Guille served steak and beans with a local goat cheese. I was very hungry, and the food tasted wonderful. After we were finished, the women and children ate, and the men went back out to the clear night and the sounds of the river. The talk was quieter now. A train passed in the distance.

I thought we were staying in the Baca's empty house, but Guille made up a double bed for me in the living room, and I crawled into it gratefully. Juan's collection of birds and animals, which seemed to come alive at night, kept me awake for awhile. Juan likes wild creatures, and usually has a miscellaneous collection around, many brought in by neighbors. When the family moved into the center of town years later, someone brought him a fawn to share the enclosed yard with a sheep and the dog. As it grew, it developed horns and became too aggressive for the various grandchildren playing in the yard, so Juan and his boys took it into the mountains. A few months later someone brought him another fawn.

For a while, I wondered whether Juan's parrot and the guinea pig, which was running laps in the kitchen, also might be better off far away in the mountains, but I finally went to sleep. Early in the morning, I pulled a heavy

Weaver Señor José Camacho with one of his wool blankets, 1990.

wool blanket over me from the foot of the bed. Later in the trip, I met the weaver of the blanket, Señor José Camacho, an elderly man from Saltillo, who lived and worked in one of the old boxcars next to the tracks. Camacho wove saddle and bed blankets from raw wool bought from sheep ranchers. He carded it by hand, and spun the yarn on a crude spinning wheel. The patterns were simple stripes, primarily browns and grays, of the natural wool colors. Occasionally he would jazz up a piece with a pink or orange stripe from commercial yarn.

When we visited Camacho, he was just finishing the dinner he had cooked on his little wood stove. He was very pleased to show us his work area with its handmade loom and rich lanolin smell from the stacks of raw wool. He showed us how he used his tools, and Tom suggested that he should card the wool more thoroughly to get all the stickers out. Camacho said there were no stickers and rubbed a blanket against his cheek saying in Spanish that it was as soft as a baby's behind. Tom replied that once he had been in bed with a beautiful lady under one of Camacho's blankets, and she rolled over on a sticker, leaped out of bed, and he had not seen her since. Señor Camacho laughed and choked so hard we began to worry about him.

I woke early to find Guille already in the kitchen, separated from the living room by only a curtain. From the outhouse behind the new corral, came the voices of Juan's younger boys cleaning this edifice, so I decided to take a

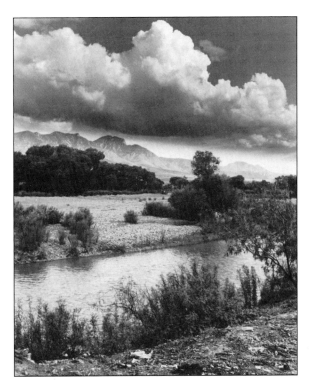

*The Palanganas River
and El Indio.*
Photo: Trudy Adler

walk in the mesquite. I returned to a breakfast of coffee, canned juice, fried eggs, and tortillas. As we lingered over the second cup of coffee, that day's visitors began to arrive. The first was the mechanic, Señor Martínez, to repair a tire on Juan's truck. A lug had been twisted off in the process of removing the wheel.

Señor Martínez is a true shade-tree mechanic, working under a large tree behind his house. He keeps the village's old pickups going over the rough roads, and several times he revived Spencer's Datsun. Martínez's family lives closer to town between the arena and the school. Several of his children and grandchildren have become very competent potters.

In 1986, Tom hired Martínez to help transport ISOMATA students from Mata Ortiz to the Cave of the Olla, a rough four-hour drive into the mountains. His pickup, built from junked parts, had no matching fenders or door, a windshield with a hole patched with a glass plug and resin, and an interior decorated with fringe, a statue of Our Lady, and decals. On the way, a shock absorber fell off and one tire blew which hardly dampened an otherwise glorious overnight excursion. Later that year, Señor Martínez painted the pickup light blue — with a brush — carefully outlining the letters for CHEVROLET in white.

The next to arrive was carpenter-electrician-policeman Simón López to discuss a carpentry problem. Simón is the husband of Juan's sister Reynalda, one of the prominent potters in the village. He arrived in the horse-drawn wagon he had made years ago, essentially a large rectangular box on old car axles and wheels. Simon later built many things for Tom — benches, tables, outhouses — in preparation for the various on-site classes.

Today's problem was the roof. Juan was not satisfied with the light inside his workshop. After much discussion, Tom suggested a slanting roof with a north-facing window on top to admit light. Everyone thought it was a great idea; however, the roof never changed. Juan continued to rely on a tangle of cords and bulbs inside to give him adequate light for painting.

During this discussion, three North Americans from Santa Fe drove into the yard looking for pots. They had heard about Juan and had an idea of buying a thousand pots with old designs for a few dollars each to be sold as gifts for children. Although Juan and everyone else was amused at the idea of his pots being sold this way, Juan wanted to accommodate them, perhaps hoping that one of his family could make money. However the amount offered was unrealistic. Then a young man named Carlos rode by on horseback carrying three pots in a sack. Carlos was a beginner and his quality poor, but the men finally bought all three for $20. Juan gave the Americans directions to other potters, but in about an hour, they passed the house on the way out of town, apparently without their thousand childrens' gifts.

After a lunch of potato soup and tortillas, Juan invited Tom and me for a ride in his pickup. We got in the cab, and Junior rode in the back. As he turned on the ignition, Juan told us he was a terrible driver, and he began the first of several stories of near calamities. He said all of his family think he is *"loco"* behind the wheel. In fact, in later years as the family prospered and cars became more common, Juan rarely drove. Whether this was his choice or by popular demand was never clear.

This time he drove straight out across the prairie, turning here and there through the grazing cattle in accordance with Junior's shouted instructions from the back. This was Juan's first cattle inspection since his return. Junior knew each of his father's animals by sight as they grazed among the others on the *ejido* land. At a hole in the ground, one of Juan's sources of clay, we interrupted the inspection trip to dig and fill a sack. This hole was a small blank spot in a solid carpet of yellow flowers stretching clear to the hills to the northwest. Farther on along an arroyo, we collected more clay where it had been exposed by flood waters. Then Junior pointed out a calf which was not branded, and we began a hot pursuit. Back and forth across the flowers we drove. The calf's mama would try to run interference, and Juan would try to get between them close enough for Junior to throw his lasso from the back of the truck. But the calf was too quick, veering off at the last instant or running straight in front of the truck, creating an ineffective tail chase.

Finally, Junior jumped out of the truck, got a clear shot, and skillfully threw the rope over the running calf's head. We jumped out of the cab as Junior flipped him over. They did not have a branding iron, so Juan took out his pocketknife and notched the calf's ear for identification, then castrated him. The job done, the bawling calf ran off to his mama. We continued the census, stopping briefly at a *moctezuma*, or prehistoric mound, riddled with holes left by pot hunters. Shards were scattered about, along with a broken *metate* and a large *mano* stone. Just beyond, Junior found another beautiful little white-faced calf. The chase was on again, but this time Mama was a much better blocker, and she led the truck into a rough area full of mesquite. We chased the animals on wheel and foot until we were exhausted. We never got close enough to rope the calf. Finally, Juan collected us all, and we headed back joking about the futile effort. All agreed this clearly was a job for horses.

By the time we arrived back at Juan's house it was dusk. Hot and sweaty, Tom and I went down to bathe in the river near a place behind some willows where concrete work diverted part of the water into a small irrigation canal. Although running water serviced the central section of the village, Juan's house had only the well at that time. The women and children bathed in wash tubs inside the house, and the men used either the tubs or the river. In spite of the lack of fancy porcelain, everyone kept very clean. The children walking down the dirt road to school each morning in their pastels and whites looked like little scrubbed and combed fashion models.

After a dinner of tacos and guacamole, the men took us into town to see the bulls which had been gathered for the next day's *jaripeo*, a Chihuahua-style rodeo and part of the fiesta celebrating the holiday of *16 de Septiembre*.

In town, we crossed to a large, divided corral near the railroad station with horses on one side and bulls and steers on the other. Young boys ran about, playing on the fences. Cowboys came and went, greeting friends and commenting on the quality and condition of the bulls. We went back to an alley where a number of men stood around in the dusty gloom. Beer sales had been banned in Mata Ortiz, but because of the holiday a temporary cantina had been set up in an old adobe building. Tom charged in to see what was happening. I followed him into a scene from a Western movie — hazy smoke, bare walls, and cowboys in hats and boots leaning on the plank bar drinking *Carta Blanca* beer. I was a little nervous. Perhaps I had seen too many Westerns, and it took two or three *Carta Blancas* before I felt calm enough to melt into the scene. Tom, however, had a great time.

The Jaripeo

Riders passed by the Quezada house all the next morning on their way to town for the *jaripeo*. While Tom and Juan mixed and strained the clay collected the previous day, the rest of the family prepared for the fiesta. Noe dressed up and left on the family horse to join the other young people.

September 16 is Mexico's Independence Day. On that day in 1810, Father Miguel Hidalgo Y Costilla, the parish priest of Dolores, Guanajuato, began the revolt against the Spanish — the hated *gachupines* — by ringing the church bells and inciting the people with a speech that has come through history as the "Grito de Dolores." Every year, each town and village in Mexico celebrates with a fiesta which culminates in some form of the *grito* given by the mayor or other appropriate dignitary.

On this date in 1988, the ISOMATA on-site class was camped high in the Sierra Madre near the Cave of the Olla. That night, next to a huge campfire the irrepressible Pino stood on a bench straight as a soldier and gave the *Grito*, in this case a series of *viva Mexicos*, echoed by the assembly of students, Quezada family members, camp helpers, and local farmers. Afterwards the students danced by the fire to tapes played in the truck cassette player. This caused an already weak battery to go completely dead, but fortunately not until the party was over.

For other holiday fiestas with *jaripeos,* notably November 20, the celebration of the Revolution of 1910, a queen and court members are selected to ride in a parade and to preside over the evening dance. The parade features children dressed as Pancho Villa-type revolutionaries.

After lunch, the family made ready to go to the *jaripeo.* The little girls wore bright dresses, the boys cowboy gear. All piled into the pickup and headed to the large circular arena. People arrived from all directions, some in pickups and others on horseback. The arena was probably two hundred yards in diameter, surrounded by a brick wall with glass shards set in the top. Inside, back end to the wall, were parked all of the pickups. These provided the grandstands, the elder members in the cab and everyone else in back. In some places where there was no glass, the top of the wall itself provided a seat. The wall was just high enough for a man on horseback to see over. This allowed dozens of boys and young men to ride and gallop outside without missing anything important inside. A large truck served as a band stand, flanked by a smaller truck dispensing beer and another dispensing ice cream. The beer truck always had a large crowd around it. Later in the afternoon, one fighting drunk was removed after his mother came down to bawl him out.

Behind the arena stood the corral with the bulls, bull riding being the major event of the *jaripeo.* The bulls had been driven there in the morning through the mesquite from the railroad station. Inside the corral, six to eight young men ran around in great clouds of dust yelling and hitting the bulls with ropes to drive them into a chute leading to the arena. The system looked very inefficient but the boys were having a great time. The event started with a young rider mounting a small bull in the chute and grasping a leather strap buckled around its middle. The gate opened and the boy rode the bucking bull for a few seconds, ending on his back in the dirt or if more fortunate, pulled off by supporting horsemen. Then the band played wildly, and the real act began. Chasing the bull, the horsemen roped forelegs and hind legs separately, threw him, undid the strap, and returned it to the judges' stand for the next bull. One *vaquero,* on a dancing black horse with three white stockings, always undid the strap. Holding it in his hand above his head, he would gallop pell-mell straight for the judges' stand, pull his horse to a skidding stop at the last instant, and toss the strap to the stand — always with a cigarette drooping from the corner of his mouth.

Sometimes a bull got away from the horsemen, and wedged himself between the pickups, scattering the spectators until the *vaqueros* could work them out again. While the bulls and horses dashed about, people walked around casually visiting and buying ice cream. When a bull got too close or between the trucks, children got into the act, throwing clods and empty cans at the stampeding animal.

The shadows grew longer, projecting distorted sombreros against the brown dirt of the ring. The rodeo played itself out in the distance.

All of a sudden there was a wrenching scream. Across the ring a wiry figure had become detached from the bull he was trying to ride, cartwheeled, and landed on his head. He lay spread-eagled on his back, twitching. His mother broke away from the crowd wailing and ran toward the now motionless figure. The band stopped playing. Several other people went out and stood around the young man and his kneeling mother. Her screams were the only sounds that reached us. Others milled around, but no one did anything. I thought the boy was probably dead, but there was no doctor in the village. Finally, several men picked up the young man, whose name turned out to be Antonio, age 18, and carried him to the back of a pickup truck. If he had back injuries he was done for, I thought. Men held long discussions around the truck. The mother, María Ortega, continued to sob, comforted by Juan's sister Consolación, but there was no action. The band began to play and gradually the activities of the rodeo picked up again.

Discussion around the pickup continued. Juan, a respected man in the town, was consulted at length. María made passionate exhortations. Finally a group detached itself from the crowd around the truck and approached me. Tom translated.

"They want you to take the boy to Nuevo Casas Grandes (an hour away) to find a doctor."

"But why don't these people take him? There must be a hundred pickup trucks right here in the ring," I said.

"Because they don't think it will do any good," he replied. "The doctor's office will be closed. The pharmacies will be closed. The boy will die anyway, so why should they leave the rodeo? All of these things, I guess. The mother begged Juan, and he thinks every effort should be made to get the boy to a doctor."

I agreed to go. Juan immediately climbed to the top of the wall from the truck bed and surveyed the line of riders outside the wall. He called one over. "Give this man your horse," he said in Spanish. I climbed over the wall and onto the horse and rode to Juan's house where the car was parked.

I returned driving dramatically through the main entrance across the ring, to the side where the boy sat slumped over in the pickup. He was not dead. In fact he was conscious and sitting up, but he was a very sick cowboy. We helped him in the back of the car, and then everyone else tried to get into the vehicle. Finally, María, two others, and Juan crowded in, and we left. Tom, the only one that could translate, was pushed aside and never got close to getting in the vehicle.

Immediately, Antonio was sick. Juan and I got him out of the back just in time to avoid a mess. This time we put him in the front with the seat way back where he was more comfortable. He was sick twice more but seemed slightly better.

We spent a long time in Colonia Juárez and Casas Grandes looking for a doctor. Finally they found a small clinic staffed by a woman. She examined Antonio, concluded he had a concussion, gave him a shot, prescribed some medicine, and sent us on. We then proceeded to drive all over Nuevo Casas Grandes for a long, long time looking for an open pharmacy. After many tries, someone opened up, and the prescription was filled.

It was long after dark when we returned. Everyone seemed to think the trip successful. María was vastly relieved. Juan was very tired and went to bed. The rest of us talked and wondered about the events of the day. As for Antonio, the rumor was that he went on to the dance.

The next day, the whole town seemed a bit hung over. Tom and Juan spent the morning planning the upcoming on-site class. They met with Oscar, Consolación's eldest son, to discuss cleaning and painting a vacant house in the center of town to use as classrooms and student quarters. A long list was finally prepared and we spent the rest of the day in Nuevo Casas Grandes shopping for paint, cement and groceries. A fan belt broke in the Chrysler coming out of a flooded wash but did not seem to affect the operation of the vehicle. We could not find the correct size belt, but a mechanic said it was for the smog device and not critical.

Guille served us a delicious dinner that night of fish soup, or *caldo*, to which we added fresh lime juice. Juan left and then rushed in a short while later to get us to drive him to the center of the village. Tom could not explain. Something about Indians he said. Without asking more questions, we drove off to Nicolás' workshop. Inside, we saw three Tarahumara Indians sitting on the floor. They had walked to Mata Ortiz from Nuevo Casas Grandes, and Nicolás had invited them to sleep in his shop.

The Tarahumara live in the mountain area to the south made famous by the great canyon system known collectively as "Copper Canyon" or *Barranca del Cobre.* In earlier times their territories extended into northern Chihuahua. Apache incursions and Spanish settlements forced them into the present rugged terrain that was only pierced by the railroad in 1961. Today they will travel north on foot to Nuevo Casas Grandes to sell their baskets and herbs or to beg. There on the streets they add bright color to the mix of Mexican shoppers, Mennonites, Mormons, and *vaqueros*.

The three in Nicolás' workshop wore cast-off clothing, one with a patch on his shirt that said "Oyster Bay, New York." Their hair hung long, held by a band of red cloth. On their feet, they wore tire-tread sandals, held by a single thong through the first two toes attached to another thong around the ankle. The top of each foot was callused where the thong rubbed; the rest of their skin shone a polished brown.

The oldest Indian lay on the floor, eyes closed. The other two stood while ten of us including children crowded into the room. Juan, who must have seen them often before, seemed fascinated. He talked with them in Spanish about their travels, their baskets, etc., occasionally eliciting a laugh. When we left, the Indians went to sleep.

I got up early to go back and see them, but they had left. So I spent some time browsing in Nicolás' workshop. He had made several large open bowls or *cazuelas* done in Mimbres style. Juan had done several of these lately, and Nicolás had followed his lead. Bobby Rodríguez said that when he began coming to Mata Ortiz in 1983 it was common for all of the family members except Reynaldo to emulate whatever Juan was doing. A few years later, however, most had developed their own techniques and styles.

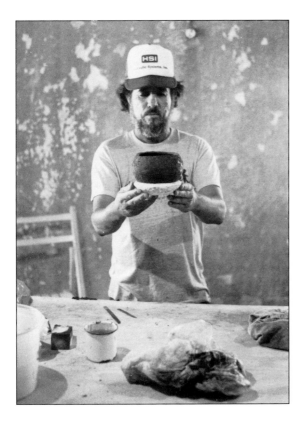

*Nicolás Quezada examines a
pot for symmetry, 1990.*

Nicolás' workshop served as an exhibition space for his pots and for a work space. He began this addition to the east side of his house above the river in 1980. He prepared his own plans and did much of the work. Spencer said the plans were ingenious and quite different from conventional architectural drawings. When he finished this two-room space the following year, Nicolás hosted a celebration complete with business cards, printed in Nuevo Casas Grandes, announcing the *"Galería de los Artes Palanganas."* It was undoubtedly the only gallery between Ciudad Juárez and Chihuahua City.

Nicolás' party was on December 12, 1981, the day of the Virgin of Guadalupe and of the Matachine dances. Nicolás and his wife Gloria served *bizcochos,* a kind of biscuit, and *tesgüino,* a non-alcoholic drink made from fresh corn sprouts ground lightly on a *metate* stone and then boiled for twelve or so hours. This is a traditional Tarahumara drink for saints' day celebrations. They often allow it to ferment and then drink it during long periods of dancing, with outstanding results. Usually in northern Chihuahua it is not kept long enough to ferment.

Ten years later, Nicolás completely remodeled a large building across the street from his house. Again, he did much of the work. The corner brick fireplace and chimney were beautifully made, showing that his manual skills are not limited to pottery. In 1991 Nicolás moved to the newly remodeled home, allowing his oldest son, José, with his new wife and baby, to occupy the older

Consolación, Juan's oldest sister, 1990.

home. All of the family potters — Nicolás, José, and younger son Leonel — continue to use the workshop.

Later that morning we visited the home of Consolación, the eldest of the eleven Quezada brothers and sisters. Her pòttery styles are unique and can readily be identified. On some of her pieces, she alternates incised bands with bands of polychrome design. On others she slips the entire pot with an unusual wine-colored liquid clay. On this surface she paints black designs. The material for this slip, a soft red rock, was found by her son-in-law, Pedro, husband of her daughter Dora. He found this unusual rock near their home in La Junta, the junction of the north-south and east-west railroads 200 miles to the south. He forwards the raw rock regularly via the railroad. This color is exclusively Consolación's, and imitators have always failed. Also, Consolación's pots are usually large, sometimes very large. Juan said that for a long time he and Consolación were the only ones who could form such large pots. Others would not work fast enough, and the bottoms would dry and crack while the top was still wet. Also others could not "see" the large pot, and it would be out of shape when finished.

Consolación works hard, doubling as a housekeeper and potter. Her husband, Lupe, who grows beans, potatoes, and corn on two plots of ground or *labores,* helps process her clay. Her daughter-in-law, Marta, from next door often helps with the firing, apparently a variant of the tradition of the daughter-in-law helping in the mother-in-law's kitchen. Like most Mexican families, the Quezadas are close. Nicolás takes his morning coffee very early each day in Consolación's kitchen. Other family members drop by daily. When Consolación started potting, she could form the pots but not paint well. Nicolás painted her early pieces, all the while encouraging her to learn. Her first designs were copies of Nicolás' work. However, sometime between 1976 when Spencer arrived and 1984, she perfected her painting skills and developed her own style.

At the end of the week I had to leave. Tom decided to stay longer so I returned alone in the big Chrysler. In old Casas Grandes I turned off the pavement to the ruins of Paquimé, where I wandered completely by myself for an hour.

This first trip was a prototype for more than forty trips made over the years by me, Tom, and a small cadre of *aficionados* who loved the scene. We switched to four-wheel-drive vehicles (the Chrysler never returned), and there were many variations, but the basic format remained the same, although never as special as the first time.

Selling Juan Quezada

In September, 1985, Tom Fresh conducted an on-site class with Juan in Mata Ortiz. The students lived and worked right in Juan's crowded house. Four women slept in one bedroom that had been set up for them, and the rest of us slept in the workshop, one on the table and two underneath. Simón López, Reynalda's husband, built a shower that Tom designed, consisting of a large wooden frame with a wooden slatted floor, the walls and door covered with black plastic. The water came from plastic "sun shower" bags. It was a great success, and the family continued to use it until a strong wind blew it apart.

One of the students was Judith Anderson, who had participated in several Native Arts classes in Idyllwild. She enjoyed a good rapport with students and instructors and began to assist Tom with the details of his classes, becoming a "regular" on trips to Mata Ortiz.

After a few days of the on-site class, Tom and Judith became aware that Juan was concerned about selling his work. Spencer McCallum, Bobby Rodríguez and others had helped establish his reputation, but now he had no regular buyer and was dependent on the irregular visits of traders. After much discussion, the three of us — Tom, Judith, and I — agreed to buy Juan's pots on a regular basis and represent him in the United States.

People often ask why we became involved. The distances were awesome. Buying, selling, packing, unpacking, transporting, and negotiating all were expensive, time consuming and often frustrating. We did it because it was a special privilege to be involved with a great artist. If we had been asked to help Picasso 80 years ago, would we have refused? This is how we felt about Juan.

We called our new venture "The Art of Juan Quezada." Each month we purchased a certain dollar amount of pots, and we began a selling program.

Our objective was to help Juan reach what we felt was his rightful place in the pantheon of great ceramic artists. To do this we had to sell pots. However, we always maintained that we were not in the pottery business, but rather in the business of selling Juan Quezada.

One who helped us a great deal was John Wingate from Riverside, California. A veteran Baja traveler, he loved to drive anything — a car, four-wheel drive, boat, or airplane. The rough roads of Chihuahua were a particular attraction. He became a good friend of Pino (José Molina), and they made several trips together, including one across the rugged Sierra Madre near the Copper Canyon where the maps show no roads. Since Pino spoke no English and John little Spanish, the trips had more than one challenge. John's interest was the travel, and he never was directly involved with the pottery. His mechanical skills and willingness to drive or fly long distances provided strong support to those of us working with the potters and the various sales outlets.

At this time in the mid 1980's, Juan was making a variety of pots. Each trip we looked forward to seeing his latest creations. It addition to the basic *olla* forms, he made pots in the form of fish, frogs, owls and human effigies. The effigies often featured exaggerated mouths and stomachs with arms and legs protruding from the side of the pot. Some pots had exquisitely modeled bear or ram heads on the sides or lizards with their tails winding in and out of the pot rim. He did one series of Mimbres-style pieces and another of *olla*s with long necks. This gave great variety to our early inventories. Later Juan became more interested in painting and pure design and therefore concentrated on the classic *olla* shapes.

Our first major sales show of "The Art of Juan Quezada" was in February, 1986, at the Squash Blossom Gallery in Palm Desert. Juan and Guille came for three days for the opening of the show. The gallery owners, Bud and Joan Towne, were affable hosts and held a grand dinner party at their home honoring Juan and two other artists. The show was well attended, but we learned a valuable lesson.

Juan and Guille attended the Friday night opening party at the gallery and remained faithfully in or near the gallery for the entire opening weekend. This turned out to be a waste of Juan's talents and terribly boring for them both. Juan's great charisma did not come across best in a conversational setting especially if only English was being spoken. We realized that the relationship of Juan and his admirers came alive when he was actually working. The act of forming a lump of raw clay into a perfectly symmetrical pot fascinated an audience. Questions and answers began to flow via a translator and an intimacy was established as everyone became involved with the pot evolving before their eyes. This was the lesson. Juan could not be expected to hold court like an artist in a Parisian salon. But if he formed or painted a pot, everyone went home feeling that they *knew* Juan Quezada.

From then on, if Juan was to be present at an opening, we tried to arrange a demonstration or workshop.

Juan returned to ISOMATA to teach in 1986. His class was accompanied by an exhibit in the Todd Gallery on campus. This was followed by an exhibition in a sales gallery in San Diego. A pattern began to emerge of a yearly round of sales gallery shows, demonstrations, and Indian shows, punctuated by special events such as museum exhibitions. This round was capped each summer by the ISOMATA-sponsored classes and exhibitions.

Selling at Indian shows was Hermann Knechtle's idea. Hermann was a young man from a family of artists and furniture makers in Switzerland. He came to this country a few years ago and eventually established his own business in Pasadena as a maker of molds for special airplane parts. In the course of events he met and married Marisa Nava of Nuevo Casas Grandes. A recent Brigham Young University graduate, Marisa was working as an interior designer in Los Angeles. On a trip to Nuevo Casas Grandes to visit Marisa's parents, Hermann discovered the pottery. No one in the family could tell him much about it, but Marisa's brother offered to guide the young couple to Mata Ortiz and to Juan's house. Juan and Guille greeted them hospitably as they do all guests, and Juan showed them a beautiful array of his work. Hermann was overwhelmed by what he saw. The fine-line designs and precise work appealed to his artistic sense as well as to his Swiss sense of order. Juan took him to see other potters, and he bought the best of what he saw.

Back at Juan's house, Hermann was shown one of my business cards, and when he returned to Pasadena he called me. We spent an evening together talking pottery. He had seen a large Indian show in Pasadena and wanted to participate in similar shows. These typically are sponsored by promoters who take over large halls like the Pasadena or Santa Monica convention centers. The promoter advertises the event, and traders, galleries, artists and anyone else with Indian art to sell rent booths to exhibit their merchandise. Antique and other collector shows follow this same format. I was dubious, but Hermann's enthusiasm won me over. "The Art of Juan Quezada" joined forces with Hermann Knechtle, and we went on to do fifteen shows over the next three years.

Each time, I provided Juan's pots for the booth, and Herman provided what we referred to as the "best of the rest" from other good potters in the village. Overall the pottery sold better than I expected. Juan's work was expensive for the casual visitor, and most just looked. However, hundreds passed the booth over a three-day show to be stopped by the beauty and obvious quality of the pots. They were fascinated by Juan's story, and often purchased a less-expensive piece by another potter. We added them to our mailing list which was based on an updated list of Spencer's and began to see familiar faces at succeeding shows. Sooner or later at a show, at a gallery, or at Idyllwild, these people would return with enough money so they could own "just one Juan pot."

As the mailing list grew, I decided to send a newsletter, another Spencer MacCallum idea. He had sent seven between 1978 and 1982. My first, headed "The Art of Juan Quezada," was dated November, 1987. The purpose was to update Juan's story for the intervening years. The response was so encouraging that I sent one each spring and fall for four years. Letters and calls came from all over the country from people wanting more information or who were just anxious to pick up the threads of the story.

We continued with sales gallery shows, two of which stand out. By 1987, Juan's first two prints (discussed on page 67), *Mis Animales* and *Liebre con Tarahumar*, had been shown at ISOMATA in Idyllwild, but three newer prints had never been exhibited. Lysbeth Anderson, who owned the entire editions of these three, *Relámpagos, Mis Garzas*, and *Los Pericos*, arranged with the Sun Bird Gallery in Los Altos, California for the first exhibit of these prints. The show opened on May 2, 1987. Lysbeth had selected a number of pots with complimentary color and designs to display with the prints.

The following year the prestigious Gallery 10 in Scottsdale, Arizona wanted to feature Juan's work in one of their winter shows. In February, 1988 the gallery opened a show which included Juan in conjunction with three famous Southwest Indian artists: Grace Medicine Flower of Santa Clara, Dorothy Torivio of Acoma, and Russell Sanchez of San Ildefonso. This was an important step in meeting our objective of placing Juan among prestigious potters of the world. However, there was a condition, one that was to change our business relationship with Juan.

Lee Cohan, the owner of Gallery 10, wanted to make sure he had an exclusive in the Scottsdale and Santa Fe area if he was to sell Juan's work. We had always purchased most of Juan's pots, but certainly not all, and it was entirely possible that the pieces we did not buy could find their way to some of the many competing galleries in the area. Cohan wanted a guarantee this would not happen. At the time we felt our relationship with Gallery 10 was extremely important, and we therefore needed an exclusive arrangement with Juan.

On our next trip to Mata Ortiz, Tom explained this concept in detail to Juan. He considered it and agreed to sell only to us. This had many ramifications, one being that Juan would not have pots to sell to others after they made the long trip to his door. We had learned that people like to become directly involved with the artist when they buy art. Juan was concerned about this too. Later when the exclusivity concept with Cohan and others became less important, Juan readily took back pots from us in order to have an inventory at home. Years later, he had become so well known that he and I agreed that he could do just as well by selling to all comers from his house and eliminate agents, contracts and other entangling arrangements altogether.

Such arrangements are contrary to Juan's independent nature anyway. Beginning with Spencer MacCallum, Juan had entered into a series of business agreements which would go well for awhile, but then would begin to chafe. When that happened, the arrangement had to change or fall apart. Juan is self reliant and does not work well with or within the traditional institutional framework—church, government or big business. Years before, he had stood up to his boss on the railroad. Juan had been popular with the men who had worked for him on the track-repair crews, but he would not stand for abuse from above, nor would he play the political or *mordida* games.

In 1984, some politically and socially prominent people in Nuevo Casas Grandes wanted to include Juan in an exhibition. Juan was reluctant because he had very few pots, but he felt forced to do it. Bobby Rodríguez helped by providing pots from his inventory. Juan attended the opening party which included among the guests the wife of the Governor of Chihuahua. As a gesture, Juan held up two of his pots and asked her to select one. She replied that she wanted them both. Juan told this story many times to illustrate his disdain for high-handed institutions.

But there is a sidelight to this story. This show in Nuevo Casas Grandes was the first formal exhibition of Juan's work in Mexico. Prior to this, virtually all of his fame was north of the border. Central Mexican art critics tended to dismiss him as more of a phenomenon of the American Southwest than a true "Mexican" artist. This show was the beginning of critical recognition for Juan in his own country. From then on Mexican newspapers and TV journalists traveled to Mata Ortiz to do stories on Juan and the miracle happening there. In November, 1990, the Governor of Chihuahua hosted an exhibition featuring Juan's work in Chihuahua City to celebrate the opening of a large bank building, *Servicio Pan Americano De Protección SA de CV*.

From 1986 into 1990, Juan had seemed satisfied with his arrangement with us and our pattern of visits to Mata Ortiz, Indian shows, gallery openings and ISOMATA classes. He had always made the long trip to teach or demonstrate when we asked. He understood the importance of museums in establishing his reputation, and he now urged us to get more such exhibitions. This was easier said than done.

The Museum World

Art museums are different entities from commercial sales galleries. Museum shows have a specific educational purpose, and sales are incidental. Such shows are few in number, and usually are planned long, sometimes years, in advance. They often are funded by outside sources which must be sought by formal application. However, when successful, a show at a prestigious institution can bring credibility and even fame to the artist or subject of the show. The five-museum traveling show of 1979-80 had done both for Juan and the potters of Mata Ortiz. But several years had now passed.

In 1987, the Southwest Museum in Highland Park near Los Angeles invited Juan to demonstrate as part of their visiting "Native American Artisan" series. He was featured along with famous Indian artists including Art Thompson, a Northwest Coast (Nootka) wood carver and graphic artist; Blue Corn, a San Ildefonso potter; and Kalley Musial, a Navajo weaver. Juan drew good crowds, including a sizable number of Mexican-Americans curious about this potter from Chihuahua. The Museum staff invited him back each year for the next three years. Nicolás came in his place in 1990.

Although it was an honor to demonstrate before so many people at this important institution, it still was not the same as an exhibition. Several museums were interested, but funding grant problems and budget cutbacks delayed the process.

Then, early in 1989, the curators of the Centennial Museum at the University of Texas, El Paso (UTEP), came up with a unique idea which ultimately resulted in a fine double exhibition. Tom O'Laughlin, the Curator of

Olla, *Juan Quezada, 1980.*

Exhibits and Collections, and Florence Schwein, the Curator of Education were working on an exhibit of UTEP's prehistoric Casas Grandes collection. They decided to juxtapose Juan's work in an adjoining gallery—the modern in contrast to the prehistoric. Juan liked it and agreed to demonstrate the full process — forming, painting, and firing — at the opening of the show. I would supply the pots, and John Wingate offered to fly them to El Paso right after Juan's class at ISOMATA ended.

The class was over on Saturday, July 8. After Juan had helped the last student finish firing, I drove him, Guille, and Pino to my house in Riverside. In the early evening, Juan sat outside on a low brick wall and sanded off the designs from an unfired pot he had painted in Idyllwild. Since he now usually lets a pot dry before painting, he needed an unpainted pot for Sunday's demonstration at the Southwest Museum. I understood the problem, but it gave me pause to see his designs ground to dust.

In the morning we drove to the Museum, located just off of the old Pasadena Freeway in Highland Park. There, Juan formed a new pot from wet clay for the first part of the demonstration and painted or repainted the much-traveled dry pot from Idyllwild. He worked with his usual concentration as an audience of over a hundred crowded around to watch and to get angles for photographs. Spencer MacCallum was a surprise guest, and after introductions stepped smoothly into his old role of moderator and translator.

The following morning relatives of Guille's from El Paso picked up Juan and Guille and toured them around Southern California before returning with them to Mexico. John Wingate, Pino and I went to the Riverside Airport. We loaded John's old Bellanca Super Viking with boxes of pots, filling the small cargo space and one backseat to the overhead. I rode in the other backseat with a ceramic fish in a large box on my lap. All I could see between the boxes on the four-hour flight to Albuquerque was John's right ear and Pino's left ear.

John had agreed to fly Pino to Albuquerque to see his son, who was an accountant there. After letting Pino off, I replaced him in the right front seat for the two-hour trip down the Rio Grande to El Paso. We passed over the hills of *El Paso del Norte*, the historic pass between old and new Mexico and landed at dusk. Tom O'Laughlin met us, and together we transported the pots to the museum, a beautiful institution done years ago in an unusual Tibetan architectural style. The next day, John and I flew back to Riverside.

I returned to El Paso via commercial airline the following week for the opening. Tom and Florence had done a good job. Entitled "Legends in Clay: Potters of Casas Grandes," the show took up two galleries. The first, "Ancient Potters of Casas Grandes," held the widest variety of prehistoric pottery I had ever seen, displayed in recessed cases between which large panels with maps and explanations interpreted the Casas Grandes culture. In the cases were vessels, animals, and anthropomorphic forms. One held what appeared to be Anazasi pots from the prehistoric culture in northern New Mexico but were in fact Casas Grandes done in the Anazasi style. Even the ancients did a little plagiarizing.

In the second gallery, "A Legend in Clay, Juan Quezada of Casas Grandes," the curators had displayed Juan's pieces on free-standing pedestals. His framed prints hung on the walls interspersed with pictures of him forming a pot.

Juan, assisted by Juan Junior, Pino, and nephew Nolbie, worked all day both inside and outside before a large appreciative crowd. Juan and the potters of Mata Ortiz were by now well known in El Paso. Many in the audience owned pottery and some had been to Mata Ortiz. A few brought in old unsigned pieces for Juan to identify. These had been distressed and all looked prehistoric, but Juan was sure that each one had been made by this or that member of his family. Late in the day, we visited Dr. and Mrs. James Spiers' home to see their Quezada pots collected about 1980.

The El Paso newspapers and television thoroughly covered the event. Florence Schwein was quoted in the *Prospector* describing Juan's work as "the best pottery coming out of Mexico." Robbie Farely Villalobos, the Arts and Entertainment Editor of the *El Paso Herald Post*, interviewed Juan and Guille in Spanish for her article which appeared (in English) on July 21. An article in *Horizons,* entitled "Chips Ain't Chips," described Florence's journey out to the farm to find cow chips for the demonstration firing. As has been seen, Juan is very particular that his fuel source is a grass-fed animal. A frantic search led to a buffalo farm near El Paso where she spent the morning before the opening filling plastic bags with dried buffalo pies. The article said that Juan preferred buffalo chips, but he was just being polite; he told me pri-

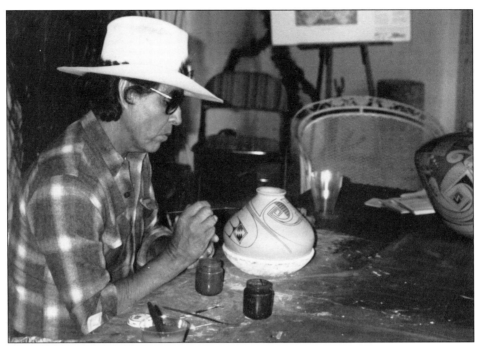

Juan demonstrates before an audience at Tohono Chul Park, Tucson, 1989.

vately that buffalo is inferior to the standard grass-fed cow chip.

Both the local CBS and NBC television stations covered the event. That evening on the news, we watched commentator Robert Anthony of CBS, Channel 4, El Paso, miraculously condense six hours of taping into a very informative 90 second slot.

Later in the year, after the UTEP show, the Tohono Chul Park in Tucson exhibited Juan's work. Cathy Husted, the operator of Fiesta Tours in southern Arizona, was the catalyst for bringing Juan together with the Park.

Tohono Chul is a unique institution, located on what was a large private estate north of the city. It is dedicated to the plants, animals, and art of the Southwest. Many species of native plants and animals live on the grounds and the galleries feature exhibits of old and new art relating to the Southwest. For Juan's show the curator used pots which emphasized the modern, contemporary look of much of Juan's work. Juan came up and demonstrated forming, painting and firing before a large audience on November 24, 1989.

Tohono Chul was followed in early 1990 by an exhibit at the University of California, Riverside Art Gallery. Curated by Debbie Dozer, the show was called "The Great Spirit's Work: Ten Centuries of Native American Creation." Debbie had gathered outstanding pieces of prehistoric and modern Indian art. She selected three of Juan's pieces to include with this collection.

Grandfather Juan

The last half of the eighties was a time of many and often distracting activities for Juan and his family. The rhythm of the clay, digging, processing, forming, painting, and firing was often broken by visitors, relatives, family demands, home improvements, and outside projects.

Juan continued to buy and sell cattle. Junior looked after much of this business, tending the new calves in the spring and helping to sell the steers and excess cows to Mexican and North American buyers in the fall. Juan liked the cattle business, viewing it as a hedge against the pottery business and vice versa. Land and cattle, the traditional investments of northern Mexico, were the only types of investments Juan trusted. He once said that his father, Don José, had sold twelve cows and deposited the money in a bank, but when he withdrew the money he could only buy eight cows. While Juan liked the cattle, there were always problems with them that took his time. The late eighties were drought years, and the animals on the already over-grazed *ejido* land suffered terribly. Sick cows were brought into the corral for care. Some died, which always seemed to be a greater catastrophe than the loss of a valuable pot. In November, 1988, Juan and his boys spent two weeks rounding up cattle. The *ejido* officials had decided that there were too many cattle on the common land, and they cracked down. All of the cattle in the area had to be driven into the *jaripeo* ring so that the number of brands could be compared to the number permitted under the communal rights system, or *derechos*, per family. All of this took a great deal of Juan's time.

During this same period, Juan decided to build a house across the river on the slope of the hills leading up to El Indio, where he could escape visitors and work in solitude. He hired two men to dig a well. For days and weeks entirely by hand, they dug a shaft into the rocky earth. Juan came regularly to check on the progress of the work. The well was always dry.

He was more successful with a venture to grow corn on *ejido* land. He joined with a few other men to fence several acres which produced a good crop.

At home, he built a fireplace and chimney, added an electric pump to the well, and mounted a satellite dish on the corral. It is not clear whether the dish ever worked, but it made a startling statement on the corral between the main adobe house and the outhouse.

He also planted trees in back of his house. Juan stuck what appeared to be three tall five-inch posts with neither branches or roots into the ground and began to water them. When asked, he said they were *sauce*, willow trees, for shade. We were very dubious, but on our next trip, the "posts" had sprouted. Two years later, they had grown into full-fledged trees, providing shade for the yard just as he had said.

Meanwhile, the family grew. Daughter María Elena, "Nena," had given birth to Alondra, Juan and Guille's first grandchild, in 1981, just a year after Juan and Guille's youngest child, Laura. By 1991, they had five more grandchildren. Guille liked having her family close to her and at times it seemed as if there were tiny children everywhere in her home. Nena and her husband Daniel Lujan had added two more — Daniel, Jr. and Adrian. Mireya, the sec-

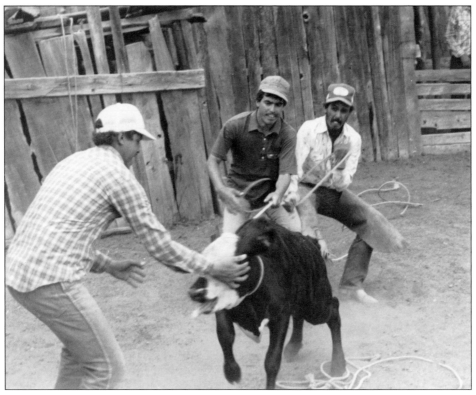

Juan Junior helps with the Ejido *roundup, 1992.*

ond daughter, had had a daughter, Marisol in 1984. Noe had married Betty Quintana and they had two girls, Guillita and Lupita. Junior married Betty Quintana's sister, Luly, and they had a daughter, Judi. At the same time Juan and Guille's three little boys, Albaro, Arturo, and Efren (Pollo), were growing into lanky teen-agers.

In 1988, to accommodate this brood and various relatives and friends, Juan bought a house in the center of town on the main street facing the rail-road station and tracks. This large single-storied building had been a hotel in earlier times, the Hotel Colón. It had many rooms and a large enclosed yard. Nena and Daniel moved into Juan's old house by the river. Noe, Junior, Mireya, and their families moved into the new house with Juan, Guille, Laura, and the three teen-age boys.

Nena had become an accomplished potter over this period. Her early small figures or *monos* were popular and easy to sell. But as her skills increased, she concentrated on more traditional *olla* shapes. For much of the time in the early years of their marriage, Daniel had worked in a meat pack-ing plant in Colorado. Nena had visited him there. In telling the story of her adventures in the United States, she lifted the edges of her skirt and tiptoed to demonstrate how she crossed the border. By the late eighties, however, the pottery business was good enough for Daniel to remain at home to help Nena and to work cattle on the *llano*.

Mireya also improved her ceramic skills, usually producing small polychrome *ollas*. She often worked with another potter, a school teacher, Elías Javier Pérez Dávila, who was nicknamed "Profie."

While other members of the family were involved with cattle, baseball and other pursuits, Noe concentrated on his pottery. When Spencer visited in 1986, he was amazed by Noe's work. When Juan and Spencer had ended their relationship, Noe had been a boy who, as far as Spencer remembered, had never made a pot. By 1990, he was considered one of the best in the village. Traders and tourists sought him out, and often it was difficult to obtain his work. He made enough money to remodel completely an old adobe beyond Juan's former house and close to the river. It was adjacent to a large cement slab reputed to be the floor of a barracks (or barn) used by Pancho Villa's men. Noe, Betty and their two little girls moved out of the "Hotel Colón" and into their own home in the summer of 1991.

Junior and Luly continued to live in the family house. In contrast to Noe, Junior has a multitude of interests: cattle, fighting roosters, horses, old cars, baseball and, when there is time, pottery.

Spencer described Albaro, Juan's third son, as a likable mischievous imp, but he grew up to be a very serious young man. He works diligently as a potter, often taking his ideas from Noe. By 1991, his younger brothers Arturo and Efren were taking some interest in potting. Little sister Laura, a pretty blithe spirit, was still in school with only the interests of little girls to worry about.

By the end of 1991, Guille still had at least nine for dinner every night.

Prints—Another Art Form

As a boy, before beginning his long romance with clay, Juan had experimented with painting and wood carving. Hanging in Don José's house is an oil painting he did of a bridge across the river in Copper Canyon. He carved little animals of wood and herons of cow horn to give to friends or to sell to passengers at the train station. Once he carved a Mexican peso so realistically that it passed at the local grocery store. A friend scared him by saying he could get into real trouble, and he never did it again. In Idyllwild one summer he carried a pine knot into the forest for a few hours, and returned with a small Indian head, a Tarahumara, carved into the knot. He gave this exquisite miniature to Judith Anderson.

After Juan discovered clay and became proficient with it, he did little in other mediums until the summer of 1984. This was his third summer at ISOMATA, and he had seen other artists at work. Printmakers Nick Capaci and Jondi Northcutt showed him some of their processes. These two had been working for years with all forms of prints in their studio, Bluestone Editions, in Anaheim, California. Juan was intrigued, and they encouraged him. Nick, Jondi, and Tom Fresh wanted to see if Juan could adopt his complex pottery designs to a two-dimensional surface. They gave Juan a copper

Juan's first print, "Mis Animales," 1984.

plate and showed him the techniques of marking on it to produce an image.

After experimenting with the first plate, Juan took a second and with a stylus started at one edge and worked to the other, creating the basic design for what became his first print, *Mis Animales*. The entire composition was in balance within a fraction of an inch. The final image, printed by Nick and Jondi, was a combination etching and aquatint, printed from three separate plates. Each print on handmade archival paper from France had to be pulled from the press three times. One hundred and twenty five numbered prints plus eight artist's proofs were made. This was the standard number for Juan's subsequent prints. Most of *Mis Animales* were sold to individuals, although a few were sold to investors for resale.

Then Tom had the idea of ISOMATA publishing a portfolio of prints by famous Native American teachers at the campus. He invited Juan to participate. Again Juan was grouped with the "Indians," but it seemed logical. Juan liked the medium and was eager to do another print. The other artists were Lucy Lewis of Acoma, Blue Corn of San Ildefonso, and Michael Kabotie of Hopi. Michael, a multi-talented artist, had done prints, but this was a first for the famous potters Lucy Lewis and Blue Corn. Juan's print was the black and white *Liebre con Tarahumar*, featuring a Mimbres-style rabbit and Tarahumara Indians. Mexican Indians were thus his contribution to the "Indian" portfolio.

Later Tom formed a partnership of Nick, Jondi, Juan and himself to pub-

68

"Remolino," one of three prints completed by Juan in 1990.

lish three more of Juan's prints. This resulted in the very popular black print, *Relámpagos* or "Lightning" which echoes the black-on-black pottery prized by North Americans. It was an aquatint, a form of etching whereby the areas of the plate which are not to receive the ink (the negative areas) are painted. An acid process etches the unpainted area, making a surface which will receive and hold the ink until it is transferred to the paper in the press. The other two prints were the wine-colored *Mis Garzas,* featuring stylized water birds and *Los Pericos,* featuring parrots.

Juan produced more prints after entering into a formal contractual arrangement with a Japanese group in the spring of 1990. He drew designs on six copper plates which were then delivered to printer Robert Blanchard of Albuquerque. Blanchard is a master printer, trained at the University of New Mexico's Tamarind Institute of Lithography.

Three of the copperplates were etched and proof prints made. Juan signed the proofs, and Blanchard printed the editions by hand, one at a time. An edition consisted of 25 artist's proofs and 125 numbered prints.

The numbered prints all went to Japan, and Juan and his family sold most of the artist's proofs. The arrangement with the Japanese group dissolved before the second group of three images were printed. In 1992, the plates remained in Albuquerque waiting for someone to step forward to finance the printing and distribution.

La Lucha del Barro

In 1989, Michael Williams, a Canadian working on his master's degree in anthropology at Arizona State University, learned of Mata Ortiz. He made a visit and decided to do his thesis on the economics of the pottery families. After review, he elected to study the families of Nicolás Quezada, Consolación Quezada, and Roberto Bañuelos. He did not include Juan because the situation of the original *maestro* was less typical of the village.

Nicolás, the closest brother to Juan, was known as one of the best potters in the village. His teenage son, José, an excellent craftsman, was just then beginning to break away from his father's style. Two other children, Dora and Leonel, were beginners.

In contrast to Nicolás' small family, his older sister Consolación, a few doors away, was the matriarch of a large family of potters including daughters-in-law and their relatives.

Roberto Bañuelos and his wife, Angela, lived completely outside the Quezada family circle. They were examples of skilled artisans who learned their craft many years after the Quezadas began.

Mike came to know these families well, and his interest expanded from the economics of ceramics to the pottery designs and techniques and to the potters themselves. He spent many hours watching Nicolás preparing clays and paint mixes, firing each test piece until he found the right combination. Mike gathered clay with Consolación and her extended family and spent hours in conversation with them. His thesis evolved into a study of the technical, esthetic, and economic struggle of the potters, with emphasis on "the struggle" or *la lucha*. The struggle was to create an art object from mud fired in dung and then sell it to put food on the table and survive.

This concept was dramatically demonstrated in an exhibition at Arizona State's Museum of Anthropology in April, 1991. It was called *La Lucha del Barro*, "The Struggle of the Clay," and was supported in part by a grant from the Arizona Humanities Council. Mike curated the exhibition and showed only the work of the three families he had studied — thirteen potters in all. This in itself was a first. Never had there been a museum exhibition of the new Casas Grandes pottery that did not feature Juan's work, although his place and importance were noted in the interpretive material.

Another departure here from earlier shows was the emphasis in the interpretive material on the potters themselves and their *lucha* rather than the history and esthetics of the art form. Mike used photographs, text, and quotations which introduced the viewer directly to the potters and the difficulties of their lives and their craft. Below a picture of Consolación working, she is quoted, "We had nothing before making pottery. The first thing I bought with the money from my *ollas* was a wood stove." Angela Bañuelos says of her husband, Roberto, "Before he made pottery, he did little. Our lives were humble."

Mike also displayed raw clay, paint materials, and the simple tools used by the potters. Nicolás and Mauro demonstrated at the opening reception assisted by Hilario, Mauro's brother.

Mike felt that he had received so much from his experience in Mata Ortiz that he wanted to give something back. He did not want to be just another visitor who took what he needed and left. So he developed a small hotel, or *posada*, in the village. He thought that a *posada* would encourage visitors and provide jobs for some who were not potters. A dilapidated old adobe building that had once housed a cinema and boxing ring — the site of Juan's three boxing matches — was totally rebuilt by local workers into a five-room inn. *La Posada de las Ollas* began taking guests in the summer of 1991.

Double Olla *or* Cuate *by Juan Quezada.*

72

CHAPTER 4
THE JAPANESE CONNECTION

The Pope's Pot

During the winter of 1990, we began to hear rumors that Juan was involved with a group from Japan. Juan had not had many pots for us since November. He told us he was having trouble with the large pieces cracking in the firing. A trader, Joe Garcia, called me in February to say that Juan was working on five for me, but when Tom called Mata Ortiz — not an easy thing to do — there were no pots ready. Tom called again in March, still no pots. That same month a trader at an Indian show said that he had heard that Japanese buyers had visited Juan.

We were very curious as to what was going on. A few weeks later in April, Tom, John Wingate, and I decided to go to Mata Ortiz whether Juan had pots or not. Tom needed to prepare for his summer classes, and he wanted to start accumulating an inventory of pots from other Mata Ortiz potters for the campus gallery.

In Mata Ortiz, Juan told us that a Japanese man had purchased a pot for $2,000. He had taken this back to his group or "society," and now he wanted all of the work that Juan could do. We spent two days walking the village with Juan meeting new potters, but nothing more was said about the Japanese.

Tom was changing the gallery format at ISOMATA, and he wanted a variety of pots from the village. In the past the teachers were the featured artists in a small gallery for the period of time they were on campus. For the summer of 1990, a much larger gallery would be available, and Tom needed more inventory than typically would have been provided by the teacher-artists. Juan had always been a featured artist. Tom explained that this would happen again in 1990, but he needed to purchase additional inventory to stock the larger gallery for the total period of time it was open. Juan had no problem with this and was very helpful. However, he did not want to make any final decisions on arrangements for his classes. Tom did not press. There was still plenty of time until July.

In May, Tom talked by telephone with Guille. Enrollment in Juan's Idyllwild class was still slow, but Tom thought he had communicated that he intended the class to go as scheduled.

In late June, Spencer MacCallum called with an amazing story. He had not had any direct contact with the Quezada family for years, but a few days before he had been called by Juan and asked to help with a new venture.

The Pope had visited the City of Chihuahua on his tour of Mexico in May. The Bishop Hilario Chávez Joya of the Diocese of Nuevo Casas Grandes

Opposite: *Large* Olla *by Juan Quezada, 1980.* Photo: N. Prasad had commissioned Juan to make a pot for presentation to the Pope. Guille's brother-in-law showed a picture of this pot to a Japanese businessman in Chihuahua City. At first the Japanese showed little interest, but later when he saw an actual pot, he became very enthusiastic. He made a special trip to Mata Ortiz, bringing along another man, Yoichi "Stanley" Kitao. This was probably the Japanese that Juan told us about in April. Kitao was so impressed with Juan's work that he contacted his superior, Mrs. Reiko Horiguchi of the Tokyo firm, Fuji Project Co. Ltd. As reported later by the *El Paso Herald-Post,* Mrs. Horiguchi was the founder and president of this company which was involved in projects throughout the Pacific Rim, including a hotel in Canada, a building in Saipan, real estate in California and a coffee plantation in Jamaica. She also was reported to own buildings, a botanical garden, and a gallery in Tokyo. She was a major art collector and the patron of Japanese painter Tsugu Kohashikawa. According to the newspaper article, her personal collection included work by French painters Auguste Renoir, Claude Monet and Georges Braque.

The Japanese appreciate ceramic art as much or more than any group in the world. This national consciousness, in addition to her eye for good art, caused Mrs. Horiguchi to recognize immediately that Juan was a significant artist.

In late May Mrs. Horiguchi and Stanley Kitao traveled to Albuquerque to meet with Juan and Guille at the home of Guille's sister, Susanna Olivas Reyes and Susanna's husband Andy Martínez, also known as "Luis Reyes." Mrs. Horiguchi proposed a contractual arrangement whereby she would purchase the exclusive right of first refusal of all of Juan's work and that of his children. Juan agreed to this, and a few days later they all met again to formalize the arrangement with contracts.

A company was formed called the "Fine Arts of Juan Quezada." With Susanna as president (taking instructions from Andy), the company would be responsible for all of the logistics — receiving, packing, shipping, and banking — in the U.S. One contract was between "Fine Arts of Juan Quezada" and "Paideia Overseas Co. LTD," represented by Yoichi Stanley Kitao, either a subsidiary of Fuji or a separate operation set up by Mrs. Horiguchi.

The contract had two parts. The first gave the right to Paideia to sell the Quezada work, splitting the "profit" 60 percent to Paideia and 40 percent to Fine Arts. "Profit" was not defined. The second part dealt with Juan's compensation. He was to receive flat amounts for agreeing to the exclusive contract, for producing prints and for an existing group of 106 pots. These pots were made by Juan and his children: Nena, Mireya, Noe, Juan Jr., and Albaro plus Juan's nephew, Nolbie. Another set of contracts, prepared by a Mexican lawyer in Spanish, spelled out the relationship of each of the family members with Fine Arts. These latter documents, one for each potter, were simple and clear. However, the language of the first contract was confusing, particularly about Juan's compensation for new prints. This led to problems later.

Part of the plan was for Juan to prepare plates for a new series of prints. An agreement was reached with the Albuquerque printer Robert Blanchard. As told earlier in Chapter 3 under *Prints — Another Art Form,* Juan ultimately prepared six plates, three of which were printed by Blanchard.

Figures by Noe Quezada, 1989.

The news of this arrangement burst on the Southwest with a blaze of publicity. In June, major articles appeared in the *Albuquerque Journal,* the *El Paso Times,* and the *El Paso Herald-Post.* Mrs. Horiguchi was interviewed by columnists, and she talked of her respect for the natural purity of Juan's materials and his aversion to modern techniques. In describing her admiration for Juan's work, she compared it to the centuries-old tea ceremony in Japan in which the host serves and the guest admires and discusses the beauty of the exquisite tea cup.

After announcing the exclusive arrangement in El Paso on June 2, Mrs. Horiguchi traveled to Mata Ortiz and spent two days visiting Juan's home and family. Afterwards she was quoted in one of the papers as saying she wanted to model a museum in Tokyo after the Quezada's home and workshop.

There were more grand plans: to market Juan's work in the major cultural centers of the world; to build a museum for his work in Tokyo; to bring Juan and his family to Japan for a major exhibition; and to produce up to 20 prints. The headline in the *El Paso Times* read, "NOW FOR THE REST OF THE WORLD."

East Meets Oeste

All of this happened very fast. The Pope visited Chihuahua on May 10, 1990, and Mrs. Horiguchi visited Mata Ortiz on June 4 and 5, after the contracts had been signed and the press notified. Kitao must have seen the picture of the Pope's pot and gone to Mata Ortiz before the Pope's visit. The time line is vague, but there is no doubt that Juan and the family had time to complete a large number of pots for the first shipment to Japan. The contract specifically mentioned 106. These were brought to Albuquerque, and Susanna Reyes made arrangements for packing and shipping them to Japan. For the next several months this was the pattern. After receipt of the shipment in Japan, Mrs. Horiguchi's museum specialist inspected the pots and made arrangements for payment to Fine Arts of Juan Quezada, which in turn forwarded the Quezadas' share to Mata Ortiz. All of this took time.

Juan also started right into the print project. By the middle of July, two were in the proof stage, and a few copies were ready for Juan's signature in the fall.

During the fall and winter, plans were made and discarded for Juan and Guille to travel to Japan. Finally a trip was scheduled for February to attend the opening on February 14 of an exhibition of Quezada work in Tokyo. A beautiful invitation was printed and a copy sent to Juan. However, the outbreak of the Iraqi war caused the trip to be canceled.

All of us who had been involved with Juan felt this was a big opportunity for him and his family. However, events had moved so fast that some were left behind, if only temporarily. After Spencer called with the news in June, Tom renewed his efforts to communicate with Juan via the single telephone in Mata Ortiz and by calls to Albuquerque. Several students had signed up for the class in Idyllwild which was scheduled to start in less than two weeks. Also deposits had been received for the August on-site class. When he finally got through to Guille, she said that Juan was under the impression that the class had been canceled for lack of enrollment. When Tom protested, Susanna came on the line to explain that the representatives of Mrs. Horiguchi felt that a master potter should not teach.

Here was a dilemma that had to be solved quickly. Not only was Juan scheduled for the two ISOMATA classes, the Southwest Museum had publicized his fourth annual demonstration which was expected to draw a big crowd. Should Tom cancel everything or risk a substitute? Tom made his decision and talked with Nicolás Quezada, who agreed to come north on this very short notice. The officials at the Southwest, Margery Thomason, Mary Jo Minturn, and Barbara Alves, also agreed to the change. As it turned out, both the class and the demonstration went very well, a credit to Nicolás' skill and careful if hurried preparation.

Juan continued to forward shipments of pots to Albuquerque but, apparently, not fast enough. Stanley Kitao pushed for more. However the museum "experts" in Japan were becoming more particular. Sometime after the first of the year, they notified Juan that they only wanted his and Noe's work.

During this period, Juan concentrated on the painted-design aspect of his pots. He formed large white *ollas* with classic shapes for the background to his intricate geometric patterns and swirls. He used the whitest of the white clays, and his paint mixes resulted in the purest black and red colors. Noe also began making just *ollas,* departing from his previous preoccupation with animal and fish shapes.

By April, 1991, many pots had been shipped and paid for; however, Juan was now concerned about the terms of the contract. He had prepared images on six copper plates and been paid for three. Although the second three had not been printed, he felt he had done his part, and under the contract, should receive at least a partial payment. The response to his queries from Fine Arts was that the prints had not been "approved." He asked Tom to review the contract, but the language was too confusing to clarify Juan's position. Mrs. Horiguchi later said that the money for all six prints was sent, but she never received the second group of three.

Juan's concerns were compounded by the cumbersome communication from Mata Ortiz to Susanna and Fine Arts in Albuquerque to Stanley Kitao and Paideia at a number of locations, and finally to Mrs. Horiguchi's representatives in Tokyo and then back again. Many of the details are not known, but it is clear that Stanley Kitao and Susanna's wheeler-dealer husband, Andy (the power behind Susanna) had their own separate agendas throughout this arrangement. Kitao's performance finally became so unacceptable that Mrs. Horiguchi had to fire him. To further complicate matters, Andy was arrested and sent to prison.

In spite of the difficulties, Juan was looking forward to signing a new contract in June, 1991. Mrs. Horiguchi had sent him up to $1,500 each for most of the work she received and as much as $2,500 for the larger pieces. He expected to continue to ship to Japan all he could produce for similar prices — prices higher than in the United States. He had earlier expressed interest in teaching again, but in June he told Tom that he wanted to concentrate on producing pots for Mrs. Horiguchi under the expected new contract. However, this did not happen. There had been too much confusion.

In late July, I received a call from Guille (the first ever) asking when I was returning to Mata Ortiz. I told her I was planning to attend an archaeology conference at Paquimé in August. She said to come as soon as I could because Juan wanted to renew our business relationship. This was a great surprise, and I had many questions. All I could find out was that the arrangement with the Japanese was over.

Two weeks later, I sat with Juan in his house across from the old railroad station and heard his version. He expressed frustration with Stanley Kitao and Fine Arts. He had made many useless trips to El Paso and Albuquerque, payments were slow, and the final blow was a $3,000 shipping charge he had to pay for rejected pots returned from Japan. Also, he wanted to teach and demonstrate in the United States, and the contract would not permit it. It was clear that once again the constraints of a contractual arrangement had rubbed too hard.

Another Chapter

The Japanese experience was over, and as I sat with Juan, it was clear to me that he did not need agents or contracts. He offered to renew our relationship by giving me first refusal on all his work. I said I would think about it and let him know before the end of the trip, but I already knew the answer. A few days later we talked again. I told him he was *un hombre muy independiente* and was now well enough known that he did not need to entangle himself in arrangements which would soon chafe. I suggested that he sell to everyone on a first come basis. I would help in any way possible with exhibitions and demonstrations in the United States as in the past. He agreed with

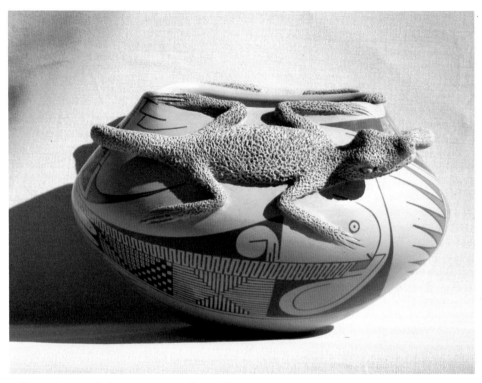

Olla *with Lizards by Juan Quezada, 1988.*

my assessment and thanked me for offering the future help.

I left Juan's house and walked back toward the Posada, where I was staying. This trip to Mata Ortiz had been made in part to attend the 64th annual "Pecos Conference" of Southwestern archaeologists hosted by Dr. R.B. Brown at Paquimé. Many of Juan's old North American friends were in the village plus many newcomers. One conference activity was a tour conducted by John Davis, an old friend of the village potters. Both Spencer MacCallum and Mike Williams attended, making formal presentations to the conference. The Posada's five rooms were full. Just the fact that there was a Posada at all in the village caused me to reflect on the changes in the lives of the people here as a direct result of Juan's talent and inquiring mind. I passed Mauro's house, and I could see him through the window painting a pot on his "Sears and Roebuck" kitchen counter. Down a block, Nicolás and another man sat on the porch of his new house. He yelled a greeting and a joke I did not get, and I yelled something back. I knew a chapter in Juan's career had ended and another begun. Whatever was to come, this part of his legacy was secure. Through his skills and artistry, he had given his family and neighbors the opportunity for a better life. The final chapter will be written another time.

Red Clay Olla *by Juan, 1988.*

Effigy by Juan, 1977.

Photo: N. Prasad

80

Noe Quezada

CHAPTER 5
THE VILLAGE OF MATA ORTIZ

The Economic Miracle

By 1980, the pottery of Mata Ortiz had received considerable attention in the United States. The pottery had sold well, and many traders, both American and Mexican, had found their way to Mata Ortiz. Because the village was so poor, Spencer thought everyone immediately would climb on the bandwagon and begin making pottery. Wages on the railroad or in the fields were a few dollars per day. Even in 1990, wages in the apple orchards were just $5 per day. The sale of one $25 pot would be equal to a week's wages!

However, by 1980 only a few had joined the early group that was working when Spencer arrived in 1976. (See page 12.) This puzzled Spencer, but he concluded that the high degree of skill required and the long learning period were at least partial answers.

The serious lack of meaningful employment for the villagers had concerned both Spencer and Juan. Together they had investigated the possibility of starting a tile factory in Mata Ortiz, incorporating the abundance of good clay and Juan's designs. The idea did not go anywhere, and it turned out not to be necessary.

It is not completely clear how the phenomenon occurred, but between 1980 and 1990, the idea of potting as a serious vocational endeavor caught on. By 1990 there were perhaps as many as 300 potters working in Mata Ortiz. Many of these appear to have begun as late as 1987 or 1988.

A few Quezadas and their neighbors in the central part of the village joined the group, most notably Noe, Juan's oldest son. A great ceramist, Noe in his late teens and early twenties became one of the best three or four potters in the village. He started doing animals, and some of his small four-legged *imaginario* animals are now collector's items. For a long time his fish figures with their precise "circuit-board" designs, intricate layouts of small squares and circles, were his trademark.

However, by far the largest quantity of pottery leaving Mata Ortiz was from the Porvenir neighborhood across the arroyo. Felix Ortiz had influenced many potters there including a group of brothers also named Ortiz, who were distantly related to him. The Ortiz brothers, also working musicians, became very good potters. They in turn influenced many others. By the early eighties

Opposite: Olla *by Felix Ortiz.* Photo: N. Prasad

great quantities of pottery were being produced in Porvenir. Much of it was low quality. Discount traders, such as the famous "El Paso Saddle Blanket" store of El Paso, bought truckloads. So-called "Casas Grandes" pottery began to appear in "Indian" stores throughout the West. This low-quality high-volume syndrome seemed to peak in the mid-nineteen eighties. Even the work of some of the better potters declined into a downward spiral of price and quality. These potters had fallen into the trap of lowering prices when they needed money and then trying to produce more to make up the difference. This led to lower quality, lower prices, and the need for even higher production.

Juan has always been concerned about quality. In the beginning he could withhold paint and other materials to the few potters working under his influence. However, this phenomena of the eighties was beyond anyone's control. He and the members of his immediate family, especially Noe and daughter Nena, continued to innovate and grow. However much mediocre work left Mata Ortiz. Then in the latter half of the decade, things began to change again.

The number of potters accelerated rapidly in this time period, but amazingly enough so did the quality. By 1990, traders could select pieces from several villagers producing good work on a regular basis. Some were within the Quezada family, but many more were not.

The reasons for these changes in the number of potters and the quality of their work are complex. Certainly Spencer's thoughts about the difficulties in becoming proficient are valid. Working with clay is referred to in the village as *La Lucha*, "the struggle." For many it had taken years to reach a level of competency approaching that of the basic Quezada group. After years of producing low-quality work, their skills improved and they reversed the downward spiral. But there are other factors. The traders played a part. There always have been volume operators bargaining for lower prices, but there had been also those who wanted only the best pieces. In fact some traders simply refused to buy anything they did not feel was quality work. If there were five pots displayed on the kitchen table or bedspread in the potter's home, the trader would pick the best two and leave the rest. The potters realized that with a little more effort and attention, they could produce work that could bring many times the return from an appreciative trader or tourist.

It appears that the firing technique developed by Juan had inadvertently promoted quality. Michael Williams, in his anthropological studies, compared the pottery industry in Mata Ortiz to other pottery centers in Mexico. He pointed out that in other areas, the potters accumulated their green ware and fired large quantities in kilns, while in Mata Ortiz most pieces were fired individually. The first practice encouraged a conservative approach. Losing a large batch of pots in a single firing was an economic disaster while losing one pot was only unfortunate. As a result, the Mata Ortiz potters had been more willing to experiment, to innovate, to take chances, which in the long run improved the quality of their work.

All of these reasons for the increase in number and proficiency of the potters are significant, but the key may be the emergence of the second generation. Mauro Quezada was ten when the decade began. He was helping his mother, Consolación, as a little boy, and by his late teens he was an accomplished potter. This second generation — the sons, daughters, nieces, nephews, daughters-in-law, and sons-in-law of Juan, Nicolás, Consolación and Reynalda — grew up with their hands in clay. By the late eighties, they were entering adulthood. They did not leave the fields or the railroad to become potters like the first generation. When it was their turn to earn a living, they went directly into what they already knew well.

All of these young potters have individual stories. Noe was a natural artist like his father, Juan, and there was no question of another occupation. Nicolás had to have a man-to-man talk with his oldest son, José, to point out the economic realities of life. José heard the message, and is now a superb potter.

Manuel Rodrígues was a boyhood friend of Juan Junior. He certainly saw what was going on in the Quezada household as he grew up. He began to make small *monos* or effigy figures of humans and animals. His human figures represent to Manuel what the prehistoric people looked like. They are usually seated, performing a task—carving, skinning, potting, etc. They caught on immediately with the traders. An older brother, Armando, wanted to learn, and by the time Manuel was 18, three of his brothers and two of his sisters were producing figures. Manuel at a young age became in effect the mentor of a sub-school of Mata Ortiz potters.

The net result is a large number of talented young people producing good pottery. These young people and the others in the village that have turned to pottery did so because it pays. They take pride in their work, and some are fine artists, but their purpose is to earn more than is available to them any other way. For most of the women, there is no other way to make money.

The growing numbers increased the competition, which worried some of the older potters. However, the number of buyers, traders and tourists seems to have kept pace. There is no organized marketplace; most of the pots are sold out of the potter's homes. One of the pleasures for visitors is walking the dusty streets of the village and receiving invitations to enter the homes of craftsmen. At the doorways there is always the gracious request to *pásale* into the coolness of the adobe interior and then to *siéntese* at the kitchen table or edge of the bed where the resident artist's work is displayed after being retrieved from various cupboards and boxes.

Some of the traders buy for their own galleries. Most buy for resale to various stores and galleries in the western United States. Very little is resold in Mexico. A few Mexican traders sell from their homes in Nuevo Casas Grandes, and one gallery in Ensenada regularly sells ware from Mata Ortiz. More and more tourists travel to the village to buy directly, some on tours and some on their own. A few southwest tour companies now make Mata Ortiz a regular stop on trips to Paquimé, Copper Canyon, and Chihuahua City.

From time to time various potters in addition to Juan have been asked to demonstrate or give workshops in the United States. Usually this provides an opportunity to sell to a receptive audience. These experiences have led some

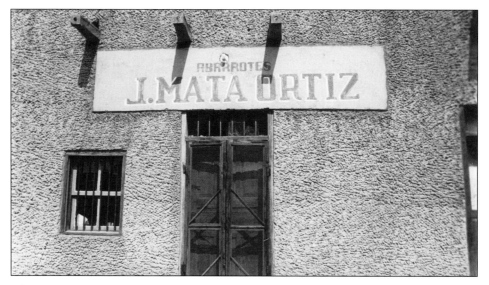

The grocery store.   Photo: Beth Thomas

potters to try selling directly in the United States on their own. Usually they find the costs of trips beyond the border towns outweigh any price advantage from direct selling.

To the casual observer Mata Ortiz still appears to be a quiet, decaying Mexican village with cattle grazing on the edges. This is deceptive. Behind the crumbling adobe and the old signs is a vigorous cottage industry, dominated by young people who know their craft, know what it means to them economically, and who find a ready market at their doorstep.

Juan's earnings per year are at the level of the highest paid Mexican professional. Nicolás, Noe, and others are able to afford pickup trucks, indoor plumbing, color television, VCRs, etc. The prevalent means of transportation has shifted from the horse and cart to cars and pickups.

This is the economic miracle of Mata Ortiz. In this remote, unlikely place, Juan Quezada developed a unique ceramic ware based on the remnants of a prehistoric culture. This showed a way to his family and neighbors to work out of the grinding poverty that was otherwise their destiny.

Why Is It There?

The pueblo of Mata Ortiz seems an unlikely place for a major ceramic revival. It is far from any of the art or craft centers of modern Mexico, and its economic base had all but disappeared by the 1960s. It is not an ancient town with roots in prehistoric or even Spanish Colonial times, as is Casas Grandes a few miles to the north. Most of the residents trace their family origins to other places. It is unlikely that many if any of them are descended from the prehistoric Indians of the Casas Grandes culture in spite of some overly enthusiastic gallery promotional material to the contrary. The Quezada family itself came from Santa Bárbara Tutuaca far to the south in 1941.

Olivia Domínguez Rentería and her mother Lidia Rentería Cota, 1990.

Mauro Quezada, 1990.

Reynalda Quezada, 1990.

Goyo Silviera, 1990.

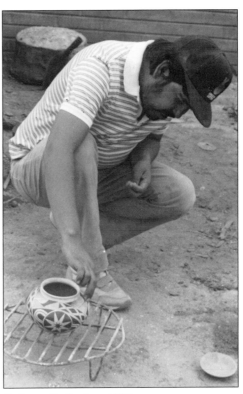

Roberto Bañuelos, 1990.

Spaniards in the seventeenth century found some nomadic Indians such as the Opatas living in the area, but for years before and after the Conquest, raiding Apaches hampered settlement by either Indians or Spaniards. It was not until 1884, after General Crook's peace mission across the border and into the heart of the Sierra Madre, that the last Apaches finally were herded into reservations in Arizona and New Mexico.

Although the area was still considered dangerous, A.F. Bandelier explored the area around the Casas Grandes ruins that spring of 1884. He described the virtues of the area and the Apache problem in a monograph published six years later in 1890.

> "Admirably fitted for a centre of subsistence on a small scale, the region of Casas Grandes could not fail to attract all tribes within grasp of its superior natural advantages. It did not so much allure the aborigines to roam over its tracts as to settle on them. Its surroundings are not inviting to the marauding savage except in the west, where the eastern branch of the Sierra Madre rises like an unbroken wall clad in somber green. There he found profusion of game, abundance of limpid brooks and streams, majestic pine forests, and innumerable lurking places. There for nearly two hundred years the Apaches had their favorite lairs, harassing the Spaniards to such a degree that twice the latter almost completely abandoned the valley of Casas Grandes."

The mountainous area Bandelier describes is just to the east of Mata Ortiz and its immediate neighbor, the much older village of San Diego. Later in the article he described the sites of these communities as he looked back after he began his climb into the mountains:

> "A broad plain separates the former hacienda of San Diego, where the Casas Grandes River is formed, from the eastern front of the Sierra Madre. This plain is about ten miles wide and alive with antelopes."

Bandelier goes on to describe prehistoric dwellings and mounds along the hills at the edge of the mountains in the same locations that Juan later found shards while tramping the hills with his burros.

With the elimination of the Apaches, the area expanded into a cattle empire. By the end of the nineteenth century, most of the land was part of a vast feudal-like holding belonging to Luis Terrazas. A Spaniard, Don Luis Terrazas, had fought against the French in Mexico and had been rewarded by President Benito Juárez with land which he parlayed into a huge ranch empire in northern Chihuahua. By the turn of the century, he was one of richest cattlemen in the world, reputed to have ninety-nine haciendas across Chihuahua. Probably the figure was closer to thirty, but they included fifteen million acres! One was the old rancho of San Diego where he built a grand mansion, large stables and a storehouse, just three miles north of the present site of Mata Ortiz. Cattle by the thousands took over the plains from the antelope. Don Luis lived like a grandee, and became the governor general of Chihuahua.

In spite of his power and wealth, he was ultimately to be destroyed by the Revolution and its chief executioner in *El Norte,* Pancho Villa. To many Americans and Europeans, Terrazas was a sophisticated gentleman of the world with whom they could do business. To Villa — whose family were virtual serfs — he was the personification of evil oppression.

Terrazas was a military man, but once Villa started his raids, Terrazas could never catch him (neither could Pershing). Pancho the Puma and his *banda* rode freely, killing Terraza's men and destroying his herds. Some of the cattle they gave away or sold to finance their operations, but most they killed and left. They killed and killed until Don Luis Terrazas was ruined. He died a broken man, cursing "Villa the Villain."

In the meantime, with the elimination of the Apaches and the impetus of the machine age, other types of development and settlement started. In 1885, thirty-two Mormon families crossed the border with their plows, children, and furniture in wagons to escape the U.S. marshals enforcing the new anti-polygamy laws. They came to the high-plains country of Chihuahua and set-tled in the little valleys near old Casas Grandes. Eventually thousands more were "called" by the church to join these expatriates. They dammed the rivers to irrigate their peach and apple orchards and developed a major agri-cultural and packing industry. This became an important source of employ-ment in later years for the men of Mata Ortiz.

Lumber entrepreneurs began to exploit the vast forests of the Sierra Madre. In 1890, Carl Lumholtz on one of his expeditions to study ancient ruins and "primitive" Indians, described a small lumber mill in Pacheco, a mountain village that still exists in the Sierra Madre near the Cave of the Olla.

Lumber and agriculture were feasible now because of the railroad system that gradually expanded from the border south. Financed mostly by foreigners encouraged by the Porfirio Díaz regime in Mexico City, the railroads by the early part of the twentieth century connected central Mexico with the markets in the midwestern United States.

Mata Ortiz began in about 1907 as a tent camp for workers building the railroad. Two years later, a consortium organized by F.S. Pearson of Canada and Enrique Creel, Terrazas' son-in-law, extended the Rio Grande, Sierra Madre and Pacific railroad to the Mata Ortiz site. There they prepared to build a large lumber mill to exploit the virgin timber of the Sierra Madre. The growing village site was called "Pearson," a name that stuck until the politics of the Revolution required a change. The railroad line also had more than one name; later called the *Noroeste* (the Mexican Northwestern Railroad) and still later the *Chihuahua al Pacífico.*

The entrepreneurs built the mill and hauled logs to it out of the Sierra Madre via a narrow gauge railroad that crawled up the side of the mountain. Today diesel trucks haul logs and lumber (from a small mill in Zaragoza or "Willy" a few miles from the old mill site at Pacheco seen by Carl Lumholtz in 1890) down a dirt road that follows in part the old narrow gauge track bed.

Lumbering in the Sierra Madre above Mata Ortiz about 1910.

Pearson expanded. The railroad, lumber mill, and orchards provided the work, and the houses, stores, cantinas and workshops, built in long rows opposite the railroad tracks, served the influx of workers and their families. However, throughout Mexico, not enough people were benefiting from this type of foreign investment. Most lived in such hopeless poverty that in the fall of 1910, they rose up against President/Dictator Porfirio Díaz and drove him into exile. For awhile, the new leader, the intellectual-idealist Francisco Madero, held the country together, but it turned out to be easier to start a war than to administer the peace. The Revolution degenerated into essentially a civil war. The man who emerged as the powerful leader in Chihuahua was Francisco "Pancho" Villa. Villa was loyal to Madero, and after the latter was assassinated, Villa fought all of his successors back and forth across Chihuahua and Durango.

The revolutionaries roamed the high plains confiscating entire trains when they needed them and blowing up others. The tragedy known as the Cumbre Tunnel Disaster occurred in February 1914, just south of Pearson. A train of the Mexican Northwestern Railway was dynamited inside a tunnel; all fifty-one passengers, including some Americans, burned to death in the explosion. To the north Villa fought two major battles in Casas Grandes. The old people in Mata Ortiz still tell tales of the days when Villa rode the *llano.*

Everyone in the area with anything to lose lived in fear of the "Villistas." Some of the Mormon farmers began to leave. The foreign owners of the railroads tried to keep their tracks open and equipment running, but as Villa took control of many of the installations, the foreigners left. Finally even the lumber mill closed. It stood with its doors locked for years until 1948 when the government permitted the local people to dismantle it. All that is left now are some sections of concrete to the north of the *jaripeo* ring.

After the Revolution wound down in the 1920s, stability gradually returned to northern Chihuahua. The Mormons rebuilt their farms, the railroad lines reopened, and a large railroad repair facility was established in Pearson. This helped offset the loss of the mill, except that the town was not called "Pearson" any more. With the foreign investors gone and the big land holdings broken up, foreign names for towns were *passe.* Many communities were renamed after heroes of the revolution (the politically correct heroes), but Pearson received its new name in May, 1925, after an earlier hero, an army officer that helped defeat the Apaches led by the famous Victorio. The officer's name was Juan Mata Ortiz.

Much of the land around Mata Ortiz now belonged to a lumber company called "Bosques de Chihuahua." In the 1930s, the Federal Government put this land and other land owned by the railroad into communal ownership and formed the *Ejido* of Juan Mata Ortiz. The old ranch of San Diego was also formed into an *ejido.*

The *ejido* is a form of municipal organization that traces its roots to the *Reconquista* in Spain of the Christians over the Moors, which was finally finished by Ferdinand and Isabella in the late fifteenth century. The Christian nobles who fought for the crown were given tracts of land formerly held by the Moors. The ordinary people on the land were organized into towns with common areas or *ejidos* at the entrance to the towns for grazing. This same system was used in the New World when the Spanish kings awarded land to their representative conquerors there. The new landowners attempted to organize the scattered Indians into concentrated towns for administrative purposes. These towns, following the Spanish example, had commonly-owned land or *ejidos.*

This system continued in Mexico for over 300 years into the nineteenth century until the great Mexican reformer, Benito Juárez, became President. His reform laws, the *Ley Lerdo* of 1863 and the *Ley de Reforma* of 1867, turned church and *ejido* land over to individual owners. The idealistic objective was for the peons to work their individual parcels. In fact, the illiterate individuals were not able to offer the same protection to the land as had the community as a whole. Much of the property was eventually sold for debt and was concentrated again into large land holdings or *haciendas.*

In part, the Revolution of 1910 was a reaction to the feudal-like system that resulted. In 1917 the new constitution offered *Restitución* of the *ejido* lands to those communities that could prove communal ownership prior to the 1860s. Often the original sixteenth and seventeenth century Spanish document provided this proof. As the Revolution progressed through various stages, much more land was added to the communal system. This accelerated in the 1930s when Lázaro Cárdenas was elected President. The government organized *ejidos* on hundreds of former haciendas in states from Baja California to Yucatán. Mata Ortiz was one of those new *ejidos.*

Train carrying lumber from "Pearson" (Mata Ortiz) about 1910.

In its heyday the village had cantinas, dance halls, a movie theater, and the Hotel Colón, all contained within its flat-roofed adobe walls. However, in the early 1960s, the railroad yard was moved to Nuevo Casas Grandes, depriving the community of most of its economic base. The occupations that remained involved cattle for those who could afford to buy cows or day labor on distant railroad tracks, in the orchards, or to the north across the border. By the 1970s Mata Ortiz was remote, poor, and seemed destined to further decay and oblivion.

None of this background suggests that Mata Ortiz was fertile ground for a major artistic movement. There was no traditional art and few crafts that could be considered folk art except for leather work and saddle-blanket weaving associated with horses and cattle. The great pool of artistic tradition in Mexico lapped only at the edges of *El Norte.* Then came Juan.

Who Was Pearson?

The villagers sometimes still use Mata Ortiz's earlier name. The local oral history has it that a "Lord Pearson" from England established the lumber mill and extended the railroad through the village to the next major town on the line, Madera. He abandoned the mill during the chaos of the Revolution, and left Mexico for other adventures, eventually sinking with the Titanic. This story, told many times, points directly to Mexico's greatest foreign entrepreneur, Weetman Pearson, First Viscount Cowdray, who was given that title by the King of England for his significant engineering and contracting achievements throughout the world. Pearson spent years in Mexico, and the name, the title, the reputation, and the time period all point to him as the namesake of the village. The only problem is that he died in bed at his estate in England, not on the Titanic.

Dr. R.B. Brown, the Paquimé archaeologist, became intrigued with this

90

bit of historical trivia. On one of his many trips to Chihuahua City to deal with the authorities, he researched the question. In obscure books about early railroading in Mexico, he found references to a Canadian engineer and businessman (not an English lord), Dr. Frederick Stark Pearson, who had bought the Rio Grande, Sierra Madre, and Pacific Railroad in 1909 in collaboration with Enrique Creel. Using English capital, Dr. Pearson bought and extended other lines under the name "Mexico Northwestern Railroad." At the railroad camp at the end of the line, which subsequently took the name of "Pearson," he established a large lumber mill. Clarence Cooper, described as a brilliant engineer who also may have been one of the owners, was hired to build and operate it. From the growing village of "Pearson," Dr. Pearson extended the

Lumber mill at "Pearson" (Mata Ortiz) about 1910.

railroad line south over the mountains completing the rail line loop through the lumber country from Ciudad Juárez to Chihuahua. This research by Dr. Brown seems to indicate that the man we are looking for as the namesake of "Pearson" is Dr. F.S. Pearson and not Weetman Pearson, the great Lord Cowdray.

During the turmoil of the Revolution, Dr. Pearson struggled to keep his rail lines open and operating. He appealed to the United States for help, but because he was Canadian, he received little support. Finally in 1914, when Pancho Villa took control of most of his installations, Pearson sold or abandoned his Mexican mill and railroad investments. He pursued other developments in Spain and the Caribbean but never again in Mexico. Also he did not die on the Titanic. He went down with the Lusitania, torpedoed by the Germans in 1917.

The Battle of Tres Castillos

The next obvious question is, "Who was Juan Mata Ortiz?" His story is more dramatic than that of Dr. Pearson. In the early 1880s the Apaches under their leader Victorio were causing even bigger problems than usual. Pressured by settlement and the United States Army across the border, they penetrated deep into Chihuahua and stayed for long periods of time raiding and killing. The governor general of Chihuahua, the grand landholder Don Luis Terrazas, was angry and frustrated, but his military chief said he had no one to fight the marauders. Don Luis turned to his nephew, Colonel Joachim Terrazas and appointed him commander of a special expedition to raise an army and drive out the Apaches. The second in command was Major Juan Mata Ortiz, an experienced older soldier. The two officers traveled to villages all over Chihuahua and recruited and armed 600 men willing to fight, including several Tarahumara Indians. Although ordinarily peaceful people, this group had suffered greatly from the Apaches.

This force rode into the sierra and began to clear out the marauders. They caught up with Victorio and his main group at a place called Tres Castillos to the east of Mata Ortiz in the *Municipio* of Coyame. Terrazas and Ortiz and their men attacked and fought all day. Most of Victorio's fighters were killed or wounded, and ironically, he himself died under the vengeful hand of a Tarahumara Indian. By the end of the day, there were seventy-two Apaches dead and 200 wounded. The remainder were rounded up — men, women and children — and marched into Chihuahua City with lassos around their necks. The victors paraded the prisoners through the city along with Victorio's head stuck on a lance. After being displayed as a curiosity, the Indians marched under guard hundreds of miles north to reservations in the United States.

The Apaches were not completely eliminated for two more years, but Colonel Terrazas and Major Ortiz became the heroes of the Battle of Tres Castillos. Years later, in 1925, when it was time to eliminate North American place names, it was also politically correct to bypass the Terrazas name, and change the Anglo name of Pearson to that of the old Indian fighter, Juan Mata Ortiz.

The Great City of Paquimé

A hundred years ago when Adolph F. Bandelier paused in his ascent of the Sierra Madre to look back over the broad plain toward the present-day site of Mata Ortiz, he noted the "aboriginal ruins ... recalling isolated houses of clay peculiar to the Casas Grandes Valley." From these same ruins, most no more than mounds, came the shards that were to have such influence on Juan Quezada and his family and neighbors. Juan and the other locals call the ruin sites *moctezumas,* and there are at least a thousand spreading out for miles along the rivers and into the plains, foothills, and mountains surrounding the core of the Casas Grandes Valley.

The ceramic style of the shards, the unusual "T" shaped doors, the "rammed earth" walls, and other features and artifacts all indicate that these ruins were satellite habitations of the "Casas Grandes" culture centered in the great city of Paquimé. The remnants of this city — multi-story adobe walls, pillars, cisterns, ball courts, and huge stone platforms — are located near the river in the Casas Grandes Valley about 15 miles north of Mata Ortiz, adjacent to the old town of Casas Grandes.

The first Spaniard to see the "Big Houses" was a young explorer, Francisco de Ibarra, in 1565, during an arduous three-year exploration of northern Mexico. His chronicler, Baltasar de Obregon, called the city "Paquimé" and wrote that the city "contains buildings that seemed to have been constructed by the ancient Romans. It is marvelous to look upon."

Paquimé, the center of the Casas Grandes culture.   Photo: Hermann Knechtle

Ibarra and Obregon camped among the buildings which, at that time, had been abandoned for only about 225 years. Undoubtedly these structures were in much better condition than when the city was excavated and studied almost 400 years later. The site covered about 400 acres including spacious courtyards, ball courts, and large apartment-style structures. The walls were of thick adobe but not adobe bricks. They were apparently poured in place using forms and then covered with plaster after drying. The forms for these so-called "rammed earth" walls were placed a section at a time which has the effect of creating huge blocks. As the walls deteriorated in later centuries these blocks have become evident. Roofs and second stories were supported by horizontal beams made of tree trunks. Walls and pillars still standing suggest that some of the buildings were four or more stories.

For reasons that have never been determined, the doors were the so-called "T" shape. Perhaps it was a defensive measure, no one knows. The living quarters inside had raised cooking hearths, stairways, and sleeping platforms.

Other interior rooms had workshops for ceramics, copper, feathers, weaving, and stone work. A system of stone-lined ditches and cisterns provided water and perhaps drainage or waste removal.

The ancient planners carefully located their city on the west bank of the Casas Grandes River in one of the most fertile valleys in northern Chihuahua. The river begins a few miles to the south in San Diego at a point

Prehistoric Casas Grandes pot.
Photo: N. Prasad

were the Palanganas River, which flows by Mata Ortiz, joins the Piedras Verdes River which flows by Zaragoza and the Cave of the Olla, high in the Sierra Madre mountains. The river flows on to the northwest and empties into Lake Guzman.

About three miles to the west is a steep, bald hill, called Cerro de Moctezuma. On top are the remains of an ancient circular watch tower with stone walls two feet thick. Below the tower are ruins which might have been the residences for the garrison of this strategic hilltop. From this vantage point, lookouts could see a long distance in every direction. Bandelier reported that well-used trails descended in every direction: towards the east to the city; to the north and northeast; to the west to the villages along the Piedras Verdes River; and to the southwest and south to the villages along the Palanganas River.

When Bandelier, Carl Lumholtz, and the other 19th century explorers saw the ruins, the roofs had fallen in and the spaces between the walls were filled with a fine, powdery debris from the gradual decay and collapse of the roofs and upper stories. Within the soft debris they found pieces of a beautiful ceramic ware. Lumholtz described the pieces as "far superior in quality and decoration to anything now made in Mexico." Lumholtz also described beautifully-made stone implements including well-finished *metates* used for grinding corn. These ancient implements were prized by the local Indians and were still used in the late nineteenth century whenever one was found.

When Paquimé was excavated, the archaeologists found one room full of skulls each with a hole punched through it and missing the jawbone. In another they unearthed thousands of sea shells, later traced to the Pacific Coast area way to the south. They discovered turkey, macaw, and parrot bones in rows of small compartments which must have been cages. Circles of carved stone with a stone plug in the center formed the doors to the cages, possibly to withstand the gnawing of heavy beaks.

Also in the debris were human skeletons, some in obvious burials and others sprawled about as if left from a massacre. Burned posts and beams suggested a terrible fire and intentional destruction.

All of this says that a few hundred years ago a sophisticated culture existed in northern Chihuahua centered in a large city. It appeared, flourished, declined, and disappeared. Beyond this, its history is guesswork, even though it is educated guesswork by trained anthropologists and archaeologists. Who these people were, where they came from, how they interrelated with other cultures, and what was their fate, no one really knows. Dr. R.B. Brown, the archaeologist at Paquimé, calls it a "three-dimensional jigsaw puzzle, missing 90 percent of the pieces."

The major excavations and study of Paquimé and the surrounding Casas Grandes cultural area were made between 1958 and 1961 by a team headed by Dr. Charles C. DiPeso, Director of the Amerind Foundation in Arizona. The results of this work were published in 1974 by Dr. DiPeso in three large volumes supported by five other reference volumes of notes and source material. The total work is called *CASAS GRANDES: A Fallen Trading Center of the Gran Chichimeca.* The first volume subtitled the "Viejo Period" describes the hunter/gatherers and early agriculturists who wandered for thousands of years in the American Southwest and the Mexican El Norte, an area DiPeso calls the *Gran Chichimeca.* The second volume, the "Medio Period" covers the flowering of the Casas Grandes as an agricultural and trading culture. The third volume, "Tardio and Espanola" covers the decline and fall of the culture and the period after the arrival of the Spanish.

This important work formed the framework for all study of the Casas Grandes culture. Scientists and students either agree or disagree with DiPeso; none ignore him.

The standard thinking based on DiPeso and others is that human hunter/gatherers existed in the Gran Chichimeca for at least ten thousand years before the birth of Christ. They survived the demise of the mammoths and mastodons and continued their wandering ways leaving behind some stone spear points here and there. About the time of Christ, a few groups began rudimentary agriculture. Gradually some of these moved into simple pit-house villages, making pottery and introducing different crops. DiPeso feels that by AD 700 a portion, probably less than one half, of the people had adopted some form of sedentary living.

In the meantime, in southern Mexico and Guatemala, a general area referred to as "Mesoamerica," very sophisticated cultures had developed. Some features of these more advanced cultures spread north to the *Gran Chichimeca.* The experts disagree as to how. Some subscribe to the "diffusion" theory or the "pebble-in-the-pond" whereby the ever-diminishing ripples spread out from the big splash in the middle. DiPeso had another theory. He believed that traders or *puchtecas*, representing business interests in Mesoamerica, came up from the south and established trade centers in strategic locations with certain of the indigenous peoples. These centers became islands of advanced culture whose influence spread into surrounding areas as they prospered. There are many versions in Mesoamerican and Gran Chichimecan iconography of the figure with a hump or burden on his back, including the famous Hopi figure Kokopelli. Some of these figures may represent the *puchteca* trader on the trail to new markets.

In any case, the area around Paquimé changed rapidly. The pit house villages were covered over by walled rooms and compounds. Later in the city itself, massive, multi-storied buildings grew up, surrounded by a complex of ceremonial structures, plazas, and ball courts. The more sophisticated residents created a fine pottery and established elaborate bird facilities. Traders packed the pottery and bird feathers over trails that went in all directions to other islands of emerging civilization. The return trip brought turquoise, sea shells, salt, copper, and perhaps better strains of corn, perhaps slaves, perhaps peyote, but certainly news of developments beyond the mountains. Work became specialized as craftsmen used shell, copper, wood, stone, bone, feathers, and various fibers to create utilitarian, decorative, and ceremonial objects. Mesoamerican religious forms appeared such as plumed serpent motifs of the god Quetzalcoatl.

Most impressive to archaeologists was the vast agriculture and irrigation system surrounding Paquimé. They found evidence of this over hundreds of miles in the mountains, high plains and river bottoms. A series of thousands of arroyo check dams of rock, terraces and trenches protected the top soil and directed the water to crop-growing areas. Remnants of this system, *trincheras,* can be seen all around the Mata Ortiz/Casas Grandes area.

One of the most unique of the Casas Grandes satellite agricultural areas is located in Cave Valley high in the Sierra Madre, four hours by truck from Mata Ortiz. Through this little valley flows the Piedras Verdes River on the way to its junction with the Palanganas to form the Casas Grandes River. For hundreds of years to the present, corn, squash, and other crops have been grown in the river bottom, while the caves in the sides of the valley provided shelter for the prehistoric farmers. Dwelling walls, shards, and stone tools in the Casas Grandes style abound. Juan and Nicolás once found a mummy while exploring one of the caves. Under the lip of one large cave, referred to as the Cave of the Olla, is a huge, jar-shaped structure. Made of adobe and straw, it is over twelve feet high. It may have been a granary, but there is nothing quite like it north or south of the border. The Cave of the Olla has been the location of several of Juan's on-site classes. Students fortunate enough to come and work in this remote spot are haunted by the memory of this giant *olla.*

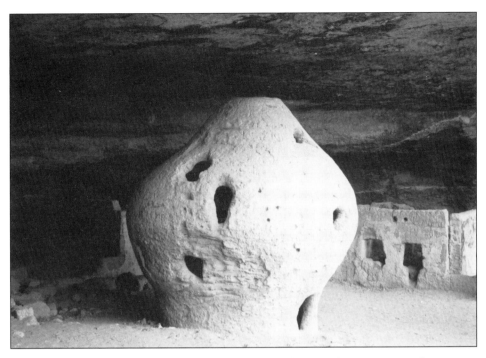

Cave of the Olla, ruins from the Casas Grandes culture in the mountains above Mata Ortiz.

By the mid 13th century the Casas Grandes culture had reached its zenith. Its influence had spread over thousands of square miles of northwestern Chihuahua and northwestern Sonora. As many as a thousand villages adopted various aspects of the culture and looked to Paquimé as the trade and cultural center. Barely one hundred years later, the culture was dead and the city and outlying communities abandoned to occasional wanderers seeking shelter.

No one knows what happened. Similar centers of culture such as Mesa Verde and Chaco in the *Gran Chichimeca* were abandoned at roughly the same time. Experts develop theories including drought, revolt from within, and challenges from strong enemies, but none satisfactorily account for such a rapid demise. Perhaps Casas Grandes was gradually weakened by a loss of agriculture production that allowed nomadic enemies to overcome it.

There is evidence of a single cataclysmic event at Paquimé with hundreds of men, women, and children killed, shrines defiled, and the city burned. DiPeso identifies 1340 as the year of the destruction. Dr. Brown says that recent studies indicate that all Casas Grandes dating may have to be moved forward 100 to 200 years and this final disaster probably occurred later. Whatever the date, DiPeso's studies show that the Paquimé had been declining for a couple of generations before the decisive destructive event. Trade goods were still manufactured, but few repairs were made of the buildings and new work was slovenly. After the final blow, the survivors left.

No one knows where they went. When the Anasazi left Mesa Verde and the other centers of the Four Corners area, many relocated in places that today can be identified as the Zuni, Hopi, and the northern Rio Grande Pueblos. The prehistoric Hohokam of the Casa Grande in Arizona can be traced to the modern Pima and Papago tribes. Undoubtedly after Paquimé was abandoned, many people lived on in the satellite villages. Spanish explorers found some Indians living in rammed earth buildings in outlying regions on the fringes of the Casas Grandes area of influence. DiPeso makes an argument that these were survivors of the culture. However, the Casas Grandes people cannot or at least have not been traced to any specific post Spanish-contact tribe, and certainly no one today claims any Casas Grandes ancestry. The indigenous peoples first encountered around Paquimé were nomadic late-comers.

This is important when evaluating Juan Quezada's achievements. Sometimes he erroneously is characterized in the same way as the Pueblo Indian artists with roots deep in a prehistoric culture. However, the Casas Grandes people had been displaced by others around Mata Ortiz hundreds of years before Juan's family or any of the ancestors of any of the current inhabitants arrived in the area. Casas Grandes had no direct or indirect influence on Juan except for the shards he found in the ground. The inspiration of the shards combined with his artistic genius produced the ceramic miracle in Mata Ortiz, not an inherited tradition.

For 500 years, Paquimé moldered and melted. Poor squatters rebuilt some of the old walls into homes. No one noticed. At the start of the 20th century, the ruins of the American Southwest were receiving serious attention from archaeologists. Also, the great civilizations of central and southern Mexico were the subject of international study. Paquimé was ignored.

Finally, in the late 1950s, Dr. Charles DiPeso convinced enough people on both sides of the border that Paquimé was a very important prehistoric city, and the Casas Grandes was a major culture of the *Gran Chichimeca*. He received funding, assembled an international team, obtained permits, relocated the squatters, and began excavation and study. Three years later in September, 1961, the site was turned over to the protection of the *Instituto Nacional de Antropología e Historia*. For the next 13 years, the Amerind Foundation studied the massive amounts of data and artifacts collected by the DiPeso expedition which culminated in the publication of the eight-volume study in 1974.

DiPeso's was a major effort, but after the team left, Paquimé was again left virtually alone. The *Instituto* assigned one of Dr. DiPeso's assistants, Eduardo Contreras, to the site. Contreras represented the Mexican government on the DiPeso expedition and made important contributions to that work during the entire three years of the project. For the next several years with very limited resources, he did his best to protect and preserve the ruins. He performed some reconstruction and stabilization of the steadily deteriorating adobe walls and supervised the visitors, who found their way to the tiny building at the entrance to the site. In 1988, Dr. R.B. Brown took over this assignment.

A dedicated Englishman, originally from Newcastle, Ben Brown trained at the University of Arizona and the Colegio del Bajío in León, Mexico. He holds forth from rooms in a hotel in Nuevo Casas packed with books on archaeology and history. With only a few laborers to help, he is responsible for guarding, maintaining, preserving, restoring, and interpreting Paquimé as well as serving as guide, host, and advisor to the travelers who knock on his door or find him supervising a repair on site.

He is very knowledgeable on his subject and can answer most questions about Paquimé ...except, who were the people who lived there? ...and, what really happened to them?

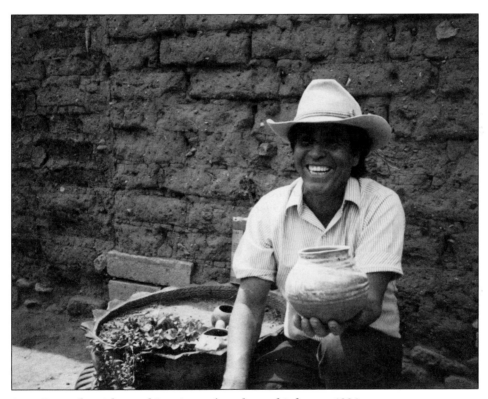

Juan Quezada with a prehistoric pot found near his house, 1986.

CHAPTER 6
CLAY AND FIRE

Nicolás Quezada

Finding and Processing the Clay

Pottery making in all traditions from all ages can be broken down into four distinct steps. One, the clay is found and processed. Two, the pot is formed from the processed clay. Three, the pot is decorated by painting or incising. Four, the pot is heated to a certain temperature to harden or vitrify the clay. Techniques and styles may vary, but all ceramics, from primitive earthenware to sophisticated porcelains, one way or another go through these four steps.

Juan worked out each step by trial and error and careful thought. First, he reasoned that if the ancient people made pots there must be clay, and there is — lots of it. Much of the earth's crust is alumina silicate, the basic ingredient of clay formed over eons by wind, water and ice pulverizing cooled molten rock. The trick is to find relatively pure concentrations which can be readily processed into a usable plastic material. This is not difficult around Mata Ortiz.

Clay can be found in veins or "lens" along arroyos, in flat areas on the *llano,* and in the mountains. The most common is *amarillo,* a gray clay that fires to a yellowish, beige color. The classic Mata Ortiz polychrome pot is made from this clay.

Juan initially looked for the purest clays, reasoning that pure clay could be worked better. This led to many cracked pots until he discovered that clay with a natural "temper" worked better. As all experienced potters know, clay needs a certain amount of an inert additive to give it structure as it dries and is fired. Temper can be sand or "grog," which is ground-up fired clay added to the clay in various proportions.

In most of the clays around Mata Ortiz, temper appears naturally in the form of volcanic ash. When Juan examined the edges of the fired prehistoric shards, he could see the temper. He thought the ancient people used such clay because it occurred naturally, but after many experiments, he concluded that it must have been a conscious decision.

Red clay is often used to make the highly polished black pots because of its high iron content. In the "reduction" firing described later, this red clay turns to a deep black. In a regular "oxidation" firing it stays a beautiful brick red. The red clay can be mixed with *amarillo* or white clays to create various shades of salmon.

The rarest and most difficult-to-use clays are the whites. It was years before Juan found white clay. He knew it existed because he found white clay shards of what appeared to be the best prehistoric pieces. When he finally

Opposite: *Juan forms a lip for the* olla, *1989.* Photo: Topi Arvi

101

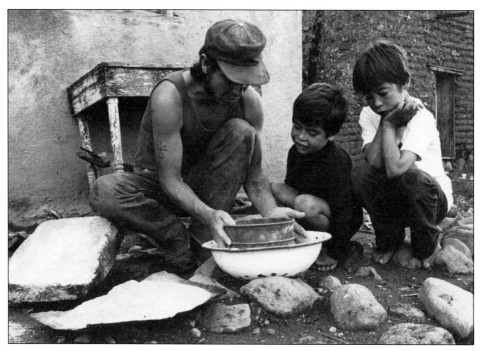

Juan sifts the clay ground on the metate *while Juan Junior and Noe watch, 1977.*
Photo: Bobby Furst

found some, he kept it secret from everyone except his brother Nicolás. Later Nicolás found his own sources in the mountains. On one trip to collect white clay, Nicolás noticed two men following him, watching from a distance. He avoided the white clay site and took a circular route home. The next trip he was followed again. This time he went into a different area, stopped, and loaded his pickup with "kaliche," hauled it home, and dumped it into the river. Kaliche is a soil common in the area. It has interesting properties such as drying into a very solid mass. That made it very useful to the ancient people as a building material. However, no matter how it is handled, it will not fire into a pot. On Nicolás' third trip for white clay, he was not followed. He returned via the kaliche site and noticed recent evidence of heavy digging!

Not only is the white clay rare, it is extremely difficult to work. Stiff and brittle, it is the opposite of the plastic *amarillo*. The chorus of curses from experienced American potters working with Juan or Nicolás is vocal testimony to the problem. However in the hands of skilled masters, the whites form some of the most dramatic pieces.

For a long time, only Juan and Nicolás used white. Nicolás particularly has made it something of a specialty. His fine black lines and solid red designs against the dead-white surfaces result in some of his best work. Other potters have found white clay and use it well, but it is still not common. Juan

102

and Nicolás continue to search the hills for the "whitest of the white."

The clays are found in all forms from solid chunks to soft earth. Juan at one early point used rock-hard chunks from a particular site. This had to be broken up and ground before it could be soaked to release the clay. He laughs because he later found softer versions of the same thing. But those who spied on him are still laboriously breaking up the big ones into little ones.

The raw clay is placed in buckets or tubs of water to soak. Later it is poured through a strainer, usually an old dress or table cloth. Only the portion is used that has dissolved in the bucket and passed through the strainer. The resulting solution is allowed to settle. The clear water is poured off, and the residue of clay is poured out on plaster of Paris slabs to dry partially. When the clay is sticky and malleable, it is wadded up (wedged) and packed into plastic bags.

The potters agree that aging the clay makes it easier to work; however, most do not have time to wait. As Nicolás says, *"Tenemos que comer,"* or "We have to eat," so the new clay is used as soon as it is needed.

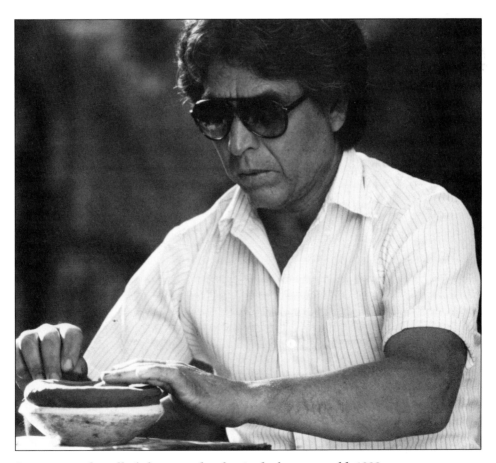

Juan presses the roll of clay onto the clay in the bottom mold, 1989.

Photo: Topi Arvi

103

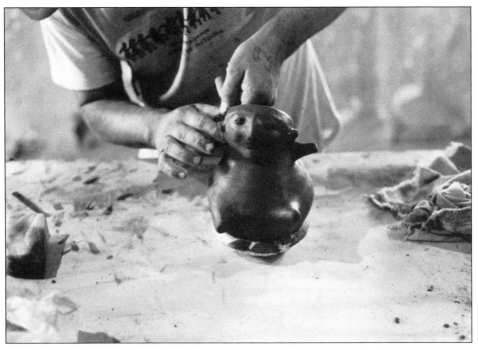

Nicolás forms an effigy figure, 1990.

Forming the Pot

One of the misconceptions about the potters of Mata Ortiz is that there is a standard way of forming a pot. It is thought that Juan developed a technique, taught his brothers and sisters who taught others, and the ripples went out evenly from the center splash. However communication in a small Mexican village, even among family members, is different and far less open than in the typical Anglo society. Teaching in the classic teacher/pupil relationship does not happen very often. Most in Mata Ortiz have learned their skills almost surreptitiously, by observation and experimentation. It is common for potters to respond when asked that they taught themselves and had no teachers. After a few such responses, one is given the impression that this original knowledge sprang from the head of the potter, and it is a mere coincidence that several dozen of his neighbors are doing the same thing. However it is true that no one sat the potter down and showed him the process step by step. A casual glance over a shoulder, an oblique question, and a clue here or there over time is the more likely way he or she learned. Some aspiring potters sent their children to look for throwaways around the Quezadas' houses that could be studied. Some of the potters will acknowledge a debt to a mentor, as do all of Consolación's children. Juan certainly showed his family, and others such as Taurina Baca, his basic concepts. Still, observation and trial-and-error rather than instruction seem to be the standard way to learn the craft. Therefore, instead of the expected uniformity among the village potters, there is a surprising diversity of technique for forming a pot.

Everyone uses certain of Juan's basic steps. The first is to use a plaster-of-Paris mold to form the pot bottom. All Mata Ortiz pots start out with round bottoms formed in a mold. If the bottom of a finished pot has a flat place to make it stand securely, it has been pressed gently on a flat surface when the clay was still wet.

To begin a pot, a piece of clay is kneaded into a round lump and then rolled out flat with a rolling pin-like tool into a flat tortilla. This is placed gently into a mold that has been coated with vegetable oil. The top edges of the tortilla are folded into pleats to allow the bottom and sides of the tortilla to be pressed into the mold. The clay is pressed gently from the sides down. It is tempting to press the middle first which can cause invisible cracks. The excess clay is trimmed with a knife or hacksaw blade, the universal tool.

The next step is to place a fat coil or doughnut of clay directly on top of the edge of the tortilla in the mold. This *chorizo* is carefully attached to the tortilla edge and then pinched up to form the pot. This is not the coiled pot of the American Indian Southwest where many small coils are built up and then smoothed into shape with a gourd rib. This is actually more like wheel-thrown pots. Here the pot is pinched up, rotated, pinched up again, rotated over and over until the clay is pulled up to the desired form. The difference is that wheel-thrown pots are pulled up in a continuous motion as the clay is mechanically rotated.

If done skillfully, the pinched pot will have a uniform thickness and shape, and the opening at the top will be even all around. To this top Juan often adds a second tiny coil from which he forms the lip.

This so-called "single coil" method developed by Juan is the basic technique used by potters all over the village. However as noted, there are interesting individual variations. Nicolás, some experienced ISOMATA students were surprised to learn, always uses two coils and sometimes three or more. At the other extreme is Ramiro Veloz, Juan's next-door neighbor, who uses no coils at all. He pinches up the entire pot from a very fat tortilla in the mold. The result is an extremely thin porcelain-like pot. Ramiro's pots were exquisitely painted by his wife Sylvia until her tragic death from cancer in July, 1991. Ramiro, Jr., 13, began painting his father's pots in 1993. Felix Ortiz and some of his followers have always used many coils, particularly on large pieces. Jaime Domínguez and Jesús Lozano, prolific makers of beautiful black pots, simply trim off the top edge with a knife, similar to trimming a wheel-thrown pot with a needle, something never done by the Quezadas.

Generally, the only tool used is the hacksaw blade. Right after the pot is formed, the surfaces are gone over with the toothed edge of the blade to even out the clay, redistributing clay from high to low places and from thick to thin places. This is called *segueteando* which literally means "hacksaw blading." The serrations in the clay caused by the teeth are then smoothed with the flat side of the blade. It is likely that the ancient potters used a piece of gourd for this step. The finished pot is wiped carefully with a sponge and left to dry to a leather-hard condition. The pot is then removed from the mold and any roughness on the bottom or mold joint smoothed with the flat side of

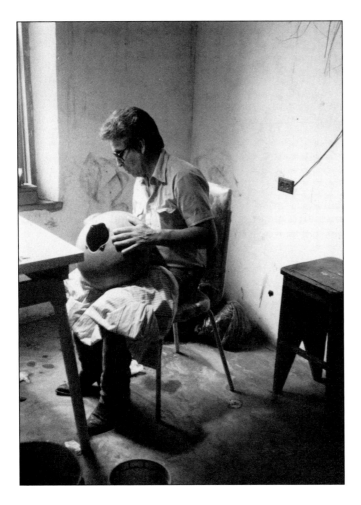

Juan sands the pot surface, 1991.

the hacksaw blade.

Juan, Nicolás, and the other family members used to paint their pots at this stage before they dried. The painted designs were set into the wet clay body with a polishing stone. The result was different, but it was more difficult to control the paint on the wet surface. Now the most common technique is to let the pot dry completely and then sand it perfectly smooth. The dry surface permits the artist to paint very fine lines without bleeding. The drawback is that when water in the form of wet paint is reintroduced to the sides of the dry pot, it can cause a weak spot, particularly in large thin-walled pieces. These weak areas can crack later in the firing. Juan thinks the prehistoric pots were painted wet. They were physically stronger because the clay was compressed with the polishing stone. This was important for pots which were used domestically. Juan says that if he made a pot to hold water or for cooking, he would polish it inside and out while wet to compress and help seal the clay. The Mata Ortiz pots are used primarily for decorative purposes, and therefore the point is to prepare a surface which will lend itself to the best designs.

After the pot is dry and sanded, vegetable oil is applied with a piece of clean plastic or brush. It is rubbed with the bare hands until the shine from the oil is gone, then rubbed with a slightly damp cloth which helps seal the exterior. This process is repeated. After the pot dries, it is polished with a cloth again. The result is a satin matte finish which can be painted, or the pot can be polished with a stone to obtain a higher sheen.

Polishing with a stone is a technique dating to prehistoric times. A very smooth round stone is gently rubbed over the surface. The goal is to obtain a uniform sheen without creating a mass of streaks. This is difficult and takes just the right touch. It is not uncommon to find a patient wife polishing the pots of her more celebrated potter husband. If the pot is to be fired black, then it is polished a third time with clean plastic, such as a wad of Saranwrap, without using oil. Now the pot is ready to paint.

Painting and Design

Forming clay into a thin, symmetrical vessel with a uniform sheen is a demanding process. However it is wasted if the piece is not well painted. Although most Mata Ortiz potters make and paint their work, it is not uncommon to find one family member forming the pot and another painting.

Most of the paints used are reds from iron oxides and blacks from manganese. Both minerals occur naturally in various forms around Mata Ortiz and are available to the artists. Other colors used occasionally — such as white — are liquid clay or slip. Juan, Nicolás, and the other leading potters are always experimenting with paints just as they do with clay. The objectives are rich, intense blacks and reds. In late 1991, Juan showed visitors some test pots painted with his best black ever which he had just developed. He said the paint had some *azul* or blue in it. This must have been some impurity which helped give the paint a deep blackness with no thin spots on the fired piece.

As noted, the classic Quezada technique is to paint directly on the burnished clay. The alternative, common in the pueblos of the American Southwest, is to "slip" the pot: that is to paint the surface of the pot with a liquid clay. This forms the base for the painted designs. Felix Ortiz slips many of his pieces, and the technique is common in the Porvenir barrio. However in "El Centro" where Juan and the other Quezadas live, only Consolación regularly uses a special wine-colored slip which has become her trade mark.

The paint brushes are made from a few very straight strands of human hair, usually from a child. These are tied to the end of a stick, the brush handle, with common thread. The hairs of the brush are one and one half to two inches long. The technique is to lay the long strands loaded with paint on the pot surface and pull it through to create a line. This is in contrast to attempting to make a line with the tip of the brush.

To insure symmetry the designs are usually either duplicated on both sides of the pot or the pot is divided into thirds with three sets of identical designs. The painter will mark a point on one side of the pot, turn it 180 degrees, and paint a line. Then the pot is turned back to the original dot, and the line is duplicated. The painter will continue adding lines and duplicating them on the other side until the design is complete.

Nervous students are told to take a deep breath, check to see that there are no drops on the brush hair, and touch the surface with the tip of the brush. Then the long strand is laid down on the surface and pulled through the line. Every line is gone over twice. Straight lines are relatively easy; tight curves, or *caracoles*, are hard. It was his ability to paint long curving patterns down the sides and bottoms of his pots that enabled Juan to first break away from the traditional geometric Casas Grandes designs.

The outlines of the design are filled in with a thicker brush, floating the paint into the spaces much like water-color technique. The outlines are often repainted after being filled in. It is important to keep the paint constantly mixed so that it covers flat and even, but thick enough so that the clay surface does not show through after firing.

After the paint has dried, the pot is polished for a final time to set the paint. Each potter has a favorite stone and sometimes even a favorite place on the stone. John Davis from Deming, New Mexico, has brought dozens of polished stones from rock shops in the United States to his friends in the village as very welcome gifts. Polishing stones have been used for centuries in various cultures and their use is standard procedure in the American Indian Southwest. However, conventional techniques do not always satisfy Juan. In the fall of 1991 he discovered that deer bone made a superior polishing tool. It was more forgiving and less likely to cause streaks. The beautiful pieces made that fall with the blue-black paint previously noted were all polished with the end of a four-inch long deer bone.

Occasionally, some of the lesser potters will use shoe wax to obtain a bright sheen on their pot. This is not considered an appropriate technique by the better potters, and any mediocre piece with a bright polish is suspect. Once a few years ago, Noe, Juan's oldest son, accompanied us as we visited potters throughout the village. In one house, he started picking up each shiny pot and sticking his nose in it, verifying the presence of wax by the lingering smell.

Pots that will be fired black with the "black on black" designs are painted after they are polished in the same way. However, the point of this painting is only to disrupt the polished surface. Therefore it is not necessary to paint the lines twice. After the pot is fired black, the painted design is a slightly roughened matte area, while the remainder of the surface is shiny black. It would be technically possible to create black-on-black designs by painting with just water. However, the artist must use pigmented paint in order to see the designs he creates. Spencer says it was Lydia that developed this black-on-black technique, one of the most popular in the village.

After the final polish, the pot is ready for the fire.

Juan paints a thin line while daughters Nena and Mireya watch, 1977.

Photo: Bobby Furst

Firing, the Last Step

Firing is the moment of truth. Before this, the pot, no matter how beautifully decorated, is still just dried clay. In the firing, as the temperature increases, then decreases during the cooling phase, many complex chemical changes take place that permanently alter the state of this clay. The material is fused together causing a decrease in porosity and a considerable increase in strength.

This is a violent process for a thin globe of dried clay. A few molecules of air or water trapped in the clay body will expand as the temperature rises and crack the piece or blow a hole in the side. The chemical reaction itself can cause cracks if the temperature increases or decreases too rapidly.

To prepare for the firing, the Mata Ortiz potters make very sure the ground is dry. Sometimes a fire is built on the firing place to insure dryness. The pot is usually pre-heated in the kitchen oven or next to an open fire. When it is ready, it is placed on three pieces of brick on the ground. A cover is placed over it, usually either a bucket or a large terra-cotta flower pot. This is the "kiln," or *quemadora.* Around this, dried cow chips are stacked carefully in a beehive shape. Kerosene is splashed on the beehive and lighted. The cow chips burn like a bonfire for 20 to 30 minutes. Then the potter begins knocking away the residue of the fuel with a rake or stick until the *quemadora* is completely exposed. Juan used to let the pot cool for a few minutes, then lift off the *quemadora* and with a hook, pick up the pot and rush it into the kitchen oven. There it cooled gradually. This sprint to the kitchen was very exciting, but after dropping a few pieces, Juan found that it worked almost as well to let the pot cool for 20 or so minutes under the *quemadora*. When it is time to remove this cover, the pot is revealed in the debris like a new-born baby, an exciting moment even for those that have witnessed it a thousand times.

A pot that survives the firing is now ready for use. Mata Ortiz ware is fired at a higher temperature than most pottery from the American Indian Southwest. In theory, the Mata Ortiz ware could be used to hold water or to cook beans, particularly if they were polished inside. However most pots were created as individual art pieces, and water jugs can be found elsewhere today. Nevertheless, the Mata Ortiz potters maintain the integrity of the process just as though they made utilitarian pieces.

Blackware

Most pots in Mata Ortiz are fired one at a time. Sometimes two or three black pots will be fired together. However, black pot firing involves an additional step. After the fire reaches a certain temperature, it is smothered, usually with dried horse manure, so that the pot inside is without oxygen. In this so called "reduction" atmosphere, a chemical reaction takes place, and the clay body color changes to black.

A fascinating characteristic of the reduction process is that it is reversible. In exhibitions, it is a great trick to show a painted beige pot, then fire it black. After the black "jewel" is shown to the crowd, the pot is refired in an oxygen atmosphere. The crowd always gasps as the pot in its original color is revealed under the *quemadora.*

The local prehistoric people made black pottery, a fact Juan knew from the shards he found. Like his other discoveries, he patiently experimented until he had worked out the techniques, although he does not understand the chemical reaction. His practical education does not extend to atoms and molecules. However, he knows exactly how to create the reaction, and he has a number of variations to create different effects.

Black pots are popular and sell well. Also they are easier to make. Painting errors are less obvious, and there is no problem with fire marks (usually caused by partial reduction on one spot of the pot's surface) or uneven color. Therefore many potters concentrate only on black-pot production and never attempt polychrome pieces.

Some that specialize in blackware use graphite to give a brilliant sheen to the surface. Powdered graphite is mixed with water, oil, and kerosene and applied to the pot with brush, sponge, or rag. These pots must be fired at a high temperature for a longer time because the graphite tends to insulate the clay. The results are dramatic, but the pot is softer in spite of the additional firing. Water and natural oils from handling can damage the designs and shiny surface.

Macario Ortiz and his brothers have developed another technique by adding a red lead mineral — they call it *almagre* — to their paint. Using

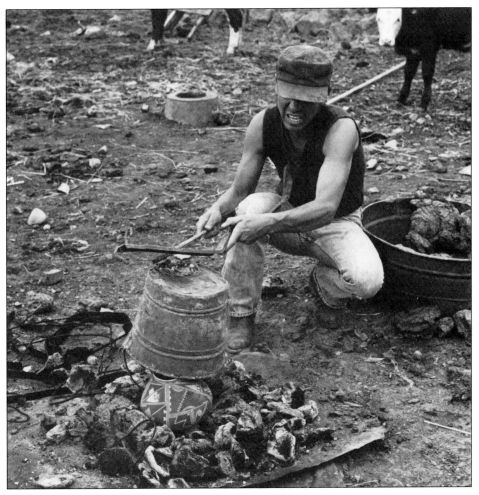

Juan removes the cover that protected the pot from the burning cow chips, 1977.
Photo: Bobby Furst

graphite and *almagre,* they can fire in an oxygen atmosphere and obtain brilliant black pieces with a reddish cast in the painted design.

The popularity of black pottery increases, and it is probably the most common product produced in Mata Ortiz.

Identification

Virtually all of the potters etch their signatures into the bottoms of the pots. Only very poor pieces are occasionally found unsigned. The signature not only identifies the potter, but clearly states that it was the intent of that potter to create a new art object, not a fake prehistoric or American Indian piece. Some potters include a date which is very useful for the collector. Juan began dating some of his pots in 1990.

Effigies by Manuel Rodríguez.

EPILOGUE

More of the Miracle

This book was written to tell the story of Juan Quezada and the early development of the ceramic art movement in Mata Ortiz. Others continued to chronicle the artistic and economic miracle as it gained acceptance in the art markets and as more and more villagers turned to pottery. However, none — writers, traders, collectors, or researchers — foresaw the incredible expansion of the art movement in the late 1990s. Since the first printing of this book in 1993, hundreds of villagers and members of nearby communities have begun working with the clay, producing high quality imaginative art beyond the dreams of the most enthusiastic *aficionados.* An increasing number of traders have joined the scene to open markets for the ware throughout the United States and in other countries.

If one must pick a date and place for the beginning of this rapid blossoming, it would be March, 1995, at the exhibition in the Fine Arts Gallery of the University of New Mexico. For nineteen years the word had been slowly spreading about this remarkable pottery from this obscure village in northern Chihuahua. Then all seemed to come together in this "fine arts" gallery to create a defining moment. Old collectors and new collectors mingled with anthropologists and art students viewing and discussing the work. Curator Bill Gilbert from the university ceramics department had selected the best from a broad range of master potters. This was not an exhibition just about Juan Quezada but about a number of artists doing unique, aesthetically-pleasing work. Nicolás Ortiz's now famous rabbit stood out like fine cloisonné in the museum setting along with Manuel Rodríguez's Escher-like pieces, and Hector and Graciela's Gallegos' superbly-crafted wedding jar. Many of the artists represented had been babies or children when Juan began. They had grown up playing and working with clay. When it was time to make a living, they turned directly to potting with years of experience behind them. This exhibition seemed to announce that the new generation had arrived with new ideas, shapes, and designs.

Through the rest of the nineties and into the new century, a series of exhibitions and special events followed one after another in prestigious museums throughout the United State and even in Mexico. Recognition in Mexico had always been minimal, particularly in the art circles of Mexico City. However, in the summer of 1999, the Franz Mayer Museum launched a spectacular exhibition with an opening party attended by over 400 people. At the same time the leading art magazine, *Artes de Mexico,* devoted an entire issue to the pottery. These activities culminated in December, 1999, when Juan Quezada received the *Premio,* the Mexican equivalent of the Nobel prize for Traditional and Popular Arts. Juan stood in the *Palacio Nacional* before a crowd of over one thousand to receive the gold medal from the hand of the President of Mexico.

The growth and success of the pottery movement has affected the Mata Ortiz villagers in different ways. Pickups, television sets, and cell phones are obvious symbols of economic improvement. Less obvious is the fact that children stay in school longer. Indoor plumbing and appliances ease the chores for women, and women potters can stay in their homes earning significant money while still carrying out their traditional tasks.

Mata Ortiz ceramic art continues to unfold before us. It seems logical that at some point this art movement, like others, should reach a plateau and stagnate. This has not happened yet. Virtually every trip to the village reveals a new artist or an established artist with an exciting new idea. Some of the best work is still out there, waiting to be created.

APPENDIX

The Potters of Mata Ortiz

Usually the buyer or admirer of a pot knows only the name on the bottom. However, even the most beautiful piece becomes more interesting when we learn something about the potter and where he or she fits into the village scheme of things. To that end, this list attempts to identify as many of the potters as possible. Many of the names are familiar and have been signed on hundreds of pots over the years, and some names have appeared on just a few pieces.

The Quezada family remains the dominant overall pottery group in Mata Ortiz. So much so that some relatives with other surnames use "Quezada" on their work, much to the amusement of Juan's immediate family. The most important Quezada potters of the first generation are Juan's brothers, Nicolás and Reynaldo, and his youngest sister, Lydia. Older sisters Consolación, Reynalda and Genoveva, brother Jesús and sister Rosa follow these. About twenty-five second generation Quezadas are now working, along with at least three of Consolación's grown grandchildren representing the third generation.

Beyond the Quezada family, no one knows exactly how many potters work in Mata Ortiz. It is even hard to define what is meant by the word "potter." Those who work full time at potting are easy to identify. However, some work only occasionally, spending most of their time at other pursuits. Others help the main potter of the family, performing certain tasks either regularly or occasionally. To define a "potter" for this list, we have followed the lead of the famous Indian potter, María Martínez. She began the practice of signing the pots. Even though potting in her pueblo was a group or family activity, the signer got the credit. Therefore, the following list includes those who sign pots.

All in the village acknowledge Juan as the master, and in general they follow his techniques and styles of forming, painting, and firing the pots. However some, over time, have developed styles of their own, and around the better of these, subgroups have formed following the style of the leader. There is no pattern to these groups. Often they are composed simply of family members or friends that live nearby.

One large group of potters with a distinct style has grown up at the other end of the village, across an *arroyo* draining into the Palanganas River. This neighborhood or *barrio* is called Porvenir. It was originally a migrant camp when the sawmill was in production at the turn of the century. There, soon after Juan started making pots, Felix Ortiz began developing his own style. He usually makes larger pots from thin coils which he covers with clay paint (slip) prior to painting with his own designs. So many of his neighbors have emulated him that Porvenir for years has produced a large amount of pottery. One with the same name as Felix but no relation is Nicolás Ortiz, a fine and well-known artist. Nicolás's four brothers, particularly Macario and Eduardo, are also good potters. The Ortiz brothers used to be musicians, playing regularly in a group, *Los Hermanos Ortiz.* Now they concentrate on pottery, and the three mentioned are among the best known in the village.

Mexican names can be confusing to *Norteamericanos* who do not understand the system. Men's names are formally expressed this way:

First name	Surname	Mother's maiden name
Juan	Quezada	Celado

Some (including Juan) drop their mother's maiden name for everyday usage. Women use the same form until they are married. Then they drop their mother's maiden name, keep their father's surname, and add their husband's name after the word *de.* Therefore Juan's wife's full name is expressed this way:

First name	Father's surname	Husband's surname
Guillermina	Olivas	de Quezada

Male potters usually, but not always, sign their work with first and surnames, sometimes adding the first letter of their mother's name. Women may use any combination of their maiden or married names. Anyone with Quezada as any part of their name will sign that as their surname. Nicknames add to the confusion. They are very common and often used in the pot signatures.

This list of potters is in alphabetical order by surname, and the names are expressed the way the potter usually signs the pot:

Aurelia Aldavas de López

Many of the extended López family live or lived in Barrio Adobe (also called Barrio López), a cluster of houses next to the cemetery a bit north of the main village. Aurelia Aldavaz de López and her husband Vincente moved from Barrio Adobe to the El Centro neighborhood, possibly to be near the little fundamentalist church there. They have several adult children involved with pottery including Edmundo, Eleazar, Nena, Silvia, and Susana. Nena married the well-known Macario Ortiz, who showed many of the López family the basics of pottery making.

Salbador Almazan

Salbador "Chava" Almazan Burciago learned from Pilo Mora in a workshop across from Humberto Ponce in Nuevo Casas Grandes. Chava's pots are often of white or mixed clay with designs similar to Pilo's. He painted some pots that Pilo formed when Pilo was having eye problems.

Angel Amaya

Angel Amaya Mora and his wife Abelina Corona live in the Porvenir section of the village. She forms small delicate white-clay pieces that Angel paints with fine curvilinear designs. The Amayas were influenced by the highly-regarded Pilo Mora who lived near them before he moved to Nuevo Casas Grandes.

Fernando Andrew

Fernando is the brother of Octavio Andrew and makes similar black pieces.

Octavio Andrew

Octavio Andrew Bugarini lives across the street from Consolación Quezada. In 1988 at age 18, he began working with Reynaldo, Juan's youngest brother. He makes only black pots which are quite good. Octavio is an example of a journeyman doing a limited thing well.

Alvaro Arrieta

Alvaro Arrieta Rodríguez, the son of Flora Rodríguez de Arrieta, is a kindergarten teacher in Cuauhtemoc, a village between Mata Ortiz and Colonia Juárez. The sales of his small well-painted polychrome *ollas* pay for his continuing education to be a primary teacher.

Flora Rodríguez de Arrieta

From Barrio Porvenir, she is the wife of Natividad Arrieta. She and Natie have worked together since about 1984. She makes the pots, he paints. Their three sons help with the sanding and polishing. The pottery is their main source of income, although Natie also farms a plot of land. All of the pots are signed by Flora.

Carmen Fierro de Baca

Carmen and her husband, Luis Baca, make black pieces with long thin necks, painted white with delicate thin-line designs.

Luis Baca

Luis Baca Carbajal is a cousin of Taurina Baca. He began potting about 1988 after learning from Mauro and Hilario Quezada. He still works as a *vaquero* for Taurina's father.

Salbador Baca

Salbador was born in Mata Ortiz but now lives with his wife Virginia Lozoya in Nuevo Casas Grandes. As a team, they produce quality polished blackware and polychrome pieces. Virginia forms very light thin-walled pots and wedding vases that Salbador paints and signs. Neighbor Jorge Quintana helped Salbador learn his painting skills. Salbador is a second cousin of the well-known Taurina Baca.

Taurina Baca

For years Taurina Baca Tena has been one of the best-known potters from Mata Ortiz. She was Juan's first non-family pupil and was featured along with Juan and his family in some of the earliest shows in the United States. A few years ago, she moved to Nuevo Casas Grandes and began a family. She continued to pot, sometimes making very large pieces, but her output was low and was usually purchased immediately by traders who knew her work. In 1991, she moved back to the village, and began making more pottery of yellow, white, and mixed clays, painted with classic Quezada-style designs. Her work appeared in the first traveling exhibit in 1979-80 mentioned on pages 22-24. Her picture is on page 32.

Roberto Bañuelos

Roberto Bañuelos Guerraro is another potter that openly acknowledges his respect and debt to Juan Quezada. However, he has had little direct contact with Juan, learning his craft instead from two of his wife's sisters, Gloria Isela López and Rosa López de Cota, sisters-in-law of Reynalda Quezada. Before Roberto started working with the clay, he had a family to feed and little else. He worked where he could, usually in the orchards of Colonia Juárez. *Por necesidad* he became a potter. He sold his first pots in a group in 1987 for two dollars. Roberto makes a variety of pot shapes and uses different designs. At first he was most noted for his Mimbres-style designs on plates. These he obtained from books on the American Southwest that traders gave him. However, Roberto is a natural artist, and his best work now is polychrome with his own designs. His wife, María de Los Angeles, "Angela," helps with various steps of the process and actually forms the *ollas*. Roberto forms the plates and other shapes. Occasionally Angela adds her signature to a pot, resulting in a rare two-signature piece. Bañuelos' work was included in the prestigious exhibition at the University of New Mexico Art Museum in the spring of 1995, the Franz Mayer exhibition in Mexico City in 1999, and the Exhibits USA *Potters of Mata Ortiz* traveling exhibition, 1999-2001.

César Bugarini

César Bugarini Soto is the son of Yolanda Soto and Miguel Bugarini. At age 14 in 1997, he was making and signing his own pieces, usually using red clay with small cone-shaped bottoms.

Elvira Bugarini Cota

An older sister of the popular Laura Bugarini, Elvira also paints the pieces her mother, Guadalupe Cota de López, makes. Her husband is Jesus Pedregón.

Enrique Bugarini

Enrique began potting in 1995. Encouraged by American artist Debi Flanigan, he produces a variety of work including unusual animals and nativity figures as well as more typical village pottery.

Laura Bugarini Cota

By the time Laura was 18 in 1995, she was an excellent painter. She lives in Barrio Adobe with her mother, Guadalupe Cota de López, who along with Rosa López makes most of the pots Laura paints. She has developed a unique style of tiny fine-line designs repeated over the entire pot, a sort of Chinese blind stitch. Two of her pieces appeared in the Exhibits USA *Potters of Mata Ortiz* traveling exhibition, 1999-2001.

Liliana Bugarini

Liliana Bugarini Ríos, the daughter of Teresa Ríos de Bugarini, makes primarily small black pots.

Loranzo Bugarini

Loranzo works with his wife Lucila Mora. He signs the lesser work, she signs the best. He learned from his mother-in-law, Jesús Maria Sandóval, about 1986.

Miguel Bugarini

Miguel is married to Yolando Soto. The Bugarinis and the Sotos live in the southwest corner of Barrio Porvenir and are associated by intermarriages. Miguel's house is next to Gloria Hernández. Most of the families are farmers as well as potters. Miguel makes large pieces with stripes, checks, and intricate banded designs.

Teresa Bugarini de Ríos

Teresa, a sister of Enrique and Miguel, lives in the Seccion area of the village which is next to the *arroyo* between the Porvenir and El Centro neighborhoods. She makes small, flat bottom black pots, assisted by her husband, Reymundo.

Yolanda Soto de Bugarini

Yolanda is the daughter of Lilia Velo de Soto and the sister of Guadalupe Soto de Mora and Chamin Soto de Núñez. Her husband is Miguel Bugarini. She makes extra large pots probably more suited for outdoor use.

Adalberto Calderón

Adalberto is a teacher in the village school. In addition to pottery, he makes Tarahumara-style drums and reproductions of stone tools.

Gris Camacho

Griselda Camacho de Silveira is married to Juan Silveira, the son of one of the old-time potters in Porvenir, Rojelio Silveira. Gris and Juan work together, but Gris signs all of their pieces.

Susana Camacho

From Barrio Porvenir, Susana Camacho de Villa and her family have been making pots since about 1989. Her husband, Benjamín Villa, paints much of their work, incorporating Indian motifs and snakes into his designs.

Ivan Castillo

Ivan lives in Nuevo Casas Grandes where he makes sgraffito-style pots.

Bertha Chacón

Bertha Chacón de Ortiz is married to Santos Ortiz, one of *Los Hermanos Ortiz.* Berta and Santos work as a team producing a commercial product, using the same designs and shapes repeatedly.

Jorge Cordero Luruena

Jorge is the son of Jorge Cordero Palacios. His work, like that of his father, often has unusual shapes and designs.

Jorge Cordero Palacios

Jorge is an agronomist who supplements his income making pottery. He lives in Nuevo Casas Grandes and has no direct family connections in Mata Ortiz. He learned from Pilo Mora. Jorge's pieces often have unusual shapes and designs reflecting his interpretation of the spirituality of the prehistoric people.

Alfredo Rodríguez Corona

While Alfredo's surname is Rodríguez, he is included here with his mother Sara's family.

Abelina Corona

Abelina Corona de Amaya is Mauro Quezada's niece. He taught her to pot. She forms small but elegant thin-walled pieces, often with long necks, spouts or handles, from white clay. Her husband, Angel Amaya, usually paints and signs these pieces, but Abelina does paint and sign some of her own work.

Florencia Corona

Florencia was 17 in 1997 and making small pieces with finely-detailed designs.

Guillermina Corona de López

Guillermina lives near Ana Trillo and her small red-clay pots with black designs reflects the work done by Ana and others in the neighborhood.

Jesús Corona

Jesús Corona González typically makes white pots with tightly-painted checkerboard designs. His brother is Jorge Corona González.

Jorge Corona

Jorge Corona Guillén is the brother of Abelina and Vidal Corona. He lives in Barrio López near Vidal. There are two unrelated Jorge Coronas.

Jorge Corona González

Another Jorge Corona, the son of Picole Corona, the watchman for the train station, lives in Barrio El Centro and makes primarily white polychrome pieces. He learned from Manuel Rodríguez as a teenager, and some of his fish designs follow Manuel's style.

Lupe Corona

Guadalupe "Lupe" Corona Jr., the father of Abelina, Jorge, and Vidal, lives in Barrio López. He makes white fish-shaped pieces and white double pots, called *cuates.* In 1997, he was the village sheriff. Lupe's father, Guadalupe Sr. was the former husband of Consolación Quezada and father of Mauro and Hilario Quezada. This connects the Quezada and Corona families, and some like Abelina Corona learned pottery from Mauro Quezada.

Sara Corona Rentería

Sara is a friend and sister-in-law of Ana Trillo and lives near her in Barrio Americano. Sara's work includes small red clay pieces similar in style to Ana's.

Vidal Corona

Vidal Corona Guillén, brother of Abelina and Jorge and a half brother of Hilario and Mauro Corona Quezada (his teacher), makes inventive polychrome and black *ollas.* He often makes pots for others to complete. His wife Luz Elva Gutiérrez helps him.

Gerardo Cota

Gerardo Cota Guillén lives at the north end of the village near the river where Juan and other Quezadas once lived. Gerardo was very much influenced by the Quezada family, and he began working with clay about 1986. He has emerged as one of the outstanding young potters of the village, although his production is low. His work appeared in the University of New Mexico Art Museum exhibition in the spring of 1995 and in the Exhibits USA *Potters of Mata Ortiz* traveling exhibition, 1999-2001

Jesús Cota

Jesús, a cousin of Gerardo Cota, lives in Barrio López (also called Barrio Adobe), a cluster of houses north of the village near the cemetery.

José Cota

José, a pupil of Reynaldo Quezada, makes good quality black pots.

Lupita Cota

In the late 1970s, Juan and Consolación Quezada taught pottery to a group of villagers which included Guadalupe "Lupita" Cota de López (identified as Lupita Cota Delgado on p. 12). Like most in this early group, she did not immediately try to make a living with pottery. She moved to Juárez to clean houses. However, when her daughters, Laura and Elvira Bugarini and Luci López, became teenagers, she returned to Mata Ortiz and began making pots with them so they would not have to leave home to work.

Martín Cota

Martín Cota Guillén, a younger (23 in 2000) brother of Gerardo Cota, is a creative young potter, doing imaginative work with irregular backgrounds and pot surfaces.

Ricardo Delgado

Ricardo Delgado Cruz lives in the *El Centro* area of the village. He does sgraffito work, carving animals into the surfaces of his pots in the manner of Leonel López Sáenz. However, he may have learned this technique from Oscar Rodríguez, who experimented with it years ago.

Angélica Domínguez

Angélica Domínguez Martínez, 23 years old in 2001, is the daughter of Tony Domínguez and Martha Martínez. She and her younger sister, Brenda, make small nicely-painted white pots similar to their mother's work and the work of others in the extended Martínez family. In the fall of 1995, the two girls were in the first class in the new *secondario* or high school in Colonia Juárez, a few miles from Mata Ortiz.

Antonio Domínguez

Tony is part of two well-known potting families. He is the older brother of Jaime and

César Domínguez, and his wife is Martha Martínez. He makes black graphite-style pots. He and Martha operated a small store, restaurant, and telephone service from the front of their home.

Brenda Domínguez
Brenda Domínguez Martínez, 20 years old in 2000, is the sister of Angélica and does similar work. She helps in the family store and runs the telephone service there.

César Domínguez
César Domínguez Alvarado is the older half-brother of the Jaime Domínguez. However, César concentrates on polychrome pieces while Jaime is known for his blackware. César's wife, Gaby, forms the pots, and César paints and signs them. In 1991 he and his brother-in-law Humberto Ponce moved their families to Nuevo Casas Grandes. César teaches school there as well as producing pottery with Gaby of sufficient quality to be included in the exhibition at the University of New Mexico Art Museum in the spring of 1995, where they were honored guests. Their work appeared in the Franz Mayer exhibit in Mexico City in 1999 and in the Exhibits USA *Potters of Mata Ortiz* traveling exhibition, 1999-2000. César and Gaby have taught classes at Idyllwild Arts (see page 39) for several summers.

Chela Domínguez
Martha Andrew de Domínguez, "Chela," is the matriarch of the extended Domínguez family, and the mother of Jaime and the stepmother of César and Tony. The Domínguezes are an old family in the village. When the railroad repair yards were located there, Chela's husband had a large store on the plaza. After the yards were moved to Nuevo Casas Grandes and the store closed, the family stayed and survived the hard economic times that followed. Now they concentrate almost exclusively on pottery. Chela makes small black *calabazas* or pots with fluted sides like winter squash.

Gaby Domínguez
María Gabriela Almeida Gallegos de Domínguez, "Gaby," the wife of César Domínguez, has always formed the pots for her husband. Occasionally she does paint and sign her own pieces. She is the niece of the well-known Hector Gallegos. Gaby has traveled many times to the United States to teach and demonstrate along with César.

Jaime Domínguez
Jaime Domínguez Andrew lives in the El Centro neighborhood of the village near the plaza. He is married to Dalia, a sister of Jesús Lozano. For years, he and Jesús were part of a subgroup producing small to medium, well-painted, well-polished black-on-black pieces. In the late 90s, he began making graphite-style black pieces, probably because of the influence of Jesus' brother Rubén Lozano, who lives nearby. Jaime runs the billiard parlor where the old family store used to be. However, he concentrates on his pottery and therefore does not open the parlor very often.

Manuela Domínguez
A cousin of Chela Domínguez, Manuela lives in Anchondo, a small village along the river northeast of Mata Ortiz. She learned from her neighbor Chela López and began making pots about 1991.

Francisco Enriques
Francisco Enriques Silva and his younger brothers, Tito and Beto, make polychrome pots which they sell in the old Casas Grandes village in a shop behind the square. The family moved from Mata Ortiz in 1993.

Beto Enriques
Nolberto "Beto" Enriques learned to pot from his brother Francisco who sells their work from a shop which can be seen on the left just before entering the square in old Casas Grandes.

Tito Enriques
Tito is Francisco Enriques' youngest brother and participates in the family pottery shop in old Casas Grandes.

Ishmael Flores

Ishmael Flores Ledesma is a cousin of the well-known Manuel Rodríguez, who was his teacher. He is also influenced by his relative and friend, Jorge Quintana. Ishmael grew up as a wood worker and furniture maker, following his father's trade. Now he supports his family by painting good-quality polychrome pieces that his wife Maria Loya forms.

Ishmael Flores Jr.

Ishmael's son and namesake makes and signs his own white polychrome pieces.

Graciela Gallegos

In 1988, some visitors were passing by the Gallegos house in the Barrio Americano area of the village when one of Graciela's children invited them in to *"comprar ollas."* On her table, she had some small, simple figurines which the visitors bought. Graciela "Chela" Martínez Flores de Gallegos is a very nice person, and they enjoyed talking with her and meeting her large, hulking cowboy husband, Hector. Almost two years later, these same visitors came by again and were amazed to see some outstanding pieces. The best were *cuates,* double pots joined by a handle. They were of a pure white clay with excellent painting. All of the work was signed by Graciela. In another visit, the visitors discovered that Hector did the painting. Here was a situation where the wife formed the pots, the husband painted them, and the wife signed them. Later Hector began signing their pieces and by the early nineties, his name became one of the best known in the village after the Quezadas. In 1995, Graciela began painting and again signing a few of her own pieces.

Guadalupe Gallegos

Guadalupe Gallegos Garcia, a nephew of Hector Gallegos, began potting in 1992 at age fifteen after watching Juan Quezada. He now produces creative, quality work. One of his techniques involves covering a white pot with red paint, adding Mimbres-style animal figures in black, and then scratching through the red paint to create an attractive mottled background.

Hector Gallegos

Hector Gallegos Esparza, somewhat reluctantly, started painting some of Graciela's pots in 1989. In an amazingly short length of time, this team was producing high-quality work. Hector still farms and works his cattle on the *llano* during the day, and in the evening, he paints intricate black and red designs, often with Mimbres-style animals, on the white-clay *ollas* made by Graciela. Hector's work is some of the most sought after in the village, and his pieces have appeared in most major exhibitions including the University of New Mexico Art Museum exhibition in the spring of 1995, the Exhibits USA *Potters of Mata Ortiz* traveling exhibition, 1999-2001, the Franz Mayer exhibition in Mexico City, August, 1999, and the *The Road to Aztlan* exhibition at the Los Angeles County Museum of Art in the summer of 2001.

Hector Gallegos, Jr.

Young Hector has helped his parents Hector and Graciela since childhood. In 1996 at age 14, he began painting some of the pots made by his mother. He struggled at first, but within a year produced good work, some with his own creation, little splotches of red paint covering the background of the design.

Miriam Gallegos

Miriam Gallegos Martínez is the daughter of the well-known Hector and Graciela Gallegos. She has helped her parents since childhood. In 1994, when she was eighteen, she began making small delicate white ware, painted with designs similar to her father's.

Aide González

Aide González Betancourt comes from a family that for years has formed pots for others to paint and sign. Jorge Quintana taught her to paint in 1999 when she was 13. Soon she was producing such quality work that it caused a minor sensation among the regular Mata Ortiz traders.

Carolina Marín González

Carolina lives with her parents in the center of the village just off of the main plaza. She is the registrar for the pueblo, recording births, deaths, and marriages. She makes black pottery.

Daniel González

Daniel González Villapando is a young man from Barrio Porvenir making very large pieces somewhat in the Felix Ortiz style. While not finely executed in the classic Quezada manner, Daniel's best pieces, covered with animals, real and imaginary, have an exuberant charm.

José González V.

José is Daniel's brother. He is primarily a farmer, but he makes pottery when time permits.

Martha González

Martha González de Rodríguez makes small, whimsical animals in the early style of her neighbors and husband's nephews, Manuel and Armando Rodríguez, from whom she learned.

Grupo Pearson

In 1996, an agency of the Mexican government organized a group of lessor-known women potters in the village into two cooperatives, Grupo Pearson and Grupo Paquime. The most visible, Grupo Pearson, now has a sales gallery in Mata Ortiz, and all members share in the sales proceeds. The original fifty-two members are listed here. Some are not regular potters, and others, over one half of the total, are well enough known to be mentioned separately in this appendix.

Aurelia Aldavaz de López, Guadalupe Amaya Mora, Antonia Andrew de Lucero, Nury Andrew Hernández, Liliana Bugarini Ríos, Bertha Chacón de Ortiz, Avelina Corona Guillén, Tomasa Díaz de Cano, Cayetana Escalante Corona, Martha González de Rodríguez, Luz Elva Gutiérrez Orozco, Maria Teresa Ibarra Ortiz, Juana Jurado Núñez, Silvia Lidia López Aldavaz, Maria de Lourdes López de Corona, Abigail López de Marin, Parricia López de Mora, Maricruz López Escalante, Lidia Lucero Sandóval, Irene Luján de Heras, Amelia Martínez de Tena, Martha Elena Martínez Domínguez, Mary Claudia Martínez Rentería, Velia Mora de López, Amelia Mora Ozuna, Tomasa Mora Osuna, Lucia Mora Sandóval, María Antonia Mora Sandóval, Dina Moreno Márquez, Teodora Ortiz Rodríguez, Celia Ortiz Sandóval, Marisela Ortiz Sandóval, Dora Imelda Pedregón Ortiz, Luz Elva Ramírez Carbajal, Lidia Rentería de Cota, María Teresa Ríos Fierro, Flora Rodríguez de Arrieta, Reyna Patricia Rodríguez González, Rosi Rodríguez González, Silvia Rodríguez González, Yoli Rodríguez González, Eduwiges Rodríguez Rodríguez, Guadalupe Sandóval de Lucero, Sofia Sandóval de Tena, Otila Sandóval de Ortiz, Paz Silva de Ramírez, Yolanda Soto de Bugarini, Guadalupe Soto Velo, Lilia Velo de Soto, Cruz Celia Villa Ortiz, María Anatasia Villa Ortiz, Delia Vizcarra Rascón

Bety Guillén

Bety Guillén Ramírez makes both black and polychrome pots and signs them with her maiden name. She is married to Victor Loya Jacques, and they live in Nuevo Casas Grandes.

Servando Gutiérrez

Servando Gutiérrez Mendoza was one of Humberto Ponce's first pupils.

Nancy Heres de Martínez

Nancy is the daughter of Lalo Heres, who operates the *Posada de Las Ollas* inn. She is married to Luis Martínez from whom she learned to make pots. Her work reflects his style, using a combination of squares and Mimbres figures.

Elda Hernández

Elda is the wife of Daniel González and sister of Gloria Hernández. She was one of the first to make clay pot rings.

Gloria Hernández

The large pots by Gloria Beatriz Hernández Hernández (her maiden name) are examples of some of the better work done at the Porvenir end of the village that sell for reasonable prices. Her designs, usually including animals, lizards, or birds in a geometric setting, are quite different from the classic Casas Grandes style. She says that she does not copy Paquime designs but just paints what comes into her head. Gloria uses her maiden name, but is married to Goyo Silviera, a prolific potter for many years, who was her teacher. They are an example of a couple who independently form and paint their pots. However Goyo does all of the firing. Gloria began making pots about 1983.

Nora Isela Mendoza
Nora learned to make pottery in 2000.

Teresa Jaquez
Teresa Veloz de Jaquez lives near the school and is married to Socorro Jaquez. They work primarily in white clay.

Irma Juárez S.
Irma was from Barrio Adobe, a cluster of houses north of the village near the cemetery. She moved to Chihuahua City, and in 1995 still made pottery which she sold in Mata Ortiz.

Juana Jurado Núñez
Juana lives in Barrio Porvenir. She learned to make pots from Flora Rodríguez, starting in 1991. Juana speaks good English and often guides tourists in the village.

Arturo Ledezma
Arturo Ledezma Veloz began making small figures and animals in about 1990, following his friend Manuel Rodríguez's early style. His work has evolved into nicely-formed *ollas*, usually with an intricate checkerboard pattern. Arturo in turn has influenced his four brothers Santos, Gerardo, Rafael, Efrén, and other members of the Veloz branch of the extended Ledezma family. One of Arturo's pots was selected for the Exhibits USA *Potters of Mata Ortiz* traveling exhibition, 1999-2001.

Efrén Ledezma
Efrén Ledezma Veloz, the youngest of the five Ledesma brothers, often paints designs consisting of small parallel bands with alternating geometric designs.

Elsa Ledezma
Elsa Ledezma de Ponce is Humberto Ledezma's (Olga's husband) sister.

Gerardo Ledezma
Gerardo is a younger brother of Arturo Ledezma, who taught him his pottery skills. Gerardo makes polychrome pots with variations of checkerboard and cross hatch designs.

Javier Ledezma
Javier Ledesma Diaz is a cousin of Arturo Ledezma.

Jorge Ledesma
Jorge Alejandro Ledesma Loya is the son of Santos Ledesma.

Juana Ledesma
Juana Ledesma Veloz is a sister of Santos, Arturo, Gerado, Rafael, and Efrén. She follows the Ledesma family style, decorating her pots with checkerboard patterns.

Julio Ledezma
Julián (Julio) Ledezma Jacquez is the brother of Humberto Ledezma, and makes pots in the red and black checkerboard style of Humberto and Olga Quezada. Julio's wife, Rosa Ponce, assists him. She is from the small village of Santa Rosa along the track south of Mata Ortiz.

Manuela Ledesma
Manuela is the sister of Carmen Veloz. However, she learned to pot from Blanca Ponce in Nuevo Casas Grandes.

Rafael Ledezma
Rafael is the brother of Arturo Ledezma and makes pots similar to his, usually with intricate checkerboard designs. However, he often paints the rim of his pots which distinguishes his pieces from those of Arturo and his other brothers.

Santos Ledezma
Santos Ledezma Veloz is Arturo, Gerado, Rafael, and Efrén Ledezma's older brother. He makes pots in the general style of the Ledezma family, usually featuring checkerboard designs. His wife is potter Rosa Loya.

Yoly Ledezma

Yolanda Ledezma Jacquez is Humberto Ledezma's sister. Her pots originally followed Humberto's and his wife Olga's checkerboard style. Later, she developed her own designs, based on Mimbres images. One of her pieces received first place in the Mimbres category in the August, 2000 *Concurso*, the fourth government-sponsored competition of Mata Ortiz pottery.

Baudel López

Baudel López Corona began potting in about 1993 at age 15. He makes primarily red pieces with black designs.

Chela López

Celia "Chela" López is Reynalda Quezada's sister-in-law, from whom she learned to pot, probably in the late 1970s. She now lives in Anchondo, a village a few miles from Mata Ortiz. Chela's work is mostly blackware. In recent years, she has created unusual pieces by engraving birds and animals on the sides.

Edmundo López

Edmundo López Aldaváz, Nena Ortiz's brother, is also a cousin of Angela Bañuelos and a nephew of Simon López, Reynalda Quezada's husband. He cannot remember exactly when he starting potting but probably about 1985. Now it is his full-time occupation. He learned from watching Macario Ortiz, his brother-in-law, and most of his production is well-made graphite-style blackware. One of Edmundo's pieces was selected for the Exhibits USA *Potters of Mata Ortiz* exhibition, 1999-2001.

Eleazar López

Eleazar is a brother of Edmundo López and Nena López de Ortiz. While he makes pots, he has begun to specialize by preparing clay for others to use. Olivia Juarez de López, his wife, also makes black pots both natural and graphite in the manner of this branch of the López family.

Estela S. de López

Estela is the wife of Juan Quezada's nephew Samuel López Quezada. She makes small well-polished black pots, usually with an animal or lizard form sculptured into the clay.

Gaby López

Abigail López de Marín is the sister of Nena Ortiz. She learned pottery from Nena's husband Macario Ortiz. She is married to Pepe Marín. Gaby became part of the Grupo Pearson co-op in 1997. Later that year, *FONART*, the agency that promotes regional art, sent one of her pieces to an international competition in Columbia where she won a $5,000 prize. This caused a problem because all 52 of the co-op members wanted to share the prize.

Gloria Isela López

Gloria Isela López de Mora has been potting for 17-18 years, a long time in Mata Ortiz. She is a niece of Simon López, Reynalda Quezada's husband, and learned to pot from various members of the López family — Rosa, Chela, etc. She is married to Anastacio Mora, a cousin of Manuel and Pilo. She is a sister of Angela Bañuelos and helped teach pottery to Angela and Roberto.

Leonel López Sáenz

Leonel began working with clay in 1993, and in a short time he was producing red *ollas* with well-painted black designs. Then he developed an unusual sgraffito technique, etching animals and landscape scenes into the surfaces of his pieces. These have become very popular with traders, and other potters have adopted this style, called *calcado* in the village. Leonel is married to Elena Rodríguez of the well-known Rodríguez family (Manuel, Oscar, etc.), and he learned to pot from them. As is true of other young potters in the village, he is a better painter than potter. Therefore, he often buys pieces from others to paint and etch. His work appeared in the Exhibits USA *Potters of Mata Ortiz* exhibition, 1999-2001.

Lety López

Lety López Sáenz is one of the sisters of the well-known Leonel López and makes pottery similar to their sister Lourdes López.

Lourdes López

María Lourdes López de Corona used to live in Barrio Adobe (also known as Barrio López). She is a sister of Leonel and Uriel López Sáenz. In 1997, she married Armando Corona and moved to Barrio Americano near potter Ana Trillo de Corona. Lourdes makes good red clay and white-clay pots in the style of Ana Trillo.

Luci López Cota

Luci, nineteen years of age in 2001, is the younger half sister of Laura and Elvira Bugarini. She usually makes small polychrome pieces.

Nely López Sáenz

Nely is one of the sisters of the well-known Leonel López and follows sister Norma's style.

Norma López Sáenz

Norma is another sister of Leonel López and learned to make pots from Leonel's wife Elena. She follows the latter's style, producing nicely-painted checkerboard designs. Her husband is Jose L. Martínez Cano and they live in San Diego, three miles north of Mata Ortiz.

Maribel López

Maribel López Guillén, Uriel López's daughter, in her early 20s in 2001, belongs to the extended López family in Barrio Adobe (also called Barrio López). Sometimes she decorates her pots with old Paquime designs. On others, she paints tiny repetitive designs she learned from Laura Bugarini. Her mother Jesus Guillén forms the pots.

Miguel López

Miguel López Mora is Lourdes López's brother and makes red clay pieces in her style.

Olivia López

Olivia López Quezada (her maiden name) is Reynalda Quezada's daughter. A skilled potter, she primarily makes black pieces in her mother's style. Her husband Hector makes pots that Olivia signs. Olivia does not use the Quezada surname, just signing her pots "Olivia López," a unique practice among the extended Quezada family.

Rosa López de Cota

Rosa has been potting for many years and helped teach her sister and brother-in-law, the well-known Angela and Roberto Bañuelos. She learned to pot from her sister-in-law, Reynalda Quezada. Her work includes Mimbres-style bowls.

Silvia López

Silvia Lidia López Aldavaz is the sister of Nena Ortiz, Macario's wife. Silvia makes blackware in the general style of her family.

Uriel López Sáenz

Uriel looks like his well-known brother, Leonel, and does similar work with sgraffito designs of cactus and yucca on the sides of his pots.

Walter López Corona

Walter, the brother of Baudel López, makes small red pots, painted with black designs. He lives in Barrio Americano and was 26 in 2000. A former lady teacher of Walter's mother gave him this rather unusual name for Mexico.

Carlos Loya

Carlos now lives in Nuevo Casas Grandes. He makes pottery pieces with very simple, clean, modern designs. These are finely finished with even the inside surfaces carefully smoothed. In 2001, he had been working seriously for only about one year. However, in the early 1980s, he was married to Mireya Quezada and had learned the basics from the Quezada family. Carlos is the brother of Jose and Rosa Loya.

José Loya

José Loya Jaquez is a brother of Rosa Loya. He makes well-painted white pieces with intricate designs somewhat reminiscent of Noe Quezada's work. José learned from watching Juan and other members of the Quezada family.

Rosa Loya

Rosa Isela Loya Jaquez de Ledezma makes medium-sized polychrome pieces, often with a checkerboard design. She lives with her husband Santos Ledezma in Barrio Americano, the neighborhood in the northwest corner of the main village where so many of the good potters of the Gallegos, Rodríguez, Ledesma, and Martínez families live.

Jesús Lozano

Jesús Lozano Lucero lives near Jaime Domínguez, his brother-in-law. Both have done very well making small highly polished black pieces. Family members and others have emulated this style which is very popular with North Americans.

Rubén Lozano Lucero

Rubén is a brother of Jesús Lozano and the brother-in-law of Jaime Domínguez. As a boy, he lived in Mexicali, coming to Mata Ortiz when he was fifteen. Although he lived in the central part of the village, he was influenced by Macario Ortiz from Barrio Porvenir. Rubén is very creative, and he does not rely on a set formula learned either from his own family members or from Macario. While most of his work is black, he has made some very interesting polychrome pieces using white slip and a green copper oxide as paint colors. In 1993, Rubén won a first prize for a black polished pot in the National Exhibition of Folk Art. He received his award directly from President Salinas in Mexico City. The pot is proudly displayed in a plastic case in Rubén's house. One of his pieces was selected for the Franz Mayer exhibition in Mexico City in 1999. Rubén's wife Anastacia Villa Ortiz is also a potter.

Gloria Lozoya

Gloria Lozoya de Veloz has been making pots for several years. Most of her production is small black *ollas*. She says she used to make figures but their prices were the same as the *ollas* and more work.

Efraín Lucero

Efraín makes black pots of fairly good quality. He learned from Macario Ortiz and Rubén Lozano (his cousin). In 2000, he began making graphite-style black pieces with matte and polished surfaces decorated with red designs. Efraín's sons, Efraín Jr. and César, make small generally wide-mouthed black and polychrome pots. César married Miriam Gallegos in 1999, and his work now reflects some of Gallegos' style as well as that of his father.

Jorge Lucero

Jorge was formerly a student of Julien Hernandez of the Francisco Villa school in Nuevo Casas Grandes. In 2001, he was working with Humberto Ponce doing white-clay pieces.

Lidia Lucero

Elida Lucero Sandóval de Mora is married to Pepito Mora, the brother of Tomasa Mora. Lidia is part of the Sandóval family in Porvenir and she and Pepito both were potters before their marriage. Now they work together making medium-sized polychrome pieces which she signs.

Rosa Lucero

Rosa was one of the promising early potters. In 1981 when she was 16, she attended the NCECA conference in Wichita, Kansas, with Spencer MacCallum, Juan, and other members of the Quezada family. However, later she married and moved to Juárez and gave up potting.

Hugo Macias

Hugo learned from Manuel Rodríguez. He makes well-painted, thin-walled pieces.

Pepe Marín

Jose "Pepe" Marín lives in the *El Centro* neighborhood of the village. He began working with Macario Ortiz about 1990 and makes both polychrome and black graphite-style pots. He also works with Eleazar López, preparing clay to sell to other potters.

Quico Márquez
Quico learned to make pots from his wife Lupe Sandóval. They live in the center of the village not far from Juan Quezada. Quico usually uses red clay which he decorates with black designs.

Amelia Martínez
Amelia is a sister of Graciela Gallegos, and her work, like that of many in the Martínez family, reflects the Gallegos' influence. She often makes small, oval flat plates with Mimbres designs. She is married to Ernesto Tena, the pharmacist.

Jesús Martínez R.
Jesús "Chuey" Martínez Rentería makes nicely-painted polychrome pots following the Quezada style. María del Socorro Amaya Mora, his wife, forms the pot and Chuey paints. He learned painting from Mauro Quezada, and she learned to work the clay from her cousin Pilo Mora. Chuey is part of the extended Martínez family. His grandfather is Señor José Martínez, the village mechanic. Chuey's pots appeared in the University of New Mexico Art Museum exhibition in the spring of 1995, and one large white piece was selected for the Exhibits USA *Potters of Mata Ortiz* traveling exhibition, 1999-2001.

José Martínez
José Martínez López, the grandson of mechanic José Martínez and the brother of potter Luis Martínez, learned to pot from his aunt, Graciela Martínez de Gallegos. He makes black pots and polychrome pots decorated often with a checkerboard pattern or the classic Mimbres feather pattern (sometimes called the knife pattern in Mata Ortiz). His wife is Susana, the daughter of Aurelia Aldavaz de López.

Luis Martínez
Luis Martínez López has been potting since his mid-teens. He is the nephew of Graciela Martínez de Gallegos and Martha Martínez de Domínguez and the brother of José Martínez. His father, Pepe Martínez, operates the only public bus which passes through the village to and from Nuevo Casas Grandes. Luis makes well-formed and well-painted polychrome pots and effigy figures, usually with white clay and often with Mimbres-style designs on square-shouldered jars.

Martha Martínez de Domínguez
Martha is the sister of Graciela Gallegos and both are daughters of the older José Martínez, the village mechanic. In 1988 Señor Martínez showed us some crude pieces by Martha. Now she is an accomplished craftsman, making primarily small to medium polychrome pieces. Antonio "Tony" Domínguez, her husband, assists Martha.

Nancy Heres de Martínez
Nancy is the wife of Luis Martínez and makes finely-executed pieces in his style with square shoulders and Mimbres designs. Nancy's father is Lalo Heres, who operates the *Posada de las Ollas*, Mata Ortiz's first inn to welcome traders and tourists.

Susy Martínez
Susana López Aldavaz de Martínez is José Martínez's wife and Aurelia López's daughter. She learned from the Gallegos family and generally makes small polychrome pieces.

Rubén Meledez
Rubén is another of the small but growing group of potters from the tiny village of Santa Rosa, along the tracks south of Mata Ortiz. At the beginning of 2001, he had been working about a year producing sgraffito-style pots in the manner of Leonel López Sáenz.

Benito Meras G.
Benito lives in the Seccion area of the village near where the railroad crosses the *arroyo*. He originally came from Durango. He works as a team with his wife, Manuela Josefino Estrado, a cousin of *Los Hermanos Ortiz.* Benito signs all of their work.

Maupel Molina
Maupel usually makes effigy figures in the old Casas Grandes style.

Anastacio Mora

Anastacio (Tacho) Mora Sandóval lives in Porvenir and makes large pots in the typical Porvenir style. In 1997, he began making clay masks in molds. A former school teacher from the area, Adalberto Pérez Meillón, who buys pottery for his gallery in Ensenada, has encouraged Anastacio in this unique endeavor.

Antonia Mora de Heres

Maria Antonia Mora Sandóval is the sister-in-law of Manuel Rodríguez and is also a cousin of Pilo Mora.

Beny Mora

Beny is the husband of potter Paty López and the cousin of Pilo Mora. He makes both polychrome and graphite-style black pieces.

Juan Mora

Juan Mora Sandóval Jr. worked with his wife, Guadalupe, his brother Julio, and sister Lucia making small white pots until Juan and Guadalupe moved to Phoenix and gave up potting. Later they returned and opened a grocery store and began potting again. They also purchase lower-quality pottery for resale in Arizona. Juan's brothers and sisters include Julio, Anastacio, Lucia, Olivia, Belia, and Antonia. Their late mother, Jesus María Sandóval de Mora, was an important factor in the development of her children as potters.

Julio Mora Sandóval

Julio worked with his brother and sister, Juan Jr. and Lucia Mora, making low-quality pieces until about 1990 when they began to work with white clay. Now Julio produces small well-painted pieces with intricate designs. This group of Moras are cousins of Pilo Mora, and although they never worked with him directly, they certainly observed his success doing quality work.

Lucy Mora

Lucia Mora Sandóval de Bugarini is the sister of Juan and Julio Mora. Lucy began potting several years before her brothers and now concentrates on large, intricately-painted white and red pieces. Lucy is influential in local politics and is the Municipio (county) registrar. She rents videos and engages in other small business activities.

Manuel Mora

Jesús Manuel Mora Villalba is the brother of the well-known Pilo Mora from whom he learned ceramics. He began potting in 1989 and progressed rapidly. He teaches in the elementary school, and does not have much time for potting. However, the work he produces is unique, usually a matte surface with subtle colors obtained by mixing brown, yellow, and white paint with the traditional red and black. He also makes blackware. Manuel has invented a unique double *quemadora* system which allows him to fire several pots in sequence in the same fire.

María Mora

María learned to make pots from her sister Tomasa Mora. She produces a nicely-made Porvenir-style pot. She now lives in Santa Rosa, the tiny village south of Mata Ortiz.

Pilo Mora

Porfirio "Pilo" Mora Villalba lived in Barrio Porvenir before moving to Nuevo Casas Grandes. Although his teacher was Ermeterio Ortiz from Porvenir, his fine-line painting style shows much more of the Quezada influence. Pilo was one of the best of the new group of artists that appeared in the late 1980s, and his work was sought after by traders and other buyers. However, in 1992, he suffered an eye injury while pounding nails on a community school project. He gradually lost his sight in this eye. He continued to paint, but it was difficult to produce the very fine lines for which he was known. Often he made pots for others to paint. In 2000, trader/collector Nick Brown of Redlands arranged for eye surgery in Riverside, California. The doctor removed a black cataract caused by a tiny piece of iron from a nail, and Pilo could see again — another miracle of Mata Ortiz. Pilo has taught many young potters who are working successfully today. His work appeared in exhibitions at: the University of New Mexico Art Museum in the spring of 1995; the Franz Mayer Museum, Mexico City in 1999; and the Exhibits USA *Potters of Mata Ortiz* traveling exhibition, 1999-2001.

Tomasa Mora

Tomasa Mora de Silveira, a niece of Pilo Mora, married into the prolific Silveira family of Barrio Porvenir. She and her husband Armando Silveira help the family produce a large volume of ordinary-quality, medium-to-big pieces.

Dulces Nombres Meleros

This young man, eighteen years old in 1995, became a student of Nicolás Quezada after Nicolás moved to Nuevo Casas Grandes. Dulces has learned to work the difficult white clay and produces well-painted pieces. In 2000, he began making unusual animal and bird figures following the style of Nicolás Ortiz, completely different from that of his original mentor, Nicolás Quezada.

Benito Muñoz

Benito and his wife Manuela live in Porvenir.

Cruz Núñez

Cruz Núñez de Soto is married to Benjamín "Chamin" Soto. They work as a husband and wife team in Barrio Porvenir.

Luisa Núñez González

Luisa started working in 1994 making white pieces with primitive animal designs.

Candelaria Olivas H.

Candelaria, Cipriano, and Maricela Olivas Hernández all live in Barrio Porvenir near the Silviera family from whom they learned potting.

Cipriano Olivas H.

Cipriano is married to Tomasa Mora's sister Amalia. He builds his pots directly from the tortilla in the mold without adding a coil.

Ines Olivas

Ines Olivas Hernández lives with his family in the *Seccion* neighborhood next to the *arroyo*. Earlier he made mostly small black pots like his sister Matilde, who is married to Hilario Quezada. However in about 1998, he began making unusual fish effigy pots of white clay, painted with red and black designs. His brother Roberto makes white double-spouted *matrimonio* pots. A sister María also makes pots.

Ivonne Olivas

Ivonne is the niece of Guillermina Quezada, Juan's wife. She learned from Juan, beginning in 1995. Her husband Florencia Sanchez often forms the pieces that she paints.

Maricela Olivas H.

The sister of Candelaria and Cipriano Olivas, Maricela uses her maiden name on her pottery even though she is married to potter Luis Armando Ortiz of Barrio Porvenir.

Martín Olivas

Martín Olivas Chacón is related to Isidro Ortiz. He lives in Nuevo Casas Grandes and makes black pots.

Celia Ortega Ledesma

Celia is the daughter of Yoly Ledesma. She won first place in the "miniatures" category in the fourth *Concurso* in August, 2000.

Hector Ortega

Hector is a brother-in-law of Eduardo "Chevo" Ortiz. He sometimes makes red pots with large round depressions on the sides, similar in style to Chevo's popular graphite-black pieces. Hector also makes black pots with nicely sculptured ram or bear heads on the rims. Hector is married to potter Olivia López Quezada, Reynalda's daughter.

Naty Ortega

Natividad Ortega is the brother of Hector Ortega. Nati makes the swirled "turbino" pieces originated by Eduardo Ortiz, his brother-in-law.

Santiago Ortega

Santiago Ortega Ledesma makes excellent miniature pieces. He won first place in the forth *Concurso* in August, 2000. The son of Yoly Ledesma, he also makes graphite-style black pots and other larger pieces with sgraffito decoration.

Anastacia Villa Ortiz

Anastacia is the daughter of potter Ramón Villa of Porvenir and the wife of Rubén Lozano. She makes medium-sized black pieces.

César Navarete Ortiz

César "Chester" is a nephew of Macario Ortiz (his mother is Macario's sister). He worked with Macario for about three years before he began working alone in 1994. At first he used his mother's maiden name, Ortiz, on his intricately-painted graphite-style black pots because the name was so well known. Now he uses his full name. This César should not be confused with his cousin, the Julio César Ortiz López, Macario's son.

David Ortiz

David Ortiz Sandóval is a cousin to *Los Hermanos Ortiz.* He has been making pots since about 1988. His work initially was crude, but he has evolved a simple, refined style, resulting in good, affordable pottery. In 1995, he moved to Nuevo Casas Grandes.

Eduardo Ortiz

Eduardo "Chevo" Ortiz Estrada is one of the well-known *Los Hermanos Ortiz,* a group of brothers from Barrio Porvenir, who used to be musicians as well as potters. He used to make polychrome pieces but now concentrates on blackware, using graphite to create brilliant, metallic-like surfaces. His wife, Hortencia "Tencha" Domínguez, helps throughout the process, particularly with the polishing. His work has appeared in most of the major exhibitions, and one of his unique *ollas* with concave depressions on four sides was shown in the University of New Mexico Art Museum exhibition in the spring of 1995. Two pieces were selected for the Exhibits USA *Potters of Mata Ortiz* traveling exhibition, 1999-2001.

Eduardo Ortiz, Jr.

Eduardo Junior makes large graphite-style black pots. Sometimes he signs his pots with his nickname "Lalo."

Ermeterio Ortiz R.

The late Ermeterio Ortiz Rodríguez was an older brother of Felix Ortiz, one of the first and most important potters in Barrio Porvenir. The two worked together on the first pots made in Porvenir. One story has it that Ermeterio actually studied with Juan Quezada and Consolación in an early group of students that included Felix and Lupita Cota. In the 90s, Ermeterio did not make many pots but those he did make were interesting because they reflected the styles used in Porvenir years ago. He died in January, 1998, but he will be remembered as one of the early potters and one who taught many in Porvenir, including Pilo Mora and Sabino Villalba.

Eli Ortiz

Eli Navarete Ortiz is a brother of César Navarete Ortiz and did graphite-style black-ware, typical of the Ortiz family in Porvenir. He began using red and even green and blue paints to enhance the typical black-on-black designs of black pottery. Reynaldo Quezada had showed Eli and César green paint made from copper oxide. They experimented and were among the first to use it successfully on blackware. Eli is an exceptional painter, and by 2001, his multicolored black pots were in great demand by traders and collectors. He originally lived in Barrio Porvenir but in 2000 moved to old Casas Grandes. One of his pieces was selected for the Exhibits USA *Potters of Mata Ortiz* traveling exhibition, 1999-2001.

Felix Ortiz R.

Felix Ortiz Rodríguez represents one of the important influences in Barrio Porvenir. Very early, he developed his own style which clearly distinguished his followers from those of Juan Quezada. These distinctions have broken down somewhat but are still evident. Felix uses multiple coils instead of the single-coil method to make his pots which are often very large and painted with bold asymmetrical designs. His work was shown in the landmark traveling exhibition of 1979-80 referred to on pages 22-24.

Isidro Ortiz

Isidro Ortiz Chacón is the son of the potting team of Bertha Chacón and Santos Ortiz, one of *Los Hermanos Ortiz*. The family produces medium quality pieces in the general Porvenir style.

Julio César Ortiz López

César is Macario and Nena Ortiz's son and has worked with the clay intermittently.

Luis Ortiz

Luis Armando Ortiz Sandóval is the brother of David Ortiz and the husband of Maricela Olivas. Luis often uses red clay for his pots.

Macario Ortiz

After Nicolás, Macario Ortiz Estrada is the best known of *Los Hermanos Ortiz*. Most of his pots are lustrous black-on-black pieces sometimes with a slight reddish cast. He does not use reduction firing. He achieves this surface by painting the entire pot with graphite and *almagre*, then firing it in an oxidation atmosphere. *Almagre* is a red ocher the Ortiz brothers dig from an old mine on the way to Ciudad Juárez. Macario also has experimented with green and blue colors. He has traveled to the U.S. and to Ensenada for exhibitions, and his success has enabled him to build the first two-story house in Mata Ortiz. He is the businessman of the family and made all of the arrangements for the band of which he was the lead singer. His work appeared in the University of New Mexico Art Museum exhibition in the spring of 1995, and in the Exhibits USA *Potters of Mata Ortiz* traveling exhibition, 1999-2001.

Nena Ortiz

Maria Elena López de Ortiz, "Nena", is Macario's wife. She helps him with his work and also makes her own good-quality blackware.

Nicolás Ortiz

Nicolás Ortiz Estrada is an accomplished artist and musician. Before he was inspired to pot, he did sculpture, painted, and led the popular local band known as *Los Hermanos Ortiz*. At almost seven feet, he is by far the tallest man in the village. Nicolás makes a wide variety of pots and enchanting figures — rabbits, snails, turtles and others in both polychrome and blackware. His work has influenced many in Barrio Porvenir. Three of his animal figures were selected for the University of New Mexico Art Museum exhibition in the spring of 1995. His work appeared in the Franz Mayer exhibition in Mexico City in 1999, and the Exhibits USA *Potters of Mata Ortiz* traveling exhibition, 1999-2001.

Otila de Ortiz

Otila Sandóval de Ortiz is the wife of the pioneer Barrio Porvenir potter, Felix Ortiz. Otila has helped Felix from the beginning and also makes and signs her own pieces.

Osbaldo Ortiz

The late Osbaldo was one of *Los Hermanos Ortiz* (he played guitar). He and his wife Theresa used to work as a team before their divorce. Later he worked with his teenage children Alonzo and Flor. Often their pieces included animal figures in bas-relief on the sides and tops, following one of brother Nicolás' styles. Osbaldo signed all of the pots. He died of diabetes in the late 1990s.

Paty Ortiz

The daughter of Salbador Ortiz, Paty and her husband Cruz Santillan make together mixed clay pieces with good, traditional Paquime designs, which she signs.

Raquel Ortiz

Raquel Ortiz Sandóval (her maiden name), the daughter of Felix and Otila Ortiz, by her marriage to César Navarete Ortiz, helped link the two well-known but separate Ortiz potting families of Barrio Porvenir.

Rosa Ortiz

Rosa is a daughter of Salvador Ortiz and produces a typical Porvenir polychrome pot with red and black designs on a beige surface.

Salbador Ortiz E.

Salbador was the oldest of the Ortiz family that included Nicolás, Macario, and the others of *Los Hermanos Ortiz*. Primarily a farmer, Salbador knew well the plains, mountains and caves of the area. He usually made effigy figures or very small pots. There is no direct connection between the two large Ortiz pottery families in Barrio Porvenir, but Salbador's widow, Eduviges "Vicki," is the half-sister of Felix Ortiz, the best-known potter of the other Ortiz family.

Salbador was killed while hitchhiking from Nuevo Casas Grandes to Mata Ortiz in January, 1997.

Santos Ortiz E.

Santos is another of *Los Hermanos Ortiz*. For years, he has worked as a team with his wife Berta Chacón, producing medium-quality pots with bold designs.

Tomás Ozuna

Tomás lives in Barrio Porvenir, where he makes and signs his own pottery. However, he also makes large pots for other well-known potters to paint, polish, fire, and sign. Tomás works with his wife, Silvia, daughter of Nicolás Silveira.

Enrique Pedragón

Enrique Pedragón Ortiz, the son of Teodora and Reynaldo Pedragón and nephew of Felix Ortiz, does original, intricately-lined designs on his polychrome *ollas* and fish shapes. Some designs have an oriental cloisonne look. On small pieces, he signs "Enrique P.O."

Gerado Pedragón

Gerado Pedragón Ortiz, the brother of Enrique Pedragón, is married to Macaria Ortiz, the daughter of Nena and Macario Ortiz. This marriage links again the two well-know Ortiz pottery families. Gerado paints red and amarillo-clay pots that he purchases from others, notably the family of Aide González.

Jesús Pedregón

Jesús is a cousin of Enrique and is married to potter Elvira Bugarini Cota.

Rene Pedregón

The son of Yolanda and Santiago Ledesma, Rene makes a variety of ware including graphite-style black, large "bayas" or beige-clay polychrome, and miniatures. He won second place in the miniature classification in the forth *Concurso* in August, 2000.

Reynaldo Pedregón Luján

Reynaldo lives in Barrio Porvenir. He is the uncle of Rubén Lozano. His wife is Teodora Ortiz, the sister of Felix Ortiz.

Teodora Ortiz de Pedragón

Teodora is the sister of Felix Ortiz and the wife of Reynaldo Pedragón. Spencer MacCallum bought several miniature pieces from her as early as 1980.

Lorenzo Elias Peña

Elias is part of a small group of potters living and working in the tiny village of Santa Rosa along the railroad a few miles south of Mata Ortiz. Elias paints the quaint bird and animal figures that his brother-in-law Manual Molina forms. They learned from Andres Villalba. Elias has entered large *bayas* or beige-clay polychrome pieces in all of the *Concursos*, winning third place in the fourth event held in August, 2000.

Javier Pérez

Javier Pérez Olivas, 18 in 1997, worked in Pilo Mora's studio in Nuevo Casas Grandes along with Salbador Almazan. He painted pots that Pilo formed, often using colors other than the classic red and black. One of his pieces was selected for the Franz Mayer exhibition in Mexico in 1999.

Mária Pérez

Mária "Mary" Pérez de Zuniga lives in Nuevo Casas Grandes. She often makes large black imaginary figures and double-necked polychrome "wedding jars."

Rodrigo Pérez

Rodrigo learned pottery from Pilo Mora in a workshop in Nuevo Casas Grandes along with Javier Pérez and Salvador Almazon. He produces polychrome pieces of white and mixed clays.

Eleuterio Piña

Eleuterio Piña Aguirre is a brother-in-law of Jorge and Eduardo Quintana, the latter his teacher. He etches his pots following Eduardo's style. He does good quality work considering that in 2001 he had been making pots for about one year. His wife Antonia Quintana form the pots and occasionally paints and signs a piece. Their son Humberto Eleuterio Piña Quintana, 12 years old in 2001, also makes etched or sgraffito-style pots. The family lives in Nuevo Casas Grandes.

Blanca Ponce

Blanca Noelia Almeida Gallegos de Ponce is the wife of Humberto Ponce. She usually forms pots for Humberto to paint. However, occasionally she paints and signs pieces.

Carlos Veloz Ponce

The son of Lidia Ponce de Veloz and the nephew of Humberto Ponce, Carlos was reputed by some (probably incorrectly) to be the youngest potter in Mata Ortiz in 1997. He was seven and making and selling tiny shiny-black pieces.

Humberto Ponce

Humberto Ponce Avalos paints the pots that his wife, Blanca, forms. They both learned from César and Gaby Domínguez, Blanca's brother-in-law and sister. Humberto paints beautiful polychrome designs, sometimes incorporating Mimbres motifs. He is a school teacher, and in 1991, he and César Domínguez moved their families to Nuevo Casas Grandes. His work appeared in the University of New Mexico Art Museum exhibition in the spring of 1995, in the Franz Mayer exhibition in Mexico City in 1999, and in the Exhibits USA *Potters of Mata Ortiz* traveling exhibition, 1999-2001. Blanca occasionally forms, paints, and signs her own work.

Jorge and Luis Ponce

Jorge and Luis live in the tiny village of Santa Rosa south of Mata Ortiz. Their work reflects the checkerboard designs of the Ledesma family.

Lazaro Ponce

Lazaro is Humberto Ponce's brother and paints mixed-clay pieces somewhat in Humbertos's style. Marta Ledesma, his wife makes the pots. This husband and wife team also make naturally-polished black ware. Marta is the sister of Carmen Veloz, but she learned to form pots from Humberto's wife, Blanca. Lazaro and Marta live in Nuevo Casas Grandes.

Lidia Ponce de Veloz

Lidia is a sister of Humberto Ponce and makes small black and polychrome pieces.

Maribel Ponce

Maribel, a beautiful young woman, lives and works in Nuevo Casas Grandes with her mother, Manuela, and sister Mayra. Manuela is a sister of the well-known Humberto Ponce. She forms the pots that her daughters paint and sign. This branch of the Ponce family learned much of their art from Manuela's sister Martha, Rubén Rodríguez's wife. They usually makes black pieces with checkerboard designs with a clear, bright natural polish, reflecting Rubén's influence.

Martha Ponce de Rodríguez

Martha is married to Rubén Rodríguez of the well-known Rodríguez family of potters. Her brother is Humberto Ponce, another well-known potter. She won third place in the miniature category in the forth *Concurso* in August, 2000.

Mayra Ponce

Mayra is a sister of Maribel Ponce. Like Maribel, she paints and signs black pieces her mother Manuela forms. Both sisters use their mother's maiden name.

Albaro Quezada

Albaro Quezada Olivas is Juan's third son. A tall serious young man, his work obviously reflects his father's styles. His work also shows the influence of brother Noe's particular shapes and intricate designs.

Alondra Quezada

Alondra Luján Quezada is the daughter of Juan Quezada's oldest daughter Nena. While Alondra was born in Mata Ortiz, her family moved to a village near Janos called Pancho Villa when she was a little girl. However, her mother is a very good potter, and Alondra has learned to make white-clay polychrome pots following the classic Quezada style.

Arturo Quezada

Juan's two youngest sons, Arturo and Efrén, grew up helping their father and older brothers dig and process clay. About 1993 in his teens, Arturo began taking a more serious interest in the family profession. His work reflects Juan's and older brother Noe's styles.

Betty Quezada

Betty Quintana de Quezada is Noe Quezada's wife. She has learned to make basic Quezada-style white pieces. She uses Noe's and father-in-law Juan Quezada's paint, so the reds and blacks are intense and cover well.

Blanca Quezada

Blanca is not part of Juan's extended family. Along with her husband, Cruz Rentería, she makes plates often with Mimbres figures surrounded by delicate fine-line designs. Blanca also makes pots, usually from white clay.

Consolación Quezada

Consolación Quezada de Corona, Juan's oldest sister, is one of the matriarchs of the village and of the ceramic movement there. By Mata Ortiz standards she has been making pots for a long time. Juan and Nicolás taught her about 1973-74. She is known for her large pieces, particularly those slipped with a red pigment unique to her. Consolación recognized very early the importance of the pottery to her family and village. She encouraged her children and for years was their chief salesperson from her home. Now Oscar, Manuel, Dora, Hilario, and Mauro all support their own families with their pottery. Consolación's picture is on page 56.

Damián Quezada

Damián Escársega Quezada is Genoveva's son and Juan's nephew. He did not grow up in Mata Ortiz, and in 1992 he moved to Nuevo Casas Grandes and began making pots under the tutelage of cousin Oscar and uncle Nicolás Quezada. He is a natural painter and in less than a year was producing outstanding polychrome *ollas* in the classic Quezada style. Damián's wife, Elvira Antillón, often makes the pieces he paints. Damián takes pride in dividing his symmetrical designs in to seven or more segments instead of the typical 2-4 segments. His work was shown at the Franz Mayer Exhibition in Mexico City in 1999, and one of his tall vases was selected for the Exhibits USA *Potters of Mata Ortiz* exhibition, 1999-2001.

Dora Quezada

Dora Quezada de Valenzuela is Consolación Quezada's only daughter. She began helping her mother sand and polish pots when she was twelve. After marrying, she moved to La Junta, about a six-hour train ride south, where her husband, Pedro, was a mechanic. There she made *ollas,* usually blackware with incised designs. A friendly railroad custodian enabled her to send her pots by train to her mother to sell. Dora returned to live in Mata Ortiz to help her mother and continues to produce good-quality blackware.

Dora Quezada Talamontes

Another Dora is the daughter of Nicolás Quezada and a cousin of the other Dora Quezada. She has been working for about five years producing white pieces with classic Quezada designs.

Efrén Quezada

Juan's youngest son, Efrén, known to the world as "Pollo," has grown up around pottery production. He began making his own pots to sell in about 1993, but did not make a commitment to the family profession at that time. He left the village to work in the United States. He returned to the village and to potting in 1999.

Elida Quezada

Elida Quezada Talamontes is the daughter of Nicolás Quezada. She forms pots which her husband Ramon López paints. She signs their work.

Genoveva Quezada

Genoveva Quezada de Escársega, Juan's third sister after Consolación and Reynalda, has lived for years in a town several miles south of Mata Ortiz called Barras Barbicora. She began potting about 1990 and makes black *ollas* similar in style to those of Reynalda and other Quezada family members.

Hilario Quezada

Hilario "Lalo" Corona Quezada, Consolación's third son, is a competent potter, who supports his wife, Matilde, and family primarily with this work. However, unlike his younger brother Mauro, he did not take to potting naturally. As a teenager, he preferred working in the fields with his father, Lupe Corona, and today still enjoys that work. Before turning to potting *por necesidad,* he tried crossing the border twice to work and was returned by immigration authorities both times. He worked in Ensenada for six months, but returned to Mata Ortiz to work in the orchards in Colonia Juárez. Finally when he was past 20, he began to take seriously the pottery he had been around all of his life. He started working with his mother, Consolación, and also with his brothers Mauro and Oscar. By 1990 after four years, he was prospering and his work was popular with traders and tourists. He uses his mother's maiden name as a surname.

Imelda Quezada

Imelda Quezada is Jesús Quezada's daughter and Juan's niece. She makes primarily small black or polychrome pieces often with bird or animal heads.

Ivona Quezada

Ivona Escársega Quezada is Genoveva's daughter and Juan's niece. She makes black *ollas* similar in style to those of her mother, her aunt, Reynalda, and other Quezada family members.

Jaime Quezada

Jaime is one of Jesús Quezada's sons and makes primarily blackware of good quality. One of his pieces was selected for the Franz Mayer exhibition in Mexico City in 1999.

Javier Quezada

Javier is a son of Oscar Quezada. He made both polychrome and black pottery until 1997 when he turned 18. He began work in a *maquiladora,* and his production of pottery has been low.

Jesús Quezada

Jesús Quezada Celado is a younger brother of Juan's. He lives in Nuevo Casas Grandes where he makes primarily black pottery, somewhat in Reynalda's style.

José Quezada Talamontes

José is Nicolás Quezada's son. By 1990, at eighteen, he was already an excellent potter. He emulated his father's style closely, using the difficult white clays and painting long curving designs. Later he began experimenting with his own shapes and designs, generating even higher quality work. José should not be confused with his cousin, José Luis Quezada, Jesús's son, who makes primarily black pots. A tall vase of José's was selected for the Exhibits USA *Potters of Mata Ortiz* traveling exhibition, 1999-2001.

José Luis Quezada Camacho

José is another of Jesús Quezada's sons. He makes primarily black pottery. He should not be confused with Nicolás's son, José Quezada Talamontes, who usually makes polychrome pieces.

Juan Quezada

Juan is the acknowledged master and originator of the ceramic art movement in Mata Ortiz.

Juan Quezada Junior

Juan "Junior" Quezada Olivas is the cowboy of Juan's family. He spends much of his time working with horses or with his father's cattle. At one time Juan had over two hundred head, most of which Junior could identify individually in the herds on the *llano.* He has many other interests including baseball, mechanics, and fighting roosters. Junior is often one of the ropers in the local rodeos or *jaripeos.* In addition to his other activities, Junior is a competent potter in the classic Quezada style. However, because of his other interests, his output is low.

Leonel Quezada

Leonel "Chonel" Quezada Talamontes is the second son of Nicolás Quezada. He began potting in 1989 at age 12, the same year he finished primary school. He decided to become a potter, *"como mi papa."* Some of his pieces were shown in the 1991 exhibition *"La Lucha del Barro"* in the Museum of Anthropology at the University of Arizona.

Luli Quezada

Lourdes "Luli" Quintana de Quezada is Juan Jr.'s wife and the sister of Noe's wife Betty. Since her marriage, she, Junior, and the two children have lived with or next to Juan and Guille and have been constantly exposed to the potting cycle. In the mid 90s, she began making small polychrome pieces.

Lydia Quezada

Lydia Quezada de Talavera is Juan's youngest sister. Her picture appears on pages 20 and 26. She always has been considered one of the best potters in the Mata Ortiz tradition. She makes all types: polychrome, black, figures, etc. She did some of the original innovative work with black-on-black pottery, now so popular throughout the village. She now lives and works in Nuevo Casas Grandes with her husband Rito Talavera, who also is a potter. Her work has appeared in every major exhibition dating back to the traveling exhibition of 1979-80 referred to on pages 22-24. This includes the University of New Mexico Art Museum exhibition in 1995, the Franz Mayer exhibition in Mexico City in 1999, and the Exhibits USA *Potters of Mata Ortiz* traveling exhibition, 1999-2001

Manuel Quezada

Manuel Quezada González is one of Consolación's older sons. He concentrates on black pottery.

Martha Martínez de Quezada

Mauro Corona Quezada is Consolación Quezada's youngest son and an excellent potter. After their marriage, his wife Martha began making small pots painted in the basic Quezada style. At first she struggled with painting, saying she had no patience for it, and she let Mauro paint her first pieces. She has progressed and now does her own painting. She also helps Mauro polish his finer work, takes care of their children, sells clothing, and helps her mother-in-law, Consolación. She is the sister of Jesús Martínez and the niece of Graciela Gallegos.

Mary Quezada

Mary is a daughter of Juan's brother Jesús. She makes polished black pots in the style of this branch of the Quezada family.

Mauro Quezada

Mauro is one of the best examples of the second generation in Mata Ortiz. He was three when his mother began potting and seven when his uncle Juan was discovered by Spencer MacCallum. He started making pots as a youngster, and that is all he has ever wanted to do. A good artist and technician, he makes all types of pots and figures. Usually he paints intricate black and red designs (polychrome) on white clay *ollas* or figures. Some of his animal shapes follow the style of his cousin Noe. Mauro's picture is on page 85. His work appeared in the Franz Mayer exhibition in Mexico City in 1999, and in the Exhibits USA *Potters of Mata Ortiz* traveling exhibition, 1999-2001.

Matilde de Quezada

Matilde Olivas de Quezada is Hilario's wife. A sister of Ines Olivas and a cousin of Gloria Hernández, she makes small black *ollas, chiquitas negras,* which she signs Matilde de Quezada. She also helps Hilario in the production of his work.

Mireya Quezada

Mireya, Juan's second daughter, has been producing quality work of and on since the mid 1980s. In recent years, she has produced large pieces with modern irregular lips, somewhat in the style of her brother Noe. In the late 80s and early 90s, she worked as a team with a local teacher, Elias Javier Pérez Davila, producing excellent pieces but in her father's basic style. From time to time, she has followed other pursuits, including running a small restaurant in Nuevo Casas Grandes, and then has returned to the clay.

Nena Quezada

Maria Elena Quezada de Luján, "Nena", is the first of Juan's eight children. Years ago she began making little pots and little whimsical figures *("monos")* with which she had good success. In spite of the responsibilities of tiny children, she concentrated on her pottery, and in the 1990s her work improved dramatically, reflecting the styles of her father and brother Noe. In 1993, she and her husband Daniel moved their family to a small community near Janos, called Pancho Villa. They farmed there, and Nena did not pot for a year. Then she started making her *monos* again which are sold from Juan's house in Mata Ortiz. One of her pots with an checkerboard design was selected for the Exhibits USA *Potters of Mata Ortiz* traveling exhibition, 1999-2001.

Nicolás Quezada

Nicolás Quezada Celado is Juan's brother and one of the major figures among the Mata Ortiz potters. Many of his pieces are of museum quality, particularly his large extremely-thin white bowls painted in black and red. Nicolás has exhibited and taught in the U.S. and his pots are in museum collections. His work has been exhibited in all of the major exhibitions including the traveling exhibition of 1979-80 mentioned on pages 22-24, the University of New Mexico Fine Arts exhibition in the spring of 1995, the Franz Mayer exhibit in Mexico City in 1999, the San Diego Museum of Man retrospective *The Magic of Mata Ortiz* in 2000, and the Exhibits USA *Potters of Mata Ortiz* exhibit, 1999-2001. Nicolás' picture is on page 55.

Noe Quezada

Juan's oldest son, Noe, is one of the best in the village, and has established his own reputation as a ceramic artist. He literally has grown up working with the clay, and his fine-line, "computer board" painting is virtually unmatched in technique and original design. Several honor him by copying his work. Noe's trademark used to be figures, particularly fish or frogs. However, in recent years, he has concentrated on classic *olla* shapes. His work has been shown several times in the United States, including a fish figure and two *ollas* in the prestigious University of New Mexico Art Museum exhibition in the spring of 1995, and large *ollas* in the Franz Mayer exhibit in Mexico City in 1999, the San Diego Museum of Man retrospective *The Magic of Mata Ortiz* in 2000, and the Exhibits USA *Potters of Mata Ortiz* exhibit, 1999-2001.

Noelia Quezada

Noelia Hernández Quezada is Rosa Quezada's daughter and Juan's niece. Twenty-five years of age in 2000, she has been making good, lustrous black pots since childhood.

Nolbie Quezada

Nolberto Olivas is Juan's nephew, the son of Guille's brother. He does not live in Mata Ortiz, but sometimes stays with Juan's family and works with Juan's younger sons making *ollas* in the style of Juan and Noe. He signs his pieces with the Quezada surname.

Octavio Quezada

Octavio "Tabo" Gonzales Camacho, signs his pots with his grandmother Consolación's maiden name, "Quezada." This is the son of Oscar Quezada that was eligible for the university. However, instead of continuing his studies, he married and decided to take up the family business working with the clay. He often produces well-painted canteens.

Olga Quezada de Ledezma

Olga is married to Humberto Ledezma Jacques, a cousin of Arturo Ledezma. Humberto forms the pieces and Olga does the painting. They learned from Gerardo Cota in about 1988. Because Humberto continued to work in the fields, Olga signed their first pieces, and they stayed with that practice. The couple lives in the neighborhood, called Barrio Iglesia, north of the plaza near the church. Olga is not a relative of the Juan Quezada family. Much of the couple's work consists of thin beautifully-made pieces with a black checkerboard pattern painted on red clay with a unique square, fluted rim. Such pieces were included in the prestigious University of New Mexico Art Museum exhibition in 1995 and in the Exhibits USA *Potters of Mata Ortiz* exhibition, 1999-2001.

Oscar Quezada

Oscar Gonzales Quezada is Consolación's oldest son by her first husband. After Oscar finished school at 14, he started working in the orchards. This was not long before his mother began potting. She soon was teaching him, and he sold his first pot that year. However, he went back to work in the orchards and made pots on a part-time basis. He married his wife, Concha, and moved to other areas looking for conventional jobs. Finally he returned to Mata Ortiz and began to work as a full-time potter. He does both polychrome and black pieces of good quality. Concha helps him, particularly with the polishing. The couple moved to Nuevo Casas Grandes in the late eighties so that their sons could receive a better education. This has made it harder to make pots, but the effort paid off in 1994 when Octavio, their oldest son, completed high school and was eligible for the university.

Oscar Quezada Jr.

Oscar Gonzales Camacho is another son of Oscar Quezada, and he also signs his pots with his grandmother Consolación's maiden name, "Quezada."

Paty Quezada

Paty Hernández Quezada is Rosa Quezada's daughter. She makes primarily black ware.

Paty Quezada

This Paty lives in Nuevo Casas Grandes and is not related to the extended Juan Quezada family although she paints in the basic Quezada style. Her good friend is Blanca Ponce, Humberto's wife, who often makes the pots Paty paints.

Pedro Quezada

Pedro Valenzuela Quezada, named after his father, is Dora Quezada's son. He began potting in about 1996 making mixed clay, *mezclado,* pieces.

Reynalda Quezada de López

Very early, Juan's sister Reynalda began turning her pots into fat turtles, bats, and other creatures by adding heads, legs, and tails to the basic pot. In other versions lizards and snakes were worked into the top of the pot. These whimsical pieces were very successful and her daughters Yolanda and Olivia, her son Samuel, and several others followed Reynalda's style. Reynalda made nice polychrome pieces, but now she concentrates mostly her popular blackware. Her picture is on page 85.

Reynaldo Quezada

Reynaldo Quezada Celado is Juan's youngest brother. Spencer MacCallum considered him to be one of the best natural artists of the early group of potters. His best work was on a par with that of Juan, Nicolás, or Lydia. In the late seventies and early eighties, he spent much time in the U.S. teaching and giving demonstrations with Spencer and others. In recent years, he has concentrated on blackware, usually incised overall with Reynaldo's special *tejido* or cloth-texture design. One of these was shown in the Exhibits USA *Potters of Mata Ortiz* exhibition, 1999-2001. His work has been in several other major exhibitions including the early traveling exhibition in 1979-80 mentioned on pages 22-24, the Franz Mayer exhibition in Mexico City in 1999, and the San Diego Museum of Man retrospective, *The Magic of Mata Ortiz,* in 2000. Reynaldo's picture is on page 31.

Rosa Quezada

Rosa Quezada de Hernández is a younger sister of Juan. She did not begin potting as early as the rest of the family. However now she makes very nice black *ollas.* Her daughters Noelia and Paty do similar work.

Samuel López Quezada

Samuel is Reynalda's and Simon's son. He has been involved with the potting process all of his life, and in 1989 at age 17, he began potting full time. He makes good black pieces in Reynalda's style.

Yolanda L. Quezada

Yolanda López de Talavara (her married name) is Reynalda Quezada's daughter. She has been making and selling black pots in Reynalda's style for several years. Her work has been sold in galleries throughout the West and Southwest.

Zulema Valenzuela Quezada

Zulema is the daughter of Dora Quezada. In 1995 at age 19, she began making good corrugated blackware in her mother's style.

Eduardo Quintana

Eduardo "Lalo" Quintana Rodríguez is a brother of Jorge. He usually makes pots with sgraffito or carved surfaces, called *calcado* in the village. His primary occupation has been as a carpenter specializing in carved doors and furniture. Because of the influence of brother Jorge, he now also makes pottery. Lalo has helped several other potters get started including his nephew Martin Quintana and Juan Carlos Villalba Rodríguez.

Jorge Quintana

Jorge makes quality polychrome pottery with a variety of designs: checkerboard, Mimbres, Casas Grandes, and even Zapotec and Aztec. When In his early twenties, he spent considerable time at Juan Quezada's house with other young people learning to make pots. After he married his wife Leticia, he followed his own family tradition and became a carpenter. He returned to potting to help Pilo Mora when Pilo began having eye problems. Since then, Jorge and has become a major figure on the Mata Ortiz pottery scene as an artist, teacher, trader, and friend to many, collectors, and tourists. With the help of trader Jerry Boyd, he opened a small inn, Casa Adobe, in Mata Ortiz in 1998. Jorge has demonstrated pottery making many times in the U.S., including exhibitions at the Southwest Museum in Los Angeles and at the Exhibits USA *Potters of Mata Ortiz* traveling exhibition in Riverside, California in November, 1999.

Leticia Quintana

Leticia Cota de Quintana is the wife of Jorge Quintana, She makes small polychrome pieces.

Martín Quintana

The nephew of Jorge and Eduardo Quintana, Martín worked with both of his uncles. However, he is most influenced by the carved surface sgraffito style of Eduardo.

Rocio Quintana

The daughter of Jorge and Leticia Quintana, Rocio attended a technical college in Nuevo Casas Grandes in 2000. When she has time, she makes small polychrome pots.

Tomás Quintana

Tomás occupies a unique position in the Mata Ortiz pottery phenomena. He does not live in Mata Ortiz but rather in Cuatemoc, a village a few miles away. He has had minimal contact with the potters, yet learned to work the clay and now makes interesting animal figures, particularly iguanas from white clay, painted with red and black designs.

Fernando Ramírez

Fernando González Ramírez, the son of Luz Elva Ramírez, began potting seriously at age 18 in 1996. He makes good well-painted blackware. He speaks English and often guides visitors to the village. Fernando uses his mother's name for his pot signature.

Luz Elva Ramírez

Luz Elva Ramírez Carbajal is married to Edmundo López, the well-known graphite blackware potter. Luz Elva (sometimes Luz Elba) also does good blackware. Her teenage sons Fernando and Miguel González Ramírez by another marriage are well on their way to becoming good potters.

Miguel González Ramírez

Miguel, four years younger than his brother Fernando, has been working the same length of time and does similar work, except that he signs his pots with his full, formal name.

Paz Silva Ramírez

This Ramírez family lives across the arroyo in Barrio Porvenir. All work on the pots with Paz Silva de Ramírez signing most. However, daughter Veronica and sons Alonso and Ernesto sign some. They learned from Alonzo Ortiz, the son of the late Osbaldo Ortiz. They make unusual polychrome pieces using green and light red paints. They also make black graphite pots with colored designs. Paz is a member of Grupo Pearson.

Cruz Rentería

Cruz is from a large family of farmers. He is married to potter Blanca Quezada (not a relation of Juan's family). He usually makes plates with extremely fine-line patterns surrounding Mimbres figures.

Lidia Rentería

Lidia Rentería de Cota and her husband, Francisco Cota, lived near Juan and had been working almost ten years when Francisco passed away in 1993. They had developed a black pot style somewhat reminiscent of Reynalda Quezada's work. They occasionally did polychrome pieces. Lidia formed and polished and Francisco painted. Lidia signed most of the pots. After a year of mourning, Lidia began potting again alone. Her picture is on page 85.

Olivia Domínguez Rentería

Olivia is Lidia Rentería's daughter. She began potting about 1988 at age 18. In 1994, she moved to Nuevo Casas Grandes where she continued to make small well-polished black *ollas* and polychrome *ollas* which she brought back to her mother's house to sell. Her picture is on page 85.

Beto Reyes

Beto lives in Barrio López near Leonel López Sáenz from whom he learned the sgraffito style. He etches through green and other unusual paint colors to create various landscape scenes.

Manuel Reyes B.

Manuel lives in the Seccion area of the village. He and his wife, Benita, have been working since the late 80s making a low-cost ware. They learned from Ermeterio Ortiz. Their daughter, Yolanda, and son, Manuel, also make pottery.

Martín Ríos

Martín makes polychrome and black figures — animals, fish, and birds. He learned from Ermeterio Ortiz of the Barrio Porvenir even though he lives in the El Centro neighborhood.

Mary Ríos Lechuca

Mary makes small black and polychrome pieces. She learned from her uncle, Martín Ríos.

Alfredo Rodríguez

Freddy was 16 in 1997 and making imaginative animal figures unique to him.

José Antonio Rodríguez González

Tonio is the son of Martha González and the cousin and neighbor of the well-known Manuel Rodríguez. He began making pots about 1995, following Manuel's style.

Armando Rodríguez

One of Manuel's older brothers, Armando Rodríguez Guillén, is a cowboy who supported his family with a few cattle on the *llano*. When Manuel began selling his figures, Armando started making similar pieces. He now mostly makes polychrome pots which he paints with checkerboard designs. Olivia Mora de Rodríguez, his very outgoing wife, helps Armando, and the two have prospered, adding a room and a porch to their house.

Elena Rodríguez

Elena Rodríguez de López, a sister of Manuel Rodríguez, used to make small human figures like some of the original work of her talented brother. She now concentrates on *ollas* with tiny op-art designs. Elena is married to potter Leonel López Sáenz.

Juan Carlos V. Rodríguez

Juan Carlos is a half brother of Jorge and Eduardo Quintana. Following Eduardo, he carves his pieces in the sgraffito style, called *calcado* in the village.

Lety Rodríguez

Leticia "Lety" Rodríguez Mora is the daughter of Armando and Olivia Rodríguez. She makes small polychrome pots with fine, intricate designs, often with a Mimbres animal on the bottom.

Manuel Rodríguez

Manuel Rodríguez Guillén, "Manolo," is a friend of Juan Junior, Juan's second son. They were on the same baseball team. This boyhood relationship with Junior and the Quezada family undoubtedly influenced Manuel. As a teenager, he began making small animal figures painted with Casas Grandes-style designs. However, it was his little human figures, representing his version of the ancient peoples, which gained him early success. He taught his older brothers, Armando, Rubén and Oscar, his sisters, Tere and Elena, and various neighbors to make similar figures. This created a little subgroup around Manuel and his parents' home in Barrio Americano in the northwest area of the village. Apparently North Americans lived in this area in the lumber mill days. In the early 1990s, Manual stopped making figures and began the making *ollas* painted with exquisite animals cavorting among abstract Escher-like forms in asymmetrical designs. This change thrust Manuel into the forefront of the artists of Mata Ortiz. He is one of the best of a young group that has taken Mata Ortiz pottery to a new level of excellence. Four of his pieces, figures and *ollas,* appeared in the University of New Mexico Art Museum exhibition in 1995. His *ollas* also appeared in the Franz Mayer exhibit in Mexico City in 1999 and in the Exhibits USA *Potters of Mata Ortiz* traveling exhibition, 1999-2001.

Olivia Mora Rodríguez

Olivia has helped her husband, Armando Rodríguez, for years, and about 1996 began making and signing her own pieces. Her brother is Juan Mora.

Oscar Rodríguez

Oscar Rodríguez Guillén is two years older than his brother Manuel. In 1990, he began making small human and animal figures like his brother. By 1994, he progressed to painting such beautiful polychrome *ollas* that he is now counted among the best painters in the village. He sometimes obtains pots from others to paint, particularly Tomás Ozuna, in order to concentrate on his special skill. His pots appeared in the University of New Mexico Art Museum exhibition in 1995 and in the Exhibits USA *Potters of Mata Ortiz* traveling exhibition, 1999-2001.

Rey Rodríguez

Rey and his wife Lupe make up a husband and wife team producing high-quality polychrome canteens and plates. They live in Nuevo Casas Grandes.

Rubén Rodríguez

Rubén is the oldest brother of Manuel, Oscar and others in the Rodríguez family. He makes a variety of polychrome and blackware pots including a specialty — small, brilliantly-polished black *ollas.*

Tere Rodríguez

Teresa "Tere" is Manuel Rodríguez's sister and follows his early style, making small human figures. Her personal touch is that her figures are usually women. She also makes small well-formed pots, sometimes with fluted sides.

Yolanda Rodríguez

Yolanda "Yoli" Rodríguez González is the daughter of Martha González and a cousin of Manuel Rodríguez, Yoli makes small flat-topped seed pots.

Reidesel Reyes Roque

Reidesel was taught by Salvador Ortiz, and makes small pieces with good Mimbres designs.

Adrian Rojas

Adrian is the son of Patrocinio Rojas, who is involved in civic affairs and is in charge of the village water pump and system. Adrian makes white-clay pots and fish shapes.

Arminda Sáenz

Arminda is the wife of Saúl Veloz and the cousin of Leonel López Sáenz.

Chela Sandóval

Chela and her husband, Lucio Soto, produce very large graphite-style blackware. Chela is the daughter of Chevo Sandóval.

Chevo Sandóval

Eusebio "Chevo" Sandóval lives in Barrio Porvenir next to Eduardo Ortiz and is much influenced by the latter's work. He makes polychrome and black pieces.

Ernesto Sandóval

Ernesto Sandóval Ortega is the son of María Ortega, who is featured with another son Antonio in the *Jaripeo* story on page 53. Ernesto makes both polychrome and black pottery.

Israel Sandóval

Israel Sandóval Tena makes large graphite-style blackware. His father is Chevo Sandóval.

Socorro Sandóval

There are many potters in the extended Sandóval and Silveira families that live in Barrio Porvenir near Felix Ortiz and the Ortiz brothers. Socorro Sandóval de Silveira was married to the late José Silveira but has always used her maiden name. Her pots are often large with the body covered with red slip and an incised decoration around the tan, unslipped rim, a characteristic of Porvenir pottery.

Armando Silveira

Armando is the son of Nicolás Silveira and the husband of Tomasa Mora. He usually makes large red pots. He sometimes makes pots for others to paint.

Arminda Silveira

Arminda Silveira Sandóval de Olivas, the daughter of Nicolás Silveira, does large well-painted pots in the general style of the Sandóval/Silveira/Ortiz families.

Fabiola Silveira

Fabiola is the daughter of Gloria Hernandez and Goyo Silveira.

Goyo Silveira

There are several Silveiras and Silbeiras (the same family uses different spellings) working in Barrio Porvenir. Gregorio "Goyo" Silveira Ortiz is one of the best known. For several years, he has been producing large pots for a lower-priced market. He is married to Gloria Hernández. These two are an example of a couple who work together but have different styles. They sign their own pieces. When they work on the same piece, whoever paints it signs it. Goyo learned from his brother Rojelio. Other brothers are Nicolás and José. His son, also called Goyo, makes smaller pots in the same style. Goyo's picture is on page 85.

Israel Silveira

Israel, the son of Rojelio Silveira, makes very large well-made black pieces that are reasonably priced.

José Silveira O.

José died of cancer in 2000. He was married to Socorro Sandóval and was a brother of Goyo, Nicolás and Rojelio. His work followed the general style of his family, including an incised rim. His son, Saúl, makes excellent rings for holding pots.

Lila Silveira

Lila and her sister Trini are daughters of José Silveira and Socorro Sandóval. They began making pots in the early 1990s when they were about 13-14 years old. They worked together, Lila forming and Trini painting. Lila signed the work. In 1997, they were still working together even though Lila married Carlos Carillo in 1995. Lila taught Carlos the art of potting. Later Carlos and Lila had the opportunity to study with Juan Quezada. Now they work as a team, both forming and painting in a style that directly reflects their time with Juan. Trini continues to make her own pots separately in the Porvenir style.

Nicolás Silveira

Nicolás is the oldest of the four Silveira brothers living and working in the Barrio Porvenir. His wife, Genoveva Sandóval, and most of their eight sons and daughters are also potters, all working together producing large quantities of low-cost pottery.

Octavio Silveira

Octavio "Tavo" Silveira Sandóval is the son of Nicolás Silveira. His well-made pieces, a combination of Porvenir and El Centro styles, are a departure from the standard Silveira family product.

Rafael Silveira

Rafael, the son of Rojelio Silveira, usually makes small pots with old Casas Grandes designs.

Rojelio Silveira

Rojelio is the oldest of the four Silveira brothers making pottery in Barrio Porvenir. It is unclear when he began, but there is no doubt that he was one of the very early potters. He says that he, Felix Ortiz, and Salvador Ortiz made a few pots in the early 70s. They painted the pieces with Casas Grandes designs, buried them in the ground for awhile, and then sold them to a Mormon rancher in Colonia Juarez. Rojelio left the village for 12 years, returned, and eventually began making large primitive pieces typical of Porvenir in the 1980s. Now he makes mostly human or animal effigy pieces.

Trini Silveira

Trinidad Silveira Sandóval used to make pots with her sister Lila. Now she works independently, producing Porvenir-style polychrome pieces.

Silvia Silveira

Silvia Silveira de Ozuna is a daughter of Nicolás Silveira. She and husband Tomás Ozuna work as a team.

Veronica Silveira

Veronica (or Beronica) Silveira de Villalba is the daughter of Nicolás Silveira and the wife of potter Sabino Villalba.

Benjamín Soto

Benjamín "Chamin" Soto works as a team with his wife, Cruz Núñez.

Rito Talavera

Rito is married to Lydia Quezada. They live in Nuevo Casas Grandes. Rito at first helped Lydia, for years considered to be one of the best Mata Ortiz potters. However, he has developed his own blackware similar to that of his sister-in-law, Reynalda Quezada. Rito's *ollas* usually feature lizards or snakes in relief around the rim.

Antonia Tena

The Tenas are another extended family of potters in Barrio Porvenir. Antonia Tena de Mora is the sister of Beto Tena and the mother of Bonifacia, Rosa, Nena, Manuel, and Laulo. She was taught by her sister-in-law Sofía Tena, and has been working since about 1991.

Beto Tena

Roberto "Beto" Tena López from Barrio Porvenir is the husband of Sofía. They both do competent work, large *ollas* and figures, following Felix Ortiz's style.

Bonifacia Mora Tena

Bonifacia is the daughter of Antonia. She began potting in 1990 when she was 17. She works with her husband, Efrien.

Esperanza Tena S.

Esperanza Tena de Sandóval is the sister of Antonia and Beto and is married to Chevo Sandóval. She makes and paints her own black graphite-style pots.

Ernesto Tena

Señor Tena is the pharmacist in Mata Ortiz. His whimsical pots are clearly a sideline in contrast to the other potters for whom pottery sales are a major source of income.

Fito Tena

Adolfo Tena Sandóval, "Fito," is the son of Beto and Sofía Tena and works in their style.

Gerardo Tena

Gerardo Tena Sandóval lives next to Gloria Hernández and Goyo Silveira. He makes large and small polychrome pots of good quality, using an original painting style. His wife, Nora Hernández, helps in the process.

Sofía de Tena

Sofía Sandóval de Tena is the wife of Beto Tena and the sister of Felix Ortiz's wife Otila Sandóval de Ortiz. She learned to pot by watching her sister.

Ana Trillo

Ana Trillo de Corona lives behind the elementary school in Barrio Americana. She is not from a family of potters, but she has been making well-made polychrome, red-clay, and black pieces since the late 1980s. Often her pots are formed into a double necked or "wedding jar" shape. She learned from Elvira Antillón, the wife of Damián Quezada. Her husband, Monico Corona, the uncle of Mauro and Hilario Quezada, sands and polishes Ana's work. Ana has influenced several other potters in her neighborhood.

Hector Trillo

Hector is Ana's brother. In 1999, he had been working about three years. His wife Bety forms the pots that he paints.

Diego Valle

In 1999-2000, Diego rode a bus every day to the new high school in Colonia Juarez. He was in the second class of Mata Ortiz students to be transported to the school. He began potting in 1999 and by the middle of the following year made quite acceptable seed pots.

Carmen Veloz

Carmela (she signs "Carmen") Ledezma de Veloz and her husband, Jesús (a cousin of Saúl and Ramiro Veloz), live between the church and the orange railroad bridge in a nice house with arched doorways—a house that pottery built (or at least remodeled). She, assisted by Jesús, makes small beautifully-painted double-necked "wedding" jars as well as seed pots and small *ollas*. This couple learned by watching neighbor Gloria Lozoya. They have done well and have conducted many demonstrations and classes. Carmen is named after her father, Carmelo Ledezma, a famous Chihuahuan baseball player. The rodeo/baseball stadium in Mata Ortiz is named after him.

Celia Veloz

Celia is a daughter of Saúl Veloz. She now lives in Porvenir. She typically paints her long-necked jars with tight, detailed designs, characteristic of her family's work.

Fabiola Veloz

Fabiola is Saúl Veloz's daughter. She usually makes red *ollas* with black checker-board designs.

Ramiro Veloz Casas

In 1993, young Ramiro, age twelve, took over the duty of painting his father's pots after his mother died of cancer. When Ramiro Senior suffered a stroke, Ramiro Junior learned to form the pots as well as the other steps in the process in order to support his father and sister.

Ramiro Veloz

Ramiro Veloz Gutiérrez lives next door to Juan Quezada. He and his wife Sylvia

Casas made beautiful ware with very thin walls and detailed painting. Sylvia painted the pots Ramiro formed until she died of cancer in July, 1991. About a year and a half later, twelve-year old Ramiro Jr. began painting his father's pots. Young Ramiro has talent, so much so that his father told him to sign all of their work. He signs "Ramiro Veloz Casas," omitting the "Junior." Unfortunately, Ramiro, a robust, handsome man, suffered a stroke that left him partially paralyzed and unable to work. Since then Ramiro Jr. has filled the gap, making and selling pots to support the family.

Saúl Veloz

Saúl Veloz Gutiérrez is Ramiro's brother. For many years, he has made small well-painted polychrome *ollas*, with designs showing the influence of his brother and Juan Quezada.

Adan Villa

Adan lives in Barrio Americano. He learned pottery from his friend Julio Mora and makes small pieces and miniatures like Julio.

Anastacia Villa Ortiz

María Anastacia, originally from Barrio Porvenir, lives now in El Centro with her well-known potter husband Rubén Lozano. Her father is Ramón Villa. Anastacia usually makes small blackware.

Benjamín Villa López

Benjamín is from Barrio Porvenir. He is married to Susana Camacho and is the brother of Ramón and Tomás Villa.

Benjamín Villa Ortiz

This Benjamín is the nephew of the other and the son of Ramón. He and his wife María López work together with white clay making many different shapes and designs.

Cruz Celia Villa

Cruz Celia Villa de Camacho is another daughter of Ramón Villa. She has been a potter since childhood and now produces good-quality marbleized pots with the help of her husband Alvaro Camacho.

Deonicio Villa Corona

When he was only 13 years old in 1997, Deonicio made small white pieces with detailed designs including lizards, birds, and animals. These were very popular with visitors to the village. His father, Tomás Villa, helped in the process. Some of the pieces were signed "Dionicio."

Ramón Villa

Ramón, a brother of Tomás and Benjamín Villa López, makes pottery with his wife, Celia, and son, Rito.

Tomás Villa

From Barrio Porvenir and the brother of Ramón Villa, Tomás makes small white pieces. Some of his work is painted by his son, Deonicio.

Adriana Villalba de Andrew

Adriana, in spite of being the daughter of the well-known Andres Villalba, makes small polychrome and black pots in the style of her husband Fernando Andrew.

Andres Villalba

The late Andres Villalba Pérez and his son Caby used to make pots together. Their pieces were generally of the Ortiz or Porvenir style, and were signed "Caby." When they began working independently in the late 1980s, Andres' work improved dramatically. He had a deep respect for Juan, and his newer work with its fine symmetrical lines reflected Juan's influence. However, instead of gradually growing away from the basic prehistoric Casas Grandes style, Andres took pride in maintaining the old shapes and designs. The bishop in Nuevo Casas Grandes sent one of Andres' and one of Juan Quezada's pots to the Pope as gifts when he visited Chihuahua City in May, 1990. Andres' work was selected for the prestigious University of New Mexico Art Museum exhibition in 1995, and for the Exhibits USA *Potters of Mata Ortiz* traveling exhibition, 1999-2001. Andreas died of cancer in the spring of 2001 but not before he had composed a song, a *corrido,* thanking his friends for their kindness during his illness.

Carlos Villalba

Another son of Andres Villalba, Juan Carlos Villalba does good quality work, producing some pots in the traditional Casas Grandes style like his father and others in the black graphite style.

Sabino Villalba

Andres Villalba's son, Sabino "Caby" Villalba Hernández actually taught his now well-known father potting when Caby was a teenager. He used to sign all of his work "Caby," but changed at the request of long-time Mata Ortiz trader Adalberto Pérez Meillón. By 2001, Sabino was making pots in the prehistoric Casas Grandes style like his late father.

Lourdes Villalba

The youngest daughter of Andres Villalba, María de Lourdes (Luly) Villalba Hernández makes traditional Casas Grandes-style pots following her father's style.

Gerónimo Villapando

Gerónimo lives in the Seccion area of the village and works as a team with his wife Socorro Reyes, making both polychrome and black *ollas.*

INDEX

This Index does not include the potters listed in the Appendix except for those potters specifically mentioned in the text of the book.

RIZONA

NEW MEXICO

Douglas

gua Prieta

Deming

Columbus

El Paso

Ciudad Juarez

TEXAS

Janos

Nuevo Casas Grandes

C. Juarez

Paquime

Mata Ortiz

Cave of the Olla

SONORA

CHIHUAHUA

Chihuahua

Creel

Copper Canyon

151

Potters' Autographs

IN QUEST OF

The Universe

SIXTH
EDITION

Theo Koupelis
Edison State College

JONES AND BARTLETT PUBLISHERS

Sudbury, Massachusetts

BOSTON   TORONTO   LONDON   SINGAPORE

World Headquarters
Jones and Bartlett Publishers
40 Tall Pine Drive
Sudbury, MA 01776
978-443-5000
info@jbpub.com
www.jbpub.com

Jones and Bartlett Publishers Canada
6339 Ormindale Way
Mississauga, Ontario L5V 1J2
Canada

Jones and Bartlett Publishers International
Barb House, Barb Mews
London W6 7PA
United Kingdom

Jones and Bartlett's books and products are available through most bookstores and online booksellers. To contact Jones and Bartlett Publishers directly, call 800-832-0034, fax 978-443-8000, or visit our website, www.jbpub.com.

Substantial discounts on bulk quantities of Jones and Bartlett's publications are available to corporations, professional associations, and other qualified organizations. For details and specific discount information, contact the special sales department at Jones and Bartlett via the above contact information or send an email to specialsales@jbpub.com.

Production Credits
Chief Executive Officer: Clayton Jones
Chief Operating Officer: Don W. Jones, Jr.
President, Higher Education and Professional Publishing: Robert W. Holland, Jr.
V.P., Sales: William J. Kane
V.P., Design and Production: Anne Spencer
V.P., Manufacturing and Inventory Control: Therese Connell
Publisher, Higher Education: Cathleen Sether
Acquisitions Editor: Molly Steinbach
Senior Editorial Assistant: Jessica S. Acox
Editorial Assistant: Caroline Perry
Production Manager: Louis C. Bruno, Jr.
Senior Marketing Manager: Andrea DeFronzo
Text Design: Anne Spencer
Cover Design: Scott Moden
Illustrations: Precision Graphics, Carlisle Communications, Elizabeth Morales, and Graphic World, Inc.
Senior Photo Researcher: Christine Myaskovsky
Composition: Graphic World, Inc.
Cover and Title Page Image: Courtesy of Gemini Observatory/Association of Universities for Research in Astronomy
Printing and Binding: Courier Kendallville
Cover Printing: Courier Kendallville

Library of Congress Cataloging-in-Publication Data
Koupelis, Theo.
  In quest of the universe / Theo Koupelis. — 6th ed.
    p. cm.
  ISBN 978-0-7637-6858-4 (alk. paper)
  1. Astronomy—Textbooks. I. Title.
QB45.2.K84 2010
520—dc22   2009027210

6048

Printed in the United States of America
14 13 12 11 10   10 9 8 7 6 5 4 3 2

About the cover: The Gemini North Laser Guide Star (LGS) system in Maunakea, Hawaii.

To Alex and Billy, for shining so bright.

BRIEF CONTENTS

CONTENTS

BOXED FEATURES

ADVANCING THE MODEL

HISTORICAL NOTE

TOOLS OF ASTRONOMY

ACTIVITIES

I recognize that many students using this text are not planning to become astronomers or perhaps even scientists in general. Yet, I strongly believe in the importance of every student (and every person, for that matter) understanding how science operates and how we know what we know about our world. Without an understanding of the basic concepts of science, we cannot understand the scientific and technological progress around us. We cannot contribute informed and useful opinions on how this progress is used. Above all, we cannot distinguish science from pseudoscience. A habit of skeptical thought and a reliance upon observation and testing to verify an idea are valuable not just for scientists but for everyone. Towards that end, this book was written as an introduction to astronomy, as well as an introduction to the general methods of science.

Astronomy is presented in this text in the traditional order of solar system, stars, and galaxies. This gives me the opportunity to emphasize the historical development of science and technology as well as to proceed from the more familiar to the less familiar. It also allows students to expand their sense of astronomical dimensions gradually, from the sizes of planets to the distances between the stars to the vast spaces between the galaxies. I frequently stop our tour of the universe to discuss how new scientific theories gradually replaced older ones, building upon established information by adding new observations and new insights into how the universe works.

Updated Content

Even though the basic goals of the book have remained the same as in the fifth edition, this edition represents a thorough rewrite of the book that includes a rethinking of every argument and an update of all the information presented in all its forms (text, numbers, tables, and figures). New information can be found throughout the book, but the following are some of the major changes and updates:

- An expanded discussion of non-optical telescopes is included in Chapter 5, where space telescopes are now discussed in a *Tools of Astronomy* box.

- Chapter 8 includes new information on Venus and Mars based on the latest data from satellites, especially the *Phoenix* lander and *Venus Express*.

- In Chapter 9, the discussion on Saturn's moons, especially Titan and Enceladus, has been expanded based on *Cassini* data.

- In Chapter 10, the discussion on the Kuiper belt and Oort cloud has been expanded, based on the discoveries of new trans-Neptunian objects. Also, the section on the "Importance of the Solar System Debris" includes an in-depth discussion of the connections between meteoritic material and life in our solar system.

- Based on observations by *TRACE, SOHO,* and *Hinode*, new insights into how the Sun's magnetic field controls the release of mass and energy into the solar atmosphere are presented in Chapter 11.

- The discussion on various methods of distance measurements has been expanded in Chapters 14 and 17.

- Based on observations by *HST, XMM-Newton*, and *Chandra*, new insights on the distribution of dark matter are described in Chapter 17, along with new information on early star formation based on *Spitzer* data.

- A clear and in-depth description of all the latest findings on cosmology is included in Chapter 18. These new results have signaled the dawn of the era of precision cosmology.

- A great number of new images are included from a variety of sources that cover the entire electromagnetic spectrum and are the result of many international collaborative efforts. I have tried to select pictures that are useful as well as exciting, illustrating many of the awesome events that take place throughout the cosmos.

Pedagogical Features

- *Data Pages* on individual planets, the Moon, and the Sun should help students in reviewing the material and focusing on important concepts; these data pages can be found in Appendix C. A data page for planetary nebulae is included in Chapter 14.

- *Marginal definitions* and *marginal notes* are located throughout the text. Definitions appear next to key terms highlighted in the text; these definitions are collected in the Glossary at the end of the book. Marginal notes often refer to relevant material in other chapters or provide additional facts about the topic under discussion.

- *Quotations* appear in the margin to give students an idea of what astronomers and physicists themselves thought about science or about their work. Other quotations show what people in other disciplines or other cultures think about the issues involved in astronomy.

- *Student misconceptions* are addressed by placing in the margin typical questions often asked by students. Each such question appears in the chapter section that provides the answers to the question. Students can use these questions as guidelines for review, making sure they understand the correct explanation for each question.

- *Historical Note* boxes discuss historical developments and biographies of astronomers.

- *Advancing the Model* boxes discuss concepts covered in the text in more depth and/or cover additional material.

- *Tools of Astronomy* boxes discuss mathematical and observational tools astronomers use to describe the universe.

- *Worked Examples* illustrate how astronomers determine some of the data we now accept as accurate descriptions of celestial objects.

- *Try One Yourself* problems involve a more mathematical understanding of astronomy.

- A built-in *Study Guide* at the end of each chapter provides three sets of exercises. New exercises have been added and some old ones have been revised. Answers to even-numbered exercises are included at the end of the book.

Aristotle lived from about 384 to 322 BC but still influences today's thinking.

Every physicist thinks he knows what a photon is. I spent my life to find out what a photon is and I still don't know it.

Albert Einstein

Is an arcminute or an arcsecond a unit for measuring time?

- *Recall Questions* are mostly multiple choice but also include other review questions.

- *Questions to Ponder* are generally more complex than the Recall Questions and sometimes ask students to relate material in the chapter to ideas from earlier chapters. Some questions ask students for personal evaluations of issues or to research topics in other resources.

- *Calculations* pose numerical problems for students to solve, based on examples in the
chapter.

- *Activities* are also included in the Study Guides, featuring observational astronomy and drawing of scale models, among other things.

Ancillary Materials

To assist the instructor with teaching this course and provide students with the best in teaching aids, Jones and Bartlett Publishers has prepared a complete ancillary package. All the electronic materials are compatible with Windows and Macintosh systems. Additional information and review copies of any of the following items are available through your Jones and Bartlett publisher's representative.

For the Instructor

WebAssign® is the premier online independent teaching and learning environment, guiding over three million students through their academic careers since 1997. It was developed by teachers, for teachers, allowing you to:

- Create and distribute assignments using questions specific to this textbook

- Grade, record, and analyze student responses and performances instantly

- Offer practice exercises, quizzes, and homework

- Upload resources to share and communicate with your students seamlessly

For more detailed information and to sign up for free faculty access, please visit www.webassign.net. To find out how students can purchase access to WebAssign bundles with this textbook, please contact your Jones and Bartlett publisher's representative.

The *Instructor's Media CD-ROM* provides instructors who have adopted the text with the following traditional ancillaries:

- The **PowerPoint® Image Bank** provides a library of all the illustrations, photographs, and tables, to which Jones and Bartlett Publishers holds the copyright or has permission to reprint digitally, inserted into PowerPoint slides. Instructors can easily copy individual images into existing PowerPoint slides or add more images to the PowerPoint Lecture Outline Slides.

- The **PowerPoint Lecture Outline Slides**, prepared by Gregory J. Black of the University of Virginia, combine text and images into a presentation that is both educational and engaging. Using the Microsoft® PowerPoint program, instructors can modify and edit the slide show to fit individual presentation needs.

- Seventy **animations of key illustrations** in the text have been created, expanding the reach of the figures beyond the static page. Illustrations in the text accompanied by the icon ◯ indicate that a corresponding animation is on the Instructor's Media CD-ROM and on the Starlinks student companion Web site. Because so many concepts in astronomy involve motion, these animated illustrations are invaluable tools for helping students understand the concepts.

Online Instructor's Resources

- The **Instructor's Manual**, prepared by David J. Ennis of Ohio State University, contains chapter summaries and outlines, learning objectives, teaching suggestions and classroom activities, questions to test student understanding, and answers to all of the end-of-chapter questions that appear in the book.

- The **Test Bank**, prepared by George Spagna of Randolph-Macon College, features nearly 3000 questions in plain text files that can be easily integrated with your existing course management software.

For the Student

Increase your in-the-field observing success with the ***Starry Night® Pro version 6 DVD***, provided free with this text. Use the Events Finder to choose targets, or make your own Observing List for a specific night or for specific objects of interest. Print out three-view starhopping charts customized to your equipment that effortlessly guide you to challenging objects. With extensive data sets, advanced telescope control, and comprehensive observational tools, Starry Night Pro is a powerful program designed for the serious astronomer. Transform your computer into a sophisticated virtual observatory!

Starlinks is the Jones and Bartlett Web site that accompanies *In Quest of the Universe, Sixth Edition*. This site, http:// physicalscience.jbpub.com/starlinks, hosts a wide array of additional resources and activities for independent study, review, and research.

> **Quest Ahead to Starlinks:**
> http://physicalscience.jbpub.com/starlinks
>
> **Starlinks** is this book's online learning center. It features **eLearning**, which contains chapter quizzes and other tools designed to help you study for your class. You also can find **online exercises**, view numerous relevant **animations**, follow a guide to **useful astronomy sites** on the Internet, or even check the latest **astronomy news** updates.

- A **Study Guide** includes learning objectives and summaries for each chapter of the book, which you can download and use as note-taking guides.

- A set of original **Animations** that correspond to images in the book will help you to visualize the key concepts of motion in astronomy.

- An **Interactive Glossary**, on-screen **Flashcards**, and electronic **Crosswords** offer fun and easy ways for you to review the key terms.

- To help with reading comprehension and exam preparation, **Study Quizzes and Short Answer Quizzes** for each chapter provide you with short Web-based tests, the results of which can be submitted directly to your instructor.

- Additional **NetQuestions** are Web-based exercises that encourage independent research.

- **Web Explorations** recommends external Web sites that provide further information about topics covered in the text.

Acknowledgments

Good teachers learn from their students. Attention to students' questions helps instructors to discover which concepts are most difficult and require special explanation. The same is true for textbook writers, and I thank my students over the years for their questions.

Although it is the author's name that appears on the cover of a textbook, all textbook writers know that "their" book is far from theirs alone. The sweat of many brows moistens the pages of every book. My thanks to the Jones and Bartlett team for all their excellent work, and especially Louis Bruno for his infinite patience and dedication to this project.

Special thanks to Karl Kuhn for giving me the opportunity to work with him and learn from him. I hope future editions of this text will do justice to his original vision for it.

I owe a debt of gratitude to my teachers through the years, great teachers and friends—examples that have been very hard to follow. I thank them for everything they taught me and for providing me with a never-ending challenge.

My support and guidance during the entire process of revising/updating this text came from the two stars in my sky, Alex and Billy. Thank you for being there, for everything you are teaching me every day, and for making the world such a beautiful place.

Reviewers play a major role in the success of a book. I would like to thank all those reviewers who have spent time commenting on the revisions and page proofs for *In Quest of the Universe*, Sixth Edition.

Jill Bechtold, University of Arizona

Peter A. Becker, George Mason University

John H. Bieging, University of Arizona

Gregory J. Black, University of Virginia

Juan Cabanela, Minnesota State University, Moorhead

Michael W. Castelaz, University of North Carolina, Asheville and Pisgah Astronomical Research Institute

Peter Deutsch, Pennsylvania State University, Beaver Campus

David B. Green, Pepperdine University

David Goldwater, Community College of Southern Nevada

Bruce Gronich, University of Texas, El Paso

David Heiden, Fairfield High School

Michael Inglis, SUNY Suffolk

Douglas R. Ingram, Texas Christian University

Jonathan Keohane, Hampden Sydney College

Lauren Likkel, University of Wisconsin, Eau Claire

Joe Mast, Eastern Mennonite University

Mark McConnell, University of New Hampshire

Jim Mihal, Milwaukee Area Technical College

Scott Miller, University of Louisville

Slawomir Piatek, New Jersey Institute of Technology

Pamela Peterson, Anoka-Ramsey Community College, Cambridge Campus

Cameron Reed, Alma College

Sheldon Schafer, Bradley University

George Spagna, Randolph-Macon College

Walther Spjeldvik, Weber State University

Martin Steinbaum, Iona College

Rosemary Walling, University of Alaska Southeast

Marguerite Zarrillo, University of Massachusetts, Dartmouth

I invite instructors using *In Quest of the Universe* to contact me directly with comments and suggestions. It is you who know best what should be changed in future editions. For any questions and suggestions about the ancillary materials, please contact Jones and Bartlett Publishers at info@jbpub.com

Theo Koupelis
Edison State College
tkoupelis@edison.edu

The Quest Ahead

Comet Shoemaker-Levy 9 was broken by Jupiter's gravitational forces into more than 20 fragments (bottom photo), all following the same path toward a collision with Jupiter. This photo of Jupiter (top photo) shows the impact spots left by some of the fragments.

ON THE NIGHT OF MARCH 23, 1993, AMATEUR ASTRONOMER David Levy photographed part of the sky near the planet Jupiter. His friends, fellow astronomers Carolyn Shoemaker and her husband Eugene Shoemaker, spotted something unusual in the picture: a comet that had broken up into about 20 pieces. The comet became known officially as Comet Shoemaker-Levy 9 (the ninth comet discovered by these three sky-watchers) and unofficially as the "string of pearls" comet.

When astronomers announced the news of the comet on June 1, 1993, they had traced its path closely enough to tell that it had come under the influence of Jupiter's powerful gravitational field. They had deduced that the comet was pulled apart by Jupiter's gravity in July of 1992. They predicted that the comet would crash into Jupiter on or about July 25, 1994.

By October 1993, astronomers had refined their predictions. The comet was then stretched out over a distance of 3 million kilometers (1.8 million miles) in orbit around Jupiter. The first piece was predicted to hit Jupiter at 4:01 PM (Eastern daylight savings time in the United States) on July 16, and the last piece was predicted to hit at 4:00 AM on July 22, 1994; however, nobody knew whether the impacts would be big or small or even observable by telescopes on Earth.

All cross references to chapters, sections, figures, and tables pertain to the main text, *In Quest of the Universe, Sixth Edition. In Quest of the Solar System* contains Chapters 1–11 and 19 of the main text. *In Quest of the Stars and Galaxies* contains Chapters 1–5 and 11–19 of the main text.

By the time of the predicted impacts, the entire world was watching, linked together by the Internet and the television. The *Hubble Space Telescope* was trained on Jupiter, as was the *Galileo* space probe then approaching the Jupiter system, as well as most major observatories around the world and untold numbers of amateur telescopes. It has been said that more telescopes were aimed at the same spot—Jupiter— than ever before or since, and the viewers were not disappointed.

Fragment A of the comet hit Jupiter at 4:11 PM Eastern daylight time, only 10 minutes off the prediction made 10 months earlier. Traveling at 60 kilometers/second (130,000 miles/hour), each fragment created a fireball in Jupiter's upper atmosphere reaching up as high as 3000 kilometers (1900 miles) and leaving darkened areas in the atmosphere as wide across as the diameter of the Earth. Scientists estimated that some of the larger impacts, caused by fragments about 3 kilometers across, released energy equivalent to 6 million megatons of TNT. (The largest nuclear bomb ever detonated produced a blast equivalent to about 5 megatons.) The event made front-page headlines around the world, featuring photographs of fireballs and dark impact spots across the giant planet.

How were astronomers able to predict the time of impact with such accuracy? What did they learn from observing the aftereffects of this stupendous collision? Many scientists believe that a similar collision with an asteroid occurred on Earth 65 million years ago, heralding the end of the age of dinosaurs. Since seeing the visible proof of such collisions on Jupiter, many people worry about the chances of further catastrophes on our own planet. Astronomers say that the chances of such an event happening here are roughly once in 300,000 years, but how can they make such a prediction?

You will learn the answers to some of these questions in this book. You will find that although collisions of comets and planets are very rare in our immediate neighborhood of space, the vast regions of the universe show tremendous activity. Stars are born in dense clouds of gas while other stars explode, spewing forth gas back into space. Galaxies collide over periods of millions of years, hurtling stars around at fantastic speeds. The universe is a wild and fabulous showcase, and we will see some of its highlights, looking out from our quiet corner called Earth.

Astronomy is the oldest of the sciences, but it is still changing rapidly today. It is a study rich in interesting personalities and exciting discoveries. Its long history and recent advances make it an excellent example of the progressive nature of science.

Science is fundamentally a quest for understanding, and in the case of astronomy, the subject of the quest is the entire universe. The study of astronomy covers the full range of matter from smallest to largest. On the small end, it includes atoms and their internal workings, for astronomers need to know about the nuclear reactions that make **stars** shine; this knowledge one day may lead to peaceful applications of thermonuclear reactions. Astronomers also study Earth's neighbors, the planets, and in doing so help us solve problems right here on Earth. For example, a study of weather patterns on Venus and Jupiter has advanced our understanding of weather on Earth. In addition, studying Mars and Venus helps us understand the past and future of our own planet. Information we collected using unmanned spacecraft and Earth-based telescopes has revolutionized our understanding of how our solar system formed billions of years ago and has evolved since then. In particular, our neighborhood was and, to a lesser extent, still is a shooting gallery; we can see the scars of collisions on the surfaces of Mercury, the Moon, and other planetary satellites. Understanding the composition of the objects in our vicinity may one day prove extremely valuable in our efforts to find additional sources of materials for our own survival. The apparent weightlessness and very low density of space may one day lead to the manufacture of exceptional substances. In some cases, astronomy's results are more trivial but nevertheless practical: materials developed for the *Apollo* missions to the Moon are now used in tennis rackets.

Astronomers also study the largest groupings of billions of stars, and they ask big questions, the answers to which tell us something about ourselves, both as individuals and as a species. Our studies of stars and ***nebulae*** help us better understand the

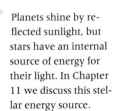

Six million megatons is about 600 times the estimated arsenal of the world.

Nothing is rich but the inexhaustible wealth of nature. She shows us only surfaces, but she is a million fathoms deep.
Ralph Waldo Emerson

star A self-luminous celestial object.

Planets shine by reflected sunlight, but stars have an internal source of energy for their light. In Chapter 11 we discuss this stellar energy source.

nebula (plural **nebulae**) An interstellar region of dust and/or gas.

natural cycle of the formation of a star, its evolution, its death, and the recycling of some of its material into a new star.

Our studies of *galaxies* help us better understand the creation and evolution of our universe. Studying astronomy causes us to change our basic outlook as we better appreciate where humans fit into the magnificent universe. Our species and our planet seem to be dwarfed by the immensity of the cosmos. In a sense, astronomy teaches humility.

At the same time, one marvels that humans have been able to learn so much about the universe in which we live and that such tiny beings are able to comprehend the huge, complex universe. From this we may decide that size is not so important after all—at least not when compared with the intelligence and spirit of our species. We should take pride in our accomplishments but also continue pushing the frontiers of knowledge.

> **galaxy** A group of gravitationally bound stars, ranging from a billion to perhaps a thousand billion stars.

1-1 The View from Earth

In our modern world, few of us can escape from city lights to sit under a clear sky and enjoy its splendors. Fortunately, our ancestors had the time and inclination to do so. The sky on a clear, dark night is a wondrous sight, and before electric lights and television, watching the sky must have been a very popular activity.

As your eyes adjust to the darkness, perhaps the most impressive spectacle that you see is the myriad of twinkling stars in the sky, ranging from dim to bright and from lone stars to clusters of many stars (**FIGURE 1-1**). What is truly astounding is that each of these stars is simply another sun, shining by the same processes that take place in our Sun.

The nature of the Sun and the tremendous energy it produces have been mysteries through the centuries, but now we know that the Sun is a sphere made up almost entirely of hydrogen and helium and that its energy comes from nuclear fusion reactions in its core. As you sit under the stars some night, try to think of each of them as a sun, and imagine how far away they must be to look as dim as they are.

The Sun is described in Chapter 11.

We discuss the stars in Chapters 12 through 15.

FIGURE 1-1 The night sky illuminates a fir tree in this photo. Brighter stars appear larger in a photograph because they overexpose the film. Their apparent size is not related to their actual size. Return to this figure after you gain some experience in recognizing stars and constellations on the night sky, and try to find the Southern Cross, Carina, and alpha and beta Centauri; these are some of the most significant southern stars and constellations.

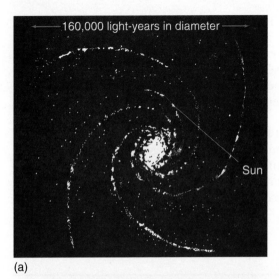

160,000 light-years in diameter

Sun

(a)

Looking out of the disk

Looking along the disk

(b)

FIGURE 1-2 (a) Our Sun is one of a few hundred billion stars that form a spiral disk somewhat like this simplified, face-on drawing of our Galaxy. (b) This simplified edge-on drawing of the Milky Way shows that when we see it in the sky, we are looking along its disk, and distant stars are not distinct but instead appear as a bright haze. When we look in other directions, we see right out of the Galaxy. (c) This wide-angle photo shows the Milky Way [in the constellations Sagittarius (left) and Scorpius (right)].

(c)

Nebulae are involved in both the birth and the death of stars.

FIGURE 1-3 This is a photo (not a painting!) of a small area of the sky. The Eagle Nebula is a very luminous cluster of stars surrounded by dust and gas. The three pillars at the center of the image were made famous in an image by the *Hubble Space Telescope*.

How many stars are there? Only about 5000 can be seen with the naked eye from Earth, but telescopes reveal hundreds of billions of stars clustered in a giant disk that we call the Galaxy (**FIGURE 1-2a**). The wondrous *Milky Way*, a hazy white area that stretches across the sky, is caused by our view along the disk of the Galaxy (Figure 1-2b and c).

Besides the Milky Way you can see a few smaller patches of dim light in the sky. We call them nebulae (**FIGURE 1-3**) because of their intrinsic, nebulous appearance. They are giant clouds of gas, illuminated by light from stars within them. Though we compare them with clouds, we know today that the gas within them is extremely sparse, sparser than a laboratory vacuum here on Earth. A nebula is visible to us only because it is very large; our line of sight passes through so much material that although any given part of it provides only slight illumination, the nebula as a whole is visible.

Other objects that were formerly called "nebulae" are separate galaxies from ours, groups of millions to hundred of billions of stars (**FIGURE 1-4**). They appear to the eye as tiny, hazy splotches only because they are so far from us.

The patient observer is likely to see a meteor, a quick flash of light across the sky. Once called "falling stars," meteors are caused by (mostly) rocky visitors from beyond the Earth that glow as they burn in our atmosphere. A few times in your life, you will be able to see a comet, which will probably appear as the largest object in the sky.

If you watch for a few hours, you will see that the stars are not stationary at all, but move across the sky, most of them rising in the east and setting in the west (FIGURE 1-5). The entire sky seems to be on a bowl rotating around us. You will make another observation as you watch the sky through the seasons: different stars are visible at different times of the year because the entire sky shifts to the west very slightly from night to night. Why are we privileged to be at the center of this majestic spectacle?

As you watch the sky from night to night and begin to remember patterns of the positions of stars, you will see that a few "stars" do not stay in the same place relative to the others. These are the **planets**—wanderers on an apparently irregular path across the sky. If the Moon is visible, it represents a magnificent view, varying from night to night but always interesting.

What we know about these celestial objects would have astounded our forefathers. We know that the Moon is a solid planet-like object about one fourth the diameter of the Earth. The planets range in size from tiny Mercury, with a diameter about 38% of Earth's, to Jupiter, a giant more than 11 times wider than Earth. As for the Sun, the celestial object most important to us, its diameter is about 10 times Jupiter's and 109 times Earth's.

If you have the opportunity to use binoculars or a small telescope to view the heavens, a myriad of sights will be available. As we proceed with our quest for understanding in this text, we will point out many of the objects that are accessible to the backyard astronomer.

FIGURE 1-4 This distant spiral galaxy (named NGC-2997) is in the constellation Antlia. Although this galaxy is not visible to the naked eye, a few other galaxies are. The bright stars in the photo are in our Galaxy and are much closer to us than NGC2997.

Galaxies are the subject of Chapters 16 and 17.

planet Any of the eight (Mercury to Neptune) large objects that revolve around the Sun, or similar objects that revolve around other stars.

The Moon is discussed in Chapter 6 and the planets in Chapters 7 through 10.

Pluto's diameter is about 19% of Earth's. Pluto's designation as a planet was changed in 2006 (see Chapter 10).

FIGURE 1-5 Night sky at ESO-Paranal in Chile. This time exposure shows the motion of the stars. The lines are actually parts of circles, whose center is not in the picture. You can make photographs like this with any camera capable of taking time exposures. Choose a dark, starry night, and point the camera toward the part of the sky that you want to photograph. Fix the camera so that it won't move, and open the shutter for an hour or two. (See margin note by Figure 1-8 on page 7.)

1-2   The Celestial Sphere

As we watch the sky during the night from any mid-latitude location on Earth, we see some stars rising in the east and setting in the west. Stars above the poles of the Earth move in concentric circles, centered on a spot in the sky above each pole (FIGURE 1-6).

Another observation that can be made by even a casual observer is that the stars stay in the same patterns night after night. The Big Dipper seems to retain its shape through the ages as it moves around the North Star; in reality, its shape is very slowly changing, as we describe in the next section. It is easy to see why the ancients concluded that the stars act as if they were glued on a huge sphere that surrounds and rotates around the Earth. FIGURE 1-7 illustrates this *celestial sphere*.

Its axis of rotation passes through the sphere at the center of the circles of Figure 1-6, and at the center of similar circles for the stars in the Southern Hemisphere. The photograph in Figure 1-6 was taken from the Northern Hemisphere, and the point at the center of the circles, the *north celestial pole*, is exactly above the North Pole of the Earth.

celestial sphere The imaginary sphere of heavenly objects that seems to center on the observer.

celestial pole The point on the celestial sphere directly above a geographic pole of the Earth.

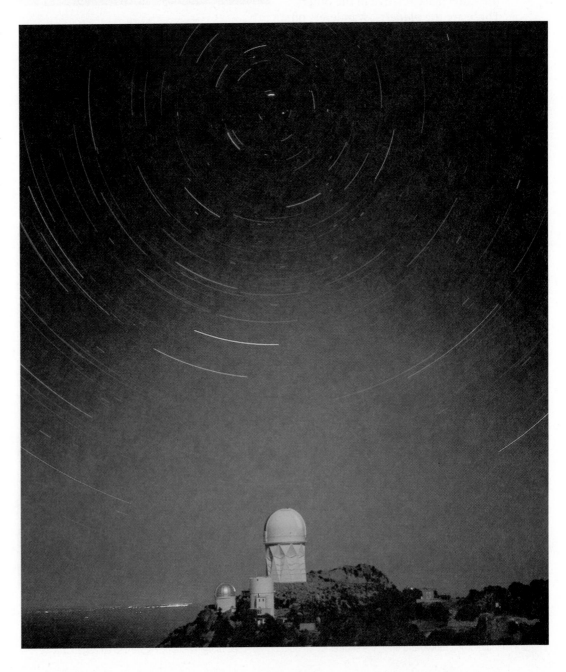

FIGURE 1-6 The stars in this time exposure of the northern sky seem to move in a counterclockwise direction around one point. Polaris, the North Star, formed the short, bright streak near the center of the circles. Polaris also moves around this center because our North Star is not located exactly above the Earth's rotation axis. Color differences between the streaks were caused by variations in brightness, not by the stars' actual colors.

Above the Earth's South Pole, we find a corresponding point on the celestial sphere called the *south celestial pole*. The motions of the stars make it appear that the Earth is sitting still at the center of the celestial sphere as it rotates around us. To picture the motion of the celestial sphere, you might think of it as spinning on rods that extend straight out from the Earth's North and South Poles. These rods would connect to the celestial sphere at the north and south celestial poles.

Constellations

It is natural, when we look at the sky, to look for order—for a pattern. This desire for order is basic to science. Indeed, we can see (or imagine) patterns in the stars. The ancients saw similar patterns and identified them by associating them with beings in their particular mythology. **FIGURE 1-8a** is a photograph of the *constellation* Orion, and Figure 1-8b shows a drawing of the hunter Orion in Greek mythology. He is fighting off Taurus, the bull at the upper right. From the Northern Hemisphere, if you look at the evening sky in December, January, February, or March, you will see the stars of Orion. You may find it easy to imagine the three closely spaced stars as the belt of the hunter. And if you have a good dark sky, you can see the stars that form his sword's sheath hanging from the belt as well as the stars forming his upraised arm.

The mythological creatures of most other constellations are much more difficult to imagine. Ursa Major—Latin for Great Bear—is a prominent constellation of the northern sky (**FIGURE 1-9**). This group of stars will likely not remind you of a bear, but you might recognize the pattern of stars in the bear's rear and tail: the Big Dipper. The group of stars that form Ursa Major was identified as a bear by ancient civilizations

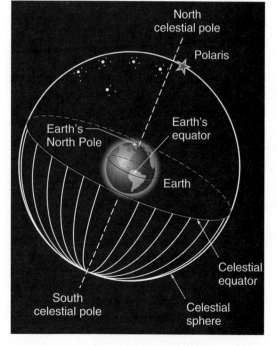

FIGURE 1-7 Because of their daily motion, objects in the sky appear to be on a sphere surrounding the Earth. (The celestial sphere is an imaginary sphere whose size is really much larger compared with Earth than it appears in this diagram.)

The word *constellation* comes from Latin, meaning "stars together."

constellation An area of the sky containing a pattern of stars named for a particular object, animal, or person.

Trails of stars that are on the celestial equator are straight lines. The rise and set points of such stars mark true east and west, and the angle that the trail of such a star makes with the horizon reveals the geographic latitude from which the picture was taken. A star that is almost exactly on the celestial equator is Mintaka (delta Orionis), the rightmost of the three stars in Orion's belt, as shown in Figure 1-8. (See Figure 1-5.)

(a)

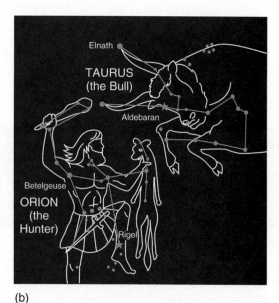

(b)

FIGURE 1-8 (a) From the Northern Hemisphere, the stars of the constellation Orion are visible high in the winter sky. (b) Ancient Greeks pictured Orion as a hunter warding off Taurus the Bull.

FIGURE 1-9 This hand-colored engraving of Ursa Major by Johann Bayer appeared in *Uranometria* in 1603. This was the first attempt at a celestial atlas and began the practice of naming stars after the constellation in which they appear.

Do the shapes of constellations change through time?

in North America, Europe, Asia, and Egypt. Historian Owen Gingerich has suggested that the labeling of these stars as a bear may have originated in Asia or Europe as far back as the Ice Age and then gradually spread to other cultures. The Greeks associated it with a bear before the time of Homer, and the constellation is mentioned in the *Odyssey*. According to the Greek story of the origin of the constellation, the bear once had been a nymph who attracted the attention of Zeus, the father of the other gods. This caused Hera (the wife of Zeus) to be jealous and to change the nymph into a bear. Finally, to protect the bear from hunters, Zeus grabbed it by the tail and flung it into the sky. This is why Ursa Major has a longer tail than earthly bears. One legend in Native American culture held that hunters had chased the big bear onto a mountain from which it leaped into the sky. The bowl of our Big Dipper is now the bear, and the handle is made up of the hunters who followed.

We know that as early as 2000 BC the Sumerians had defined several constellations, including a bull and a lion. Today we realize that the constellations have no real identity. They are accidental patterns of stars, much the same as patterns you might have seen in the clouds when you were a young dreamer watching them pass overhead. The stars don't change their patterns as quickly as the clouds, however; so perhaps it was natural for ancient peoples to attribute real meaning to them. Besides, the stars were in the "heavens," and their association with the gods seemed natural.

Why do we say that the patterns are accidental? First, the various stars are located at different distances from Earth. This means that if the Earth were in a greatly different position, we would see different patterns. For example, the stars of Orion are not all close to one another. Consider the two stars Rigel and Betelgeuse (Figure 1-8b). Rigel is nearly two times as far from Earth as is Betelgeuse. In addition, stars gradually move relative to one another along different directions and at different speeds. Given enough time, the shape of any constellation will change, but the distances from Earth of the stars in a constellation are so large that thousands of years must pass for a change in shape to be easily recognized. FIGURE 1-10 shows how the Big Dipper is changing.

Despite their artificial nature, constellations are used by astronomers today to identify parts of the sky. For example, Halley's Comet was in the constellation Aquarius on Christmas Day in 1985. The ancient Greeks had no constellations in areas of the sky that did not have bright stars nor in areas they could not see from their location

50,000 years ago

Today

50,000 years from now

FIGURE 1-10 The center drawing shows the Big Dipper as it is today; the arrows indicate the direction of motion of its stars as seen on the sky. From these motions, we can conclude that it once had the shape shown in the left drawing and will some day have the shape shown in the right one.

in the Northern Hemisphere; as a result, others have had to be added to their list. In addition, the constellations of ancient cultures had poorly defined boundaries, and thus, modern astronomers have had to establish definite ones. By international agreement of astronomers, the entire celestial sphere has been divided into 88 regions ("constellations") with specific boundaries. About half of these regions correspond to constel-

FIGURE 1-11 The constellation Cygnus was seen as a swan, but we often call it the Northern Cross, as outlined here. The official boundaries of Cygnus are shown as white lines. Draco, Lyra, Vulpecula, and Lacerta are neighboring constellations. (From the Northern Hemisphere, you can find Cygnus in the evening sky in late summer and early fall.)

lations identified by the ancient Greeks, and the names we know them by are Latin translations of the original names. FIGURE 1-11 shows the constellation Cygnus and its boundaries.

Measuring the Positions of Celestial Objects

When people speak of objects in the sky, they sometimes talk about how far apart they are. What they are probably referring to is their *angular separation*, or the angle between the objects as seen from here on Earth. FIGURE 1-12 illustrates this angle. We say, for example, that the angular separation of the two stars at the ends of the arms of the Northern Cross (Figure 1-11) is about 16 degrees. As FIGURE 1-13 indicates, this says nothing about the actual distance between the two stars.

It is often necessary in astronomy to discuss angles much smaller than one degree. For this purpose, each degree is divided into 60 *minutes of arc* (or 60 *arcminutes*, or 60′), and each minute is divided into 60 *seconds of arc* (or 60 *arcseconds*, or 60″). Although these units are very similar in definition to units of time, they are not units of time, but units of angle. As an example of the use of these smaller units, a good human eye can detect that two stars that appear close together are indeed two stars if they are separated by about 1 arcminute or more. In Chapter 5 we explain how the use of a telescope allows us to detect such double stars if they are separated by as little as one arcsecond—3600 times smaller than one degree.

There is an easy way to estimate angles in the sky. Make a fist and hold it at arm's length. The angle you see between the opposite sides of your fist is about 10 degrees (FIGURE 1-14a). For estimating smaller angles, the angle made by the end of your little finger held at arm's length is about one degree (Figure 1-14b). You can use these rules to estimate the angular separations of stars.

angular separation The angle between lines originating from the eye of the observer toward two objects.

minute of arc One sixtieth of a degree of arc.

second of arc One sixtieth of a minute of arc.

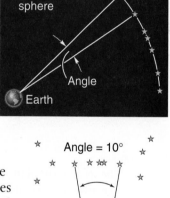

FIGURE 1-12 The two stars, when viewed from Earth, have an angular separation as shown.

Is an arcminute or an arcsecond a unit for measuring time?

(a)   (b)

FIGURE 1-13 The angular separation of stars says nothing about their distances apart. All of the stars that lie along line *X* have the same angular separation from the stars that lie along line *Y*.

FIGURE 1-14 (a) Your fist held at arm's length yields an angle of about 10°. (b) Your little finger held at arm's length cuts off an angle of about 1°. Both the Sun and the Moon have a diameter of about 0.5°.

EXAMPLE

Mizar and Alcor are two stars in the Big Dipper that can be distinguished by the naked eye (FIGURE 1-15). They are separated by 12 arcminutes. Mizar, the brighter of the two, reveals itself in a telescope to be two stars, separated by 14 arcseconds. Express each of these angles in degrees.

FIGURE 1-15 The Big Dipper is part of the constellation Ursa Major. (Refer to Figure 1-9 to see the full drawing of Ursa Major, the Big Bear.)

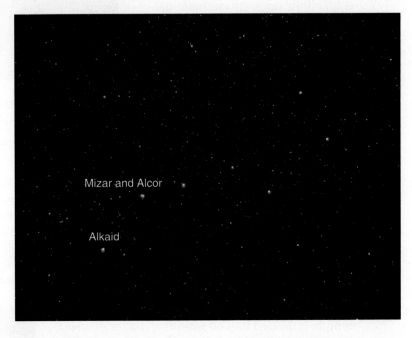

SOLUTION   Because 60 arcminutes equals one degree, we can create the conversion factors

$$\frac{1°}{60'} = 1 \qquad \text{and} \qquad \frac{60'}{1°} = 1.$$

We choose the form of the conversion factor that causes the given unit to cancel, giving us the unit we want. In this case, multiply the 12 arcminutes by the first ratio, thus converting its value to degrees:

$$12' \times \frac{1°}{60'} = 0.20°.$$

The second part of the problem is done in like manner, but another conversion factor is needed to convert arcseconds to arcminutes:

$$14'' \times \frac{1'}{60''} \times \frac{1°}{60'} = 0.0039°.$$

TRY ONE YOURSELF
The top star in the head of Orion (Figure 1-8b) is a double star with a separation of 4.5 arcseconds. Express this angle in degrees.

The answers to each Try One Yourself is in Appendix H.

Celestial Coordinates

To describe the location of an object on Earth, we use the coordinate system of longitude and latitude whose center is the center of the Earth. The use of these two numbers uniquely defines the position of the object on Earth for anyone. Similarly, astronomers specify locations of objects in the sky by using a coordinate system

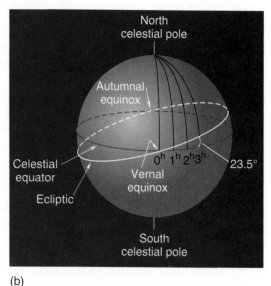

(a)

(b)

FIGURE 1-16 (a) Declination measures the angle of a star north or south of the celestial equator. Angles north are positive, and angles south are negative. (b) Right ascension measures the angle around the celestial equator eastward from the vernal equinox; as we see in the next section, this point is where the Sun crosses the equator moving northward. Angles are expressed in hours and parts of an hour, with 24 hours encompassing the entire circle. The ecliptic is the apparent path of the Sun on the celestial sphere; the angle between the planes of the ecliptic and the celestial equator is about 23.5 degrees.

inscribed on the celestial sphere, the imaginary sphere centered on the Earth. The equatorial coordinate system describes the location of objects by the use of two coordinates, *declination* and *right ascension*.

The declination of an object on the celestial sphere is its angle north or south of the *celestial equator* (**FIGURE 1-16a** and Figure 1-7). Angles north of the equator are designated positive, and those south are negative. Thus, the scale ranges from +90 degrees at the North Pole to −90 degrees at the South Pole. For example, Sirius (the second brightest star in our sky after the Sun) has a declination of −16°43′.

The right ascension of an object states its angle around the celestial sphere, measuring eastward from the vernal equinox; as we see in the next section, this is the location on the celestial equator where the Sun crosses it moving north. Instead of expressing the angle in degrees, however, it is stated in hours, minutes, and seconds (Figure 1-16b). These units are similar to units of time, with 24 hours around the entire circle. Sirius has a right ascension of 6h 45m 9s, or—as it is usually written—$6^h45^m.15$, as 9 seconds is 0.15 minutes.

declination A star's angle north or south of the celestial equator.

right ascension A star's angle around the celestial equator measuring eastward from the vernal equinox.

celestial equator A line on the celestial sphere directly above the Earth's equator.

1-3 The Sun's Motion Across the Sky

Like the stars, the Sun and Moon also seem to move around the Earth as the hours pass, rising in the east and setting in the west. Watching the Sun's motion over a few days might lead us to conclude that it is moving at the same rate as the stars, but if we carefully observe the stars in the sky immediately after sunset, we will see that they change as the weeks and months go by. We can show this by mapping the stars that surround the Earth, and locating the position of the Sun on this map by observing the stars that appear just after the Sun sets and again just before the Sun rises. The Sun is between those two groups of stars. If we do this again 2 weeks later, we would find that the Sun has moved and is now farther toward the east on our map. Thus, it appears that the Sun moves around the Earth, but not as fast as the sphere of stars. Instead, it seems to move constantly eastward among the stars.

You may want to see Figure 2-14, which shows how today's model explains the apparent motion of the Sun among the stars.

How long does the Sun take to get all the way around the sphere of stars? You could determine the approximate time by drawing the pattern of stars you see in the western sky after sunset tonight and then waiting until you see that same pattern again. If you did this over a number of cycles, perhaps you could determine that the time is about 365 days. Being an alert observer, you would undoubtedly notice that this cycle coincides with the cycle of the seasons on Earth. Finally, you—or perhaps your descendants to whom you hand down your data—would decide that the time for the Sun's cycle through the stars exactly fits the cycle of the seasons and that 365 days is the length of the year. (The time the Sun takes to return to the same place among the stars is actually not a whole number of days. It is about 365.25 days. Every 4 years we add 1 day to our year to make up for this difference. This is our leap year.)

See the Advancing the Model box on page 16 for more details on leap years.

Early in history, people noticed that certain star patterns appear in the sky at the same time every year. Even before the development of the calendar, the arrival of these patterns was used as an indication of a coming change of seasons. For example, the arrival of the constellation Leo in the evening sky meant that spring was coming, and this alerted people that even though the weather might not yet indicate it, warm days were on the way.

The Ecliptic

For an observer on Earth, as the Sun moves among the stars, it traces the same path year after year.

FIGURE 1-17a is a map of the stars in a band above the Earth's equator extending 30 degrees on either side of the equator. Figure 1-17b shows the relationship of these stars to the Earth. In fact, the dashed line drawn straight across the map is directly above the Earth's equator and is the celestial equator. The other line on the map corresponds to the Sun's apparent path among the stars and shows that it is sometimes north of the celestial equator and sometimes south. The apparent path that the Sun takes among the stars is called the ***ecliptic***, and it is not the same as the celestial equator. (The name comes from the fact that an eclipse can occur only when the Moon is on or very near this line. This is discussed further in Section 1-5.)

ecliptic The apparent path of the Sun on the celestial sphere.

The constellations through which the Sun passes as it moves along the ecliptic are called constellations of the ***zodiac***.

FIGURE 1-18 shows the 12 major constellations of the zodiac. (Actually, the Sun spends almost 3 weeks in a 13th constellation, Ophiuchus, which is a much longer time than it spends in Scorpius.)

zodiac The band that lies 9° on either side of the ecliptic on the celestial sphere.

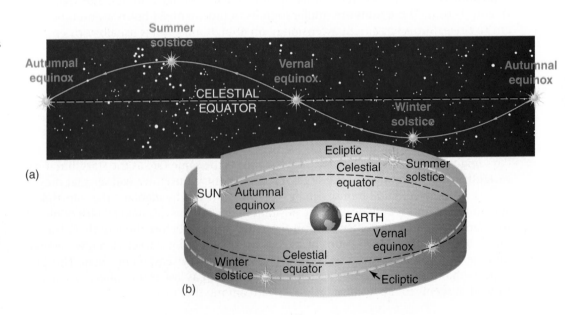

FIGURE 1-17 (a) A map of the stars within 30 degrees of the equator. Picture this map wrapped around the Earth as shown in (b). Compare (b) with Figure 1-16b.

FIGURE 1-18 The constellations of the zodiac lie along the ecliptic. In addition to the 12 zodiacal constellations that most people are familiar with, there is a 13th—Ophiuchus—that the Sun passes through. You may want to look at Figures 2-14 and 2-15 for an explanation of the Sun's apparent motion among the stars.

The months indicated on the ecliptic show the Sun's locations at various times. On March 21, the Sun is in the constellation Pisces and is crossing the equator on its way north. The changing position of the Sun on the celestial sphere is related to the changing of the seasons, as we now explain.

The Sun and the Seasons

There are three easily observed differences between the behavior of the Sun in winter and summer:

Why do we have seasons?

- For an observer in the Northern Hemisphere, the Sun rises and sets farther north in the summer than in the winter. FIGURE 1-19 shows the Sun's rising and setting points at various times of the year as well as the Sun's path across the sky in each case. Although we may say that the Sun rises in the east, it actually rises exactly east only when it is on the celestial equator—at a particular time in March and again in September.

- The Sun is in the sky longer each day in summer than in winter. Figure 1-19 shows why this happens, for the Sun's path above the horizon is much longer in June than in December. This effect is one reason for the seasons. Because the summer Sun is in the sky longer, we collect more solar energy during the daytime, and less time is available at night for our surroundings to lose the energy they have gained.

- The third difference in the Sun's observed behavior results in two more reasons for our seasonal differences. As Figure 1-19 illustrates, the Sun reaches a point higher in the sky in summer than in winter, and FIGURE 1-20 emphasizes this by showing the Sun's path and its location at midday in late June and in late December. When the Sun is higher in the sky, its light hits the surface at an angle that gets closer to 90 degrees. Consider shining a flashlight directly down onto

(a) December

(b) March and September

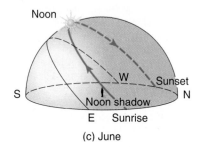

(c) June

FIGURE 1-19 The Sun's apparent path across the sky of the Northern Hemisphere in (a) December, (b) March or September, and (c) June. The Sun rises and sets at different places on each date, and its noontime altitude differs in each case.

(a) June   (b) December

FIGURE 1-20 The Sun's apparent path across the sky in the Northern Hemisphere in (a) summer and (b) winter. In each case we have drawn a line from south to north straight over the person's head (the **meridian**). The Sun moves across the sky along the yellow line and reaches a much higher position in the sky in summer than it does in winter.

a surface in one case and shining it at an angle to the surface in another (**FIGURE 1-21**). In the second case, the same amount of light is spread over more surface area, and thus, each portion of the surface receives less light. The same is true for sunlight; thus, a given area, in a given amount of time, receives more energy from the Sun in June than in December. In addition, because the Sun is never high in the sky in winter, its light must pass through more atmosphere in winter than in summer. As a result, each portion of the lit surface receives less direct light, as more of it is scattered and absorbed in the atmosphere. (See Figure 8-2 for this effect.)

If you live in the Southern Hemisphere, you know that this explanation is backward for your part of the Earth. In the Southern Hemisphere, the Sun gets higher in the sky in December than in June, and the seasons are reversed from those in the Northern Hemisphere. While people are enjoying summer in Canada, Australians are feeling the chill of winter.

It is logical for someone to believe that the difference in seasons is directly related to the change in distance of the Earth from the Sun. That is, you may believe that when we are closer to the Sun we have summer, and when we are farther from the Sun we have winter. After all, you do feel warmer when getting closer to a fireplace; however, if this were the only reason for the seasons, then how could we have two different seasons, for the two hemispheres, at the same time? In reality, the distance of the Earth from the Sun does not vary too much during a year, at least as a percentage of its average distance. (Also, the Earth is closer to the Sun in January and farther from the Sun in July.)

By analogy, suppose you were standing at a distance of 1 meter from a fireplace and then walked toward or further from it by less than 2 centimeters. It obviously would not make too much of a difference in the amount of energy you received from the fireplace. Thus, even though in principle the amount

You may want to see Figure 2-15, which shows that according to today's model, the tilting of the Earth's axis with respect to its orbital plane explains the seasons.

Is the change of our distance from the Sun an important factor that causes seasons?

FIGURE 1-21 (a) The light from the flashlight shines perpendicularly onto the surface, whereas in (b) it strikes the surface at an oblique angle. The fact that the same amount of light illuminates more surface in (b) means that each little part of the surface is less illuminated in that case. Relate this to the noontime Sun's position in the sky in summer and winter.

(a)   (b)

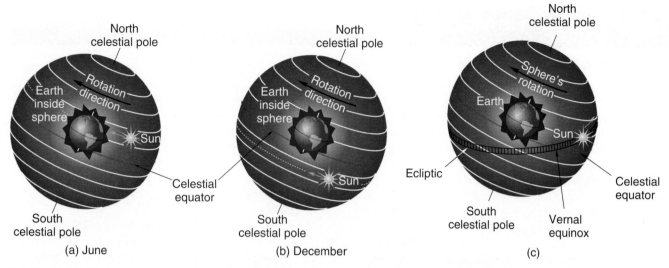

FIGURE 1-22 The height the Sun reaches in the sky is explained by its position on the celestial sphere. The dashed lines correspond to the Sun's apparent path in the sky on June 21 (a) and December 21 (b). (c) The Sun acts as if it follows a path along the ecliptic on the celestial sphere. The sphere rotates toward the west as the Sun gradually moves along it toward the east.

of energy we receive from the Sun does depend on how far we are from it, in the case of our planet, distance is not an important factor and it does not really influence the seasons. The important factor in this case is the orientation of the Earth with respect to the Sun, as shown in the previously mentioned observations.

To see how the path of the Sun along the ecliptic relates to the seasons, refer to the star map of Figure 1-18. The Sun is at its northernmost position on about June 21. If you picture the celestial sphere circling the Earth in late June, you can see that it will carry the Sun to a much higher position in the sky of North America. The Sun reaches its southernmost position on about December 21, and on that date, it reaches the least **altitude** in the sky of the Northern Hemisphere (**FIGURE 1-22**).

The two dates discussed in the last paragraph are unique. During the spring the Sun gets higher in the midday sky. Then about June 21—at the **summer solstice**—it stops climbing, and after that it starts getting lower again. The reverse happens about December 21—at the **winter solstice**. (The word *solstice* is a conjunction of the Latin words "sol" meaning "Sun" and "sistere" meaning "to stand still.") These dates were given this name because at the solstice the Sun *seems to stop* and reverses its direction.

The star map reveals two more unique events each year: Around March 21 the Sun crosses the celestial equator moving north, and about September 22 it crosses the equator moving south. On these dates every location on Earth experiences equal periods of day and night. The events are called the **vernal equinox** and the **autumnal equinox**, respectively. (*Equinox* means "equal night.")

We estimate each of the four previously mentioned dates rather than state them exactly because they may vary a day or so from year to year. The fact that there are not exactly 365 days per year causes our calendars to get out of synchronization with astronomical events until a leap year allows us to catch up. In addition, your "today" may be the previous day or the next day somewhere else on the Earth.

A Scientific Model

The idea of the stars residing on a giant celestial sphere is a **scientific model** that explains the observation of the daily motion of the stars. Likewise, the changing position of the Sun in the sky explains the changing of the seasons.

A scientific model is not necessarily a physical model, in the sense of a model airplane; it is basically a mental picture that attempts to use analogy to explain a set of

altitude The height of a celestial object measured as an angle above the horizon.

summer and winter solstices The points on the celestial sphere where the Sun reaches its northernmost and southernmost positions, respectively.

vernal and autumnal equinoxes The points on the celestial sphere where the Sun crosses the celestial equator while moving north and south, respectively.

scientific model An idea, a logical framework, that accounts for a set of observations and/or allows us to create explanations of how we think a part of nature works.

ADVANCING THE MODEL

Leap Year and the Calendar

People in early times began keeping records of celestial events because they realized that certain cycles observed in the sky corresponded to familiar events in their surroundings, such as the arrival of migratory birds and the ripening of fruits. The agricultural revolution that began around 10,000 BC led to the need to better understand the celestial cycles and to predict the seasonal changes. Observational evidence collected through the years showed that there is a correlation between the seasons and the apparent motion of the Sun among the stars. As a result, the first calendars were created by the end of this period. The Indians of the American Southwest followed a lunar calendar (of 29.5 days average per lunar cycle), resulting in a 29.5 × 12 = 354-day year, which obviously needed an annual adjustment. A solar calendar (of 360 days) was used in Mesopotamia and Egypt. The 360-day year follows a Babylonian practice of using the sexagesimal (60-based) system, instead of our current decimal (10-based) system. (Our division of the circle into 360 degrees is probably a result of this Babylonian approximation for the year and the fact that 360 is divisible by the numbers 2, 3, 4, 5, and 6.)

Observations of solstices and equinoxes offered a way for early civilizations to reset the calendar every year. Archaeological evidence suggests that numerous astronomical traditions of keeping a "calendar" sprang up independently around the world—for example, at Stonehenge, England around 2800–2200 BC, and by the Plains Indians of Wyoming around 1500–1760 AD. Such evidence includes special alignments or designs of temples that mark solstices or other events, legends, and historical records of observation ceremonies carried out at the sites. Buildings designed with astronomical orientations were also built by the Egyptians (the great pyramids around 3000 BC), the Aztecs, Mayans, and Incas.

Our present calendar comes primarily from the Roman calendar. This calendar started its year in March; the Latin words for the numbers 7 through 10 are "septem," "octo," "novem," and "decem." By the time of Christ, January and February had been added, giving us the 12 months we have now. The months of the calendar were based on the Moon's period of revolution around the Earth and alternated in length between 29 and 30 days to match the average of 29½ days between full Moons. Twelve of these lunar months totaled only 354 days, which was defined as the length of the standard year. To make up for the fact that this calendar quickly got out of synchronization with the seasons, an entire month was inserted about every 3 years—a sort of "leap month."

No single authority controlled the calendar, and by the time of Julius Caesar (100–44 BC), the date assigned to a specific day differed widely between different communities. In some countries, nearby communities did not even agree on what year it was. Caesar reformed the calendar in 46 BC, making the months alternate between 31 and 30 days, except for February, which had 29. Thus, the *Julian calendar* had 365 days, and (almost) like ours, it added 1 day at the end of February every 4 years to make it correspond more closely to the time the Sun takes to return to the vernal equinox.* This latter time determines the seasons and is called the *tropical year*. Thus, the Julian year had an average of 365.25 days.

The tropical year is 365.242190 days long. This means that the seasons on Earth repeat after that period of time, and the difference between the tropical year and the average 365.25 days of the Julian calendar caused the calendar to gradually get out of synchronization with the seasons. The difference between the Julian and tropical years is about 0.0078 days per year, which corresponds to about 3 days for every 400 years. By the year 1582, the vernal equinox occurred on March 11 rather than March 25, as it had when Julius Caesar instituted the calendar. It was time for more reform. Pope Gregory XIII declared that 10 days would be dropped from the month of October so that October 15 followed October 4 that year. That restored the vernal equinox to March 21, which corresponded to what the Catholic church wanted for establishing the date of Easter each year. To keep the calendar from having to be adjusted this way again, Pope Gregory instituted a new leap year rule: every year whose number was divisible by four would be a leap year—as in the Julian calendar—unless that year was a century year not divisible by 400 (such as 1800 or 1900). Thus, 1700, 1800, and 1900 were not leap years, but the year 2000 was a leap year. This rule takes care of the 3 days per 400 years discrepancy mentioned previously here. Thus, the Gregorian year has an average of 365.2425 days.

Roman Catholic countries accepted the *Gregorian calendar*, but most other countries chose to stick with the old calendar. England changed in 1752, at which time it was necessary to omit 11 days. Russia did not adopt the Gregorian calendar until 1918.

The Gregorian calendar reform, however, is also an approximation, albeit a better one than the Julian calendar reform. Because the difference between the Gregorian and tropical years is about 0.0003 days per year, there is a difference of about 1 day for every 3300 years. As a result, a proposal has been made to include an exception to the Gregorian calendar: the years 4000, 8000, 12,000, and so on will not be leap years, as they would have been according to the original Gregorian calendar. Such a calendar will have an average of 365.24225 days and will be accurate enough that it will not have to be revised for about 20,000 years.

* The vernal equinox, defined in this chapter, determines the moment when spring begins.

observations in nature. We thus are able to say that the stars appear as if they are on a sphere rotating around the Earth. Later in the book, we encounter some scientific models that cannot be represented well by a physical construction.

We can combine our explanation for the seasons with our model of the celestial sphere. Imagine a path *along the ecliptic* (Figure 1-22c). As the celestial sphere rotates around the Earth, the Sun moves along this path following the sphere's general motion on a daily basis, as shown in Figures 1-22a and b. Gradually, however the Sun creeps back eastward along the track. As the months pass, the Sun changes its position among the stars. It moves along the path with such speed that in about 365 days it is back to where it started.

The Sun in our model moves from north to south of the equator and back again. This corresponds to the observed motion of the real Sun. We are not saying that there is actually a real track on which the Sun moves, but our model provides this picture that helps us describe the motion of the Sun. That is one of the functions of a scientific model: to allow us to make sense of a set of observations. Our model does not actually explain the Sun's motion in the sense of telling us why it occurs, but it provides a mechanism that allows us to say, "OK, that makes sense now."

The model we have constructed is a *geocentric model*—an Earth-centered model. In Chapter 2 we examine reasons why this model has been replaced (but not entirely abandoned).

geocentric model A model of the universe with the Earth at its center.

1-4 The Moon's Phases

Like the stars and the Sun, the Moon also *seems* to orbit the Earth, but it does so in such a way that its same face points toward Earth at all times. At first thought, you might be tempted to say that the Moon does not *rotate*, but this is not so.

Consider FIGURE 1-23. The Moon is shown with a spot on its surface. In (a), you see that if the Moon did not rotate, this spot would always face the same way in space. In (b), that spot continues to face the Earth as the Moon goes around its orbit, but this means that the Moon must rotate once for every *revolution* around the Earth.

The fact that the rotation period and revolution period of the Moon are exactly equal seems remarkable and cannot be attributed to mere coincidence. In fact, this is another phenomenon that can be explained by the law of universal gravitation, as will be described in Chapter 3.

The photographs in FIGURE 1-24 show the *phases* of the Moon at various times during a period of about a month. The cause for the Moon's phases has been known since antiquity; to explain them we need only consider three objects: the Earth, the Sun, and the Moon.

The Moon circles the Earth, completing one orbit in slightly less than a month. This causes its position in the sky, relative to the Sun, to change with time. Figure 1-24a shows various positions of the Moon in its orbit around the Earth. The Sun is out of the picture, far to the left. The drawings of the Earth and the Moon are dark on the side away from the Sun because sunlight does not reach that side of them. Consider the Moon in position *A*. Most of the side that faces the Earth is dark, and only a small portion of that side is lit by the Sun. Figure 1-24b(A) shows how the Moon appears from Earth when it is in position *A*. We call such a Moon a *waxing crescent* Moon.

When the Moon is at position *B* on its monthly

rotation The spinning of an object about an axis that passes through it.

revolution The orbiting of one object around another.

phases (of the Moon) The changing appearance of the Moon during its revolution around the Earth, caused by the relative positions of the Earth, Moon, and Sun.

FIGURE 1-23 The Moon rotates as it revolves. If it did not rotate, a dot on its surface would always point in the same direction in space, as in (a). Instead, the Moon always keeps the same face pointed toward Earth (b). (The Moon-Earth system is not drawn to scale.)

FIGURE 1-24 The Moon in various phases. (a) Seen from above the Earth's North Pole, no light reaches the half of the Moon shown as black. The half of the Moon's surface facing the Sun is always lit; the portion shown in white can be seen by an observer on Earth, whereas the lined portion cannot be seen. The elongation of the Moon, stated as an angle either east or west of the Sun, is indicated for the waxing gibbous phase and for the waning crescent phase. We are viewing the system from above the north, and thus, east is counterclockwise. (The Moon–Earth system is not drawn to scale.) (b) These photos of the Moon in phases correspond to the positions shown in (a). The Earth-Moon distance is not the same for each photo.

Terms related to the phases of the Moon are defined based on their elongation as shown in **TABLE 1-1**.

elongation The angle of the Moon (or a planet) from the Sun in the sky. The angle of elongation is illustrated in Figure 1-24a.

(a)

(b)

TABLE 1-1

Terms Relating to Moon Phases

Phase	Elongation (in degrees)
Waxing	0–180° east
Waning	0–180° west
Crescent	0–90° east or west
Gibbous	90°–180° east or west
New	0
First quarter	90° east
Full	180°
Third quarter	90° west

trip around the Earth, we call it a ***first-quarter*** Moon, for if we start the cycle when the Moon is at position *H*, it is now one quarter of the way around.

From Earth, a ***waxing gibbous*** Moon will appear as in the photograph of Figure 1-24b(C). The word "waxing" is derived from an old German term that means "growing." Between points *H* and *D*, the Moon is waxing; the visible portion is growing nightly from a thin crescent near *H* toward the ***full Moon*** (when the Moon is at position *D*). When we see the Moon in a gibbous phase, most of its sunlit side is facing the Earth.

Observe the photograph of the Moon when it is in position *E*. It is again in a gibbous phase, but here the gibbous phase is called ***waning gibbous*** because from night to night the lit portion that we observe is decreasing (waning) in size.

At position *F* the Moon is again in a quarter phase, the ***third quarter***, or ***last quarter***. Then around position *G* we have the ***waning crescent*** phase, and, finally, the Moon is back to where we start the cycle, at position *H*. Because we (arbitrarily) begin the cycle here, we call this a ***new Moon***. In this position, the Moon is not visible in our sky because no sunlight strikes the side facing Earth. Only at this phase can an eclipse of the Sun occur. Because it takes about a month for the Moon to revolve around the Earth, you may expect to see a solar eclipse approximately once a month. This does not occur, as you may know from personal experience. In the next section we see why such an eclipse does not occur every time there is a new Moon; before you read it, try to think of a reason why this may be so. (Also, check the activities at the end of this chapter to get a better understanding of the Moon's phases and of eclipses.)

Because the Earth moves in its orbit while the Moon revolves around it, we must distinguish between two revolution periods of the Moon. Refer to **FIGURE 1-25**. At position *A*, the Moon is full, and an imaginary line connecting the Earth and the Moon is pointing to the right of the figure toward the distant stars. About 27.3 days later, the Earth reaches point *B*, whereas the Moon, as it revolves around the Earth, is at such a position that an imaginary line connecting the Earth and the Moon is pointing again to the right of the figure toward the distant stars. The time interval between these

quarter (phase) The phase of a celestial object when half of its sunlit hemisphere is visible.

gibbous (phase) The phase of a celestial object when between half and all of its sunlit hemisphere is visible.

full (phase) The phase of a celestial object when the entire sunlit hemisphere is visible.

crescent (phase) The phase of a celestial object when less than half of its sunlit hemisphere is visible.

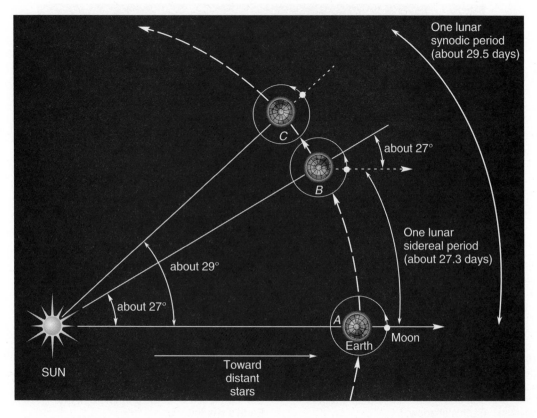

FIGURE 1-25 This drawing shows the difference between the Moon's sidereal period and its synodic period. When the Earth is at point *A*, the Moon is full. At point *B*, the Moon has completed one sidereal period, but about 2 more days are required for it to reach full phase again (which occurs when the Earth is at point *C*), at which time one synodic period will have been completed.

sidereal period The amount of time required for one revolution (or rotation) of a celestial object with respect to the distant stars.

synodic period The time interval between successive similar alignments of a celestial object with respect to the Sun.

lunar month The Moon's synodic period, or the time between successive similar phases.

◆ The lunar month is 29^d 12^h 44^m 2^s.9.

lunar eclipse An eclipse in which the Moon passes into the shadow of the Earth.

umbra The portion of a shadow that receives no direct light from the light source.

two successive similar alignments between the Earth, Moon, and distant stars is the **sidereal period** of the Moon (about 27.3 days).

Notice, however, that the Moon is not full at this time. A certain amount of time must pass for the Earth and Moon to reach an alignment with the Sun (at position *C*) so that the Moon is again full. The time interval between two successive similar alignments between the Earth, Moon, and Sun is the **synodic period** of the Moon (about 29.5 days, a **lunar month**).

A calculation at the end of the chapter shows you how to find the difference of about 2 days between the sidereal and synodic periods. (Keep in mind that the Earth covers 360° around the Sun in about 365 days, whereas the Moon covers 360° around the Earth in about a month. That is, the Earth moves about 1° per day and the Moon moves about 12° per day on the sky.)

1-5 Lunar Eclipses

During its orbit of the Earth, the Moon sometimes enters the Earth's shadow; when this occurs, sunlight is blocked from reaching the Moon. This phenomenon is known as a **lunar eclipse** (FIGURE 1-26). You might wonder why this doesn't happen at the time of every full Moon. There are several reasons. First, as we have seen, the Moon and Earth are very small compared with their distance apart: the Moon is 30 Earth diameters away. Thus, it is unlikely that they will align so accurately that one eclipses the other. Think of trying to align a grapefruit, a Ping-Pong ball 12 feet away, and a distant object.

Second, the Earth's full shadow—called the **umbra**—tapers down to a point in a direction opposite to the Sun. Along this direction, the Earth's umbra is smaller than the Earth. This is because the source of light—the Sun—is so much larger than the Earth. At the distance of the Moon (at point *A*, for example), the width of the umbra is only three fourths of the diameter of the Earth. The Moon thus is less likely to pass

FIGURE 1-26 (a) Point *A* is in the umbra of the Earth's shadow. Point *B* is in the penumbra, where light from part of the Sun hits it. Distances are not to scale in the drawing. (b) View from point *A*. This observer is looking at the Earth and Sun from point *A*, in the umbra of the Earth's shadow. (c) View from point *B*. This observer is looking at the Earth and Sun from point *B*, in the penumbra of the Earth's shadow.

This observer is looking at the Earth and Sun from point *A*, in the umbra of the Earth's shadow.

This observer is looking at the Earth and Sun from point *B*, in the penumbra of the Earth's shadow.

through the shadow than if the shadow were the size of the Earth. If the Moon is at point *B* of Figure 1-26, on the other hand, it is only in partial shadow, for light from the left part of the Sun (as seen from the Moon) is hitting it. When the Moon is here, in the **penumbra**, it will not receive the full light from the Sun and will appear dim to Moon watchers on Earth. The penumbral shadow increases in size at greater distances from Earth, but it is not equally dark across its width. Right next to the umbra, the shadow is very dark, but it gets brighter and brighter out toward its edge. When the Moon passes through the outer penumbra, we don't even notice the darkening.

The third and most important factor in explaining why a lunar eclipse does not occur at each full Moon is that the Moon's plane of revolution is tilted relative to the Earth's plane of revolution around the Sun. Consider FIGURE 1-27, which shows both the Earth's and the Moon's orbits. The tilt of the Moon's orbit with respect to the Earth's is actually only 5 degrees, but we have exaggerated it in the drawing. When the Earth is at positions *B* and *D*, its shadow cannot hit the Moon. In fact, only when the Earth is near points *A* and *C* can the Moon pass through its shadow. These points represent the two **eclipse seasons** that occur each year.

Thus, in most cases of a full Moon, the Moon will not be in the Earth's shadow but will be either north or south of it. The plane of the Moon's orbit changes relatively little as the year progresses, and so eclipses can only occur about twice a year.

Types of Lunar Eclipses

At the Moon's average distance, the umbra has a diameter of about 9200 kilometers. Because the diameter of the Moon is less than 3500 kilometers, the Moon can easily be covered by the umbra; however, the Moon might not pass right through it. FIGURE 1-28 shows three possible paths of the Moon through the shadow of the Earth. If the Moon moves along path *A*, it only passes through the penumbra, producing a **penumbral lunar eclipse**. In this case, it darkens slightly as it does so, but such an effect is not obvious from Earth and is only noticeable if the Moon passes into the darkest part of the penumbra, near the umbra.

If the Moon follows path *B*, it slowly darkens as it moves toward the umbra. FIGURE 1-29 is a triple exposure of the Moon during an eclipse. The Moon is moving along a path such as path *B*, and the exposure at the right side of the photo shows the Moon while only part of it is in the Earth's umbral shadow. As the Moon continues to move into the umbra, the shadow slowly moves across its surface until the Moon appears as it does in the center exposure, where we see a **total lunar eclipse**.

Depending on the Moon's distance from Earth, it may take an hour from the time of first contact with the umbra until the eclipse reaches totality. The Moon can stay in the shadow for up to about 1.5 hours. On the left side of Figure 1-29, we see the Moon leaving the Earth's umbra again.

Why don't we have a lunar eclipse every month?

penumbra The portion of a shadow that receives direct light from only part of the light source.

eclipse season A time of the year during which a solar or lunar eclipse is possible.

penumbral lunar eclipse An eclipse of the Moon in which the Moon passes through the Earth's penumbra but not through its umbra.

total lunar eclipse An eclipse of the Moon in which the Moon is completely in the umbra of the Earth's shadow.

Eclipse seasons occur when the Earth is at points *A* and *C* in Figure 1-27. Eclipse seasons are slightly less than 6 months apart because the orientation of the Moon's orbit changes slightly as time passes.

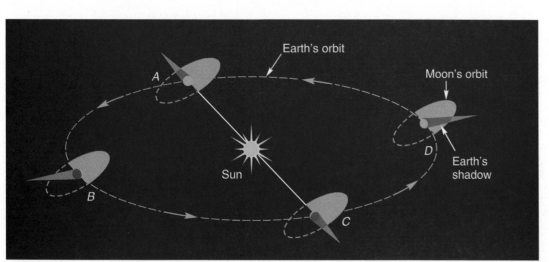

FIGURE 1-27 When the Earth is very near either *A* or *C*, lunar eclipses can occur, but when it is at other points in its orbit, the Moon does not pass through its shadow. If the Earth's orbital plane around the Sun were this page, then the dashed half of the Moon's orbital plane around the Earth would be under this page and the other half would be above this page.

(Figure labels: Earth's orbit, Moon's orbit, *A*, *D*, *B*, *C*, Sun, Earth's shadow)

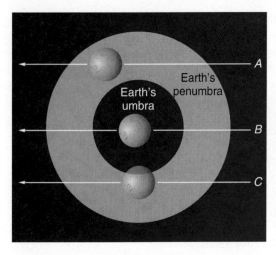

FIGURE 1-28 Three of the possible paths of the Moon through the Earth's shadow. Path *A* produces only a penumbral eclipse. Path *B* produces a total eclipse, and *C* produces a partial eclipse.

FIGURE 1-29 This is a triple-exposure photo of the Moon taken before (left), during (middle), and after (right) the total eclipse of August 28, 2007. This composite image is centered on the same sky background to show how much the Moon moved during the eclipse.

partial lunar eclipse An eclipse of the Moon in which only part of the Moon passes through the umbra of the Earth's shadow.

If the Moon follows path *C* of Figure 1-28, it is never entirely covered by the umbra, and we see only a ***partial lunar eclipse***. The dark shadow creeps across the Moon, covering (in the case shown) only the top part of the Moon.

An eclipse of the Moon, especially a total eclipse, is a beautiful sight. The totally eclipsed Moon is not completely dark, however. Even when the Moon is completely in the umbra, some sunlight strikes the Moon. This light has been refracted (and scattered) by the Earth's atmosphere, as shown in FIGURE 1-30. As the light passes through the atmosphere, however, the blue end of the spectrum is scattered away more than the red is, and thus, the light that makes it to the Moon is more reddish. After reflection from the Moon's surface, this light must again pass through the Earth's atmosphere; thus, the light seen by an observer on the ground is mostly red. For this reason the eclipsed Moon appears a dark red color (as in the middle image in Figure 1-29).

TABLE 1-2 shows the dates of coming lunar eclipses. You cannot be sure that you will be able to see any particular lunar eclipse, however, for two reasons. First, to be able to see it, you must be on the dark side of the Earth when the eclipse occurs. This means that, on the average, only half of the people on Earth have a chance to see a given lunar eclipse. For this reason, the last column of the table indicates where each eclipse will be visible. Second, there is the weather factor. A cloudy night can ruin a long-planned eclipse-viewing party.

FIGURE 1-30 Though the Moon is in total eclipse, some light is refracted toward the Moon by the Earth's atmosphere. As the light passes through the atmosphere, however, the blue end of the spectrum is scattered away more than the red is, so the light that makes it to the Moon is more reddish. After reflection from the Moon's surface, this light must again pass through the Earth's atmosphere and thus the light seen by an observer on the ground is mostly red. (This selective scattering also explains why the Sun looks red at sunsets and sunrises and why the sky is blue.)

TABLE 1-2

Dates of Total/Partial Lunar Eclipses, 2009-2012

Date	Type	Visible from the Following Regions
Dec. 31, 2009	Partial	Europe, Africa, Asia, Australia
June 26, 2010	Partial	East Asia, Australia, Pacific, West Americas
Dec. 21, 2010	Total	East Asia, Australia, Pacific, Americas, Europe
June 15, 2011	Total	S. America, Europe, Africa, Asia, Australia
Dec. 10, 2011	Total	Europe, E. Africa, Asia, Australia, Pacific, N. America
June 4, 2012	Partial	Asia, Australia, Pacific, Americas

1-6 Solar Eclipses

We have seen that a lunar eclipse occurs when the shadow of the Earth falls on the full Moon. An eclipse of the Sun—a *solar eclipse*—occurs when the Moon, in its new phase, passes directly between the Sun and the Earth so that the Moon's shadow falls on the Earth. There is a major difference between these events, however. The Earth's size is such that its umbral shadow reaches back into space nearly a million miles, and at the distance of the Moon, it is easily large enough to cover the entire Moon. The umbral shadow of the Moon, however, reaches only about 377,000 kilometers (234,000 miles). Compare this with the average distance from the Earth to the Moon of about 384,000 kilometers (239,000 miles). If the Moon stayed at this average distance, its dark shadow (its umbra) would never fall on the Earth.

The Moon, however, follows an eccentric orbit, coming as close as 363,300 kilometers (218,000 miles) to Earth. So it does get close enough that its umbra can reach the Earth. When this occurs, we can experience one of the most spectacular of natural phenomena, a *total solar eclipse*. FIGURE 1-31 shows two cases of the Sun, Moon, and Earth being aligned when the Moon is close enough for its umbra to reach the Earth. Even when the Moon is at its closest, the width of its umbral shadow at the Earth's distance is only about 130 kilometers (80 miles). The width of the shadow depends on where it hits the Earth's surface, but it seldom exceeds 400 kilometers (250 miles).

This explains why relatively few people ever experience a total solar eclipse. As the Moon moves along, its shadow swings in an arc across the surface of the Earth (Figure 1-31). This strip may be many thousands of kilometers long, and you have to be within this strip at the exact moment of totality, in clear weather, to see the total eclipse of the Sun. At totality, the sky is dark enough that planets and the brightest stars can be seen in the sky. The appearance of the Sun is shown in FIGURE 1-32. What you see around the dark disk where the Moon blocks out the Sun is the glowing

solar eclipse (or **eclipse of the Sun**) An eclipse in which light from the Sun is blocked by the Moon.

total solar eclipse An eclipse in which light from the normally visible portion of the Sun (the photosphere) is completely blocked by the Moon.

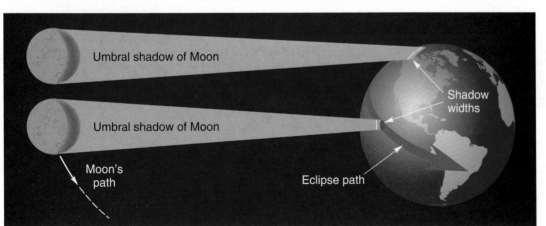

FIGURE 1-31 If the Moon's umbra strikes the Earth at an angle, a wider area on Earth will experience a total eclipse. The Moon's motion causes the path of a total solar eclipse to sweep across the Earth. The lower eclipse shown moves primarily across water and, therefore, would be seen by few people.

Umbral shadow of Moon

Umbral shadow of Moon

Moon's path

Shadow widths

Eclipse path

FIGURE 1-32 During a total solar eclipse, the glowing light of the Sun's outer atmosphere—the corona—is visible. This photo of the June 30, 1992 eclipse was taken from the window of a DC-10 30,000 feet above the ground.

corona The outer atmosphere of the Sun. (We discuss the Sun and its corona in Chapter 11.)

partial solar eclipse An eclipse in which only part of the Sun's disk is covered by the Moon.

TABLE 1-3		
Dates of Total/Annular Solar Eclipses, 2009-2012		
Date	Type of Eclipse	Visible from the Following Regions
July 22, 2009	Total	India, Nepal, China, Central Pacific
January 15, 2010	Annular	Central Africa, India, Myanmar, China
July 11, 2010	Total	South Pacific, Easter Island, Chile, Argentina
May 20, 2012	Annular	Asia, Pacific, N. America
November 13, 2012	Total	Australia, New Zealand, S. Pacific, S. America

outer atmosphere of the Sun, called the **corona**. This is a layer of gas that extends for millions of miles above what normally appears to be the surface of the Sun. The gas glows because of its high temperature, but the glow is so much dimmer than the light we receive from the main body of the Sun that it is observed only during an eclipse. The opportunity to observe the corona is one of the scientific values of an eclipse, although today we are able to block out the Sun by artificial means to observe its outer layers.

A total solar eclipse is truly an awesome experience. If you get a chance to travel to the path of totality of a solar eclipse (**TABLE 1-3**), don't pass it up. It is one of nature's grandest spectacles. The next total solar eclipse to cross the continental United States will occur on August 21, 2017 (and the next after that will be on April 8, 2024).

The Partial Solar Eclipse

FIGURE 1-33 shows not only the Moon's umbra, but also its penumbra. Within the penumbra one sees a **partial solar eclipse**. The penumbra covers a much greater portion

(a)

(b)

(c)

FIGURE 1-33 (a) A person at point *X* sees a total solar eclipse, whereas a person at *Y* sees a partial solar eclipse, with only the southern part of the Sun blocked by the Moon. (Compare to Figure 1-26a for a *lunar* eclipse.) (b) This series of photos shows the progression of a partial solar eclipse as would be seen by a person standing at point *Y*. (c) The umbra and penumbra in the Moon's shadow can clearly be seen in this true-color image of the November 13, 2003 total solar eclipse over Antarctica. The tip of the roughly 500-km long shadow is pointing toward Africa. The Sun was about 15° above the horizon, just rising over Antarctica, when this image was taken from space.

FIGURE 1-34 When the Moon is far away during a solar eclipse, the eclipse will be annular. The person at point *A* sees the annular eclipse, whereas the person at *P* sees a partial eclipse. (Compare to Figure 1-26a for a *lunar* eclipse.)

of the Earth's surface, stretching about 3000 kilometers (2000 miles) from the central path of totality, and thus, most of us have the opportunity to see a few partial solar eclipses during our lifetimes.

In a partial solar eclipse, the dark disk of the Moon moves across the Sun, but its path is not perfectly aligned with the Sun and it does not move across the center of the Sun. The closer you are to the path of totality, the more of the Sun is blocked out by the Moon.

The Annular Eclipse

A total solar eclipse can occur only when the Moon is directly between the Sun and the Earth, and the Moon is close enough to the Earth that its umbral shadow reaches the Earth. When the Moon is at its average distance from the Earth, it is a little too far away to cause a total eclipse on Earth. Therefore, somewhat fewer than half the solar eclipses that occur are total. FIGURE 1-34 illustrates what happens when the Moon is too far from Earth to allow a total eclipse: its disk is not large enough to cover the Sun, even when it is directly centered on the Sun. As a result, an observer at point *A* would see at eclipse maximum something similar to that shown by the photograph in FIGURE 1-35. The Latin word *annulus* means ring, and from the figure you can see why such an eclipse is called an ***annular eclipse***. Note the spelling; this is not an annual eclipse. Slightly over half of the solar eclipses are annular.

annular eclipse An eclipse in which the Moon is too far from Earth for its disk to cover that of the Sun completely, and thus, the outer edge of the Sun is seen as a ring.

There are about twice as many total or annular solar eclipses as total lunar eclipses, but you are much less likely to see a solar eclipse because of the narrow path of the shadow.

(a)

(b)

FIGURE 1-35 (a) During an annular eclipse, we can see the entire ring—annulus—of the Sun around the Moon. This photo shows the annular eclipse of May 30, 1984. The irregularity of the ring is due to mountains and valleys on the Moon's surface. (b) This series of photos shows the progression of the Moon's motion across the Sun during an annular eclipse.

1-7   Observations of Planetary Motion

Why is East on the left on sky photographs?

Thus far we have barely mentioned the other major class of objects in the sky: the planets. Without a telescope we can see five planets: Mercury, Venus, Mars, Saturn, and Jupiter. "Planet" comes from a Greek word meaning "wanderer," and wander they do. Like the Sun and Moon, the planets move around among the stars on the celestial sphere. The Sun and Moon always move eastward among the stars, but the planets sometimes stop their eastward motion and move westward for a while. They lack the simple, uniform motion of the Sun and Moon.

FIGURE 1-36a shows the path that Mars followed on the sky between May and November 2003. Mars moved eastward (to the left) and southward (downward) between May and late July 2003 but then started moving backward, heading west! It moved westward until late September 2003 and then resumed its eastward motion for about 2 years, at which time (September 2005) it began another of its backward "loops" (Figure 1-36b). We call this backward motion **retrograde motion**. Retrograde motion is characteristic of planets, including those discovered in modern times.

retrograde motion The east-to-west motion of a planet against the background of stars.

Although the planets move among the stars in a seemingly irregular manner, there are limits to where they move, for they never get more than a few degrees from the ecliptic. Mercury and Venus have an additional limitation on their motion. These two never appear very far from the position of the Sun in the sky. We only see them either in the western sky shortly after the Sun has set or in the eastern sky shortly before sunrise. Mercury appears so close to the Sun that it is hard to find, even if we know where to look. This is because even when Mercury is at its maximum *elongation*, we have to look for it in the semibright sky during dawn or twilight.

elongation The angle in the sky from an object to the Sun.

You never see Mercury or Venus high in the sky at night. Any model of the planets must explain not only their observed retrograde motion, but why they stay near the ecliptic as well as the peculiar behavior of Mercury and Venus.

(a)   (b)

FIGURE 1-36 (a) Mars' retrograde motion in 2003. If you charted Mars' position on the night sky you will find that, in general, Mars moves eastward from one night to the next; however, every 2 years or so, Mars changes direction and moves westward for about 2 months before resuming its eastward motion again. Courtesy NASA/JPL-Caltech. (b) Mars' retrograde motion in 2005. To understand why maps and photographs of the sky show east and west reversed from Earth maps (on which north is at the top, east on the right, and west on the left), think of yourself lying face down on the ground with your head toward the north. Your right arm points toward the east. Suppose you now turn over to look up to the sky; your right arm is now toward the west! Thus the difference occurs because when we look at a map of the Earth we are looking down, but when we view a map of the sky we are looking up. Courtesy NASA/JPL-Caltech.

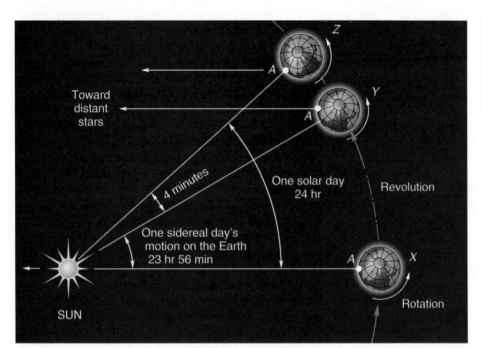

FIGURE 1-37 When the Earth has rotated once with respect to the stars, it has not completed a rotation with respect to the Sun. Thus, the sidereal day is shorter than the solar day. (The drawing greatly exaggerates the distance the Earth moves in one day.)

1-8   Rotations

As a planet revolves around the Sun, it also rotates around its axis. In discussing the rotation periods of the planets, we must distinguish between a solar day and a sidereal day. The **solar day** is defined as the time between successive passages of the Sun across the **meridian** so that the length of a solar day on Earth is 24 hours; however, this is not the same amount of time that the Earth takes to complete one rotation. With respect to the stars, the Earth rotates once in 23 hours, 56 minutes.

Refer to **FIGURE 1-37** to see why there is a difference between the solar day and the **sidereal day**, which is the amount of time required for an object to complete one rotation with respect to the stars. In that figure, we have designated a particular location on the Earth as *A*. When the Earth is at location *X* in the figure, point *A* faces the Sun directly. When the Earth has rotated once with respect to the stars, moving from *X* to location *Y*, a *sidereal day* would have passed. At this location, point *A* does not face the Sun directly; for this to occur again, the Earth must rotate an additional angle of about 360/365 degrees. This is because the Earth moves about 360/365 degrees per day around the Sun as it rotates; we have exaggerated this motion in the figure so that you can see the effect. Because it takes about 24 hours to rotate through 360 degrees, this additional rotation requires 24/365 hours or 4 minutes. The Earth's sidereal period is 23 hours and 56 minutes, but the Earth has to rotate for another 4 minutes to complete a *solar day* (location *Z*).

From the point of view of an observer on Earth, it is the Sun and the stars that move around the Earth. As such, a star will rise 4 minutes earlier from one night to the next.

solar day The amount of time that elapses between successive passages of the Sun across the meridian.

meridian An imaginary line that runs from north to south, passing through the observer's zenith.

sidereal day The amount of time that passes between successive passages of a given star across the meridian.

1-9   Units of Distance in Astronomy

In everyday life we use different units of distance for different types of measurements. We might use centimeters and meters (or inches and feet in the United States) to measure distances around the house. Although it would be possible to continue to

1 mile is about 1.6 kilometers. 1 yard is about 0.9 meters.

astronomical unit A distance equal to the average distance between the Earth and the Sun. This is about 150 million kilometers or 93 million miles.

light-year The distance light travels in a year.

Is a light-year a unit of time or distance?

use these units when we describe distances across the country or across the Earth, it is much more convenient to use kilometers (or miles) in these cases.

To measure distances in the solar system, kilometers and miles are too small to be convenient. In this case we use the ***astronomical unit (AU)***, which is defined as the average distance between the Earth and the Sun. We thus are able to say that Mars is 1.5 AU from the Sun and that Venus gets as close as 0.3 AU to the Earth.

When we go from considering distances within the solar system to distances between stars, the astronomical unit is too small to be very useful. A unit that is handy in this case is the ***light-year***, defined as the distance light travels in 1 year.

The speed of light is tremendous—a bit less than 300,000 kilometers/second or about 186,000 miles/second—so a light-year is indeed a great distance. Because a year has approximately

$$365 \text{ days} \times \frac{24 \text{ hours}}{\text{day}} \times \frac{60 \text{ minutes}}{\text{hour}} \times \frac{60 \text{ seconds}}{\text{minutes}} = 3.2 \times 10^7 \text{ seconds},$$

a light-year is about

$$300,000 \frac{\text{km}}{\text{second}} \times 3.2 \times 10^7 \text{ seconds} = 9.6 \times 10^{12} \text{ km},$$

or about 9.6 trillion kilometers or about 63,000 AU. This is about 6 million million miles, or 6 trillion miles. (See the accompanying Tools of Astronomy box for an explanation of this notation. You see here the reason it is needed.)

1-10   The Scale of the Universe

It is difficult for us to appreciate the sizes of objects in the universe and the distances between them (**FIGURE 1-38**). To try to get a sense of the objects that are the subject of astronomy, let us construct an imaginary scale model of part of the universe.

Suppose in our model we represent the Sun by a basketball, as in **FIGURE 1-39**. (A "standard" basketball is 9.4 inches in diameter.) On this scale, the Earth is the head

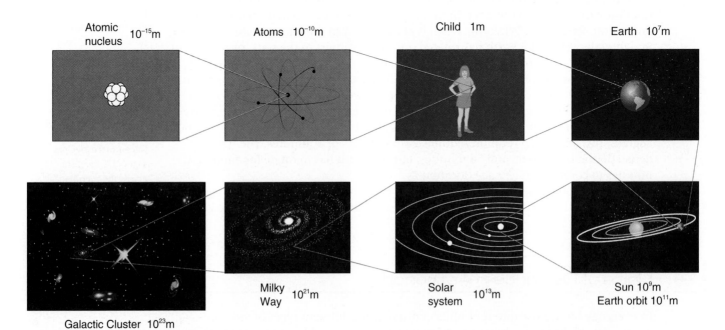

FIGURE 1-38 The use of powers-of-ten notation (see the Tools of Astronomy box) makes it much easier to describe the sizes of astronomical objects, but the notation should not obscure the tremendous differences in size.

of a pin, about 84 feet away and invisible in the photo. The Moon is a dot the size of a period on this page and is about 2.6 inches from Earth. Jupiter, the largest planet, is the size of a grape about 146 yards away—almost one and a half football fields away. Pluto is a grain of sand about six tenths of a mile away. Thus, the entire solar system inside Pluto's orbit occupies an area of about 1.2 miles in diameter with a basketball-size Sun at the center.

Where is the nearest star (other than the Sun)? About 4460 miles away! If our model solar system is located in Detroit, Michigan, the nearest star might be in Honolulu, Hawaii (FIGURE 1-40). This is about the average distance between stars in our Galaxy; thus, we must imagine basketballs spread around randomly with approximately 4460 miles between adjacent ones. The diameter of the Galaxy on this scale would be about 164,000,000 miles.

By developing such models, we begin to appreciate the distances involved in the real universe. Such imaginary scale models will be constructed throughout the text. If you try to imagine the distances involved each time, the repetition will not be boring, but instead will be mind expanding.

FIGURE 1-39 If the Sun is a basketball, the Earth is the head of a pin 84 feet away.

Simplicity and the Unity of Nature

It is our human nature to try to simplify things. In the sky we see a tremendous variety of objects and phenomena. Astronomy provides a method of seeing order in the apparent confusion. The more we learn about the objects that make up the universe, the more patterns we see, and the more order we find. As our knowledge of the universe expands, we become more and more aware of the unity of the cosmos.

Each of the natural sciences studies a different aspect of the universe, but because the unity exists, the various sciences overlap in many areas. Astronomy is particularly close to physics, with the two fields becoming indistinguishable at times. Likewise, astronomy and geology combine as we attempt to understand the formation, evolution, and surface features of the planets. Chemistry and biology become areas that astronomers are concerned about as they study the compositions of astronomical objects and the possibility of extraterrestrial life, and meteorology aids the astronomer in studying weather patterns on other planets.

The application of physics in astronomy is now so common that *astrophysics* is often used synonymously with "astronomy."

astrophysics Physics applied to extraterrestrial objects.

1-11   Astronomy Today

We live in exciting times. During six Apollo spaceflights (1969–1972) humans walked and drove a vehicle on the Moon. In 1997, a robot vehicle sent us pictures from the surface of Mars. In 2004, two rovers at two different sites on the surface of Mars started searching for and collecting information on a range of rocks and soils that hold clues to the planet's past water activity. In 2008, another rover started digging down to the ice of a Martian arctic plain, sampling soil and ice for evidence of past

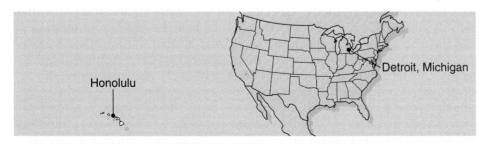

FIGURE 1-40 If our solar system with its basketball Sun is located in Detroit, the nearest star is at the distance of Honolulu.

A Model Universe with Sun as Basketball

Earth	Head of pin, 26 m from Sun
Moon	Dot, 7 cm from Earth
Jupiter	Grape, 134 m from Sun
Pluto	Grain of sand, 1 km from Sun
Nearest star	7180 km from Sun
Our Galaxy	260,000,000 km diameter

TOOLS OF ASTRONOMY

Powers of Ten

Numbers in science—and particularly in astronomy—are sometimes extremely small or extremely large. For example, the diameter of a typical atom is about 0.0000000002 meters, and the diameter of the Galaxy is about 1,000,000,000,000,000,000,000 meters. Both are rather awkward numbers to use. We can avoid such clumsy numbers by using a variety of units, such as the astronomical unit within the solar system and the light-year for distances between stars, but sometimes it is inconvenient to switch units simply to avoid large and small numbers. Instead, scientists use *powers-of-ten* notation, also called *scientific* notation, or *exponential* notation. (The exponent is the power to which a number is raised.)

Scientific notation is simple because when the number 10 is raised to a positive power, the exponent is the number of zeros. For example:

$$10^1 = 10,$$
$$10^2 = 100,$$
$$10^3 = 1000.$$

Written in meters, the diameter of the Galaxy contains 21 zeros, thus, it is written as 10^{21} meters.

If the number to be expressed in this notation is not a simple power of 10, it is written as follows:

$$2100 = 2.1 \times 1000 = 2.1 \times 10^3,$$
$$305,000 = 3.05 \times 100,000 = 3.05 \times 10^5.$$

To change a number from scientific notation to regular notation, you simply move the decimal point to the right by a number of places equal to that indicated by the exponent, filling in zeros if necessary.

Rather than explain negative exponents, we will just give some examples and let you see the pattern:

$$10^0 = 1,$$
$$10^{-1} = \frac{1}{10^1} = 0.1,$$
$$10^{-2} = \frac{1}{10^2} = 0.01,$$
$$10^{-3} = \frac{1}{10^3} = 0.001,$$
$$2 \times 10^{-8} = \frac{2}{10^8} = 0.00000002,$$
$$4.67 \times 10^{-5} = \frac{4.67}{10^5} = 0.0000467.$$

In this case, the same rule is followed, moving the decimal point by a number of places equal to the number indicated by the exponent, but this time moving it to the left and supplying any needed zeros.

When two numbers written in scientific notation are multiplied, to get the final answer you multiply the coefficients of the two powers of ten and add their exponents. For example:

$$(3.2 \times 10^5) \times (2 \times 10^2) = (3.2 \times 2) \times 10^{(5+2)} = 6.4 \times 10^7$$

and

$$(4.2 \times 10^5) \times (3 \times 10^{-2}) = (4.2 \times 3) \times 10^{[5+(-2)]}$$
$$= 12.6 \times 10^3 = 1.26 \times 10^4.$$

In the case of a division, you divide the coefficients of the two powers of ten and subtract their exponents. For example:

$$\frac{3.2 \times 10^5}{2 \times 10^2} = \frac{3.2}{2} \times 10^{5-2} = 1.6 \times 10^3$$

and

$$\frac{4.2 \times 10^5}{3 \times 10^{-2}} = \frac{4.2}{3} \times 10^{[5-(-2)]} = 1.4 \times 10^7.$$

life on the planet's surface. After a 7-year journey, the *Cassini* orbiter entered Saturn's orbit in July 2004 and, 6 months later, released its attached *Huygens* probe for descent through the thick atmosphere of Saturn's largest moon, Titan. Farther afield, we've detected planets around distant stars. The *Hubble Space Telescope* is returning amazing images to us, images of things never seen before (FIGURE 1-41). Numerous new telescopes are under construction or being put into operation. Through the use of new instrumentation and new methods, we are discovering celestial objects that were undreamed of a few decades ago. The most distant galaxies are being observed and studied, and answers are being sought to questions as basic as the origin and the fate of the universe. Discoveries can be made only once, and the generations of people now alive are witnessing some of the most exciting discoveries ever.

Of what value is the science of astronomy? Will it help us advance toward worldwide prosperity? Probably not. Technological advances (sometimes beneficial and sometimes not) have followed almost every scientific advance. This, however, is not astronomy's purpose. Astronomy is a pure science rather than an applied science, and astronomers seek knowledge because knowledge is a reward in itself. Asking and answering questions is one of the things that make humans different from the other animals with whom we share our Earth. We are curious because we are human; we study the heavens because we are curious.

Conclusion

We know today that the universe is more wondrous than the most imaginative dreamer of old could have envisioned. To fully appreciate the wonder, however, one must understand the questions asked, the methods used, and the results produced by modern astronomy.

In our quest to understand the universe, we will journey through the solar system, to the stars, and then to distant galaxies, and we will come to appreciate that although our Earth is but a tiny rock circling an ordinary star, we humans have significance in the universe. The significance lies not in our size, but—at least in part—in the fact that our tiny brains have the ability to comprehend the spacious universe.

FIGURE 1-41 The "Eskimo" nebula, first spotted by William Herschel in 1787, looks like a face in a fur parka when seen through ground-based telescopes, but the *Hubble Space Telescope* shows it to be an inner bubble of gaseous material being blown into space by a dying star, surrounded by a ring of comet-shaped objects. The nebula is about 5000 light-years from Earth. Glowing gases in the nebula produce the colors in this image: nitrogen (red), hydrogen (green), oxygen (blue), and helium (violet).

STUDY GUIDE

1. The Milky Way that we observe with the naked eye is
   A. the path planets take across the sky.
   B. debris left by the motions of planets.
   C. debris left by comets.
   D. the asteroid belt.
   E. stars in the galaxy of which the Sun is a part.
   F. sunlight scattered from water vapor in the atmosphere.

2. The smallest planet is _____ and the largest is _____.
   A. Earth . . . Saturn
   B. Mercury . . . Earth
   C. Pluto . . . Earth
   D. Mercury . . . Jupiter
   E. Earth . . . Jupiter

3. In astronomical units, how far is the Earth from the Sun?
   A. 0.5
   B. 1.0
   C. 1.5
   D. 3.0
   E. 93,000,000

4. Which choice lists the objects in correct size from smallest to largest?
   A. Earth, Sun, solar system, Galaxy
   B. Sun, Earth, solar system, Galaxy
   C. Earth, Sun, Galaxy, solar system
   D. Earth, Galaxy, Sun, solar system
   E. [None of the above.]

RECALL QUESTIONS

5. Polaris is unique because it
   A. moves in a different direction than any other bright star.
   B. is the brightest star in the sky.
   C. twinkles more than any other bright star.
   D. is fairly bright and shows very little motion when viewed from Earth.
   E. [The premise is false. Polaris is not unique at all.]

6. In ancient times, people distinguished the planets from the stars because
   A. planets appear much brighter than any star.
   B. features on planets' surfaces could be seen whereas no star's features could be seen.
   C. planets move relative to the stars.
   D. planets differ in color from the stars.
   E. planets can be seen during the day.

7. Which of the following choices can be seen from Indiana?
   A. Stars near the north celestial pole.
   B. Stars near the ecliptic.
   C. Stars near the celestial equator.
   D. [All of the above can be seen from Indiana.]
   E. [None of the above can be seen from Indiana.]

8. On the first day of spring, the Sun rises
   A. north of east.
   B. directly east.
   C. south of east.
   D. [Any of the above, depending upon your location on Earth.]

9. What causes summer to be hotter than winter?
   A. The Earth is closer to the Sun in summer.
   B. The daylight period is longer in summer.
   C. The Sun gets higher in the sky in summer.
   D. [Both B and C above.]
   E. [All of the above.]

10. The Sun's apparent path among the stars
    A. is south of the celestial equator.
    B. is right on the celestial equator.
    C. is north of the celestial equator.
    D. is south of the celestial equator part of the time and north of it part of the time.
    E. crosses the north celestial pole once each year.

11. The Sun crosses the celestial equator on the first day of
    A. winter.
    B. spring.
    C. summer.
    D. fall.
    E. [Two of the above.]

12. Which of the following planets appear(s) to move through the background of stars?
    A. Venus
    B. Mars
    C. Jupiter
    D. [Both A and B above.]
    E. [All of the above.]

13. The ecliptic and celestial equators intersect at two points called the
    A. equinoxes.
    B. solstices.
    C. tropics.
    D. sidereal points.
    E. poles.

14. A minute of arc is
    A. a measure of how far the Sun moves during 1 minute of time.
    B. one-sixtieth of a degree.
    C. how far the Earth turns on its axis in 1 minute.
    D. 60 degrees.
    E. the angular diameter of the Sun.

15. Thirty arcminutes is about _____ degrees.
    A. 0.008
    B. 0.5
    C. 180
    D. 1800
    E. [None of the above.]

16. If the Moon was new last Saturday, what phase will it be this Saturday?
    A. Waning crescent.
    B. Waxing gibbous.
    C. At or very near first quarter.
    D. At or very near full.
    E. [Any of the above, depending upon other factors.]

17. If you observe the Moon rising in the east as the Sun is setting in the west, then you know that the phase of the Moon must be
    A. new.
    B. first quarter.
    C. full.
    D. third quarter.
    E. [Any of the above, depending upon other factors.]

18. Suppose that astronauts land somewhere on the Moon when it is new for Earth-bound observers. Which of the following statements would be true?
    A. Earth would appear full to the astronauts (assuming that they could see it).
    B. Around the landing site there might be bright sunlight.
    C. The landing site might be dark.
    D. [All of the above.]
    E. [None of the above.]

19. A lunar eclipse can occur
    A. only around sunset.
    B. only near midnight.
    C. only near sunrise.
    D. at any time of day or night.

20. The Sun is _____ during an annular eclipse as/than during a total solar eclipse.
    A. farther from Earth
    B. closer to Earth
    C. the same distance from Earth
    D. [No general statement can be made.]

21. You are likely to see more of which type of eclipse during your lifetime?
    A. Solar eclipse.
    B. Lunar eclipse.
    C. [No general statement can be made.]

22. Name at least seven types of celestial objects that are visible to the naked eye.

23. What causes the Milky Way we see in the sky?

24. What is a galaxy?

25. What causes a meteor?

26. How do stars near Polaris appear to move as we watch them through the night?

27. What is the ecliptic?

28. What are the approximate dates of the summer and winter solstices and what is their significance?

29. What is the origin of the word planet?

30. In what direction across the background of stars do the planets normally move?

31. Define *retrograde motion* of a planet.

32. Name the planets that are never seen far from the Sun in the sky.

33. In what part of the sky must you look to find the planets Mercury and Venus?

34. What is meant by the *elongation* of a planet?

35. Name eight different phases of the Moon in the order in which they occur.

36. Define umbra and penumbra.

37. Total (and annular) solar eclipses occur more frequently than do total lunar eclipses. Why, then, will you probably observe many more lunar eclipses than solar eclipses during your lifetime?

38. Why are penumbral lunar eclipses not easily detectable?

39. Why are some solar eclipses annular rather than total?

1. The text states that astronomy is "still changing rapidly" today. Report on a new discovery or new hypothesis in astronomy that you find in the news during the next 2 weeks. Suggested sources include national television news, newspapers, and news magazines.

2. Some people argue that astronomy does not produce anything useful for our lives and, therefore, it does not deserve public funding. How do astronomers answer this? What do you think?

3. Figure out a method not mentioned in this chapter that would allow you to measure the length of the year by astronomical observations.

4. Specify the two coordinates by which we describe locations in the sky. List the units of each and the maximum and minimum value of each.

5. How does our calendar adjust for the fact that the year is about 365.25 days long rather than an even 365 days?

6. The star in Orion's left leg (Rigel) is much farther away than the other bright stars in the constellation (see Figure 1-8). If you look at Orion in the sky, and then move far into space in the direction to your left, how will that star shift relative to the others?

7. Identify the position of the vernal equinox, autumnal equinox, and the two solstices on Figure 1-18.

8. Why do people who live near the equator not experience major seasonal changes? (The answer, "It is always hot there" is not sufficient.)

9. Find the Arctic Circle on an Earth globe. What is the astronomical significance of this line? Where is the Tropic of Capricorn and what is its significance?

10. If you look at the Moon tonight and then again tomorrow night at the same time, will it be farther east or farther west on the second night? If you observe it at 8 PM tonight and then again at 9 PM, will it appear farther east or farther west at the later time? Explain the discrepancy.

11. At about what time does the first quarter Moon rise? Set?

12. Will the Moon appear crescent or gibbous when it is at position *X* in **FIGURE 1-42**? At position *Y*? At about what time will the Moon rise if it is at position *Y*?

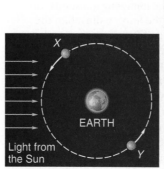

FIGURE 1-42 (Question 12)   FIGURE 1-43 (Question 17)

13. If you see the Moon high overhead shortly before sunrise, about what phase is it in?

14. At the same time that people in Chicago see a total solar eclipse, what type of eclipse is seen by people in Evansville, Indiana? (Evansville is about 250 miles south of Chicago.) Answer the same question for a total lunar eclipse.

15. Even at the midpoint of most total lunar eclipses, the Moon is not uniformly illuminated. Instead, one edge of the Moon is usually much brighter than the rest. Why is this? What would be necessary in order for the red color to appear uniform across the Moon?

16. Discuss the danger involved in viewing a solar eclipse and describe four ways to view such an eclipse safely. (Hint: See the Activity "Observing a Solar Eclipse.")

17. **FIGURE 1-43** is a multiple exposure of the Moon and Venus as they set one night over Tulsa. Explain why the Moon's distance from Venus changes as time passes.

18. The expression "Once in a Blue Moon" is commonly used to describe a rare phenomenon. It was thought

that the origin of this expression had to do with the rare occurrence of two full Moons in the same month, the second one being called "Blue Moon." However, this is not the case. A literature search suggests that the term "Blue Moon" was assigned to the third full Moon in a season that had four full Moons. During which month(s) can we not have a "Blue Moon" if we adopt the first (erroneous) explanation? During which month(s) do you expect to get "Blue Moons" if we adopt the second explanation? (Hint: You may want to consult *Sky & Telescope*; the magazine was actually the source of the erroneous modern convention for the meaning of the expression.)

CALCULATIONS

1. Using powers of ten, evaluate the following expressions:

$$(2 \times 10^{-2}) \times (3 \times 10^3)$$

and

$$\left(\frac{4 \times 10^{-4}}{2 \times 10^{-3}} \right)^2.$$

2. Verify that one light-year is about 63,000 AU.

3. The speed of light is about 300,000 kilometers/second and the average distance between Earth and Sun (1 AU) is about 150 million kilometers. How long does it take light to travel from the Sun to Earth? (Hint: An object moving at a speed v for a time t covers a distance d given by $d = v \times t$).

4. Using scientific notation and data found in the appendices of the book, answer the following questions: (a) How many times greater is the Sun's radius than the Earth's? (b) The stars Rigel and Betelgeuse are both in the constellation Orion. Are they at the same distance from us? What does your answer suggest about the constellations? (c) How long does it take light to travel from Rigel to Earth? What does that tell you about the *current* state of this star?

5. The Crab Nebula is the remnant of a supernova explosion that was first seen by the Chinese in 1054 AD. The distance of this nebula from Earth is about 6000 light-years. In what Earth year did the explosion actually occur?

6. Express an angle of 15 arcseconds in degrees.

7. Four degrees of angle is how many arcminutes?

8. Suppose one star is 3 arcminutes from another. What is this angle in degrees?

9. Given that the angle between the celestial equator and the ecliptic is 23.5 degrees, what is the declination and right ascension of the vernal equinox? Of the autumnal equinox? Of the winter solstice? Of the summer solstice?

10. Compare the distances reached by the umbral shadows of the Moon and the Earth. Compare the diameters of the two bodies. Discuss any relationship you see.

11. To show that the Moon's synodic period is about 2 days larger than its sidereal period, refer to Figure 1-25 and consider the following steps. (a) During one sidereal period (27.322 days), how many degrees has the Earth covered on its orbit around the Sun, from point *A* to point *B*? (Hint: The Earth covers 360° in about 365 days.) (b) Let us assume that we need an additional *x* days for a synodic period to be completed. During this period, both the Earth and the Moon move on their respective orbits. How many degrees does the Earth cover on its orbit around the Sun in this period? (c) To find *x*, set up a ratio by taking into account that the Moon covers 360° in a sidereal period.

ACTIVITIES

1. Building a Replica of the Solar System

Let us assume that we can build a replica of the solar system in which the Earth has a diameter of 1 mm. (Use relevant data from the appendices in your text.) In this replica, find the following: (a) the Sun's diameter (in cm), (b) the Earth-Moon distance (in cm), (c) the distances between the Sun and the planets (in m), (d) the distance to the nearest star other than the Sun (in km). Consult a map of your area (for example, from a phone book), and plot on it the positions of the planets (and the Moon), assuming the Sun is located at your school.

2. Star Charts and Observations

Obtain one of the star charts published monthly in astronomy magazines such as *Astronomy* and *Sky & Telescope*. On a clear, cloud-free night, use the star chart to locate as many constellations of the zodiac as you can. Can you locate the celestial equator? The ecliptic? Spend some time outdoors and see whether you could clearly distinguish the motion of the stars toward the west. Has Polaris moved? What is the overall pattern that the stars follow?

3. The Rotating Earth

On a clear dark night, find a good observing location, and draw a quick sketch of some stars high over your head. Look for a pattern so that you can remember these stars later. If you can, mark your map so that it shows which stars are toward the north, east, south, and west.

Take about 2 hours off; then go back to your observing location and find the stars you drew. How has their position changed? You probably know what this answer should be from having read the text. Your real job, however, is to stand under the stars and imagine that their motion is due to the rotation of the Earth. Try to "feel" the Earth turning under the stars. Which is easier to imagine, the stars on a sphere rotating around the Earth or the Earth spinning under the stars?

Finally, spend a half hour watching either a sunrise or a sunset. Better yet, watch the Moon rise or set, particularly when it is full or nearly full. Now picture this phenomenon as explained by the heliocentric system. Try to think of the Earth turning instead of the Sun or Moon moving. Imagine yourself on a little ball that is turning so that the place where the Sun's light hits the ball changes.

4. Do-It-Yourself Phases

This is an important activity that is worth the trouble if you want to understand the phases of the Moon. We will simulate the Sun/Earth/Moon system as it is shown in Figure 1-24. For the Moon you will need something like an orange, a grapefruit, or a softball. The softball would be best because it is rounder than the other choices. For the Sun, you can use a bright light across an otherwise dark room. (You could go outside and use the real Sun, but you must be careful not to look directly at it. This method would work best when the Sun is low in the sky.) Your head will be the Earth, and one of your eyes will be you.

Hold the ball (your Moon) out at arm's length so that it is nearly between you and your Sun. Now observe it as you move it around to the left until it is at 90 degrees to the Sun, the first-quarter position, as shown in **FIGURE 1-44**. Did you see its growing crescent as you were moving it? Continue to move it around your head and observe it as it changes phase. (When it gets directly behind you from the Sun, you will eclipse it.)

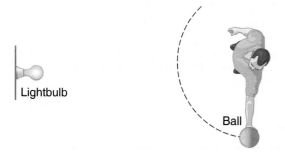

FIGURE 1-44 The person is holding a ball that represents the Moon at first quarter. When doing this, you should put the lightbulb farther away than indicated here, perhaps 10 to 15 feet away.

Now fix the Moon at the first-quarter position by laying it down on something in that position. Turn your head (and body) slowly around and around toward the left to simulate the Earth rotating. When the Sun is directly in front of you, it is noontime. As you lose sight of the Sun, it is sunset, about 6:00 PM. It is midnight when the back of your head is toward the Sun. When the Moon is at first quarter and it is sunset on Earth, where do you see the Moon?

Put the moon in various other positions and observe it as you rotate your head to simulate different times of day. Answer the following questions:

a. If the Moon is at third quarter, at about what time will it rise? At about what time will it set?

b. At about what time will a full Moon appear highest overhead?

c. If you see the Moon in the sky in mid-afternoon, about what phase will it be?

5. Observing the Moon's Phases

This exercise will take several nights. Find a calendar or daily newspaper that lists Moon phases, or ask your instructor for this information so that you can begin your observations 3 or 4 nights after the new Moon. Observations should start at sunset or shortly thereafter. At least four observations should be made, continuing for at least 3 more clear nights during the 2 weeks following your first night.

It is important that the observations be made from exactly the same place and at exactly the same time of night. Stand at the same place, not just in the same parking lot, for example. You might even go so far as to mark your location with chalk.

a. On each night of your observations, after you have arrived at your observing location, use a full sheet of paper to make a sketch of the position of the Moon relative to buildings, trees, and the like on the horizon. This sketch should show how things look to you and should not be a map. Label the buildings, such as "Student Union." Also include prominent stars you see near the Moon. Draw the Moon in the shape it appears and with the correct apparent size relative to objects on the horizon. Finally, write the date and time on your paper.

b. On one of the nights, repeat the observation after waiting about an hour. Use the same sketch and show the new position of the Moon.

c. When you have finished your four (or more) observations, make a general statement about how the Moon changed position and phase from one night to another. Look for a pattern in the Moon's behavior and explain that pattern based on the Moon's motion around the Earth.

6. Observing a Solar Eclipse

There is a misconception that the Sun emits especially harmful rays of some kind during a solar eclipse. This is a particularly anthropomorphic idea, for it would mean that somehow the Sun knows when Earth's Moon is about to block sunlight from the Earth. Naturally, the radiation emitted by the Sun during an eclipse is no different from that emitted at any other time.

Like most misconceptions, however, there is an element of truth in this idea. In fact, the Sun continuously emits radiation that is harmful to our eyes: infrared radiation.* If you were to look at the Sun anytime, this radiation would harm your eyes, but normally you are not able to look at the Sun. If you attempt it, your eye will quickly close because of the intense light. When the Sun is nearly totally eclipsed, however, its light is dim enough that you are able to look at it. Thus, during an eclipse it would be possible for a person to stare directly at the Sun for some time, all the while unknowingly absorbing the harmful infrared rays in his or her eyes.

There are a few safe methods of observing the Sun during an eclipse. First, we might use a telescope with a solar filter attached. This is a filter that blocks out some 99.99% of the Sun's light, allowing just enough through for us to see the Sun.

A more convenient way to use a telescope to observe an eclipse is illustrated in **FIGURE 1-45**, which shows the use of a telescope to project the partially eclipsed Sun onto a screen. In this case, a reflecting device was mounted on the telescope to cause the image to appear off to the side. This photo was taken when the Moon had progressed much of the way across the solar disk. It was near noon at the time, but the sky had still not darkened noticeably. Even a little of the Sun's light is enough to give us a bright day on Earth.

FIGURE 1-45 The telescope has a mirror (called a *star diagonal*) attached to it so that it projects the image of the partially eclipsed Sun onto the screen at the side.

A third method of safely observing a solar eclipse—one requiring little equipment—is by pinhole projection. To use this method, all that you need is a piece of cardboard with a hole in it and a piece of paper to use as a screen. **FIGURE 1-46** illustrates the method. Try holes of different sizes, from 1 millimeter to one made with a paper punch. (A hole made by a pin will probably be too small.) To see the image better, you might use large pieces of cardboard to shield your screen from reflected light or work in a dark room that has an opening facing the Sun. Block all of the opening except for your pinhole.

A fourth method of observing an eclipse is to obtain a safe filter through which you can view the Sun directly.

FIGURE 1-46 A pinhole projector can be used to view a solar eclipse, but you must shield your screen better from scattered light than is done here.

Extreme care must be exercised here, however. If your filter does not block the Sun's infrared radiation, it may damage your eyes. (Smoked glass is definitely not recommended.) To avoid the possibility of injury, it is recommended that you be very sure of your filter or that you use one of the other methods.

* The Sun also emits ultraviolet radiation that can harm the eyes; however, the primary danger during solar eclipses is infrared radiation.

---

1. The book *The Measure of the Universe*, by I. Asimov (Harper and Row, 1983), will take you for a trip through the universe using powers of ten.

2. The book *Powers of Ten* by Philip and Phylis Morrison (W. H. Freeman, 1982) also will take you for a tour through the universe using powers of ten. There is also a video based on the book (Pyramid Film and Video, 1989).

3. Read the article, "Solar Eclipses That Changed the World," by B. E. Schaeffer, in *Sky & Telescope* (May, 1994).

4. The Web sites for the magazines *Sky & Telescope* and *Astronomy* (and the magazines themselves), which

cover the latest developments in astronomy for a general audience, have information about upcoming eclipses. An authoritative site for eclipses is maintained at NASA's Goddard Space Flight Center. At the same Center you also can find information about past, current, and future NASA missions (including *Lunar Prospector*) and pages devoted to our planet and the Moon.

5. *Spinoff* is a NASA publication that features successful transfers of NASA technology to the private sector, resulting in the development of numerous commercial products and services. Since the 1950s, space technology has been applied to tens of thousands of commercial products.

Quest Ahead to Starlinks:
http://physicalscience.jbpub.com/starlinks

Starlinks is this book's online learning center. It features **eLearning**, which contains chapter quizzes and other tools designed to help you study for your class. You also can find **online exercises**, view numerous relevant **animations**, follow a guide to **useful astronomy sites** on the Internet, or even check the latest **astronomy news** updates.

ACTIVITIES

EXPANDING THE QUEST

STARLINKS

From an Earth-Centered to a Sun-Centered System

ANCIENT OBSERVERS WONDERED ABOUT THE OBJECTS AND PHENOMENA we described in Chapter 1. Through the methods of astronomy, we are answering questions asked by those ancient observers as well as questions far beyond their imagining. Our search toward understanding the universe fills us with awe and provides us with an endless stream of new questions. In this text, we try to describe not only the answers to some of the questions but also the methods used in the search.

Studying the methods that astronomers use actually means studying scientific methods in general, for although each of the sciences uses different instruments, the basic methods of inquiry are similar for all of the natural sciences. We thus explore the very nature of the scientific endeavor, showing how astronomers gather data, how those data are developed into theories, how various theories compete against one another, and how and why some theories are retained and others abandoned. Data and theories are the working materials of all of the sciences, and examples of the interplay between data and theory will be an essential part of our study.

All cross references to chapters, sections, figures, and tables pertain to the main text, *In Quest of the Universe, Sixth Edition. In Quest of the Solar System* contains Chapters 1–11 and 19 of the main text. *In Quest of the Stars and Galaxies* contains Chapters 1–5 and 11–19 of the main text.

The *International Space Station* moves away from the space shuttle *Atlantis*; in the backdrop, Earth's horizon and the blackness of space.

2-1   Science and Its Ways of Knowing

scientific method A never-ending cycle of hypothesis, prediction, data gathering, and verification.

Science is a very human endeavor, and the science that a particular culture produces is in part a reflection of the characteristics of that culture. In astronomy, the human aspects of science are very visible.

Science is about discovering the orderliness of nature and the rules that govern this order. It is also the body of knowledge about nature that represents the collective efforts of people throughout history. Science progresses through the interaction of observations and experiments with theory. With our theories we make predictions, while our observations and experiments support, disprove, or place constraints on these theories. This information provides a means of determining the best description of nature. The characteristics of good science include the continuous search for new knowledge, the ability to make predictions and test them against observations, and the ability to repeat and verify any experimental result. Learning from observations and experiments and, as a result, refining our theories are not weaknesses in science—they are strengths.

hypothesis An educated guess made in describing the results of an experiment or observation. A hypothesis can be widely speculative but must be testable.

It is said that the ***scientific method*** is the best approach for doing good science. This method is used to gain, organize, and apply new knowledge and was first introduced in the 16th century. Essentially, it involves the following series of steps: (1) recognize a problem; (2) make an educated guess, called a ***hypothesis***, about the problem's solution; (3) predict the consequences of the hypothesis; (4) perform experiments to test the predictions; and (5) find the simplest general rule that organizes the hypothesis, prediction, and experimental outcome into a ***theory***.

theory A synthesis of a large body of information that encompasses well-tested (by repeatable experiments) and verified hypotheses about certain aspects of the natural world. No theory can be proved true, but data can prove a theory to be false.

The scientific method is a never-ending cycle of hypothesis, prediction, data gathering, and verification. In reality, this method is not always used. For example, some of the most important discoveries in science were accidental, such as Becquerel's discovery of radioactivity by noting that a chunk of uranium ore caused a photographic plate to turn cloudy. The important ingredient is the continuous comparison between observations and theory.

It is important to emphasize again that a hypothesis is nothing but an educated guess made in explaining the results of an experiment or observation. A hypothesis must be testable and, at least in principle, it must be susceptible to being shown wrong. A useful hypothesis is one that makes predictions about nature that can be confirmed or refuted by observations. It is only considered to be a ***fact*** after it has been demonstrated by experiments.

fact Generally, a close agreement by competent observers of a series of observations of the same phenomenon.

In everyday life, the word *fact* implies something that is absolute. In science, however, it simply implies a generally close agreement among most competent scientists about a series of observations of the same phenomenon. Something that in science was considered a fact a few decades ago, thus, may turn out to be wrong. For example, we used to consider it a fact that the universe is static, whereas our current observations clearly show that we live in an expanding universe.

law or principle When a hypothesis has been repeatedly tested and has not been contradicted, it may become known as a law or principle.

When a hypothesis has been tested over and over again and has not been contradicted, it may become known as a ***law*** or ***principle***. In science we describe reality using ***models***, which are developed sets of ideas used to describe some aspect of nature and are composed of hypotheses that are supported by observations and experiments. A model gives us a description of a phenomenon and allows prediction of future events, but it is not necessarily the truth or reality.

scientific model An idea, a logical framework, that accounts for a set of observations and/or allows us to create explanations of how we think a part of nature works.

Finally, a theory is a synthesis of a large body of information that includes related hypotheses (which have been repeatedly tested and verified), giving us a self-consistent description of a certain aspect of the natural world. A theory can never be proven to be true, but data can prove a theory to be false. In everyday usage the word *theory* implies something that is nothing but a wild guess that has little to do with reality. In science, however, a *theory* represents a coherent framework describing an aspect of nature very well. For example, you might hear someone refer to Einstein's theory of relativity and say, "Well, it is *only* a theory," meaning that you must not put too much faith in it. Einstein's theory of relativity is indeed a theory but one that is well founded and has been experimentally verified many times.

Criteria for Scientific Models

Three criteria are applied to scientific models today.

- The first criterion is that the model must fit the data. It must fit what is observed.

- The second criterion is that the model must make predictions that allow it to be tested and that it must be possible to disprove the model—that is, to show that it needs to be modified to fit new data or perhaps needs to be discarded entirely. In other words, a scientific model must contain the potential seeds of its own destruction. If a model's prediction turns out to be correct, this serves as further evidence that the model is good, but it does not "prove" it. On the other hand, further evidence can always prove a model wrong. We can disprove a model, but we can never absolutely prove one. "Prediction" here does not necessarily refer to the future. It means that the theory itself indicates an observation that will either support it or disprove at least part of it. Sometimes the observation has already been made and needs only to be checked against the theory.

    Not all models make predictions that allow them to be tested and possibly be proven wrong. For example, suppose someone presents a model that says the planets appear to move the way they do because of a divine plan. Using this model, whatever we later find out about a planet can be explained by saying that it was a part of this divine plan. There would be no way to prove this model wrong. This model cannot be accepted as a good scientific model because it does not contain within itself predictions that allow it to be disproved.

- The third and final feature of a good model is that it should be aesthetically pleasing. This concept is difficult to define. It generally means that the model should be simple, neat, and beautiful. Today's idea of beauty in a scientific model is more along the lines of symmetry and simplicity. A model should be as simple as possible; that is, it should contain the fewest arbitrary assumptions. The philosophical choice that among two or more competing theories (which explain all known observations equally well) the best theory is the one that requires the fewest assumptions is known as **Occam's razor**. It is named for a 14th-century Franciscan monk–philosopher who stressed that in constructing an argument one should not go beyond what is logically required. Using Occam's razor, one "cuts out" extraneous suppositions.

Occam's razor The principle that the best explanation is the one that requires the fewest unverifiable assumptions.

2-2 From an Earth-Centered to a Sun-Centered System

We currently have good explanations for what we see in the sky, and we understand the Earth's relationship to other astronomical objects. The search for this understanding began long before telescopes were invented. Even though many civilizations contributed in different ways to our understanding of the observed motions of stars and planets, our starting place will be two major theories that explain these motions, one of which is nearly 2000 years old. We examine these theories for two different purposes: first, to answer the question of where the Earth fits into the scheme of things, and second, to see how well they match the criteria for a good scientific theory. Finally, we show how and why one of these theories won out over the other and how the understanding of nature provided by the successful theory eventually allowed humans to travel beyond the Earth and leave footprints on the Moon.

Why does an astronomy text begin by looking back into history instead of plunging into today's astronomy? Furthermore, why start with an outmoded theory? There is good reason. To understand how astronomy—and science in general—works, we must look at how it progresses with time. We must see what led up to today's ideas. Science is a dynamic enterprise and the continual refinement of theories is one of its strengths. Every advance in science is necessarily incomplete and may well be partly inaccurate; this is a natural result of the fact that science is a human activity and thus includes people's biases. Looking back and understanding how a certain idea evolved allow us to better appreciate all of the specific influences on that idea from people of different times and nationalities. We can also better understand the basis of the idea and see how the scientific "knowledge filter" works, at least ideally, by recognizing and removing weaknesses such as personal biases during the different evolutionary stages of the idea.

2-3   The Greek Geocentric Model

Aristotle lived from about 384 to 322 BC but still influences today's thinking.

To trace the evolution of our present model of the system of the heavens, we begin with the advanced Greek culture that lasted from about 600 BC until about 200 AD. Before looking directly at the Greek model, however, it is necessary to begin with a discussion of the world as seen by some of the ancient Greek philosophers, especially Aristotle.

There is a fundamental difference between the contributions to astronomy made by the ancient Greeks and those made by the other ancient civilizations. The Babylonians studied the heavens mostly because they were interested in interpreting daily events, in the same way as some people do today with astrology. The ancient Egyptians studied the heavens because they were interested in making predictions for agricultural purposes. The ancient Chinese believed in a kind of astrology in which events in the heavens influenced events on Earth; thus, they were very good at recording celestial events. The ancient Greeks, however, were interested in astronomy because of a pure philosophical desire to understand how the universe works. They believed in, and looked for, a sense of symmetry, order, and unity in the cosmos. They took the first steps in creating a unified model of the universe.

Had we never seen the stars, the sun, and the heavens, none of the words we have spoken about the universe would have been uttered. But now, the sight of day and night and the revolutions of the years have created number and given us a concept of time as well as the power of inquiring about the nature of the universe, and from this source we have derived philosophy. No greater good ever was or will be given by the gods to mortal men.
Plato, in Timaeus

Thales of Miletus (about 600 BC) believed that rational thought can lead to understanding of the universe. He also speculated that the Sun and stars were not gods, as was then usually thought, but balls of fire. Pythagoras (about 530 BC), one of the first experimental scientists, believed that nature can be described by numbers (that is, mathematics) and was the first to propose that Earth is spherical. His students, called the Pythagoreans, proposed around 450 BC that the universe is spherical, with a central "fire" containing a force that controls all motion. Around this fire, in order outward from the center, move Earth, the Moon, the Sun, the five planets, and the stars. This system predates by more than 2000 years Nicolaus Copernicus' revolutionary model of the planets moving around the Sun. The Pythagoreans were also the first to use the observed roundness of the Earth's shadow on the Moon as a supporting argument for the Earth being a spherical body. Plato (about 380 BC) taught the ideas of Thales and believed that the planets are spheres moving in circular orbits. He reasoned that astronomy contributed to the civilization of humanity.

Aristotle rejected the idea of the Pythagoreans that the Earth moves around a central "fire" and placed it back at the center of the solar system. Even though to us this choice seems to be obviously wrong, we must keep in mind that Aristotle's reasoning was supported by the observational evidence of his time. He argued that if Earth were moving, we ought to be able to see changes in the relative positions of the various stars in the sky, just as, if you drive down a highway, you see changes in the relative positions of nearby and distant trees. Such a shift in position due to motion is called *parallax*.

Hold your thumb in front of your face while you close one eye and look at the wall across from you (**FIGURE 2-1**). Now, without moving your thumb, view the wall with the other eye. Wink with one eye and then the other. You will see that your thumb seems to move from one spot on the wall to another. Also, the closer your thumb is to your face, the greater the shift is in its position with respect to the background. The explanation, of course, is that you are looking at your thumb from a different location each time you change eyes. In general, if our observing location changes, nearby objects will appear to move with respect to distant objects. This observation is given the general name ***parallax***.

parallax The apparent shifting of nearby objects with respect to distant ones as the position of the observer changes.

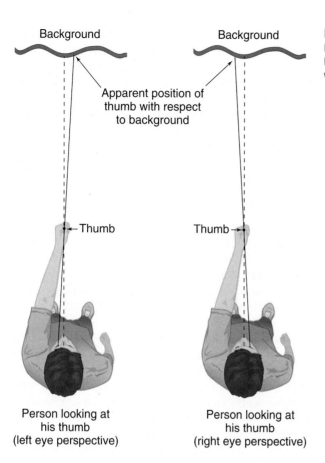

Background   Background

Apparent position of
thumb with respect
to background

←Thumb   Thumb→

Person looking at
his thumb
(left eye perspective)

Person looking at
his thumb
(right eye perspective)

FIGURE 2-1 To observe parallax, hold one thumb in front of you and look at it first with one eye and then with the other.

FIGURE 2-2 shows the Earth at two positions on opposite sides of its orbit. Just as your thumb shifted its apparent position when you alternately winked your eyes, if stars differ in their distances from Earth, a nearby star would be expected to shift its position relative to very distant stars. Such ***stellar parallax*** was first observed in 1838. All of the stars are so far away, however, that the greatest annual shift observed is only 1.5 arcseconds (corresponding to Proxima Centauri, the nearest star to the Sun), and this is why stellar parallax was not observed earlier.

A visual survey of the stars and constellations over time showed no evidence of such shift, and thus, Aristotle concluded that Earth must not move. This is a great example of how a perfectly correct logical argument can lead to wrong conclusions if based on incomplete data. One can hardly blame Aristotle for not being able to observe parallax, as the stars are so much farther away from Earth than anyone of his time could imagine.

Aristotle thought the Moon is spherical, probably by noticing that the line separating the lit side of the Moon from the unlit side changes its curvature as the phases progress. He believed that the Sun is farther away than the Moon because the Moon's

stellar parallax The apparent annual shifting of nearby stars with respect to background stars, measured as the angle of shift.

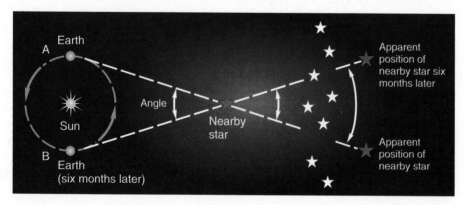

FIGURE 2-2 As the Earth goes around the Sun, we see parallax of a nearby star as it shifts its position against background stars. The amount of parallax (half of the angle shown) is very much exaggerated here. For the nearest star, Proxima Centauri, the angle shown is only about 1.5 arcseconds (0.0004°). Accurate stellar parallaxes can currently be measured for stars up to about 1600 light-years away (corresponding to angles of about 4×10^{-3} arcseconds).

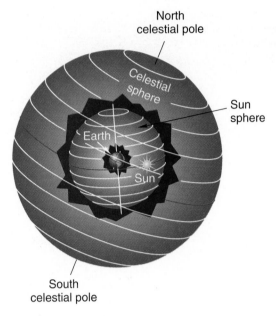

North celestial pole

Celestial sphere

Sun sphere

Earth

Sun

South celestial pole

FIGURE 2-3 To account for the Sun's path around the Earth (and among the stars), the Greek model located the Sun on a sphere that moves around the stationary Earth inside the celestial sphere of stars. The axis of the Sun's sphere is tilted with respect to the axis of the celestial sphere to account for the apparent path of the Sun in the sky.

Ptolemaic model The theory of the heavens devised by Ptolemy.

FIGURE 2-4 Ptolemy.

crescent phase shows that it passes between the Earth and Sun and that the Sun appears to move more slowly in the sky than the Moon. Aristotle used three observations to argue that the Earth is spherical, saying that only on a sphere do all falling bodies seek the center; that as a traveler goes north, more of the northern sky is exposed while the southern stars sink below the horizon; and that during lunar eclipses, the edge of the Earth's shadow is always circular.

Aristotle's system of the world made a great distinction between earthly things and the things of the heavens. He observed that matter on Earth and matter in the sky seem to behave fundamentally differently. For example, objects on Earth have an undeniable tendency to fall to the ground; they fall *down*. In fact, we might define the word "down" as the direction things fall. Objects in the sky don't do that; instead, they seem to move in circles around the Earth. Aristotle said that it is "natural" for earthly objects to move downward, that they seem *naturally* to seek the downward direction. On the other hand, it seems reasonable that heavenly objects move in circles. Something in the very nature of the objects seems to make them behave differently.

Aristotle saw another basic difference between the two types of objects: Although earthly objects always seem to come to a stop, heavenly objects just keep going. Thus, the "natural" motion of the two classes of objects appears to be different. This idea from Aristotle was a basic part of the world view of the Greeks, and it can be seen in their celestial models. They believed that there were two different sets of rules: one for earthly objects and one for celestial objects.

A celestial model developed by Greek thinkers before the time of Aristotle placed the stars on a sphere, similar to the model we described in Chapter 1. Instead of having the Sun move on a path on that sphere, however, the Sun was placed on another sphere that rotates around the Earth inside the sphere of the stars, as shown in FIGURE 2-3. To account for the fact that the Sun is sometimes seen north of the celestial equator and sometimes south, the Sun's sphere was thought to turn on a different axis from the one on which the stellar (celestial) sphere rotates. The difference between the tilts of the two spheres is shown in Figure 2-3.

There was good reason for the Greeks to use a sphere to carry the Sun, and the reason is linked to their admiration of geometry, which is traceable to the time of Pythagoras, the discoverer of the Pythagorean theorem. They sought geometric explanations for all natural phenomena. The Greeks then carried the idea of spheres much further and developed a model of the Earth, Sun, Moon, and planets using many spheres rotating around one another. For example, in Aristotle's model of the universe, every celestial object was attached to one of 55 crystalline spheres, each sphere having the Earth at the center and moving at different (but constant) speed around it. In order of distance from the Earth, Aristotle positioned the spheres carrying the Moon, Mercury, Venus, Sun, Mars, Jupiter, Saturn, the fixed stars, and finally the sphere of the Prime Mover. The Prime Mover caused the outermost sphere to rotate at constant speed, which in turn caused the next sphere to move, and so on. This model, however, could not explain the observations of retrograde motion and varying planetary brightness.

The Greek model we discuss most thoroughly is that of Claudius Ptolemy (FIGURE 2-4), who lived around 150 AD. In his book (which we call the *Almagest*), he presented a comprehensive model that lasted for almost 1400 years after his death. Today we know this geocentric model as the ***Ptolemaic model***. Ptolemy abandoned the spheres of earlier Greek models, for he saw no need to imagine actual physical objects carrying the Sun, Moon, and planets. He still spoke of the stars, however, as being on the celestial sphere.

In accordance with the thinking of Aristotle, people of Ptolemy's time thought that things in the sky (the "heavens") must be perfect. It seemed reasonable that the heavens would feature the circle, a symmetrical shape with no beginning and no end. Indeed, the stars seem to move in circles around the Earth. It seemed natural that they would lie in a spherical arrangement and that the sphere would move around us at a constant speed. As we discussed in Chapter 1, the Moon changes its position among the stars from day to day just as the Sun does (but at a different speed).

The Moon fits the Ptolemaic scheme perfectly. All that is necessary is that it moves around the Earth as the closest heavenly body. In fact, the Moon fit the overall Greek philosophical approach. Being the closest to the imperfect Earth, the Moon might be expected to have imperfections on it. Indeed, it has dark and light areas. It is somewhere between the imperfect Earth and the perfect heavens.

The observed eastward motion of the planets also fits the Ptolemaic model. (In Section 1-7, we described the eastward and southward motion of Mars. The model can also account for the southward motion of Mars if the planet's orbital plane is placed at an angle with the celestial equator. Mars moves northward again later in the year. This is similar to how the model explains the Sun's motion.)

Any model of the planets must explain not only their observed retrograde motion, but also why they stay near the ecliptic and also the peculiar behavior of Mercury and Venus, which can never be seen high in the night sky. How did the Greeks account for the planets' unique motions? Were the heavens perhaps imperfect, with the planets not moving uniformly in a smooth circle?

A Model of Planetary Motion: Epicycles

Ptolemy was indeed able to use circles to make a model that fit the planets' motions. It simply took more than one circle for each planet. (Though this idea was originally used by Hipparchus, who lived about 300 years before Ptolemy, he did elaborate on it, and he is generally given credit for it.) FIGURE 2-5 shows Mars moving uniformly on a small circle (the **epicycle**) whose center moves uniformly around the Earth. By a correct choice of rotation speeds, an observed motion for Mars such as that shown in Figure 2-5 can be produced.

A person on Earth viewing Mars' motion among the stars sees the planet moving eastward most of the time. This corresponds to the eastward motion of the epicycle's

The Greeks listed the Sun and Moon as planets. This made seven planets, and this is the origin of our week having 7 days.

Having set ourselves the task to prove that the apparent irregularities of the five planets, the sun and the moon can all be represented by means of uniform circular motions, because only such motions are appropriate to their divine nature. We are entitled to regard the accomplishment of this task as the ultimate aim of mathematical science based on philosophy.
Ptolemy

epicycle The circular orbit of a planet in the Ptolemaic model, the center of which revolves around the Earth in another circle.

FIGURE 2-5 Mars' motion on its epicycle results in a looping path, which—when seen from Earth—appears as retrograde motion.

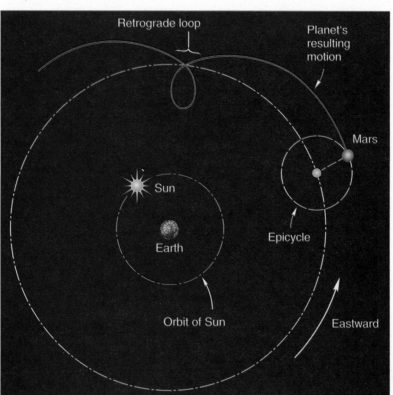

center around the Earth. Occasionally, however, the planet retrogrades. This occurs when the planet is inside the circular path of the epicycle's center and thus closer to the Earth. In this way, Ptolemy was able to preserve the idea of perfect circles and perfect uniform speeds for the heavenly objects. He could also explain why planets seem brightest when they are at the midpoint of their retrograde motion.

How, then, does the model explain why the planets never move far from the ecliptic? The answer is that the plane of their circular motion lies very close to the plane of the Sun's motion. The greater the angle between these two planes, the farther the planet will move from the ecliptic as it moves among the stars.

The different behavior of Mercury and Venus was explained by having the centers of their epicycles remain along a line between the Earth and the Sun (FIGURE 2-6). Although the center of other planets' epicycles could be anywhere on their circle around the Earth without regard to where the Sun is, Mercury and Venus are special cases.

The Ptolemaic model had many features that we look for in a scientific model. Even though the criteria for scientific models we discussed earlier in this chapter were not the standards of Ptolemy's times, it is instructive to apply them to the Ptolemaic model.

- The Ptolemaic model fits the data pretty well in that it gives an explanation for the motions of the heavenly objects. The stars' motions were explained by the rotation of the celestial sphere on which they reside. The Sun and the Moon were theorized to move in circles around the Earth. Explanation of the planets' motions required the use of epicycles and special treatment for Mercury and Venus, but when these features were included, the planets' motions were accounted for.

- The Ptolemaic model includes many testable predictions. The model made predictions for the locations of the planets at times in the future. One could use the model to predict that Jupiter would be at a particular place in the sky at a particular time the next year. Also, the Ptolemaic model holds that the Earth is stationary. It would predict that as knowledge advances and new methods are found to measure the motion of the Earth—either rotational motion or motion through space—no motion would be found. If further experimentation did not confirm this, the model would have to be adjusted drastically or abandoned.

- In the Ptolemaic model we find a form of symmetry in the sense that all objects travel in circles, and they basically obey the same rules as they move from east to

Actually, to make the model fit the data more accurately, Ptolemy either had to make the planets vary their speeds along their paths, or he had to move the Earth off-center among the planets' paths. He chose the latter method. After this and a few similar adjustments, the model fit pretty well but became even less aesthetically pleasing.

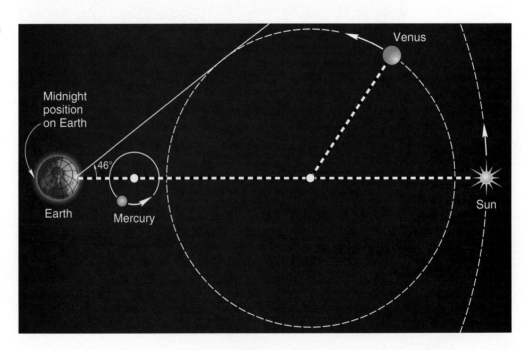

FIGURE 2-6 In the Ptolemaic model, the centers of Mercury's and Venus' epicycles stay between the Earth and the Sun. This accounts for the fact that the planets are never seen far from the Sun. Venus reaches a maximum of 46-degrees elongation. The drawing is not to scale.

west around the Earth. The model required the use of epicycles to explain retrograde motion, however, and included different rules for Mercury and Venus. The need for different rules for certain planets means that the model lacks an aspect of simplicity.

Remember, however, that the primary rule for a good model is that it fits the observations. An aesthetically pleasing model that did not come close to the real world would be almost useless. The Ptolemaic model did fit the data of the time, but to do so, it had to be continuously adjusted during the 1400 years of its reign.

2-4 Aristarchus' Heliocentric Model

About 400 years before Ptolemy, around 280 BC, the Greek philosopher Aristarchus had proposed a moving-Earth solution to explain the motions of the heavens. According to this model, the reason the sky seems to move westward is that the spherical Earth is spinning eastward. Although Ptolemy was aware of Aristarchus' model, he argued that if the Earth turned on an axis, it would be moving through the air around it, and, therefore, a tremendous wind should be observed in the opposite direction. Ptolemy referred to the moving-Earth model as being a "simpler conjecture." He saw that it was more aesthetically pleasing, but he believed it was not a good model because it presented obvious contradictions with the observation that the air stays where it is, along with everything loose on Earth. Ptolemy was unable to see that the Earth might be carrying the air and everything on it along as it rotates.

Aristarchus' model was a *heliocentric* model, constructed about 1800 years before Copernicus proposed the one that we use today (in a modified form). Aristarchus visualized the Moon in orbit around a spherical Earth and the Earth in orbit around the Sun. One could argue that Aristotle's argument, based on the lack of observable parallax for the stars, clearly shows that Aristarchus' heliocentric model is wrong. Why, then, did Aristarchus propose such a model? As shown below, the answer lies in the results he obtained about the relative distances and sizes of the Earth, Moon, and Sun.

Relative Distance to the Sun When the Moon is exactly half lit, Aristarchus correctly stated that the angle between the Earth-Moon-Sun is 90 degrees (FIGURE 2-7). However, for the angle Moon-Earth-Sun, he used 87 degrees, instead of the correct value of 89.85 degrees. (A calculation at the end of the chapter offers a possible method that Aristarchus could have used to measure this angle.) Knowing the angles in the right triangle Earth-Moon-Sun, he was then able to obtain a relationship between

The gods did not reveal, form the beginning, all things to us; but in the course of time, through seeking, men find that which is better. But as for certain truth, no man has known it, nor will he know it; neither of the gods, nor yet all things of which I speak. And even if by chance he were to utter the final Truth, he would himself not know it; for all is but a woven web of guesses.
Xenophanes, Greek Historian, 6th century BC

heliocentric Centered on the Sun.

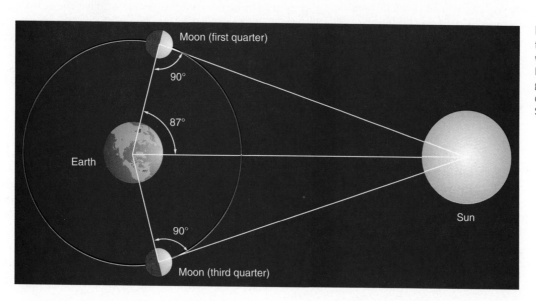

FIGURE 2-7 The positions of the Earth, Moon, and Sun when the Moon is exactly half lit. Aristarchus used this geometry to find the relative distances of the Moon and Sun from Earth.

Moon (first quarter)

90°

87°

Earth

Sun

90°

Moon (third quarter)

ADVANCING THE MODEL

Astrology and Science

Astrology is the belief that the relative positions of the Sun, planets, and Moon affect the destiny of humans. It is often used to determine the nature of a person's personality or of certain circumstances in the future. To discover the astrological effect on an individual, an astrologer designs, or "casts," a horoscope.

Casting a horoscope involves determining the positions of significant heavenly objects at the moment of the person's birth. To do so, the zodiac is divided into 12 equal-sized *signs*, which have the same names as the 12 principal constellations of the zodiac, but differ from them in two ways. First, the constellations differ from one another in size, whereas all signs are the same size. The constellation Cancer, for example, is much smaller than Virgo or Pisces, but their signs are the same size. Second, the signs are at different locations in the sky from the constellations. At one time the positions corresponded fairly well, but because of *precession* (to be discussed in Chapter 3), the signs and constellations are now "off" by about one position. The sign of Aries, for example, is located mostly in the constellation Pisces. This means that a person born on March 22 is said by astrologers to be an Aries, while the Sun actually appeared to be in the constellation Pisces at the person's birth. (Some astrologers, called sidereal astrologers, use the constellations rather than the signs.)

Astrologers divide the sky above us into 12 *houses*, starting with the eastern horizon and proceeding around the sky. The houses do not rotate with the stars, but remain in the same position relative to Earth. Thus, the first house stays above the eastern horizon. The houses are arbitrarily associated with various areas of our lives, such as children, health, and enemies. Likewise, the planets are associated with various good or evil influences. Mars, for example, is associated with war.

When the previous information is determined for the moment of a person's birth, we have what is called the *natal chart* for that person. This chart could be made by anyone who knows the sky and has tables of solar, lunar, and planetary positions. It might be determined, for example, that the planet Mars was just above the eastern horizon at the time of your birth. This is where the astrologer's interpretation comes in, telling you about your personality and life pattern.

Scientific Criteria Applied to Astrology

Having briefly described the nature of astrology, we will now apply to it the criteria for a good scientific theory.

- **Does astrology fit the observations?** It claims to be able to account (at least in part) for our personalities and our characteristics. Can this be true? This question has been tested many times. Invariably, the tests show that astrologers are unable to identify the personality traits of people or to predict future events. (For example, read the report in the December 5, 1985, issue of *Nature* concerning the research done by Shawn Carlson at the University of California.) After numerous tests, we must conclude that astrology fails our first criterion.

- **Does it make verifiable predictions that could possibly prove the theory wrong?** In Carlson's study, astrologers claimed that if enough cases were considered, they could make verifiable predictions. Astrologers would say that it is not fair to test the accuracy of a horoscope of an individual person because it only predicts tendencies, and people do not necessarily follow their tendencies. In other words, you might be very different from what is predicted by your horoscope and still not contradict astrological predictions. If this is the case, there is no way that astrology can be proved incorrect. It therefore fails the second criterion.

- **Simplicity and aesthetics.** Astrology does not pass this test because it is not a single, unified theory at all, but instead is a group of arbitrary rules as to the effect of heavenly objects on people. One could hardly call it aesthetically pleasing.

Because astrology is a faith system, it cannot be disproved to those who believe. People who believe in it do not care whether scientists can explain the belief.

Scientists do not accept astrology as a valid theory. Some scientists strongly object to the publication of astrological columns in newspapers, but others claim that astrology does no harm if people use it only as a pastime and do not let it actually determine what they do with their lives.

the distances Earth-Moon and Earth-Sun. He found that the Sun is about 20 times farther from the Earth than the Moon is, instead of the correct value of about 390. However, this large difference of a factor of about 20 is due to the difference of only about 3 degrees in the choice of the angle Moon-Earth-Sun. What is important here is not the quantitative error, but the power and simplicity of the argument he used to find, 2000 years before anybody else, the relative distance to the Sun.

Relative Sizes of the Moon and Earth From the time it takes the Moon to move through the Earth's shadow during a total lunar eclipse, Aristarchus concluded that the Earth's diameter is about three times larger than the Moon's diameter (the correct ratio is about 3.7). The geometry by which he estimated the relative sizes of the Moon and Earth is shown in FIGURE 2-8. The fact that total solar eclipses just barely occur leads to the conclusion that the angular diameters of the Moon and Sun are about the same as seen from Earth. Aristarchus measured this angular diameter to be 0.5°, and thus he represented Earth's shadow by lines leading away from Earth and converging at an angle of 0.5°. These criteria specified the position and size of the Moon in the Earth's shadow.

Relative Sizes of the Moon and Sun Because the angular diameter of the Moon and the Sun are the same (0.5°) as seen from Earth, Aristarchus correctly concluded that

$$\frac{\text{radius of Moon}}{\text{radius of Sun}} = \frac{\text{distance from Earth to Moon}}{\text{distance from Earth to Sun}}.$$

Using the calculations mentioned here, he found that the Sun is about 20 times larger than the Moon, instead of the correct ratio of about 390; this error is the result of the difference of only 3 degrees in the choice of the angle Moon-Earth-Sun shown in Figure 2-7.

These calculations clearly showed the Sun being much bigger than Earth. As a result, Aristarchus concluded that the Sun, not Earth, must be the central body in the solar system, thus proposing the first heliocentric system. For this, an outraged critic declared he should be charged with impiety.

Aristarchus had made a map of the solar system but did not have the scale for it. If he knew the radius of the Earth and the distance to the Moon, then he could accurately find how big the Moon and Sun were and their exact relative distances.

Measuring the Size of the Earth

The first person to understand clearly the shape and approximate size of the Earth, 1700 years before Columbus, was Eratosthenes (276–195 BC). His calculation of the radius of the Earth is very simple (FIGURE 2-9).

Eratosthenes knew that at noon, during the summer solstice, the Sun shone directly down a well near Syene (the present city of Aswan, in Egypt), casting no shadow. This implied that the Sun was directly overhead, or at the *zenith* at that time.

In his city of Alexandria, on the same day, he noted that the Sun's direction was off the vertical by about 7 degrees. Because he was aware of Aristarchus' results, Eratosthenes could safely assume that the Sun is far away from the Earth, and thus, its light travels in almost parallel rays toward the Earth. He realized that the difference of 7 degrees had to be due to the curvature of the Earth. Because 7 degrees is about 1/50 of a full circle (7/360), Eratosthenes concluded that the Earth's circumference was about 360/7 or 50 times the distance from Alexandria to the site of the well. This distance was about 5000 stadia, where a stadium was a unit of distance equivalent to about 0.15 to 0.2 kilometers. If we assume that one stadium was 1/6 km, then the distance between the two cities is about 830 kilometers. Eratosthenes thus calculated the Earth's circumference to be 50 × 830 = 41,500 kilometers and thus the Earth's radius to be 41,500/2π or about 6600 km. This is amazingly close to the correct value of 6378 kilometers! Combining the calculations of Aristarchus and Eratosthenes, the ancient Greeks had, for the first time,

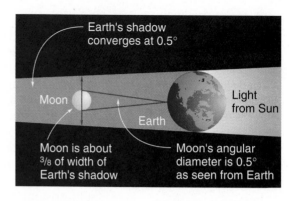

FIGURE 2-8 Aristarchus used the time it takes for the Moon to go through the Earth's shadow to find the relative size of the Earth and Moon.

zenith The point in the sky located directly overhead.

FIGURE 2-9 Eratosthenes calculated the size of the Earth by comparing the Sun's direction off the vertical at two locations at the same time. When the Sun was overhead at Syene, it was 7 degrees from the zenith at Alexandria.

solar system The system that includes our Sun, planets and their satellites, asteroids, comets, and other objects that orbit our Sun.

measurements of the radii of the Earth, Moon, and Sun and the relative distances between them. Even though later astronomers obtained more accurate measurements, we would have to wait until 1769 AD to obtain the actual value of the astronomical unit and thus the true dimensions of the *solar system*.

What is important here is not the accuracy of the measurements. It is the fact that simple logical arguments allowed the ancient Greeks to have a very good sense of the solar system more than 2000 years ago. Sometimes an idea is so revolutionary that it takes a long time for others to become convinced. In this case, the lack of observable parallax for the stars allowed the Ptolemaic model (instead of Aristarchus') to be the accepted model for the heavens for almost 1400 years, until a little after the time of Copernicus. Parallax of stars was successfully measured around 1838 AD. As a result, Aristotle's argument convinced one of the greatest observers of all times, Tycho Brahe (1546–1601), to believe in a geocentric universe decades after the Copernican revolution.

There is a tendency to think that Greek science was bad science because it is not today's science. This is simply not true. It is true that the Ptolemaic model is more primitive than today's. The Greeks did not have the accurate observations and extensive data we have today. Their model, however, did fit the data they had. In fact, it fits the casual observations of most people today. Can you think of any direct evidence obtainable without a large telescope that contradicts Ptolemy's model? What observations can you personally make, without relying on reference materials, which will show the 2000-year-old Ptolemaic model to be a poor model?

2-5   The Marriage of Aristotle and Christianity

During the 13th century, Saint Thomas Aquinas (1225–1274 AD), one of the greatest theologians and philosophers of the Christian church, incorporated the works of Aristotle and Ptolemy into Christian thinking. Aquinas insisted that there must be no conflict between faith and reason, and he blended the natural philosophy of Aristotle with Christian revelation. For the Aristotelian and Ptolemaic ideas we have discussed, the blend was an easy one. The idea of an Earth-centered universe fit comfortably with literal biblical interpretation, for it placed humans at the center of God's creation—the ultimate expression of the divine will (FIGURE 2-10).

The idea of a central, unmoving Earth was natural for early humans. Through the work of Aquinas, this easily accepted idea was shown to fit perfectly with Christian beliefs. So Aristotle's science—and with it the Ptolemaic model—became even more entrenched in Western culture. It was no longer just a natural, normal way of thinking about the world, but was part of Christian thinking and religious dogma.

Why have we presented material that seems to be more closely related to Church history than to science? The reason is that science does not exist apart from human culture. Science and scientists are part of the society in which they live, and it is necessary to know something of the flavor of an age to appreciate the work of the thinkers of that age—including those thinkers who today might be labeled as scientists. It, therefore, is important to emphasize that after the 13th century, the teachings of Aristotle and the Ptolemaic model were an ingrained part of Western thinking.

A very important characteristic of the Middle Ages was a great reliance on authority, particularly on authorities of the past. Today most of us have a much greater tendency to rely on our own thoughts, observations, experiences, and feelings than did people of the times we are discussing. Aquinas relied

FIGURE 2-10 A medieval illustration from a world atlas of 1661, showing a model of the universe with the Earth at its center. This was the model approved by the Catholic Church, which had the power to punish anyone who argued against this model. Each planet is shown being carried by a chariot drawn by winged horses.

on the authority of the Bible, the authority of earlier churchmen, the authority of his superiors in the Church, and the authority of Aristotle. Arguments were often settled by reference to authorities rather than by personal experience or independent experimentation. Into this world came a man who was to cause a revolution in the way people think.

2-6 Nicolaus Copernicus and the Heliocentric Model

At the time when Columbus was journeying to America, a brilliant Polish student was studying astronomy, mathematics, medicine, economics, law, and theology. As was common for scholars of that time, Nicolaus Copernicus did not limit himself to studies in a particular discipline as we do today (perhaps necessarily). He is known today, however, for initiating the revolution that finally resulted in replacing the geocentric system of Ptolemy with a heliocentric—Sun-centered—system.

Copernicus worked on his heliocentric system for nearly 40 years. Even after all this work, he was slow to publish it. It was eventually published with the title *On the Revolutions of the Heavenly Spheres*, but it is often called *De Revolutionibus*, a shortened form of the original Latin title (**FIGURE 2-11**).

Copernicus apparently decided to develop and publish his model for three primary reasons. First, as the centuries had passed, it was found that Ptolemy's predicted positions for celestial objects were not in agreement with the carefully observed positions. For example, Ptolemy's model could be used to predict the position of Saturn on some night in the future. The prediction of its position for a night a few years later was accurate enough, but when the prediction was made for a few centuries in the future, the predicted position might differ from the carefully observed position by as much as 2 degrees. This difference corresponds to about four times the angular diameter of the Moon as observed from Earth. Ptolemy's model had been updated several times through the years so that it would be fairly accurate for awhile. These corrections were not refinements in the way it worked, but were "resettings" of each planet's position that were made to fit the latest observations. As we discussed in Section 2-1, a good model would not require such updating. Copernicus recognized this and sought a more accurate model.

A second reason Copernicus sought another model was that he became convinced after studying the ancient writings that a Sun-centered system would not only provide better data for use by the Church and by astrologers, but that it would also be a more aesthetically pleasing system. He linked astronomy very closely with his religious faith, arguing that placing the Sun at the center of everything is completely logical because the Sun is the source of light and life. The Creator, he said, would naturally place it at the center.

Finally, it has long been known that planets change their brightnesses as they shift positions among the stars. The Ptolemaic system accounted for this with its epicycles, for they would cause a planet to change its distance from the Sun and from Earth. Copernicus noticed, however, that Mars seemed to change in brightness even more than would be predicted by that model. The epicycles of Ptolemy were simply not large enough to explain the great changes in Mars' brightness (Figure 2-5). Thus, Ptolemy's model explained the basic phenomenon, but it did not explain it very precisely when

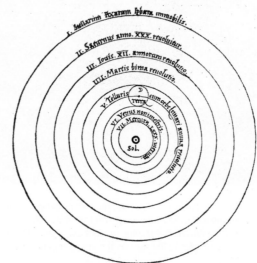

FIGURE 2-11 The Sun-centered model of the Universe that appeared in Copernicus' *De Revolutionibus*. It is said that a copy of the printed book was rushed to Copernicus so that he could see it as he lay on his death bed.

North
celestial pole

North
celestial pole

South
celestial pole

South
celestial pole

(a)

(b)

FIGURE 2-12 (a) The celestial sphere rotating toward the west around a stationary Earth produces the same observed motion of the stars as (b) the Earth rotating toward the east under a stationary celestial sphere.

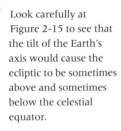

Try the first Activity at the end of this chapter to appreciate the change in outlook as one switches from a geocentric to a heliocentric system.

Look carefully at Figure 2-15 to see that the tilt of the Earth's axis would cause the ecliptic to be sometimes above and sometimes below the celestial equator.

accurate data were used. It was this observation that first prompted Copernicus to reconsider the heliocentric system of Aristarchus, which had lain hidden in obscurity for 2000 years.

We return to a discussion of the criteria for a good model after we have described the model developed by Copernicus.

The Copernican System

Copernicus' system revived many of the ideas of Aristarchus (FIGURE 2-12). In answering Ptolemy's argument that a rotating Earth would produce a great wind, Copernicus stated as an assumption that the air around the Earth simply follows the Earth around. How high above the Earth does this air extend? Copernicus did not answer this question, but his theory requires that the air does not extend all the way to the stars, or even to the Moon.

In Copernicus' heliocentric system, the Earth assumes the role of just another one of the planets, all of them revolving around the Sun. FIGURE 2-13 shows the order of the planets that were known in the 16th century. If we consider the view of Figure 2-13 to be that of someone far out in space above the Northern Hemisphere of the Earth, the planets all move around in a counterclockwise direction, as shown by the arrows in this figure.

FIGURE 2-14 shows the Earth in a circular orbit around the Sun. Its path and the band of stars around the Sun do not appear as circles in the drawing because we are seeing them at an angle. (Remember, we are describing Copernicus' model, not today's model.) In the drawing, when viewed from Earth, the Sun can be thought of as located among certain stars. As the Earth moves around the Sun, the position of the Sun seems to be moving across the background of the stars, which is what we observe. Ptolemy explained it by having the Sun revolve around the Earth independent of the celestial sphere. Copernicus explained it by having the Earth move around a stationary Sun.

Recall from Figure 1-18 that the Sun appears to move from among the stars south of the equator to those north of the equator and back again. To fit this observation, Copernicus' model had the plane of the Earth's equator tilted with respect to the plane of its orbit around the Sun (FIGURE 2-15). (In Chapter 1 we discuss how and why this tilt causes the seasons on Earth.)

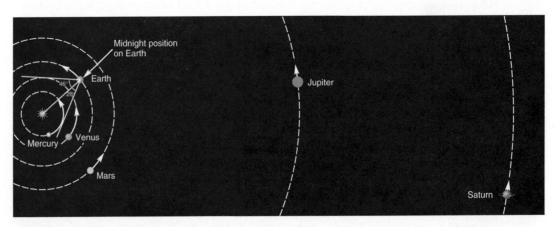

FIGURE 2-13 The planets that can be seen by naked-eye observations, shown in order from the Sun. Their relative orbital speeds are indicated by the lengths of the arrows. Planetary sizes and relative distances from the Sun are not to scale. This figure illustrates the heliocentric model's explanation for the fact that Mercury and Venus never get far from the Sun and can never be seen in the sky late at night. Compare it with Figure 2-6.

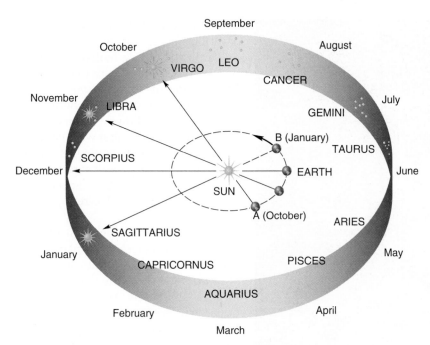

FIGURE 2-14 As the Earth moves around the Sun during the year, the Sun appears to move among the background stars. For example, when the Earth is in position A on its orbit (on October 1), the Sun appears to be in Virgo. (Of course, we cannot see the stars in Virgo or any stars for that matter during daytime.) On this date, however, an observer on Earth's midnight position sees Pisces all night long. Similarly, when the Earth is in position B (on January 1), the Sun appears to be in Sagittarius; however, an observer on Earth's midnight position sees Gemini all night long.

The Moon appears to complete about one revolution around the Earth each month. Copernicus accounted for this in his model by having the Moon on a sphere that revolves around the Earth in that time. For Copernicus, everything else circles the Sun, but the Moon revolves around the Earth.

We stated in Chapter 1 that someone watching the planets from Earth would see that these wanderers spend most of their time moving eastward against the background of the stars, but occasionally, according to a regular schedule that is different for each planet, they move in the opposite direction. Ptolemy explained this motion using epicycles. How does Copernicus' model handle retrograde motion? **FIGURE 2-16** shows several equally spaced positions of the Earth in its orbit, along with the corresponding positions of Mars. This is because Copernicus—like Ptolemy—assumed that the planets move at

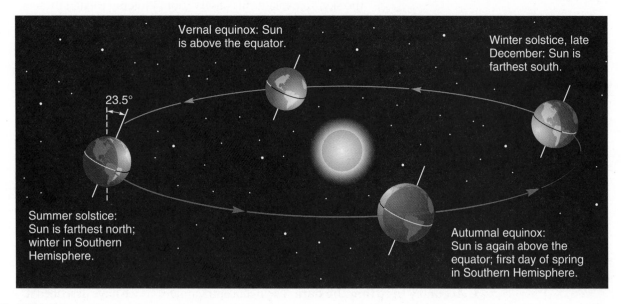

FIGURE 2-15 The Copernican model explains the Sun's apparent motion north and south of the equator by having the Earth's equator tilted with respect to the planet's orbit around the sun.

FIGURE 2-16 This drawing corresponds to Mars' 2003 retrograde motion. While Earth moves from position 1 to position 3, Mars appears to be moving eastward among the background stars. Then as Earth passes Mars, Mars appears to move backward before resuming its eastward motion. This is how the heliocentric model explains retrograde motion. At position 4, Mars is in the middle of its retrograde motion and closer to Earth; as a result, Mars looks brighter.

To picture how this works, think of running circular laps at constant speeds with a friend; you are running on the inside track and faster than your friend who is running on an outer track. Watch your friend against a distant background.

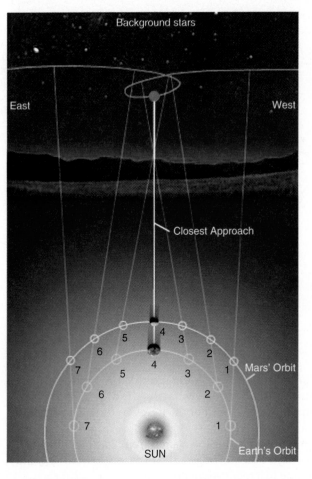

constant speeds. The lines from Earth to Mars illustrate the direction in which we on Earth see Mars. As both planets move on their orbits, Mars seems to move eastward (for the first three positions) among the background stars. Between locations 3 and 5, however, Mars follows a retrograde motion, after which it resumes its eastward motion. Mars reaches its closest distance to Earth at position 4, which explains why the planet looks brighter in the middle of its retrograde motion.

Copernicus was able to calculate the relative distances of the planets from the Sun. Two activities at the end of this chapter show the calculations for Mars and Venus. By such methods, Copernicus predicted that Mars is 1.5 times farther from the Sun than the Earth is. Similar calculations for the other planets yielded for Copernicus the values shown in the center column of **TABLE 2-1**. The table also shows today's measurements. Copernicus had a map of the solar system but without a scale; he did not know the value of the astronomical unit. How do we know the actual distances today? One way to determine distance is to bounce a radar beam from a planet and measure the time it takes for the beam to return. Knowing the speed of the radar signal, we can calculate the distance to the planet and from this the value of the astronomical unit.

Mercury and Venus never get very far from the Sun in the sky. To explain this observation, Ptolemy treated these planets as special cases by requiring that the centers of their epicycles remain along a line between the Earth and the Sun (Figure 2-6). As shown in Figure 2-13, in the Copernican system neither planet can get very far from the Sun as seen from Earth simply because they orbit the Sun at a distance less than the Earth's distance. No matter where Venus is in its orbit, it can never appear farther than 46 degrees away from the Sun as viewed from Earth. There is no way for an observer located at the midnight position on Earth to see Mercury or Venus at midnight.

TABLE 2-1

Planetary Distances: Copernicus' Values versus Today's Values

Planet	Sun-to-Planet Distances	
	Copernicus' Values (AU)	Today's Values (AU)
Mercury	0.38	0.387
Venus	0.72	0.723
Earth	1.00	1.000
Mars	1.52	1.524
Jupiter	5.2	5.204
Saturn	9.2	9.582

2-7   Comparing the Two Models

In Section 2-1 we discussed the scientific criteria for deciding the value of a proposed model. Let's use these criteria to compare the Copernican and Ptolemaic models.

1. Accuracy in fitting the data. The heliocentric model, as we have described it, is able to account qualitatively for the observed motions of the stars, the Moon, and the planets; however, there were differences between the predicted and observed planetary positions. Copernicus sought to increase the accuracy of his model by inserting small

HISTORICAL NOTE

Copernicus and His Times

Mikolaj Koppernigk (or Nicolaus Copernicus by his Latinized name; FIGURE B2-1) was born in Torun, Poland and was educated in Poland and Italy. During most of his life he worked for the Church, serving as canon of the cathedral of Frauenberg, Poland. He lived during an exciting and disturbing time, as a list of some of his contemporaries suggests: Henry VIII, Martin Luther, Michelangelo, Leonardo da Vinci, Christopher Columbus, and Raphael.

Copernicus entered the University of Bologna (Italy) in 1496 and was liberally educated in several subjects. His great interest in astronomy can be attributed to the close link between astronomy and religion at the time. There were two reasons for this link: First, it was important to the Church that its feast days be celebrated at the right time, and this required a correct calendar—a matter for astronomers. (The dates of Easter and the feasts that follow it depend even today upon accurate determination of the time of the vernal equinox.) Second, at the time of Copernicus, astrology was considered a more important study than astronomy, but astrology cannot function without accurate astronomical data.

FIGURE B2-1 Nicolaus Copernicus (1473–1543).

Copernicus lived about 100 years before the invention of the telescope. Measurements of the heavens had to be made with the naked eye, and yet accurate measurements were necessary. One important measurement was the exact time that a celestial object crossed the *meridian*. Copernicus made this measurement by having his house constructed with a narrow slot in one of its walls. By placing himself at the correct location and looking through the slot, he could determine accurately when a given object was crossing (or *transiting*) the meridian.

epicycles for the celestial objects to move on. This was necessary because he assumed—like Ptolemy—that the planets move at a constant speed. In fact, the observed motions did not correspond exactly to planets moving at constant speed. Copernicus' epicycles were smaller than Ptolemy's, and the motion of the planets around them was much slower so that each planet moved in a somewhat elongated circle.

Why did Copernicus not abandon the idea of circles altogether? The reason lies partly in the fact that the circle had such a long tradition and partly in Copernicus' belief that because the motions in the heavens are repetitive, "a circle alone can thus restore the place of a body as it was."

Even with his epicycles, Copernicus' model resulted in errors in predicting planetary positions of about 2 degrees over a few centuries of planetary motion. This is about the same error as in Ptolemy's model. No definitive observation could be made in the 1500s that would decide which of the two competing models fit the data more accurately. For that reason, using the evidence available in the 1500s, we must call our comparison of the models a draw, based on the criterion of data fitting. (Observing stellar parallax, for example, would have clearly shown that the Earth moves and thus supported the heliocentric model. Such observations would also have provided evidence that stars are not all at the same distance from Earth, something that both models assumed; however, stellar parallax was not observed until 1838, and the question had been settled by that time as a result of the contributions of Kepler and Galileo, which we discuss shortly.)

2. Predictive power. Both models made testable predictions. The Ptolemaic model predicted that stellar parallax should not exist, whereas the Copernican model predicted that it would; thus, both pass this test. (A prediction that is eventually disproved by new data is as acceptable as a prediction that is eventually supported by new data.)

The calculations of planetary distances based on the heliocentric model serve as an example of testable predictions made by the model. If later measurements had shown the distances to be wrong, the theory would have suffered a setback.

In the center of everything rules the sun; for who in this most beautiful temple could place this luminary at another or better place whence it can light up the whole at once?...In this arrangement we thus find an admirable harmony of the world, and a constant harmonious connection between the motion and the size of the orbits as could not be found otherwise. Copernicus

As the example of parallax shows, predictions are inherent in models. They need not be stated by the model's designer.

◆ Venus is often called the "morning star" or "evening star" because it is so bright and easily seen in the morning or evening sky. It outshines all surrounding stars.

◆ A person on Mars would never see Mercury, Venus, or Earth around midnight.

◆ Ptolemy's model actually contained further complications, such as the Earth being slightly off-center of the planets' paths. This contributed to Copernicus' conviction that his own system was simpler.

3. Simplicity: Mercury and Venus. Copernicus, and other thinkers of his time and the years following his death, preferred the heliocentric model to the Ptolemaic model even though it had no particular advantage as far as the criteria we have discussed so far. The main reason for this preference was due to our third criterion for a good model: simplicity. To make the comparison, it is instructive to see how the two models treated the motions of Mercury and Venus and the observed retrograde planetary motions.

Both models are able to explain why the observed motions of Mercury and Venus differ from those of the other planets, and both models are able to explain why Mercury and Venus are never seen high in the night sky.

The Ptolemaic model, however, required a special rule to bring this about (Figure 2-6). In the Copernican model, this was a natural consequence of the fact that Mercury's and Venus' orbits are inside the Earth's orbit (Figure 2-13).

Ptolemy used epicycles to explain retrograde motion. Each planet was assigned an epicycle of a certain size, a speed for its motion around the epicycle, and another speed for the center of the epicycle moving around the Earth. The speeds that were assigned did not form a pattern, and as we have seen, Mercury and Venus were special cases. Copernicus, on the other hand, saw a pattern in planetary speeds. According to his model, the farther from the Sun a planet is, the slower it moves in its orbit. This rule of motion was all that was needed to account for retrograde motion. (Copernicus found epicycles necessary to make his model more accurate but did not use them to explain retrograde motion.)

Overall, the descriptions of planetary motions offered by the heliocentric model were simpler, and Copernicus (and others) felt that his was a better model for explaining the heavens. But when one considers both models in their full detail, the final verdict in favor of the heliocentric model seems less than overwhelming.

Why were people of Copernicus' time concerned with how simple and orderly a theory is? This concern arose from a religious belief that a Creator would not have created a disorderly, overly complicated universe. Scientists today would express their desire for simple models in different terms, but the desire is still present. One reason scientists search for a simple model is that our experience since the time of Copernicus tells us that when there are two competing models, the simpler one is more likely to fit new data—data from observations not yet made (Occam's razor). The belief that this pattern will continue with new models is a faith different from that of Copernicus and his supporters. It is a faith in the unity and beauty of nature, based on past experience.

Copernicus died in 1543, just as *De Revolutionibus* was being released. This single book started such an upheaval in people's thinking that the word "revolution" took on a second meaning—an upheaval, as in a social or political revolution. Copernicus began the revolution, but it was up to others to carry it forward to completion.

2-8   Tycho Brahe: The Importance of Accurate Observations

◆ People of Tycho's time are often known by their first names. For example, do you know the last name of Michelangelo?

Three years after Copernicus died, Tycho Brahe (pronounced "bra" or "bra-uh") was born in Denmark (**FIGURE 2-17**). When he was a teenager studying law, he developed an interest in astronomy and learned that both the Ptolemaic and Copernican models were based on recorded planetary data that were inaccurate. That is, he found discrepancies between different tables of observed planetary positions. He was convinced that before a decision could be made about which model was better or before a completely new and better model could be devised, there was a need for more accurate observations of the positions of the planets as they move across the background of stars.

At this time, the telescope had not yet been invented, and thus, all of Tycho's observations were made with the naked eye. In an observatory built for him by King Frederick II of Denmark, Tycho built the largest observing instruments yet constructed. The mural in **FIGURE 2-18** shows some of his equipment. Because of the large size of this equipment, Tycho was able to measure angles to an accuracy of better than 0.1°, far more accurate than any measurements made before his time and close to the limit the human eye can observe.

In addition to making such accurate measurements, Tycho was careful to determine the accuracy of each individual measurement. For example, he would not only state the position of a particular planet, but would also give a value indicating the amount of uncertainty in his measurement. Because of this statement of uncertainty, when such data are later compared with the predictions of a particular model to test the model for accuracy, we can tell how close the predictions

FIGURE 2-17 Tycho Brahe (1546–1601).

of the model should be expected to come to the reported measurements. For example, if Tycho stated that a particular measurement was accurate to 0.1° of angle, then we should expect a model's predictions to come within 0.1° of that measurement. On the other hand, if the model did not make the prediction within 0.1° of the measurement, it would have to be considered not accurate enough. The inclusion of a statement concerning the accuracy of measurements is now a common practice in science, but it was not in Tycho's time.

One tenth of a degree is the angle intercepted by a quarter when viewed face-on from a distance of 50 feet (15 meters).

Tycho's Model

You might expect that the quality of Tycho's observations would convince him of the correctness of the Copernican model. Exactly the opposite was true, for a reason having to do with parallax. Tycho argued that if the Earth were in motion around the Sun, as the Copernican model suggested, then nearby stars should show parallax as the Earth revolved around the Sun. Because he failed to observe any such parallax, he concluded that the Earth must be at the center of the universe and that the Copernican model was wrong. Tycho became famous for his observations of two very important phenomena early on in his career. In 1572 he observed a bright "star," what we now call a supernova explosion, which suddenly appeared in the sky and was observable for about 18 months, and in 1577 he observed a bright comet. What is important about these observations is that Tycho tried to measure the parallax of each of these two objects, but failed. As a result, he concluded that these objects must be very far from the Earth, showing that change occurs in the heavens, a view contrary to thousands of years of traditional belief.

Tycho's model of the heavens was a mix between the Ptolemaic and Copernican models (**FIGURE 2-19**). He positioned the Earth at the center with the Sun revolving around it, but he argued that the other planets were revolving around the Sun. Tycho's conclusion was wrong, but his argument for placing the Earth at the center was a very good one. It was the

FIGURE 2-18 This mural depicts Tycho's quadrant, which was designed to measure the time and the elevation angle of an object crossing the meridian. The quadrant itself consists of the slot at upper left and the large quarter circle. Tycho is shown as the observer at the edge of the mural at right center. In addition, he had himself painted on the quadrant (the large figure on the wall near center) to remind his assistants that he was watching. Tycho's quadrant had a radius of over 2 meters. The large quarter circle in the foreground is drawn to the scale of the people in front. The person shown partially on the drawing at right center is looking past a pointer on the degree markings and through the slot in the wall at upper left.

(a) Ptolemy's Model

(b) Ptolemy's Model (modified)

(c) Copernicus' Model

(d) Tycho's Model

FIGURE 2-19 The models of Ptolemy, Copernicus, and Tycho. The drawings are not to scale. (a) Ptolemy's Earth-centered epicycle theory (around 100 AD) of the layout of the universe, according to which the five visible planets move on epicycles around the Earth. The epicycles of the two innermost planets, Mercury and Venus, are centered on the line joining Earth to the Sun. (b) In this modification of his model, Ptolemy has the Earth displaced slightly from the center of the *deferent* (the circle on which the center of a planet's epicycle moves). The center of the epicycle moves at a constant speed as seen from the equant but not as seen from the Earth or the center. (c) Copernicus' Sun-centered theory of the layout of the universe, 1543 AD. The diagram is simplified; the planets all move on epicycles, similar to those in Ptolemy's theory, but here there are far fewer epicycles. Furthermore, Copernicus used no equants. (d) Tycho Brahe's Earth-centered model of the universe.

same argument used by the ancient Greeks, based on the lack of observable parallax for the stars; as we now know, even the nearby stars are so far away from us that their parallax is very difficult to measure. However, this clearly shows the importance of having many independent observations of the same phenomenon and the difficulty in understanding the universe based on data that will always be incomplete.

Night after night for 20 years, Tycho recorded data concerning the positions of the planets, with particular emphasis on Mars. This data will prove invaluable to Johannes Kepler, an assistant Tycho hired in 1600, the year before he died.

2-9 Johannes Kepler and the Laws of Planetary Motion

During his studies of theology, Kepler learned of the Copernican system and became an advocate for it. As Tycho's assistant, Kepler was assigned the job of working on models of planetary motion. After Tycho's death, Kepler took over most of Tycho's records, and 4 years later, after trying 70 different combinations of circles and epicycles, he finally devised a combination for Mars that would predict its position—when compared to Tycho's observations—to within 0.13° (about one fourth the diameter of the Moon). Recall that before this, a typical error between predicted positions and observed positions was about 2°; however, the error of 0.13° still exceeded the likely error in Tycho's measurements. Kepler knew enough about Tycho's methods to know that an error of 0.13° in the data was too much, and he sought a model that would fit the data to the limits of its precision. This is a tribute both to Kepler's persistence and to his belief in the accuracy of Tycho's careful measurements.

Finally, Kepler decided to abandon the idea of circular orbits for the planets and to try other shapes. He tried various ovals, with the speed of the planet changing in different ways as it went around the oval. After 9 years of work, he found a shape that fit satisfactorily with the observed path of Mars. What's more, he found that the same basic shape worked not just for Mars, but for every planet for which he had data. The shape? An **ellipse**.

The Ellipse

At first glance, an ellipse is nothing more than an oval, but it is more specific than that; not every oval is an ellipse. FIGURE 2-20 shows how to draw an ellipse. Each point where we placed a tack is called a focus of the ellipse. The plural of this word is "foci," so an ellipse has two foci.

Ellipses can be of various **eccentricities (e)**, from $e = 0$ to $e = 1$. The eccentricity of an ellipse is defined as the ratio of the distance between the foci to the longest distance across the ellipse (the major axis). Essentially, the eccentricity tells us how "flat" the ellipse is. For example, if the tacks coincide, the ellipse would be a circle and its eccentricity would be zero (FIGURE 2-21a). If the tacks are a small distance apart, the ellipse would have a small eccentricity and might look like Figure 2-21b. If the

> **ellipse** A geometrical shape of which every point (P) is the same total distance from two fixed points (the foci). (That is, in Figure 2-20, $PF_1 + PF_2 = $ constant = major axis.)

> **eccentricity of an ellipse** The result obtained by dividing the distance between the foci by the longest distance across an ellipse (the *major axis*).

FIGURE 2-20 To draw an ellipse, start with two tacks, a pencil, and a string. Stick the two tacks into a board some distance apart and put a loop of string around them. Then use a pencil to stretch the string as shown. Finally, keeping the string taut, move the pencil around until you have completed the ellipse. Every point (P) on the ellipse is at the same total distance from the two fixed points F_1, F_2 (the foci); that is, $PF_1 + PF_2 = $ constant. Half of the major axis is called the semimajor axis (a) and is what we have previously referred to as the average distance from a planet to the Sun. The semiminor axis is usually denoted by b. The eccentricity can be calculated by $e = \sqrt{1 - (b^2/a^2)}$ or by $e = F_1F_2/2a$.

FIGURE 2-21 (a) An ellipse with zero eccentricity ($e = 0$), that is a circle. (b) An ellipse with a small eccentricity ($e = 0.4$). (c) A more eccentric ellipse ($e = 0.9$).

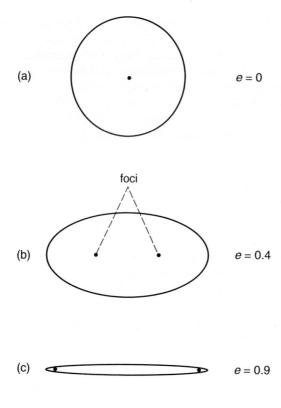

(a) $e = 0$

foci

(b) $e = 0.4$

(c) $e = 0.9$

tacks are farther apart or the string is shorter, the ellipse would have a greater eccentricity and might look like Figure 2-21c. Although different ellipses have different eccentricities, it is important to see that a definite rule governs the shape of an ellipse; that is, every point (P) on the ellipse is at the same total distance from the foci: $PF_1 + PF_2 =$ constant $=$ major axis. Compare this with the definition of a circle, where every point on the circle is at the same distance from a fixed point, the circle's center. In this case, F_1 and F_2 coincide and thus $e = 0$.

An example of an elliptical shape you see every day is that of a circle seen at an angle. FIGURE 2-22 shows a round object seen in perspective. The shape the artist drew to represent the rim of the basket correctly is an ellipse. The eccentricity of such an apparent ellipse is changed by changing your angle of viewing the rim. Viewing it from below, you see a circle, but by viewing it at an angle, you see its apparent shape become more eccentric.

Kepler's First Two Laws of Planetary Motion

Kepler published his first model of planetary motion in 1609 in his book, *The New Astronomy*. Today we summarize his findings for planetary motion into three laws, the first of which is as follows:

> KEPLER'S FIRST LAW: **Each planet's path around the Sun is an ellipse, with the Sun at one focus of the ellipse.**

FIGURE 2-23a shows an elliptical path of a planet around the Sun. We have exaggerated the eccentricity of the ellipse to make it more obvious. Most planets in our solar system move on nearly circular paths.

The second law tells us about the speed of a planet as it moves around its elliptical path. Kepler found that a planet moves faster when it is closer to the Sun and slower when it is farther away. He was able to make a more definite statement than this, however, one that would allow a calculation of the speed:

> KEPLER'S SECOND LAW: **A planet moves along its elliptical path with a speed that changes in such a way that a line from the planet to the Sun sweeps out equal areas in equal intervals of time.**

Suppose we consider the Earth moving in an elliptical path, such as that shown in Figure 2-23b. (The eccentricity of the Earth's orbit in this figure is greatly exaggerated.) Further suppose that point *A* in the figure represents the position of the Earth on December 19, and point *B* is its position on January 18. The yellow-shaded area (area *X*) represents the area "swept out" during this 30-day time period. Then suppose that on June 19 the planet is at point *C*. Kepler's second law tells us that in the next 30 days, the line from the Earth to the Sun must sweep out an area equal to *X* (area *Y* in the figure). Thus, the Earth can only get to point *D* by July 19. To understand this, recall that the area of a triangle is equal to half the product between its base and the height to that base. Even though we are not dealing with perfect triangles here, you see from the figure that the

To solve the problem of how to determine Mars' unknown orbit while riding on planet Earth, whose orbit was also unknown, Kepler selected observations of Mars on the same day in different years. This effectively froze the Earth in position. Then he did the same thing in different *Martian* years to map the orbit of Earth. Clever!

FIGURE 2-22 A circular shape, such as the rim of a basketball hoop, appears elliptical when viewed at an angle.

(a)

(b)

FIGURE 2-23 (a) Kepler's first law states that a planet moves in an elliptical orbit with the Sun at one focus of the ellipse. The orbits of actual planets are much more circular than the ellipse shown here. (b) Kepler's second law: A line from the Sun to a planet sweeps out equal areas in equal times. In the drawing, area *X* = area *Y*.

Earth is closer to the Sun at points *A* and *B* than at points *C* and *D*. The height of the "triangle" corresponding to area *Y* thus is greater than that for area *X* and, therefore, it must have a smaller "base" in order for both triangles to have the same area; that is, the path *CD* is shorter than *AB*. However, the Earth took the same amount of time to cover the paths *AB* and *CD*. We conclude then that the Earth's speed on its orbit is slower when it is farther from the Sun.

In this example, we considered the Earth and a time period of 30 days as it revolves around the Sun. The point of Kepler's second law, however, is that no matter what planet or time interval is selected, the area swept out during that time interval by the imaginary line connecting the planet and the Sun will be the same everywhere on the elliptical journey of the planet.

In essence, Kepler's second law describes how the orbital speed of a planet changes as the planet revolves around the Sun. A planet moves fastest when it is at the nearest point to the Sun (called the ***perihelion***), whereas it moves most slowly at its farthest point from the Sun (called the ***aphelion***).

perihelion/aphelion The closest/farthest point from the Sun on a planet's orbit.

Kepler's Third Law

Kepler went further than Ptolemy and Copernicus in his search for a working model for the heavenly motions. He also asked *why* the planets should have such motions. It was Kepler—not Isaac Newton, whom we discuss in the next chapter—who first hypothesized that there was a force that kept the planets near the Sun: a force we now identify as gravity. In addition to this force, however, Kepler felt that there must be a force sweeping the planets around the Sun. Just like the gravitational force, this force should become weaker with distance. That is why, he argued, the more distant planets move around the Sun more slowly. It was his consideration of this sweeping force that led him to his third law. Although no such sweeping force exists, it helped Kepler find a rule that later led Newton to discover the forces that *do* exist. Kepler's third law allows us to compare the speed of one planet along its path to that of another.

> KEPLER'S THIRD LAW: **The ratio of the cube of the semimajor axis of a planet's orbit to the square of its orbital period around the Sun is the same for each planet.**

The third law is most easily understood when it is expressed in symbols. Let

a = semimajor axis of planet's elliptical orbit =
   (approximately) average distance of a planet from the Sun,

and

P = the planet's orbital period = the time it takes the planet to complete a
   full orbit around the Sun, relative to the stars (called the ***sidereal period***),

then

$$a^3/P^2 = C,$$

The distance in Kepler's third law—that is, the *semimajor axis*, or half the length of the major axis of the orbit—is very nearly the same as the planet's average distance from the Sun.

sidereal period The time it takes a planet to complete a full orbit around the Sun, relative to the stars.

HISTORICAL NOTE

Johannes Kepler

FIGURE B2-2 Johannes Kepler (1571–1630).

Johannes Kepler (FIGURE B2-2) was born in a small town in southern Germany in 1571. When he was 4, he contracted smallpox. The disease left him with poor eyesight, a condition that prevented him from becoming an observer and enjoying the astronomical sights reported to him by Galileo. Instead, his contributions to astronomy resulted from his great mathematical abilities and his insights to the observational data collected by others. Tycho hired Kepler in the hope that the mathematician would be able to verify Tycho's Earth-centered model, but Kepler apparently took the position with the idea of gaining access to the accurate data he needed to test his own ideas.

Kepler was a mathematician of some note; his work on determining volumes of objects by using approximations (inspired by trying to find the most convenient proportions for wine barrels) was an important early contribution to the development of calculus. Today we know Kepler for his three laws of planetary motion, but these laws seem to have been developed almost accidentally as he searched for other, deeper patterns in the heavens. For example, his first great endeavor was to try to find out why the planets are spaced apart as they are. When he was about 24 years old and working as a professor of mathematics, an idea occurred to him while he was lecturing. He was discussing the size of the largest circle that could be drawn inside a triangle and the smallest that could be drawn outside the triangle when he wondered if this could possibly be the basis for the spacings of the planets. After working with various shapes, he decided that it was not two-dimensional figures that were significant, but three-dimensional solids. It was known that only five symmetric solids were possible (the 4-sided tetrahedron, 6-sided cube, 8-sided octahedron, 12-sided dodecahedron, and 20-sided icosahedron). That number is exactly what would be needed to fill the spaces between six planets. FIGURE B2-3 shows a construction that illustrates the plan Kepler finally worked out. Kepler might have saved a lot of time if all of today's planets had been known then, for he would have had too many planets for the five solids.

Kepler's personal life was very difficult, and he was forced to cast horoscopes to support himself and his family. His consolation was that he believed his mathematical and scientific findings were important and would be recognized after he died.

FIGURE B2-3 Kepler worked out a plan using the five regular three-dimensional figures to fix the spheres of the six known planets at their correct distances.

where C is a constant whose value depends on the physical units used for a and P. In using Kepler's third law, any units of measure can be used for the period and the distance. We choose units that make the calculation simple, expressing time in years and average distance in astronomical units (AU). Thus, for the Earth, $a = 1$ AU and $P = 1$ year. Applying Kepler's third law to the Earth we get

$$a^3/P^2 = (1 \text{ AU})^3/(1 \text{ year})^2 = 1 \text{ (AU)}^3/(\text{year})^2.$$

That is, the numerical value of the constant C in Kepler's third law is 1 for all planets in our solar system, as long as we measure the planet's orbital period in years and the semimajor axis of its orbit in astronomical units.

Kepler was very careful to use the sidereal period of a planet in his third law. This is the true orbital period of a planet as it revolves around the Sun, as seen by someone above the solar system, and it differs from its *synodic period*, which is the time it takes for the planet and Sun to be in the same configuration when seen from Earth.

synodic period The time between two successive identical configurations between a planet and the Sun, as seen from Earth.

EXAMPLE

Use the fact that Mars' orbital period is 1.88 years to calculate the average distance of Mars from the Sun.

SOLUTION The third law says that a^3/P^2 is also equal to 1 for Mars when the above units are used. After rewriting the equation, we substitute the value of Mars' period and solve for its distance from the Sun.

$$a^3/P^2 = 1 \ (AU)^3/ \ (year)^2,$$
$$a^3/(1.88 \ year)^2 = 1 \ (AU)^3/ \ (year)^2,$$
$$a^3 = 3.53 \ (AU)^3,$$
$$a = 1.52 \ AU.$$

This agrees with the measured value of the average distance of Mars from the Sun.

TRY ONE YOURSELF
Calculate the radius of Venus' orbit using the fact that its period of revolution around the Sun is 0.615 years. (Venus' orbit is very close to circular and, thus, its average distance from the Sun is essentially the radius of its orbit.)

TABLE 2-2 shows modern data for each of the planets known to Kepler. For completeness, it also includes data for Uranus, Neptune, and Pluto. In each case, Kepler's third law tells us that *to the limits of the accuracy of the data*, the distance cubed is equal to the sidereal period squared. (It is not completely accurate because planets are influenced not only by the Sun but also by the gravitational tug of the other planets.) But it is the synodic period, not the sidereal, that is easily measured from observations. How did Kepler find the sidereal period of a planet? We show how he did it in two calculations at the end of the chapter.

Kepler had fairly accurate data for the orbital periods of the planets. The actual distances to the planets from the Sun were unknown to him, but remember that the

TABLE 2-2				
Testing Kepler's Third Law				
Object	Distance from Sun (AU)	Sidereal period (years)	Distance cubed (AU³)	Sidereal period squared (yr²)
Mercury	0.387	0.241	0.0580	0.0581
Venus	0.723	0.615	0.378	0.378
Earth	1.000	1.000	1.000	1.000
Mars	1.524	1.881	3.540	3.538
Jupiter	5.204	11.862	140.9	140.7
Saturn	9.582	29.457	879.8	867.7
Uranus	19.201	84.011	7079.0	7057.8
Neptune	30.047	164.790	27,127	27,156
Pluto*	39.236	247.68	60,402	61,345
* Dwarf planet.				

In the first place, lest per-chance a blind man might deny it to you, of all the bodies in the universe the most excellent is the sun, whose essence is nothing else than the purest light, than which there is no greater star; it is...called king of the planets for his motion, heart of the world for his power, its eye for beauty, and which alone we should judge worthy of the Most High God.
Kepler

I measured the skies, now the shadows I measure. Skybound was the mind, earthbound the body rests.
Kepler's epitaph, as he composed it.

Copernican system allows us to calculate the *relative* distances to the planets. For example, it was known that Mars is 1.52 times farther from the Sun than the Earth is. This, however, is all that is needed to do calculations with Kepler's third law because 1.52 is the radius of Mars' orbit in AU. So Kepler didn't need to know the actual distances. To the limits of the accuracy of Brahe's data, Kepler's third law fit.

2-10 Kepler's Contribution

Kepler's modification to the Copernican model brought it into conformity with the data; finally, the heliocentric theory worked better than the old geocentric theory. To achieve this fit to the data, however, it had been necessary to abandon the long-held idea of perfect circles in the heavens. Kepler's only reason for proposing ellipses for planetary motion was that they worked.

Our understanding of the solar system would be very unsatisfactory if it had remained where Kepler left it. At the time of Kepler, our scientific understanding of the world was just beginning to take major steps forward, and a man who was a contemporary of Kepler—Galileo Galilei—provided what was needed for the next leap in understanding. The discussion of Galileo's contributions will be left to the next chapter, in which we show how they led, in turn, to the crowning achievements of Isaac Newton.

Conclusion

In this chapter we presented models of the heavens from antiquity to about 1600 AD (FIGURE 2-24), including the two major models of Ptolemy (geocentric) and Copernicus (heliocentric). Both models had simple explanations for the daily motion of the stars and for the annual motion of the Sun, but their explanations of planetary motions were more complicated. Copernicus' model had an aesthetic advantage in that it explained all planetary motions in the same way, whereas Ptolemy's model had special rules for Mercury and Venus; however, when the models were compared in the most important of scientific criteria—fitting the data—the heliocentric system of Copernicus was not significantly better than the old geocentric system. To accept Copernicus' model would mean taking an entirely different view of the world, for his model moved the Earth from its central position and reduced it to being just one of the planets.

Kepler's revision of Copernicus' model solved its data-fitting problem by using ellipses rather than circles and by presenting simple rules for the speeds of planets. Using the criteria for scientific models, we judge Kepler's model a better one than

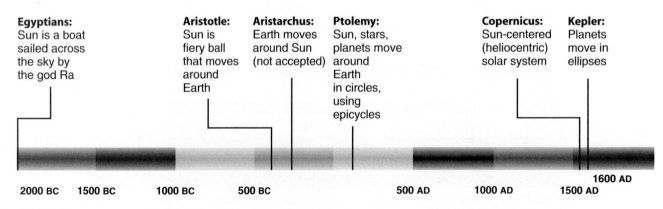

Egyptians: Sun is a boat sailed across the sky by the god Ra

Aristotle: Sun is fiery ball that moves around Earth

Aristarchus: Earth moves around Sun (not accepted)

Ptolemy: Sun, stars, planets move around Earth in circles, using epicycles

Copernicus: Sun-centered (heliocentric) solar system

Kepler: Planets move in ellipses

2000 BC   1500 BC   1000 BC   500 BC   500 AD   1000 AD   1500 AD   1600 AD

FIGURE 2-24 Models of the universe have changed over the past 4000 years with most changes coming in the last 500 years. Chapter 2 takes us only to about 1600 AD.

Ptolemy's. Kepler's revision suffered one flaw, however: the laws he proposed did not "make sense" in that they did not correspond to anything else in nature. They made the model fit the data, and they were reasonably "neat and clean," but they seemed to have been pulled out of thin air. Before the heliocentric system could be fully accepted, it would have to be tied successfully to other phenomena in our experience.

STUDY GUIDE

1. It is _____ to observe Venus in the sky throughout the entire night from central United States.
   A. sometimes possible
   B. always possible
   C. never possible

2. It is _____ to observe Jupiter in the sky throughout the entire night from a point on the Earth's surface.
   A. sometimes possible
   B. always possible
   C. never possible

3. If the plane of the Earth's equator were not tilted with respect to the ecliptic plane,
   A. the daylight period on Earth would be the same year-round.
   B. there would be no seasonal variations on Earth.
   C. Earth's poles would not experience 6-month-long nights.
   D. [All of the above.]

4. Which of the following choices is *not* a criterion for a good scientific theory?
   A. A theory should be aesthetically pleasing.
   B. A theory should be agreed on by all knowledgeable scientists.
   C. A theory should fit present data.
   D. [None of the above; all are criteria for a good theory.]

5. The Copernican model explained retrograde motion as due to
   A. planets moving along epicycles.
   B. planets stopping their eastward motion, moving westward a while, and then resuming their eastward motion.
   C. different speeds of the Earth and another planet in their orbits.
   D. [Both A and B above.]
   E. [None of the above; the Copernican model was unable to explain retrograde motion.]

6. Why was Copernicus forced to use epicycles in his model?
   A. To account for retrograde motion.
   B. To account for phases of the Moon.
   C. To predict accurately the position of a planet.
   D. [Both A and B above.]
   E. [All of the above.]

7. The observation that Mercury and Venus never get high in the night sky was explained by
   A. the geocentric model only.
   B. the heliocentric model only.

   C. both the geocentric and heliocentric models.

8. Which of the following choices could be calculated from the Copernican model but not from the Ptolemaic model?
   A. The length of the day on each planet.
   B. The actual distance from the Sun to each planet.
   C. The relative distance from the Sun to each planet.
   D. The approximate position of a given planet in the sky a few years in the future.

9. If you lived on Jupiter, which of the following planets might you see high overhead during the night (assuming that your sky was clear enough that you could see the stars)?
   A. Mercury and Venus only.
   B. Mercury, Venus, Earth, and Mars only.
   C. All of the planets except Mercury and Venus.
   D. All of the planets except Mercury, Venus, Earth, and Mars.

10. The Sun appears to move among the stars. The Copernican model accounts for this as being due to
    A. the Earth's rotation on its axis.
    B. the Earth's revolution around the Sun.
    C. the actual motion of the Sun against distant stars.
    D. the Earth changing speed in its orbit.
    E. different planets moving at different speeds.

11. If the Earth's diameter were double what it is, stellar parallax would be
    A. easier to observe.
    B. more difficult to observe.
    C. the same, for stellar parallax does not depend on the Earth's diameter.

12. Why did the existence of stellar parallax not convince people of Copernicus' time that his model was better than the geocentric model?
    A. Few people understood stellar parallax.
    B. Stellar parallax was understood, but ignored.
    C. Although most people understood the phenomenon, it was not clear that it provided evidence of the heliocentric theory.
    D. The phenomenon actually provides evidence for a geocentric theory.
    E. Stellar parallax had not yet been observed.

13. According to the heliocentric model, the reason the planets always appear to be near the ecliptic is that
    A. the ecliptic is only 23.5 degrees from the celestial equator.
    B. the planets revolve around the Sun in nearly the same plane.

C. compared with the stars, the planets are nearer the Sun.

D. the planets come much nearer to us than does the Sun.

14. The apparent motion of the planet Jupiter in the sky during a single night as seen by an Earthbound observer is

A. from west to east, then backward a while, and then wet to east again.

B. a west-to-east motion throughout the night.

C. an east-to-west motion throughout the night.

D. [None of the above, for no motion is observed.]

15. According to Kepler's laws, a planet moves

A. at a constant speed through its orbit.

B. fastest when nearest the Sun.

C. fastest when farthest from the Sun.

D. [None of the above, for there is no simple rule.]

16. The primary reason that it is hotter in Australia in December than in July is that

A. the Southern Hemisphere is tilted toward the Sun in December.

B. the Earth is closer to the Sun in December than in July.

C. the Earth is moving faster in its orbit in December than in July.

D. the Earth is on the hotter side of the Sun in December.

E. [Both B and C above.]

17. If the Earth were in an orbit closer to the Sun, the

A. day would be longer.

B. day would be shorter.

C. year would be longer.

D. year would be shorter.

E. [Two of the above are correct.]

18. Kepler's law of equal areas predicts that a planet moves fastest in its orbit when

A. it is closest to the Sun.

B. it is closest to the Earth.

C. the Earth, Moon, and Sun are in a line.

D. it is farthest from the Sun.

E. [None of the above; the law makes no predictions as to speed.]

19. If there were another planet between Mercury and Venus,

A. its "day" would be shorter than Earth's.

B. its "year" would be shorter than Earth's.

C. its speed in orbit would be less than Earth's.

D. [Both A and C above.]

E. [Both B and C above.]

20. From the law of equal areas, one can predict that the Earth

A. moves the same distance in January as in July.

B. moves faster when it is closer to the Sun.

C. spins faster when it is closer to the Sun.

D. [Both A and C above.]

E. [Both B and C above.]

21. If a planet were found at a distance of 3 AU from the Sun, its sidereal period would be

A. about 2.1 years.

B. 3 years.

C. about 5.2 years.

D. 9 years.

E. about 0.3 years.

22. If a new planet were found with a period of revolution of 6 years, what would be its average distance from the Sun?

A. About 2 AU.

B. About 3.3 AU.

C. 6 AU.

D. About 9 AU.

E. 36 AU.

23. Ptolemy's system of epicycles was used to explain the apparent

A. daily motion of the stars.

B. annual motion of the Sun around the sky.

C. backward motion of the Moon through the sky.

D. changing speeds and directions of the planets among the stars.

E. motion of the Sun north and south of the celestial equator.

24. In science, what is the difference between a *theory* and a *hypothesis*?

A. A hypothesis is more fully developed than a theory.

B. A theory is more fully developed than a hypothesis.

C. A hypothesis is based on a model, while a theory isn't.

D. There is essentially no difference. The words are interchangeable.

25. Eratosthenes calculated the size of the Earth from

A. angles to the Sun from locations a measured distance apart.

B. angles to the Moon from locations a measured distance apart.

C. its angular size and distance from the Sun.

D. its orbital speed and distance from the Sun.

E. its calculated rotational speed.

26. In what century did Ptolemy live?

27. What observation convinced Pythagoras that the Earth was spherical?

28. What is an epicycle and what did the use of epicycles enable us to explain?

29. Define *geocentric*.

30. List three criteria for a good scientific model.

31. Which of the criteria for a scientific model is the most important?

32. Explain how Eratosthenes measured the diameter of the Earth.

33. Identify or define: heliocentric, geocentric, astronomical unit, *De Revolutionibus*.

34. How did the Copernican model explain the daily motion of the heavens?

35. How did the Copernican model explain retrograde motion?

36. Why was Copernicus forced to use epicycles in his model?

37. Name a discovery made in the 19th century that the Copernican model fits (or can be made to fit), but the Ptolemaic model does not.

38. What rule did the Copernican model have concerning the speed of one planet compared with another?

39. How did each model explain why Mercury and Venus are never seen in the night sky?

40. Explain how to draw an ellipse, including how to draw one with more or less eccentricity.

41. State and explain Kepler's second law, the law of equal areas.

42. List the planets known in Kepler's time in order of their speeds in orbit. List them in order of their distances from the Sun.

43. Copernicus had stated that planets farther from the Sun move slower than nearer ones. What did Kepler's third law add to this statement?

1. Science never arrives at a final answer. As it answers one question, it just finds more. Why then should we continue doing science?

2. The ancient Greeks believed that "the universe is comprehensible" and that it can be described using mathematics. We consider this to be one of their most important contributions. What do you think we mean by saying that "nature is rational"?

3. What is meant by saying that one criterion for a good scientific model is its aesthetic quality?

4. Ptolemy's model placed the Sun on a sphere whose axis was not the same as the axis of the celestial sphere. Why was it necessary for the Sun's sphere to have a different axis?

5. Why did Ptolemy include epicycles in his model?

6. Explain why the Greeks used circles and spheres to account for heavenly motions.

7. What observation forced the Ptolemaic model to locate the center of Venus' and Mercury's epicycles on a line between the Earth and the Sun?

8. Name the three criteria for a good scientific model and discuss their relative importance.

9. Describe one observation that would disprove the Ptolemaic model and explain why it would conflict with the model.

10. We sometimes speak of the sky as being "the Heavens," and it is traditional in Christian circles to speak of a spiritual heaven as being up above us. Cite a pre-Christian historical reason for this link between the sky and heaven.

11. Explain the concept of Occam's razor by giving an example of its use in distinguishing which is the better of two hypotheses. (You may make up two hypotheses about some everyday event if you wish.)

12. Ptolemy observed parallax of the Moon against the distant stars. Explain how this can be observed. (Hint: It is not due to the motion of the Moon or of the Earth around the Sun.)

13. Was Ptolemy's model based on his own observations? Discuss the origin of the ideas in his model.

14. According to the Copernican model, what causes the Sun to change its position periodically from south of the equator to north of the equator and back again?

15. Compare the Copernican and Ptolemaic models as to their accuracy in fitting the data available in the 16th century.

16. What is Occam's razor and why is it important in considering the value of a scientific theory?

17. Explain why Copernicus was dissatisfied with Ptolemy's model.

18. Compare the Ptolemaic and Copernican models as to how each explains the Sun's apparent motion among the stars.

19. What observation led Tycho Brahe to develop his own model of the solar system? Describe his model.

20. It might be possible to prove a theory false, but it is never possible to prove it true. Explain.

21. When you read how each of the models explained retrograde motion, you may have found it easier to understand the explanation of the Ptolemaic model than the explanation of the Copernican model. If so, how can Copernicus' explanation for retrograde motion be called the simpler one?

22. Suppose that you have a friend across the Atlantic with whom you converse on the telephone. Describe a measurement that the two of you might make that would allow you to calculate the distance of the Moon. (Assume that you know how far apart the two of you are.)

23. When observed from Earth, Mercury and Venus have different motions than other planets. Describe this difference. (Hint: We can NOT observe directly that these planets are closer to the Sun than other planets.) Compare Copernicus' explanation for this difference with Ptolemy's explanation.

24. What is meant by the "eccentricity" of an ellipse? What is the eccentricity of a circle?

25. The Earth is closest to the Sun in January. Then why do we not experience our hottest weather in January?

1. Calculate the radius of Jupiter's orbit (in astronomical units) from data available to Copernicus. Data: Jupiter's sidereal period is 11.86 years, and quadrature occurs 87.5 days after opposition. (Hint: see the activity "The Radius of Mars' Orbit.")

2. Jupiter's semimajor axis is 5.2 AU. What are the smallest and largest distances possible between Earth and Jupiter?

3. A comet moves around the Sun on a highly eccentric orbit. Assume that its distance from the Sun at perihelion is 0.1 AU. The comet's period is 729 years. Use Kepler's third law to find the average distance of the

comet from the Sun and the largest distance between the comet and the Sun.

4. Mercury's period of revolution is 88 days, or 0.24 years. Use Kepler's third law to calculate its average distance from the Sun in astronomical units.

5. The planet Uranus was discovered in 1781. The semi-major axis of its orbit is 19.2 AU. Calculate its period of revolution around the Sun.

6. A quarter at 50 feet spans an angle of about 0.1 degrees. About how many quarters could be placed side by side around a circle with a radius of 50 feet?

7. The eccentricity of Pluto's orbit is 0.24. Use a drawing of an ellipse to explain what this means quantitatively.

8. Suppose you live on planet X. One day the Sun is directly over a place 500 km to your south, while at your position the Sun's direction is 10 degrees off vertical. What is the radius of planet X?

9. The time between successive similar phases for the Moon is on the average about 29.53 days. (In Chapter 1, we defined this time period as a *lunar month* or the *synodic period* of the Moon.) If it takes the Moon an average of 1.2 hours more to go from first to third quarter than to go from third to first quarter, show that the angle Moon-Earth-Sun in Figure 2.7 is about 89.85 degrees.

10. **Synodic versus sidereal period.** FIGURE 2.25a shows the circular (as assumed by Copernicus) orbits of Jupiter and Earth. The time the Earth takes for a complete orbit with respect to the distant stars is its sidereal period (P_E), which is 1 year. The time Jupiter takes for a complete orbit is its sidereal year (P_{sid}). The time it takes Jupiter between successive similar alignments (for example, between **oppositions**, when the Sun and

Jupiter are on opposite sides of the Earth) is its synodic period (P_{syn}). Between two successive oppositions, the Earth covers an angle of $(360°/P_E) \cdot P_{syn}$, while Jupiter covers $(360°/P_{sid}) \cdot P_{syn}$. However, the Earth has covered a full 360 degrees more than Jupiter has. Therefore, $(360°/P_E) \cdot P_{syn} = (360°/P_{sid}) \cdot P_{syn} + 360°$. Show that $P_{sid} = P_{syn}/(P_{syn} - 1)$. Using the observed synodic period of Jupiter (398.9 days), show that its sidereal period is 11.86 years. Also show that the angle θ in the figure is about 33 degrees. (Watch for the conversion between days and years.) Copernicus used the same logic to find the sidereal periods of Mars and Saturn.

11. **Synodic versus sidereal period.** Figure 2-25b shows the circular (as assumed by Copernicus) orbits of Earth and Venus. The time the Earth takes for a complete orbit with respect to the distant stars is its sidereal period (P_E), which is 1 year. The time Venus takes for a complete orbit with respect to the distant stars is its sidereal period (P_{sid}). The time it takes Venus between successive similar alignments (for example, between **inferior conjunctions**, when the Sun and the Earth are on opposite sides of Venus) is its synodic period (P_{syn}). Between two successive inferior conjunctions, the Earth covers an angle of $(360°/P_E) \cdot P_{syn}$, while Venus covers $(360°/P_{sid}) \cdot P_{syn}$. However, Venus has covered a full 360 degrees more than Earth has. Therefore, $(360°/P_{sid}) \cdot P_{syn} = (360°/P_E) \cdot P_{syn} + 360°$. Show that $P_{sid} = P_{syn}/(P_{syn} + 1)$. Using the observed synodic period of Venus (583.9 days), show that its sidereal period is 224.7 days. Also show that the angle θ in the figure is about 215 degrees. (Watch for the conversion between days and years.) Copernicus used the same logic to find the sidereal periods of Mercury.

(a)

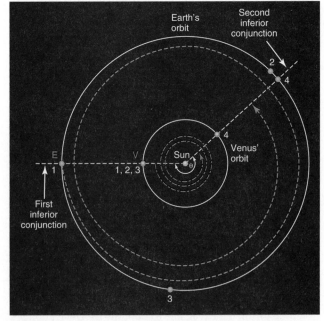

(b)

FIGURE 2-25 These diagrams show the relationship between the synodic and the sidereal period of the planet. The orbits are not in scale; however, for the cases shown, the corresponding positions of each planet (shown by numbers) are accurate.

ACTIVITIES

1. Calculating the Earth's Radius

Let us assume that you would like to repeat Eratosthenes' calculation of the radius of the Earth. However, neither you nor your friend who volunteered to help you live at a place where the Sun is directly overhead at any day of the year. You decide to give it a try anyway. Both of you set a stick vertically in the ground and around noontime on the same day you measure the smallest shadow that the stick makes on the ground. You know the size of your stick and therefore, by drawing a scale of a right triangle (vertical stick and horizontal ground) you are able to determine the angle that the Sun's direction makes with the vertical. You also know the direct, north-south distance between your locations. Do you have enough information to find the size of the Earth? If yes, how would you calculate it?

2. The Radius of Venus' Orbit

In this activity, we measure the orbital radius of Venus. This is the method used by Copernicus to measure the orbital radius of the two **inferior planets**, Venus and Mercury (called this because their orbits are smaller than Earth's).

Mark a location for the Sun on the right side of a piece of paper, and draw an arc of a circle about halfway across the paper, representing the orbit of the Earth. The radius of this circle represents 1 AU. Make a scale drawing and assume that the Earth and Venus move in circular orbits. Then draw a line from the Sun horizontally across the paper and mark its intersection point with the Earth's orbit as the position of the Earth. Copernicus measured the angle between the Sun and Venus, when Venus was at its **greatest elongation**. This is the farthest from the Sun that Venus is seen to be in the sky from Earth. Therefore, when an inferior planet is at its greatest elongation, it means that the line connecting it with the Earth is tangent to the planet's orbit. The angle measured by Copernicus for Venus was 46 degrees.

Center a protractor on the Earth so that the Sun is at 0 degrees. Mark a point at 46 degrees and draw a line from the Earth to that point, extending it a bit further. Draw the perpendicular to this line from the Sun. This perpendicular distance is the radius of Venus' orbit. Using a compass you can now draw the orbit of Venus. Measure the radius of Venus' orbit; divide this by the Earth's distance to the Sun and compare your result with that in Table 2-1. Are you close?

3. The Radius of Mars' Orbit

Let us determine the radius of Mars' orbit from data available to Copernicus. To do so, we start by making a scale drawing, assuming that the Earth and Mars move in circular orbits. Mark a location for the Sun on one side of a piece of paper. As in **FIGURE 2-26a**, draw an arc of a circle about halfway across the paper to represent the orbit of the Earth. Then draw a line from the Sun horizontally across the paper. Suppose that when the Earth crosses your horizontal line, Mars is also crossing it, so the Sun and Mars are on opposite sides of the Earth. (Mars is then said to be in **opposition**.) Mars and the Earth are now moving in the direction shown in Figure 2-26a. Now suppose that Mars is observed night after night until it is at **quadrature**, which is defined as the position when Mars is 90 degrees from the Sun in the sky (seen from Earth), as shown in Figure 2-26c. This is observed to occur 106 days after opposition. This observation, along with the sidereal period of Mars (1.88 years), is all that we need to determine the radius of its orbit.

To draw your figure to scale, you must first calculate the angle through which the Earth moves in 106 days. This is obtained by dividing 106 days by 365 days and multiplying by 360 degrees. Draw a line from the Sun at the angle you have calculated (angle X in Figure 2-26b), and determine the position of Earth (point E) when Mars is at quadrature.

Because Mars is at quadrature when the Earth reaches point E, you should start at E and draw a line toward the right 90 degrees from the line to the Sun. This line points to the planet Mars. You don't know yet where Mars is located on this line. You can determine this by calculating the angle Mars moves through in 106 days. Use its period of 1.88 years to calculate this angle. (Because 1.88 years is 686 days, Mars moves 106/686 of a complete circle in 106 days.) Starting from the Sun, draw a line at the angle you have calculated

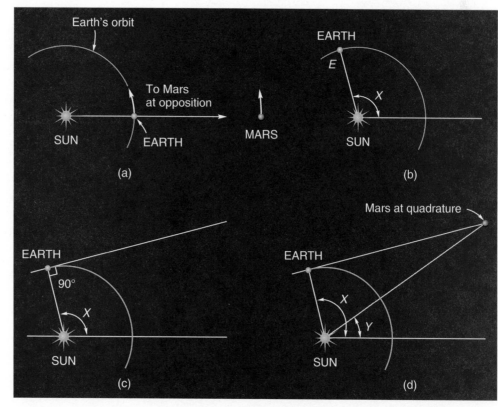

FIGURE 2-26 Steps involved in determining the radius of an outer planet's orbit. This figure is not drawn to scale, as yours must be.

(angle *Y* in Figure 2-26d). Because Mars lies along this line, it must be located where the two lines cross.

Measure the distance from the Sun to Mars, divide this by the Earth's distance to the Sun, and compare your result with that in Table 2-1. Are you close? This was the method used by Copernicus to measure the radius of not only Mars' orbit but also the orbital radius of every **superior planet**, that is, of every planet with an orbit larger than Earth's.

1. M. Caspar: *Kepler* (Dover, 1993).

2. O. Gingerich: *The Great Copernicus Chase, and Other Adventures in Astronomical History,* a collection of essays including the period of Copernicus and Kepler (Sky Publishing/Cambridge University Press, 1992).

3. "Observing the Occasion" by E. C. Krupp, a short biography of Tycho, in *Sky & Telescope* (December 1996).

4. "Copernicus and Tycho" by O. Gingerich, in *Scientific American* (December 1973).

5. A simple description of archaeoastronomy is given in "Archaeoastronomy: Past, Present, and Future" by A. Aveni (*Sky & Telescope*, November 1986, p. 456).

6. A recounting of Eratosthenes' experiment is given by Carl Sagan in *Cosmos* (Random House, 1980), in the chapter entitled, "The Shores of the Cosmic Ocean."

7. "From Aristarchus to Copernicus" by O. Gingerich, in *Sky & Telescope* (November 1983, p. 410).

8. An award-winning history of the development of astronomical thought is given by T. Ferris in *Coming of Age in the Milky Way* (Morrow, 1988).

9. The book *Introductory Readings in the Philosophy of Science, 3rd ed.* (edited by E. D. Klemke, R. Hollinger, D. Wyss Rudge, and A. D. Kline; Prometheus Books, 1998) has a number of interesting articles on science, including P. Thagard's "Why Astrology is a Pseudoscience."

Quest Ahead to Starlinks
http://physicalscience.jbpub.com/starlinks

Starlinks is this book's online learning center. It features **eLearning**, which contains chapter quizzes and other tools designed to help you study for your class. You can also find **online exercises**, view numerous relevant **animations**, follow a guide to **useful astronomy sites** on the Internet, or even check the latest **astronomy news** updates.

EXPANDING THE QUEST

STARLINKS

Gravity and the Rise of Modern Astronomy

3

ON JULY 20, 1969, HUMANS LANDED FOR THE FIRST TIME on another astronomical object. From the Moon's Sea of Tranquility they reported to mission headquarters in Texas, "Houston, Tranquility Base here. The Eagle has landed." Shortly thereafter, Neil A. Armstrong stepped onto the surface of the Moon saying, "That's one small step for a man, one giant leap for mankind." (Historians might note that although the words quoted here are what Armstrong meant to say, he actually left out the word "a.")

Armstrong and Edwin (Buzz) Aldrin, Jr., stayed on the Moon for 21.6 hours. When they left the lunar module, each wore a 90-kilogram spacesuit. On Earth this weighed about 200 pounds, but on the Moon it weighed a mere 33 pounds. During their 2.5 hours of walking on the Moon outside the lunar module, they deployed several instruments to measure various features of the Moon and unveiled a plaque that reads, "Here Men From Planet Earth First Set Foot Upon the Moon. July 1969 AD. We Came in Peace For All Mankind." As they left the Moon to rejoin Michael Collins in the command module and return to Earth, the plaque remained behind to express for ages to come a lofty ambition of the human race.

Apollo 11 astronaut Buzz Aldrin stands next to a lunar seismometer, looking back toward the lunar landing module.

All cross references to chapters, sections, figures, and tables pertain to the main text, *In Quest of the Universe, Sixth Edition. In Quest of the Solar System* contains Chapters 1–11 and 19 of the main text. *In Quest of the Stars and Galaxies* contains Chapters 1–5 and 11–19 of the main text.

The flight to the Moon and back was made possible by many people and many discoveries, some of which we discuss in this chapter. Perhaps the most basic discovery of all was that the laws of physics that describe motion on the Earth are the same laws that describe motion on the Moon and, indeed, everywhere else in the universe. Neil Armstrong's step onto the lunar surface was the last step in a sequence of events dating back over 300 years, with contributions from some of the greatest scientific minds of all time. Their work led to the exploration of space as well as to the rise of modern astronomy.

Although Kepler's laws succeeded in adding accuracy to the heliocentric system, it was the work of Galileo Galilei and Isaac Newton that led to the final triumph of that system. We usually credit the beginning of modern science to Galileo, while the work of Newton helped describe gravity and the causes of planetary motions. Newton formulated some of the fundamental laws of physics, and his work not only helped us understand the force of gravity, but also sparked the technological developments of the Industrial Revolution. In the 20th century, Albert Einstein changed our understanding of such basic concepts as space, time, and mass, refining Newton's laws to make them applicable to the vast regions and exotic objects that we find in a universe much larger and more wondrous than Newton envisioned.

In this chapter we look first at how Galileo's use of the telescope established the validity of the heliocentric system. Then we examine how Newton's new description of mechanical motion and his law of gravitation successfully explained the motions of celestial objects so that only a few unsolved problems remained. Those remaining problems were not solved until Einstein proposed an entirely new theory, the general theory of relativity.

3-1   Galileo Galilei and the Telescope

The contributions of Galileo Galilei to our understanding of the solar system consisted both of observations and theory. His observations were of particular value because he was the first person to use a telescope to study the sky. Galileo built his first telescope in 1609, shortly after hearing about telescopes being constructed in the Netherlands.

Several of Galileo's observations with his telescope affected the comparison between the geocentric and heliocentric theories, as we discuss later:

- Mountains and valleys on the Moon
- Sunspots—dark areas on the Sun that move across its surface
- More stars than can be observed with the naked eye
- Four moons of Jupiter
- The complete cycle of phases of the planet Venus (similar to the Moon's phases)

◆ The word *moon* is not capitalized here. In this book, when talking in general about satellites of planets, we will use lowercase letters. Earth's satellite is named "Moon"; thus, we capitalize its name.

FIGURE 3-1 Even a small telescope reveals features such as mountains and craters on the Moon. This photo was taken with an 8-inch aperture telescope.

Observing the Moon, the Sun, and the Stars

The first three observations in the list provide no data that completely rule out either theory. However, they cast doubt on basic assumptions of the geocentric theory. The Ptolemaic idea of the perfection of the heavens was at the heart of the geocentric system, yet Galileo's telescope (like the small telescope used for **FIGURE 3-1**) revealed Earth-like features on the Moon, such as mountains and craters. Also, in the case of the Sun, the existence of dark spots did not fit at all with the idea of perfection in the celestial realm (FIGURE 3-2).

Galileo's telescope also revealed that the sky contains many more stars than had previously been imagined. Thomas Aquinas had incorporated the Ptolemaic model into Christian theology. Part of this idea was the centrality of humans, not only in position, but in importance. Passages in the first book of the Bible can be interpreted to indicate that the stars were put in the sky for the exclusive purpose "to shed light on the Earth" (Gen. 1:17). Why, then, do stars exist that are so dim that they cannot even be seen by the unaided eye? What is their purpose? The existence of these stars seemed to undermine the Ptolemaic model, and with it a literal interpretation of the Bible. For this reason, many people in Galileo's time simply refused to look through a telescope at the stars.

Jupiter's Moons

In January 1610, Galileo turned his attention to Jupiter. Near the planet, he saw three very faint "stars." They were all in line, two east of the planet and one west. As he continued to observe them night after night, he noted that there were four "stars," rather than three, and it became clear to him that they were not stars at all, but natural satellites—moons—of Jupiter. He concluded that they were objects that revolve around the planet, just as the planets themselves revolve around the Sun in the heliocentric model. (Today we call these four satellites the **Galilean moons** of Jupiter.)

The fact that they never appear north or south of the planet indicated to Galileo that their orbital plane is aligned with the Earth. FIGURE 3-3 shows that someone viewing Jupiter's satellites from Earth would see them moving back and forth from one side of the planet to the other.

The Ptolemaic model held that everything revolves around the Earth, a special object in the model. Galileo's observation of Jupiter's satellites indicated otherwise.

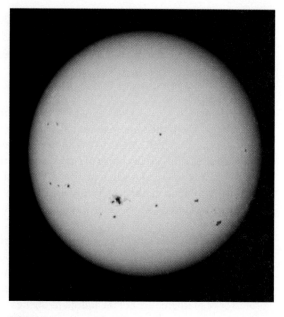

FIGURE 3-2 Sunspots appear as dark spots on the Sun's surface. See Chapter 11 for more details on sunspots.

Galilean moons The four natural satellites of Jupiter that were discovered by Galileo. Their names, starting closest to Jupiter, are Io, Europa, Ganymede, and Callisto.

(a)

(b)

(c)

FIGURE 3-3 (a) The orbits of Jupiter's Galilean satellites as seen face on. (b) The same satellites and orbits seen almost edge on. From Earth, this is how this system appears. (c) This 1979 photo from the *Voyager 2* spacecraft shows the moons Io (left) and Europa (right) in front of Jupiter.

HISTORICAL NOTE

Galileo Galilei

Galileo Galilei (FIGURE B3-1) was born in Pisa, Italy on February 15, 1564, the same year that Shakespeare was born (and Michelangelo died). At age 12 Galileo went away to school, studying the usual course of Greek, Latin, and logic. He entered medical school when he was 17, but lost interest in it and took up mathematics. However, he was forced to leave school after 4 years, before graduating, because of a lack of money.

While in medical school, he invented a pendulum device for measuring pulse rates. After leaving school, he continued to study mathematics, applying it to the physics of motion and of liquids. At the age of 25, he was appointed professor of mathematics at Pisa and spent the next 2 decades as a college professor.

In his early years, Galileo had little interest in astronomy, but medical students whom he taught were required to learn some astronomy for use in medical astrology. He therefore became quite familiar with the Ptolemaic model. In 1597, however, he obtained a book published by Kepler concerning the Copernican theory. Galileo apparently preferred the Copernican theory from the time he learned of it, but kept these ideas secret (except from Kepler and a few others) to avoid controversy. Not until his publication of *Letters on Sunspots* in 1613, well after many of his telescopic discoveries had been made, did he openly espouse Copernicus' ideas.

Galileo's announcement of support for the heliocentric system started an uproar that would cause him—and society in general—much grief. One factor contributing to the opposition engendered by the *Letters* was that Galileo did not write them in Latin, the "international" language at the time in which most scholarly writings were written and which was understood by well-educated people in all countries. Instead, Galileo chose Italian, his native language and that of the ordinary literate person, because he was convinced that people other than scholars could understand his arguments and his evidence that the Copernican system was correct.

Primarily because of this controversy, in 1616 the Roman Catholic Church declared that the Copernican doctrine was "false and absurd" and issued a proclamation prohibiting Galileo from holding or defending it. Why did the church make such a strong statement? We must recall the times and the fact that the Ptolemaic theory and Aristotelian physics were a definite part of both religious doctrine and the general culture.

The Catholic Church was not alone in voicing opposition to the Copernican theory. Martin Luther, who was a contemporary of Copernicus, had called Copernicus "the fool who would overturn the whole science of astronomy." John Calvin asked, "Who will venture to place the authority of Copernicus above that of the Holy Spirit?" To appreciate why religious leaders were so concerned about this issue, we must realize that they considered the spiritual salvation of the individual of paramount importance—more important than answering the question of what is the best theory of the universe. They feared that the idea of a nongeocentric model might seem to undermine the supremacy of humans in God's plan, thereby confusing people and threatening their chance of salvation.

FIGURE B3-1 Galileo Galilei (1564–1642).

An Inquisition court sentenced Galileo, at the age of 70, to house arrest for life; it also banned his book *A Dialogue on the Great World Systems*, published in 1632, in which two fictional characters debate whether or not the Earth is at the center of the universe. Galileo was forced to abandon publicly "the false opinion" that the Sun is at the center of the universe, thus avoiding the fate of Giordano Bruno (a mystic and astronomer who also believed in the heliocentric model), who was burned at the stake 33 years earlier. In the end, the church was not able to stop the spreading of the new ideas, and in 1992, Pope John Paul II formally accepted that it was a mistake to condemn Galileo. He also proclaimed that knowledge obtained by science is soundly based on evidence and that this knowledge "reason can discover by its own power."

The important point in Galileo's story is not what the church did, but that similar things happen in cultures and societies around the world. (Actually, the Catholic Church supports the work of many professional astronomers and the Vatican Observatory, one of the oldest astronomical institutes in the world). There are many examples in our history, in many fields, where the status quo defends a specific ideology against new ideas that turn out to be true. It takes courage to defend one's ideas and to be open to the possibility of being proved wrong.

(a)

(b)

(c)

(d)

FIGURE 3-4 When viewed through a telescope, Venus exhibits a full set of phases, including (d) full, (c) gibbous, and (a and b) crescent. The planet's apparent size changes as it goes through its phases.

In the heliocentric system, everything revolves around the Sun. The Earth is just one of the planets, and Galileo's observation of a "solar system" in miniature does not contradict the model. In addition, the fact that Jupiter is able to move through space without leaving its satellites behind conflicts with the Aristotelian/Ptolemaic view, which held that if the Earth moved through space it would leave the Moon behind.

The Phases of Venus

The observation that Galileo found most convincing in supporting the heliocentric theory was that of a complete set of phases for the planet Venus. **FIGURE 3-4** shows four photographs of Venus at different times. It exhibits phases, similar to the Moon. To the naked eye, Venus appears as a dot of light, but Galileo's telescope revealed its phases. When the entire disk of Venus is seen lit, Venus is said to be in *full* phase (Figure 3-4d). (A full Moon is similar; we see the entire Moon lit.) When more than half but less than the entire disk of Venus is seen lit, it is said to be in a *gibbous* phase (Figure 3-4c). Venus is said to be in a *crescent* phase when less than half of its lit disk is visible (Figures 3-4a and b).

Repeated observations of Venus lead us to conclude that Venus never gets far from the Sun in the sky. It always appears either in the east shortly before sunrise or in the west shortly after sunset, and it is never seen high overhead at night. Ptolemy explained this by saying that the center of Venus' epicycle always remains on a line that joins the Earth and the Sun (**FIGURE 3-5a**).

What phases of Venus would we see according to the Ptolemaic model? In Figure 3-5a, the sunlit side of Venus never faces the Earth. At times we should be able to see

full (phase). The phase of a celestial object when the entire sunlit hemisphere is visible.

gibbous (phase). The phase of a celestial object when between half and all of its sunlit hemisphere is visible.

crescent (phase). The phase of a celestial object when less than half of its sunlit hemisphere is visible.

(a)

(b)

FIGURE 3-5 (a) Venus' motion according to Ptolemy. (b) This is how Venus would appear from Earth when it is at each of the three points shown in part (a).

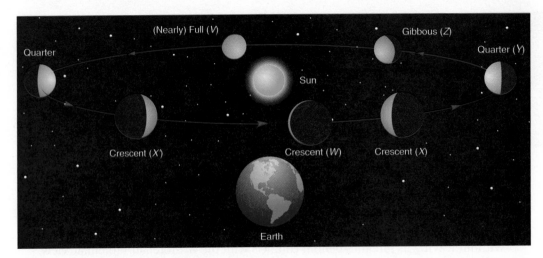

○ **FIGURE 3-6** Venus at various places in its orbit, according to the Copernican, heliocentric model. This drawing shows how the model predicts that all phases are possible and correspond to what is actually observed. Compare the phases of Venus marked by *V*, *Z*, *X*, and *W* with those in Figure 3-4. Venus is brightest at positions *X* and *X'* as we explain in the Advancing the Model box on "Our Changing View of Venus" in Chapter 8.

◆ Additional concepts such as **interior** and **superior planets**, **quadrature**, **greatest elongation**, and **opposition** are covered in *Activities 2 and 3* at the end of Chapter 2.

The Holy Spirit intended to teach us in the Bible how to go to Heaven, not how the heavens go.
Galileo

I do not feel obliged to believe that the same God who has endowed us with sense, reason, and intellect has intended us to forgo their use.
Galileo

part of its illuminated surface, but never much of it. Venus should never get beyond a crescent phase. Galileo, however, saw Venus in a gibbous phase, an observation that is unexplainable by the Ptolemaic model, but can be accounted for by the heliocentric model as shown in **FIGURE 3-6**. At point *X*, Venus would be seen in a crescent phase by an Earth-bound viewer. As it moves farther around and reaches point *Y*, it should appear in quarter phase. Then when it reaches point *Z*, it should appear in a gibbous shape, similar to the gibbous Moon.

We thus finally have an observation that gives us data for choosing the heliocentric system over the geocentric one. The heliocentric model explains all of the phases and therefore becomes the model of choice. In addition, it explains the correlation between the phases and the corresponding observed sizes of Venus. When Venus is in gibbous phase, it looks smaller than when it is in crescent phase. According to the heliocentric model, this happens because at gibbous phase Venus is farther from the Earth than when it is in crescent phase.

Galileo was a leader in breaking the bonds of Aristotelian and Ptolemaic thought. He and Kepler gave a new direction to the methods of stating natural laws, for their laws were stated in a manner that allowed measurement and testing by the methods of mathematics. In addition, Galileo referred constantly to experiments that would test his hypotheses. This was a new procedure in the study of nature. Even though experimentation was not a new idea (experiments were conducted by some ancient Greek scholars), the synthesis of Aristotle's ideas into religious belief by Aquinas resulted in an almost complete dependence on "authoritative" opinions. Today, a reliance on observation and experimentation, rather than on authority, is a cornerstone of science. Its beginning is usually credited to Galileo.

One problem remained after Galileo's observations: There seemed to be no logic supporting the laws of Kepler, except that they work. Galileo wrote that he had "opened up to this vast and most excellent science, of which my work is merely the beginning, ways and means by which other minds more acute than mine will explore its remote corners." Indeed, Isaac Newton, born the year Galileo died, was the person who synthesized Galileo's findings into one expansive theory of motion.

3-2   Isaac Newton's Grand Synthesis

Can a moving object slow down and stop by itself?

Today we summarize Newton's conclusions concerning force and motion in three laws, known as "Newton's laws of motion."

Newton's First Two Laws of Motion

The first of Newton's laws was built directly on conclusions (though incomplete) that Galileo had reached. Newton stated that an object at rest tends to stay at rest, whereas a moving object has a tendency to continue moving in a straight line at the same speed. A stationary object starts to move only when something causes it to move. A moving object changes direction or stops only because something causes it to change direction or stop. The tendency of an object to maintain whatever speed and direction of motion it has is called *inertia*, and Newton's first law is often called the *law of inertia*.

> **NEWTON'S FIRST LAW (THE LAW OF INERTIA): Unless an object is acted upon by a net, outside force, the object will maintain a constant speed in a straight line (if it were initially moving), or remain at rest (if initially at rest).**

Newton's first law is a basic observation about motion and cannot be directly proven or derived. Still, the law of inertia is a powerful tool that emphasizes cause and effect. It indicates that a force is needed to change the speed and/or the direction of an object's motion—that is, to *accelerate* it. Newton's second law quantifies and extends the first law. It tells us how much force is necessary to produce a certain *acceleration* of an object.

Consider the brick shown in FIGURE 3-7 and imagine that the wheels allow the brick to move without friction. The brick is at rest in part (a), and because it has inertia, it will stay at rest. In (b), you give the brick a push. While you are pushing, the brick accelerates. The amount of force you exert determines how great the acceleration is. As you increase the force, so does the brick's acceleration (c). This idea gives us the first part of Newton's second law: The acceleration of an object is proportional to the force exerted on it. "Proportional to" actually goes beyond what we deduced from our thought experiment. It tells us that twice the force will cause twice the acceleration.

Refer to FIGURE 3-8. Here we show one hand pushing on a frictionless brick as before and another hand pushing on a stack of two identical bricks. If the hands push with equal force, which hand will cause the most acceleration? It should be intuitive that the greater acceleration will be produced by the hand pushing on the single brick. It is important to see that friction has nothing to do with this. It is tougher to accelerate two bricks than one simply because the two have more inertia. In fact, two identical bricks have twice as much inertia as one brick. This is an idea we didn't discuss previously here: Some objects have more inertia than others. So before continuing with the second law, we must introduce the property of an object that determines its inertia—its *mass*.

An Important Digression—Mass and Weight

Mass, like inertia, is one of those terms that is used in everyday language but has a very specific definition in science. An object's *mass* is the measure of its inertia. Instead of saying that one object has twice the inertia of another, we normally say

---

inertia The tendency of an object to resist a change in its motion.

The "net" force acting on an object is the sum of all forces, taking into account both their magnitudes and their directions. Equal forces in opposite directions, acting on the same object, cancel one another.

accelerate To change the speed and/or direction of motion of an object.

acceleration A measure of how rapidly the speed and/or direction of motion of an object is changing.

The question of the origin of inertia has not yet been resolved. Newton believed that inertia is an intrinsic property of matter. Some today believe that it arises from the interaction of all matter in the universe, whereas others are exploring alternative ideas.

mass The quantifiable property of an object that is a measure of its inertia.

(a)

(b)

(c)

FIGURE 3-7 (a) The wheeled brick will accelerate (b) if a force is exerted on it. (c) If twice as much force is exerted on it, it will accelerate at twice the rate.

FIGURE 3-8 The same amount of force will give twice as much mass only half the acceleration.

HISTORICAL NOTE

Isaac Newton

To give an idea of the importance of Isaac Newton (FIGURE B3-2) to the history of thought, we quote the English poet Alexander Pope, who lived at the same time as Newton:

> Nature and nature's laws lay hid in night.
> God said, Let Newton be! and all was light.

Newton was born on Christmas Day, 1642, in a small village in England. His father, a farmer, had died before Isaac was born, and his mother decided that he was too frail to become a farmer. He was not a particularly good student, however, "wasting" much of his time tinkering with mechanical things, including model windmills, sundials, and kites that carried lanterns and scared the local people at night. When her second husband died, Isaac's mother called him home from school to help on the farm, where he spent most of his teenage years.

At the age of 19, Newton was admitted to Cambridge University. There he studied mathematics and natural philosophy (known today as science). In 1665, after Newton had received his degree and was serving as a junior faculty member, England was swept by the bubonic plague. This incurable disease killed more than 10% of the population of London in only 3 months, and those who could afford to do so escaped it by moving away from population centers. Newton returned to his mother's home at Woolsthorpe. There he worked feverishly on science for the next 2 years. These must have been two of the most productive years in the history of science, for during this time Newton made discoveries in light and optics, in force and motion, and in gravitation and planetary motion. He also devised a theory of color. To solve a problem in gravitation, he invented calculus. During this time he outlined what would become his major book, *Philosophiae Naturalis Principia Mathematica*, usually called *The Principia*. In later years, Newton wrote, "All this was in the two plague years of 1665 and 1666, for in those days I was in the prime of my age for invention, and minded Mathematics and Philosophy more than at any time since."

Newton's manner of attacking a problem was simply to concentrate his mind on it with such intensity that he finally solved it. As a young man, Newton was not interested in publishing his work. He seemed to want to discover the mysteries of nature simply for his own curiosity, and his friends often had to persuade him to publish his findings. Besides, he did not like having to defend his

FIGURE B3-2 Sir Isaac Newton (1642–1727) worked in many fields. In this painting, he is shown experimenting with a prism to investigate the nature of light.

views against criticism, and he wanted to avoid getting involved in arguments over who was the first to make certain discoveries. Nevertheless he *did* get involved quite fiercely in such disputes, including one with Gottfried Leibniz over which of them first developed calculus. This dispute lasted long after both had died. (Today they are both credited for discovering calculus independently.)

Newton had a very practical side as well as being a theoretician. He served as Warden of the Mint, and while in this office, he began the practice of making coins with small notches around their edges. (Check the quarters in your pocket.) This was done to discourage people from illegally shaving off and retaining the valuable metal of the coins.

Newton received many honors for his work and was given positions of authority. From 1703 until his death in 1727, he was president of the Royal Society, an organization of scientists. In 1705 he was knighted, the first scientist to receive this honor. When he died, Sir Isaac Newton was buried in Westminster Abbey after a state funeral.

---

that it has twice the mass. Mass is an intrinsic property of an object and remains the same independent of where the object is located in the universe.

Mass is *not* volume. Suppose that the brick in Figure 3-7 is a piece of styrofoam made to look like a brick. If you do not know this, however, you will be quite surprised when you push on it because it will accelerate much more than you expected. Why? Because a styrofoam brick has much less mass than a real brick, even though they both have the same volume.

Mass also is *not* weight. In our examples of pushing the frictionless bricks, the weight of the brick was not a factor. The brick's weight is the downward force experienced by the brick as a result of its gravitational interaction with the Earth. (See Section 3-4.) Weight did not oppose the pushing hand. This is a subtle distinction, but a very important one.

◆ Rotational inertia—the inertia of a spinning object—involves more than just mass and is discussed in Chapter 7.

Is mass the same thing as weight?

The worldwide unit of mass measurement is the kilogram. At the International Bureau of Weights and Measures near Paris is a platinum cylinder that has, by definition, a mass of *exactly* 1 kilogram. Even though a kilogram weighs about 2.2 pounds at the surface of the Earth, it is not correct to say that a kilogram is about equal to 2.2 pounds because a pound is a unit that expresses weight and a kilogram is a unit that expresses mass. The weight of an object depends on where the object is located in the universe.

Back to Newton's Second Law

Figure 3-8 shows one hand pushing on one brick and another hand pushing on two bricks. We stated that if the two applied forces were equal, the acceleration of the two bricks would be smaller. In fact, measuring the accelerations would show that if the forces are equal, the acceleration of the two bricks is exactly half that of the single brick, and the same force applied to three bricks results in one third the acceleration. Thus, for a given force, acceleration is inversely proportional to the mass being accelerated.

We have thus far discussed the relationships between force and acceleration and between mass and acceleration. We can sum them up in a single statement.

> **NEWTON'S SECOND LAW: A net external force applied to an object causes it to accelerate at a rate that is proportional to the force and inversely proportional to its mass.**

The second law is usually written as

$$\text{Force} = \text{mass} \times \text{acceleration or } F = ma.$$

The second law also makes it apparent that if the net external force is zero, there is no acceleration, which agrees exactly with Newton's first law.

Newton's Third Law

Newton's third law is simple to state:

> **NEWTON'S THIRD LAW: When object *X* exerts a force on object *Y*, object *Y* exerts an equal and opposite force back on *X*.**

This law seems very simple, but its implications are great. It is sometimes stated as this: "For every action there is an equal and opposite reaction." The implication is that it is impossible to have a single, isolated force. Forces always occur in pairs.

When you sit on a chair, you exert a force downward on the chair (**FIGURE 3-9**). The third law states that the chair exerts an equal force upward on you. We may call the force you exert on the chair the *action* force and the force of the chair on you the *reaction* force, but these labels can be assigned in an arbitrary way. The point is that one of these forces cannot exist without the other and neither "comes first."

The statement of Newton's third law indicates that two objects (called *X* and *Y* here) are *always* involved in the application of forces. A force cannot be exerted without an object to exert it and an object on which it is exerted. The word "object" here might refer to an individual atom, or it might refer to a collection of atoms; the collection might be a gas or a liquid as well as a solid object. For example, if you hold your hand out of the window of a moving car to feel the force of air resistance, it is the air that exerts a force on your hand. The third law tells us that your hand exerts a force on the air. This is not easy to see, but we know that your hand must deflect the air as it comes by and a force is necessary to do so. Calling the air an object may seem odd, but air is simply a collection of objects—atoms.

Force of chair on body

Force of body on chair

FIGURE 3-9 When you sit, you exert a downward force on the chair, and the chair exerts an upward force on you. By Newton's third law, these forces are equal in magnitude and opposite in direction, but they do not cancel each other because they are exerted on different objects.

Is a kilogram a unit of weight?

A kilogram on the Moon weighs only about one third of a pound.

The concept of force is a fundamental one. It is reasonable to think of force as pushes and pulls, but this is subjective and not always accurate. We see the changes produced by a force and maybe the best way of describing force is as *the agent of change.*

In Newton's second law, force and acceleration are always in the same direction.

In using Newton's second law, we assume that the speeds involved are much less than the speed of light; otherwise, Einstein's theory of relativity comes into play.

3-3   Motion in a Circle

Does accelerating an object always cause it to speed up or slow down?

You might try the Activity "Circular Motion" (at the end of the chapter) now.

centripetal force The force directed toward the center of the curve along which the object is moving.

Newton's second law says that a net external force acting on an object always produces an acceleration.

Consider what happens if you whirl a rock on a string. You are exerting a force on the rock toward the center of its circular motion as you pull inward on the string (FIGURE 3-10a). If you are careful, you might be able to make the rock go around you with a constant speed. Where is the acceleration that, according to Newton's law, must be produced by the force you are exerting? If the rock moves at a constant speed, the force is not causing a change in speed. Instead, it changes the *direction* of the rock's motion. Motion of an object in a circle at constant speed is an example of acceleration causing a change in direction; the acceleration is in the direction of the force—toward the center of the circle.

Parts (b) through (e) of Figure 3-10 show several potential paths for the rock when the string breaks. Based on Newton's laws, which of these paths is the way you expect the object to travel? Once the string breaks, there is no horizontal force (that is, parallel to the ground) on the rock. If this is the case, there can be no horizontal acceleration of the rock. According to Newton's first law, it thus will continue in a straight line (Figure 3-10d). When the rock was moving in the circle, the only horizontal force on it was exerted by the string. (The rock's weight pulls down, but we are considering only horizontal forces and horizontal motions.) The horizontal acceleration produced was therefore due only to the string.

A force is necessary to make something move in a curve. We give this force a name, calling it the ***centripetal*** (meaning "center-seeking") ***force***. This is *not* a new kind of force, but rather the name we apply to a net force if that net force is causing something to move in a curve. For example, the centripetal force involved when you were whirling the rock was the force exerted by the string on the rock. The centripetal force on a car rounding a curve on a level roadway is the frictional force of the road acting on the tires in the direction toward the center of curvature. The roadway exerts a force on the car, keeping it in the curve. Do not think of centripetal force as another type of force, similar to a push, a pull by a string, or a friction force. It might be any of those three or other single forces or combinations of them; it is what we call the net force responsible for an object's motion along a curved path.

Now let us consider the force that causes the Moon to move around the Earth.

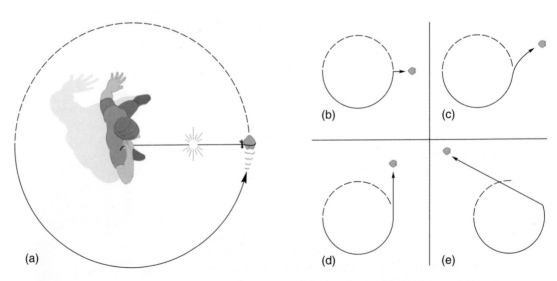

(a)

(b)   (c)

(d)   (e)

FIGURE 3-10   (a) The string breaks as the rock is whirled in a circle. (b–e) Which way does the rock go after the string breaks?

3-4   The Law of Universal Gravitation

The importance to astronomy of Newton's three laws of motion becomes evident when they are combined with another of his accomplishments: the law of universal gravitation, or "the law of gravity."

Newton's first law states that an object continues at the same speed in the same direction unless some unbalanced external force acts on it. This law is applicable to objects on Earth, but what about objects in the sky? Aristotle believed that earthly laws do not hold in the heavens, but Newton sought to apply his laws of motion there, too. It was during his great, productive years of 1665 and 1666 that, in Newton's words, he "began to think of gravity extending to the orb of the Moon." The Moon follows a nearly circular path around the Earth, so if the laws of motion apply to the Moon, a force must be exerted on it toward the center of its circle—a centripetal force.

Newton hypothesized that there is a force of attraction between the Earth and the Moon and that this serves as the centripetal force. What causes this force? Newton didn't know, but he hypothesized that it is the same force that causes an object here on Earth to fall to the ground. The insight that all matter (hence the term "universal") interacts gravitationally developed gradually. Even Copernicus had made a similar, but incomplete, proposal. Newton's formulation of this idea is as follows.

THE LAW OF UNIVERSAL GRAVITATION: Between every two objects there is an attractive force, the magnitude of which is directly proportional to the mass of each object and inversely proportional to the square of the distance between the centers of the objects.

In equation form, this is

$$F = G \frac{m_1 m_2}{d^2},$$

where m_1 and m_2 are the masses of the two objects, d is the distance between their centers, and G is a constant number that depends on the units used.

According to Newton, *every* object in the universe attracts every other one. Because Newton's law of gravitation applies to every two objects, you may wonder why you are not gravitationally attracted to the person sitting next to you in the classroom. If we use Newton's law and substitute appropriate numbers for your mass, the mass of your classmate, and the approximate distance between you, we get a force that is about equal to the weight of a small flea. This tiny force, combined with the presence of frictional forces, explains why people are not attracted to each other (gravitationally, anyway). When one of the attracting objects is the Earth, however, one of the masses is enormous, and the force we experience in this case is what we call *weight* (FIGURE 3-11).

More than 100 years after Newton published his law, Henry Cavendish was able to measure the gravitational force between two ordinary objects in a laboratory. This experiment enabled him to determine the numerical value of $G = 6.67 \times 10^{-11}$ N · m²/kg². (1 N, one newton, is a unit of measurement for force. The weight of an average apple on the surface of the Earth is about 1 N.)

weight The gravitational force between an object and the planetary/stellar body where the object is located.

(a)   (b)

FIGURE 3-11 An object's mass doesn't change from one location to another, but its weight can change. An object that weighs 12 pounds on Earth (a) would weigh 2 pounds on the Moon (b), but its mass is the same.

EXAMPLE

Let us now apply Newton's law of gravity to compare the force required to keep the Earth orbiting the Sun, F_{ES}, to the one required to keep the Moon orbiting the Earth, F_{ME}. The masses of the three objects and their relative distances can be found in the appendices of this book.

SOLUTION

You might think that the force from the Sun on the Earth will be the greater one because the Sun has much more mass than the Moon; however, keep in mind that the gravitational force decreases as the *square* of the distance between two objects, and the Sun is much farther from the Earth than the Moon is. Applying Newton's law of gravity for both pairs we have

$$F_{ES} = G\frac{m_E m_S}{(d_{ES})^2} = 6.67 \cdot 10^{-11}\,\frac{N \cdot m^2}{kg^2} \cdot \frac{5.97 \cdot 10^{24}\,kg \times 1.99 \cdot 10^{30}\,kg}{(1.50 \cdot 10^{11}\,m)^2} = 3.52 \cdot 10^{22}\,N,$$

and

$$F_{ME} = G\frac{m_M m_E}{(d_{ME})^2} = 6.67 \cdot 10^{-11}\,\frac{N \cdot m^2}{kg^2} \cdot \frac{7.35 \cdot 10^{22}\,kg \times 5.97 \cdot 10^{24}\,kg}{(3.84 \cdot 10^{8}\,m)^2} = 1.98 \cdot 10^{20}\,N.$$

Taking a ratio of the two expressions, we get

$$\frac{F_{ES}}{F_{ME}} = \left(\frac{m_S}{m_M}\right)\left(\frac{d_{ME}}{d_{ES}}\right)^2 = \left(\frac{1.99 \cdot 10^{30}\,kg}{7.35 \cdot 10^{22}\,kg}\right)\left(\frac{3.84 \cdot 10^{8}\,m}{1.50 \cdot 10^{11}\,m}\right)^2 \approx 180.$$

Indeed, the force from the Sun on the Earth is greater by about a factor of 180 than the force from the Earth on the Moon.

TRY ONE YOURSELF

At the surface of the Earth, a distance of about 6400 km from the Earth's center, an astronaut's weight is about 160 pounds. This is the attractive force on the astronaut from Earth. What is the value of this attractive force on the astronaut if he were at a height of 300 kilometers above the surface of the Earth? Taking account of your answer, how do you explain the fact that astronauts in the Space Shuttle, orbiting at 300 km above the Earth's surface, feel no weight?

According to Newton, the attractive force of gravity not only makes objects fall to Earth, but keeps the Moon in orbit around the Earth and keeps the planets in orbit around the Sun. Newton proposed that this law, along with his laws of motion, could explain the motions of the planets as well as the falling of objects on Earth. If he could explain the planets' motions, this would clear up the mystery of why Kepler's laws worked and bring the motions of the heavenly planets within the realm of our scientific understanding.

Arriving at the Law of Universal Gravitation

Kepler believed that the planets were pushed along their orbits by a force that spread out from the Sun and, therefore, decreased with distance.

How did Newton arrive at his formulation of the law of gravity? Kepler (in 1609) was the first to suggest that two objects placed in space would attract gravitationally and "come together . . . each approaching the other in proportion to the other's mass. . . ."

This is easy to test—in one case, anyway. A 10-kilogram object has twice the *mass* of a 5-kilogram object. The law of gravity predicts that a 10-kilogram object has twice the *weight* of a 5-kilogram object, and indeed it does. Weight is proportional to mass, so the law seems to work when one of the objects is the Earth. That is, the gravitational attraction between the Earth and an object is proportional to the object's mass (say m_1). According to Newton's third law, however, the object is also attracting the Earth with an equal and opposite force. Therefore, the gravitational force between the Earth and an object is also proportional to the Earth's mass (say m_2). Thus, the force is proportional to the product of the masses of the two objects, that is, $F \propto m_1 m_2$.

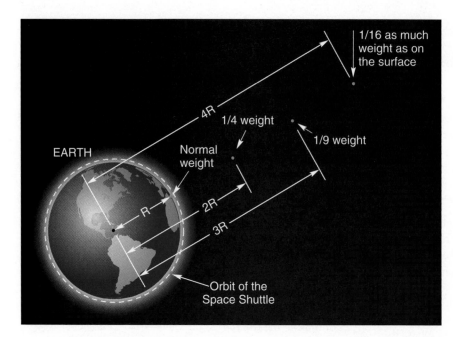

Because of today's sensitive instruments, we can now measure differences in weight at different locations on Earth. As expected, the measurements confirm Newton's law of gravitation.

To test gravity's dependence on distance, we must be able to compare forces on objects at different distances from each other. The law states that the force is inversely proportional to the square of the distance between the objects' centers. For example, if the two objects are the Earth and your book and if you take your book to a location twice as far from the center of the Earth as it is now, the law says that the book will weigh only one fourth (which is $(1/2)^2$) as much. At three times as far from the Earth, it will weigh one ninth as much (**FIGURE 3-12**).

Newton, of course, was unable to change an object's distance from Earth's center significantly. He could have taken an object up on a mountain and measured its weight, but his theory predicted that the weight change in this case would be so small that it would not be measurable with the methods he had available. Instead, he used an object already in the sky: the Moon. And rather than comparing forces directly, he compared accelerations produced by the forces, as they should change in the same way that forces do.

As we explain in Chapter 6, Ptolemy used parallax to determine that the distance from the Earth to the Moon is 27.3 Earth diameters, very close to today's value of 30.17 for the average distance to the Moon.

Even though the Moon's orbit around the Earth is slightly elliptical, Newton assumed that the Moon circles the Earth at a distance of about 60 Earth radii under the influence of the centripetal force provided by Earth's gravity. He also knew that the Moon's sidereal period is about 27.3 days. As we show in one of the calculations at the end of the chapter, this information was enough for Newton to show that the Moon's centripetal acceleration is 0.0027 m/s², about $(1/60^2)$, or 1/3600 of the acceleration of gravity on Earth's surface, which is about 9.8 m/s².

The surface area of a sphere of radius R is $4\pi R^2$. Anything that diffuses outward from a central point, filling all space uniformly in all directions, therefore, becomes less concentrated by a factor of $1/R^2$.

We can reach the conclusion that gravity decreases inversely with the distance squared $(1/d^2)$ if we assume that gravity "spreads out" from an object uniformly in all directions. Indeed, this outward diffusion has to pass through successive imaginary spheres centered on the object. Because the surface area of a sphere of radius d is $4\pi d^2$, as gravity spreads out from the object filling all space uniformly in all directions, it must become less "concentrated" by a factor of $1/d^2$.

3-5 Newton's Laws and Kepler's Laws

One had to be a Newton to see that the Moon is falling, when everyone sees that it doesn't.
Paul Valery (French poet and philosopher, 1871–1945)

Kepler's laws were not derived from fundamental principles of nature; they were accepted because they seemed to work. Based on his laws of motion and his law of gravity, Newton was able not only to prove Kepler's laws but also expand beyond them. **TABLE 3-1** summarizes the types of motion as they were analyzed by Newton.

ADVANCING THE MODEL

Travel to the Moon

The technology to launch satellites was not developed until the second half of the 20th century. But 300 years earlier, Newton developed the required gravitational theory and predicted the possibility of artificial satellites. He presented the following argument for placing an object in orbit around the Earth, based on his laws of motion and his law of universal gravitation:

> If a mountain could be found that extends above the Earth's atmosphere, and if a cannonball were fired from the summit, the ball's path would be somewhat as shown in FIGURE B3-3, line *A*. If a greater charge were used to shoot the cannonball, the ball might follow path *B*. Shoot harder yet and get path *C*. With careful adjustment (and a very powerful cannon!) the ball can be made to go around the Earth and return to where it started (line *D*). Then it will continue around again in the same path; the cannonball will be in orbit.

The gravitational aspects of a flight to the Moon are not vastly more complicated than those of Earth orbit. The mission begins with the spacecraft orbiting the Earth. As indicated in FIGURE B3-4, a rocket then launches the spacecraft out of Earth's orbit to begin its trip to the Moon. As the spacecraft gets farther from the Earth and nearer the Moon, the gravitational pull of the Moon becomes significant. The law of gravity tells us that every object in the universe attracts every other. At one point, the gravitational pulls toward Earth and Moon exactly cancel one another. Up until this point, the force pulling the craft toward the Earth has been greater than that pulling it toward the Moon, and the spacecraft has been slowing down. After passing that point, the pull toward the Moon is greater, and the spacecraft speeds

up. Finally, when the spacecraft has reached the appropriate point in its journey (at about *X* in Figure B3-4), a rocket is fired to slow it down so that it remains in orbit around the Moon. Without this firing, the craft would have so much speed that it would swing right past the Moon. For most of the trip the astronauts feel weightless, as they are in free fall, coasting along with the craft.

FIGURE B3-4 A craft sent to orbit the Moon starts out in Earth orbit. A rocket is fired at point *K* to send it toward the Moon. At point *X*, a rocket is fired to put it in Moon orbit. The arrows along the path illustrate the changing gravitational pull on the craft from the Earth and Moon. Distances are vastly out of scale here.

Once in orbit around the Moon, the lunar module disconnects from the command/service module that remains in orbit, fires its rockets to slow down, and descends to the Moon's surface. The lunar module does not have to be very large and does not need particularly powerful rockets. This is because the force of gravity on the surface of the Moon is only one sixth of that on the Earth; thus, the fall toward the Moon is not as fast, and the lift-off requires much less energy. In addition, the Moon does not have an atmosphere, so the frictional effects of an atmosphere need not be considered, as they do for takeoff and landing on Earth.

To leave the Moon, part of the lunar module is left behind when a rocket launches the small remaining craft into lunar orbit to reconnect ("dock") with the command module. Then, at the appropriate point, rockets fire again to send the craft out of lunar orbit and back toward the Earth.

Very little of the trip to and from the Moon is spent with the rockets firing. They are needed only to begin and end each portion of the trip and to make minor midcourse corrections. On one of the missions to the Moon, an astronaut spoke with his son by radio. His son asked who was driving. The reply was that Isaac Newton was doing most of the driving at the time.

The first manned *Apollo* flight took place in October 1968. In December of that year, three astronauts orbited the Moon, but did not land. Their mission provided the first whole-Earth photos ever made. In July 1969, astronauts Neil A. Armstrong and Edwin (Buzz) Aldrin, Jr., guided their lunar module "Eagle" onto the Moon at the Sea of Tranquility and uttered the famous words, "Tranquility Base here. The Eagle has landed." In all, 12 men visited the Moon between July 1969 and December 1972, when *Apollo* 17 blasted off from the Moon.

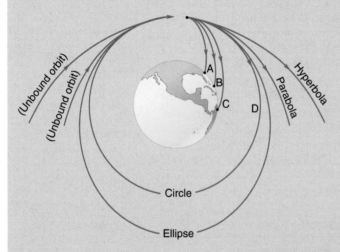

FIGURE B3-3 Newton drew a figure similar to this to illustrate how an artificial satellite would circle the Earth. Under the influence of gravity, the orbit of an object moving around a stationary body can be a circle, an ellipse, a parabola, or a hyperbola.

TABLE 3-1

Summary of Types of Motion

Motion	Type of Acceleration	Direction of Force and Acceleration
Linear	Change in speed	Forward (to speed up) Backward (to slow down)
Circular	Change in direction	Toward center of circle
Orbital	Change in speed and direction	Toward the object being orbited

As the poet Lord Byron (1788–1824) said of Newton, "When Newton saw an apple fall, he found in that slight startle from his contemplation . . . a mode of proving that the earth turn'd round in a most natural whirl, called 'gravitation.'" Indeed, Newton's major insight that gravity operated in the same way in the heavens as it did on Earth was the final blow to the Aristotelian ideas; the idea that the laws of nature as we uncover them on Earth apply in a similar fashion to the rest of the universe is now a basic assumption in astrophysics.

Newton took the Sun as the source of the force responsible for the motion of the planets. Using calculus, he showed that a planetary orbit will be elliptical if, and only if, the centripetal force varies as $1/d^2$ from the Sun, which is located at one of the foci. In other words, he proved Kepler's first law. He also showed that under the influence of the gravitational force between an object (such as a comet) and a stationary body (such as a star), the object's orbit could be elliptical (which includes circular), parabolic, or hyperbolic (Figure B3-3).

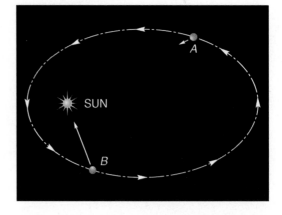

Newton showed that Kepler's second law results from the fact that the gravitational force acting on an object orbiting the Sun (or any other stationary body) always points toward the Sun. Without using math, here is how we can show that Newton's laws make Kepler's second law seem reasonable. Consider a planet moving on an (exaggerated) elliptical path around the Sun (FIGURE 3-13). When the planet is at position A, moving closer to the Sun, the gravitational force exerted on the planet by the Sun (shown by the arrow pointing toward the Sun) is not perpendicular to the motion of the planet; it is not simply a centripetal force. If it were a centripetal force, it would be exerted perpendicular to the motion of the planet, and it would have only one effect: to cause the planet to curve in its path. Instead, it has two effects: It causes the planet to curve, and it also causes the planet to speed up. This is because it pulls *forward* as well as sideways on the planet.

FIGURE 3-13 At point A, the planet is moving closer to the Sun, and the gravitational force on it causes it to speed up as well as curve from a straight line. At point B, the force of gravity slows the planet as well as curves its path.

At location B in the figure, the planet is moving away from the Sun. Here the gravitational force pulls both backward and sideways on the planet, thus slowing it down as well as curving its path. We thus see that as the planet moves toward the Sun, it speeds up, and as it moves away, it slows down. This motion is incorporated in Kepler's second law.

Finally, using his laws of motion and his law of gravity, Newton modified Kepler's third law, which now can be used for any two objects orbiting each other as a result of their mutual gravitational attraction. Using standard units (meters for distance, seconds for period, and kilograms for mass), Newton's formulation of Kepler's third law for a **binary system** is

$$\frac{a^3}{P^2} = \frac{G}{4\pi^2} \cdot (m_1 + m_2),$$

where a = semimajor axis of the orbit, P = period of the orbit, m_1, m_2 = the masses of the two objects, and G = gravitational constant.

binary system A system of two objects orbiting each other due to their mutual gravitational attraction.

In some cases, however, it is easier to measure the semimajor axis a in AU and the period P in years; then

$$\frac{a^3_{(AU)}}{P^2_{(yrs)}} = \frac{m_1 + m_2}{m_{Sun}}.$$

For the case of a planet (of mass m_1) orbiting the Sun (of mass $m_2 = m_{Sun}$), Newton's version of Kepler's third law actually simplifies to the original version by Kepler. This is the case because the mass of any planet is very small compared with the mass of the Sun; that is, $m_1 \ll m_{Sun}$, so the expression on the right side of the equation is essentially equal to one. For all objects orbiting the Sun, we thus get Kepler's original version: $a^3_{(AU)}/P^2_{(yrs)} = 1$.

EXAMPLE

Let us now examine the case of two stars orbiting each other. Suppose observations suggest that the orbital period of this system is 4 years and that the average distance between the stars is 8 AU. Substituting these numbers into Kepler's third law, we find

$$\frac{8^3}{4^2} = 32 = \frac{m_1 + m_2}{m_{Sun}}.$$

The total mass of both stars thus is 32 times the mass of the Sun. Without any additional information, we cannot find the mass of each star. We come back to this problem at the end of the next section.

TRY ONE YOURSELF

An artificial satellite is orbiting the Moon with period $P = 11.5$ hours (or 1.3×10^{-3} years) and at an average distance from the Moon's center of 5960 km (or 4×10^{-5} AU). What is the mass of the Moon? (The Sun's mass is about 2×10^{30} kilograms. Make sure you use the appropriate units for the period and average distance.)

3-6   Orbits and the Center of Mass

center of mass The average location of the various masses in a system, weighted according to how far each is from that point.

Newton's third law tells us that when one object exerts a gravitational force on another, the second object exerts an equal force back on the first. We thus should not expect that one of the objects just remains still whereas the other orbits around it. Instead, the two objects orbit about a point between them, called the **center of mass** of the objects. (Even though an object's center of mass is not always the same as its center of gravity, for almost all the cases we discuss the two points will be considered to be identical.) As a child, you probably played on a seesaw (or teeter-totter) with someone whose weight was greater than yours. This person had to sit closer to the pivot point to balance. In fact, both persons on a seesaw must position themselves in such a way that their center of mass is at the pivot point of the seesaw if they are to balance on it. Suppose person A weighs 50 pounds and person B weighs 150 pounds. Because person A's weight is three times smaller than B's, person A must sit three times farther from the pivot of the seesaw.

FIGURE 3-14 The two balls at the ends of the rod balance at the center of mass of the device, where the string is connected.

FIGURE 3-14 shows a large ball and a small ball connected by a rod and held by a string tied to the rod. The two balls balance because the string is connected at the center of mass

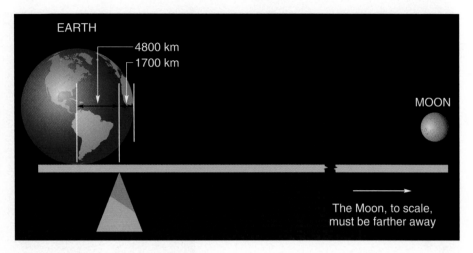

of the objects. If this contraption were thrown into the air with a spinning motion—like a baton—it would spin around the center of mass. A planet and the Sun are somewhat like the two balls on the rod, but instead of being held together by a rod, they are held by the force of gravity. For the case of the Sun–Earth system, the Sun is 330,000 times more massive than the Earth and, thus, the center of mass of this system is essentially at the center of the Sun. However, for the case of the Earth–Moon system, the Earth's mass is only 81 times that of the Moon. Therefore, the Moon is 81 times farther from the center of mass of this system than the Earth. This means that the center of mass is about 4800 kilometers from Earth's center (380,000 kilometers from the Moon) or about 1700 kilometers below the Earth's surface (FIGURE 3-15).

It was the relationship between the distances of the Earth and Moon from the system's center of mass that allowed us to calculate the mass of the Moon. Today we know the Moon's mass more accurately by observing its gravitational effect on space probes that have flown by it, but until the space age, the method described above was the most accurate. In Chapter 12 (and the example later), we show that the center-of-mass method is what allows us to calculate the masses of stars.

Historically, the center of mass of the Earth-Moon system was determined by observing parallax of nearby planets due to Earth's motion around the center of mass.

EXAMPLE

In the previous example we found that the total mass of the binary system is 32 solar masses. Suppose observations suggest that one star (say star X) is three times farther from the center of mass than the other star (star Y). Star Y, therefore, has three times the mass of star X. As a result, we find that the mass of star X is 8 solar masses and the mass of star Y is 24 solar masses.

When an entire system moves under the influence of a net external force, it moves according to Newton's second law, behaving as if all of its mass were concentrated at the center of mass (FIGURE 3-16a). It thus is the center of mass of the Earth–Moon system that follows an elliptical path around the Sun (Figure 3-16b).

3-7   Beyond Newton

Science seeks to show that the various phenomena we observe are not independent of one another, but are instead manifestations of a relatively few basic principles. In the previous sections, we saw how Newton's work succeeded in describing planetary motions based on a few basic ideas on motion and gravity. In addition, Newtonian ideas explained a wide range of observations: In Chapter 6 we describe how they explain the tides and the Earth's precession; in Chapters 9 and 10 we mention that they

I do not know what I may appear to the world; but to myself I seem to have been only like a boy playing on the seashore, and diverting myself in now and then finding a smoother pebble or a prettier shell than ordinary, whilst the great ocean of truth lay all undiscovered before me.
Newton

FIGURE 3-16 (a) The center of mass of a thrown hammer follows a smooth path as the hammer rotates around that point. (b) Likewise, it is the center of mass of the Earth–Moon system that orbits the Sun in an elliptical path. (By holding a straight edge up to the paths drawn, you can see the Earth and Moon are always curving toward the Sun during the orbit. This is because the Sun's gravitational force on either object is stronger than the gravitational force from the other object.)

(a)

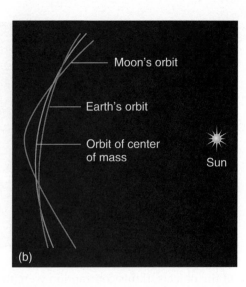

Moon's orbit

Earth's orbit

Orbit of center of mass

Sun

(b)

were used to predict the existence of the planet Neptune, and the return of comet Halley, respectively.

From these examples, you might conclude (correctly) that Newton's laws are more fundamental than Kepler's. They explain motions in a measurable, mathematical manner; they fit the data and make predictions that can be checked, and they fit with other laws to make an overall theory that is a simple, unified package. (This package is called "Newtonian mechanics" or "classical mechanics," to distinguish it from the mechanics of Einsteinian relativity. FIGURE 3-17 shows a timeline of how our ideas on gravity have changed through the years.)

Newton was not the first to consider laws that hold both for Earth and the heavens; the idea of the unity of nature began to take shape from the time of Galileo; however, it was Newton who first created a unified model. The word universe begins with the prefix "uni," meaning "one, single" (*unit, unify, unique*, and so on). Our modern science of astronomy could not exist without the basic understanding of the unity of nature. In addition, Newton's work confirmed the belief of the ancient Greeks that nature is explainable—that if we work hard at it, we have the ability to understand the many seemingly mysterious things that occur in nature.

As we found out in the 20th century, however, Newton's laws cannot be applied to all situations. In the next section we describe Einstein's special theory of relativity and his general theory of relativity, which go beyond Newtonian ideas to describe what happens at high speeds and in places where gravity is extremely strong. In Chapter 4, we discuss quantum mechanics, which better describes what happens inside an atom.

All things by immortal power,
Near or far,
Hiddenly
To each other linked are,
That thou canst not stir a
*   flower*
Without troubling a star.
Francis Thompson
(1859–1907)

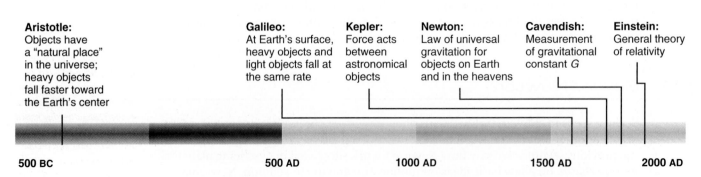

Aristotle:
Objects have a "natural place" in the universe; heavy objects fall faster toward the Earth's center

Galileo:
At Earth's surface, heavy objects and light objects fall at the same rate

Kepler:
Force acts between astronomical objects

Newton:
Law of universal gravitation for objects on Earth and in the heavens

Cavendish:
Measurement of gravitational constant G

Einstein:
General theory of relativity

500 BC   500 AD   1000 AD   1500 AD   2000 AD

FIGURE 3-17 Aristotle's explanation of gravity lasted for almost 2000 years, before it was replaced by scientific models based on observation and experiment.

3-8 General Theory of Relativity

Mass was defined earlier in this chapter as the measure of the inertia of an object. In stating the law of gravity, however, Newton proposed that mass is also the quantity that determines the strength of gravitational attraction. Why should the same quantity be the measure of two seemingly different physical properties? It is certainly not obvious that *inertia* (the resistance to a change in motion) should have anything to do with *gravitational attraction*. Yet the measures of these two properties are not just similar; experiments show that they are identical to at least one part in 1 trillion. Can this be simply a coincidence?

Scientists do not like such coincidences. They believe that if two things are so similar, there must be a reason. The attempt to explain this apparent coincidence is what led Albert Einstein to develop his general theory of relativity more than 200 years after Newton stated his law of gravity. The theory begins with a statement of the equivalence of gravity and acceleration, and fundamentally changes the way we look at the phenomenon of gravity.

The woman in FIGURE 3-18a has dropped a book on the surface of the Earth. In part (b), she drops the same book while in a spaceship that is far from Earth (and any other gravitational influences) and accelerating in the direction shown. If her spaceship is accelerating at the same rate that falling objects accelerate here on Earth, she will observe the book falling toward her feet in exactly the same way as it did on Earth's surface. She won't be able to tell the difference between "falling" caused by the ship's acceleration and falling caused by gravity. If she steps on a scale in such a spaceship, the scale will register the same weight as a scale on the Earth's surface. The ***principle of equivalence*** of Einstein's general theory of relativity tells us that there is no experiment whatsoever that she can do to distinguish between the two conditions. This principle forms the cornerstone of the theory in which the similarity of the effects of gravity and acceleration are explained by considering the curvature of space.

Space curvature is not easy to imagine because the world we experience is three dimensional, and we cannot imagine what dimension our world can curve into. We say that our world has three dimensions because we use three directions to specify the exact location of something. We can state these directions as north–south, east–west, and up–down. For example, you might state that to get from the library to your bed at home, you must go 4325 feet north, 5843 feet west, and 12 feet up to the second floor. Although other choices might be made for the three coordinates that specify the location of an object relative to your position, you must always give three pieces of information in our three-dimensional world.

Imagine some tiny two-dimensional creatures on a large, expanding balloon. The creatures have no height, and they only know of the two dimensions of their universe; they can perceive north–south and east–west, but have no conception of up–down. You might object that the surface of the balloon is not really two dimensional,

The spaceship is far enough from Earth (and other objects) that there is no observable gravitational force.

principle of equivalence
The statement that effects of acceleration are indistinguishable from gravitational effects.

(a)

The book accelerates downward

Gravity acts toward the center of the Earth

(b)

The book has the same acceleration as it did on Earth

Acceleration of spaceship is equal to that of a dropped object on Earth

FIGURE 3-18 Whether on Earth or in a spaceship far from Earth and any other gravitational influences, accelerating at the acceleration due to gravity, the book will "fall" in the same way.

FIGURE 3-19 According to the general theory of relativity, matter curves the space around it. This curvature, in turn, influences the motion of objects in the vicinity. To visualize the curvature of three-dimensional space, in this figure we show how (a) a two-dimensional space (the surface of a waterbed) curves around a massive object (a heavy bowling ball), and how (b) the resulting distortion, in turn, affects the paths taken by light and other objects passing by. (Changes in the paths have been exaggerated for clarity.)

This idea is borrowed from *Flatland*, written by Edwin A. Abbott in 1884. This book is a classic illustration of multiple dimensions in space, but even more than that, it's great fun to read.

We will see later in the text that space curvature also explains black holes.

but if the balloon is large enough compared with the size of the creatures, they would not easily perceive the balloon's curvature. If one creature realizes that his universe is curved, how can he explain this idea to his contemporaries?

Saying that their universe is curved "downward" would have no meaning, because they have no conception of "up" and "down." We humans see that the balloon's surface is curved into the third dimension, but it would take a great stretch of the creatures' imagination to think of a third dimension, for it is not part of their everyday world.

By a similar analogy, we picture the curvature of *our* space. Suppose that the presence of a massive object causes space to be warped. We can picture space near the Sun as being warped analogous to the way the surface of a waterbed is warped by a bowling ball placed at its center (**FIGURE 3-19**). The waterbed's surface would be distorted so that a straight line following the surface would have to follow the distortion. Similarly, a beam of light passing near a massive object would follow the curvature of space caused by the massive object. Let us also imagine the motion of a small ball on this waterbed. Far from the distortion, the surface of the waterbed is fairly flat and thus the ball will move in a straight line; however, the closer the ball gets to the distortion, the more it will curve toward it. If the ball's speed is chosen appropriately with respect to the distortion, the ball may end up moving in an orbit around the sides of the distortion, in the same way a planet moves around the Sun. We can say that matter (in our case, the heavy bowling ball) tells space (the surface of the waterbed) how to curve and that the space curvature (or distortion) tells matter (the small ball) how to move.

3-9   Gravitation and Einstein

In Newton's view of gravity, interacting objects act at a distance; one object influences another across the empty space between them. If I let go of an apple that I hold in my hand, it *immediately* starts falling toward the Earth's surface, but how does it know when to start falling and how strong the Earth's influence is on it? Einstein proposed that instead of thinking of gravity as an attractive force between two objects acting at a distance, we think of space as being curved by the presence of mass so that objects move because of the curvature. In this section we describe four of the many experimental tests of the general theory of relativity; they clearly show that it provides a better description of gravity than Newton's theory.

Test 1: The Gravitational Bending of Light

As shown in Figure 3-19, according to the general theory of relativity, a light beam passing by a massive object will be deflected from its original straight path. This gravitational bending of light (which we discuss in more detail in Chapter 15) was predicted by Einstein in 1915, and observations made during a solar eclipse in 1919

HISTORICAL NOTE

Albert Einstein

The young Albert Einstein (FIGURE B3-5) found the formal, disciplinary schools of Germany at the end of the 19th century intimidating and boring, and he dropped out before completing high school. He studied at home, however, and learned to play the violin well enough that he became an accomplished violinist. His studies of geometry and science led him to conclude, at age 12, that the Bible is not literally true. That shock implanted in him a deep distrust of authority of any kind—a distrust that he carried with him throughout life.

On his second try, Einstein was granted admission to the Swiss Federal Institute of Technology in Zurich. While there, he often preferred to study on his own, reading the classical works of theoretical physics. He was granted a Ph.D. in 1900, but it was 2 years before he found regular work—as a patent examiner in the Swiss Patent Office.

Like Newton, Einstein's most revolutionary work was done during a short period in his early 20s. In 1905, Einstein published four important papers in the prestigious German physics journal *Annalen der Physik*. Although the paper for which he is best known is the one introducing special relativity, he was awarded the Nobel Prize for another, concerning the photoelectric effect of light. Many physicists quickly recognized the importance of his work, but it was not until 1909 that he was given a full-time academic position at the University of Zurich.

In 1903, Einstein married his college sweetheart, Mileva Maritsch, and they had two sons. Mileva's influence on Einstein's ideas is still debated. Their forced separation during World War I resulted in a divorce in 1919. Later that year, Einstein married his cousin Elsa.

In 1916, Einstein published his general theory of relativity, but his theories were slow to gain acceptance because of the lack of experimental verification. In 1919, however, the Royal Society of London announced that its scientific expedition to observe the solar eclipse of that year had verified Einstein's prediction of the gravitational deflection of starlight as it passes near the Sun. The international acclaim that followed changed Einstein's life, for he was suddenly considered a genius.

FIGURE B3-5 Albert Einstein (1879–1955) had several hobbies; one of his favorites was sailing.

Although Einstein continued his scientific work until he died in 1955, his fame also allowed him to exert influence in world affairs. Though a Jew and a critic of the political situation in Germany, he escaped the Nazis because he was visiting California when Hitler assumed power in 1933. Einstein renounced his German citizenship and never returned to his home country. The next year he became an American citizen.

It is ironic that Einstein's name is so closely linked to the atomic bomb. Although his theories predicted that mass could be converted to energy, which was the idea that led to the development of nuclear weapons, Einstein was an avowed pacifist who worked untiringly to prevent war, which he saw as the ultimate scourge of humanity. He argued that the establishment of a world government was the only permanent solution.

confirmed this prediction. Newton's theory predicts no gravitational effect on light, as light has no mass, and light is not observed to respond to gravity in our everyday world. The bending of light is observed only around very massive objects, and because Newton's theory had never been checked in such cases, no one realized that it makes incorrect predictions.

Suppose a total solar eclipse occurs while the Sun—as seen from Earth—is between two bright stars. (When the Sun is totally eclipsed by the Moon, stars can be seen in the sky.) FIGURE 3-20a shows the stars as they normally appear. During the eclipse, shown in part (b) of the figure, as light from the stars passes near the Sun before reaching Earth, it bends and, thus, it makes the stars appear slightly farther apart, as shown in part (c). The maximum predicted gravitational bending of light is very small, only 1.75 arcseconds, but the observations made during the 1919 expedition produced results in agreement with the theory, providing the first experimental support for the general theory of relativity.

Test 2: The Orbit of Mercury

In 1859, 14 years after predicting the existence of Neptune, Urbain Le Verrier reported that Mercury's elliptical orbit *precesses*; that is, it does not keep the same orientation in space. FIGURE 3-21 illustrates a greatly exaggerated precession, showing the

If we were to use Newtonian mechanics to describe the motion of a photon as a particle (of mass *m* and speed *c*) in a gravitational field, we would find that the photon's path is deflected by an angle that is half the size predicted by the general theory of relativity.

precession (of an elliptical orbit) The change in orientation of the major axis of the elliptical path of an object.

FIGURE 3-20 Light from the two stars is bent as it passes near the Sun, causing the stars to appear farther apart.

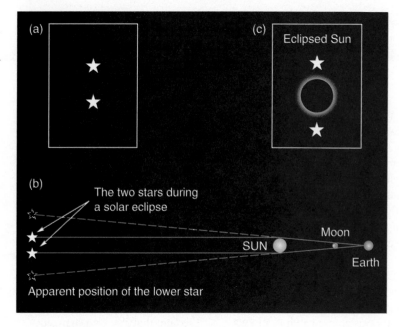

near point in the orbit (the perihelion) gradually sliding around the Sun. Mercury's orbit precesses at the rate of 574 arcseconds per century, which is less than a degree per century. Calculations show that Newton's theory of gravity can account for the basic effect because gravitational pulls by other planets, particularly Venus and Jupiter, would cause it. However, the total precession accounted for by these gravitational tugs amounts to only 531 arcseconds per century.

The unaccounted-for 43 arcseconds of precession per century presented a mystery for astronomers. One hypothesis held that there is another planet in the inner solar system that is responsible for the extra precession. This planet was named Vulcan. Extensive searches for it were carried out, but it was never found.

Einstein applied his general theory of relativity to the problem of the precession of Mercury's orbit and found that it accounted precisely for the 574 arcseconds of precession. He later wrote that, "for a few days, I was beside myself with joyous excitement."* Like Newton's theory, general relativity predicts the precession effect caused by the other planets, but unlike Newton's theory, it predicts additional precession due to properties of curved space. The Sun itself thus caused the extra 43 arcseconds of precession.

*The quotation is from Clifford M. Will, *Was Einstein Right?* (New York: Basic Books, 1993).

Additional Tests

gravitational wave
Ripples in the curvature of space produced by changes in the distribution of matter.

According to Einstein's theory of gravity, massive objects warp not only space around them but also time. Time slows down in the presence of gravity, and the greater the strength of gravity, the more time slows down. This effect (which we discuss in more detail in Chapter 15) was experimentally tested in 1960, and the results were in complete agreement with the general theory of relativity.

Finally, the general theory of relativity predicts the existence of ***gravitational waves***. Consider Figure 3-19 and imagine that the massive object at the center of the curved space was made to move up and down. As a result, ripples will be produced in the curvature of space, and these waves will propagate outward at the speed of light. Even though we have not yet directly observed such waves, strong indirect evidence comes from observations of a binary system of two stars, as we discuss in Chapter 15. Newton's theory of gravity

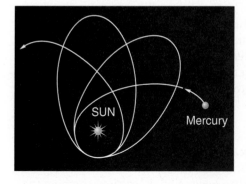

FIGURE 3-21 This illustration exaggerates the actual precession of the perihelion (the closest point to the Sun) of Mercury's orbit.

ADVANCING THE MODEL

The Special Theory of Relativity

About 10 years before he developed the general theory of relativity, Einstein proposed the special theory of relativity, which is based on two postulates, the first of which states:

- All laws of physics are the same for all nonaccelerating observers, no matter what the speed of those observers.

People once thought that the laws of nature that govern objects here on Earth are different from those that rule the heavens. Then Newton showed that the same laws work for both—at least, the mechanical laws of force and motion. Einstein's first postulate completes the progression; he begins with the assumption that *all* laws, including those of electricity and magnetism, are the same everywhere. The first postulate abolishes the idea of absolute rest and therefore absolute motion. Motion is relative, as it is not possible to distinguish experimentally between two different uniformly moving observers.

Einstein's second postulate concerns the speed of light:

- The speed of light (*c*) is the same for all nonaccelerating observers, no matter what their motion relative to the source of the light.

Compare this behavior of light to that of ordinary objects in our experience. For example, when we catch a baseball, we see it coming at us faster if we are moving toward the thrower than if we are standing still. If the postulate is true, this doesn't happen for light. FIGURE B3-6 shows an imaginative case in which people on fast-moving spaceships are measuring the speed of light that comes from an Earthling's flashlight. Technological advances since Einstein's time have allowed us to repeatedly confirm the second postulate; we now consider the constancy of the speed of light a law of nature.

On the basis of his two postulates, Einstein showed that Newton's laws of motion become increasingly inaccurate with increasing speed. The special theory of relativity predicts that (1) the observed length along the line of motion of a moving object becomes less than its length when measured at rest; (2) the observed passage of time becomes slower for the moving object; and (3) the observed inertia of an object becomes greater than its inertia when at rest. Special relativity shows that the three spatial dimensions and the time dimension are intimately bound, and thus it makes sense to describe them together as a four-dimensional continuum: *spacetime*. The framework of the special theory of relativity, however, is such that it does not include a consistent description of gravity; the theory's realm is flat spacetime. Gravitation, being a manifestation of the curvature of spacetime, is described by the general theory of relativity, which involves special relativity, the equivalence principle, and the local nature of physics.

One more conclusion based on the postulates of special relativity should be mentioned: mass (*m*) can be transformed to energy (*E*) and vice versa. The conversion between the two is governed by the equation $E = mc^2$. The equation was dramatically verified in 1945 by the first explosion of a nuclear bomb, for the energy of these bombs comes from the conversion of mass to energy. A more peaceful example of mass–energy conversion is provided by nuclear power plants, which produce electrical energy based on Einstein's theory. (We see in Chapters 11 and 12 that nuclear energy is the source of the energy of the stars.) The predictions of the special theory of relativity become significant only at speeds greater than those attained in everyday life. Every time a test has been conducted to check the theory, the theory has passed the test.

FIGURE B3-6 According to the special theory of relativity, the speed of light is the same regardless of the motion of the observer.

does not include any effect that gravity might have on time and does not predict the existence of gravitational waves.

All tests of Einstein's relativity theory have confirmed it, and the theory forms the basis of modern astronomy. We still talk about Newtonian ideas, however, for the same reason we still use a geocentric view of the world when we talk about "sunrises" and "sunsets." Newton's theory works very well in the realm of our everyday experiences and is more easily understood than Einstein's. You will see little mention of curved space in this text until the discussion of black holes, where Einstein's theory is essential.

Conclusion

correspondence principle
The idea that predictions of a new theory must agree with the theory it replaces in cases where the previous theory has been found to be correct.

 The correspondence principle is usually credited to Niels Bohr, whom we discuss further in Chapter 4.

There is a general principle in science concerning the replacement of old theories by new ones. The *correspondence principle* states that the predictions of the new theory must agree with those of the previous theory where the old one yields correct results. This is entirely reasonable. In the previous chapter, we discussed two primary models: Ptolemy's geocentric model and the heliocentric model, as presented by Copernicus and revised by Kepler. In this chapter, we discussed how Galileo's telescopic observations supported Kepler's results and how Newton expanded on the work of his predecessors by offering us a more unified view of the world around us.

We now find that Newton's ideas have been supplanted by Einstein's. Even though the theory of relativity does not seem to fit our everyday experiences, it is firmly established in science, and perhaps someday it will become part of our everyday thinking. It is also not only possible but likely that at some point in the future Einstein's theories will be supplanted by new theories that more accurately describe the universe.

STUDY GUIDE

1. Using his newly invented telescope, Galileo discovered all of the following except
   A. moons of Jupiter.
   B. phases of Venus.
   C. sunspots.
   D. stellar parallax.
   E. mountains on the Moon.

2. Which of the following planets can be seen (from Earth) in a crescent phase?
   A. Mercury.
   B. Venus.
   C. Mars.
   D. [Two of the above.]
   E. [All of the above.]

3. Which of the following observations by Galileo was most convincing in deciding between the two opposing theories of our planetary system?
   A. Moons of Jupiter.
   B. Mountains on the Moon.
   C. Phases of Venus.
   D. Sunspots.

4. Suppose you are riding as a passenger in a car when the car stops suddenly. What pushes you forward?
   A. Inertia.
   B. Your weight.
   C. The car's forward motion.
   D. Nothing pushes you forward.

5. If the same net force is applied to two different objects, one with a mass of 1 kilogram and the other with a mass of 2 kilograms,
   A. the 1-kilogram mass will have twice the acceleration of the other.
   B. the 1-kilogram mass will have more acceleration than the other, but not necessarily twice as much.
   C. both objects will have the same acceleration, for the force determines the acceleration.

6. If the mass of the Earth magically decreased with no change in its size, your weight (as you stand on the surface) would
   A. increase.
   B. not change.
   C. decrease.

7. According to Newton, the natural motion of an object is
   A. a circle.
   B. an ellipse.
   C. a straight line.
   D. retrograde motion.

8. If the distance between two objects is tripled, the gravitational force exerted by one on the other will be
   A. the same.
   B. one third as much.
   C. one ninth as much.
   D. three times as much.
   E. nine times as much.

9. The gravitational attraction between an object and the Earth
   A. stops just beyond the Earth's atmosphere.
   B. extends to about halfway to the Moon.
   C. extends about five sixths of the way to the Moon.
   D. extends to infinity.

10. The mass of the Moon is about 1/81 that of the Earth. If you were on the Moon, however, you would weigh 1/6 of your weight on Earth. Why do you weigh more than 1/81 of your Earth weight?
    A. The Moon is made of different materials than Earth.
    B. The Moon has a different density than Earth.
    C. The Moon has no atmosphere, whereas Earth does.
    D. The Moon is much smaller than Earth.
    E. [Both A and B above.]

11. Which statement best describes the relationship between Newton's laws and Kepler's laws?
    A. Newton proved that Kepler was wrong.
    B. Newton's laws and Kepler's laws are now considered equally valuable.
    C. Newton's laws are more fundamental and more powerful than Kepler's laws.
    D. Neither Newton's laws nor Kepler's laws have any modern applications.

12. When you whirl a rock around on the end of a string, centripetal force
    A. pulls outward on the rock.
    B. pulls inward on the rock.
    C. pulls outward on your hand.
    D. [Both A and B above, and the two forces balance.]
    E. [All of the above, for all of the forces are equal.]

13. Kepler's third law states that the ratio of the cube of a planet's semimajor axis to the square of the planet's period of revolution is equal to a constant. Newton found that the value of that constant depends on
    A. the sizes of the two objects.
    B. the masses of the two objects.
    C. the velocities of the two objects.

14. Newton checked his hypothesis concerning an inverse square law of gravitation by calculating
    A. the Moon's acceleration toward the Earth.
    B. the time required for the Moon to complete one orbit.
    C. the mass of the Earth.
    D. the mass of the Moon.
    E. [Both C and D above.]

15. The force of gravity is responsible for
    A. the weight of an object on Earth.
    B. the mass of an object on Earth.
    C. the tides.
    D. holding the Earth in its orbit.
    E. [All of the above.]

16. If the Earth's radius magically decreased with no change in its mass, your weight (as you stand on the surface) would
    A. increase.
    B. not change.
    C. decrease.

17. If the Earth were magically moved farther from the Sun but kept in orbit around it, the length of the year would
    A. increase.
    B. not change.
    C. decrease.

18. If the Sun's radius magically doubled but everything else remained the same, the Earth's orbital period would
    A. increase.
    B. not change.
    C. decrease.

19. If a small asteroid is found to orbit the Sun on the same orbit as Earth, the asteroid's orbital period will be
    A. about the same as Earth's.
    B. much greater than Earth's.
    C. much smaller than Earth's.

20. The principle of equivalence of the general theory of relativity tells us that
    A. effects of gravity are equivalent to effects of acceleration in the opposite direction.
    B. speeds measured in any location are equivalent.
    C. the speed of light is the same for all observers.
    D. Newton's laws are equivalent to Kepler's laws.
    E. Newton's laws are equivalent to Einstein's theories.

21. Which of the following choices confirmed a prediction made by the general theory of relativity?
    A. Observations of Jupiter's satellites.
    B. Observations of phases of Venus.
    C. Calculations of the orbit of Mercury.
    D. Calculations predicting the existence of Mars' moons.
    E. [None of the above; general relativity has not been successful in astronomical applications.]

22. The correspondence principle states that
    A. predictions made by a new theory must agree with those of the theory it replaces where the old theory fit the data.
    B. all predictions made by a new theory must agree with those of the theory it replaces.
    C. no predictions made by a new theory are expected to agree with those of the theory it replaces.
    D. effects of gravity are equivalent to effects of acceleration in the opposite direction.

23. List the following men in the order in which they lived: Copernicus, Aristotle, Ptolemy, Kepler, Galileo, Brahe. (Hint: You may have a "tie" between two of them.)

24. Most of Galileo's observations argued *against* the Ptolemaic system rather than *for* a heliocentric system. What was the exception?

25. Which of the phases of Venus could not be explained by the Ptolemaic model?

26. Define inertia and give an example of its action.

27. Which is the more fundamental quantity, mass or weight? Describe an observation that confirms your answer.

28. State Newton's three laws and cite an example of each.

29. How was the mass of the Moon (compared with Earth's mass) first determined?

RECALL QUESTIONS

30. What determines the magnitude (strength) of the gravitational force between two objects?

31. How did Newton use an astronomical object to check his hypothesized law of gravitation?

32. Explain how the law of gravitation accounts for the fact that planets move fastest when they are closest to the Sun.

33. Did Newton's laws conflict with Kepler's laws? Explain.

34. What provides the centripetal force to keep the Earth in orbit around the Sun?

QUESTIONS TO PONDER

1. What events took place during the century before Galileo that contributed to the revolutionary flavor of his times?

2. Neither the geocentric nor the heliocentric system made a direct prediction about whether Jupiter has moons. Why, then, did Galileo's discovery of moons have an impact on the choice of a model?

3. Figure 3-4 shows that Venus appears to be larger when it is in certain phases. Why does this occur?

4. Mars exhibits phases. What phase(s) would you expect to see in viewing Mars? In what phase(s) would Mars never appear when viewed from Earth?

5. Explain the distinction between mass and weight, showing that the difference is more than just a matter of what units are used.

6. Newton's laws tell us that no force is needed to keep something moving. Why, then, when we are driving on level ground, don't we turn off the engine of our car?

7. It seems presumptuous to call the law of gravitation "universal." What evidence did Newton have that the law applies beyond the Earth?

8. Explain why the work of Newton had implications beyond science.

9. Kepler held that the center of the Earth orbits the Sun in an elliptical path. Newton's laws tell us that this isn't exactly true. Explain.

10. Why do we teach Newton's law of gravitation even though general relativity is a more up-to-date explanation of the phenomena involved?

11. What causes weight?

12. Give an example of the correspondence principle in the case of the heliocentric theory replacing the geocentric theory.

13. Some people even today oppose the theory of evolution on religious grounds. Compare this position with the conflicts of Copernicus and Galileo with the church establishment.

CALCULATIONS

1. Suppose that you move three times as far from the center of the Earth as you are now. By what factor will your weight change?

2. On Earth's surface, Big Al is about 6500 kilometers from its center. If the force of gravity on Big Al here is 250 pounds, how much will it be on him at a distance of 13,000 kilometers from the Earth's center?

3. Two planets (A and B) orbit a star S. Planet B is three times farther from the star than A is and has three times the mass of A. The force from the star on planet A is x. What is the force, in units of x, from the star on planet B?

4. In the preceding problem, suppose that the orbital period of planet A is two years and that it orbits the star at an average distance of 2 AU. What is the mass of the star compared to that of our Sun? (Assume the planets have small masses.) What is the orbital period of planet B?

5. Using data for Jupiter and its Galilean satellites (Io, Europa, Ganymede, and Callisto) given in the appendices of your book, show that these data agree with Newton's form of Kepler's third law.

6. The average center-to-center distance between the Earth and Moon is 3.84×10^8 m. The sidereal period of the Moon is 27.32 days. Assuming a circular orbit, show that the Moon moves on its orbit with a speed (v) of about 1020 m/s. (Hint: During one orbit, the Moon covers a distance equal to the orbit's circumference; also, speed is distance divided by time.) It can be shown that the centripetal acceleration of an object moving at constant speed on a circular orbit of radius r is given by v^2/r. Show that the Moon's centripetal acceleration is 0.0027 m/s^2 or 1/60^2 of 9.8 m/s^2, which is the acceleration of gravity on Earth's surface.

ACTIVITIES

1. Circular Motion

This activity should be done outside, away from anything breakable. Tie some object such as a shoe to the end of a fairly long (6 or 8 feet) string or rope. Now whirl the object in a horizontal circle around you. Feel the pull you must exert to keep the object in the circle. Whirl it faster. Do you have to increase the force you exert on the string?

Now let go of the string and carefully observe the path taken by the object. Forget the downward motion (caused by gravity) and concentrate on how the object travels horizontally. Figure 3-10 shows several potential paths for the object. Which of these did your object take?

2. Observing Venus

If you have a small telescope and Venus happens to be visible in the evening sky, observe the planet once a week for a month. In essence, you will be repeating Galileo's observations. Do your observations show that the observed shape of the planet is changing? If yes, can you tell if it is coming toward us or moving away from us?

The following books and articles will give you a sense of the impact that Galileo, Newton, and Einstein had on our understanding of the universe.

1. "Newton's Discovery of Gravity," by I. B. Cohen, in *Scientific American* (March, 1981).

2. "Newton's Principia: A Retrospective," by G. Christianson, in *Sky & Telescope* (July, 1987).

3. "How Galileo Changed the Rules of Science," by O. Gingerich, in *Sky & Telescope* (March, 1993).

4. J. Fauvel, et al., *Let Newton Be!* (Oxford University Press, 1988).

5. O. Gingerich, *The Great Copernicus Chase, and Other Adventures in Astronomical History*, a collection of essays including the period of Galileo and Newton (Sky Publishing/Cambridge University Press, 1992).

6. Clifford M. Will, *Was Einstein Right?* (Basic Books, 1986).

7. Lewis Carroll Epstein, *Relativity Visualized* (Insight Press, 1985).

8. George Gamow and Roger Penrose, *Mr Thompkins in Paperback* (Cambridge University Press, reissue edition, 1993).

9. George Gamow, *The Great Physicists from Galileo to Einstein* (Dover Publications, 1988).

10. Galileo Galilei, *Discoveries and Opinions of Galileo*, Stillman Drake, translator (Anchor Books/ Doubleday, 1957).

11. James Reston, *Galileo, audio cassette*, Jeff Riggenbach, narrator (Blackstone Audio Books, 1996).

12. Gale E. Christianson, *Isaac Newton and the Scientific Revolution. Oxford Portraits in Science* (Oxford University Press, 1998).

13. John L. Heilbron, *The Sun in the Church: Cathedrals as Solar Observatories* (Harvard University Press, 1999)

14. "Relativity Turns 100," by R. Panek, in *Astronomy* (February, 2005).

Quest Ahead to Starlinks
http://physicalscience.jbpub.com/starlinks

Starlinks is this book's online learning center. It features **eLearning**, which contains chapter quizzes and other tools designed to help you study for your class. You can also find **online exercises**, view numerous relevant **animations,** follow a guide to **useful astronomy sites** on the Web, or even check the latest **astronomy news** updates.

atomic hydrogen

radio continuum (2.5 GHz)

molecular hydrogen

infrared

mid-infrared

near infrared

optical

x-ray

gamma ray

4

Light and the Electromagnetic Spectrum

The Milky Way seen at 10 wavelengths of the electromagnetic spectrum.

JAMES CLERK MAXWELL WAS BORN IN EDINBURGH, SCOTLAND IN 1831. His genius was apparent early in his life, for at the age of 14 years, he published a paper in the *Proceedings of the Royal Society of Edinburgh*. One of his first major achievements was the explanation for the rings of Saturn, in which he showed that they consist of small particles in orbit around the planet. In the 1860s, Maxwell began a study of electricity and magnetism and discovered that it should be possible to produce a wave that combines electrical and magnetic effects, a so-called electromagnetic wave. His analysis of this hypothetical wave showed that its speed would be 300,000 kilometers/second. Because this is the speed of light, Maxwell concluded that he had discovered the nature of light: Light is an electromagnetic wave.

In 1888, 9 years after Maxwell's death, radio waves were discovered by Heinrich Hertz and were shown to have properties similar to those of light. This verified Maxwell's prediction. The importance of Maxwell's work is indicated in the following quotation from the Nobel Prize winner Richard Feynman:

> *From a long view of human history—seen from, say ten thousand years from now—there can be little doubt that the most significant event of the 19th century will be judged as*

All cross references to chapters, sections, figures, and tables pertain to the main text, *In Quest of the Universe, Sixth Edition. In Quest of the Solar System* contains Chapters 1–11 and 19 of the main text. *In Quest of the Stars and Galaxies* contains Chapters 1–5 and 11–19 of the main text.

The Feynman Lectures on Physics. Vol. 2 (Reading, Mass.: Addison-Wesley Publishing Co., 1964).

Maxwell's discovery of the laws of electrodynamics. The American Civil War will pale into provincial insignificance in comparison with this important scientific event of the same decade.

An important part of your study of astronomy is to learn about the objects in our universe, but perhaps more important is to see how astronomy functions by learning *how* we know what we know about these objects. The only thing we obtain from them is the radiation they emit. This radiation, including not only visible light but many other types of radiation, carries to us a tremendous amount of information. To understand how astronomers analyze radiation to answer questions about celestial objects, it is necessary to learn something about radiation itself.

In this chapter, we examine the nature of light and show how we measure three major properties of stars: their temperatures, their compositions (that is, the chemical elements of which they are made), and their speeds relative to the Earth. Recall that we already have a tool, in the form of Kepler's third law (see Chapter 2), which allows us to find the total mass of a binary system. In addition, there are other tools, described in later chapters, which allow us to learn more about the stars (for example, how far away and how big they are).

4-1 The Kelvin Temperature Scale

Light transmits energy. We know this because we can clearly feel the warmth of sunshine. When we think of the Sun as an energy source (even though very different from other energy sources, such as a fireplace or a very hot iron bar), an obvious question to ask is how "hot" it is. What is its temperature? Even more important, what do we mean by the term "temperature," and how do we measure it? It should not be surprising that we started measuring temperatures long before we understood what temperature is. Check the accompanying Tools of Astronomy box where we describe the temperature scales currently in use.

The commonly used temperature scale in science is the *Kelvin scale*; its zero point corresponds to the lowest temperature possible (absolute zero), about −273°C. The intervals on the Kelvin scale are the same size as on the Celsius scale and, thus, in Kelvin temperature, the freezing point of water is 273 K and the boiling point is 373 K. (No degree symbol is included; the latter temperature is stated as "373 kelvin.") Figure B4-1 includes the Kelvin temperature scale on the right.

We now recognize that temperature is a fundamental quantity, as are mass and time. As such, it cannot be expressed in terms of other quantities; however, it is a good approximation for us to say that given the temperature of an object, such as a pot of water on a stove, we can calculate the average speed of each of its constituent particles; that is, temperature is a measure of their average *kinetic energy*. As the temperature of an object increases, each of its constituent particles moves faster, whereas as the temperature decreases, the particle speed also decreases (although not in a linear fashion). At absolute zero, we have a state of minimum atomic motion.

Kelvin temperature scale A temperature scale with its zero point at the lowest possible temperature ("absolute zero") and a degree that is the same size (same temperature difference) as the Celsius degree. $T_K = T_C + 273$.

kinetic energy An object's energy due to motion. For an object of mass m and speed v, its kinetic energy is equal to $(1/2)mv^2$.

EXAMPLE

A star's surface temperature is 6000 K. What is its temperature in degrees Celsius and Fahrenheit?

SOLUTION   In degrees Celsius, the star's temperature is 6000 − 273 = 5727°C. In degrees Fahrenheit, it is

$$\frac{9}{5}(5727)+32=10{,}341°F.$$

TOOLS OF ASTRONOMY

Temperature Scales

Around 1592, Galileo invented the first device indicating the "degree of hotness" of an object. The invention of the thermometer, in 1631, is credited to J. Rey, a French physician. The scale in common use in the United States is the Fahrenheit scale, but most of us are at least somewhat familiar with the Celsius temperature scale. The freezing point of water is defined as 0°C or 32°F, whereas the boiling point of water is defined as 100°C or 212°F. Because 180 divisions on the Fahrenheit scale correspond to 100 divisions on the Celsius scale, a Fahrenheit degree is smaller than a Celsius degree by a factor of 180/100 = 9/5. Thus, the two scales are related by

$$T_F = 32 + \frac{9}{5}T_C \quad \text{or} \quad T_C = \frac{5}{9}(T_F - 32).$$

The first two thermometers of Figure B4-1 compare the Fahrenheit and Celsius scales, from extremely low temperatures up to the boiling point of water, but let's think for a minute about what these temperature scales can and cannot tell us. What does it mean to say that object A is two (or a thousand) times hotter than object B, which is at 0°F? What is then the temperature of object A? The obvious answer is 0°F, but we know there is something wrong with this. (We could ask a similar question using 0°C.) Neither scale—nor, for that matter, any other scale that defines its zero mark arbitrarily—has anything to do with what temperature "is." Clearly, we would like to have an "absolute" temperature scale, one on which the zero mark is associated with the lowest temperature possible (absolute zero). Such a scale exists (FIGURE B4-1). It is called the **Kelvin** scale and is the one commonly used in science; it was first proposed by William Thompson (1824–1907), a British physicist and engineer who was made a baron in 1892, taking the title Lord Kelvin. He contributed important ideas across the entire range of physics.

FIGURE B4-1 A comparison of temperature scales.

For a large enough Kelvin temperature, we can approximate its Celsius equivalent by the same number, while its Fahrenheit equivalent is approximately twice as large in value.

TRY ONE YOURSELF

Two objects A and B are identical except that B is at 0°C and A is twice "as hot" (meaning its temperature is twice as large). What is the temperature of object A? (Hint: You must work with the Kelvin scale for both objects.)

4-2   The Wave Nature of Light

Our understanding of the nature of light has changed several times over the years. Two lines of thought about light came to us from the ancient Greeks. The first suggested that light is a stream of extremely small, fast-moving particles and that our vision is the result of the interaction between our eyes and this stream. The second idea, suggested by Aristotle, pictured light as an "aethereal motion." Aristotle added *aether* as the fifth element to his four elements of nature (fire, air, earth, and water) and imagined that it fills all space. According to this idea, our vision is the result of movement of the aether produced by the object we perceive.

The first step away from Aristotle's idea was taken by Newton, who theorized that light consists of tiny, fast-moving particles. FIGURE 4-1 shows a beam of white light passing through a glass prism. The emerging light is separated into colors—into a *spectrum*. Newton showed that the prism does not add color to the light, as was previously thought, but rather that color is already contained in white light and that the prism merely separates the light into its colors. He showed this by using a second prism to recombine the colors produced by the first. In a separate experiment, Newton allowed one color of the spectrum created by a prism to pass through a second prism. Because each color of the spectrum remained unchanged by the second prism, he was able to show that color is a fundamental property of light. We see in later chapters that analysis of the spectrum of light from stars is extremely important in astronomy.

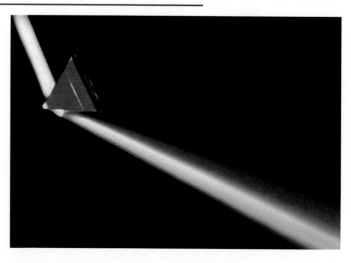

FIGURE 4-1 A prism separates white light into its component colors. This is shown by the beam emerging from the base of the prism and moving toward the bottom right in the image. In the case shown, however, there is an additional beam that emerges from the right of the prism and moves toward the upper right of the image. Why do we not see colors in this beam?

spectrum The order of colors or wavelengths produced when light is dispersed.

Characteristics of Wave Motion

Light acts like a wave. FIGURE 4-2 is a simplified drawing of a wave indicating that the distance between successive peaks (crests) of the wave is called the *wavelength* (λ). Waves you make by dipping your hand in a swimming pool might have a wavelength of about 2.25 inches.

A wave does not sit still, however. Imagine yourself fishing while sitting on a pier, watching waves pass underneath. As the waves move by, they cause the cork on the fishing line to move up and down. This indicates that the water itself moves up and down, rather than along the direction of the wave's motion. As the wave travels along the surface, the water's motion is *primarily* in the vertical direction and not along the direction of the wave. If you count the number of times the cork moves up and down, you might find that it moves through a complete cycle 30 times each minute. We say that the *frequency* of the cork's motion is 30 cycles per minute and therefore that the frequency of the wave is 30 cycles/minute. (Frequency is often reported in units of *hertz*, abbreviated Hz, where 1 hertz = 1 cycle/second.)

Now suppose you measure the wavelength of the waves and find it is 20 feet. Because each wave, from crest to crest, is 20 feet long and 30 of these waves pass by you each minute, the waves must move at a speed of 600 feet/minute. We multiply wavelength by frequency to obtain the speed of the wave. In equation form,

$$\text{wave speed} = \text{wavelength} \times \text{frequency},$$

or, using symbols,

$$v = \lambda \times f,$$

where v = wave speed, λ = wavelength and f = frequency.

wavelength The distance from a point on a wave, such as the crest, to the next corresponding point, such as the next crest.

frequency The number of repetitions per unit time.

hertz (abbreviated **Hz**) The unit of frequency equal to one cycle per second.

FIGURE 4-2 Wavelength is the distance between successive crests of a wave.

This equation applies to all types of waves, including light and sound waves. An application of its use for sound waves is shown in the next example. If you do the suggested exercise in this example, you will see that a sound of higher frequency has a shorter wavelength, as the speeds are the same. In the example, we use sound rather than light because sound waves have frequencies, velocities, and wavelengths within our everyday experience, whereas light waves do not. Now let's return to light and the spectrum produced when white light shines through a prism.

EXAMPLE

Sound travels at a speed of about 344 meters/second in air at room temperature. What is the wavelength of a sound that has a frequency of 262 Hz? (This is the frequency of the note C in music.)

SOLUTION   We start with the equation,

$$\text{wave speed} = \text{wavelength} \times \text{frequency, or}$$

$$344 \text{ m/s} = \lambda \times 262 \text{ cycles/s}.$$

We now solve the equation for the wavelength of the sound wave and do the calculation:

$$\lambda = \frac{344 \text{ m/s}}{262 \text{ cycles/s}} = 1.31 \text{ m}.$$

TRY ONE YOURSELF
What is the wavelength of a sound that has a frequency of 4000 Hz? (Hint: The speed of sound is the same for all frequencies, about 344 meters/second in air at room temperature.)

Light as a Wave

It only takes light 8.3 minutes to reach us from the Sun, but for faraway objects, we see them the way they were millions or even billions of years ago.

Can anything travel faster than the speed of light in a vacuum?

nanometer (abbreviated **nm**) A unit of length equal to 10^{-9} meter.

The color we see is not a property of the light itself but a manifestation of the system that senses it, that is our eyes, nerves, and brain.

White light is made up of light of many different wavelengths, all traveling at the same speed in a vacuum (and interstellar space is essentially a vacuum). The speed of light (c) is 300,000 kilometers/second (186,000 miles/second). If a light beam could be made to travel around the Earth's surface, it would circle the globe seven times in one second. According to Einstein's special theory of relativity (which we discussed in Chapter 3), the speed of light in vacuum is always measured as the same speed and is the fastest speed possible in the universe. Check the accompanying Advancing the Model box to find out how we measure this incredibly high speed.

We perceive light of different wavelengths as different colors. The wavelength of the reddest of red light is about 7×10^{-7} meters, or 0.0000007 meters. The wavelength decreases across the spectrum from red to violet, and the wavelength at the violet end of the spectrum is about 4×10^{-7} meters. In describing the wavelengths of visible light, a meter is much too long to be convenient, and thus, scientists use another unit—the **nanometer**. One nanometer (abbreviated nm) is 10^{-9} meters. So the shortest violet wavelength and the longest red wavelength are about 400 nm and 700 nm, respectively.

Using the equation $c = \lambda \times f$ to calculate frequencies of light waves, we obtain extremely high frequencies: 400 nm corresponds to 7.5×10^{14} Hz, and 700 nm corresponds to 4.3×10^{14} Hz.

The particular frequency or wavelength of light in vacuum determines its color; however, because color is so subjective and people are unable to distinguish between two very similar colors, scientists describe light by referring to wavelength in vacuum (or frequency, as the two quantities are related) rather than color (**TABLE 4-1**). They might mention the color in some cases, but this is to help us better picture the situation: Light can be described more accurately than by simply calling it "red" or "green."

4-3 The Electromagnetic Spectrum

The waves we see—visible light—are just a small part of a great range of waves that make up the ***electromagnetic spectrum***. Waves somewhat longer than 700 nm (the approximate limit of red) are called *infrared* waves. **FIGURE 4-3** shows the entire electromagnetic spectrum. The infrared region of the spectrum goes from 700 nm at the border of visible light up to about 10^{-4} meters, which is a tenth of a millimeter or 100,000 nm. Electromagnetic waves longer than that are called *radio* waves. Going the other way, from visible light toward shorter wavelengths, we first encounter *ultraviolet* waves and then *X-rays* and *gamma rays*.

It is important to emphasize that all of these types of waves (or rays, as certain portions of the spectrum are known) are essentially the same phenomenon. They differ in wavelength, and this causes some of their other properties to differ. For example, visible light is just that—visible. Ultraviolet is invisible to us, but it kills living cells and causes our skin to tan or burn. On the other hand, we perceive infrared as "heat" radiation, and yes, the radio waves in the spectrum are the same radio waves we use to transmit messages on Earth. They are handy for carrying messages containing sound and pictures (in the case of television) for several reasons, including the fact that they pass through clouds and bend around obstacles. All of these various waves are electromagnetic waves, just as visible light is. We give the various regions different names because of their properties and the uses we have for them.

The electromagnetic spectrum is important to astronomers because celestial objects emit waves in all the different regions of the spectrum. Visible light is a very small fraction of the entire spectrum. We humans tend to regard it as the important part, but this only reveals our limited outlook. Astronomers learn a great deal from the *invisible* radiation emitted by objects in the heavens.

TABLE 4-1

Approximate Vacuum Wavelength* Ranges for the Various Colors

Color	l (nm)
Violet	380-455
Blue	455-492
Green	492-577
Yellow	577-597
Orange	597-622
Red	622-720

* From now on, whenever we refer to the wavelength of light, we mean its wavelength in vacuum. As light travels from one medium to another, its speed and wavelength change but its frequency remains the same.

electromagnetic spectrum
The entire array of electromagnetic waves.

The waves are called "electromagnetic" because they consist of combined, perpendicular, oscillating electric and magnetic fields that result when a charged particle accelerates (see Figure B4-9b).

It is probably not worth memorizing these wavelengths of light waves, but it is handy to remember that the wavelength of visible light ranges from 400 (violet) to 700 (red) nanometers.

Is most of the electromagnetic spectrum made up of visible light?

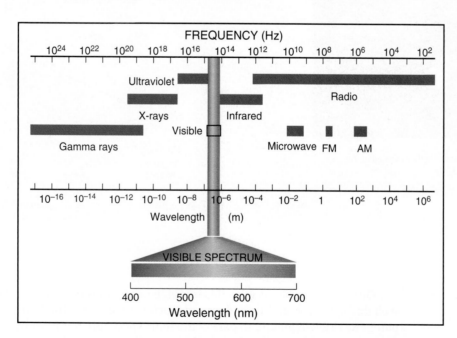

FIGURE 4-3 The electromagnetic spectrum is divided into several regions, depending upon the properties of the radiation. Region boundaries are not well defined. Notice the small portion of the spectrum occupied by visible light.

ADVANCING THE MODEL

Measuring the Speed of Light

Today we know that the speed of light c is 2.9979×10^8 m/s. How do we know that? You can't exactly time a light beam with a stop watch. Our understanding of light and its speed parallels the development of the technology that was used to measure this speed.

In the early 1600s, Galileo attempted to measure the speed of light by using his pulse-beat and comparing the time between opening his lantern while on a hilltop and seeing the light from his assistant's lantern from a distant hilltop. His attempts were not successful, but he correctly concluded that light is simply too fast to be measured by the slow human reaction.

Around 1675, the Danish astronomer Ole Roemer made the first accurate measurement of the value of c (FIGURE B4-2). Roemer had made many careful observations of Jupiter's moon Io and knew that Io's orbital period is about 1.76 days. As a result, he expected that he could predict Io's eclipses accurately. He was astonished to find that Io seemed to be behind its predicted position when the Earth was farther away from Jupiter (point A) and ahead when the Earth was closer (point B). Roemer correctly attributed this effect to the time required for light to travel from Jupiter to Earth. Light takes about 16.5 minutes to travel across the diameter of the Earth's orbit (2 AU); Roemer's actual measurement was 22

minutes. Using today's value for the AU (as it was not accurately known during Roemer's time) we find

$$c = \frac{\text{distance}}{\text{time}} = \frac{2 \times 1.5 \times 10^{11}\,\text{m}}{16.5 \times 60\,\text{s}} = 3 \times 10^8\,\text{m/s}.$$

(Roemer's actual calculation gave $c = 2.14 \times 10^8$ m/s.)

In 1849, French physicist Armand Fizeau measured the speed of light using the arrangement shown in FIGURE B4-3. His idea was to bounce a light beam between two mirrors, passing through a rotating toothed wheel in each direction. By choosing an appropriate rotation speed, the light beam can be made to pass through one gap on its way to the far mirror and the very next gap on its return to the observer. From the rotation rate, Fizeau calculated the time for the wheel to move from one gap between teeth to the next; this was the time during which light traveled from the wheel to the mirror and back. Dividing the distance by the time, Fizeau calculated $c = 3.15 \times 10^8$ m/s.

We can now routinely make accurate measurements of c in the laboratory. The speed of light in vacuum is now defined to be $c = 299,792.458$ km/s. Light has a smaller speed when going through other transparent media, but unless otherwise specified, we use $c = 300,000$ km/s.

FIGURE B4-2 Roemer's method of measuring the speed of light. The scale of the orbits of Earth and Jupiter has been changed to exaggerate the effect.

FIGURE B4-3 Fizeau's method of measuring the speed of light.

One of our problems with this invisible radiation is that most of it does not pass well through air and, thus, it does not reach the surface of the Earth. Our air is transparent to visible light and to part of the radio spectrum, but most of the rest of the electromagnetic spectrum is blocked to some degree. The chart in FIGURE 4-4 shows the relative absorbency of the atmosphere to various regions of the spectrum. Where the graph line is highest, the least amount of radiation gets through. Not much ultraviolet radiation, which damages living cells, penetrates to the surface.

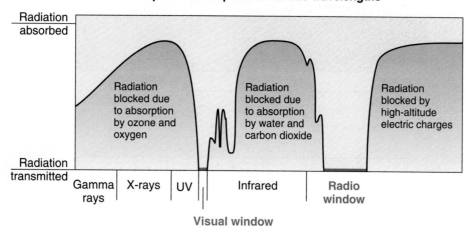

Atmospheric absorption at various wavelengths

FIGURE 4-4 The height of the curve indicates the relative amount of radiation of a given wavelength blocked by the atmosphere from reaching Earth's surface. The atmosphere is transparent to two regions of the spectrum: visible light and part of the radio region.

Astronomers, however, wish to detect and examine these nonpenetrating radiations from space. They accomplish this by using balloons to carry detectors high into the atmosphere or by using artificial satellites to take detectors completely above the atmosphere. This will be covered in the next chapter.

Astronomers refer to *windows* in the atmosphere, saying that there is a visual window and a radio window. This means that our atmosphere allows radiation in these two regions of the spectrum to penetrate to the surface.

4-4   The Colors of Planets and Stars

How do we analyze the light spectrum from a celestial object to determine some of the object's properties? This analysis can be divided into two parts. First, we look at the overall spectrum, from which we typically determine the color of the object; however, when we look at the spectrum, we are really examining the actual wavelengths of light rather than just the color. The second analysis, discussed later in this chapter, involves examining individual regions of the spectrum.

Color from Reflection—The Colors of Planets

When you see a visible spectrum spread out on a screen, you see a particular color at a given location on the spectrum. This is because a wave whose wavelength is associated with that color is coming to your eye from that spot; however, the color we see in most objects does not correspond to a single wavelength. FIGURE 4-5a might be the spectrum of light from some lemons. It contains many different wavelengths of light; however, there is no violet or blue light, and the center of the spectrum is indeed in the yellow. Part (b) of the figure shows a graph that indicates the intensity of light of each wavelength. Where the graph is higher, the light of the corresponding color

Spectrum of light from lemons

(a)

(b)

FIGURE 4-5 An example of reflected color. (a) If light reflected from the lemons were sent through a prism to reveal its spectrum, we would see that the lemons reflect mostly yellow light. (b) This graph indicates the relative intensity of the various wavelengths of light from the lemons.

FIGURE 4-6 An example of transmitted light. (a) The spectrum of light from the taillight of this particular car (right). The lightbulb emits white light, but the plastic cover over the bulb absorbs much of the light, letting pass some wavelengths in the red, orange, and yellow regions of the spectrum. (b) This graph indicates the relative intensity of the various wavelengths of light in this case.

Spectrum of light from taillights

(a)

(b)

is brighter. Lemons have this spectrum because when white light strikes them, they absorb some of the wavelengths of the white light, especially blue and violet. They reflect only those we see in their spectrum (the wavelengths centered on the color yellow). This is what determines their color.

Planets have their colors because of a process like that described for the lemons. The rusty red color of Mars, for example, occurs because the material on its surface absorbs some of the wavelengths of sunlight and reflects a combination of wavelengths that looks rusty red to us.

FIGURE 4-6 shows the color spectrum and graph of intensity versus wavelength for the light from the red taillight of a car. The spectrum includes not only many wavelengths in the red part of the spectrum but also some orange. In this case, the bulb inside the taillight emits white light, but part of that light is absorbed by the plastic cover. The light that gets through the cover has the spectrum in the figure.

In the case of the Sun and other stars, light from the star is produced by emission within the star and some light is absorbed as it passes through the star's outer layer. The effect of this absorption on the color of the star is minimal, but nevertheless, the process is somewhat similar to that described for the taillight of the car. We will look at this in more detail later.

Color as a Measure of Temperature

We want you to imagine a dark room because in a well-lit room, the lamp and stove element reflect light and you can see them even if they are turned off.

The light emitted by the Sun and other stars can be compared with light coming from a lightbulb or from the element of an electric stove in an otherwise dark room. Consider what happens when you turn the burner of an electric stove to a low setting. It glows a dull red. The bottom curve in **FIGURE 4-7** is a graph of intensity versus wavelength for this case. This graph includes not only the visible portion of the spectrum, but quite a lot of the infrared. Recall that we experience infrared radiation as heat. In fact, the graph indicates that more infrared radiation is being emitted than visible radiation, and the graph reaches its peak in the infrared portion of the spectrum. Some red light is emitted, but very little light from the center and violet end of the visible spectrum.

Astronomers usually call the graph of intensity versus wavelength for a star its *thermal spectrum.*

Now turn up the heat on the stove. The burner begins to take on an orange glow. The second curve from the bottom in Figure 4-7 is a graph of intensity versus wavelength for this burner. Compare it with the bottom curve (the red-hot burner). First, the orange burner is emitting more radiation of all wavelengths. This should correspond to your experience, for you can feel that more infrared is being emitted and see that more light is coming from the burner. Second, the peak of the graph has moved over toward the visible portion of the spectrum, toward the shorter wavelengths.

This is about as far as you can go with an electric stove burner. If you have an object with a temperature you can control, you can increase its temperature so that the object emits most of its light in the yellow part of the spectrum. The third curve from the bottom is a graph of such an object. It actually corresponds to the Sun. The fourth

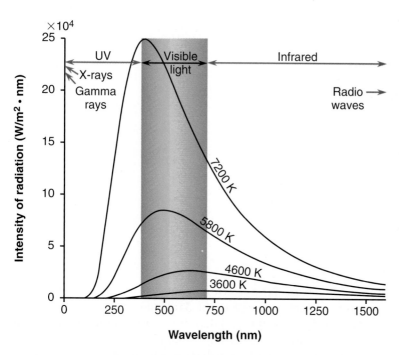

FIGURE 4-7 The bottom curve represents an object (at 3600 K with $\lambda_{max} = 805$ nm) that emits mostly infrared radiation. The next curve corresponds to an object (at 4600 K with $\lambda_{max} = 630$ nm) that emits most of its light in the orange part of the spectrum. The third curve from the bottom corresponds to the Sun (at 5800 K with $\lambda_{max} = 500$ nm). The 7200 K object would most likely seem "blue" because it emits most of its light in the violet part of the spectrum ($\lambda_{max} = 403$ nm). Recall that color is subjective.

blackbody A theoretical object that absorbs and emits all wavelengths of radiation, so that it is a perfect absorber and emitter of radiation. The radiation it emits is called **blackbody radiation**.

continuous spectrum A spectrum containing an entire range of wavelengths, rather than separate, discrete wavelengths.

Beta Cygni (named Alberio) is the second brightest star in the constellation Cygnus. It is the brighter of a closely spaced pair of stars with obvious color differences.

curve from the bottom of Figure 4-7 corresponds to an object of even higher temperature. You see that it emits most of its light in the violet part of the spectrum.

The temperatures indicated in Figure 4-7 are typical of surface temperatures of stars. As their sequence indicates, the higher the temperature of a star, the shorter the wavelength at which the star emits most of its energy. The relationship between an object's temperature (T) and the wavelength at which maximum emission occurs (λ_{max}) was discovered in 1893 by the German physicist Wilhelm Wien. **Wien's law** is expressed as

$$\lambda_{max(in\ nm)} = \frac{2.9 \times 10^6}{T_{(in\ K)}},$$

where λ_{max} is in nanometers and the temperature is in kelvin. You can check that this equation applies to the curves of Figure 4-7.

FIGURE 4-8 is an image of one of the coolest stars ever found. We often refer to stars by color as a quick way to indicate their temperature: A "white" star is hotter than a "red" star. In practice, of course, a "red" star does not appear red like a Christmas tree bulb, but it definitely has a red tint. To the unpracticed naked eye, color differences between stars are not at all obvious; however, if you have the opportunity to use a telescope to observe pairs of closely spaced stars, you can see this color difference easily.

The important point is that by examining the intensity versus wavelength curve for a star and using Wien's law, we can determine the star's surface temperature without ever visiting it!

Blackbody Radiation. Wien's law was derived from theoretical calculations about the radiation that would be emitted from an object that absorbs (or emits) all wavelengths completely. Such an ideal object is called a *blackbody*, and the radiation it emits is called *blackbody radiation*. A blackbody emits a *continuous spectrum*, which has a peak at a certain wavelength λ_{max}, but some energy is emitted at all wavelengths, as shown by the blackbody curves in Figure 4-7. It was found that although the stars are not perfect blackbodies, the theory applies very closely to them, as shown by **FIGURE 4-9**. This figure shows the intensity of the measured solar radiation outside the Earth's atmosphere from 300 to 830 nm; the Sun's

FIGURE 4-8 The *Hubble Space Telescope* imaged one of the lowest-temperature stars ever seen (upper right). It is a companion to the dwarf star at lower left. The surface temperature of the cool star may be as low as 2300 degrees Celsius. (The white bar is an effect produced by the camera.)

FIGURE 4-9 The Sun is almost an ideal blackbody at 5800 K. The measurements of the Sun's intensity were made above the Earth's atmosphere.

FIGURE 4-9 The Sun is almost an ideal blackbody at 5800 K. The measurements of the Sun's intensity were made above the Earth's atmosphere.

spectrum peaks in the visible part of the electromagnetic spectrum, where our eyes have become most sensitive. Superimposed to the data is a curve obtained by assuming that the Sun is a blackbody at 5800 K and that its intensity is measured outside Earth's atmosphere. Compare this curve with the 5800 K curve in Figure 4-7; as we discuss in Section 4-8, radiation from a source decreases in intensity as the inverse square of the distance from the source.

The Stefan-Boltzmann Law. Figure 4-7 indicates that the hotter an object is, the more radiation it emits. In 1879 an Austrian physicist, Josef Stefan, discovered the mathematical relationship between temperature and energy emitted, based on data published 14 years earlier. In 1884, another Austrian physicist, Ludwig Boltzmann, used a theoretical argument to show why the relationship occurs. This rule, now called the *Stefan-Boltzmann law*, is

$$F = \sigma T^4,$$

where T is the object's temperature on the Kelvin scale, F, called the energy flux, is the energy it emits per unit time per unit area, and σ (the Greek letter sigma) is a constant, called the *Stefan-Boltzmann constant*, that relates the two quantities. This law tells us that the energy flux of an object is directly proportional to its temperature to the fourth power. If the temperature of an object were to double, its energy flux thus would be 2^4, or 16, times greater than it was before.

As we see in Chapter 12, the Stefan-Boltzmann law allows us to find the radius of a star. (From observations, we can find a star's temperature and the total energy it emits each second. Recall the meaning of energy flux and the fact that the surface area of a sphere is proportional to the square of its radius.)

4-5   Types of Spectra

The spectrum of visible light shown in Figure 4-1 is a *continuous spectrum*. Such a spectrum is produced when a solid object (in this case the filament of a lamp) is heated to a temperature great enough that the object emits visible light. Not all spectra are of this type, as was discovered nearly 200 years ago.

Kirchhoff's Laws

In 1814, Joseph von Fraunhofer, a German optician, used a prism to produce a solar spectrum. He noticed that the spectrum was not continuous but had a number of dark lines across it (**FIGURE 4-10**). Fraunhofer had no explanation for these dark lines, but it was later discovered that they were the result of the sunlight passing through cooler gases (in the Sun's and the Earth's atmospheres). Then, in the mid-1800s, several

Hydrogen

Neon

Calcium

Strontium

400 nm   500 nm   600 nm

FIGURE 4-11 The visible bright line spectrum of four different chemical elements. Each element emits specific wavelengths of light when it is heated. This applies not only to visible light (shown here) but also to infrared and ultraviolet. Such a spectrum is called an emission spectrum.

German chemists discovered that if gases are heated until they emit light, neither a continuous spectrum nor a spectrum with dark lines is produced; instead, a spectrum made up of *bright* lines appears. Further, they discovered that each chemical element has its own distinctive pattern of lines (FIGURE 4-11). This proved to be a very valuable way of identifying the makeup of an unknown substance and was soon developed into a standard technique that allows us to identify the chemical composition of matter.

In the 1860s, Gustav Kirchhoff formulated a set of rules, now called *Kirchhoff's laws,* which summarize how the three types of spectra are produced:

1. A hot, dense glowing object (a solid or a dense gas) emits a continuous spectrum (Figure 4-1).

2. A hot, low-density gas emits light of only certain wavelengths—a bright line spectrum (Figure 4-11).

3. When light having a continuous spectrum passes through a cool gas, dark lines appear in the continuous spectrum—a dark-line spectrum (Figure 4-10).

The dark lines that result when light passes through a cool gas (process 3) have the same wavelengths as the bright lines that are emitted if this same gas is heated (process 2).

Kirchhoff's laws tell us how to produce the various types of spectra, but the science behind the laws—the connection between the laws and the nature of matter—remained a mystery in the 19th century. The connection was finally made in 1913, when a young Danish physicist, Niels Bohr, proposed a new model of the atom.

Gustav Kirchhoff (1824–1887) was a German physicist and astronomer whose primary work was in the field of spectroscopy, the study of spectra.

4-6   The Bohr Model of the Atom

The atomic model accepted at that time was due primarily to the New Zealand physicist Ernest Rutherford. His model described the atom as having a *nucleus* with a positive electrical charge, circled by *electrons* with a negative electrical charge. Positive and negative electrical charges attract one another, and this electrical force holds the electrons in orbit around the nucleus. As an electron orbits the nucleus, it continuously changes direction and thus accelerates; however, according to classical theory,

nucleus (of atom) The central, massive part of an atom.

electron A negatively charged particle that orbits the nucleus of an atom.

HISTORICAL NOTE

Niels Bohr

Niels Bohr (1885–1962) was born into a very cultured Danish home. His father's interest in science led Niels to that subject, and he became known as a student who gave his utmost to every project—a reputation that continued throughout his life.

In 1922 Niels Bohr was awarded the Nobel Prize in physics "for his services in the investigation of the structure of atoms and of the radiation emanating from them." In his acceptance speech, he emphasized the limitations of his theory, and indeed, he seems to have been more aware of its limitations than other scientists who worked with the theory.

Niels' son Aage followed his father in the study of physics and won the Nobel Prize in 1975. One major project on which Niels and Aage Bohr worked together was the development of the atomic bomb. Niels' mother was Jewish, and after Hitler's army overran Denmark, Niels' family (FIGURE B4-4) fled their native land to avoid arrest. Niels and Aage came to the United States and helped with the Manhattan Project (the code name for the bomb development effort).

Bohr's contribution to science goes far deeper than the development of the Bohr model of the atom, as important as that is. His philosophical ideas on the nature of physical theory are perhaps his greatest contribution. Many important

FIGURE B4-4 Niels Bohr and his sons.

ideas of modern physics were clarified through the friendly arguments between Bohr and Einstein. Einstein would try to imagine situations in which the new ideas of quantum mechanics (the modern description of matter and energy) did not work, and Bohr would always figure out how quantum mechanics did explain these situations. It is a classic example of how science can progress through the informal discussions between scientists.

any charged particle moving in a curved path or accelerating in a straight-line path will emit electromagnetic radiation, thus losing energy. Therefore, what keeps the electrons from simply spiraling into the nucleus, leading to collapse of the atom? Bohr's model attempted to answer this question.

Before describing his model, we must emphasize that today we have a much more powerful model of matter and energy (called **Quantum Mechanics**); however, just like we still use Newtonian ideas to describe gravity even though we have the theory of relativity, we still use Bohr's model because many of its conclusions are essentially valid and it provides the basic conceptual tools in understanding atomic structure. Wherever appropriate, we mention important differences between the two models.

The **Bohr atom**, as Niels Bohr's model is called, is based on three postulates:

1. Electrons in orbit around a nucleus can have only certain specific energies. To imagine different energies for the electrons, imagine electrons orbiting at different distances from the nucleus. The negatively charged electrons are being attracted to the positively charged nucleus; thus, to pull an electron farther away from the nucleus requires energy. Because only certain energies are possible, we speak of "allowed" orbits for the electrons. The element hydrogen has only one electron, but many possible energy levels and therefore many allowed orbits. The drawing in FIGURE 4-12a depicts the hydrogen atom with its electron in the lowest orbit (the ground state) and also shows, as an example, the next orbit this electron might have. The point of Bohr's first postulate is that the electron can have only specific energies and therefore specific orbits. This is far different from the solar system, where there are no limitations on possible positions of orbits.

Bohr atom The model of the atom proposed by Niels Bohr; it describes electrons in orbit around a central nucleus and explains the absorption and emission of light.

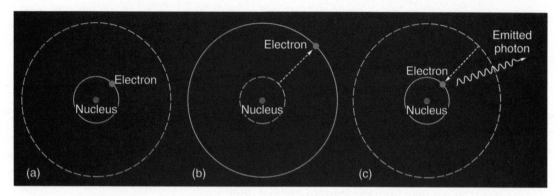

FIGURE 4-12 (a) The electron is in the lowest possible energy state—the ground state. (b) When the atom gains energy (perhaps by collision with another atom), the electron jumps up to a higher orbit. (c) The electron then quickly falls down to its original orbit and, as it does, emits energy in the form of a photon of electromagnetic radiation. The orbits are not drawn to scale.

Bohr simply assumed that an atomic electron in one of the allowed circular and stable orbits did not radiate any energy. (In the modern view of Quantum Mechanics, the wave-particle duality of light is extended to all entities, including matter. That is, there is a wave aspect associated with an electron, and therefore, there is a wavelength associated to a moving electron. This provides an interesting interpretation of Bohr's model of an atom; an allowed circular orbit has a circumference that is an integer multiple of the electron's wavelength. Also, according to Quantum Mechanics, we can calculate the probability that an electron of a given energy will be at some distance from the nucleus; Bohr's orbit for the same electron simply corresponds to the most probable distance.)

2. An electron can transit from one energy level to another, changing the energy of the atom. In terms of electron orbits, when energy is added to an atom, the electron moves farther from the nucleus. On the other hand, the atom loses energy when an electron moves from an outer orbit to an inner orbit. This lost energy leaves the atom in the form of electromagnetic radiation.

Our previous discussion of waves and light assumed that light acts as a simple long wave, similar to the waves you can make in a swimming pool. However, as we discuss in the Advancing the Model box on pages 112 to 113, light has a wave-particle duality. In the Bohr model, light is emitted not as continuous waves, but in tiny bursts of energy; each burst is emitted when an electron moves to an orbit closer to the nucleus. These tiny bursts of electromagnetic energy are called ***photons***. The energy of the photon depends on the spacing between electron orbits.

3. The energy of a photon determines the frequency of light that is associated with the photon. The greater the energy of the photon, the greater the frequency of light, and vice versa. A photon of violet light thus has more energy than a photon of red light. The relevant equation is

$$E = hf,$$

where E = the energy of the photon, h = a constant (called *Planck's constant*), and f = the frequency of the light.

Emission Spectra

The Bohr model of the atom can be used to explain why only certain wavelengths are seen in the spectrum of light emitted by a hot gas. In its normal, lowest energy state, the electron of a hydrogen atom is in its lowest possible orbit, as indicated in Figure 4-12a. If this atom is given enough energy (perhaps by collisions with other atoms), the electron will jump to the next allowed orbit. Figure 4-12b illustrates this jump. An atom will not stay in its energized state long. Quickly, the electron falls down to a lower orbit, emitting a photon as it does, as shown in Figure 4-12c.

The wave particle duality of light is discussed in the corresponding Advancing the Model box on pages 112–113.

photon The smallest possible amount of electromagnetic energy of a particular wavelength.

Every physicist thinks he knows what a photon is. I spent my life to find out what a photon is and I still don't know it.
Albert Einstein

◆ The lowest energy state of an atom is usually called the *ground state*, and the energized states are called *excited states*.

The energy of this photon is exactly equal to the energy difference between the two orbits. Finally, because the energy of the photon determines the frequency of the radiation, the radiation coming from this atom must be of the corresponding frequency (and color).

We have described one atom emitting one photon. In an actual lamp that contains hot hydrogen gas, there are countless atoms gaining energy and countless atoms emitting photons as they lose energy. Different atoms will have different amounts of energy, depending on the energy they have absorbed (from a collision with another atom, for example). If a particular atom's energy corresponds to the electron being in the third orbit, the atom might release its energy in a single step, as shown in FIGURE 4-13a, or in two steps as shown in Figure 4-13b. That is, there are two different ways for an electron to move from the third to the first orbit.

Let us now assume that enough energy is available to cause electrons to move to even higher orbits. Using similar drawings, you should be able to show that there are four different ways for an electron to move from the fourth to the first orbit, eight different ways to move from the fifth to the first orbit, and so forth. Each jump of an electron for each of the steps involved in each different path corresponds to a certain specific energy and therefore to a certain specific frequency of emitted radiation. The electrons of some atoms will fall by some paths, and the electrons of other atoms will fall by other paths. As a result, radiation of several different frequencies will be emitted from the entire group of atoms. Not all frequencies will be emitted, however—just those that correspond to the electron jumps.

Hence, the spectrum from a heated, low-density gas is not a continuous spectrum. It contains only certain definite frequencies. We call such a spectrum an **emission spectrum**—the bright line spectrum mentioned earlier.

Refer back to Figure 4-11, which shows the emission spectra of four elements. Each spectrum is different because the allowed energy levels of the atoms are different for each chemical element. No two chemical elements have the same set of energy levels, and thus, no two chemical elements have the same emission spectrum. This provides us with a valuable method of identifying elements, as each has a unique spectral "fingerprint." This process has some important applications here on Earth, but because in this book we are more interested in the stars, we look at a stellar application.

emission spectrum A spectrum made up of discrete frequencies (or wavelengths) rather than a continuous band.

Continuous and Absorption Spectra of the Stars

Kirchhoff's laws tell us that dark line spectra result from light with a continuous spectrum passing through a cool gas. Let us examine this in the case of the Sun.

The visible surface (the **photosphere**) of the Sun emits a continuous spectrum. Even though the Sun, in most ways, is more like a gas than a solid, it produces a continuous spectrum rather than an emission spectrum. This is because as atoms are

photosphere The region of the Sun from which mostly visible radiation is emitted.

FIGURE 4-13 (a) The electron may fall directly from orbit 3 to orbit 1, emitting a single photon. (b) The electron may fall from orbit 3 to orbit 1 in two steps, emitting two photons whose energies sum to that of the single photon emitted in part (a). The orbits are not drawn to scale.

The Balmer Series

In Figure 4-11, notice the pattern to the spacing of bright lines in the hydrogen spectrum—they become progressively closer as they approach the blue end of the spectrum. The mathematical relationship that expresses this pattern was found in 1885 by Johann Jacob Balmer, a Swiss teacher. The lines visible in the figure are therefore called the **Balmer series** of spectral lines. This series served as the foundation for Bohr's work, and it is easily explained by Bohr's model of the atom. In FIGURE B4-5, the spacing of the lines depicting the orbits of the hydrogen atom represents the relative energy of each of the levels. According to Bohr's model, there is less difference between the energy levels as orbits get farther from the nucleus. The levels thus are spaced closer together toward the top of the figure.

Suppose that an electron is in the lowest energy level, the ground state. This electron will jump to a higher state when a photon of the appropriate energy strikes it. Look at the left side of FIGURE B4-6. Five arrows point upward from the ground state, representing electron jumps to higher orbits. On each arrow is printed the wavelength of the photon corresponding to the jump indicated. Each of these wavelengths is less than 400 nm, the shortest wavelength of visible light. They are in the ultraviolet region of the spectrum.

As a gas becomes hotter, more of its atoms have electrons in energy levels above the ground state. Suppose that hydrogen is at a temperature at which a significant number of its electrons are in energy level 2. The middle of Figure B4-6 shows the wavelengths of photons that would cause electrons at this level to jump to a higher level. The wavelengths of the photons that cause jumps from the second level are within the visible range—from 400 to 700 nm—and because energy levels are more closely spaced toward the top of the figure, the wavelengths toward the blue end of the spectrum are closer together. These wavelengths correspond to the wavelengths of the Balmer series.

The first set of wavelengths described previously, those in the ultraviolet region of the spectrum, form the *Lyman series*. As Figure B4-6 indicates, there is another series that falls in the infrared portion of the spectrum, called the *Paschen series*.

Thus far, we have discussed the absorption of photons to produce an absorption spectrum. As we noted in the text, the emission spectrum of hydrogen is produced when electrons fall from higher energies to lower. The spectrum shown in Figure 4-11 thus is an emission spectrum that resulted from electrons falling from higher energies to lower levels of the atom.

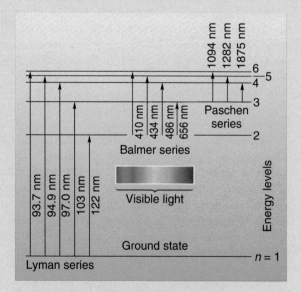

FIGURE B4-5 The energy levels of the hydrogen atom (not drawn to scale). The levels are progressively closer in energy as they are farther from the nucleus. The length of each arrow corresponds to the energy involved in the process. An atom is *ionized* when an electron absorbs enough energy and escapes.

FIGURE B4-6 Electrons that transit from the ground state to higher energy levels do so by absorbing photons of the wavelengths shown. Electron jumps for the first three series of the hydrogen atom's spectrum are represented here.

ADVANCING THE MODEL

Evidence for the Wave-Particle Duality of Light

In the 1660s, English scientist Robert Hooke challenged Aristotle's particle model of light for the first time. He proposed a simple wave theory in which light was the manifestation of fast oscillations in the aether. He reasoned that this model better explained the color patterns observed in thin transparent films, such as soap bubbles. On the other hand, Newton favored the particle model for light and suggested that light has a dual nature and that it is a stream of particles that can induce oscillations in the aether. Newton, however, misunderstood how waves behave. He expected that if light were a wave, it should clearly spread out after passing through an opening, instead of producing the observed narrow beams. In his opinion, the particle model for light better explained how light propagates along straight lines and why shadows are sharp. The problem is that light *does* spread out as Newton expected, but this can be seen only if the opening is of the same approximate size as the wavelength of the light, which is extremely small (at least for visible light, which was what he used at the time).

Both the particle and wave models for light explained two of the most common phenomena we observe. Light reflects—it bounces like a tennis ball off a flat surface. Also, light refracts—it changes direction when going from one medium (such as air) to another (such as water). The particle model of light, however, gained acceptance for more than a century, mainly because of Newton's reputation and authority.

Around 1801, Thomas Young first proposed a simple but convincing experimental test to distinguish between the two competing models. Young's experiment was to shine light of a specific wavelength (from a single source) through two narrow parallel slits, close to each other. The light then fell on a screen a certain distance away (FIGURE B4-7). Young observed a pattern of light and dark bands on the screen, called interference fringes, which he explained by assuming that light is a wave. As light waves go through the slits, they *diffract* (they spread out) in a series of crests and troughs. When the waves meet, they add up algebraically as shown in FIGURE B4-8. Bright (dark) fringes appear on the screen in places where the waves interfere constructively (destructively). Young used this *double-slit experiment* (actually he used pinholes instead of slits) to measure the wavelength for violet (400 nm) and red light (700 nm).

The experiments of the French physicist Augustin Fresnel (1788–1827) helped put the wave model of light on a firm mathematical basis. The interference of light clearly

FIGURE B4-7 Young's double-slit experiment. The colors used for the light areas on the screen are for illustration purposes only and correspond to decreasing intensity of the light.

showed its wave nature, but what was the nature of the waves? In the early 1860s, the Scottish mathematical physicist James Clerk Maxwell (1831–1879) succeeded in unifying what was then known about electricity and magnetism into four equations, which today are named after him. He found that his equations described the existence of *transverse* waves (such as the up-and-down waves traveling on a stretched rope) that combine electromagnetic effects and move at a speed that is almost the same as the then known speed of light. To understand this, consider a small sphere carrying a uniform charge Q. If we place a tiny positive test-charge q_0 anywhere in the space around Q, it will experience a force of a specific direction and strength. We say that there is a *field* of force around charge Q. To represent visually this electric field, we draw continuous lines that are tangent to all of the "specific directions of force," as shown in FIGURE B4-9a. Now consider what will happen if we make charge Q oscillate; if you visualize the field lines as made of rubber bands, you can see that the oscillation will set up waves propagating outward. Indeed, the changes in the strength of the field that occur due to the motion of charge Q propagate outward like

FIGURE B4-8 (a) Waves interfering constructively. (b) Waves interfering destructively.

ADVANCING THE MODEL

Evidence for the Wave-Particle Duality of Light *(Cont'd)*

waves with a speed equal to *c*. Maxwell found that magnetic fields can be formed not only by moving charges but also by changing electric fields, and that electric fields form not only by charges but also by changing magnetic fields (Figure B4-9b). Maxwell wrote that "we can scarcely avoid the inference that light consists in the transverse modulations of the same medium which is the cause of electric and magnetic phenomena." Nine years after Maxwell died, the German physicist Heinrich Hertz (1857–1894) produced radio waves in his lab, which confirmed all the properties of light known at the time. At the close of the 19th century, the wave model for light seemed to be very successful; however, some unanswered questions still remained. The most important ones dealt with the continuous spectrum of blackbody radiation and with the emission and absorption spectra.

In 1900, while trying to explain the continuous spectrum of blackbody radiation, the German physicist Max Planck (1858–1947) discovered an equation that fit the blackbody curve. In an effort to understand its meaning, Planck was forced to accept that electromagnetic waves can only have discrete (*quantized*) energy values that are integer

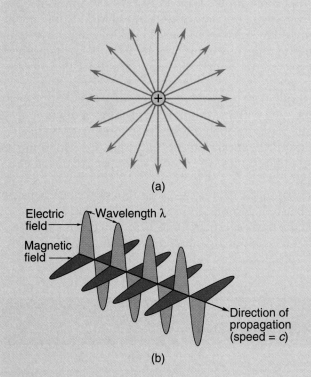

(a)

(b)

FIGURE B4-9 (a) Electric field lines around a positive charge. If the charge were negative, the lines would be pointing toward the charge. Keep in mind that this is a three-dimensional field. The field is stronger where the concentration of lines is denser. (b) Electromagnetic radiation (from radio waves to X-rays) consists of oscillating electric and magnetic fields, perpendicular to each other, moving through space at the speed of light.

multiples of a minimum energy value, called a *quantum* of energy. This quantum of energy is given by *hf*, where *f* is the frequency of the wave and *h* is Planck's constant. Today we consider *h* to be a fundamental constant of nature, like the gravitational constant *G* and the speed of light *c*. It is also the basis of *Quantum Mechanics*, which is the modern description of matter and energy; however, the quantum idea did not fit at all with the prevailing wave model of light.

The quantum nature of light was taken seriously by Einstein, who in 1905 used it to explain a very puzzling phenomenon, known as the *photoelectric effect*. When light of a certain frequency shines on a metal surface, electrons are ejected from it with a range of energies. (This is the basis of today's photocells in door openers, bar code scanners, and hundreds of other applications.) However, the maximum kinetic energy of these electrons does not depend on how bright the source of light is! According to the wave model of light, if we increase the rate of light energy falling on the surface, individual electrons will absorb more energy and will be emitted with larger kinetic energies. This is not what is observed. Increasing the brightness of the light source results in more electrons being emitted, but it doesn't affect their maximum kinetic energy. In addition, there is a minimum frequency that the light must have in order for any electrons to be emitted. This is also in contrast to the wave model for light, according to which if we wait long enough, the electrons will be able to absorb enough energy to be emitted, independent of the frequency of the light source.

Einstein's explanation was based on the assumption that light energy striking the metal surface is quantized in small bundles. These bundles behave as if they are a stream of massless particles that today we call *photons*. The energy of each photon is equal to *hf*. Convincing evidence that light indeed shows its particle nature when it interacts with matter was provided by the American physicist Arthur Compton in 1922. He measured the change in the wavelength of X-ray photons as they were scattered by free electrons (an observation now called the *Compton effect*) and found it to be exactly as predicted by the theory of a collision between two particles.

What, then, is the nature of light? It seems that light has a *wave-particle duality*. When it propagates through space, light can be described by a wave model (as shown by the double-slit experiment). When it interacts with matter, light can be described by a particle model (as shown by the photoelectric effect and the Compton effect). We cannot say whether light *is* particle or wave. This is not an either/or situation; light seems to be both particles and waves and thus is probably neither.

pushed together, their energy levels are broadened (as if slightly different orbits are allowed). As atoms become more and more tightly pressed together, their energy levels begin to overlap so that a full range of orbital energies is possible. An entire range of photon energies thus is emitted by the atoms, and instead of separate, distinct spectral lines appearing in the spectrum, an entire range of frequencies appears.

Before the light from the Sun gets to us on Earth, it must pass through the relatively cooler atmosphere of the Sun as well as through the atmosphere of the Earth. The Sun does indeed have an atmosphere and, as we will see in a later chapter, its atmosphere is much deeper than Earth's. As the light passes through these gases, atoms of the gases absorb some of it. This absorption of energy raises an atom's energy level, but because only certain specific energy levels are possible, only certain amounts of energy can be absorbed by the atom. This results in the reverse of what we had before: instead of an atom emitting a photon as it releases energy, it absorbs a photon as it absorbs energy. Just as a hot, low-density gas emits photons of certain energies, the same gas when in a cooler atmosphere absorbs photons of the same energies.

FIGURE 4-14a represents the emission spectrum of some element. Figure 4-14b shows the ***absorption spectrum*** that results when white light is passed through the cool gas of this same element. The dark lines of the absorption spectrum correspond exactly to the bright lines of the emission spectrum.

You might point out that after the cool gas has absorbed radiation, it must re-emit it. Shouldn't this then cancel out the absorption? No. As FIGURE 4-15 shows, the re-emitted light is sent out in all directions. Certain frequencies of the light that was originally coming toward the Earth thus are scattered by the atmosphere of the Sun. This results in less light of those frequencies reaching us, and we observe an absorption spectrum.

The spectrum of the light that is re-emitted is an emission spectrum. During a total eclipse of the Sun, light from the main body of the Sun is blocked out, and astronomers can see the light emitted by the Sun's atmosphere and examine its emission spectrum. It was by examining the emission spectrum from the gas near the Sun that astronomers first discovered the element helium (from the Greek *helios*, the Sun).

The Sun, and other stars as well, has various chemical elements in its atmosphere (that is, different kinds of atoms, each with its own pattern of electron orbits and spectral lines). As the white light passes through this gas, many frequencies are absorbed, corresponding to the various chemical elements of the gas. By examining the complicated absorption spectrum that results, we are able to deduce what elements are present in the star's atmosphere.

We thus answer a question that, just a century ago, was thought to be unanswerable. We now know what the surface layers of stars are made of! As you might appreciate from the complexity of the Sun's spectrum (look back at Figure 4-10), the analysis is fairly complicated, but it is now a common one in astronomy.

We discuss the Sun in Chapter 11.

---

absorption spectrum A spectrum that is continuous except for certain discrete frequencies (or wavelengths).

Absorption spectra are the dark line spectra of Kirchhoff's laws.

The elements in the Earth's atmosphere also absorb radiation, the frequencies of which depend on what elements are in our atmosphere, but we know what those elements are and can take them into account.

(a)

(b)

FIGURE 4-14 (a) The emission spectrum of an element; (b) the absorption spectrum of the same element. The absorbed wavelengths in (b) are the same as the emission lines in (a).

FIGURE 4-15 Consider a beam of light leaving a point on the Sun and moving toward the Earth. As it passes through the Sun's atmosphere, some wavelengths are absorbed and then re-emitted in random directions. This results in the solar spectrum being an absorption spectrum. Light from the Sun's atmosphere is an emission spectrum.

4-7 The Doppler Effect

Have you ever stood near a road and listened to the sound of a siren on a car as it sped by you? Recall how the sound changed when the siren passed, going from a higher pitch down to a lower pitch. This phenomenon has a very important parallel in astronomy. To understand it, we first consider water waves.

FIGURE 4-16a is a photo of waves spreading from a disturbance on the surface of water. The waves move away from the source in a regular way and appear the same in all directions from the source. Figure 4-16b was made by moving a vibrating object toward the right as it makes waves on water. Look at the difference between the waves in front of and behind the moving source. Four important points can be made about this case, although only one of them is apparent in the photo.

1. Even though the source of the waves is moving, the waves still travel at the same speed in all directions. The source's motion does not push or pull the waves. The source just disturbs the liquid, and the disturbance moves away at a speed that depends only on the liquid's characteristics—water, in this case.

2. The wavelengths of the waves in front of the moving source are shorter than they would be if the source was stationary, and the wavelengths behind the moving source are longer. For waves traveling at the same speed, the wavelength is

(a)

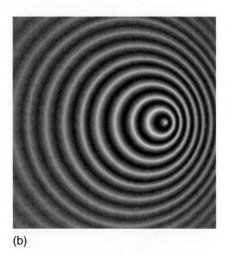

(b)

FIGURE 4-16 (a) Waves spread evenly from their source. (b) If the source is moving to the right, the waves are compressed in front of the source and stretched behind it.

inversely proportional to the frequency. This means that if there were corks on the water, the corks in front of the moving source would bounce up and down with a greater frequency than if the source were not moving, and corks behind the moving source would bounce with a lower frequency.

This change in wavelength is the same effect that causes the sound frequency of a siren to change as the car passes. The siren emits sound waves just as the vibrating object produces water waves. When you are in front of the car, you are in the region of shorter wavelength and higher frequency. In the case of sound, high frequency means high pitch. After the siren has passed, its sound waves are stretched in wavelength, causing you to hear a lower pitch.

This effect, which we see here both in water waves and in sound waves, is called the **Doppler effect**, named after the Austrian physicist Christian Doppler (1803–1853), who first explained it. Before we apply it to light waves and astronomy, let's continue the list of important things to know about it.

3. The sound does indeed get louder as a siren approaches (and the water waves get higher as the vibrating object approaches a bobbing cork), but this is *not* what the Doppler effect is about. The Doppler effect refers only to the *change in wavelength* (and therefore frequency) of the wave.

4. The frequency does *not* get higher and higher as the source approaches at a uniform speed. Rather, the frequency is observed to be higher than the source's (but constant in value) as the source approaches and lower than the source's (but constant in value) as it recedes.

The Doppler Effect in Astronomy

The Doppler effect also occurs for electromagnetic waves, which is what we receive from the stars. This means that if an object is coming toward us, the light we receive from it will have a shorter than normal wavelength, and from an object moving away we will receive a longer than normal wavelength. The reason you can't observe this for moving objects here on Earth is that the amount of the shortening and lengthening of the wave depends on the speed of the object *compared with the speed of the wave*.

For water waves, which move fairly slowly, you observe the Doppler effect even for a slow-moving wave source. In the case of sound, which has a speed much greater than water waves, you notice the Doppler effect only for fairly fast objects. A car going 70 miles/hour is moving at about 10% of the speed of sound.

In the case of light, you don't perceive the Doppler effect for a car traveling at 70 miles/hour because it is moving at only one ten-millionth the speed of light. To describe the Doppler effect for light, consider a spaceship with a lamp emitting green light. If the spaceship is moving away from us at a great enough speed, the wavelength of the light we see from the lamp is stretched so that the light appears red. The light is *redshifted*. If the spaceship is approaching, the light is *blueshifted*.

The spaceship example does illustrate the Doppler effect, but it is very misleading in an important respect: Except for very distant galaxies, objects in the heavens do not move with speeds great enough to actually change their colors appreciably. The redshift or blueshift caused by the Doppler effect is very small in most cases. If the spectra of stars were continuous spectra, there would be few cases in which the Doppler effect could be used to detect motion. It is the spectral lines (usually the absorption lines) that make the Doppler effect such a powerful tool.

As an example, imagine that we record the spectrum of hydrogen gas in the laboratory (FIGURE 4-17a). Figure 4-17b represents the spectrum of a star having only hydrogen in its atmosphere (which is unrealistic, but this is a simplified example). The absorption lines in the star's spectrum do not align exactly with the emission lines of the laboratory spectrum. Instead, the absorption lines are shifted slightly toward the red. This indicates that the star is moving away from us.

There are three major differences between our example and a measurement of a real star: First, a real star's spectrum has many more spectral lines. Second, the Doppler shift is almost always much smaller than that indicated in the example. When we later show photos of actual spectra, they will usually be a magnified por-

Doppler effect The observed change in wavelength of waves from a source moving toward or away from an observer.

By *normal* we mean the wavelength of the emitted light as measured by someone traveling with the source.

redshift A change in wavelength toward longer wavelengths.

blueshift A change in wavelength toward shorter wavelengths.

(a)

(b)

FIGURE 4-17 (a) Emission spectrum of hydrogen when the source is stationary with respect to the observer. (b) Absorption spectrum of hydrogen for a receding source (at 0.7% of the speed of light). Note the shift of all lines toward redder colors.

tion of a small part of the visible spectrum. Third, astronomers do not normally use color film in recording the spectrum. This may seem odd, but color is not easy to describe accurately, whereas wavelength is. The wavelengths of absorption lines can be measured very accurately and compared with the lines from a laboratory spectrum to determine the existence and the precise amount of the Doppler shift.

The Doppler Effect as a Measurement Technique

Thus far, we have described the Doppler effect as a method for detecting whether a star is moving toward or away from us, but it is more powerful than this. From measurements of the *amount* of the shifting of the spectral lines, we can determine the **radial velocity** of the star relative to Earth. The radial velocity is the star's velocity toward or away from us and must be distinguished from its **tangential velocity**, which is its velocity across our line of sight.

FIGURE 4-18 distinguishes the two velocities. To measure tangential velocity, we must look for motion of the star across our line of sight (like the yellow car in Figure 4-18), and this motion can be detected only for relatively nearby stars. To measure radial velocity, we use Doppler shift data and the following equation:

$$\frac{\Delta\lambda}{\lambda_0} = \frac{v}{c},$$

where $\Delta\lambda = \lambda - \lambda_0$ = wavelength difference, λ = observed wavelength, λ_0 = wavelength of spectral line from stationary source, v = radial velocity of object, and c = velocity of light.

If we solve this equation for what we are usually calculating—that is, the velocity of the object—we obtain

$$v = c\left(\frac{\Delta\lambda}{\lambda_0}\right).$$

When an object is approaching the observer, the wavelength difference is negative and so is the radial velocity. When an object is moving away from the observer, the wavelength difference is positive and so is the radial velocity.

An object's velocity is a quantity that gives us the object's speed and its direction of motion.

radial velocity Velocity along the line of sight, toward or away from the observer.

tangential velocity Velocity perpendicular to the line of sight.

This equation applies if the object is moving much slower than the speed of light, as is the case for most galaxies other than the very distant ones. For distant galaxies, a slightly more complex equation is needed, as relativistic effects become important.

EXAMPLE

The wavelength of one of the most prominent spectral lines of hydrogen is 656.285 nanometers (this is in the red portion of the spectrum). In the spectrum of Regulus (the brightest star in the constellation Leo), the wavelength of this line is observed to appear greater by 0.0077 nanometers. Calculate the speed of Regulus relative to Earth, and determine whether it is moving toward or away from us.

SOLUTION   First, the data indicate that the wavelength of the line in the spectrum of

FIGURE 4-18 The red car has a radial (to-or-fro) velocity with respect to the observer, while the yellow car has a tangential (side-to-side) velocity. The Doppler effect cannot be used to detect tangential velocity.

Regulus is *longer* by 0.0077 nanometers. This means that the star is moving *away* from us. To determine its speed, we substitute the given values in the equation that relates Doppler shift and speed:

$$v = c\left(\frac{\Delta\lambda}{\lambda_0}\right) = (3.0\times10^8\,\text{m/s})\times\left(\frac{0.0077\,\text{nm}}{656.285\,\text{nm}}\right)$$
$$= 3500\ \text{m/s} = 3.5\ \text{km/s}.$$

Regulus thus is moving away from the Earth at a speed of about 3.5 kilometers/second. This is about 2 miles/second, or 8000 miles/hour, a typical speed for nearby stars. Because the Earth's speed in its orbit around the Sun is about 30 kilometers/second, the Earth's motion would have to be taken into account in making the measurement. Our calculation assumed that the Earth was between the Sun and Regulus so that the Earth had no motion toward or away from the star.

TRY ONE YOURSELF

The nearest star to the Sun that is visible to the naked eye is Alpha Centauri. With Earth's motion removed, the 656.285 nanometers line of hydrogen has a wavelength of 656.237 nanometers in Alpha Centauri's spectrum. Calculate the radial velocity of this star relative to the Sun, and tell whether it is moving toward or away from the Sun.

The annual variation in the Doppler shift observed in stellar spectra provides evidence for the Earth's motion around the Sun. The evidence was not available, of course, when the question was controversial.

Police radar measures motorists' speeds by bouncing waves from their cars and detecting the Doppler shift in the reflected waves.

binary star (system) A pair of stars gravitationally bound so that they orbit one another.

This understanding of the relativity of motion is called *Galilean relativity* (or *Newtonian relativity*). Einstein's theory of relativity goes much further than this.

Other Doppler Effect Measurements

The use of the Doppler effect is not limited to measuring the speeds of stars. Other applications include the following:

1. Measuring the rotation rate of the Sun. Galileo was the first to observe that sunspots move across the Sun, thus providing a method to measure the Sun's rotation rate. The Doppler effect gives a second method. The measurement is done by examining the light from opposite sides of the Sun. Light from the side moving toward us is blueshifted and light from the other side is redshifted.

2. In a similar manner, the rotation rates of distant stars, other galaxies, planets, and the rings of Saturn can be measured. The fact that the light in the case of planets has been reflected by the planet (or rings) rather than emitted by it does not matter; the light is still shifted by the Doppler effect. In fact, the rotations of Mercury and Venus were first revealed by reflected radar waves.

3. Many stars are part of a two (or more) star system in which the stars orbit one another. If their orbits happen to be aligned so that each star moves alternately toward and away from us, we can detect this motion by the blueshift and redshift of each star's spectrum. When we discuss such **binary stars** in Chapter 12, we will see that they are very important in our quest to learn more about stars.

Relative or Real Speed?

The speed measured by the Doppler effect is the object's speed *relative to the speed of the Earth*. We, therefore, must take the Earth's speed into account in any calculation made with the Doppler effect, but even then we are only measuring the speed of the object with respect to the Sun. What about the object's *real* speed? There is no such thing because all speeds are relative to something. When you say that a car is moving at 50 miles/hour, you mean "relative to the surface of the Earth." When you walk up the aisle of a moving plane, you have one speed relative to the seated passengers, another relative to the Earth, another relative to the Sun, and so on.

Just as all motion is relative, all nonmotion is relative, too. When we say that something is at rest, we *usually* mean that it is at rest relative to the Earth. It is meaningless to say that something is absolutely at rest. Thus, there is no loss of meaning to our finding the velocity of an object relative to the Earth and then correcting for the Earth's motion around the Sun. All motion is relative.

FIGURE 4-19 As light spreads from a star, its intensity decreases as the inverse square of the distance.

4-8 The Inverse Square Law of Radiation

Everyone has experienced the fact that the intensity—that is, the brightness—of light decreases when we move farther from its source. The decrease in intensity follows an ***inverse square law***, a relationship that states that radiation spreading from a small source decreases in intensity as the inverse square of the distance from the source.

We can reach the conclusion that light intensity (just like gravity) decreases inversely with the distance squared ($1/d^2$) if we assume that light "spreads out" from its source uniformly in all directions. Indeed, this outward diffusion has to pass through successive imaginary spheres centered on the source. Because the surface area of a sphere of radius d is $4\pi d^2$, as light spreads out from the source filling all space uniformly in all directions, it must become less "concentrated" by a factor of $1/d^2$ (**FIGURE 4-19**).

In Chapter 12, we discuss how we use this inverse square law to find how much energy a star really emits if we know its distance from us and its apparent brightness.

inverse square law Any relationship in which some factor decreases as the square of the distance from its source.

The inverse square law applies only to small sources of light, but this requirement is easily met in most astronomical cases.

Conclusion

One of the major differences between Astronomy and other disciplines is that the subject of our studies, the universe, is beyond our control. Stars are born and die continually, galaxies collide and, most important of all, when we look at an object we see it as it was when it emitted the light we now see. One of the means to learn about the cosmos is by unlocking the information in the radiation we collect. In this chapter, we examined the evolution of our ideas on light since antiquity (**FIGURE 4-20**). We also discussed how the spectra of stars are used in two very different ways. First, the spectra are treated as continuous spectra, and we examine their graphs of intensity versus wavelength. By measuring the wavelength of the maximum intensity of radiation, we can determine the temperature of a star's surface. In doing this analysis, we ignore the absorption lines. Recall that these lines are very narrow, and their presence does not change the overall pattern of the blackbody curve.

Second, we examine the absorption lines within the spectrum. These lines allow us to determine the chemical composition of stars. In addition, when we measure the Doppler effect, the shift in the lines allows us to calculate the radial speeds of stars relative to Earth, as well as the speeds of rotation and revolution of celestial objects.

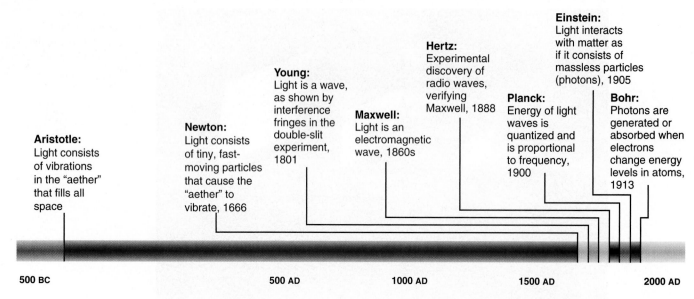

FIGURE 4-20 Over the years, explanations for the nature of light went back and forth between wave models and particle models. As we saw in the Advancing the Model box on pages 112–113, today we talk about the wave-particle duality of light; it propagates through space as a wave but interacts with matter as a stream of particles.

STUDY GUIDE

1. The frequency of visible light falls between that of
   A. infrared waves and radio waves.
   B. X-rays and cosmic rays.
   C. ultraviolet waves and X-rays.
   D. short radio waves and long radio waves.
   E. ultraviolet waves and radio waves.

2. Infrared radiation differs from red light in
   A. intensity.
   B. wavelength.
   C. its speed in a vacuum.
   D. [All of the above.]
   E. [None of the above.]

3. The frequency at which a star emits the most light depends on the star's
   A. distance from us.
   B. brightness.
   C. temperature.
   D. eccentricity.
   E. velocity toward or away from us.

4. In an infrared photo taken on a cool night, your skin will appear brighter than your clothes.
   A. Correct.
   B. Wrong, it depends upon the color of your clothes.
   C. Wrong, your clothes will appear brighter.
   D. Wrong, they will be equally bright.

5. Light waves of greater frequency have
   A. shorter wavelength.
   B. longer wavelength.
   C. [Either of the above; there is no direct connection between frequency and wavelength.]

6. Which of the following choices does not have the same fundamental nature as visible light?
   A. X-rays.
   B. Sound waves.
   C. Ultraviolet radiation.
   D. Infrared waves.
   E. Radio waves.

7. As an electron of an atom changes from one energy level to a higher energy level by absorbing a photon, the total energy of the atom
   A. increases.
   B. decreases.
   C. remains the same.

8. Which of the following choices is produced when white light is shined through a cool gas?
   A. An absorption spectrum.
   B. A continuous spectrum.
   C. An emission spectrum.
   D. [All of the above.]
   E. [None of the above.]

9. The solar spectrum is which of the following?
   A. An absorption spectrum.
   B. A continuous spectrum.
   C. An emission spectrum.
   D. [All of the above.]
   E. [None of the above.]

10. The spectrum of light from the Sun's atmosphere *seen during a total solar eclipse* is
    A. an emission spectrum.
    B. an absorption spectrum.

C. a combination of emission spectrum and absorption spectrum.

D. a continuous spectrum.

E. a combination of all three types of spectra.

11. Analysis of a star's spectrum *cannot* determine
    A. the star's radial velocity.
    B. the star's tangential velocity.
    C. the chemical elements present in the star's atmosphere.
    D. [More than one of the above.]

12. According to the Doppler effect,
    A. sound gets louder as its source approaches and softer as it recedes.
    B. sound gets higher and higher in pitch as its source approaches and lower and lower as its source recedes.
    C. sound is of constant higher pitch as its source approaches and of constant lower pitch as its source recedes.
    D. [Both A and B above.]
    E. [Both A and C above.]

13. The Doppler effect causes light from a source moving away to be
    A. shifted to shorter wavelengths.
    B. shifted to longer wavelengths.
    C. changed in velocity.
    D. [Both A and C above.]
    E. [Both B and C above.]

14. We can determine the elements in the atmosphere of a star by examining
    A. its color.
    B. its absorption spectrum.
    C. the frequency at which it emits the most energy.
    D. its temperature.
    E. its motion relative to us.

15. Which list shows the colors of stars from coolest to hottest?
    A. Red, white, blue.
    B. White, blue, red.
    C. Blue, white, red.
    D. Red, blue, white.
    E. Blue, red, white.

16. The Doppler effect is used to
    A. measure the radial velocity of a star.
    B. detect and study binary stars.
    C. measure the rotation of the Sun.
    D. [Two of the above.]
    E. [All of the above.]

17. Sound waves cannot travel in a vacuum. How, then, do radio waves travel through interstellar space?
    A. They are extra-powerful sound waves.
    B. They are very high frequency sound waves.
    C. Radio waves are not sound waves at all.
    D. The question is a trick, for radio waves do *not* travel through interstellar space.
    E. Interstellar space is not a vacuum.

18. The energy of a photon is directly proportional to the light's
    A. wavelength.
    B. frequency.

C. velocity.
D. brightness.

19. In the Bohr model of the atom, light is emitted from an atom when
    A. an electron moves from an inner to an outer orbit.
    B. an atom gains energy.
    C. an electron moves from an outer to an inner orbit.
    D. one element reacts with another.
    E. [Both A and B above.]

20. The intensity/wavelength graph of a "blue-hot" object peaks in the
    A. infrared region.
    B. red region.
    C. yellow region.
    D. ultraviolet region.

21. The emission spectrum produced by the excited atoms of an element contains wavelengths that are
    A. the same for all elements.
    B. characteristic of the particular element.
    C. evenly distributed throughout the entire visible spectrum.
    D. different from the wavelengths in its absorption spectrum.
    E. [Both A and D above.]

22. Each element has its own characteristic spectrum because
    A. the speed of light differs for each element.
    B. some elements are at a higher temperature than others.
    C. atoms combine to form molecules, releasing different wavelengths depending on the elements involved.
    D. electron energy levels are different for different elements.
    E. hot solids, such as tungsten, emit a continuous spectrum.

23. The speed of sound is 335 meters/second. What is the wavelength of a sound that has a frequency of 500 cycles/second?
    A. 0.67 meters.
    B. 1.49 meters.
    C. 165 meters.
    D. 835 meters.

24. Suppose the speed of a water wave is 12 inches/second and the wavelength is 4 inches. What is the frequency of the wave?
    A. 48 cycles/second.
    B. 18 cycles/second.
    C. 8 cycles/second.
    D. 3 cycles/second.
    E. 1/3 cycles/second.

25. Define *wavelength* and *frequency* in the case of a wave.

26. Which has the higher frequency, light of 400 nanometers or light of 450 nanometers?

27. Approximately what are the least and greatest wavelengths of visible light?

28. Name six regions of the electromagnetic spectrum in order from longest to shortest wavelength. (Do not list the colors of visible light as separate regions of the spectrum.)

29. Which parts of the electromagnetic spectrum penetrate the atmosphere?

30. Define the following terms: electron, nucleus, photon.

31. State the three postulates on which the Bohr model of the atom is based.

32. How is the energy of the photon related to the frequency of the light?

33. Why do the various elements each have different emission spectra?

34. Name the three different types of spectra, and explain how each is produced.

35. Explain how we know what elements are in the atmospheres of the stars.

36. Carefully explain what the Doppler effect is. For light waves, does the Doppler effect tell us anything about the intensity of the light in front of and behind a moving light source?

37. Distinguish between the way a spectrum is used to determine the temperature of a star and the way it is used to determine the star's composition and/or motion toward or away from us.

1. Why do we have three different temperature scales instead of one? What are the advantages (if any) of each?

2. Two people are having fun in the ocean. One is surfing, and the other is floating up and down. Their different motions could be used to illustrate two quantities in the equation $v = \lambda \times f$. Which two?

3. The period of a wave is defined as the amount of time required for the wave to complete one cycle. What, then, is the relationship between the period and the frequency of a wave?

4. It is especially easy to get a sunburn when skiing high in the mountains. How does the high altitude contribute to the danger of sunburn?

5. Why can't we hear radio waves without using the device that we call a "radio"?

6. Nowadays, radio waves (both for radio and TV) are striking your body all the time, but you are not allowed to get too many X-rays in one year. Why is this so? After all, both radio waves and X-rays are a part of the electromagnetic spectrum.

7. What does an object do to light to give the object its color? How does this differ from the color of an object that emits its own light?

8. Draw a graph of intensity versus wavelength for a red star and another for a white star. Describe two ways in which the graphs differ.

9. The text explains that cool stars are redder than hot ones. However, couldn't the red color result instead from the Doppler effect if the star is moving away from us? Explain.

10. If absorption lines were to be included in the graph of intensity versus wavelength for a star, how would this change the graph?

11. How would Figure 4-10 be different if it were the spectrum of a red star?

12. How do we know what chemical elements are in the atmosphere of the Sun? Explain.

13. What is the Doppler effect and why is it important to astronomers?

14. Figure 4-18 greatly exaggerates color differences for the two cars. If it showed a car coming toward you, what color would the car be, using the same exaggeration?

1. If the speed of a particular water wave is 12 meters/second and its wavelength is 3 meters, what is its frequency?

2. The speed of sound in air at room temperature is about 344 meters/second. What is the wavelength of a sound wave with a frequency of 256 Hz?

3. Express 500 nanometers in meters.

4. The 656.285 nanometers line of hydrogen is measured to be 656.305 nanometers in the spectrum of a certain star. Is this star approaching or receding from the Earth? Calculate its radial speed relative to the Earth.

5. If a certain star is moving away from Earth at 25 km/s, what will be the measured wavelength of a spectral line that has a wavelength of 500 nm for a stationary source?

6. Suppose the Kelvin temperature of blackbody X is three times as great as that of blackbody Y. Compare the energy released by equal areas of the two objects.

7. Use Wien's law to determine the wavelength at which an object at body temperature (98.6°F) emits most of its energy. (Hint: Make sure you find the corresponding temperature in kelvin.) What kind of radiation is this? Can you see it?

8. Two thermometers, one marked in °F and the other in °C, are placed in the same container. At what temperature will both thermometers read the same?

9. Matter falling toward a black hole gets compressed and heated to about 10^6 K. In what part of the electromagnetic spectrum would you search for black holes?

10. A star has five times the surface area of the Sun, but its surface temperature is smaller by a factor of three. Does this star emit more energy than the Sun or less? Explain.

11. (a) We said that light takes 8.3 minutes to reach us from the Sun. Show that this is the case. (b) When we are observing an object that is 5000 light years away, do we see it as it is now? Explain.

12. Compare the light we receive from a 100-watt lightbulb that is 30 feet away with the light from a similar bulb that is 10 feet away.

ACTIVITIES

EXPANDING THE QUEST

STARLINKS

Doppler Effect Measurement

Figure 4-17a shows a hydrogen emission spectrum (in the visible part of the spectrum) when the source is stationary with respect to the observer, whereas Figure 4-17b shows a corresponding hydrogen absorption spectrum for a receding source. In general, spectra are much more complicated, including many lines from different elements; however, let us imagine that we have isolated the hydrogen lines in this spectrum. In addition, consider the spectrum as a "map," exactly as is. We would like to calculate the speed of the source, using the Doppler effect.

For a map to be useful, it must include the correct scale. The lines in Figure 4-17a correspond to the following wavelengths from right to left: 656.3 nm (red), 486.1 nm (blue-green), 434.0 nm (violet), and 410.1 nm (violet). Measure the distances between the lines in millimeters (mm), and calculate the scale with units nm/mm.

Now compare the position of the lines between the two spectra. For example, by how many millimeters has the 656.3-nanometer line shifted to the right (toward longer wavelengths)? Using the scale you found in the previous step, translate this shift (redshift) into nanometers. This is the change between the observed and laboratory-based wavelength for this hydrogen line ($\Delta\lambda$). Using $\lambda_0 = 656.3$ nanometers and the Doppler equation, show that the speed of the receding source is 0.7% of the speed of light.

1. "The Duality in Matter and Light," by B.G. Englert, M. O. Scully, and H. Walther, in *Scientific American* (December, 1994).
2. "The Truth About Star Colors," by P. C. Steffy, in *Sky & Telescope* (September 1992, p. 266).
3. "Unlocking the Chemical Secrets of the Cosmos," by O. Gingerich, in *Sky & Telescope* (July, 1981).
4. "The Electromagnetic Spectrum," by H. Augensen and J. Woodbury, in *Astronomy* (June, 1982).
5. "Beyond the Rainbow," by J. B. Kaler, in *Astronomy* (September, 2000).
6. "Starlight Detectives," by A. W. Hirshfeld, in *Sky & Telescope* (August, 2004).

Quest Ahead to Starlinks
http://physicalscience.jbpub.com/starlinks

Starlinks is this book's online learning center. It features **eLearning**, which contains chapter quizzes and other tools designed to help you study for your class. You can also find **online exercises**, view numerous relevant **animations**, follow a guide to **useful astronomy sites** on the Web, or even check the latest **astronomy news** updates.

5

Telescopes: Windows to the Universe

The Crab nebula as seen in ultraviolet (inset) and (clockwise from the right) in X-ray, visible, and radio radiation.

Looks can be deceiving. During the past few decades, astronomers have come face to face with this old saying. Up until the middle of the 20th century, almost all of our knowledge of the sky came from visible light waves. Therefore, photographs of the sky showed what our eyes see, just adding detail because telescopes can detect very dim light and magnify the image. Still, it seemed that "what we see is what we get."

Then along came detectors of radiation in other parts of the spectrum. The chapter-opening photo shows four views of the Crab nebula, which is the leftover debris of a star that exploded almost a thousand years ago (1054 AD). The bottom left image was taken with an optical (visible-light) telescope. The larger image was taken by the *Chandra X-Ray Observatory*, which is in orbit around the Earth. It shows the spinning, top-like structure that may provide the energy for the glowing gases seen in visible light. Which image shows reality? The answer is "both, and more!" for the same picture taken in radio or ultraviolet radiation looks different still. We must conclude that our eyes don't tell us the whole story. In astronomy, what we see is just part of what we get.

All cross references to chapters, sections, figures, and tables pertain to the main text, *In Quest of the Universe, Sixth Edition. In Quest of the Solar System* contains Chapters 1–11 and 19 of the main text. *In Quest of the Stars and Galaxies* contains Chapters 1–5 and 11–19 of the main text.

124

124

To understand the universe, we rely heavily on observations. As with any branch of science, we need observational data to test existing theories or develop new ones. The distances between us—the observers—and the objects of our studies are vast, and the cosmos is very dynamic in nature. All we can do is passively collect the radiation sent from these objects and try to decipher the information it carries. The most useful tools for collecting radiation are telescopes.

Galileo Galilei was the first to use a telescope to study the heavens systematically, as we discussed in Chapter 3. Much was learned before Galileo's time by naked-eye observations, but Galileo's telescope changed astronomy—and our outlook on the universe—tremendously. As we make telescopes larger and take them into space, above the distortions of the Earth's atmosphere, we realize that we are just beginning to learn about the mysteries of our universe.

The past century has brought a multitude of telescopic tools, and our view of the skies has expanded to all parts of the spectrum well beyond visible light. We begin this chapter by describing some properties of light that are important to the understanding of visible-light telescopes. Then we discuss the use of such telescopes. Finally, the chapter concludes with a look at some of the nonvisible-light telescopes that are so indispensable to modern astronomy.

O telescope, instrument of much knowledge, more precious than any scepter!
—Kepler, in a letter to Galileo

5-1 Refraction and Image Formation

The discussion of light thus far has concentrated on its wave properties. The effect of these properties is examined later in this chapter, but for the moment, we concentrate not on the nature of light, but on the path that light travels. That path is usually very simple, for light travels in a straight line as long as it remains in the same (uniform) *medium*. It may, however, change direction upon entering a second medium. FIGURE 5-1 shows a ray of light passing through a wedge of glass. We see that the light travels in a straight line before and after passing through the glass and that it travels in a straight line inside the glass; however, the ray bends when it passes through each surface of the glass. The phenomenon of the bending of a wave as it passes from one medium into another is called *refraction*.

Two factors determine the amount of refraction that occurs when light crosses from one material into another. The first factor is the relative speeds of light in the two materials. In Chapter 4, we stated that the speed of light in vacuum is about 3×10^8 m/s. In air, light's speed is just slightly slower. In glass, however, light travels at about 2×10^8 m/s, depending on the type of glass. Because of the change in speed, a ray of light may bend significantly when going from air into glass.

For a simple analogy, consider what happens when you roll a pair of toy wheels connected by an axle from a smooth wooden floor onto a carpet. If the wheels cross the interface between the two surfaces perpendicularly (face-on), then they will slow down but will continue moving in the same direction. If, on the other hand, they cross the interface between the two surfaces nonperpendicularly, the wheel that first hits the carpet will slow down while the other wheel, still on the smooth floor, will continue moving at its original speed. As a result, the axle will turn; it will change direction. In a similar way, light changes direction when it crosses the interface between two different media nonperpendicularly (FIGURE 5-2a). Figure 5-2b shows an everyday example of refraction.

To understand the second factor in refraction, consider FIGURE 5-3a, which shows several rays of light (that came from beyond the left side of the page) passing through a lens-shaped piece of glass. Notice that the rays that strike the surface of the glass (the interface between the two media) at a glancing angle (farther from the perpendicular) bend more than those rays that hit the glass more "head-on." The central ray strikes the glass perpendicularly and does not bend at all. This is a general rule: the larger the angle between the ray of light and the perpendicular line to the interface, the more the light bends on passing through the surface.

The word *medium* refers, in a generic way, to the "material" though which light travels, such as air, glass, water, or the almost perfect vacuum in the far reaches of the universe.

refraction The bending of light as it crosses the boundary between two materials in which it travels at different speeds.

FIGURE 5-1 When light passes through a wedge of glass, it is bent from its straight-line path. The smaller the angle of the wedge, the less the bending. (The "wedge" is really a prism, but we are concentrating here on the bending of the light rather than its separation into colors.) The bending occurs both when the light enters the glass and when it emerges.

FIGURE 5-2 (a) As a light beam crosses the interface between two different media (such as from air into water, which is optically denser), it bends because of the change in the speed of propagation (as shown in Figure 5-1). This is similar to the change in direction when a pair of toy wheels travels from a smooth floor onto a rough carpet; however, if we consider two light rays instead of two wheels, both rays change direction at the interface and the distance between them increases by an amount that depends on the type of media. (b) The pencil in a cup of water appears bent because of the refraction of light. As the light rays from the submerged part of the pencil rise toward the observer, they bend at the interface.

image The visual counterpart of an object, formed by refraction or reflection of light from the object.

focal point (of a converging lens or mirror) The point at which light from a very distant object converges after being refracted or reflected.

focal length The distance from the center of a lens or a mirror to its focal point.

 Refraction of light in raindrops is a part of the process that gives us the rainbow.

Refer again to Figure 5-3a. The surfaces of the lens have just the right curvature to cause all of the rays of light shown in the figure to pass through the same spot. We could even block some of the incoming light rays (for example, the one labeled X) and still get an *image* of the object, although a bit dimmer. This is important later in this chapter in our discussion of a class of telescopes.

To see how a lens forms an image, imagine that each ray in the figure came from a distant star, which we treat as a point. A point light source emits light rays in all directions; if this source is far from our telescope, only a few of these rays will enter the telescope, and they will be essentially parallel to each other. If we put a piece of paper at the point where the light rays come together, all the light from that star that passes through our lens will come to a single point on the piece of paper. In fact, the rays of light coming from other stars will likewise come to a focus on the paper, forming an *image* of that area of the sky (Figure 5-3b).

The *focal point* of a lens is that point where light from a very distant object comes to a focus. This is the point where the rays converge in Figure 5-3.

The *focal length* of the lens is the distance from the center of the lens to the focal point. Depending on the curvature of their surfaces, different lenses have different focal lengths.

Refraction has important consequences for observations involving the Earth's atmosphere. When light passes from the (almost perfect) vacuum of space into Earth's atmosphere, it continuously refracts as it moves through the air. Each thin layer in the atmosphere is under different conditions and therefore behaves as a different medium. As a result, objects appear higher in the sky than they really are (FIGURE 5-4a), and the amount of refraction depends on the object's altitude above our horizon. We must take this into account when measuring positions of celestial objects. This phenomenon also explains why the Sun looks "flattened" when it is closer to the horizon. Its lower edge, being closer to our horizon, is shifted upward more than its upper edge (Figure 5-4b).

FIGURE 5-3 (a) A lens bends incoming rays of light toward a single point. When the incoming rays are parallel to the axis (as shown here), they cross at the lens' focal point. (b) Light rays from two different stars are focused into two separate images.

(a)

(b)

FIGURE 5-4 (a) A simplified picture of atmospheric refraction. The position of the observed object seems to be higher in the sky than it really is. (b) The Sun appears flattened at sunset because the lower edge is refracted higher than the upper edge. As shown in part (a), the amount of refraction depends on the altitude above the horizon. As a result, the Sun appears more flattened the closer it is to the horizon.

5-2   The Refracting Telescope

Lenses are at the heart of the refracting telescope. (The reflecting telescope will be discussed later in this chapter.) The simplest use of a telescope (in principle, anyway) is as a lens for a camera (FIGURE 5-5a). The camera is using the long-focal length lens of the telescope in place of its regular lens (Figure 5-5b). The telescope lens simply replaces the regular camera lens and brings the image to a focus on the film. As we see later, telescopes can be mounted so that they can track stars across the sky and allow astronomers to take long time exposure photographs of the heavens. Long time exposures allow us to photograph much fainter objects than can be seen by simply looking through a telescope. The use of a telescope with a camera thus is much more important to a professional astronomer than its use for direct viewing.

Figure 5-5c shows how a small telescope is used for direct observation. The primary lens—the lens through which the light passes first—is called the *objective lens*, or simply the *objective*. This lens brings the light to a focus at the focal point, which is where the film is placed when the telescope is used with a camera. This is where the image is located. For direct viewing, a second lens, the *eyepiece*, is added just beyond the focal point. This lens simply acts as a magnifier to enlarge the image.

objective lens (or objective) The main light-gathering element—lens or mirror—of a telescope. It is also called the primary lens.

eyepiece The magnifying lens (or combination of lenses) used to view the image formed by the objective of a telescope.

Chromatic Aberration

A prism separates white light into its colors because different wavelengths of light are refracted different amounts. Except for the ray of light that goes straight through the center of a lens, rays go through a lens in much the same way as they go through a prism. Light passing through a lens separates into colors, and this causes the lens to

(a)

(b)

(c)

FIGURE 5-5 (a) A simple way to use a telescope for photography is to let the telescope serve as the camera's lens. (b) The image is focused directly on the film by the telescope's main lens. (c) When a telescope is used for direct viewing, the eyepiece magnifies the image formed by the objective lens. This image is formed at the objective's focal point.

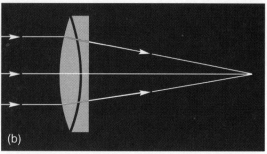

FIGURE 5-6 (a) Chromatic aberration. A lens exhibits a prism effect, separating white light into its colors. The lens therefore focuses each color at a different place. Only red and blue are shown here. (b) A lens can be corrected for chromatic aberration by the proper combination of lenses of different types of glass. Here the second lens brings the separated colors back together at the image.

chromatic aberration The defect of optical systems that results in light of different colors being focused at different places.

have a slightly different focal length for each wavelength of light (**FIGURE 5-6a**). As a result, there is no single place where an image is exactly in focus. If the film of a camera is placed at the point where the red light focuses, the other colors will be out of focus, and the result will be an image with a fuzzy, bluish edge. This phenomenon, called **chromatic aberration**, occurs not just in telescopes, but in regular cameras as well. Fortunately, it can be corrected, at least in part.

achromatic lens (or achromat) An optical element that has been corrected so that it is free of chromatic aberration.

The amount of color separation that occurs when light passes through a lens depends not only on the curvature of the glass but also on the type of glass. Some kinds of glass separate the colors more than other kinds. Telescope and camera manufacturers use this fact to correct for chromatic aberration. In all but the cheapest toy-store telescopes, the objectives of refracting telescopes are made of two lenses instead of one. As Figure 5-6b shows, the second lens has reverse curvature from the first. This curvature is not enough to undo all of the converging effect of the first lens, however, and the light is still brought to a focus. The second lens is made of a different type of glass than the first, and although it does not cancel out the bending of the light, it does cancel out most of the color separation. Such a combination of lenses is called an **achromatic lens**.

5-3   The Powers of a Telescope

Do telescopes just magnify things?

When most people think of a telescope's power, they think of magnification. Magnification, however, is the least important of the three major powers of a telescope (the other two being the light-gathering power and the resolving power). After all, magnifying a blurry image will not show any more details. Again, we describe small telescopes, but the same ideas apply to large telescopes used by professional astronomers. In fact, the reasons for using such large telescopes are related to the powers of telescopes.

angular size (of an object) The angle between two lines drawn from the viewer to opposite sides of the object.

Angular Size and Magnifying Power

The **angular size** of an object is the angle between two lines that start at the observer and go to opposite sides of the object. **FIGURE 5-7a** shows this angle for the case of someone looking at the Moon. (Angular size is defined very similarly to angular separation in Chapter 1. Angular size measures the apparent size of one object, whereas angular separation measures the apparent angular distance between two objects.) The angular size determines, for example, how big the image of the Moon is on the retina of your eye.

magnifying power, or **magnification** (of an instrument) The ratio of the angular size of an object when it is seen through the instrument to its angular size when seen with the naked eye.

For a telescope (as well as binoculars and several other optical instruments), **magnifying power** or **magnification** is defined as the ratio of the angular size of an object when it is seen through the instrument to the object's angular size when seen with the naked eye. Figure 5-7b shows the angular size of the Moon as seen through

FIGURE 5-7 (a) The Moon seen by the naked eye. (b) In a telescope, the angular size of the Moon is apparently larger. The magnification of the telescope is the ratio of the two angular sizes.

a particular telescope. You might estimate from the angles in the figure that this telescope has a magnification of about four; that is, the telescope magnifies the object four times.

The magnification of a particular telescope depends on the focal lengths of the objective and the eyepiece. It can be calculated using the following formula:

$$\text{magnifying power} = \frac{\text{focal length of objective}}{\text{focal length of eyepiece}} \quad \text{or} \quad M = \frac{f_{\text{obj}}}{f_{\text{eye}}}.$$

This means that the greatest magnification can be achieved by having a long-focal length objective and a short-focal length eyepiece.

EXAMPLE

The telescopes used in an introductory astronomy laboratory have objectives with focal lengths of 1250 mm. One eyepiece has a focal length of 25 mm. What is the magnification produced by this telescope? What is the angular size of the Moon as seen through this telescope, using the 25-mm eyepiece? (The naked-eye angular size of the Moon from Earth is about 0.5°.)

SOLUTION   To calculate the magnification, we use the equation that relates it to focal lengths:

$$M = \frac{f_{\text{obj}}}{f_{\text{eye}}} = \frac{1250 \text{ mm}}{25 \text{ mm}} = 50.$$

The magnifying power of the telescope thus is 50. We say that the magnification is 50 times, or 50×.

Now, because the Moon's angular size as seen by the naked eye is 0.5° and the telescope magnifies the Moon 50 times, the Moon's angular size in the telescope will be 50 × 0.5° = 25°.

TRY ONE YOURSELF

What is the magnification produced by a telescope having an objective with a focal length of 1.5 meters when it is being used with an eyepiece that has a focal length of 12 millimeters. (Hint: In doing the calculation, you must express the two lengths in the same units: either meters or millimeters.)

FIGURE 5-8 Increasing the magnification decreases the field of view and makes the image darker. The entire telescopic view is shown in each case.

(a) 50×   (b) 100×   (c) 250×

As we hinted in both the example and the suggested problem, you might use an eyepiece of a different focal length. Indeed, it is a minor matter to change the eyepiece of a telescope. An eyepiece costs relatively little so it is common to have a few different eyepieces for a telescope to have different magnifications available. The obvious question is, "Why not always use the greatest magnification?" There are several answers to this question.

The first answer is that as the magnification increases, the **field of view** of the telescope decreases (FIGURE 5-8). Field of view refers to how much of the object is seen at one time. This is entirely reasonable, for if the object appears larger, not as much of it will be contained within the view of the telescope. When viewing the Moon, for example, you may wish to see all of it rather than just a portion. If so, you need an eyepiece with a long focal length, thus producing less magnification.

The other reasons why we do not always use the greatest magnification relate to the other powers of a telescope.

field of view The actual angular width of the scene viewed by an optical instrument.

Light-Gathering Power

Notice in the three views in Figure 5-8 that the more magnified the image, the darker it is. To see why this occurs, consider the region of the Moon we see in view (c). The light from this region was concentrated in a small segment of the image shown in view (a), but it is now more spread out in the more magnified view. That is, the same light that covers only part of the image in view (a) has to illuminate the entire image in view (c). The image is therefore darker. There are two ways to make the image brighter and still retain this magnification. If we are taking a photograph, a longer time exposure can be used. When we do this, we allow the light's effect to accumulate on the film over a longer time, and the film becomes more exposed. The other way is to capture more light from the Moon in the first place. This can only be done by using a larger objective, which brings us to the second power of a telescope: the **light-gathering power**, which is often the most important power.

light-gathering power A measure of the amount of light collected by an optical instrument.

The light-gathering power of a telescope refers to the amount of light it collects from an object. Most objects that are observed with a telescope are very faint, and to obtain an image, we need to capture as much light from them as possible. This is true whether we are using the telescope for photography or for direct viewing.

A telescope does not literally "gather" light. It simply captures the light that hits the objective and brings that light to a focus.

The major way to gather more light is to use a telescope with a larger objective. The amount of light that strikes the objective simply depends on its area. This is the primary reason that it is desirable to have a telescope with a large-diameter objective and why the size of the objective is one of the features specified when discussing a telescope. For example, we might describe a particular telescope as a refractor with a 12-centimeter objective of focal length 140 centimeters; however, although we state the *diameter* of the objective, it is the *area* that is important. Because the area of a circle is proportional to the square of the diameter, we must be careful in making comparisons of light-gathering power.

EXAMPLE

How does the light-gathering power of a telescope with a 6-inch objective lens compare with that of a telescope with a 9-inch objective?

SOLUTION   The area of a circle depends on the square of its diameter and, thus, the squares of the diameters of the telescopes must be compared to compare their light-gathering power. We set up a ratio of the squares of the two diameters:

$$\frac{9^2}{6^2} = \frac{81}{36} = 2.25.$$

The light-gathering power of the larger telescope thus is more than twice that of the smaller.

TRY ONE YOURSELF

Compare the light-gathering power of a small telescope, with an objective lens of diameter 10 centimeters, with that of a fully dark-adapted human eye with a pupil of diameter 5 millimeters.

The desire to be able to see fainter and fainter objects in space has led us to make larger and larger telescopes. Before discussing large telescopes, however, another advantage of size, the third and last power, must be considered.

Resolving Power

One property of light that we assume in our everyday life is that it travels in straight lines (unless it reflects from a mirror or is refracted at an interface). If we could not assume this, we would be unsure whether an object we see is in front of us or behind us. Yet there are exceptions to this rule: Light does not always travel in straight lines. The exceptions are usually unimportant, but look at FIGURE 5-9. This is a magnified photograph of the shadow of a regular household screw. The shadow was made by holding the screw a few meters from a screen and illuminating it with a small, bright light source. The edges of the shadow are not distinct; there are light and dark fringes near the edges.

In this case, the light passing near the edge of the object (the side of the screw) has "spread out" slightly. The effect is small and is difficult to see in everyday life. We do not discuss the reason that light acts this way except to point out that water waves behave similarly; they bend around corners. This phenomenon is called *diffraction*.

The amount of diffraction that occurs when light passes through an opening depends on the wavelength of the light and the size of the opening. The longer the wavelength, the more diffraction, and the larger the opening, the less diffraction.

In a telescope, the objective itself forms the opening through which the light passes. The effect is small, but it is there: Light that should bend regularly and accurately according to the laws of refraction fans out a slight amount. This results in the image not being exactly clear. The image of a star that should appear as a single point is blurred into a small spot. If we increase the magnification, we simply make the blurred spot bigger and fainter.

FIGURE 5-10a is a photograph of the Big Dipper and indicates what seems to be a single star in the Dipper's handle. If you have fairly good eyes and look at the Dipper in a clear dark sky, you can see that this star is not one, but two stars (named Mizar and Alcor). We say that your eyes and the clarity of

diffraction The spreading of light upon passing the edge of an object.

FIGURE 5-9 If an extremely small light source is used, the shadow of an object will have light and dark fringes at its edge. This is due to diffraction of light. (A laser was used to make this photo, but laser light is not necessary to produce the effect.)

FIGURE 5-10 (a) Mizar and Alcor, stars in the handle of the Big Dipper, are seen as a single star by many people, but can be resolved into two stars by those with better eyesight. (b) Even a small telescope resolves Mizar into two stars (lower right). Alcor is at the upper left.

Mizar and Alcor

(a)   5°

Alcor

Mizar

(b)   0.1°

resolving power (or resolution) The smallest angular separation detectable with an instrument. It thus is a measure of the instrument's ability to see detail.

the sky allow you to *resolve* the pair of stars. Someone with poorer eyesight may be unable to resolve the pair. Figure 15-10b shows what you would see if you looked at this pair of stars with a small telescope. The photograph shows three stars, two of them very close together. In fact, the two stars that are close together were seen as one star (Mizar) when viewed with the naked eye; it was the brighter of the naked-eye pair. The fainter of the naked-eye pair, Alcor, is the third star in the photograph, at the opposite side of the field of view. The telescope is able to resolve the group of stars into three.

The **resolving power** of an instrument is the smallest angular separation between two stars that can still be resolved as two by the instrument. Resolving power thus is described in terms of an angle.

What is it about a telescope that determines its resolving power? Naturally, the quality of the lenses is a major factor, but even with perfect optical components, the resolving power of a telescope is limited by diffraction. Because less diffraction occurs with a large objective, the maximum resolving power can be achieved by a telescope with a large-diameter objective.

Assuming that diffraction is the only limitation, a telescope's resolving power can be calculated by using the expression

$$\theta \approx 2.5 \times 10^5 \times \frac{\lambda}{D},$$

where θ = angular resolution in arcseconds, λ = wavelength of the light used, in meters, and D = diameter of the telescope objective, in meters.

EXAMPLE

What is the resolving power of a human eye?

SOLUTION   Assuming that a fully dark-adapted human eye has a diameter of 5 millimeters = 5×10^{-3} meters, for visible light of wavelength λ = 600 nanometers = 6×10^{-7} meters, we get

$$\theta \approx 2.5 \times 10^5 \times \frac{\lambda}{D} = 2.5 \times 10^5 \times \frac{6 \times 10^{-7}}{5 \times 10^{-3}} = 30'' = 0.5' = 1/120 \text{ of a degree}.$$

TRY ONE YOURSELF
The *Hubble Space Telescope* has a 2.4-m primary mirror. (The expression for the resolving power of a telescope works for both refracting and reflecting telescopes.) Show that its resolving power for visible light of 600 nanometers is about 0.06" or 1/60,000 of a degree. This is about the equivalent of the angle subtended by a quarter from 80 kilometers (50 miles) away.

Based on size alone, the largest telescopes should have a resolving power far greater than the best backyard telescope, but in fact, the lack of clarity of the Earth's atmosphere becomes a major factor in limiting the resolution of large telescopes. This lack of clarity is caused by turbulence of the air and air pollu-

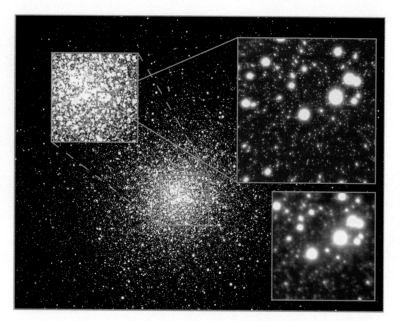

FIGURE 5-11 M-13 is a cluster of more than 100,000 stars about 23,000 light-years away orbiting the center of our Galaxy. The image at top right was obtained using adaptive optics (resolution of about 0.06 arcseconds), whereas the image of the same field at bottom right was obtained without adaptive optics under exceptional conditions (seeing of about 0.26 arcseconds). The field of view is about 20 arcseconds.

tion—the latter caused by modern civilization or simply by dust. Recall that light is refracted as it passes from one material into another if there is a difference in its speed in the two materials. In fact, light travels at slightly different speeds in air at different temperatures and densities. Our atmosphere always contains some amount of turbulence, and this causes air at various temperatures to move across the line of sight of a telescope. This results in the image moving slightly in nearly random directions, causing the image of a point source to become blurred. This blurring and twinkling of the image caused by the Earth's atmosphere is called **astronomical seeing**, and it is commonly measured by the diameter of the seeing disk ("*seeing*"). This is the diameter of the fuzzy image obtained while observing a point-like source (such as a star) through the Earth's atmosphere and corresponds to the best angular resolution that can be achieved. Atmospheric seeing places a limit on the resolution of even the largest telescope. The largest telescopes on Earth have a practical resolving power of about 0.5 arcseconds, improving to about 0.25 arcseconds on the best nights. To improve on the limit the Earth's atmosphere places on resolving power, astronomers place telescopes in space or use new observing techniques (such as adaptive and active optics and interferometry, which we discuss later in this chapter). FIGURE 5-11 shows how such techniques improve the quality of an image.

This atmospheric turbulence is what causes the *twinkling* of the stars when they are viewed with the naked eye. Most planets do not seem to twinkle because their angular size is larger than the scale of the atmospheric turbulence, and the distortions are averaged out over the size of the image.

> **astronomical seeing** The blurring and twinkling of the image of an astronomical light source caused by Earth's atmosphere.

> **seeing** The best possible angular resolution that can be achieved.

5-4   The Reflecting Telescope

An inwardly curved mirror will bring rays of light to a focus, just like a lens (FIGURE 5-12a), allowing us to use such a mirror as the objective of a telescope. Figure 5-12b shows the arrangement devised by Isaac Newton. A small flat mirror is arranged in front of the objective mirror to deflect the light rays out to the eyepiece or camera body.

The largest refractor in existence is the 40-inch diameter telescope at Yerkes Observatory at Williams Bay, Wisconsin (FIGURE 5-13). Reflecting telescopes are made much larger than this, however, and they are less expensive. Astronomers prefer to build and use reflecting telescopes instead of refracting ones for the following reasons.

1. To be achromatic, a refractor requires two lenses. This means that four surfaces of glass have to be shaped correctly. A front-surface mirror, on the other hand, has

An inwardly curved mirror is said to be *concave* and, thus, the objective mirror of a telescope is concave. A mirror with an outward curvature—such as the passenger-side mirror on many cars—is said to be *convex*.

○ **FIGURE 5-12** (a) A curved mirror can bring incoming light rays to a focus. Again, the focal point is defined as the point where incoming rays that are parallel to the axis of the mirror converge. (b) The Newtonian focal arrangement places a small flat mirror in the path of the reflected rays so that they are bounced off to the side and into the eyepiece (or camera or other instrument).

Newtonian focus The optical arrangement of a reflecting telescope in which a plane secondary mirror is mounted along the axis of the telescope to intercept the light reflected from the objective mirror and reflect it to the side.

FIGURE 5-13 The 40-inch diameter Yerkes Observatory refractor. The telescope tube is nearly 20 meters (60 feet) long, indicating that the focal length of the objective is about that long. The telescope was completed in 1897. The floor of the observatory can be raised so that the eyepiece is within reach.

only one critical surface, thus simplifying the construction of the objective. How "perfect" must the surface be? We typically want to keep any deviations from the desired shape of the surface to be less than about $\lambda/20$. For example, if we are observing in the visible part of the spectrum and set $\lambda = 500$ nanometers, any deviations must be kept less than 25 nanometers. Such a small deviation for, say, a 10-meter diameter surface, corresponds to requiring that the largest mountain—deviation from a flat surface—on Earth be smaller than about 5 centimeters (2 inches) in height.

2. It is impossible to correct lenses completely for chromatic aberration. When light reflects from a mirror, however, all wavelengths reflect in exactly the same way; thus, reflectors automatically eliminate chromatic aberration problems.

3. Because a reflector's mirror is front surfaced, the light does not pass through the glass of the mirror. The glass thus does not need to be as perfect as that used for a refractor. It is difficult (and therefore expensive) to make large pieces of glass without tiny air bubbles or other imperfections. In addition, a fraction of the light going through the lens of a refracting telescope gets absorbed, and this is especially true for short-wavelength light. Reflecting telescopes do not have this problem, as light simply reflects off the mirror.

4. For a refracting telescope, light must pass through the objective lens; thus, the lens must be supported from its edges. However, as the size of the lens is increased in order to collect more light, its weight increases, and gravity will deform its shape. In addition, this deformation will change with the orientation of the telescope. For a reflecting telescope, we can support the mirror's weight by a support structure, in a honeycomb form, behind the reflecting surface. This also allows the use of a computer-controlled active system of pressure pads that can slightly change the mirror's shape to accommodate for distortions caused by gravity or the atmosphere.

For all of these reasons and others, a large reflector is much less expensive and more practical than a large refractor. As a result, all really large telescopes are reflectors; however, even reflectors have some image distortions.

Large Optical Telescopes

A reflecting telescope with an eyepiece arrangement like that in Figure 5-12b is called a *Newtonian telescope*, or is said to have a **Newtonian focus**. The Newtonian focus is a common one for small telescopes. **FIGURE 5-14** shows an arrangement common in

FIGURE 5-14 (a) In the Cassegrain focal arrangement, the secondary mirror is curved outward (convex), and the light is reflected back through a hole in the objective or primary mirror. (b) This is a 5-inch diameter Cassegrain telescope.

large telescopes, the ***Cassegrain focus*** (invented by G. Cassegrain, a French optician who lived at the time of Newton). The eyepiece or camera body is at the back of the telescope. In this arrangement, the secondary mirror is not a flat mirror but has an outward curvature. The effect of the curved secondary mirror is that an objective that actually has a short focal length can be given a longer effective focal length and thus can be contained in a short telescope.

In very large telescopes, observing is often done at the ***prime focus***. This is the point where the light from the objective mirror comes to a focus, the focal point. FIGURE 5-15 shows the 200-inch (5-meter) Hale telescope on Mount Palomar. The observer's "cage" is at the prime focus of the instrument, located at the top end of the telescope. The astronomer can sit in the cage and be carried around with the telescope as it moves. The observer's cage does block some light to the objective mirror, but only a small fraction of it.

Losing some light because of reflection from the objective mirror back along the direction of incoming light is a drawback of reflecting telescopes; however, if the secondary mirror or the observer's cage is small enough, only a fraction of the incoming light is lost. Consider the case of a 5-meter objective mirror and a 1.5-meter cage. The amount of light received is proportional to the area of the objective mirror, while we lose an amount of light proportional to the area of the cage. Both areas are proportional to the squares of their diameters and, thus, we lose about $1.5^2/5^2$ or about 10% of the incoming light.

FIGURE 5-16 shows another design, the ***Coudé telescope***. This is a useful design for the case when large and heavy equipment, such as a spectroscope, is used for observing through the telescope. The equipment is set at the focal point, which is outside the main telescope tube and thus does not exert a weight on the telescope that must be compensated for. This design also increases the focal length substantially, which can be very useful for high-resolution observations.

New telescope technology has produced telescopes larger than the Hale telescope. The Tools of Astronomy box on p. 139 describes how a laboratory at the University of Arizona is making mirrors in a radically different way than ever before. The world's most powerful single telescope is currently the Large Binocular Telescope on Mount Graham, Arizona. The telescope (the result of a collaboration between institutions in the United States, Italy, and Germany) consists of two 8.4-meter mirrors on a common mount, making it equivalent in light-gathering power to a single 11.8-meter mirror (because $2 \times 8.4^2 = 11.8^2$).

Cassegrain focus The optical arrangement of a reflecting telescope in which a convex secondary mirror is mounted so as to intercept the light reflected from the objective mirror and reflect the light back through a hole in the center of the primary.

prime focus The point in a telescope where the light from the objective is focused. This is the focal point of the objective.

Coudé focus The optical arrangement of a reflecting telescope in which two mirrors are used to reflect the light coming from the objective to a remote focal point.

FIGURE 5-15 The Hale telescope on Mount Palomar. The objective mirror is right above the two people pointing at it. The observer's cage is at the top left of the image.

A new generation of extremely large ground-based telescopes is under study. The first such telescope to start construction is the Giant Magellan Telescope, to be completed by 2016 at a site in northern Chile. It will have seven 8.4-meter mirrors and thus the light-gathering power of a single 22-meter telescope.

To achieve the best viewing conditions, it is advantageous to locate telescopes high in the mountains in dry, clear climates. This greatly reduces but does not eliminate the blurring effects of the atmosphere. These effects are reduced even further by using new techniques, as described in the following section.

And now our hundred inch... I hardly dare to think what this new muzzle of ours may find. Come up, and spend that night among the stars.
—British poet Alfred Noyes, in *Watchers of the Skies*, written during the first observations with the 100-inch Mt. Wilson telescope, Nov. 1, 1917.

active optics A technology that works by "actively" keeping a telescope's mirror at its optimal shape against environmental factors such as gravity and wind. It works on timescales of a second or more.

Active and Adaptive Optics

To collect more light, the objective mirror must be as large as possible, but the problem with making a large mirror is that it tends to bend and sag when the telescope moves. As a result, the mirror's changing surface destroys image quality. To avoid this problem, new large reflecting telescopes use very thin mirrors together with an array of actuators (little motor-driven pistons) behind the mirror that keep it in an optimal shape. This new technology is called *active optics* and works as follows: Sensors on the mirror send information about the mirror's shape to a computer, which then drives the actuators to keep the mirror in perfect shape as it moves or is affected by the wind.

The first fully active telescope was the 3.6-meter New Technology Telescope of the European Southern Observatory (ESO); it entered into operation in 1989 at La Silla, Chile, and served as a test case for ESO's Very Large Telescope (VLT) (**FIGURE 5-17a**). The mirrors of VLT's four 8.2-meter telescopes are flexible, and the image they produce is constantly monitored by a computer. To keep the image sharp under different conditions, the computer controls about 200 actuators that push and pull on the back of each mirror to adjust its shape. When the four telescopes work in combined mode, their total light-gathering power is that of a 16.4-meter single telescope.

Active optics is also used for the Keck telescope (operating since 1993) on the 4200-meter summit of Mauna Kea in Hawaii. The Keck I telescope (Figure 5-17b)

FIGURE 5-17 (a) The four telescopes of the VLT in Paranal, Chile. VLT's useful wavelength range extends from the near ultraviolet up to 25 μm in the infrared. (b) The 36 mirrors of the Keck I telescope are reflecting the underside of the prime focus cage, where the 1.4-meter secondary mirror is mounted. The hole at the center of the objective is for the Cassegrain focus. (c) A yellow laser beam is coming out of one of the four telescopes of the VLT. The Milky Way is shining on the left. One of the Magellanic Clouds, a satellite galaxy to our own, is visible on the right.

has a 10-meter aperture consisting of 36 hexagonal mirrors; each mirror is 1.8-meters across, weighs 880 pounds, is mounted separately, and is controlled by a computer.

Active optics works on scales of a second or more and differs from ***adaptive optics***, which works on much shorter scales to compensate for the effects of atmospheric distortion. An adaptive optics system includes a sensor that measures atmospheric distortion on a timescale of a few milliseconds, a deformable mirror that is located in the path of the light from the source, and a computer that controls and reshapes the mirror so that the distortion is eliminated. But how does the computer know what the appropriate shape of the mirror should be? The computer must know both the distorted and undistorted image of the observed object.

One method to accomplish this is to use as a reference a bright star that is near the position of the observed object. Light from both the reference star and the observed object is affected similarly by astronomical seeing; however, we know that the undistorted image of a star should typically be a point that shows no details. From the distorted and undistorted images of the reference star, the computer calculates the effects of atmospheric distortion and uses that information to correct the image of the observed object. The problem with this method is that it is limited to only the study of objects that are near bright reference stars. An alternative method involves the use of a laser beam to generate an artificial star; for example, the naturally occurring layer of sodium atoms about 90 km (56 miles) above the Earth's surface can be excited by laser light at 589 nm and thus serves as a reference artificial star almost anywhere in the sky (Figure 5-17c).

Active and adaptive optics are now used in many of the world's large telescopes.

Telescope Accessories

Telescopes have many other astronomical uses besides obtaining images of celestial objects. Three of these applications and their corresponding accessories are described here.

- Even though a camera can be attached to a telescope to take photos, photographic film is not a very efficient detector of light, for only about 5% of the light hitting the film causes the chemical reaction that results in an image. For this reason, astronomers often use various electronic light detectors, particularly the ***charge-coupled device (CCD)***.

  This device, about the size of a postage stamp (FIGURE 5-18a), is divided into small squares, each capable of detecting the intensity of the light that hits it. Just as a black-and-white newspaper photo (or the screen of an electronic game) is made up of many individual pixels, a CCD may have more than 4 million pixels. Figure 5-18b is a highly magnified CCD image in which individual pixels are visible.

  The intensity of light collected in each pixel of a CCD is stored as a number in a computer. The data can then be used to show what the object would "look like" in a regular photograph, or they can be used to produce a false-color image that reveals some other aspect of the object (Figure 5-18c). For example, a false-color image may illustrate the intensity of radiation from the object by showing each brightness level as a different color. Most modern astronomical "photos" are actually CCD images, not film-based photographs. CCDs have revolutionized the way astronomers count photons. These devices not only can count almost all the incident photons but also can detect a wide range of wavelengths. When viewing objects of very different intensities simultaneously, CCDs can differentiate between them. Finally, CCDs have a linear response; that is, the signal increases linearly with the number of incident photons.

- One important measurement made of celestial objects is the intensity of light that is received at various wavelengths, a procedure called ***photometry***.

  In the past, this was done with a device similar to the light meter of a camera, but today, a CCD is normally used. The measurement can be made by placing filters in front of the light detector that allow only the wavelength of interest to pass through.

adaptive optics A technique that improves image quality by reducing the effects of astronomical seeing. It relies on an active optics system and works on timescales of less than 0.01 seconds.

charge-coupled device (CCD) A small semiconductor chip that serves as a light detector by emitting electrons when it is struck by light. A computer uses the pattern of electron emission to form images.

The devices used in digital cameras are similar to CCDs.

photometry The measurement of light intensity from a source, either the total intensity or the intensity at each of various wavelengths.

FIGURE 5-18 (a) A CCD (charge-coupled device) is a rectangle of the semiconductor silicon. This one contains nearly 164,000 electric circuits that detect the intensity of light striking them. A computer analyzes the resulting data and produces an image. (b) This CCD image has been magnified so much that the individual pixels are obvious. (c) This false color image of the Moon not only emphasizes slight natural color differences, but also compresses the spectrum from the ultraviolet to the near infrared so that it all shows as visible. The image was made from images from the spacecraft *Galileo*.

(a)

(b)

(c)

spectrometer An instrument that measures the wavelengths present in electromagnetic radiation. (A **spectrograph** is a spectrometer that produces a photograph of the spectrum.)

- In Chapter 4, we pointed out that a tremendous amount of information about celestial objects is obtained by spectral analysis—the examination of light that has been separated into its various wavelengths. To obtain data for such an analysis, a *spectrometer* is connected to a telescope. This instrument uses a prism—or, more commonly, a *diffraction grating*—to separate light into its colors. A spectrometer produces either a photograph of the spectrum or numerical data about the intensity of light at various wavelengths. The data can then be converted into a graph of intensity versus wavelength, as shown in **FIGURE 5-19**.

diffraction grating A device that uses the wave properties of electromagnetic radiation to separate the radiation into its various wavelengths.

5-5 Radio Telescopes

Thus far the discussion has concentrated on optical telescopes—telescopes that gather visible light. Besides visible light, the type of radiation from space that best penetrates the atmosphere is radio waves. In 1932, Karl Jansky, working on radio transmission for Bell Laboratories, noticed that static received by his antenna originated in the Milky Way. (See the Historical Note box on page 143.) When better radio receivers were designed (largely during World War II), astronomers were able to pinpoint the sources of celestial radio waves, and the field of radio astronomy was born.

FIGURE 5-19 This drawing shows two different ways of representing a spectrum. The dark absorption lines in the photograph correspond to the dips in the intensity versus wavelength graph.

Two problems arise in examining radio waves from space. First, the intensity of radio waves from a star is much less than the intensity of visible light. Second, because the wavelengths of radio waves are a million times longer than the wavelengths of visible light, there is a corresponding de-

TOOLS OF ASTRONOMY

Spinning a Giant Mirror

The 5-meter (200-inch) mirror for the Hale Telescope was cast at the Corning Glass Works in 1934. It was nearly 60 years before a mirror this large was made again in the United States. Then, in 1992, the Steward Observatory Mirror Laboratory at the University of Arizona in Tucson transformed 10 tons of glass into a 6.5-meter mirror blank.

The Steward Laboratory is making mirrors in a radically different way than ever before. In the past, mirrors were made by melting glass to form large pieces with flat surfaces. Then, after the glass hardened, the working surface of the glass was carefully ground into a curve to form a concave mirror surface. For the 6.5-meter mirror, that would have meant starting with more than twice the weight of the finished mirror, with 12 tons of glass then to be ground away, taking a year of extra work. Under the stands of the University of Arizona football stadium, technicians of the Steward Laboratory form the mirror surface by spinning the mirror as the glass melts (FIGURE B5-1).

Rotating the furnace—a technique called spin-casting—saves time and money in the production of large telescope mirrors. It shapes a natural curve in the surface of the molten glass in the same way that swirling a liquid in a glass causes a curved surface. The curvature created this way is close to the mirror's final parabolic shape, the rotation speed determining the amount of curvature. To create the 6.5-meter mirror, the furnace was spun at 7.4 revolutions per minute. This may seem slow, like a merry-go-round or carousel, but remember that the mirror was 6.5 meters—21 feet—across.

The new mirrors use much thinner glass than in the Hale telescope mirror, making them much lighter. The 6.5-meter mirror has 64% more light-gathering area than the Hale telescope mirror, but weighs half as much. The glass facesheet of the mirror surface averages only a little more than an inch thick; strength is provided by a honey-comb structure cast all in one piece with the facesheet and extending back nearly 30 inches at the edge of the mirror and half that at the center.

FIGURE B5-1 In the spin-casting technique, molten glass is placed in a rotating furnace to form a mirror with a curved upper surface. Increasing the rotation rate increases the amount of curvature.

Another advantage to spin-casting is a deeply curved, parabolic surface with a focal length much shorter than conventional mirrors. The shorter focal length means that the mirrors require a much shorter, less expensive enclosure.

The first 6.5-meter Steward Observatory mirrors have been installed at the Multiple Mirror telescope on Mount Hopkins in southern Arizona and at the Magellan Project telescope on Las Campanas, Chile. Two 8.4-meter mirrors were also installed on the Large Binocular Telescope on Mt. Graham, Arizona.

crease in the resolution of images made with radio waves. (Diffraction is greater with longer wavelengths.)

Both of these problems are solved in the same way—by making radio telescopes extremely large. The spherical mirror of the world's largest radio telescope, located in Arecibo, Puerto Rico, is fixed on the ground; however, its various antennas, suspended on a track above the mirror, enable it to receive radio emissions from different parts of the sky. Shown in FIGURE 5-20, it is a telescope constructed by perforated aluminum panels supported by steel cables stretched across a natural bowl between hills. This telescope is 300 meters (1000 feet) in diameter and scans the sky as the telescope moves along with the Earth. Changes in the direction from which it detects radio signals can be achieved by moving its antenna, which hangs from the cables suspended above the bowl.

FIGURE 5-20 The radio telescope near Arecibo, Puerto Rico, is the world's largest. Its radio detectors are part of a 900-ton platform suspended above the reflecting surface.

Radio telescopes are similar in principle to optical reflecting telescopes and to the satellite dishes we use to receive television signals from Earth satellites. In each case the reflector simply directs waves to a small detector located at the reflector's focal point. You can see the supports for the detector in Figure 5-20.

At Green Bank, West Virginia, the first of a modern generation of radio telescopes was completed in 2001. In a regular radio telescope, the detector and its supports not only block out a small portion of the waves, but they also cause diffraction effects. The detector of the new Green Bank Telescope (GBT) is located off to the side (FIGURE 5-21). This is done by constructing the reflecting surface in the shape of part of a much larger reflector. The surface of the GBT is not symmetrical. It is a 100- by 110-meter section of an imaginary giant 208-meter symmetric radio telescope and consists of 2004 separate panels, each of which is computer controlled. This adaptive capacity, the first use of adaptive optics for radio telescopes, permits the surface to be adjusted as the metal supports flex because of the telescope's motion. The resulting surface accuracy allows the GBT to be useful at shorter wavelengths than would otherwise be possible.

The image formed by a radio telescope is not a normal photograph. The radio telescope simply detects the intensity of radio signals from the area of the sky toward which it is pointed. One way to display and examine the data received is to plot a graph of the intensity of the radiation as the telescope moves across a small portion of the sky. FIGURE 5-22a shows what such a plot might look like. A more complete image of the radio-emitting object can be obtained by scanning the radio telescope back and forth across the celestial object and feeding the data into a computer that is programmed to represent the various intensities of the radio waves as different colors. Parts (b) and (c) of Figure 5-22 were produced in this manner and indicate the intensity of radio waves from a small portion of the sky. FIGURE 5-23 illustrates the different appearance of the same object (a galaxy) when seen in visible light, infrared, and radio waves.

5-6   Interferometry

The resolution formula is

$$\theta = 2.5 \times 10^5 \times \frac{\lambda}{D}.$$

FIGURE 5-21 The GBT is the first radio telescope to take advantage of adaptive optics. A computer controls each of the panels making up the surface of the reflecting dish. The GBT is the world's largest fully steerable radio telescope. The weight of the moving part of the telescope is 16 million pounds (7300 metric tons). The GBT is 485 feet (148 meters) tall—taller than the Statue of Liberty.

The resolution of a telescope depends on both the diameter of the telescope and the wavelength of the radiation. The greater the diameter of the telescope, the better the resolution (assuming "seeing" is not a factor), but the greater the wavelength, the poorer the resolution. Even though radio telescopes are very large, radio waves are so long that the best resolution from a single radio telescope is of the order of a number of arcminutes. A radio source the size of a star thus would still appear in a radio telescope to be a blur as large as half the diameter of the Moon.

The solution to this problem lies in the fact that a giant radio telescope would retain the same resolution if only two portions of its outer surface were being used, as shown in FIGURE 5-24a. Astronomers take advantage of this idea by combining two radio telescopes so that they act as one: In a sense, the two telescopes substitute for two portions of the outer part of a giant telescope, as in Figure 5-24b. In this way, they are able to obtain resolutions equal to that of a single large telescope.

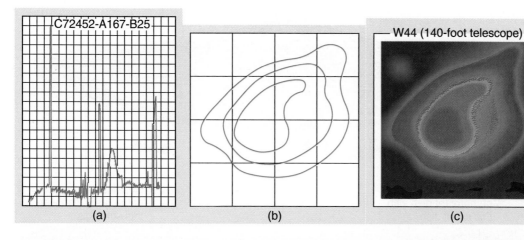

C72452-A167-B25

(a)

(b)

W44 (140-foot telescope)

(c)

FIGURE 5-22 (a) A typical graph made by one scan of a radio telescope across a source. (b) A contour map can be made from a number of such scans. The strength of the radio signals is greatest in the center. (c) Color has been added to the contour to produce a false color image.

(a)

(b)

(c)

FIGURE 5-23 (a) The Andromeda galaxy, shown here in visible, is a close neighbor to our Galaxy. (b) This view of Andromeda from NASA's *Spitzer* infrared telescope combines images taken at 24 microns (blue, showing the warmest dust), 70 microns (green), and 160 microns (red, showing the coolest dust). (c) A radio image of Andromeda shows that most radio waves are emitted from its spiral arms and its center.

Using two telescopes to act as one is not a simple matter. To understand the problem, refer to FIGURE 5-25. Radio waves from a distant source are shown striking the dish of a radio telescope. They are reflected so that a single wave gets to the detector (located at the focal point of the dish) at the same time from all areas of the dish. This feature must be retained when two (or more) radio telescopes are used as one. Waves from each single dish must be combined in the correct relationship. We say that the waves from the telescopes "interfere" with one another when they combine; therefore, the technique of linking two (or more) telescopes so that they act as one is called ***interferometry***. If the telescopes are close enough that they can be directly con-

interferometry A procedure that allows several telescopes to be used as one by taking into account the time at which individual waves from an object strike each telescope.

FIGURE 5-24 Two small radio dishes (b) can be made to have the same *resolution* as a large radio telescope (a) that has a diameter equal to the distance between the two small ones. The *strength* of the signals detected will be much greater in the case of the single large telescope.

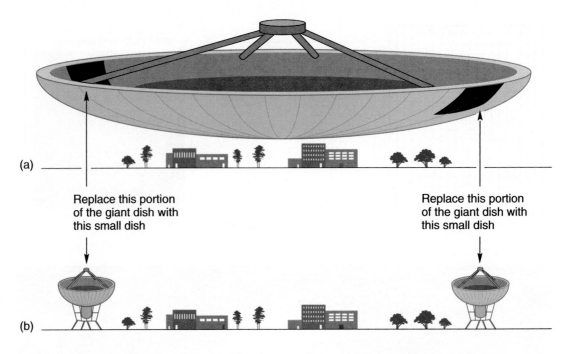

(a)

Replace this portion of the giant dish with this small dish

Replace this portion of the giant dish with this small dish

(b)

(a)   Incoming radio waves

Detector

Waves reflected from dish

(b)   Incoming radio waves

11   11
10   10
9   8 9
8 7 6 5 4 3 2 1   3 4 5 6 7

Signals relayed to correlator

Radio telescope dish

Radio telescope dish

FIGURE 5-25 (a) All portions of an incoming wave reach the detector of a radio telescope at the same time. (b) If two radio telescope dishes are to function as a single telescope, the waves must likewise reach the detector at the same time, or at least the time difference must be corrected for. (This drawing shows an obvious and oversimplified case of waves whose difference in reception times must be accounted for by the correlator.) As the Earth rotates, it causes a change in the difference in path from the source to the telescopes; as a result, the signals from a point radio source alternately arrive in phase and out of phase producing interference fringes. Also, if the source has a finite angular size, then different parts of the source are at different distances from the telescopes. High-speed computers and appropriate software are needed to obtain images from interferometric data.

Radio Waves from Space

In 1927, Karl Jansky received his B.A. in physics from the University of Wisconsin. After 1 year of graduate study, he was hired by Bell Laboratories to do research on radio communications. By this time, the first telephone service across the Atlantic had opened, and the telephone signal was sent by radio. Static was a common problem, however, and Jansky was assigned the task of designing and building an antenna to find the source(s) of the static (FIGURE B5-2). He had no specific experience in radio or electrical engineering, but after much study and some dead ends, he built a 100-foot-long antenna with which he was able to detect weak radio signals and to determine the direction from which they came.

In January 1932, Jansky wrote in his monthly report that he detected "...a very steady continuous interference—the term 'static' doesn't quite fit it. It goes around the compass in 24 hours. During December this varying direction followed the sun." As the early months of 1932 passed, he found that the direction from which the signals came seemed to move around, getting farther from the Sun. He anticipated that after the summer solstice, the apparent source would move closer to the Sun again, but instead, it continued to move around the sky during the year. By August 1932, Jansky decided that the static was coming from a fixed place among the stars; it was some type of "star static."

Jansky's star static was the first detection of radio waves from space. The source of the waves was the center of our Galaxy. Jansky had been slow to recognize the celestial

nature of the source in part because he did not know astronomy well. Astronomers, in turn, were slow to recognize the significance of his work because they were unfamiliar with electronics and radio, and they did not imagine that celestial objects emit radio waves. Radio astronomy did not grow quickly after Jansky went on to other things, but today it is a major branch of astronomy and provides us with information about the heavens that could not be learned in other ways.

FIGURE B5-2 Jansky's "merry-go-round" antenna could rotate to pinpoint the source of the radio signal.

nected, then the signals from the telescopes can be directly sent to the correlator. If the telescopes are widely separated, then extremely accurate atomic clocks are used for synchronization, and the signals from the telescopes are recorded on magnetic tape and then sent to the correlator.

In the New Mexico desert is an array of radio telescopes used for observations by interferometry. FIGURE 5-26 is a photograph of part of this Very Large Array. The telescopes ride on a double pair of railroad tracks arranged in a Y shape so that they can be moved and the arrangements changed.

The farther apart the telescopes, the better the resolution that can be obtained by interferometry. To achieve a longer baseline—distance between telescopes—some telescopes across the world are being used as part of a single array. For example, the Very Long Baseline Array consists of 10 radio telescopes across the United States (from Hawaii to the Virgin Islands), whereas the European Very Long Baseline Interferometry (VLBI) program includes an array of 18 radio telescopes that span the globe from Arecibo to China and from Finland to South Africa. Radio telescopes in space can be used as part of the VLBI program. Such long baseline programs achieve resolutions of fractions of milliarcseconds. An angle of one milliarcsecond is less than the angular diameter of a dime at 1000 miles!

Interferometry is also being employed in the newest optical telescopes. ESO's VLT is actually four separate telescopes, rather than mirrors, that focus light at the same point.

CHARA, at Georgia State University, has built an optical stellar interferometer, an array of six telescopes of only 1-m aperture each. They are placed in a Y-shaped array contained within a 400-m diameter circle on Mount Wilson, CA. Because each telescope is relatively small, this system costs much less than most new telescopes while producing a limiting resolution of 0.2 milliarcseconds in the visible range.

FIGURE 5-26 The Very Large Array is spread over 15 miles of the New Mexico desert.

To use the four telescopes as one, the signals from each must be combined using techniques similar to those originally developed for radio telescopes. Because the wavelength of visible light is much shorter than radio waves, matching waves from different sources is more critical for visible light waves. Therefore, optical interferometry is more difficult than radio interferometry. Using the four 8.2-meter telescopes together with four 1.8-meter auxiliary telescopes, the VLT can reach an angular resolution of less than a milliarcsecond in the visible, 50 times better than the *Hubble Space Telescope*, and provide astrometry at 10-microarcseconds precision, equivalent to that of a 130-meter telescope!

5-7 Detecting Other Electromagnetic Radiation

Visible light and radio waves pass through our atmosphere, and these two portions of the electromagnetic spectrum were the first that astronomers used in their quest to understand the heavens. (Examine again Figure 4-4, which shows atmospheric absorption at different wavelengths.) But celestial objects emit radiation over the entire range from radio waves to gamma rays, and modern astronomy has tools that study each region of the spectrum. (See the following Tools of Astronomy box where we describe a number of space telescopes.)

In the range of wavelengths from about 1200 to 40,000 nm (40 μm) (called the *near infrared*) are several narrow wavelength regions whose radiation penetrates to the surface of the Earth. Because water vapor is the chief absorber of radiation in the infrared, infrared observatories are located on mountains where the air is dry. The extinct volcano Mauna Kea is an ideal location for infrared telescopes, and two major observatories are located there.

⬩ These wavelengths are called "near infrared" because they are the part of the infrared region that is near the visible portion of the spectrum.

Radiation in the far infrared region—wavelengths greater than about 40 μm—is emitted by cooler celestial objects, such as planets and newly forming stars, and is very valuable in the study of these objects. Far infrared does not penetrate our atmosphere as deeply as shorter wavelengths, and we must therefore locate our instruments higher to detect it.

As we move from infrared to wavelengths shorter than visible—shorter than about 400 nanometers—we come upon ultraviolet, X-rays, and gamma rays. Ozone is the chief absorber of most of this radiation, and our atmosphere has a layer of ozone at altitudes between about 20 and 40 kilometers. Therefore, telescopes designed to detect this range of radiation must be located in space.

In building X-ray telescopes we cannot use mirrors because X-ray light is very energetic, and unless it hits the surface of the mirror at grazing angles it gets absorbed by the mirror (FIGURE 5-27).

FIGURE 5-27 This drawing shows how the mirrors in X-ray telescopes collect and focus light.

Paraboloid surfaces   Hyperboloid surfaces

X-rays

X-rays

Focal point

Just imagine what happens when you throw stones toward the surface of a pond; only the stones thrown at grazing angles will skip across the surface. That is why telescopes such as the *HST* cannot be used to observe objects in the X-ray part of the spectrum.

TOOLS OF ASTRONOMY

Space Telescopes

Infrared Telescopes

The SOFIA (Stratospheric Observatory For Infrared Astronomy) project involves a modified Boeing 747-SP aircraft carrying a 2.7-meter reflecting telescope at altitudes as high as 12,000 meters (45,000 feet), above 99% of the atmosphere's water vapor. The telescope's wavelength range is between 0.3 μm and 1600 μm. SOFIA, a joint NASA/German Space Agency effort, began operations in early 2009–2010 winter and is expected to be fully operational in 2014 and have a 20-year lifetime.

The *Spitzer Space Telescope* was launched in August 2003. It is a 0.85-m infrared telescope that observes the universe in the range of 3 to 180 μm. The telescope has a shield to protect it from the Sun and the Earth's infrared radiation, and it is cooled to a temperature only 5.2°C above absolute zero, by a tank of 360 liters of liquid helium, so that it can observe infrared signals from space without interference from its own heat. Infrared light can penetrate the regions in space that are filled with dense gas and dust clouds, giving us a unique view of star-forming regions, planetary systems, galactic centers, and cool objects too dim to be detected at visible wavelengths. FIGURE B5-3 shows a *Spitzer* image of the "mountains of creation" in the W5 star-forming region.

The GALEX Ultraviolet Telescope

NASA's *Galaxy Evolution Explorer (GALEX)*, launched in 2003, is an orbiting 0.5-m space telescope that observes galaxies in

FIGURE B5-3 An image composite comparing *Spitzer's* infrared image of the W5 star-forming region to a visible-light picture of the same region taken by the Digitized Sky Survey (inset). The "mountains of creation" reveal dust glowing in the infrared because they have been warmed up by the stars inside them.

FIGURE B5-4 A composite image of the nearby spiral galaxy M101. The *GALEX* image (in blue) shows the presence of young stars (only 10 million years old) in the galaxy's spiral arm. The two Digital Sky Survey images in visible light trace stars that have been living for more than 100 million years (in green) or more than a billion years (in orange).

UV light (130–300 nm). *GALEX* is looking for clues on how the earliest galaxies evolved and probes the causes of star formation during the early period of our universe. FIGURE B5-4 is an example of *GALEX*'s impact on the study of galaxy evolution by showing how we can trace the evolution of star formation in a galaxy such as M101.

X-Ray Telescopes

NASA's *Chandra X-ray Telescope* started operating in 1999 and has four nested mirror shells as shown in Figure 5-27. (The name "Chandra" was the nickname of the Indian physicist S. Chandrasekhar, who shared a Nobel Prize for his theoretical work on the structure and evolution of stars.) It is one of the most sophisticated observatories ever built and has an unusual elliptical orbit that takes it more than a third of the way to the Moon; its closest approach to Earth is 10,000 km. *Chandra* is designed to observe X-rays from high-energy regions of the universe, such as hot gas in the remnants of exploded stars. *Chandra*'s chapter opening image of the Crab Nebula is an example of how X-ray images provide different information than visible-light images of the same object.

ESA's *X-ray Multi-Mirror Satellite (XMM-Newton)*, launched in 1999, does not have the resolution of *Chandra* but can "see" further back in the universe's history because it can collect more light. It has 58 nested mirror shells, and its 0.3-m optical monitor with UV capabilities gives *XMM-Newton* a multi-wavelength capacity (FIGURE B5-5). Together with the joint US/Japan *Suzaku X-ray Telescope* (launched in 2005), these telescopes are already revolutionizing our un-

TOOLS OF ASTRONOMY

Space Telescopes *(Cont'd)*

FIGURE B5-5 A UV image of the M81 galaxy obtained by *XMM-Newton's* Optical Monitor. It covers a region of one quarter of a degree square; M81 is at least 22,000 light-years across.

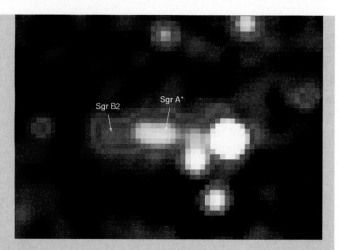

Sgr B2   Sgr A*

FIGURE B5-6 This is a false color image of the central region of the Milky Way. Sgr A* indicates the position of the supermassive black hole and Sgr B2 that of a molecular cloud at a projected distance of 350 light-years away. The cloud is currently being exposed to gamma rays emitted by the black hole 350 years ago during one of its active stages. Other gamma-ray emitters are also shown in the image.

derstanding of supernova remnants, active galactic centers, galaxy clusters, and black holes.

Gamma-Ray Telescopes

Since its 1991 launch and up to its deorbiting in 2000, the *Compton Gamma Ray Telescope* has provided high-quality data on subjects ranging from solar flares to supernova explosions to accreting black holes of stellar mass. The *Compton Observatory* was designed to map the gamma ray sky to solve some of the outstanding questions that earlier missions had posed and—perhaps most importantly—to watch for the unexpected. One of its most important findings was that gamma-ray burst sources are distributed in a manner consistent with a cosmological population.

The *International Gamma-ray Astrophysics Laboratory (INTEGRAL)*, launched in October 2002, is a collaboration involving ESA, NASA, and Russia. It carries four scientific instruments: an imager (giving sharp images of gamma-ray sources), a spectrometer (measuring gamma-ray energies), an X-ray monitor, and an optical camera (for identifying the sources). All four instruments observe the same region of the sky at the same time, allowing for a clear identification of the gamma-ray sources. *INTEGRAL* has already made enormous contributions to our understanding of extremely energetic phenomena such as supernova explosions and com-

pact objects such as black holes and neutron stars. **FIGURE B5-6** is an *INTEGRAL* observation of the central region of our Galaxy and reveals that the supermassive black hole (Sgr A*) at the center was much more active in the past.

The *Fermi Gamma-ray Telescope*, which was launched in 2008, is the result of an international collaboration between NASA, the U.S. Department of Energy, and institutions in Japan and Europe. It will investigate gamma-ray bursts, the composition of dark matter, and the acceleration mechanism responsible for the high speeds of outflows (jets) from black holes.

The Hubble Space Telescope

The *Hubble Space Telescope (HST)* is mainly an optical telescope but can observe across the spectrum from the near infrared to the near ultraviolet regions (115–2500 nm). The *HST* (**FIGURE B5-7**) has a modular design so that on subsequent shuttle missions astronauts can replace faulty or obsolete parts with new and/or improved instruments. This was fortunate because soon after its 1990 launch astronomers discovered that the objective mirror of the *HST* was slightly misshaped. The telescope has performed flawlessly after a repair mission in late 1993, during which corrective optics packages were installed. During the fourth repair mission in 2009, astronauts installed new gyros and batteries (which extend *HST's* life through 2014), a new wide-field camera (which improves *HST's* sensitivity by 10–30 times), a new spectrograph, and made necessary repairs to existing equipment.

TOOLS OF ASTRONOMY

Space Telescopes *(Cont'd)*

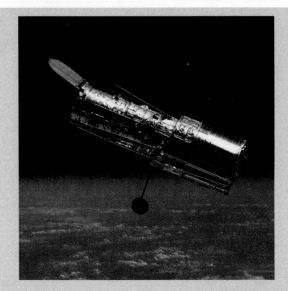

FIGURE B5-7 The crew of the Shuttle mission STS-82 took this photo of the *Hubble Space Telescope* after they had released it.

The *HST* has a 2.4-meter primary mirror and is roughly cylindrical in shape, 13.1 meters end to end and 4.3 meters in diameter at its widest point. Radiation enters the telescope through an opening below the open door at upper left in Figure B5-7.

It takes about 95 minutes for the *HST* to complete one orbit around the Earth. Only part of this time is spent observing, with the remainder spent on "housekeeping" functions, such as receiving command loads and sending data to Earth, turning the telescope to find a new target or avoid the Sun or Moon, and similar activities. To keep the telescope operating efficiently, commands are sent to the *HST* several times a day.

The *HST* is a unique instrument, a cooperative program of NASA and ESA, and an invaluable resource for all astronomers. The following are but a few of its contributions: It has uncovered evidence for the existence of supermassive black holes and evidence in support of the Big Bang theory, uncovered details of the processes involved in the formation of planets, stars, and galaxies, and is helping astronomers calculate the age of the universe.

The successor to the *HST* is the *James Webb Space Telescope* (*JWST*). It is scheduled to launch in 2013 for a 5- to 10-year mission. Its range is from visible green light through the invisible midinfrared (0.6–28 μm) and has a 6.5-m primary mirror. The *JWST* will see objects 400 times fainter than those currently observed by large infrared telescopes. Its goal is to observe the first stars and galaxies in the universe and to give us a better understanding of the dark matter problem.

The shortest wavelength in the electromagnetic spectrum corresponds to gamma radiation. As a result, gamma rays are too energetic to be reflected by mirrors, making gamma-ray detection an integral part of astronomy only since the 1960s. New detectors, using advanced solid-state technology, are slowly catching up in resolution with detectors at other wavelengths, giving us an increasingly sharper view of the universe at high energies.

Conclusion

In this chapter, we showed how refraction and reflection of light allow us to gather radiation from dim stellar objects and focus it to form an image. We saw that the powers of a telescope include not only magnification, but also light-gathering power and resolving power. This analysis showed the importance of large telescopes and led to a discussion of reflecting telescopes, which can be made much larger than refractors.

The importance of nonoptical telescopes in our quest to understand the universe cannot be underestimated. They permit us to observe objects that are invisible to the eye yet emit vast quantities of electromagnetic energy. New and different telescopes—including space telescopes—have provided us with information that was impossible to obtain by other means. The Chapter 4 opening images clearly show the different appearances an object—in this case our entire Galaxy—can have when observed at different wavelengths. These differences provide us with an enormous amount of information that was not available from ground-based observations centered on visible light. As later chapters show, entirely new celestial objects have been discovered in recent years by the new generation of telescopes. Undoubtedly, telescopes of the future will continue to bring us new and unexpected results and open whole new areas of exploration in astronomy.

Galileo's telescope began a revolution in astronomy nearly 400 years ago. Today the *HST* and other new telescopes are producing a comparable revolution. We do indeed live in exciting times.

STUDY GUIDE

1. The best site for an optical telescope is a place where the air is
   A. thin and dry.
   B. thick and dry.
   C. thin and moist.
   D. thick and moist.

2. Which of the following features determines the light-gathering power of a telescope?
   A. The diameter of the objective.
   B. The focal length of the objective.
   C. The focal length of the eyepiece.
   D. [Two of the above.]

3. Which of the following features determines the resolving power of a telescope?
   A. The diameter of the objective.
   B. The focal length of the objective.
   C. The focal length of the eyepiece.
   D. [Two of the above.]

4. Which of the following features determines the magnifying power of a telescope?
   A. The diameter of the objective.
   B. The focal length of the objective.
   C. The focal length of the eyepiece.
   D. [Two of the above.]

5. When the magnification of a telescope is increased by changing eyepieces,
   A. the apparent angular size of the object is increased.
   B. the field of view is decreased.
   C. the brightness of the object is decreased.
   D. [All of the above.]
   E. [None of the above.]

6. Which of the following telescopes has the greatest light-gathering power?

Telescope	Focal Length of Eyepiece	Focal Length of Objective	Diameter of Objective
A	24 mm	150 cm	12 cm
B	6 mm	100 cm	8 cm
C	18 mm	125 cm	20 cm
D	12 mm	90 cm	6 cm
E	12 mm	100 cm	10 cm

7. Which of the telescopes in question 6 has the greatest magnification?

8. The objective of most radio telescopes is similar to the objective mirror of a reflecting optical telescope
   A. in being concave in shape.
   B. in its approximate diameter.
   C. in being made of Pyrex glass.

9. The field of view of a telescope is
   A. the range of distance from the telescope over which it is in focus.
   B. the particular object being viewed by the telescope.
   C. the range of practical magnifying powers for the telescope.
   D. the range of wavelengths that can be detected by a particular telescope.
   E. the actual angular width of the scene viewed by the telescope.

10. Why are achromatic lenses used in optical telescopes?
    A. They reduce diffraction.
    B. They reduce color fringing.
    C. They produce greater magnification.
    D. They allow more light-gathering power.

11. Which of the following choices puts a limit to the useful magnification of a given telescope?
    A. Diffraction of light.
    B. Redshift of distant objects.
    C. The limit to how well lenses can be made.
    D. Reflection of light from parts of the telescope.

12. The resolving power of a telescope is a measure of its
    A. magnification under good conditions.
    B. overall quality.
    C. ability to distinguish details in an object.
    D. [All of the above.]

13. The light-gathering power of a telescope is determined by
    A. the telescope's magnification.
    B. the diameter of the objective of the telescope.
    C. the clarity of the sky.
    D. [All of the above.]
    E. [None of the above.]

14. Radio telescopes need not have finely polished surfaces because
    A. we are not interested in detail in the radio image.
    B. the speed of radio waves is less than that of light.
    C. the speed of radio waves is greater than that of light.
    D. radio telescopes can be used during the day.
    E. radio waves have longer wavelengths than light waves.

15. The primary purpose of a typical radio astronomer's work is to
    A. look for signals from other beings.
    B. send out radio waves to other beings.
    C. send out radio waves to be reflected back from stars and galaxies.
    D. receive radio waves sent out by radio sources.
    E. [All of the above.]

16. The eyepiece of a telescope is primarily used
    A. to collect as much light as possible.
    B. as a magnifier.
    C. as a prism to break light into its component colors.

17. A 40-inch telescope has _____ times the light-gathering power of a 10-inch telescope.
    A. 4
    B. 8
    C. 16
    D. 40
    E. [Either A, B, or C, above, depending on the eye-piece used.]

18. The Keck telescope is
    A. a large ground-based optical telescope.
    B. an orbiting telescope.
    C. a single radio telescope.
    D. an array of radio telescopes.

19. The Hubble telescope is
    A. a large ground-based optical telescope.
    B. an orbiting optical telescope.
    C. a single radio telescope.
    D. an array of radio telescopes.
    E. an orbiting infrared telescope.

20. The Arecibo telescope is
    A. a large ground-based optical telescope.
    B. an orbiting optical telescope.
    C. a single radio telescope.
    D. an array of radio telescopes.
    E. an orbiting infrared telescope.

21. Interferometry is used to increase
    A. magnifying power.
    B. resolving power.
    C. light-gathering power.
    D. [All of the above.]
    E. [None of the above.]

22. Which of the following effects is reduced by using a larger telescope?
    A. Diffraction.
    B. Refraction.
    C. Reflection.
    D. Chromatic aberration.
    E. [All of the above.]

23. Define refraction, chromatic aberration, and diffraction.

24. How is an achromatic lens made? Describe the defect it corrects.

25. Define magnifying power. Why do we not always use the highest magnification available?

26. What is meant by light-gathering power, and what is it about a telescope that determines its light-gathering power?

27. Explain what is meant when we say that a certain telescope can "resolve" a particular pair of stars.

28. Sketch a Newtonian reflecting telescope, showing the relative positions of the primary mirror, the secondary mirror, the eyepiece, and the image produced by the objective.

29. About how large is the largest refracting (visible light) telescope? The largest reflecting (visible light) telescope? Explain why one type can be made larger than the other.

30. Why do we not have to correct the objectives of reflectors for chromatic aberration?

31. Why must radio telescopes be made so large? About how large is the largest?

32. Why are most research telescopes located on mountains?

33. What is interferometry, and what is its advantage?

34. What is the primary advantage of locating a telescope in space?

35. What is spectroscopy?

---

1. Define and distinguish between reflection and refraction, and explain how each phenomenon is used in telescopes.

2. Consider the following telescopes:

Telescope	Focal Length of Eyepiece	Focal Length of Objective	Diameter of Objective
A	24 mm	150 cm	12 cm
B	6 mm	100 cm	8 cm
C	18 mm	125 cm	20 cm
D	12 mm	100 cm	10 cm

Which telescope has the greatest light-gathering power? Which one has the greatest magnification? What is the magnification of that telescope?

3. What determines the resolving power of a telescope? The magnification? The light-gathering power?

4. In the drawings showing light rays that come from very distant objects, the rays are represented as being parallel. If two rays come from a single point, how can they ever be parallel? A drawing may be helpful.

5. If the magnification of a telescope can be changed by changing eyepieces, why don't we use an eyepiece that will magnify objects thousands of times?

6. If radio telescopes use the principle of reflection, why do they not require a shiny reflecting surface?

7. Describe some special features of two recently constructed telescopes.

QUESTIONS TO PONDER

8. Why are the telescopes of the Very Large Array arranged so far apart? It would seem more convenient to have them in a tight cluster.

9. Write a report on the future plans that NASA has for space observatories. (You might begin with articles in *Sky & Telescope* or *Astronomy*. Also, visit NASA's Web page.)

10. Why are all large telescopes reflectors?

11. Some of the largest telescopes in the world are located on Mauna Kea in Hawaii, at an altitude of 4.2 km. What are some of the factors that astronomers consider when deciding the location for a telescope?

12. Suppose you and your neighbor each have a satellite dish to receive television signals from a satellite, but the signals from each dish are weak. Suppose that you decide to solve your problem by combining the signals from the two dishes to produce a signal twice as strong. Why won't this work well?

CALCULATIONS

1. Suppose you have lenses of the following focal lengths: 30, 10, and 3 centimeters. If you wish to construct a telescope of maximum magnification, which two lenses would you use? Which would be the objective and which the eyepiece? What magnification would this telescope produce?

2. The pupil of your eye is the opening through which light enters. The maximum diameter of the pupil of a human eye is about 0.5 centimeters. How does the light-gathering power of two eyes compare with that of a telescope with a 10-centimeter objective?

3. The telescope at Mount Pastukhov in Russia has a 6-meter objective. Compare its light gathering power with that of the 5-meter Hale telescope on Mount Palomar.

4. To have four similar mirrors with the same light-gathering power as one 16-meter circular mirror, what must be the diameter of each of the four?

5. The *HST* has a 2.4-meter objective mirror. If we would like to use it to observe Pluto in the visible, could we distinguish any of Pluto's features? (Diameter of Pluto = 2390 kilometers. Closest distance of Pluto from Earth ≈ 38 AU, at which distance Pluto's angular size is about 0.08 arcseconds.)

6. In the text, we discussed the concept of using a space radio telescope in conjunction with ground-based radio dishes in order to increase the baseline. An 8-m space radio telescope is at a distance (from Earth's surface) of about 21,000 kilometers at apogee and 560 km at perigee. Observations are made at 18, 6, and 1.3 centimeters. What is the best possible angular resolution that we can achieve?

ACTIVITIES

1. Making a Telescope

To build your own simple telescope, you will need two cardboard tubes that fit tightly together. You may even use kitchen paper tubes, as long as one tube fits tightly inside the other and you can roll the small tube in and out of the larger one. You will also need two converging lenses: the first, the objective, should be the size of the opening of the large tube, and the second, the eyepiece, should be about half the size of the opening of the smaller tube. Both lenses should have their flat sides facing out of the tubes and their curved sides facing in. The objective can be held in place with a piece of tape wrapped around the tube. To keep the eyepiece in place, you may use a foam ring (a piece of foam that fits inside the smaller tube and has its central region cut so that it plays the role of the eyepiece holder). By moving the smaller tube, you can focus on a specific object. Find the magnification of the refracting telescope you just built and use it to observe objects near and far.

2. Making a Spectroscope

To make a simple spectroscope you will need a small piece of diffraction grating, some black construction paper, tape, scissors, and a box. (Plastic diffraction grating is available for a few dollars from Edmund Scientific Co., http://www.scientificsonline.com.) The simplest box that works for this purpose is a toothpaste box, which has at each end a "tongue" that folds in and a pair of "ears" that cover the opening. Cut off the ends of the ears so that there is an opening about half an inch wide between them. Cut a piece of the black construction paper so that after rolling it and inserting it in the box it fits loosely inside. Also, cover the inside face of each tongue of the box with this paper by using some tape. The purpose of the paper is to create a dark interior, reducing extra reflected light. Punch a hole at the center of one tongue, and cover this hole with the small piece of diffraction grating by taping the edges of the grating on the inside face of the tongue. On the other tongue you will create a thin slit by making two parallel and closely spaced cuts along the tongue (from the tip of the tongue to the body of the box). Close the box. Tape around the edges of the tongues, and your spectroscope is ready. Use it to look at any light source by putting the end with the grating close to your eye. Compare the spectra you see when looking at an ordinary incandescent light bulb, a fluorescent light source, a mercury vapor streetlight and the sky. (**Warning: Never look directly at the Sun**.)

1. The book *Observing the Universe: A Guide to Observational Astronomy and Planetary Science* (2004, Cambridge Univ. Press) introduces a range of useful techniques and skills for those wanting to do observational work.

2. The article "Untwinkling the Stars" by R. Fugate and W. Wild in *Sky & Telescope* (May, 1994, p.24 and June, 1994, p.20) discusses adaptive optics.

3. The book *Great Observatories of the World* by S. Brunier and A-M. Lagrange (2005, Firefly Books Ltd.) includes a history of and the technology used in 56 professional astronomical observatories.

4. If you are interested in buying a telescope, you may want to read the article "Buying the Best Telescope" by A. Dyer in *Sky & Telescope* (December, 1997).

5. "2MASS: Unveiling the Infrared Universe," by M. Skrutskie, in *Sky & Telescope* (July 2001).

6. "Seeing in Infrared," by A. Swafford, in *Astronomy* (August 2002).

7. "Telescopes 101," by M. E. Bakich, in *Astronomy* (June 2005).

8. "Giant Telescopes of the Future," by R. Gilmozzi, in *Scientific American* (May 2006).

9. "Hubble's Top 10," by M. Livio, in *Scientific American* (July 2006).

10. "Window on the Extreme Universe," by W. B. Atwood, P. F. Michelson, and S. Ritz, in *Scientific American* (December 2007).

11. "Next Light: Tomorrow's Monster Telescopes," by J. Lowe, in *Sky & Telescope* (April 2008).

Quest Ahead to Starlinks
http://physicalscience.jbpub.com/starlinks

Starlinks is this book's online learning center. It features **eLearning**, which contains chapter quizzes and other tools designed to help you study for your class. You can also find **online exercises**, view numerous relevant **animations**, follow a guide to **useful astronomy sites** on the Web, or even check the latest **astronomy news** updates.

EXPANDING THE QUEST

STARLINKS

The Earth-Moon System

6

The rising Earth as viewed by Apollo 8 astronauts as they came from behind the Moon during a lunar orbit.

*Interview with Aleksei Leonov, March 18, 1987, Zvyozdny Gorodok, USSR. By permission of Michael Woods, Senior Editor, the *Toledo Blade.* Quoted in *The Home Planet,* Kevin W. Kelley, Ed. (Reading, MA: Addison-Wesley and Moscow: Mir Pubishers, 1988).

"WHAT STRUCK ME MOST WAS THE SILENCE. It was a great silence, unlike any I have encountered on Earth, so vast and deep that I began to hear my own body: my heart beating, my blood vessels pulsing, even the rustle of my muscles moving over each other seemed audible. There were more stars in the sky than I had expected. The sky was deep black, yet at the same time bright with sunlight.

The Earth was small, light blue, and so touchingly alone, our home that must be defended like a holy relic. The Earth was absolutely round. I believe I never knew what the word 'round' meant until I saw Earth from space."*

These are the words of Russian cosmonaut Aleksei Leonov, describing what it was like for him to walk free in space. For a time, he was a human satellite of Earth.

In previous chapters we laid the groundwork for our study of the cosmos. We presented the historical development of some fundamental ideas in astronomy and described some of the tools that we use in our efforts to understand celestial phenomena. We are now ready to begin our voyage. We must not forget that our explorations are based on the very important assumption that the physical laws derived from and supported by our experiments and observations are valid throughout the universe. This is a bold assumption, but seems to be supported by the data.

All cross references to chapters, sections, figures, and tables pertain to the main text, *In Quest of the Universe, Sixth Edition. In Quest of the Solar System* contains Chapters 1–11 and 19 of the main text. *In Quest of the Stars and Galaxies* contains Chapters 1–5 and 11–19 of the main text.

If we are to understand our universe, we must be able to understand first our immediate environment. The knowledge we have about the Earth–Moon system serves as a basis for our studies of the entire solar system. On the other hand, information we obtain about other planets and satellites helps us better understand our own past and future. We thus begin our quest of the universe by first examining our home planet and its satellite.

6-1 Measuring the Moon's Distance and Size

Astronomers have learned a great deal about the Earth and Moon since the advent of the space program in the late 1960s, but simple naked-eye observations had allowed people to calculate the size of the Earth long before we even journeyed around it. In Section 2-4 we described how Eratosthenes measured the size of the Earth more than 2000 years ago. We begin this chapter by describing how the Moon's distance and size were measured.

The Distance to the Moon

Recall the discussion of parallax in Section 2-3. The Moon exhibits parallax when seen from different positions on the Earth. For example, if a person in Chicago and another person in Paris, France happen to be looking at the Moon at the same time, they will observe it in slightly different positions against the background of stars (FIGURE 6-1).

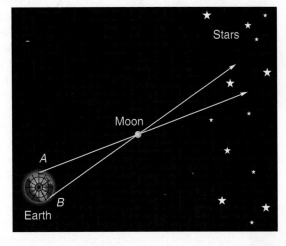

FIGURE 6-1 When viewed from two different places on Earth (*A* and *B* in the figure), the Moon seems to be at two different places among the stars. The effect is greatly exaggerated in the drawing.

In reality, the Moon is far enough away that its parallactic shift among the stars is very small. The shift can be observed, however, and the observation allows us to measure the distance from the Earth to the Moon. Using parallax, Ptolemy determined that the distance from the Earth to the Moon is 27.3 Earth diameters—very close to today's value of 30.13 for the average distance to the Moon. Ptolemy's measurement is significant not only because it is so close to the correct value, but also because it shows how close the ancient Greeks were in having a realistic map of the solar system about 2000 years ago. If Aristarchus' heliocentric model had been accepted, then Ptolemy's determination of the Earth–Moon distance would have provided the final clue in having realistic sizes for the Earth–Moon–Sun system. Recall from the information in Section 2-4 that Aristarchus had calculated the relative sizes of these three objects and their relative distances, thus providing a map, albeit one without a scale. Eratosthenes' and Ptolemy's measurements provide the missing scale and thus a realistic map of the solar system.

Today we know that Earth's diameter is about 12,800 kilometers and that the Moon is about 380,000 kilometers (or 240,000 miles) from Earth.

The Size of the Moon

The diameter of the Moon can be calculated from data related to spacecraft orbiting the Moon, for example, by knowing the spacecraft's speed and orbital time, but it can also be calculated by knowing the distance to the Moon. FIGURE 6-2 illustrates the idea.

When we look up at the Moon from Earth, we have no way of judging its actual size. Suppose you see two objects like those in FIGURE 6-3a. Could you tell how large they are? One looks larger than the other, but in fact, they are the same size and one

FIGURE 6-2 Both characters are right. To determine size, one must know the distance, and the word "looney" comes from "lunar."

By permission of Johnny Hart and Creators Syndicate, Inc.

(a)   (b)

FIGURE 6-3 (a) It is difficult to judge the real size of the two balls here. They are actually the same size. (b) Here we can use the surroundings to judge the size of the balls.

FIGURE 6-4 The Moon's angular diameter is about 1/2 degree.

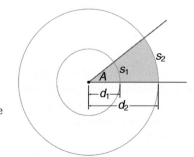

FIGURE 6-5 The angular size and diameter of an object are related to its distance from the observer.

looks smaller simply because it is farther from the camera. When we view an object at a distance, we estimate its size in several ways. One way is by comparing it with objects of known size that are near it. That makes the judgment of the size of the two balls in Figure 6-3b easier.

When we look at the sky, there are no familiar objects near the things we see. In this case, we can estimate the size of an object only if we know how far away it is. By combining knowledge of its angular size and its distance, we can determine the object's size.

An object's angular size is the angle between two lines that start at the observer and go to opposite sides of the object. For example, the angular size of the Moon seen from Earth is very close to 0.5° (**FIGURE 6-4**). As you look at the two balls in Figure 6-3a, the angular size of the ball on the left is less than that of the ball on the right. Not knowing its distance, you thus would say that it looks smaller.

The distance to the Moon and the angular size of the Moon (as seen from Earth) can be used to calculate the Moon's diameter. This can be done with a simple equation, called the small-angle formula, which relates the angular size, the distance, and the width of an object. (The term *width* is used here instead of diameter so that the equation will be general for all objects. In the case of the Moon, the width is about equal to its diameter.)

The Small-Angle Formula

If we have two circles (**FIGURE 6-5**) with the same center and radii d_1 and d_2 and we draw an angle A from the center, then the angle "cuts" arcs s_1 and s_2 from the two circles. Clearly, the larger the radius of the circle, the larger the arc that subtends the angle A.

Because 360 degrees correspond to the circumference of a circle of radius d (that is, to a length $2\pi \cdot d$), then an angle A corresponds to an arc of length s. In mathematical terms this implies the following relationship:

$$\frac{360°}{A} = \frac{2\pi \cdot d}{s} \Leftrightarrow s = \frac{2\pi \cdot A}{360°} \cdot d.$$

In astronomy, however, the angles subtended by an object are, in general, very small. For example, for the Sun and Moon the angle is about 0.5°. A more convenient unit is the arcminute (where 1° = 60′) and the arcsecond (where

$1' = 60''$). If we measure our angles in arcseconds (and write A'' as a reminder), then 360 degrees correspond to about 1.3×10^6 arcseconds and thus $360°/2\pi$ is about $206,265''$. Also, the length s of the arc is approximately equal to the diameter (or width) D of the object we are observing. The previous equation, therefore, now takes the simpler form

$$D \approx \frac{A''}{206,265} \times d \quad \text{(the small-angle formula)},$$

where D = diameter (width) of an object, d = distance from observer, and A'' = angular size of object (in arcseconds).

This equation cannot be used accurately for large angles (more than about 5 degrees), but in most cases in astronomy, angular sizes are much less than 1 degree. Before using the equation for the Moon, let's use it in a terrestrial example.

This "small-angle formula" is very convenient and is used again later in the book.

EXAMPLE

Suppose you look at a photograph on the wall across a large room. You happen to have a device with you that allows you to measure the angular width of the photo, and you determine it to be 1.5 degrees. Suppose further that you know that the photo is 5 meters away from you. How wide is the photograph?

SOLUTION   Substituting into the small-angle formula:

$$D \approx \frac{A''}{206,265} \times d = \frac{1.5 \times 60 \times 60}{206,265} \times 5 \text{ m} \approx 0.13 \text{ m or } 13 \text{ cm}.$$

TRY ONE YOURSELF
Use the small-angle formula to calculate the diameter of the Moon, using the fact that the Moon's angular size is 0.52 degrees and its distance is 384,000 kilometers (more accurate values than given above). Why does your answer differ from the known diameter of 3476 kilometers?

If we use the most accurate data, an exact calculation yields 3476 kilometers (2160 miles) for the Moon's diameter. This is very close to one fourth of the diameter of the Earth. FIGURE 6-6 shows two balls, one four times the diameter of the other. Form a mental image of these two balls. You would probably not say that the large one is four times the size of the small one. The word *size* is an indefinite term; you can't tell whether it refers to diameter, area, or volume. *Size* will not be used in a quantitative sense here; that is, an object that has four times the diameter of another will not be described by saying that its *size* is four times greater. For the two balls in Figure 6-6, the larger one has a volume $4^3 = 64$ times greater and, assuming they are made of the same material, 64 times more mass than the smaller ball.

To appreciate the scale of the Earth–Moon system, imagine the Earth to be a large grapefruit (about 5 inches in diameter). On this scale, the Moon would be a Ping-Pong ball 12 feet away. Between the Earth and Moon, there would be nothing but (almost) empty space.

FIGURE 6-6 The larger ball has a diameter four times the smaller. Would you say that its size is four times larger? Its volume is actually 64 times greater.

Summary: Two Measuring Techniques

As our study of astronomy proceeds, we describe some important relationships that allow us to measure features of objects in the heavens. Two have been introduced so far (FIGURE 6-7). First, we used parallax to measure the distance to the Moon. This method is often called **triangulation** because it involves using a triangle to find a distance. As we explain in a later chapter, this method is also used to measure distances to nearby stars. Using this method involves a relationship among three quantities: the

triangulation The use of parallax to determine the distance to an object.

FIGURE 6-7 Two techniques for measuring features of celestial objects.

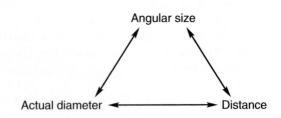

size of the baseline, the angle of parallax, and the distance to the object. Knowing any two of the three, you can calculate the third. A second relationship (the small-angle formula) involves angular size, actual diameter, and distance. Again, if you know any two of the quantities, you can calculate the third. This is an important relationship, and in later chapters, we explain its use in measuring the diameters of planets.

perigee/apogee The point in the orbit of an Earth satellite where it is closest to/farthest from Earth.

The Moon's Changing Size

FIGURE 6-8 shows two photographs of the full Moon taken at two different times by the same camera. The photographs show that the apparent diameter of the Moon changes but that it depends on distance and actual diameter.

The actual diameter of the Moon does not change, of course; thus, our distance from the Moon must change. This occurs because the Moon's orbit is an ellipse, just like the orbits of all orbiting objects, and the Moon's orbit is fairly eccentric; that is, it is not very circular. The larger apparent diameter occurs when the Moon is at its *perigee*, or closest distance to the Earth, about 363,300 kilometers. The smaller apparent diameter occurs at the Moon's maximum distance from Earth, 405,500 kilometers—when the Moon is at its *apogee*. (Note the similarity to the terms "perihelion" and "aphelion," which refer to the distances closest to and farthest from the Sun, as discussed in Section 2-9.)

FIGURE 6-8 These are two photos of the Moon put side by side; one was taken when the Moon is closest to Earth, the other when it is farthest.

6-2   The Tides

If you live near the seashore or visit it often, we don't need to describe the tides to you, but "landlubbers" don't often get a chance to experience the tides. FIGURE 6-9 shows a seashore at low and high tide; the difference in depth of water is obvious. Most locations on the Earth experience a high tide about every 12 hours and 25 minutes and a low tide midway between high tides. On most days, thus there are two high tides and two low tides.

Newton realized that the force of gravity between the Earth and an object is not really a single force exerted by the entire Earth, but the result of all the forces of gravitational attraction between the object and each part of the Earth—each little mass within the Earth. This idea applies to the force of gravity between the Earth and the Moon. The Moon exerts a gravitational force not on the Earth as a whole, but on each individual part of the Earth. FIGURE 6-10a uses arrows to indicate the force of gravity between the Moon and a small mass at three different locations within the Earth. The mass at point A feels the greatest lunar gravitational force, as it is closest to the

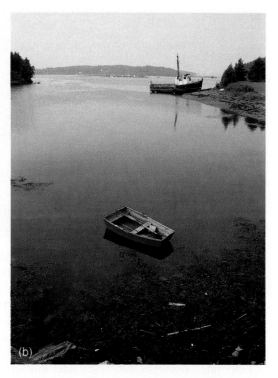

FIGURE 6-9 Those of us who don't often get to the coast may not be familiar with the phenomenon of tides. Observe how much deeper the water is at high tide. Part (a) shows low tide at a bay of Campobello Island, Canada and (b) shows the same bay at high tide.

Moon. The mass at point B, the center of the Earth, feels less force toward the Moon, and the mass at the far side of the Earth (point C) feels the least force. Specifically, the mass at point A feels a gravitational force from the Moon that is about 3% greater than the force on the mass at point B, which in turn is about 3% greater than the force on the mass at point C (see a Calculation at the end of this chapter).

Now, each of these three parts of the Earth responds to the gravitational force toward the Moon, but because there is more force toward the Moon on one kilogram of mass at point A than at point B, the mass at the surface feels pulled away from the center. Water covers most of the Earth, and because it is liquid and free to flow, some water flows toward the area under the Moon. As the water becomes deeper at that point, it causes a high tide. The high tide on the other side of the Earth occurs because 1 kilogram of mass at the center of the Earth feels a greater force toward the Moon than at point C. The main body of the Earth thus is pulled away from that water, creating another high tide there (Figure 6-10b).

These **tidal forces** result in two areas of the Earth experiencing high tides. The water that went to making those high tides has been pulled away from other parts of the Earth and, thus, a low tide lies midway around the Earth between the areas of high tides.

You might think that because the Earth completes one rotation a day, there would be exactly two high tides each day. Instead, about 12 hours and 25 minutes pass between successive high tides, so that if a high tide occurs on my beach at 10:00 this morning, the high tide tomorrow morning will be at about 10:50 AM. The reason for this is that the Moon is not stationary as the Earth rotates. Instead, the Moon moves through about 1/30 of its cycle each day. Therefore, the Earth must turn for the additional 50

tidal force A gravitational force that varies in strength and/or direction over an object, causing it to deform.

(a)   (b)

FIGURE 6-10 (a) The gravitational force exerted by the Moon on a given amount of Earth's mass is greatest on the side nearest the Moon, less on the mass at the center of the Earth, and least on the mass on the side farthest from the Moon. Arrows here represent the forces, and their differences have been exaggerated. (b) Imagine that these points represent people standing on a tiled floor, experiencing different forces to the right, such that person 3 moves three tiles to the right, persons 2, 4, and 5 move two tiles to the right, and person 1 moves 1 tile to the right. As a result, the original "round" distribution has turned into an "oval" shape. In the case of the Earth–Moon system, the gravitational forces result into a motion around the common center of mass and the differences in the forces result into tides.

FIGURE 6-11 The Earth is seen here from above the North Pole. Because the Moon moves in its orbit, the Earth must make more than one complete rotation for a point on its surface to return to the same position with respect to the Moon. About 24 hours and 50 minutes pass between the two positions shown.

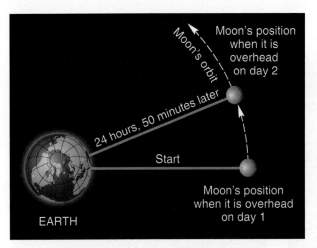

spring tide The greatest difference between high and low tide, occurring about twice a month, when the lunar and solar tides correspond.

neap tide The least difference between high and low tide, occurring when the solar tide partly cancels the lunar tide.

The next time you are at the seashore, notice that high tide occurs after the Moon is highest in the sky.

minutes, which is about 1/30th of 24 hours, before a spot on the Earth returns to the same position with respect to the Moon. This is also what causes the Moon to rise (or set) about 50 minutes later each day (FIGURE 6-11).

In addition, the Sun causes tides on the Earth. As we showed in the example in Section 3-4, the Sun's gravitational pull on 1 kilogram of Earth's mass is about 180 times stronger than the corresponding pull from the Moon; however, the Sun is about 390 times farther from the Earth than the Moon is and therefore its pull is almost the same on every kilogram of Earth's mass. Specifically, if we were to substitute the Moon with the Sun in Figure 6-10a, the mass at point A feels a gravitational force from the Sun that is 3%/390 or about 0.01% greater than the force on the mass at B, which in turn is about 0.01% greater than the force on the mass at C. As a result, the difference in the Moon's pull on opposite sides of the Earth is 2.2 times greater than the difference in the Sun's pull (see Calculations at the end of this chapter). Therefore, the tides due to the Sun are small and are not noticed independently of the Moon's tides; however, when the tides due to the Sun correspond to the Moon's tides (near the times of new and full Moon), we see extreme tides on Earth; these are known as *spring tides* (FIGURE 6-12). On the other hand, when the Sun's tides are 90° from the Moon's (near quarter Moon), they tend to partially cancel the Moon's, and this causes the change from low to high tide to be less than normal; such tides are called *neap tides*.

Rotation and Revolution of the Moon

The period of the Moon's rotation exactly matches its period of revolution. As a result, the Moon keeps the same face toward Earth at all times. This effect is caused by tidal forces. To understand it, recall that as the Earth rotates, it interacts with tides in the water. If there were no friction between the solid Earth and its oceans, one area of high tide would stay exactly under the Moon and another would be on the opposite side of the Earth. The land masses, however, exert forces on the water as the Earth rotates, causing the point of highest tide to be pushed from directly under the Moon (and directly opposite the Moon). FIGURE 6-13 illustrates this behavior.

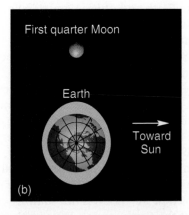

FIGURE 6-12 The Moon exerts a tidal force on Earth that is 2.2 times greater than the Sun's tidal force. (a) During a new Moon, the tidal forces from the Moon and Sun add up to give us enhanced (or spring) tides. The same is true during a full Moon. (b) During first quarter Moon, the two tidal forces cancel partially, giving us smaller (or neap) tides. The same is true during third quarter Moon. Spring (neap) tides are about 20% higher (lower) than average.

If the land masses exert a force on the tidal bulges as the Earth turns, it follows from Newton's third law that the bulges exert an equal and opposite force on the land masses. This results in the Earth's rotation being slowed down because of the *tidal friction* exerted on it. The Earth is indeed turning more slowly today than it was years ago. Our days are very slightly longer than Shakespeare's were, increasing by about 25 billionths of a second every day. Billions of years from now, the Earth's rotational period will increase to the point that the Earth will always keep the same face turned toward the Moon.

FIGURE 6-13 The Earth's rotation tends to drag the tides along with it so that a high tide is not directly under the Moon but instead is farther to the east.

Just as the Moon and Sun cause tides on Earth, the Earth and Sun cause Moon tides, similar to the tides on the solid Earth. The Moon's surface may move as much as 4 inches (10 centimeters) over a month, and just as tides on Earth are causing it to change its speed of rotation, the tides on the Moon have resulted in a change in its speed of rotation. At one time in the past, the Moon must have had a rotation period different from its revolution period. Through millions of years, the tides have slowed the Moon's rotation until it now keeps its same face toward the Earth. As a result of the tidal interactions between the two objects, the Moon is also pushed farther away from the Earth at a rate of about 4 centimeters per year.

Tides also occur on the dry land. In this case, the rocks and dirt actually stretch to allow the surface to rise and fall. Parts of a continent may move as much as 20 inches (half a meter) in a day.

As you might suspect, the actual tidal phenomenon is more complicated than we have just described. The Earth is rotating, and its land masses disturb the flow of water. The shape of the shoreline, the depth of the water, and the location of the Moon all play a part in determining exactly when high and low tides occur at a particular location on Earth and just how high and how low those tides are. For example, in the deep ocean, the difference in tides is usually less than 1.6 feet, but in the Bay of Fundy (Nova Scotia, Canada), tides have a range of about 45 feet (14 meters).

tidal friction Friction forces that result from the movement of tides on a rotating object caused by its gravitational interactions with another object.

Precession of the Earth

Think of what happens when you spin a child's top on a smooth table. The axis of the top does not stay in the same orientation (unless you were able to begin the rotation around a perfectly vertical axis). Instead, the top wobbles around. What causes the wobble? The mathematics to describe this effect is far from simple; in simple terms, the top has a tendency to fall over, and its rotation prevents this from happening. Instead, the top wobbles around, keeping the same angle with the table's surface until friction slows it down. Any time a spinning object feels a force trying to change the orientation of its axis, it will wobble. The wobble is called *precession*.

The Earth also spins on its axis. It might seem that the Earth would not precess because there is nothing below it trying to pull it over. There is, however, a force on the Earth tending to change the orientation of its axis of rotation. FIGURE 6-14a shows the Moon's gravitational force at three points on the surface of an exaggerated "flattened" Earth. (The measure of how much a planet is "flattened" [*oblate*] is called its *oblateness*).

Because point *A* is closer to the Moon than point *C*, the Moon exerts a greater force on a particle at *A*. This results in an overall force seeking to change the tilt of the spinning Earth's axis. The Earth's axis does indeed precess as a result of the gravitational forces from both the Moon and the Sun, although very slowly. Although the child's top may complete a precession in about a second, the Earth requires about

precession The conical shifting of the axis of a rotating object.

oblateness A measure of the "flatness" of a planet, calculated by dividing the difference between the largest (d_{large}) and smallest (d_{small}) diameter by the largest diameter:

$$\text{oblateness} = \frac{d_{large} - d_{small}}{d_{large}}.$$

FIGURE 6-14 (a) The Earth is flexible enough that its spinning causes its diameter to be about 26 miles (43 km) greater across the equator than from pole to pole. (Imagine what would happen if you made a ball of wet clay and set it spinning.) The differences in the gravitational forces from the Moon on different parts of the Earth cause the Earth's precession. (The drawing is not to scale.) (b) As the Earth spins, its axis precesses with a period of about 26,000 years, pointing to different "pole stars" over the centuries. The radius of the precession circle covers an angle of about 23.5° in the sky.

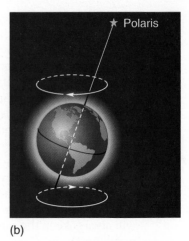

(a)

(b)

26,000 years (Figure 6-14b)! If the Earth were not spinning, the result of the forces from the Sun and Moon would be to have the Earth's bulges on the Sun–Earth orbital plane.

What effect does precession have on what we see in the sky? Right now, Polaris is the closest bright star to the Earth's north celestial pole, but it will not remain so forever. The pole will gradually change, and about 12,000 years from now the star Vega will be our "North Star."

A corresponding effect is that the positions of the equinoxes and solstices change over the centuries. For example, the summer solstice now appears in the constellation Gemini, but about 2000 years ago it was in Cancer; that is why the latitude at which the Sun is directly overhead on the summer solstice is called the Tropic of Cancer. Also, the vernal equinox, now in Pisces, is slowly drifting toward Aquarius (heralding to some the "age of Aquarius"), thus introducing a difference between the sidereal year (measured with respect to the distant stars) and the tropical year (measured with respect to the Sun).

The ancient Greek astronomer Hipparchus of Nicea (around 130 BC) first suggested that the Earth is precessing. During equinoxes, the Sun is at the intersections of the ecliptic and the celestial equator, and it rises exactly in the east and sets exactly in the west. Because one cannot easily observe the position of the Sun among the stars, Hipparchus concentrated on the Earth's shadow on the Moon. During a lunar eclipse, the center of the Earth's shadow is located exactly opposite the Sun. By comparing observations in the preceding 150 years or so to his own, Hipparchus concluded that the intersections of the ecliptic and celestial equator have moved about 2 degrees (or 1/180 of a full circle) and, therefore, that they will return to the same positions after about 180 × 150 or 26,000 years.

FIGURE 6-15 The tilt of the Earth's axis oscillates with a period of 41,000 years by about 1.3° around its average value of 23.3°.

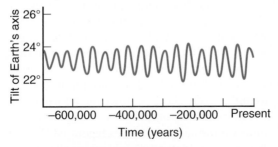

Compared with the influence of the Sun and Moon, the planets have a very small gravitational effect on the Earth, but they nevertheless cause its orbit to precess (with a period of 71,000 years) and the ellipticity of its orbit to oscillate. Overall, the tilt of the Earth's axis oscillates around its average value of 23.3 degrees (FIGURE 6-15).

6-3   Earth

The next few chapters focus on the details of the objects that make up the solar system. Before moving outward from the Earth and Moon, however, a close examination of these two objects is presented to provide a basis for comparison.

The Interior of the Earth

How do we know what is inside the Earth? One of the first properties of the interior that would aid our quest is the *density* of the Earth. The density of an object is defined as the ratio of the object's mass to its volume. As we have seen, the diameter of the Earth, and thus its volume, has been known for centuries, and of course, the space program has greatly increased the accuracy of our measurements of the Earth's size and shape.

The mass of the Earth was first determined by applying Kepler's third law (as revised by Newton) to the period and radius of the Moon's orbit. We saw in Chapter 3 that the period of revolution of an orbiting object depends only on the size of the orbit and total mass of the objects. Today we can calculate the gravitational pull on orbiting satellites and use this to further refine our values for the Earth's mass. Values of the mass and diameter of the Earth are given in Appendix C.

Using the mass and volume of the Earth, we calculate its average density to be 5.52 grams per cubic centimeter (g/cm³) or 5520 kilograms per cubic meter (kg/m³). For comparison, the density of water is 1 g/cm³, of aluminum is 2.7 g/cm³, and of iron is 7.8 g/cm³.

Knowing the density of a celestial object allows us to make a reasonable guess about its composition. For example, assume that you discover a planet whose average density is 5.5 times that of water. The surface of this planet seems to be rocky and is mostly covered by water. Based on this information, what can you say about the interior of this planet? Because the density of water is 1 g/cm³ and that of rock about three times larger, the interior must have elements whose densities are greater than the density of rock. This is necessary for the average density to be 5.5 g/cm³. You may reasonably guess that the interior must have metals—iron and nickel, for example. Even though we cannot accurately predict the ratios at which the different elements exist in the interior, the simple knowledge of the average density of the planet allows us to say something reasonable about its interior. A comparison closer to the situation of the Earth is a snowball with a rocky–metallic interior. Like the Earth, the snowball is made up of different materials at different levels of its interior.

The interior of the Earth is made up of three layers, as shown in FIGURE 6-16. The *crust*, which is the outer layer, extends to a depth of less than 100 kilometers and is made up of the common rocks with which we are familiar here on the surface. The density of the crust is about 2.5 to 3 g/cm³.

The *mantle* extends nearly halfway to the center of the Earth, about 2900 kilometers below the surface. This layer, although solid, is able to flow very slowly when steady pressures are exerted on it; however, it can crack and move suddenly under extreme sudden pressures. The mantle is denser (3 to 9 g/cm³) than the crust and, therefore, the crust floats on top of the mantle.

The *core* of the Earth seems to be divided into two parts: a liquid outer core and a solid inner core. The core is even denser than the mantle, ranging from 9 to 13 g/cm³. Because of its high density, the core of the Earth is thought to be made up primarily of iron and nickel, the most common heavy elements.

The pattern of increasing density of materials within the Earth tells us something of the Earth's past, for such *chemical differentiation* could only have come about when the Earth was in a molten state, when the heavier elements would have sunk through the less dense layers. (The molten state must have resulted from heating during the formation of the planet and from energy released by radioactive elements early in the Earth's history.) As a result of this differentiation, according to the popular "late-veneer hypothesis," most of the Earth's original iron-loving (siderophile) elements (such as gold, platinum, iridium, and palladium that bond easily with iron) would have been removed from the Earth's crust and mantle over tens of millions of years. The amounts of these elements that we see today, therefore must have been supplied to Earth late in its formation by meteorite bombardment, which also added other materials essential to life such as water and carbon. However, recreating in the laboratory the conditions experienced by matter at a depth of about 500 km from the Earth's surface, researchers have recently found palladium in the same relative

density The ratio of an object's mass to its volume.

For example, if you take a cube of metal 1 centimeter on each edge (1 centimeter³ of metal) and determine that its mass is 5 grams, then its density is 5 grams/centimeter³.

The applicable equation is

$$\frac{a^3}{p^2} = \frac{m_1 + m_2}{m_{Sun}},$$

where *a* is the orbital semimajor axis in AU, *P* is the orbital period in years, and m_1 and m_2 are the masses of the objects—the Moon and the Earth in this case. See Chapter 3 for how we know what fraction of the total mass of the Earth-Moon system is the Earth's.

crust (of the Earth) The thin, outermost layer of the Earth.

mantle (of the Earth) The thick, solid layer between the crust and the core of the Earth.

core (of the Earth) The central part of the Earth, consisting of a solid inner core surrounded by a liquid outer core.

chemical differentiation The sinking of denser materials toward the center of planets or other objects.

FIGURE 6-16 The interior of the Earth, showing its primary layers.

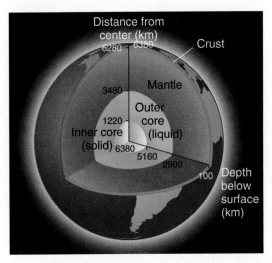

proportions between rock and metal as is observed in the natural world. This suggests that the millions of years of meteorite bombardment is not the only explanation for the distribution of siderophile elements in the Earth's mantle.

Looking at Figure 6-16 naturally brings up the question of how we know the internal structure of our planet to such a degree. After all, the deepest wells only go down a few kilometers from the surface, and the information we get from volcanic eruptions takes us only a bit deeper. We learn about the makeup of the Earth's interior primarily by detecting two types of waves that result from earthquakes. These waves travel through the Earth, and by analyzing their times of travel from distant earthquakes, geologists can deduce some properties of the materials that lie deep within the Earth. The first type of seismic waves, called primary or **P waves**, are analogous to the waves produced by pushing a spring back and forth. The second type, called secondary or **S waves**, are analogous to the waves produced by shaking a rope, attached to a wall, up and down. Just as light refracts when traveling from one medium into a different one, seismic waves refract when they travel from one region inside the Earth into another region of different composition. Using seismographs at many locations around the Earth, we can measure at a specific location whether the observed wave has P or S characteristics and also determine its travel time from the center of the earthquake. Taking into account that S waves cannot travel far through liquids, the absence of S waves at certain regions and the strength of P waves in general allows us to draw the internal structure of the Earth as shown in Figure 6-16. Analyzing the speeds of seismic waves and how they damp out from their source, researchers have recently discovered a large amount of water (about an Arctic Ocean's worth) in the Earth's lower mantle under eastern Asia. Water is important for life but also acts as a lubricant in the process of mantle convection, which drives plate tectonics, as we discuss next.

P waves Seismic waves analogous to the waves produced by pushing a spring back and forth.

S waves Seismic waves analogous to the waves produced by shaking a rope, attached to a wall, up and down.

continental drift The gradual motion of the continents relative to one another.

rift zone A place where tectonic plates are being pushed apart, normally by molten material being forced up out of the mantle.

Plate Tectonics

You may have noticed while looking at a map of the Earth that there seems to be a rough fit between the eastern edge of the American continents and the western edge of Europe and Africa (**FIGURE 6-17a**). Early in the 20th century it was proposed that the continents were once in contact. No acceptable mechanism for continents moving relative to one another (**continental drift**) was obvious, however, and the idea was put aside. (Alfred Wegener, a German meteorologist, is credited with first developing the idea of continental drift.)

Later, geologists discovered that there is a line near the center of the Atlantic Ocean where lava flows upward, called the **rift zone**, forming an extensive range of

FIGURE 6-17 (a) The Earth today and (b) about 200 million years ago. The motion of the continents in (b) is indicated by arrows.

(a)

(b)

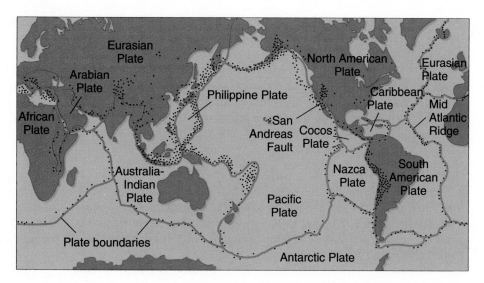

FIGURE 6-18 The major tectonic plates of the Earth. The dots represent earthquake locations. Earthquakes tend to occur near plate boundaries. If the Atlantic Ocean were drained, we could see the Mid-Atlantic Range of mountains and the rift down its center. As lava is forced out of the rift, the plates are pushed aside, causing continental drift.

underwater mountains (FIGURE 6-18). They discovered further that as the lava solidified, magnetic material in it oriented in specific directions, depending on the direction of the Earth's magnetic field at the time. (We see later in this section that the magnetic field of the Earth has changed through the ages.) From the magnetic properties of the material, they were able to determine roughly when it solidified. Then, by examining the sea floor at various distances from the center of the rift zone in the mid-Atlantic, they learned that the sea floor has gradually spread from the rift. Finally, laser light was bounced from satellites to detect any relative motion between continents, and it was discovered that Europe and North America are moving apart at the rate of 2 to 4 centimeters/year. From this evidence, our present theory of **plate tectonics** developed. The Earth has about a dozen tectonic plates that extend about 50 to 100 kilometers deep. Figure 6-18 shows the major plates.

If the plates are spreading from places where lava flows from beneath the crust, they must be jamming together at some other places. FIGURE 6-19 shows how one plate might be pushed below another at such a location. South America is on a plate that is moving westward from the rift zone in the mid-Atlantic. At the western boundary of South America, this plate is forced against the Nazca Plate (Figure 6-18), which is moving eastward. Consequently, the Nazca Plate gets pushed under the South American continent. Two major effects have resulted from these movements: (1) A deep ocean trench has opened off the western coast of South America. (2) As the material of the Nazca Plate is pushed downward, it melts and low-density rock is forced upward, erupting from the Earth's surface as volcanic lava. Over millions of years, this volcanic action has raised the Andes mountain range that runs the length of the western side of the continent. The volcanoes of the west coast of North America and those of Japan were formed in the same manner.

In some places, plates are slipping by one another. This is the primary motion that occurs between the Pacific Plate and the North American Plate. The slippage

plate tectonics The motion of sections of the Earth's crust (plates) across the underlying mantle.

It is just as if we were to refit the torn pieces of a newspaper by matching their edges and then check whether the lines of print run smoothly across. —Wegener

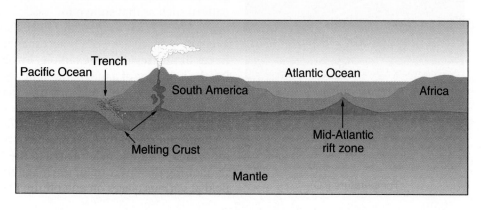

FIGURE 6-19 As the South American Plate is pushed westward (to the left here) from the mid-Atlantic rift, it is pushed against the Nazca Plate under the Pacific Ocean. This forces that plate down into the mantle, resulting in the volcanoes of the Andes Mountains.

is not smooth and continuous, however. Instead, forces build up over a number of years until motion occurs very suddenly, causing an earthquake.

By projecting the motion of the plates backward in time, we can conclude that some 200 million years ago, a map of the Earth's continents looked somewhat like that in Figure 6-17b. Today's continents started separating shortly after that and continue to move apart today. The great mountains, the canyons, and indeed the continents that may appear to us as permanent monuments are instead transitional stages of an ever-changing planet.

Earth's Atmosphere

Compared with the Earth's radius of 6378 km, the atmosphere reaches a very small distance above the surface (**FIGURE 6-20**). The atmosphere gets thinner and thinner farther from Earth, and thus, it is impossible to put a definite boundary on it, but at a distance of 100 or 150 km above the surface, the atmosphere is essentially nonexistent.

Our atmosphere consists of about 78% nitrogen and 21% oxygen by volume. Other constituents, such as water vapor, carbon dioxide, and ozone, make up a very small percentage of the atmosphere, even though they are very important to life on Earth. We discuss the atmospheric importance of carbon dioxide when we discuss the planet Venus in Chapter 8.

Most of the mass of the atmosphere—about 75%—lies within 11 kilometers (7 miles) of the surface. This portion of the atmosphere, called the *troposphere*, is where all of our weather occurs. It receives most of its heat from infrared radiation emitted by the ground, so it is cooler as one gets higher. Figure 6-20 illustrates the temperature of the atmosphere at different heights.

Centered at about 50 kilometers above the surface is the ozone layer. Ozone is a molecule containing three oxygen atoms, and it is an efficient absorber of ultraviolet radiation (UV) from the Sun. This absorption is the reason that temperature reaches a peak at the ozone layer.

The ozone layer is extremely important to life on Earth, for most life has developed while being sheltered from all but a little UV. Ultraviolet radiation breaks apart molecules that make up living tissue, as you have experienced if you have ever been sunburned (a condition resulting from a fairly small amount of UV). As we are frequently warned, too much exposure to UV can cause skin cancer. Modern civilization releases into the atmosphere chemicals that are reducing the amount of ozone, primarily chlorofluorocarbons from aerosol cans and chlorine from various sources. Even if we suddenly and drastically reduce the release of these gases, the problem will not be solved, for chlorofluorocarbons remain in the atmosphere for over a hundred years, continuing to damage the ozone layer.

Earth's Magnetic Field

If a piece of hard paper is laid over a magnet and iron filings are sprinkled on the paper, a pattern such as that shown in **FIGURE 6-21** appears. We say that a *magnetic field* exists in a region of space if we can detect magnetic forces in that region; for example, by observing the behavior of a magnetic compass.

When a magnet is suspended so that it is free to rotate near the Earth, it always aligns so that its opposite ends point in specific directions, indicating that the magnet is aligning with a magnetic field related to the Earth. By plotting the direction of the magnetic field at various places on and off the Earth's

troposphere The lowest level of the Earth's (and some other planets') atmosphere.

 Commercial planes fly at the top of the troposphere to avoid the turbulence of weather in that layer.

magnetic field A magnetic field exists in a region of space if magnetic forces can be detected in that region.

FIGURE 6-20 The temperature of the atmosphere varies with altitude because of the way solar energy is absorbed by the different layers. The temperature at altitudes of 200 to 300 kilometers (where satellites and the space shuttle orbit) is much larger than on the surface. This poses no threat because atmospheric density at these altitudes is extremely small (although there is still enough air resistance in the lower thermosphere to affect a satellite's motion and eventually cause it to reenter and burn up in Earth's lower atmosphere).

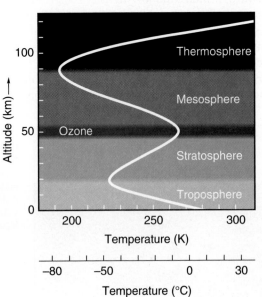

surface, we can determine that the Earth's magnetic field has a shape similar to that of a bar magnet, as shown in FIGURE 6-22.

The poles of the Earth's magnetic field—those points toward which the magnetic field converges—are located near (but not exactly at) the poles of the Earth's rotation axis. As shown in FIGURE 6-23, the Earth's magnetic north not only does not coincide with the Earth's geographic north (fixed by our planet's spin axis), but can actually wander hundreds of miles. In addition, we have a terminology problem as the Earth's magnetic north is actually a "south" pole (and the Earth's magnetic south is actually a "north" pole). This is why a magnetic compass points north, because the north-seeking pole of its needle is attracted to the Earth's magnetic south pole (which is located north)! Actually a magnetic compass rarely points exactly north. In New York it points about 15° west of north. In Los Angeles it points about 15° to the east of north, whereas in Chicago it points almost due north.

Even though you might picture the Earth as containing within it a bar magnet that is not quite aligned with its rotation axis, this is not the case. First, the Earth's core is too hot to remain magnetic, which means we are not dealing with a solid magnetic region. Second, magnetic fields decay, and unless there is a mechanism that regenerates it, the Earth's current field will disappear in about 15,000 years.

The most likely mechanism for generating the magnetic field is analogous to a *dynamo* (generator), a device that converts mechanical to electrical energy. To understand how it works, consider again Figure 6-16. The Earth's core is solid under the immense pressures that exist in that region and contains mostly iron. At the core–mantle boundary, the temperature is high enough for the outer core to be in a liquid state. Because of the Earth's rotation and convection (as the lighter elements move upward and the heavier elements freeze on the inner core), the outer core is under constant motion. These conditions inside Earth satisfy the three main conditions for generating a magnetic field:

* We must have a seed magnetic field.
* We must have a conducting fluid.
* We must have an energy source to move the fluid in an appropriate pattern.

After the process starts (and the Sun's field played the role of the original "seed" field) and the molten conducting fluid passes through the field, an electrical current is generated, which in turn creates a magnetic field. Under appropriate conditions between the field and the flow, the generated magnetic field can reinforce the existing one.

Numerical models of dynamos driven by convection have been very successful in reproducing many of the observed characteristics of the Earth's magnetic field. They also indicate that the solid core plays a vital role in providing the energy needed to

FIGURE 6-21 A magnetic field pattern made by iron filings. Notice in particular the pattern the filings form beyond the magnet.

FIGURE 6-22 The magnetic field of the Earth is similar in shape to that of a bar magnet.

A magnetic compass is simply a magnet that is free to rotate so that it can align with a magnetic field.

dynamo model The model that explains the Earth's (and other planets') magnetic fields as due to currents within a molten iron core.

FIGURE 6-23 The Earth's magnetic poles are not located at its poles of rotation. The location of the magnetic north (magnetic "south" pole) is shown here; also, its location changes with time.

FIGURE 6-24 (a) The Van Allen belts are regions where the magnetic field of the Earth traps charged particles from the Sun (the solar wind). The belts surround the Earth except near the poles. (b) Charged particles move in spirals around the lines of a magnetic field. This causes them to become trapped in the Earth's field.

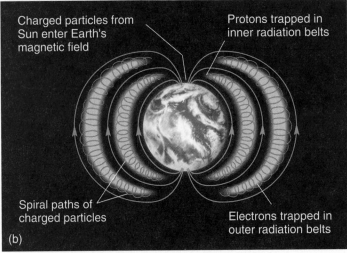

FIGURE 6-24 (a) The Van Allen belts are regions where the magnetic field of the Earth traps charged particles from the Sun (the solar wind). The belts surround the Earth except near the poles. (b) Charged particles move in spirals around the lines of a magnetic field. This causes them to become trapped in the Earth's field.

FIGURE 6-25 An aurora is caused by charged particles trapped in the Earth's magnetic field striking atoms in the upper atmosphere.

aurora Light radiated in the upper atmosphere due to impacts from charged particles.

drive the convection in the liquid outer core and in providing a barrier for the flow. Also, measurements of travel times of seismic waves generated by earthquakes occurring near each other but at different times indicate that the inner core is currently spinning slightly faster than the mantle and crust; the current rate is of the order of 1 degree per year, but it probably varies over time.

Sediments that record the Earth's magnetic field when deposited and dating techniques, such as layer counting and carbon dating, allow us to track changes in the Earth's field. We know that the location of the Earth's magnetic poles wandered in the past (Figure 6-23) and that the magnetic field has undergone complete reversals. The reversal rate varies over time; we had about 300 reversals in the past 170 million years, the last time about 780,000 years ago. A field reversal takes thousands of years to occur and is the result of complex, not well-understood changes in the Earth's core. Simulations show that the shape of the field is an important factor that controls the rate for reversals; this shape, in turn, depends on how energy flows at the boundary between the core and the mantle.

One effect of the Earth's magnetic field became the first scientific discovery of the space age. Early spacecraft discovered the existence of electrically charged particles swarming in doughnut-shaped regions high above the Earth's surface (**FIGURE 6-24a**). The reason for these "Van Allen belts" is well understood. Just as an electric current (moving electric charges) causes a magnetic field, a magnetic field exerts a force on charged particles. When charged particles enter a magnetic field, they are forced to move in a spiral around the lines of the field, as shown in Figure 6-24b. In the case of the Van Allen belts, the charged particles (protons and electrons) come primarily from the Sun (the "solar wind") and have been captured by the magnetic field of the Earth.

We see the effect of the particles trapped within the Earth's magnetic field in the *auroras* that are often visible in the skies near the North and South Poles of the Earth (**FIGURE 6-25**). These beautiful displays of light are the byproducts of violent events on the Sun's surface, as a result of which streams of very energetic protons and electrons are sent out into space. Some of these particles manage to penetrate the Earth's magnetic field (our "shield") but are forced by the field to spiral toward the magnetic north and south poles. These energetic particles collide with atoms and molecules in our atmosphere, exciting them to high energy levels. The atoms and molecules then release this energy as visible light. The displays of northern or southern lights can be breathtaking. (In Chapter 11, we discuss the reason for the violent events on the Sun's surface.)

6-4   The Moon's Surface

The Earth is a planet of rich diversity, with interior heat and motion, plate tectonics, a rich atmosphere, and the only known life forms in the universe. The Moon is a very different place. It is cold and lifeless, with little interior heat and no plate tectonics. The Moon has an extremely tenuous and "transient" atmosphere; it is continuously being produced by evaporation of surface materials, which either escape into space or return back onto the surface, but there is much to learn about the solar system from studying the rocks and surface of the Moon.

The surface of the Moon can be divided into the *maria* (singular *mare*) and the mountainous, cratered regions. From Earth, the maria appear darker than the other regions. The far side of the Moon, first seen when a Soviet spacecraft photographed it in 1959, is covered almost completely with craters.

Until the middle of the 20th century, it was assumed that lunar craters were formed the same way almost all Earthly craters are, by volcanic action, instead of by impacts of *meteorites* from space. There were two primary reasons for thinking that the craters were volcanic: (1) Because almost all craters on Earth were thought to have formed that way, it was reasonable to assume that lunar craters were similar. (2) Lunar craters are very circular, but if you form a crater by throwing a rock into sand, the crater will only be circular if the rock is thrown straight down. Otherwise the crater will be elongated. Because meteorites would be likely to hit the Moon's surface at various angles, one would expect many impact craters to be somewhat elliptical in shape if they were formed by meteorite impact.

Two observations, on the other hand, provided evidence against a volcanic origin for the craters: (1) The floors of lunar craters are lower than the surrounding surface (as we can tell by measuring the shadows cast by the crater walls). Volcanic craters typically occur at the top of volcanic mountains, and their floors are higher in elevation than the surrounding territory. (2) The presence of overlapping craters suggests an impact origin.

We now realize that almost all (and perhaps all) lunar craters are the result of impacts. The arguments against an impact origin are answered as follows:

1. Craters produced far back in Earth's history have been eroded so that they are no longer noticeable. Lunar craters, on the other hand, do not suffer erosion on the airless Moon. Now that we have observed the Earth from space, we have found many more impact craters on Earth. Also, Earth has few impact craters because its atmosphere prevents any but the largest meteoroids from reaching its surface. Small meteoroids burn up in the air or are slowed enough by the air that they do not produce craters.

2. The argument that we would expect some impact craters to be elongated does not apply to lunar craters because they are not formed simply from material being "splashed" away by the impact. Instead, a meteoroid that collides with the Moon strikes with such great speed that it penetrates below the surface, compressing and heating the Moon's material until an explosion occurs. Such an explosion is similar to a nuclear bomb ignited below the surface of the ground; it results in a circular crater in spite of the angle of the meteoroid's fall.

Much of the material thrown upward by the explosion falls back into the crater and forms its floor. Other material is thrown away from the crater to form the *rays*

maria (singular **mare**) Any of the lowlands of the Moon or Mars that resemble a sea when viewed from Earth.

meteorite An interplanetary chunk of matter that has struck a planet or moon.

Until about 1940, Meteor Crater in Arizona (see Chapter 10) was thought to have a volcanic origin.

lunar ray A bright streak on the Moon caused by material ejected from a crater.

TOOLS OF ASTRONOMY

The Earth from Space

We Earthlings have learned much about neighboring planets by sending spacecraft past them, putting craft into orbit around them, and sending landers to their surfaces. Let us consider what could be learned about Earth if we lived on another planet and used similar technology to study the Earth.

The cloud layer of the Earth's atmosphere hinders detailed viewing of the surface from afar. Inhabitants of nearby planets, however, could detect differences between our continents and oceans, and they could see the Earth's white polar caps (as we see those on Mars). To determine what makes up the continents, oceans, and polar caps, our neighbors could analyze the spectra of light reflected from these areas. They would be able to determine that most of our planet is covered by water, that our polar caps are frozen water, and that our ever-changing cloud cover also consists of water.

Could they detect signs of life? Probably not. Although we think of ourselves as important, we have not changed our planet in a way that would be obvious to an observer on another planet or moon. The only sign of life they are likely to detect from afar is our radio and television broadcasts.

As an alien spacecraft approached Earth and went into orbit around it, it would obtain views such as those in FIGURE B6-1a. Now its occupants might be able to see signs of life. Perhaps their first visible evidence of life would come when they viewed the dark side of our planet, for urban areas would be visible at night because of the wasted light that escapes from them into space (Figure B6-1b).

If landers were sent to Earth to look for life, their ease in finding it would obviously depend on where they landed, but if they were equipped like our *Viking* missions that landed on Mars to search for life, they would not only be capable of photographing our large animals, but they also would be able to detect organic molecules in the soil (or ice) no matter where they landed.

(a)

(b)

FIGURE B6-1 (a) A composite image of our beautiful planet taken by the *Rosetta* spacecraft. Australia can be seen at the bottom. (b) A composite of several hundred photos showing the Earth from space at night.

that are seen radiating from some craters (FIGURE 6-26a). The peaks found in the center of many craters (Figure 6-26b) are caused by a rebound of the surface after the explosion. Both the low floor levels and the central peaks are in accord with the idea that the craters are impact craters.

Volcanic eruptions did occur in the Moon's past, however, and they resulted in the Moon's maria. They were caused by the flow of dark lava onto lowland areas of the Moon. Most of the maria are roughly circular, leading us to believe that they were originally the floors of very large craters. We know, however, that the dark lava that fills them was not produced by the impacts that formed the craters, for within the maria are old, smaller craters that have themselves been mostly covered by lava. Thus, the lava flowed from beneath the surface after the small craters had been formed inside the giant ones.

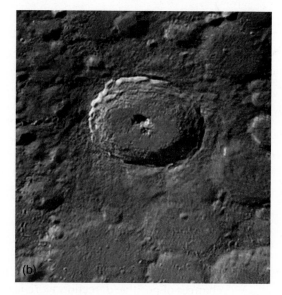

FIGURE 6-26 (a) Light-colored rays can be seen radiating from the prominent crater (named Tycho) near the bottom of this photo of the full Moon. They were formed by material ejected from the crater. (b) A close up of Tycho shows that it has a prominent central peak, the result of its surface rebounding after the impact of the meteorite that caused it. Such peaks can be seen through a telescope from Earth.

The top few centimeters of the Moon's surface are made up of loose powdery lava, small rocks, and mostly spherical pieces of glass, the result of bombardment by countless meteorites through the ages. FIGURE 6-27 is a photograph of a footprint made in the dust of the Sea of Tranquility during the first visit to the Moon by a human, on July 20, 1969.

The crust of the Moon (FIGURE 6-28) ranges in depth from about 60 to 100 kilometers and is thinner on the side facing the Earth than on the other side. When the maria were formed, molten lava released from within the Moon flowed toward the side with the thinner crust. It is no accident that the side of the Moon with more maria faces the Earth, for lava has a greater density than the rocks of the highland areas. Tidal forces are what caused the Moon to slow its rotation. These same forces acted on the Moon's uneven distribution of mass to cause the denser side to face the Earth.

If you have studied geology, you know that Earthly mountains were formed by the motion of plates within the Earth and by volcanic action. The lunar mountains were formed differently. They are simply the results of millions of ancient craters, one on top of another. Mountain ranges that border maria are the walls of giant craters whose floors are now covered with lava.

The density of the Moon is 3.35 g/cm³. Because this is close to the average density of rocky material, we conclude that if the Moon has an iron core, that core must be small. In addition, the magnetic field of the Moon is less than one ten-thousandth of the Earth's, and thus, this also indicates that the Moon cannot have a large molten iron core. It is thought that any iron core must be less than about 700 to 800 km in diameter. Questions remain, however: First, we are not certain that planetary magnetic fields are due to molten iron cores, and second, some rocks brought back by Apollo astronauts were magnetized more than we would have expected in such a weak magnetic field. Perhaps the Moon's field was stronger in the past, or perhaps these rocks were magnetized by the Earth's or the Sun's magnetic field.

Even though we still do not have answers to these questions, we have better data to work with thanks to the *Lunar Prospector*, a small spacecraft sent on a polar-orbiting mission to the Moon. The science objectives of the mission

Many of the glassy spheres resulted from the melting and solidification of rock upon ejection from a crater.

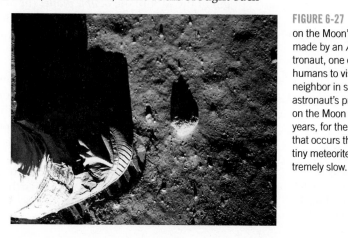

FIGURE 6-27 This bootprint on the Moon's surface was made by an *Apollo 11* astronaut, one of the first two humans to visit our nearest neighbor in space. The astronaut's prints will remain on the Moon for millions of years, for the only erosion that occurs there is due to tiny meteorites and is extremely slow.

60 km Crust

Mare (lava flows)

Iron-rich core?

100 km Crust

To Earth

740 km   1740 km

Partially molten?

Mantle

Lunar Prospector was launched in January 1998. Its mission ended with a planned dive into a shadowed crater near the Moon's south pole in July 1999.

The Moon's equatorial plane is tilted only 1.5° from the ecliptic. There are no seasons on the Moon, and some places in steep-walled craters near the poles have been shaded from the sun (at –200°C throughout the long lunar day).

The objectives of *Lunar Reconnaissance Orbiter*, launched in 2009, are explorative in nature; it will study and map the lunar surface to prepare for the return of astronauts on the Moon.

The sensors on the Moon that measure the intensity of quakes are called *seismographs*.

double planet (or **co-creation**) **theory** A theory that holds that the Moon was formed at the same time as the Earth.

were (a) to study the lunar atmosphere and crust for resources, such as minerals, certain gases, and water ice; (b) to learn more about the Moon's core, its size and content; and (c) to map the Moon's gravitational and magnetic fields.

Tentative results from data collected by *Lunar Prospector*'s instruments suggest that there is water ice in some polar craters, thus answering a question first raised in the early 1970s and later by a 1994 mission. It is estimated that a few billion metric tons of water ice exist at each pole; however, this is indirect evidence, as the instrument detects hydrogen levels from which we infer water ice. The planned crash of the spacecraft was meant to liberate water vapor and dust, which could be observed by instruments on Earth. No such signature was seen, but then the chances of positive detection were less than 10%. The question thus is still open as to whether ancient impacts by comets on the Moon deposited water ice that still exists in the permanently shadowed polar regions.

A precise gravity map of the entire lunar surface indicates the existence of a lunar core, probably iron, with a diameter of more than about 600 km. Also, even though the Moon does not have a global magnetic field such as Earth's, we now know that strong magnetic fields exist locally and that they are diametrically opposite large young impact basins on the surface. Could it be that an object such as the Moon can acquire magnetic characteristics from impacts, such as with asteroids and comets? Finally, the *Lunar Prospector* provided us with the first global map of abundances of 10 key elements, several of which give us clues to the Moon's formation and evolution.

Other sources of information about the Moon are the sensors left there by the *Apollo* missions to measure moonquakes. Some of these quakes were artificially produced by striking the Moon at various places, but we have detected about 3000 natural moonquakes a year, far fewer than the hundreds of thousands detected on Earth every year. These moonquakes were much weaker than our earthquakes, but they tell us that there is very little activity in the interior of the Moon. There is no evidence for plate tectonics on the Moon's surface, and the cause of these quakes is the tidal interactions between the Earth and Moon.

6-5   Theories of the Origin of the Moon

In this section we describe some of the evidence indicating that the Moon formed about 4.6 billion years ago. Until recently, there have been three theories of the origin of the Moon: the *double planet* (or *co-creation*), the *fission*, and the *capture* theories. We briefly describe each of them and look at the evidence to see which best fits the data. Then we introduce a modern theory that seems to work better than any of the other three.

- The **double planet theory**, which was suggested in the early 1800s, is the oldest. It holds that as the Earth formed from a spinning disk of material, not all of that material coalesced to form the Earth. A small part of it was left orbiting the Earth and formed into the Moon. In Chapter 7, we discuss theories of the origin of the solar system and see that this idea is entirely consistent with those theories.

A simple density comparison seems to rule out the double planet theory, for if the Moon formed along with the Earth, the two bodies should have about the same density. The Earth's density, however, is 5.52 g/cm³, much greater than the Moon's 3.35 g/cm³.

- In 1878, the astronomer Sir George Howard Darwin, son of the biologist Charles Darwin, proposed that the Moon was once part of the Earth and broke (or *fissioned*) from it due to forces caused by a fast rotation and solar tides. This ***fission hypothesis*** proposed that the large basin of the Pacific Ocean was the place from which the Moon was ejected.

The difference in density between the Earth and the Moon might seem to rule out the fission theory along with the double planet theory, but the crust of the Earth does have a density close to that of the Moon. If the Moon formed from material from the Earth's crust, we would expect its density to be just as we find it.

There is a problem with the fission theory, however. Astronomers have difficulty explaining how an object as massive as the Moon might have been pulled out of—or thrown off from—the Earth. No satisfactory mechanism for this event has been proposed. In addition, the Moon does not orbit in the plane of the Earth's equator, as it should if it were ejected from a spinning Earth.

- Early in the 20th century, another theory was proposed. It holds that the Moon was originally a separate astronomical object that happened to come near the Earth and was captured by the Earth's gravitational field so that it settled into orbit as the Moon. This is the ***capture theory***.

There are also problems with the capture theory. If one astronomical object comes close to another, each of their paths will be changed by the gravitational force between them (**FIGURE 6-29**); however, one will not capture the other unless there is contact between the two or unless a third object is involved so that the interaction of the three objects results in one of them being slowed down to an orbital speed. Such a near collision between three objects seems highly unlikely.

Although we have known the density of the Moon for a long time, its chemical composition was not well known until the *Apollo* astronauts brought back soil and rock samples. These new data posed new problems for the three theories. In many ways, the Moon's chemical composition is similar to that of the Earth's crust, for both have about the same proportions of some of the major elements: silicon, magnesium, iron, and manganese. The Moon, however, has smaller proportions of easily vaporized (*volatile*) substances (such as potassium and sodium) and higher proportions of nonvolatiles (such as aluminum and titanium), which require a very high temperature to vaporize than does the Earth's crust. The differences between terrestrial and lunar rocks suggest that the Moon was formed out of material that was at higher temperature than the material from which the Earth formed. This offers an additional argument against the fission theory.

The differences between the rocks could support the capture theory if the Moon were formed elsewhere, such as closer to the Sun. In addition, the plane of the Moon's orbit is closer to the ecliptic than to the plane of the Earth's equator, supporting the idea that the Moon was orbiting the Sun before the Earth captured it. The conditions for such capture, however, are very improbable.

In order for the double planet theory to explain the differences between the rocks, we must assume that the Moon was formed by rocky debris orbiting the Sun in the plane of the ecliptic. This debris lost its volatile elements because of the solar heat and later coalesced to form the Moon, a very unlikely scenario.

None of these three theories for the origin of the Moon thus gave a satisfactory answer to the question "how did the Moon get there?"

The Large Impact Theory

In the 1970s, A. G. W. Cameron and William Ward of Harvard proposed a new theory of Moon formation. They proposed that early in the Earth's history, our planet was struck at a glancing angle by a large object. The impact resulted in a fusion of the two objects, and material was thrown off from the combined object to

fission theory A theory that holds that the Moon formed when material was spun off from the Earth.

capture theory A theory that holds that the Moon was originally solar system debris that was captured by Earth.

volatile Capable of being vaporized at a relatively low temperature.

FIGURE 6-29 If the Earth and another object (in this figure, a smaller one) had a near collision, each object's path would be altered, but they would not begin to orbit one another.

ADVANCING THE THEORY

The Far Side of the Moon

FIGURE B6-2 is an image that includes most of the far side of the Moon, the side that is never seen from Earth. Although the image is in false color, you can see immediately that this side is different from the side that faces Earth (see Figure 5–18c). The most obvious difference is that the far side has fewer maria. (The large green area is not really a mare. If you look closely, you can see that it is filled with craters. The colors are explained below.) To understand the reason for the lack of maria, refer to Figure 6-28, which shows a cross section of the Moon. The crust is thicker on the side opposite Earth. Maria are thought to have formed as the result of volcanism between 4 billion and 2.5 billion years ago. Lava is more likely to be forced to the surface where the crust is thinner, and because the side of the Moon that faces Earth has a thinner crust, that is where most of the volcanism occurred.

The image of Figure B6-2 is a composite of images made by *Mariner 10* in 1973 (as it passed the Moon on the way to Venus and Mercury) and the Jupiter-bound *Galileo* spacecraft in December 1990. The image was made from separate photos that were taken with different filters on the cameras. This technique allows astronomers to determine the mineral content of the surface. For example, areas in red are associated with the cratered lunar highlands and are relatively poor in titanium, iron, and magnesium. The other colors are associated with the ancient volcanic lava flows of maria, with green, yellow, and light orange signifying basalts low in ti-

tanium but rich in iron and magnesium, whereas blue areas are rich in titanium. Knowing the mineral composition of each location helps astronomers in their quest to understand the Moon's past.

FIGURE B6-2 The far side of the Moon is shown here in false color. The prominent bull's-eye crater toward the left is called Mare Orientale. Different colors represent different mineral abundances, as explained in the text.

large impact theory A theory that holds that the Moon formed as the result of an impact between a large object and the Earth.

form the present Moon (**FIGURE 6-30**). Computer simulations of such collisions show that if the impacting object has a mass nearly as great as Mars, heat resulting from the collision would vaporize material and eject enough of it into orbit to account for the mass of the Moon, once the material coalesced in its orbit around the Earth. The ***large impact theory*** (or ***collisional ejection theory***), as it is called, is able to explain both the similarities and the differences in the compositions of the Earth and the Moon. Because the impact would have vaporized the rocks, they should be depleted in water and volatile

FIGURE 6-30 (a) According to the large impact theory, the young Earth was hit by a large object, perhaps as big as Mars. (b) The two objects fused together, but much material was thrown off and went into orbit around the new Earth. (c) Eventually, the material coalesced into the Moon.

elements, in agreement with observations. If the collision occurred after the Earth was chemically differentiated, then the resulting Moon would have proportionally much less iron than the Earth, which is the case, as has been recently confirmed by the *Lunar Prospector*. If the plane of the impacting object were close to the ecliptic, so would be the plane of the resulting debris and thus the Moon, again in agreement with observations. The impact would most likely tip the Earth's rotation axis in the process.

Since the mid-1980s, a consensus has been building among astronomers that the large impact theory fits the data better than the other three theories. Recent theoretical work on the formation of the planets indicates that without large impacts, the Earth would rotate once every 200 hours instead of every 24 hours. A glancing impact by a large object would explain its present rotation rate. Like all new theories, the large impact theory needs to be tested against both existing data and new data as the years pass. Although it will probably have to undergo modification, it appears that astronomers may finally have found the answer to the age-old question of the origin of the Moon.

Computer simulations suggest that the process of forming the Moon from the material ejected after the collision is not very efficient; therefore, more material must be ejected at a greater distance from Earth than was previously believed.

6-6 The History of the Moon

The history of the Moon can be pieced together in several ways. For example, when we observe that one crater overlaps another (FIGURE 6-31), we know that the overlapping crater was formed after the other. Likewise, we know that the crater Tycho was formed relatively recently because its rays overlap the craters around it. Lunar rays darken with time, providing more information on the order of lunar events; however, such examination of the surface only provides information about the order of events; it does not allow us to determine how long ago the events happened. Reliable assessments of time scales had to wait for the *Apollo* missions and the 840 pounds of lunar material they brought back to Earth. The accompanying Advancing the Model box describes a procedure that uses radioactivity of rocks to determine their age. Such *radioactive dating* techniques have been indispensable in forming a model of the Moon's history.

The Moon formed about 4.6 billion years ago. (The oldest rocks we found there are 4.42 billion years old.) We know that its surface was molten a few million years after the Moon was formed and conclude that the surface was probably molten from its formation, in agreement with the large impact theory. As the Moon cooled and solidified, cratering marked its surface. Most craters were formed between 4.2 and 3.9 billion years ago. Giant impacts that occurred near the end of the cratering period produced the areas where we see maria today. After most of the cratering ended, the interior of the Moon became hot enough (probably because of radioactivity) that molten lava flowed from beneath the surface and gathered in the floors of the giant craters. Rocks that astronauts gathered from the maria are between 3.1 and 3.8 billion years old, leading us to believe that this volcanic stage ended about 3.1 billion years ago.

The darkening is caused by sunlight and bombardment by tiny meteorites.

radioactive dating A procedure that examines the radioactivity of a substance to determine its age.

The volcanic action described here consisted of lava seeping through cracks in the surface, so volcanic mountains did not form.

Cratering continues today, but at a much reduced rate from the Moon's early history. Three rocks have been found on Earth that are thought to have been ejected from the Moon by impacts within the past few million years. Our region of the solar system has been swept clear of most large chunks of matter, however, so meteorites large enough to produce noticeable craters on the Moon are now infrequent. We see in Chapter 10 that the Earth is constantly being struck

FIGURE 6-31 In this photo, a small crater overlaps a larger one (named Gassendi), so that we know that it was formed after Gassendi. Note that Gassendi has a central peak.

ADVANCING THE MODEL

Measuring the Ages of the Earth and Moon

From rocks brought back from the Moon by *Apollo* astronauts (**FIGURE B6-3**), we know that the Moon is at least 4.5 billion years old. We have found rocks on Earth that are 3.9 billion years old. How do we determine the age of these rocks—how do we "date" them? The method used is called *radioactive dating*, and to understand it, we must first look at the makeup of the nuclei of atoms.

FIGURE B6-3 Astronaut Jack Schmitt collects rock samples during the *Apollo 17* trip to the Moon. The astronauts brought back 243 pounds of rock on this mission alone.

There are two primary particles within the nucleus: protons and neutrons. The number of protons in a nucleus determines what element the atom is. For example, any atom with only one proton in its nucleus is necessarily hydrogen; two protons, helium; and so forth, up to uranium, which has 92 protons, more than any other naturally occurring element. Although different atoms of the same element all have the same number of protons, the number of neutrons in their nuclei may differ. Such different forms of an element are called *isotopes*. To specify which isotope we are talking about, we state the name of the element and the total number of protons and neutrons the nucleus contains. Uranium-238, thus, has a total of 238 protons and neutrons in its nucleus (and it has 92 protons because every uranium nucleus has 92 protons).

The nuclei of some isotopes are unstable, in that their nuclei change spontaneously. When this happens, some isotopes emit a gamma ray, and others emit a nuclear particle. The gamma ray or particle emitted is the radiation that comes from a radioactive material. We say that the isotope *decays*, but the term *decay* here does not refer to deterioration, such as the process that wood undergoes when it decays. Rather, it simply means that the isotope spontaneously emits radiation and in doing so changes to another isotope. For example, when rubidium-87 undergoes radioactive decay, it changes into strontium-87. Each isotope has its own characteristic rate of decay, which is called the *half-life* of the isotope—the amount of time needed for *half* of the isotope to emit radiation and change to another isotope. Half-lives range from tiny fractions of a second to billions of years. Isotopes with long half-lives are the ones that are useful in dating geological samples. We are making an important as-

sumption here, however, one that does seem to be supported by the observations. We accept that an atom that is thousands of years old is identical to an atom of the same species that is 1 second old. We accept that an unstable nucleus decays spontaneously, that there is no way to predict when it will decay, and that identical atoms behave, by themselves, in nonidentical ways that follow rules of statistics.

The basic idea of radioactive dating is quite simple. Consider uranium-238, which has a half-life of 4.5 billion years. If we begin with a pure sample of uranium-238, we know that in 4.5 billion years half of it will have decayed to another isotope (and then, by a series of quicker decays, to lead-206). By comparing the percentage of uranium-238 and lead-206 in a sample that was once pure uranium-238, we, therefore, can tell how much time has passed since the sample was pure. The problem, of course, is that we must know that the sample was pure at the beginning.

There are several radioactive dating techniques, all of which depend on an assumption about the original condition of the matter. One technique uses the fact that when molten material solidifies, the crystals that are formed have certain specific chemical elements in them. If uranium is present when crystallization takes place, certain types of newly formed crystals will contain uranium but no lead. If we examine rocks containing such crystals and find lead-206, we can be confident that this resulted from radioactive decay of uranium-238. The relative percentages of the two isotopes then allow us to calculate the time elapsed since the crystals formed.

Fortunately, the dating of a sample of rock does not depend on just one isotope. For example, the radioactive isotope rubidium-87 (whose half-life is known) is found in some crystals, along with its decay product strontium-87. By comparing the concentrations of these isotopes to that of strontium-86, which is stable and not created by radioactive decay, a second value can be found for the age of the sample. This value does not depend on whether the sample was initially pure and thus provides a way to check the value found by uranium dating. Other techniques depend on other isotopes; for example, potassium-40 decays into argon-40 with a half-life of 1.3 billion years.

Radioactive dating does not actually tell us the age of the Moon or the Earth, but only the minimum age, because the Moon and Earth existed before the rocks solidified. Knowledge about the solidification of matter and theories of planetary formation are used to determine how much time elapsed between the formation of the planetary body and the solidification of its surface rocks.

by debris from space, but much of it burns up in the atmosphere and never reaches the surface. The Moon has no atmosphere, however, and thus, meteorites large enough to produce small craters must still strike it occasionally, although no new crater has ever been observed. In addition, *micrometeorites* strike the Moon's surface, further pulverizing its soil.

> **micrometeorite** A tiny meteorite.

Except for these impacts—and some recent visits by humans and their machines—the surface of the Moon changes very little. This is fortunate for astronomers, for the surface becomes a book in which we can read the Moon's distant history.

> In Chapter 7 we discuss the formation of the solar system and the sweeping up of its original matter into planets and moons.

Conclusion

To determine the diameter of the Moon, we must first know its distance, and to determine this distance, we must know the diameter of the Earth. By measuring the position of the Sun as seen from different locations on Earth, Eratosthenes in the 3rd century BC was able to measure the Earth's diameter (see Chapter 2). A few centuries later, Ptolemy successfully used the method of parallax to measure the distance to the Moon, and he was therefore able to calculate its diameter.

Tidal interactions between the Earth and the Moon affect both their shapes and their motions. Understanding the Moon and the Earth allows us to better understand our immediate neighborhood, the solar system, and in return better understand our place in it. With the aid of what we learned from the *Apollo* missions, we are able to explain the features on the surface of the Moon and are becoming more and more confident that it originated in a tremendous impact between some object and the Earth. We are also piecing together an outline of the Moon's history from the information we have obtained from telescopic observations, from visits during the 1960s and 1970s, from the *Lunar Prospector* mission, and now from the *Lunar Reconnaissance Orbiter*.

STUDY GUIDE

RECALL QUESTIONS

1. Knowledge of which of the following quantities will allow us to calculate the diameter of the Moon?
   A. The Moon's distance and speed.
   B. The Moon's angular size and speed.
   C. The Moon's angular size and distance.
   D. All three—distance, speed, and angular size—must be known.
   E. [None of the above.]

2. Suppose some object is known to be 6 kilometers away and is observed to have an angular size of 0.25 degrees. What is its actual size?
   A. 26 kilometers.
   B. 57.3 kilometers.
   C. 60 kilometers.
   D. 1.5 kilometers.
   E. [None of the above.]

3. If the Moon were covered with water, the number of tidal bulges on it would be
   A. one.
   B. two.
   C. [None.]

4. Tides on the Earth are primarily caused by the mutual gravitational attraction between the Earth and
   A. the Moon.
   B. the Sun.
   C. Jupiter.
   D. [None of the above.]

5. How many high tides are observed most days at most seaports on Earth?
   A. One, caused by the Moon.
   B. Two, because the Sun and the Moon each cause one.
   C. One or two, depending on the relative positions of the Earth, Moon, and Sun.
   D. Two, roughly 12 hours apart.

6. The gravitational force due to the Moon is exerted
   A. only on the side of the Earth nearest the Moon.
   B. only on the point on the Earth nearest the Moon.
   C. on the center of the Earth only.
   D. on the entire Earth.
   E. on the water surfaces of the Earth but not on the land surfaces.

7. The average density of an object is defined as
   A. its thickness.
   B. how much solid material the object contains.
   C. its mass.
   D. its volume.
   E. the ratio of its mass to its volume.

8. The Earth's atmosphere is made up of about
   A. 80% oxygen and 20% nitrogen.
   B. 50% oxygen and 50% nitrogen.
   C. 20% oxygen and 80% nitrogen.
   D. equal amounts of oxygen, nitrogen, and carbon dioxide.
   E. equal amounts of oxygen, hydrogen, and carbon dioxide.

9. Auroras result from
   A. the Earth's magnetic field and its rotation.
   B. the Earth's magnetic field and its revolution around the Sun.
   C. the Earth's magnetic field and the solar wind.
   D. the solar wind and the Sun's rotation.
   E. the motion of the Moon around the Earth.

10. Maria are
    A. lunar mountains.
    B. lunar highlands.
    C. flat plains.
    D. near the lunar poles, and nowhere else.
    E. [More than one of the above.]

11. Which of the following theories of the Moon's origin seems to fit the data best?
    A. The capture theory.
    B. The fission theory.
    C. The double planet theory.
    D. The large impact theory.
    E. [Either A or C above.]

12. The fact that the average density of the Moon is somewhat different from that of the Earth is an argument against which theory of the origin of the Moon?
    A. The capture theory.
    B. The fission theory.
    C. The double planet theory.
    D. The large impact theory.
    E. [Both B and C above.]

13. When we see an unfamiliar object at a distance, how can we judge its size?

14. What is the angular size of the Moon? How does this compare to the angular size of the Sun?

15. Is it just coincidence that the Moon's periods of revolution and rotation are the same? If not, explain the cause.

16. Venus is the greatest contributor to Mercury's orbital precession because the two are neighbors. The planet causing the next most effect is not Earth, however, but Jupiter. Hypothesize as to why this occurs.

17. Show on a sketch the relative positions and sizes of the Earth's core, mantle, and crust.

18. What is a magnetic field and how can one be detected?

19. What are the Van Allen belts, and what causes them?

20. List some evidence for the theory of plate tectonics.

21. Name and describe four theories for the origin of the Moon. Which best fits present data?

22. What caused the craters and rays on the Moon?

23. Explain how we can determine the relative order in which events occurred in the formation of the Moon's surface.

24. Explain why there are two areas of high tide on Earth rather than one.

1. Because Ptolemy lived long before instant distant communication was possible, he was not able to coordinate his observations of the Moon with someone far around the Earth. Propose a method by which he might have been able to observe parallax of the Moon.

2. If you observe the Moon with first one eye and then the other, do you detect a parallax shift against the stars? Why or why not?

3. Suppose that you see an object in the sky that you have never seen before. You estimate that it is 100 feet long. Another person sees the same object and estimates that it is 20 feet long. Explain how this can happen. (Hint: Each of you is making a different assumption about some other factor.)

4. If the Moon were twice as big as it is, but four times as far away, how much smaller or larger would its angular size be?

5. Describe some features of the Earth's surface that are direct consequences of the motion of tectonic plates.

6. Craters have been formed on the Earth and on the Moon by meteorite impact. The Earth has a much stronger gravitational field than does the Moon, and yet we find more craters on the Moon. Explain this apparent contradiction.

7. What leads us to conclude that the Moon does not have a large iron core?

8. Name and describe three different theories of the formation of the Moon. Which of these theories is considered most likely correct? Describe the evidence that leads us to that conclusion.

1. You just bought a telescope that allows you to see clearly two separate stars if the angular distance between them is at least 1 arcsecond. What is the diameter of the smallest crater you can see on the Moon?

2. At what distance could we see clearly an asteroid of diameter 200 kilometers if the best telescope on Earth could give us a resolution of 0.25″?

3. Consider Figure 6-10. Let d_{EM} be the distance between the center of the Earth and that of the Moon. Using Newton's law of gravity, write the expression for the gravitational force between the Moon (of mass m_{Moon}) and a small mass m on the Earth's surface, a distance R from the center of the Earth, for each of the three points A, B, and C. Label these forces F_A, F_B, and F_C, respectively. Using appropriate values for d_{EM} and R, and the approximation $d_{EM} \gg R$, show that $F_A/F_B \approx F_B/F_C \approx 1 + (2R/d_{EM})$ or 1.033. That is, show that F_A is 3.3% greater than F_B, which in turn is 3.3% greater than F_C.

4. Repeat Calculation 3 but with the Sun in the place of the Moon. Let d_{ES} be the distance between the center of the Earth and that of the Sun. Using appropriate values for d_{ES} and R and the approximation $d_{ES} \gg R$, show that $F_A/F_B \approx F_B/F_C \approx 1 + (2R/d_{ES})$ or 1.00009. That is, show that F_A is about 0.009% greater than F_B, which in turn is 0.009% greater than F_C.

5. In Calculations 3 and 4 you used the expressions for the gravitational force from the Moon and the Sun on a mass m at points A and C on Earth's surface (Figure 6-10). By dividing, show that the difference $(F_A - F_C)$ between the forces acting on points A and C due to the Moon is 2.2 times that difference due to the Sun. That is, show that the Moon is mainly responsible for the tides.

6. Consider a drawing similar to Figure 6-10 but with Jupiter and its moon Io. Using data from Appendix D, compare the tides on Io due to Jupiter with the tides on Earth due to the Sun.

The Moon Illusion

When the Moon is low on the horizon, it sometimes appears to be much larger than when it is high in the sky. This phenomenon does not involve refraction, as refraction would tend to "flatten" the Moon. If anything, the Moon's angular size is a bit smaller closer to the horizon, as in this case you are a bit farther from it than when it is at your zenith. This is a purely "psychological" illusion.

One explanation involves the inverted "railroad track" illusion. (In this illusion, a set of "parallel" tracks is drawn on a piece of paper so that they converge in the distance, due to perspective. If we put two equal-size blocks between the tracks, one "farther down" the tracks than the other, then the farther block will appear larger because the "background" influences our perception of the "foreground" objects—the two blocks.) In this scenario, the illusion depends on our perception that the "horizon sky" is farther away than the "zenith sky"; when we view the horizon over a typical landscape, the familiar objects we see (mountains, trees, etc.) form distance-cue patterns that signal "very far" for objects at the horizon, whereas such patterns are absent when we view the "zenith sky." When we see the Moon "against" an apparently more distant sky, it thus will appear larger than when we see it "against" an apparently closer one.

To verify this explanation, use a tube to observe the Moon close to the horizon and high in the sky. The tube blocks light from other objects. Do you see the Moon at its "normal" size? Another way is to turn your back to the Moon when it is close to the horizon and look at it from between your legs. An argument against this explanation is based on the fact that for some people the horizon Moon looks larger but also closer than, or at the same distance as, the zenith Moon. Also, airline pilots flying at very high altitudes sometimes experience this illusion without any objects in the foreground. A better understanding of this illusion thus will come from considering together the ideas of angular size, linear size, and distance.

A second explanation is based on how our eyes focus on an object. For the Moon, which has a fixed linear size, located at approximately a fixed distance from us, its approximately constant angular size will look slightly smaller when our eyes are focused and converged to a closer distance than the Moon's (the zenith Moon case), whereas it will look slightly larger when our eyes are adjusted to a greater distance (the horizon Moon case). The reason for the change in focus and convergence of the eyes is that, as in the first explanation, there are different distance cues because of the background. To test this second explanation, while observing the horizon Moon, deliberately "cross" your eyes, thus focusing at a closer point. This, of course, will create blurring and double vision, but do you notice a decrease in the Moon's angular size? Do you also see a change in either the Moon's apparent linear size or distance? Please contact us and let us know what you think about this illusion.

EXPANDING THE QUEST

1. Check the site of NASA's Goddard Space Flight Center where you can find information about past, current, and future NASA missions (including *Lunar Prospector*) and pages devoted to our planet and the Moon.

2. "The Evolution of Continental Crust," by S. R. Taylor and S. M. McLennan, in *Scientific American* (January, 1996).

3. "The Dynamic Aurorae," by S.-I. Akasofu, in *Scientific American* (May, 1989).

4. "The Scientific Legacy of Apollo," by G. Jeffrey Taylor, in *Scientific American* (July, 1994).

5. *The Mystery of the Moon Illusion*, by Helen Ross and Coernelis Plug (OUP Oxford, 2002).

6. "The New Moon," by P. D. Spudis, in *Scientific American* (December 2003).

7. "When Methane Made Climate," by J. F. Kasting, in *Scientific American* (July 2004).

8. "A Cool Early Earth," by J. W. Valley, in *Scientific American* (October 2005).

9. "The Evolution of Earth," by C. J. Allègre and S. H. Schneider, in *Scientific American* Special Edition (July 2005).

10. "Sculpting Earth from Inside Out," by M. Gurnis, in *Scientific American* Special Edition (July 2005).

11. "The Core-Mantle Boundary," by R. Jeanloz and T. Lay, in *Scientific American* Special Edition (July 2005).

12. "Probing the Geodynamo," by G. A. Glatzmaier and P. Olson, in *Scientific American* (April 2005).

13. "Impact from the Deep," by P. D. Ward, in *Scientific American* (October 2006).

14. "Hot Spots Unplugged," by J. A. Tarduno, in *Scientific American* (January 2008).

STARLINKS

Quest Ahead to Starlinks
http://physicalscience.jbpub.com/starlinks

Starlinks is this book's online learning center. It features **eLearning**, which contains chapter quizzes and other tools designed to help you study for your class. You can also find **online exercises**, view numerous relevant **animations**, follow a guide to **useful astronomy sites** on the Web, or even check the latest **astronomy news** updates.

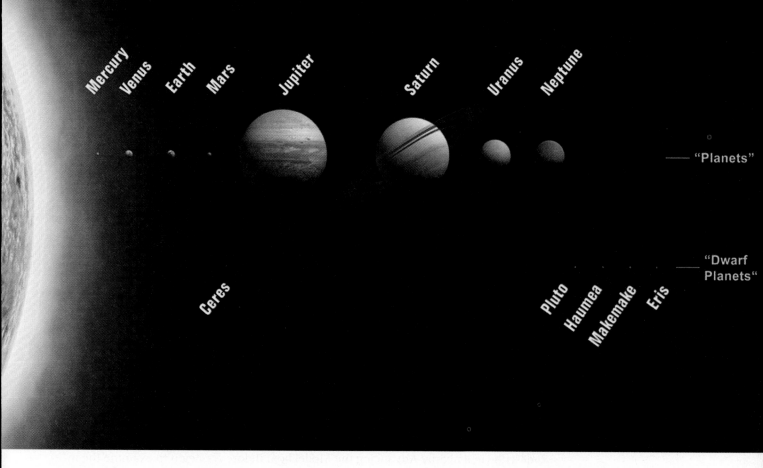

Mercury Venus Earth Mars Jupiter Saturn Uranus Neptune — "Planets"

— "Dwarf Planets"

Ceres Pluto Haumea Makemake Eris

A Planetary Overview

7

A reclassification of the objects in our solar system by the International Astronomical Union reduced the number of planets to eight; asteroid Ceres, Pluto, Haumea, Makemake, and Eris are members of the "dwarf planet" category.

Kuiper belt A disk-shaped region beyond Neptune's orbit, 30–1000 AU from the Sun, closer to the solar system than the Oort cloud and presumed to be the source of short period comets.

WHAT'S IN A NAME? Amazingly, we did not have a scientific definition of what a planet is until August 24, 2006. Between 1930, when Pluto was discovered, and the early 1990s, we talked about the four terrestrial planets, the four Jovian planets, and Pluto, an odd planet that did not fit the other two categories. Discoveries of icy objects from hundreds to over 1000 km across in the region beyond Neptune forged a different picture of our solar system, one in which Pluto is but a nearby representative of the very populous class of icy dwarfs found in the **Kuiper belt** (the disk-shaped region between Neptune's orbit and 30–1000 astronomical units [AU] from the Sun). A few of these icy objects have similar sizes to Pluto, and at least one of them is a bit larger. We discuss this class of objects and their region in Chapter 10.

What should we call these new objects? The International Astronomical Union (IAU) is the only body that can decide, and a fierce debate was reignited about the definition of a planet. At the end, the IAU resolved that objects in our solar system were classified into three categories as follows:

1. A *planet* is a celestial body that (a) is in orbit around the Sun, (b) has sufficient mass for its self-gravity to overcome rigid body forces so that it assumes a hydrostatic equilibrium (nearly round) shape, and (c) has cleared the neighborhood around its orbit.

All cross references to chapters, sections, figures, and tables pertain to the main text, *In Quest of the Universe, Sixth Edition. In Quest of the Solar System* contains Chapters 1–11 and 19 of the main text. *In Quest of the Stars and Galaxies* contains Chapters 1–5 and 11–19 of the main text.

2. A *dwarf planet* is a celestial body that (a) is in orbit around the Sun, (b) has sufficient mass for its self-gravity to overcome rigid body forces so that it assumes a hydrostatic equilibrium (nearly round) shape, (c) has not cleared the neighborhood around its orbit, and (d) is not a satellite. *Plutoids* are dwarf planets with a semimajor axis greater than that of Neptune.

3. All other objects except satellites orbiting the Sun shall be referred to collectively as *small solar-system bodies*.

As a result of this classification, there are now only eight planets in our solar system: Mercury, Venus, Earth, Mars, Jupiter, Saturn, Uranus, and Neptune. Pluto is now a dwarf planet, along with the asteroid Ceres and Eris, an object a bit larger than Pluto in the Kuiper belt. The IAU will establish a process to assign borderline objects into either dwarf planet or other categories. The third category above includes most of the asteroids, most of the objects beyond the orbit of Neptune, comets, and other small bodies.

As expected, not everyone is happy with the new definition. The wording is indeed not precise, and most arguments are about the meaning of an object "clearing its neighborhood around its orbit." The process of "clearing" is a continuous one and is related to how much an object dominates the dynamics of other objects in its neighborhood. The wording might need to be fixed still, but the concept is clear. The arguments have given us another example of how science is done, and along with our observations and the new discoveries of more Pluto-sized icy objects in the Kuiper belt that will surely follow, a new and exciting view of our solar system is emerging.

Much of what we know about the outer planets in our solar system and many of the photos of them in this book are the result of the *Voyager* missions, which we describe in a nearby Advancing the Model box. Before we begin to examine the individual planets and satellites in our solar system, we need to develop a common framework to understand similarities and differences among these objects. We cannot possibly expect to understand the universe by simply describing in detail all known characteristics of all its objects. The information we collect must be used to develop an understanding (a model) of how these characteristics developed and why certain objects (or groups of objects) seem to have similar or different characteristics from others in the same system. Such knowledge will allow us to make reasonable generalizations about similar systems everywhere in the universe.

In previous chapters we have pointed out some patterns among the planets of our solar system. For example, Kepler's third law tells us of the relationship between a planet's distance from the Sun and its period of revolution. Before turning to the individual planets, an examination of other patterns of similarities and differences among the planets will be helpful. In this chapter, we present our current understanding of our own planetary system and of how such systems form around stars. In the next three chapters, we study in detail the major objects in it.

A possible new mnemonic for the eight planets is the following: *My Very Educated Mother Just Served Us Noodles.*

7-1   Sizes and Distances in the Solar System

The Sun contains almost all the mass (about 99.85%) of the solar system and is about 10 times larger in diameter than the largest planet (Jupiter). FIGURE 7-1 shows the planets drawn to scale. At the bottom of the drawing, you see the partial disk of the Sun. If the Sun had been drawn as a complete circle fitting the page, many of the planets would have been too small to see. The Sun's diameter is about 1,390,000 kilometers, whereas the Earth's diameter is about 13,000 kilometers. The diameter of the Sun, therefore, is about 110 times that of Earth. To picture this better, think of the Sun as an object the size of a basketball, a sphere 9.4 inches in diameter. On this scale the Earth would be about the size of the head of a pin, a tenth of an inch in diameter (FIGURE 7-2). Jupiter is the largest planet, with a diameter about 11 times that of the Earth. On our scale, Jupiter would have a diameter of about an inch. The dwarf

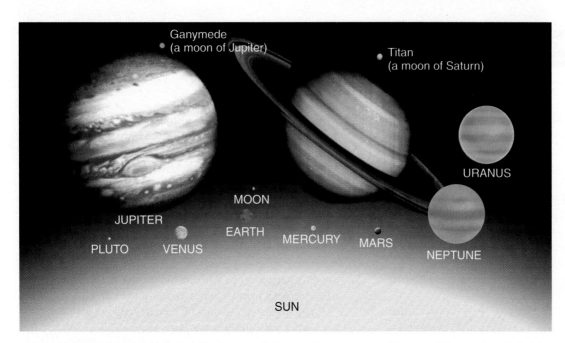

planet Pluto has a diameter about one fifth that of Earth. In our scale model it would be a grain of sand, about 1/64 inch across! Appendix C lists the actual sizes of the planets, along with their sizes compared with the Sun and the Earth.

Now let us consider the distances between the planets. **TABLE 7-1** shows the average distance of each planet from the Sun in astronomical units and according to our model. To continue the model in which the Sun is a basketball, we might put the basketball at one end of a tennis court. A pin at the opposite end of the tennis court would be the Earth. A 1-inch ball, one and a half football fields away would be Jupiter. Pluto would be a grain of sand a kilometer away! Between these objects we put nothing—or almost nothing. There are only the other planets, all smaller than Jupiter, and some even smaller objects.

More than 4000 *asteroids* that are too small to include in our scale model have been discovered in the solar system. The largest of these asteroids has a diameter of about 1000 kilometers, or 600 miles. Perhaps another 100,000 much smaller asteroids orbit the Sun, most of them in the asteroid belt between Mars and Jupiter. In

As we discuss the sizes of solar system objects and the distances between them, try to form a mental picture of the relative distances rather than just memorizing the values.

asteroid Any of the thousands of minor planets (small, mostly rocky objects) that orbit the Sun.

TABLE 7-1			
Average Distances of the Planets and Pluto from the Sun			
		On Our Scale	
Object	Distance from the Sun (AU)	Mean Diameter	Distance from Sun
Sun	—	9.4 inches (23.88 cm)	—
Mercury	0.39	0.03 inch (0.08 cm)	33 feet (10 m)
Venus	0.72	0.08 inch (0.21 cm)	61 feet (19 m)
Earth	1.0	0.09 inch (0.22 cm)	84 feet (26 m)
Mars	1.52	0.05 inch (0.12 cm)	128 feet (39 m)
Jupiter	5.20	0.97 inch (2.45 cm)	438 feet (134 m)
Saturn	9.58	0.81 inch (2.07 cm)	807 feet (0.15 mile) (246 m)
Uranus	19.20	0.35 inch (0.88 cm)	1616 feet (0.31 mile) (493 m)
Neptune	30.05	0.33 inch (0.85 cm)	2530 feet (0.48 mile) (771 m)
Pluto	39.24	0.02 inch (0.04 cm)	3303 feet (0.63 mile) (1007 m)

FIGURE 7-2 If the Sun were the size of a basketball, the Earth would be the size of the head of a shirtpin.

ADVANCING THE MODEL

The *Voyager* Spacecraft

In the period 1976–78, an astronomical event took place that only occurs about once every 177 years. During this time the large outer planets Jupiter, Saturn, Uranus, and Neptune were bunched closely together looking out from Earth, as they traveled their orbits around the Sun. This had not happened since the time of Napoleon. Starting in 1972, NASA scientists and engineers planned to take advantage of this situation by sending out two space probes to explore these planets (**FIGURE B7-1**). *Voyager 1* was launched on September 5, 1977, on a faster trajectory than *Voyager 2*, which was launched 16 days earlier. Over the next few years they revolutionized our understanding of the solar system.

Keeping in touch with the two tiny spacecraft turned out to be a trial in overcoming adversity and avoiding disaster. *Voyager 2*'s onboard computers often detected emergencies when none existed. For example, during the initial launch of the rocket from Earth, the computers interpreted the rapid acceleration of the spacecraft as outside normal operation and tried to reprogram the thrusters to slow it down. Later, the craft's radio receiver blew a fuse and the craft could receive only a limited range of signals from Earth. NASA engineers overcame these problems, and the two space probes continued on their way.

Voyager 1 arrived at Jupiter in March of 1979, about 4 months earlier than *Voyager 2*, and the two craft sent back unprecedented views of the planet during the spring and summer. They discovered the rings of Jupiter, which had never before been seen, and then went on to explore the large moons Io, Ganymede, Callisto, and Europa.

Voyager 1 began making discoveries about Saturn in October 1980, when it was still 30 million miles away from the planet. *Voyager 2* followed in August of 1981. Between them, the spacecraft sent back images of the complex structure of

Saturn's rings and the violent storms in Saturn's atmosphere and detected an atmosphere on Titan, Saturn's largest moon.

Four and a half years passed before *Voyager 2* reached Uranus, making its closest approach in January 1986. It sent back photos of the Uranian rings and its major moons, before the craft was reprogrammed for the trip to Neptune. *Voyager 2* passed within 3100 miles of Neptune in August 1989 and then went on into deep space. (You might think 3100 miles is a large distance, but remember that Neptune is 30,800 miles across and almost 2700 million miles from Earth. Sending a space probe that close to Neptune is like using a rifle to shoot a penny 2 miles away—and hitting it!)

The spacecraft are now on an extended mission, searching for the outer limits of the Sun's magnetic field and outward flow of the solar wind (the heliopause boundary). After the spacecraft cross this boundary, they will be able to take measurements of the interstellar fields, particles, and waves without being influenced by the solar wind.

Voyager 1 has already passed the termination shock; this is the region where the solar wind meets the interstellar gas, thus quickly slowing down, becoming denser and hotter. *Voyager* scientists were surprised to find that the speed of the solar wind beyond the shock was much less than predicted and that at times it seemed to be flowing backward, suggesting a possible correlation with the less active phase of the solar cycle (which we discuss in Chapter 11). They also found that the direction of the interplanetary magnetic field beyond the shock varies much slower (every 100 days or so) than expected (every 13 days or so, half of the Sun's rotational period); this field is carried out by the solar wind, with the alternating directions forming a pattern of stripes. More surprisingly, the shock region does not seem to be the source of ***cosmic rays***; these are energetic charged particles that originate in outer space; they travel at nearly the speed of light and strike Earth from all directions. The intensity of these rays has been steadily increasing as the spacecraft moves farther from the shock, suggesting that their source is even farther from the Sun.

The *Voyager* spacecraft continue to make surprising discoveries and have shown that the Sun's interaction with the surrounding interstellar matter is more complex than we had imagined. In May 2009, *Voyager 1* (*Voyager 2*) was at a distance of 110 AU (89 AU) from the Sun, escaping the solar system at a speed of about 3.6 AU/year (3.3 AU/year), 34° out of the ecliptic plane to the north (29° south). By about 2015, *Voyager 1* is expected to cross into interstellar space, beyond the heliopause, followed by *Voyager 2* about 5 years later. Electrical power on the *Voyager* spacecraft is produced from the heat generated by the natural decay of plutonium. The spacecraft have enough power to operate at least until 2025.

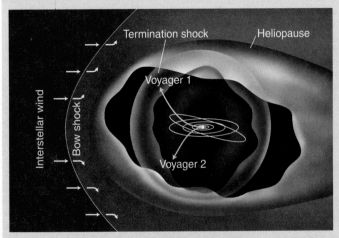

FIGURE B7-1 The *Voyager 1* and *Voyager 2* spacecraft started their Grand Tour from Earth to the outer planets in 1977.

addition, trillions of ***comets*** orbit the Sun in a huge shell at a distance of about 40,000–100,000 AU. We discuss these objects in more detail in Chapter 10.

Figure 7-1 shows the planets as disks, but they are actually spheres. In trying to imagine their comparative sizes, keep in mind that the volume of a sphere is proportional to its radius cubed. For example, the Sun's diameter is about 110 times that of Earth, but the Sun's volume is about 110^3 or 1.3 million times that of Earth's. Similarly, Jupiter's volume is about 11^3 or 1400 times that of Earth's.

Measuring Distances in the Solar System

In Chapter 2 we discussed how Copernicus used geometry to calculate the relative distances to the planets. That is, he was able to calculate that Mars is 1.5 ***astronomical units (AU)*** from the Sun, although he could not determine the value of an astronomical unit. Today we can measure the distances to planets using radar. We send radar signals to a planet and measure the time required for the signal to reach the planet and bounce back. Then, knowing that radar signals travel at the speed of light (3×10^8 m/s, or 3×10^5 km/s), we can calculate the distance to the planet.

When the nearest planet, Venus, is closest to Earth, a radar signal still requires nearly 5 minutes to get there and back. The great distances in the solar system become clearer when we realize that if such a signal could be emitted in New York City and reflected from something in Washington, D.C., only 0.002 seconds would be required for the round trip.

comet A small object, mostly ice and dust, in orbit around the Sun.

astronomical unit (AU) A unit of distance equal to the average distance between the Earth and the Sun.

The radar signal is typically a burst of 400 kilowatts of power, but the returning signal is only 10^{-21} watt, which is so weak that it is very difficult to detect.

EXAMPLE

Suppose we bounce a radar signal off of Mars. The signal returns to Earth 22 minutes after being transmitted. How far away is Mars?

SOLUTION

First, we realize that 22 minutes is the time the signal takes to reach Mars and return to Earth. So a one-way trip requires 11 minutes. Now let's change 11 minutes to seconds (as our signal speed is given in kilometers/second).

$$11 \text{ min} \times \frac{60 \text{ s}}{1 \text{ min}} = 660 \text{ s.}$$

Now,

$$\text{distance} = \text{velocity} \times \text{time} = (3.0 \times 10^5 \text{ km/s}) \times (660 \text{s}) = 2.0 \times 10^8 \text{ km.}$$

To check that this is a reasonable answer, recall that one astronomical unit is 1.5×10^8 kilometers. Our calculated distance, thus, is 1.33 AU. Because the orbit of Mars is 1.5 AU from the Sun, the distance from Earth to Mars varies from about 0.5 to 2.5 AU. At some point in its orbit, it is, therefore, possible for Mars to be at our calculated distance from Earth.

TRY ONE YOURSELF
When Venus is at its closest distance to Earth, it requires about 4.7 minutes for a radar signal to travel to Venus and back. What is the distance to Venus? Convert the answer to astronomical units and check it with the correct distance given in Table 7-1.

7-2 Measuring Mass and Average Density

How do we know the masses of the Sun and planets? To answer this we must return to Kepler's third law, as modified by Newton, which relates each planet's distance from the Sun to its period of revolution. Using standard units (meters for distance,

The Titius-Bode Law

As we pointed out in Chapter 2, the relative distances to the planets (from Mercury to Saturn) were known in Copernicus' time. We saw that Kepler used these data to formulate his third law. From the time of Copernicus, people have wondered if there is a pattern to the distances of the planets from the Sun.

In 1766, a German astronomer named Johann Titius found a mathematical relationship for the distances from the Sun to the various planets. The rule was publicized by Johann Bode, the director of the Berlin Observatory, in 1772, and is known today as the Titius-Bode law or simply Bode's law. **TABLE B7-1** illustrates how the law works. Column 1 shows a series of numbers starting with zero, jumping to three, and then doubling in value thereafter. Column 2 was obtained by adding 4 to each of those values. Finally, to get column 3, we divide each of the column 2 values by 10. Now compare these figures with the measured distances (in AU) of each of the planets from the Sun.

The table shows that the Titius-Bode law fits fairly well, except that there is a gap: The law seems to indicate that there should be a planet between Mars and Jupiter and, further, that the planet should be 2.8 AU from the Sun. In addition, the law predicts that if other planets were found beyond Saturn, the next one would be about 19.6 AU from the Sun. Indeed, in 1781, the planet Uranus was discovered at a distance of 19.2 AU from the Sun by William Herschel in England.

With this confirmation of the validity of the Titius-Bode law, a group of German astronomers (who called themselves the Celestial Police) divided the zodiac into regions, planning to assign a specific region to each of a number of astronomers who would systematically search for the missing planet at 2.8 AU. The searchers did not find it, however. Instead, a monk who was working on a different project discovered the largest of the asteroids at the distance predicted for Bode's missing planet. (See the Advancing the Model box on page 190.) Although it was first thought that this was the missing planet, the discovery within a few years of other objects at about the same distance made it obvious that things were not this simple. The Titius-Bode law could not account for the large number of "planets" between Mars and Jupiter. (However, it is possible that tidal interactions from Jupiter did not allow all these objects to coalesce and form a planet at this distance from the Sun.)

Neptune and Pluto were discovered after the discovery of the asteroids. How well do they fit the Titius-Bode law? Neptune does not fit the prediction at all, but Pluto's distance of 39.24 AU comes fairly close. (Because Pluto's characteristics are more like those of a satellite than a Jovian planet, it has been suggested that early in the history of the solar system, collisions and close encounters between the outer planets and Pluto-like objects could have changed Pluto from being a satellite to being a planet, while knocking Uranus on its side and moving Neptune closer to the Sun; however, recent work has all but ruled out the idea that Pluto was originally a satellite of Neptune. The suggested explanations for the rotation of Uranus, and for that matter Venus, are still at the speculative stage.)

Relationships such as the Titius-Bode law are said to be *empirical*. This means that they are found to work, but they are not related to any theoretical framework; we don't know why they work. The Titius-Bode law isn't a particularly good empirical law, however. The law is not accurate even for the planets it fits; it does not fit Neptune at all, and it is not internally consistent. (The number in column 1 of Table B7-1 is not doubled in one case.) In this chapter, we show that theories proposed for the formation of the solar system account for the fact that the more distant a planet is from the Sun, the farther it is from other planets. Astronomers may be able to judge the significance of the Titius-Bode law better when, at some future date, they are able to observe planetary spacing around other stars.

TABLE B7-1

Planetary Distances According to the Titius-Bode Law Compared with Today's Values

A Series of Numbers	Add 4	Bode's Law Prediction	Today's Measured Distance (AU)	Object
0	4	0.4	0.39	Mercury
3	7	0.7	0.72	Venus
6	10	1.0	1.00	Earth
12	16	1.6	1.52	Mars
24	28	2.8	2.77	Ceres
48	52	5.2	5.20	Jupiter
96	100	10.0	9.58	Saturn
192	196	19.6	19.20	Uranus
384	388	38.8	30.05	Neptune
			(39.24	Pluto)

seconds for period, and kilograms for mass), we saw in Chapter 3 that Newton's formulation of Kepler's third law is

$$\frac{a^3}{P^2} = \frac{G}{4\pi^2} \cdot (m_1 + m_2),$$

The semimajor axis of a planet's elliptical orbit is essentially its average distance from the Sun.

where a = semimajor axis of the orbit, P = period of the orbit, m_1, m_2 = the masses of the two objects, and G = the gravitational constant.

In some cases, however, it is easier to measure the semimajor axis a in AU and the period P in years; then

$$\frac{a^3_{(AU)}}{P^2_{(yrs)}} = \frac{m_1 + m_2}{m_{Sun}}.$$

Let us now consider the case of a planet orbiting the Sun. Because the mass of even the largest planet, Jupiter, is less than 0.001 times the mass of the Sun, the sum of the two masses is essentially equal to the mass of the Sun ($m_1 + m_2 = m_{planet} + m_{Sun} \approx m_{Sun}$). For objects in orbit around the Sun, we can write the preceding equation as

$$\frac{a^3}{P^2} \approx \frac{G}{4\pi^2} \cdot m_{Sun}, \quad \text{or} \quad \frac{a^3_{(AU)}}{P^2_{(yrs)}} \approx 1.$$

Because the Sun's mass is constant, the value on the right side of Newton's equation is very nearly the same for each of the planets, just as Kepler said. Newton's statement of the law, however, allows us to calculate something else—the mass of the Sun. All we need to know to do this is the semimajor axis of one planet's elliptical orbit and that planet's period of revolution around the Sun.

Even more important, Newton's formulation of Kepler's third law applies to *any* system of orbiting objects. For example, Jupiter's system of moons resembles the solar system; here the equation lets us calculate the mass of Jupiter, which is the central object in this case. As we discuss in Section 7-4, every planet except Mercury and Venus has at least one natural satellite. To calculate the mass of one of these planets, we, therefore, only need to know the distance and period of revolution of at least one of its satellites.

This is an example of the *correspondence principle*, which states that a new theory must make the same predictions as the old one in applications where the old one worked. (See page 92.)

EXAMPLE

The average distance of the Earth from the Sun is a = 1 AU $\approx 1.5 \times 10^{11}$ m and the Earth's orbital period is P = 1 year $\approx 365 \cdot 24 \cdot 60 \cdot 60$ seconds $\approx 3.15 \times 10^7$ s. Using Kepler's third law as modified by Newton, find the mass of the Sun.

SOLUTION

The mass of the Earth is much smaller than the mass of the Sun. Therefore,

$$\frac{a^3}{P^2} = \frac{G}{4\pi^2} \cdot (m_{Earth} + m_{Sun}) \approx \frac{G}{4\pi^2} \cdot m_{Sun},$$

and, thus,

$$\frac{(1.5 \times 10^{11})^3}{(3.15 \times 10^7)^2} \approx \frac{6.67 \cdot 10^{-11}}{4 \cdot (3.14)^2} \cdot m_{Sun}.$$

Therefore,

$$m_{Sun} \approx 2 \times 10^{30} \text{ kg}.$$

TRY ONE YOURSELF

The Moon orbits the Earth with a period of 27.32 days (which is 2.36×10^6 seconds), and its semimajor axis is 3.844×10^8 meters. Assuming that the Moon's mass is negligible compared with the Earth's, use this data to calculate the mass of the Earth. When you check your answer in Appendix C, remember that the Moon's mass is not really negligible compared with the Earth's.

TABLE 7-2	
Percentages of the Total Mass of the Solar System	
Object	%
Sun	99.85
Jupiter	0.095
Other planets	0.039
Satellites of planets	0.00005
Comets	0.01 (?)
Asteroids, etc.	0.0000005 (?)

What about Mercury and Venus, which have no moons? Their masses have been calculated on a few occasions by observing their effects on the orbits of passing asteroids and comets. No asteroid or comet has passed close enough to provide highly accurate data, however, and thus the accuracy of the calculations was limited until space probes flew by these planets. If a space probe is put into orbit around a planet, the previous equation applies to it and allows us to calculate the mass of the planet. In practice, the space probe does not actually have to be put into orbit. By analyzing how the gravitational force of the planet changes the direction and speed of a probe during a flyby, we can calculate the planet's mass, although by a more complicated method than the equation we have used.

When we consider the masses of the objects that make up the solar system, we should be impressed by the fact that the Sun comprises almost the entire system. TABLE 7-2 shows the masses by percentages of the total; the Sun's mass is almost 99.9 percent of the total. Jupiter makes up most of the rest, having more than twice as much mass as the remainder of the planets combined.

Calculating Average Density

The density of an object is defined as the ratio of the object's mass to its volume. In the previous section, we discussed how we could calculate the mass of a solar system object. We have also discussed (in Section 6-1) how to use the small-angle formula to find the diameters of objects if we know their distances from Earth and their angular size. Unless the object is too small, its angular size can be measured with observations. The object's distance from Earth can be obtained by using the methods described in Section 7-1.

Knowing the mass (m) and radius (R) of an object, its average density is given by

The formula for the volume of a sphere of radius R is

$$V = \frac{4}{3} \pi R^3.$$

$$\text{average density} = \frac{\text{mass}}{\text{volume}} = \frac{m}{\frac{4\pi}{3} \cdot R^3} = \frac{3}{4\pi} \cdot \frac{m}{R^3},$$

where we assumed that the object is approximately spherical.

EXAMPLE

When Venus is close to Earth, we measure its angular size to be about 54 arcseconds. Its distance from Earth at that point is 44.8 million kilometers. Using the small-angle formula (Section 6-1), we find that Venus' diameter is 12,100 kilometers, and therefore, its radius is about 6050 kilometers. Kepler's third law allows us to find Venus' mass, about 4.87×10^{24} kilograms. Now we are ready to calculate Venus' average density.

$$\text{average density} = \frac{3}{4\pi} \cdot \frac{4.87 \times 10^{24} \text{ kg}}{(6,050,000 \text{ m})^3} = 5250 \text{ kg/m}^3.$$

This is equal to 5.25 g/cm³, in good agreement with the value of 5.24 g/cm³ found in Appendix C.

TRY ONE YOURSELF

The angular size of the Moon is 0.52 degrees and its distance from the Earth is 384,000 kilometers. The Moon's mass is 7.35×10^{22} kilograms. Using all of these data, find the average density of the Moon and compare it with the value given in Appendix D.

As we mentioned in Section 6-3, after we know the average density of an object, we can compare it with the densities of well-known materials such as water, rock, and iron. This allows us to make a reasonable guess about its composition. For example, the average density of Jupiter is 1.33 g/cm³, barely greater than that of water (1 g/cm³) and less than silicate rock (about 3 g/cm³). We can infer that Jupiter consists mostly of low-density materials (gas, liquids) with a small (compared with its overall size) core of iron, rock, and water; however, knowing the value of an object's average density does not mean we can accurately predict its exact composition. Different combinations of materials can result in the same average density and an object's gravity can affect the density of certain materials; however, even though there are limitations, we can gain reasonable insights into the makeup of an object by calculating its average density.

7-3 Planetary Motions

FIGURE 7-3 illustrates the orbits of the planets, drawn to scale. They are all ellipses, as Kepler had written and most are very nearly circular. For comparison, the orbit of the dwarf planet Pluto is eccentric enough that it overlaps the orbit of Neptune. In 1979, Pluto moved to a location in its orbit where it was inside Neptune's orbit. Until 1999 it remained closer to the Sun than Neptune. For the next 220 years Pluto will be farther from the Sun than Neptune.

All of the planets revolve around the Sun in a counterclockwise direction as viewed from far above the Earth's North Pole. Their paths are very nearly in the same plane. This means that we can draw them on the same piece of paper without having to change their paths to view them face-on. **FIGURE 7-4** illustrates the angles between the planes of the various planets' orbits and the plane of the Earth's orbit (this angle is known as the planet's *inclination*). For comparison, Pluto's inclination is greater than that of the planets. We will see that Pluto is unusual in several other ways.

In Section 2-9 we showed that the eccentricity of an elliptical orbit is a measure of how much the orbit is less than perfectly circular. The eccentricities of the planets' (and Ceres' and Pluto's) orbits are given in Appendix C. Notice how much Pluto and Mercury differ from the other planets in eccentricity.

All of the planets except Mercury and Venus have natural satellites revolving around them, just as the Earth does. The direction of revolution of most of these satellites is also counterclockwise, although there are some exceptions. Finally, as we see in the next section, most of the planets also rotate counterclockwise about an axis.

inclination (of a planet's orbit) The angle between the plane of a planet's orbit and the ecliptic plane.

FIGURE 7-3 The orbits of the planets are ellipses, according to Kepler's first law, but most are very nearly circular. For comparison, the orbit of the dwarf planet Pluto is eccentric enough that it overlaps Neptune's. For about 20 years of its 248-year period, Pluto is closer to the Sun than Neptune.

FIGURE 7-4 The orbits of most of the planets are in the same plane as the Earth's (the ecliptic), but Mercury's plane is inclined at 7 degrees and Pluto's at 17 degrees.

The fact that the planets have their orbits in basically the same plane, that they all orbit in the same direction, that most of them rotate in that same direction, and that most of their satellites revolve in that direction cannot be coincidence. We will recall these similarities when we discuss theories concerning the formation of the solar system; we must be sure that the theories explain these properties.

7-4 Classifying the Planets

In Latin, "earth" is "terra." Also, Jupiter was named after the most powerful of the Roman gods. "Jove" is another form of the name "Jupiter" and "Jovian" is an adjective form of the name.

When we examine the properties of individual planets in the following chapters, it will be clear that they divide easily into two groups. It is convenient to classify the four innermost planets—Mercury, Venus, Earth, and Mars—in one group, which we call the terrestrial planets because of their similarity to Earth. The next four planets—Jupiter, Saturn, Uranus, and Neptune—are called the Jovian planets because of their similarity to Jupiter. As already noted, Pluto is unusual in several ways and it has been classified as a dwarf planet.

Size, Mass, and Density

The diameters of the planets are given in Appendix C. Although the four terrestrial planets differ quite a bit from one another, they are all much smaller than the Jovian planets. The dwarf planet Pluto is out beyond the Jovian planets but it has a size more like the terrestrials.

The masses of the planets, given in Appendix C, present even bigger differences between the terrestrial and Jovian planets. Many people have a tendency to skip over tables and graphs. You are not expected to memorize the values given, but a few minutes looking at patterns and thinking of their meaning will yield much knowledge about the solar system. Study the values of the planets' masses in terms of Earth's mass. Notice the great difference between the two classifications of planets. Earth is the most massive of the terrestrial planets, but the least massive Jovian planet has more than 14 times the mass of Earth. Again, Jupiter stands out as the giant.

Density values, given in Appendix C, differ between the terrestrial planets and the Jovian planets. The terrestrials are denser. This is because they are primarily solid, rocky objects, whereas the Jovians are composed primarily of liquid. At one time Jovian planets were commonly called "gas planets," but now we know that they actually contain much more liquid than gas. The average density of the four terrestrial planets is about 5 g/cm³ (or five times that of water), whereas the average density of the four Jovian planets is about 1.2 g/cm³.

Satellites and Rings

TABLE 7-3 shows the number of natural satellites of each planet. Although there is no obvious pattern, the Jovian planets have more satellites. More details of the planetary satellites are found in Appendix D and in discussions of the planets in future chapters.

Table 7-3 also indicates that all Jovian planets have rings. A planetary ring is simply planet-orbiting debris, ranging in size from a fraction of a centimeter to several meters. Motions of particles within the rings are extremely complex, due largely to gravitational interactions with nearby planetary satellites. In a sense, each particle of

TABLE 7-3	
The Number of Known Planetary Satellites	
Planet	Known Satellites*
Mercury	0
Venus	0
Earth	1
Mars	2
Jupiter	63 + r
Saturn	47 + r
Uranus	27 + r
Neptune	13 + r
Pluto†	3

* An "r" indicates that the planet has a ring system
† Dwarf planet

FIGURE 7-5 The tilt between a planet's axis of rotation and its orbital plane varies among the planets in our solar system. Venus, Uranus, and dwarf planet Pluto rotate in a direction opposite that of Earth's as seen from far above the Earth's North Pole. The arrows point in the direction of the planets' north poles, and the direction of rotation is also shown. If you grab a planet with your right hand in a manner such that your fingers point in the direction of its rotation, then your thumb will point to the planet's north pole. This "right-hand rule" is used in many applications in physics and astronomy.

a ring may be considered a satellite of the planet, but if we do so, counting satellites becomes meaningless. We, therefore, continue to speak only of the larger "moons" as being planetary satellites.

Rotations

We discussed planetary rotations in Section 1.8. The sidereal periods of planetary rotations are given in Appendix C. The sidereal rotational periods of the terrestrial planets differ considerably from one another; they range from Earth's period of about 23.9 hours to Venus' period of about 243 days; however, all of the Jovian planets rotate faster than Earth. They range from Jupiter's period of about 9.9 hours to Uranus' period of about 17.2 hours.

As we saw in Section 7-3, every planet revolves around the Sun in a counterclockwise direction when viewed from above the Earth's North Pole. We know from previous chapters that when viewed from this perspective, the Earth rotates on its axis in this same counterclockwise direction and that the Moon also orbits the Earth in a counterclockwise direction. We might ask if this pattern holds elsewhere in the solar system. The answer is yes, in most cases. As shown in FIGURE 7-5, all of the planets except Venus and Uranus (and dwarf planet Pluto) rotate in a counterclockwise direction as seen from far above the Sun's North Pole.

7-5   Planetary Atmospheres

Long before people visited the Moon, we knew that it contained no air and no liquid water. This had been predicted by applying Newton's law of gravity, and the same law can also be applied to make predictions concerning planetary atmospheres. To see the connection between the law of gravity and an object's lack of atmosphere, we first discuss how to escape from Earth's gravity. This discussion leads to an idea that will help us understand not only why some planets have no atmosphere, but also—in Chapter 15—what a black hole is.

We start by imagining an Earth with no air. On such an Earth, if we throw something upward, it is not slowed by air friction. It still feels the effect of gravity, however, and thus, it slows down, stops, and then falls back to Earth. So we throw it harder. It rises farther, and as it gets higher, the force of gravity on it is less. Its rate of slowing—its *deceleration*—thus is less at greater heights. Could we throw the object fast enough so that Earth's gravity could not stop it and bring it back down? The answer is yes. We can calculate from the laws of motion and gravitation that the minimum speed needed to escape Earth's gravity, assuming we start at the surface, is about 11 km/s; this is much greater than the speed of sound in air at the Earth's surface (which is about 0.3 km/s). An object fired upward from Earth at this speed or

Even though we use the terms "speed" and "velocity" as if they are the same, they are not. An object's velocity tells us not only how fast it is moving (its speed), but also the direction of its motion.

ADVANCING THE MODEL

The Discovery of the Asteroids

Johannes Kepler once proposed that there might be an undiscovered planet between Mars and Jupiter, because the large distance between their orbits does not follow the pattern of other orbits. The Titius-Bode law also seemed to predict such a planet. This led Francis von Zach, a German baron, to plan a systematic search for the planet. Giuseppe Piazzi, a Sicilian astronomer and monk, was one of the astronomers who had been chosen to search in one of the sectors into which von Zach had divided the sky. Before he was notified where he was to search, however, Piazzi discovered (on January 1, 1801) what he first thought was an uncharted star in Taurus. The object was far too dim to see with the naked eye. He named it Ceres after the goddess of the harvest and of Sicily. Continuing to observe it, he saw that it moved among the stars, and by January 24, he decided that he had discovered a comet. He wrote two other astronomers (including Bode) of his discovery, but on February 11, he became sick and was unable to continue his observations. By the time the astronomers received their letters (in late March), the object was too near the Sun to be observed.

Bode was convinced that the hypothesized new planet had been discovered, but he also realized that it would not be visible again until fall. By that time, it would have moved so much that astronomers would have a difficult time finding it again. This was because relatively few observations had been made of the object's position, not enough for the mathematicians of the time to calculate its orbit. Fortunately, a young mathematician named Carl Friedrich Gauss, one of the greatest mathematicians ever, had recently worked out a new method of calculating orbits.

He worked on Bode's project for months and was able to predict some December positions for the object. On December 31, 1801, von Zach rediscovered the object.

The elation over finding the predicted planet did not last long, however, for another "planet" was found in nearly the same orbit about a year later. Its discoverer, Heinrich Olbers, was looking for Ceres when he discovered another object that moved. He sent the results of a few nights' observations to Gauss, and the mathematician calculated its orbit. The object was given the name Pallas, and a new classification of celestial objects had been found: The new objects were called *asteroids*.

By 1890, about 300 asteroids had been found using the tedious method of searching the skies and comparing the observations to star charts, looking for uncharted objects. In 1891, a new method was introduced: A time exposure photograph of a small portion of the sky was taken, and the photograph was searched for any tiny streaks. The streaks (**FIGURE B7-2**) would be caused by objects that did not move along with the stars. These objects were then watched very closely and their orbits determined. Using such methods, well over 4000 asteroids are now known and named, and it is predicted that some 100,000 asteroids are visible in our largest telescopes.

FIGURE B7-2 The two streaks (arrows) on the time exposure photo are caused by the motion of two asteroids as the camera follows the stars' apparent motions across the sky.

---

escape velocity The minimum velocity an object must have to escape the gravitational attraction of another object, such as a planet or star.

greater will continue to rise, slowing down all the time, but never stopping. We call this speed the ***escape velocity*** from Earth.

The reason that we imagined an Earth without air friction is that, in practice, if we fired an object from the surface at 11 km/s, it would be slowed—and probably destroyed—by air friction. In the space program we have sent probes into space with a velocity exceeding escape velocity; the probes were not destroyed by air friction because rockets carried them above the atmosphere before increasing their speed to escape velocity (**FIGURE 7-6**).

The escape velocity of a projectile launched from an astronomical object depends on the gravitational force at the object's surface (or from whatever height we are launching the projectile). The gravitational force at the Moon's surface is only one sixth of that at Earth's surface; a 120-pound astronaut weighs only about 20 pounds on the Moon. The escape velocity from the Moon is therefore less than that from

Earth. It is only about 2.4 km/s. The escape velocity from Phobos, a Martian moon, is only 50 km/hr (30 mi/hr). If you have a good arm, you could throw a ball from Phobos so that it would never return.

To see what escape velocity has to do with the question of the atmosphere of an astronomical object, we must briefly discuss the nature of a gas.

Gases and Escape Velocity

There are three states of matter in our normal experience: solid, liquid, and gas. Some understanding of the gaseous phase is necessary to understand planetary atmospheres. To envision a gas, picture a great number of molecules bouncing around in a container (**FIGURE 7-7**). We must keep in mind the following about the molecules of a gas:

1. The average distances between molecules are greater than their sizes.

2. Compared with the volume occupied by the gas, the volume of a molecule is much smaller.

3. Molecules move in straight lines until they collide, either with one another or with the walls of the container. Then they bounce off and move in straight lines again.

4. There is empty space between the molecules.

5. As gas molecules bounce around, at any given time, different molecules have different speeds. Some will be moving fast and some will be moving slow.

6. The average speed of the molecules depends on the temperature of the gas. Gases at higher temperature have faster moving molecules.

7. At the same temperature, less massive molecules have greater speed. For example, because a molecule of oxygen has less mass than a molecule of carbon dioxide, in a mixture of oxygen and carbon dioxide gases, the oxygen molecules will, on the average, be moving faster.

Now let's consider the Earth's atmosphere, which is held near the Earth by gravitational forces. Consider a molecule at great heights above Earth where the atmosphere has a low density. This means that the molecules are much farther apart than down here at the surface. Suppose that at some instant a particular molecule up there happens to be moving away from Earth. There are very few other molecules around; thus, a collision is unlikely and our molecule acts just like any other object moving away from Earth. The force of gravity slows it down. Whether the molecule returns to Earth or escapes depends on how the speed of the molecule compares with the Earth's escape velocity. If the molecule's speed is greater than escape speed, the molecule is gone, never to return to Earth.

The fact that the Earth has an atmosphere means that the velocities reached by virtually all molecules of the air do not exceed escape velocity. Recall, however, that molecules of lower mass have greater speeds. It is, therefore, no coincidence that there is little hydrogen in the Earth's atmosphere: Hydrogen molecules have less mass than those of any other element, and the temperature of the upper atmosphere is high enough for hydrogen molecules to escape. Any pure hydrogen that is released into the Earth's atmosphere is eventually lost. The chemical element hydrogen does not exist

FIGURE 7-6 Sixty seconds after takeoff, the main engines on the space shuttle cut back to 65% thrust to avoid stress on the wings and tail from the Earth's atmosphere. When the shuttle reaches thinner air at higher altitudes, the engines resume full power until the shuttle reaches orbiting speed.

In fact, the temperature of a gas is defined as a measure of the average energy of motion of the gas molecules: average kinetic energy $= 3/2 \cdot k_B \cdot T$, where T is the temperature in kelvin and k_B is Boltzmann's constant.

Does the Earth keep all of its atmosphere forever?

FIGURE 7-7 Atmospheric gas molecules move at different speeds and in random patterns, but molecules are very tiny; their average speed depends on temperature; and less massive molecules have higher speeds.

The escape velocity of a projectile at a distance *r* from the center of a celestial object of mass *M* is given by

$$v_{esc} = \sqrt{\frac{2 \cdot G \cdot M}{r}}$$, where

G is the gravitational constant.

alone in our atmosphere, but only as part of more massive molecules (such as a molecule of water vapor).

As noted earlier, the escape velocity from the surface of the Moon is about 2.4 km/s. At the temperatures reached on the sunlit side of the Moon, all but the most massive gases attain speeds greater than this, and therefore, the Moon has essentially no atmosphere. The *Apollo* astronauts were not surprised to find no air to breathe when they landed on the Moon.

The Atmospheres of the Planets

The average speed of a particular type of molecule depends on the temperature of the atmosphere, but at any given time, some molecules are traveling faster than average. This means that although the average speed of a molecule of a particular gas in the atmosphere may be less than the escape velocity from a planet, the atmosphere may still gradually lose some of the gas because the speed of a small fraction of the gas molecules exceeds the escape velocity. Because of this, we must use a multiple of the average speed in considering whether or not a gas will escape from a planet. Theory shows that rather than the average speed, the value we should use in determining whether the planet will retain the gas for billions of years is about 10 times the average speed of the molecules of that gas.

FIGURE 7-8 is a graph of the average speeds of various molecules versus their temperatures. The dashed lines represent 10 times the average molecular speed. All of the planets, including Pluto as well as some planetary satellites, are plotted on the graph at their respective temperatures and escape velocities. A planet can retain a gas if the planet lies *above* the dashed line for that gas. Find the Moon on the graph and notice that the average molecular speed for every gas is greater than escape velocity. The planet Mercury is similar. On the other hand, only hydrogen and helium escape from Earth and Venus. The four Jovian planets retain all of their gases, including hydrogen and helium.

Even though a graph such as the one in Figure 7-8 is a powerful tool, we can only accurately find the chemical composition of an object's atmosphere by using spectroscopy. This is necessary because we have directly examined atmospheric samples of only a small number of objects in our solar system. Spectroscopy, the analysis of reflected sunlight from a distant object, allows us to find the chemical composition of the object's atmosphere.

As light from the Sun penetrates a planet's or satellite's atmosphere before it gets reflected back into space, some of its wavelengths are absorbed. The spectrum we observe from the reflected light has absorption lines. As we discussed in Chapter 4, every element has its own unique spectral "fingerprint"; thus, by studying the specific absorption lines we can infer the chemical composition of the atmosphere. (Of course, we must take into account that some of these lines result from absorption that occurs in the atmospheres of the Sun and Earth.)

If an object does not have an atmosphere, we can still use spectroscopy to get useful information about the chemical composition of the object's surface. In this case, the observed absorption lines are broad, instead of the sharp lines produced by molecules in a gas.

TABLE 7-4 summarizes the differences we have discussed between the terrestrial and

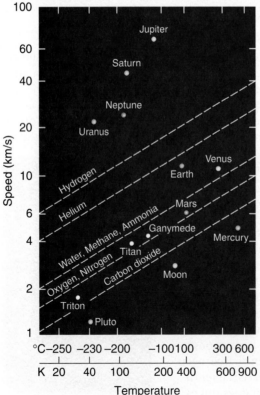

FIGURE 7-8 This graph shows how the speeds of the atoms (or molecules) of various gases depend upon their temperatures. The dashed lines represent 10 times the average speeds. All of the planets, Pluto, and some planetary satellites are indicated at their corresponding temperatures and escape velocities.

Jovian planets. You should keep these differences in mind as we discuss theories of the origin of the solar system, as any successful theory must be able to explain these differences.

TABLE 7-4

Characteristics of the Jovian and Terrestrial Planets

Terrestrials	Jovians
Near the Sun	Far from the Sun
Small	Large
Mostly solid	Mostly liquid and gas
Low mass	Large mass
Slow rotation	Fast rotation
No rings	Rings
High density	Low density
Thin atmosphere	Dense atmosphere
Few moons	Many moons

7-6   The Formation of the Solar System

More than 5 billion years ago, the atoms and molecules that now make up the planets—and our own bodies—were dispersed in a gigantic cloud of dust and gas. In Chapter 13, we examine how such an interstellar cloud condenses to form a star, but with what we have learned about the patterns within the solar system, we can discuss its formation. A study of the beginnings of the solar system is interesting as an example of the way science in general (and astronomy in particular) progresses, because the theory is still in its early development and many gaps remain. The search for answers here resembles a mystery story where there are many clues; new ones appear all the time and some of the clues seem to contradict others.

There are two main categories of competing theories to explain the origin of the solar system: evolutionary theories and catastrophe theories. This section examines the evidence for each and shows why one is gaining favor among astronomers.

Evidential Clues from the Data

As we discussed earlier, any successful theory of the solar system's origin must explain the patterns exhibited by its members and should also be able to account for exceptions to the patterns. Here is a list of significant data that must be explained.

1. All of the planets revolve around the Sun in the same direction (which is the direction the Sun rotates), and all planetary orbits are nearly circular.

2. All of the planets lie in nearly the same plane of revolution.

3. Most of the planets rotate in the same direction as they orbit the Sun, the exceptions being Venus and Uranus.

4. The majority of planetary satellites revolve around their parent planet in the same direction as the planets rotate and revolve around the Sun. In addition, most satellites' orbits are in the equatorial plane of their planet.

5. There is a pattern in the spacing of the planets as one moves out from the Sun, with each planet being about twice as far from the Sun as the previous planet.

6. The chemical compositions of the planets have similarities, but a pattern of differences also exists, in that the outer planets contain more volatile elements and are less dense than the inner planets.

7. All of the planets and moons that have a solid surface show evidence of craters, similar to those on our Moon.

8. All of the Jovian planets have ring systems.

9. Asteroids, comets, and meteoroids populate the solar system along with the planets, and each category of object has its own pattern of motion and location in the system.

10. The planets have more total angular momentum (to be described later in this section) than does the Sun, even though the Sun has most of the mass.

11. Planetary systems in various stages of development exist around other stars.

Any successful theory of the origin of the solar system must explain these clues and should be consistent with the theory of star formation.

We are concerned here only with the formation of the solar system and not the formation of the Galaxy or the origin of the universe, both of which occurred much earlier. These questions are considered in Chapters 16–18.

First of all there came Chaos... From Chaos was born Erebos, the dark, and black night, And from Night again Aither and Hemera, the day, were begotten...
Kesiod (Theogony), about 800 BC.

The pattern of the spacing of planets was discussed in an Advancing the Model box, The Titius-Bode Law, near the beginning of this chapter.

Evolutionary Theories

The French mathematician and philosopher René Descartes (1596–1650) is best known for developing the most common coordinate system used in geometry; however, his ideas about motion and the nature of the universe were influential in the 17th century, particularly for Isaac Newton.

There is no single evolutionary theory for the solar system's origin, but there are several theories that have in common the idea that the solar system came about as part of a natural sequence of events. These theories have their beginning with one proposed by René Descartes in 1644. He suggested that the solar system formed out of a gigantic whirlpool, or vortex, in some type of universal fluid and that the planets formed out of small eddies in the fluid. This theory was rather elementary and contained no specifics as to the nature of the universal fluid. It did, however, explain the observation that the planets all revolve in the same plane, the plane of the vortex.

After Isaac Newton showed that Descartes' theory would not obey the rules of Newtonian mechanics, Immanuel Kant (in 1755) used Newtonian mechanics to show that a rotating gas cloud would form into a disk as it contracts under gravitational forces (FIGURE 7-9). To explain the disk aspect of the solar system (our clue #2), Kant thus changed the philosophical "universal fluid" of Descartes into a real gas subject to the natural laws of mechanics. Later, in 1796, the French mathematician Pierre Simon de Laplace found that such a rotating disk would break up into rings similar to the rings of Saturn. He suggested that perhaps these rings could form into the individual planets while the Sun was coalescing from material in the center.

However, application of Newtonian mechanics to such a contracting gas cloud caused another problem. To understand this problem, consider what happens when a spinning ice skater pulls in his arms: His rotation speed increases greatly (FIGURE 7-10). This increase in speed is predicted by Newton's laws and is a result of the law of ***conservation of angular momentum***. We do not define angular momentum mathematically, but simply state that the ***angular momentum*** of a rotating (or revolving) object is a direct measure of how fast the object rotates (or revolves) and how far it is from its axis of rotation (or revolution). In other words, an object's angular momentum is greater if the object is rotating (or revolving) faster or if the object is farther from the axis of its rotation (or revolution). As the skater pulls in his arms, he decreases their distance from the axis of rotation; in the process, he decreases their angular momentum. To make up for this, his entire body increases its rotation speed, keeping the total angular momentum approximately constant ("conserved"). (The total angular momentum would remain perfectly constant if it were not for air resistance and small friction forces with the ice.)

The law of conservation of angular momentum must also apply to a contracting, rotating cloud of gas. Like the ice skater, the cloud speeds up its rotation as its parts come closer to the center of rotation. When calculations are made for a cloud contracting to form the Sun and planets, we find that the Sun should rotate much faster than it does; it should spin around in a few hours instead of the observed period of rotation of about a month. This means that the angular momentum possessed by the Sun is much less than the theory predicts. In fact, the total angular momentum of the planets (because of their greater distance from the center) is observed to be much

angular momentum An intrinsic property of matter. A measure of the tendency of a rotating or revolving object to continue its motion.

conservation of angular momentum A law that states that the angular momentum of a system does not change unless there is a net external influence acting on the system, producing a twist around some axis.

FIGURE 7-9 As a cloud contracts, its rotational motion causes it to form a disk.

(a)   (b)

FIGURE 7-10 If an ice skater begins a spin with his arms extended (a), he will spin faster and faster as he draws his arms in (b). This effect is explained by the law of conservation of angular momentum.

greater than the angular momentum of the Sun. This should not occur, according to Newton's laws.

The contradiction of these well-established laws caused the evolutionary theories to lose favor early in the 20th century. The alternative theory was a catastrophe theory.

Catastrophe Theories

In contrast to what the name may imply, a *catastrophe theory* does not refer to a disaster, but rather to an unusual event—in this case, the formation of the solar system by an unusual incident. In 1745, Georges Louis de Buffon proposed such an event: the passage of a comet close to the Sun. Buffon suggested that the comet pulled material out of the Sun to form the planets. In Buffon's time, comets were thought to be quite massive, but in the 20th century, we learned that a comet's mass is not great enough to cause this breakup of the Sun; however, his basic idea—that a massive object exerted gravitational forces on the Sun, pulling material out and causing it to sweep around the Sun until it eventually coalesced to form the planets—still seemed a reasonable hypothesis. Such an event as the passage of a massive object so near the Sun would be very unusual, but not impossible.

More recently, it was suggested that the Sun was once part of a triple-star system, with the three stars revolving around one another. As we see, such star systems are common, and thus, this in itself is not a far-fetched idea. This particular catastrophe theory holds that the configuration was unstable and that one of the stars came close enough to cause a tidal disruption of the Sun, producing the planets. The close approach of this star also caused the Sun to be flung away from the other two stars.

Starting around the 1930s, astronomers began to find major problems with catastrophe theories. First, calculations showed that material pulled from the Sun would be so hot that it would dissipate rather than condense to form planets. A second problem involved deuterium, an *isotope* of hydrogen. Even the outer portions of the Sun are too hot for deuterium to be stable, and thus, not much deuterium exists in the Sun; however, much more deuterium is found on the planets than in the Sun, indicating that the material of the planets could not have been part of the Sun.

Finally, as we discuss later, we now know that other nearby stars have planetary systems around them. A catastrophe theory would predict that such systems are rare because they are produced by unusual events. If we find planetary systems elsewhere, there is probably some common process that forms them.

At the same time as these problems were becoming apparent, a solution appeared for the angular momentum problem of the evolutionary theories; as a result, catastrophe theories have been nearly abandoned in favor of modern evolutionary theories.

Present Evolutionary Theories

In the 1940s, the German physicist Carl von Weizsäcker showed that a gas rotating in a disk around the Sun would rotate differentially (the inner portion moving faster than the outer). This would result in the formation of eddies, as shown in **FIGURE 7-11**. As the figure shows, the eddies would be larger at greater distances from the Sun. According to his view, these eddies are the beginnings of planet formation, and the eddies therefore explain the pattern of distances between the planets.

A real breakthrough occurred when it was realized that a mechanism exists to account for why the Sun does

catastrophe theory A theory of the formation of the solar system that involves an unusual incident, such as the collision of the Sun with another star.

The evolution of the world may be compared to a display of fireworks that has just ended: some few red wisps, ashes and smoke. Standing on a cooled cinder, we see the slow fading of the suns, and we try to recall the vanished brilliance of the origin of the worlds.
G. Lemaître (1894–1966), Astronomer and Catholic priest

isotope One of two (or more) atoms whose nuclei have the same number of protons but different numbers of neutrons.

FIGURE 7-11 Carl von Weizsäcker showed that eddies would form in a rotating gas cloud and that the eddies nearer the center would be smaller.

FIGURE 7-12 (a) The bright bluish stars visible in the Rosette nebula are apparently hot, young ones forming from dense dust clouds. The nebula is about 3000 light-years away. (b) Hodge 301, at lower right, is a cluster of massive, brilliant stars in the Tarantula nebula, about 160,000 light-years away. Many of the stars in the cluster have exploded as supernovae, blasting material into the nebula at high speed. These explosions compress the gas into filaments, seen at upper left. Near the center of the image are small, dense gas globules and dust columns where new stars are being formed today.

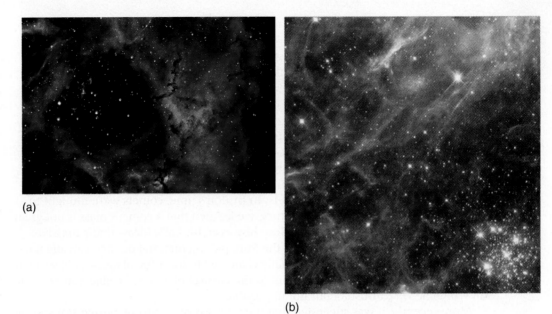
(a)

(b)

not rotate faster than it does. First, however, let's consider the beginning of the scenario that today's theory envisions.

In Chapter 13 we explain that new stars form from enormous interstellar clouds of gas and dust. FIGURE 7-12 shows the Rosette nebula and the Tarantula nebula, which are stellar nurseries where newly formed stars can be seen. When an interstellar dust cloud collapses, any slight rotation that it had at the beginning, before the collapse, results in a greatly increased speed of the central portion (explained by the conservation of angular momentum). The material in the center becomes a star—the Sun in the case of our solar system. During the few million years that this is occurring, the matter surrounding the newly forming Sun is condensing into a disk.

As the gases in the disk cool, they begin to condense to liquids and solids, just as water vapor condenses on the cool side of an iced drinking glass. Nonvolatile elements such as iron and silicon condense first, forming small chunks of matter, or dust grains. Each of these grains has its own elliptical orbit about the center, and as time passes, more matter condenses onto its surface. The orbits of these tiny objects are elliptical so that they intersect one another. The resulting collisions between particles have two effects: (1) particles involved in gentle collisions (as if they were rubbing shoulders with one another as they orbit) occasionally stick together and form larger particles, and (2) particles are forced into orbits that are more nearly circular.

As the matter sticks together, small chunks grow into larger chunks. Their increased mass causes nearby particles and molecules of gas to feel a greater gravitational force toward them. Because this force is still very small, the coalescing is a very slow process, but over a few hundred thousand years, larger particles—now called *planetesimals*—sweep up smaller ones. Some planetesimals, resembling miniature solar systems, have dust and gas orbiting them—material that eventually condenses to become the moons we know today.

As the force of gravity shrinks a celestial object, gravitational energy causes it to heat up. A simple case of gravitational energy being converted to thermal energy occurs whenever you drop something. The object hits the floor and heats up slightly. (The heating is very slight, and to experience it, you should probably cheat and *throw* an object, such as modeling clay, down to the floor a few times.) Perhaps you can visualize a release of heat when an object falls from the heavens onto a planet, but the same effect occurs when gravitational forces cause the collapse of a cloud of gas and dust. The material heats up as it falls toward the center.

This heating effect occurs with our solar system-in-formation. The material that falls inward to form the Sun gets hot, and the high temperatures near the new Sun do not allow for condensation of the more volatile elements. It thus is difficult for

planetesimal One of the small objects that formed from the original material of the solar system and from which a planet developed.

◆ In Chapter 9 we present evidence that Jupiter has not yet lost all of the excess thermal energy that resulted from its formation.

a planet-in-formation near the Sun to accrete gases; as we discussed earlier, higher temperatures result in higher speeds for gas particles, which allows them to overcome the gravitational pull of the planet. As a result, the planet does not increase its mass by accretion as quickly as a planet at great distances from the Sun, where the temperatures are lower. In addition, lower masses result in weaker gravitational pulls, which makes it even harder for planets near the Sun to increase their sizes. This explains why the terrestrial planets are smaller in size than the Jovian planets and why they are primarily composed of nonvolatile, dense material, compared with the mostly gaseous Jovian planets.

The differences in densities between the forming planets have an interesting effect on their oblateness (that is, how "flattened" they are). Under spherically symmetric conditions, a nonrotating self-gravitating cloud will end up as a perfectly spherical object; every particle will move on radial lines toward the center of the cloud; however, as we discussed earlier, rotation will tend to flatten the object in a direction perpendicular to the rotation axis (Figure 7-9). The more gaseous the planet, and the faster it rotates, the greater its oblateness. Even the least oblate Jovian planet, Neptune, is five times more oblate than Earth.

According to Newtonian mechanics, the gravitational influence of the new Sun (the *protosun*) gets weaker with distance; at greater distances matter orbits at a more leisure pace, and the swirling eddies around protoplanets are more prominent. The situation at this time is illustrated in **FIGURE 7-13**.

A particularly large outer planet, Jupiter, gravitationally stirs the nearby planetesimals of the inner system so that the weak gravitational forces between them cannot pull them together. Today's asteroids are the remaining planetesimals.

While planet formation is taking place, the Sun continues to heat up. It heats the gas in the inner solar system and causes electrons there to leave their atoms, forming charged atoms (*ions*) and electrons. A magnetic field does not exert a force on an uncharged object, but if a magnetic field line sweeps by a charged object, a force is exerted on that object. This is what must have slowed the Sun's rotation; the magnetic field of the rapidly rotating Sun exerted a force on the ions in the inner solar system, tending to sweep them around with it; however, Newton's third law tells us that if the Sun's magnetic field exerts a force to increase the angular speed of these particles, they must exert a force back on the Sun to decrease its angular speed. It thus is the magnetic field of the Sun, discovered rather recently, that provides the explanation for why the Sun rotates so slowly—a fact that was once a stumbling block for evolutionary theories.

The solar system of our story is getting close to what we see today; however, gas and dust were still more plentiful between the planets than in today's solar system, and the inner solar system of our story contained much more hydrogen and other volatile gases than exist there today. To help answer the question of how these gases were moved to the outer solar system and how, in general, the system was "cleaned up," we can again look into space at interstellar dust clouds.

In these clouds we see stars at various stages of formation. There is evidence that many newly forming stars go through a period of instability during which their **stellar wind** increases in intensity. The stellar wind, called the solar wind in the case of our Sun, consists of an outflow of particles from the star. It continues throughout a star's lifetime, as we explain in Chapter 14. If the instabilities we observe in other stars occurred during the formation of the Sun, the pulses of solar wind would sweep the volatile gases from the inner solar system. Even without this

The oblateness value for each planet is included in the planet's Data Page.

ion An electrically charged atom or molecule.

A charged particle moving in a magnetic field experiences a force unless it is moving parallel to the magnetic field lines.

stellar wind The flow of particles from a star.

FIGURE 7-13 At the stage of development shown here, planetesimals have formed in the inner solar system, and large eddies of gas and dust remain at greater distances from the protosun.

increased activity, it is expected that the solar wind would gradually move this material outward, but if the Sun did go through this active period, there is certainly no difficulty explaining why hydrogen and helium exist on the outer planets but not the inner. Once in the outer system, this material would gradually be swept up by the giant planets there. Also, recall Figure 7-8 and our discussion in Section 7-5 about planetary atmospheres: The proximity of the terrestrial planets to the Sun and their weak gravitational fields (as compared with the Jovian planets) make it easier for gases such as hydrogen to escape the pull of the terrestrial planets.

Explaining Other Clues

As millions of years passed, remaining planetesimals crashed onto the planets and moons, resulting in the craters we see on these objects today.

Comets are thought to be material that coalesced in the outer solar system, the remnants of small eddies. These objects would feel the gravitational forces of Jupiter and Saturn, and many would fall onto those planets. (Recall the discussion at the start of Chapter 1 of Comet Shoemaker-Levy 9 crashing onto Jupiter.) Small objects that formed beyond the giant planets' orbits, however, would be accelerated by Jupiter and Saturn as those planets passed nearby and would be pushed outward. As we explain in Chapter 10, there is reason to think that great numbers of comets exist in a region far beyond the most distant planet.

The evolutionary theories explain that nonvolatile elements would condense in the inner solar system, but volatiles would be swept outward by the solar wind. This accounts for the differences in the planets' chemical composition. In fact, astronomers find that when compression forces are taken into account in calculating density, planets closest to the Sun contain the most dense and least volatile material, as would be expected from the theories.

Further confirmation of evolutionary theories is found in Jupiter's Galilean satellites. As we point out in Chapter 9, these satellites also decrease in density and increase in volatile elements as we move outward from Jupiter. The formation of Jupiter and its moons must have resembled the formation of the solar system; thus, we see the same density pattern in Jupiter's system.

In the next two chapters we examine each planet in turn and point out some exceptions to the patterns described here. Some of the exceptions are easy to explain using evolutionary theories. Others cannot be explained by these theories and require a hypothesis of collisions—"catastrophes"—within the early solar system.

Catastrophes may well have played a part in the formation of the solar system, as in the formation of our Moon (Section 6-5), but it was a fairly minor part, involving relatively few objects. The overall formation of the system in which we live was evolutionary in nature. Nonetheless, the origin of the solar system is poorly understood. Pieces continue to fall into place, but we still have much to learn.

For information on the distant shell of comets, refer to the Oort cloud in Chapter 10.

7-7   Planetary Systems around Other Stars

Is the existence of our planetary system unusual, or is it common for stars to have planets? Until recently, it has been very difficult to answer this question. Direct observation of extrasolar planets (or exoplanets) is necessarily based on light reflected by these objects (or weak infrared light emitted by their cool surfaces); however, planets are very small, and the light emitted from their companion star overwhelms their light. For example, our Sun is 10 billion times brighter than Earth at visible wavelengths. However, in the infrared, the brightness of the star is reduced while the brightness of a planet peaks, allowing us to detect a planet more easily in the infrared. In most cases, we have to use indirect methods to search for exoplanets. Different categories of evidence can help answer the question we asked. We examine each category in turn.

- *Direct observation/Infrared companion.* The first direct image of an exoplanet was obtained in April 2004 using adaptive optics at ESO's VLT (**FIGURE 7-14a**). The planet,

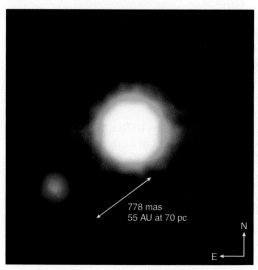

778 mas
55 AU at 70 pc

N
E ←

(a)

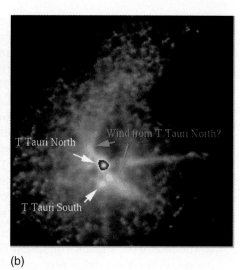

T Tauri North

Wind from T Tauri North?

T Tauri South

(b)

FIGURE 7-14 (a) A composite image in the infrared of the brown dwarf 2M1207 (about 25 times as massive as Jupiter) and its planet (about 5 times as massive as Jupiter and more than 100 times fainter than the brown dwarf). The planet's spectrum shows strong signature of water molecules. (b) A false-color image of the T Tauri system, a prototype laboratory for the formation of low mass stars like our Sun. The binary system consists of the star T Tauri North and its companion T Tauri South.

five times as massive as Jupiter, orbits a **brown dwarf** about 230 light-years from the Sun in the direction of the constellation Hydra. This system is only about 8 million years old, making the planet hotter and brighter than similar objects orbiting much older stars like our Sun and thus easier to detect.

In March 2005, scientists using the *Spitzer Space Telescope* measured directly the infrared radiation from two previously detected (using the transit method, described later) Jupiter-like planets orbiting Sun-like stars. When the planet dips behind the star, the star's infrared light is measured and then subtracted from the total infrared light of both the planet and star; this corresponds to the planet's own infrared radiation and allows a measurement of the planet's temperature. The planets (HD209458b and TrES-1) orbit their stars with periods of about 3 days, at distances of about 0.04 AU, and have temperatures of about 1100 K. *Spitzer* has also detected the presence of dust grains orbiting a number of brown dwarfs, suggesting that planet formation around these failed stars proceeds along steps similar to those for normal stars.

The star T Tauri has a companion (Figure 7-14b) that emits significant radiation only in the infrared region. The companion has too little mass for it to become a star itself, yet its infrared radiation indicates that it has a high temperature. A possible explanation for this high temperature is that it is a giant planet in the process of formation, with dust and gas still falling into it. If so, this scenario lends support for evolutionary theories of planet formation—at least, for large Jupiter-size planets.

- *Dust disks.* Disks of dust and gas about the size of the solar system have been detected around several stars. The most obvious case is that of β Pictoris (**FIGURE 7-15**). Studies of the disk around the star at midinfrared wavelengths suggest that

brown dwarf A star-like object that has insufficient mass to start nuclear reactions in its core and thus become self luminous.

β is the Greek letter beta.

FIGURE 7-15 This is an *HST* visible-light view of β Pictoris. The star itself has been blocked out, and the disk of particles around it is visible up to 300 AU from the star. β Pictoris is a young star (12 to 20 million years old), 63 light-years away. A secondary disk is seen tilted by a few degrees from the primary disk, providing circumstantial evidence for the presence of a planet in a similarly inclined orbit.

it contains fine dust with an icy consistency. The presence of dust, which is usually either blown out of the system or accreted by the star over a period of a few hundred thousand years, suggests that it is replenished continually, most likely by collisions among planetesimals orbiting the star in belt-like regions at specific distances (about 6, 16, and 30 AU). The lack of dust between 6 and 16 AU from the star suggests the presence of a planet at about 12 AU from the star. This is a system that is still in the process of forming planets.

In early 2005, the *Spitzer Space Telescope* detected gaps in the dusty disks around two very young stars. The gaps are empty and sharp edged, suggesting the presence of Jupiter-like planets. These findings support the idea that Jupiter-like planets form faster than previously thought. One of the stars, GM Aurigae, is very similar to our Sun and at a mere 1 million years of age provides us a unique opportunity to understand how our solar system formed.

- *Pulsar companion.* In 1992 astronomers reported that they had found variations in the rate of the signals from the pulsar PSR 1257 + 12 (about 2630 light-years away). **Pulsars** are stellar remnants that result from supernova explosions and emit beams of radio waves. When these beams sweep past the Earth, we observe them as radio pulses that normally are very constant in their frequency of pulsation. The variations in the frequency of a pulsar can be explained if it has one or more companion objects, such as a planet. We now have a confirmed detection of three planets around this pulsar. Two of these exoplanets have masses about four times that of Earth, while the third is about twice as massive as the Moon. Since 1994, we have another confirmed observation of a planet 2.5 times as massive as Jupiter around pulsar PSR B1620 – 26 (about 12,400 light-years away).

  Other observations, which have not been confirmed yet, suggest that planets may be orbiting two other pulsars. As additional pulsars are examined for similar evidence, and if any of these observations are confirmed, we will have more pieces to add to the puzzle of how common are planetary systems.

- *Binary systems and visual wobble.* As we showed in Chapter 3, gravitationally bound objects revolve around their common center of mass. The case we discussed there was the Earth–Moon system. Among the stars, we observe many cases of **binary star systems**, in which two stars revolve around one another in this manner. In some cases, only one star of a binary system is visible, but we can deduce the existence of the dimmer star from the motion of the visible one. If we see a star that appears to wiggle in its position or that exhibits an elliptical motion, we can conclude that it is in orbit with another object. This provides us with a possible method of detecting the presence of a large planet in orbit around another star. If we hope to find a planet by such means, we must look at nearby stars, whose motion is easier to observe.

  A star named Barnard's star is the second-closest star to the Sun. In the first half of the 20th century, a back-and-forth motion was reported for this star; however, the motion is very slight and detecting it involved comparing photographs taken over long periods of time. Most astronomers considered the data very suspect, for the photographs were taken under different conditions with instruments that had been changed over the course of the observations; however, measurements of changes in the *radial* velocity of Barnard's star agreed with the original conclusions and indicated that the star may indeed have at least one planet of 1.5 times the mass of Jupiter revolving around it at a distance of 4 AU. (Large planets, of course, would cause the star to move more than small ones would.) Measurements on this object are continuing, as even recent observations with the *Hubble Space Telescope (HST)* have not yet confirmed the existence of any planets around this star.

  Detecting the wobble of a star by carefully measuring its position in the sky relative to other stars is not easy (FIGURE 7-16a). For example, if we were to look at the wobble of our Sun (mainly due to Jupiter) from 30 light-years away, the

---

pulsar A celestial object of small size (typical diameter of 30 kilometers) that emits beams of radio waves, which, when sweeping past the Earth, are observed as pulses of radio waves with a regular period between a millisecond to a few seconds.

 Pulsars are described in Chapter 15.

binary star system A pair of stars that are gravitationally bound so that they orbit one another.

 Radial velocities are measured by the Doppler effect, and radial motion therefore can be measured with greater sensitivity than can tangential motion.

(a)

FIGURE 7-16 Different methods of detecting exoplanets. (a) The astrometric method. The presence of a planet around a star results in a to-and-from motion for the star: Both the star and the planet move around their common center of mass. This method requires very precise measurements of the position of the star. The drawing is not to scale. (b) The Doppler (radial-velocity) method. Astronomers measure the Doppler shift in the star's spectrum and use the shift to determine the star's orbit. This in turn allows us to determine the orbit of the unseen companion (planet-like object). (c) The transit photometry method. When a planet passes directly between its star and an observer's line of sight, it blocks out a portion of the star's light. The shape of the light curve allows us to find the sizes of the orbit and of the planet. (d) The gravitational microlensing method. Light rays from a background star bend when they pass through space that is warped by the mass of a foreground star and its planet, which act as lenses briefly increasing the background star's apparent brightness.

(b)

(c)

(d)

small circle made by the Sun would appear to be about the size of a quarter seen from a distance of 6000 miles. Measurements made using this direct method must be extremely accurate and must be made over long periods of time to capture the orbital period of the star's motion. The advantage of this *astrometric* technique is that it allows us to find the mass of the planet because the star's motion is detectable in two dimensions.

- *Binary systems and Doppler wobble.* Another method for detecting the wobble of a star due to the presence of planets around it involves measuring the Doppler shift of the star's spectrum as it alternately wobbles toward and away from the Earth (Figure 7-16b). Such shifts are tiny because the star's motion is very slow in its orbit: For example, Jupiter causes the Sun's speed to vary with an amplitude of 12.5 m/s (or 28 miles/hour); Saturn's effect is the next largest, with an amplitude of 2.7 m/s (or 6 miles/hour). The current precision achieved by researchers using this radial-velocity technique is 1 m/s, allowing them to find Jupiter-like (but not yet Earth-like) planets orbiting Sun-like stars. The wobble motion of a star can provide a wealth of information about its planetary companion, such as its

astrometry The branch of astronomy that deals with the measurement of the position and motion of celestial objects.

mass, distance, and orbital period. This method has proven to be very success-ful. In 1995, astronomers used this method to discover the first planet orbiting a normal, Sun-like star, 51 Pegasi. Since then, many groups of researchers have discovered several exoplanets. As of early 2009, about 285 stars have been dis-covered to have planet-like objects (including some stars with orbiting brown dwarfs), and for some of them we detected multiple planets (for a total of about 335). The majority of the exoplanets known so far have been discovered using the Doppler method; the current precision limitations of this method result in a bias toward finding massive, Jupiter-like planets at close distances from their stars. Also, many of these planets have large eccentricities. This is very unlike the planetary orbits in our solar system. The first two Saturn-sized planets were dis-covered in March 2000, suggesting that as time goes on we should be able to de-tect even smaller planets; this discovery supports our current theory that planets form in a disk of dust and gas by a snowball effect of growth.

Even though this radial-velocity (Doppler) method has proven to be very successful, precise measurements require a large number of spectral lines; be-cause the hottest stars have far fewer spectral features than cooler Sun-like stars, this method cannot be used for the hottest stars. It also does not allow us to find the exact mass of the planet but only a lower limit to it, because the angle at which we observe its orbit is unknown. Finally, finding Earth-like planets in Earth-like orbits with this method is beyond our current capabilities.

- *Stellar occultation*. When one celestial object passes in front of another, we say that an **occultation** occurs. In late 1999 astronomers observed the dimming of star HD209458, caused by its planet passing in front of it (such a passage is called a *transit*). This confirmed the earlier discovery, made using the Doppler method, that this star has a Jupiter-size planet. The star's intensity dims by only 1.5% dur-ing occultation. This method is very useful in confirming previously discovered planets. An advantage of this method is that it is not sensitive to the planet's mass; we are looking for the amount of starlight the planet obscures and not the planet's gravitational pull on its star (Figure 7-16c). It is clear that this method can be used only in cases where the Earth lies in or near the orbital plane of an exoplanet; however, this method is very efficient because within the field of view of a telescope there are thousands of stars that can be surveyed. In January 2003, astronomers announced the first detection using the transit method of a Jupiter-sized planet (OGLE-TR-56b) orbiting a *normal* star about 5000 light-years away, in the Sagittarius arm of our Galaxy.

    NASA's *Kepler Mission*, launched in 2009, uses a space-borne telescope to search for Earth-like (or even smaller) exoplanets using the transit method. Because a planet transits its star in a periodic fashion, all transits produced by the same planet last the same amount of time (the orbital period) and result in the same drop in the star's brightness; from such observations we can deter-mine the size of the orbit and the size of the planet. From the orbital size and the star's temperature (which can be found from spectroscopy), we can calculate the planet's characteristic temperature and thus find out if the planet is in principle habitable. The 0.95-meter diameter telescope has a 105-square degrees field of view and can continuously monitor the brightnesses of more than 100,000 stars at the same time. ESA's *Corot* satellite, a 0.3-m telescope launched in 2006, uses the transit method to detect rocky exoplanets, several times larger than Earth. While looking at a star, *Corot* is able to detect "starquakes," allowing astronomers to find the star's mass, age, and chemical composition.

- *Gravitational* **microlensing**. When a massive object passes between the observer and a distant source of light (say a star), the gravity of the object will bend the light according to the general theory of relativity. The massive object plays the role of a lens, causing the source to appear to slowly brighten to a few times its usual intensity over a period of time. For the case of a star and its planet(s), their individual gravitational fields act as a lens magnifying the light of a distant back-

occultation The passing of one astronomical ob-ject in front of another. The passage of a planet in front of its star is called a *transit*.

The star's intensity dims by 15% when observed at a specific UV transition of atomic hydrogen. This sug-gests that a hydrogen atmosphere envelops the planet extending beyond its gravitational reach; thus, some of the hydrogen atoms are escaping.

microlensing The effect of a temporary brighten-ing of the light from a distant star orbited by an object such as a planet. Light rays from the star bend when they pass through the planet's gravity, which acts as a lens.

ground star (Figure 7-16d). This method can only be used when the star and its planet(s) pass almost directly between the observer and the background star. Both stars and Earth are moving relative to each other during the microlensing event, which lasts for a few days or weeks. Even though these events cannot be repeated, this method can be used to find how common Earth-like planets are in our Galaxy because it allows for such planets to be discovered with available technology. In early 2006, astronomers discovered a small, icy planet with a mass only five times that of Earth using this technique.

All of the methods described previously are currently used from the ground, and they are increasingly used from space. Astronomers are also exploring additional methods. For example, spectroscopy can be used to detect elements expected to be present in the atmospheres of planets such as water vapor and sodium. Indeed, using the *HST*, astronomers detected atomic sodium in the atmosphere of HD209458b; also, using the *Spitzer Space Telescope*, and analyzing the transit of the gas giant HD189733b across its star, astronomers discovered the presence of water vapor in the planet's atmosphere. Spectra also show the presence of molecules of methyl formate (a product of alcohol and formaldehyde, commonly used as an insecticide) in the dust clouds in our Galaxy; the average ratio between such molecules to hydrogen molecules is about 1 to a billion, but a typical dust cloud would still contain about 10^{27} gallons of the chemical condensed into liquid form. We do not yet know what role this and other molecules play in the formation of stars and planets. The *Spitzer Space Telescope* has detected significant amounts of icy dusty particles coated with carbon dioxide, water, and methanol, in the dusty disks around young stars in the constellation Taurus. Such materials may be the building blocks for comets. Finally, organic gases such as acetylene and hydrogen cyanide were detected in the disk around the young star IRS46. In the presence of water, these gases form amino acids and adenine, one of the four chemical bases of DNA. Such gases are found in our solar system, on comets, and in the atmospheres of the Jovian planets and Saturn's moon Titan.

The Formation of Planetary Systems

In Section 7-6 we discussed the *core-accretion model* of planetary formation: Planets start as small chunks of rock, dust, and debris and grow through a series of collisions among planetesimals and accretion of dust and gas from the disk. In this model, Jupiter-like planets form if their rocky core is more massive than a few Earth masses, but it takes tens of millions of years for such cores to grow. This contradicts the observed lifetimes of the accretion disks, which tend to evaporate as a result of the stellar wind or influences from nearby stars in only a few millions of years. A substantial gas reservoir is needed to complete the formation of a Jupiter-like planet, whereas Earth-like planets can continue growing in a gas-free environment.

Observations suggest that for Sun-like stars, planetary formation peaks between 1 and 3 million years after the process starts. Infrared and radio data show that planet-forming disks around stars older than about 10 million years are very rare. (It is possible, however, for some stars to have massive dust clouds around them up to hundreds of million of years after they are formed; such clouds have been observed using the *Spitzer Space Telescope* and can form from collisions between young, terrestrial-like planets.)

According to a competing model, the *disk-instability model*, dense regions forming in the disk accrete more material and suddenly collapse to form one or more planets. In this model, giant planets can form in only a few hundreds of years; however, such instabilities require massive disks (more than 10% of the star's mass), which are not commonly observed.

Many Jupiter-sized exoplanets are observed very close to their parent star. The high temperatures and lack of raw materials at these distances make it unlikely that these planets formed at their current locations. It is possible that planets form at large distances from their star but migrate inward. Because a newly formed planet separates the dust disk around the star into two regions, the protoplanet and the disk's inner region will lose energy and angular momentum to the outer region of the disk. As a result, the protoplanet will migrate inward toward the star. The protoplanet may finally reach a stable orbit close to the star as a result of tidal interactions with it or because the inner disk region is cleared out by the star's magnetic field or if the protoplanet manages to accrete the material in the outer disk before it gets destroyed by the star. (In our solar system, the migration of Jupiter lasted a very short time, which allowed Earth to remain in its orbit; as we discuss in Chapter 10, our solar system formed in a cluster of stars that did not allow for a massive accretion disk.) Numerical simulations of planetary migrations show that in most cases protoplanets are trapped into a series of resonances and migrate inward together in less than a million years; this suggests that understanding how giant planets form is still a major challenge.

The mass of a red dwarf ranges from about 8% to 60% of the Sun's mass. At least 70% of the stars in our Galaxy are red dwarfs.

Observations suggest that the size of the largest planet formed around a star is directly related to the size of the star. That is, super-Earths form in the disks around small, red dwarf stars, Jupiter-like planets form in the disks of Sun-like stars, whereas brown dwarfs may form in the disks of bigger stars. For example, low-mass stars tend to have less massive disks, resulting in smaller amounts of raw material to form planets; in addition, planets form gradually in such disks, allowing the gas in the disk to dissipate before large planets form. Spectroscopic surveys also suggest that there is an almost linear relationship between the likelihood that a planetary system will form around a star and the star's abundance of heavy elements such as iron, nickel, titanium, silicon, and sodium. Because a star will have the same chemical composition as its surrounding disk of gas and dust, such surveys support the idea that heavier elements coalesce easier, allowing the formation of planetesimals and therefore planetary systems.

Theoretical calculations suggest that it is easier to form small, cold planets than larger ones around low mass stars. Because about two thirds of the stars in our Galaxy are small, red dwarf stars, it is likely that planetary systems with super-Earths are three times as common as systems with Jupiter-like planets.

Current observational data coupled with theoretical work suggest that at least 25% of Sun-like stars have planetary systems; this means that just in our Galaxy there are tens of billions of stars with planetary systems. This does not guarantee, however, that these planetary systems are as stable as our own solar system; planet–planet interactions during the early stages of formation may result in highly eccentric orbits for the planets, as is the case of many of the exoplanets observed so far.

It is possible that the mechanism that formed some of these planets is different from that which operated in our solar system and that some of these objects are actually brown dwarfs that follow a different evolutionary path.

The properties of the exoplanets found so far have defied expectations and are forcing us to reexamine our ideas of how planets form. Infrared observations of the Orion Nebula suggest that what we once thought to be an obstacle in forming a planet, namely ultraviolet radiation from a nearby star, may actually promote the formation of planets; such radiation can remove the gas from a disk, allowing large dust grains to grow and slowly form planetesimals. Our own solar system was formed in an Orion-like environment, as we learned from the study of primitive materials in meteorites. Theoretical work suggests that planetary systems can form around binary stars in much the same way that they form around single stars like our Sun. Finally, computer simulations suggest that we need to consider not only the role of collisions between embryonic planets but also the role of close encounters between them; tidal interactions between such objects can have dramatic effects, such as melting, stripping material away, decompressing, and of course annihilating the smaller object.

It is too early for us to draw any conclusions based on the newly discovered exoplanets. After all, the recent discoveries seem to suggest two contradictory ideas. On one hand, we now know that planets are more plentiful than we once thought, and therefore, it is more likely that Earth-like planets exist where life could develop. On the other hand, life on Earth could be unique, as all planetary systems discovered so far are not suitable for life. We do not yet have the ability to detect Earth-like objects, and the few discovered objects may be exceptions to the general rules of planetary formation. There is no doubt that in the next few decades we will discover many more exoplanets as our telescopes and instruments allow us to make even more precise observations; for example, using adaptive optics at the Gemini Observatory, astronomers were able in 2008 to *directly* image a family of planets around a normal star outside our solar system (FIGURE 7-17). A planned space-borne interferometer (such as ESA's *Darwin* mission) might be able to detect other Earths as early as the next decade, and it should be able to use spectroscopy to determine the chemical composition of their atmospheres or surfaces, looking for any signatures of life on them. Already in 2007, astronomers combined observations and theoretical models of the habitable zone around the dwarf star Gliese 581 (20 light-years away) and discovered that one of the three confirmed planets around the star lies in the star's habitability zone, making this super-Earth the first candidate for a habitable planet.

During the 4th century BC, Aristotle argued in favor of the uniqueness of our planet, as it was at the center of the universe. Another great philosopher at the time, Epicurus, argued that the universe must be infinite and therefore must contain an infinite number of other worlds. For about 2400 years we have been trying to answer the question of whether our solar system is truly unique. We are getting very close.

FIGURE 7-17 Shown in this image are two of the three planets orbiting the young star HR8799 (1.5 solar masses, 130 ly from Earth, with a massive disk of cold dust). They are at 40 and 70 AU from the star and have masses of 7 and 10 times that of Jupiter, respectively. The third planet is at 25 AU from the star, which has been blocked in order to increase the planets' visibility.

In Chapter 13, we study how the material in interstellar space forms stars and planetary systems.

The European Space Agency has two planet-search missions in development. *Gaia* (December 2011) is an astronomy mission that will conduct a survey of a billion stars in our Galaxy. *Darwin* (2015) is a flotilla of eight spacecraft that will use interferometry to survey 1000 of the closest stars looking for the most likely places for life to develop.

Conclusion

In this chapter, we showed that our solar system contains a myriad of objects, vastly different from one another. Similarities are also present, however, and enable the planets to be divided into two categories: terrestrial and Jovian.

One of the most important topics discussed during our overview of the solar system was how we measure some of the properties of the objects circling the Sun, including distances between them, their sizes, and their masses.

The patterns we observe in the solar system, along with what we know about the formation of stars, allow us to put together a reasonably detailed story of the origin of the solar system. Although many questions remain, observations of newly forming stars are confirming our theories of the development of our system. Recent observations of exoplanets lend support to an evolutionary development of planetary systems, while bringing forward many new questions about the process.

The reasoning is as follows. If catastrophic processes are necessary for the formation of planetary systems, relatively few such systems would be expected, as the special circumstances needed are, by their nature, rare. On the other hand, if stars form by the process described by evolutionary theories, we would expect planetary systems to be common. Although the formation of planetary systems by catastrophic events is unlikely, this in itself is not an argument against such a scenario in the case of the solar system. If there is any possibility at all that a catastrophic event can cause a planetary system, it could well have happened here; however, there is now clear evidence that evolutionary development of planetary systems is common, and it lends support for hypotheses that postulate that this is what occurred in our own system.

In the next three chapters we examine each of the planets in more detail and look at the lesser objects within the solar system—comets, meteoroids, and asteroids.

In some worlds there is no Sun and Moon, in others they are larger than in our world, and in others more numerous. In some parts there are more worlds, in others fewer...; in some parts they are arising, in others failing. There are some worlds devoid of living creatures or plants or moisture.

Democritus (~460–370 BC)

STUDY GUIDE

1. Which planet is most massive?
   A. Mercury.
   B. Mars.
   C. Earth.
   D. Jupiter.
   E. Saturn.

2. The object whose orbit is more eccentric than Mercury's is
   A. Saturn.
   B. Earth.
   C. Pluto.
   D. Venus.
   E. Neptune.

3. Whether a planet or moon has an atmosphere depends on the planet's (or moon's)
   A. orbital speed.
   B. temperature.
   C. escape velocity.
   D. [Both A and C above.]
   E. [Both B and C above.]

4. Which planet has its equatorial plane tilted most with respect to its plane of revolution?
   A. Uranus.
   B. Earth.
   C. Venus.
   D. Mars.
   E. Mercury.

5. Venus might be called Earth's sister planet because it is similar to the Earth in
   A. size.
   B. mass.
   C. rotation period.
   D. [Both A and B above.]
   E. [Both A and C above.]

6. Saturn is one of the _____ planets.
   A. Jovian
   B. inner
   C. inferior
   D. minor

7. Which of the following statements is true of all of the planets?
   A. They rotate on their axes and revolve around the Sun.
   B. They rotate in the same direction.
   C. They have at least one moon.
   D. Their axes point toward Polaris.
   E. [More than one of the above is true of all of the planets.]

8. Saturn's density is
   A. less than that of Jupiter.
   B. more than that of Jupiter.
   C. similar to the Earth's.
   D. greater than that of Earth.
   E. [Two of the above.]

9. Which of the following choices lists the four planets from smallest (in radius) to largest?
   A. Mars, Mercury, Earth, Uranus
   B. Mercury, Uranus, Mars, Earth
   C. Uranus, Mercury, Mars, Earth
   D. Mercury, Mars, Earth, Uranus
   E. [None of the above.]

10. Compared to Jovian planets, terrestrial planets have a
    A. more rocky composition.
    B. lower density.
    C. more rapid rotation.
    D. larger size.
    E. [More than one of the above.]

11. Which of the following statements is true of Jovian planets?
    A. They have low average densities compared to terrestrial planets.
    B. Their orbits are closer to the Sun than the asteroids' orbits.
    C. They have craters in old surfaces.
    D. They have smaller diameters than terrestrial planets do.
    E. They have fewer satellites than terrestrial planets do.

12. Most asteroids orbit the Sun
    A. between Earth and Mars.
    B. between Mars and Jupiter.
    C. between Jupiter and Saturn.
    D. beyond the orbit of Saturn.
    E. [None of the above. No general statement can be made.]

13. Distances to the planets are measured today by the use of
    A. geometry.
    B. calculus.
    C. spacecraft flybys.
    D. analysis of the motion of their moons.
    E. radar.

14. The mass of Jupiter was first calculated
    A. using its distance from the Sun and its revolution period.
    B. using its angular size and distance from the Earth.
    C. using data from spacecraft flybys.
    D. by analysis of the motion of its moons.
    E. [Two of the above.]

15. Which is a longer time on Earth?
    A. A sidereal day.
    B. A solar day.
    C. [Either of the above, depending on the time of year.]
    D. [Neither of the above, for they are the same.]

16. At a greater distance from the surface of a planet, the escape velocity from that planet
    A. becomes less.
    B. remains the same.
    C. becomes greater.
    D. [Neither of the above, for the behavior of different planets is different in this regard.]

17. At the same temperature, the average speed of hydrogen molecules is _____ that of oxygen molecules.
    A. less than
    B. the same as

C.   greater than

D.   [No general statement can be made.]

18. The escape velocity from the top of Earth's atmosphere is _____ the escape velocity from the surface of the Moon.

A.   less than

B.   the same as

C.   greater than

D.   [No general statement can be made, for the escape velocity depends upon temperature.]

19. Which planet (of those listed) gets closest in distance to the Earth?

A.   Jupiter.

B.   Mercury.

C.   Venus.

D.   Saturn.

E.   Mars.

20. If planetary systems are caused as proposed by the catastrophe theories, there should be

A.   many planetary systems besides ours.

B.   few planetary systems besides ours.

C.   [Neither of these; the theories would make no predictions in this regard.]

21. Evolutionary theories now account for the slow rotation rate of the Sun by pointing to

A.   the interaction between its magnetic field and charged particles in the inner solar system.

B.   friction within the gases involved, which would prevent the Sun from rotating fast.

C.   the effect of the inner planets on the Sun.

D.   the effect of the large planets—particularly Jupiter—on the Sun.

E.   the conservation of angular momentum, which predicts a slowly rotating Sun when it formed.

22. Which of the following observations cannot be accounted for by evolutionary theories of solar system formation?

A.   All of the planets revolve around the Sun in the same direction that it rotates.

B.   All of the planets revolve in nearly the same plane.

C.   Planets farther from the Sun are farther apart.

D.   The outer planets contain more volatile elements than the inner planets do.

E.   [All of the above are accounted for by evolutionary theories.]

23. After the evolutionary theory of the formation of the solar system was proposed, it was almost dismissed because it seemingly could not explain

A.   planetary masses.

B.   planetary distances from the Sun.

C.   the existence of comets.

D.   why some planets—particularly Jupiter—have a strong magnetic field.

E.   the observed rotation rate of the Sun.

24. According to the evolutionary theories of solar system formation, the outer planets contain much more hydrogen and helium than the inner planets because these elements

A.   never fell in near the Sun.

B.   condensed quickly to liquids and solids and remained far from the Sun.

C.   were blown away from the inner solar system by the solar wind.

D.   [Both A and B above.]

E.   [All of the above.]

25. Astronomers are now reasonably confident that the planets of the solar system

A.   formed when a comet pulled material from the Sun.

B.   formed when another star passed very close to the Sun.

C.   evolved from a rotating disk when the Sun was forming.

D.   [None of the above. There is currently no satisfactory explanation for the origin of the planets.]

26. In a previous chapter, we saw that Kepler's third law relates a planet's period to its distance from the Sun. This law was expanded by Isaac Newton to include what other quantity?

27. How does the Sun's mass compare with the total mass of all other objects in the solar system?

28. What is the largest planet, and how does it compare in size and mass with the Earth?

29. What was the first celestial object discovered after Bode's law was proposed? Did it fit predictions made by the law? (Hint: See the Advancing the Model box on page 190.)

30. How do we know the masses of the planets?

31. Distinguish between a sidereal day and a solar day. Which is longer on Earth?

32. The planets' directions of rotation and revolution have certain features in common. Describe these features. Which planets have an unusual direction of rotation?

33. Name the terrestrial planets and the Jovian planets. Why are the latter called Jovian?

34. In what ways are the terrestrial planets similar to one another but different from the Jovians?

35. How does the eccentricity of the Earth's orbit compare with that of other planets?

36. How does the Earth compare with the other planets in density?

37. What is meant when we say that the escape velocity from the Earth is 11 kilometers per second?

38. What two factors determine the speed of the molecules of a gas?

39. Explain why hydrogen escapes from the Earth's atmosphere but carbon dioxide does not.

40. How do evolutionary theories explain the pattern of chemical abundance among the planets?

41. We now have definite evidence that planetary systems exist around other stars. Does this lend support to either the catastrophe or evolutionary theories? If so, which?

42. How do evolutionary theories account for asteroids? The Oort cloud?

43. Describe the evidence that planetary systems exist around other stars.

1. Copernicus did not know the distance from the Earth to the Sun. Yet the text states that he calculated the relative distances to the planets. Explain.

2. How do we measure the distances to the planets today?

3. Is density the same thing as "hardness"? (What additional information is gained by calculating an object's density compared to simply stating its mass?)

4. Name the planet in our solar system that
   A. has the most eccentric orbit.
   B. has the greatest diameter.
   C. has the least density.
   D. has the most mass.
   E. has the most moons.
   F. has the least atmosphere.

5. If a planet rotates slowly in a retrograde direction (clockwise as seen from above the Sun's north pole), which will be longer, its sidereal day or its solar day? Explain.

6. Is the escape velocity from Earth the same whether we are considering a point just above the atmosphere or a point higher up? Explain.

7. How do evolutionary theories explain observations 1, 2, and 4 as listed in the section "Evidential Clues from the Data"? How do catastrophe theories explain these observations?

8. Explain the problem the law of conservation of angular momentum presents for evolutionary theories and describe how today's theory accounts for the observations.

9. Explain in your own words why there is a pattern of changes in the composition of planets as we move from those close to the Sun to those far away.

10. What techniques are used to detect planets that orbit other stars? Name some limitations to these techniques.

11. If we wish to find planets near other stars, why not just use telescopes to look for the planets directly?

1. The eccentricity of Pluto's orbit is 0.24. Use a drawing of an ellipse to explain what this means quantitatively.

2. If another planet were found beyond Pluto, how far would Bode's law predict it to be from the Sun (assuming it is the next planet in his scheme).

3. At a time when Jupiter is 9.0×10^8 kilometers from Earth, its angular size is 33 seconds of arc. Use these data to calculate the diameter of Jupiter, and then check your answer in Appendix C.

4. Suppose that we bounce a radar signal off of Jupiter. It returns to Earth 100 minutes after being sent. How far away is Jupiter at the time of the measurement?

5. The escape speed of an object from a planet or star of mass m and radius R is proportional to $\sqrt{m/R}$. The escape speed from Earth's surface is about 11 kilometers/second. Using data from Appendices B and C, find the escape speed from the Sun's surface and compare your result with that given in Appendix B.

6. Phobos is a small satellite orbiting Mars. The average distance between the two objects (from center to center) is about 9400 kilometers and the orbital period is 0.319 days (see Appendix D). What is the mass of Mars? What assumption did you make to get this answer? As Mars' radius is 3400 kilometers, what is its average density? What can you say about its chemical composition?

1. "Other Suns, Other Planets?" by D. C. Black, in Sky & Telescope (August, 1996).

2. "Searching for Life on Other Planets," by J. R. P. Angel and N. J. Woolf, in Scientific American (April, 1996).

3. "The Diversity of Planetary Systems," by G. Marcy and R. P. Butler, in Sky & Telescope (March, 1998).

4. "The Formation of the Earth from Planetesimals," by G. W. Wetherill, in Scientific American (June, 1981).

5. Peter Ward and Donald Brownlee, Rare Earth: Why Complex Life Is Uncommon in the Universe (Copernicus Books, 2000).

6. "Bonuses of the Microlensing Business," by M. Mateo, in Sky & Telescope (September 1997).

7. "The Hidden Members of Planetary Systems," by D. R. Ardila, in Scientific American (April 2004).

8. "The Genesis of Planets," by D. N. C. Lin, in Scientific American (May 2008).

9. "Improbable Planets," by M. W. Werner and M. A. Jura, in Scientific American (June 2009).

10. "The Planetary Air Leak," by D. C. Catling and K. J. Zahnle, in Scientific American (May 2009).

Quest Ahead to Starlinks
http://physicalscience.jbpub.com/starlinks

Starlinks is this book's online learning center. It features **eLearning**, which contains chapter quizzes and other tools designed to help you study for your class. You can also find **online exercises**, view numerous relevant **animations**, follow a guide to **useful astronomy sites** on the Web, or even check the latest **astronomy news** updates.

The Terrestrial Planets

8

THE MARS *PATHFINDER* MISSION TOOK OFF FROM EARTH on December 4, 1996, and landed on Mars July 4, 1997. Cameras on the lander took pictures of the Martian landscape for almost 3 months, until contact was lost. The photos showed a bone-dry landscape that might once have been a flood plain, though when floods of water existed on Mars is still not known, but the star of the *Pathfinder* show was its robot rover, named *Sojourner.*

Sojourner rolled down a ramp from *Pathfinder* and started crawling around the Martian surface at a rate of 2 feet/minute, guided by cameras and laser range-finders. At a size of 2 feet long and 1 foot wide, *Sojourner* looked like a child's remote-control car, bumping along from rock to rock (see Figure 8-24). *Pathfinder* sent back pictures of *Sojourner* that headlined newspapers and television broadcasts around the world. NASA engineers made up whimsical names for each rock that *Sojourner* stopped to study, including Barnacle Bill, Yogi, and Scooby Doo. When *Sojourner* bumped into the rock called Yogi, headlines reported the first "fender bender" on Mars. Weather reports noted morning temperatures on Mars of −76°F (−60°C), with a forecast of 10°F (−12°C) for an afternoon high.

The X-ray analysis of rocks and soil completed by *Sojourner* supported theories of geological convulsions through much of Mars' history. It's no accident that the largest volcano and the largest canyon known in the solar system are both on Mars. Yet the

This color composite image of Mars was taken by the *HST* on August 27, 2003, when Mars was at its closest distance to Earth in about 60,000 years. It reveals the southern polar ice cap, the largest volcano in the solar system (Olympus Mons, the oval-shaped feature above center), and a system of canyons (Valles Marineris, right of center). When this image was taken, Mars' Northern (Southern) hemisphere was in the midst of winter (summer). Clouds cover the region around the northern polar cap, while the orange streaks show dust activity above the southern polar cap.

All cross references to chapters, sections, figures, and tables pertain to the main text, *In Quest of the Universe, Sixth Edition. In Quest of the Solar System* contains Chapters 1–11 and 19 of the main text. *In Quest of the Stars and Galaxies* contains Chapters 1–5 and 11–19 of the main text.

rocks also appeared to be more like those of Earth than are the lunar rocks brought back by the *Apollo* missions. Geologists reported that the landing site was a true "rock festival," but not really a nice place to visit.

Our trip to the planets begins with the planet closest to the Sun and then proceeds outward. As we discuss each planet in turn, you should compare that planet with Earth and with planets previously discussed. Concentrate on remembering patterns and comparisons between planets rather than memorizing numerical facts.

8-1   Mercury

Mercury as Seen from Earth

In legend, Mercury was the god of commerce and travel, the Roman counterpart of the Greek god Hermes, the messenger of the gods. It is for this speedster that the fastest planet of the solar system is named.

Although Mercury was one of the planets known to the ancients, it is the planet least seen by people on Earth without a telescope. Because it is so close to the Sun, it can be seen with the naked eye only either shortly after sunset in the western sky or shortly before sunrise in the eastern sky (FIGURE 8-1).

Looking at Mercury through a telescope, we are able to see that it exhibits phases like Venus and the Moon. Surface detail is difficult to discern, however, primarily because when Mercury is near the horizon, its light is passing through so much of the Earth's atmosphere (FIGURE 8-2). The best telescopic views of Mercury actually are made when it is high overhead during the day; however, even then, surface features are not well defined, and the telescope shows only that Mercury's surface contains bright and dark areas. Details of Mercury's surface features were not seen clearly until the planet was visited by space probes.

Mercury—Comparison with the Moon

Mariner 10's mission to, and flybys of Mercury in the early 1970s provided us with more than 4000 photographs. However, achieving an orbit around Mercury required advances in engineering and design that finally made feasible the *MESSENGER* mission. After three flybys of Mercury (two in 2008 and one in 2009), the spacecraft will begin orbiting the planet in 2011.

FIGURE 8-3 is a mosaic of *Mariner's* views of Mercury. Notice its similarity to our Moon; both are covered with impact craters produced by debris from space. We find, however, that the walls of the craters of Mercury are less steep than those of the Moon so that Mercury's craters are less prominent than the Moon's (FIGURE 8-4). This was expected because Mercury's surface gravity is about twice that of the Moon and loose material does not stack as steeply under the greater gravitational force. We also find that ray patterns of material ejected from craters are less extensive on Mercury than on the Moon. When craters were formed by meteorite impacts, the greater

(a)   (b)

FIGURE 8-1 (a) Mercury can only be seen from Earth either shortly before sunrise (shown) or shortly after sunset. Mercury's maximum elongation (its maximum angle from the Sun) is about 28 degrees. (b) Possible positions of Mercury and Venus in the evening relative to the horizon. Mercury never appears in a really dark sky.

FIGURE 8-2 Light from an object near the horizon must pass through more atmosphere than light from an overhead object. The dot on the Earth's surface is the location of the observer. The thickness of Earth's atmosphere is not to scale.

FIGURE 8-3 A mosaic of photos of Mercury taken by *Mariner 10*.

FIGURE 8-4 Craters on the Moon have steeper walls than those on Mercury, and because of the greater surface gravity on Mercury, material ejected from the crater does not travel as far.

gravitational force on the surface of Mercury kept the material from being thrown as far from the craters.

Mercury lacks the large maria we see on the Moon. Instead, Mercury's craters are fairly evenly spread across the surface, separated by smooth plains. This difference between the two surfaces is related to differences in the rate at which the objects cooled after formation. As we discussed in Chapter 7, the terrestrial planets and the Moon began as balls of molten rock. As they cooled, a solid crust formed on their surfaces. Debris falling from space struck the crust with enough energy to penetrate it and let lava flow up through the break. The results of these lava flows are obvious on the Moon, where large maria were formed from the lava that welled up from beneath the surface.

A larger object cools more slowly than a small one, however, and thus, Mercury's crust formed more slowly than the Moon's. To understand this, consider the amount of energy included in the volume of a cooling object. This energy is released into space through the object's surface. The larger the surface area, the easier it is for the object to release energy into space and cool down; however, the larger the volume of the object, the more energy it has to release. In other words, the time it takes for an object to cool is directly related to the ratio of the object's volume to its surface area. For a spherical object, this ratio is simply proportional ($\propto$) to the object's radius:

$$\text{time to cool} \propto \frac{\text{volume}}{\text{surface area}} = \frac{(4\pi/3) \cdot R^3}{4\pi \cdot R^2} \propto R.$$

EXAMPLE

The radius of Mercury is 1.4 times the radius of the Moon. Considering only this difference between the two objects, which would take longer to cool and what would be the ratio of their cooling times?

SOLUTION

The previous equation tells us that the cooling time of a sphere depends directly on its radius. Because Mercury is larger, it will take longer to cool. In fact, its radius is 1.4 times as great, and thus, its cooling time will be 1.4 times as long.

TRY ONE YOURSELF

Jupiter and Earth were both hot when they were formed, but although Earth has cooled as much as it will, Jupiter is still cooling. Considering only their sizes (included in Appendix C), what would be the ratio of their cooling times?

FIGURE 8-5 (a) A long scarp in this *MESSENGER* image extends from the upper left to the lower right. Scarps are much more extensive on Mercury than on the Moon. Some are hundreds of kilometers in length and up to 3 kilometers high. (b) It is estimated that Mercury's radius decreased by about 1 kilometer after its crust hardened, causing the cliffs to be formed along fault lines.

(a)

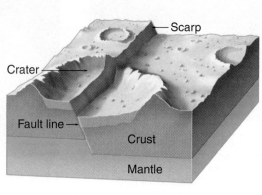

(b)

Because Mercury is so close to the Sun, is its surface completely molten?

scarp Transition zone from one series of sedimentary rocks to another of a different age and composition. They are found on Mercury, Earth, Mars, and the Moon.

FIGURE 8-6 The center of the Caloris Basin lies just out of the photo toward the left. Notice the ring pattern that was formed by the impact of a large object (now buried under the surface). The basin is about 1550 kilometers (960 miles) in diameter, the size of Texas. The diameter of Mare Orientale on the Moon is only about 1000 km (620 miles).

The Latin word *calor* means *heat*. A unit for measuring heat is the *calorie*.

The larger the object is, the longer it takes for the object to cool. As a result, Mercury's crust formed more slowly than the Moon's. For a long time after the crust started forming, meteoritic debris was still able to penetrate it, allowing lava to flow out and obliterate older craters. This resulted in the smooth plains we see between the evenly spread craters.

Another difference between Mercury's surface and the Moon's is the great number of long *scarps* (involving high and long cliffs) that are found on Mercury (FIGURE 8-5). These are found at many locations around the planet and suggest that after its crust hardened during its formation, Mercury shrank a little, causing the cliffs to be formed.

Mariner photographs revealed a large impact crater, named the Caloris Basin, on Mercury's surface (FIGURE 8-6). It consists of several rings somewhat like those of Mare Orientale on the Moon (Figure B6-2), although the Mercurian feature is larger. Both "bull's eyes" were caused by large objects striking the surfaces; the impacts resulted in shock waves that caused the rings of cliffs. On the opposite side of Mercury from Caloris Basin is a jumbled, wavy area, strange enough that it has been dubbed "weird terrain." This was probably the outcome of the shock wave that was sent around the planet as a result of the Caloris Basin impact. When the waves met on the other side of the planet, they caused a permanent disruption of the surface there. We see another consequence of the Caloris Basin impact when we discuss Mercury's motions.

Data from *Mariner* confirmed that Mercury has negligible atmosphere, as was expected considering the escape velocity from Mercury's surface and the high daytime temperatures caused by its proximity to the Sun. The thin atmosphere (composed mostly of oxygen) is created by the ejection of atoms from the planet's surface, a process that also occurs on our Moon. Refer to Figure 7-8 and notice that although the escape velocity from the surface of Mercury is greater than from the Moon, Mercury's temperature is higher; therefore, we would expect none of the gases shown to be found on Mercury.

Structural Characteristics

Mercury is the smallest of the eight planets. In fact, there are two natural satellites in the solar system that are larger than tiny Mercury (FIGURE 8-7). With a diameter of about 4880 km, Mercury's total surface area is only slightly greater than that of the Atlantic Ocean.

The mass of Mercury, accurately determined from its gravitational pull on the *Mariner 10* probe, is only 0.055 of the mass of the Earth. Its average density is 5.43 times the density of water, slightly less than the Earth's 5.52.

The density of an astronomical object is determined not only by the material of which it is composed, but also by how much that material is compressed by the gravitational field of the object. For example, an object on the surface of Mercury feels less gravitational pull downward than it would on Earth. If Mercury were made up of the same elements as the Earth, matter below the surface thus would be less compressed by material above, and Mercury would have a density considerably less than the Earth's. The fact that Mercury's average density is only slightly less than Earth's means that Mercury has a higher concentration of heavy elements than the Earth does; however, evidence from *Mariner* indicates that the rocks on Mercury's surface are similar to Earth rocks, so this higher density material must be below the surface. The answer must be that Mercury has a very large core (composed of mostly iron with some nickel), one that accounts for as much as 65% to 70% of the planet's mass. In FIGURE 8-8 we show Mercury's theorized interior and compare it with Earth's. Astronomers speculate that early in Mercury's history a catastrophic collision with a large asteroid blasted away much of Mercury's rocky mantle, leaving behind a planet with a greater than normal percentage of iron.

Before the *Mariner 10* mission, Mercury was thought to have no magnetic field. To understand why, recall that the Earth's field is caused by the rotation of the planet and its liquid metallic core. The Earth's rotation period is about 24 hours, whereas Mercury's is about 59 days. As a result, Mercury's rotation rate was thought to be too slow to produce a magnetic field.

Mariner 10 did detect a global magnetic field on Mercury (confirmed by *MESSENGER*), although it is not very strong—about 1% as strong as the Earth's field. The field appears to be shaped like the Earth's, with magnetic poles nearly aligned with the planet's spin axis. The presence of the magnetic field has been a puzzle since it was detected in 1974. First, it led astronomers to hypothesize that Mercury's metallic core is molten, because

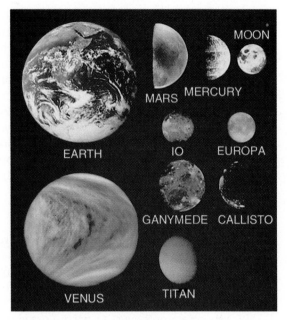

FIGURE 8-7 The diameter of Mercury compared with the mean diameters of some other solar system objects, including Jupiter's Galilean moons (Io, Europa, Ganymede, and Callisto) and Saturn's moon Titan. Mercury is about the size of Callisto but smaller than Ganymede and Titan.

4880 kilometers = 3033 miles.

FIGURE 8-8 Mercury's core occupies a greater portion of the planet's volume than does Earth's core. Mercury's core is about the size of the Moon.

dynamo effect The generation of magnetic fields due to circulating electric charges, such as in an electric generator.

the *dynamo effect* (see Section 6-3)—the predominant explanation for planets' magnetic fields—requires molten magnetic material within the planet. But measurements indicate that Mercury does not release more heat than it receives from the Sun. Therefore, the planet's interior must no longer retain heat from its formation, making it difficult to imagine a completely molten core. Many astronomers still think that some form of the dynamo effect is responsible for the magnetic field, but the question remains open. Since 2002, Earth-based radar measurements of Mercury's rotation have shown small variations in the planet's spin, which rule out a completely solid body and support the idea that the core is at least partially molten. This could be the result of impurities such as sulfur, which would lower the temperature at which the metal would solidify, or tidal interactions between Mercury and the Sun.

Mercury's Motions

◆ 48 km/s is about 107,000 miles/hour.

Being the closest planet to the Sun, Mercury circles the Sun in less time (about 88 days) than any other planet and moves faster in its orbit than any other (average speed: 48 km/s). Mercury's orbit is the most eccentric of the eight planets: Its distance from the Sun varies from 46 to 70 million kilometers. Careful observations made in the 19th century showed that Mercury's orbital path could not be exactly explained using Newton's laws. As we discussed in Section 3-9, Einstein's General Theory of Relativity correctly explains Mercury's motions.

◆ If Mercury's orbit were circular, with the Sun at the center, Mercury would keep the same face toward the Sun.

Because of Mercury's proximity to the Sun and its elongated orbit, it exhibits an interesting effect: One solar *day* on Mercury lasts 2 Mercurian *years*. To explain this, recall that because of tidal effects, the Moon keeps the same face toward the Earth. Astronomers once thought that Mercury likewise points the same face toward the Sun at all times; however, radar observations indicate that this is not the case. They show that Mercury rotates on its axis once every 58.65 Earth days, which is precisely two thirds of its orbital period of 87.97 days. This means that the planet rotates exactly 1.5 times for every time it goes around the Sun.

perihelion (aphelion) The point in its orbit when a planet (or other object) is closest to (farthest from) the Sun.

Why would this pattern occur? The answer is that Mercury is not perfectly balanced; one side is more massive than the other. Because of this, the Sun exerts a torque on the planet, especially when it is closest to the Sun (at *perihelion*). After countless revolutions, this has resulted in the rotational period of the planet being coupled with its orbital period. FIGURE 8-9 shows this situation; the light spot on Mercury's surface illustrates that opposite sides of the planet face the Sun at each perihelion passage. This spot could represent Caloris Basin because it falls directly under the Sun at every other perihelion position. This is unlikely to be a coincidence. Astronomers have hypothesized that the object that hit Mercury's surface and created the Caloris Basin must have been made of dense material and that the object remains under the planet's surface, causing Mercury to be lopsided and therefore to have its periods of rotation and revolution coupled as they are.

FIGURE 8-9 Mercury's rotation period is such that a point on its surface that is under the Sun at one perihelion position is opposite the Sun at the next. If Mercury's orbit were circular, however, the planet would always be facing the Sun just like the Moon always faces the Earth.

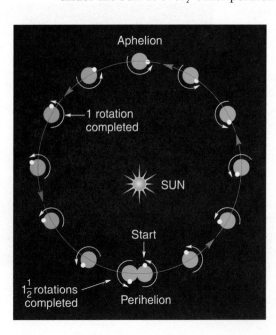

Mercury's solar day is far different from its sidereal day. Refer again to Figure 8-9 to see why. After two thirds of an orbit, Mercury has completed one rotation with respect to the distant stars, a sidereal day. However, Mercury does not complete one rotation with respect to the Sun, a solar day, until 176 Earth days have passed. A person standing at the light spot when the planet is at the position marked "start" would see the Sun at its highest point in the Mercurian sky. As time passes, the Sun would get lower, finally setting when the planet has completed half a revolution. When Mercury reaches "start" again, it is midnight for that person. It takes 88 days for Mercury to complete its orbit and that constitutes only half of a day for the person on the planet. A solar *day* on Mercury thus lasts 176 Earth days (or two Mercurian *years*) as mentioned earlier!

Imagine the Earth with almost no atmosphere to shield us from the Sun and with a daylight period lasting 88 of our days. This is the situation on Mercury. Daytime temperatures there reach as high as about 450°C (or 840°F). The element lead melts at about 330°C, and thus, lead would be molten at midday on Mercury.

On the other hand, the nighttime side of Mercury gets as cold as −180°C (or −300°F) as there is no atmosphere to hold in the heat during its long nights. Mercury's temperature variations are much greater than any other planet's.

Mercury's poles are thought to remain in constant cold because the planet's equator aligns almost exactly (within a few arcminutes) with its orbit. This means that Mercury has no seasons, as we define seasons on Earth. Therefore, even if the polar surface were perfectly smooth, only a very small amount of sunlight would strike it; however, the surface isn't smooth, and the bottoms of some craters never receive sunlight. There are indications that the surface temperature inside these polar craters hovers forever at around −180°C, about the same temperature reached by the nighttime side of the planet.

Radar results from Mercury show a very high **albedo** for the polar regions (**FIGURE 8-10**). The most plausible explanation for the reflections is that Mercury has ice at its poles; however, even cold ice should evaporate over the ages, and the question of why it still exists remains a mystery. *MESSENGER* and future missions to Mercury (such as ESA's *BepiColombo*) could provide us with more details about the origin, evolution, and general properties of this planet.

FIGURE 8-10 Radar reflections from Mercury show strong reflectivity from the planet's north pole. The reflections (using 3.5-centimeter wavelength radar) can be explained if ice exists at the pole.

albedo The fraction of incident light that an object reflects.

8-2 Venus

Venus is never seen farther than 46 degrees from the Sun and, like Mercury, it is visible only in the evening sky after sunset or in the morning sky before sunrise. Except for the Sun and Moon, however, Venus can be the brightest object in our sky. Seeing such a bright object above the horizon has fooled many people into thinking they were seeing something else. During World War II, pilots of fighter planes sometimes shot at Venus, thinking that it was an enemy plane. Today, reports of UFOs often increase when Venus is at its brightest in the sky.

Venus is such a beautiful sight that it is little wonder that the ancients named it after the goddess of beauty and love; however, we will see that as a possible home for a human colony, it is not such a beautiful planet after all.

Adjectives for Venus include "Venusian," "Venerian," and "Cytherean," the latter from the Greek island of Cytherea that was associated with the goddess Aphrodite.

Structural Characteristics

Historically, Venus has been known as the Earth's sister planet. It is similar to Earth in many ways: Its diameter is 95% of Earth's; its mass is 82% of Earth's, and of all the planets, its orbit is located closest to us. From the values for its diameter and mass, we can calculate that Venus has a density 5.24 times that of water—not much different from Earth's 5.52. It would have a slightly higher density if its material were compressed as much as Earth material. Soviet spacecraft that landed on Venus have shown that its surface rocks have about the same composition as Earth rocks, and we therefore conclude that to have a density as high as it does, Venus must have a very dense interior and is probably differentiated, with a metallic core.

No magnetic field has been detected on Venus, and based on the sensitivity of the instruments that have searched for it, if one does exist, its strength must be less than 1/10,000 of Earth's. Because of Venus' slow rotation (about 243 days), we would not

In some drawings of Venus' magnetic field, a shock structure and a magnetotail are shown around Venus. These features result from the interaction of the solar wind with Venus' upper atmosphere.

expect it to have a strong magnetic field; however, according to present theories for the origins of planetary magnetic fields, Venus' field should be strong enough for us to detect. Earth's field is known to have reversed its direction in the geologic past. Perhaps the magnetic field of Venus is now in the process of reversing, which would explain why it is so weak.

Venus' Motions

Venus orbits the Sun in a more nearly circular orbit than any other planet. Its period is about 225 days, resulting in a very nearly constant orbital speed of about 35 km/s.

The surface of Venus is covered by dense clouds, and thus, it is not visible from Earth; however, radar waves can penetrate Venus' cloud cover. Since 1961 we have been bouncing radar signals off its surface, and this is how we first learned about its rotation rate and its surface features.

The use of radar to study Venus told us that it rotates *backward* compared with the direction of rotation of most other objects in the solar system. That is, if we view the solar system from far above the Sun's North Pole, we see that all planets circle the Sun counterclockwise and that all the planets except Venus and Uranus rotate in this same direction. This backward rotation could be the result of a large collision early in the process of planetary formation. (Recall from Chapter 7 that as the original solar cloud collapsed to form the solar system, the directions of orbital motion and rotation for each planet are expected to be the same as the initial angular momentum of the solar cloud; however, a large collision, or a number of collisions during the accretion of planetesimals, or tidal effects, could affect the final direction of motion.) Venus' rotation is very slow, with a sidereal rotation period of 243 days. Its period of revolution around the Sun, however, is only 225 days. These rotation and revolution rates result in the solar day on Venus being about 117 Earth days.

Tables showing the tilt of Venus' equator relative to its orbital plane list an angle of 177°. Because a tilt of 180° would turn a planet completely over, wouldn't a tilt of 177° be the same as a 3° tilt? Not really. To show the difference, we first need to define what we mean by the north pole of a planet. After all, only the Earth has its axis oriented so that Polaris, the North Star, is nearly above its North Pole. To decide which pole of a planet is to be called north, imagine standing on the planet facing one of its poles. When we do this, if the rotation of the planet carries us around to our right, we are facing the north pole. The north pole of Venus, as defined in this manner, lies on the other side of the plane of the ecliptic from the Earth's North Pole. FIGURE 8-11 illustrates this difference. We, therefore, usually list the tilt of Venus' axis as 177° rather than 3°. The fact that the angle is greater than 90° tells us that Venus has a backward rotation compared with most objects in the solar system.

Another way to define the north pole of a planet is to imagine grabbing the planet with your right hand in a manner such that your fingers point in the direction of its rotation. Your thumb will then point to the north pole.

Through a telescope, Venus looks as smooth as a big white cue ball. No markings are visible. Images like the one in Figure 8-11 greatly exaggerate slight color variations.

FIGURE 8-11 An arrow on Earth's surface indicates its rotation. Venus' rotation arrow points in the same direction around its pole as does Earth's arrow (the "right-hand" rule).

The Surface of Venus

Since 1962, many spacecraft have visited Venus, none of them with humans aboard. From 1962 to 1975, three *Mariner* spacecraft from the

FIGURE 8-12 This photo of the surface of Venus was taken by *Venera 13*. The object at the bottom is part of the lander.

United States flew by the planet, obtaining data as they did so. The former Soviet Union landed 11 spacecraft on Venus, and some of them produced close-up photos of the surface (FIGURE 8-12). The photos indicate that the surface is rock strewn, at least at the landing sites. They showed that rocks in some locations are more weathered than in others, indicating that they have been on the surface for a longer period of time. The sharp-edged rocks were a surprise to scientists studying Venus until they realized that the wind is fairly calm at the surface. If there had been great winds at the surface, the dense atmosphere (see the next section) would have caused considerable dust movement and erosion of the rocks.

Venus' surface is not visible from above its atmosphere, but radio waves can penetrate the atmosphere; thus, we were able to make maps of Venus' surface from Earth using the characteristics of the returned signals. Radar data from spacecraft orbiting Venus are of much higher quality. Just as radar from airport control towers is used to determine the distances to airplanes, radar from Venus orbiters can determine the distances from the orbiter to points on the planet's surface. The *Magellan* orbiter mapped 98% of Venus' surface to such a resolution that objects smaller than 100 meters were detected (FIGURE 8-13).

Pioneer Venus I started orbiting Venus in 1978 and sent data until 1992. The *Magellan* orbiter sent data from 1990 to 1994.

FIGURE 8-13 This *Magellan* three-dimensional image enhances the height of structural features of the Venusian crater Golubkina. The central peak, terraced inner walls, and surrounding ejected material are characteristic of impact craters on the Earth, Moon, and Mars.

About two thirds of the surface of Venus is covered by rolling hills, with craters here and there. Highlands occupy less than 10% of the surface and lower-lying areas make up the rest. Remember that maps of the surface (FIGURE 8-14) are made from radar data, and the colors used simply indicate altitude. The blue/violet regions in Figure 8-14 are very low in altitude: All of Venus, including the rolling plains that make up most of its surface, is dryer than the driest desert on Earth.

Venus has about a thousand craters (FIGURE 8-15a) that are larger than a few kilometers in diameter. This is many more than are found on Earth, but far fewer than are found on the Moon. We know that the terrestrial planets experienced more frequent cratering early in the history of the solar system than they do now, for there was much more interplanetary debris. The cratering rate decreased as this debris was swept from space. Assuming that Venus has been struck by impacts at about the same rate as other objects in its vicinity (such as the Moon or Mercury), we can compare

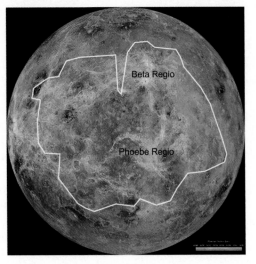

Beta Regio

Phoebe Regio

FIGURE 8-14 This infrared *Venus Express* image is a color-coded map of Venus' surface showing the highest elevations in brown/red and the lowest in blue/violet. Almost all Venusian features are named for women, as is the planet. Beta Regio and Phoebe Regio represent some of the oldest terrain on Venus.

ADVANCING THE MODEL

Our Changing View of Venus

Galileo was the first person to observe the phases of Venus. As discussed in Chapter 3, he argued that the fact that Venus exhibits a gibbous phase proves that it orbits the Sun and not the Earth. Although its phases are not visible to the naked eye, they have a definite effect on how bright Venus appears to us. When Venus is between the Earth and the Sun, it is closer to us than any other planet gets; however, it is then in a new phase and cannot be seen from Earth. Just before and just after the new phase, its crescent is so small that the planet appears dim to the naked eye. Also, when it is nearly full and we see almost its entire disk, it is on the other side of the Sun from us and is so far away that it appears dim again. Venus appears brightest at an intermediate position, when it shows less than a full face but is fairly close to Earth (FIGURE

B8-1). This position occurs when Venus is 39 degrees from the Sun, about 36 days before and after its new phase.

In a telescope, the angular diameter of Venus varies from 10 arcseconds when it is most distant to 66 arcseconds when it is closest. The photographs of the planet in Figure 3-4 show the great change in its angular diameter as seen from Earth.

It was during Venus' solar transits in 1761 and 1769 (when Venus passed in front of the Sun) that combined observations from different sites on Earth allowed us to measure the actual distance between Earth and Venus using the method of parallax. As a result, we finally had the actual value of the astronomical unit and, thus, the true dimensions of our solar system, compared with only knowing the relative sizes of the planetary orbits.

FIGURE B8-1 Venus is most brilliant when its elongation is 39 degrees, which occurs about 36 days before or after (shown here) its new phase. (A planet's elongation is the angular distance between the planet and the Sun as viewed from Earth.)

the number of impact craters found on Venus with that on the Moon. This allows us to determine the age of a planet's surface, for volcanic action and motion of tectonic plates remove old craters. Venus has no craters older than about 500 million years, and we conclude that the average age of the planet's surface is no more than about 500 million years. This is about twice as old as Earth's, but much younger than the Moon's. Also, as a surface becomes smoother due to weathering, it becomes a poorer reflector of radio waves, allowing us to compare the age of lava flows over the planet. Some *Magellan* radar data suggest that there are regions of very young lava flows on Venus, less than 10 million years old (Figure 8-15b).

Additional evidence for recent volcanic activity is provided by the decrease in the amount of sulfur dioxide, a volcanic gas, over the past few decades and the detection of radio bursts (thought to be lightning). Because sulfur dioxide is converted to sulfuric acid by ultraviolet radiation in the upper Venusian atmosphere, the decrease in sulfur dioxide suggests that a major eruption may have occurred in the 1970s. The presence of volcanism suggests that Venus has a molten interior. In the case of

Earth, the molten interior gives rise to plate tectonics, which, along with volcanism, ensures the smooth dissipation of energy from the planet's interior. For Venus, however, we have no evidence to suggest the existence of plate tectonics, while all of the observational data points to a geologically active planet that experienced a global resurfacing in the last 500 million years. This suggests that in the interior of Venus instabilities build up until eruptions occur on the planet's entire surface, erasing signs of past activities and older craters.

Venus Express also has measured highly variable quantities of sulfur dioxide in Venus' upper atmosphere, reviving the debate on whether active volcanoes exist on Venus. It is possible that the volcanic eruptions occurred about 10 million years ago and that on Venus the sulfur dioxide takes a long time to react with surface rocks, in contrast to Earth where sulfur compounds do not stay in the atmosphere for long. We do not yet understand why relatively large quantities of sulfur dioxide exist at high altitudes in Venus' atmosphere and why it is highly variable.

Notice how the shapes of some rocks in Figure 8-12 indicate that they fit together like pieces of a puzzle. Apparently, these are pieces of lava that fractured as it cooled and solidified. Most of the surface of Venus is covered with lava rock. Venus has no large tectonic plates. If it did, we would see mountain ranges as we find on Earth. One explanation is that Venus' wrinkled surface is the result of a thin crust that moves and flexes over most of its area. This thin crust is not strong enough to form large tectonic plates. Another explanation is that the crust is relatively thick, but Venus' molten interior is not moving fast enough so that convection stresses are relieved in many relatively small surface areas instead of plate boundaries as on Earth.

(a)

(b)

FIGURE 8-15 (a) The thick atmosphere of Venus shields the surface from small interplanetary debris, but impacts of larger objects result in craters such as these. The foreground crater is 37 km wide. Most of the floors of the craters are flat because lava has flooded them. (b) The lava near Maat Mons is the youngest crustal material yet found on Venus. The mountain is 8 km high, exaggerated 10 times in this image made from *Magellan* radar data.

The Atmosphere of Venus

The length of a day on Venus and the lack of water on its surface are not the only features that make the planet a poor candidate for the title of Earth's twin sister. The Soviet *Venera* landers confirmed what we had already begun to learn about the unusual atmosphere of Venus.

The Earth's atmosphere consists of nearly 80% nitrogen and 20% oxygen, with small amounts of water, carbon dioxide, and ozone. Venus, on the other hand, has an atmosphere made up of about 96% carbon dioxide, 3.5% nitrogen, and small amounts of water and sulfuric acid—the same acid used in car batteries. In fact, the clouds we see on Venus are made up in large part of sulfuric acid droplets. Chemical reactions between the sulfuric acid in the atmosphere and fluorides and chlorides in surface rocks result in some very corrosive substances that can dissolve even lead. Venus is indeed inhospitable.

Probes landed by the former Soviet Union (between 1966 and 1983) contained instruments to measure the composition of the Venusian soil and rocks.

Because Venus is covered with clouds, does that mean it's a wet planet?

360 km/hr is about 225 mi/hr.

Computer models suggest that dragging from Venus' heavy atmosphere changed the planet's rotation from its original Earth-like mode to its current slow backward rotation.

The density of the gas in Venus' atmosphere is so high that if we could survive its hazards, we could strap on wings and fly.

ESA's *Venus Express* arrived at Venus in April 2006.

At the level of the cloud tops in Venus' lower atmosphere, the winds reach speeds up to 360 km/hr. The wind blows in the direction of the planet's rotation, but the planet is rotating very slowly. As one moves lower in the atmosphere, the wind velocity decreases until it is nearly zero at the surface. We do not fully understand the causes of Venus' wind patterns. Undoubtedly, the slow motion of the Sun across Venus' surface (because of its slow rotation rate) is the basic cause, but the details are not known. Further study of the weather on Venus would not only help us understand that planet better, but would also increase our understanding of weather patterns on Earth.

As the space probes descended through the atmosphere of Venus, they encountered hazards from more than the acidic atmosphere and the great winds. The space probes were also subjected to tremendous pressures. The atmospheric pressure on the surface of Venus is about 90 times that on the surface of Earth, about the same as the pressure at a depth of 1 kilometer in Earth's oceans. As if the acidic atmosphere and high pressure were not enough, Venus is also inhospitable because of its high temperatures: about 464°C (867°F) near the surface.

The clouds of Venus form a layer between altitudes of about 50 and 70 kilometers (FIGURE 8-16). A layer of haze extends from the cloud layer down to about 30 kilometers. From there to the ground, the Venusian atmosphere is surprisingly clear; however, the light that filters through the clouds has a distinct yellow/orange hue, caused primarily by the sulfur dust in the clouds. Refer back to Figure 8-12 and note the color of the rocks at the base of the spacecraft. This color is not the natural color of the objects, but is the same result you would get if you turned out all the white lights in a room and lit only a yellow light—everything would have a yellow tint. If the surface of Venus were lit with white light, it would appear gray.

In addition to carbon dioxide and water vapor, *Venus Express* has detected carbon monoxide deep in the planet's atmosphere and hydroxyl at high altitudes. Carbon monoxide can be used as a tracer to monitor circulation patterns. Hydroxyl is a very reactive molecule and is closely linked to the abundance of ozone. We know that in earth's atmosphere, ozone plays an important role by absorbing the Sun's ultraviolet radiation. The amount of the radiation absorbed plays a key role in driving the heating and dynamics of the planet's atmosphere. The same might be true for Venus, where the amount of hydroxyl is highly variable. As such, at ultraviolet wavelengths, the cloud-covered world of Venus shows a very dynamic nature, including temporary dark and bright stripes across the planet. A dramatic example of the changes in Venus' atmosphere is its south polar vortex (FIGURE 8-17). It is thought that this hurricane-like feature is formed when air from the equatorial regions, heated by the Sun,

FIGURE 8-16 At the top of Venus' atmosphere, the temperature is about 170 K (−100°C). It increases smoothly to about 737 K (464°C) at the surface. The cloud layer causes the surface to appear orange.

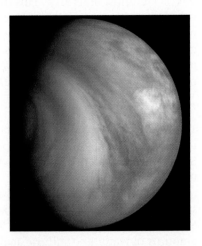

FIGURE 8-17 This *Venus Express* false color image (in the ultraviolet) shows Venus' southern hemisphere from equator (right) to the pole. A dark oval feature surrounds the south pole. Elsewhere we see streaky clouds and a bright mid-latitude band. There is a similar structure on Venus' north pole.

rises and moves toward the poles, where it begins to cool and sink, spiraling downward. The vortex changes shape within a matter of days, and it does not penetrate into the lower atmosphere because of the high density of the gas there. It seems that the vortex drives the planet's cloud dynamics at all altitudes.

A Hypothesis Explaining Venus/Earth Differences

As noted earlier, both Earth and Venus have small amounts of water vapor in their atmospheres. However, Venus' atmospheric water is about all the water that exists on the planet; if condensed, it would create a layer just 3-cm thick around the planet. (For comparison, all the water in Earth's oceans and atmosphere would create a layer of about 3-km thick around the planet.) Why is this planet, so close to the size of the Earth, so different from Earth?

Terrestrial planets get much of their atmospheres from gases released from their interiors, primarily through volcanic action. These gases were presumably trapped (accreted) during planetary formation. Volcanoes on Earth release large amounts of both water vapor and carbon dioxide, and it is likely that this is also the case for volcanoes on Venus. Both planets are theorized to have once had water on their surfaces and substantial amounts of carbon dioxide in their atmospheres. Most of the carbon dioxide on Earth is now dissolved in the oceans and in rocks such as limestone, which is found in the oceans. Venus, however, would have had a higher surface temperature due to its position nearer the Sun; as a result, any liquid water on the planet's surface quickly evaporated, and the carbon dioxide remained in the atmosphere. The clouds of water vapor, along with large amounts of carbon dioxide, resulted in an effect we experience only to a mild degree here on Earth: the greenhouse effect.

Did you ever notice that our coldest nights occur when the sky is clear? When we have cloudy skies at night, the difference between day and night temperatures is minimized. The reason for this is that in order for the Earth's surface to cool down at night, it must radiate into space a portion of the energy it gained during the day. The primary energy loss occurs in the form of infrared radiation. However, infrared radiation does not readily pass through water vapor, and as a result the clouds block the infrared waves from escaping into space, thus forming a sort of blanket for the Earth.

Early in Earth's and Venus' history, both planets experienced this blanketing effect, but because of Venus' higher temperature, it had more water vapor than Earth did. In addition, Venus had large amounts of carbon dioxide in its atmosphere. This gas is also opaque to infrared radiation. Visible light, on the other hand, is not blocked by carbon dioxide. Although most of the visible light from the Sun was reflected by the clouds of Venus, some of it passed through the atmosphere and was absorbed by the surface, causing the surface to heat up. Meanwhile, high in Venus' atmosphere, ultraviolet radiation from the Sun was breaking water molecules into their constituents: hydrogen and oxygen. The hydrogen escaped from the planet, and the oxygen combined with other elements in the atmosphere. Evidence for this comes from the abundances of ordinary hydrogen and deuterium (a hydrogen isotope that has a neutron in its nucleus): On Earth, the ratio is 1000 to 1, whereas on Venus, it is only 100 to 1. On the average, the heavier deuterium atoms stay closer to the surface than the lighter ordinary hydrogen atoms. Assuming that initially the two planets had the same ratio, it is likely that the Sun's ultraviolet light is responsible for the preferential loss of ordinary hydrogen. As a result of the loss of water, Venus could not develop plate tectonics like the Earth and any biological evolution would have stopped.

This left the atmosphere with large amounts of carbon dioxide, which continued to trap infrared radiation. In contrast, on Earth, carbon dioxide dissolves in the oceans and is chemically bound into carbonate rocks such as limestone and marble. The hotter Venus' surface got, the more infrared radiation it emitted. Because of the carbon dioxide in the atmosphere, however, much of this radiation could not escape; therefore, the planet continued to heat up. The high surface temperature on Venus baked more carbon dioxide out of the surface rocks. So a chain reaction resulted: The more carbon dioxide released, the hotter the surface became and the more carbon dioxide was released.

Recall our discussion of the blackbody curve in Chapter 4. The Earth's surface temperature is such that most of its emitted energy is in the infrared part of the spectrum.

FIGURE 8-18 Some visible light penetrates the atmosphere of Venus and reaches the surface, heating it. Most of the infrared radiation emitted by the surface, however, is reflected back by the atmosphere, causing Venus to be very hot.

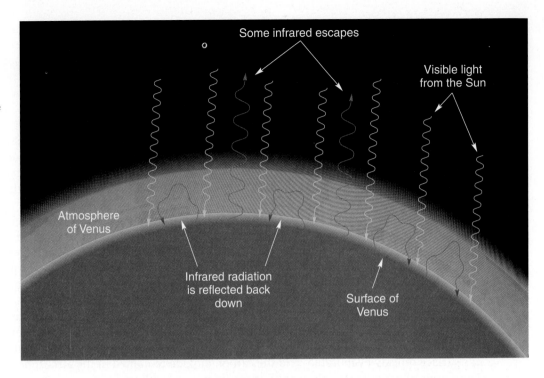

greenhouse effect The effect by which infrared radiation is trapped within a planet's atmosphere through the action of particles, such as carbon dioxide molecules, within that atmosphere.

◆ The Stefan-Boltzmann law (see Section 4-4) allows us to calculate the energy radiated from the Earth due to its temperature.

◆ The effect illustrated in Figure 8-18—the greenhouse effect—is a well-established theory; however, the explanation for why Venus developed an atmosphere so different from Earth's is not fully accepted. Even though it seems likely that at least a portion of a terrestrial planet's atmosphere results from volcanic activity, it could be that comets and meteorites have delivered significant fractions of these atmospheres.

The planet did not continue heating forever, of course. The atmosphere was not *completely* opaque to infrared. A small fraction of the infrared radiation that entered the atmosphere was re-emitted into space and that energy was lost to the planet. The amount of solar energy being absorbed by Venus was constant, whereas the amount being released depended on the temperature of the planet. Venus continued to heat up until the amount of radiant energy leaving it was equal to the amount striking it. At this point an equilibrium condition was reached. **FIGURE 8-18** illustrates the situation.

The heating due to trapped infrared radiation is called the ***greenhouse effect*** because it is somewhat similar to what happens in greenhouses on Earth. Sunlight penetrates the glass of a greenhouse's roof and walls and is absorbed by the plants and soil within. These surfaces then emit infrared radiation. Glass, like water vapor and carbon dioxide, is a poor transmitter of infrared radiation, and thus, the air in a greenhouse is kept warmer than the outside air. A very important factor in the heating of greenhouses, however, is that the walls prohibit the warm air inside from mixing with the cooler outside air. Because this trapping of the air is not a factor on a planet, the heating of Venus and of a greenhouse are not truly similar. A similar phenomenon to a greenhouse is what happens inside a car whose windows are closed during a hot summer day.

The greenhouse effect is also at work in Earth's atmosphere. If we calculate what Earth's temperature should be due to the amount of solar radiation that strikes it and the energy it emits into space due to its temperature, we obtain a temperature 35°C colder than it actually is. The greenhouse effect, primarily caused by water and carbon dioxide, makes up the difference. As humans burn more and more fossil fuel, we add more carbon dioxide to the atmosphere. The carbon dioxide (and other greenhouse-causing chemicals) in Earth's atmosphere is increasing at a rate of about 0.5% per year, and many scientists fear the effect this may have in the future. Computer simulations of the effect of an increase in carbon dioxide depend greatly on what assumptions are made, but various studies indicate that if we double the amount of carbon dioxide in the atmosphere, we will cause an increase in Earth's temperature of somewhere between 2.8°C and 5.2°C.

The great disparity between conditions on Venus and on Earth appears to be due to a fairly slight difference in temperature far back in their histories. This difference was magnified by the greenhouse effect so that now Venus' atmosphere might be compared with an inferno. We know that an increase of just a few degrees in Earth's temperature would cause major disruptions in our way of living because of changes in growing conditions; however, the greater fear is that a change of just a few degrees may cause a runaway greenhouse effect, destroying Earth as we know it. More study is needed before we know at what point a runaway greenhouse effect would begin.

During the last few decades we have experienced, worldwide, some of the warmest years in the last century. Climatologists are trying to determine whether this represents a chance fluctuation or if it is due to the greenhouse effect. If the greenhouse effect is responsible, significant changes in our lifestyles may be necessary to reverse the process.

Another factor in the evolution of Venus' atmosphere and another difference between Venus and Earth is the absence of any intrinsic magnetic field on Venus. The only magnetic field present on Venus is that induced by the solar wind and maybe some local surface magnetism. As we discussed in Chapter 6, the Earth's magnetic field is generated by movements in its liquid metallic core and its relatively fast rotation; however, Venus' rotation is very slow and its core may be solid. As a result, Venus has no protection against the solar wind; this could have resulted in the loss of atmospheric gases and therefore the different evolutionary path followed by Venus' atmosphere as compared with Earth's.

Data from *Venus Express* will help us answer many of the questions about Venus' atmosphere and ultimately better understand the evolution of Earth's long-term climate.

8-3   Mars

Mars as Seen From Earth

The amount of surface detail that is visible on Mars' surface depends on several factors. First, the surface of Mars is often obscured by its dust storms. Second, surface visibility varies greatly depending on Mars' distance from Earth.

As you might expect, Mars is best seen when it is directly opposite the Sun in the sky. When a planet is in such a position, 180° from the Sun as seen by an observer on Earth, it is closest to Earth and is said to be in **opposition**. This happens about every 2.2 years for Mars, but Mars' orbit is eccentric enough that the distance from Earth to Mars at opposition might be as little as 55 million kilometers or as great as 100 million kilometers.

FIGURE 8-19 shows a view of Mars taken by the *HST*, a day before Mars' closest approach to Earth on October 2005. The red color of the light areas is obvious. Before the advent of color photos, some observers claimed that the darker areas appear green. These markings were observed as early as 1660, and the rotation rate of Mars was determined from their motion. In addition, you can see a white cap at the pole of the planet. Observing this cap as Mars orbits the Sun, we can watch it diminish in size as that pole faces the Sun and then grow again when that pole faces away from the Sun. This effect is similar to the Arctic and Antarctic areas on Earth. The tilt of Mars' axis is very similar to Earth's, and we are observing these poles as they experience the Martian summer and winter.

Other seasonal changes can be observed on Mars. Large parts of the planet change periodically from a dark to a light color and back, depending on the position

Plant growth has the effect of decreasing atmospheric carbon dioxide; however, humans are destroying tropical forests at the rate of 1 acre per second.

So much solar radiation is reflected from the clouds of Venus that if Venus had no greenhouse effect, its atmosphere would be cooler than Earth's.

If we don't change the direction in which we are going, we are likely to end up where we are headed.
—Chinese proverb

The ancient Greeks called the fourth planet from the Sun "Ares," the name of their mythical god of war, perhaps because of the association of its red color with blood. In Roman mythology, however, the god of war is Mars.

opposition The configuration of a planet when it is opposite the Sun in our sky. That is, the objects are aligned as Sun-Earth-planet.

FIGURE 8-19 The bright, red, cloudy region in the middle of this October 2005 color composite *HST* image is a large regional dust storm. Bluish water-ice clouds are seen at the top (the north, winter, polar region), whereas the south polar ice cap has mostly sublimated due to the approaching summer.

of the planet in its orbit. This color change led to speculation that there is vegetation on the planet and that it changes color in response to seasonal growth. If there is vegetation, could there be animal life on Mars? What about intelligent life, then?

Early Speculations on Life on Mars

Speculation about life on other planets—particularly Mars—is nothing new. The famous mathematician Carl Friedrich Gauss was so convinced that intelligent life existed on Mars that in 1802 he proposed that a huge sign be marked in the snows of Siberia to signal the Martians.

During the favorable (close) opposition of Mars in 1863, Father Angelo Secchi, an Italian astronomer, observed Mars and drew a colored map of the planet's surface including some lines that he called *canali*, an Italian word best translated as channels. Then in 1877, the director of the Rome Observatory, Father Giovanni Schiaparelli, observed Mars and drew a more elaborate map showing many *canali*. In translation to English, however, *canali* became *canals*, rather than channels, giving the implication of artificial waterways. This struck a responsive chord with the public, and his findings were taken as confirmation of an intelligent race of beings on Mars.

In 1894, American astronomer Percival Lowell (1855–1916) built an observatory on a hill near Flagstaff, Arizona to concentrate on the study of Mars and its supposed intelligent life. Lowell's drawings of Mars include as many as 500 canals. White polar caps are easily visible on Mars, and they change in size according to the season. Lowell believed that the canals were built to transport water from the polar caps to the drier parts of the planet.

Other astronomers failed to see canals, however, even though some of them were using telescopes much larger than Lowell's and Schiaparelli's. In 1894, as Lowell was completing his observatory, the astronomer Edward Barnard said, "To save my soul I can't believe in the canals as Schiaparelli draws them." Barnard was probably the keenest telescopic observer of his day, and he reported to friends that he saw craters on Mars. For fear of ridicule, he did not publish his drawings. Lowell's assistant, Vesto Slipher, also believed that he saw Martian craters, but he also did not publish his views.

In 1898, H. G. Wells wrote *The War of the Worlds*, describing a fictional invasion of Earth by Martians. When Orson Welles dramatized this novel in a very realistic radio broadcast in 1938, he made it appear that a radio music show was being interrupted frequently to report on the invasion as it occurred. Many people did not hear (or forgot about) the announcement at the beginning of the show that it was a dramatization, and there was widespread panic, especially in New Jersey, where the invaders were supposed to be landing.

Invasion and Its Results

A series of Martian invasions did start in the late 1960s and is still in progress. The invasion, however, is proceeding in the opposite direction than H. G. Wells envisioned, and it is a peaceful endeavor, although competition between major political powers has certainly been a factor. In 1965 *Mariner 4* passed by Mars, sending back 22 pictures of the surface. These pictures ended speculation about canals, for none was observed. The planet was seen to be covered by deserts and craters. Other questions were raised, however, for the pictures confirmed that major dust storms are common on Mars, yet the surface contains numerous craters—craters that should have been worn down by the constant pounding of wind and dust. We know now that erosion does not occur very quickly because the atmosphere of Mars is extremely thin, so that the pressure at the surface is about 1/160 of the air pressure at Earth's surface. Dust stirred up by this thin atmosphere must be extremely fine and not at all like a sandstorm in one of our deserts.

Mariner 4 was followed in 1969 by *Mariners 6* and *7* and in 1971 by *Mariner 9*. The latter spacecraft provided us with a wealth of information about Mars' surface, particularly about the spectacular canyons and volcanoes. In 1997, the *Pathfinder* spacecraft landed on Mars. The *Mars Global Surveyor (MGS)* started mapping the planet's surface in 1999. *Mars Odyssey* started orbiting Mars in 2001 and began studying the radiation environment as well as mapping the amount and distribution of chemical elements and minerals on the planet's surface. The twin *Mars Exploration Rovers* (*Spirit* and *Opportunity*) landed on Mars in 2004 and are studying its surface. ESA's *Mars Express* began collecting data in 2005, while NASA's *Mars Reconnaissance Orbiter (MRO)* arrived at Mars in 2006; the two spacecraft have complementary ground-penetrating radars that provide information about Mars' subsurface structure. NASA's *Phoenix* lander studied the history of water in Mars' arctic region for five months in 2008. More missions are in the planning stages, showing our immense interest in understanding Mars.

Structural Characteristics

Figure 8-7 compares Mars with Mercury, Venus, Earth, and the Moon. Mars has a diameter about half of Earth's. This makes the surface area of Mars about one fourth that of Earth and its volume about one eighth of Earth's. Now recall that both Mercury and Venus have densities comparable to Earth's. If Mars were to follow this pattern, its mass should have been about one eighth that of Earth's. The mass of Mars, however, is only one tenth of Earth's, and its density is only 3.93 times that of water, about 0.7 of Earth's density.

Everything we know about the interior of Mars comes from data from its surface, its overall characteristics, and its tidal interaction with orbiting spacecraft. Mars' surface rocks are rich in iron and silicon. The planet rotates almost as fast as the Earth, but has no global magnetic field. From these data and the planet's relatively low density, we conclude that a significant fraction of Mars' iron is probably distributed throughout the planet's body instead of being concentrated in a dense core.

This is consistent with computer models and geologic evidence suggesting that core formation, and therefore the accretion process, for the terrestrial planets was complete in the first 30 million years of the solar system. The geologic evidence is based on the decay of the radioactive element hafnium-182 to tungsten-182 for all objects for which we have samples, namely Earth, Mars, the Moon, and the asteroid Vesta. Also, high-temperature, high-pressure laboratory experiments support the idea that the planetesimals that formed the terrestrial planets were already separated into a metal core and a silicate shell. Measurements of the tidal interactions between Mars and the *Mars Global Surveyor (MGS)* spacecraft suggest that the planet's interior may be more like Earth's than previously thought. It seems that Mars has not cooled to a completely solid iron core but that there is at least a layer of liquid outer core surrounding the solid inner core. Also, the core has a significant fraction of a lighter element, such as sulfur, and its overall size is about half the size of the planet.

FIGURE 8-20 is a magnetic field map that covers Mars' entire surface and is based on 4 years of data taken by the *MGS*. The stripes at the bottom of the image are evidence of plate tectonics early in the planet's history. The alternating stripe colors indicate changes in field direction that result when molten rock coming up from the mantle pushes apart plates; as it spreads and cools, the material becomes magnetized in the direction of the magnetic field that exists at the time. We find similar stripes on Earth.

On Mars' surface we currently find only remnants of its once active planetary-scale magnetic field, scattered around its surface in areas of highly magnetized rock. Observations suggest that Mars probably lost its magnetosphere about 4 billion years ago, and since then, the planet's atmosphere has been feeling the full force of the Sun's solar wind. Observations by *Mars Express* show that the solar wind penetrates deeply into the Martian atmosphere, eroding it and contributing to its loss of water. The observed remnant fields could have played an important role in the evolution of the planet's atmosphere by shielding parts of it from being swept away by the solar wind. Even though the strongest of these remnant fields is 50 times weaker than the field at the surface of the Earth, auroras are commonly observed on Mars as its local fields interact with solar wind particles.

Area depends on the square of the diameter and $(1/2)^2 = 1/4$. Volume depends on the cube of the diameter and $(1/2)^3 = 1/8$. Also, mass = density $\times$ volume.

FIGURE 8-20 Mars' crustal magnetism. The colors represent the strength and direction of the field. The Tharsis volcanoes, located along a straight line, could have formed just as the Hawaiian islands on Earth—from the motion of a plate over a hotspot in the mantle below. Valles Marineris, the largest canyon in the solar system, looks like a rift that forms while a plate is being pulled apart.

Mars' Motions

 The eccentricity of Mars' orbit is 0.093, whereas Earth's is 0.017.

You should be able to figure out why the two periods are nearly the same for Mars.

Mars orbits the Sun at an average distance of 1.524 AU. Its orbit, however, is fairly eccentric, and its distance from the Sun varies from about 210 to 250 million kilometers. From Kepler's third law we can calculate that Mars requires 1.88 years to complete its orbit around the Sun.

We saw that a solar day on Mercury was 176 Earth days, and on Venus 117 Earth days. In this sense, it is Mars that should be called Earth's sibling, for it has a sidereal rotation period of 24 hours and 37 minutes, whereas its day is 24 hours and 40 minutes.

The equator of Mars is tilted 25.2 degrees with respect to its orbital plane. This is very close to Earth's 23.4 degrees. Because the tilt of a planet's axis causes opposite seasons in the planet's two hemispheres, we expect such seasons on Mars, and indeed, this is the case; however, another feature of Mars' motion affects its seasons. The eccentricity of Mars' orbit causes it to be much closer to the Sun at some times of its year than at others. It turns out that Mars is 19% closer to the Sun during the northern hemisphere's winter than during its summer (FIGURE 8-21). Being closer to the Sun in winter and farther away in summer means that seasonal temperature variations are moderated in the northern hemisphere.

In the southern hemisphere, the reverse is true. Mars is closer to the Sun during summertime and farther from the Sun in winter. The southern hemisphere, therefore, experiences greater seasonal temperature shifts than the northern hemisphere.

The same effect occurs for Earth, which is closest to the Sun in January (wintertime in the northern hemisphere). The Earth's orbit is so nearly circular, however, that we are only about 3.3% closer to the Sun at one time than the other (rather than 19%).

FIGURE 8-21 Mars is closer to the Sun during summer in its southern hemisphere. In this drawing both the tilt of Mars' axis and the change in its distance from the Sun are exaggerated.

The Surface of Mars

 The base of Olympus Mons has a diameter of 400 miles and the collapsed depression at its top is 50 miles across and 2 miles deep.

The largest of the Martian volcanoes, and the largest mountain known in the solar system, is Olympus Mons. FIGURE 8-22a shows the gigantic cliffs around its base, and Figure 8-22b compares it with two of the largest mountains on Earth. Its height of 15 miles is twice that of our largest mountain, and its base would cover much of the area of Washington and Oregon (Figure 8-22c).

Venus also has at least one mountain (Maat Mons) larger than any mountain on Earth. Why do these planets have such tall volcanoes? On all three planets,

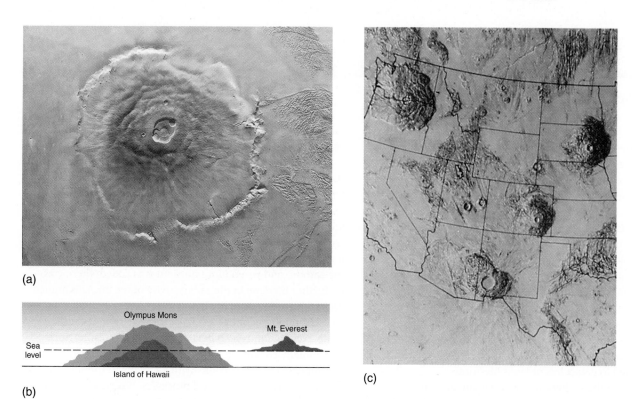

(a)

(b)

(c)

FIGURE 8-22 (a) A computer-enhanced photo of Olympus Mons at latitude 18° north. (b) Olympus Mons compared to Mount Everest and the volcanic island of Hawaii. (c) A composite photo of Olympus Mons and three companion volcanoes has been overlaid on the western United States to show comparative sizes.

volcanoes are formed above hot spots that lie deep within the planets. From time to time, material wells up from these hot spots, spilling out lava and building up the volcanoes. The reason that Mars and Venus have larger mountains than Earth has to do with the motions of their crusts. On Earth, the crust is divided into plates that move across the underlying material. This means that the crust moves across a given hot spot and the volcanic action slowly shifts along the surface. This is why we often find volcanoes on Earth in a straight line, with only the volcano on the end being active. The crusts of Venus and Mars do not contain large tectonic plates and, thus, the same part of the crust stays above a particular hot spot. This causes the volcano to grow higher and higher. Mars is a small planet and therefore its interior cooled quickly. Its crust may now be thick enough that it is too strong to be broken into individual pieces. Recall, however, our discussion on Mars' magnetic field and Figure 8-20.

Stretching away from the area of Olympus Mons is a canyon that more than matches the volcano. If placed on Earth, *Valles Marineris* (named for the *Mariner* spacecraft) would stretch all the way across the United States, as shown in FIGURE 8-23a. Part (b) of the figure shows its size relative to the Grand Canyon.

The first close-up photographs of the Martian surface (Figure B8-2), taken by *Viking 1*, showed the landscape near the lander in approximately true color. The red color we see from Earth is real! Immediately after its landing, the *Pathfinder* spacecraft sent back photos that showed the surrounding rock-strewn area. The next day, its roving robot, named *Sojourner*, began a slow journey to investigate the composition of some of the many rocks in the area (FIGURE 8-24). The major surprise from this mission has been that Mars is more similar to Earth than had been thought. The first rock investigated turned out to be rich in silica, the quartz material found in sand. Such a rock may have been brought to the surface by volcanic action or by meteorite impact.

We'll see the reason for the red color later.

TOOLS OF ASTRONOMY

Viking's Search for Life

In the late summer of 1975, *Viking 1* and *Viking 2* were launched toward Mars. After traveling to Mars, each spacecraft separated into two parts, one part staying in orbit and another descending to a soft landing on the planet. *Viking 1* lander touched down on Mars on July 20, 1976, and on August 7, *Viking 2* lander touched down nearly on the other side of the planet.

One of the primary purposes of the *Viking* mission was to look for signs of life on our neighboring planet. Various tests were conducted toward this end. The first was made by a television camera that scanned the area for any signs of plant or animal life or even for footprints. Scientists did not really expect that such large life-forms existed on Mars, and thus, the negative results were not particularly disappointing. The other tests, however, were more sophisticated and were designed to detect less obvious life-forms.

To perform these experiments, each lander contained an arm with a scoop at its end (FIGURE B8-2) so that it could retrieve some soil from the surface. The first of these experiments was called the "labeled release experiment." It was performed by taking about a teaspoon of soil and dampening it with a rich nutrient that should have been absorbed by any organism in the soil. Some of the carbon atoms in this nutrient were carbon-14, a radioactive form of carbon. It was thought that after an organism absorbed nutrients, it should release carbon into the air, including some of the radioactive carbon. Such radioactivity can be easily detected.

To try to ensure that a positive result from this experiment would be due to biological processes rather than chemical processes, other soil samples were heated to 300°F before being fed the nutrient. This was done to sterilize the soil and kill any living matter that might be in it. In this way, the investigators could see whether the unheated soil acted differently from soil that had been heated to kill life forms. (In a procedure like this, the sample that was sterilized is called the *control*. Such a procedure allows a comparison to be made and is common in all branches of science.)

When the labeled release experiment was tried on unsterilized soil by both *Viking 1* and *2*, the radioactivity of the air increased quickly. In the case of the control, the change in radioactivity was much less. The experiment thus seemed to indicate that life was present, but there was a problem: The radioactivity showed up *too* quickly, faster than should occur if it had been caused by an organism absorbing and releasing the carbon, and when more nutrient was added, there was no further increase in the radioactivity of the air. This argued *against* the presence of life in the soil.

Although the initial results of the experiment caused some excitement, researchers monitoring the results from Earth finally concluded that the release of carbon was caused by simple chemical reactions with elements in the soil and did not involve any biological processes. It seems likely that hydrogen peroxide, a water molecule with an extra oxygen atom, is present in the soil and that this chemical reacted with the carbon to produce carbon dioxide, which was then detected by the radiation monitors. (Indeed, hydrogen peroxide, used as antiseptic on Earth, was first observed in the Martian atmosphere in 2004.) Once the reaction used up the hydrogen peroxide from the Martian soil, the reaction stopped and no more carbon was released. The reason the control sample did not show the activity was that the heat broke down the hydrogen peroxide before it was exposed to the nutrient containing carbon.

Another experiment aboard the *Viking* was a test for respiration. Here, the soil sample was put in a container with inert gases (gases that don't react chemically), and a nutrient was added.

Finally, the gas was examined for changes in its chemical composition. If the living organism released any gases, they would be detected. When the experiment was performed, no more new gases appeared than would be expected from normal chemical reactions.

A common procedure in laboratories on Earth is to use a *mass spectrometer* to search for very small quantities of given chemicals in a sample. (A mass spectrometer is a device used to measure the masses of isotopes.) The *Viking* landers contained mass spectrometers capable of finding organic molecules even if they made up only a few billionths of the sample. All life on Earth contains these very large molecules that use carbon as their foundation. No such molecules were found.

Since the *Viking* missions, scientists have simulated the environment on Mars' surface in the laboratory and found that the combination of ultraviolet light, dry conditions, atmospheric oxygen, and mineral grain surfaces produce oxi-

FIGURE B8-2 *Viking 1*'s sampler scoop is at the end of the arm extending from right.

TOOLS OF ASTRONOMY

Viking's Search for Life *(Cont'd)*

dants, which can destroy organic molecules. The failure of the *Viking* landers to find any organic molecules does not absolutely show that life does not exist on Mars. Life might still exist beneath the planet's surface or in places protected from oxidants. The latest observations of Mars clearly suggest that there are vast amounts of water ice under the planet's surface, and wherever there is water and energy, there is a good chance that life exists.

Our technology has improved greatly since the 1970s, and we now know that organisms thrive under extreme conditions on Earth, in places where the *Viking* instruments would not have been able to detect organic compounds. If future missions do find life on Mars, we would gain a tremendous amount of knowledge examining it, and it would then be a small step for us to believe that life might be common in the universe. If the Martian conditions were once right for life, but we find no evidence for it, it would support the idea that life is special.

(a)

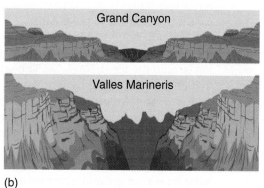

(b)

FIGURE 8-23 (a) Valles Marineris would stretch nearly across the United States. It is 4000 km long, 7 km deep, and up to 600 km wide. (b) In width and depth, Valles Marineris dwarfs the Grand Canyon, which is 450 km long, 1.6 km deep, and up to 29 km wide. It is the product of stresses in the Martian crust, not of erosion by flowing waters, as is a canyon.

FIGURE 8-24 This photo was taken soon after the *Sojourner* rover moved onto the Martian surface at the Carl Sagan Memorial Site. The rock that *Sojourner* is examining was dubbed Yogi.

The *Viking* orbiting modules confirmed something that had been seen by *Mariner 9*: It appears that running water was once common on Mars. FIGURE 8-25 shows dry riverbeds that look very similar to the arroyos found in the southwestern U.S. deserts. Arroyos are formed on Earth by infrequent flows of large amounts of water from

FIGURE 8-25 What appear to be dry riverbeds on Mars lead us to believe that water once flowed on the surface.

rainstorms. At present, however, there can be no rainfall on Mars because atmospheric pressure on Mars is much too low for liquid water to exist. The Martian arroyos are so similar to those found on Earth that we conclude that at one time there must have been liquid water flowing on Mars, but most of the evidence for water is 3.8 billion years old. Early in its history, Mars lost most of its atmosphere and all of its surface liquid water. Where would the water have gone? The answer lies, at least partly, in those white polar caps.

The polar caps of Mars consist of two parts: a water ice base that is covered during the winter by frozen carbon dioxide. In summer, the carbon dioxide evaporates, leaving behind the ice (FIGURE 8-26). The temperature on Mars does not rise high enough to melt that ice. If it did, there would still be only a small fraction of the water found on Earth. This "freezing out" of carbon dioxide from the atmosphere in the form of dry ice frost and snow is the most important seasonal change on Mars; it involves up to 30% of the atmosphere and results in large variations in surface pressure over the entire planet.

Other water seems to be hidden in permafrost below the surface of Mars. We have no way at present of knowing exactly how much water is there and whether this water and the water in the polar caps are enough to have provided the moisture for a warmer, more hospitable Mars at some time in its history. An alternative hypothesis is that the riverbeds were formed in brief, cataclysmic periods when ice was melted by meteorite impacts or volcanic heating. In the Advancing the Model box on page 232, we discuss the surface conditions on Mars and the case for water on this planet. The channels, gullies, and layers of sedimentary rock discovered on Mars clearly suggest that the planet was very different 3.8 billion years ago than it is today. Liquid water seems to have played an important role in shaping the planet's surface, but it is likely that it was not the only force at play. Other factors such as volcanism, tectonic shifts, ice, and strong winds almost certainly contributed to the features we see today. Examples of such factors are shown in FIGURE 8-27. The hourglass-shaped structure in Figure 8-27a was most likely formed by glaciers. Such features, when coupled with climate models and calculations on the tilt of Mars' orbit, suggest that Mars goes through climate shifts. The greater the tilt of the axis, the more illumination is received at the north polar cap and the sublimation of the polar ice increases. This ice will accumulate at lower latitudes and form glaciers several hundreds of meters thick after a few thousand years. The valley shown in Figure 8-27b is thought to have formed from water that escaped through the cracks under the surface causing the ground above it to collapse; this left a winding channel similar to stream valleys on Earth.

Spectroscopic data from *Mars Express* show that two different classes of minerals that contain water in their structure are present over large and isolated areas on Mars' surface. This implies

◆ The amount of water vapor in Mars' atmosphere would barely fill a small pond; however, the water volume in the ice on Mars' north polar cap is about 4% of the Earth's south polar ice sheet.

FIGURE 8-26 This *Mars Express* image (in almost natural colors) shows water ice on the floor of a crater near the north pole of Mars; faint traces of water ice are also visible around the rim and on the walls. The crater is 35 km wide and has a maximum depth of about 2 km from the rim. The image was taken during late summer in the Martian northern hemisphere.

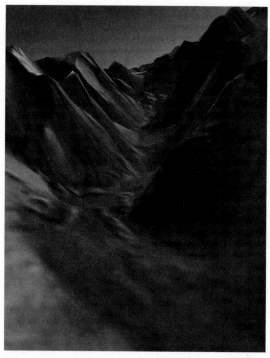

(a)

(b)

FIGURE 8-27 (a) This hourglass-structure, taken by *Mars Express'* high-resolution stereo camera, is in Promethei Terra, at the eastern rim of the Hellas Basin. (b) This Odyssey image in the infrared shows a winding valley feeding into Valles Marineris.

that large amounts of liquid water existed at some point on the surface. These data, coupled with methods to calculate the relative ages of surface features by counting craters, suggest that Mars experienced three geological periods in its history. The first period, from Mars' birth to about 4 billion years ago, is described by the formation of thin-layered silicates. These minerals form when rocks originating from magma come into a long-term contact with water; an example of such a mineral is clay. The second period, between 4 and 3.5 billion years ago, is described by the formation of sulfate minerals that form as deposits from salted water; these minerals point to a more acidic environment. The third period, which began about 3.5 billion years ago and continuous today, involves little water, and Mars' tenuous atmosphere is slowly altering the planet's surface. The presence of liquid water during the third period is supported by *MRO* observations of a new category of minerals (hydrated silica, commonly known as opal) spread across large regions of Mars.

Verifying the presence of water on Mars was one of the mission objectives of the Mars *Phoenix* lander. For five months in 2008 the lander tested the soil in a northern region of Mars (FIGURE 8-28). The instruments on Phoenix "baked and sniffed" the soil to find volatile ingredients, observed the soil under a microscope, and took many landscape images. The lander confirmed the presence of water ice, detected snow falling from Martian clouds, found evidence (in the form of calcium carbonate) that liquid water has interacted with the soil's minerals in the past, and documented that the soil is mildly alkaline and

FIGURE 8-28 The robotic arm of the *Phoenix* lander carries a scoop of Martian soil toward the spacecraft's microscope for examination.

ADVANCING THE MODEL

Surface Conditions and the Case for Water on Mars

The geological information collected by NASA's rovers, *Spirit* and *Opportunity*, supports the idea of an ancient Martian environment that included periods of wet but highly acidic and oxidizing conditions. *Opportunity* has found evidence of long-standing salty water, whereas *Spirit* examined many rocks and found mineral fingerprints of water. Examining layers of bedrock, the two rovers found evidence for cyclical changes, perhaps 3.5 to 4 billion years ago, between wet and dry conditions based on the sequence of layers deposited as underwater sediments or windblown dunes. *Opportunity* also found many scattered small spheres, gray in color, embedded in outcrop rocks, which probably formed from minerals (mostly hematite) precipitating out of a porous, wet rock (FIGURE B8-3). Similar spheres are also found on Earth in

areas where minerals precipitate from flowing groundwater; however, it is possible that the layered rock outcrops formed long ago by volcanic ash reacting with traces of acidic water and sulfur dioxide gas or by meteorite impacts; these alternative scenarios challenge the notion of a wet and warm young Mars.

Observations from the *MGS* also show features that suggest there may be current sources of liquid water at or near Mars' surface (FIGURE B8-4). These features look like gullies formed by flowing water and the deposits of soil and rock transported by these flows. The gullies appear to have been formed in the recent past, and they are seen at some of the coldest places on Mars. Almost all of them are in latitudes between 30° and 70°, mostly in the southern hemisphere

FIGURE B8-3 A mosaic close-up image of the small spheres (nicknamed "blueberries") found by *Opportunity* at Meridiani Planum.

(a)

(b)

FIGURE B8-4 These *MGS* images are providing tantalizing evidence that liquid water from an underground source *may* flow on the surface of Mars for short periods of time. They show that new deposits appear and gully sites change on Mars' surface over a period of a few years. (a) The image on the left shows a gully (on the wall of a crater in Terra Sirenum) as it appeared on December 22, 2001. (b) The mosaic of two images on the right (from August 26 and September 25, 2005) shows new light-toned deposit in the gully. The Sun illuminates the area from the top left.

ADVANCING THE MODEL

Surface Conditions and the Case for Water on Mars *(Cont'd)*

surface because of the extreme cold temperatures. This frozen permafrost acts like a cap on a soda bottle. A burst of internal planetary heat can trigger a dramatic release of gas and water under the permafrost, just as in the case of a capped soda bottle when heated. During such episodes, an ocean can form over the northern hemisphere, while the released carbon dioxide promotes the greenhouse effect that keeps liquid water stable near the surface. Because Mars lacks a soil layer like Earth's, when it rains, water removes carbon dioxide from the atmosphere and filters underground. As a result, Mars cools to the point that permafrost forms again and enters another long-lasting cold and dry period.

Another important *MGS* discovery is the lack of carbonates, at least on the planet's surface. This is important because atmospheric carbon dioxide is supposed to be locked up in carbon-rich sediments, after being dissolved by rainfall early in the planet's history. This is one of the two ways that carbonate rocks are formed on Earth. The second is by marine organisms that produce carbonates for shells or other hard parts; when these organisms die, the accumulated material eventually forms a carbonate deposit at the bottom of the water. (An example of such carbonate is blackboard chalk.) So far we have not discovered similar deposits on Mars' surface and that is a discouraging observation about the possibility of life on Mars; however, carbonate patches have been found on Martian meteorites. *MGS* did discover the presence of carbonate in Martian dust in quantities between 2% and 5%. These trace amounts probably did not come from marine deposits but are instead the result of the interaction between tiny amounts of water in Mars' atmosphere with dust. This finding is pointing to a cold and icy Mars through its history (because otherwise the carbonate rock layers formed in oceans should be observable). To understand this result we may have to wait for the discoveries to be made by future missions.

Observations made by *Mars Odyssey* suggest that there is enough water (in the form of ice) just a few feet under the surface of Mars to cover the entire planet ankle deep. These observations were based on the detection of hydrogen on the surface of the planet (FIGURE B8-7). The hydrogen-rich areas are also very cold, and water ice should be stable in such regions. It is then likely that this hydrogen is in the form of water ice. But how did water get into the soil and rocks under the surface of the planet? This is an area of active research, and we simply mention two possible theories. The first theory is based on the results of numerical modeling of the changes in the tilt of Mars' equator to its orbital plane; these results show that about a million years or so ago Mars' axis was tilted about 35°. This could have caused the polar icecaps to evaporate and for a short time create enough water in the atmosphere to make ice stable over the entire planet. The soil and rocks then absorbed this thick layer of frost. According to the second theory, the source of the water is the vast water icecaps at the poles. Their thickness is such that they could bottle up enough geothermal energy from below, resulting in melting of their bottom layers, which could then supply a global water table.

(a)

(b)

FIGURE B8-7 The images are equatorial projections of the Martian surface and show epithermal neutron flux, which is sensitive to the amount of hydrogen present. (a) A view during late summer in the south. The magenta region in the south implies large amounts of water ice (60% by volume) buried less than 1 meter beneath the surface. At this time a thick cap of dry ice covers the north. (b) A view during early summer in the north. The thick dry ice frost has disappeared and the water ice regions are now visible. The water ice in the north is greater than in the south. At this time the water ice regions in the south are beginning to be covered by dry ice.

ADVANCING THE MODEL

Surface Conditions and the Case for Water on Mars *(Cont'd)*

and usually on slopes that get the least amount of sunlight. Because there is a very low surface atmospheric pressure on Mars, if liquid water were to get exposed at the planet's surface, it would begin to boil in a violent and explosive way. (However, using a planetary environmental chamber to simulate conditions on Mars, scientists found that the evaporation rates of brine solutions expected to be found on Mars are two orders of magnitude lower than those for pure water.) How then can these gullies form? One explanation assumes the existence of a ground water supply, similar to an aquifer, located near the surface. The location of the gullies indicates that ice plays a role in protecting the liquid water from evaporating until enough pressure builds for it to be released catastrophically down a slope. In an alternative explanation for the gullies, liquid carbon dioxide vaporizes as it comes out from the ground, expands and cools quickly, and forms carbon dioxide snow. This snow, together with rock debris, forms slurry that acts like a liquid. No explanation to date has been universally accepted, and new possibilities are being examined. One such possibility is supported by observations made by the *Mars Odyssey* spacecraft. FIGURE B8-5 shows gullies on crater walls that may be carved by water melting from remnant snow packs. As the snow melts and evaporates in the thin atmosphere of Mars, the gullies are being exposed. According to this scenario, Mars goes

through 100,000-year climatic cycles. At the beginning of a cycle, ice packs form as a result of snowfall. Sunlight warms the snow, which begins to melt from below, creating liquid water that flows downhill forming the gullies over a 5000-year period. A layer of snow above the liquid water protects the melt from evaporating immediately.

Layers of sedimentary rocks discovered on Mars (FIGURE B8-6) reveal clues about the planet's early history, when impact craters were forming more frequently than today. This history may have included warm, wet climates that lasted for millions of years, with many crater lakes filled with liquid water. On Earth, layered rock structures are commonly found in lakes; over long periods of time, sediments settle to the lake bottom and form sheets of rock, like a stack of pancakes. But it is also possible that these rocks are providing evidence for a drier and much colder Martian surface, which went through many climate changes and thick deposits of airborne dust. This view of a cold and dry Mars through its geologic history is supported by the abundant presence on the planet's surface of the mineral olivine, an iron–magnesium silicate that weathers easily by water. It is also possible that Mars is cold, dry, and quiet for hundreds of millions of years and then it becomes actively warmer and wetter during brief episodes, triggered by internal planetary heat that lasts thousands of years. In such a scenario, water and volatiles remain frozen under the planet's

FIGURE B8-5 This *MGS* image shows gullies on Martian crater walls (33.3°S, 92.9°E). The arrow shows the remnant of the snow pack proposed to be the source of the water that eroded the gullies. The image covers an area of 2.8 km by 4.5 km.

FIGURE B8-6 The picture covers an area of 1.5 km by 2.9 km and shows a large number of layers on the floor of the West Candor Chasma. Each layer has about the same thickness, estimated at about 10 meters.

ADVANCING THE MODEL

Surface Conditions and the Case for Water on Mars *(Cont'd)*

Mars Express is already providing us with direct information about the deep subsurface of Mars. Studying the echoes of the radio waves emitted by its radar, the spacecraft can probe different layers under the planet's surface, finding buried impact craters and distinguishing between the different deposits. To date, we do not have strong evidence for the existence of *liquid* water under the surface. But we do have an estimate for the amount of *frozen* water in Mars' south polar region; it is enough to cover the planet in a liquid layer about 11 meters deep.

Differences between Mars' Hemispheres

Since 1999, the *MGS* has produced detailed three-dimensional maps of Mars' surface that show differences between the planet's hemispheres (FIGURE B8-8). The northern hemisphere seems to consist of young plains, on average 6 km lower in elevation than the mainly ancient cratered highlands in the southern hemisphere. (In the southern hemisphere of the planet, there is an enormous impact crater, the Hellas Basin, 2300 km in diameter and more than 9 km deep.) Scientists were able to probe beneath the planet's

surface by combining high-resolution topographic maps of Mars (like the ones shown in Figure B8-8) with measurements of Mars' gravity. They found that the crust thins progressively from the south pole toward the north pole (FIGURE B8-9). Beneath the southern highlands the crust is about 45 miles thick, whereas the northern lowlands have a crust of uniform thickness, about 22 miles thick. *Mars Express'* measurements suggest an explanation for the striking difference between the heavily cratered highlands of the southern hemisphere and the smooth and low in elevation features of the northern hemisphere; the presence of an abundance of buried impact craters in the northern hemisphere suggests that they are very old, and that they were filled by volcanic lava and sediments carried by wind and episodic flood waters. *MGS* measurements also show evidence for large channels (buried under tons of sediment) that could have formed from the flow of large quantities of water from the southern highlands to the northern lowlands, which could have created early oceans on Mars. These subsurface channels, about 125 miles wide and over 1000 miles long, continue the path begun by the Valles Marineris canyon that is visible on the surface (FIGURE B8-10). The differences

(a)

(b)

FIGURE B8-8 These maps show features on the surface of Mars. The false colors in the images show elevation, from white (highest elevation) to red to green to blue (lowest elevation). The images were made possible by bouncing a laser off the surface of the planet and calculating the distance traveled by the beam of light. (a) Olympus Mons is shown on the upper right side of the map and the Hellas basin on the bottom left side. (b) Olympus Mons is shown on the upper left side of the map and Valles Marineris on the right, with the Tharsis rise between the two.

FIGURE B8-9 This visualization shows a cross-section of the planet's skin, with surface features and crustal thickness displayed in relative (but exaggerated) sizes to each other. The crust on the right side of the cross-section (the Martian south pole) appears significantly thicker than the crust on the left (the Martian north pole). This could be the result of subcrustal erosion by a large-scale mantle convection cell or one large impact (or multiple impacts) in the lowlands.

ADVANCING THE MODEL

Surface Conditions and the Case for Water on Mars *(Cont'd)*

FIGURE B8-10 This is a flat topographic map, showing Olympus Mons as a white area at upper left and Valles Marineris in the middle of the map. The image shows a channel draining from Valles Marineris into the wide, flat area of the north.

between the two hemispheres on Mars are very similar to the differences between the oceans and continents on Earth. These measurements also provide information on how Mars cooled over time, which in turn is related to the climate and history of water on the planet. It seems that early in Martian history there was high heat loss from the planet's interior through the northern lowlands; this was probably the result of a period of plate recycling and strong convection inside Mars. During this period, large amounts of gases and water or ice trapped in the interior could have been released in the atmosphere, so the planet could have had a warmer climate, with liquid water flowing on the surface and a strong global magnetic field protecting the planet's surface.

Differences also exist between the two polar regions on Mars (FIGURE B8-11). The north polar cap, about the size of Greenland, has a flat and pitted surface, resembling cottage cheese, and the residual cap (the part that survives the summer) is made mostly of water ice. The south polar cap, about 10% the size of the north polar cap, has larger pits and troughs, giving it a holey swiss-cheese appearance; the residual cap is made mostly of dry ice. This supports the idea that a large ocean once covered most of the northern part of the planet. The latest observations by the *MGS* and *Mars Odyssey* show that the pitted layer is dry ice but that water ice makes up the bulk of both polar caps. The main difference between the two poles is the thickness of their dry ice cover; the north polar cap has a 1-meter covering of dry ice whereas the south pole dry ice cover is about 8 meters deep and does not disappear completely during summertime. These new findings present new mysteries. Planetary scientists have assumed that Earth, Venus, and Mars were formed with similar

total amounts of carbon dioxide. Earth's carbon dioxide is mostly in the form of marine carbonates, whereas Venus' is in the atmosphere causing the greenhouse effect. The latest observations suggest, however, that the total amount of carbon dioxide on Mars is a small fraction of that found on Earth and Venus.

In late 2002, scientists confirmed the presence of water ice at the surface of the southern polar regions of Mars using thermal emission images made by Odyssey and temperature data from the *MGS*. Infrared observations by *Mars Express* directly confirmed in 2004 that water ice is present at Mars' south pole in the form of permafrost. We now split this region in three parts: the south polar cap itself (a mixture of 85% dry ice and 15% water ice), steep slopes (made almost entirely of water ice) from the polar cap to the surrounding plains, and the vast permafrost regions that stretch away from the slopes.

(a)   (b)

FIGURE B8-11 (a) An *MGS* picture of the residual (summertime) north polar cap, covering an area of 1.5 × 3 km. The surface of the cap is covered by pits (estimated to be less than 2 meters deep), cracks, small bumps, and knobs. The summertime temperature at the north cap is usually close to the freezing point of water, and water vapor has been observed by the orbiters. (b) An *MGS* picture, covering an area of 3 × 9 km, of the residual (summertime) south polar cap. The cap has been eroded, leaving flat-topped regions (mesas) standing as high as 4 meters, into which there are circular depressions.

that it contains salts that could be nutrients for life, such as magnesium, potassium, sodium, and perchlorate (an oxidant).

Possible evidence for life on Mars comes from meteorites. About 34 meteorites found on Earth have been identified by astronomers as having come from Mars (based on their composition and on gases trapped inside). The meteorites are causing controversy among scientists. Some who study the meteorites claim to find evidence that some of them were under water while they were on Mars. Furthermore, they claim that the meteorites contain the remains of single-cell organisms, showing that life once existed on Mars. Other scientists, however, claim that the evidence can be understood by simply considering inorganic reactions in Mars' atmosphere and contamination, not biological processes. Also, by using geochemical techniques on a few of the Martian meteorites to find the maximum long-term average temperature they were subjected, some scientists conclude that during the last 4 billion years Mars has never been warm enough for surface liquid water to flow for extended periods of time.

Atmospheric Conditions

Near the Martian equator, noontime temperatures reach as high as 30°C, a comfortable temperature for humans. At night, however, the temperature at the same location might drop to −135°C. The thin atmosphere is the reason for this extreme difference in temperature. As we saw in the discussion of Venus and Earth, a planet's atmosphere shields it from the Sun during the day and serves as a blanket at night by reflecting back some infrared radiation toward the surface. The amount of shielding and reflection is determined by the amount and type of atmosphere. The atmosphere of Mars is 95% carbon dioxide, and one might suppose that Mars would have a greenhouse effect as Venus does; however, the low atmospheric pressure at the surface of Mars means that there is simply too little atmosphere of any type to significantly moderate the temperature.

The escape velocity from Mars is 5 km/s, less than half of Earth's escape velocity. Even though Mars is colder than Earth, almost all of the water vapor, methane, and ammonia have escaped the atmosphere, along with the less massive gases. (Refer again to Figure 7-8.)

If we assume that the primitive atmospheres of Mars and Earth were similar, their current differences are due to their different evolutionary paths (FIGURE 8-29).

30°C corresponds to 86°F, and −135°C corresponds to −210°F.

FIGURE 8-29 A comparison of the atmospheres of three of the terrestrial planets. Mercury is omitted because it has almost no atmosphere.

As we discussed for Earth and Venus, the atmosphere's carbon dioxide gets locked up in carbonate rocks after being washed out by rainfall; however, because Mars did not exhibit a continuous plate tectonic activity, the recycling of carbon dioxide through volcanic activity stopped. This resulted in a permanent depletion of carbon dioxide from the atmosphere and the destruction of the greenhouse effect. As Mars got colder, water could not exist in liquid form.

Another difference between Mars and Earth is that Earth has a layer of ozone that prevents most of the Sun's ultraviolet radiation from reaching the surface. Mars has little ozone, and thus, the Sun's intense ultraviolet radiation passes through the atmosphere and breaks up water vapor into hydrogen and oxygen. The hydrogen escapes and the oxygen enters into chemical reactions with other elements. Also, the absence of a global magnetic field on Mars results in additional depletion of Mars' atmosphere because of its interaction with the solar wind.

One of the elements with which the oxygen combines is iron. The surface of Mars is rich with iron, and when oxygen and iron react, we get a compound that is usually a nuisance to us on Earth—rust. It is this rust that gives Mars its characteristic red color. The views of Mars in FIGURE 8-30 were taken by the *HST* when Mars was in opposition in 1997, at a distance of 60 million miles. The photos show different views of Mars and make the red, rusty color obvious.

From the *Viking* landers, we also learned what causes the seasonal color variations. The fine grains that make up the dust storms are a lighter color than the underlying surface. In the springtime, this dust is stripped away by the wind, exposing the darker surface. Global dust storms on Mars, larger than any seen on Earth, have been observed by the *HST* and *MGS* to last for months. Such events provide a laboratory for observing global warming in real time. The dust traps sunlight and warms the upper atmosphere (by as much as 80°F), while the planet's surface cools under the cloud shroud.

There is no vegetation on Mars. In fact, as we discussed in the Tools of Astronomy box on *Viking*'s Search for Life in this chapter, the *Viking* landers found no signs of *current* life on Mars. This is not the same as saying they found evidence that there was never life on Mars. Perhaps our experiments were too limited in what they were searching for, or perhaps we simply need to look in other locations.

Spectroscopic data in 2004 from the *Mars Express* orbiter indicated the presence of methane in the Martian atmosphere in concentrations that overlap significantly those of water vapor close to the planet's surface over three equatorial areas. These are the same areas where *Odyssey* has detected a layer of water (in the form of ice or

FIGURE 8-30 The three views of Mars (taken by the *Hubble Space Telescope*) show its northern polar cap during the transition from spring to summer in the Martian northern hemisphere.

hydrated minerals) a few tens of centimeters thick below the surface. This suggests a common underground source for both water and methane. Methane is an important greenhouse gas, and it might have played an important role in the environmental changes on Mars. The presence of methane, however, does not necessarily imply the presence of life on the planet because it can be produced just as easily by inorganic processes.

The history of Mars may be more complicated than our current models allow. All of these new data make comparisons between Earth and Mars even more interesting. Current and future explorations underway will continue to change the way that we think of our neighbor, the red planet.

The Moons of Mars

Mars has two natural satellites, named Phobos and Deimos. Both are small and irregularly shaped. Phobos, for example, is 27 km across its longest dimension, but it is 22 km and 18 km across its other dimensions. It thus is shaped like a potato. Deimos is even smaller and is similarly shaped.

Phobos' dimensions are 17 × 14 × 11 miles. Deimos' dimensions are 9 × 8 × 6 miles.

The surfaces of both Martian moons are very dark, similar to those of many asteroids. Their densities are 1.9 and 1.8 times that of water (for Phobos and Deimos, respectively), also similar to the densities of the rocky asteroids. Such similarities lead us to believe that these satellites are captured asteroids rather than objects that were formed in orbit around Mars during the formation of the solar system. A capture like this could have taken place as the asteroid passed very close to Mars and was either slowed by friction with the Martian atmosphere, by collision with a smaller asteroid, or by gravitational pull from another asteroid. Such an event may not seem likely, especially for Phobos because it orbits above Mars' equator, a very special case, but given the number of asteroids that have passed by Mars over billions of years, it is certainly a possibility. In an alternative scenario, each moon could be the byproduct of a meteorite impact on Mars, which resulted in a number of Martian rocks blasting into space and then coalescing to form a rubble pile.

The masses of Phobos and Deimos are so small that you would weigh almost nothing standing on their surfaces. A 120-pound person on Earth would weigh about 1 ounce at the lowest point on Deimos. Escape velocity from Deimos is about 13 miles/hour (21 km/hr), so you could easily throw a ball completely off this moon, never to return. If you threw a ball at a lower speed, it would go into orbit, circling the moon in about three hours. A baseball game on Deimos would be quite strange.

The Martian moons are not only small, but they orbit very close to the planet and have short periods of revolution, about 0.3 days for Phobos and 1.3 days for Deimos. Both revolve in the same direction as most other solar system objects, counterclockwise as seen from a point above the solar system, north of Earth.

The counterclockwise motion of our Moon results in it moving slowly eastward among the stars as viewed from Earth; however, as we watch the Moon during a single night, this eastward motion is overwhelmed by its apparent westward motion that results from the rotation of the Earth. The eastward motion is far from obvious to the casual observer during one night. Things would be quite different for a Martian. Mars rotates with a period of about 24.5 hours in a counterclockwise direction; however, Phobos takes only about 8 hours to circle Mars. As a result, an observer on Mars would see stars move across the sky just as we do on Earth, but that person would see Phobos rise in the west and move across the sky toward the east! Deimos would hover overhead for long periods of time, moving only very slowly toward the west.

Mars has an oblateness of 0.006, which means that its polar diameter is 0.6% smaller than its equatorial diameter. Mars is the most oblate of the terrestrial planets, and, thus, these planets are all very nearly perfectly spherical. We have seen that Phobos and Deimos are far from spherical. Before explaining why they are not spheres, we should first explain why one might expect celestial objects to be spherical.

HISTORICAL NOTE

The Discovery of the Martian Moons

Although Johannes Kepler made important contributions to science, he was very nonscientific in some ways. One of the patterns he saw in the heavens concerned the numbers of satellites of the various planets. Mercury and Venus have none, Earth one, and Jupiter four (known at that time). Between Earth and Jupiter was Mars, and Kepler proposed that Mars must have two moons if it is to fit the pattern. From the time of Kepler, popular thought held that Mars must have two moons circling it. The idea appears a few times in literature, most notably in Jonathan Swift's *Gulliver's Travels*, where Swift makes up such details as the moons' size (small) and orbital periods.

There was no evidence for the existence of any satellites of Mars until 1877 when Asaph Hall, the astronomer of the newly constructed U.S. Naval Observatory near Washington, D.C., decided to search very near the planet for moons. To do so, he used a disk that blocked the planet's brightness from his view. According to Carl Sagan, Hall was unsuccessful for the first few nights and was about to quit when his wife encouraged him to continue searching. He did find the two moons and named them Phobos (Fear) and Deimos (Terror), the names of the horses that pulled the chariot of the Greek god of war. FIGURE B8-12 is a *Mars Express* image of Phobos showing the Mars-facing side of the moon.

The actual orbital periods of the two moons are 7.7 and 30.3 hours. Although Swift had predicted 10 and 21.5 hours, he hit close enough to the actual times that some people believe that he had special knowledge of some sort. Actually, it was reasonable for him to assume that the moons—if they existed—must be close to the planet and must be small.

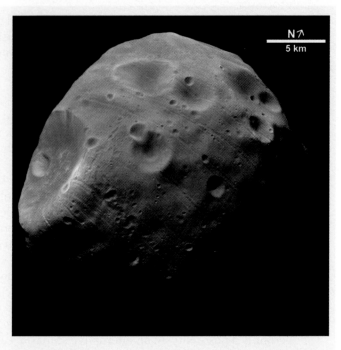

FIGURE B8-12 This color image of Phobos was taken by *Mars Express* from a distance of less than 200 km. The scale bar is only valid for the center of the image.

Otherwise they would already have been discovered, and if they are close to the planet, Kepler's laws tell us that their periods of revolution must be short. There is no reason to hypothesize strange explanations for Swift's guesses. He just knew about Kepler's work.

◆ We explain why the equatorial diameter of a planet might be greater than its polar diameter when we discuss Jupiter, a noticeable out-of-round planet.

◆ Most asteroids are likewise nonspherical.

A celestial object tends to be spherical because the force of gravity pulls its parts toward its center. As a result, the object takes the shape that will give it the smallest possible surface area. This shape is a sphere. Consider what would happen if the Earth were a cube. In this case, a rock at a corner of the cube could get closer to Earth's center by moving to the center of one face of the cube. In that event, the Earth would not remain a cube. Earthly mountains, which are formed by geological phenomena within the Earth (such as volcanic action), are forever being disturbed by wind and rain so that their parts can be pulled closer to the center, making the planet a more perfect sphere.

The same tendency exists in the case of Phobos and Deimos, but the gravitational force toward the center is too small to form these small objects into a spherical shape. The strength of the rock of which the moon is made resists the weak gravitational force that tends to reshape it.

Phobos and Deimos are more interesting to us than their size might seem to indicate. In fact, we may visit them some day. When people go to Mars, some plans call for using Phobos as a landing area before proceeding to the surface of the planet. The moon's weak gravitational field will make landing and taking off easy.

8-4 Why Explore?

The Martian invasion continues. Despite failures of some (1999) missions to Mars, ambitious plans are being made for its further exploration. For example, the *Mars Science Laboratory* is the next Rover mission planned to arrive at the red planet in late 2012; it will collect and analyze soil and rock samples in greater detail than ever before, and it will be able to identify organic compounds and atmospheric gases that are associated with biological activity. In 1989, President G. H. W. Bush established a goal of a human expedition to Mars. This venture will probably be international in scope, and it may be preceded by an unmanned mission that returns samples from the planet.

We have learned much about our planetary neighbors by observing them from Earth, but there is a limit to what we can learn without sending spacecraft to visit these worlds. Some people question the value of using our resources for these endeavors. There are two answers to their questions.

First, seeking knowledge about our universe is one of the things that separates humans from any other known creature. It is our nature to explore, just as it is our nature to enjoy music and art. If we never achieve one practical benefit from planetary exploration, such exploration would be valuable simply because seeking new knowledge is one of our highest aspirations. The amount of money that should be spent on such endeavors might be a subject for discussion, but when we compare the total amount of money spent on the basic sciences with what is spent on warfare or entertainment, we see that the money spent on space exploration is trivial.

Second, planetary exploration offers many practical benefits. Few would argue that knowledge of Earth is without practical benefit, but many people do not realize that a study of other planets is a valuable source of knowledge about our Earth. If we did not study other planets, we would be severely limited in what we would know about our own planet. For example, by learning more about the greenhouse effect on Venus and the lack of such an effect on Mars, we will find out how serious the threat of a runaway greenhouse effect is here on Earth. We cannot afford to experiment with our planet, but an examination of other planets provides us with just such an experiment. By studying weather systems on other planets, we learn about our own. Was there once life on Mars? If so, why does it not seem to be there now? Could the same thing happen on Earth? Surely such knowledge is of practical benefit.

Imagination will often carry us to worlds that never were. But without it we go nowhere.
—Carl Sagan

Conclusion

Throughout history, people have wondered about the planets. With the advent of telescopes, particularly the larger ones, we began to learn something about their surfaces; however, it was the planetary visits of the space age that made us think of these planets as *places*, rather than as celestial objects. We now have detailed maps of their surfaces, and landers have invaded Venus and Mars to begin exploration.

As we learn more about the other terrestrial planets, we are finding that in many ways they are similar, for they share a common history of formation, but we also find major differences. Some of the differences exist because the planets differ in size and mass. These factors determine whether a planet will retain an atmosphere, and the atmosphere of a planet determines such properties as the planet's range of temperature. Other differences occur simply because of the planets' different distances from the Sun.

In the next chapter, we move out to the Jovian planets. Each of these giants forms another piece of the puzzle of how the solar system—including the inhabitants of its third planet—came to be.

STUDY GUIDE

1. Mercury's atmosphere is
   A. mostly hydrogen.
   B. mostly hydrogen and helium.
   C. mostly nitrogen and oxygen.
   D. virtually nonexistent.

2. Mercury's rotation and revolution are linked so that Caloris Basin is
   A. directly under the Sun at every perihelion passage.
   B. directly under the Sun at alternate perihelion passages.
   C. never directly under the Sun.

3. Mercury's surface is difficult to map from Earth because
   A. Mercury is such a small planet.
   B. Mercury rotates so slowly.
   C. the surface is hidden below a thick cloud cover.
   D. Mercury is always close to the Sun.
   E. [All of the above.]

4. Mercury's diameter is about
   A. one fifth of Earth's.
   B. one third of Earth's.
   C. the same as Earth's.
   D. twice that of Earth's.
   E. more than twice that of Earth's.

5. The property of Mercury that makes its temperature variations greater than those of any other planet is primarily
   A. its lack of an atmosphere.
   B. its proximity to the Sun.
   C. its small size.
   D. the carbon dioxide in its atmosphere.
   E. [The statement is false; Mercury is so close to the Sun that it is always hot.]

6. *Mariner* spacecraft found that Mercury has _____, and this leads us to conclude that the planet _____.
   A. no magnetic field . . . rotates very slowly
   B. no magnetic field . . . has little or no iron in it
   C. a magnetic field . . . rotates faster than we had thought
   D. a magnetic field . . . has a metallic core
   E. [Both A and B above.]

7. The greenhouse effect heats a planet because
   A. more sunlight strikes the planet's surface than normal.
   B. the surface of the planet is darker than normal.
   C. infrared radiation is trapped by the planet's atmosphere.
   D. cloud cover prevents the atmosphere from escaping.
   E. cloud cover prevents visible light from striking the surface.

8. In which of the following ways is Venus most like the Earth?
   A. Its period of rotation.
   B. Its average surface temperature.
   C. Its average density.
   D. The length of its day.
   E. The composition of its clouds.

9. When we see Venus in the sky, the light we receive is sunlight reflecting from
   A. its oceans.
   B. its solid surface.
   C. the top of its cloud layer.
   D. [Both A and B above.]
   E. [All of the above.]

10. A planet that has a high albedo
    A. is necessarily a large planet.
    B. is necessarily a small planet.
    C. has water or ice on its surface.
    D. has clouds in its atmosphere.
    E. reflects a relatively high percentage of the light that hits it.

11. The primary constituent of Venus' atmosphere is
    A. oxygen.
    B. water vapor.
    C. nitrogen.
    D. sulfuric acid.
    E. carbon dioxide.

12. Mars is least similar to Earth in
    A. the tilt of its equator to its orbital plane.
    B. its period of rotation.
    C. that Mars' surface is not hard.
    D. its atmosphere.

13. The two moons of Mars are named
    A. Ceres and Pallas.
    B. Io and Europa.
    C. Galileo and Copernicus.
    D. Helios and Juno.
    E. Phobos and Deimos.

14. The seasonal color changes on Mars probably result from
    A. vegetation.
    B. rain.
    C. dust movement.
    D. dry ice.
    E. [Both A and B above.]

15. The Martian polar caps
    A. are all water ice.
    B. are all frozen carbon dioxide ("dry ice").
    C. are a combination of carbon dioxide and water ice.
    D. completely disappear during the Martian summer.
    E. [Two of the above.]

16. Which of the following statements about the Martian satellites is true?
    A. Both are large satellites (nearly the size of Earth's Moon).
    B. Both are small satellites compared with Earth's.
    C. One is very large and the other is small.
    D. Mars has only one satellite.

17. The main source of erosion on Mars today is
    A. flowing liquids in the channels.
    B. ice flows that cover the entire planet in winter.
    C. microscopic organisms in a layer just below the surface.
    D. giant dust storms.
    E. [The statement is false; there is no erosion on Mars.]

18. The channels of Mars (observed in the 19th century) were found to be
    A. irrigation ditches dug by now-extinct Martians.
    B. faults in the Martian crust.
    C. straight mountain ranges.
    D. optical illusions.

19. Mars' moons are not spherical like Earth's Moon because
    A. of cratering.
    B. their gravitational force is not strong enough.
    C. they are much older than our Moon.
    D. they are much younger than our Moon.
    E. [The statement is false; they are spherical.]

20. Olympus Mons has a base _____ miles in diameter and a height of _____ miles.
    A. 5000 . . . 40
    B. 400 . . . 15
    C. 20 . . . 2
    D. 10 . . . 1

21. Why do Venus and Mars have larger volcanoes than Earth?
    A. Differences in atmospheres result in volcanoes being larger.
    B. Movement of the Earth's crust has prevented our volcanoes from growing as large as those on the other planets.
    C. Erosion on Earth is more prominent than on either of the other planets.
    D. [The statement is false; Earth's volcanoes are larger.]

22. Water is thought to be present on Mars
    A. in its polar caps.
    B. in permafrost below its surface.
    C. in liquid form on its surface.
    D. [Both A and B above.]
    E. [All of the above.]

23. If we list the terrestrial planets in order of increasing atmospheric pressure at the surface, the list should read
    A. Mercury, Venus, Earth, Mars.
    B. Mercury, Earth, Venus, Mars.
    C. Mercury, Earth, Mars, Venus.
    D. Mercury, Mars, Earth, Venus.
    E. Mars, Mercury, Earth, Venus.

24. The escape velocity from the surface is least for which of the following planets?
    A. Mercury.
    B. Venus.
    C. Earth.
    D. Mars.

25. Which is the smallest of the terrestrial planets?

26. Which planet is most similar to the Earth in size? In rotation period?

27. Why is the surface of Mercury difficult to see from Earth?

28. What is unusual about the revolution and rotation rates of Mercury and why has this occurred?

29. How was the most accurate value for Mercury's mass obtained?

30. Explain why Mercury's surface experiences such great extremes of temperature.

31. In what ways is Venus the Earth's sister planet? In what ways is it different?

32. What is the greenhouse effect? Why is the effect not an exact analogy to a greenhouse on Earth?

33. Describe the surfaces of Mercury, Venus, and Mars.

34. How does the tilt of Mars' axis compare with Earth's?

35. What is meant by a planet being in opposition? In inferior conjunction?

36. Of what are Mars' polar caps composed?

37. Why can't liquid water exist on Mars? What is the evidence that liquid water once flowed on Mars?

38. How do the daily temperature changes on Mars compare with those on Earth? Why does this difference exist?

39. Explain why large celestial objects tend to be spherical and how some small ones avoid that fate.

1. What is unusual about Mercury's period of rotation? What is the hypothesized explanation for this regularity of motion?

2. What causes Mercury's temperature variations to be so great?

3. Why do we not expect Venus to have a strong magnetic field?

4. Why is Venus' orbital tilt usually shown as 177°, as this would seem to be the same as saying it is tilted 3°?

5. Describe the evidence that Venus is—or recently has been—volcanically active.

6. We see hot-spot volcanoes on Venus but not in "linear chains" like the Hawaiian chain on Earth. What does this mean about the differences in tectonic activity between the two planets?

7. What would be the effect on a planet's temperature if its atmosphere reflected most of the visible light striking it but let infrared radiation pass through?

8. The difference between the length of the solar day and the sidereal day is much greater for Earth than for Mars. Why?

9. Mars has no ozone layer protecting its surface from ultraviolet radiation. Our industrial society may be destroying the ozone layer here on Earth. Report on the latest research concerning depletion of the Earth's ozone layer.

10. Why is it reasonable to assume that Venus, Earth, and Mars started with roughly the same primordial atmospheres? Why are the atmospheres of the three planets so different today?

11. In discussing our search for life beyond Earth, researchers point out that "absence of evidence is not evidence of absence." Explain this statement.

1. If a planet has a diameter one third of Earth's, how does its surface area compare with Earth's? Its volume?

2. Jupiter's diameter is 11 times Earth's diameter. Compare the volume of Jupiter with the volume of Earth.

3. If planet X has a diameter four times that of planet Y, and both start at the same temperature, which will cool faster? By what factor?

4. You are observing Mercury using a telescope that can resolve features as small as 1 arcsecond. Observing con-ditions are good and the planet is at about 1 AU away from Earth. Using the small-angle formula, find the size of the smallest surface features you could see on Mercury. Compare your answer with the size of Caloris Basin, shown in Figure 8-6.

5. Using Figure 8-1, show that Mercury never rises (or sets) more than about 2 hours before (or after) the Sun.

6. Mars' semimajor axis is 1.524 AU. Using Kepler's third law, show that the planet's sidereal orbital period is 1.88 years.

Viewing Mercury, Venus, and Mars

Helpful advice for observing Mercury, Venus, and Mars is available for the amateur astronomer in several monthly magazines, particularly *Astronomy* and *Sky & Telescope*. They include diagrams of planetary locations and hints on viewing.

Within about 45 minutes of sunrise and sunset, the sky is so bright that Mercury is particularly difficult to see with the naked eye. If you are viewing in the morning, you thus should begin your search at least an hour before sunrise. In the evenings, there is no need to begin searching until about 45 minutes after sunset. Mercury is never easy to find for the first time, and you must have a very clear sky and a low horizon.

Venus should be easy to find any time the sky is clear. Venus is bright enough that you can find it as close as 20 minutes to sunrise or sunset.

If a telescope is available to you, use it to observe the planets. You should be able to see the phases of Venus (and perhaps Mercury).

You can find information about current explorations of our solar system at NASA's homepage (http://www.nasa.gov).

1. "Mercury: The Forgotten Planet," by R. Strom, in *Sky & Telescope* (September, 1990).

2. "The New Face of Venus," by E. R. Stofan, in *Sky & Telescope* (August, 1993).

3. "What Makes Venus Go?" by R. Burnham, in *Astronomy* (January, 1993).

4. "Global Climate Change on Venus," by M. A. Bullock and D. H. Grinspoon, in *Scientific American* (March, 1999).

5. "Welcome to Mars!" by C. C. Petersen, in *Sky & Telescope* (October, 1997).

6. "Mars Global Surveyor: You Ain't Seen Nothin' Yet," by S. Parker, in *Sky & Telescope* (January, 1998).

7. "Global Climatic Change on Mars," by J. S. Kargel and R. G. Strom, in *Scientific American* (November, 1996).

8. "On Mars, a Second Chance for Life," by Richard A. Kerr, in *Science* (December 17, 2004).

9. "Global Climate Change on Venus," by M. A. Bullock and D. H. Grinspoon, in *Scientific American* Special Edition (Septemeber 2003).

10. "Mercury: The Forgotten Planet," by R. M. Nelson, in *Scientific American* Special Edition (September 2003).

11. "The Spirit of Exploration," by G. Musser, in *Scientific American* (March 2004).

12. "The Transit of Venus," by S. J. Dick, in *Scientific American* (May 2004).

13. "The Many Faces of Mars," by P. R. Christensen, in *Scientific American* (July 2005).

14. "The Red Planet's Watery Past," by J. Bell, in *Scientific American* (December 2006).

15. "The Mystery of Methane on Mars and Titan," by S. K. Atreya, in *Scientific American* (May 2007).

16. "The Planetary Air Leak," by D. C. Catling and K. J. Zahnle, in *Scientific American* (May 2009).

Quest Ahead to Starlinks
http://physicalscience.jbpub.com/starlinks

Starlinks is this book's online learning center. It features **eLearning**, which contains chapter quizzes and other tools designed to help you study for your class. You can also find **online exercises**, view numerous relevant **animations**, follow a guide to **useful astronomy sites** on the Web, or even check the latest **astronomy news** updates.

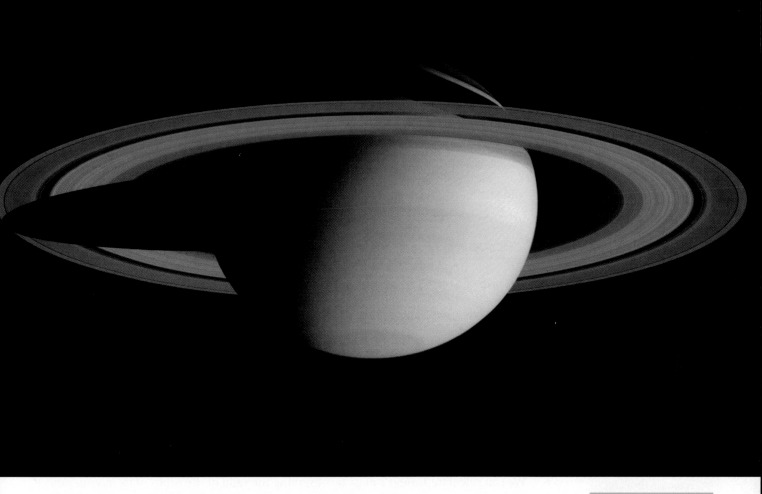

The Jovian Planets

9

IN OCTOBER 1997, THE SPACECRAFT *CASSINI* was launched toward Saturn. (It was named for astronomer Giovanni Cassini, who in 1675 observed that Saturn's rings were separated by a gap, now called the Cassini Division.) *Cassini* (with a mass of about 5650 kilograms, the mass of a small school bus) was launched toward Venus rather than Saturn in order to take advantage of a "gravitational assist," which uses the gravitational field of a planet to increase the speed of a passing spacecraft. *Cassini* got two assists from Venus, one from Earth, and one from Jupiter before finally arriving at Saturn in July 2004. Without such assists, *Cassini* would have taken decades to get to Saturn. (Gravitational assists come with a price. When the *Voyager* spacecraft got an assist from Jupiter, *Voyager* gained 36,000 miles/hour at a cost of slowing down Jupiter by 1 foot every trillion years!)

Nineteen days before arrival at Saturn, *Cassini* passed close to Phoebe, Saturn's most distant satellite. Of all the moons in the solar system, Phoebe is one of the most curious. Its inclined, retrograde orbit suggests that the moon may be a captured object, perhaps an old comet or asteroid that wandered close to Saturn in ages long past.

The tour of Saturn is ongoing, as *Cassini* makes tens of orbits with various orientations, from as close as three Saturn radii to more than seven. It is collecting large amounts of data about the planet, its rings, and its moons, and it is making many

This 2004 image is a composite of many *Cassini* images of Saturn and its rings in natural color. The planet's shadow on the rings is seen on the left; ring shadows are seen against the planet's blue northern hemisphere; blue-grey storms are seen on the right, in the planet's southern hemisphere.

All cross references to chapters, sections, figures, and tables pertain to the main text, *In Quest of the Universe, Sixth Edition. In Quest of the Solar System* contains Chapters 1–11 and 19 of the main text. *In Quest of the Stars and Galaxies* contains Chapters 1–5 and 11–19 of the main text.

flybys of Saturn's moon Titan—the second largest moon in the solar system. On December 25, 2004, *Cassini* dropped the *Huygens* probe (supplied by ESA) to Titan; the probe landed on January 14, 2005, and explored Titan's clouds, atmosphere, and surface.

In this chapter, we turn our attention to the planets of the outer solar system—the Jovian planets. (The dwarf planets will be reserved for the next chapter.) Although Mercury, Venus, and Mars are certainly strange worlds for us, in this chapter we show that the outer planets are even stranger. We consider these planets in order as we continue our journey out from the Sun. There is still a lot that astronomers do not know about our neighboring worlds, and you will see that as we get farther and farther from our home base, less and less is known about the objects there.

The *Cassini-Huygens* venture includes the *Cassini* orbiter and the *Huygens* probe. It is a collaboration of three space agencies (NASA, ESA, ASI) and scientists and engineers from 15 countries on both sides of the Atlantic.

9-1   Jupiter

The size of a planet is not apparent to the naked eye, but long before the invention of the telescope, Copernicus had deduced that Jupiter was larger than Venus, even though Venus at its brightest is brighter than Jupiter. From the two planets' relative brightnesses and distances, he concluded that because Jupiter is so much farther away, if it shines only by reflected light it would have to be much larger to appear so bright. Galileo observed the planets' angular sizes with a telescope and was able to determine that Jupiter was indeed larger, for he could use their angular sizes and relative distances to calculate their relative sizes. Today we know that Jupiter is the largest object in the solar system besides the Sun. It is appropriate, then, that it is named after the king of the Roman gods.

Copernicus simply assumed that every planet reflects the same percentage of the light that hits it.

Jupiter as Seen From Earth

We can calculate Jupiter's mass by observing the radii of the orbits of its moons and their periods of revolution, as explained in Chapter 7. Jupiter has more than twice the combined mass of all the other planets, their moons, and the asteroids. When compared with the Earth, Jupiter is 318 times more massive.

In size, Jupiter is even more remarkable. Look back at Figure 7-1 to see how it compares in size with the other planets. Jupiter's diameter is about 11 times that of the Earth, making its volume about 1400 times that of Earth. Because Jupiter's volume relative to Earth is so much greater than its mass relative to Earth, you might deduce that its density must be less than that of Earth. That's exactly right; Jupiter's density is only about one fourth of Earth's. This means that Jupiter must be composed of a higher percentage of light elements than is the Earth.

Although the Earth's density is about twice as great as common rock, Jupiter's density is 1.3 times that of water.

You might have a tendency to picture Jupiter as a lumbering, slow-moving giant. Indeed, it is 5.2 astronomical units (AU) from the Sun and takes nearly 12 years to circle the Sun; however, its rotation rate is not slow. This gigantic planet spins on its axis once every 9 hours and 55 minutes. This is the first Jovian planet we have studied, and we will find that fast rotation is common for Jovians. Their rotational speeds are much greater than those of the terrestrial planets.

Things are not quite this simple, however. Through even a small telescope we can see that Jupiter has dark- and light-colored bands parallel to its equator. The photograph in **FIGURE 9-1**, which was taken with an Earth-based telescope, shows obvious parallel bands around the planet. Observations show that the bands near the equator rotate slightly faster than those nearer the poles. The band at Jupiter's equator has a rotation period of 9 hours, 50 minutes. Bands closest to the poles complete one rotation in 9 hours, 56 minutes. This "spreading" of the rota-

FIGURE 9-1 The bands around Jupiter are easily visible in this photo taken from Earth. The red spot (lower left) is called "the Great Red Spot." The circle has been drawn to show the oblateness of Jupiter.

tion, or **differential rotation**, indicates that the visible surface of Jupiter is not solid. Instead, it must be at least partially fluid. Like a pot of liquid when stirred, different regions of Jupiter take different amounts of time to rotate around the planet's axis.

Another thing about Jupiter that can be observed fairly easily is that it is slightly flattened at the poles (**oblate**). A circle has been drawn on the photo of Figure 9-1 to make it obvious that Jupiter's equatorial diameter is definitely greater than its polar diameter. In fact, it is 6.5% greater. Both Earth and Mars are oblate, but not nearly as much as Jupiter. The cause for the greater oblateness of Jupiter is its great rotation rate. (Picture a spinning ball of Jello; its spin would cause it to flatten out.)

Jupiter as Seen From Space

We learned a lot about Jupiter from the *Pioneer* and *Voyager* missions in the 1970s; in addition to taking thousands of photographs, the spacecraft contained instruments to detect charged particles, radiation from the planet, and Jupiter's magnetic field.

Galileo orbited Jupiter and its moons between 1995 and 2003, before it finally plunged into Jupiter's atmosphere. Upon reaching Jupiter, *Galileo* dropped a probe into the planet's atmosphere, and some of the information that follows has been learned from *Galileo* and its probe.

As we pointed out in Chapter 8, if we knew more about weather on Venus, we would know more about weather on our own planet. Jupiter may provide an even better study of weather systems than does Venus, for weather patterns in the upper atmosphere of Jupiter are far removed from any solid surface that Jupiter may have and, therefore, are almost unaffected by complications produced by surface irregularities. This is probably what allows Jupiter's weather patterns to last for such long periods. (The practice of examining a simple system to form a working hypothesis about a complicated one is common in science.) The prime example of this is the giant Red Spot on Jupiter (FIGURE 9-2). This spot was seen as early as the mid-1600s, and thus, it has lasted for more than 350 years. The spot is about 40,000 kilometers in length and nearly 15,000 kilometers across. When we realize that the Earth is about 13,000 kilometers in diameter, we can appreciate the immensity of this feature. From time to time over the centuries, the Red Spot has faded in intensity, but it has never disappeared completely.

Data from Jupiter indicate that the Red Spot is a storm system of rising high-pressure gas whose cloud tops are colder and about 8 kilometers higher than the surrounding regions. It is similar to the much smaller Earth systems reported by your local weather forecaster. High-pressure systems in Earth's Northern Hemisphere rotate in a clockwise direction, and in the Southern Hemisphere, they rotate in the opposite direction. The Red Spot is in Jupiter's southern hemisphere, and indeed, it rotates counterclockwise, with a period of about 6 days. As shown in FIGURE 9-3, the winds to the north and south of the Great Red Spot move in opposite directions. The motion of the gas in this region resembles that of a wheel spinning between two surfaces moving in opposite directions. Figure 9-2 is a close-up view of part of the spot; we can see the swirling currents at its edges.

The light-colored bands (called **zones**) around the planet mark the tops of low-pressure, low-temperature, high-altitude regions. These clouds formed by gas that, after being warmed by heat from the planet's interior, rose from inside Jupiter and cooled. The dark-colored bands (called **belts**) mark the tops of high-pressure, high-temperature, low-altitude regions. These clouds formed by gas that gets warmer as it descends (FIGURE 9-4). Jupiter's

differential rotation Rotation of an object in which different parts have different periods of rotation.

oblate Flattened at the poles.

zones/belts The light-colored/dark-colored bands that mark Jupiter's atmosphere.

FIGURE 9-2 Jupiter's Great Red Spot (at upper right) is seen with the fierce turbulence around it. Wind speeds in this system reach 500 km/hr. Earth is superimposed at the same scale to help us appreciate the size of the spot. Another feature that persisted for a long time in Jupiter's atmosphere is seen near the Great Red Spot: it is a white oval region where winds also flow counterclockwise. This is probably an area of high-altitude, cold clouds.

FIGURE 9-3 (a) Jupiter's turbulent and dynamic atmosphere is shown in this *HST* image. The Little Red Spot (LRS) is shown below and to the left of the Great Red Spot (GRS). (b) Jupiter in the near-infrared. The LRS (under the GRS in this image) is the byproduct of three white-colored storms that merged together.

(a)

(b)

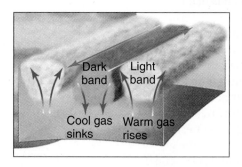

FIGURE 9-4 The light and dark bands on Jupiter are each thousands of kilometers wide, blowing around the planet at 300 to 500 kilometers/hour. The dark bands (belts) are sinking cool gas; the light bands (zones) are rising warm gas. The white patches are ammonia ice.

◆ The Red Spot is difficult to see in a small telescope. Its color is assumed to be the result of a chemical reaction of the Sun's ultraviolet light and cloud material the storm has brought from low altitudes.

◆ The winds in Jupiter's bands move in alternate directions. The strongest winds are on the equator; they move easterly with speeds of up to 170 m/s.

◆ These percentages correspond to the number of particles of each element in the atmosphere.

differential rotation moves the regions around the planet so that it has a banded appearance. This has been the standard interpretation of atmospheric motion in the bands and is based on our experience with Earth's atmosphere, in which many clouds form where air is rising; however, pictures from the *Cassini* spacecraft show that almost without exception individual storm cells of upward-moving bright-white clouds exist in the dark-colored bands. This suggests that the dark-colored bands are the regions of net upward-moving gas motion in Jupiter's atmosphere, with the implication that the light-colored bands correspond to a net downward-moving gas motion. This is exactly the opposite of our current interpretation, shown in Figure 9-4. We still have a lot to learn about the atmospheres of the Jovian planets. In any case, measurements made by *Voyager* show that at the boundaries of each band, the wind velocities are different and in opposite directions. As a result of these different speeds, there is considerable swirling at the boundaries between bands. The stormy nature of these swirls is obvious in the view of the bands in Figures 9-2 and 9-3.

Jupiter's atmosphere goes through global upheavals during which entire bands of clouds change colors over periods of a few months. Such upheavals have been seen many times but it is yet unclear as to what powers them. They could be powered by the Sun, as is the case for Earth. However, three-dimensional computer simulations suggest that convection driven by internal heat sources may be responsible for the complex system of bands and that the wind system may reach as deep as 7000 km into the planet's atmosphere. On the other hand, data obtained by *Galileo* support the idea that lightning storms beneath the upper cloud cover are the energy source for Jupiter's colorful weather patterns. Observed at depths of 80 to 100 kilometers, lightning indicates the presence of water, as nothing else can condense at those depths. As is the case on Earth, lightning may occur in water clouds where positive and negative charges separate as a result of turbulent upward and downward motions of partially frozen ice droplets. Lightning then points to areas where swirling currents occur, which in turn get pulled apart by shear flow and give up their energy to the large-scale features observed on Jupiter. Scientists have also observed the merging of giant storms that had lasted for decades to a single, bigger storm. It is possible that a similar merger took place centuries ago giving us the Great Red Spot.

The Composition of Jupiter's Atmosphere

The terrestrial planets consist mostly of hard, rocky material. Jupiter is different. The compositions of Jupiter and the other Jovian planets are more similar to the Sun than to the terrestrial planets. The *Galileo* probe measured Jupiter's atmospheric composition to be about 90% hydrogen and 10% helium, with small amounts of methane, ammonia, and water vapor. This is similar to the composition of the original solar nebula. *Galileo* detected small amounts of heavier elements (carbon, nitrogen, and sulfur) at concentrations about three times higher than the solar composition, suggesting that meteorites and other small bodies have contributed to the planet's composition. Few complex organic compounds were evident, and thus, the likelihood of finding life as we know it here on Earth is extremely remote.

The *Galileo* probe did not detect the thick, dense clouds that were expected, despite the fact that data received from the probe go down to about 150 kilometers below the top of the atmosphere. Infrared images from Earth-based telescopes and by *Galileo* indicated that the site where the probe descended is not typical.

The probe found that Jupiter has the same helium content as the outer layers of our Sun, but only a 10th of the Sun's neon concentration. Because the outer layers of our Sun lose helium, these observations suggest that there must be a mechanism on Jupiter that removes helium and neon from its upper atmosphere. It is possible that there is helium rain in Jupiter's atmosphere, with neon dissolving in the helium raindrops under certain conditions. Also, the concentration of deuterium—one of the heavy forms of hydrogen—was found to be similar to that of the Sun, but very different from that of comets or of Earth's oceans. This finding minimizes the possible effect that comets may have had on the composition of Jupiter's atmosphere.

The *Galileo* probe also found that the concentrations of the noble gases argon, krypton, and xenon are two to three times higher than the solar composition. The only way for Jupiter to get such quantities of these gases is to trap them by condensation or freezing, which requires very cold temperatures, colder than what we find on the surface of Pluto. This challenges our current theory of planetary formation, as described in Chapter 7. According to this theory, Jupiter and the other giant planets were built up with material found in the original solar nebula. Planetesimals clumped together to form a protoplanet that, after growing to a critical size, started sweeping up gas directly from the nebula. Jupiter's original composition thus was similar to the early Sun's. Since then, the planet has been shaped by continuing collisions with space debris and by its internal differentiation; however, the data suggest that the material that makes up Jupiter must have originated at a much colder place than Jupiter occupies today. It is possible that the original solar nebula was much colder than we currently think, or that planetesimals could have started forming even before the original cloud of dust and gas collapsed to form our solar nebula. It is also possible that Jupiter formed farther from the Sun and then drifted inward. The latter is a very tempting possibility because we have now discovered many planetary systems in which large planets are very close to their stars, as we discussed in Chapter 7. As is usually the case, new observations provide new insights while creating new and exciting problems.

The colors seen in Jupiter's upper atmosphere are thought to be the result of chemical reactions induced by sunlight and/or by lightning in its atmosphere, but this is still an open question. Another possibility is that impurities (possibly in the form of sulfur or phosphorus) in the cloud droplets of water, ammonia, and ammonia sulfides result in the distinctive colors.

In addition to direct observations and the data we received from *Galileo* and its probe, we had an opportunity to learn a great deal about Jupiter's atmosphere by observing a spectacular show in July 1994. During the week of July 16–22, 23 fragments of the comet Shoemaker-Levy 9 crashed into Jupiter's atmosphere, as we discussed at the beginning of Chapter 1. As each fragment entered the atmosphere, the resulting shock wave vaporized it, resulting in a huge, hot fireball that sent millions of tons of material up to 3000 kilometers (1900 miles) above Jupiter's clouds. As the material cooled and fell back to the atmosphere, it left a signature of dark-colored blotches, some of which were the size of the Earth (FIGURE 9-5). Unfortunately, there is no consensus as to the makeup of the fragments or the depth to which they penetrated the atmosphere. As a result, the analysis of the fireball spectra has not provided conclusive information about the chemical composition of Jupiter's atmosphere.

FIGURE 9-5 The *HST* took this ultraviolet image of Jupiter on July 21, 1994, which shows the blotches formed by impact from fragments of the Shoemaker-Levy 9 comet. Many dark patches are seen from different impacts. The reason the spots are dark in the ultraviolet is because sunlight gets absorbed by the large quantity of dust deposited high in Jupiter's atmosphere as a result of the fireballs.

Jupiter's Interior

The gaseous atmosphere of Jupiter is fairly thin, only a few thousand miles in depth. Naturally, the lower you go in the atmosphere, the greater the pressure is (because the gas at lower elevation supports the gas above). On Jupiter, the pressure soon becomes so great that the hydrogen molecules are forced very close together, resulting in liquid hydrogen. On Earth we have a gaseous atmosphere above a liquid ocean; however, on Jupiter there is no distinct boundary between the liquid and the gas. If we could travel inward from the top of the gaseous atmosphere, we would find ourselves in thicker and thicker gas until we finally decided that we were no longer in a gas but were in a liquid.

At perhaps 15,000 kilometers below the cloud tops, another change in Jupiter's composition occurs, caused by the increasingly greater pressures and temperatures. At these depths, electrons move easily from one atom to another, making the hydrogen a good electrical conductor. Because it conducts electricity like a metal, we call it *liquid metallic hydrogen*. Hydrogen in this form cannot be produced on Earth because we cannot create such a combination of high temperature and high pressure, but it is predicted by atomic theories. As FIGURE 9-6 indicates, most of the planet is made up of this state of matter. The latest theoretical calculations show that under the great temperatures and pressures deep inside Jupiter's atmosphere (reaching at the core 70 million times Earth's atmospheric pressure), hydrogen and helium atoms could mix forming a liquid metal alloy; this is a more homogeneous mix than we previously suspected.

Figure 9-6 shows a core of heavy elements at the center of Jupiter. We have no direct evidence that such a core exists, but it is hypothesized on the basis that there must have been heavy elements in the original material of which Jupiter is made. These heavy elements exist on the moons of Jupiter, and there is good reason to think that they also exist on the planet. If so, they would have sunk to the center of Jupiter. The size of this portion of the planet is unknown, but it is thought to have a diameter perhaps as small as Earth's or as much as a few times Earth's diameter. In any case, it makes up a very small portion, perhaps 1%, of the entire planet.

When the *Pioneer* spacecraft passed Jupiter, we learned of that planet's very strong magnetic field. *Voyager* provided more data, and then in February 1992, the *Ulysses* spacecraft passed by the planet and found that Jupiter's magnetic field is even larger and stronger than had previously been thought. Jupiter's magnetic field is nearly 20,000 times stronger than Earth's!

Recall from Chapters 6 and 8 that the dynamo theory of planetary magnetic fields holds that in order for a planet to have a strong magnetic field, two conditions are necessary: rotation and electrically conductive material within the planet. The terrestrial planets appear to have iron (or nickel-iron) cores that are good electrical conductors. Jupiter does not depend on its core to produce its magnetic field, for the liquid metallic hydrogen that makes up much of the planet is responsible—along with Jupiter's fast rotation—for its strong magnetic field.

Like the Earth's magnetic field, Jupiter's field deflects the solar wind around the planet, as well as trapping some of the charged particles of the wind in belts around it. Volcanic eruptions on Jupiter's moon Io also add large quantities of particles (such as hydrogen, oxygen, sulfur, and sulfur dioxide) into Jupiter's **magnetosphere**. The magnetosphere extends to perhaps 15 million kilometers from the planet, enveloping most of Jupiter's satellites. (The field has presented problems to the electronic circuits of spacecraft that passed through it.) FIGURE 9-7a illustrates the radiation belts and magnetosphere of Jupiter. The belts are flattened by the planet's rapid rotation; compare them with the Van Allen belts shown in Chapter 6. Jupiter's magnetosphere is so large that if you could see it from Earth it would cover an area in the sky about three times larger than the full Moon.

Jupiter's magnetic field accelerates the charged particles in the magnetosphere to high speeds. As a result, the temperature of this hot, gas-like mixture of charged particles can reach 400 million kelvin. This is about 25 times larger than the temperature

70,000 km

Hydrogen/ helium gas

Liquid hydrogen — 50,000 km

Liquid metallic hydrogen

10,000 km — Heavy element core

40,000K
11,000K
700K

FIGURE 9-6 The interior of Jupiter consists mostly of liquid metallic hydrogen, possibly with a core made up of heavy elements.

The *Ulysses* spacecraft was built by ESA. In 1992, it used a gravitational assist from Jupiter to go into a polar orbit around the Sun, where it arrived in 1994. After three polar orbits around the Sun the mission ended in 2009.

magnetosphere The volume of space in which the motion of charged particles is controlled by the magnetic field of the planet, rather than by the solar wind.

(a)   (b)

FIGURE 9-7 (a) Three features are sketched in to provide context in this *Cassini* image of Jupiter's vast magnetosphere: a black circle showing the size of Jupiter, lines showing Jupiter's magnetic field, and a cross-section of a doughnut-shaped ring of charged particles circling Jupiter at about Io's orbit. The magnetosphere is normally invisible; however, fast-moving ions within the magnetosphere can pick up electrons to become neutral atoms and thus escape Jupiter's magnetic field. *Cassini's* ion and neutral camera detects these atoms and derives information about their source. The angle between Jupiter's rotational axis and magnetic axis is about 11°. (b) A radio image of Jupiter at a wavelength of 21 centimeters. The bright features beyond the disk are due to synchrotron radiation, which is mainly concentrated along Jupiter's magnetic equator. The radiation is also seen at higher magnetic latitudes as indicated by the two "horns." Rotate this image by about 45° counterclockwise and compare it to part (a).

at the center of our Sun! However, you should not expect nuclear reactions to occur in Jupiter's magnetosphere, as the average density of this gas is very low. In order to have nuclear reactions, we need both high densities and high temperatures; however, the fast-moving charged particles trapped in Jupiter's magnetic field do emit radiation, which is observed at radio wavelengths (Figure 9-7b).

As you might expect, powerful auroras form close to Jupiter's poles, a thousand times more powerful than on Earth (**FIGURE 9-8**). Contrary to Earth's auroras, which are caused by solar storms, Jupiter creates its own auroras. The planet's fast rotation and strong magnetic field generates millions of volts around its poles; these strong electric fields force charged particles to spiral along the magnetic field lines and crash into Jupiter's upper atmosphere at high speeds. As a result, violent winds blow in these regions of the auroras, producing lots of energy (due to friction) as they interact with the rest of Jupiter's atmosphere. This might explain why the temperature at the top of Jupiter's atmosphere is about 1000 K, much hotter than expected for a planet so far away from the Sun.

Is the center of our Sun the "hottest" place in our solar system?

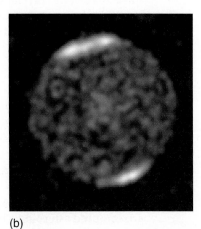

(a)   (b)

FIGURE 9-8 (a) In this 1998 *HST* ultraviolet image the auroral lights are the bright emissions above the dark blue background. (b) The *Chandra* image shows Jupiter's intense X-ray emission associated with auroras in the polar regions. The charged particles are primarily oxygen and sulfur ions.

Energy From Jupiter

Several puzzles concerning Jupiter remain besides the composition of its interior. One such puzzle results from the fact that Jupiter emits more energy than it absorbs from the Sun. This was known before the *Pioneer* and *Voyager* missions, and those missions only confirmed the observations. Let's explain why this is a problem.

We would expect the radiation coming from a planet to be simply the sum of the solar radiation that is reflected from the planet and the infrared radiation that is emitted as the planet re-emits the absorbed solar radiation. We don't expect a planet to have an energy source of its own. It is easy to calculate the amount of solar energy that strikes any planet. In Chapter 4 we discussed the inverse square law of radiation—the fact that as light emitted by the Sun spreads out in a spherical volume, the amount of energy collected per unit area decreases as the square of its distance from the Sun. We, therefore, can use our knowledge of how much solar energy strikes a square mile of Earth's upper atmosphere, along with the inverse square law, to calculate the energy that strikes a square mile of another planet's surface (or atmosphere). Then we multiply this value by the cross-sectional area of the planet to get the total solar energy that strikes that planet.

When the energy that strikes a planet is compared with the energy reflected and emitted from the planet, we expect to find that the energy coming from the planet is the same as the energy absorbed. If it isn't, the planet must either be heating up as it gains energy or cooling as it loses energy.

Jupiter, however, does not behave as expected; it emits about twice as much energy as it absorbs. There are three possible ways for it to do this. One possibility is that it may have an internal energy source, such as chemical reactions or a source of radioactivity, within it. There is no reason to believe that much energy is produced in Jupiter by either of these methods. It was once hypothesized that Jupiter acts like a miniature star, with significant nuclear fusion reactions going on within it. (Nuclear fusion reactions provide the energy of the stars.) However, further calculations showed that Jupiter is not massive enough and does not have sufficient internal pressures or temperatures to support fusion reactions.

A second possibility: recall from Chapter 7 that as an object shrinks due to gravitational force, it heats up. Calculations show that Jupiter may still be shrinking and producing heat; however, if this were the case, the amount of shrinking would still not be enough to explain all of the extra energy from Jupiter.

It is possible that the excess energy from Jupiter is energy left over from its formation. By now, the smaller planets have lost most of their excess energy, but Jupiter's immense size has served to insulate its interior so that it cools slowly, and the cooling continues even today. Computer models show a temperature of about 40,000 K for Jupiter's center and a density about 20 times larger than the density of water. However, a comparison between *Cassini* measurements of the solar wind and simultaneous *HST* observations of Jupiter's auroras in the ultraviolet shows that there is a strong correlation between the behavior of Jupiter's polar auroras and the strength of the solar wind. It seems that Jupiter receives substantial amounts of energy from the solar wind.

Jupiter would have to be nearly 80 times more massive to support nuclear fusion.

Do not get the idea that Jupiter gets significantly cooler from year to year. The planet is so large that the extra energy emitted from it corresponds to an extremely small temperature change.

Jupiter's Moons

Jupiter's family of 63 moons (as of June 2009) can be divided mainly into three groups. The first group includes four moons that are very close to Jupiter, inside Io's orbit. These satellites are generally referred to as fragmented moonlets. The second group includes the four Galilean satellites (Io, Europa, Ganymede, and Callisto) orbiting in nearly circular orbits. The third group includes the remaining 55 moons; the majority of the outermost of these moons orbit in a clockwise direction, different from the rest of Jupiter's moons (and most objects in the solar system), and their orbits are fairly eccentric. Astronomers hypothesize that the moons in the third group are captured asteroids. That is, they once orbited the Sun but came close enough to the Jovian system that they were captured by the planet's gravity. In its early history,

Jupiter probably had a more extensive atmosphere, which might have been sufficient to slow down the asteroids so they could be captured. The moons have black surfaces, as do many asteroids, providing further support for the hypothesis. It has been suggested that these outer moons are divided into two groups orbiting in opposite directions because only two asteroids were captured, each of which broke into pieces when it hit Jupiter's atmosphere.

Among the Galilean satellites, Europa, the smallest, is 7000 times more massive than the largest of the non-Galilean moons. FIGURE 9-9 shows the relative sizes of the four Galilean moons. Because of the large gravitational forces exerted by Jupiter, the Galilean moons keep the same face toward Jupiter as they move in their orbits. In addition, the three moons closest to Jupiter influence each other's orbital period, with Io orbiting Jupiter twice for each orbit of Europa and Europa orbiting Jupiter twice for each orbit of Ganymede.

1. Io. The Galilean moon nearest Jupiter is Io. FIGURE 9-10 shows Io's strange, mottled surface. Its yellow-orange color is caused by the element sulfur, which covers its surface. During the *Voyager* mission, the biggest surprise to astronomers came when Linda Moribito of NASA, while examining *Voyager* photographs, discovered an active volcano on Io. *Galileo* and the two *Voyager* craft photographed many more active volcanoes or geysers (FIGURE 9-11). The circles and dark spots you see in the photograph of Io are not impact craters; they are the results of volcanoes. In fact, the volcanoes explain the lack of impact craters, for the surface of Io is constantly changing by the release of hot sulfur and sulfur dioxide from below the surface. (Sulfur dioxide is a gas on Earth, but on Io it can be either a solid or a gas at the surface, or a subsurface liquid.) Sulfur can take many different colors if heated and then suddenly cooled, and this probably explains the many colors on Io. Originally, *Voyager* images suggested that the lava flows on Io's surface were mostly molten sulfur; however, sulfur vaporizes at about 700 K, whereas *Galileo* has observed lava flows at temperatures as high as 1800 K—about

FIGURE 9-9 This is a "family portrait" that includes Jupiter (with its Great Red Spot) and its largest moons. From top to bottom the Galilean moons shown are Io, Europa, Ganymede, and Callisto.

The term *geyser* is more appropriate than *volcano* because the eruptions do not come from mountain tops. The propulsive agent here is sulfur dioxide, which changes from liquid into high-pressure gas in Io's interior.

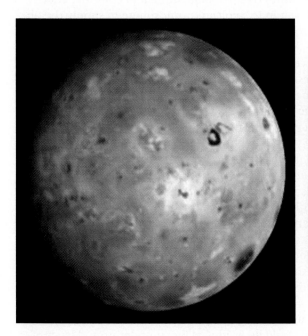

FIGURE 9-10 Io, the innermost of the Galilean satellites, has several active volcanoes on its surface. This *Galileo* image is color enhanced with data taken in the near-infrared, green and violet filters.

FIGURE 9-11 This *Galileo* image shows two volcanic plumes on Io. One plume (at the edge of the moon and at upper right inset) is 140 km high. The second plume (at center and at lower right inset) is 75 km high and may have been continuously active for more than 18 years. We now recognize at least 120 different active volcanoes on Io.

---

ing in this environment, as they do deep in Earth's oceans near volcanic vents. As a result, Europa is a major target of our searches for life in the solar system.

There are few craters on Europa. We know of only about 10 impact craters with diameters greater than 20 kilometers. Again, this does not indicate that meteoroids have not struck Europa, but rather that its surface is young and active so that craters do not remain visible for long. Although it is farther from Jupiter than Io, Europa also experiences tidal heating. There appears to be at least one volcano on Europa, although what looks like a volcano may simply be water spraying out through a crack in the moon's crust, forced out by pressure resulting from tidal flexing. The cracks in Europa's surface are hypothesized to be another result of this flexing.

3. Ganymede. Ganymede is the largest moon in the solar system; it is larger than the planet Mercury. On its surface (FIGURE 9-14) we see ice, but notice how different Ganymede is from Europa. There are craters, indicating that its surface is not as active. Its ice is also darker than Europa's. This darker color is due to dust from meteorites that spreads across the surface of the satellite after impact. On Europa, the surface is constantly being refreshed with water from below, causing the meteorite dust to be spread through a much deeper layer of the satellite. The less active surface of Ganymede, on the other hand, leaves the dust on the surface; however, there are light-colored streaks on Ganymede, the origins of which are clearly tectonic. These are where cracks have formed and icy slush from below has welled up to fill the cracks. Data from *Galileo* suggest that Ganymede has a small iron or iron/sulfur core, surrounded by a rocky mantle and a shell of ice (maybe 800-km thick) at the surface. *Galileo's* data also suggest that Ganymede generates its own magnetic field, most likely due to a thick layer of liquid, salty water deep under its icy crust.

Is Earth the only place in the solar system where liquid water can exist?

4. Callisto. The outermost of the Galilean moons is Callisto (FIGURE 9-15). Now we see a more familiar cratered surface. At its greater distance from Jupiter, Callisto experiences little tidal heating and has a very inactive surface. It actually has the most cratered surface of any observed object in the solar system. The newer craters are the whitest, showing where a meteorite impact has brought clean ice to the surface. The large white crater near the top of the photograph is named Valhalla and is the largest impact crater known in the solar system. Callisto seems to have a relatively uniform mixture of ice (40%) and rock (60%), with the percentage of rock increasing toward the center. Observations of the region exactly opposite to the Valhalla crater on the moon's surface do not show any signs of such an impact. Such signs are seen on similar-sized worlds, like Mercury and our Moon. It is then possible that a liquid layer exists under Callisto's crust acting as a shock absorber.

Galileo's magnetometer data support the idea that Callisto may have a liquid layer under its crust.

FIGURE 9-14 Ganymede is larger than Mercury. The craters on the surface appear bright, possibly due to clean ice at lower depths.

FIGURE 9-15 Callisto, the Galilean satellite that is farthest from Jupiter, has the least active surface.

Summary: The Galilean Moons

As one moves from the innermost Galilean moon to the outermost, patterns of change are obvious. The farther the moon is from Jupiter,

1. The less active the surface,
2. The lower the average density of the moon, and
3. The greater the proportion of water (frozen and liquid).

Points 2 and 3 listed here are related, for because water has a lower density than most other substances on the moons, the more water on a moon, the lower its density.

According to the standard model describing the formation of the Galilean moons, the moons formed from a disk orbiting Jupiter. The combined mass of the moons suggests that the mass of this disk was 2% of Jupiter's mass. The model assumes that the disk formed first and then the moons formed within it; however, the patterns of change we mentioned previously are not consistent with such a model. The temperatures in such a massive and gas-rich disk would be too high for ice to exist for long enough periods for Ganymede and Callisto to form. A new model is emerging in which the material necessary to form the moons is delivered to the disk over a long period of time as Jupiter itself is growing by accreting gas and particles from the original solar nebula. According to this model, the Galilean moons formed slowly, over 100,000 to 1 million years, in a disk where the temperatures remained low enough for ice to exist naturally.

FIGURE 9-16 The ring system of Jupiter was imaged by the *Galileo* spacecraft in 1996. The rings clearly show a structure that had only been hinted at in the *Voyager* images.

Jupiter's Rings

A surprising discovery by *Voyager 1* was that Jupiter has rings. **FIGURE 9-16** shows the rings as photographed by *Galileo*. The photograph was made when the camera was in Jupiter's shadow. The light that reached the camera from the rings was therefore scattered forward by the material of the rings; because large chunks of matter cannot scatter light in this manner, the rings are known to be made of very tiny particles (as small as particles of cigarette smoke). The rings are fairly close to Jupiter, extending to about 0.8 planetary radius from the planet's surface.

Calculations indicate that the particles of Jupiter's rings could not have been there since the formation of the solar system because radiation pressure from the Sun as well as forces from Jupiter's strong magnetic field would gradually send some particles down to the planet and others away into space. The rings, therefore, are thought to be continually replenished, probably by meteoroid impacts on small moonlets within it or near it; two of these moonlets, Adrastea and Metis (Jupiter's innermost moons), orbit through the outer portion of the rings. We discuss planetary rings further when we discuss Saturn and its very prominent system of rings.

The age of a typical ring is a few hundred million years. The lifetime of a ring increases as a result of the recycling of material from moonlets destroyed by impacts.

In Roman mythology, Saturn was the god of agriculture and the father of Jupiter.

9-2   Saturn

As shown in the chapter opening image, Saturn is probably the most impressive object visible with a small telescope. Galileo, who first observed it in 1610, called Saturn "the planet with ears" and was unable to explain what appeared to be bumps on opposite sides of it. Some 50 years later, Christian Huygens recognized that the "ears" were due to rings around the planet.

Huygens (1629–1695) was a Dutch physicist and astronomer who made major advances in the field of optics. He also discovered Saturn's moon Titan. The probe dropped on Titan from the *Cassini* spacecraft was named *Huygens* in his honor.

Size, Mass, and Density

Saturn has an equatorial diameter of 120,000 kilometers, not much smaller than Jupiter's and more than nine times that of the Earth (**FIGURE 9-17**). Except for its obvious rings, Saturn is in many ways similar in appearance to Jupiter; however, Saturn's density is about half that of Jupiter and only 0.7 as that of water. As we see later, the low density of Saturn is probably due to a less dense core and a lower percentage of liquid metallic hydrogen.

The composition of Saturn's atmosphere is about the same as Jupiter's: approximately 96% hydrogen and 3% helium, with only about 1% of heavier materials. This is about the same as the composition of the Sun. The similarity is not a coincidence, for all of these objects formed from the same material—the interstellar cloud that collapsed to form the solar system. Recall from Chapter 7 that the reason the terrestrial planets have less hydrogen and helium is that these volatile gases were swept away from the hot, inner portions of the system.

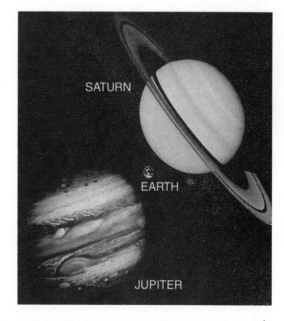

FIGURE 9-17 Here photos of Saturn, Earth, and Jupiter are reproduced to scale. Jupiter's diameter is 11.2 times Earth's, whereas Saturn's diameter is 9.5 times Earth's.

These percentages correspond to the number of particles of each element in the atmosphere.

Saturn's Motions

Saturn orbits the Sun at an average distance of 9.6 AU; its distance from the Earth varies from about 8.5 AU to 10.5 AU. Its appearance from Earth varies greatly, but not because of changes in distance. **FIGURE 9-18** shows several views of Saturn taken between 1996 and 2000, about a sixth of its 29.5-year period of revolution. To see the reason for the change in appearance of its rings, think of Saturn revolving at its great distance from the Earth and Sun, as shown in **FIGURE 9-19**. The rings of Saturn are in the plane of the planet's equator, and the planet is tilted 27 degrees with respect to its orbital plane. Saturn keeps this same tilt while moving around the Sun (and the Earth), and thus, when it is viewed from the Earth, we see the rings at different orientations at different times.

Saturn

FIGURE 9-18 These *HST* images show Saturn from 1996 (bottom left: rings almost edge-on) to 2000 (top right: rings nearly fully open) as it moves from fall to winter in its northern hemisphere.

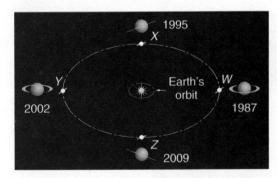

FIGURE 9-19 Saturn is shown at four points in its orbit. The outer drawings show its appearance from Earth with respect to the background stars when it is at each of those locations. At points X and Z the rings are edge-on to Earth. At position W, we see the "top" of the rings, whereas at position Y, we see the "underside" of the rings. The cycle repeats every 29.5 years.

Saturn's oblateness is about 0.1, meaning that its equatorial diameter is 10% greater than its polar diameter.

Saturn's magnetic field is only 5% as strong as Jupiter's, which makes it only 1000 times stronger than Earth's!

When we consider the rotation of Saturn, we find two more similarities to Jupiter. The various belts of Saturn's atmosphere rotate at different rates, just as in the case of Jupiter, and its equatorial rotation rate of about 10 hours and 40 minutes is close to Jupiter's 9 hours and 50 minutes.

Jupiter's oblateness was explained by its high rotation rate. Saturn has a similar rotation rate, but is even more oblate. This is because the gravitational field at its surface is weaker than at Jupiter's; because there is less gravitational force tending to keep the planet in a spherical shape, Saturn is more oblate than any other planet.

Pioneer, *Voyager*, and *Cassini*

We have learned much about Saturn from space probes (*Pioneer 11*, *Voyager 1*, *Voyager 2*, and *Cassini*). Knowledge gained from each of these probes was used to guide scientists in decisions concerning the following ones.

Because Saturn is smaller, one must descend deeper into its interior to reach a pressure great enough for hydrogen to form a liquid metallic state. Whereas liquid metallic hydrogen extends out about two thirds of the way to Jupiter's cloud tops, it extends only about halfway to Saturn's clouds (**FIGURE 9-20**). As a result, Saturn has a weaker magnetic field than does Jupiter.

Simultaneous *HST* and *Cassini* observations show similarities and differences between Saturn's auroras (**FIGURE 9-21**) and those of Earth. Dramatic brightening of the auroras can last for days on Saturn compared with a few minutes on Earth. As on Earth, radio waves are generated at the brightest auroral spots, as electrons spiral around field lines toward the atmosphere. Unlike on Earth, the solar wind pressure is the dominant force in driving Saturn's magnetosphere, whereas the solar magnetic field plays a smaller role than expected.

In some places, Saturn's magnetosphere resembles water-based plasmas around comets. That is so because Saturn's rotation controls the flow of plasma in a large volume around the planet that includes its rings, Titan, and many icy moons. As a result, collisions between solar ultraviolet light, along with electrons and ions in the plasma, and the icy surfaces of the rings and moons, release and ionize water and nitrogen molecules, which in turn are accelerated by Saturn's field and regenerate the plasma.

Except for its rings, Saturn appears much blander than Jupiter for two reasons. First, because of its greater distance from the Sun, Saturn's atmosphere is much colder than Jupiter. The extreme cold inhibits the chemical reactions that give Jupiter's atmosphere its varied colors. Second, a layer of methane haze above Saturn's cloud tops blurs out color differences; however, *Voyager* photos show that Saturn has atmospheric

FIGURE 9-20 Saturn's interior resembles Jupiter's, but Saturn contains a smaller percentage of liquid metallic hydrogen. The rocky core contains silicates, minerals, and hydrogen compounds under tremendous temperature and pressure. As for the case of Jupiter, Saturn's interior structure is inferred from models and extrapolation of data from the outer layers.

features similar to Jupiter and that its winds reach speeds three to four times faster than Jupiter's.

A comparison of wind speeds in Saturn's equatorial region measured by the *Voyager* spacecraft, *HST*, and *Cassini* shows that they decrease with height ranging from about 275 m/s (615 miles/hour) at high altitudes to 400 m/s (900 miles/hour) deeper in Saturn's atmosphere. These winds have subsided since the *Voyager* era (when speeds of 470 m/s were measured), whereas wind speeds have remained very stable elsewhere in the planet's atmosphere. What drives these winds? In addition to sunlight, which is the

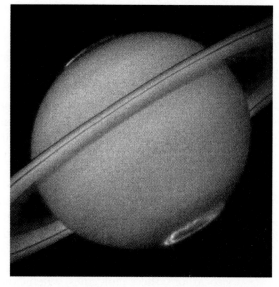

FIGURE 9-21 This 1998 *HST* photo in the extreme ultraviolet range shows glowing auroras at the north and south poles of Saturn, reaching as high as 1200 miles above the top clouds. (This photo could not be taken from an Earth-based telescope because the Earth's atmosphere would absorb the ultraviolet radiation.)

primary energy source for winds on the terrestrial planets, internal heat provides an additional source of energy in the case of Jupiter and Saturn; however, the exact role of this internal heat in sustaining the strong winds is not well understood. Also, in the case of Saturn, the long seasonal cycle (about 30 Earth years) and the shadow of the planet's rings on the equatorial regions could play a role in the slowing down of the equatorial winds.

FIGURE 9-22a is a color-enhanced photo taken by the *HST* showing two major storms (the white areas) near Saturn's equator. Storms lasting for months or even centuries are common in the Jovian planets, as is the merging of smaller storms into a larger one and the presence of intense lightning activity. Figure 9-22b shows a giant vortex at Saturn's south pole. A similar giant cyclone was observed at the planet's north pole having a more hexagonal shape. It appears that both vortices have been long-lasting and they do not depend on the amount of sunlight received at the polar regions; after all, the north polar vortex has survived the 15-year-long winter that started in 1995. We still do not understand what drives the global motion of Saturn's atmosphere.

Saturn's Excess Energy

Like Jupiter, Saturn radiates more energy than it absorbs. We once thought that the source of the energy is the same as Jupiter's—leftover energy from the planet's formation—but calculations show that because of its smaller size, Saturn would have cooled quickly enough that it would not still be radiating excess energy.

Saturn also has another unusual feature that astronomers must explain: analysis of data obtained by the *Voyager* spacecraft showed that Saturn has less helium in its upper atmosphere than Jupiter. By mass, Saturn's upper atmosphere contains 11% helium, much less than the nearly 20% on Jupiter. Astronomers had expected Saturn to have about the same composition as the original material of the solar system—the composition of Jupiter and the Sun.

An interesting hypothesis explains both of these anomalies. Some astronomers propose that the cooling of Saturn's atmosphere causes helium to condense to liquid form and rain downward. This would explain the low percentage of helium in the upper atmosphere. In addition, as the helium droplets fall, they lose gravitational energy, and this energy is converted to

FIGURE 9-22 (a) This 1998 false-color image of Saturn, taken by the *HST*'s infrared camera, shows two violent storms near the planet's equator. In this photo, blue indicates clear atmosphere or ammonia ice; green and yellow indicate atmospheric haze; and red and orange indicate clouds high in Saturn's atmosphere. (b) At the center of this 2007 *Cassini* near-infrared false-color image of Saturn's south polar region there is a hurricane-like vortex powered by Earth-like storm patterns.

Saturn's cloud tops have a temperature of −180°C.

thermal energy. This thermal energy, the hypothesis holds, results in Saturn emitting more energy than it absorbs. However, the latest theoretical calculations suggesting a more homogeneous mixing between helium and hydrogen under the atmospheric conditions found deep in Jupiter and Saturn may make this hypothesis unlikely.

Enceladus and Titan

Refer to Appendix D for details concerning the moons of Saturn as well as other moons in the solar system.

Saturn has 61 moons, most of which consist of dirty ice such as we see on some of Jupiter's moons. Each of Saturn's moons is unique; most of them are the leftover pieces of the disintegration of pre-existing moons as a result of powerful collisions. The subsequent accretion of material from the disk gave these moons their unique sizes and shapes.

Cassini observations suggest that most of Saturn's inner moons have low densities, about that of water ice. However, the density of Phoebe (**FIGURE 9-23a**), 1.6 grams/cm³, suggests a composition of ice and rock similar to that of Pluto and Neptune's moon Triton; its density, dark color, and retrograde orbit suggest that this moon was formed in the outer solar system and was captured by Saturn's gravitational field. *Cassini* also revealed that Hyperion (Figure 9-23b) has cup-like craters filled with hydrocarbons; these molecules, when exposed to ultraviolet light while in an environment that includes water, form new molecules of biological significance.

Enceladus (**FIGURE 9-24a**) is covered in water ice. As a result, it reflects almost all of the sunlight that strikes it, and its surface temperature is about −200°C (−330°F). Parts of its surface are covered with craters no larger than 35 km, whereas other parts are very smooth, suggesting that in the geologically recent past (less than 100 million years ago) the moon experienced major resurfacing events. The moon's surface features suggest that its interior may be liquid today. Indeed, *Cassini* images (Figure 9-24b) show plumes of water vapor, ice water particles, and minor amounts of gases (including nitrogen) over the moon's south polar region. Tidal interactions with Saturn (due to the moon's eccentric orbit) and the decaying radioactive elements within the moon set into motion the forces that power the moon's geysers. Besides

(a)

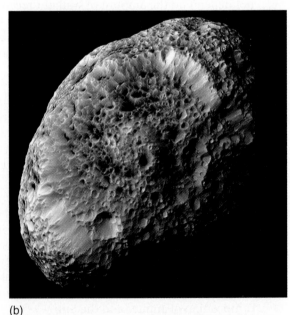

(b)

FIGURE 9-23 The enhanced-color views of Phoebe and Hyperion were created by *Cassini* images in UV, visible, and infrared. Both moons have surfaces of water ice. (a) Phoebe (220 km) is probably an ice-rich body coated with a thin layer of dark material. The small bright craters on Phoebe are probably fairly young features; as a result of collisions, fresh material (probably ice from underlying layers) has been brought to the surface. (b) Hyperion (370 × 280 × 226 km) is irregular in shape and tumbles as it orbits Saturn. For this view, the reddish tint that appears naturally was toned down in order to enhance color variations.

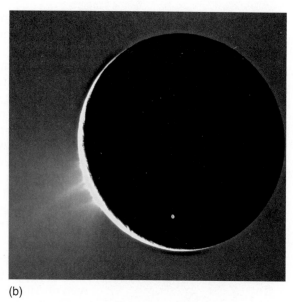

(a)

(b)

FIGURE 9-24 (a) This 2006 enhanced-color view of Enceladus, 500 km in diameter, was created by *Cassini* images in the ultraviolet, visible, and infrared. Craters, fractures, folds, and ridges are seen on the moon's surface. (b) The plumes seen above Enceladus' edge over its south polar region in this 2005 *Cassini* image are believed to be geysers erupting from pressurized reservoirs of liquid water below the moon's surface.

Earth, Io, and possibly Neptune's moon Triton, Enceladus is the only known object in the solar system where active volcanism exists.

In addition to water, carbon dioxide, methane, and other simple carbon-based molecules have been detected in the atmosphere of Enceladus. The plumes provide a continuous source of particles to the moon's atmosphere, which would not otherwise have lasted long because the moon's gravity is not strong enough to hold it. Even though most of the particles in the plumes fall back to the surface, those that escape go into orbit around Saturn forming the planet's E ring; there they collide with the more than 11 moons orbiting the planet within this ring, resulting in their bright appearance. The weight of these charged particles also seems to affect Saturn's magnetic field lines, which are forced to slip relative to the planet's rotation. As a result, the rhythm of the natural radio signals from the planet changes, making an accurate determination of Saturn's rotational period elusive.

Titan (FIGURE 9-25) may turn out to be the most interesting moon in the solar system; with a diameter of 5150 km, it is the second largest moon after Ganymede. Its atmosphere extends 10 times further into space than Earth's, and a thick methane haze from an altitude of 150 km down to the surface obscures the view of the moon's surface from space. Titan's atmosphere can be compared with Earth's in its very early history; it is mostly nitrogen, with a few percent methane and argon. There are also traces of water and organic compounds such as ethane and carbon monoxide.

Solar ultraviolet light breaks down the methane in Titan's atmosphere, forming in the process organic molecules that slowly drift down to the surface. (This is similar to a thicker version of the smog found over large cities.) It would take only a few tens of millions of years for Titan's atmosphere to be depleted of methane. The fact that methane is still present suggests that it is probably locked with water ice in a crust above an ocean of ammonia and

FIGURE 9-25 This *Cassini* composite image of Titan is in ultraviolet and infrared wavelengths. The pale orange hue of Titan is natural.

liquid water, and that during outgassing events methane is released in Titan's atmosphere. Support for the existence of such an ocean comes from comparing images of prominent features on Titan's surface taken by *Cassini* during different flybys. The features seem to shift in position by 30 km, implying that the icy crust is decoupled from the moon's core by an internal ocean about 100 km under the crust.

The *Huygens* probe landed in an area with the consistency of loose wet sand. Surface images (FIGURE 9-26) show small (a few centimeters wide) rounded pebbles, whose composition is more like dirty water ice than silicate rocks. Images taken during the probe's descent show that Titan's surface includes bright highlands with deep channels and dark lowlands that look like dried lake or river beds (FIGURE 9-27a).

Sand dunes and prominent features that appear to be impact craters (but could also be calderas or volcanoes) are seen on Titan's surface. The shapes of these features are important because they provide us insight into the structure of the crust beneath the moon's surface. It seems that, just like Earth, Titan's surface is shaped by winds, liquid flows, and tectonic activity, except that the conditions are a bit more exotic. Just like water on Earth, methane, measured to be three times more abundant at lower altitudes than in Titan's stratosphere, is playing an important role in shaping Titan's surface. Liquid methane drizzles are a constant feature on the moon's surface, closing the methane cycle and keeping the surface wet and muddy.

Cassini radar imaging data suggest that large bodies of liquid (methane and ethane) exist over the high latitudes surrounding the moon's north pole (Figure 9-27b). The amount of liquid hydrocarbons on Titan is estimated to be hundreds of times greater than all the known oil and gas reserves on Earth.

Studies of isotopic ratios of nitrogen as measured by *Huygens* suggest that Titan's early atmosphere was five times denser than it is now; this implies that Titan is losing material from the top of its atmosphere to space. Titan is inside Saturn's magnetosphere, and thus, the top of its atmosphere is being bombarded by highly energetic

(a)

(b)

FIGURE 9-27 (a) This panoramic view of Titan's surface was made by images taken by *Huygens* during its descent. A network of possible channels, as shown by the narrow dark markings, cuts through the brighter terrain and suggests a methane rain and possibly springs. (b) *Cassini* radar imaging provides evidence for hydrocarbon lakes. In this false-color image, lakes are darker than the surrounding terrain.

particles. *Huygens* data also indicate that Titan's surface is rich in organic compounds not seen in the atmosphere. The moon has experienced in the past and is probably still experiencing internal geological activity, as indicated by the presence of Argon-40 at the surface.

Huygens data suggest that winds in Titan's atmosphere flow in the direction of the moon's rotation at high altitudes but in the opposite direction (and at lower speeds) closer to the surface; it is possible that convection at low altitudes disconnects local winds from Titan's main wind patterns.

The clouds on Titan show a very complicated structure. They are highly localized (found in a band at latitude 40° south). They contain storms that form and dissipate quickly, and they cause strong methane rains. It is possible that a combination of out-gassing from volcanoes and rising air due to global circulation at this latitude blocks air from mixing between southern latitudes and the rest of Titan's atmosphere; this causes smog to build up and form a cap over the moon's south pole.

Titan's average density of almost twice that of water was first determined using data from the *Voyager* spacecraft. It is likely that the composition of the moon's interior is a combination of rock and ice. The absence of a detectable magnetic field suggests that Titan does not have a liquid metallic core.

Titan is only slightly larger than Mercury, which has no appreciable atmosphere. Titan, however, has a denser and more massive atmosphere than Earth's. How can this be? An object can retain an atmosphere only if the escape speed from its surface is greater than about 10 times the speed of gaseous molecules there. The escape speed from Titan is somewhat less than from Mercury (see Figure 7-8); however, the difference in temperature between the two objects allows Titan to retain an atmosphere. On Mercury's Sun side, we find temperatures up to 450°C, but the temperature of Titan's surface is only about −180°C. The speed of the gas molecules on Titan thus is much less than the escape speed for this moon, and it has retained its atmosphere.

Planetary Rings

As shown in Figure 9-18, the rings of Saturn are less visible when they are more edge-on to us. This is because they are very thin, a few tens of meters across. The rings, however, are not solid sheets but are made up of small particles of water ice mixed with smaller amounts of rocky and organic matter. The great amount of empty space between the particles in the rings means that if they were compressed, their thickness would be reduced to less than a meter, and the resulting single object would be less than 100 km across.

In proportion to their diameter of about 275,000 km, Saturn's rings are no more than 1.5 km thick; much flatter than a compact disk.

Each of the particles that make up the rings of Saturn revolves around the planet according to Kepler's laws. Thus, particles nearer the planet move faster than those farther out. Each of the particles is, in a sense, a separate satellite of Saturn.

Three distinct bands are visible from Earth, and long before the advent of space flight they were named (from outer to inner) rings A, B, and C. Photographs from space indicate that there are many more rings than these, as is evident in **FIGURE 9-28**.

Are Saturn's rings solid?

FIGURE 9-28 This *natural color* mosaic of six images was taken by *Cassini* in 2004 from under Saturn's rings; it covers the distance from 15,000 km to 77,000 km as measured from Saturn's outer surface along the ring plane. The color variations in the rings are the result of differences in chemical composition from the outer A ring to the inner C ring. The Cassini division is seen between the A and B rings. In addition to gaps, also present are gravitational resonances and wave patterns, like ripples on a pond, caused by small moons in the ring system.

Several reasons have been given for the existence of the spaces between the rings, and it is now evident that different spaces have different causes. Some explanations are quite complicated, but others are much simpler.

One of the spaces that is easily explained is the one between rings A and B, known as *Cassini's division* after the astronomer G. D. Cassini. To explain this space between rings, we must compare the motion of a particle in the Cassini division with the motion of Mimas, one of Saturn's moons. A particle in Cassini's division would orbit the planet with a period of 11 hours, 17.5 minutes. This is just half of the orbital period of Mimas. Any particle found in the division, thus, will be at the same place in its orbit each time Mimas passes near it. Each time this happens, Mimas exerts a slight gravitational tug on the particle, deflecting it slightly from its path. If Mimas did this at random times during the orbiting of the particle, the gravitational effect would be random and the particle's path would not be severely affected; however, as a result of the synchronous relationship between the periods, the tug is repeated regularly, and the overall effect is to pull the particle out of its orbit. This is what happens to particles that drift into Cassini's division, and it is the reason the division exists.

If such synchronous gravitational tugs were the only mechanisms at work determining the structure of Saturn's rings, Cassini's division might be completely clear of particles, but in fact, it is not. Many other forces are at work, including gravitational forces from other moons and particles as well as electromagnetic forces from Saturn's magnetic field.

Other features of the rings are explained by the existence of small moons orbiting near the rings. These satellites, called *shepherd moons*, cause some of the rings to keep their shape. Shepherd moons are discussed in an Advancing the Model box in this chapter. Still other features of the rings seem to be similar to spiral wave patterns seen in galaxies. Various hypotheses have been used to explain the various features of the rings, but no comprehensive theory has yet been proposed. There are many similarities between the observed structures in the rings and those seen in numerical models of the early stages of planetary formation; in this sense, *Cassini* is providing us with tools to understand the origin of planets.

The Origin of Rings

The origin of the rings of Saturn is not well understood. The most likely scenario is that an icy moon (or moons) once orbited near Saturn and was shattered in a collision with a passing asteroid or comet. Another possibility is that an object from the outer solar system came too close to Saturn and was torn apart by the planet's gravity. The particles of the shattered moon eventually dispersed in a ring around the planet. This event may seem unlikely, but in fact, we know that small objects in orbit around a planet do arrange themselves in a flat ring. Whether or not this is the true origin of the rings, we do understand why the rings have not formed into moons. To see why, we must review the effect of tides.

Recall how the gravitational force between the Earth and the Moon causes tides on both the Earth and the Moon. It is not simply the existence of a gravitational force that causes the tides, but the fact that there is a *difference* in the amount of gravitational force exerted on masses that are at different places on the Earth (or the Moon). We considered tides in Chapter 6, but we now look at them in another way, focusing here on Kepler's laws.

According to Kepler's third law—expanded to apply to planets and moons—if two objects are orbiting a planet, the object closer to the planet must move faster in its orbit if it is to stay in that orbit. FIGURE 9-29 illustrates a moon in a circular orbit around a planet, but in the figure, we have divided the moon into three parts, each at a different distance from the planet. Kepler's law tells us that if the three parts of our moon were not connected, part *X* would have to move faster. If it were to move at the same speed as part *Y*, it would fall inward toward the planet. Likewise, part *Z* should travel

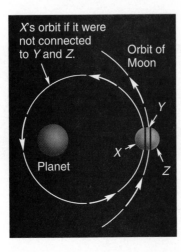

FIGURE 9-29 The moon is divided into three parts for analysis. Part *X* is closer to the planet than the rest of the moon and would have to move faster if it were a separate satellite. If there were no attractive force toward the rest of the planet, at *X*'s present speed, it would fall inward and begin an eccentric orbit.

X's orbit if it were not connected to *Y* and *Z*.

Orbit of Moon

Planet

X

Y

Z

more slowly than Y, and if it were to travel at the same speed as Y, it would fly out of Y's orbit. This, in fact, is just another way to look at the cause of tides, for each part of the moon tends to do what we have just described.

Why doesn't a moon fly apart because of this tidal effect? The answer is that the moon has its own forces holding it together. A rock on its surface is pulled by the force of gravity toward the center of the moon. Artificial satellites, on the other hand, are held together by the strength of the materials of which they are made.

It is important to see that it is the *relative difference* in distance from the planet that causes the effect. If a moon is far from its planet, the outside edge may be only a fraction of a percent farther from the planet than the center of the moon. If the same moon is located close to its planet, the difference in distance between the moon's outer edge and its center will be a greater fraction of the moon's distance from the planet. This causes the effect of tides to be greater if a moon is nearer a planet. There is a critical distance, called the **Roche limit**, inside which the tidal force on a moon will be greater than the moon's own gravitational force. Inside this distance, a large moon will be unable to hold itself together.

Now we come to Saturn. Until 1859 it was thought that Saturn's rings might be solid sheets of material, but calculations of Saturn's Roche limit showed that they are inside that limit and therefore the gravitational force between particles within the rings is less than the tidal force that tends to pull them apart. That they are made up of separate particles was experimentally confirmed in 1895 by means of the Doppler effect, which showed that different parts of the rings have different speeds. Because the rings are inside the Roche limit, no moons have formed from the particles.

The particles of the rings vary in size from small grains to irregularly shaped pieces as big as a bus (**FIGURE 9-30**). It is interesting to note that if all of the material of the rings of Saturn were formed into a single moon, the moon would be about the mass of Janus (one of the smallest of Saturn's moons) and only 1/20,000 the mass of the Earth's Moon.

Cassini has provided us with direct evidence that the objects in the rings are made mostly of pure ice covered with various amounts of dust (rocky or organic) from pulverized moons or meteoroids. Spectroscopic observations point to the presence of impurities between the rings; this material is similar to that found on Phoebe, which suggests that the objects responsible for Saturn's rings formed at the outer solar regions.

As in the case of Jupiter's rings, Saturn's rings are continually replenished. *Cassini* observations show that particles in the A ring continually assemble and are then torn apart by tidal interactions with Saturn. The spacecraft also observed a massive eruption of atomic oxygen from the outer rings, which may have been caused by meteoroid impacts on small moonlets within the ring system or near it. The presence of oxygen is not surprising because hydroxyl was discovered during earlier *HST* observations; both chemicals are the product of water chemistry. The ring system seems to have its own atmosphere, composed mostly of molecular oxygen. The great variations in the ages of the different rings and the continuous recycling of the material in them suggest that Saturn has its ring system for a long time.

Roche limit The minimum radius at which a satellite (held together by gravitational forces) may orbit without being broken apart by tidal forces.

FIGURE 9-30 Saturn's rings consist of thousands of fragments of water ice covered with rocky and organic dust.

9-3 Uranus

Uranus was unknown to the ancient Greeks even though they undoubtedly saw it, for it is barely visible to the naked eye under perfect viewing conditions. It was plotted on star charts made by telescope as early as 1690; however, in anything but large, high-resolution telescopes, Uranus appears only as a speck of light rather than a disk.

In Greek myth, Uranus (YOOR-uh-nuss) was the earliest supreme god, the farther of Cronus (Saturn). The name was suggested by Johann Bode (of Bode's law fame); the planet's discoverer, William Herschel, had suggested "Gregorium Sidus" (the Gregorian star), after King George III.

Seeing is in some respect an art, which must be learnt.
William Herschel

occultation The passing of one astronomical object in front of another.

51,000 km is about 32,000 mi. This is four times Earth's diameter.

This, coupled with the fact that it moves very slowly, caused it to go unnoticed as a planet until 1781, when the English astronomer William Herschel (1738–1822) noticed that this particular "star" seemed to have a size. He thought at first that it was a comet, but after calculations showed that this object's orbit was nearly circular, Herschel realized that he had discovered a new planet.

The first reliable determination of the diameter of Uranus was made in 1977 when Uranus was observed passing in front of a star. Such an event, when a moon or planet eclipses a star, is called an ***occultation*** and provides us with a valuable measuring method. Because the speed of Uranus in its orbit was known, all that had to be measured during the occultation in order to calculate Uranus' diameter was the time during which the star was occulted.

The diameter of Uranus is 51,000 kilometers, about half the diameter of Saturn and one third that of Jupiter. Long before *Voyager 2* passed Uranus in 1986, the mass of the planet had been calculated by applying Kepler's third law to its five major satellites known at the time. Its density is then calculated to be 1.27 times that of water—greater than Saturn but slightly less than Jupiter. Taking into account the surface gravity on Uranus (which is less than on Saturn or Jupiter), we can calculate what Uranus' density would be if the planet were made up entirely of hydrogen and helium. Astronomers once thought that a dense, rocky core about the size of the Earth was necessary to produce Uranus' measured density, but recently, researchers have subjected material that matches the composition of Uranus to a pressure 2 million times that of Earth's atmosphere and found that it becomes dense enough to account for the planet's density. It thus may be that Uranus has a very small rocky core or no core at all (**FIGURE 9-31**).

The atmosphere of Uranus is similar to those of Jupiter and Saturn, consisting primarily of hydrogen and helium, with some methane. **FIGURE 9-32** is a *HST* photo of Uranus. The reason for the planet's blue coloring is that the methane absorbs red light and reflects the rest of the spectrum. The atmospheres of Jupiter and Saturn also contain methane, but they have high cloud layers that reflect sunlight before it reaches the higher concentrations of methane. Uranus does not have these cloud layers. **FIGURE 9-33** shows that Uranus has zonal flow patterns parallel to its equator. Many atmospheric phenomena observed on Uranus vary in size, duration, and brightness; the larger of these may be giant hurricane-like vortices.

The purpose of the Uranus observations during the occultation of 1977 was to determine the planet's size more accurately; however, a surprise was in store for the observers. A short while before Uranus was expected to occult the star, the light from the star blinked five times. Then, after the occultation, similarly timed blinks were observed,

FIGURE 9-31 A model of Uranus' interior.

26,000 km
13,000 km
Atmosphere H + He
Water
Rocky core

FIGURE 9-32 This 2003 *HST* image of Uranus was made using filters sensitive to red, green, and blue light. This is how the planet would appear if we could see it through a telescope. The south pole of the planet is on the left.

FIGURE 9-33 This *HST* false-color view of Uranus shows its atmospheric flow patterns, four of the rings and several moons. Differences in color correspond to differences in thickness and altitude of clouds and hazes. The colors have the same interpretation as in the photo of Saturn in Figure 9–22a.

HISTORICAL NOTE

William Herschel, Musician/Astronomer

William Herschel, who has been called the greatest observational astronomer ever and the Father of Stellar Astronomy, was a musician. He moved to England at age 19 from Hanover (a province in the former state of Prussia in Germany) and spent most of his young adult life teaching, performing, and composing music.

He inherited from his father an interest in astronomy. He began to build his own telescopes, and after teaching music lessons during the day, he would spend the evenings observing the heavens. By 1778 he had built an excellent reflecting telescope about 6 inches in diameter. This was no easy task, for construction of the mirror involved metal casting. Herschel's life changed after March 13, 1781. On that night he saw a hazy patch in the sky and after observing it over a few nights, he saw that it moved. What he thought was a comet turned out to be the first planet to be discovered in recorded history.

William Herschel was not immediately accepted by the scientific community. His telescopes were of such quality that he was able to see things in the heavens that other astronomers couldn't, and many did not believe his claims about the details of what he was seeing; however, Herschel's skills as a telescope maker and as an observer won out, and

his discovery of Uranus could not be denied. He was soon recognized and celebrated by scientific societies. Within a year after he discovered Uranus, he received a pension from King George III so that he could devote full time to astronomy, his former hobby. In 1787 he discovered two moons of Uranus and soon after found two smaller moons of Saturn.

Together with his sister Caroline, they made the first thorough study of stars and nebulae (faint, hazy objects not understood at the time). One important discovery they made was the existence of double stars—stars in orbit about one another. After Herschel's death, the orbits of these stars were analyzed in enough detail to determine that the stars obey Newton's laws of motion and gravitation, an indication that these laws are valid not only in our solar system but even among the distant stars.

Herschel continued serious observing until he was nearly 70. After his death at the age of 84, Caroline compiled a large catalog of his observations and received many honors for her own astronomical work. She discovered eight comets from her own observations and was one of the first two women elected to honorary membership in the Royal Astronomical Society.

---

but in the opposite order. From this, astronomers concluded that Uranus has at least five rings that are invisible from the Earth but are dense enough to obscure the light from a star behind them. By comparing the results obtained by several observatories, details of the rings' orientations and sizes could be determined. FIGURE 9-34, taken by *Voyager*, indicates the complexity of the ring system.

The rings of Uranus cannot be seen from the Earth because they reflect only about 5% of the sunlight that hits them. The rings must be made of material as dark as soot. By comparison, Saturn's rings reflect 80% of the light that hits them.

FIGURE 9-34 In this backlit view, *Voyager's* photograph of the rings revealed a great number of ringlets. The camera is on the opposite side of the rings from the Sun so that the light we see has been scattered in passing through the rings.

William Herschel might have observed Uranus' rings in 1797 but he was not able to confirm his sightings.

Uranus' Orientation and Motion

Venus is unusual in that it rotates in a backward direction: clockwise as observed from north of the Sun. Except for Venus, every other planet we have studied so far rotates normally: counterclockwise as observed from the north. In addition, all planets we have studied, including Venus, have their equatorial plane tilted less than 30 degrees to their plane of revolution around the Sun. Here is where Uranus is unique. Its equatorial plane is tilted nearly 90 degrees to its plane of revolution. (The tilt of

As of August 2007, the total number of rings around Uranus is 13. The rings contain many smaller ringlets, as shown in Figure 9-34.

FIGURE 9-35 Uranus' axis is tilted 98°, which tells us that the planet has retrograde rotation.

FIGURE 9-36 Uranus' axis is tilted so that its poles point nearly directly at the Sun at times.

The corresponding angle between the rotation axis and the magnetic dipole axis for Earth is currently 11.5°.

Do all planets rotate so that the equator lies in the plane of revolution?

FIGURE 9-37 Some of Uranus' moons compared in size with Earth's.

Uranus' orbit is listed as 98°, indicating its retrograde rotation. See FIGURE 9-35.) This means that during its 84-year orbit, its north pole at one time points almost directly to the Sun and at another time faces nearly away from the Sun. FIGURE 9-36 illustrates this fact. Recall from Chapter 1 that the tilt of Earth's axis is what causes Earth to have seasons. One might think that the large tilt of Uranus' axis would have a great effect on its weather; however, data from *Voyager* reveal that Uranus has a fairly uniform temperature over its entire surface (about −200°C), indicating that the atmosphere is continually stirred up, with winds moving from one hemisphere to another. (On Earth, there is little air exchange between the Northern and Southern Hemispheres.)

The axial tilt of Uranus was thought to be the result of a glancing impact with another object; however, Uranus' moons are still orbiting the planet in its equatorial plane, which is an unlikely result of such a short-lived interaction. It is possible that the impact occurred during a very early stage of the formation of the moons. Computer simulations, however, show that Uranus' axial tilt (and that of the other Jovian planets) can arise naturally as a result of the strong gravitational interactions present during the early stages of the formation of our solar system—specifically, as the newly forming planets were changing orbits and were interacting with the remaining material in the solar nebula.

Features of Uranus' surface are not visible from the Earth and, thus, until *Voyager* approached Uranus, there was uncertainty about its period of rotation. *Voyager* photographs told us that, as on Jupiter and Saturn, there are various bands of clouds on Uranus and that these bands rotate with different periods—from 16 hours at the equator to nearly 28 hours at the poles. Uranus has about the same chemical makeup as Jupiter, about 83% hydrogen with most of the remainder helium.

Uranus' magnetic field is comparable to Saturn's. Probably it originates in electric currents within the planet's layer of water. The magnetic field is unusual in that its axis is tilted 59 degrees with respect to the planet's rotation axis. No other planet has such a large angle between the two axes, although Neptune's—at 47 degrees—is close.

Five moons of Uranus (FIGURE 9-37) were known before *Voyager*, and now we know of 27 (as of January 2009). All are low-density, icy worlds. The innermost, Miranda, is perhaps the strangest looking object in the solar system. FIGURE 9-38 shows its varied terrain. One possible explanation for the strange features of Miranda is that it experienced a tremendous collision with another object and was broken into pieces that later fell back together.

Two of Uranus' moons are shepherd moons (see the Advancing the Model box), keeping one of the rings in for-

FIGURE 9-38 Miranda. It is hypothesized that an impact once tore Miranda apart. The V-shaped feature is called the Chevron. The cliff at the upper right is 5 kilometers high.

ADVANCING THE MODEL

Shepherd Moons

The 1977 occultation that resulted in the discovery of Uranus' rings showed that they are very narrow and that their edges are well defined. Soon after this discovery, two astronomers—Peter Goldreich and Scott Tremaine—proposed a mechanism to explain why a ring might stay in a narrow band rather than spread out over space.

They hypothesized that there are a pair of moons, one orbiting just inside and another just outside the narrow ring (FIGURE B9-1). Kepler's third law tells us that the moon closer to the planet moves faster than the particles of the ring. As that moon catches and passes the particles on the inside portion of the ring, the gravitational pull from it increases the particles' energy just a little, causing them to move outward in their orbit. (This energy comes from the moon and, therefore, the moon loses energy and moves inward a bit; however, the moon is so much more massive than the particles that the change in its path is almost insignificant.)

In an opposite manner, as particles on the outside edge of the ring pass the more distant moon, they lose energy and move inward. The effect on each particle is very small. Nevertheless, Goldreich and Tremaine showed that the effect is significant enough that as the moons continue to orbit near the rings, they force the particles together; in other words, the moons act as shepherds for the flock of particles in the ring.

The scientific community awaited *Voyager's* passing by the rings of Uranus to see if it found such moons. The answer came earlier than expected. *Voyager 2* at that time had not yet passed Saturn. When it did, it photographed Saturn's rings, and on each side of Saturn's narrow F ring was a moon (FIGURE B9-2). Calculations showed that the two moons near the F ring would indeed perform the function of shepherds for that ring.

In January 1986, *Voyager 2* passed Uranus and returned a remarkable photograph (FIGURE B9-3) of the epsilon ring

FIGURE B9-1 As the inner moon passes the inner portion of the ring, it forces ring particles outward. The outer moon forces particles inward. The effect is greatly exaggerated here.

of Uranus along with two shepherds. Other rings around Uranus exist without the aid of shepherd moons, and thus, although Goldreich and Tremaine were right in their prediction of the action of shepherd moons, this mechanism is only a part of what is happening in planetary ring systems.

Inside the Roche Limit?

The shepherd moons of Saturn's F ring and those orbiting Uranus are within the Roche limit of each planet. How can they exist there without being pulled apart by gravitational

FIGURE B9-2 *Voyager* photographed these shepherd moons near the F ring of Saturn. *Cassini* data show that Prometheus is gravitationally pulling material away from the F ring and is responsible for kinks seen in the ring.

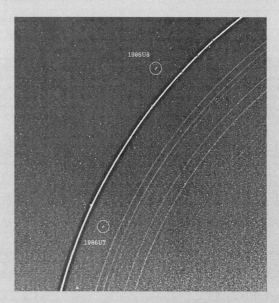

FIGURE B9-3 Moons 1986U7 and 1986U8 were photographed shepherding a ring of Uranus.

ADVANCING THE MODEL

Inside the Roche Limit? *(Cont'd)*

forces? There are several answers to this question. First, it is an oversimplification to refer to a single Roche limit. For a smaller moon, the limit is closer to the planet than it is for a larger moon. The shepherds are small moons. Second, the position of the limit depends on the density of the moon. Most important, however, the Roche limit concerns only moons that are held together by gravitational forces. A single large rock can exist inside the Roche limit, for it is held together by cohesive forces within the material. Each shepherd moon may well be a single large rock rather than being made of smaller particles held together by gravity.

Chaotic Motions

In the mid-1990s, observations of the two shepherd moons in Figure B9-2 found them far from where they should

have been based on *Voyager* data in the early 1980s. It seems that the best explanation for this discrepancy is based on chaotic interactions between the moons and the rings. The movements of the moons are not predictable because a very small difference in starting conditions can result in a big difference in later positions. Pandora pushes the particles in the ring inward toward Saturn, whereas Prometheus pushes them outward; by the principle of action and reaction (Newton's third law), the two moons are slowly pushed away from the ring. (The influence of Saturn's A ring on the moons is even more important in pushing them outward.) This is the first observation of chaotic *orbital* motions in our solar system. (However, it has been known since 1984 that Saturn's moon Hyperion exhibits a chaotic *rotational* motion.)

mation; however, material in the rings is very sparse—so much so that there is more material in Cassini's division of Saturn's system than in all of the rings of Uranus!

9-4   Neptune

Neptune's size and composition matches that of Uranus, and its blue color (FIGURE 9-39) has the same cause—methane in its upper atmosphere; however, light penetrates deeper into Neptune's atmosphere, resulting in a deeper blue than Uranus. The other major difference in appearance is that while Uranus is almost featureless, Neptune exhibits strong weather patterns.

It has parallel bands that change in brightness over time. *Voyager 2* images revealed a Great Dark Spot, an Earth-sized storm system similar in appearance and relative size to Jupiter's Great Red Spot that was varying in size during the flyby; winds near this storm system were measured up to 2400 km/hr! The Dark Spot had vanished when the *HST* viewed Neptune in 1994, but another similar storm appeared in the planet's northern hemisphere. The wispy white clouds seen on Neptune (FIGURE 9-40) are thought to be crystals of methane; these clouds cast shadows in the direction opposite the Sun, suggesting that they are at a higher altitude than the surrounding atmosphere. It has very strong winds and storm systems. *HST* observations from 1996 to 2002 of strong winds and storm systems suggest that Neptune shows seasonal changes; this is remarkable considering that the planet receives only 1/900 as much solar energy per unit area as Earth. A year on Neptune lasts about 165 Earth years and thus a season lasts about 40 years. This long period allows the temperature at each pole during their summer season to increase enough that methane, which should be frozen

FIGURE 9-39 The left image is a 2005 *HST* image of Neptune and its satellites in natural color (using filters sensitive in red, blue, and green light). The other two images, obtained using color enhancement and different filters, show high-altitude clouds.

HISTORICAL NOTE

The Discovery of Neptune

The discovery of Neptune is especially interesting because it reveals some very human aspects of science. After Uranus was discovered in 1781, astronomers examined old star charts and found that it had been plotted on charts as far back as 1690. Those who had plotted it had mistaken it for just another star, but the positions they marked allowed later astronomers to calculate the planet's orbit. As time went on, however, it was clear that Uranus was not following the orbit predicted by Newton's laws, even with the gravitational effects of Jupiter and Saturn taken into account. Most astronomers thought that an unknown planet was disturbing Uranus' orbit, but others thought that perhaps the law of gravity is different at great distances from the Sun.

John C. Adams, a 26-year-old British mathematician, took up the problem of calculating the position of the hypothesized planet. In late September 1845, after 2 years of calculations, he tried to get his results to Sir George Airy, the British Astronomer Royal, telling him where the planet would be found. Airy was one of the astronomers who doubted the existence of the new planet, thinking that Newton's laws were inexact at the distance of Uranus. As a result, when Airy finally got one of Adams' messages, he refused to use valuable time on the large telescope for what he thought would be a fruitless search. Adams' youth and inexperience also seem to have contributed to Airy's skepticism. Adams was rather unsure about the exact location of the planet and his predictions ranged over as much as 20°.

During the same period, and not knowing about Adams' work, the French mathematician Urbain Le Verrier was making similar calculations of Uranus' orbit. In November 1845, Le Verrier published the first part of his calculations in a scientific journal. Then in June 1846, he published his final results. Similar to Adams' experience with his own countrymen, Le Verrier was unable to get French astronomers to search for the planet. Finally, on September 23, 1846—one year after Adams had first requested a search—Le Verrier asked Johann Galle in Berlin to look for the planet. Galle quickly convinced the director of the observatory where he worked of the worthiness of the project, and the new planet was discovered on the very first night of searching within 1° of Le Verrier's prediction and 10° of Adams'.

Credit for scientific discovery usually goes to the first person who documents his or her results. (Today such documentation normally takes the form of publication in a scientific journal.) For years, controversy swirled about the priority of prediction. In this case, not only was the reputation of the two mathematicians involved, but also national prestige. (Similar disagreements have arisen in the 20th century concerning scientific discoveries made in the United States and the former Soviet Union).

in the upper part of the planet's atmosphere, can leak out into space. An overall temperature difference of 10°C was indeed observed by astronomers in 2007 using ESO's Very Large Telescope (VLT).

Neptune radiates more internal energy than Uranus, although the cause of the energy is not understood. This energy, however, is what drives the weather on Neptune, stirring the liquids and gases of the planet so that winds reach speeds of 700 miles/hour.

The rotation rate of Neptune was uncertain until *Voyager* measured it. Like the other gas planets, Neptune exhibits differential rotation: near the equator it rotates in 18 hours but near the poles its rotation period is only about 12 hours; however, these great differences are confined to the upper few percent of the atmosphere. Neptune's magnetic field rotates with a period of 16 hours, 7 minutes. Because the magnetic field is thought to result from electric currents in liquid layers deeper within the planet, this is taken as Neptune's basic rotation rate.

The temperature of Neptune's surface is fairly uniform at about −218°C. This is another similarity to Uranus and was a surprise to astronomers, for Neptune's axis is tilted 28 degrees to its orbit, rather than the 98-degree tilt of Uranus. The reasons for many of the similarities and differences between these two planets remain unknown.

FIGURE 9-40 The Great Dark Spot of Neptune. The narrow clouds are made up of crystals of methane and they are at a higher altitude than the surrounding atmosphere.

FIGURE 9-41 Neptune's interior is probably similar to that of Uranus (Figure 9-31), although Neptune may have a larger core.

FIGURE 9-42 The southern part of Triton has been exposed to sunlight for some 30 years, and erupting volcanoes (not obvious here) were photographed by *Voyager*.

Neptune is presumed to have an interior much like that of Uranus, but its central rocky core is probably larger, thus resulting in its greater average density. **FIGURE 9-41** illustrates one model of Neptune's interior.

Neptune's Moons and Rings

Before *Voyager's* visit, Neptune was known to have two moons, both unusual. Triton, its largest moon (and the seventh largest in the solar system), revolves around the planet in a clockwise direction as seen from the north. Although some smaller moons of the Jovian planets move in retrograde orbits, Triton is the only major moon to do so. The other moon known prior to *Voyager*, Nereid, orbits in the "right" direction, but it has the most eccentric orbit of any known moon in the solar system; its distance from the planet is five times greater at some times than at others. Its 360-day orbital period is the longest of any moon of its size (340-kilometer diameter) in the solar system.

Voyager showed us that the surface of Triton is as unusual as its orbit. **FIGURE 9-42** shows the region surrounding its south pole, which is near the bottom of the photograph in an area of very irregular terrain. Other parts of the moon are much smoother, as seen in the top part of the photograph. The surface consists primarily of water ice, with some nitrogen and methane frost. Three observations lead us to believe that the surface is very young: (1) It is very light in color. When methane is exposed to sunlight for a long time, darker organic compounds are formed. (2) There are very few craters, indicating that they have been obliterated by surface activity. (3) Active geysers have been seen on the moon.

A current hypothesis explains many of the unusual properties of Triton and Nereid. The mass of Triton was determined by its gravitational influence on *Voyager*, and we find that its density (about 2 g/cm^3) is about the same as the density of Pluto. It could be that both Triton and Nereid are objects that were captured by Neptune after the initial formation of the solar system. If so, then Triton probably once had an eccentric orbit like Nereid. If its orbit came very close to Neptune, tidal forces would eventually cause it to settle into a circular orbit such as the one in which we find it. In addition, the tidal forces would heat the interior of Triton by continually distorting its shape. This heat would result in the volcanic action that has covered old craters. Much more remains to be learned about Neptune's unusual moons before we can be confident of this hypothesis.

Voyager discovered six more moons orbiting Neptune, one of them larger than Nereid. It had not been seen from Earth because it is very close to the planet. The other five moons are very small.

◆ Jupiter's Galilean moons, our Moon, and Saturn's Titan are larger than Triton. All seven of these moons are larger than Pluto.

◆ Data on Neptune's moons can be found in Appendix D.

Stellar occultations observed in 1984 had revealed that Neptune has rings; *Voyager* photographs revealed that they are indeed complete rings (FIGURE 9-43) but "lumpy," perhaps as a result of undiscovered moons orbiting with them. We thus find that each of the Jovian planets has a ring system.

Conclusion

The Jovian planets certainly are different from the worlds of the inner solar system. Compared with the terrestrial planets, the Jovians are larger, more massive, more fluid (rather than solid), less dense, and rotate faster. Their many moons are vastly different from one another; the differences are caused at least partly by their distances from the Sun and from their planet.

As we learn more about the Jovian planets, we are even more amazed at these beautiful giants. We see great similarities among them, but we also see great differences. Jupiter, Saturn, Uranus, and Neptune are similar enough that we classify them into a single group, but each is an individual world with its own history.

In the next chapter we discuss the dwarf planet Pluto and various small objects that are part of our solar system.

FIGURE 9-43 Neptune's rings are seen clearly in this photo. Note their "lumpiness."

STUDY GUIDE

RECALL QUESTIONS

1. The most abundant constituent of Jupiter's atmosphere is
   A. helium.
   B. carbon dioxide.
   C. ammonia.
   D. hydrogen.
   E. sulfuric acid.

2. The Great Red Spot is
   A. a continent.
   B. a storm.
   C. an optical illusion.
   D. a shadow of one of Jupiter's moons on its surface.
   E. a mountain protruding above Jupiter's atmosphere.

3. The chemical composition of Jupiter is most similar to which of the following?
   A. The Earth.
   B. The Sun.
   C. Mars.
   D. The Moon.
   E. Venus.

4. A planet is said to have differential rotation if
   A. it changes speed when orbiting the Sun.
   B. it changes its rate of spin from time to time.
   C. different parts of it have different rotation periods.
   D. its rotation rate is far different from the planets closest to it.
   E. most of its moons revolve around it in a different direction than it rotates.

5. Jupiter's weather patterns should be simpler than Earth's because
   A. Jupiter is so large.
   B. Jupiter is so massive.
   C. Jupiter is made up primarily of hydrogen.
   D. Jupiter has a small ring.
   E. Jupiter's core is a small fraction of the total planet.

6. The bands around Jupiter are due to the fact that the planet
   A. rotates differentially.
   B. has a fairly low rotation rate.
   C. has so many moons.
   D. is made up primarily of hydrogen.
   E. has no solid core.

7. Most of the extra energy that Jupiter emits is thought to be energy
   A. left over from its formation.
   B. that results from the fact that it is still shrinking.
   C. that results from radioactive materials within it.
   D. that results from the greenhouse effect.
   E. [All of the above are considered about equally responsible.]

8. The energy for the volcanic activity on Io results from
   A. radioactive substances within it.
   B. chemical reactions.
   C. tidal action.
   D. energy radiated from Jupiter and the Sun.
   E. [Both A and B above.]

9. Saturn's rings are
   A. composed of ice particles.
   B. in the plane of the planet's equator.
   C. within the planet's Roche limit.
   D. [All of the above.]

10. Titan is able to retain an atmosphere even though it is just slightly larger than Mercury because it is
    A. close to Saturn.
    B. very dense.
    C. far from Saturn.
    D. far from the Sun.
    E. [Three of the above.]

11. Saturn has rings instead of additional moons because of
    A. magnetic fields.
    B. tidal forces.
    C. electrical forces.
    D. radiation.
    E. the proximity of Jupiter.

12. Saturn is unique in that it
    A. is the only planet with rings.
    B. is the brightest planet in our sky.
    C. is the only Jovian planet with more than four moons.
    D. has the least average density of the planets.
    E. [Three of the above.]

13. Liquid metallic hydrogen
    A. can exist only at great pressures.
    B. exists both in Jupiter and Saturn.
    C. is a conductor of electricity.
    D. [Two of the above.]
    E. [All of the above.]

14. Uranus is unique in that
    A. it has the least average density of the planets.
    B. its poles point nearly toward the Sun at some times.
    C. it is the most distant of the Jovian planets.
    D. its north pole is south of its orbital plane.
    E. it has a more eccentric orbit than any other planet.

15. The fact that Uranus has a fairly uniform temperature over its surface indicates that
    A. it has a great angle between its equatorial plane and its orbital plane.
    B. it has no solid core.
    C. it has a large solid core.
    D. its winds move from one hemisphere to the other.
    E. [Both A and B above.]

16. The oblateness of Jupiter and Saturn is caused primarily by
    A. expansion forces from within.
    B. rotation.
    C. revolution around the Sun.
    D. tidal forces from their moons.
    E. storms in their atmospheres.

17. Observation of the occultation of a star by a planet allows us to determine
    A. a planet's diameter.
    B. whether a planet has rings.
    C. the chemical composition of a planet.

D. [Both A and B above.]
E. [Both B and C above.]

18. The existence of Neptune was proposed
    A. on the basis of photographs.
    B. because of its effect on Pluto's orbit.
    C. because of its effect on Uranus' orbit.
    D. on the basis of Bode's law.
    E. [None of the above; it was discovered by accident.]

19. Which of the following is a spacecraft that analyzed Jupiter's atmosphere?
    A. *Viking*
    B. *Galileo*
    C. *Skylab*
    D. *Mariner*
    E. *Mir*

20. A Satellite passes by Jupiter at a distance of ten planetary radii. As viewed by the satellite, what is the angle subtended by Jupiter?
    A. 0.2 degrees
    B. 11.5 degrees2
    C. 11.5 arcseconds
    D. 10 degrees
    E. 10 arcseconds

21. Even though we are inside Earth's Roche limit, we are not torn apart by tidal effects. This is because
    A. we are held together by gravitational forces.
    B. we are held together by electrical forces.
    C. we are held together by tidal forces.
    D. tidal forces do not apply to humans.
    E. [The question is misleading because we are outside Earth's Roche limit.]

22. We say that Jupiter has a rotation rate of 9 hours, 50 minutes. What is it on the planet that has this rotation rate?

23. What is the *Galileo* probe?

24. Starting at the cloud tops and descending downward, describe Jupiter's interior. What leads us to think that Jupiter has a core made up of heavy elements?

25. What causes the swirling between the bands we see in Jupiter's atmosphere?

26. Explain why, as the years go by, Saturn appears so different when viewed from the Earth.

27. Describe the rings of Saturn and explain the Roche limit.

28. Describe two ways the diameter of a planet can be measured from the Earth.

29. Why were the rings of Uranus not observed directly from the Earth? How were they observed?

30. What is unusual about the orientation of Uranus?

31. How do the densities of the Jovian planets compare to the densities of the terrestrial planets?

32. What causes the heating of the inner Galilean moons that results in volcanism? On which moons is this most prevalent?

33. In what ways are Triton and Nereid unusual?

1. What causes a planet to be spherical (rather than some other shape, like a pancake, for instance)? What causes Jupiter to be a "flattened" sphere?

2. Analysis of data from the *Galileo* probe has produced some surprising results regarding the composition of Jupiter. Explain why these results are causing astronomers to re-evaluate today's theories of the formation of the solar system.

3. It would seem that a planet should absorb and release the same amount of energy. Jupiter doesn't. Describe the situation and list possible explanations.

4. Among the terrestrial planets and their moons there are several cases of gravitational linkage between rotation and revolution. In this chapter we have encountered another. Describe at least three such linkages among terrestrial planets/moons and one that involves a Jovian planet and its moon(s).

5. What is the source of energy for the geysers on Io?

6. Do you think it is possible for Europa to harbor some sort of life? What kind of life would you expect and what energy source would it use?

7. Why does Saturn appear so different year to year when viewed with a telescope?

8. Report on the status of the *Cassini* mission. (The Internet and the magazines *Sky & Telescope* and *Astronomy* are suggested sources.)

9. How can it be that Titan has an atmosphere, while Mercury (only slightly smaller) has almost none?

10. Describe a theory that explains why some planets have rings and others do not.

11. How can we determine the sizes of Uranus and Neptune?

12. Name each Jovian planet and in each case describe at least one property of the planet that makes it unique from other planets (for example, the biggest planet, the hottest planet, etc.).

13. Does one pole of every planet point to Polaris? What is meant by the direction *north*? What defines which pole of a planet is its north pole?

14. Each of the Jovian planets has differential rotation. Kepler's third law might lead you to expect that the rotation period at a planet's equator would be greater than near a pole, but the opposite is true. Explain why the rotation of a gas planet is fundamentally different from a situation that is covered by Kepler's third law.

1. If an object has a diameter equal to four times the Earth's diameter, how would its volume compare with the Earth's?

2. If an object has a mass equal to three Earth masses and a volume five times that of the Earth, how would its density compare to the Earth's?

3. Suppose a planet has an angular diameter of 11 arcseconds when it is 7.5 AU from the Earth. Use the small-angle formula to calculate its diameter.

4. Estimate the wind speeds in the Great Red Spot, assuming that it is approximately circular with radius 10,000 kilometers.

5. Choose relevant data from Appendix D for a Jovian satellite and calculate Jupiter's mass.

6. Io is losing material into Jupiter's magnetosphere at a rate of 1000 kg/sec. How long would it take to lose 1% of its mass? Is your answer larger or smaller than the age of the solar system (about 5 billion years)?

7. Material of density ρ orbits a planet of mass M. An *estimate* for the radius of the Roche limit for a planet is given by $R_{Roche} = (4M/\rho)^{1/3}$. The greater the density of the material that is trying to hold itself together, the closer the material can be to the planet without being destroyed. It is logical to assume that the density of the material just forming around a planet is lower than that of the planet. Therefore, a conservative estimate for the radius of the Roche limit is given by using the value of the planet's density. Use the data in Appendix C and calculate the radius of the Roche limit for Saturn. Compare you result to Saturn's radius. Repeat your calculations for the other planets.

8. Consider a planet of radius R and black-body temperature T at a distance d from the Sun. Using the Stefan-Boltzmann law and the inverse square law for radiation, show that the ratio between the energy given off by the planet to that received by the planet from the Sun is given by the expression $4(T/T_{sun})^4 (d/R_{sun})^2$. Use the data in the appendices and show that for Jupiter (with $T = 125$ K) this ratio is 1.3. In reality, this ratio is even greater, why?

Observing Jupiter and Saturn

Jupiter and Saturn are beautiful objects to observe if you have access to a telescope. Even with binoculars you may be able to see the four Galilean moons of Jupiter and the rings of Saturn. Make a careful sketch of the location of Jupiter's moons and then view them a few hours later or the next night. You will be able to see that they have moved. In addition, see if you can tell that Jupiter and Saturn are not perfectly round. Look for dark bands across the disk of Jupiter.

Pick up an issue of either *Astronomy* or *Sky & Telescope*, two monthly magazines (or *SkyNews*, a bimonthly Canadian magazine) that contain maps and hints for viewing the planets and other celestial objects.

EXPANDING THE QUEST

Expanding the Quest

You can find information about current explorations of our solar system at NASA's home page (http//www.nasa.gov).

1. "Galileo in Retrospect," by S. J. Goldman, in *Sky & Telescope* (December, 1997).

2. "Europa: Distant Ocean, Hidden Life?" by M. Carroll, in *Sky & Telescope* (December, 1997).

3. "Big Blue: The Twin Worlds of Uranus and Neptune," by T. Cowling, in *Astronomy* (October, 1990).

4. "Uranus," by A. P. Ingersoll, in *Scientific American* (January, 1987).

5. "The Rings of Uranus," by J. N. Cuzzi and L. W. Esposito, in *Scientific American* (July, 1987).

6. "Into the Giant," by J. Beatty, in *Sky & Telescope* (April, 1996).

7. "Voyage of the Century," by B. Smith, in *National Geographic* (August, 1990).

8. "Bound for the Ringed Planet," by J. Rogan, in *Astronomy* (November, 1997).

9. "The Hidden Ocean of Europa," by R. T. Pappalardo, J. W. Head, and R. Greeley, in *Scientific American* Special Edition (September 2003).

10. "The *Galileo* Mission to Jupiter and its Moons," by T. V. Johnson, in *Scientific American* Special Edition (September 2003).

11. "Saturn at Last!" by J. I. Lunine, in *Scientific American* (June 2004).

12. "The Case of the Pilfered Planet," by W. Sheehan, N. Kollerstrom, and C. B. Waff, in *Scientific American* (December 2004).

13. "The Mystery of Methane on Mars and Titan," by S. K. Atreya, in *Scientific American* (May 2007).

14. "The Restless World of Enceladus," by C. Porco, in *Scientific American* (December 2008).

STARLINKS

Quest Ahead to Starlinks
http://physicalscience.jbpub.com/starlinks

Starlinks is this book's online learning center. It features **eLearning**, which contains chapter quizzes and other tools designed to help you study for your class. You can also find **online exercises**, view numerous relevant **animations**, follow a guide to **useful astronomy sites** on the Web, or even check the latest **astronomy news** updates.

Largest known Kuiper Belt objects

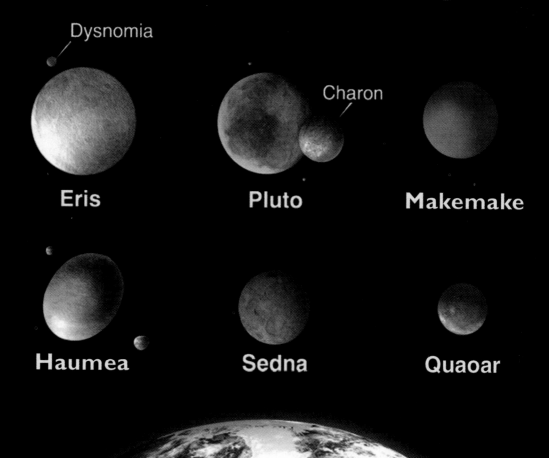

Dysnomia

Charon

Eris   **Pluto**   **Makemake**

Haumea   **Sedna**   **Quaoar**

Dwarf Planets and Solar System Debris

10

THE FACT THAT ASTRONOMERS were able to predict the existence and location of Neptune, based on irregularities in the orbit of Uranus, led them to try the method once more. (See the Historical Note on the discovery of Neptune in Chapter 9.) Analysis of the orbital data of Uranus led to the conclusion that although the gravitational pull from Neptune accounted for about 98% of the variation from Uranus' expected orbit, there still were unexplained irregularities. Some astronomers used the data to predict a ninth planet. Percival Lowell made his prediction of the existence of the new planet in 1905. He used the Lowell Observatory telescope to search for the disc of "Planet X" until he died in 1916, but he had no success.

In the 1920s a new photographic telescope, donated by Percival Lowell's brother, was installed at Lowell Observatory. On April 1, 1929, Clyde W. Tombaugh started a new search for the predicted planet. Tombaugh, however, used a different method of searching. Instead of looking for a small, faint disk, he concentrated on looking for the motion a planet must exhibit.

Tombaugh searched for the moving planet with the aid of an instrument called a *blink comparator*. This instrument is essentially a microscope containing a mirror that can be flipped quickly, allowing the observer to look alternately at two different photographs of the sky. The astronomer takes photographs of the same area of the

All cross references to chapters, sections, figures, and tables pertain to the main text, *In Quest of the Universe, Sixth Edition. In Quest of the Solar System* contains Chapters 1–11 and 19 of the main text. *In Quest of the Stars and Galaxies* contains Chapters 1–5 and 11–19 of the main text.

This illustration shows a comparison between some of the largest currently known Kuiper belt objects. Eris, the largest of the known dwarf planets, is named after the Greek goddess of discord and strife; its satellite Dysnomia is named after the demon goddess of lawlessness and the daughter of Eris.

This is the same Percival Lowell, a successful businessman-turned-astronomer, who found evidence for life on Mars. He built an observatory near Flagstaff, Arizona in 1894.

(a)   (b)

FIGURE 10-1 These are the two photos on which Tombaugh discovered Pluto. Notice how difficult it is to detect the change in Pluto's position, which is indicated by the arrows.

After the discovery of Pluto was confirmed by other astronomers, young Tombaugh went to college, enrolling as a freshman at the University of Kansas.

Neptune's discovery was not an accident, of course, but a triumph of the ability of Newton's theories to make predictions.

sky a few days apart. The two photographs are then arranged in the comparator so that the stars in each photograph appear at the same place as the photographs are viewed one after the other. If a moving object such as a planet is in the photographs, it will appear to jump from one spot to another as the astronomer changes views.

Searching for an object in this manner is very tedious work because the comparator must be scanned slowly over one pair of photographs after another. Tombaugh's search was especially difficult because the predicted position of Planet X was in the constellation Gemini, which is near the Milky Way and therefore in a region with a great many faint stars. As a result, each photograph contained some 300,000 star images. Nevertheless, Tombaugh was successful.

On February 18, 1930, more than 10 months after he began, Tombaugh detected a difference, indicated by the arrows in the two photographs in FIGURE 10-1. Consider that in searching for the planet, even with the help of the comparator, Tombaugh had to examine not just this pair of photographs but numerous pairs. Tombaugh announced the discovery of the new planet on March 13—the 75th anniversary of Lowell's birth and the 149th anniversary of the discovery of Uranus. It was named Pluto after the mythical Greek god of the underworld.

Pluto was discovered nearly 6 degrees from where Lowell had predicted, and it soon became clear that Pluto's size was so small that its mass must also be small—too small to cause the irregularities that had been seen in Uranus' orbit. More recent analysis of the orbital data used by Lowell and his contemporaries indicates that the irregularities they perceived were not caused by another planet at all, but were simply variations caused by the limited accuracy of the data. This is an example of the importance of knowing the amount of uncertainty involved in a measurement.

We thus must conclude that Pluto was discovered by accident; however, if Lowell's calculations and predictions had not been made, the search would not have been carried on so diligently, and the planet probably would not have been discovered until much later.

We devoted a chapter to the four terrestrial planets and another to the four Jovian planets. That leaves only the dwarf planets, of which we will discuss first Pluto, before moving on to the debris of the solar system: the asteroids, comets, and meteoroids.

10-1 Pluto

Kuiper belt A disk-shaped region beyond Neptune's orbit, 30–1000 AU from the Sun, closer to the solar system than the Oort cloud and presumed to be the source of short-period comets. The main Kuiper belt extends from 30–50 AU.

Pluto is so far away from the Earth that less is known about it than any of the eight planets. This will change when the *New Horizons* spacecraft, launched in 2006, will pass by Pluto in 2015 and give us the first close-up images of the planet and its moons; after that, the spacecraft will continue its exploration of objects in the *Kuiper belt* at the outer solar system until 2020.

Pluto as Seen From Earth

From 1979 to 1999 Pluto was inside Neptune's orbit. Refer back to Figure 7-3.

Pluto was as close to Earth in 1989 as it has been for 248 years, but its image in a telescope was very small and fuzzy even then. Its orbit is more eccentric than any of the eight planets, so that although its average distance from the Sun is about 40 astronomical units (AU), its distance ranges from 30 AU to about 50 AU. Recall from Chapter 7 that Pluto's orbit has another unusual aspect: it is tilted 17 degrees to the ecliptic, whereas none of the orbits of the eight planets is tilted more than 7 degrees.

Stellar occultations revealed that Pluto has an atmosphere, and spectroscopic examination of the light from Pluto indicates the presence of nitrogen with traces of methane and carbon monoxide. It is probable, however, that this atmosphere is not present during Pluto's complete orbit, for when Pluto is at aphelion, it receives so little energy from the Sun that its surface is probably below the temperature at which methane freezes. Its atmosphere thus may be a temporary phenomenon that occurs only when it comes within a certain distance of the Sun. Comparing observational data from successive Pluto occultations, astronomers discovered that its atmosphere is undergoing global cooling, whereas its surface is getting slightly warmer. Only a part of this change can be explained by the motion of Pluto on its eccentric orbit around the Sun. It seems that Pluto is a more complex system than expected. Also, the planet's surface temperature is not uniform. The coldest regions have a temperature of about −235°C, whereas the warmest may reach −210°C.

In 1956, astronomers observed that Pluto's brightness changes slightly every 6.4 days, leading to the conclusion that it has a dark area on its surface and that its period of rotation is 6.4 days. Observations of an occultation in 1965 had placed an upper limit on the planet's size, but not until the discovery of Pluto's moon Charon did we have an opportunity to learn much about Pluto's mass and size.

Pluto and Its Moons

In 1978, James W. Christy of the U.S. Naval Observatory was analyzing data and noticed that Pluto seemed to have a bump on one side. FIGURE 10-2a shows this bump and indicates the limited resolution of photographs of this distant, tiny planet. Continued observation showed that the bump moved from one side to another, and it was concluded that Pluto has a moon. The moon was named Charon (pronounced KEHR-on), after the mythical boatman who ferried souls to the underworld to be judged by Pluto, and after Christy's wife, Charlene. The ground-based CCD photo of Pluto and Charon (Figure 10-2b) shows two separate objects, while Figure 10-2c is an *HST* image in which we see two obviously distinct objects.

Charon's orbit is tilted at 61 degrees to Pluto's orbit around the Sun. Its orbital period around Pluto is 6.4 days, the same as both Charon's and Pluto's rotational period. These two objects thus rotate synchronously with their orbital motion and always keep the same face toward each other. As a result, each one of these two objects seems to hover in the sky, as seen from the other, never rising or setting. FIGURE 10-3a shows the orbits of Charon and Pluto in 1978. As Pluto continued to move to the left in its orbit, our view of the system shifted so that between 1985 and 1990, Charon occulted Pluto during each revolution (Figure 10-3b). The duration of each occultation allowed astronomers to calculate the sizes of the two objects with greater accuracy. Still, a lack of knowledge of the nature of Pluto's atmosphere limits the accuracy of measurements of the planet's diameter. Its diameter may be as little as 2300 km (if the atmosphere is clear and we are seeing through it) or as great as 2340 km (if the atmosphere is hazy).

Pluto's mass is about 8 times that of Charon, but only a fifth of our Moon's mass. Its density (about 1.92 g/cm³) leads us to conclude that its interior is probably a mixture of ice (about 30%) and rock (about 70%), similar to Triton. Charon's diameter and density are known with more precision than Pluto's. Data taken during a very

Aphelion refers to the point in an object's orbit when the object is farthest from the Sun.

An increase in temperature of 1.5°C leads to a doubling of the density of Pluto's atmosphere.

Is Pluto always the farthest object from the Sun?

Our Moon was the first case where we saw synchronous rotation and revolution.

This series of occultations occurs only twice during each of Pluto's orbits of the Sun. (Each orbit takes 248 years.)

(a)

(b)

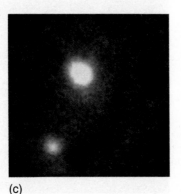
(c)

FIGURE 10-2 (a) James Christy concluded from a photo such as this that Pluto has a moon, although Pluto and Charon could not be seen as separate objects. Charon causes the "bump" at the lower left. (b) In this Earth-based CCD photo, two objects can definitely be seen. (c) This 1991 image was made by the *HST*.

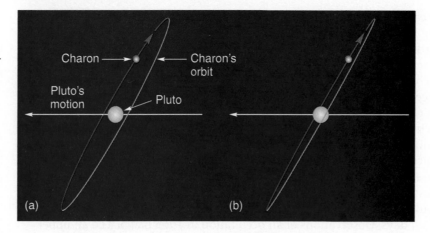

FIGURE 10-3 The plane of Charon's orbit is tilted at a great angle with respect to Pluto's path around the Sun. (a) This represents the view from Earth when Charon was discovered. (b) A decade later Pluto had moved such that Charon passed in front of and behind Pluto. Pluto and Charon are not drawn to scale.

FIGURE 10-4 These 1996 images of Pluto, based on *HST* data, show the planet during the course of a solar day. They indicate polar ice caps and bright features near the equator.

rare stellar occultation (a star passing behind Charon) suggest a diameter of 1212 km and a density of 1.63 g/cm³. This density indicates that Charon has a rocky core with a crust that is a mixture of ice and rock. Observations provide evidence that Charon's surface is coated in ice crystals and ammonia hydrates. This suggests that liquid water, with the help of ammonia, is pushed to the surface from deep within Charon. Because Charon is a typical Kuiper Belt object, it is likely that other objects in the belt of similar size and composition could have water reservoirs beneath their surfaces.

The two images of Pluto in **FIGURE 10-4** were constructed through computer image processing on *HST* data and are the first to reveal surface features on the planet. Some of these variations in surface reflectivity may be due to topographic features such as basins or fresh impact craters; however, most of these surface features, including the prominent northern polar cap, are likely produced by the complex distribution of frost that migrates across Pluto's surface with its orbital and seasonal cycles. The frost is a byproduct deposited out of Pluto's nitrogen-methane atmosphere.

Two additional moons of Pluto, 140 and 125 km in diameter, were discovered by the *HST* in 2005. **FIGURE 10-5** shows the motions of Pluto's moons over a 2-week period. All three moons are essentially the same neutral color, reflecting sunlight with equal efficiency at all wavelengths, just like Earth's Moon. (In contrast, Pluto has a reddish hue, the result of sunlight's effect on its methane and nitrogen surface ices.) The new moons are in the same orbital plane as Charon, and they are in near orbital resonance with Charon. All of these results, coupled with Charon's large mass and its lack of any substantial atmosphere, support the idea that Pluto and its moons formed as a result of a giant collision between two objects, 1600 to 2000 km in diameter, in a process similar to the one that gave us the Earth and the Moon.

FIGURE 10-5 The motions of Pluto's moons are seen over a 15-day interval by the *HST* using a red filter. The moons move counterclockwise, with Charon completing a bit less than three full revolutions.

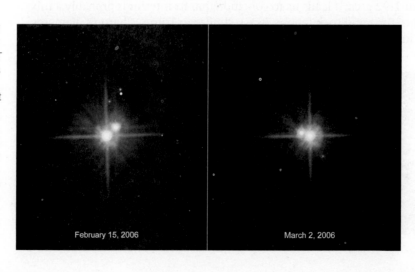

A Former Moon of Neptune?

For several reasons, including Pluto's very eccentric orbit, the similarity in its bulk properties with Triton, and the fact that it is so much smaller than any Jovian planet, some astronomers have proposed that Pluto was once a moon of Neptune. Jupiter, Saturn, Neptune, and the Earth all have moons that are larger than Pluto. Perhaps a collision or near passage of some unknown celestial object caused Pluto to be ejected from the Neptunian system. Such a collision would be highly unlikely, but not impossible. However, the discovery of Pluto's moons makes it unlikely that Pluto was once a moon of Neptune.

An alternative hypothesis is based on the overall similarities between Charon and Pluto. In contrast to other planet–moon systems in our solar system, Pluto and Charon have comparable sizes and masses. It now seems likely that this system was formed when Pluto collided with a similar object, leaving behind enough mass to form Charon, and other moons which were then captured by Pluto's gravity.

> Although the orbits of Neptune and Pluto intersect on a two-dimensional drawing, the two objects don't actually cross paths.

> Recall the "double planet" and "capture" theories for the origin of our Moon, discussed in Section 6-5.

10-2 Solar System Debris

Pluto and Charon are now classified as merely two of the largest examples of a group of objects orbiting in the Kuiper belt. We study this disk-shaped region past the orbit of Neptune (roughly 30 to 1000 AU from the Sun) later in this chapter. The IAU decision on the planetary status of Pluto (which we discussed in Chapter 7) indicates arbitrariness in our classification of celestial objects. Nature is unified; we divide objects within it into discrete groups only to help our understanding.

One dictionary defines *debris* as "an accumulation of fragments of rock," which is similar to how we conceptualize it in the rest of this chapter. It could be said that the solar system is made up of one large object (the Sun), some medium-sized objects (the planets), and a lot of debris. The medium-sized objects (as well as some smaller moons) were discussed in the preceding two chapters and the large object is discussed in the next chapter. Now we look at the debris.

The material of which the debris is composed is not basically different from that which makes up the planets. Rather, it is material that did not become part of the Sun or the planets when the solar system was formed. The debris comes in several forms, including asteroids, meteoroids, comets, and dust.

> Ceres was named for the patron goddess of Sicily by its discoverer, Giuseppe Piazzi. German astronomers wanted to call it Juno or Hera, whereas some French astronomers wanted to call it Piazzi. Piazzi the man won out over Piazzi the name.

10-3 Asteroids

Since the first night of the 19th century, when Father Giuseppe Piazzi discovered Ceres (see Advancing the Model: The Discovery of the Asteroids, in Chapter 7), we have discovered several hundred thousand asteroids. The photograph in FIGURE 10-6 shows the motion of two asteroids across the background of stars; it is from photographs like this that most asteroids are discovered and their orbits analyzed. These objects traditionally have been called *minor planets*, indicating their stature as objects that orbit the Sun. Only when the orbit of an asteroid is determined well enough that its location can be predicted on succeeding oppositions do we give it a name. Because calculations of asteroid orbits are no trivial task and usually are of no great value to astronomical knowledge, most asteroids go nameless.

Ceres is now classified as a dwarf planet and is by far the largest "asteroid," with a diameter of about 930 km (580 miles). Two others (Pallas and Vesta) have diameters greater than 500 km, about 30 more are between 200 and 300 km in

FIGURE 10-6 The telescope was following the stars during this time exposure. The two streaks (identified with arrows) are asteroids.

diameter, and about 100 are between 100 and 200 km. There are probably a few million asteroids with diameters of about 1 km. All the rest are smaller. Observations of Ceres and studies of its properties show evidence of a planet-like shape and suggest an internal structure that consists of a rocky core, icy mantle, and a crust of carbon-rich compounds and clays. Theoretical models suggest that the icy mantle may contain more frozen water than all of Earth's fresh water. Ceres makes up about a third of the entire mass of all asteroids. The Moon is more massive than all the asteroids combined and about 85 times more massive than Ceres. The masses of the three largest asteroids have been calculated by observing the perturbations they cause on smaller asteroids passing nearby. Masses of other asteroids have been estimated based on their sizes and expected densities.

Asteroids are classified in a number of ways, but the main two schemes involve either the position of the asteroids in the solar system or their type (based on chemical composition and albedo). In the first scheme, asteroids are classified as the objects in the ***asteroid belt*** (located between Mars and Jupiter), as near-Earth asteroids (those that come close to the Earth), and as Trojan asteroids (found near two special points on Jupiter's orbit, one 60° ahead and the other 60° behind Jupiter). There are also some asteroids in the outer solar system that orbit between the Jovian planets, but their orbits are unstable.

According to the second scheme, asteroids are classified as follows. The S-type asteroids are bright reddish, metallic nickel-iron, mixed with iron- and magnesium-silicates, and more reflective than the Moon. Bright nonreddish asteroids are M type, which are pure nickel-iron. Most of the known asteroids are the dark C type, which have a chemical composition similar to the proportions of metals within the Sun and are similar to the carbonaceous chondrite meteorites.

The brightness of most asteroids changes with periods that are typically a few hours as a result of their irregular shape, which causes them to reflect different amounts of light toward Earth as they rotate. In 1990, the *Galileo* spacecraft passed 16,000 km from the asteroid Gaspra and took many images (**FIGURE 10-7a**) that show that this 19 × 12

asteroid belt The region between Mars and Jupiter where most asteroids orbit.

FIGURE 10-7 (a) The asteroid Gaspra was photographed by *Galileo* on the spacecraft's trip to Jupiter. Gaspra is about 19 km (12 miles) end to end. (b) *Galileo* also photographed the asteroid Ida, which is orbited by a tiny satellite named Dactyl. Ida is 56 km (33 miles) in its longest dimension; Dactyl is 1.4 km across. (c) This picture of Eros was taken by the *NEAR* spacecraft. (d) The size and shape of Eros are close to that of Manhattan Island, but would you really want to live there? (e) A mosaic of four images of Eros taken by *NEAR Shoemaker* from about 100 km (62 miles) above the asteroid.

(a)   (b)

Size comparison
Manhattan Island (New York City)   Eros (Asteroid)
8 Miles   21 Miles

(c)   (d)   (e)

× 11–kilometer asteroid rotates with a period of about 7 hours. It is an S-type asteroid apparently covered with about a meter of dusty, rocky soil. Figure 10-7b is an image of asteroid Ida, which has a tiny satellite of its own. Figure 10-7c shows asteroid Eros, which was the target of a spacecraft exploration that began in February 2000 and lasted for a year (see Advancing the Model: The Mission to Eros). The spinning rate and orbit of small asteroids is influenced by the absorption and emission of sunlight over millions to billions of years. This re-radiation of sunlight acts as a propulsion engine that affects the motion of the asteroids. Exposure to solar and cosmic radiation and the heating effect of impacts also affect the color of asteroids. Understanding this "space weathering" is important because the color of an asteroid can be correlated to its age. Such a correlation explains why the most numerous meteorites (the ordinary chondrites) are bluish in color even though they are supposedly released from asteroids that are reddish in color. Asteroids get more reddish with time; Figure 10-7b shows the differences between the bluish areas of asteroid Ida, which are associated with freshly exposed surfaces, and the reddish regions that correspond to old craters and smooth areas that have remained undisturbed for a long time.

The goal of the University of Arizona's Catalina Sky Survey is to discover and track, by the end of 2010, more than 90% of the 1-km or greater in diameter, potentially hazardous asteroids and comets that could approach Earth. A collision between a 300-meter asteroid and Earth will generate 1400 megatons of energy.

The Orbits of Asteroids

The direction of motion of all of the asteroids, like that of the planets, is counterclockwise as viewed from north of the solar system. Most of their planes of revolution are near the plane of the ecliptic, although we know of one with a plane of revolution 64 degrees from Earth's.

Most of the asteroids orbit the Sun at distances from 2.2 to 3.3 AU (in the *asteroid belt*). This corresponds, by Kepler's third law, to orbital periods of about 3.3 to 6 years. Most of the asteroids in the asteroid belt have fairly circular orbits, although not as circular as the orbits of the major planets.

If the about 100,000 asteroids that are large enough to appear in photographs were in exactly the same plane and were spread evenly across the asteroid belt, neighboring asteroids would be separated by 2 million kilometers, or more than a million miles. In reality, this separation distance is a low estimate because the asteroids are irregularly spaced in the asteroid belt and are not all in the same plane. There are many more asteroids smaller than this, but even so, the asteroids present no major hazard to spacecraft. Compared with the popular picture of a crowded asteroid belt, the belt is almost empty. To illustrate this, imagine a scale model in which the largest asteroid—Ceres—is the size of a grain of sand. In this case, a normal-size asteroid would be 1 meter away and would be too small to be seen.

Is there a major risk of collision when a spacecraft passes through the asteroid belt?

As the orbits of more and more asteroids were calculated during the 19th century, it became clear that they are not evenly distributed across the asteroid belt. At certain distances from the Sun, gaps occur in the belt; these are regions where the density of asteroids is significantly lower than the average in the belt. FIGURE 10-8 illustrates the situation. One very prominent gap occurs at 2.50 AU and another at 3.28 AU. Daniel Kirkwood, an American astronomer, first explained these gaps in 1866. He noticed that 3.28 AU corresponds to a period of revolution of 5.93 years, which is just half of Jupiter's period of 11.86 years. An asteroid at 2.50 AU would orbit the Sun in 3.95 years, which is one third of Jupiter's period. We saw a similar situation in Chapter 9 in the explanation for Cassini's division in Saturn's rings. In both cases, synchronous tugs from a large object on smaller particles gradually move those particles out of their orbits and result in gaps.

FIGURE 10-8 Kirkwood gaps appear where asteroids would have periods of one third and one half of Jupiter's. The gaps are not totally devoid of asteroids.

ADVANCING THE MODEL

The Mission to Eros

The *Near Earth Asteroid Rendezvous (NEAR)* mission was the first to orbit an asteroid and the first that involved a controlled descent to and elegant landing on the surface of an asteroid (even though the spacecraft was not built as a lander). *NEAR* was launched in 1996, and after a 5-year, 2-billion-mile journey it began a yearlong orbit of Eros in 2000. Renamed *NEAR Shoemaker*, the spacecraft provided the most detailed profile yet of a small celestial object.

The mission provided astronomers with about 160,000 images covering the asteroid's entire surface, which includes craters, boulders, and dust. Data from millions of laser pulses that were bounced on the asteroid's surface resulted in a detailed shape model of Eros. The mission also provided infrared, X-ray, and gamma-ray readings on Eros' composition and spectral properties, along with data on its weak gravity and solid but cracked interior.

We now know that Eros has a composition similar to the most primitive rocks in the solar system, the chondritic meteorites (the building blocks of the terrestrial planets). It is a homogeneous mixture of heavy and light materials, with aluminum, magnesium, and silicon having the same relative abundances that they do in the Sun. This suggests that Eros was never exposed to intense heating and thus never subjected to melting. It is a relic from the dawn of our solar system, a planetesimal that was not captured by a growing protoplanet.

On the surface of Eros there are many craters smaller than 1 kilometer in diameter, while the largest one is 5.5 kilometers wide. There are also many rocks and boulders, 30 to 100 meters across, created by impacts. There are fewer young craters on Eros than expected from our experience with our Moon, and more boulders than expected. Some small craters have flat, smooth floors, as if a fine-grain material is covering the surface. It is possible that dust grains levitate downhill into the bottom of craters due to static electricity, which results from the bombardment of the dust grains by the solar wind.

The asteroid lacks a measurable magnetic field, and its density is similar to that of Earth's crust. The gravity on Eros is very weak but enough to hold a spacecraft. A 90-kg person (200 pounds) on Earth would weigh about 2 ounces on Eros, making it possible for a person on the surface to escape into space. Eros is about 21 by 8 by 8 miles (33 by 13 by 13 km) in size, orbits the Sun once every 1.76 Earth years, and spins on its shortest axis once every 5.27 hours. The rotation axis appears to remain steady as the asteroid moves in space, as if Eros were a football thrown in a perfectly tight spiral pass. Eros is a "near-Earth asteroid," its next close approach to Earth being in 2012 at a distance of only 0.18 AU, but there is no chance that it will collide with our planet.

Jupiter has cleared out other regions of the asteroid belt where it exerts a regular gravitational pull on objects that may once have been there. Besides the gaps at locations corresponding to one third and one half of Jupiter's period, there are also major gaps corresponding to two fifths and three sevenths of the period of the giant planet.

Not all asteroids orbit the Sun between Mars and Jupiter. About 2000 are currently known to have orbits eccentric enough that they cross the Earth's orbit; these are near-Earth asteroids known as **Apollo asteroids**. About 70 of these are potentially hazardous to Earth, in the sense that they are larger than 1 km in diameter and their orbits bring them closer than 0.05 AU to Earth. Some of these have passed fairly close to the Earth in recent history. On May 19, 1996, an asteroid passed within about 450,000 km of the Earth, which is slightly more than the distance of the Moon from Earth. The predicted closest encounter by a potentially hazardous asteroid through the 21st century will occur on August 7, 2027, at a distance of about 400,000 km. When we discuss meteors later in this chapter, we describe what happens when a large asteroid hits the Earth.

Apollo asteroids
Asteroids that cross the Earth's orbit and have semi-major axes larger than Earth's.

The Origin of Asteroids

Astronomers once thought that asteroids are the remains of the explosion of a planet. This theory has been abandoned today for two reasons. First, there is no known mechanism by which a planet could explode. Second, if all of the asteroids were combined into one object, that object would be only about 1500 km in diameter—much less than the 3500-kilometer diameter of our Moon. Such a small object does not fit the pattern of planetary sizes.

Are asteroids pieces of a destroyed planet?

You Can Name an Asteroid

So you want to name an asteroid? That sounds like a magazine advertisement. The fact is, however, that only about 3000 of the perhaps 100,000 asteroids that appear on photographs (and thus have a diameter of about 1 km or greater) have been named. Why? To name an asteroid, you must know its orbit accurately. You determine its orbit by taking photographs of it and perhaps searching photographs taken by others studying different objects. After you have determined the orbit, you must wait until the asteroid has completed at least one more cycle around the Sun to check your predicted orbit.

If you have indeed calculated a reliable orbit, you will be given the privilege of naming the asteroid. The object's official name will include not only the name you give, but a number indicating the order of discovery. For example, 1 Ceres and 2 Pallas. These first asteroids were named after gods of Roman and Greek mythology. Names from mythology quickly ran out, and today, almost any name is acceptable. Asteroid number 1001 is Gaussia, named after the mathematician who discovered the method of calculating orbits. As you can verify in the internationally accepted catalog of asteroids, the *Minor Planet and Comets Ephemeris*, asteroid number 1814 is named for Bach and 1815 for Beethoven. Others are named Debussy, McCartney, Clapton, and Elvis. Some of the more recently named asteroids honor the seven astronauts lost in the *Challenger* explosion in January 1986.

It is considered much more probable that the asteroids are simply primordial material that never formed into a planet. There is a good reason that the material in the asteroid belt did not form into a planet: The gravitational pull from Jupiter causes a continual stirring effect on the objects in the asteroid belt. This prevents the small gravitational forces that exist between the asteroids from pulling them together to form a larger object.

Even today, there is evidence that Jupiter causes collisions between asteroids that result in their fragmentation. In fact, some of the asteroids that have orbits outside the main belt are thought to have resulted from such collisions. Analyses of the orbits of such asteroids have identified groups ("families") whose orbits, when traced backward, indicate that they were once together. They apparently broke apart as the result of a collision with another asteroid, caused by the gravitational force of Jupiter.

In 2006, for the first time, a breakup event in the asteroid belt was positively linked to a large quantity of interplanetary dust deposited on Earth. A spike in the concentration of helium-3, a rare isotope of helium, was found in sediments in oceanic core samples, indicating that the Earth was blanketed 8.2 million years ago by dust; computer simulations of the orbits of a cluster of asteroid fragments show that they are the byproduct of an impact that blew apart the 160-km asteroid Veritas, creating in the process the dust found in the sediments.

It is estimated that about 40,000 tons of the interplanetary dust continually ejected from comets or produced by collisions between asteroids get deposited on Earth each year. This estimate is based on measurements of the helium-3 and helium-4 flux of dust particles preserved in the Antarctic snow. Observations of dust clouds forming from an asteroid burning up in Earth's atmosphere and theoretical models suggest that micron-sized particles in such dust may actually influence our weather more than previously believed.

Asteroids are discussed again later in the chapter when we cover the origin of meteoroids. Now we turn to another category of solar system debris: comets.

10-4 Comets

One of the most spectacular astronomical sights available to the naked eye is a comet. People who have not seen a comet commonly assume from photographs such as FIGURE 10-9, which shows Comet Hale-Bopp, that the comet streaks across the sky at

Does a comet move visibly across the sky?

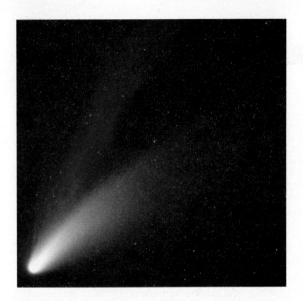

FIGURE 10-9 In this photo of Comet Hale-Bopp, the blue ion tail is obvious. It is straight and streams directly away from the Sun. The white dust tail is curved.

Wherefore if according to what we have already said [the comet] should return again about the year 1758, candid posterity will not refuse to acknowledge that this was first discovered by an Englishman.
Edmund Halley

SOHO (*Solar Heliospheric Observatory*), launched in 1995, is a collaboration between ESA and NASA. Its mission is to investigate the Sun from its deep core through its outer atmosphere.

nucleus (of comet) The solid chuck of a comet, located in the head.

coma (KOH-mah) The part of a comet's head made up of diffuse gas and dust.

tail (of comet) The gas and/or dust swept away from a comet's head.

great speed in the direction opposite to its tail. In fact, if you see a comet in the sky, you observe no rapid motion at all. Unless you observe carefully, the comet appears to stay in the same place among the stars, having only the motion across our sky caused by the rotation of the Earth. (It does move among the stars, of course, and its motion can easily be seen over a few days.) Don't confuse a comet with a meteor, which *does* streak across the sky, as we discuss later.

Cometary Orbits—Isaac Newton and Edmund Halley

Isaac Newton proposed that comets orbit the Sun according to his laws of universal gravitation and motion, just as do the planets. He concluded that because comets are visible from Earth for only short periods of time (typically a few months), their orbits are very elongated.

Edmund Halley, a friend of Newton's, used Newton's methods, his own observations, and descriptions of previous comet sightings to calculate the orbits of several comets. Halley noticed that the orbits of the comets of 1531, 1607, and 1682 were very similar and suspected that they might be the same comet; however, he was at first confused by the fact that the time that elapsed between one appearance of the comet and the next was not always the same. When he realized that the comet's path would be changed slightly by the gravitational pull of a planet—particularly Jupiter or Saturn—when the comet passed nearby, he hypothesized that these three comets were in fact three appearances of the same comet. In 1705, Halley predicted that the comet would reappear in 1758.

On Christmas night of 1758, the comet was sighted. In honor of its predictor, it was named Halley's comet. The brilliant Edmund Halley, however, had died 16 years earlier at the age of 85 and was unable to see his hypothesis verified. By investigating reports of comets in literature, we can now trace Comet Halley back as far as the year 239 BC.

SOHO, a satellite whose mission is to actually study the Sun, is the greatest comet hunter ever, responsible for almost half of all recorded comets (FIGURE 10-10). The planes of revolution of comets are not limited to the ecliptic plane, but are randomly oriented and, thus, comets pass the Sun from all directions. Not surprisingly, a comet's visibility depends on the relative positions of the Earth and the comet, with respect to the Sun, at the time of the observation.

The Nature of Comets

We normally think of a comet as having three parts (FIGURE 10-11a). What is commonly called the head of a comet consists of the **nucleus** and the **coma**. Sweeping away from the coma is the comet's **tail**, which varies greatly in size and appearance from comet to comet. The coma of a comet may be as large as a million kilometers in diameter—almost as large as the Sun. Some comet tails have been as long as an astronomical unit.

In 1950, Harvard astronomer Fred L. Whipple proposed what remains today as the basic model of a comet: The nucleus resembles a dirty snowball

FIGURE 10-10 The Sun-grazing comets *SOHO* 54 and 55 (at bottom right) were discovered in 1998. The satellite's coronagraph produces an artificial eclipse of the Sun. Comet *SOHO* 1500 was discovered in 2008.

(a)   (b)

made up of water ice, frozen carbon dioxide, a few other frozen substances, and small solid grains—the "dirt." Observations of comets since that time have slightly modified his model to include a crusty layer on the surface of the nucleus, with the ices and "dirt" inside. Figure 10-11b shows a cross-sectional view of the nucleus of a comet. When the comet is far from the Sun, the nucleus (which is only a few miles in diameter) is all there is. As the comet approaches the Sun, it becomes warmer and the ices inside melt and vaporize. These materials then break through the crust, forming a jet. These gases, along with dust particles that have been torn away, hover near the nucleus, held there by the small gravitational field of the nucleus. This is what makes up the coma.

FIGURE 10-12a is a close up of the coma of Comet Hale-Bopp. This comet has a fairly large nucleus (25 miles across); as it spins around about once every 12 hours, parts of it shoot away in a few geysers. As the ejected material spirals away from the nucleus, it causes the appearance of rings around the nucleus. These are the "layers" seen in the photo. They were visible even in small telescopes in early 1997.

The coma and tail of a comet are mostly empty space. When Comet Halley came through the inner solar system in the late 1980s, ESA launched the spacecraft *Giotto* to intercept it. *Giotto* passed within 600 km (350 miles) of the nucleus (Figure 10-12b), going right through the coma. *Giotto* found that the coma is billions of times less dense than the atmosphere of Earth at sea level. It observed the abundances of chemical elements and confirmed that the comet was composed of material as primitive as the original solar nebula. *Giotto* also showed that there were two major groups of particles. The first group was rich in mineral-forming elements such as silicon, calcium, and magnesium. The second group was composed mainly by organic grains made of carbon, hydrogen, oxygen, and nitrogen.

The spacecraft *Giotto* was named after the Italian artist who included Comet Halley as the star of Bethlehem in his fresco of the nativity scene. He had just seen a return of the comet a few years earlier, in 1301. *Giotto* was launched in 1985 and encountered Comet Halley in the night between March 13 and 14, 1986.

(a)   (b)

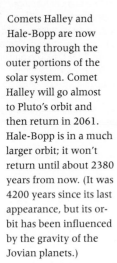

Comets Halley and Hale-Bopp are now moving through the outer portions of the solar system. Comet Halley will go almost to Pluto's orbit and then return in 2061. Hale-Bopp is in a much larger orbit; it won't return until about 2380 years from now. (It was 4200 years since its last appearance, but its orbit has been influenced by the gravity of the Jovian planets.)

The entire mass of a typical comet is less than one billionth the mass of the Earth, and more than 99.99% of this mass is in the nucleus. The reason that we can see the coma at all is that its molecules and dust particles reflect sunlight to us. In addition, ultraviolet light from the Sun causes the molecules to fluoresce, in much the same manner that a "black light" poster glows in ultraviolet light. There are very few molecules and dust particles in any particular volume of the coma, but the coma is extremely large—hundreds of thousands of kilometers in diameter—so there is a lot of material along any particular line of sight.

Astronomers have observed not only ultraviolet radiation from comets but also intense X-ray emission from the gas surrounding the nucleus of a comet. It was an unexpected and puzzling result when energetic X-rays (100 times more intense than anyone had predicted) were first observed in 1996 coming from the vicinity of Comet Hyakutake. Since then, satellites have detected such radiation from a number of comets, including Comet Hale-Bopp. The most probable explanation to the phenomenon of X-rays from cosmic snowballs is the following. Highly ionized elements in the solar wind (such as oxygen, nitrogen, and carbon) interact with the gas being released by the comet. The strong positive charge of the ions attracts electrons from the atoms and molecules from the comet. The electrons that leap from the neutral atoms to the ions emit X-rays as they move from high- to low-energy orbits of the ions.

The high brightness of Comet Hale-Bopp allowed astronomers to detect the presence of a noble gas, argon. This is important because noble gases do not interact chemically with other elements and are easily lost from comets at low temperatures. The high abundance of argon in Comet Hale-Bopp suggests that it has always been cold and, therefore, was most likely formed in the zone around Uranus and Neptune or possibly farther out. The presence or absence of such gases thus provides a tool for measuring the thermal history of comets. Another tool is provided by the structure (amorphous versus crystalline) of the dust that comets carry. Astronomers now believe that comets could have formed at different times during the evolution of our solar system. Comets whose dust is amorphous formed very early on, while the presence of crystalline dust signifies that the comet formed later, as the dust clouds were heated by the forming Sun.

Comet Tails

As indicated earlier, the tail of a comet does not necessarily follow the head through space. Rather, a comet's tail always points away from the Sun. After a comet has passed the Sun, its tail thus actually *leads* it through space (**FIGURE 10-13**). This takes some explaining.

Comets usually have two tails, although one or both may be very small and they may change greatly as time passes. The drawing in Figure 10-11a and the photo of Comet Hale-Bopp in Figure 10-9 show the ion and dust tails of a comet. The straight tail consists of charged molecules (*ions*) being swept away from the comet by the solar wind—charged particles that are always being emitted by the Sun. These molecules move away at a great speed and form a straight tail.

The curved tail is caused by grains of dust in the coma being pushed away by the weak pressure of solar radiation. This radiation pressure is not detectable by us in everyday life, but light indeed does exert a tiny force on objects it strikes. In the weak gravitational field of the comet's nucleus, the force is great enough to move dust particles away from the head; however, they move much more slowly than the molecules that form the ion tail, and

FIGURE 10-13 In general, a comet's tails point away from the Sun. This led Ludwig Biermann to predict the existence of the solar wind a decade before it was discovered in 1962 by *Mariner 2*. The tails are largest shortly after the comet has passed the Sun.

ion A charged atom or molecule resulting from its loss or gain of at least one electron.

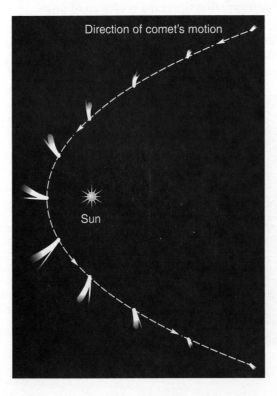

Direction of comet's motion

Sun

Astronomer Maria Mitchell, A Nineteenth-Century Feminist

Maria (pronounced ma-RYE-a) Mitchell (1818–1889) grew up on Nantucket Island, Massachusetts and learned astronomy both from her schoolteacher father and from her readings while she worked as a librarian. In 1847, while observing the sky from her rooftop, she discovered a comet. The discovery resulted in her becoming the first woman elected to the American Academy of Arts and Sciences (although the all-male membership refused to name her a "fellow," calling her instead an "honorary member").

At that time, the king of Denmark awarded a gold medal to each discoverer of a comet, and receiving the medal brought Mitchell some fame. Her astronomical work remained on the amateur level, however, until her mother died, when finally, at the age of 40, she sought a professional career. Vassar College had just been founded, and Maria Mitchell was hired to teach.

Mitchell was an early believer in women's rights and saw astronomy and science as an avenue for liberation and a way for women to break from domestic tradition. Her outspoken nature was revealed on one occasion when her wish to observe the Moon as it occulted a star conflicted with something her college president wanted her to do. She wrote the following note to him*:

My good natured President, I want to hear you preach tomorrow, and I also want to see the moon pass over Aldebaran. Can't you let me do both? Will you stop at eleventhly or twelfthly? Or, why need you show us *all* sides of a subject? The moon never turns to us other than the one side we see, and did you ever know a finer moon? If I could stop the moon and do no more harm than Joshua did, I wouldn't ask such a favor of you, knowing, as I do, what a difficult thing it is for you to pause, when you are once started, and knowing also, that I never want you to do so—*except this once*. Yours with all regret, even if it doesn't appear—M. Mitchell. (Mitchell's italics)

*This story is from E. A. Daniels, "Maria Mitchell, the Star of Vassar College," *Star Date*, November/December, 1989. To subscribe to this delightful magazine, write Star Date, RLM 15.308, University of Texas at Austin, Austin, Texas 78712.

FIGURE 10-14 shows why this results in the dust tail being curved. Dust particles that left the comet when it was at location X have reached X', those that left at Y are at Y', and so on.

Sometimes only one tail of a comet is visible because one is behind the other as seen from Earth. In addition, some comets are not as dusty as others and do not contain a prominent dust tail.

In general, the tails of comets point away from the Sun regardless of the motion of the comet nucleus because the agents responsible for forming the tails (the solar wind and light) are emitted radially from the Sun. Comet tails are typically 10^7 to 10^8 kilometers long and may be as long as 1 AU.

Because a comet loses material as its gas and dust are pushed off to form its tails, comets have limited lifetimes. Comet Halley spews about 25 to 30 tons of its mass through its jets each second when it is close to the Sun. This sounds like a great deal, but it means that the nucleus loses less than 1% of its mass on each pass of the Sun. Comet Halley is now on its way toward the outer portion of its elliptical orbit, and because its jets are now inactive, it is no longer losing mass.

Comets do gradually lose their ices, however. It is thought that some comets evaporate away all of their nuclei and just fizzle out. Other comets, after they lose all of their volatile materials, become simple chunks of rock and probably would be

Is it dangerous for Earth to pass through a comet's tail?

FIGURE 10-14 Dust that was blown off the comet when it was at point X is now at X'. Dust blown off at Y is at Y'. This causes the dust tail to be curved.

This dust left the comet when it was at point Z

To Sun

classified as asteroids. A third way that comets die is to fall into the Sun; a comet that comes close to the Sun is slowed by the Sun's atmosphere, and after several passes, it becomes slowed enough that it falls into the Sun. Finally, a comet can disintegrate either by gravitational forces, as was the case of Comet Shoemaker-Levy 9 (discussed in Chapter 1), or by the Sun's heat, which could crack a comet's crusty outer layer and release gases that split the comet apart.

Missions to Comets

ESA's *Giotto* mission to Comet Halley and NASA's *Deep Space 1* encounter of Comet Borrelly in late 2001 were only the start of our efforts to understand comets.

NASA's *Deep Impact* spacecraft flew by and released a probe that crashed on the nucleus of Comet Temple 1 in 2005, producing a crater and a plume of ejected gas and material. The comet was chosen because its stable orbit around the Sun (between the orbits of Mars and Jupiter) had created a protective layer of dust around the icy dirt-ball interior. Ground and spacecraft observations showed that the comet's interior is similar to the exterior of comets that have not passed close to the Sun as often as Temple 1; they also detected a mix of water, organic compounds, and silicates (including large amounts of olivine, a compound of iron, magnesium, and other elements) that is similar to what is observed in the long-period comets from the Oort cloud, which we discuss in the next section. It is possible that these comets had a common origin, the region of the solar system between Uranus and Neptune, and were scattered early in the history of the solar system due to the migration of the planets, as we discussed in Chapter 7.

The presence of organic chemicals in the ejected material, including ethane and methyl cyanide, a key player in reactions that form DNA, has strengthened the notion that comets delivered to Earth many of the chemical building blocks of organic life. Observations also showed an increase in the rate of water production, from 16,000 to 40,000 tons per day, as a result of the impact. This increase lasted for about a week; a comet's water cycle and supply provide clues about these objects and the possibility that they delivered water to Earth early in its history.

NASA's *Stardust* mission plunged through the coma of Comet Wild 2 in 2004. The images (FIGURE 10-15a) show the presence of boulders, cliffs, and impact craters. The rough terrain is an indication that solar heating has not yet molded this comet and that it is a very recent arrival to the inner solar system. The spacecraft collected samples of the coma material and returned them to Earth, along with a sample of interstellar dust collected during the journey. Analysis of the samples so far has shown the presence of olivine, nitrogen-rich organic molecules, and high-temperature minerals rich in aluminum and calcium. The latter suggests that comets are not composed only of volatile-rich materials that formed at cold temperatures at the outer reaches of the solar system; they also include material that formed at places near the early Sun and was propelled outward or was collected by the comet during its lifetime. The entire collected sample contains less than a few hundredths of a gram of material; however, a comparison of the structure and chemistry of this material to that of interstellar dust and meteorites will help us better understand the history and evolution of our solar system.

ESA's *Rosetta* mission, launched in early 2004, will meet its target, Comet Churyumov-Gerasimenko, in 2014, and be the first ever to land on a comet. The lander will be ejected from the spacecraft from a small height above the nucleus, fire a harpoon into the ground to avoid bouncing off the surface while landing, drill into the crust, collect and analyze mate-

Stardust was launched in 1999. It collected samples from Comet Wild 2 in early 2004, and the sample-return capsule parachuted to the Utah desert in January 2006.

Rosetta's name comes from the "Rosetta Stone," which helped decipher Egyptian hieroglyphics 200 years ago. The spacecraft will receive four gravitational assists during its mission, one from Mars and three from Earth.

FIGURE 10-15 (a) This composite image of Comet Wild 2 was taken by *Stardust* on January 2, 2004. It shows a rough and active terrain and jets of gas and dust. The comet is about 5 km in diameter. (b) A dust mote (the bright dot at the end of the trail from the lower right to the upper left) from Comet Wild 2 is seen in this small piece of aerogel extracted from the *Stardust* collectors. Aerogel is a very lightweight, porous, silicon-based material that is ideal for slowing down and collecting fast-moving dust particles.

rial from the comet's nucleus, and thus determine the structure of the comet's surface and the chemical composition of the comet sample. The spacecraft will continue studying the comet for more than a year as it approaches the Sun and grows its coma and tail.

10-5   The Oort Cloud and the Kuiper Belt

Comet Halley is one of many short-period comets—those with periods of less than 200 years. Most comets have much longer periods and approach us from far beyond the orbits of the planets.

In 1950, the Dutch astronomer Jan Oort revived the idea that great numbers of comets, all of which orbit the Sun, exist in a region of space that lies from 10,000 to 100,000 AU from the Sun (**FIGURE 10-16**). This hypothesis was based on three observations. First, no comet has been observed that is not gravitationally bound to the Sun. Second, the orbits of long-period comets show a strong tendency to have aphelia at distances around 50,000 AU. Finally, as new long-period comets continually join the inner solar system, they show they come from no preferential direction. This shell of comets surrounding the solar system has come to be known as the ***Oort cloud***. Naturally, the Oort cloud is too far away for its comets—which are simply nuclei at that distance—to be visible from Earth.

Many of the comets we observe are in elliptical orbits with extremely long periods. Because they obey Kepler's second law, they move at extremely low speeds when they are far from the Sun. As a result, they spend the overwhelming majority of the time well beyond planetary distances. For example, a comet with a period of 500,000 years would spend about 499,998 of those years beyond the orbits of the planets. Many of the comets in the Oort cloud thus are there simply in accordance with Kepler's laws.

In addition, there must be many comets in the Oort cloud whose orbits never approach the inner solar system. This would not necessarily mean circular orbits, for a comet could vary from 10,000 to 100,000 AU from the Sun and still remain in the Oort cloud. From time to time, one of the comets of this category must pass near another comet, causing it to change its path. This may result in a more circular path, or it may result in the comet being moved into an orbit that takes it toward the inner solar system. In addition, although the outer Oort cloud stretches only about one third of the way to what is now the nearest star, every few million years a star passes closer to the Sun than this, and gravitational forces from the star cause changes in the orbits of comets. Astronomers believe some comets are deflected into the inner solar system by this method. These comets from the Oort cloud become long-period comets. Statistics imply that the Oort cloud may contain up to a trillion comets, with a total mass of more than the mass of Jupiter.

> **Oort cloud** The theorized spherical shell, lying between 10,000 and 100,000 AU from the Sun, containing billions of comet nuclei. The inner Oort cloud lies between 1000 and 10,000 AU.

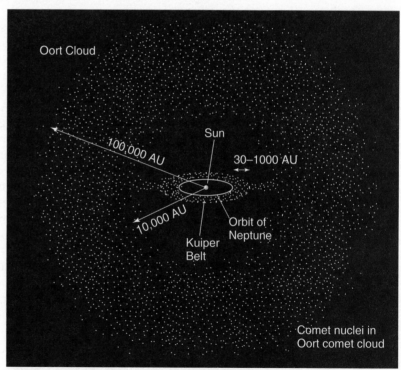

FIGURE 10-16 Long-period comets are believed to originate in the Oort cloud, a *spherical shell* between 10,000 and 100,000 AU surrounding the Sun. The inner Oort cloud extends from 1000 to 10,000 AU. The Kuiper belt is a *disk-shaped* region, 30 to 1000 AU from the Sun (past the orbit of Neptune), containing many small icy objects. The main Kuiper belt extends from 30 to 50 AU. It is believed to be the source of the short-period comets. Distances are not to scale.

HISTORICAL NOTE

Jan H. Oort, 1900–1992

On November 5, 1992, Jan Oort died at the age of 92 in his home country, The Netherlands. Although he is best known for the cloud of comets that bears his name, he considered his work with distant comets a sidelight to his other astronomical work. He first drew international attention in 1927, when he and Bertil Lindblad of Sweden discovered that the Milky Way Galaxy rotates (see Chapter 16). Later he established that the Sun is about 30,000 light-years from the center of the Galaxy, moving in an orbit around the center with a period of about 225 million years.

Oort's accomplishments are numerous. He was among the first to realize the value of radio astronomy and was the driving force behind the Westerbork Radio Telescope. His work resulted in establishing the link between the Crab nebula that we observe and the supernova observed by the Chinese in 1054 (see Chapter 15). Oort served as director of the Leiden Observatory from 1945 until his retirement in 1970.

The Oort cloud does not explain all comets, however, and in 1951, Gerard Kuiper proposed that a second, smaller band of comets must exist inside the Oort cloud. This disk-shaped region is beyond the orbit of Neptune, from about 30 to 1000 AU from the Sun. The first object in this *Kuiper belt* was discovered in 1992 (FIGURE 10-17). Since then, about 1000 objects have been discovered, mostly confined within a thick band around the ecliptic.

Their sizes range from about 100 km to 1000 km, and their surfaces are believed to be composed of dust and ice. It is estimated that there are a billion short-period comets in the Kuiper belt and about 100,000 small icy worlds greater than 100 km in diameter, compared with the 200 asteroids in the asteroid belt known to be that large. The total mass of the Kuiper belt objects is estimated to be about a tenth of the Earth's mass.

The chapter opening illustration shows the largest currently known Kuiper belt objects. Eris, the largest of the known dwarf planets, is about 5% larger than Pluto, which since 2006 is also considered to be a member of the Kuiper belt. Eris has a mass of 1.27 times that of Pluto and a density of 2.3 g/cm³. Spectral observations of Eris show it is very similar to Pluto, with strong signatures of methane ice. Its highly eccentric orbit ranges from 38 to 97 AU from the Sun and is inclined by 44° to the ecliptic plane, probably as a result of gravitational interactions with Neptune.

Haumea is a cigar-shaped object with a very fast 4-hour rotation period and a surface of water ice, whereas Makemake is like Pluto, with a surface covered in frozen methane.

Sedna is unlike Pluto, showing no evidence for a large amount of either water or methane ice. It is the second reddest object in the solar system after Mars. It has a highly eccentric orbit that brings it no closer than 75 AU to the Sun, and its orbital period of 10,500 years corresponds to a semimajor axis of about 480 AU. As such, it does not belong to the inner Kuiper belt but it can be considered as an inner Oort cloud object. Because of its extreme distance from the Sun, Sedna's surface has probably not been influenced for millions of years by anything other than cosmic rays and solar ultraviolet radiation, which turned the planetoid's original icy surface into a hy-

Haumea is named after the goddess of fertility and childbirth in Hawaiian mythology. Makemake is named after the creator of humanity and god of fertility in the mythology of the Rapanui, the native people of Easter Island. Sedna is named after the Inuit goddess of arctic sea life.

FIGURE 10-17 The arrows point to an object that moved during a 2-hour period on August 30, 1992. The object was given the name 1992 QB1 and is thought to be the first trans-Neptunian object to be discovered after Pluto and Charon.

drocarbon-rich substance similar to asphalt. It is possible that Sedna's unusual orbit is the result of gravitational interactions due to a companion star to our Sun.

The field of study of the Kuiper belt objects is rapidly evolving. Astronomers are trying to understand the origin of the observed differences between groups of these objects; these differences include orbital inclinations, physical properties, and probable regions of formation. The history of the early solar system is likely frozen into the properties of these objects.

The Origin of Short-Period Comets

The age of the solar system is about 5 billion years. Why have the known comets with periods of less than 200 years not evaporated away their ices so that they are no longer observed? The answer must be that these short-period comets are relative newcomers to the inner solar system. We must ask where they come from, and an obvious hypothesis is that long-period comets sometimes become short-period comets. How might this occur?

If the path of a comet depended solely on its gravitational attraction toward the Sun, there would be no way in which its orbit could be changed to make it a short-period comet; however, other objects (particularly the massive Jupiter) affect a comet's orbit. The combined effects of the gravitational forces from a Jovian planet and the Sun can cause one of these comets to change its orbit so that it becomes a short-period comet. FIGURE 10-18 illustrates one way this could occur. All of the short-period comets were captured in the inner solar system by such a mechanism. On the other hand, the Sun and a planet can have the effect of changing the orbit of a comet so that it leaves the solar system and the Oort cloud entirely.

The word *cloud* in reference to comets in orbit around the Sun can be misleading. When you think of a cloud on Earth, you may think of a volume fairly crowded with water droplets, but the Oort cloud and Kuiper belt are far from crowded. We pointed out that the asteroid belt is mostly empty space, but it is crowded compared to the Oort cloud. If the Oort cloud contains a trillion comets—a high estimate—there would still be an average distance of 16 AU (1.5 billion miles) between comets. A future interstellar traveler stranded in the middle of the Oort cloud with a telescope probably would not be able to find a comet nucleus.

It seems that objects in the Oort cloud formed closer to the Sun than objects in the Kuiper belt. Objects that formed at the distance of Jupiter and Saturn were either accreted by these massive planets or ejected from the solar system as a result of a gravitational slingshot. Objects that formed farther out, at the distance of Uranus and Neptune, were deflected outward when they passed too close to these planets; they now make up the Oort cloud. Finally, objects that formed beyond the orbit of Neptune never combined to form a planet; they now make up the Kuiper belt. It is almost certain that these objects are "leftover" material from the original cloud that formed our solar system. Understanding how these objects are distributed and what they are made of will put important constraints on models describing the formation and early evolution of our solar system.

In addition to the cold comet reservoirs of the Oort cloud and the Kuiper belt, where the equilibrium temperatures are about 10 and 40 K, respectively, comets are also found in the asteroid belt. Optical data showing an atmosphere of dust particles around some asteroids suggest that they are actually comets whose subsurface ices have been exposed to solar heating due to collisions in the recent past. Because objects in the asteroid belt have been in the region for billions of years, studies of the ices in these comets could lead to a better understanding of the changes in the ice composition early in the history of the solar system. The discovery of these comets, announced in 2006, supports the idea that asteroid-belt objects could be a major source of water on Earth.

The large range in estimates illustrates how little we know of the Oort cloud.

Suddenly a blazing stream of fire pierced the sky, lighting the landscape as though Nature had pressed a giant electric switch. The blade of light vanished with equal suddenness, leaving a darkness seeming thicker than before.
Meteorite collector Harvey Nininger, upon seeing a fireball November 9, 1923.

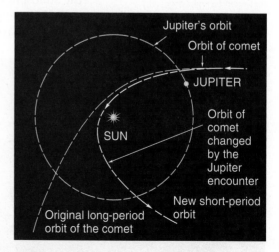

FIGURE 10-18 Gravitational attraction to a planet—Jupiter, here—can cause a comet to alter its orbit, perhaps changing a long-period comet to a short-period one.

Finally, density calculations of a known Trojan asteroid binary system suggest that both objects are probably composed of water ice covered by dirt. It is likely that this system was formed in the Kuiper belt and was captured in one of Jupiter's Trojan points about 650 million years after the formation of the solar system, during a period when the inner solar system was intensely bombarded by comets. If more such objects are found, it could mean that many of the probably thousands of Jupiter's Trojan asteroids are actually Kuiper belt objects.

10-6 Meteors and Meteor Showers

meteor The phenomenon of a streak in the sky caused not only by the burning of a rock or dust particle as it falls but also by the air molecules in the particle's path that, after being excited, then give off light as they de-excite.

Almost everyone has seen the flash of light in the sky that is sometimes called a *falling star* or *shooting star*. This phenomenon is better termed a *meteor* because obviously it is not a star. (Recall the size of our Sun—a typical star—compared with the Earth.) The streak of light in the photograph in FIGURE 10-19 is a meteor. The nature of these sudden flashes of light across the sky must have been of great concern to people since the beginning of time. The idea that they are caused by rocks falling from the heavens can be found in ancient writings of the Greeks, the Romans, the Chinese, and in the Old Testament, but some people found the idea hard to accept.

The first confirmation by modern science that rocks do indeed fall from the heavens occurred on April 26, 1803. Citizens of the small town of L'Aigle, France, saw an exceedingly bright meteor that exploded and formed a shower of 2000 to 3000 fragments that fell to Earth. Reportedly, some fragments were still warm when found. The French Academy of Science sent the respected physicist J. B. Biot to investigate the incident, and his report confirmed the ancient writings.

meteoroid An interplanetary chunk of matter smaller than an asteroid.

Before describing the stones and the flashes of light in any more detail, some definitions are in order. A meteor is the phenomenon of the flash of light; it is not the object itself. The object out in space that causes the meteor in our atmosphere is called a *meteoroid* and is in orbit around the Sun. Finally, if the object survives its fall through the atmosphere and lands on Earth, it is called a *meteorite*.

meteorite An interplanetary chunk of matter that has hit a planet or moon.

Meteors

Most meteors are very dim. You might see one out of the corner of your eye and wonder whether you saw something. Others, however, known as *fireballs*, are very bright and might cause a long streak across the sky.

fireball An extremely bright meteor. (More than 10,000 fireballs can be seen each day over Earth.)

In fact, the brightest are brighter than a full Moon. The light is the result of the meteoroid burning itself up as it passes through our atmosphere. As the stone enters the atmosphere, it experiences friction caused by the molecules of air. This heats up the object as well as the air it passes through. At first glance, this may seem odd to you if you have held your hand out of a car window and experienced the *cooling* effect of the air striking your hand. The difference is in the speeds of the objects—your hand and the meteoroid. A meteoroid's speed is typically 50 km/s (100,000 miles/hour). The air molecules, thus, are striking the object at tremendous speeds, causing the surface of the object to heat up until it vaporizes, streaming its atoms in its wake. These atoms, along with the similarly heated air, glow like the gas in a fluorescent lamp and present us with the phenomenon known as a meteor.

It is difficult for an individual observer to estimate the height or speed of a meteor, but if two observers at different locations each record the same meteor on a photograph, they can use triangulation to calculate these quantities. By means of such measurements, it has been determined that the typical meteor begins to glow at a height of about 130 km (80 miles) and burns

FIGURE 10-19 The streak of light in this photograph is a Perseid meteor.

out at about 80 km (50 miles). The speed of a meteoroid as it enters the Earth's atmosphere might be anywhere from about 10 km/s to about 70 km/s.

Meteoroids

Most meteoroids vaporize completely in the atmosphere and never reach the Earth's surface. The energy source that produces the light we see is simply the kinetic energy of the meteoroid. By calculating how much light is emitted from the meteoroid as it burns up and by estimating how much of its original kinetic energy changes to light (rather than thermal energy), we can calculate the mass of the original meteoroid. Most meteors are produced by meteoroids with masses ranging from a few milligrams (a grain of sand) to a few grams (a marble-size rock).

Under ideal viewing conditions, a person looking for meteors can see an average of five to eight meteors per hour. Because a meteor can be seen only if it is within 150 to 200 kilometers of the viewer, we can calculate that over the entire Earth there must be about 25,000,000 meteors a day bright enough to be seen by the naked eye. The number visible in telescopes would be hundreds of billions. Although the average meteor may have a mass of only a fraction of a gram, it is estimated that 1000 tons of meteoritic material hit the Earth each day.

If a meteor trail is recorded from more than one location, its path can be determined accurately enough to calculate the path of the original meteoroid before it was slowed by the atmosphere. In this way we find that, as expected, most meteoroids are simply tiny particles orbiting the Sun. Meteoroids differ from asteroids in that most asteroids orbit the Sun close to the plane of the ecliptic, whereas the orbits of small meteoroids around the Sun may be in any orientation. A majority have very eccentric orbits rather than the nearly circular orbits of most asteroids.

However, this does not rule out the asteroid belt as the origin of these meteoroids. It is thought that many small meteoroids are debris from collisions between asteroids. Such collisions would break the asteroids into smaller pieces, including pieces as small as sand grains. These tiny pieces would emerge from the collision in all directions and move in elliptical orbits at all orientations with the ecliptic.

Many meteors, however, are from a source other than the asteroids—they are due to material evaporated from a comet's nucleus and then blown off the comet by the action of the Sun. This leads us to a discussion of meteor showers.

Meteor Showers

On some nights, we see many more meteors than normal, and if we observe closely, we see that there is a pattern to the directions of the meteors. FIGURE 10-20 is a long-time exposure photograph showing this phenomenon. The streaks are meteors. They seem to point to (or rather, originate *from*) one point in the sky. This phenomenon is called a **meteor shower** and is caused by the Earth passing through a swarm of small meteoroids, as illustrated in FIGURE 10-21a. A cluster of tiny particles is shown in the Earth's path. These tiny meteoroids cause the shower.

To see why the meteor seems to originate in a certain constellation, think of the Earth moving through space. When it encounters the swarm of meteoroids, the meteor trail seems to originate from a specific direction in the sky; this direction is the result of the combination of the directions and speeds of motion of the Earth and the meteoritic material around the Sun (Figure 10-21b). Meteor showers are named after the constellation from which they seem to originate. The meteors in Figure 10-20 seem to radiate from a single point off to the upper right of the photograph (this point is known as the **radiant**). They appear to come from within the constellation Leo, and the shower is therefore known as the Leonid meteor shower. The meteor shower about to occur in Figure 10-21b will likewise be a Leonid shower.

The particles that cause a meteor shower strike the Earth along nearly parallel paths, yet they appear to diverge from a point. The reason for this apparent contradiction is the same as the reason that the parallel sides of a long, straight highway seem to diverge as they near a viewer standing in its center

These speeds correspond to 20,000 and 150,000 miles/hour.

It has been estimated that only 1 in 1 million meteoroids that hit the atmosphere survives to reach the surface. Even at a rate of 1000 tons per day, it will take 160 trillion years to increase the Earth's mass by 1%.

meteor shower The phenomenon of a large group of meteors seeming to come from a particular area of the celestial sphere.

radiant (of a meteor shower) The point in the sky from which the meteors of a shower appear to radiate.

FIGURE 10-20 This photo shows the Leonid meteor shower of November 1966. The streaks radiating from one area of the sky are all part of the shower.

FIGURE 10-21 (a) The Earth passes through a swarm of meteoritic particles, left over from a comet. The plane of the original comet's orbit is inclined to the Earth's orbital plane. (b) The meteor trails seem to originate from a specific constellation. The Earth's speed around the Sun is about 30 km/s. In the case of the Leonid showers, the speed of the meteoritic material is about 70 km/s. As shown in Table 10-1, the orbit of Halley's Comet intersects Earth's orbit at two points; the orbits of the other comets associated with major meteor showers intersect Earth's orbit at one point. (Differences in color for the particles and for Earth's orbit are used to clarify their locations in space.)

(a)

(b)

(**FIGURE 10-22**). The particles forming the shower are coming into the Earth's atmosphere along parallel paths, but as they near us, they seem to be spreading out.

For centuries we have known that some meteor showers repeat regularly each year, but the origin of the showers was not known. Then, in 1866, it was shown that the particles that cause the Perseid meteor shower (which occurs around August 12 and appears to originate in the constellation Perseus) have almost exactly the same orbital path that an 1862 comet had. Astronomers concluded that the meteoroids of the shower were simply particles that had long ago come from the comet and formed its tail. Those particles were in orbit about the Sun when their paths intersected the Earth's. Today we are able to associate most of the major annual meteor showers with some comet. **TABLE 10-1** lists the major showers and their associated comets.

Table 10-1 also indicates the average number of meteors expected to be seen during the maximum of the shower; however, the intensity of some showers changes greatly from year to year. Figure 10-21a shows why this occurs. If the particles that had been blown from the comet are spread fairly evenly around the comet's orbit, each time the Earth passes through this orbit about the same number of particles strike our planet. However, if the particles are clumped in one region of the comet's orbit, and the Earth and this swarm happen to meet, we see much greater meteor activity.

FIGURE 10-22 (a) Meteors in a meteor shower seem to come from a single point in the sky. (b) The divergence of the meteors is the same phenomenon seen by a person standing on a long, straight highway. The road seems to diverge as it comes toward the observer.

(a)

(b)

As an example, the Leonid showers are irregular in intensity from year to year. In 1833, 1866, and again in 1899, the Earth passed through a major swarm of particles in the comet's orbit, and nearly 100,000 meteors could be seen in an hour. The maxima of the Leonid showers occur about every 33 years, which is just the period of the comet from which they originated. As the years go by, the particles spread out more and more along their orbit, but the display was spectacular in November 1966, when Figure 10-20 was taken. Another beautiful display of the Leonids was seen in 1999, when observers in Europe saw up to 2500 meteors/hour. The Leonids can be very active for 3–4 years after the Comet's passage.

Many meteor showers occur every year; Table 10-1 lists only the major ones. The best time to observe a meteor shower (assuming a clear, moonless night and an observing site far from city lights) is in the early morning hours. As the activity at the end of the chapter explains, this results from the Earth's rotation and its motion through the swarm of particles left behind by the comet.

10-7 Meteorites and Craters

Meteorites are traditionally classified in three categories: iron meteorites (or *irons*), which are made up of 80 to 90% iron (most of the rest being nickel); stony meteorites (*stones*), which are just what their name implies, but often contain flakes of iron and/or nickel; and *stony irons*, about half iron and half rock. FIGURE 10-23 shows an iron and a stony meteorite.

About 95% of all meteorites are stones, but if you find a meteorite, it will likely be an iron. The reason for this apparent paradox is that stony meteorites are very similar to regular Earthly stones, especially after the meteorites have weathered for a few years. They are thus difficult to recognize. Irons, however, can be found by using metal detectors and are different in appearance from regular Earthly rocks.

TABLE 10-1

Some Major Meteor Showers

Shower	Date of Maximum*	Associated Comet	Expected Hourly Rate
Quadrantids	Jan. 3	??	40
Lyrids	April 21	Comet Thatcher	15
Eta Aquarids	May 4	Comet Halley	20
Delta Aquarids	July 30	??	20
Perseids	Aug. 12	Comet Swift-Tuttle	50
Draconids	Oct. 9	Comet Giacobini-Zinner	15
Orionids	Oct. 21	Comet Halley	20
Leonids	Nov. 17	Comet Tempel-Tuttle	15
Geminids	Dec. 13	Asteroid Phaethon**	50

*The dates given are for the approximate date of maximum and may vary slightly from year to year.
**This asteroid is in the same orbit as the meteoroids and is thought to be the remains of the comet's nucleus.

Stars can be seen equally well at any time during the night; are meteors the same in this regard?

(a)

(b)

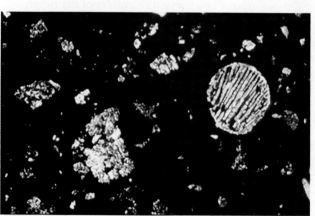
(c)

FIGURE 10-23 (a) A part of an iron meteorite that fell in Canyon Diablo, Arizona. (b) The sawed face of the stony Martian meteorite ALH84001,0. It is the oldest Martian meteorite, a sample of the early Martian crust, with a crystallization age of 4.5 billion years. As a result of a collision between Mars and an asteroid (or comet) about 16 million years ago, the rock wandered in space until about 13,000 years ago, when it fell on the Antarctic ice sheet, where it was found in 1984. (c) A thin section from a C2 chondrite meteorite.

How do we know, then, that most meteorites are stones? Meteorites can be found in the Antarctic, where they become exposed when snow is blown away from them. Here, where there are no natural rocks to cause confusion, 95% of the meteorites we find are stones.

Chondrites comprise a very important class of stony meteorites. They are the most abundant class, making up about 91% of the approximately 24,000 known meteorites. They originate from asteroids that were never large enough to undergo melting and differentiation. As a result, they formed early in the history of our solar system and remained mostly unchanged since. Chondrites are thought to be the building blocks of the planets. As shown in Figure 10-23c, they consist mostly (up to 80%) of *chondrules*, which are millimeter-sized rock spheres, in a mix of other mineral or metal grains (including calcium, aluminum, and other interstellar grains formed around other stars in the solar neighborhood).

Carbonaceous chondrites comprise the most important subclass (but only about 3.5% of the total) of chondrites. They contain high levels of water, organic compounds (mainly silicates, oxides, and sulfides), and minerals such as olivine. Their composition suggests that they have not undergone significant heating since they formed, and thus, they represent the chemical composition of the original solar nebula.

The largest meteorite ever found, the Hoba meteorite, weighs about 65 tons and is in Namibia, in southwestern Africa. Iron meteorites such as this are much stronger than stones and therefore do not break up in the atmosphere as stones do. The Hoba meteorite barely disturbed the surrounding surface of the Earth, apparently because it entered the atmosphere at a very small angle and was greatly slowed down before reaching the surface.

The second largest meteorite is on display in New York City. This 34-ton giant was hauled from Greenland in the 1890s by the explorer Robert Peary and is now in the Hall of Meteorites of the American Museum of Natural History.

What happens when a meteorite strikes the Earth? Quite naturally, it makes a hole larger than the meteorite. You can confirm this by throwing a rock into mud to simulate a meteorite strike. FIGURE 10-24 is a photograph of one of the most prominent impact craters on Earth, Meteor Crater near Winslow, Arizona. The crater is in the desert about 40 miles east of Flagstaff. The crater, nearly a mile across, is 180 meters deep, and has a rim rising 45 meters above the surrounding desert ground. To appreciate the size of the crater, look at the right center of Figure 10-24 and find the parking lot and guest building.

Some 25 tons of iron meteorite fragments have been found around the crater, some as far as 4 miles away. The meteorite that formed Meteor Crater is estimated to have had a total mass of 300 million kilograms (300,000 tons) and to have been about 45 meters across. It struck about 25,000 years ago at a speed of about 13 km/s (28,600 miles/hour), releasing an energy equivalent to a 2.5-megaton bomb.

About 160 meteorite craters of diameter larger than 1 km have been found so far on Earth, but most are far less impressive than Meteor Crater because weather has worn them down or they are under the sea. Meteor Crater is not only the most recently formed major crater, but it is also well preserved because of its location in the dry Arizona desert.

It has been estimated that a meteorite larger than 1 km in diameter strikes the Earth once every few hundred thousand years, on the average. A hit by a meteorite 1 km in diameter would be equivalent to a 5000-megaton bomb and would produce a crater 10 km in diameter. Such an explosion would have effects far beyond the area of impact because it could send enough dust into

The Hoba meteorite was named after the name of the farm on which it lies. It was discovered in 1920 and has not been moved since it landed on Earth about 80,000 years ago. It is composed of 84% iron and 16% nickel with some traces of cobalt.

One megaton corresponds to about 60 times the size of the bomb that destroyed Hiroshima in 1945.

FIGURE 10-24 This view of Meteor Crater shows the guesthouse and entrance road at the lower edge of the crater. The crater is 600 feet deep and rises 150 feet above the surrounding ground.

ADVANCING THE MODEL

Hit by a Meteorite?

Something spectacular fell in Tunguska, Siberia on June 30, 1908. The fireball was bright enough to be seen in daylight, and the sound that resulted from its explosion some 10 km above the Earth was heard as far away as 1000 km (600 miles). The explosion, which was equivalent to about a 15-megaton bomb, knocked down trees as far as 30 km away (FIGURE B10-1), and a man 80 km away was knocked down by the shock wave from the explosion.

FIGURE B10-1 These trees were broken like matchsticks by an explosion in 1908 in the Tunguska region of Siberia.

Recent work on the fate of asteroids as they plunge through the atmosphere indicates that the object that caused the Tunguska event was an asteroid. There is still debate about the details, but astronomers calculate that an asteroid at least 50 meters across traveling at about 20 km/s would have broken up violently in the atmosphere and caused the disruption at Tunguska in 1908.

Human bodies take up a small portion of the Earth's surface and, thus, it is unlikely that a person will be hit by a meteorite or even see one land. There is an unconfirmed report of a monk being killed by a meteorite in 1650 in Milan, but no good evidence that a meteorite has ever killed anyone. In 1954, a meteorite came through the roof of a house in Sylacauga, Alabama, and hit a woman on the bounce, severely bruising her hip. In 1971, a house in Wethersfield, Connecticut was hit by a meteorite, and in an extremely unusual coincidence, a house about a mile away was hit just 11 years later. These meteorites were a few inches across and

did no major damage to the houses (if puncturing the roof and ceiling is not major damage).

On August 31, 1991, in Noblesville, Indiana, two boys were standing by the sidewalk when they heard a whistle followed by a thud. Twelve feet from them they found a meteorite in a crater about 9 centimeters wide and 4 centimeters deep. They reported that the rock felt slightly warm when they picked it up.

Another close call occurred when a meteorite plunged through the rear of a car about 40 miles north of New York City on October 9, 1992 (FIGURE B10-2). The football-sized meteorite had a mass of 27 kilograms (about 60 pounds). The fireball caused by the meteorite (or from the larger one from which it broke) had been seen from as far away as Frankfort, Kentucky.

On September 23, 2003, a large meteorite (about 20 kg) fell in downtown New Orleans. It went through the roof of a house, penetrated the upstairs room floor, and then punctured a hole through the bottom floor of the house before shattering into many pieces on the ground.

FIGURE B10-2 Michael Apoute shows neighbors the damage done to his friend's parked car in Peekshill, New York, by a stony meteorite. The meteorite was found in a small crater under the car in the driveway.

the atmosphere to block out a significant amount of sunlight. A hypothesis put forward in 1980 suggests that such a meteorite strike was responsible for the extinction of the dinosaurs. (See the Advancing the Model box on page 301.)

The main Kaali crater (one of nine in all), shown in FIGURE 10-25, was formed about 4000 years ago. The 110-meter wide and 22-meter deep crater was caused by an iron meteorite that at impact was moving at about 15 km/s and had a mass of about 50 tons. The impact resulted in burned forests within a radius of 6 km.

10-8 The Importance of the Solar System Debris

In this chapter we discussed a number of missions to investigate asteroids and comets. Astronomers are interested in what seems to be nothing but debris for several reasons.

FIGURE 10-25 This 110-meter wide crater was formed in Saaremaa, Estonia about 4,000 years ago by a 50-ton iron meteorite.

Hayabusa is a Japanese word for falcon. This ambitious mission launched in 2003 and rendezvoused with the near-Earth asteroid Itokawa in 2005. It was supposed to survey the asteroid's surface, collect samples, and return them to Earth for analysis but it has been beset with a number of technical problems. Its return to Earth is scheduled for mid-2010.

During the early period of the formation of the solar system, many collisions occurred between the planets and this debris. We believe that life on Earth started at the end of this period, about 3.8 billion years ago. This seems plausible because carbon-based molecules could not have survived the intense heat resulting from the collisions. There is evidence for biological activity at the end of the heavy bombardment period and known fossils on Earth date as far back as 3.5 billion years ago. This very short, on a geological scale, time period during which life formed on our planet raises the question of how it could have started during a time when most of the water in Earth's oceans was still vapor and there were few carbon-based molecules around. It has been suggested that the building blocks of life could have been delivered to Earth by asteroid and comet impacts. These collisions supplied the Earth with large supplies of water, volatiles, and carbon-based molecules. Understanding the chemical makeup of asteroids and comets opens a window to our understanding of the composition and conditions from which our planet formed 4.6 billion years ago.

The following are but a few examples of the possible connections between meteoritic material and life in our solar system.

- Most meteorite carbon molecules are PAHs (polycyclic aromatic hydrocarbons), the most common carbon-rich chemical compounds in the universe, found from oil deposits, engine soot, grilled meat, to the distant galaxies. These molecules are very similar to the molecules that make up living things. Under the influence of ultraviolet light they become soluble in water and they were very likely a part of the primordial sea.

- Iron meteorites may have played a critical role in supporting the evolution of life on Earth by providing the necessary amounts of phosphorus. Phosphorus forms the backbone of DNA and RNA. It is vital to metabolism and is found in cell walls and the bones of vertebrates. It is much more common in living organisms than in the environment and understanding its behavior early in the history of the Earth could give us clues to understanding the origin of life.

- The stony Martian meteorite ALH84001 (Figure 10-23b) has caused a controversy among scientists about the possibility that the crystals found in it might be of biological origin. The study of another Martian meteorite (which landed in Egypt in 1991 and is called Nakhla) shows a series of microscopic tunnels very similar to tracts left on Earth rocks by feeding bacteria.

- Amino acids have been found in carbonaceous chondrites and in interstellar clouds. Eight of life's 20 amino acids are found in meteorites, and all of them, except glycine, have a left-handed molecular structure that is favored by life on Earth. In Chapter 19, we discuss the Miller-Urey experiment, which showed that amino acids can be formed in the absence of living organisms through only physical and chemical process; however, the amino acids formed in this experiment are of equal amounts of the left-handed and right-handed molecular structure.

It is ironic that asteroid and comet impacts may have brought the building blocks of life to Earth, whereas similar collisions later on may have wiped out many developing species and significantly modified our planet's biosphere. Such drastic changes

ADVANCING THE MODEL

Meteorites and the Death of the Dinosaurs

Sixty-five million years ago, dinosaurs became extinct. In fact, nearly 75% of all species on Earth became extinct during the same short time period (as geological time is measured). The reason for this mass extinction has been debated by scientists for some time, and several different catastrophes have been hypothesized as the cause for the extinctions.

In 1980, astronomy entered the picture. In that year, geologists Walter Alvarez, Frank Asaro, Helen Michel, and Luis Alvarez (Walter's physicist father) proposed a solution for which they had real evidence. At Gubbio, Northern Italy, they found a layer of clay that contained the elements iridium, platinum, and osmium in much greater abundance than normally found on Earth. (Similar layers were later discovered at several other sites around the Earth.) How could this layer have been deposited? These elements are much more abundant in meteorites than in the crust of the Earth. Perhaps a giant meteorite—an asteroid—struck the Earth, exploded, and sent its debris high into the atmosphere to fall to Earth and form the layer. To account for the thickness of the layer found around the world, the meteorite must have been about 10 kilometers in diameter—not an unusual size for an asteroid. The debris, which also would have included Earthly material pulverized by the impact, would spread as a cloud around the Earth and then gradually settle to form the layer found by the Alvarez team.

The energy released by such an impact would correspond to a few billion megaton bombs. But could this explosion have wiped out entire species all around the Earth? No, not directly. Consider, however, what effect a giant cloud of dust, soot from global fires, and sulfate aerosols produced from impacted rocks would have on vegetation on Earth. Such a cloud could remain in the atmosphere for more than a year, darkening the Earth below. Much vegetation would die, along with many animal species that depended on vegetation for food. Dinosaurs as well as many other species are included in this category; however, small creatures such as rodents that could forage for seeds and nuts could survive, and, indeed, the fossil record shows that such creatures did survive this period.

One test of this asteroid hypothesis is to find out how long ago the clay layer was formed. If you have studied geol-

ogy, you know that such dating of past events is a common procedure. The result? The clay was deposited about 63 million years ago, remarkably close to the value given for the mass extinction as shown by the fossil record. Another test is to find the location of such an impact. Observations suggest that the 180-kilometer crater buried below the jungle near Chicxulub, in the Yucatan Peninsula, is the likely impact site, based on its size, age, and the deposits found in its surrounding area (**FIGURE B10-3**).

Since 1980, when the Alvarez team presented their data, their hypothesis has become more and more accepted. (In fact, it is usually referred to as a theory, in accordance with the practice of calling an idea a theory only after it has gained some acceptance, as was discussed in the first few chapters.) However, a number of scientists believe that this mass extinction was not the result of a single event. Instead, they suggest that an intensive period of volcanic eruptions in addition to a number of asteroid impacts stressed the Earth's ecosystem to the breaking point. They also suggest that the Chicxulub impact was not as powerful as originally believed and probably occurred 300,000 years before the mass extinction. (See the references at the end of the chapter.)

FIGURE B10-3 The Chicxulub crater off the Yucatan coast of Mexico measures 180-km across, making it one of the largest craters formed in the inner solar system during the last 4 billion years. It is not completely visible from above, but was detected by measuring slight variations in Earth's gravitational pull—measurements made originally for oil exploration.

probably allowed only species capable of quickly adapting to the new conditions to continue evolving and possibly opened the way for mammals to dominate our planet.

Understanding the chemical composition of the debris in our solar system can help us better understand how it formed and how its different components are related.

- An analysis of the isotopic composition of hydrogen and nitrogen in insoluble organic matter found in some carbonaceous chondrites shows that the asteroids from which these meteorites originated contain primitive organic matter similar to that found in interstellar dust particles of cometary origin. As we mentioned before, it is possible that comets and asteroids are more similar in origin than we previously thought.

- Using numerical simulations and chondrites as their models and as the building blocks of the planets, scientists have shown that Earth's early atmosphere was full of methane, ammonia, hydrogen, and water, the same mix used in the Miller-Urey experiment. This contradicts the conclusion reached by geologists of an atmosphere poor in hydrogen but rich in carbon dioxide, based on models of gases from volcanic eruptions.

- The presence of the short-lived radioactive isotopes chlorine-36, aluminum-26, and iron-50 in chondritic meteorites provides direct evidence that these isotopes were present early in the history of our solar system. This supports the idea that the Sun formed in a cluster of stars and not in an isolated environment; the abundances of the isotopes require a nearby supernova explosion, which contaminated the solar system. Also, an analysis of isotopes in an igneous-rock meteorite found in the Sahara Desert suggests that its age is only a million years younger than the age of the solar system. Therefore, asteroids, the parent objects of many meteorites, must have formed in a few hundred thousand years before melting as the result of the heat provided by short-lived radioactive isotopes.

There is another strong reason for interest in solar system debris. Most of the meteorites reaching Earth's surface originate as fragments of collisions between asteroids and are small in size. The larger the size of the asteroid, the less frequent a possible collision; however, even though the probability of a catastrophic collision is small, the consequences are such that it becomes imperative that we understand their structure, composition, and orbits to better protect our planet. Catastrophic collisions happened in the past and they will happen again. For example, the discovery of iridium and high concentrations of molecules that form under high pressures and temperatures at many archaeological sites in North America suggests that about 13,000 years ago a large asteroid (about 5 km across) exploded over North America. The energy of the explosion melted a large portion of an ice sheet. The resulting amounts of fresh water that flowed in the Arctic and Atlantic oceans would have disrupted the circulations in these oceans, while the resulting wildfires across the continent would have killed off the food supply of many of the larger mammals. This led to a quick atmospheric cooling and the extinction of large mammals. The cooling lasted for about 1000 years and happened during an inter-glacial warm period.

Finally, asteroids and comets will most likely play an important role in any future exploration and colonization of the solar system. Comets can supply water and carbon-based molecules necessary to sustain life. Liquid hydrogen and oxygen obtained from the water can be used to generate rocket fuel. Asteroids are rich resources of raw materials that we can use to build space structures. This may sound like science fiction now, but what was science fiction yesterday is the reality of today. Colonization of the inner solar system will most likely occur in the 21st century, and solar system debris may play an integral part in our efforts.

Conclusion

The solar system is indeed a collection of diverse objects. As our space probes venture out to study it in more detail, we are continually surprised by the beautiful diversity we find. As the last few chapters have shown, great differences exist not only among planets, asteroids, comets, meteors, and satellites, but even between objects within these various categories. On the other hand, we cannot help but be impressed by the similarities we see—even between objects we place in different categories.

As we explained in Chapter 7, the objects in our solar system formed at about the same time, and their formation and differentiation were determined by the conditions that existed at the time. We are beginning to understand why they are different and why they are the same, but we have a long way to go. That is what makes the study of the solar system exciting.

STUDY GUIDE

1. The connection between comets and meteors is demonstrated when one sees
   A. sporadic meteors on almost any night.
   B. a comet in one part of the sky and meteors in another part of the sky on the same night.
   C. a predictable shower of meteors.
   D. [None of the above; there is no connection.]

2. Which of the following statements about Pluto is true?
   A. It has two moons (that we know of).
   B. Its orbit is within 2 degrees of the plane of the Earth's orbit.
   C. Its orbit is as circular as the Earth's orbit.
   D. We are confident that it was once a moon of Neptune.
   E. [None of the above is true.]

3. The search for Pluto was undertaken based on
   A. Bode's law.
   B. calculations concerning the orbit of Uranus.
   C. perturbations in the orbits of asteroids.
   D. [None of the above, for it was discovered accidentally.]

4. Pluto was discovered by
   A. William Herschel in England in the 19th century.
   B. Percival Lowell in Arizona in 1905.
   C. Clyde Tombaugh in Arizona in 1930.
   D. James Christy in Arizona in 1978.
   E. Asaph Hall in California in 1921.

5. Pluto's mass has been calculated from
   A. its effect on passing spacecraft.
   B. its effect on passing asteroids.
   C. the motion of Charon.
   D. [All of the above.]
   E. [None of the above.]

6. How was Ceres discovered?
   A. It was discovered by accident, during a search for comets.
   B. It was observed when it fell to Earth.
   C. It has been known since antiquity and, thus, the manner of its discovery is unknown.
   D. It was found during a search for a "missing planet."
   E. It was found accidentally as a streak on a stellar photo.

7. The discovery of asteroids depends on the fact that, compared with the stars, the asteroids
   A. look bigger.
   B. look brighter.
   C. move.
   D. vary in brightness.
   E. are a different color.

8. The largest asteroid is closest to _____ in diameter.
   A. 6 feet
   B. 600 feet
   C. 6 miles (10 kilometers)
   D. 600 miles (1000 kilometers)
   E. 60,000 miles (100,000 kilometers)

9. The total radiation reflected and radiated by an asteroid depends on
   A. its size.
   B. the total radiation it receives from the Sun.
   C. its speed in orbit.
   D. [Both A and B above.]
   E. [All of the above.]

10. The Kirkwood gaps result from
    A. radiation pressure from the Sun.
    B. the previous passage of a comet through the asteroid belt.
    C. regular gravitational pull from the largest of Jupiter's moons.
    D. regular gravitational pulls from Jupiter.
    E. previous explosions of asteroids at points in the asteroid belt.

11. The masses of the *largest* asteroids are measured by observing
    A. their motions as they come closest to Jupiter.
    B. perturbations they cause on smaller asteroids.
    C. the motion of spacecraft passing nearby.
    D. the total radiation received from them.
    E. their orbital speed and distance from the Sun.

12. Which of the following statements about the *Voyager* spacecraft that passed through the asteroid belt is true?
    A. They were guided from Earth so that they did not collide with asteroids.
    B. They had their own guidance system to prevent collisions with asteroids.
    C. They passed through the asteroid belt with no collision-avoidance system.

13. Which of the following statements best describes cometary orbits?
    A. They are circular, lying in the plane of the ecliptic.
    B. They lie between the orbits of Mars and Jupiter.
    C. They are elongated ellipses, lying within one astronomical unit of the Sun.
    D. They are very elongated ellipses tens to hundreds of astronomical units across.
    E. They are within the orbit of Mercury.

14. When a comet is visible in the night sky, it appears to the naked eye to
    A. move so rapidly across the sky that it is easily missed if one is not looking in the right direction.
    B. stay in the sky for a week or more, with only slight shifting among the stars each night.
    C. [Either of the above, depending on the particular comet's motion.]

15. The nucleus of most comets is
    A. much smaller than the Earth.
    B. slightly smaller than the Earth.
    C. slightly larger than the Earth.
    D. much larger than the Earth.

16. A comet's tail results when
    A. part of the comet drifts in the direction opposite to the motion of the comet.
    B. the solar wind carries some of the gas of the coma away from the Sun.
    C. gravitational force pulls loosely held material from the Sun.
    D. tidal forces tear the comet apart.

17. The best-known comet was named after Halley because
    A. he was the first to see it.
    B. he first calculated its orbit.
    C. although he had nothing to do with the comet, he was a famous astronomer and it was named to honor him.
    D. Galileo discovered it and named it after him.
    E. [Both C and D above.]

18. A comet's tail
    A. precedes its head through space.
    B. follows its head through space.
    C. is farther from the Sun than its head is.
    D. is closer to the Sun than its head is.
    E. [None of the above.]

19. The Oort cloud is located
    A. between the orbits of Mars and Jupiter.
    B. just beyond Pluto's orbit.
    C. far beyond the orbit of Pluto.
    D. at about the distance of the nearest star.

20. Why do many comets appear brighter after passing the Sun?
    A. They are more massive after the passage.
    B. The Sun starts nuclear reactions in them.
    C. They are moving faster after passing the Sun.
    D. Their head and tail are larger after passing the Sun.

21. Short-period comets are hypothesized to
    A. be permanent parts of the inner solar system similar to asteroids.
    B. be formed when the orbits of long-period comets are changed.
    C. be formed in the inner solar system and then ejected, becoming long-period comets.

22. Why do most meteoroids not reach the surface of the Earth?
    A. They bounce off the atmosphere and go back into space.
    B. They burn up in the air.
    C. They are light enough that they remain suspended in the air.
    D. They land in the ocean (as oceans cover most of the Earth).
    E. [The statement is false; almost all reach the Earth, but they are not found.]

23. Meteor showers are caused by
    A. the Earth crossing the asteroid belt.
    B. a comet's nucleus striking the atmosphere.
    C. the eccentricity of the Earth's orbit.
    D. meteorite impacts on the Earth's surface.
    E. the Earth crossing a meteoroid stream.

24. Meteors are most easily seen after midnight because
    A. the sky is darker then.
    B. the Sun is closer to rising.
    C. you are then on the "leading" side of the Earth.
    D. meteor showers occur then.
    E. [The statement is false; they are seen equally well anytime.]

25. List two ways in which Pluto's orbit is unusual compared with the other planets.

26. We cannot determine the size of Pluto from the size of its image in a telescope. How, then, can we know its size?

27. What did the discovery of Charon allow us to calculate about Pluto?

28. Why have we not named all of the asteroids that have been observed?

29. What causes the Kirkwood gaps?

30. Why have the asteroids not formed into a planet between Mars and Jupiter?

31. Why do we think that it is unlikely that the asteroids are the remains of a planet that exploded?

32. Describe the three main parts of a comet. Include approximate sizes of each part for a typical comet.

33. Describe the modified "dirty snowball" model of a comet's nucleus.

34. What causes a comet to have two tails? Why are they different shapes?

35. What is the Oort cloud?

36. We cannot hope to see the Oort cloud. What makes us think that it exists?

37. Explain why the passing air heats a meteoroid, whereas a wind cools a person.

38. What causes a meteor shower and why do the meteors appear to come from just one part of the sky?

39. Name and describe the three main types of meteorites. Which is most common? Which is easiest to find? Why?

1. Charon occulted Pluto during the time that Pluto was closest to the Sun. Astronomers (and police detectives) do not like coincidences. Propose a reason that Pluto and Charon act this way.

2. List reasons why Pluto should be considered a planet and other reasons why it should not.

3. In early 2006, NASA's *Stardust* mission returned samples of coma material from Comet Wild 2. Use *Astronomy* and/or *Sky & Telescope* magazines to write a report on the latest results from this mission.

4. Objects in the Oort cloud cannot be seen, even with the best telescopes. Why, then, do we believe it exists?

5. If a comet is seen in the west shortly after sunset, in what direction will its tail point—toward or away from the horizon? In what direction will it point if it is seen in the east in the morning sky?

6. What effect on the motion of a comet would you expect to result from the jetting of material from its nucleus?

7. Compare the size and shape of Mars' moon Phobos with that of the nucleus of Halley's comet.

8. Comets are generally brighter during the few weeks after they pass perihelion than during the few weeks before perihelion. Why? (Hint: How well does water ice retain heat?)

9. Use *Astronomy* and/or *Sky & Telescope* magazines and information from NASA's Web site on "Asteroid and Comet Impacts Hazards" to write a report on the latest efforts to counter a possible catastrophic impact. Compare an impact with a 10-kilometer asteroid to the destruction resulting from a global thermonuclear war.

10. Write a report about a meteor crater in your part of the country or the world. The geology department of your college is a suggested source of information.

11. Find out more about the "theory" that a catastrophic impact led to the extinction of the dinosaurs. Do you think that there is enough observational support for it? Are there any competing theories? If so, describe them.

12. Assume that the dinosaur-extinction-by-meteorite theory is correct. If the impact had not occurred 65 million years ago, would mammals still have risen to the point of dominating our planet? Discuss.

13. Based on what you know about the makeup of the solar system debris and their constant bombardment of the planets, what effect do you think the debris had on the evolution of life on our planet?

1. Assume that 1000 metric tons (one million kilograms) of meteoritic material strikes the Earth each day. Calculate the area of the Earth and determine how much material strikes each square meter each day.

2. Use the answer to calculation 1 to determine how long it would take to build up a layer of meteoritic material weighing 1 kg on a desktop that has an area of 2 m².

3. Assume that the period of Halley's comet is 76 years. What is, approximately, the farthest distance that this comet gets from the Sun? (Hint: Use Kepler's third law and ignore the comet's distance from the Sun at perihelion.)

4. Imagine that we have just observed an asteroid on an orbit that will bring it somewhere within 400,000 km from Earth. What is the probability that this asteroid will actually hit Earth? (Hint: Look at this problem from the point of view of the asteroid. You have a dartboard of radius 400,000 km and the bull's-eye has a radius of 6400 km.)

5. Consider two comets that get very close to the Sun at perihelion, while their aphelion distances are 100 AU and 100,000 AU, respectively. Assume that the comets can survive only 100 passages around the Sun. What is the lifetime of each comet? How does it compare with the age of our solar system?

6. Assume that a 1-km asteroid is on a direct collision course with Earth, moving at about 10 km/s relative to the Earth. We first observe this object at a distance of 10 million km. How much warning time do we have? How long would it take for this object to pass through our atmosphere (about 100 km thick)?

7. Assume we have the technology to mine asteroids. Consider a small asteroid of radius 100 meters, which is made of mostly nickel-iron of density 8000 kg/m³. If the cost for 1 kg of this alloy is $1, how much money can we make by mining this asteroid?

Observing Meteors

To observe meteors, you should have a clear sky away from city lights and, thus, your first step is to get out into the country. Second, you must avoid a night with a bright Moon that will light up the sky so that you have difficulty viewing. Finally, the best time for observing is after midnight, preferably from around 2 AM until the beginning of morning twilight.

The reason for choosing a time after midnight can be seen by referring to **FIGURE 10-26**. In this figure, the Sun (not shown) is to the left and the Earth is moving toward the top of the figure. The half of the Earth lined in blue thus is on the leading edge as the Earth moves through space. Now

FIGURE 10-26 The Earth is moving upward in the drawing and strikes most meteoroids on its leading edge. Those striking it from behind must catch up. It is midnight at point *A* and sunrise at point *B*.

consider a car driving through a rain shower and you see why most meteoroids hit the Earth on this leading side. The analogy is not quite exact because different meteoroids have very different motions through space, whereas raindrops all fall in about the same direction. Meteoroids are able to catch up with the Earth from behind and hit the trailing half of the Earth. Still, many more strike the Earth's leading edge as the Earth sweeps them up.

Referring again to the figure, you see that it is midnight for a person standing at point *A* and that the Sun is rising for a person at *B*. Meteors, then, are better observed in the early morning hours.

After you have found your observing location, you must wait for your eyes to adapt to the darkness. Unless you have chosen a night of a heavy meteor shower, you must

be patient. Lie back and relax. (Did you bring a lawn chair?) Patience should reward you with a streak of a meteor across the sky. It is likely that you will see the meteor in some direction other than where you are looking—out of the corner of your eye. There is a good reason for this: The part of your retina that sees things out of your direct line of sight is more sensitive to motion and to changing light. An experienced observer takes advantage of this effect when looking, for example, for the motion of a satellite in the sky. The observer looks to the side of where the object is expected to be seen.

The best advice to the person looking for meteors is to pick a night when a meteor shower is expected. Table 10-1 lists the dates of the most prominent annual meteor showers.

You can find information about current explorations of our solar system at NASA's home page (http//www.nasa.gov).

Mike Brown's group has discovered most of the new Kuiper belt objects discussed in the text. Additional information can be found at http://www.ifa.hawaii.edu/faculty/jewitt/kb.html.

For more information about the Alvarez theory and the extinction of the dinosaurs check http://www.ucmp.berkeley.edu/diapsids/extinction.html.

1. "Killer Crater in the Yucatan?" by J. K. Beatty, in *Sky & Telescope* (July, 1991).
2. "The Origins of the Asteroids," by R. P. Binzel, M. A. Barucci, and M. Fulchignomi, in *Scientific American* (October, 1991).
3. "The Oort Cloud," by P. Weismann, in *Scientific American* (September, 1998).
4. "The Kuiper Belt," by J. X. Luu and D. C. Jewitt, in *Scientific American* (May, 1996)
5. "Journey to the Farthest Planet," by A. S. Stern, in *Scientific American* Special Edition (September 2003).

6. "The Origins of Water on Earth," by J. F. Kasting, in *Scientific American* Special Edition (September 2003).
7. "The Oort Cloud," by P. R. Weissman, in *Scientific American* Special Edition (September 2003).
8. "The Small Planets," by E. Asphaug, in *Scientific American* Special Edition (September 2003).
9. "The Day the World Burned," by D. A. Kring and D. D. Durda, in *Scientific American* (December 2003).
10. "What Heated the Asteroids," by A. E. Rubin, in *Scientific American* (May 2005).
11. "Impact from the Deep," by P. D. Ward, in *Scientific American* (October 2006).
12. "Unlocking the Solar System's Past," by D. A. Kring, in *Scientific American* (August 2006).
13. "What is a Planet?" by S. Soter, in *Scientific American* (January 2007).
14. The Tunguska Mystery," by L. Gasperini, E. Bonatti, and G. Longo, in *Scientific American* (June 2008).

Quest Ahead to Starlinks
http://physicalscience.jbpub.com/starlinks

Starlinks is this book's online learning center. It features **eLearning**, which contains chapter quizzes and other tools designed to help you study for your class. You can also find **online exercises**, view numerous relevant **animations**, follow a guide to **useful astronomy sites** on the Internet, or even check the latest **astronomy news** updates.

The Sun

THE CHAPTER-OPENING PHOTOGRAPH, WHICH WAS TAKEN FROM SPACE, shows prominences on the Sun's surface, giving us a hint of the tremendous energy within. Over the years, many well-known physicists tried to explain where all of this energy comes from. In 1854, Hermann von Helmholtz hit on the idea of gravitational contraction as the source of the Sun's heat. He calculated that the Sun could have existed for 25 million years this way, which was not long enough to match the findings of geologists of the time concerning the age of the Earth. In 1862, Lord Kelvin, one of the most imposing figures in science, refined the calculations to say that the Sun could have been shining for 500 million years, but no more. By this time, Darwin's theory of evolution was being debated all over Europe, and for evolution to be correct, the Earth (and Sun) had to be much older than this. Kelvin, however, obtained the same result in several versions of the same calculation, always basing his work on gravitational contraction. His only concession to the possibility of error was to say, "I do not say there may not be laws which we have not discovered."

There is such a law: radioactivity. Henri Becquerel announced his discovery of radioactivity in 1896, touching off a flood of research activity. One result was the work of young Ernest Rutherford, who showed that radioactive materials could produce large amounts of energy. This energy could provide additional heat in the Earth and

Prominences on the Sun are huge eruptions of gas that often form arches along magnetic field lines. The entire Earth could easily fit beneath one of these arches.

All cross references to chapters, sections, figures, and tables pertain to the main text, *In Quest of the Universe, Sixth Edition. In Quest of the Solar System* contains Chapters 1–11 and 19 of the main text. *In Quest of the Stars and Galaxies* contains Chapters 1–5 and 11–19 of the main text.

FIGURE 11-1 The Sun is the ultimate source of oil (including that pumped by this rig) and of all energy on Earth except nuclear and geothermal energy.

the Sun that would mean these objects are far older than Kelvin's results—billions of years older, in fact. Here is Rutherford's description of the address he gave on this topic at a meeting of England's Royal Institution:

I came into the room, which was half dark, and presently spotted Lord Kelvin in the audience and realized that I was in for trouble at the last part of my speech dealing with the age of the earth, where my views conflicted with his. To my relief, Kelvin fell fast asleep, but as I came to the important point, I saw the old bird sit up, open an eye and cock a baleful glance at me! Then a sudden inspiration came, and I said Lord Kelvin had limited the age of the earth, provided no new source [of energy] was discovered. That prophetic utterance refers to what we are now considering tonight, radium! Behold! the old boy beamed upon me. (From A.S. Eve, *Rutherford*, Cambridge, UK: Cambridge University Press, 1939, p. 107.)

In fact, we now believe that the source of energy in the Sun is not due to the energy of radioactive decay, but comes from reactions of nuclei in the hot, dense core. We discuss these reactions in this chapter.

In our quest to understand our universe, we started by first examining the basic tools we have for deciphering the information we get from celestial objects. Then we used these tools to understand the formation and evolution of our own planet and that of the remaining objects in our neighborhood—the solar system. We now study the Sun, the most important member of our solar system. Without it, life on Earth would not be possible. It is also the closest laboratory for studying how other stars evolve and, thus, it is a logical next step in our quest to understand the physical universe.

Although the Sun is the celestial object of most importance to life on Earth (FIGURE 11-1), it is just an ordinary star. The cosmic importance of the Sun is limited to the fact that it is the central object of the planetary system in which we live. Many other stars are bigger and brighter. Many are more interesting and unusual, and most will far outlive the Sun.

We begin this chapter with a brief overview of the major properties of the Sun. Then we examine the source of the Sun's energy, along with various theories for the production of that tremendous energy. Finally, we describe the Sun in more detail, starting at its center, where energy production takes place, and proceeding outward.

11-1 Solar Properties

FIGURE 11-2 If the Earth were at the center of the Sun, the Moon would orbit about half-way to the Sun's surface.

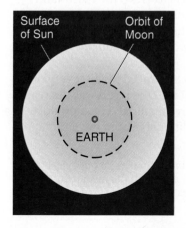

As viewed from Earth, the Sun has an average angular diameter of 31'59", just barely less than 32 minutes of arc. By taking 1.50×10^8 kilometers as the average distance from Earth to Sun and by using the small-angle formula (the relationship between angular size, distance, and actual size discussed in Section 6-1), we can calculate that the Sun's diameter is 1.39×10^6 kilometers, about 110 times Earth's diameter and about 10 times Jupiter's. FIGURE 11-2 illustrates the great size of the Sun. (Activity 1 at the end of the chapter shows how you can measure the diameter of the Sun.)

From Kepler's third law (as revised by Newton), we calculate that the mass of the Sun is 1.99×10^{30} kilograms. This is about 333,000 times the mass of the Earth! The Sun's average

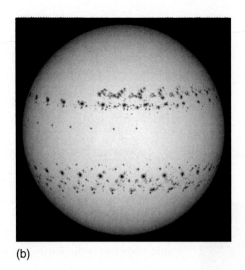

(a)   (b)

FIGURE 11-3 (a) Sunspots appear as dark spots on the Sun's surface. (b) This composite image shows the Sun's visible surface for most days of August 1999; the same sunspots appear many times as the Sun's rotation carries them across its surface.

density, then, is 1.41 g/cm³, about the same as the density of Jupiter. This is just the first of several similarities we will see between the Sun and some of the planets in our solar system.

Nearly 400 years ago, when Galileo first used a telescope to view the Sun, he observed dark spots moving across its face (FIGURE 11-3a). Figure 11-3b is a series of photographs of the motion of such **sunspots**. Galileo concluded from sunspot motions that the Sun rotates with a period of more than a month. Today we know that the Sun exhibits differential rotation; it rotates with a period of 25 days at its equator and nearly 35 days near its poles. Recall from Chapter 9 that the equatorial regions of the Jovian planets also rotate faster than their polar regions.

sunspot A region of the Sun's surface that is temporarily cool and dark compared with surrounding regions.

11-2   Solar Energy

The Sun emits energy in all portions of the electromagnetic spectrum. A valuable piece of information about the Sun is the rate at which it emits its energy, or total power output. Fortunately, this is not too difficult to determine.

We start by measuring the rate at which solar energy strikes the Earth's atmosphere. This determination was made long ago by measuring the amount of energy from the Sun that strikes an area on the Earth's surface and then correcting for the energy absorbed by the atmosphere. Today it is done most accurately from satellites above the atmosphere. Measurements show that solar energy strikes the upper atmosphere of the Earth at the rate of about 1370 watts per square meter. This value is used in the following example to show that the Sun's **luminosity**—the energy the Sun radiates into space per second—is 3.85×10^{26} **watts**. (If the Sun were a lightbulb, this would be its "wattage.") This is an awesome amount of **power**. The energy that the Sun releases *in 1 second* is about the same as the energy released by the simultaneous explosion of 4 trillion atomic bombs! The solar energy received by the surface of the Earth, assuming we could collect and harness it efficiently, is enough to cover the energy needs of the entire world population 10,000 times over.

The example also illustrates nicely why the inverse square law applies to radiation from the Sun (or any distant object). The surface area of a sphere that is centered on the Sun depends on the square of the sphere's radius. A sphere twice the distance from the Sun thus has a surface area four times as great, and only one fourth as much energy strikes a square meter on the surface of this more distant sphere.

luminosity The rate at which electromagnetic energy is emitted.

watt A unit of power that corresponds to a specific amount of energy each second. (Imagine how dim a 1-watt light bulb would be.)

power The amount of energy exchanged per unit time.

The Source of the Sun's Energy

It has been estimated that a 1% change in solar luminosity would result in a temperature change on Earth of 1°C or 2°C (about 2°F to 4°F). When we consider that the last major ice age on Earth resulted from a temperature decrease that averaged only

5°C across the planet, we see how critical it is that the Sun maintain a uniform rate of energy production. In reality, this rate is not uniform; the amount of solar energy that strikes the Earth varies with time, the variations over the centuries being of the order of fractions of a percent. The more we study the interaction between the Sun's energy output and our planet, however, the more it seems that even these small variations have consequences for life on Earth. What is the source of this energy, which must have remained approximately constant far into the past?

EXAMPLE

Calculate the energy output of the Sun in watts, given that solar energy strikes the Earth at the rate of 1370 watts/meter² and that the Sun is 1.496×10^8 kilometers from Earth.

SOLUTION   First, because we have expressed the area on Earth in square meters, we should also express the Earth-Sun distance in meters:

$$1.496 \times 10^8 \text{ km} \times \frac{1000 \text{ m}}{1 \text{ km}} = 1.496 \times 10^{11} \text{ m}.$$

Imagine a sphere around the Sun at the Earth's distance. We must calculate how many square meters are on that surface (FIGURE 11-4). To do this, use the equation for the area of a sphere, with 1.496×10^{11} meters being the radius of the sphere in the calculation:

$$\text{area of sphere} = 4\pi r^2 \quad (r = \text{radius of the sphere})$$

$$= 4 \,(3.14)\,(1.496 \times 10^{11} \text{ m})^2 = 2.81 \times 10^{23} \text{ m}^2.$$

Each of these square meters receives 1370 watts of solar power. Therefore,

$$\text{total solar power} = (1370 \text{ watts/m}^2) \times (2.81 \times 10^{23} \text{ m}^2)$$

$$= 3.85 \times 10^{26} \text{ watts}.$$

TRY ONE YOURSELF
How many watts of power strike one square meter of Mars' surface? (Mars is 2.3×10^{11} meters from the Sun.) Solve this by using the total solar power calculated in the example and the area of a sphere at Mars' distance.

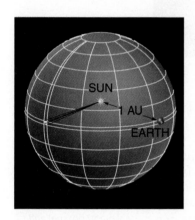

FIGURE 11-4 An imaginary sphere is shown drawn around the Sun at the distance of the Earth. It is a simple matter to calculate the area of such a sphere and to determine the solar energy that strikes each square meter of it.

 Given the power striking the Earth's surface, you could use the inverse square law of radiation, discussed in Section 4-8, to calculate this number.

Calculation 3 takes you through the steps for proving this statement.

Before the 20th century, several hypotheses had been suggested to explain the source of the Sun's energy. All have now been rejected, based on additional data. For example, it was proposed that chemical reactions (such as the burning of a fuel) are the source of the Sun's energy. We now know that this cannot be the case, simply because if the Sun were made of a fuel such as coal or oil, it would burn out in a few centuries at the rate that it is releasing energy.

In the mid-19th century, Hermann von Helmholtz and Lord Kelvin proposed that the source of the Sun's energy is a very slow gravitational contraction. Such contraction compresses the gases inside the Sun, raising their temperature. This is similar to the air in a bicycle tire getting warmer when you compress it with a pump. When the Sun's gases got hot enough, they started radiating energy out into space. The calculations of Helmholtz and Kelvin showed that gravitational contraction could have produced the Sun's energy output with a reduction in the Sun's diameter of only a few tens of meters per year—so slight that it would not have been enough to notice in recorded history. Assuming that the Sun was formed from a large diffuse cloud, however, they calculated that gravitational contraction could not have started more than a few hundred million years ago. This time period seemed long enough in the 19th century, as the Earth was thought to be much younger. Their theory seemed to be a good one; it fit the available data.

Then, in the 20th century, geologists discovered that the Earth's age is not a few hundred million years, but rather a few *billion* years—10 times longer. The contraction theory had to be abandoned, and the source of the Sun's energy was again an open question.

In the first decade of the 20th century, as a result of Einstein's special theory of relativity, we started considering mass and energy as interconvertible. That is, one can be transformed into the other. In the late 1920s, it was hypothesized that this process could be the source of energy in the Sun. Then during the 1930s, Hans Bethe at Cornell worked out the theory that today explains how the Sun has produced its tremendous power for the past 4 to 5 billion years and how it will continue this production for another similar period of time.

Solar Nuclear Reactions

Recall from Chapter 4 that the Bohr model of the atom proposed that the atom consists of a nucleus surrounded by orbiting electrons (FIGURE 11-5). That nucleus is our focus now. An atom's nucleus makes up about 99.98% of the mass of the atom and consists of two kinds of particles: *protons* and *neutrons*.

Protons have a positive electrical charge and neutrons have no electrical charge. The number of protons in the nucleus determines what element the atom is. For example, if the nucleus of an atom contains 1 proton, that atom is necessarily an atom of hydrogen. If it contains 2 protons, it is helium; if 6, carbon; if 92, uranium. A nucleus of hydrogen, on the other hand, is not limited to a specific number of neutrons. Although most hydrogen nuclei contain no neutrons, some have one neutron, and a few have two.

It is important to distinguish nuclear reactions from chemical reactions. Chemical reactions, which we encounter in everyday life, involve atoms changing the ways in which they are combined with other atoms. When we burn paper, for example, the paper's carbon atoms combine with oxygen atoms from the air, producing carbon dioxide molecules. FIGURE 11-6 illustrates this reaction and emphasizes that this is a *chemical bond*, formed by the sharing of electrons between the carbon atom and each of the oxygen atoms. The forces involved here are electromagnetic in nature. Forces responsible for the structure of the nuclei are not involved in chemical reactions.

Nuclear reactions, on the other hand, involve forces between nuclear particles; orbiting electrons are not part of these reactions. There are many types of nuclear

The relationship between the amount of energy (E) that can be created from a certain amount of mass (m) is $E = mc^2$. The conversion factor c is the speed of light in vacuum.

Bethe was awarded the Nobel Prize in 1967 for his theory that the source of the energy from stars is thermonuclear reactions from which hydrogen is converted into helium.

proton The positively charged particle in the nucleus of an atom.

neutron The nuclear particle with no electric charge.

Do not confuse the terms *proton* and *photon*; they are very different. Refer to Section 4-6 for a description of photons.

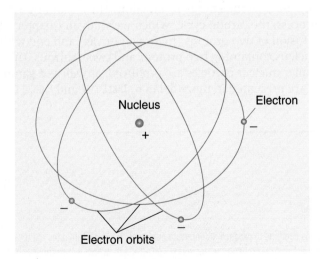

FIGURE 11-5 The Bohr atom, with electrons (which have a negative charge) circling the positive nucleus. If the atom were this size, the nucleus would still be too small to see. Drawings such as this one are used only as visualization tools. The orbits shown for the electrons correspond to the most probable distances from the nucleus at which electrons are observed.

FIGURE 11-6 A carbon dioxide molecule (like all molecules) is held together by chemical bonds, in this case involving the sharing of electrons between two oxygen atoms and one carbon atom. Nuclear forces do not come into play in the bonding. Drawings such as this one are used only as visualization tools.

reactions, but only one will be of interest to us: the *fusion* reaction. In a nuclear fusion reaction, two nuclei combine to form a larger nucleus. They "fuse."

The core of the Sun is too hot to allow for complete atoms to exist. Instead, nuclei and electrons are separate from one another and bounce around at great speeds. The primary source of energy in the Sun (and in all stars during most of their lifetimes) is a series of nuclear fusion reactions in which four hydrogen nuclei are fused to form one helium nucleus. In the process, a small fraction of the mass of the nuclei is changed into energy. This is where Einstein's theory comes into play. Let's look at the process.

Most hydrogen nuclei consist simply of one proton. Before the fusion reaction, we have four hydrogen nuclei, and after the reaction, there is one helium nucleus. Let us subtract the mass of one helium nucleus (6.6447×10^{-27} kg) from the mass of four hydrogen nuclei (each having a mass of 1.6726×10^{-27} kg):

$$\begin{aligned} \text{mass of 4 hydrogen nuclei} &= 6.6905 \times 10^{-27} \text{ kg} \\ - \text{ mass of 1 helium nucleus} &= 6.6447 \times 10^{-27} \text{ kg} \\ \hline \text{difference} &= 0.0458 \times 10^{-27} \text{ kg}. \end{aligned}$$

The difference between the mass of the original matter and the resulting matter is very small, not only in terms of the actual amount (less than 10^{-28} kg per reaction), but also in that the "lost" mass (which has been completely converted to energy) is only seven tenths of 1% of the original mass of four hydrogen nuclei. Not even 1% of the mass is changed into energy. In fact, the energy produced by a trillion such fusion reactions is only enough to lift up this book by about a foot.

If the energy produced per fusion reaction is so small, how does the Sun produce an output of 3.85×10^{26} watts? The answer lies in the huge number of fusion reactions occurring in the Sun's core every second—about 10^{38} reactions per second. This implies that nearly 5 million metric tons of matter must be completely converted into energy each second. This involves the transformation of some 626 billion kilograms of hydrogen to about 622 billion kilograms of helium every second. Although this is a tremendous amount of matter by human standards, it is almost insignificant when compared with the Sun's total mass. If the Sun were originally pure hydrogen, it would take about 100 billion years for the Sun to convert its entire mass to helium at the present rate of consumption. (As we discuss later in the chapter, only the inner portion of the Sun—about 30% of its mass—is involved in the reaction and is converted to helium.)

In practice, the process by which hydrogen is converted into helium incorporates three steps, called the *proton–proton* chain. (This chain is the main fusion process in the Sun, responsible for 98.5% of the energy production. The remaining 1.5% is produced by a different process, the carbon cycle, which we study in Chapter 14.) The reactions start with a fusion of two protons (hydrogen nuclei) and end with the production of a helium nucleus containing two protons and two neutrons. During the process, two other smaller nuclear particles are produced, as well as a gamma ray. The solar fusion reactions are presented in more detail in **TABLE 11-1** and FIGURE 11-7.

TABLE 11-1

The Proton-Proton Chain

Reaction	Explanation
$^1_1H + ^1_1H \rightarrow ^2_1H + e^+ + \nu_e$	Two protons combine to produce a deuterium nucleus (^2_1H; the 2 indicates the total number of protons and neutrons in the nucleus), a positron (e^+, which is a positively charged electron), and an electron neutrino (ν_e).
$^2_1H + ^1_1H \rightarrow ^3_2He + \gamma$	A deuterium nucleus joins with another proton to produce a helium nucleus (^3_2He, containing two protons and one neutron) and a gamma ray (γ).
$^3_2He + ^3_2He \rightarrow ^4_2He + 2 \cdot ^1_1H$	Two helium nuclei fuse to form the common type of helium (^4_2He) and two protons.

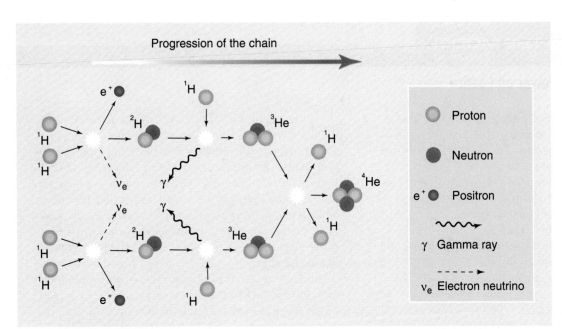

Progression of the chain

Proton
Neutron
e⁺ Positron
γ Gamma ray
νₑ Electron neutrino

FIGURE 11-7 The proton-proton chain begins with four protons and ends with a helium nucleus. The four protons are shown at left combining in separate reactions to produce two deuterium nuclei (each with a proton and a neutron).

Look at the first reaction in the table. Here, two hydrogen nuclei fuse to form the nucleus of another type of hydrogen, called *deuterium*, which has a neutron in its nucleus along with the proton. In addition, two other particles are formed, and these two particles fly away from the reaction at great speeds. One of them, the positive electron, or *positron*, combines with an electron and completely annihilates into gamma-ray photons. The other particle, the electron *neutrino*, escapes from the Sun and does not cause significant heating within the Sun. This particle is discussed later in this chapter.

In reality, only about 85% of the Sun's energy is produced by the chain described previously. The remaining 15% is produced by two other, similar chains, where the third step involves the temporary formation of the element beryllium before finally producing a helium nucleus. These additional two chains are important because they produce electron neutrinos with larger energies than the chain shown in Figure 11-7. In the next section, we discuss the importance of these neutrinos in our understanding of the interior of the Sun.

Hydrogen exists throughout the world. Yet it does not, on its own, fuse into helium. The reason for this is that all nuclei have a positive electric charge and, therefore, they repel one another. This electrical repulsion force acts over great distances, at least compared with the very short distances over which nuclear forces act. This means that the particles are unable to get close enough together for the attractive nuclear forces to take over unless they happen to be moving toward one another at a great speed (**FIGURE 11-8**). Because the temperature of a gas is determined by the speed of its particles, the particles of hot hydrogen are more likely to fuse than those of cool hydrogen. Significant fusion occurs only in high-temperature matter.

In addition, as we have seen, a great number of fusions of hydrogen nuclei must occur each second to produce the Sun's power. We thus know that the density of matter must be extremely high in the region of the Sun where fusion occurs. To see how and where this happens, let us investigate the Sun's internal structure.

deuterium A hydrogen nucleus that contains one neutron and one proton.

positron A positively charged electron emitted from the nucleus in some nuclear reactions.

neutrino An elementary particle that has little rest mass and no charge but carries energy from a nuclear reaction.

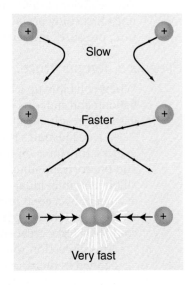

Slow

Faster

Very fast

FIGURE 11-8 Nuclei moving toward one another at too slow a speed will be repelled because of their positive charges; however, if they are moving fast enough, electrical repulsion will not be strong enough to prevent them from colliding and fusing.

ADVANCING THE MODEL

Fission and Fusion Power on Earth

The dream of unlimited energy has been with us at least since the beginning of the Industrial Age, and humans wondered at the tremendous power of the Sun long before that. We now know that nuclear fusion reactions are the source of the Sun's energy, and just a few decades ago humans harnessed this energy (if *harnessed* is an appropriate word here) in the hydrogen bomb. The bomb's name comes from the fact that it uses a form of hydrogen (deuterium) as its fuel. The nuclear reaction in the H-bomb is similar to that in the Sun; it produces helium from hydrogen.

Peaceful uses of fusion power have not yet been developed, although much research has taken place over the last 6 decades and is still in progress. A hint at the problems of controlling fusion can be seen by considering the tremendous temperatures and pressures that are necessary to produce fusion in the centers of stars. On the other hand, such reactions have an essentially unlimited supply of fuel—deuterium—and therefore, controlled energy production from fusion is a very attractive goal.

Although fusion is much more common than fission in the universe as a whole, humans developed fission first. Fission involves the release of energy when a large nucleus is broken into two medium nuclei, with mass being converted into energy in the process. The atomic bomb (poorly named, for it uses the energy of the nucleus rather than the energy of the outer atom) was the first application of fission power. Since the development of the A-bomb, we have learned to control this reaction, and today we use the energy of fission to produce electricity in nuclear power plants. In contrast to the ready availability of fuel for fusion, the uranium that must be used for fission power is definitely limited. Many people, scientists and nonscientists alike, question the wisdom of building and using fission power plants. Fission power must be viewed as only a temporary solution to the problem of finding a long-range source of energy on Earth. (See the references at the end of this chapter for more information on nuclear fission and fusion.)

11-3 The Sun's Interior

Obviously, we cannot examine the interior of the Sun directly; however, astronomers have learned much about its interior by computer modeling, based on observations of the Sun's surface and our knowledge about the behavior of matter at the temperatures and pressures necessary to sustain fusion reactions. We know that at temperatures as high as the Sun's, matter must exist as a gas rather than as a solid or a liquid, and this fact makes the analysis easier, for gases are much simpler than liquids or solids. As is discussed later, the temperature on the surface of the Sun is about 5800 K, and it increases greatly below the surface. At these temperatures, solids and liquids cannot exist, and most electrons are stripped away from their nuclei. As a result, most of the material of the Sun's interior consists of free nuclei and free electrons. The behavior of this material, however, is similar to that of a simple gas, and thus, we must first study properties of gases. The properties of importance to us are temperature, pressure, and ***particle density***.

particle density The number of separate atomic and/or nuclear particles per unit of volume.

Pressure, Temperature, and Density

When you blow up a balloon, the gas inside exerts a pressure on the rubber of the balloon and supports it against its tendency to contract. The pressure exerted by the gas is the result of collisions of the individual gas molecules with the rubber surface. FIGURE 11-9a illustrates this. Each molecule, as it strikes the rubber wall and rebounds, exerts a tiny force on the wall. Although we cannot detect each individual bounce and the corresponding force, the overall force exerted by the gas is simply the total of all of these individual tiny forces. To see this, imagine tiny grains of sand being fired at a board by a great number of sand throwers, as in Figure 11-9b. The force exerted on the board by a single grain of sand might seem negligible, but the overall result could be a force great enough to cause the board to move.

pressure The force per unit of area.

This discussion sometimes refers to force and other times to pressure. ***Pressure*** is defined as the amount of force exerted per unit area and might be expressed as newtons per square meter or pounds per square inch. When we think of a single grain of sand or a single atom rebounding from something, it thus is more natural to speak of the force exerted by the particle. On the other hand, when we think of many sand grains or many atoms striking over a large area, we speak of the force exerted on each unit of area, or the pressure.

What then determines the pressure of a gas? There are two factors: the speed of the molecules of the gas and their particle density. To see that each of these factors is important, think again of the gas molecules in the balloon. If we heat this gas while keeping the balloon's volume constant, then the molecules will start moving faster. Each collision with the inside surface of the balloon will be more violent, exerting more force on the wall of the balloon. In addition, a greater speed results in more collisions. For these two reasons, the total force exerted on one square centimeter of the wall will be greater; that is, the pressure exerted by the gas will be greater. On the other hand, if the gas is cooled, it will exert less pressure. We thus can conclude that the pressure and temperature of a gas are related. More rigorous analysis shows that in fact a direct mathematical relationship exists between them, so that one changes proportionately to the other.

To appreciate the effect of particle density on pressure, imagine that twice as much gas at a given temperature is somehow put into the balloon without allowing it to expand. If this is done, twice as many molecules will be striking the inside walls of the balloon, exerting twice as much pressure. This is what causes the balloon to expand when more gas is added without restraining the volume. We thus can conclude that pressure and density of a gas are related. In fact, a direct mathematical relationship exists between them so that one changes proportionately to the other.

Pressure, density, and temperature thus are interrelated. If one changes, one or both of the others must change. Now let's turn back to the Sun and consider how these factors determine the character of the Sun's interior.

FIGURE 11-9 The walls of a balloon (a) are held out by numerous collisions by molecules inside the balloon, in the same way that a great number of tiny sand throwers (b) could exert a force on a board and topple it backward.

Molecules bouncing from balloon surface

(a)   (b)

One newton is a unit of force (about 0.225 lb, the weight of an average apple.)

Under ideal conditions, pressure is proportional to density times temperature.

Hydrostatic Equilibrium

The force of gravity holds the solar material to the Sun just as the force of gravity holds the atmosphere of the Earth near its surface. In this respect, the Sun is merely a big ball of gas. Earth's atmosphere is denser near the surface, not simply because the force of gravity is greater there than higher up, but also because the pressure exerted by the gas above compacts the lower layers. Gases lower in the atmosphere have to support the gases above. The same logic applies to the Sun. At any particular depth below the Sun's surface, the pressure of the gas at that point must be enough to support the gas above. It therefore is convenient to think of the Sun as having layers, like the various layers of an onion, as shown in **FIGURE 11-10a**. Keep in mind, however, that in the Sun there are no distinct boundaries between layers, but rather a continuous change as we move toward or away from the center.

Because the Sun is in a state of equilibrium (that is, neither noticeably contracting nor expanding), the pressure downward on any thin layer must be equal to the pressure exerted upward on that layer (Figure 11-10b). Knowing the total mass of the Sun, we can calculate the weight of gas above any particular layer and thus the pressure that is needed within the layer to support the gas above.

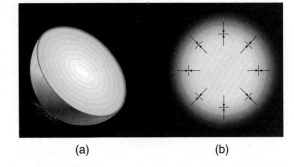

(a)   (b)

FIGURE 11-10 (a) You can think of the Sun as consisting of multiple layers, like those of an onion, except that there is no distinct boundary between the Sun's layers. (b) Within the Sun, the pressure upward on any layer must be the same as the pressure downward.

The density at the Sun's center is about 150 g/cm³, approximately 20 times the density of iron. The temperature there is about 15.6 million K.

The equilibrium conditions in the Sun are known as *hydrostatic equilibrium*. The name is almost self-explanatory: "Hydro" refers to the fluid state. This is basically just a more complex case of the situation we discussed with the inflated balloon. In that case, the stretched rubber holds the air inside in a compressed state. As long as the outward pressure of the compressed air inside is enough to support the inward pressure of the rubber, equilibrium is maintained.

Because the gas at the center of the Sun is supporting the weight of the gas all the way out to the surface, we should expect great pressures at the center. In fact, the pressure there is calculated to be about 2.5×10^{11} times that on the surface of the Earth. This tremendous pressure pushes protons close enough together that hydrogen fusion can take place. Only near the center of the Sun are the temperature and density of hydrogen great enough to support fusion. The solar core, where fusion is taking place, extends out to perhaps 25% of the radius of the Sun.

The fusion reactions in the core provide a heat source that must be taken into account when calculating conditions within the Sun. As we discussed earlier, when a gas is heated, it tends to expand. A balloon expands when its temperature rises, but then it stabilizes at a new equilibrium condition. Likewise, the Sun exists in a state of equilibrium, with the force of gravity balanced by forces tending to expand the gas.

To see how hydrostatic equilibrium works, imagine that the Sun could somehow be compressed artificially. Under compression, the pressure within the Sun would increase. The fusion rate would then increase, raising the temperature and pushing the Sun back out to another equilibrium position. As our discussion of the life cycle of stars in Chapter 14 explains, once the energy production of a star slows and the core cools, contraction of the core begins; however, as long as energy production is stable, the star remains in equilibrium.

To see what happens to the energy produced in the core of the Sun, we must look at energy transport within the Sun.

Energy Transport

We observe that energy is radiated from the Sun's surface; however, the fusion reactions in the Sun occur at its core, where the temperatures and pressures are greatest. The energy produced at the core must then be transported out to the surface in one (or more) of the three possible methods: conduction, convection, and radiation. These same three processes occur here on Earth and, indeed, everywhere in the universe.

If you put one end of a spoon on the burner (or in the flame) of a kitchen stove and hold the other end, you'll feel your end of the spoon gradually getting warmer. Energy is being transferred by vibration through the metallic crystal structure of the spoon. This method of transfer is called *conduction*. Imagine the atoms near the end of the spoon in the fire. As that end heats, the atoms vibrate at greater speeds (FIGURE 11-11); however, these atoms exert forces on adjacent atoms of the metal and cause those atoms to start vibrating faster. Gradually, the increased vibration spreads up the spoon until the atoms at the other end are also vibrating more rapidly than they were. In transferring energy by conduction, atoms do not move from one region to another, but vibrational energy—thermal energy—is transferred.

Conduction requires that the particles of the substance be in close contact, as are the atoms in a solid. In a star, this is not the case, except in some extremely dense stars, and thus, conduction is not a significant factor in transporting energy from within the Sun.

Convection occurs when the atoms of a warm fluid (liquid or gas) move from one place to another. Put your hand about a foot above a hot stove burner. You will feel hot air rising from the burner. This takes place because heated air is less dense than cooler air and, therefore, the hot, less dense air rises. The result is that energy is transferred upward from the stove by the motion of the hot gas. In forced-air central heating/cooling systems, the motion of the hot (or cool) air is caused by fans. On Earth, convection currents (thermals) enable hang gliders and gliding birds to travel long distances, carried along with the rising air.

Atoms at hot end vibrate faster

Atoms at cool end vibrate slowly

FIGURE 11-11 The fast-vibrating atoms at the end of the spoon in the fire cause atoms next to them to vibrate faster. This continues until atoms at the far end are also vibrating fast, meaning that this end also becomes hot.

In a star, convection between adjacent layers is significant only when the temperature difference is great compared with the pressure difference. In the case of our Sun, this condition is met only in the region within about 200,000 kilometers of the surface (FIGURE 11-12). In this region, convection constantly mixes the solar material as hot gas rises and cooler gas descends. Deeper within the Sun, convection is almost inconsequential, and mixing does not occur to a great degree.

FIGURE 11-12 This figure illustrates the relative thicknesses of the three energy-transport zones of the Sun.

The final method of energy transfer is by *radiation*. If you hold the palm of your hand exposed to the stove burner, you can tell that your hand is being heated by another method besides rising hot air. To emphasize this, hold your hand off to the side, where it is not in the stream of hot air, and you will still feel your hand being heated. Radiation of energy occurs in all portions of the electromagnetic spectrum. Its effect on another object depends only on whether the receiving object absorbs the particular wavelengths of radiation emitted by the radiator. The air of your kitchen, for example, is transparent to most electromagnetic radiation produced by the stove burner, and thus, it does not absorb the radiation and is not heated by it directly. Your hand, however, being opaque to the radiation, absorbs it and is heated by it.

radiation The transfer of energy by electromagnetic waves.

Inside the Sun and most stars, radiation is the principal means of energy transport. If the Sun were transparent, the electromagnetic radiation produced in the core would travel outward at the speed of light and reach the surface in about 2 seconds. In reality, the material in the Sun's radiative zone is too hot for atoms to exist and thus the radiation coming from the core scatters as it encounters free electrons and atomic nuclei. On the other hand, the material in the convective zone is cool enough for some atoms to exist (such as carbon, nitrogen, oxygen, calcium, and iron) and, thus, the radiation coming from the core gets absorbed and then reemitted, absorbed, reemitted, and so on, with a typical distance between successive absorptions of 1 centimeter (FIGURE 11–13). The reemissions occur in random directions, and as a result, energy that began perhaps as a gamma ray photon resulting from the proton–proton chain travels a very circuitous path and may take hundreds of thousands of years to reach the surface. This seems an impossibly long time for something traveling at the speed of light, but keep in mind both the multitude of scatterings, absorptions, and reemissions taking place and the extreme length of the roundabout path taken by the energy. As a result, any information about the Sun's core carried by the photons produced there is lost to us. This is similar to what happens when you forward a message by fax, using a fax you received from a friend, who did the same thing before you, and so on. The end result is that the final recipient will most likely not be able to read the message.

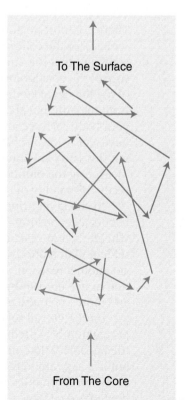

To The Surface

From The Core

FIGURE 11-13 A photon is absorbed and reemitted numerous times as it travels from the Sun's core. Each reemission is in a random direction.

Can we tell what happens in the Sun's core by analyzing the light produced there?

Figure 11-12 shows the various portions of the interior of the Sun: the core, the radiative zone, and the convective zone. The temperature at the Sun's core, where the nuclear reactions occur, is about 15.6 million K, and the density is about 150 times that of water. Both temperature and density decrease as we move toward the radiative zone, which starts at about 25% of the distance from the center to the Sun's surface. The temperature here is about 7 million K, and the density is about 20 times that of water.

The radiative zone extends to about 70% of the distance to the surface, where the temperature is about 2 million K and the density is 0.2 times that of water. Across the thin layer between the radiative and convective zones (occupying the region from 69 to 71% of the distance to the surface), there is a change in the chemical composition and also the flow speed of the material. These changes in flow speeds are thought to generate the Sun's magnetic field.

The convection zone occupies the region within 200,000 km from the surface, where the temperature is about 5800 K and the density 2×10^{-7} times that of water. As we mentioned before, the presence of atoms in this layer makes it harder for the radiation from the core to escape; as a result, the trapped heat makes the material unstable and gives rise to convection currents, which carry energy quickly to the Sun's surface. After the energy of the Sun reaches the surface, it is again radiated outward. The energy from the Sun is released primarily as ultraviolet, visible, and infrared radiation, but it also comes in two less familiar forms: charged particles and neutrinos. As we explain in Section 11-5, the charged particles flowing outward from the Sun have observable effects on Earth. Neutrinos, however, are very difficult to detect because the probability of them interacting with matter they pass through is very low. This presents astronomers with a major problem.

Nevertheless, neutrinos can tell us about the *current* conditions in the Sun's core because they move very close to the speed of light in vacuum (*c*). (Until late in the 20th century, neutrinos were thought to be massless and thus moving at *c*. The first evidence for neutrino mass was seen in 1998. The latest experiments suggest that neutrinos have a very small mass, less than a billionth the mass of a proton; as such, their speed is very close to *c*.)

Solar Neutrinos and the Standard Solar Model

Recall from Figure 11.7 that the proton–proton chain produces two electron neutrinos for each helium atom produced.

There is almost no doubt about the fundamental ideas of the solar model just described, for the concepts of pressure and density are well understood, and we are confident that the Sun's energy is produced by nuclear fusion; however, we are less sure of the details of the workings of the Sun's interior. The generally accepted theory of the Sun is called the **standard solar model**; it predicts that so many neutrinos flow from the Sun that about 65 billion of them pass through every square centimeter of your body each second. These neutrinos do not affect your body because neutrinos have a very low probability of interaction with whatever matter they pass through, but this same low interaction rate makes them difficult for astronomers to detect. Measuring the number of solar neutrinos that reach the Earth allows us to check directly the validity of the standard solar model.

To shield neutrino detectors from cosmic rays and natural radioactivity, the detectors must be located far underground. Otherwise, the other radiation would overwhelm the few reactions caused by neutrinos. In addition, because neutrinos react so seldom with matter, a neutrino detector must contain a large amount of material to get enough reactions to detect. The world's first solar-neutrino detector began operation in the late 1960s; a number of other experiments have been conducted since, and more are in the planning process.

Until 1998, all solar neutrino experiments were finding 30 to 60% of the expected numbers predicted by the standard solar model. These results did not rule out the possibility that our theories concerning the detection of neutrinos were in error, but it is very unlikely that all experiments were wrong, as they all used very different detection techniques and were thoroughly tested. Also, the neutrinos produced in the Sun's core have a wide range of energies. The different detectors were sensitive to different energy ranges, and the measured neutrino deficit depends on the energy of the neutrino. The discrepancy between the observed and predicted numbers of neutrinos was commonly referred to as the *"solar neutrino problem."*

This discrepancy gave scientists two choices. The first choice was that the standard model was not correct. Many modifications of the model were proposed, but none gave a satisfactory solution to the "solar neutrino problem." Also, the model has been so successful in helping us understand the Sun, and therefore the stars in general, that in the absence of a better model there was no compelling reason to abandon it. When experimental data contradict the predictions of a theory, the theory could be wrong; however, it is also possible that there is some "new physics" that once understood could become an integral component of the existing theory. (Refer to our discussion on science, geocentrism, and heliocentrism in Chapter 2 and the evolution of our ideas on light, matter, and gravity covered in earlier chapters.)

The second choice was that during their 8-minute flight from the Sun's core to Earth, solar neutrinos oscillate between different types of neutrinos that the experiments at the time could not detect. (Indeed, according to the standard model of particle physics, neutrinos come in three types related to three different charged particles: the electron, and its lesser known relatives, the muon and the tau.) This is precisely what physicists Stanislaw *Mikeyev*, Alexei *Smirnov*, and Lincoln *Wolfenstein* proposed; however, for neutrinos to oscillate they must have mass. The so-called MSW theory was put to the test in experiments around the world.

As described in the Tools of Astronomy box on Solar Neutrino Experiments, the first evidence for neutrino oscillations was seen in 1998 by the Super-Kamiokande experiment. In early 2002, results from the Sudbury Neutrino Observatory (SNO) showed with great certainty that solar neutrinos change their type en route to Earth and that the total number of neutrinos observed by SNO is in excellent agreement with the number predicted by the standard solar model. Strong support for neutrino oscillations came in late 2002 from the KamLAND project and in 2006 by the MINOS experiment.

Neutrino oscillations are real, and they seem to explain the solar neutrino problem; however, so far we can only measure about 0.005% of the total number of neutrinos emitted by the Sun. The remaining neutrinos are difficult to detect because they are at lower energies. Additional experiments have been proposed in a concerted effort to solve this very serious problem.

There is at least one other possibility. The prediction of the total number of neutrinos produced by the Sun is based on the energy we receive from the Sun; however, as we have seen, the solar energy that comes to us as electromagnetic radiation requires millions of years to get from the core of the Sun to the photosphere where it is radiated away. The energy we receive had its beginning millions of years ago, but solar neutrinos from the core reach us in only about 8 minutes. Could it be that the core of the Sun has decreased its energy production since it released the electromagnetic energy we are now receiving? If so, then the change in solar activity will not have an effect on Earth until thousands or millions of years from now, when it will cause another ice age.

Understanding solar neutrinos is a very important problem in astronomy. At stake is not just the accuracy of a model for the Sun. If the standard solar model is accurate, which now seems to be the case, then we can be confident about our understanding of not only our Sun but of all stars. This obviously has ramifications for our understanding of galaxies and the overall evolution of the universe. The latest results suggest that neutrinos do have mass, and thus, being the most numerous entities in the universe other than photons, they contribute to a small degree to its overall mass and influence its evolution.

11-4   Helioseismology

In 1962, scientists discovered that the Sun is vibrating. Doppler shift measurements indicate that parts of the *photosphere* move up and down about 10 km with a period of about 5 minutes. Since then, many other vibration frequencies have been

There is something wrong either with the Sun or with the neutrinos—or with what we think we know about them. John Bahcall, co-leader of the Homestake mine neutrino experiment

photosphere The visible "surface" of the Sun. The part of the solar atmosphere from which mostly visible light is emitted into space.

TOOLS OF ASTRONOMY

Solar Neutrino Experiments

The world's first solar-neutrino detector (**FIGURE B11-1a**) began operation in the late 1960s in the Homestake Gold Mine in Lead, South Dakota. This detector, operated by a group from Brookhaven National Laboratory led by Raymond Davis, Jr., and John Bahcall, used 378,000 liters (100,000 gallons) of perchloroethylene (C_2Cl_4), a dry-cleaning fluid containing chlorine. When a solar neutrino strikes a chlorine atom with enough energy, a reaction occurs, transforming the chlorine into a radioactive isotope of argon that has a half-life of 35 days. The accumulated argon atoms were collected from the tank and counted, thereby revealing the number of neutrinos involved in the reactions. The results of experiments conducted from 1970 to 1995 suggest that, on average, one radioactive argon atom was created in the tank every 3 days. This corresponds to about 30% of the number of neutrinos predicted by the standard solar model.

In an effort to confirm or improve these results, other solar-neutrino experiments followed. The Kamiokande experiment operated from 1986 to 1995 in Kamioka, Japan. This detector had the ability to provide information on the direction of the neutrinos' travel. It confirmed that neutrinos do indeed come from the Sun, giving direct evidence that nuclear reactions occur in the Sun. Like the Homestake experiment, it found fewer neutrinos than theory predicts (about 50%).

The two detectors discussed thus far were sensitive only to high-energy neutrinos, which account for a very low percentage of the total neutrino production. Two other neutrino detectors, known as SAGE (Soviet American Gallium Experiment) and GALLEX, employ the element gallium, which is able to detect the low-energy neutrinos produced by the dominant reactions in the Sun's core. In these experiments, the interaction between solar neutrinos and gallium atoms produces radioactive germanium atoms, which can be collected and counted. SAGE (1990 to 2001) was housed in a tunnel under a mountain in the northern Caucasus, near a town called Neutrino City, and detected about 55% of the number of neutrinos predicted by the standard model. Statistically more substantial results came from the GALLEX experiment (1991 to 1997), which was located in a tunnel in Italy; it detected about 60% of the predicted neutrinos.

The Super-Kamiokande experiment, a joint Japan–U.S. collaboration and a continuation of the Kamiokande experiment, started operating in 1996 (Figure B11-1b). Super K is sensitive to electron neutrinos and muon neutrinos and can distinguish between them. In 1998 it found evidence for neutrino oscillations and thus for the possibility that neutrinos may have mass. It also found about 50% of the predicted neutrinos.

The Sudbury Neutrino Observatory (SNO), in Sudbury, Canada, is a Canada-Britain-U.S. collaboration that began operating in 1999 (Figure B11-1c). By early 2002, SNO scientists were able to use the unique properties of heavy water (where the hydrogen has an extra neutron in its nucleus) to measure the total number of neutrinos of all three types reaching their detector. They found that the number of electron neutrinos observed is only about one third of the total number reaching the Earth. This shows with great certainty

FIGURE B11-1 (a) The Homestake neutrino experiment located nearly a mile under the hills of South Dakota. (b) Scientists use a boat to check the detectors in the Super-Kamiokande neutrino experiment, which uses 50,000 tons of ultrapure water. (c) An artist's view of the SNO. The SNO detector consists of 1000 metric tons of ultrapure heavy water surrounded by 9600 light sensors, which detect tiny flashes of light emitted as neutrinos are stopped or scattered in the heavy water. The detection rate is about 1 neutrino/hour. It is the size of a 10-story building, 2 kilometers underground in Inco's Creighton Mine near Sudbury, Ontario.

TOOLS OF ASTRONOMY

Solar Neutrino Experiments *(Cont'd)*

that solar neutrinos change their type en route to Earth and arrive as a mixture of electron-, muon-, and tau-neutrinos. These results imply that neutrinos have mass and that the mass differences between the three types can be calculated. These masses are minute, and for all practical purposes, neutrinos can still be thought of as traveling at the speed of light in vacuum. The total number of neutrinos observed by SNO is also in excellent agreement with calculations of the nuclear reactions powering the Sun, suggesting that the standard solar model is quite accurate in describing the inner workings of the Sun. This agreement is very impressive if we consider the fact that the predicted number of neutrinos depends on the 25th power of the temperature at the center of the Sun. We can now calculate this temperature to better than 1%.

Strong support for neutrino oscillations came in late 2002 from the KamLAND project. This detector is located at the Kamioka mine in Japan and measures antineutrinos (the antimatter equivalent of neutrinos) from all 17 nuclear power plants in the country. Because matter and antimatter are mirror images of each other, studying antineutrinos produced by the fission reactions in the power plants should be the same as studying neutrinos produced by the fusion re-

actions in the Sun's core. In this case, the amount of nuclear material generating these neutrinos is well known, and thus, physicists can observe neutrino oscillations without making any assumptions about the properties of the source of the neutrinos. The results of this experiment clearly showed that neutrino oscillations are real.

In the MINOS experiment, operational since 2005, a beam of muon neutrinos travels underground from Fermilab (in Batavia, Illinois) to a particle detector in Soudan, Minnesota, 735 km away. In 2006, scientists announced that only 52% of the muons were detected, a clear indication of neutrino disappearance and therefore neutrino mass.

Additional experiments have been proposed in a concerted effort to detect the low-energy neutrinos generated in the Sun's core. For example, the main goal of the Borexino experiment, in Gran Sasso, Italy, is to observe neutrinos of specific energy created during the nuclear chain reactions involving beryllium. According to the standard solar model, this is the second most important neutrino production reaction after the basic proton–proton chain. The flux of these neutrinos is also predicted more accurately and is about a thousand times greater than the flux measured by Super-Kamiokande and SNO.

discovered, all taking place at the same time. FIGURE 11-14a is a computer simulation illustrating a high-frequency vibration. In this figure, the blue color represents regions where material is expanding at a given instant and orange represents areas where it is contracting. On the surface, the orange areas thus are moving inward and the blue areas outward. If this were a movie, in about 2 minutes the colors would reverse. The

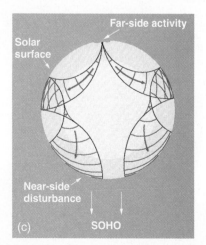

FIGURE 11-14 (a) A computer model of solar resonance that produces the observed vibrations of the photosphere. (b) An image of the actual solar surface showing oscillations; blue areas are moving toward us, and red areas are moving away from us. The motions are mainly radial (inward and outward), as shown by the fact that the signal is strongest near the center of the imaged disk of the Sun and weakest near the edge. (c) The *SOHO* satellite sees "through" the Sun by observing the disturbances at its near side as a result of the pressure waves generated by the activity (for example, a sunspot) at its far side.

pulsations are caused by waves, similar to sound waves, produced by pressure fluctuations in the turbulent convective motions of the Sun's interior. When the waves reach the photosphere, they reflect back toward the interior. These inward moving waves refract because of the changing physical conditions and eventually return to the surface. These trapped sound waves set the Sun vibrating in millions of different patterns. The combination of waves coming out and going back in produces a resonating effect, like a "gong."

Just as geologists use earthquakes to study the interior of the Earth, *helioseismology*—the study of vibrations of the Sun—is giving us insight into the Sun's interior. The Global Oscillation Network Group (GONG) has established a six-station network of telescopes around the world that obtain nearly continuous observations of the Sun's oscillations. The direct evidence we now get about the Sun's interior allows us to better test our theories of stellar structure and evolution and to find the role that magnetic fields play in the Sun's behavior. Also, a more accurate measurement of the helium abundance of the Sun put limits on cosmological models of the early universe and helped falsify a suggested explanation of the solar neutrino problem. Figure 11-14c shows how helioseismology has been used to see "through" the Sun in an effort to predict strong solar activity. In addition, it has provided us with information about flows from the Sun's equator toward the poles in the top 25,000 km of the convection zone, with the return flows being deeper in the zone. Finally, the rotation rate in the Sun was found to vary with depth and latitude; most of the variation occurs just below the base of the convection zone where we now think the Sun's magnetic field is generated.

> **helioseismology** The study of the propagation of pressure waves (similar to sound) in the Sun.

11-5 The Solar Atmosphere

FIGURE 11-15 is a combination of six photos of the Sun, each taken by a different method and in a different portion of the spectrum. The yellow "pie wedge" at the top right position shows the Sun in visible light—the way it appears in a "regular" photograph. In this case we see what we call the Sun's "surface," the photosphere, although the Sun does not have a surface in the sense that the Earth does. The Sun's photosphere is the part of the Sun from which we receive visible light.

Figure 11-15 shows that we receive different information about an object depending upon the wavelength used in taking a photograph. The photo (particularly the "pie wedge" to the left) shows that there is material beyond the Sun's surface that is not visible to our eye. This is the solar atmosphere. It is convenient to divide the atmosphere into three regions: the photosphere, the chromosphere, and the corona. We now discuss each in turn.

> Photosphere = "sphere of light."

> **limb (of the Sun or Moon)** The apparent edge of the object as seen in the sky.

The Photosphere

The photosphere is a very thin layer (about 400 kilometers thick), meaning that we can see to that depth. This thickness implies that some of the light we receive from the Sun comes from one depth within the photosphere and other light comes from other depths. When we look at an edge (the *limb*) of the Sun, we see that it appears to be "darker" than the center of the solar disk (**FIGURE 11-16a**).

This limb darkening occurs because we see to a lesser depth as a result of observing the Sun at a grazing angle. Figure 11-16b shows this effect, which is important in that it allows us to analyze light from different depths within the photosphere and therefore to determine the temperature at different depths.

FIGURE 11-15 This figure was made by combining as separate wedges six different photos of the Sun. Each photo was made using a different portion of the spectrum.

FIGURE 11-16 (a) The solar disk, the photosphere, is visible. Notice the limb darkening. (b) The light we receive from the center of the disk of the Sun originated at a greater depth than the rays we receive from near the edge. The three light rays travel an equal distance inside the photosphere; therefore, the one from the limb must originate in the upper photosphere, which is relatively cooler and thus glows less brightly. **Warning: Never look directly at the Sun**.

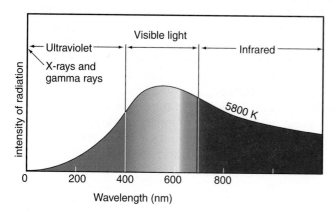

FIGURE 11-17 The intensity/wavelength graph of light from the Sun reaches a peak about the center of the visible portion of the spectrum.

We learn that the photosphere varies in temperature from about 6500 K at its deepest to about 4400 K near the outer edge. Overall, the light we receive from the photosphere is representative of an object whose temperature is about 5800 K. An intensity/wavelength graph of the radiation from the Sun (**FIGURE 11-17**) peaks near the center of the visible spectrum.

The pressure of the outer photosphere (calculated as for the inner layers, from knowing the gravitational force there and the amount of material above each layer) is only about 0.01 the pressure at the surface of the Earth. Knowing the temperatures and gas pressures of the photosphere, we calculate the density of particles there to be only about 0.0005 of the density of air at sea level on Earth (even though the gravitational field there is 28 times what it is at the Earth's surface).

When we observe the base of the photosphere (**FIGURE 11-18a**), we see irregularly shaped bright areas surrounded by darker areas, a constantly changing patchwork with individual regions appearing and disappearing with a period of a few minutes. Recall from the discussion of the intensity/wavelength diagram in Section 4-4 that a hotter object emits more radiation than a cooler object of the same size. The brighter areas of the Sun are brighter simply because they are hotter. This *granulation* of the

The solar spectrum peaks near the center of the electromagnetic region visible to us; as a result, it is reasonable to think that this is not a coincidence but that our eyes evolved so as to use the available radiation efficiently. However, see the reference at the end of this chapter on this issue.

granulation Division of the Sun's surface into small convection cells.

(a)

(b)

FIGURE 11-18 (a) This image (taken in 488 nm) of an active region near the solar eastern limb (top of the image) shows granules and sunspots (the dark areas). The tick marks are 1000 km apart. The three-dimensional nature of the photosphere is clearly seen in the elevated structures around the dark "floors" of the sunspots. Numerous bright "faculae" are also visible; these are granular structures slightly hotter than the surrounding photosphere and associated with strong magnetic fields. (b) Granules are seen where hot material from below the photosphere rises. Where it descends after cooling slightly, we see the darker edges of the granules. The flow can reach speeds of up to 15,000 miles per hour (6.7 km/s), producing sonic "booms" and other noise that generates waves on the Sun's surface.

Sun's surface is the result of convection. Granules are areas where hot material (the light areas) is rising from below and then descending (the dark surroundings). Figure 11-18b illustrates the effect and demonstrates that the photosphere is a boiling, churning region. A granule is about 1000 kilometers (600 miles) across, and thus, each granule covers an area about the size of Texas. Supergranules can be 35,000 kilometers across. Supergranules appear to move across the Sun's surface faster than the Sun rotates; however, this is an illusion similar to "the wave" done by fans at a sporting event.

Using methods described in Chapter 4, we find the chemical composition of the photosphere to be about 78% hydrogen and 20% helium (by mass). The remaining 2% consists of some 60 elements. All of these elements are known on Earth and occur in about the same proportions on Earth as in the Sun's atmosphere, with a few exceptions. The exceptions are of two types: (1) elements such as helium that have masses so low that they would have escaped Earth if they were once here in abundance and (2) elements found on Earth but whose characteristic spectra are such that they would not be detectable in the solar spectrum if the elements were as rare in the Sun as they are on Earth. As we pointed out in Chapter 7, this similarity of composition between objects as different as Earth and the Sun is not accidental, but results from the way the Sun and the solar system formed.

It is the composition of the Sun's atmosphere—not of the entire Sun—that we deduce from the solar spectrum. From our knowledge of nuclear fusion, we know that helium must be more abundant in the core of the Sun than in the atmosphere. Overall, the Sun is theorized to be about 73% hydrogen and 25% helium (by mass); this leaves only about 2% for the remainder of the elements.

The Chromosphere and Corona

The *chromosphere*, a region some 2000 kilometers thick lying beyond the photosphere, is not normally observable from Earth. It was first reported in the 17th century during a solar eclipse. It appears as a bright red flash, lasting only a few seconds, when the Moon has just covered the photosphere. During solar eclipses from 1842 to 1868, it was examined in more detail. Its spectrum was observed to be a bright line (or emission) spectrum because in viewing it we are seeing light from a hot gas with the dark sky behind it. Because the chromosphere is so much dimmer than the photosphere, it is only observed at the time of an eclipse, when the brighter portions of the Sun are blocked out (FIGURE 11-19a).

FIGURE 11-20 is a photograph of the chromosphere that was taken at a wavelength that allows us to see its structure. The *spicules* that can be seen shooting upward into the corona typically reach a height of 6000 to 10,000 kilometers and last from 5 to 20 minutes. Spicules occur periodically, every 5 minutes or so, at the same location. They are caused by sound waves of the same period that leak into the Sun's atmosphere and develop into shock waves that push these jets of plasma upward. Spicules play a very important role in how much mass is lost through the solar wind.

Today, the chromosphere and the region beyond it, the *corona*, can be observed by the use of a telescope that produces an artificial eclipse of sorts. With this instru-

---

The composition of the photosphere by volume is mainly hydrogen (91%) and helium (8.9%).

About 92% of the atoms of the Sun are hydrogen and 8% are helium. The Sun's composition changes slowly over time as hydrogen is converted to helium in the core.

chromosphere The region of the solar atmosphere between the photosphere and the corona.

Chromosphere = "sphere of color."

spicule A narrow jet of gas that is part of the chromosphere of the Sun and extends upward into the corona.

corona The outermost portion of the Sun's atmosphere.

FIGURE 11-19 (a) At the higher temperatures in the chromosphere, hydrogen emits light that gives off a reddish color (H-alpha emission). This colorful emission can be seen in prominences that project above the limb of the Sun during total solar eclipses. (b) This is an image of the Sun taken with a filter that isolates H-alpha emission.

ment we can observe the Sun's atmosphere at various depths. We learn that as one moves outward from the photosphere, the temperature increases instead of diminishing, as we would expect. It is as high as 30,000 K in the outer portions of the chromosphere and continues to increase beyond the chromosphere into the corona, where it may reach 2 million K. This change in temperature occurs rapidly in a transition region of about 300 km between the chromosphere and the corona.

Most of the radiation emitted in these regions is in the X-ray portion of the spectrum rather than in the visible. (You can show this by using Wien's law.) As a result, you might think that these regions would be extremely bright because of their high temperature; however, the chromosphere and corona have a low density of matter and, thus, hardly any matter is available to glow. The corona's density is less than one trillionth that of the Earth's atmosphere. A simple example is to consider what would happen if you were to put your hand inside a hot oven. Even though the temperature is the same for the walls and air in the oven, you would get burned much easier by touching the walls—where the matter density is large and thus provides lots of thermal energy.

The reason for the high temperatures within the chromosphere and corona is only now becoming clear. After all, the corona cools rapidly, losing its energy as radiation into space and, thus, something must be pumping energy into it from below. The prevailing theory has been that the high temperature is the result of sound waves that are produced within the convective regions of the Sun and intensify as they pass outward until they are absorbed in the chromosphere and corona, heating these regions. Recent data, however, call this explanation into question, and it is now accepted that the heating is caused by an interaction between the Sun's magnetic field and its differential rotation. Continuous changes in the Sun's magnetic field result in pressure changes at the base of the field, which allow enormous jets of gas to escape from the Sun's interior into the solar atmosphere. As a result, some of the trapped, energetic sound waves (described in Section 11-4) escape the photosphere and transfer their energy into the chromosphere and corona. FIGURE 11-21, taken by NASA's *TRACE* spacecraft in 1999, shows "solar moss," a sponge-like feature that is associated with regions where there is strong magnetic activity. The moss consists of very hot gas (about 1 million K), occurs in patches as large as 20,000 kilometers (12,000 miles) in extent, and sometimes reaches 5000 kilometers (3000 miles) high above the Sun's visible surface. This observation gives us a glimpse of how the magnetic field of the Sun becomes increasingly organized as we move from the photosphere into the corona. The transition region is very dynamic.

FIGURE 11-20 The short, dark features in the right half of this image are spicules, jets of gas shooting upward into the corona at speeds of 14 km/s (30,000 miles/hour) and then dying down within a few minutes. This 2003 image of an area toward the limb of the Sun was taken through a filter in H-alpha light (656 nm). Also visible in the upper left are some small sunspots connected by magnetic loops. The diameter of the spicules is about 500 km, and the entire area measures about 60,000 by 43,000 km on the Sun.

The word *corona* comes from the Latin word for crown.

A telescope designed to photograph the atmosphere of the Sun (when there is no eclipse) is called a *coronagraph*.

Launched in 2006, *Hinode* (Japanese for "sunrise") is studying the Sun's magnetic field and its role in powering the solar atmosphere. The mission is a collaboration between Japan, U.S. and U.K.

FIGURE 11-21 The "solar moss" (observed in the extreme UV) by the *Transition Region and Coronal Explorer* (*TRACE*) spacecraft.

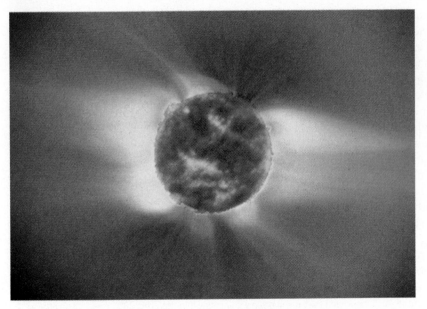

FIGURE 11-22 This is a composite photo of the Sun and its corona taken in March 1988. The surface of the Sun is a combination of X-ray and visible-light images. The photo of the corona was taken during the March 1988 eclipse. Note the irregularity of the corona and how it streams outward to form the solar wind.

An additional process that contributes to the heating of the chromosphere and corona is *magnetic reconnection*; this occurs when oppositely directed magnetic field lines interact, releasing the energy stored in the magnetic field. Observations by *TRACE*, *SOHO*, and *Hinode* are providing new insights into how the Sun's magnetic field controls the release of mass and energy into the solar atmosphere.

The corona, a region extending for millions of kilometers from the Sun, has been observed during total solar eclipses for centuries, although many people used to claim that it was just an optical illusion caused by the sudden dimming of light as the Sun is eclipsed. **FIGURE 11-22** shows its extremely irregular appearance.

The photograph on the first page of this chapter and **FIGURE 11-23** show spectacular occurrences in the Sun's atmosphere. These are ***prominences***, eruptions of solar material up into the chromosphere and corona. Some of these are relatively slow moving and remain fairly stable for as long as a few days. They may reach as high as thousands of kilometers above the photosphere. Some move much more quickly, ejecting material from the Sun at speeds up to 1500 km/s and reaching heights of nearly a million kilometers. Prominences are often associated with sunspots and the solar activity cycle to be discussed in the next section.

When we divide the Sun into regions, we must remember that the boundaries between them are artificial, for we have named them and distinguished between them on the basis of certain selected properties. For example, we consider that the process of energy transport is important, and we therefore talk of a radiative zone and a convective zone. If we emphasized another property, we might not make a division between these two parts of the Sun at all. In addition, although the boundaries between various regions appear sharp in our drawings, in reality, they are not as well defined. This is especially true of the outer limits of the corona, where the coronal material becomes the solar wind.

prominence The eruption of solar material beyond the disk of the Sun.

Yesterday I got a prominence photo good enough to prove the success of the method, and the result is that I am just now feeling pretty neat. George Ellery Hale, upon taking a photo of the Sun in the light from calcium vapor, in 1891.

solar wind The flow of charged particles from the Sun.

coronal hole A region in the Sun's corona that has very little luminous gas.

The Solar Wind

The ***solar wind*** is a continuous outflow of charged particles from the Sun, mostly in the form of protons and electrons. **FIGURE 11-24a** is an X-ray image of the Sun, in false color, showing the hottest, most dense regions as bright, and the cooler, less dense regions as dark. Such images indicate that X-ray emission is not uniform and that the active regions change appearances on a time scale of hours to days. The large dark area is called a ***coronal hole*** because it has very little luminous gas.

Coronal holes correspond to regions where the magnetic field lines are open, thus providing a corridor for charged particles to escape into space, generating the solar wind. The high coronal temperatures result in the wind particles escaping the Sun's strong gravity. These particles stream through space, taking mass away from the Sun, about 6×10^{16} kilograms every year. This corresponds to only a tiny fraction of the Sun's total mass.

Figure 11-24b shows that the solar wind is not uniform and that its speed is higher over coronal holes. Near the Earth, the solar wind normally travels at about 400 km/s and has a density of about 2 to 10 particles per cubic centimeter. Recall from Section 10-4 that one effect of the solar wind is that it causes comet tails to point away from the Sun as its particles sweep comet material along with them.

Earth shown
for size comparison

(a)

(b)

(c)

FIGURE 11-23 (a) A solar prominence. The Earth could easily fit under one of the loops shown in the picture. (b) Gas erupts in all directions from the Sun's surface in this photograph taken by the *TRACE* satellite. (c) This sequence of photos, taken from space, shows how this particular prominence progressed as charged particles were pushed from the Sun by its magnetic field.

(a)

(b)

FIGURE 11-24 (a) An X-ray image of the Sun, in false color, taken by the *Yohkoh* satellite. The large, dark area (corresponding to a cooler, less dense region) is a coronal hole. (b) A composite image of the solar wind and corona, in false color, with additional information on the solar magnetic field and speed of the solar wind. Data and images were taken by the *Ulysses* and *SOHO* spacecraft (ESA/NASA missions) and correspond to the 1994 period of sunspot minimum.

Perhaps a more dramatic effect of the solar wind is the auroras seen near the poles of the Earth. Auroras (refer back to Figure 6-25) result when the solar wind creates tears in the Earth's magnetosphere, allowing energy and charged particles to enter. This is the driving force for space weather activity around Earth. Where the Earth's magnetic field lines converge toward the surface of the Earth, the electrically charged particles strike the molecules of the upper atmosphere and cause them to emit the beautiful, eerie glow we call an aurora.

Recall the photo of an aurora on Saturn (Figure 9-21) and on Jupiter (Figure 9-8).

11-6   Sunspots and the Solar Activity Cycle

Observations of dark spots on the Sun were reported by the Chinese as early as the 5th century BC. It is sometimes possible to see very large sunspots with the naked eye if the Sun is viewed when it is very near the horizon. Europeans did not report sunspots until Galileo saw them with his telescope, perhaps because the Europeans did not have observers as astute as the Chinese, or perhaps—after Aristotelian thought was adopted—because Aristotle had proclaimed that the Sun was flawless. (We tend not to see what we disbelieve.)

In the late 18th century, Alexander Wilson hypothesized that sunspots were places where we were seeing through the outer surface of the Sun and into a cooler interior. William Herschel, the discoverer of Uranus (see the Historical Note in Chapter 9), even thought that the interior of the Sun might be cool enough to support life. Today's spectroscopic measurements of solar temperatures reveal that sunspots are indeed about 1500 K cooler than the surrounding photosphere. They are still very hot, however. At the central part of a sunspot the temperature may be as low as 3900 K. Using the Stefan-Boltzmann law (see Section 4-4), we find that the radiation emitted by a sunspot is $(5800/4300)^4 \approx 3$ times less than that from the surrounding photosphere, and as a result, the sunspot appears dark. Sunspots are temporary phenomena, lasting anywhere from a few hours to a few months.

The explanation for sunspots involves the magnetic field of the Sun, which can be measured using a technique discovered late in the 19th century. For an object in a magnetic field, the field can cause each emission line of the object's spectrum to split into two or more lines, and the strength of the magnetic field can be determined from the extent of the splitting. The splitting can be measured in the spectrum of light from individual parts of the Sun and is an important tool in studying the Sun.

Sunspots often appear in pairs, aligned in an east–west direction. Early in the 20th century it was found that the magnetic field in a sunspot is about 1000 times as strong as the magnetic field of the surrounding photosphere. In addition, we find that sunspot pairs have opposite magnetic polarities, one being north and the other south.

Sometimes the Sun contains a great number of sunspots, and sometimes few or no sunspots are seen. In 1851, Heinrich Schwabe, a German chemist and amateur astronomer, discovered that there is a fairly regular cycle of change in the number of sunspots and that the cycle lasts about 11 years. He found that although individual spots do not last long, about the same number are found on the Sun at any one part of its cycle. The cycle varies somewhat in period, but averages about 11 years between repetitions. FIGURE 11-25a is a graph showing how the number of sunspots has changed since 1880. The extended sunspot record shown in Figure 11-25b suggests that the Sun went through a period of inactivity during 1645–1715, when very few sunspots were seen on its surface (the Maunder minimum). Solar observations during this period were extensive enough that the lack of observed sunspots was well documented. This period corresponds to the "Little Ice Age" climatic period on Earth, and there is evidence that similar periods of inactivity existed in the more distant past. There is clearly a connection between the changes in solar activity and our climate on Earth.

Modeling the Sunspot Cycle and the Sunspots

At a sunspot maximum, most spots occur about 35 degrees north or south of the equator. Then, as the cycle progresses, the spots are seen closer and closer to the equator. By the time they reach the equator, the cycle is at a minimum, and new spots are beginning to form again at greater latitudes. If we plot the location of the spots as time goes by, we get the pattern shown in FIGURE 11-26, called a *butterfly diagram* for obvious reasons. It is important to point out that a given sunspot does not move from higher to lower latitudes. (The lifetime of a sunspot can be up to a few months, much shorter than the 11-year solar cycle.) Instead, the diagram tells us that as time passes and old sunspots die out, new ones form closer to the Sun's equator.

The darkest region of a sunspot may be as large as 30,000 km in diameter; this is about twice the Earth's diameter.

The splitting of spectral lines by strong magnetic fields is called the *Zeeman effect* after the Dutch physicist who discovered it.

When a large number of sunspots appear on the Sun's surface, its luminosity decreases by about 0.1%.

The reality of the [sunspot] minimum and its implication of basic solar change may be but one more defeat in our long and losing battle of wanting to keep the Sun perfect, and if not perfect, constant, and if not constant, regular. Why the Sun should be any of these when other stars are not is probably more a question for social than for physical science.
John Eddy, solar physicist, 1976.

(a)

(b)

FIGURE 11-25 (a) The number of sunspots varies with a period of about 11 years, but there is a great difference in the maximum number during each cycle. It also appears that some cycles are double-peaked. (b) The Maunder minimum (1645–1715) corresponds to a period of inactivity for the Sun and the "Little Ice Age" for Earth.

DAILY SUNSPOT AREA AVERAGED OVER INDIVIDUAL SOLAR ROTATIONS

FIGURE 11-26 This plot, called a butterfly diagram, shows the location and relative number of sunspots as the years pass. When each set of butterfly wings forms, the sunspots are at higher latitudes. Then, as new sunspots are formed, they move closer to the equator. Also, about every 11 years there is a period of very few sunspots.

The leading modern hypothesis explains the existence of sunspots and their 11-year cycle as being due to patterns of magnetic field lines, which are generated by the flow of the hot ionized gases in the thin boundary layer between the radiative and convective zones. The Sun's rotational velocity suddenly changes at this boundary, and this velocity shear drives the formation of the solar magnetic field. It is thought that groups of these lines form "tubes" threading through the Sun. When the tubes first form, they are relatively straight and buried deep within the Sun as shown in FIGURE 11-27a. The differential rotation of the Sun, however, causes the lines to wrap around the Sun, as shown progressively in parts (b), (c), and (d) of Figure 11-27. As the tubes become more and more twisted around the Sun, they are forced to the surface by convection. When they break through, we see a pair of sunspots, one with a north magnetic pole and one with a south magnetic pole.

An interesting feature of the 11-year cycle is that during one cycle, the leading sunspot of each pair in a given hemisphere of the Sun is a north magnetic pole and the trailing sunspot is a south pole. (In the other hemisphere, the opposite is true.) Then, during the next cycle, the pattern reverses, with the leading sunspot in that hemisphere being a south pole. The Sun's overall magnetic field also reverses from one cycle to another. During each cycle, the polarity of a leading sunspot in a given hemisphere is the same as the polarity of the Sun's magnetic pole for that hemisphere

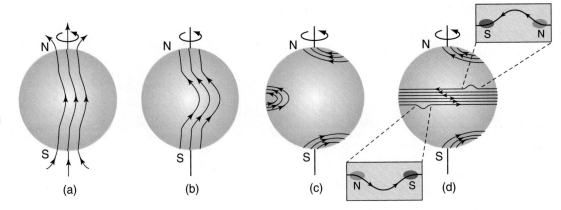

(a)   (b)   (c)   (d)

(as shown in Figure 11-27d). The entire magnetic cycle of the Sun thus has a 22-year period. The reversal of the Sun's magnetic poles happens at the middle of every 11-year sunspot cycle, during the period of sunspot maximum. Currently, the Sun's north magnetic pole points through the Sun's southern hemisphere, and it will do so until the year 2012. FIGURE 11-28 illustrates the relationship between sunspots and the Sun's magnetic field.

What causes the Sun's field to flip every 11 years? Observations made with the *Yohkoh* and *SOHO* satellites show that giant loops of hot plasma, extending into the Sun's corona, link each of the Sun's magnetic poles to sunspots of opposite polarity (trailing sunspots) near the Sun's equator. As flows from the equatorial regions of the Sun to the magnetic poles transport opposite magnetic flux, the Sun's magnetic field steadily weakens. At the same time, the leading sunspots at both hemispheres migrate toward the equator, and when they meet, their opposite magnetic polarities cancel each other out. (Recall from Section 11-4 that helioseismology has allowed us to study the flows of differentially rotating magnetic bands inside the convection zone. Magnetic bands at high latitudes migrate toward the poles, and bands from low latitudes migrate toward the equator.) At the height of sunspot maximum, the magnetic poles change polarity and the Sun's magnetic field begins to grow in a new direction. During the flip, the field is very weak and uneven across the Sun's surface, which in turn becomes very active, shooting bubbles of hot gas and energy in every direction. At the time of sunspot minimum, the Sun's magnetic field resembles that of a bar magnet (just like Earth's) and is about 100 times stronger than Earth's (or about as strong as a refrigerator magnet).

Observations made by *SOHO* are helping us understand the stormy areas on the Sun's surface where sunspots appear (FIGURE 11-29). We mentioned before that the magnetic field is very concentrated in sunspot regions, but we know from experience, playing with magnets, that magnetic fields of similar polarity repel each other. The same should be happening in a sunspot region, and as a result, the sunspot should dissipate quickly. Instead, we observe sunspots that last for weeks. How is this

(a)   (b)

possible? We know that the strong magnetic field below a sunspot behaves like a "plug" that stops the normal upward convective flow from the hot solar interior. As a result, the material above the plug cools. This includes the observable sunspot region, and that is why it looks darker than its surroundings, but as this material cools, it becomes denser. According to the *SOHO* observations, this material then plunges downward at up to 5000 km/hour, drawing the surrounding plasma and magnetic field inward toward the center of the sunspot in the process. This increases the strength of the magnetic field, which in turn prevents more energy from reaching the solar surface. As the cooling material above the plug sinks, it draws more plasma and magnetic field inward, setting up a cycle that can last as long as the field is strong enough. As Figure 11-29 suggests, the region below the plug is hot, and this is just the opposite of the conditions at the surface. It also seems that the observed outflows at the surface are confined to a very narrow layer. The *SOHO* observations give us a better understanding of the overall structure of sunspots, but we still do not have a clear picture of the details, especially at the roots of the sunspots.

FIGURE 11-29 An artist's version of the region below a sunspot. Hot regions are shown in red, cool regions in dark blue.

Sunspots can occur in large groups that cover an area tens of times the diameter of the Earth. As shown in Figure 11-18, the observed structure of a sunspot includes a dark area where the magnetic fields are locally vertical surrounded by a lighter area where the fields are locally horizontal. The release of magnetic energy can cause violent solar eruptions such as solar flares and *coronal mass ejections*, which we study next. The main sources for such activity are large clusters of sunspots. With the help of helioseismology, astronomers were able to observe strong circulation patterns near the Sun's surface that play a role in holding the clusters together. Measuring such winds may prove to be a powerful tool in predicting solar flare activity.

Solar Flares and Coronal Mass Ejections

The turbulent magnetic field of the Sun is responsible for the prominences discussed earlier, giving prominences their unique shapes, such as those in the chapter-opening photograph and Figure 11-23. It also causes the colossal flareups called *solar flares* that normally occur during sunspot maxima. Lasting from a few minutes to a few hours and reaching up to 100,000 kilometers in length, a solar flare can release the equivalent energy of a few million of our largest nuclear weapons (FIGURE 11-30). According to the model presented in the last section, these flares occur when a great number of twisted tubes of magnetic field lines release their energy at once through

coronal mass ejection
An event in which hot coronal gas is suddenly ejected into space at speeds of hundreds of kilometers per second.

solar flare An explosion near or at the Sun's surface, seen as an increase in activity such as prominences.

FIGURE 11-30 (a) An X-ray image of a solar flare. (b) A powerful flare observed by the *SOHO* spacecraft on July 2002. The flare was associated with an Earth-directed full-coronal mass ejection.

FIGURE 11-31 A coronal mass ejection. This is one frame of an ejection in progress, observed in 1997 by *SOHO* using a coronagraph. This produces an artificial eclipse of the Sun by placing an "occulting disk" over the image of the Sun, allowing us to observe the Sun for long periods of time.

the photosphere. They occur near sunspots, usually along the dividing line between areas of oppositely directed magnetic fields. In just a few seconds, flares can heat solar material to tens of millions of degrees and accelerate solar particles to very high speeds. In the case of the largest flares, these particles can reach the Earth in less than an hour. They are responsible not only for spectacular auroras but also for disruptions of Earthly radio transmissions.

Radio disruption occurs when particularly energetic particles of the solar wind strike a layer of the Earth's atmosphere called the ionosphere. The ionosphere plays a part in radio transmission because it reflects radio waves back down to the Earth's surface. Normally, the Earth's magnetic field prevents particles of the solar wind from reaching the ionosphere by deflecting and trapping them, but the high-energy particles emitted by a solar flare are able to penetrate to, and disrupt the ionosphere. As a result, communication technologies using radio waves, including the Global Positioning System, can be seriously impacted.

Coronal mass ejections (FIGURE 11-31) are often associated with solar flares and prominences but can also occur in their absence. Such ejections and flares might be just different aspects of the same phenomenon. We know they are related, with some

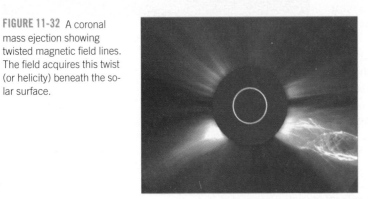

FIGURE 11-32 A coronal mass ejection showing twisted magnetic field lines. The field acquires this twist (or helicity) beneath the solar surface.

events showing more eruptive behavior, whereas others show more flare behavior. These mass ejections occur more frequently when the Sun is most active. They are huge bubbles of gas threaded with magnetic field lines that are ejected from the Sun over the course of several hours. The mass associated with these ejections can be in the billions of tons (more mass than Mt. Everest), and the speed of the charged particles can be up to 2000 km/s.

Beautiful twisted structures can be seen in coronal mass ejections (FIGURE 11-32). The twists in the magnetic field probably originate below the solar surface, and just like twisted coils of spring metal, these twisted structures contain energy that is used to blast the material into space.

We know that the active regions on the Sun's surface from which coronal mass ejections originate consist of a great number of loops filled with plasma. Such loops are shown in Figure 11-23b and in FIGURE 11-33a. The plasma that fills the coronal loops is not static. Instead, observations from the *TRACE* and *SOHO* satellites suggest that

FIGURE 11-33 (a) A *Yohkoh* image of a loop in soft X-rays. The width of the arrow's tip represents the size of the Earth. Such loops are about 50,000 kilometers in size and 450,000 kilometers long (equivalent to 40 Earths side by side). (b) A *SOHO* image of the loop in part (a) as it erupts into space.

(a)

(b)

FIGURE 11-34 A coronal mass ejection, an aurora across the United States as seen from space on July 14, 2000, and an aurora display in Alaska are shown in this composite image representing the three most visible elements of space weather.

the plasma moves in the loops at great speeds, probably because of uneven heating at their bases.

Coronal mass ejections disrupt the flow of the solar wind and produce disturbances that strike the Earth with sometimes catastrophic results (**FIGURE 11-34**). When the disturbances reach Earth, they can create a major disruption in the Earth's magnetic field, which can knock out communication satellites and cause power surges. One such power surge overload resulted in a collapse of Quebec's hydroelectric system, cutting off six million people for 9 hours in March, 1989. In 1997, a TV communication satellite was lost because of a coronal mass ejection.

Do solar flares and coronal mass ejections have other effects on the Earth and on the lives of those of us who live on this planet? As we learn more about the Sun, we may find that what seem like small quirks in the Sun's behavior are actually of major importance to life on Earth.

We mention just two possible connections. First, when high-speed protons from the Sun bombard the Earth's upper atmosphere they break up molecules of nitrogen gas and water vapor. The broken molecules form nitrogen and hydrogen oxides, which then react with ozone and reduce its amounts. Even though the overall effect of such a bombardment is minimal (on the order of 1% of the total ozone), it is important to understand and separate the natural effects on ozone from the human factor. Second, cycles of drought at the Yucatan peninsula and cycles of cooling and warming at other parts of the Earth, which can be tracked through radioactive carbon-14 dating, seem to be correlated with a known 206-year cycle in solar intensity. Small variations in the Sun's energy output, if sustained over a long period of time, could have catastrophic climate effects. The observations seem to suggest that some mechanism in our climate is amplifying these natural variations.

During the solar maximum that lasted from 2000 to 2003, solar storms knocked out power in the northern parts of Canada and Sweden and destroyed a satellite used to verify credit card payments at gas stations in the United States.

As we explained in the discussion of the formation of the solar system, the solar wind had a major function in determining the nature of today's solar system.

Conclusion

Like our ancestors, we recognize the importance of the Sun to life on Earth. We also try to understand the changes we observe and how these changes influence our planet. The Sun's luminosity varies on time scales from milliseconds to billions of years. We think that some of these variations affect our climate, but we do not yet know how. Similarly, the ultraviolet light and X-rays emitted by the Sun heat up our atmosphere. The solar wind emanating from the Sun affects the Earth's magnetic field, pumps energy into the radiation belts, and can cause power surges. As we become more dependent on satellites, we will increasingly feel the effects of space weather and the need to predict it.

To astronomers, the Sun takes on even more importance because it is by far the closest star. Because astronomers must understand stars if they are to understand the workings of the universe, the Sun becomes critical in such a study. Many physical processes occurring elsewhere in the universe can be examined in detail on the Sun. Solar astronomy teaches us much about stars, planetary systems, galaxies, and the universe itself.

STUDY GUIDE

RECALL QUESTIONS

1. The Sun's energy is generated by
   A. gravitational contraction.
   B. nuclear fission.
   C. hydrogen fusion.
   D. helium fusion.
   E. chemical reactions.

2. The layer of the Sun that is normally visible to us is the
   A. corona.
   B. chromosphere.
   C. photosphere.
   D. core.
   E. solar wind.

3. Sunspots are areas on the Sun that are
   A. hotter than their surroundings.
   B. cooler than their surroundings.
   C. brighter than their surroundings.
   D. [Both A and B above.]
   E. [Both B and C above.]

4. The energy produced in nuclear reactions in the Sun results from
   A. friction as the nuclei crash together.
   B. heat produced from the electrical effects of the reactions.
   C. the increase in mass of the particles due to the reactions.
   D. the decrease in mass of the particles due to the reactions.

5. Why is a high temperature needed for energy production in the core of the Sun?
   A. Hydrogen will not combine with oxygen at a low temperature.
   B. Energy is needed to overcome electrical repulsion.
   C. Electrons will not recombine at low temperatures.
   D. The force of gravity is greater at high temperatures.
   E. Speeds are less at high temperature, and thus, there is more time for reactions between nuclei.

6. We know that the Sun's energy does not result from a chemical burning process because
   A. of the Doppler effect.
   B. of the redshift.
   C. the Sun would have burned up already.
   D. [Both B and C above.]
   E. [Both A and B above.]

7. The two forces producing hydrostatic equilibrium in the Sun to determine its size are
   A. electrical forces and gravity.
   B. nuclear forces and gravity.
   C. electrical forces and gas pressure.
   D. electrical forces and nuclear forces.
   E. gravity and gas pressure.

8. As the Sun "burns,"
   A. its total mass decreases very slightly.
   B. its total mass increases very slightly.
   C. its energy decreases, but the Sun's mass remains the same.
   D. energy is produced, but the Sun's mass remains the same.
   E. [None of the above.]

9. During a total solar eclipse, the Sun's atmosphere becomes visible. Why?
   A. It is brighter during an eclipse because of light reflected from the Moon.
   B. The light reemitted after absorption becomes visible because the brighter Sun is blocked out.
   C. The atmosphere becomes hotter during an eclipse.
   D. [The statement is not true.]

10. The total luminosity of the Sun can be calculated from its
    A. rotation period and temperature.
    B. rotation period and diameter.
    C. diameter and distance from the Earth.
    D. diameter and the solar energy at Earth's distance.
    E. distance from Earth and the solar energy detected at Earth's distance.

11. Two factors that determine the pressure of a gas are
    A. the speed of the molecules and the particle density.
    B. the speed of the molecules and the gas' temperature.
    C. nuclear reactions in the gas and its temperature.
    D. chemical reactions in the gas and its temperature.
    E. [Both C and D above.]

12. At any particular level within the Sun, the pressure outward is
    A. less than the pressure inward.
    B. equal to the pressure inward.
    C. greater than the pressure inward.
    D. [No general statement can be made.]

13. Granulation of the photosphere is a direct result of
    A.   heat conduction.
    B.   convection.
    C.   heat radiation.

14. A prominence is
    A.   a cool spot on the Sun.
    B.   the ejection of material from the photosphere.
    C.   a fairly permanent bulge on the photosphere's surface.
    D.   a reaction within the Sun's core.

15. The solar wind extends
    A.   about to Mercury's orbit.
    B.   about to Venus' orbit.
    C.   almost to Earth's orbit.
    D.   far beyond the Earth's orbit.

16. The 11-year cycle of sunspots corresponds to
    A.   the period of change in the magnetic field of the Sun.
    B.   the rotation period of the Sun near the equator.
    C.   the rotation period of the Sun near the poles.
    D.   the revolution period of Jupiter.
    E.   [None of the above.]

17. Which of the following is the thinnest layer of the Sun?
    A.   corona.
    B.   chromosphere.
    C.   photosphere.
    D.   radiative layer.
    E.   convection layer.

18. Solar energy strikes the Earth at the rate of 1380 watts/m^2. It strikes a sphere that is 2 astronomical units from the Sun at a rate of
    A.   345 watts/meter^2.
    B.   690 watts/meter^2.
    C.   1380 watts/meter^2.
    D.   2760 watts/meter^2.
    E.   5520 watts/meter^2.

19. The primary source of energy for the Sun is a series of nuclear reactions in which
    A.   four hydrogen nuclei fuse to form a helium nucleus.
    B.   a helium nucleus fissions to form four hydrogen nuclei.
    C.   uranium nuclei fission to form several other elements.
    D.   two nuclei fuse to form uranium or plutonium.
    E.   oxygen nuclei combine to form more massive nuclei.

20. To begin nuclear fusion in a star, high temperatures are required to overcome the
    A.   nuclear force between the protons.
    B.   nuclear force between the electrons.
    C.   electrical force between the neutrons.
    D.   electrical force between the protons.

21. The photosphere is
    A.   the layer of the Sun where energy is created from mass.
    B.   the outermost layer of the Sun.
    C.   the layer of the Sun that we see when observing the Sun in visible light.
    D.   the layer of the Sun in which we see granulation.
    E.   [Both C and D above.]

22. When four hydrogen nuclei fuse to form a helium nucleus, the total mass at the end is _____ the total mass at the beginning.
    A.   less than
    B.   the same as
    C.   more than

23. The sun emits its most intense radiation in which region of the electromagnetic spectrum?
    A.   Radio.
    B.   Infrared.
    C.   Visible.
    D.   Ultraviolet.
    E.   X-ray.

24. Nuclear theory predicts that we should detect
    A.   fewer neutrinos than we do.
    B.   just the amount of neutrinos that we do, confirming the theory.
    C.   more neutrinos than we do.

25. What is meant when it is said the Sun has "differential" rotation?

26. Describe some evidence that shows that the source of solar energy cannot be chemical reactions.

27. Distinguish between chemical and nuclear reactions, giving an example of each.

28. What is it about the nucleus of an atom that distinguishes one atom from another?

29. Name the chemical element that is consumed and the element that is produced in the Sun. What produces the energy when the change occurs?

30. In what physical state is most of the material in the interior of the Sun?

31. Define and explain *hydrostatic equilibrium*.

32. How do we know how great the pressures are at certain depths below the surface of the Sun?

33. List the three methods of heat transfer, giving an example of each. What method(s) is important in which region(s) of the Sun?

34. If all electromagnetic radiation travels at the speed of light, why does radiated energy take so long to get from the center of the Sun to the surface?

35. Describe the thickness and temperature of the photosphere.

36. If the chromosphere and corona are so hot, why are they not brighter than the photosphere?

37. According to present theory, what causes sunspots?

1. Why do nuclear reactions occur only at the center of the Sun?

2. Explain, without using any math, how we measure the total energy output of the Sun.

3. What evidence do we have that the Sun's energy does not result from the burning of fossil fuels?

4. If the mass of the Sun decreases because of nuclear fusion, why don't we see the Sun decreasing in size?

5. Distinguish between force and pressure as defined in science, and give an example of units in which each can be expressed.

6. Describe the relationship among pressure, density of particles, and temperature in a gas.

7. What would happen to the Sun's core if the rate of fusion reactions decreased suddenly?

8. How do we know the pressure deep within the Sun?

9. What method of energy transport causes the handle of a poker to get warm when the business end of the poker rests in a fire?

10. We see the Sun not as it is now, but as it was 8 minutes ago. The energy we detect, however, began millions of years ago. Discuss the implications this has on what we mean by the word "now." How does this provide a possible explanation for the neutrino problem?

11. What was the solar neutrino problem, and why are astronomers so interested about solar neutrinos?

12. List and describe the layers of the Sun's atmosphere.

13. Historically, what has been the value of an eclipse in studying the Sun?

14. Until recently, the solar neutrino problem was an example of an unsolved problem concerning the Sun. Another such problem exists in explaining temperatures within the solar atmosphere. Explain the problem.

15. If the magnetic field of the Sun reverses every 22 years, what is meant when we refer to the "northern" hemisphere of the Sun?

1. Calculate the angular size of a 15,000-km sunspot as seen from Earth.

2. Verify that the average density of the Sun is about 1.4 times greater than that of water.

3. If 1 kg of coal is burned in 1 second, it will produce 2 million watts of power. How many kilograms would have to be burned each second to produce the Sun's energy output? If the Sun were made of coal, how much time would pass before it would burn out at its present rate of energy production? (In fact, oxygen would be needed for the burning—nearly three times more mass of oxygen than of coal—so only one fourth of the Sun's mass would be coal.)

4. Use Wien's law (see Section 4-4) to calculate the wavelength that corresponds to the peak of the Sun's blackbody curve. Use 5800 K as the temperature of the Sun's photosphere. What color does this wavelength correspond to? Why does the Sun appear yellow to our eyes?

5. The average power requirement for the United States is about 6×10^{12} watts. With our current technology we can collect solar power at the surface of the Earth of about 200 watts/meter². If we were to build one huge circular solar collector, what would its radius be in miles? (Hint: The area of a circle of radius R is πR^2.) Do you think this idea could lead to a solution for our energy needs?

1. Measuring the Diameter of the Sun

With simple equipment, you can measure the size of the Sun with a fair degree of accuracy. All you need is a sunny day, a piece of cardboard, a ruler, and the knowledge that the Sun is 150,000,000 kilometers from Earth. An activity in Chapter 1 discussed observing an eclipse by pinhole projection; we use pinhole projection here, also.

Punch a small hole (perhaps one eighth inch) in a piece of cardboard and hold the cardboard so that the Sun shines through the hole onto a surface behind it. (Refer to Figure 1-46.) You may have to adjust the size of the hole to get an image bright enough to see clearly, and you might use additional cardboard to shield your screen from reflected sunlight.

Making sure that the screen is perpendicular to a line from the pinhole, measure the diameter of the image of the Sun and the distance from the pinhole to the screen. Now, as shown in FIGURE 11-35, the following ratio applies:

$$\frac{\text{diameter of Sun}}{\text{distance to Sun}} = \frac{\text{diameter of image}}{\text{distance from screen to image}}$$

Use this equation to calculate the diameter of the Sun.

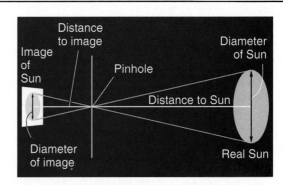

FIGURE 11-35 This drawing, obviously not to scale, illustrates the relationship between distances and sizes of the Sun and its image. Since the triangle at the left is similar to that at the right, the ratio of distance to size is the same for each.

To get a feel for the accuracy of your measurement, make several measurements with the screen at different distances. How closely do your various measurements agree? What is the largest source of error in this procedure? How does the value you obtained compare to that found in the Data Page?

2. Observing Sunspots

Sunspots were first observed by the naked eye, as described in the text, but such a method is not recommended. You would probably have to search the setting Sun for long periods of time over many years before you saw your first sunspot, and staring even at the setting Sun might damage your eyesight.

A more realistic way to view sunspots is with a telescope. **Do not, however, look directly at the Sun with a telescope.** You can obtain a solar filter to put over the front of the telescope but it is even better to use the telescope to project an image of the Sun on a screen, as described later here.

First, a caution: the intensity of sunlight is so great that you run a risk of damaging your telescope. One way to decrease this risk is to cover the objective lens with a piece of cardboard with a hole cut in it smaller than the lens. Tape it down so that it won't fall off and it will block out some of the light. If your telescope has a finderscope, you should cover it by taping a piece of cardboard (without a hole) over its objective lens. This will not only prevent eye damage to

someone who, out of habit, looks through it, but it will prevent the Sun from burning out the finderscope's crosshairs.

In using a telescope to view the Sun, set it up by first focusing on a distant object (**NOT THE SUN**). Then pull the eyepiece out just slightly. Now is the time to cover the finderscope and partially cover the objective. Point the telescope exactly at the Sun. This is not as easy as it sounds, and the best way is to move it until the shadow of the telescope tube is smallest. **DON'T LOOK THROUGH THE FINDERSCOPE.** When this is done, you should be able to see a spot on a screen held behind the eyepiece. Focus by moving the screen and eyepiece to various positions until you get the view you want. A cardboard shield around the telescope will shadow your image from direct rays and improve your view. If you have a star diagonal (which reflects the image off to the side), use it. Trace the image of the Sun and any spots you see. Then repeat your observation in a day or two and look for motion of the sunspots.

Figure 1-45 (in Activity 6 in Chapter 1) shows a small telescope being used to project the Sun's image during an eclipse.

Have fun, but be careful.

You can find information about current missions to study our Sun at NASA's homepage (http://www.nasa.gov). The "ultimate" page on neutrinos can be found at http://cupp .oulu.fi/neutrino//. An annotated bibliography for nuclear fission can be found at http://alsos.wlu.edu.

1. "How Stars Shine," by J. Trefil, in *Astronomy* (January, 1998).

2. "Where Are the Solar Neutrinos?" by J. Bahcall, in *Astronomy* (March, 1990).

3. "*SOHO* Reveals the Secrets of the Sun," by K. Lang, in *Scientific American* (March, 1997).

4. "The Sun-Climate Connection," by S. Baliunas and W. Soon, in *Sky & Telescope* (December, 1996).

5. "On the Solar Spectrum and the Color Sensitivity of the Eye," by D. K. Lynch and B. H. Soffer, in *American Journal of Physics* (vol. 67, No. 11, November 1999).

6. "Solving the Solar Neutrino Problem," by A. B. McDonald, J. R. Klein, and D. L. Wark, in *Scientific American* (April 2003).

7. "The Paradox of the Sun's Hot Corona," by B. N. Dwivedi and K. J. H. Phillips, in *Scientific American* Special Edition (September 2003).

8. "The Fury of Solar Storms," by J. L. Burch, in *Scientific American* Special Edition (September 2004).

9. "The Stellar Dynamo," by E. Nesme-Ribes, S. L. Baliunas, and D. Sokoloff, in *Scientific American* Special Edition (September 2004).

10. "The Mysterious Origins of Solar Storms," by G. D. Holman, in *Scientific American* (April 2006).

Quest Ahead to Starlinks
http://physicalscience.jbpub.com/starlinks

Starlinks is this book's online learning center. It features **eLearning**, which contains chapter quizzes and other tools designed to help you study for your class. You can also find **online exercises**, view numerous relevant **animations**, follow a guide to **useful astronomy sites** on the Internet, or even check the latest **astronomy news** updates.

12 Measuring the Properties of Stars

Mauna Kea Observatories, Mauna Kea, Hawaii. The summit (4200 meters high) houses the world's largest observatory for optical, infrared, and submillimeter astronomy.

*Sidney C. Wolff, National Optical Astronomy Observatories.

ASTRONOMER SIDNEY WOLFF AND HER HUSBAND WERE INVOLVED in the building of the observatory on Mauna Kea, a 14,000-foot high mountain in the Hawaiian Islands, in the late 1960s. In an essay in *The Scientist*, she writes:

> We had a wonderful time in those early days, developing a site without even such basic amenities as a source of water; a site where all power had to be generated locally because there was no power line, a site where blizzards raged in winter and where even in summer temperatures dipped to freezing every night. But we learned. We learned about altitude sickness and the best strategies for forcing our bodies to acclimate. We learned first aid so we could cope with accidents, since professional help was hours away. We learned how to handle heavy machinery and how to maintain generators. We learned more about telescope gears and worm drives and how to repair scored gears than we ever wanted to know. Nearly every one of us who was involved in those early days can tell—loves to tell—stories of being nearly trapped on the mountain during a blizzard, of hiking to the summit because the road was blocked by snow, of climbing to the top of the dome to remove snow so that not a moment of observing was lost. It was a great adventure, an adventure that surely I had not envisioned when I planned a life of research alone in my office.*

All cross references to chapters, sections, figures, and tables pertain to the main text, *In Quest of the Universe, Sixth Edition. In Quest of the Solar System* contains Chapters 1–11 and 19 of the main text. *In Quest of the Stars and Galaxies* contains Chapters 1–5 and 11–19 of the main text.

338

Only recently in human history have we even become aware of the astonishing fact that each of the thousands of stars we see is another sun similar to the one that rules our sky. This realization makes obvious the immense distances to those stars; just imagine how far away our Sun would have to be to appear as dim as one of these stars. Can we hope to learn much about such faraway objects? As we explained in Chapter 4, spectral analysis can be used to determine both the temperature of a star and the chemical composition of its atmosphere. Galileo and Newton would have been amazed that we can learn such things; however, temperatures and chemical compositions are only the beginning. In this chapter we discuss how parallax allows us to calculate the distances to many stars and how, after we know their distances, we can determine other properties, including their luminosities, motions, sizes, and masses. We describe relationships among the various properties that give us clues as to why one star differs from another, how stars are formed, how their lives progress, and how they die. We delay discussion of the life cycle of stars until the next chapter, turning our attention now to how we measure those properties of stars that divulge information about their life cycles.

The stars, while differing the one from the other in the kinds of matter of which they consists, are all constructed upon the same plan as our sun, and are composed of matter identical at least in part with the materials of our system.
William Huggins, 1863

Ye Stars! Which are the poetry of heaven.
Lord Byron (1788–1824)

12-1   Stellar Luminosity

When we speak of the brightness of a star, we must be careful to distinguish between its apparent brightness (**FIGURE 12-1**) and its **luminosity**. In Section 11-2 we explained how we can calculate the luminosity of the Sun if we know the Sun's distance and the amount of solar radiation striking a given area of Earth in a certain amount of time. Suppose two stars differ in apparent brightness so that different amounts of light reach the Earth from the two stars. The cause for this might be any combination of three things: (1) one star may be inherently brighter than the other (its luminosity may be greater); (2) one star may be closer, making it appear brighter; or (3) there may be more interstellar material absorbing light from one star than from the other.

In our discussion of the two quantities, *brightness* refers to the apparent brightness seen from Earth, and *luminosity* refers to the total amount of power emitted by a star. You may occasionally find the term *absolute luminosity*; this simply emphasizes that we are speaking of the radiation actually being emitted, not the radiation reaching Earth.

luminosity The rate at which electromagnetic energy is emitted.

Apparent Magnitude

One of the greatest astronomers of antiquity was Hipparchus, a Greek thinker who lived in the second century BC. Hipparchus compiled a catalog of some 850 stars, listing each star's location in the sky, along with a number that designated its brightness. To indicate the brightnesses of stars, he divided all visible stars into six groups, calling the brightest stars in the heavens *magnitude one* stars and the dimmest he could see *magnitude six* stars. Other stars fell in between, with differences between magnitudes representing equal differences in

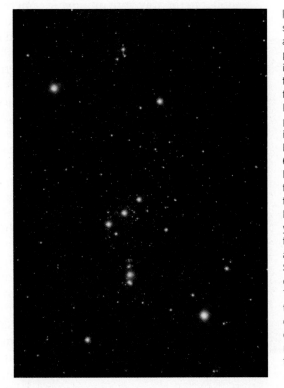

FIGURE 12-1   Some of the stars of the constellation Orion appear bright because of their proximity, whereas others are inherently so luminous that they look bright from Earth even though they are very far away. Betelgeuse, the star that appears orange at the upper left, is a variable star, about 430 light-years away, with radius 660 times that of the Sun and luminosity 4500–15,000 times that of the Sun. Rigel, the star that appears blue/white at the lower right, is about 730 light-years away, with radius 60 times that of the Sun and luminosity about 39,000 times that of the Sun. The stars appear to be different sizes in the photo. These differences are not due to the stars' actual sizes, but occur because brighter stars expose larger areas of the light-recording device. The scale of the image is 20° by 28°.

FIGURE 12-2   The basic idea of photometry is that the light from a star is focused onto a photocell, which measures the amount of light. Often a filter is used to allow only light of a certain wavelength range to enter. More modern methods use CCD technology rather than photocells.

Cassegrain telescope

The quantity described here is apparent magnitude rather than absolute magnitude, which refers to the luminosity of a star and is discussed later.

apparent magnitude A measure of the amount of light received from a celestial object.

Photometry and CCDs (charge-coupled devices) were discussed in Section 5-4.

Is our Sun the brightest star in the Milky Way galaxy?

brightness. The brightness difference between a third-magnitude star and a fourth-magnitude star on his scale thus was visually the same as that between a fifth- and a sixth-magnitude star. Although it may seem odd to assign the larger number to the dimmer star, we might appreciate his reasoning by thinking of the brighter star as a first-class star and the dimmest as a sixth-class star.

Today we use a slightly revised version of Hipparchus' *apparent magnitude* scale, for we measure the brightnesses of stars by photographic and electronic methods. Photographic techniques began to be used for such measurements in the mid-1800s. When these measurements were made, astronomers found that if two stars differ by one magnitude, we receive 2.5 times as much light from the brighter star as from the dimmer one. For example, a fifth-magnitude star is about 2.5 times brighter than a sixth-magnitude star. Moving up from fifth to fourth magnitude means that the brightness increases another 2.5 times, making a fourth-magnitude star 6.25 times brighter than a sixth-magnitude star ($2.5 \times 2.5 = 6.25$). A magnitude change of five would mean a change in brightness of 2.5 raised to the fifth power, 2.5^5, or about 100. Astronomers recreated the scale accordingly, *defining* a difference of five magnitudes as corresponding to a factor of exactly 100 in the light reaching us. This means that stars differing in apparent magnitude by one unit have a brightness ratio equal to the fifth root of 100, or 2.512.

Before electronic devices became common, astronomers measured light intensity from a star (photometry) by measuring the size and density of its image on a photograph (Figure 12-1). During the last few decades, the process used in photometry is similar to the way your automatic camera determines the brightness of the subject you are photographing. FIGURE 12-2 illustrates the idea. Today, however, video imaging is becoming common, and CCDs are used to detect and measure light intensity.

Although the eye is able to distinguish only a few different classes of stars (Hipparchus distinguished six), photometric methods allow us to discern the difference in brightness between two stars that may appear identical to the eye. The ability to measure magnitudes accurately has changed Hipparchus' unit-step system into a continuous one so that the magnitudes of stars are now measured to fractional values, to an accuracy of 0.001 magnitude or better.

When the magnitude scale is defined as described, we find that some stars in Hipparchus' first-magnitude group are much brighter than others in that group. If a star were 2.5 times brighter than first magnitude, it would have to be assigned a magnitude of zero. A star 2.5 times brighter than this would have a magnitude of −1, a negative number. Sirius, the brightest star in the night sky, is about 10 times brighter than the average first-magnitude star and has an apparent magnitude of −1.43. FIGURE 12-3 shows the approximate apparent magnitude of several objects, and Appendices E and F contain

FIGURE 12-3   Apparent magnitudes of some familiar objects.

Apparent magnitude scale:
- −25 — Sun
- −20
- −15   BRIGHT
- −10 — 100-watt bulb (at 100 feet) / Full Moon
- −5 — Venus (at brightest)
- 0 — Sirius / Saturn (at brightest)
- 5 — Naked-eye limit
- 10 — Binocular limit
- 15   DIM — Pluto
- 20 — Large telescope (visual limit)
- 25 — Large telescope (photographic limit)

TABLE 12-1

Magnitude Difference versus Ratio of Brightness

Magnitude Difference*	Ratio of Light Received	
1.0	2.5	
2.0	6.3	(2.5×2.5)
3.0	16	(2.5^3)
4.0	40	(2.5^4)
5.0	100	(2.5^5)
10.0	10,000	(2.5^{10})

* If the difference in magnitude between two stars is 3, we receive 16 times more light from one star than from the other.

tables of the brightest and nearest stars, respectively, including magnitude values. As shown in Appendix E, in addition to our Sun and Sirius, two other stars in our night sky (Canopus and Arcturus) have negative apparent magnitudes.

TABLE 12-1 shows the ratio of light received for a given difference in apparent magnitude. The following example shows how to use the chart.

EXAMPLE

The star W Pegasi is within the square of the constellation Pegasus (**FIGURE 12-4**). This star varies in brightness, getting as bright as eighth magnitude. Fomalhaut (the brightest star in the constellation Pisces Austrinus, just south of Aquarius) is a first-magnitude star. Which star appears brighter, and how many times more light do we receive from that star than from the other?

FIGURE 12-4　The great square of Pegasus is an obvious feature of the fall sky. The constellations Pegasus and Andromeda share one bright star, Alpheratz, shown as an eye of Andromeda.

SOLUTION　To answer the first question, remember that the star with the lesser magnitude is the one that appears brighter. Fomalhaut thus is the brighter star. The difference in magnitude provides the information needed to answer the second question. The difference is 7. Table 12-1 does not list a difference of 7, but the values in the table can be used to determine the light ratio. A difference in magnitude 5 corresponds to a light ratio of 100, and a difference of 2 corresponds to a ratio of 6.3. A difference of 7 thus means that the ratio of light received is 100 × 6.3, or 630. We receive 630 times as much light from Fomalhaut as from W Pegasi (when the latter is at its brightest). [The magnitudes of Fomalhaut and W Pegasi are 1.17 and 7.9, respectively. For simplicity, we have rounded them off.]

TRY ONE YOURSELF

Barnard's star has an apparent magnitude of about 10. Suppose that on some particular night Mars is measured to have an apparent magnitude of 2. How many times more light do we receive from Mars than from Barnard's star?

As indicated in the example, telescopes allow us to see stars that are much dimmer than sixth magnitude. A telescope with a diameter of 12 cm (about 5 inches) might permit one to see, under perfect conditions, stars of about 13th magnitude. With a 5-meter telescope, one can photograph stars as dim as 25th magnitude.

It is valuable to know the brightnesses—the apparent magnitudes—of stars, but this is not a quantity that is inherent in the stars. Instead, it partially depends on their distances from Earth and therefore on the position of the Earth in the Galaxy. We would like to know the *absolute luminosity* of each star, for this would tell us something about the star itself, independent of the Earth's location. To do this, however, we must know the distance to the star.

> **parallax angle**　Half the maximum angle that a star appears to be displaced because of the Earth's motion around the Sun.

12-2　Measuring Distances to Stars

Recall from the earlier discussion of the heliocentric/geocentric debate (see Section 2-3) that the *absence* of observable stellar parallax was an argument against the heliocentric system. Copernicus, however, held that it was not observed simply because the stars are too far away. Not until 1838 was stellar parallax first observed, for the maximum angular displacement of the nearest star is only 1.52 arcseconds. Although the angle between lines from opposite sides of the Earth's orbit toward the star is 1.52 arcseconds, astronomers define the ***parallax angle*** as half of that, or 0.76 arcsecond in this case. (Parallax angle is defined in this way so that there is a straightforward application of the properties of right triangles; see **FIGURE 12-5**.)

Of course, the observation of stellar parallax is now an argument in favor of the heliocentric system.

The formula used to determine the distance to a star by parallax can be written as

$$\text{distance to star (light-years)} = \frac{3.26 \text{ light-years}}{\text{parallax angle in arcseconds}}.$$

parsec The distance from the Sun to an object that has a parallax angle of 1 arcsecond.

Astronomers usually prefer to express parallax using a different distance unit, the *parsec*. With distance in parsecs, this equation simplifies to

$$\text{distance to star (parsecs)} = \frac{1}{\text{parallax angle in arcseconds}}.$$

In fact, this form of the distance equation *defines* the parsec: one parsec (abbreviated pc) is the distance from the Sun to a star that has a parallax angle of 1 arcsecond. The parsec is the unit astronomers normally use to express stellar distances. One parsec corresponds to about 3.26 light-years, or 206,265 astronomical units (AUs).

FIGURE 12-5 The nearest star has a displacement of about 1.5″. The parallax angle is defined as half of this, using one astronomical unit as the baseline. The drawing is far out of scale.

Only stars within about 120 parsecs (400 light-years) have parallax angles large enough (0.008 arcseconds) to permit accurate parallax measurements from Earth. In 1989 the European Space Agency launched *Hipparcos* (*HI*gh *P*recision *PAR*allax *CO*llecting *S*atellite), which measured the positions and parallaxes of some 120,000 stars to an accuracy of 0.001 arcseconds, and more than 2 million stars to an accuracy of 0.02–0.03 arcseconds, before its power failed. *Gaia*, the successor mission to *Hipparcos*, is named after the Greek Earth goddess, and will be launched in late 2011. Its mission is to give precise and detailed information about the billion brightest objects in the sky, thus giving us a large and precise three-dimensional map of the Milky Way. This map will allow astronomers to do an archaeological study of our Galaxy, uncovering its history and mysteries in the process. NASA is now planning *the Space Interferometry Mission* (*SIM*), scheduled for launch no earlier than 2016, which will be the first space mission with an optical interferometer as its primary instrument. *SIM* is designed to achieve an accuracy, over the whole sky, of 4 microarcseconds. This is 250 times better than the accuracy achieved by the *Hipparcos* mission. Such accuracy would revolutionize the field of astrometry—the precise measurement of the positions of stars—and allow *SIM* to probe nearby stars for Earth-sized planets.

0.001 arcseconds corresponds to the angular size of a golf ball viewed from across the Atlantic Ocean. *Hipparcos'* mirror was so smooth that if it were scaled to the size of the Atlantic Ocean, its surface bumps would be less than 4 inches high.

Having more accurate stellar distances will be very valuable to astronomers for two reasons: first, because knowledge of the distance to a celestial object is often the key to determining other properties of the object, such as its luminosity, and second, because it will help us determine the distance scale of the universe more accurately. In the next section, we explain how knowing the distance to a star allows us to calculate the star's luminosity. In a later section we explain why the accuracy of our measurements of distances to very remote objects often depends on accurate knowledge of the distances to nearby stars.

Note the similarity of Figure 12-6 to the discussion in Section 6-1 of the parallax formula and the small-angle formula. Also note that distance is a key quantity in all of these relationships.

Absolute Magnitude

In Section 11-2 we explained how we can calculate the luminosity of the Sun, using the distance from Earth to the Sun and the value of the solar power striking a square meter of the Earth. In a similar manner, we can calculate the luminosity of any light source if we know the distance to the light source and the brightness of the source. (The power striking a given area of Earth determines brightness.) We all make subconscious judgments similar to this when we look at a distant light at night—a street light, for example—and decide that the lamp is dim or bright. We subconsciously take into account how bright the light appears, as well as its distance from us, to decide (qualitatively) the wattage of the bulb. If we had the tools to measure brightness and distance quantitatively, we could calculate the lamp's power in watts.

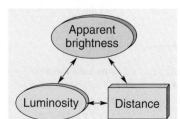

FIGURE 12-6 If any two of the three quantities are known, the other can be calculated.

FIGURE 12-6 emphasizes that if we know any two of the following three factors, we can calculate the third: apparent brightness (or, in astronomy, apparent magnitude),

TOOLS OF ASTRONOMY

Naming Stars

Most of the names of the constellations are Latin translations of the original Greek names. Most of the names of stars, however, are of Arabic origin. Ptolemy's *Almagest* (his summary of Greek astronomy, including a catalog of over 1000 stars) was preserved and passed on by Arab astronomers, who assigned names to numerous stars. The Arabic translation of the English article "the" is "al," which explains why so many names of stars begin with those letters—Alcor (in the constellation Ursa Major), Aldebaran (in Taurus), and Alpheratz (in Andromeda; Figure 12-4).

Only the brightest stars have popular names, however. Stars are assigned "official" names by several methods. The brightest stars in each constellation are given a Greek letter according to their brightness. Elnath, the second brightest star in Taurus, thus is β *Tauri*. The brightest star in Taurus is

Aldebaran, but because Aldebaran is part of a binary system (to be discussed later in the chapter), it is named α *Tauri A*, and its dimmer companion is α *Tauri B*. Dimmer stars are given English letters followed by their constellation names (for example, *W Pegasi*; Figure 12-4).

We soon run out of letters in the Greek and English alphabets, of course, and thus, most stars are known only by a catalog number. Although the brightest star in Taurus is named *Aldebaran* and α *Tauri*, it is also known as *87 Tau*. Less distinguished stars don't have popular names and don't have letter designations. One near Aldebaran just goes by the tag *75 Tau*. Only the International Astronomical Union has the authority to assign designations to celestial bodies and any surface features on them; thus, do not be fooled by companies that let you pick a name for a celestial object for a fee.

luminosity, and distance. The connection between these three quantities will be used several times in the remaining chapters. Brightness is most easily measured, and it is always one of the two known quantities. When the other known quantity is distance, we can calculate the luminosity; when the luminosity is known, we can calculate the distance. (Interstellar absorption of light does affect the observed brightness, but it is generally small enough that it can be ignored.)

The triple connection between brightness, distance, and luminosity allows astronomers to calculate the luminosity of some 1000 nearby stars; that many stars are close enough for us to determine their distance fairly accurately by parallax. If we want to know a star's luminosity in watts, we can use the procedure discussed for the Sun in Section 11-2. Usually, however, astronomers use another method to state the intrinsic luminosity of a star. The ***absolute magnitude*** of a star is defined as the apparent magnitude that the star would have if it were located 10 parsecs from the Earth. The absolute magnitude therefore becomes a way to compare a star's actual brightness; it is a very fundamental property of a star (FIGURE 12-7). A method of calculating the absolute magnitude of a star is illustrated in the next Tools of Astronomy box.

absolute magnitude The apparent magnitude a star would have if it were at a distance of 10 parsecs.

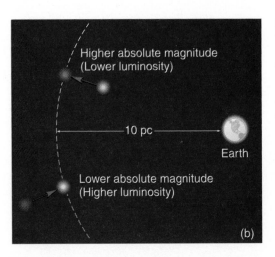

FIGURE 12-7   (a) As seen from Earth, one star may appear brighter than another star because it is closer, not because it is inherently brighter. (b) By calculating the magnitudes of stars at the same distance from Earth (10 parsecs), we can determine which stars have higher luminosity (lower absolute magnitude).

TOOLS OF ASTRONOMY

Calculating Absolute Magnitude

We can find the apparent magnitude of an object by simply observing it, but its absolute magnitude is not as easy to measure. After all, we cannot just move an object to a distance of 10 parsecs from Earth to observe it. Instead, we calculate the absolute magnitude. The relationship between an object's apparent magnitude (m), absolute magnitude (M), and distance (d, in parsecs) can be expressed as

$$m - M = 5 \times \log(d) - 5.$$

The difference ($m - M$) is called the ***distance modulus***.

To illustrate the use of this equation, let's calculate the absolute magnitude of Sirius. Sirius has an apparent magnitude of -1.43 and is 2.6 parsecs from Earth. We substitute

these values into the equation and solve for the absolute magnitude.

$$-1.43 - M = 5 \times \log(2.6) - 5$$
$$-1.43 - M = 5 \times 0.42 - 5$$
$$M = 1.47$$

What is the physical meaning of this equation? Let's use Sirius as an example. According to the inverse square law, if we "move" Sirius from its actual distance of 2.6 to 10 parsecs from us, it would appear $(2.6/10)^2$ or 1/15 times as bright. From Table 12-1 we see that this corresponds to a change in magnitude of about 2.9. Therefore, Sirius' magnitude at 10 parsecs would be about $(-1.43) + 2.9 = 1.47$, exactly the same value obtained previously.

12-3 Motions of Stars

You sometimes hear references to the "fixed stars." In fact, the stars are not fixed, but are moving relative to the Sun. This motion is obviously not visible to the naked eye, for the constellations have retained their shapes fairly well over the centuries; however, in 1718, Edmund Halley discovered that stars do move with respect to one another and therefore constellations do gradually change their shapes.

FIGURE 12-8 shows two photographs, taken 22 years apart, of a magnified portion of the sky. The arrows point to a particular star, Barnard's star, which has moved noticeably during that time. Barnard's star is the second closest star to the Sun and shows the greatest motion as observed from Earth. It moves at the rate of 10.3 arcseconds per year. Motion expressed as the angle through which a star moves each year (as seen from the Sun) is called the ***proper motion*** of the star. (You might speculate as to how a star could have improper motion, but the name comes from an old use of the word "proper" meaning "belonging to," for this is the motion that actually belongs to the star, as opposed to observed motion due to Earth's movement.) Only relatively nearby stars show proper motion and, thus, the background stars might still be called *fixed* stars, although they only appear to be fixed because their proper motion is too small to detect. FIGURE 12-9 shows how proper motion has changed the shape of the Big

> **proper motion** The angular velocity of a star as measured from the Sun.

FIGURE 12-8 (a) The arrow indicates a star named Barnard's star. (b) This photo, taken 22 years later, shows that Barnard's star has moved noticeably during that time. (The width of each photo is about 1 degree, and thus, the full Moon would cover about half the width of the photo.)

(a)

(b)

50,000 years ago   Today   50,000 years from now

FIGURE 12-9   The center drawing shows the Big Dipper as it is today; the arrows indicate the proper motions of its stars. From these motions, we can conclude that it once had the shape shown in the left drawing and will some day have the shape shown in the right one.

Dipper over the past 50,000 years and how its shape will continue to change in the future. We normally identify constellations by the stars that appear brightest, but because these stars are often the closest ones, they have the greatest proper motion. Constellations thus gradually change shape over the ages.

Proper motion does not tell us the actual velocity of a star in normal units of velocity, but we can calculate it by using the small-angle formula. (We used this formula to determine the Moon's size in Section 6-1. Instead of the width of the Moon, we calculate the distance the star moved.) Of course, one must know the distance to the star to make such a calculation (**FIGURE 12-10**). In doing the calculation, only the speed of the star *across* our line of sight—its *tangential velocity*—is being computed.

The velocity of a star toward or away from the Earth—its *radial velocity*—is easier to detect and measure than its tangential velocity. We discussed in Section 4-7 how this measurement is made and emphasized that the Doppler effect measures only the star's radial velocity.

A star's actual motion relative to the Sun—its **space velocity**—is a combination of its radial and tangential velocities. Because these two are at right angles to one another, we can use the Pythagorean theorem (**FIGURE 12-11**) to calculate the star's space velocity.

Naturally, the Earth's movement in its orbit affects the observed motions of stars and must be taken into account in calculating the velocity of a star. After this is done, we have the star's velocity relative to the Sun. We see later that there are methods for determining the Sun's movement relative to the distant, "fixed" stars. If this motion is taken into account, we can determine a star's velocity relative to the distant stars.

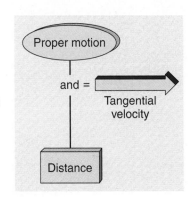

FIGURE 12-10   To calculate a star's tangential velocity, we must know both its proper motion and its distance.

space velocity The velocity of a star relative to the Sun.

FIGURE 12-11   Because radial velocity and tangential velocity are at right angles, we can use the Pythagorean theorem to add them.

EXAMPLE

Barnard's star has a proper motion of 10.3 arcseconds per year and is about 1.82 parsecs away. Using the Doppler effect, we measure the star's radial velocity to be −111 kilometers/second. (The minus sign indicates that the star is moving closer to us.) Calculate the space velocity of Barnard's star.

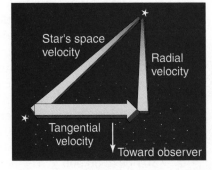

$$(Tangential\ velocity)^2 + (Radial\ velocity)^2 = (Space\ velocity)^2$$

SOLUTION   Using the small angle formula we find

$$\text{distance traveled across the sky per year} = \frac{10.3''/\text{yr}}{206,265} \times 1.82 \text{ pc}.$$

But 1 parsec is 206,265 AU, 1 AU is about 1.5×10^8 kilometers, and 1 year is about 3.15×10^7 seconds. Therefore, Barnard's tangential velocity is

$$\text{tangential velocity} = \frac{10.3''/\text{yr}}{206,265} \times 1.82 \text{ pc} \times 206,265 \frac{\text{AU}}{\text{pc}} \times \frac{1.5 \times 10^8 \text{ km/AU}}{3.15 \times 10^7 \text{ s/yr}} = 89 \text{ km/s}.$$

The star's space velocity is

$$\sqrt{89^2 + 111^2} = 142 \text{ km/s or about } 320,000 \text{ mi/h}.$$

12-4 Spectral Types

FIGURE 12-12 The colors of the stars are obvious in this photo of Orion. The photo was made from three exposures taken sequentially, so the stars are smeared in the image due to the Earth's rotation. Rigel is at lower right. The scale of the image is 19° by 21°.

Are all stars the same yellow-white color?

FIGURE 12-13 Annie J. Cannon (1863–1941), a member of the Harvard College Observatory for almost 50 years, was the founder of the spectral classification scheme in use today.

FIGURE 12-12 is a photo of Orion taken in an unusual way. During the 30-minute exposure, the camera was held steady, but its focus was changed in steps so that the stars became more and more out of focus as they drifted by toward the west (the right). This causes each star to form a fan-shaped image, and it reveals the colors of the stars. Most of the brightest stars appear as blue. The star that appears as red at upper left is Betelgeuse, and the red "star" at lower center is the Orion nebula.

As we explained in Section 4-4, the color of a star is determined by its temperature. In fact, the wavelength at which a star emits most of its energy provides an accurate way to measure the star's temperature. Refer back to the blackbody curve (intensity/wavelength graph) of the Sun in Figure 11-17, which shows that the Sun's energy output peaks near the center of the visible region and indicates a temperature of about 5800 K for the surface of the Sun.

Another method of analyzing the spectrum provides an independent measure of temperature. This method depends on the absorption of radiation at various wavelengths—the absorption spectrum. As we have seen, the absorption of certain wavelengths is what allows us to determine the chemical elements in a star's atmosphere; however, the absorption by an atom depends not only on what element it is but also on the state of its electrons (that is, whether some electrons have been moved to higher energy levels or stripped from the atom). In a gas at higher temperature, more atoms are at higher energy levels, and the transitions that occur from these atoms are different from the transitions that take place in atoms of a cool gas (whose atoms are at lower energy levels). This provides a method of determining temperature other than by the intensity/wavelength graph. The Tools of Astronomy box on page 349 explains this method in greater detail.

Annie Jump Cannon (FIGURE 12-13), an astronomer at Harvard College Observatory, devised a classification scheme for spectra and separated several hundred thousand stars according to the strength of the hydrogen lines in their spectra. The classes were first labeled alphabetically, with "A" having the strongest lines, then "B," and so forth. It was later understood, through the work of Cecelia Payne-Gaposchkin, that the classes represented stars of various temperatures. The classes were then rearranged in order of temperature, and some classes were dropped as redundant. The spectral classes used today are designated, from hottest to coolest, as O B A F G K M (FIGURE 12-14).

The hottest stars, the blue-violet O stars, range in temperature from about 30,000 to 60,000 K. The blue-white B stars have a temperature range of 10,000–30,000 K, whereas the white A stars range in temperature from 7500 to 10,000 K. The ranges for the yellow-white F stars, yellow G stars, and orange K stars are 6000–7500, 5000–6000, and 3500–5000 K, respectively. The coolest stars are the red M stars, with temperatures less than 3500 K.

Within each spectral class, stars are subdivided into 10 categories, called *spectral types*, and are indicated by attaching an integer from 0 to 9 to the original spectral class. For example, our Sun is listed as a G2 star. You need not be concerned about these subdivisions, but you should remember the classification scheme from hottest

FIGURE 12-14 The spectra of stars of various spectral types, from O to M, with their classes and subclasses shown at left. A few of the major absorption lines are identified at the top (1 nm = 10 Å).

to coolest as being O B A F G K M. The traditional mnemonic is "Oh, Be A Fine Guy/ Girl, Kiss Me," although you may want to devise your own memory aid.

The Hertzsprung-Russell Diagram

Suppose that an extraterrestrial being, unfamiliar with humans, somehow learned the age and height of each person in your neighborhood and then used these values to plot a graph, such as that shown in FIGURE 12-15. The first thing to notice in this graph is that a pattern exists: There is some relationship between height and age for humans. The graph also implies an important fact about the life cycle of humans, even though no one person had been analyzed through his or her entire life. The alien could logically hypothesize that an individual spends most of his or her life at about the same height, that height being the tallest achieved by the person. In our study of stars, we have a similar chart, called the *Hertzsprung-Russell diagram*.

Early in this century, Ejnar Hertzsprung, a Danish astronomer, and Henry Norris Russell, an American astronomer at Princeton University, independently developed the diagram now named for them and often called simply the H-R diagram. The diagram shows that a pattern exists when stars are plotted by two properties: their temperature (or spectral type) and their absolute magnitude (or luminosity). FIGURE 12-16 is similar to the diagram Russell plotted in 1913. The stars are not evenly distributed over the entire chart, but seem to group along a diagonal line. If we include many more stars than those on Russell's first diagram, we obtain a plot as shown in FIGURE 12-17. (Notice the Sun's position on the diagram.)

> **Hertzsprung-Russell (H-R) diagram** A plot of absolute magnitude (or luminosity) versus temperature (or spectral type) for stars.

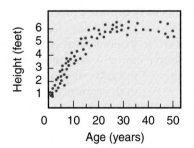

FIGURE 12-15 A plot of age versus height of people in a neighborhood might look like this. Each dot represents one person.

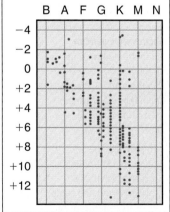

FIGURE 12-16 This graph is similar to the first H-R diagram, plotted by Henry Norris Russell in 1913. He plotted absolute magnitude versus spectral type and saw an obvious pattern in the distribution of stars. Notice that his category labeled N contained no stars.

FIGURE 12-17 A modern H-R diagram shows that stars fall into various categories, including main sequence stars, white dwarfs, giants, and supergiants. The temperature increases as you move to the left on the diagram. The purple lines show how we can calculate the absolute magnitude of a main sequence star from the H-R diagram; the star in this case is an A0 star, with a temperature of 10,000 K.

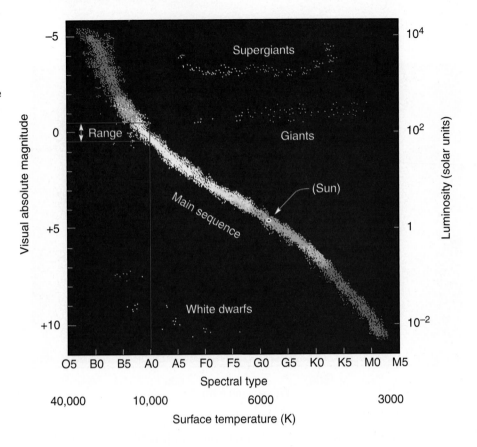

main sequence The part of the H-R diagram containing the great majority of stars; it forms a diagonal line across the diagram.

spectroscopic parallax The method of measuring the distance to a star by comparing its absolute magnitude with its apparent magnitude.

In practice, the temperature cannot be measured with absolute precision and some error thus is introduced in this manner also.

About 90% of all stars fall into a group whose properties are such that the plotted values form a band running diagonally across the H-R diagram. This band is called the *main sequence*. Other groups are named as shown in the diagram. The significance of the groups is discussed later in this chapter and in the next few chapters, along with the life cycle of stars.

Spectroscopic Parallax

As we have seen, the distances to the nearest stars can be measured using stellar parallax. The H-R diagram provides another method of measuring such distances, one that is not confined to neighboring stars. Although this method does not involve parallax, it is called *spectroscopic parallax*.

As we show later, it is possible to determine from the spectrum of a star whether that star is a main sequence star, a giant (or a supergiant), or a white dwarf. Suppose that we observe a particular star and determine that it is a main sequence star. As we have seen in our discussion of the blackbody curve and Wien's law in Section 4-4, it is a fairly routine procedure to ascertain the temperature of a star. Let's suppose that our star has a temperature of 10,000 K. The region of the main sequence where stars have such a temperature is marked on the H-R diagram of Figure 12-17. It is now a simple matter to determine that our chosen star has an absolute magnitude between about +0.5 and −0.5.

Recall the connection between absolute magnitude, apparent magnitude, and distance. If we know two of these, we can calculate the third. The use of the H-R diagram has allowed us to determine, within a small range, the absolute magnitude of the star. Because apparent magnitude is directly measurable, we can calculate the star's distance.

As indicated, we know the absolute magnitude only within a certain range, and therefore, our precision in determining distance is limited. Keep in mind, however, that this is *always* the case with a measurement. In using spectroscopic parallax, the source of the error is obvious, but as we have seen, the determination of distance by

TOOLS OF ASTRONOMY

Determining the Spectral Type of a Star

Before studying this Tools of Astronomy box, you may find it helpful to reread a related box in Chapter 4 entitled "The Balmer Series."

Hydrogen is the most common gas in the atmosphere of stars and, thus, it will serve as our example here. Each hydrogen atom has one electron in orbit around its nucleus. Suppose that the hydrogen gas near a star is cool enough that most of its electrons are in the ground state ($n = 1$ in FIGURE B12-1). When an atom with its electron in the ground state absorbs a photon, the photon's energy is such that the electron moves from the ground state to one of the other energy levels. These lines form the Lyman series, which is in the ultraviolet region of the spectrum; therefore, they do not

FIGURE B12-1 The energy levels of the hydrogen atom. If many atoms are in the $n = 2$ state, their absorption of photons will cause a dark line in the visible portion of the spectrum.

appear in the visible part of the spectrum and cannot be seen in Figure 12-14.

Now consider a hotter star, one with a significant number of atmospheric hydrogen atoms with electrons in the second energy level. For one of these atoms to absorb a photon, that photon must be of the right energy to move the electron from level 2 to higher levels. Figure B12-1 shows that the wavelengths of these photons are part of the Balmer series and are in the visible range. Look at the spectra of Figure 12-14. The hydrogen-α line is indicated at 656 nanometers, in the red part of the spectrum, far to the right of the other lines shown. The hydrogen-β line is at 486 nanometers, in the blue part of the spectrum. The other two Balmer lines shown in Figure B12-1 (hydrogen-γ, at 434 nanometers, and hydrogen-δ, at 410 nanometers) are in the violet part of the spectrum. The spectrum of the cool K5 star does not show a pronounced absorption line for the energy associated with hydrogen-β. The reason is that the star is not hot enough for many of its atmospheric hydrogen atoms to be in the level 2 state.

Look at the hydrogen-β absorption line in the hotter stars. As one moves to hotter and hotter stars, the absorption becomes more intense. In fact, the line is most pronounced in A-type stars. In the spectra of the hottest O- and B-type stars, the hydrogen-β absorption line is again less pronounced. The reason in this case is that in these very hot stars, most hydrogen atoms have so much energy that their electrons are at level 3 or the atoms are ionized. There thus are few electrons at the second level to absorb photons that correspond to the hydrogen-β absorption line.

Only one line of the Balmer series of hydrogen has been considered here. A complete analysis would require examining a number of lines of several different chemical elements. The spectral type of a star is determined by the relative intensities of these lines.

trigonometric (stellar) parallax is also limited in accuracy, both because of the difficulty in measuring the small angles involved and because other motions must be taken into account, such as the proper motion of the star being measured. All measurements contain error. The important thing in science is to recognize how great the likely error is.

Because of the limits in the accuracy of spectroscopic parallax, it is most useful when applied to groups of stars that are nearly the same distance from Earth. As we show in the next chapter, it is common for stars to be grouped with many other stars in large clusters. The stars of each cluster are very close to one another compared with their distance from Earth, and we use statistical methods to combine individual measurements of spectroscopic parallax to determine the distance to the cluster. The resulting value has much less error than the distance we calculate to any individual star.

Such averaging over a number of cases to improve accuracy is a valuable and common technique in science.

EXAMPLE

Spica, the brightest star in the constellation Virgo, is a B1-type main sequence star with a temperature of about 25,000 K. Its apparent magnitude is about 0.96. From these data, determine whether its distance from Earth is less than 10 parsecs, approximately 10 parsecs, greater than 10 parsecs, or much greater than 10 parsecs.

SOLUTION   Referring to Figure 12-17 and using the fact that Spica is a B1-type star, we determine that its absolute magnitude is between about −3 and −4.5 (although a safer range might be from −2.5 to −5.0).

Next, let's compare our absolute magnitude values with Spica's observed apparent magnitude. Spica's apparent magnitude is 0.96, and we can reason that because its apparent magnitude has a greater value than its absolute magnitude, Spica is farther than 10 parsecs away. (Remember that greater magnitude means a dimmer star and, thus, its apparent brightness is less than its brightness would be at 10 parsecs.) In fact, from the difference between +0.96 and −3 or −4, we can conclude that it would have to be moved fairly far to bring it as close as 10 parsecs. How far? The difference corresponds to about 4 to 5 magnitudes. According to Table 12-1, this means that we receive 40 to 100 times less light than if the star were at a distance of 10 parsecs. Using the inverse square law, we find that the star is about 6 to 10 times farther than 10 parsecs, or between 60 and 100 parsecs from us.

Actually, Spica is about 80 parsecs, or 260 light-years, from us. Its absolute magnitude is about −3.6.

TRY ONE YOURSELF
The star 40 Eridani is a main sequence star of spectral type K1, which means that its temperature is 4500 K. Its apparent magnitude is +4.4. (Actually, this is the magnitude of the brightest star of a triple-star system. In the example above, Spica is a binary system. Multiple star systems are discussed later.) What can you conclude about the distance to 40 Eridani?

Maury worked at Harvard College Observatory with Annie Jump Cannon and Henrietta Leavitt, who are discussed elsewhere in this chapter. Maury learned astronomy as a student of Maria Mitchell (see Chapter 10).

Do not confuse *luminosity class* with *spectral type* discussed earlier.

luminosity class One of several groups into which stars can be classified according to characteristics of their spectra.

Luminosity Classes

Recall from Chapter 4 that a solid object emits a continuous spectrum because its atoms interact with one another and thereby distort their energy levels. This smears what would be separate, discrete wavelengths into a continuous range of wavelengths. Recall also that an absorption spectrum is produced when light passes through a star's atmosphere. In the 1880s, Antonia Maury discovered that absorption lines are also subject to a smearing effect and that, in general, they are not fine lines. This discovery has become very valuable in classifying stars.

The atmosphere of a main sequence star is fairly dense, and therefore, its atoms collide frequently, distorting their energy levels; as a result, what would have been a thin absorption line turns into a broader line. Red giant stars have thinner atmospheres and, thus, the broadening does not occur to the extent seen in a main sequence star. Their spectral lines are narrower (**FIGURE 12-18**). Through the examination of the extent of line broadening, as well as other subtle differences in spectra, stars are classified into various *luminosity classes* that are located on the H-R diagram as shown in **FIGURE 12-19**.

The example of spectroscopic parallax in the preceding section involved only main sequence stars. The classification of stars into luminosity classes allows spectroscopic parallax to be used with any star. If we know a star's luminosity class and temperature, we can read its absolute magnitude (and thus luminosity) from the appropriate location on the H-R diagram.

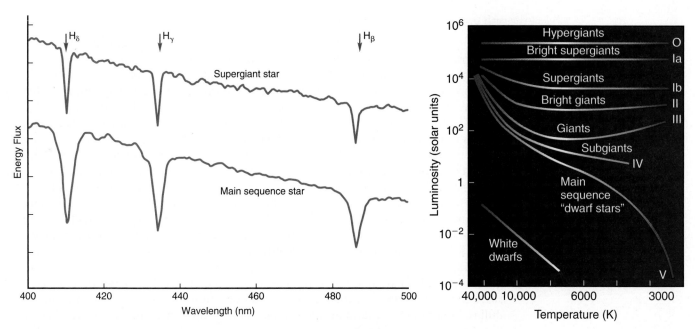

FIGURE 12-18   A comparison of the absorption spectrum of a 10,000 K supergiant star to that of a 10,000 K main sequence star. The denser atmosphere of the main sequence star results into broader hydrogen lines. The line strength and broadening depend on the number density of the atoms in the atmosphere.

FIGURE 12-19   Stars can be classified according to luminosity class, which is determined by analysis of their spectra.

Analyzing the Spectroscopic Parallax Procedure

Observe that in using the method of spectroscopic parallax to find a star's distance from us, we use two triple connections (FIGURE 12-20): By knowing the temperature of a star (that is, its spectral type) and its luminosity class, we can determine its absolute magnitude. Then, by knowing its absolute magnitude and its apparent magnitude, we can calculate its distance. This last triple connection is used in a different way than it was before. For nearby stars, distance and apparent magnitude were used to determine absolute magnitude.

Absolute magnitudes calculated for nearby stars enabled astronomers to draw the H-R diagram. Once the patterns of that diagram were known, they could be applied to stars that are too far away to permit distance measurement by parallax. We reasonably assume that these stars fit the same H-R diagram pattern as do nearby stars and, thus, we can then use the diagram to determine the absolute magnitudes of these faraway stars.

The basic procedure outlined here is often used in astronomy (and in other sciences). By observing familiar objects (nearby stars, in this case), we see patterns and formulate laws (or statements of relationships). We then assume that these patterns and laws hold for more distant objects of the same type. This allows us to use the same patterns to learn more about those distant objects. At times it appears that the whole system is a house of cards ready to fall down, but usually cross-checks are available; measurements can be taken in several ways, thereby permitting us to verify theories by independent measurements.

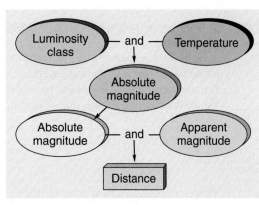

FIGURE 12-20   From the luminosity class and temperature of a star, its absolute magnitude can be determined. From this and its apparent magnitude, its distance can be determined.

Luminosity and the Sizes of Stars

white dwarf The burnt-out relic of a low-mass star. (Typical diameter is 0.01 that of the Sun—about the size of the Earth.)

Although the sizes of a few of the largest stars have now been directly detected by interferometry methods, in general a star is observed as only a point of light. How, then, can we determine the size of an object so distant that it appears to have no size?

Consider the group of stars in the lower left corner of the H-R diagram, the **white dwarfs**. These stars are hot, but their location in the lower part of the diagram indicates that they are intrinsically dim. One might think that a hot star would be bright, for this is not only the pattern seen in the main sequence, but it also follows from the intensity/wavelength graph: As an object becomes hotter, the wavelength at which the intensity of the emitted radiation is maximum becomes shorter, and the *total amount of radiation per unit area from the star increases*. How, then, can these stars be dim? The answer is that they are small. Being hot, each square meter of their surface emits more energy per second than a cooler star, but they simply have small total surface areas. (Recall our discussion of the blackbody curve and Stefan-Boltzmann law in Section 4-4.) The name *white dwarf* indicates their temperature (white-hot) and their size.

An everyday example might help here. You can adjust the burner of an electric stove to various temperatures. As the burner gets hotter, its color changes from dull red to orange-red (and perhaps to orange). At the same time, its overall brightness increases. Imagine, however, that you have a very small burner and you make it orange-hot. If it is small enough, it will emit less total radiation—it will be less bright—than a very large burner that is not as hot. The small, hot burner corresponds to a white dwarf in that its small size causes its overall luminosity to be less than average.

giant star A star of great luminosity and large size (10 to 100 times the Sun's diameter).

supergiant A star of very great luminosity and size (100 to more than 1000 times the Sun's diameter.)

On the other hand, consider the **giants** and **supergiants**. How do we know that these are large stars? Because they are very bright in spite of their low temperatures. The giants at the upper right corner of the H-R diagram are often called *red giants*, paralleling the name given the white dwarfs. (A single stove burner set to "warm" does not yield much light, but if enough of these relatively cool burners are lit, they provide quite a lot of red light.)

In these examples of white dwarfs, giants, and supergiants, qualitative reasoning was used to learn something about their sizes; however, determination of stellar sizes is not limited to these classes of stars; nor is it limited to qualitative methods. Knowing the temperature of an object, we know the amount of energy emitted each second per square meter of its surface (that is, the energy flux).

 The term "energy flux" is what we described in Section 4-4 as "energy emitted each second per square meter of area."

Then if we know the total energy emitted by the object each second (that is, the luminosity, by knowing the absolute magnitude), we can calculate the area of its surface and therefore its diameter. In other words,

Luminosity = area × energy flux ∝ radius² × temperature⁴.

A star may be very luminous and large in size but have a relatively low temperature, or it may be very luminous with an average size if it has a high temperature.

EXAMPLE

We observe the spectrum of a star and find its luminosity class and spectral type. In addition, using Wien's law and the star's spectrum, we find that it has a temperature twice that of the Sun. From the temperature and luminosity class of the star, we find, using the H-R diagram, its luminosity, which is about that of the Sun. What is the radius of this star?

SOLUTION   A star's luminosity (L) is related to its radius (R) and temperature (T):

$$L_{star} \propto R^2_{star} \times T^4_{star}.$$

This expression also holds true for the Sun:

$$L_{Sun} \propto R^2_{Sun} \times T^4_{Sun}.$$

FIGURE 12-21 (a) If a star's temperature and the total power emitted by it are known, the triple connection shown here can be used to calculate its radius. (b) This H-R diagram (the same as in Figure 12-17) includes information about the radii of stars.

In this example, we have $T_{star} = 2 \times T_{Sun}$. Also, $L_{star} = L_{Sun}$, which allows us to set the right-hand sides of the above two expressions equal to each other. We get

$$R^2_{star} \times (2 \times T_{Sun})^4 = R^2_{Sun} \times T^4_{Sun} \text{ or } R^2_{star} \times 16 = R^2_{Sun}.$$

Therefore, the radius of this star is 1/4 that of the Sun.

TRY ONE YOURSELF
Find the radius of a star if its luminosity is 10,000 times that of the Sun and its temperature is about 3870 K. (Hint: The star's temperature is about two thirds that of the Sun.)

FIGURE 12-21a illustrates the triple connection in the chain of reasoning. We find that stars on the main sequence range from about 0.1 times the Sun's diameter up to as much as 20 times the Sun's diameter. Nonmain sequence stars, however, differ in size even more: White dwarfs may be as small as 0.01 of the Sun's size and supergiants may be 100 times larger in diameter than the Sun. The H-R diagram in Figure 12-21b is similar to that of Figure 12-17, but it also includes information about the radii of stars, calculated by using the Stefan-Boltzmann law.

It is always desirable to have a second, separate method of measuring a quantity. This allows us not only to check our theories regarding the object being measured, but also to check our measurement techniques. Fortunately, there is a second method for measuring the sizes of stars, although only a few stars can be measured by this technique. To see how it works, some discussion of multiple star systems is necessary.

12-5 Multiple Star Systems

A few decades ago, astronomy books reported that about one fourth of the objects that appear to be single stars really contain two or more stars in a close grouping. Books published a decade ago reported this as about one third. A few years ago, it

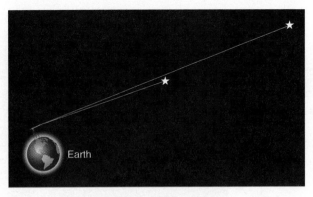

FIGURE 12-22 Two stars are said to form an optical double if they appear close together but have no actual relationship to one another.

optical double Two stars that have small angular separation as seen from Earth but are not gravitationally bound.

binary star system A system of two stars that are gravitationally bound so that they orbit one another.

visual binary An orbiting pair of stars that can be resolved (normally with a telescope) as two separate stars.

was considered to be about half. Now we can safely say that *more than half* of what appear as single stars are, in fact, multiple star systems. These systems must be distinguished from pairs of stars that appear close together as a result of being nearly in the same line of sight from Earth (FIGURE 12-22). These *optical doubles*, as they are called, are merely chance alignments of stars.

The stars in multiple star systems are gravitationally bound so that they revolve around one another. When two stars are gravitationally bound, they are said to be a *binary star system*.

FIGURE 12-23 illustrates how the two stars of a binary pair revolve about their common center of mass, in the same manner as discussed in Chapter 3 for a star and a planet. Although groups of more than two stars are common, our emphasis here will be on binary systems, as multiple star systems are simply combinations of, for example, a binary system and a single star or of two binary systems.

In 1802, William Herschel obtained the first observational evidence that some double stars orbit one another. (This was also the first direct evidence of gravitational force at work outside our solar system.) Herschel had taken an interest in double stars in hopes of using them for parallax measurements, but his discovery of binary star systems turned out to be much more important to astronomy, for it is by such systems that we are able to determine the mass of stars.

Binary systems are classified into several categories according to how they are detected. We discuss each category in turn and then explore what we can learn from binary stars.

Visual Binaries

A *visual binary* is a system in which the pair of stars can be resolved as two individual stars in a telescope. Using the largest telescopes, perhaps 10% of the stars in the sky are visual binaries. In a small telescope, only a small fraction of these can be resolved, but some are beautiful sights, particularly when the two stars are very different in color. FIGURE 12-24a is a photograph of Albireo, a visual binary in Cygnus, taken by an amateur astronomer. If you have access to a telescope, find Albireo during a clear summer night.

If two stars appear close together in the sky, how can astronomers tell if they are a binary system? The best way is simply to observe the pair over a period of time and look for signs of revolution. FIGURE 12-25 shows a binary (at the right in the photograph) that reveals obvious orbital motion over a number of years; however, things

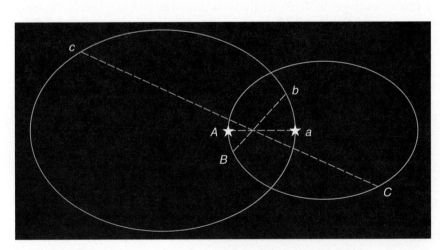

FIGURE 12-23 Binary stars orbit their common center of mass. When one star is at A, the other is at a, then B and b, and so forth. Can you tell which is the more massive star?

are not usually this easy, because in order for us to be able to resolve a binary pair, the stars must be either very close to Earth or very far apart. The Albireo pair, for example, is separated by some 4100 AU. As indicated by Kepler's laws, a great distance of separation indicates a long period of revolution, and the Albireo binary is thought to have a period of many thousands of years. Because no detectable orbital motion has occurred in the relatively short time over which we have photographic records, it is difficult to confirm that such a system is indeed a binary pair. We do know, however, that the two stars are about the same distance from us, and therefore we think that they are gravitationally bound.

A second method of determining whether a pair is indeed a binary system employs that powerful astronomical tool, the Doppler effect, which leads to the next type of binary system.

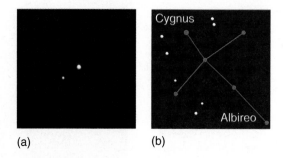

FIGURE 12-24 (a) Albireo is a binary pair that shows an obvious color difference between the two stars. (b) Albireo is the bottom star of the cross of Cygnus, about 386 light-years from Earth.

Spectroscopic Binaries

FIGURE 12-26 shows two spectra of the star κ (the Greek letter *kappa*) Arietis, taken at different times. The upper spectrum contains more lines than the lower. Look closely and you will see that this is the result of each line in the lower spectrum having broken into two lines in the upper spectrum. Continuing observations of this star reveal that the spectrum repeatedly goes through a cycle in which each line gradually breaks into two, which spread until they reach a maximum separation and then come together again. The explanation for this is that we are seeing not one, but two stars. They are revolving around one another so that the Doppler effect causes us to see separate spectral lines when one star is moving toward us and the other away. Such a binary system is called a *spectroscopic binary*.

The Doppler effect shows only the radial components of the stars' motion; that is, the motion toward or away from us. If a binary pair is oriented so that its plane of revolution is perpendicular to the line of sight from Earth, no Doppler shift is observed in its spectral lines. On the other hand, if the plane of revolution is tilted directly toward the Earth, the Doppler effect allows measurement of the stars' actual velocities during the part of their orbits when one is moving directly toward us and the other directly away (**FIGURE 12-27**). At any

FIGURE 12-25 The visual binary Kruger 60 can be seen during its 45-year period. In addition, its proper motion away from the star at the left can be seen.

spectroscopic binary An orbiting pair of stars that can be distinguished as two due to the changing Doppler shifts in their spectra.

FIGURE 12-26 Two spectra of the spectroscopic binary κ Arietis are shown here. Lines that are single in the bottom spectrum are split in the upper one. When single lines appear, the two stars are moving at right angles to the line of sight. When the lines are double, one star is moving toward us and the other is moving away. Compare this figure with the next one, and mentally note the stars' positions on their orbits to get single or double lines.

FIGURE 12-27   When the binary stars whose spectra are shown in Figure 12-26 are moving perpendicular to the line of sight, no Doppler shift is observed. The Doppler effect is seen only when the stars have a component of motion toward or away from us. The spectra shown in Figure 12-26 are snapshots corresponding to specific positions of the stars on their orbits. As the stars orbit their center of mass, the lines continually shift between these two snapshots.

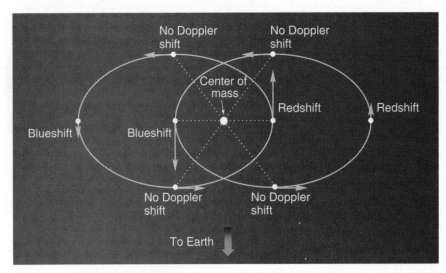

other position or any other orientation of the plane of revolution, we detect only the radial component of the stars' motions.

In the handle of the Big Dipper is a particularly interesting example of binary stars (FIGURE 12-28). As pointed out in Section 5-3, good eyesight reveals two stars at that location, the brighter one named Mizar and the dimmer one Alcor. Although it had been thought that Alcor and Mizar form an optical double rather than a gravitationally bound binary, more recent observations of their radial velocities indicate that they are orbiting one another. In any case, if you view Mizar and Alcor through a telescope, you will see that Mizar itself is two stars (Figure 5-10): Mizar A (the brighter of the two) and B are a widely separated visual binary and have a period of at least 3000 years.

In 1889, it was found that Mizar A is a spectroscopic binary with a period of only 104 days. When Mizar B was scrutinized, its spectral lines did not separate into two parts, but instead moved back and forth; first they redshifted and then blueshifted. Mizar B is indeed a binary star, but the spectrum of its companion is not bright enough to be observable. The shifting spectrum that is observed is the spectrum of the brighter star of the pair. We deduce the existence of the companion from that motion.

Mizar B is called a *single-line spectroscopic binary system* rather than a double-line system such as Alcor.

Finally, it has been found that Alcor is a spectroscopic binary. The dot in the handle of the Big Dipper thus in fact is six stars!

Eclipsing Binaries

light curve A graph of the numerical measure of the light received from a star versus time.

A special case of binary stars occurs when their plane of revolution is along a line from Earth so that one star moves in front of the other as they orbit. The star Algol, in the constellation Perseus, is a good example of an eclipsing binary. Its brightness changes periodically, and in 1783, John Goodricke, an amateur astronomer, explained the brightness change as being due to a dimmer companion passing in front of the brighter. FIGURE 12-29a shows a graph of the light received from Algol as time passes, called the system's *light curve*. Every 69 hours the apparent magnitude of Algol changes from 2.3 to 3.5. This happens when Algol A is partially eclipsed, as shown in Figure 12-29b. Midway between these dips in the light curve we see smaller dips, caused by the dimmer companion being eclipsed.

FIGURE 12-28   Even a small telescope reveals that Alcor and Mizar are three stars.

Since Goodricke's discovery that Algol is a binary star, its nature has been confirmed from

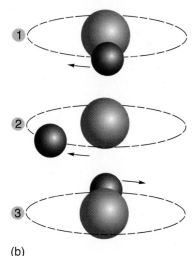

(a)   (b)

FIGURE 12-29 The light curve of Algol (a) is explained by the eclipsing of its components, one of which is much darker than the other. Positions 1, 2, and 3 in the light curve correspond to the numbers in part (b).

spectroscopic evidence. Like Mizar B, its companion is too dim to show its own spectrum, but the spectral lines of Algol A move back and forth in rhythm with its cycle of brightness changes. Like most eclipsing binaries, it can now be classified as both an eclipsing binary and a spectroscopic binary.

Other Binary Classifications

There are at least two other ways to detect binary stars. Sometimes a star is seen to shift back and forth in its position among the other stars, indicating that it is revolving around an unseen companion. Several such systems, known as *astrometric binaries*, have been found.

If one star of a binary system is much hotter than the other, their spectra differ enough from each other that it is possible to ascertain that the spectrum we see is not from a single star, but is a composite of two spectra. Such a system is called a *composite spectrum binary*. This provides another method of detecting binary stars, but nothing can be learned of the motions of the stars in such a system.

astrometric binary An orbiting pair of stars in which the motion of one of the stars reveals the presence of the other.

composite spectrum binary A binary star system with stars having spectra different enough to distinguish them from one another.

12-6 Stellar Masses and Sizes From Binary Star Data

Binary stars are interesting in themselves. For example, astronomers speculate on the stability of a planetary system around a star that is part of a binary system and on how conditions would be different on such planets because of the extra star; however, the major importance of binary stars is that they allow us to measure stellar masses. Recall from Section 7-2 that we can calculate the mass of a planet from the orbit of one of its moons and that likewise we can calculate the mass of the Sun from the orbits of the objects circling it. The calculation involves Kepler's third law as revised by Newton. Stellar masses of binary systems are calculated in the same way.

To do such a calculation, we must know two things about the orbit of one (or both) of the stars: the size of the ellipse (its semimajor axis) and the period of revolution. The period is easy to ascertain in all cases except when it is extremely long. Determining the size of the ellipse is a little more complicated.

Figure 12-23 shows the orbits of a visual binary pair as seen straight on. The center of mass of the two stars can be determined from the fact that it must always lie along a line connecting them. Each of the orbits is an ellipse, and the center of mass of the two stars is located at one of the focal points of each ellipse; however, this is not what we usually observe. The explanation for this is that we are not seeing the ellipses straight on. A circle, when viewed at an angle, yields an elliptical shape (**FIGURE 12-30**), and an ellipse

FIGURE 12-30 A circular shape, such as the basketball rim, appears elliptical when viewed at an angle.

FIGURE 12-31 This figure shows the apparent path (above) and the true path (below) of a binary star. Although both shapes are ellipses, if you turn your book, you can see that point *M* is at a focus of the lower ellipse.

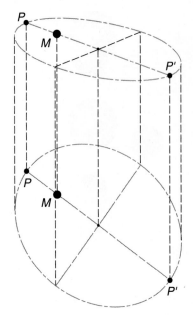

viewed at an angle also yields an ellipse, but one of a different shape than the original. The fact that the center of mass is not at one of the ellipses' foci can be used to determine how much the ellipses are tilted with respect to our line of sight (**FIGURE 12-31**).

After the true shape of the ellipse is determined, its size can be calculated using the small-angle formula. (We have to know the distance to the pair to do this calculation.) Knowledge of the size of one of the stars' ellipses, along with knowledge of the period of its motion, allows us to calculate the *total mass* of the two stars, using Kepler's third law. To determine how the mass is distributed between the two, we need only consider the ratio of the two stars' distances to the center of mass. This is analogous to the way that we can calculate the weight of each of the people on a seesaw if we know the total weight of the two people and know how far each is sitting from their center of mass if they are balanced (**FIGURE 12-32**). In Section 3-6 we worked out an example of a binary system in which we found the mass of each star by using this method.

In the case of a spectroscopic binary, if we are confident that the plane of the stars' revolution lies very close to our line of view, we can do a similar calculation. In this case, however, instead of calculating the size of the orbit with the small-angle formula, we calculate it from a knowledge of the maximum speed of the star in orbit and the period of the orbit. Because it is difficult to know the inclination of the orbit, we cannot calculate the masses; however, we can obtain valuable information about *average* masses of stars in a great number of spectroscopic systems by assuming an average inclination of the orbits. (Because any orbital inclination from 0° to 90° is equally likely, if enough systems are included in the analysis, the average inclination will be 45°.)

Eclipsing binaries that are also spectroscopic binaries provide us with a way of measuring not only the masses of the two stars but also their sizes. Because the fact that they eclipse one another means that the inclination of their orbit with our line of view is zero (or very nearly so), their Doppler shift tells us their velocities. Knowing their velocities and the time it takes to complete an eclipse, we can calculate the size and luminosity of each star. **FIGURE 12-33** shows a simplified case that illustrates this calculation. We can also determine the size of a star if we know its luminosity, distance, and apparent magnitude. Eclipsing binary systems give us an independent method of measuring star sizes.

FIGURE 12-32 Starting from the simple relationship $W_1 d_1 = W_2 d_2$, it can be shown that, if *W* is the total weight of the two people,

$$W_1 = \frac{W \times d_2}{d_1 + d_2}.$$

This same method allows us to determine the mass of each star in a binary system if we know the total mass and the distance of each star from the center of mass.

FIGURE 12-33 Suppose Doppler effect data tell us that the relative velocity of these two stars as they pass one another is 8.0×10^2 km/s (which is 6.9×10^7 km/day). Assume that in the leftmost drawing of the stars, the small one is moving to the right. At point B on the light curve, it began to be hidden by the large star. At point D it starts to emerge. From B to D is about 0.8 days, and thus, it took the small star this long to cross the large one. The diameter of the larger star must then be (0.8 days) × (6.9×10^7 km/day), or 5.8×10^7 km. In a similar manner, using the time period between points B and C, we can calculate the diameter of the smaller star.

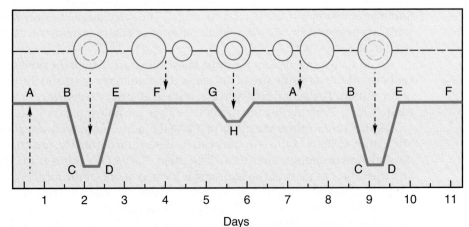

Days

12-7 The Mass-Luminosity Relationship

Suppose we plot a graph of the masses of several stars compared with their luminosities. FIGURE 12-34 shows such a graph, plotting mass in solar masses along the horizontal axis (*x*-axis) and luminosity in solar units along the vertical axis (*y*-axis). There is an obvious correspondence for main sequence stars: More massive stars are more luminous.

This ***mass-luminosity diagram*** was produced from knowledge of binary stars that are close enough to Earth to yield the necessary data; however, it is reasonable to assume that more distant stars also follow this pattern. (Otherwise, we would be claiming that we live in some special place in the universe where stars behave differently.) The graph of Figure 12-34 is empirical; that is, it is plotted from values that result directly from measurements, rather than from a theory of how mass and luminosity should be related. Because the points that represent main sequence stars lie along an approximately straight line, we can determine the mathematical equation for that line. The equation is found to be

$$L = M^{3.5} \text{ (for main sequence stars)},$$

where both L, the luminosity of a star on the main sequence, and M, the star's mass, are given in solar units.

We can use this equation to calculate the luminosity of a star that has three times the mass of the Sun:

$$L = M^{3.5} = 3^{3.5} = 3 \times 3 \times 3 \times \sqrt{3} = 46.8 .$$

This star's luminosity, thus, is about 47 times that of the Sun.

The mass-luminosity relationship is valuable to astronomers in investigating less accessible stars and in constructing and evaluating hypotheses concerning the life cycle of stars. This is discussed in the next chapter.

FIGURE 12-34   When the luminosities of stars are plotted against their masses, an obvious relationship is seen for most main sequence stars. The three at the bottom that do not fit here are white dwarfs. (The scale at the bottom is a logarithmic scale.)

mass-luminosity diagram
A plot of the mass versus the luminosity of a number of stars.

12-8 Cepheid Variables as Distance Indicators

Eclipsing binary stars are sometimes called eclipsing *variables*, as their light intensity varies over time. Other types of variable stars are also found in the heavens. One particular type is of importance to us here because it provides a method of measuring distances.

In 1784, John Goodricke (the same astronomer who explained Algol's variations) discovered that the star δ Cephei varies in luminosity in a regular way but that its variations cannot be explained by an eclipse of a binary companion. This star changes its apparent magnitude between 4.4 and 3.5 every 5.4 days, with a light curve as shown in FIGURE 12-35. Soon thereafter, other stars exhibiting this

Goodricke made his discovery when he was 19 years old, just 2 years before his untimely death.

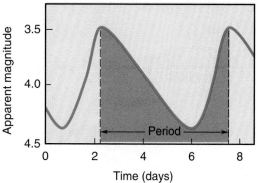

FIGURE 12-35   This is the light curve of δ Cephei, the prototype of a class of stars that have light curves with this shape and are therefore called Cepheid variables.

δ is the Greek letter "delta."

characteristic light curve—brightening quickly and then dimming more slowly—were seen. Doppler effect data show that such stars are actually pulsating—changing size—in rhythm with their changes in luminosity. It is fairly easy to identify this class of stars, now called *Cepheid variables*, or *Cepheids*.

Each Cepheid has a very constant period of variation; the periods range from about 1 day to about 3 months for different Cepheids. We discuss the reason for the pulsations of these stars in Section 14-6.

In 1908, a Harvard College astronomer, Henrietta S. Leavitt, published data on variable stars in the Small and Large Magellanic Clouds (FIGURE 12-36). She discovered that in the case of Cepheid variables, the brighter variables have the longer periods.

It may seem strange that period and *apparent* magnitude are related, for apparent magnitude is not a quantity intrinsic to the star; rather, it depends on our distance from it. The reason the relationship exists is that all of the stars of the Magellanic Clouds are about the same distance from us—at least, compared with the distance to the clouds. To see this, suppose that you are on a hill outside your town at night, observing the street lights of the town (each of which, we will assume, has the same absolute luminosity). The lights will *appear* to be many different brightnesses, depending on each light's distance from you. Now suppose that the hill is high enough so that you can use a small telescope to observe the lights of a town 200 miles away. You will find that the lights of this town all appear about equally bright, as each of them is 200 miles away, give or take only a few miles.

The stars of the Magellanic Clouds do not all have the same intrinsic (absolute) luminosity, but because they are all at about the same distance, their apparent magnitudes are related directly to their absolute magnitudes. For example, if the absolute magnitude of a certain star in the Large Magellanic Cloud is five magnitudes less than its apparent magnitude, the absolute magnitude of *each* star in the cloud will be five magnitudes less than its apparent magnitude.

Astronomers quickly realized the importance of the relationship between the magnitude and the period of Cepheids (FIGURE 12-37): The period (which is easy to determine) allows us to determine the absolute magnitude, and we can use this quantity along with apparent magnitude to determine the distance to the variable star (using the relationship between absolute magnitude, apparent magnitude, and distance that was explained in the Tools of Astronomy box on page 344). The problem was that only the *apparent* magnitudes of the Cepheids in the Magellanic Clouds were known. The absolute magnitudes of these stars could not be determined because the clouds are too far away for parallax to be observed. The apparent magnitudes of Cepheids in the clouds are around 15; they appear dim. However, it was obvious from Cepheid variables nearer the Earth that Cepheids, as a class, are very luminous stars. This provided qualitative evidence that the Magellanic Clouds are at a great distance from Earth.

All that was needed was to find one Cepheid variable near enough to the Earth that its distance could be measured by parallax, but there is none. Beginning in 1917, Harlow Shapley (to be discussed more fully when we study galaxies) worked out a complex statistical method to determine distance to Cepheids within our Galaxy. Using such methods, by the early 1950s, astronomers were confident that they had determined correct

Cepheid (pronounced SEF-e-id) **variable** One of a particular class of pulsating stars.

FIGURE 12-36 The Large Magellanic Cloud (LMC, on the right) and the Small Magellanic Cloud (SMC, on the left) are irregular galaxies, satellites to our Galaxy. They appear to the naked eye as hazy cloudlike patches in the sky of the Southern Hemisphere. They were first reported to Europeans by Magellan after his voyage around the world.

Polaris is a Cepheid variable with a small magnitude variation of between 1.9 and 2.1 and a period of 3.97 days.

FIGURE 12-37 The distance modulus of a star (the difference between its apparent and absolute magnitudes) gives us its distance in parsecs. Because the period of a Cepheid star gives us its absolute magnitude and because its apparent magnitude is easily measured, we can find the distance to the star.

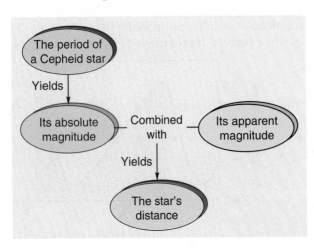

HISTORICAL NOTE

Henrietta Leavitt

Henrietta Swan Leavitt (**FIGURE B12-2**), one of seven children, was born on July 4, 1868. She graduated from Radcliffe College (then known as the Society for the Collegiate Instruction of Women) in 1892. In her senior year she took a course in astronomy, and after teaching and traveling for a few years, she joined the Harvard College Observatory in Cambridge, Massachusetts in 1895 as a student and volunteer research assistant. The quality of her work resulted in a permanent position on the staff in 1902. Soon she was named chief of the photographic photometry department.

Leavitt's primary work was with variable stars, and she discovered many of them. In 1908 she published a list of 1777 variable stars in the Magellanic Clouds; the list included a table of 16 Cepheid variables on which she had very precise data. Concerning these she inserted a comment: "It is worthy of notice that in Table VI the brighter variables

FIGURE B12-2   Henrietta Leavitt (1868–1921).

have the longer periods."[1] This brief comment went unnoticed by other astronomers. Later that year, because of ill health, she was forced to return to her family home in Wisconsin.

During her years of illness in Wisconsin, Leavitt continued her work (the observatory sent stellar photographs to her). When she returned to Cambridge in 1912, she published a report on 25 Cepheid variables. In it she stated, "A remarkable relation between the brightness of these variables and the length of their periods will be noticed."[2] She included a graph showing the relationship between period and brightness, but although she recognized the importance of the discovery, her duties at the observatory (and the nature of the work being done there) prevented her from following up on it.

Henrietta Leavitt was one of a group of some 40 women hired by Edward Pickering at the Harvard Observatory, starting in the 1880s, when it was unusual for women to work outside the home. Although women had made contributions to astronomy prior to this time, many still considered science an inappropriate field for them. Pickering was not really a progressive thinker in hiring the women; he did so because they would work for less money than men. Nonetheless, he was rewarded by the significant advances made by many members of the group, particularly Annie Jump Cannon, Antonia Maury, and Henrietta Leavitt.

Although her health was never good and her hearing was impaired from childhood, Leavitt worked at the Harvard Observatory until her death from cancer in 1921.

1. Henrietta Leavitt, "1777 Variables in the Magellanic Clouds," *Annals of the Harvard College Observatory* 60 (1908): 107.
2. Henrietta Leavitt, *Periods of 25 Variables in the Small Magellanic Cloud,* Harvard College Observatory Circular no. 173 (March 3, 1912).

distances to several Cepheids. This allowed them to plot a graph of period against *absolute* magnitude, as shown in **FIGURE 12-38**.

Brighter Cepheids have longer pulsation periods. One of the reasons that it took from 1917 to the early 1950s for astronomers to determine the correct relationship between Cepheids' periods and absolute magnitudes (the *period-luminosity relationship*) accurately is that there are actually two different types of Cepheid variables. Cepheid I stars are younger and richer in metals than Cepheid II stars. The two groups differ from each other in luminosity by about a factor of four, or 1.5 magnitudes, for the same period. We can now detect the difference between the two types, and the uncertainties surrounding the period-luminosity relationship have been greatly reduced with time.

To show how the period-luminosity chart can be used to determine distances, suppose that a Cepheid I variable has a period of 10 days and an apparent magnitude of 14. Figure 12-38 shows that a Cepheid I with a period of 10 days has an absolute magnitude of about 24. Now that both apparent and absolute magnitudes are known,

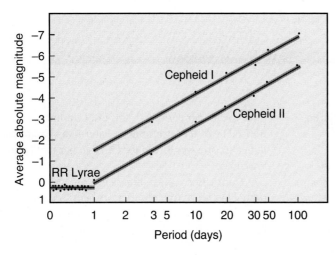

FIGURE 12-38 The period-luminosity diagram for Cepheid (and RR Lyrae) variables. Luminosity and absolute magnitude are intricately related because they are two different ways of representing the same quantity: the true energy output of a star.

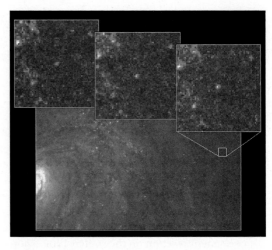

FIGURE 12-39 A Cepheid variable in the galaxy M100, seen by the *HST*. The measured period of 51.3 days indicates a distance from Earth of 56 million light-years.

we can calculate its distance. (Because the star's apparent magnitude is greater than its absolute magnitude by 18, you can see that the star must be extremely far away. In fact, using the distance modulus relationship on page 344, we find a distance of about 40,000 parsecs.) Use of Cepheid variables tells us that the Large and Small Magellanic Clouds are, in fact, 48,000 and 56,000 parsecs away, respectively.

In measuring magnitudes, however, uncertainties are introduced by the fact that the gas and dust in interstellar space absorbs and scatters starlight. These effects of the interstellar material on starlight have been well studied and can be corrected for; we examine them in Section 13-1.

A new way to accurately measure the distance to a Cepheid is based on the presence of echoes. When a Cepheid is embedded in a nebula, light from the star reaches us in two ways; first, directly from the star, and second, after reflecting from the dust of a part of the nebula. The luminosity of the star changes in a distinctive pattern (Figure 12-35). The reflected light from a blob in the nebula follows the exact same pattern but with a delay, because the star's light must first travel from the star to the nebula. This time delay, "light echo," when multiplied by the speed of light, gives us the distance between the star and the blob. Knowing this distance and the angular separation between the blob and the Cepheid we can find the distance to the star. This type of distance measurement is purely geometrical and does not depend on assumptions about the star's properties.

Figure 12-38 includes another type of variable stars, the RR Lyrae stars. They are also used to measure distances, but because they are less luminous than the Cepheid stars, they can only be seen to smaller distances. They have periods ranging from a few hours to one day, and their luminosity is approximately constant. (In Section 14-6, we examine the reason behind the variability of both Cepheid and RR Lyrae stars.)

Although astronomers have detected only a few thousand Cepheid variables, their importance greatly outweighs their number. Because they are among the very brightest of stars, we can see them not only in distant parts of our own Galaxy, but in other galaxies, giving us a method of measuring distances to these faraway worlds (**FIGURE 12-39**).

◆ Corresponding to normal metric usage, 1000 parsecs is one kiloparsec, abbreviated kpc, so the Large Magellanic Cloud is 48 kpc away.

◆ Using light echoes, astronomers measured the distance to RS Pup, a Cepheid in the constellation of Puppis, to be 6500 ± 90 light-years!

Conclusion

As we have shown in this chapter, once we know the distance to a star, many other properties become available to us. Knowing distance and proper motion, we can calculate a star's tangential velocity. The Doppler effect allows us to measure radial velocity, and from these two velocities, we can determine a star's actual motion relative to the Earth and to other stars. From distance and apparent magnitude, we can calculate a star's absolute magnitude. This knowledge can be combined with knowledge of the star's temperature to calculate its size.

On the other hand, the patterns in the H-R diagram allow us to determine a star's absolute magnitude without first knowing its distance so that we can use the distance versus absolute magnitude versus apparent magnitude relationship in reverse to determine stellar distances.

The discovery and analysis of binary stars have provided a second method of learning a star's size and also a method of measuring a very fundamental property of a star, its mass.

Finally, a particularly useful type of star, the Cepheid variable, provides a tool to measure even greater distances, opening up the entire field of galactic astronomy.

STUDY GUIDE

1. Suppose you observe a previously uninvestigated star and find its apparent magnitude. To determine its absolute magnitude, you need to know the star's
   A. distance.
   B. color.
   C. velocity.
   D. brightness as seen from Earth.
   E. Doppler shift.

2. The absolute magnitude of a star is
   A. the same as the apparent magnitude.
   B. equal to the greatest the apparent magnitude can be, in the case of a variable star.
   C. equal to the apparent magnitude if the star is 10 parsecs away.
   D. the size of a star from one side to the other.
   E. equal to the brightness of the star on the clearest night.

3. A magnitude change of 1 corresponds to a brightness change of about 2.5 times. A magnitude change of 2 corresponds to a brightness change of about
   A. 1.25 times.
   B. 2.5 times.
   C. 5 times.
   D. 6.3 times.
   E. 15.9 times.

For the next three questions, refer to the following table:

Star	Apparent Magnitude	Absolute Magnitude	Distance (parsecs)
Sirius	−1.5	—	2.7
Vega	0.0	0.5	—
Antares	0.9	−5.1	160.0
Fomalhaut	1.15	—	6.9

4. Which star appears dimmest to an observer on Earth?
   A. Sirius.
   B. Vega.
   C. Antares.
   D. Fomalhaut.
   E. [The answer cannot be determined from the information given.]

5. Which of the following is about the correct distance for Vega?
   A. 4.2 parsecs.
   B. 8.1 parsecs.
   C. 11.7 parsecs.
   D. 26.7 parsecs.
   E. [The answer cannot be determined from the information given.]

6. Fomalhaut's absolute magnitude is about
   A. 0.75.
   B. 2.
   C. 12.
   D. 22.
   E. 20.75.

7. Suppose that Star X is twice as far away as Star Y. The parallax angle of Star X is about
   A. half that of Star Y.
   B. the same as that of Star Y.
   C. twice that of Star Y.
   D. four times that of Star Y.
   E. [The answer cannot be determined from the information given.]

8. The distances to nearby stars can be measured by
   A. comparing the apparent magnitudes of several stars.
   B. bouncing radar pulses from their surfaces.
   C. measuring the time it takes light to get here from them.
   D. measuring their shifting motion against background stars through the year.
   E. [Both B and C above.]

9. Star S and Star K have the same tangential velocity, but Star S is closer to Earth. Which has the larger proper motion?
   A. Star S.
   B. Star K.
   C. They both have the same proper motion.
   D. [The answer cannot be determined from the information given.]

10. Star S and Star K have the same tangential velocity, but Star S is closer to Earth. Which has the larger radial velocity?
    A. Star S.
    B. Star K.
    C. They both have the same radial velocity.
    D. [The answer cannot be determined from the information given.]

11. If a star is 100 light-years away, what is its approximate distance in parsecs?
    A. 3000 parsecs.
    B. 900 parsecs.
    C. 30 parsecs.
    D. 9 parsecs.
    E. 1/3 parsec.

12. To use spectroscopic parallax, we must know
    A. the star's diameter.
    B. the star's temperature.
    C. the distance from the Earth to the Sun.
    D. the star's luminosity class.
    E. [Both B and D above.]

13. If the temperature of a star increases without a change in the star's size, its point on the H-R diagram moves
    A. up and to the left.
    B. up and to the right.
    C. down and to the left.
    D. down and to the right.

14. Stars on the main sequence that have a small mass are
    A. bright and hot.
    B. dim and hot.
    C. dim and cool.
    D. bright and cool.
    E. [Any of the above; there is no regular relationship.]

15. To observe spectroscopic binaries, we rely on
    A. knowing the composition of the individual stars.
    B. our knowledge of the distance separating the stars.
    C. our knowledge of the distances from Earth to the stars.
    D. the change in light intensity as the stars orbit.
    E. the Doppler effect.

16. The stars of binary star systems
    A. revolve around a point midway between their centers.
    B. revolve around a point somewhere between their centers (but not necessarily midway).
    C. revolve such that one star remains still, and the other revolves around it.
    D. do not revolve around each other.

17. Binary star systems are especially important to us because they allow us to calculate the _____ of stars.
    A. compositions
    B. proper motions

C. radial velocities
D. temperatures
E. masses

18. Which type of binary system provides the most information about its component stars' masses and sizes?
    A. Eclipsing binaries.
    B. Spectroscopic binaries.
    C. Visual binaries.
    D. Composite spectrum binaries.
    E. [All of the above about equally.]

19. We can determine the size of stars by
    A. measuring the size of their image in a telescope.
    B. a measurement using a spectroscope.
    C. calculations based on temperature and absolute magnitude.
    D. Doppler effect measurements.
    E. mass measurements.

20. Cepheid variables can be used to find distances because their
    A. luminosity is related to their period.
    B. radial velocity is related to their mass.
    C. distance is related to their mass.
    D. magnitude is related to their color.
    E. period is related to their radial velocity.

21. If the orbital plane of a certain binary star system is not parallel to our line of view, the maximum radial velocity of one of its stars measured by the Doppler effect will be
    A. less than its true velocity.
    B. greater than its true velocity.
    C. either greater or less than its true velocity, depending on other factors.

22. If a star has a parallax angle of 0.20 arcseconds, how far away is it?
    A. 0.20 parsec.
    B. 1.0 parsec.
    C. 2.0 parsecs.
    D. 5.0 parsecs.
    E. [The answer cannot be determined from the information given.]

23. When a star's spectrum is redshifted as a result of the Doppler effect, we know that the star is
    A. much cooler than average.
    B. slightly cooler than average.
    C. about average temperature.
    D. hotter than average.
    E. moving away from Earth.

24. Spectroscopic parallax allows us to measure
    A. the distances to stars using the Earth's orbital motion.
    B. the distances to stars using the Earth's rotational motion.
    C. the distances to stars using the H-R diagram.
    D. the temperatures of stars using their spectra.
    E. the radial speed of stars using their spectra.

25. Considering only stars on the main sequence, the most massive stars are the
    A. hottest and brightest.
    B. hottest and dimmest.
    C. coolest and brightest.
    D. coolest and dimmest.
    E. [No general statement can be made.]

26. To calculate (or judge) the velocity of an object moving in the sky, what quantities must we know?

27. Define and distinguish between radial velocity and tangential velocity.

28. Define and distinguish between apparent magnitude and absolute magnitude. To which is luminosity most closely related?

29. Describe the most direct method of measuring the distances to stars.

30. How is the radial velocity of a star measured?

31. What two quantities are plotted on an H-R diagram?

32. Sketch an H-R diagram, labeling the axes and showing the general location of the following: main sequence, red giants, supergiants, and white dwarfs.

33. Explain the method of spectroscopic parallax.

34. It would seem that a hot star should be a very luminous star. How can white dwarfs be dim stars?

35. Distinguish between optical doubles and binary stars. Why is one of these much more important to astronomers than the other?

36. Name and describe at least three methods of detecting binary stars.

37. Sometimes we can tell by the spectrum of a star that it is part of a binary system. Explain how this is done.

38. Describe the problem presented by the fact that the plane of revolution of a binary is unlikely to be parallel to our line of view.

39. Name two quantities that must be known to determine the absolute magnitude of a star (other than a Cepheid variable).

40. Explain how Cepheid variables are used to determine distances.

---

1. The apparent magnitude of the star Proxima Centauri (the closest nighttime star) is about 11, and the apparent magnitude of 61 Cygni B is about 6. Which star appears brighter? How many times more energy do we get from it than from the dimmer star?

2. Both "parsec" and "light-year" might sound—to non-astronomy students—to be units of time. Define each. Why do astronomers find "parsec" to be a useful unit?

3. The apparent magnitude of a star is fairly easy to determine. What else must be known to calculate absolute magnitude? Why is it important to know the absolute magnitude of a star?

4. Why do only nearby stars show measurable proper motion? In general, how does the tangential velocity of nearby stars compare to that of distant stars?

5. In Figure 12-25 (Kruger 60), the binary pair is getting farther from the single star. From this series of photographs it would be impossible to tell which has the proper motion. Still, the binary pair would be taken as the most likely candidate. Why?

6. Draw an H-R diagram, labeling the axes and including the names of at least three classes of stars.

7. It is possible for a binary star system to fall into two or more classifications (such as visual binary and eclipsing binary). Describe some situations in which this might be the case.

8. Explain why there is such a simple relationship between the apparent and absolute magnitudes of stars in the Magellanic Clouds.

9. Do you think that it is reasonable to use the H-R diagram, which is plotted from data on nearby stars, for stars much more distant from us? Why or why not?

10. In a group of stars that are gravitationally bound, we observe a red star and a blue star. Both seem to have the same radius. Which one will look brighter? Explain your answer.

11. A star's luminosity class plays an important role in determining its luminosity. What are we looking for in a star's spectrum to determine its luminosity class?

12. Why is spectroscopic parallax called "parallax" even though no angle measurement is involved?

13. Would a mass-luminosity diagram (Figure 12-34) show the same relationship if the scales were independent of the Sun instead of being multiples of the Sun's values?

14. We observe a binary system composed of two stars of the same radius and temperature. We observe their elliptical orbits edge on (so that we get full eclipses during each cycle). Sketch the light curve for this eclipsing binary. How would the light curve change if the two stars were of the same radius but one of them were blue and the other yellow?

15. Why was it important to find the distance to a Cepheid variable after Leavitt had plotted the data for Cepheids in the Magellanic Clouds?

---

1. What is the ratio of light received from stars that differ in magnitude by 15?

2. About how many times as much light reaches us from Antares, the brightest star in Scorpius (apparent magnitude +1.0), than from τ (the Greek letter "tau") Ceti (apparent magnitude +3.5)?

3. The star Ross 128 has a parallax angle of 0.30 arcseconds. How far away is it in parsecs? In light-years?

4. α (the Greek letter "alpha") Centauri is the nearest naked-eye star to the Sun. Its apparent magnitude is +0.01, and its distance is 1.35 parsecs. Is its absolute magnitude greater or less than 0?

5. Use data from the last question to calculate the parallax angle of α Centauri.

6. Altair, a star visible in the summer and fall, is on the main sequence, is spectral type A7 (8300 K), and has an apparent magnitude of +0.77. Is Altair closer than 10 parsecs, about 10 parsecs away, somewhat farther than 10 parsecs, or much farther than 10 parsecs?

7. Rigel, a bright supergiant, is a B8 Ia star with a temperature of about 10,300 K. Its apparent magnitude is +0.14. What can you conclude about its distance from us?

8. A certain main sequence star has a mass four times greater than the Sun. How does its luminosity compare with the Sun's?

9. A binary system, observed face on, has a period of 4 years and parallax 0.2 arcseconds. The length of the semimajor axis is 0.4 arcseconds. What is the total mass of the system? (Hint: You will need to first find the distance to the binary system. Then use the small-angle formula to find the length of the semimajor axis in AU. Finally, use Kepler's third law to find the total mass.)

10. Use the data given in the caption of Figure 12-33 to calculate the diameter of the smaller star.

1. "Origins of the Stellar Magnitude Scale," by J. B. Hearnshaw, in *Sky & Telescope* (November, 1992).

2. *Stars and Their Spectra*, by J. Kaler (Cambridge University Press, 1997).

3. "Reading the Colors of Stars," by C. Sneden, in *Astronomy* (April, 1989).

4. "Accretion Disks in Interacting Binary Stars," by J. K. Cannizzo and R. H. Kaitchuck, in *Scientific American* (January, 1992).

5. "Bonuses of the Microlensing Business," by M. Mateo, in *Sky & Telescope* (September 1997).

6. "Extragalactic Eclipsing Binaries: Astrophysical Laboratories," by I. Ribas, in *New Astronomy Reviews* (July 2004).

7. "The Stars that Revealed the Vastness of the Universe," by B. Dorminey, in *Astronomy* (September 2009).

Quest Ahead to Starlinks
http://physicalscience.jbpub.com/starlinks

Starlinks is this book's online learning center. It features **eLearning**, which contains chapter quizzes and other tools designed to help you study for your class. You can also find **online exercises**, view numerous relevant **animations**, follow a guide to **useful astronomy sites** on the Internet, or even check the latest **astronomy news** updates.

Interstellar Matter and Star Formation

13

When we gaze at the stars, they appear to be unchanging point-like sources of light. This was at the core of ancient beliefs about the heavens. Not until Galileo observed sunspots on the surface of our star did we start thinking of stars as changeable. We now know that all stars change, some gradually enough that we do not notice the changes during our lifetimes but others rapidly and dramatically. We know that the evolution of stars is a cyclic process. Stars are born out of the gas and dust that exist in the space between them, called the *interstellar medium*. The stars evolve and finally die and in the process return some of their mass back to the interstellar medium through explosive events and stellar winds. This recycled material will eventually form a new generation of stars.

The true-color chapter-opening image of the giant galactic nebula NGC3603 shows the entire cycle of stellar evolution. A blue supergiant star (a star at the final stages of evolution) is shown at the upper left of center, along with its grayish blue ring of glowing gas. Two jets are returning processed material back to the interstellar medium (blobs to the upper right and lower left of the star). A cluster of stars appears near the center of the image, dominated by young, hot stars and early O-type stars. A large cavity around the cluster has been created as a result of the interaction between the ionizing radiation and winds emitted from these massive stars and the interstellar

This true-color image of the giant galactic nebula NGC3603 was taken in 1999 by the *Hubble Space Telescope*. It illustrates the entire life cycle of stars. First, the Bok globules and giant gaseous pillars, then disks around protostars, followed by the evolved massive stars in the young cluster, and finally, the blue supergiant with its ring and jets. (The text here describes the positions of these objects in the photograph.)

All cross references to chapters, sections, figures, and tables pertain to the main text, *In Quest of the Universe, Sixth Edition. In Quest of the Solar System* contains Chapters 1–11 and 19 of the main text. *In Quest of the Stars and Galaxies* contains Chapters 1–5 and 11–19 of the main text.

An everyday definition of *medium* is "an intervening substance through which something is transmitted." Light is transmitted through empty space but also through the interstellar medium.

molecular cloud A cold (10–50 K), dense (10^3 – 10^6 particles/cm³), massive (from a few to a few million times the mass of the Sun) interstellar cloud; it consists mainly of molecular hydrogen, with traces of carbon monoxide and other molecules.

The Advancing the Model box on page 373 explains why this hypothesis for the dark areas was abandoned.

IRAS, a joint project of the United States, the United Kingdom, and The Netherlands, was launched in 1983. During its 10 months of operation, it detected about 350,000 infrared sources and extended infrared emission from a number of objects.

interstellar cirrus Faint, diffuse dust clouds found throughout interstellar space.

medium. This interaction is clearly shown in the form of the giant gaseous pillars to the right of the cluster. The dark clouds at the upper right (called Bok globules) are probably at an earlier stage of star formation. Finally, at the lower left of the cluster are two compact, tadpole-shaped emission nebulae. These structures may correspond to gas and dust evaporating from disks around protoplanets.

In this chapter, we discuss all but one of these objects. The image clearly shows that the interstellar medium plays a crucial role in the evolution of stars and galaxies. Stars form in **molecular clouds**, which are the densest regions of the medium and where molecular hydrogen can form; in turn, stars replenish the medium with matter and energy during their lifetimes through stellar winds, planetary nebulae, and supernova explosions (which we describe in the next two chapters). The result of this interplay affects the rate at which a galaxy depletes its gaseous content and thus its star-forming period.

In previous chapters, particularly Chapter 12, we discussed the tools and techniques by which astronomers measure the properties of stars and discern relationships among these properties. In the next few chapters, we show how these tools and techniques have enabled us to learn about the universe beyond the solar system. Astronomers study the dust and gas that exist in interstellar space and are learning how this material forms into new stars, how these stars live out their lives, and how they eventually "die."

Astronomers have amassed a tremendous amount of information about the life cycles of stars. Still, you may not be surprised to learn that many of our theories concerning stellar evolution are somewhat tentative. Many questions remain.

13-1 The Interstellar Medium

There are two seemingly contradictory truths about the space between the stars. First, a large amount of gas and dust exists in that space. Second, the space between stars is very nearly a perfect vacuum. The secret to reconciling these statements is to realize the vastness of interstellar space. Although the molecular density (the number of molecules per cubic centimeter) of the dust and gas in space is very small—smaller than the best vacuum in a laboratory on Earth—space is so vast that the total amount of material between stars is enough to affect the light that passes through it. In addition, as we explain later, this amount of material is enough to provide for the formation of new stars.

Interstellar Dust

Astronomers have been aware of dark areas in the sky (FIGURE 13-1) for ages. Although it was once thought that these dark patches are simply spaces between the stars that allow us to see into the darkness beyond, we now know that the dark areas are caused by giant clouds of interstellar dust that block light from stars behind them. In the 1930s, astronomers became aware that grains of dust exist not just in clouds, but also throughout interstellar space. The *Infrared Astronomical Satellite (IRAS)* and the *HST* have enabled astronomers to photograph the diffuse interstellar dust.

FIGURE 13-2a is an *IRAS* image of the constellation Chameleon. Figure 13-2b is an image of a region of Orion (*HST*) as it appears in near-infrared. The wispy appearance of the material in the images and its similarity to cirrus clouds on Earth lead to its name, **interstellar cirrus**. Cirrus clouds emit infrared radiation because they are warmed slightly by light that they absorb.

Wispy interstellar cirrus clouds span huge volumes of space, from parsecs to tens of parsecs across. To appreciate this size, recall that a parsec is somewhat greater than 3 light-years and that the solar system is only about 0.001 light-years across.

Interstellar dust grains make up only 1% of the mass of the interstellar medium, but dust has very definite effects on light. We have seen one of these effects, the reduction in the amount of light from distant stars—and sometimes the complete extinction of that light. Another effect results from the fact that although dust grains

(a)

(b)

(c)

(d)

FIGURE 13-1 Interstellar clouds of dust hide the stars behind them. (a) The swan-like nebula Barnard 163 is within an emission nebula complex (IC 1396) in the constellation Cepheus. (b) The dark molecular cloud Barnard 68 is 300 light-years away in the constellation Ophiuchus. Its mass is about 1.5 solar masses, at a temperature of only 10 K (one of the coldest objects in the universe). Its average diameter is about 12,000 AU. Even though molecular clouds are stellar nurseries, this one seems to be stable (except for a long-period pulsation, probably due to the influence of a shockwave from an exploding star). (c) The Horsehead nebula results from clouds of dust blocking light from a bright nebula behind (at the right center of the photo). It is in the constellation Orion, about 1500 light-years from us. The bright star at the left center is Alnitak, the easternmost star in the belt of Orion, 251 parsecs (820 light-years) from us. (d) A composite color image (in the visual part of the spectrum) of the Horsehead Nebula and its immediate surroundings. Red color is for the hydrogen (H-alpha) emission from the HII region, brown for the foreground obscuring dust, and blue-green for scattered starlight.

(a)

(b)

FIGURE 13-2 (a) A composite image, taken by *IRAS*, of the constellation Chameleon, at wavelengths of 12 micrometers (coded blue), 25 micrometers (coded green), and 60 micrometers (coded red). Stars are brighter at 12 micrometers and appear as blue dots in the picture. (b) The *HST* obtained this near-infrared image of the edge of the Orion Nebula. The image reveals the diffuse, patchy clouds of the nebula.

Is the space between the
stars empty?

The effect by which
starlight is blocked com-
pletely by interstellar
material is called *interstellar extinction*. It is due
to scattering and absorp-
tion. A similar phenom-
enon occurs when the
headlights of oncoming
cars appear dimmer
while driving in fog.

Polycyclic refers to multiple loops of carbon
atoms. *Aromatic* refers
to the types of chemical
bonds existing between
the carbon atoms.
Hydrocarbon refers to
the composition of
carbon and hydrogen
atoms.

fluorescence The process
of absorbing radiation
of one frequency and
re-emitting it at a lower
frequency.

may absorb some light, they scatter much of it, and this scattering is more efficient for light of shorter wavelengths. As a result, blue light is scattered more than red light (FIGURE 13-3). The light from distant stars thus is *reddened* by the dust through which it passes.

The *interstellar reddening* caused by scattering should not be confused with the redshift caused by the Doppler effect. In the case of interstellar reddening, the positions of the spectral lines are not changed, but in the case of Doppler redshift, the spectral lines actually shift as illustrated in FIGURE 13-4. Also, some objects might be intrinsically red and, thus, their color is not related to interstellar reddening.

How large are the interstellar dust grains? We know that they must be smaller than the wavelengths corresponding to visible light, because otherwise they would not scatter blue light more than red. This means that the dust grains are the size of particles of cigarette smoke and smaller, typically a fraction of a micron across. (You may have noticed that a cloud of cigarette smoke has a blue tint.)

What is the dust made of? Spectral analysis indicates that it contains silicate grains and carbon in the form of graphite, similar to the carbon that is found in comets. An important family of organic molecules observed in the interstellar medium is the PAHs (*polycyclic aromatic hydrocarbons*). They are common to daily life, many of them are known (or suspected) carcinogens, and they form by incomplete burning of carbon-containing fuels (such as wood, coal, diesel, and tobacco). PAH molecules *fluoresce* (absorb starlight and re-emit it at lower energies) most noticeably in the infrared part of the spectrum; this allows the *Spitzer Space Telescope* to easily observe them and, as a result, the star-forming regions in which they reside.

The presence of PAHs in dark interstellar dust clouds suggests that they are produced by the same processes as the silicon (which is like sand on Earth). These organic molecules also provide a tool to understanding the abundances of chemicals related to life. In Chapter 15, we discuss the origin of the interstellar material and the related hypotheses about the composition of the dust.

Interstellar Gas

Gas in space accounts for 99% of the total mass of the interstellar material. In most cases the gas is extremely diffuse (so that for most purposes the volume it occupies may be considered a vacuum); however, in some

FIGURE 13-3 Grains of dust scatter blue light more efficiently than red light and, thus, a star seen through a cloud of dust appears redder than it would if the dust were not present. The amount of scattering and absorption depends on the number density of particles, the wavelength of light, and the cloud thickness.

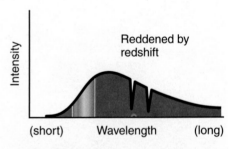

FIGURE 13-4 (top) A blackbody (intensity-wavelength) curve showing two (exaggerated) absorption lines. (middle) This is the same source with its light reddened by scattering. The absorption lines remain in the same place. (bottom) Again, the same source but with its light reddened by the Doppler shift. The entire curve is shifted to the right in this case.

FIGURE 13-5 (a) This ESO/MPG image of the central region of the emission nebula N44 in the Large Magellanic Cloud is a composite of three images taken at the H-alpha (red color), singly-ionized (blue), and doubly-ionized (green) oxygen lines. The field size is 8.5′ × 8.5′. (b) This is a mosaic of 45 images of the Orion nebula taken by the *HST*. Light emitted by oxygen is shown as blue. Hydrogen emission is shown as green, and nitrogen as red. The overall color balance is close to what an observer near the nebula would see. (c) The Tarantula nebula is the largest emission nebula in the sky, a bit less than the size of the full Moon. It is located in the Large Magellanic Cloud, about 170,000 light-years from us, and measures more than 1000 light-years across. This three-color VLT image was taken at 485 nm, 503 nm, and 657 nm. The predominantly red light comes from hydrogen atoms (the H-alpha line), and the green-blue light comes from hydrogen atoms (H-beta) and doubly ionized oxygen ions. At the heart of the nebula is a cluster of young, massive, hot stars (2 to 3 million years old) whose ultraviolet light excites the emission nebula. To its right, the reddish bubble is created by a massive star blowing material into the cloud. At the upper right is another cluster of bright, massive stars, about 20-million years old; some of the cluster's stars have already exploded as supernovae.

cases the gas clusters together into giant clouds. The gas between the stars reveals its presence in several ways.

- Clouds of gas can be seen in photographs of the sky. The red glow behind the Horsehead nebula in Figure 13-1c is a giant cloud of gas that is glowing due to ultraviolet light from hot stars within it. The glow is due to a *fluorescence* process; that is, the atoms of the gas absorb ultraviolet light from nearby hot stars, which causes the atoms to become energized, and then they lose their extra energy by emitting light at lower energies. (Recall our discussion of Kirchhoff's laws in Section 4-5.) Of particular importance is the Hydrogen-alpha line produced in the red part of the spectrum (see Figure B12-1). FIGURE 13-5 shows other examples of such bright **emission nebulae**.

  Such nebulae are direct evidence of gas atoms in the interstellar medium. A typical emission nebula temperature is about 10,000 K, and a typical mass is between 100–10,000 solar masses. The term *nebula* (plural nebulae) has its origin in the adjective *nebulous*, which means "lacking definite form or limits." This is an apt description of an interstellar cloud, for such clouds have no definite boundaries. A cloud is called a nebula if it is dense or bright enough to show up in a photograph.

- Interstellar gas causes absorption lines in stellar spectra. Astronomers can distinguish these absorption lines from the absorption lines of a stellar atmosphere in three ways. First, absorption lines due to interstellar gas tend to be narrower

emission nebula
Interstellar gas that fluoresces due to ultraviolet light from a star near or within the nebula.

FIGURE 13-6 (a) Absorption lines in the spectrum of starlight passing through an interstellar cloud can result from both the star's atmosphere and the cloud. (b) This graph is a highly magnified portion of the intensity-wavelength graph of light from a star. It shows three absorption lines. The outer two are much finer than the central one, indicating that they were caused by interstellar gas.

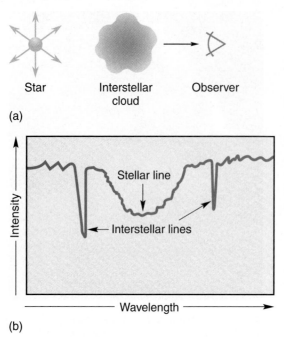

Star   Interstellar   Observer
        cloud

(a)

Stellar line

Intensity

Interstellar lines

Wavelength

(b)

As we explain in Chapter 16, the 21-centimeter radiation is very valuable to us in our efforts to map the Milky Way Galaxy.

[The Pleiades] were filled with an entangling system of nebulous matter which seems to bind together the different stars with misty wreaths and streams of filmy light all of which is beyond the keenest vision and the most powerful telescopes.
Edward Emerson Barnard, 1887, examining a long-time exposure photograph.

reflection nebula
Interstellar dust that is visible due to reflected light from a nearby star.

than those produced by a star's atmosphere (**FIGURE 13-6**). This difference occurs because the atoms of a star's atmosphere are generally moving fast in random directions, causing a range of Doppler shifts. Second, because the star and the interstellar gas typically have different velocities, the lines caused by the stellar atmosphere have a different Doppler shift than those caused by the interstellar gas. (The velocities referred to here are the overall velocities of the star and of the interstellar gas cloud, not the random molecular speeds within each gas.) Finally, the interstellar gas is generally much cooler than the gas of the stellar atmosphere. The atoms thus are in their ground state, and most of the absorption takes place in the ultraviolet region of the spectrum. (For a discussion of this phenomenon, see "Determining the Spectral Type of a Star," a Tools of Astronomy box on page 349.)

- In 1951, two American astronomers, E. M. Purcell and H. I. Ewen, used a specially built radio telescope to detect radiation emitted by interstellar hydrogen. Scientists had predicted that hydrogen atoms should emit radiation with a wavelength of 21 centimeters, but Purcell and Ewen's telescope was the first to reveal it. Hydrogen is the most common element in stars, and astronomers had expected it would also be the most common element in interstellar space. The 21-centimeter radiation confirmed this expectation and allows us to spot interstellar hydrogen at great distances, for the interstellar medium absorbs very little of the 21-centimeter radiation.

- In addition, we are able to detect radio emission lines from interstellar gases—including water, carbon monoxide, ammonia, and formaldehyde—at other wavelengths. However, these gases are much less abundant than hydrogen. Hydrogen (in neutral, ionized, or molecular form) comprises about 70% of the mass of the interstellar medium, with helium making up most of the remaining mass and other elements (such as carbon and silicon) accounting for only a few percent of the total.

Clouds and Nebulae

As we indicated earlier, the gas and dust in the interstellar material are not uniformly distributed; they tend to clump together into what we call *interstellar clouds*. The interstellar cirrus clouds are made up mostly of gas whose molecules are widely dispersed. At sea level on Earth, there are about 2×10^{19} molecules of air per cubic centimeter. The interstellar cirrus clouds contain fewer than 1000 molecules per cubic centimeter. It is difficult to determine the shape and size of these diffuse clouds, but most of them seem to be wispy sheets rather than spherical clumps. The sheets are probably less than one parsec thick, but many parsecs wide and long. The total mass of a cirrus cloud might equal the mass of a small-to-average star.

If a cloud is near a hot star, the ultraviolet radiation from the star causes the cloud to fluoresce (as in Figure 13-5), and the cloud is then known as an *emission nebula*. A diffuse cloud of dust that happens to be behind or beside a bright star may be visible to us because it refracts and reflects the star's light toward us. **FIGURE 13-7** is a photograph of such a **reflection nebula**. When we see a reflection nebula, we are seeing light that has been scattered in the cloud and, thus, the nebula appears blue. **FIGURE 13-8a** is a diagram of a star surrounded by an emission nebula with a reflec-

ADVANCING THE MODEL

Holes in the Heavens?

Sir William Herschel, the discoverer of Uranus, proposed that the dark patches we see in the sky are simply large spaces between the stars that allow us to see into the dark void beyond. How do we know that this is not the case?

Today, of course, infrared imaging allows us to detect the dust that makes up the "holes in space," but before we ever made infrared images of the dust, an argument based on geometry gave astronomers reason to doubt Herschel's idea. Stars are not all at the same distance from us; they are not on a "celestial sphere." Instead, they are spread out so that some are relatively nearby and others are very far away. For us to be able to see through gaps between the stars, the gaps thus would have to be similar to tunnels, and the tun-

nels would have to be perfectly aligned with Earth. Suppose you are deep in a forest. Even with open clearings among the trees, you might not be able to see beyond the forest. For you to see outside there would have to be straight, open trails. In the case of stars, it is extremely unlikely that so many open trails ("tunnels") would be perfectly aligned with Earth. As astronomer Arthur Cowper Ranyard put it in 1894, "The probabilities against such a radial arrangement with respect to the Earth's place in space [seem] to my mind to conclusively prove that the narrow dark spaces are due to streams of absorbing matter, rather than to holes or thin regions in bright nebulosity."

tion nebula nearby. Figure 13-8b is a photograph of a real example that is similar to the diagram. In the photograph, the pink emission nebula (the Trifid nebula, in Sagittarius) surrounds hot central stars that provide the energy to make the nebula fluoresce. Above it is a reflection nebula.

The Trifid nebula also contains dust lanes that absorb the light from the emission nebula, extinguishing this light and appearing dark. Dust clouds such as this may have densities ranging from as low as 1000 to perhaps 1,000,000 particles per cubic centimeter. (This is still not very dense compared with number densities on Earth, as

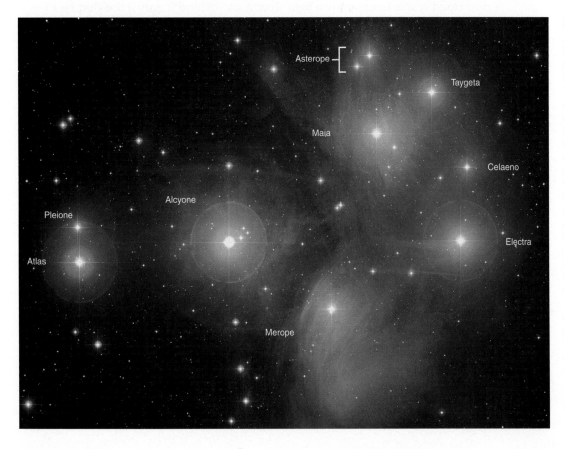

FIGURE 13-7 The reflection nebula surrounding the Pleiades (an open cluster about 436 light-years from us in the constellation Taurus). The dimmer stars are part of the cluster and at the same distance as the bright O- and B-type stars. The spikes from each star are caused by diffraction around secondary mirror supports in the telescope. The nebula is not a remnant of the cloud that formed the cluster, but a different interstellar cloud through which the cluster happens to be currently drifting. The cluster, often called the "Seven Sisters" (daughters of Pleione and Atlas), is the most famous galactic star cluster in the heavens since antiquity. According to Greek mythology, the "seven sisters" were half-sisters of the Hyades and were saved by Zeus from the pursuit of the giant Orion by being transformed into a group of celestial doves.

IRAC

(a)   (b)

FIGURE 13-8 (a) A hot star inside a cloud of gas causes the cloud to glow, so it is known as an emission nebula. When the star's light passes through the dust cloud, some of the blue light is scattered. If the Earth happens to be located to the left of the page, this dust cloud appears as a blue reflection nebula. If the Earth is located at the top of the page, and if the cloud is very thick, the star's light may not be able to penetrate it, and the cloud appears as a dark nebula. In the case shown, however, some light gets through the cloud. It is reddened in the process, making the star appear redder than it really is. (b) The Trifid nebula, 5400 light-years away in Sagittarius, is a red (or pink) emission nebula that appears to be divided into three parts by dark nebulae that form lanes blocking the light from behind. Above the Trifid nebula is a blue reflection nebula that belongs to the same molecular cloud as the Trifid nebula. The *Spitzer* false color, infrared views show bright star-forming activity where the dark lanes of dust are in the visible image. The IRAC image is a three-color composite: 3.6 μm (blue), 4.5 μm (green), and 8 μm (red); the new stars uncovered by *Spitzer* are visible as yellow or red spots. The MIPS image was taken at 24 μm and shows cool material falling on the growing young stars in the nebula. The middle panel is a combination of *Spitzer* data from both instruments. Star formation is thought to have been triggered by the massive, type-O star seen as a white spot at the nebula's center.

dark nebula An interstellar molecular cloud whose dust blocks light from stars on the other side of it.

As we will discuss later, the interstellar material is constantly in a state of flux, for it is being used up as new stars are formed and being replenished as old stars die.

air at sea level is still 20 trillion times more dense than the densest interstellar cloud.) A dust cloud is able to extinguish light from a star behind it only if the cloud is extremely large, perhaps hundreds of parsecs across. The photographs in Figure 13-1 and FIGURE 13-9 contain other examples of *dark nebulae*.

Although it is the dust of these molecular clouds that is responsible for blocking starlight, most of the particles in such nebulae are atoms, about 75% hydrogen and 23% helium, with the remaining 2% being heavier elements. The high densities and low temperatures in dark nebulae lead to the formation of molecular hydrogen.

If we take an inventory of the dust, gas, and stars in our Galaxy, we find that interstellar matter contributes about 15% of the total visible mass. In Section 16-3 we discuss how the distribution of molecular clouds in our Galaxy allowed us to infer its spiral structure.

As we mentioned earlier, a number of elements related to life have been discovered in interstellar space. In addition to PAHs, UV observations of HD124314, a reddened star in the constellation Centaurus, showed the presence of molecular nitrogen, the most prevalent element in Earth's atmosphere. Radio observations of the star-forming area W3 (OH) in our Galaxy indicate the presence of fila-

FIGURE 13-9 The reflection nebula NGC1999 in Orion. It is illuminated by the bright, young star to the left of center. The dark nebula, located right of center and in front of NGC1999, is a condensation of cold molecular gas and dust so thick that it blocks light.

Blue Skies and Red Sunsets

The same phenomenon that explains the reddening of star-light by interstellar dust also explains why the sky is blue and sunsets are red (or at least orange). As we pointed out in the discussion of interstellar reddening, dust scatters blue light more than it scatters red. A similar effect happens in the Earth's atmosphere, where the scattering of sunlight is what gives the daytime sky its color. The sky appears blue simply because particles in the air (and air molecules) scatter higher frequency (blue) light more than lower frequency light. It follows from this that light that reaches us directly from the Sun without scattering is somewhat deficient in these higher frequencies. Consequently, the Sun seen from Earth's sur-

face appears redder than it appears when viewed from a vantage point in space. From Earth, the Sun appears somewhat yellow, but from space it is closer to white.

When we look at the Sun as it is setting, the sunlight that reaches our eyes has traveled even farther through the atmosphere than sunlight at midday. Thus, even more of the high-frequency light is scattered away, and the Sun appears red. This effect is especially noticeable if the atmosphere contains significant amounts of dust. The dust that remained in the air from major volcanic eruptions in 1991 caused beautiful red sunsets for the next few years.

ments of methyl alcohol, up to 3000 AU long, wrapped around a stellar nursery. The amount of methyl formate (a product of alcohol and formaldehyde commonly used as an insecticide) in a typical dust cloud in our Galaxy is about 10^{27} gallons! Finally, *Spitzer* (infrared) observations showed the presence of significant amounts of icy organic materials (including water, methanol, and carbon dioxide) in planet-forming disks around young stars in the constellation Taurus.

13-2 A Brief Woodland Visit

Imagine that you are a visitor from another star system who has landed in a forest on Earth for a 2-day visit. What could you learn about the life cycles of the woodlands during your short visit? You would see small and large trees, but would you be able to determine that trees progress from small to large? In 2 days you would have no chance to see any growth. You would see decayed material on the forest floor, but it might not be obvious that this is what remains of once-standing trees. Perhaps you might be lucky enough to see a change take place. You might see a limb fall from a tree. Would you conclude that trees get smaller by dropping their branches? Or perhaps you might see an entire tree fall. What would that tell you?

Like an extraterrestrial forest visitor, we humans are brief tourists in the universe. During our short lifetimes, we see very little change in the heavens. As we measure time, the stars change slowly. We do have an advantage over the forest visitor in that previous generations have handed down their observations to us so that our learning cycle is longer than one lifetime. However, the earliest reports of astronomical observations are only a few thousand years old; this is a minute time period compared with the total life of the heavens.

It is possible, however, to learn about the life cycle of stars. We are fortunate that a few stellar events happen quickly enough for us to observe them over human lifetimes or (in some cases) over much shorter times. Although astronomers cannot experiment directly with their subject matter, they can observe tremendous numbers of stars in various stages of development. This, along with earthbound experiments on the material of which stars are made, allows scientists to develop theories of stellar life cycles in which we can have reasonable confidence.

13-3 Star Birth

Like other scientific theories, today's theories of star birth and star death developed slowly. Successful theories do not spring fully developed into a scientist's mind. Theories in astronomy result from long struggles with data from the heavens, often accompanied by experimentation here on Earth.

The story of today's understanding of the life cycles of stars starts early in the 20th century, with astrophysicist Henry Norris Russell playing the major role. The H-R diagram is the key to understanding the lives of stars, but it is not easy to read. Russell's early theories held that stars begin their lives as red giants, become O- and B-type main sequence stars, and then move down the main sequence, gradually dimming as they live out their lives. When new evidence arrived, particularly from H-R diagrams of clusters and from new knowledge of nuclear energy processes, Russell realized that stars live most of their lives on the main sequence with very little change in their positions and that the red giant stage is not the beginning of a star's life but is near the end. We start at the beginning.

The Collapse of Interstellar Clouds

> Astronomers estimate that there are 5000 giant molecular clouds in our Galaxy.

Stars are born in the coldest places in the Galaxy, the giant molecular clouds (GMCs) of interstellar space. These clouds have a temperature of about 20 K (−420°F) and consist mainly of molecular hydrogen. The low temperature of a GMC implies that particles in it have low speeds, and therefore, the corresponding gas pressure is small. As a result, gravity can bring interstellar material together by overwhelming the pressure pushing this material apart. All that is needed is a relatively dense region so that atoms and dust particles are close enough for gravity to take over. A typical cloud may be 50 parsecs across and may contain as much as a million solar masses of material. The densest regions in a GMC form dark nebulae where new stars are born.

FIGURE 13-10b is a picture of a very small portion of M-16, the Eagle nebula (shown in Figure 13-10a). The dark pillar-like structures are part of a GMC and, thus, they are made up of gas and dust. Intense ultraviolet radiation from hot, massive newborn stars that lie at the upper right, beyond the photo, causes the columns. FIGURE 13-11 illustrates the process. Prior to the sequence shown in the figure, a molecular cloud was fairly evenly spread throughout this region of space. In part (a) of the figure, ultraviolet radiation from the upper right is blowing the cloud back and evaporating gas outward from the cloud's surface. At the same time, the radiation illuminates the surface of the cloud, causing it to glow.

> The name EGG also fits the globules because they are embryonic stars.

Certain parts of the cloud are denser than average. In part (b), a dense globule of gas is about to be uncovered. Globules like this are called EGGs, for "Evaporating Gaseous Globules." Radiation pushes the surrounding gas away from the EGG in much the same way that a strong wind on a beach blows sand along, uncovering shells and leaving trails of sand behind the shells. Part (c) of Figure 13-11 shows most of the nebula blown away, but a snake of gas and dust remains that has been protected from radiation by the EGG. Later, the nebula will blow still farther away, leaving behind a teardrop shape, shown in part (d). Even later, all of the nebula will disappear, leaving behind only the EGG.

What is an EGG? At least in some cases, it is the beginning of a star. Within the globule, gravitational forces between individual molecules and dust particles are sufficient to draw the particles together. The globule was in the process of this contraction when the ultraviolet light began blowing away the surrounding nebula. The contraction continues within the globule. When the center of the EGG gets hot enough to give off its own radiation, it will itself blow away any remaining parts of the nebula that have not fallen inward and a star will remain. Stars born in this manner probably do not have planets around them, for the radiation that causes the pillars probably disperses the material that would have ended up as planets.

Some stars form in more isolated conditions, without nearby hot stars blowing their raw material away. In these cases, parts of the nebula that remain near the

(a) (b) (c) (d)

FIGURE 13-10 (a) The Eagle nebula in the constellation Serpens, about 7000 light-years distant and 20 light-years across. (Can you see the nebula as a landing eagle?) (b) This 1995 *HST* image shows material from a very small part of the Eagle nebula being swept away from dense areas where new stars are forming. The pillar to the left is about 1 light-year long; each pillar is a bit wider than our solar system. (c) A composite infrared image of Eagle's fiery heart, taken by ESA's *Infrared Space Observatory* (7.7 microns in blue; 14.5 microns in red). The temperature of the dust in the Eagle, seen as a "bluish fog," is about 170 K. (d) This 1999 infrared *HST* image of the Eagle nebula shows that only a small fraction of the areas that are opaque in visible, as shown in (b), remain so in the infrared. Instead of the substantial columns of material implied by the optical images, the infrared images show only isolated clumps of dust and gas.

(a) The surface of a molecular cloud is illuminated by intense ultraviolet radiation from nearby hot stars. The radiation evaporates material from the cloud's surface.

(b) A denser-than-average globule of gas (an "EGG") begins to be uncovered. Because it is denser than its surroundings, it is not evaporated as quickly and is left behind. Young stellar objects begin to form within some EGGs.

(c) The EGG is now largely uncovered. The EGG protects a column of gas behind it, giving it a finger-like appearance.

(d) Eventually, the EGG separates from the cloud in which it formed. As the EGG itself slowly evaporates, the star within it becomes visible.

FIGURE 13-11 Pillars like those in Figure 13-10 are the result of strong ultraviolet radiation striking a giant molecular cloud.

embryonic star will continue to fall into it, perhaps resulting in a very large star or revolving around the star to become a planetary system. Such isolated massive stars and compact ionized hydrogen clouds have been observed in a number of galaxies in the Virgo cluster, at the boundary between a galaxy's halo and the intercluster space, and high up in the halo of our own Milky Way.

One question remains before we consider how an EGG becomes a star. What triggers the collapse of parts of a GMC to form globules? The answer may involve collisions between GMCs. Along the boundary of such a collision, molecules would be forced closer together, perhaps close enough that gravity would take over and continue the compression. Another cause for collapse may be interstellar shock waves. As such a wave strikes the GMC, it forces parts of the cloud together enough for gravity to become dominant.

There are at least four possible sources of interstellar shock waves. We have seen one—radiation from hot, newly forming stars. Second, as we explain in the next section, very massive stars undergo a period during which they release enormous quantities of material at great speeds. These bursts are a source of shock waves in the surrounding GMC that can trigger the birth of new stars.

A third source of interstellar shock waves is a supernova—the explosion of a star as it nears the end of its life. We discuss supernovae in Chapters 14 and 15. Finally, as we discuss in Chapter 16, we know that tremendous shock waves move around the entire Galaxy, forming its galactic arms. These waves may be the most common trigger of star formation.

Protostars

Whatever causes the material within the core of a giant molecular cloud to start to collapse, once the collapse begins, the increased gravitational force causes the molecules of the core to pick up speed as they fall inward. The condition of fast-moving molecules is synonymous with high temperature and, thus, material near the center of the collapse becomes hot. Soon the higher pressure caused by the increase in temperature prevents further collapse of the central core. Material farther from the core continues falling inward, crashing down on the central core and causing a further increase in temperature.

The hot core is now called a **protostar**. It receives its energy from the infall of material, so the ultimate source of its energy is gravitational. This is similar to the way a hammer that is repeatedly lifted and dropped onto a piece of metal heats both itself and the piece of metal. Each molecule that falls onto the core converts gravitational energy into thermal energy.

As the cloud contracts and its temperature increases, about half of its gravitational energy is radiated away from the heating center. As the center gets hotter and hotter, it radiates more and more energy. In only a few thousand years, the center is as bright as the Sun; however, we cannot see the center directly because the outer portion, which continues to fall relatively slowly toward the center, blocks most of the radiation. This **cocoon**, or **cocoon nebula**, absorbs the radiation from the center, becoming warmer as it does so.

A warm object emits infrared radiation, and it is the infrared radiation emitted from the cocoon that we see from Earth and that gives evidence for the existence of protostars. FIGURE 13-12 includes two infrared photographs, which therefore are shown in false color, with each color representing a different intensity of infrared radiation. Such false-color photographs of nonvisible sources are very useful tools in astronomy, but do not be fooled into thinking that the objects have colors like the photographs.

Evolution Toward the Main Sequence

FIGURE 13-13 shows the progress of a protostar of one solar mass on an expanded H-R diagram. (The main sequence is now compressed into the left side of the figure.) The diagram had to be expanded beyond the coolest stars on the main sequence because a protostar begins its life much cooler than any main sequence star. The details of

The material flowing from stars is commonly called the *stellar wind*. The *solar wind* that we detect (and which results in auroras on Earth) is far weaker than the stellar wind bursts described here.

protostar An object in the process of becoming a star, before it reaches the main sequence.

cocoon nebula The dust and gas that surround a protostar and block much of its radiation.

In speaking of evolutionary tracks and stellar evolution, astronomers are using the term *evolution* in a very different way than biologists do. One star is said to *evolve* as it lives its life. We are not speaking of an entire species evolving through generations.

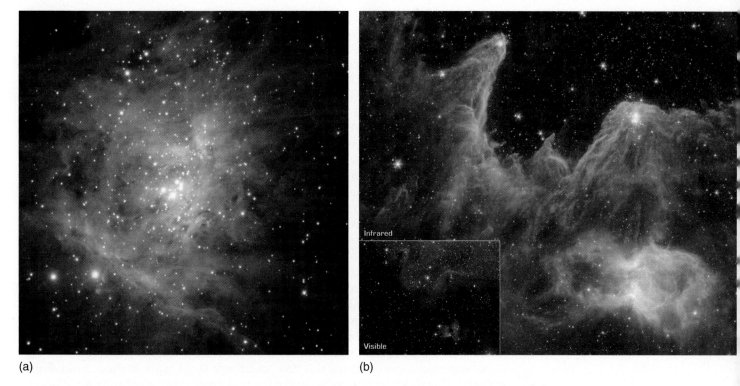

(a)   (b)

FIGURE 13-12 (a) A VLT color composite of 81 images of the central part of the Orion nebula. The image shows the Trapezium stars (near the center) and the associated cluster of about 1000 stars, about 1-million years old. This near-infrared image (1–2 microns) shows thermal radiation from the area's dust, which is heated by the intense UV and visible light from the stars. It also shows the warm, dense dust cocoons around the very young stars. (b) This is a comparison between the visible-light image (inset) and the *Spitzer* infrared image of an edge in the W5 region in the Cassiopeia constellation, 7000 light-years away. Infrared light from young stars (shown in white/yellow) inside the dusty pillars can escape and be detected, and the pillars themselves have been warmed by starlight and glow in the infrared.

this part of the star's **evolutionary track** are not known, but the protostar begins as a cool, dim object, warms up by gravitational contraction, and moves toward the main sequence. Finally, as the cocoon continues to contract, its smaller size causes it to appear dimmer and, thus, the star begins to move downward on the diagram as it nears the main sequence.

Motion on the H-R diagram does not mean the star is actually moving in space, of course. Recall from Figure 12-15, the diagram of people's height versus age, that as a person ages, his or her dot moves on this diagram. This is analogous to the motion of a star on the H-R diagram. (However, a star spends most of its life on the main sequence and, thus, its "motion" on the H-R diagram is very slow for most of its life.)

As time passes, the center of the protostar continues to shrink and become hotter, emitting more radiation all of the time. This radiation gradually blows away the outer portions of the cocoon. Some of the cocoon may not be blown away but may condense to form planets, as discussed in Chapter 7. In some stars, the cocoon is apparently blown away by sudden bursts of stellar winds. Certain stars, named ***T Tauri*** stars after the variable star T in the constellation Taurus, appear to be young stars undergoing some sort of instability that causes enormous flares. These flares are

evolutionary track The path on the H-R diagram taken by a star as its luminosity and color change.

T Tauri stars A class of stars that show rapid and erratic changes in brightness.

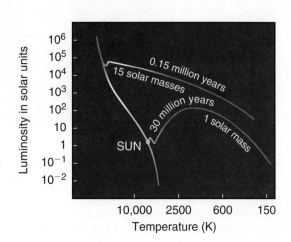

FIGURE 13-13 This H-R diagram shows temperatures much lower than on previous diagrams to include the early, cool stages of a star's formation. A more massive star ends up at a higher location on the main sequence because it is hotter and brighter. Because gravitational forces are greater on the more massive star, it spends much less time in its protostar stage.

thought to play a part in blowing away the cocoon of newly forming stars, particularly K- and M-type stars, which, being at the bottom of the main sequence, are of low mass.

Computer simulations and observations of massive star-forming regions support the idea that massive stars form in a way similar to that of less massive stars. That is, they form through gravitational collapse and mass accretion with disks. The most massive stars, the O- and B-type stars, follow a track on the H-R diagram toward the top of the main sequence (Figure 13-13). These stars are much fewer in number than stars of lesser mass; however, they are so energetic that they signal their presence by emitting ultraviolet light, which stimulates the hydrogen of their cocoon (and the nebula beyond the cocoon) to emit its own light, forming an emission nebula. **FIGURE 13-14a** is a photograph of the Orion nebula, an emission nebula lit by energy from new stars within it. The very hot blue star in Figure 13-14b is experiencing a continuous mass loss from its outer layers. The two symmetric shells of material (emission nebulae) on either side of the star were formed during past vigorous outbursts.

The infalling particles of massive stars experience much greater gravitational force than do particles in low-mass stars, and massive stars reach the main sequence much faster. M-type stars remain protostars for hundreds of millions of years. The Sun, with more mass, spent about 30 million years in this phase; however, the most massive stars remain protostars for only tens of thousands of years. Stars of low mass may undergo a period of instability just before joining the main sequence. Massive stars do likewise, but their instability is more violent; O and B stars blow off material at supersonic speeds during this time, creating a shock wave in the surrounding material. This shock wave may be one of the triggers that starts the collapse of other portions of the interstellar cloud to form more stars.

The great amount of radiation from massive stars is what limits how massive a star can be. Astronomers calculate that a star with a mass greater than about 150 solar masses emits radiation so intense that it prevents more material from falling into the star, thereby limiting the star's size. This upper limit is a conservative estimate based on *HST* observations of hundreds of massive stars in the Archer cluster, one of the densest clusters in our Galaxy, 25,000 light-years away. It is also consistent with

The Horsehead nebula of Figure 13-1d is a smaller part of this same Orion nebula. New stars are thought to be forming in the dark horse head.

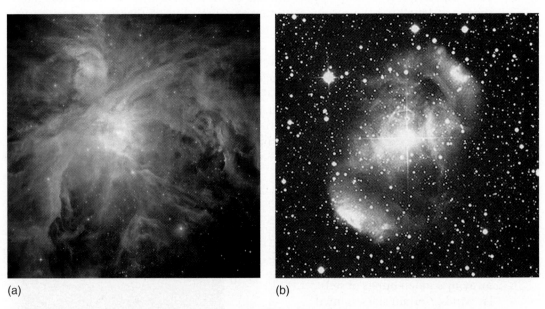

(a)   (b)

FIGURE 13-14 (a) This is a composite *HST* and *Spitzer* image of the Orion nebula, an emission nebula that is our closest massive star formation region. The Orion nebula is easily visible in small telescopes or even binoculars. The Trapezium, the collection of four massive stars, is at the cloud's center. Green reveals hydrogen and sulfur gas heated by the UV light of the Trapezium stars. Red and orange reveal organic molecules (PAHs). (b) The blue star HD148937 (the brightest in a triple-star system in the constellation Norma) is experiencing a continuous mass loss from its outer layers. The emission nebulae (NGC6164, NGC6165 on either side of the star) were formed during past vigorous outbursts.

FIGURE 13-15 Composite *HST* images, in visible light, of jets emanating from three different protostars. "HH" stands for Herbig-Haro objects, the bright knots of hot, ionized material that appear to be moving away from their corresponding protostars. (a) An edge-on disk of dust around a protostar associated with HH-30, about 450 light-years away in the constellation Taurus. The protostar is hidden behind the densest and opaque part of the disk but illuminates the disk's top and bottom surfaces. (b) The jet in HH-34 shows a beaded structure, suggesting an episodic ejection of dense parcels of material. It is about 1500 light-years away, close to the Orion nebula. (c) The protostar in HH-47 is hidden inside a dust cloud (near the left edge of the image) while its light is reflected by the white filaments on the left. The jet structure suggests that the protostar might be wobbling. It is about 1500 light-years away, at the edge of the Gum nebula.

statistical studies of clusters of smaller mass stars in our Galaxy and with observations of a massive star cluster (R136) in the Large Magellanic Cloud.

On the other hand, protostars with masses less than about 0.08 solar masses do not develop the necessary internal pressure and temperature to start hydrogen fusion. They heat up because of gravitational contraction but never become main sequence stars. Eventually, they contract as far as they can and then begin to cool, becoming planet-like objects—cold cinders in space—called brown dwarfs, which we study in the next chapter. Recall from Chapter 9 that Jupiter emits about twice as much energy as it receives from the Sun, and this comes from gravitational energy that remains from its formation.

Infrared observations have revealed that it is very common for protostars to be surrounded by disks of gas and dust. These observations fit well with the theory of the formation of the solar system and lead us to believe that planetary systems are common around stars. In addition, streams of material (jets) have been observed flowing from the poles of many protostars. FIGURE 13-15 clearly shows the presence of disks and outflows in protostars. Even though the *HST* images are of three different objects, when compared together they give us a general view of how jets from protostars behave as they propagate in space. A jet emanates from a disk surrounding a young star. The jet remains narrow and shows a beaded structure and then creates a shock wave when it interacts with the surrounding interstellar medium.

accretion The process by which an object gradually accumulates matter, usually because of the action of gravity.

On one hand, a protostar's mass may increase by the process of *accretion*, as particles in the disk surrounding the protostar lose energy and spiral closer to it as a result of collisions within the disk. On the other hand, a protostar's mass may decrease as a result of the ejection of mass along the jets (FIGURE 13-16). (In some cases the outflow occurs along only one jet, whereas in other cases, the outflow is along two oppositely directed jets.) Astronomers hypothesize that these outflows play an important part in reducing the angular

Mass ejection

Mass accretion

Protostar

FIGURE 13-16 A typical protostar strikes a balance between mass accretion from a surrounding disk of dust and gas and mass ejection in powerful jets of material.

FIGURE 13-17 (a) Close-up of protoplanetary disks in the Orion nebula. The field of view is about 9000 AU across. (b) A very young star (between 300,000 and 1 million years old) surrounded by its protoplanetary disk. There is enough material in the disk to form at least seven planets like Earth. The disk is 600 AU across or 7.5 times the diameter of Pluto's orbit in our solar system.

The problems of star formation are wonderfully complex. In a place like Orion you can see the whole region disintegrating. Supernovas, stellar winds, shocks are slamming into the molecular cloud, sweeping it back, igniting a conflagration. Things are happening wholesale. You have to be careful in applying simple models.
Patrick Thaddeus, radio astronomer

momentum of stars and allowing them to grow by accretion; particles can fall inward (toward the star) after they shed their excess angular momentum. As we discussed in Section 7-6 about the formation of the solar system, theoretical models predict that the Sun should be spinning faster than it is. If, early in the Sun's formation, material were ejected from its poles, that ejection would have resulted in reducing the Sun's rotational speed to what is observed. Much remains to be learned about the part played by the ejection of matter from the poles of protostars.

The presence of disks of gas and dust surrounding newly formed stars is also shown in FIGURE 13-17a. This *HST* image of a small portion of the Orion nebula shows five stars, four of which are surrounded by disks of gas and dust. These protoplanetary disks will probably evolve on to form planets. Figure 13-17b is an image of a very young star surrounded by a protoplanetary disk, seen in silhouette against the background of the Orion nebula. Not all stars form such disks; for example, it is likely that massive stars or some stars in binary systems do not form protoplanetary disks. As recent observations suggest, however, these disks are found around most young, low-mass stars. The duration of the different phases that a young star goes through as it evolves depends a lot on its environment. If a young star has nearby companions, their UV radiation and stellar winds may disrupt the young star's accretion disk. The longevity of the star's jets will be affected by whether or not planets start forming in the disk, clearing away gas that feeds these outflows. FIGURE 13-18 shows two examples of young stars making their presence felt in their surrounding medium.

Many details of our theories of the life cycles of stars come from computer modeling. For example, the image in FIGURE 13-19 shows the inner region of a 50-solar masses gas ball 266,000 years after it started to collapse under its own gravity. New stars are shown in white, and a dense gas disk can be seen at lower center.

FIGURE 13-18 (a) This *Spitzer* false color image of HH 49/50 (in the Chamaeleon I star-forming region) shows a tornado-like feature, a shock front created by a jet emanating from a still-forming star off the upper edge of the image. The jet slams into interstellar dust clouds, heating the dust and causing it to glow in the infrared. The shape of the feature could result from magnetic fields or eddies. It is not clear if the star at the tip of the tornado is physically related to it. (b) A bow shock around the very young star LL Ori, in Orion's Great Nebula. Such shocks can be created in space when two streams of gas collide. The star emits a strong wind, which interacts with the surrounding medium.

Such computer simulations help us understand better the processes involved in star and planetary system formation.

Star Clusters

The Pleiades (Figure 13-7) is a small cluster of some 500 stars in the constellation Taurus. The brighter stars of the cluster are visible to the naked eye and are a beautiful sight even in a small telescope. FIGURE 13-20 shows two other clusters of the same type, called *galactic clusters*, or *open clusters*.

FIGURE 13-19 A frame from a computer simulation of star formation. The original 50-solar mass ball of gas is 1.2 light-years wide. The frame shows the inner 0.08 light-years wide core.

Galactic clusters are found primarily in the disk of the Galaxy. FIGURE 13-21 shows another type of star cluster, called a *globular cluster*. Globular clusters contain hundreds of thousands of stars. They are not confined to the Galactic disk, but orbit the center of the Galaxy in all directions so that they spend most of their time outside the disk. FIGURE 13-22 shows the location of the two types of clusters relative to our Galaxy.

Clusters are important to astronomers for two reasons. First, all of the stars in a given cluster are at about the same distance from us. This means that their apparent magnitude is a direct indication of their absolute magnitude—those that look the brightest really are the brightest. Second, the stars within a cluster began their formation at essentially the same time, when their interstellar cloud began its collapse. The evidence for this conjecture is based on regularities we see in H-R diagrams of clusters such as the one for a very young cluster shown in FIGURE 13-23. This means that they formed out of the same giant molecular cloud, and therefore, it is probably safe to assume that all of them have about the same chemical composition.

Much of what we know about star formation has come from examination of clusters. The fact that the stars in a cluster began forming at about the same time allows us to learn how stars of different mass have progressed at different rates. Figure 13-23 indicates that protostars of low mass have not yet reached the main sequence. H-R diagrams of clusters provide evidence that stars of low mass spend much more time in the protostar stage than do more massive stars. As we explain in the next chapter, H-R diagrams of older galactic clusters can be used in a similar

galactic (or open) cluster A group of stars that share a common origin and are located relatively close to one another.

globular cluster A spherical group of up to hundreds of thousands of stars, found primarily in the halo of the Galaxy. Globular is pronounced "glob" (as in "mud") rather than "globe."

The history of host galaxies leaves an imprint on the properties of its globular clusters. It is possible then that, due to collisions between galaxies, not all stars in a globular cluster have the same origin.

FIGURE 13-20 Many clusters are named by their number in the New General Catalog (NGC), which was compiled between 1864 and 1908. (a) The cluster NGC457, in Cassiopeia, is called the Owl cluster and contains about 80 stars. The bright star is φ (phi) Cassiopeiae. (b) A pair of open clusters (NGC869 and NGC884) in the constellation Perseus.

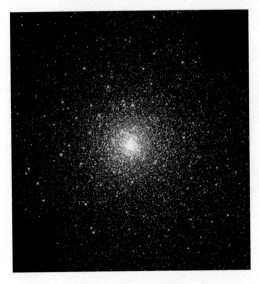

FIGURE 13-21 This is a globular cluster (M80). Globular clusters are gravitationally bound groups of hundreds of thousands of stars.

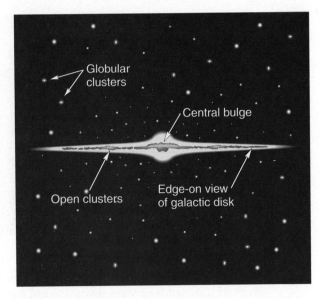

FIGURE 13-22 Galactic (open) clusters are found within the disk of the Galaxy, and globular clusters are found primarily in the halo surrounding the disk.

FIGURE 13-23 An H-R diagram of a very young cluster shows that low-mass protostars have not yet reached the main sequence. As time goes on, the H-R diagram of this cluster will look like the ones in Figure 14-6.

manner to reveal when stars end the main sequence part of their lives (see Figure 14-6).

Thus far, we have tracked the evolutionary path of stars through the protostar stage. When the core of a protostar becomes hot and dense enough, nuclear fusion begins. The new star becomes stable and begins the main sequence portion of its life. We discuss this stage of a star's life in Chapter 14.

As we observed earlier, the regularities we see in H-R diagrams such as Figure 13-23 prove the validity of the assumption that stars within a cluster began their lives at about the same time, for what other explanation could there be for the regularities? In the next chapter, we continue to examine the H-R diagrams of star clusters, for they are very valuable tools in our quest to understand stellar life cycles.

Conclusion

Interstellar space is so barren of matter that for many purposes it can be considered a vacuum; however, vast quantities of dust and gas do exist between the stars, and this material is important to astronomers for two main reasons. First, radiation from stars passes through the interstellar medium on its journey to Earth, and if astronomers are to understand the information carried by starlight, they must understand how the interstellar medium affects radiation. Second, interstellar matter is the stuff of which stars are made. If astronomers want to understand the life cycles of stars, they must first understand the substance from which the stars form. They must also use the entire spectrum to uncover details of the interstellar medium and the star-forming

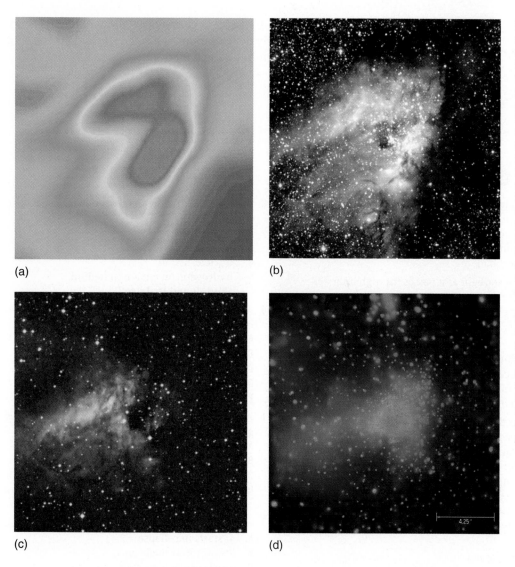

(a)

(b)

(c)

(d)

FIGURE 13-24 M17 is one of the most luminous and active star-forming regions in our Galaxy. The stars in the cloud are only a million years old. Each image is 17′ per side. (a) The VLA radio image shows the distribution of ionized hydrogen in the region, signifying active star formation. (b) The 2MASS infrared image reveals the dark molecular cloud; although it is too cold to emit visible or near-infrared light, its densest regions can still be seen as dark structures. (c) The DSS optical image shows dark regions (due to dust grains) superimposed on bright gas regions. (d) The *Chandra* X-ray image (processed to emphasize diffuse emission) shows hot gas (1.5–7 million K) flowing away from massive young stars; areas of low/high X-ray energy are shown in red/blue. The hot gas appears to have carved the horseshoe-shaped cavity in the cool gas seen in the infrared.

regions. FIGURE 13-24 shows the central region of the Horseshoe nebula (M17) in the radio, infrared, optical, and X-ray part of the spectrum.

Clouds of dust and gas in interstellar space differ in density, composition, and size. Interstellar cirrus is extremely diffuse, but some dust clouds are dense and large enough to extinguish light from stars on the other side of them. In some clouds, the processes of fluorescence and reflection provide beautiful images that can be appreciated by astronomers and nonastronomers alike.

Technological developments during the past few decades—particularly in microwave and radio telescopes—have provided many answers to questions about the interstellar medium, but, as is usual in science, they have also created additional questions. The quest to understand how stars are formed from the interstellar medium is of special interest to astronomers, and many mysteries remain, particularly about the initial steps in the formation of a star.

Whatever serves as the trigger to begin the collapse of portions of a giant molecular cloud, mutual gravitational forces between the particles continue and accelerate the compression. As the core of the cloud collapses, gravitational energy is transformed into thermal energy, which raises the temperature of the protostar. Finally, the inner portion of the collapsing matter becomes so hot and dense that nuclear fusion starts. At that time, the cloud begins its life on the main sequence of the H-R diagram. Examination of star clusters has shown the importance of a star's mass in determining how the star develops, for more massive stars become hotter and more luminous than less massive stars. In the next chapter, we show that mass is not only important in determining the early development of a star, but that it is the single most important property in determining the fate of stars.

STUDY GUIDE

1. In the densest interstellar cloud, the particle density is _____ the particle density of air at sea level on Earth.
   A. much less than
   B. about the same as
   C. much greater than

2. The reddening of starlight as it passes through interstellar dust clouds is due to
   A. the Doppler effect.
   B. fluorescence.
   C. scattering.

3. A nebula that glows due to fluorescence is called
   A. a fluorescence nebula.
   B. a reflection nebula.
   C. an emission nebula.

4. Absorption lines due to interstellar gas can be distinguished from spectral absorption lines caused by a star's atmosphere because
   A. their Doppler shifts are different.
   B. different chemical elements are found in the two different places.
   C. [The question is misleading; interstellar gas does not cause absorption lines.]

5. A protostar is
   A. a newly forming star.
   B. a main sequence star.
   C. a star nearing the red giant stage.
   D. a black dwarf.

6. H-R diagrams of young star clusters show
   A. fewer than about 10 stars.
   B. very few of the most luminous stars.
   C. that massive stars have not reached the main sequence.
   D. that low-mass stars have not yet reached the main sequence.

7. What is the primary difference between a star and a planet as each forms?
   A. Age.
   B. Mass.
   C. Volume.
   D. Chemical composition.
   E. Velocity.

8. Which of the following statements is true?
   A. Less massive protostars spend a longer time in the protostar stage than do more massive protostars.
   B. Protostars are surrounded by cocoons of gas and dust.
   C. Protostars radiate mainly in the infrared.
   D. [All of the above.]

9. Prior to reaching the main sequence, a star's energy comes from
   A. gravitation.
   B. nuclear fusion.
   C. nuclear fission.
   D. hydrogen conversion to helium.
   E. [Both B and D above.]

10. Although a star is on the main sequence, its energy comes primarily from
    A. gravitational shrinking.
    B. nuclear fusion.
    C. nuclear fission.
    D. proton instability.
    E. chemical reactions.

11. As a star is forming by the condensation of gases, the gases
    A. cool as they fall.
    B. heat up as they fall.
    C. stay about the same temperature.
    D. [Any of the above, depending upon the mass involved.]

12. A star is considered to begin its main sequence life when
    A. it starts to collapse.
    B. its protostar life begins.
    C. nuclear reactions start.
    D. it begins to move off the main sequence.
    E. its planetary system has formed.

13. The contraction of an interstellar cloud to become a star is caused by
    A. magnetic forces.
    B. electric forces.
    C. nuclear forces.
    D. gravitational forces.
    E. [Both A and B above, for they are closely related.]

14. An evolutionary track on an H-R diagram reveals
    A. the changes that occur in a star's life.
    B. the changes that occur as one star evolves into another.
    C. the motion of a star relative to others in its cluster.
    D. the motion of a star relative to others in the entire galaxy.
    E. [Both C and D above.]

15. Which of the following choices is *not* considered a possible trigger to begin the collapse of an interstellar gas cloud?
    A. A shock wave from a supernova.
    B. A shock wave occurring during the formation of very massive stars.

C. A shock wave resulting from radiation from nearby emission nebula.

D. A shock wave passing around the galaxy.

E. [All of the above are considered likely triggers.]

16. Clusters help us to learn about the evolution of stars because stars in a cluster
    A. are all about the same temperature.
    B. are all about the same mass.
    C. interact with one another and affect each other's evolution.
    D. are all about the same age.
    E. can be observed more easily than individual stars.

17. The H-R diagram for a single star cluster is different from the usual H-R diagram because all stars in the cluster have the same
    A. mass.
    B. temperature.

C. diameter.

D. rotational speed.

E. age.

18. What is a protostar?

19. List four possible events that may be responsible for triggering the collapse of interstellar clouds.

20. Which stars take longest to complete their protostar stage? Why?

21. What is the source of the energy that powers protostars?

22. Why is there a lower limit to the possible mass of a star? An upper limit?

23. Explain how galactic clusters provide observational evidence for theories of stellar evolution.

---

1. Starlight that has passed through a cloud of dust is reddened. So is starlight from a star that is moving away from us. In each case, how can we tell that the light from a star has been reddened? Perhaps what we see is the actual color of the star.

2. If light is passing through space, why does the universe look black except where we see dust, gas, or an object?

3. Describe the processes that produce each of the following types of nebulae: dark nebulae (like the Horsehead nebula), pink nebulae (like the N44 nebula), blue nebulae (like the one that appears near the Trifid nebula).

4. Explain how an examination of the H-R diagram for a large group of stars can tell us the relative lengths of the various stages of a star's life.

5. Why do astronomers feel that there must be a triggering mechanism for the beginning of an interstellar cloud's collapse? Why couldn't it happen on its own?

6. Explain the formation of "pillars" like those in Figure 13-10b.

7. Why do we think that most stars form from a *rotating* disk of gas? Couldn't it just as well be nonrotating?

8. Explain why the mass of a star determines the amount of time that the star remains a protostar.

9. The primary difference between protostars and main sequence stars is their energy source. What is the source of energy of each type of star?

10. Explain the value of star clusters to astronomers in their attempt to understand stellar evolution.

---

1. Along the line of sight to a particular star cluster, interstellar extinction allows only 20% of the light from the stars to pass through 1000 light-years of the interstellar medium. If this cluster is located 2000 light-years from us, what percentage of its light do we receive?

2. During our Sun's early stages of evolution, it had a surface temperature of 1000 K and luminosity 1000 times greater than it has now. What was our Sun's radius at this stage? Express this radius in astronomical units and as a multiple of the Sun's current radius. (Hint: 1000 K is about one sixth of the Sun's current surface temperature. Consider the Stefan-Boltzmann law.)

3. A star in Orion is located 0.1 degrees from the center of the nebula and is moving away from the center at 100 kilometers/second. How long ago did it get ejected from the center? (Hint: The distance to Orion is about 1500 light-years. Consider the small-angle formula.)

4. The temperature of dust grains in most interstellar clouds is about 300 K. Using Wien's law, calculate the wavelength at which most of the radiation is emitted by the grains. Is there a reason why astronomers are interested in using the infrared part of the electromagnetic spectrum to study these clouds?

Deep Sky Objects with a Small Telescope

Many beginning telescope users limit themselves to viewing the Moon and planets, but some interesting objects outside the solar system are accessible with a small telescope or even with binoculars. The star maps in this book can help you find the objects listed here. At the end of each listing is the time of year when the object is highest in the sky in the evening, but each may be seen in roughly the same place later at night, earlier in the year.

Orion nebula—A cloud of dust and gas 1500 light-years away. Its diameter is some 15 light-years. Find the Trapezium, four stars in a small dark area of the nebula (sometimes called the Fish Mouth). (January through March)

Alcor and Mizar—A naked-eye double star in Ursa Major. Your telescope will reveal that Mizar is itself a double star. (March through July)

Sagittarius—Such a rich area of the sky for interesting objects that if you slowly scan it with your telescope, you will find several clusters and nebulae. (July and August)

Albireo—A binary pair with obviously different colors (Figure 12-24). It is the "beak" star of the swan Cygnus, or the bottom star of the Northern Cross. (August through October)

Andromeda galaxy—A spiral galaxy similar to the Milky Way. Can you detect an oval shape? (October through December)

Pleiades—An open cluster visible to the naked eye. It contains a few hundred stars (although only six or seven are visible with the naked eye) and is about 400 light-years away. See whether you can detect the nebula around the stars. (November through February)

h and χ (the Greek letter "chi") Persei—A pair of open clusters visible to the naked eye (though not as easily as the Pleiades). In the sword handle of Perseus, they are an excellent view in binoculars. (November through February)

To enjoy your telescope (or binoculars) fully, a good star atlas is almost a necessity. The following are recommended:

The Monthly Sky Guide (8th ed.). Ian Ridpath and Wil Tirion. Cambridge University Press, 2006.

Whitney's Star Finder (5th ed.). C. Whitney. New York: Knopf, 1989.

A Field Guide to Stars and Planets (4th ed.). J. Pasachoff. Boston: Houghton Mifflin, 1999.

To keep up with developments in astronomy, you might contact the nonprofit Astronomical Society of the Pacific, whose aim is to share the excitement of astronomy with a wider public. Its members include scientists, teachers, hobbyists, and thousands of people from around the world who enjoy reading about the universe.

1. "The Stuff Between the Stars," by G. Knapp, in *Sky & Telescope* (May, 1995).

2. "The Early Life of Stars," by S. W. Stahler, in *Scientific American* (July, 1991).

3. "Interstellar Molecules," by G. L. Verschuur, in *Sky & Telescope* (April, 1992).

4. "Spying on Stellar Nurseries," by R. Jayawardhana, in *Astronomy* (November, 1998).

5. "Deciphering the Mysteries of Stellar Origins," by C. Lada, in *Sky & Telescope* (May, 1993).

6. "The Secrets of Stardust," by M. Greenberg, in *Scientific American* (December 2000).

7. "The Gas Between the Stars," by R. J. Reynolds, in *Scientific American* (January 2002).

8. "The Emptiest Places," by E. Scannapieco, P. Petitjean, and T. Broadhurst, in *Scientific American* (October 2002).

9. "Fountains of Youth: Early Days in the Life of a Star," by T. P. Ray, in *Scientific American* Special Edition (September 2004).

10. "Companion to Young Stars," by A. P. Boss, in *Scientific American* Special Edition (September 2004).

11. "Stellar Archaeology," by F. Reddy, in *Astronomy* (May 2005).

12. "Stellar Origins: From the Cold Depths of Space," by D. Shepherd, in *Sky & Telescope* (June 2007).

Quest Ahead to Starlinks
http://physicalscience.jbpub.com/starlinks

Starlinks is this book's online learning center. It features **eLearning**, which contains chapter quizzes and other tools designed to help you study for your class. You can also find **online exercises**, view numerous relevant **animations**, follow a guide to **useful astronomy sites** on the Internet, or even check the latest **astronomy news** updates.

The Lives and Deaths of Low-Mass Stars

14

THIS BEAUTIFUL *HST* IMAGE SHOWS THE "CAT'S EYE NEBULA." The image reveals that the nebula contains at least 11 concentric gas shells (each being the edge of a bubble seen projected on the sky), jets of high-speed gas, and shock-induced knots of gas. Because of its age (estimated to be 1000 years), the nebula is a visual "fossil record" of the late stages of evolution of a dying star, which is expected to collapse into a white dwarf in a few million years.

The "Cat's Eye nebula," officially named NGC6543, as seen by the *Hubble Space Telescope* (*HST*).

The observations suggest that the dying star at the center has been ejecting its outer layers in a series of pulses at 1500-year intervals. The resulting dust shells create the observed structure of layered rings around the star. It is not yet clear what creates this pattern of mass loss every 1500 years, but it seems that about 1000 years ago the pattern changed; as a result, the nebula started forming inside the dusty shells and has been expanding ever since.

Such images reveal the beauty of distant dying stars, but we hope that as we study the lives and deaths of stars, you will also admire the beauty of the theory that underlies these events.

Stars form from the material of the interstellar medium. As a portion of a giant molecular cloud collapses, the matter in its core becomes hotter and denser until

All cross references to chapters, sections, figures, and tables pertain to the main text, *In Quest of the Universe, Sixth Edition. In Quest of the Solar System* contains Chapters 1–11 and 19 of the main text. *In Quest of the Stars and Galaxies* contains Chapters 1–5 and 11–19 of the main text.

nuclear fusion begins. When this happens, the object joins the family of stars, for it is then on the main sequence of the H-R diagram, where it will spend most of its life.

In this chapter, we describe stars of relatively low mass, those toward the bottom of the main sequence (including our Sun). We show that although all stars live their main sequence lives in much the same manner, they differ greatly in the way they die. Stars with very low masses seem to fade away, "giving up the ghost" gently. Others expand to become red giants and then puff away their outer layers, thereby revealing their previously hidden white-hot cores.

As we study the amazing events in the lives of stars, keep in mind that we are describing the results of various models of stellar interiors. We cannot examine the inside of a star directly. Instead, we observe the properties of the surfaces of stars and make mathematical models of what must be occurring inside them to produce our data. Such models have improved dramatically in the last 20 years as computer capabilities have increased; the calculations that produce today's models are numerous and complex.

Theoretical models cannot be divorced from reality, of course. They must correspond to observations. For example, the major supernova of 1987 (which we study in Section 15-3) served as a case history for testing models of supernovae. The supernova excited astronomers not only because it provided another opportunity to test their theories, but—as we will see—because it confirmed most of their predictions.

14-1 Brown Dwarfs

As we explained in the previous chapter, the mass of a collapsing object determines how long the object remains in the protostar stage. After a star has completed its protostar stage and reached the main sequence, its mass continues to be the dominant property determining the steps it passes through during its life; therefore, before discussing stellar life cycles, we should examine the question of what limits the mass of a star.

The maximum mass that a star can have is probably about 150 solar masses. If a protostar has more mass than this, it collapses quickly and develops tremendous amounts of energy and internal pressure. This pressure is so large that it overwhelms gravity and blows the star apart before it can establish equilibrium on the main sequence.

On the other hand, suppose that a very small portion of an interstellar cloud becomes compressed enough for the gravitational force to take over and continue the collapse. Calculations show that if this protostar has a mass greater than about 8% of the Sun's mass, the object's core becomes hot and dense enough for nuclear fusion to begin. In that case, the object joins the main sequence as a full-fledged star. But what if the protostar has less than enough mass for fusion to begin? In this case, the object still heats up due to gravitational contraction. FIGURE 14-1a shows hypothetical evolutionary trails of five protostars on an H-R diagram. The two with the most mass become stars on the main sequence. Two other protostars on the diagram—those with masses of 0.07 and 0.02 times the mass of the Sun—heat up so that they glow with a dull red color, but nuclear fusion never starts in their cores. Their dull color gives them their name: *brown dwarfs*. After a brief initial phase where some deuterium is burned, brown dwarfs continue to cool, releasing the heat left over from their birth, and become progressively fainter. The fifth object has the mass of the planet Jupiter, which may once have emitted a small amount of visible light, but now is too cool to do so.

The question of how small an object can be and still be classified as a brown dwarf is open for discussion. In order to separate large planets from brown dwarfs, we set the lower limit for the mass of a brown dwarf to be 13.6 times the mass of Jupiter; more massive objects undergo deuterium burning, whereas those with mass greater than 65 times the mass of Jupiter undergo both deuterium and lithium burning. Brown dwarf mass limits thus are between 0.013 and 0.08 solar masses.

Brown dwarfs have been predicted since 1963, but until one was found, astronomers were not able to confirm that it is possible for such a small portion of an

brown dwarf A star-like object that has insufficient mass to start nuclear reactions in its core and thus become self-luminous.

(a)

(b)

FIGURE 14-1 (a) Protostars with masses less than about 0.08 solar masses never reach the main sequence. Of the five stars whose evolutionary paths are shown here, two become main-sequence stars, two become brown dwarfs, and one becomes a planet. (b) The small object just right of center is GL229B, a brown dwarf, photographed by the *HST* in far red light. The dwarf is a companion to a much brighter star, Gliese 229, that is off the left edge of the image. The two objects are about 18 light-years away from us in the constellation Lepus and are separated from one another by at least 4 billion miles. (c) This VLT near-infrared composite image shows the brown dwarf (2M1207a) and its companion planet (2M1207b) in the 8-million-year-old TW Hydrae association, located about 230 light-years away.

778 mas
55 AU at 70 pc

(c)

interstellar cloud to collapse. Until 1994, the only objects whose existence was confirmed that were near the required size were the planets of our solar system. The first brown dwarf was seen in October 1994, using adaptive optics with the 60-inch telescope on Mount Palomar. It appears very close to another star, a red dwarf, and a year after the discovery, astronomers confirmed that the brown dwarf is actually gravitationally bound to the nearby star. Figure 14-1b is an *HST* photograph of the brown dwarf, called GL229B; it has about 20 to 50 times the mass of Jupiter and about the same diameter as Jupiter.

Brown dwarfs bridge the gap between stars and planets. Their properties reveal new insights into how stars and planets form. Even though brown dwarfs have been discovered orbiting stars, many of them seem to be isolated. How do brown dwarfs form? Two main scenarios have been proposed for isolated brown dwarfs. According to the first scenario, brown dwarfs form just like stars, by contraction in an interstellar cloud of dust and gas. In the second scenario, when a very young star in a multiple star system gets ejected from the system, it loses access to the surrounding accretion disk; this effectively stops its further growth by accretion, and it ends up as a brown dwarf. Computer simulations that follow the collapse of an interstellar gas cloud support this scenario. Such simulations show that the process of star formation is chaotic; in new-born stellar groups the more massive objects gather more gas than lower mass objects, the latter being ejected from the groups so quickly that they do not manage to accrete enough gas to become stars.

The preponderance of evidence supports the idea that brown dwarfs form like stars, however VLT and *Spitzer* observations support the presence of dusty disks around young brown dwarfs by detecting their infrared emission. Just like young stars, the majority of brown dwarfs are surrounded by such disks at an age of about a million years, and disks are also present around brown dwarfs as old as 10 million

A red dwarf is a small-mass star with low temperature and, as a result, it appears red.

Current predictions suggest that there should be twice as many brown dwarfs as main sequence stars. As of 2009, there are about 620 known brown dwarfs.

Jets are ubiquitous in the universe. They are observed over an enormous range of masses (from young stellar objects to active nuclei of galaxies) and lengths (from a few AUs to millions of light-years).

years. Other spectroscopic observations show that the accretion of material from the disks around brown dwarfs occurs at a slower pace but is otherwise similar to that from disks around young stars. Finally, brown dwarfs have been observed in pairs, and in 2005, astronomers confirmed the presence of a 5 Jupiter-masses planet orbiting a young, 25 Jupiter-masses brown dwarf (Figure 14-1c); VLT observations in 2007 show the presence of jets emanating from this brown dwarf, a behavior similar to that of young stars. *Spitzer* has also observed the beginnings of what might become planets around brown dwarfs by detecting clumps of tiny dust grains and crystals orbiting five brown dwarfs.

After the discovery of brown dwarfs, two new spectral types were introduced below the long-known cool M dwarfs. The L and T types, loosely defined at present, cover the temperature range from 3500 to about 1000 K. Objects in this range are almost invisible at optical wavelengths, with most of their emission coming out in the infrared. As the surface of a brown dwarf cools below 1500 K, something dramatic happens that changes its appearance; large amounts of methane form, making the T-type brown dwarfs the coolest objects detected so far.

Notice that we have avoided referring to a brown dwarf as a star. The reason for this is that the word *star* is reserved for an object massive enough to sustain nuclear fusion in its core, that is, to have reached stellar maturity on the main sequence.

14-2 Stellar Maturity

Do stars simply ignite and start fusion reactions immediately?

When the center of a collapsing star becomes hot and dense enough, hydrogen fusion begins. Gravitational contraction serves as the energy source for protostars, heating them and causing the emission of radiation, but main sequence stars—including our Sun—have as their energy source the fusion of hydrogen into helium.

Stellar Nuclear Fusion

In Section 11-2, we described the fusion reactions that occur in the Sun. That series of reactions, known as the proton–proton chain, is the predominant reaction that provides the energy for stars of low mass, up to about 1.5 solar masses. For the sake of completeness, it is repeated in FIGURE 14-2.

Stars that have masses greater than about 1.5 solar masses have higher temperatures in their cores, and a different chain of nuclear reactions dominates. This series of reactions involves carbon, nitrogen, and oxygen, and is called the ***carbon cycle*** or the ***CNO cycle***. Its steps are shown in FIGURE 14-3. If you examine the steps of the CNO cycle, you will see that its overall effect is to

carbon (or **CNO**) **cycle**
A series of nuclear reactions that results in the fusion of hydrogen into helium, using carbon-12 in the process.

FIGURE 14-2 In the proton–proton chain, four hydrogen nuclei are changed to one helium nucleus, releasing energy in the process. The symbol e$^+$ denotes a positive electron, a positron. Dashed arrows indicate a nucleus taking part in the next reaction. In the third reaction, the second hydrogen-3 nucleus comes from a second occurrence of the two previous steps.

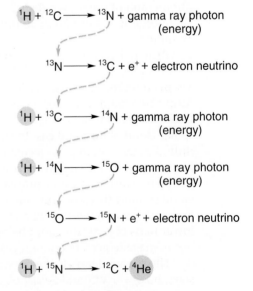

FIGURE 14-3 The CNO cycle changes four hydrogen nuclei into one helium nucleus, with an attendant release of energy.

transform four hydrogen nuclei into one helium nucleus, just like the proton–proton chain. Carbon-12 is one of the nuclei that participates in the reaction, but for each carbon-12 nucleus that enters the reaction, one is produced at the end; therefore, there is no net change in the carbon. It participates only as a facilitator. (This is similar to the role played by catalysts in some chemical reactions. The catalyst stimulates the reaction but is not used up in it.)

The Stellar Thermostat

Thermostats on the walls in our homes have two features: a thermometer to read the temperature and a switch to make the furnace or air conditioner turn on or off. If the thermometer indicates that the temperature is below some preset level, the switch turns on the furnace until the thermometer indicates that the temperature is high enough, whereupon the switch turns off the furnace. The core of a main sequence star has an analogous regulating mechanism, which controls the rate of consumption of the hydrogen fuel.

Suppose that somehow the rate of hydrogen fusion in a star begins to increase. The extra energy produced causes the temperature of the core to increase; however, when the temperature of a gas increases, the gas expands. This expansion serves as a switch to decrease the rate of fusion. This occurs because in the expanded gas, the average distance between hydrogen nuclei has increased, and the increase in distance means fewer collisions and therefore fewer fusions. The result is that the expansion causes the rate of energy production to decrease, which causes the expansion to stop. In this way equilibrium is reached, and fusion reactions occur at a uniform rate.

On the other hand, if the rate of fusion in a star's core somehow decreases, the core contracts, decreasing the distance between nuclei. This causes the fusion rate to increase. Another effect that occurs when the core contracts is the conversion of gravitational energy into heat, just as occurred when the original interstellar cloud collapsed; therefore, energy comes both from an increase in fusion and from gravitational energy, and both of these energies contribute to the thermostat that brings the star once again to equilibrium. The overall effect of the stellar thermostat is that nuclear fusion proceeds at a rate that is just enough to balance the force of gravity that tends to compress the star.

The analogy of a thermostat is an alternative description of hydrostatic equilibrium, which we discussed in Section 11-3.

When you pucker your lips and blow on your hand, your breath feels cold because it expands as it moves from inside your mouth to the outside air. Similarly, gases in a bottle of carbonated drink expand and cool when you open the bottle, creating a small cloud in the bottle's neck.

When you pump air into a bicycle tire with a hand pump, the compressed air gets warm, making the pump warm, too.

Main Sequence Life of Stars

The stellar thermostat is important during the main sequence life of a star. In a main sequence star, hydrogen in the core of the star is continually being converted to helium as the nuclear reaction occurs. This causes the number of particles in the core to decrease gradually (as *four* hydrogen nuclei are converted to *one* helium nucleus), and this results in the core shrinking slightly. In turn, the contraction causes the temperature to rise within the core, and this increases the rate of fusion; therefore, the core releases more energy, and as this energy flows outward, it causes the outer portion of the star to expand somewhat. These steps are outlined in FIGURE 14-4. We see the effects of these changes on the H-R diagram (FIGURE 14-5), for the increase in energy from the star means that it has a greater luminosity, and thus, it moves upward on the diagram. In addition, the expansion of the star causes its outer layers to cool a little,

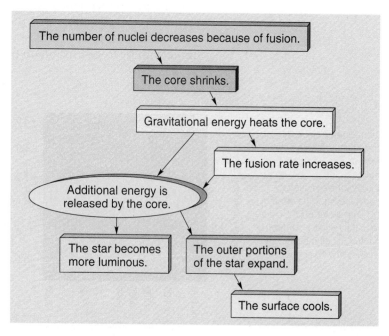

FIGURE 14-4 This diagram shows why a star becomes more luminous and cooler as it ages on the main sequence. Each arrow indicates that one event causes the next.

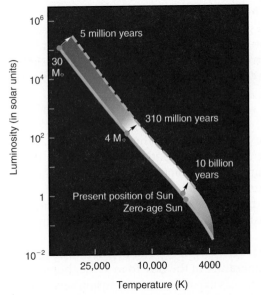

zero-age main sequence
The main sequence of newly formed stars that just started hydrogen fusion in their cores.

and this causes the star to move to the right on the diagram, toward lower temperatures. These changes are the reason the main sequence has a perceptible width. Stars start their lives as *zero-age main sequence* stars on the left side of the strip and then move up and to the right as they age.

The changes that the Sun is undergoing will have drastic effects on the Earth. The Sun began its main sequence life about 5 billion years ago, at which time its chemical composition was about 74% hydrogen, 25% helium, and the remaining 1% other heavier elements. As a result of the nuclear reactions, the Sun's core has contracted a bit. The Sun's luminosity has increased by about 40%, and its core now contains more helium than hydrogen (about 64% helium and 35% hydrogen). There is still enough hydrogen in its core for our Sun to continue on the main sequence for another 5 billion years, at which time it will be twice as luminous as it is now. This will raise the average temperature of the Earth by about 20°C (36°F), enough to melt the polar caps and drastically change the Earth's climate. Because the Sun was dimmer in the past, liquid water on the Earth's surface would have been frozen. This contradicts geological observations of sedimentary rocks, whose presence requires flowing liquid water. In order to resolve this contradiction, called the *faint young Sun paradox*, scientists have proposed that strong volcanic outgassing of greenhouse gases during Earth's early history kept the temperature high enough for liquid water to exist. It is possible, however, that the Earth experienced a number of periods when the oceans froze over completely.

Stars that are more massive than the Sun have a much greater fusion rate because their cores have greater pressures and higher temperatures—the thermostat is set higher in massive stars. This means they are more luminous. (Recall from our discussion in Section 12-7 the mass–luminosity relationship for main sequence stars: the more massive, the more luminous.) The greater fusion rate also causes these massive stars to use up their core hydrogen in a much shorter time. The most massive stars fuse hydrogen so quickly that their cores run out of hydrogen in only a few million years. Calculations for the least massive stars, on the other hand, show that they continue with hydrogen fusion on the main sequence for hundreds of billions of years.

FIGURE 14-6 (a) An H-R diagram of the Pleiades reveals that its most massive stars have started leaving the main sequence. The arrows indicate the evolutionary paths they must have taken. (b) The cluster M11 is older than the Pleiades, and stars are turning off the main sequence at a lower point.

(a)

(b)

Observational evidence for the shorter lifetimes of massive stars comes from galactic clusters. FIGURE 14-6a is the H-R diagram of the Pleiades. Although this is considered a young cluster, its most massive stars are already leaving the main sequence. Arrows on the figure indicate their evolutionary paths after they end their main sequence lives. Figure 14-6b is a similar diagram for the cluster M11, a cluster older than the Pleiades. The most massive stars have moved even farther to the right whereas stars of less mass are now leaving the main sequence. Assuming that the stars in a cluster were all formed at approximately the same time, H-R diagrams such as those shown in Figure 14-6 allow us to find the age of a cluster. Stars at the *turnoff point*, which corresponds to the top of the group of stars still on the main sequence, are just now exhausting their core hydrogen and starting to move off the main sequence; therefore, the main-sequence lifetime of the stars at the turnoff point is equal to the age of the cluster.

The name M11 means that this cluster is number 11 in the Messier Catalog of Nebulae and Star Clusters, originally developed in 1781 by the French astronomer Charles Messier (1730–1817).

14-3 Star Death

Until the end of their lives on the main sequence, the primary difference between the evolution of stars of various masses is in the amount of time they spend as protostars and as main sequence stars. For example, a one-solar-mass protostar takes about 30 million years to become a main-sequence star, whereas a 15-solar-masses protostar takes only 150,000 years. The main-sequence lifetime of a one-solar-mass star is about 10 billion years, whereas that of a 15-solar-masses star is only about 10 million years. From this point on, however, the mass of a star determines which of several very different paths its life will take. We discuss each of these paths in turn, beginning with stars of very low mass. Because mass classifications are fairly arbitrary and astronomers have not agreed on official names for the different classes, we group them in the following categories: very low mass (less than 0.4 $M_⊙$), moderately low mass (0.4–4 $M_⊙$), moderately massive (4–8 $M_⊙$), and very massive stars (greater than 8 $M_⊙$), where $M_⊙$ is the mass of the Sun.

turnoff point The point on an H-R diagram of a cluster of stars where the stars are just leaving the main sequence.

14-4 Very Low Mass Stars (<0.4 M_⊙)

Recall from the discussion in Section 11-3 of energy transport within the Sun that little convection takes place in the Sun except in the outer layers. That is why after hydrogen is used up in the core of a star like the Sun, the core is not replenished with fresh hydrogen from outside. This causes the star to move from the main sequence.

In the least massive stars (those with a mass of less than about 0.4 solar masses), however, convection occurs throughout most or all of the star's volume (FIGURE 14-7); therefore, hydrogen from throughout the star is cycled through the core, and the entire star runs low on hydrogen at the same time. When this happens, the rate of fusion in the core decreases. As described earlier, this causes the core to contract and its temperature to increase as gravitational energy is converted into *thermal energy*. In a more massive star, this thermal energy is carried outward by radiation, but a very low mass star distributes its thermal energy by convection. The result is that the entire star contracts and heats up. On the H-R diagram, the star moves toward the lower left (FIGURE 14-8) and becomes a *white dwarf*.

Computer models indicate that a star with very low mass requires more than 20 billion years to complete the nuclear burning of its hydrogen fuel and end its main sequence life. Because this is greater than the age of the universe, the white dwarfs that astronomers see could not have originated in this manner. For this reason, we discuss white dwarfs again later in this chapter.

thermal energy Energy that is due to the random motions of molecules and atoms of a substance.

white dwarf The burnt-out relic of a low mass star.

In everyday language, the word "heat" is often used when "thermal energy" would be more correct. Strictly speaking, heat is the exchange of thermal energy.

TOOLS OF ASTRONOMY

Lifetimes on the Main Sequence

The amount of time that a star spends on the main sequence depends on two things: the amount of hydrogen in its core and its rate of hydrogen consumption. The relationship can be expressed as a proportionality:

$$t \propto \frac{\text{amount of hydrogen}}{\text{rate of hydrogen consumption}},$$

where t represents the star's lifetime and the symbol "$\propto$" means "proportional to." Because all stars have roughly the same proportion of core hydrogen at equivalent points in their lives, the amount of hydrogen in a star is proportional to its mass M. The rate at which the hydrogen is consumed depends on the star's luminosity. Therefore,

$$t \propto \frac{M}{L}.$$

In Section 12-7, we explained that a star's luminosity (L) is proportional to its mass (M) raised to the power of 3.5. Thus,

$$t \propto \frac{M}{M^{3.5}} \propto \frac{1}{M^{2.5}}.$$

Using the Sun as a standard so that t_{Sun} is the lifetime of the Sun on the main sequence and M is measured in units of the Sun's mass, the previous expression can be written as an equation:

$$t = \frac{t_{Sun}}{M^{2.5}}.$$

Then the main sequence lifetime of a star with a mass of 3 solar masses can be calculated as follows:

$$t = \frac{t_{Sun}}{M^{2.5}} = \frac{t_{Sun}}{3 \times 3 \times \sqrt{3}} \approx 0.064 \times t_{Sun}.$$

A star with three times the Sun's mass thus will live on the main sequence only about 6% as long as the Sun. Because the Sun's main sequence life (t_{Sun}) is about 10 billion years, this star's life will be about 640 million years. Similarly, a star with a third of the mass of the Sun will remain on the main sequence for 16 times longer than the Sun, about 160 billion years.

FIGURE 14-7 The Sun (at left) contains a large radiative zone. A star of very low mass, on the other hand, consists of one convective zone, meaning that all of its material mixes.

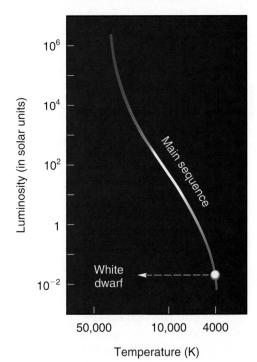

FIGURE 14-8 Very low mass stars spend their main sequence lifetimes at the very bottom of the main sequence. Although the universe is not old enough for any to have completed that stage of their life, when they do, they will slowly become hotter and join the category of white dwarfs.

14-5 Beyond the Very Low Mass Stars: The Red Giant Stage

About 90% of the stars in the sky are on the main sequence. This tells us that a typical star spends 90% of its luminous lifetime there. In all cases except for stars of very low mass (those with mass less than about 0.4 solar masses), the next step for stars leaving the main sequence is essentially the same. They become red giants.

The process of becoming a red giant starts when the core begins to run low on hydrogen fuel. Until then, the nearly constant production of fusion energy kept the core from collapsing. Now, lacking a source of energy to fight gravitational collapse, the core starts to shrink dramatically; however, just as in the case of a protostar, the contraction converts gravitational energy into thermal energy and radiation. In fact, the energy produced in the core actually increases over what it was when the energy source was fusion. The resulting increase of radiation from the core causes the shell of material around the core to heat up enough that hydrogen fusion begins there (FIGURE 14-9).

Now gravitational energy is being converted to thermal energy in the core and fusion is producing energy in a shell surrounding the core. These two sources of energy in the star's center result in a large increase in radiation from the center and cause the outer part of the star to expand. When a gas expands, it cools, and the outer portion of the star does just that. The star's surface temperature thus decreases, and the star moves to the right on the H-R diagram. At the same time, it moves upward, toward the red giant region, because its total luminosity is increasing because of the additional energy being produced in the core.

It may seem strange that a star can decrease its surface temperature and at the same time increase its luminosity, for when an object cools, it emits *less* radiation per square meter of its surface. The key to understanding this apparent contradiction is to realize just how large the red giant becomes. The Sun, at this stage in its life as a giant, will have expanded so that it encompasses the orbit of Mercury! It is true that each square meter of the Sun's cooler surface will emit less radiation, but the surface will have become so tremendously large that the total radiation emitted will be greater than before. FIGURE 14-10 illustrates how the Sun will change its position on the H-R diagram. As the Sun expands, it will move from point *A*, its turn-off point from the main sequence, toward point *B*. At this point as a red giant star, our Sun will be about 1000 times brighter than it is today, even though its surface temperature will be only about 3500 K. The outer planets will lose their atmospheres because of the

The cooling of a gas as it expands is what causes the gas escaping from an aerosol spray can to feel so cold.

FIGURE 14-9 As the core of a star shrinks, it heats up, causing additional hydrogen fusion in a shell surrounding the core. (The core and hydrogen-fusing shell are actually a much smaller fraction of the star than is shown here.)

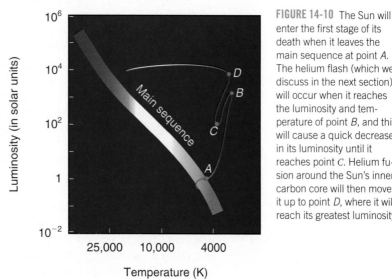

FIGURE 14-10 The Sun will enter the first stage of its death when it leaves the main sequence at point *A*. The helium flash (which we discuss in the next section) will occur when it reaches the luminosity and temperature of point *B*, and this will cause a quick decrease in its luminosity until it reaches point *C*. Helium fusion around the Sun's inner carbon core will then move it up to point *D*, where it will reach its greatest luminosity.

TABLE 14-1

A Typical Red Giant

Absolute magnitude	−1
Luminosity (solar units)	500
Mass (solar units)	1
Diameter (solar units)	200
Average density	10^{-7} g/cm³ (Sun's average density = 1.4 g/cm³)
Surface temperature	3600 K

increase in brightness and some of the inner planets will be vaporized. **TABLE 14-1** lists some properties of a typical red giant.

14-6 Moderately Low Mass Stars (0.4-4 M$_\odot$)

All main sequence stars become red giants (or supergiants, which we study in the next chapter) when they leave the main sequence. How stars change during the red giant stage, however, depends on how massive they are. We first consider the moderately low mass stars on the main sequence. This group includes stars from about 0.4 solar masses up to about 4 solar masses, and therefore, it includes our Sun. Even among members of this group, there are differences in the conditions that develop in their cores as they proceed to become red giants and in the way that the next cycle of nuclear fusion (helium fusion) begins in their cores. Because of these differences, we first consider stars with mass less than about 2 solar masses.

Electron Degeneracy and the Helium Flash

The core of a star at the end of its main sequence life consists of helium nuclei intermingled with electrons, a mixture that has properties similar to a regular gas. In this case, a simple relationship exists between pressure, temperature, and volume. For example, an increase in pressure exerted on a normal gas causes its volume to decrease and its temperature to increase. That is why gravitational pressure causes a star's core to contract and heat up when hydrogen fusion shuts down at the end of main sequence life.

As a moderately low mass star becomes a red giant, some unusual conditions start to develop in its core. Under the increasing temperatures and pressures, the free electrons in the core are forced to get very close to each other. After the density of the core reaches a certain value, the electrons are so closely packed together that any additional compression violates a very important natural law. According to this law, two electrons cannot have completely identical parameters describing their state. In a simple analogy, if we are playing a game of musical chairs, with each chair corresponding to a specific state for the electrons, only one electron is allowed to occupy each chair. As a result, the electrons produce a large pressure that resists any attempt to compress them further. At this point, the core stops contracting. The matter of the core is now said to be **degenerate**, and the pressure that supports it against gravity is called *electron degeneracy pressure*.

When a normal gas is heated, its pressure increases and the gas expands. In degenerate matter, pressure does not depend on temperature; it depends only on density. The properties of degenerate matter lead to a strange phenomenon. Refer to the graph in **FIGURE 14-11a**, which shows the relationship between the radius and the mass of a main sequence star. As you would expect, the more massive the star, the larger is its radius; however, the degenerate core of a red giant does not act this way, as shown in Figure 14-11b. The more massive the core of a red giant, the smaller is its radius!

electron degeneracy The state of a gas in which its electrons are packed as densely as nature permits.

(a)

(b)

FIGURE 14-11 (a) In the case of normal, main sequence stars, the more massive the star, the larger is its radius. (b) In the case of the degenerate core of a red giant, however, the more massive the core is, the *smaller* is its radius.

This is very different from our experience with nondegenerate—regular—matter, and it has a profound influence on the next stage of the star's evolution.

As the hot, degenerate core of a red giant radiates its thermal energy outward, hydrogen continues to fuse to helium in a shell around the core. The hydrogen-fusing shell gradually works its way outward, all the time dumping its helium "ashes" onto the core. Because of the strange relationship between the mass and the radius of a degenerate core, the increased mass falling onto the core causes the core to shrink further and further. This, in turn, causes the core's temperature to continue to rise. Finally, the temperature of the red giant's core reaches a critical value, calculated to be about 100,000,000 K. At this point, shown as point *B* in Figure 14-10, helium nuclei begin to combine, forming carbon. The first steps in helium fusion reactions that produce carbon and oxygen from helium are shown in more detail in **TABLE 14-2** and **FIGURE 14-12**. Helium fusion does not occur at lower temperatures because helium nuclei repel each other with a much stronger force than hydrogen nuclei do, as each helium nucleus contains two protons, compared with only one proton for a hydrogen nucleus. At higher temperatures, helium nuclei move faster and therefore can get close enough for fusion to occur.

A helium nucleus is also known as an *alpha particle*, and the conversion of three helium nuclei into a carbon nucleus is called the *triple-alpha process*.

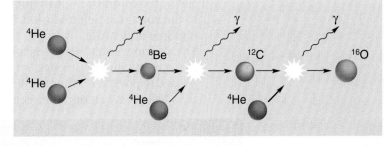

Helium fusion does not proceed smoothly, however. Degenerate matter is a good conductor of thermal energy and, thus, the additional energy produced by

FIGURE 14-12 This diagram shows schematically the steps that occur as helium fuses into carbon in the core of a red giant.

TABLE 14-2

Helium Fusion Reactions that Occur in Red Giants

Reaction	Explanation
$^4_2H + ^4_2H \rightarrow\ ^8_4Be + \gamma$ (energy)	Two helium nuclei combine to produce a beryllium-8 nucleus and a gamma ray (γ).
$^4_2H + ^8_4Be \rightarrow\ ^{12}_6C + \gamma$ (energy)	Another helium nucleus combines with the beryllium nucleus to form a carbon-12 nucleus and another gamma ray.
After sufficient carbon has been generated by the triple-alpha process, carbon nuclei can capture alpha particles (helium nuclei) to produce oxygen.	
$^4_2H + ^{12}_6C \rightarrow\ ^{16}_8O + \gamma$ (energy)	Carbon in the core fuses with helium and produces oxygen and another gamma ray (and more energy).

the new nuclear reactions spreads rapidly throughout the core. The helium in the core heats up and as a result helium fusion reactions occur faster; however, the pressure in the core does not change because the core is degenerate, and the electron degeneracy pressure does not depend on temperature. As a result, the core cannot cool by expanding and the continuously increasing core temperature causes the helium to fuse faster. The core "ignites" quickly and violently, a process known as the *helium flash*.

You might think that the violence of the helium flash would have a drastic effect on the outer portion of the star. After all, the luminosity generated by the core during a helium flash can reach 100 billion times the luminosity of our Sun, comparable to the luminosity of our entire Galaxy; however, this huge energy release lasts for only a few seconds, and most of the energy never makes it to the surface. Instead, computer models show that the helium flash changes the core drastically. Most of the energy released during a helium flash goes into heating up the core and destroying the electron degeneracy, thus restoring the stellar thermostat. The energy that escapes the core is absorbed by the layers overlying the core, which are opaque, possibly causing some mass from the surface of the star to be lost.

After the helium flash occurs, signaling the start of helium fusion in the core and providing the star with a new energy source, the star contracts slightly and its surface temperature increases. You might find this to be a very counterintuitive result. Because the core is not degenerate anymore, it expands like a normal gas. As a result, the temperature around the core decreases, and this cooling slows down the hydrogen fusion reactions in the shell around the core. Because this shell provides most of the red giant's luminosity, the resulting decrease in energy output allows the star's outer layers to contract and heat up. This stage in the evolution of the star is shown in Figure 14-10 as the movement from point *B* to point *C*.

The by-products of helium fusion reactions are carbon and oxygen nuclei. Our Sun will take about 100 million years to convert all the helium in its core to carbon and oxygen. At this point, because there is no energy source in the core, the core contracts until the electron degeneracy pressure stops the contraction again. As a result of the contraction, the temperature in a thin shell surrounding the core increases to the point that helium fusion reactions begin in this shell. While all this is happening close to the core, hydrogen fusion continues in a shell around the helium shell. The star now enters a new red giant phase. FIGURE 14-13 shows the structure of a star like our Sun during this stage of its evolution. During this time, the star evolves from point *C* to point *D* on the H-R diagram of Figure 14-10. Its size is now even larger than before. When our Sun reaches this stage, about 5 billion years from now, it will have expanded to enfold Mercury, Venus, and the Earth (FIGURE 14-14). Its luminosity will reach 10,000 times its current luminosity.

helium flash The runaway helium fusion reactions that occur in the core during the evolution of a red giant.

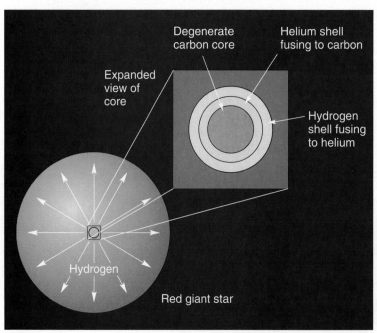

FIGURE 14-13 When a red giant reaches the stage where it has a carbon core, the heat from that shrinking core ignites helium fusion in a shell around it. At the same time, hydrogen is fusing in a second shell beyond the first. This activity occupies very little of the volume of the star.

What will happen to the Earth? As the outer layers of the red giant approach Earth, our planet will find itself speeding through the hot gas of the Sun's atmosphere. Earth's atmosphere will be ripped away. The planet will be slowed by friction and will begin falling toward the Sun's center. Meanwhile the Earth's crust will melt and then vaporize. Our planet will become one with the Sun. Mars and the Jovian planets will mostly evaporate away.

In this section, we concentrated on stars with mass less than about 2 solar masses. Computer simulations indicate that stars more massive than about 2 solar masses do not experience a helium flash. The cores of these stars get hot enough toward the end of hydrogen burning that they make a smooth transition to helium burning without becoming degenerate. When their supply of helium is exhausted, however, their carbon core shrinks and becomes degenerate just as it does for lower mass, Sun-like stars; therefore, in both cases, the interior of the new red giant has the structure of Figure 14-13.

Stellar Pulsations

During its evolution, a star continuously tries to remain in equilibrium. As its outer layers contract and expand, responding to the changes occurring in the core, the star's luminosity changes drastically, and these changes are often periodic. Astronomers have been able to deduce this behavior by using spectroscopic observations and the Doppler effect, and they have catalogued more than 20,000 pulsating stars, with periods that range from a few seconds to hundreds of days. Two types of pulsating stars are especially important to astronomers because they can be used as distance indicators. In Section 12-8 we discussed one of these groups, the Cepheid variables, which are pulsating stars with periods between 1 and 100 days. In this section, we explain the reason for the pulsations for both the Cepheids and another important group of distance indicators, the RR Lyrae variables.

As for any periodic phenomenon, a particular mechanism is responsible for the oscillations of a star's outer layers. When helium gets compressed at the outer layers of a Cepheid, the compression ionizes the helium atoms instead of increasing their temperature. Because the resulting gas of ionized helium is opaque, the layers trap heat from inside the star. This increases the pressure under the layers, forcing them to move outward. As a result of the expansion, the outer layers cool. The helium atoms are not ionized any more. The helium gas in the layers becomes transparent, and the trapped energy is released. Finally, the outer layers fall inward, compressing the helium and starting the cycle again. The conditions necessary for such pulsations to occur exist in a narrow strip on the H-R diagram, called the *instability strip* (FIGURE 14-15).

After helium fusion reactions begin in the core, a *massive* star moves across the middle of the H-R diagram. As the star crisscrosses the red-giant region of the H-R diagram, it can become unstable and pulsate while inside the instability strip, becoming a Cepheid variable. After the helium flash stage, *low mass stars* also crisscross the instability strip, but through its lower end. Some of these low mass stars become variable stars with periods shorter than a day and approximately constant luminosity (100 times that of our Sun). These low mass variables are called *RR Lyrae variables*. The relationship between the period and luminosity of RR Lyrae stars allows astronomers to find distances to globular clusters, in the same way that Cepheids are used to find distances to other galaxies.

In some cases, the pulsations of a star can be so large that the speed with which the outer layers are moving outward is larger than the escape speed from the star. As a result, the star loses its outer layers to outer space, contributing to the recycling of interstellar material through the processes of star formation and stellar evolution.

Mass Loss From Red Giants

During its main sequence life, our Sun continually sheds material as the solar wind. Orbiting X-ray and ultraviolet telescopes such as the *High Energy Astrophysical Observatories* and the *International Ultraviolet Explorer* have detected emission spectra from around other main sequence stars, indicating that stars commonly have hot chromospheres and coronas just as our Sun does. It seems safe to assume that they

FIGURE 14-14 When the Sun becomes a red giant, it will expand until its surface is somewhere between Earth and Mars. Compare this with its present size.

instability strip A region of the H-R diagram where pulsating stars are found.

RR Lyrae variables
Pulsating stars with periods shorter than a day.

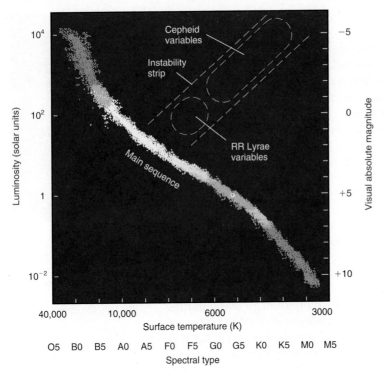

FIGURE 14-15 A section of the instability strip above the main sequence. Only two types of variable stars are shown. A star passing through this strip as it evolves becomes unstable and pulsates.

FIGURE 14-16 Star HD65750, a red supergiant, is losing material at a high rate. It is surrounded by a reflection nebula.

also have stellar winds like the Sun. The solar wind carries away about 10^{-14} of the Sun's mass each year. This is an extremely small amount, for at this rate, the Sun will lose only 0.01% of its mass in 10 billion years. Mass loss is much more important for red giants.

We are able to detect a slight Doppler shift in emission lines from gas near red giants. Based on the amount of the Doppler shift, astronomers conclude that the gas is being blown off red giants at speeds between 10 and 20 km/s, and that a typical red giant loses about 10^{-7} solar masses per year. **FIGURE 14-16** shows mass loss from HD65750, a giant star surrounded by a reflection nebula.

One reason for the greater mass loss in red giants is that these stars are so much larger than Sun-like stars that they exert less gravitational force on material near their surfaces. In addition, the helium-burning process that provides much of the energy for red giants is unstable and varies greatly in response to small changes in temperature. As a result, a red giant undergoes instabilities and pulsations as helium fusion increases and decreases. In fact, during a portion of a red giant's life, it is common for the star to pulsate with periods of less than one day, as we discussed in the previous section.

Planetary Nebulae

planetary nebula The shell of gas that is expelled by a low mass red giant near the end of its life.

The chapter-opening figure and **FIGURE 14-17** show photographs of objects called ***planetary nebulae***. Planetary nebulae were given that name decades ago because, when viewed in a small telescope, many of them have a blue-green color that resembles the color of Uranus and Neptune viewed through similar telescopes. In fact, planetary nebulae have nothing to do with planets. Spectroscopic analysis reveals—again by the Doppler effect—that these nebulae are made up of material moving outward from a very hot, low mass central star. Many planetary nebulae appear to be doughnut shaped, but this is because we are looking through a shell of material when we view them, as explained in **FIGURE 14-18**. The material glows because ultraviolet radiation from the central hot star causes it to fluoresce.

The fluorescence produces an emission spectrum, and the green color is due primarily to ionized oxygen. (Recall the fluorescence of a comet's coma and tail.)

At least two models attempt to explain planetary nebulae:

• One model holds that the pulsations in the core of a red giant continue to increase in intensity until the outer layers of the star also become unstable. With each pulse, part of the star's envelope is blown away. After perhaps 1000 years—

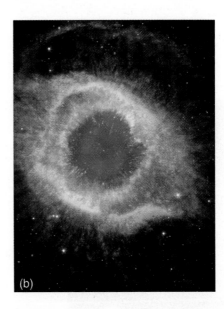

FIGURE 14-17 (a) This *HST* image of the Ring nebula (M57), in the constellation Lyra, is in approximately true colors: blue for very hot helium; green for ionized oxygen; and red for ionized nitrogen. It seems as if we are looking down a barrel of gas ejected from a dying star (with surface temperature of about 120,000 K) thousands of years ago. The nebula is about 2000 light-years away and 1 light-year in diameter. (b) The Helix nebula (NGC7293), 690 light-years away, in the constellation Aquarius. The rings are about 1.5 light-years across. In this composite *HST*/Cerro Tololo/*Spitzer* image, infrared data are shown in red and visible-light data in blue (OIII filter) and green (Hydrogen-alpha filter). The observed structure is created by a central binary system, with two gaseous disks nearly perpendicular to each other. Thousands of blobs resembling comets are seen; each holds about an Earth-mass in hydrogen and other gases and is twice the size of our solar system.

a short time by stellar standards—the entire outer portion of the star will have been ejected, forming a shell around the original core.

- A second model, now gaining in favor, holds that the stellar winds emitted from a dying star occur in definite stages. At the earliest stage, the outer layers of the star are blown off as a slow, dense wind at speeds of perhaps 90,000 kilometers/hour. This finally leaves behind a hot, dense star that emits high-energy radiation. Now the character of the wind changes so that it becomes a low-density but very fast wind at speeds of about 5 million kilometers/hour. When this second wind catches the first, it pushes the first forward, causing a region where there is a very dense wave. (To picture this, imagine that a group of walkers is being overtaken and run into by a group of runners. Where the two groups are colliding, the people are bunched very close together as the runners push the walkers into one another.) In addition, the intense radiation causes that dense area to glow, and this is the shell that we see as a planetary nebula. In the next chapter, when we discuss supernovae, we see that some hourglass-shaped planetary nebulae have been discovered that can be explained using this model.

FIGURE 14-18 Three lines of sight through the spherical shell of a nebula. Lines *X* and *Z* pass through much more of the glowing nebula than does line *Y*; thus, the nebula appears brighter here.

Whichever model is correct (or perhaps a combination of the two will be found to be the best explanation for the phenomenon), not all planetary nebulae appear as rings. The Dumbbell nebula of FIGURE 14-19a shows just a hint of a spherical structure. The *HST* image of a planetary nebula in part (b) reveals that the initial ejections from the star were periodic and fairly uniform (as evidenced by the concentric spheres). The bright inner regions of the nebula must have been produced by irregular ejections of material, and dense clouds of dust condensed from the ejected material. The "twin jet" nebula of FIGURE 14-20a is a clear example of a bipolar planetary nebula. The

In addition, a 2004 study of the central objects in eleven planetary nebulae has found that 10 of them show clear evidence for radial velocity oscillations. This indicates the gravitational influence of a companion star and provides a simple explanation for the nonspherical structures and outflows observed in many planetary nebulae.

Planetary Nebulae

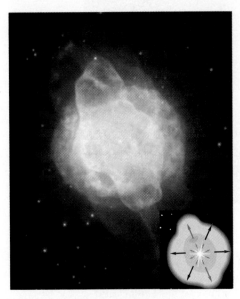

NGC3918 features an inner balloon of gas starting to break through the spherical outer envelope in two places.

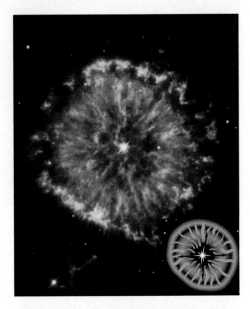

NGC6751 is 6500 light-years away. Hot blue gas forms a rough ring around the central star, pushing the cooler orange gas into an outer ring with streamers toward the central star.

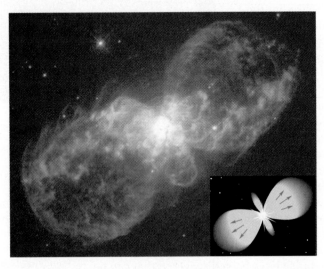

Hubble 5 is a butterfly or bipolar nebula. The lobes are fast winds of gas extending beyond the disk formed early in the star's death.

NGC7009 has a barrel-shaped envelope of material. Regions of low-density gas have shot out through each end of the barrel, glowing faintly.

QUICK FACTS

- Planetary nebulae have nothing to do with planets, but are clouds of glowing gas and dust thrown off from moderately massive stars changing from red giant stage to white dwarfs. The shapes we see depend on how the outflows interact with each other and with the star's magnetic field.

FIGURE 14-19 (a) A three-colored composite image of the Dumbbell Nebula (M27) taken by ESO's VLT. The nebula is about 1200 light-years away. (b) This *HST* image of NGC7027 is a composite of images in the visible and infrared. The central part is not solid, as it may appear in the false-color image. The dense clouds are shown in yellow.

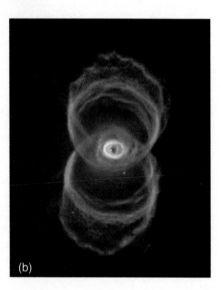

FIGURE 14-20 (a) M2-9 is an example of a "butterfly" or bipolar planetary nebula. The central star is known to be in a very tight binary system. A disk that surrounds both stars is seen in some *HST* images and has a size 10 times the diameter of Pluto's orbit. The nebula is 2100 light-years away in the constellation Ophiuchus. In this *HST* image, red corresponds to neutral oxygen, green to singly ionized nitrogen, and blue to double-ionized oxygen. (b) This is a composite of three *HST* images of the Hourglass nebula (MyCn18). Red, green, and blue represent ionized nitrogen, hydrogen, and doubly ionized oxygen, respectively. The nebula is 8000 light-years away.

measured speed of the ejected gas is more than 720,000 miles/hour. Observations show that the nebula's size increases with time, suggesting that it formed just 1200 years ago. The shape of the Hourglass nebula shown in Figure 14-20b is thought to result from the expansion of a stellar wind that moves fast inside a slowly expanding cloud (which is denser close to its equator than near its poles).

Only a few thousand planetary nebulae have been observed. Although this may seem a large number, it is very small compared with the number of stars, and this fact indicates that planetary nebulae do not last long; however, it is possible to make direct observations of cosmic evolution. **FIGURE 14-21** shows two examples of ***proto-planetary nebulae***, which represent the transition phase between the last stages of a red giant star's life and the early stages of a planetary nebula after the star has ejected most of its mass. The proto-planetary nebula phase is thought to last between a few hundred and 1000 years. The images in Figure 14-21 show that the ejected material forms complex shapes and symmetries, implying that some powerful processes are at work. It is thought that magnetic fields probably play a crucial role in creating these shapes and symmetries; support for this was provided by observations in late 2002,

proto-planetary nebula An object in transition between the last stages of a red giant star's life and its planetary nebula phase.

FIGURE 14-21 (a) In this *HST* image of the Red Rectangle, a nebula about 2300 light-years away in the constellation Monoceros, the straight features (appearing like rungs on a ladder) imply episodes of mass ejection from the central object (a close binary system) that began about 14,000 years ago and repeat every few hundred years. In a few thousand years, as the central star becomes smaller and hotter, a flood of ultraviolet light will make the nebula fluoresce, producing a planetary nebula. The surrounding dust particles are seen now because they reflect starlight from the star. Molecules mixed in with the dust emit light in the red part of the spectrum and hydrocarbons are probably forming in the cool outflow. (b) The Calabash proto-planetary nebula. It is also known as the Rotten Egg nebula because of the large amounts of sulphur compounds present, which would produce an unpleasant smell if we could smell in space. The gas (shown in yellow) has a speed of up to 1.5 million km/hour, and when it rams into the surrounding medium it forms shock-fronts on impact, which heat the surrounding gas. Light from hydrogen and ionized nitrogen arising from these shocks is shown in blue.

which showed that the magnetic field close to a number of aging stars is 10 to 100 times stronger than our Sun's.

Observations by ESA's *Infrared Space Observatory (ISO)* have found evidence that complex organic molecules form rapidly during the proto-planetary phase. It is likely that proto-planetary nebulae are huge factories of organic molecules. *ISO* also found that the dusty torus surrounding a very hot star at the center of one of the brightest planetary nebulae known, the Bug nebula (**FIGURE 14-22**), contains hydrocarbons, carbonates, water ice, and iron. The presence of carbonates (such as calcite) is very interesting because in our environment they form when carbon dioxide dissolves in liquid water and forms sediments; the observations suggest that carbonates can form through other processes in space.

FIGURE 14-23 provides two more examples of the different shapes found among planetary nebulae. The material that we see around the central star quickly dissipates into space and becomes part of the interstellar medium. As the nebula dissipates, the hot, bright core of the star begins to peek through. This core may have a temperature of 100,000 K, and its appearance causes the star to shift its position on the H-R diagram. To include this stage on an H-R diagram, the diagram must be extended toward higher temperatures than have been included in previous diagrams. **FIGURE 14-24** shows that the star moves far to the left. The core remains at its very lumi-

FIGURE 14-22 This *HST* image of the Bug nebula (NGC6302) shows the dark torus surrounding and hiding the hot (at least 250,000 K) central star, outflows, and regions of compressed gas. The nebula is 4000 light-years away in the constellation Scorpius.

FIGURE 14-23 (a) An *HST* image of the Boomerang nebula. It is a young nebula, in the constellation Centaurus, about 5000 light-years from us. The bow-tie shape of the nebula is created by a 500,000 kilometer/hour wind that results in a solar mass of material being lost every 1000 years (10 to 100 times more than other similar objects). The rapid expansion enables the nebula to be the coldest known region in the universe, just one degree warmer than absolute zero; as such, this nebula is the only object found so far that has a temperature lower than the background radiation. (b) The Ant nebula. This *HST* image shows the "ant's" body as two lobes protruding from the dying star.

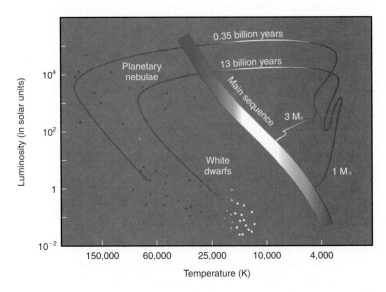

FIGURE 14-24 This H-R diagram has been expanded to the left—to higher temperatures—in order to include stars that are passing through the planetary nebula stage. The evolutionary tracks of a one-solar-mass star and a three-solar-mass star are shown.

nous stage for a relatively short time; then it quickly moves down the H-R diagram and collapses to become a white dwarf.

14-7 White Dwarfs

White dwarfs were discovered long before astronomers predicted their existence. In 1844, the German astronomer Friedrich Bessel (1784–1846) noticed that the star Sirius (in the constellation Canis Major) wobbled back and forth slightly. He hypothesized that an invisible companion orbiting Sirius causes the wobble. Bessel's calculations showed that the unseen companion (called Sirius B) has a mass about the same as Sirius (now called Sirius A). Sixteen years after Bessel had died, the American telescope maker Alvan G. Clark (1804–1877) discovered the companion of Sirius and, in doing so, became the first person to see a white dwarf. FIGURE 14-25a shows Sirius B as it appears in a much larger telescope. Figure 14-25b shows seven white dwarfs in M4, a compact cluster of stars.

A binary system in which the motion of one star reveals the presence of the other is called an *astrometric binary*. Bessel discovered, also in 1844, that Procyon, the brightest star in Canis Minor, is an astrometric binary.

FIGURE 14-25 (a) Sirius is revealed to be two stars in this telescopic view. The arrow points to Sirius B. The spikes that radiate from Sirius A are caused by diffraction around mirror supports within the telescope. (b) The image at left is a cluster of stars 7000 light-years away. The *HST* image at right is a small part of this cluster, only 0.63 light-years across. It contains seven white dwarfs (inside the blue circles) among the other much brighter stars.

(a)

(b)

More than 1000 stars have been identified as white dwarfs, but none is bright enough to be seen by the unaided eye. Astronomers estimate that about 10% of all stars are white dwarfs, but this is a rough estimate, since white dwarfs are difficult to see.

White dwarfs are the cores of red giants that remain after the outer layers of the original stars have blown away. White dwarfs that formed from low mass stars are made up of helium and carbon. White dwarfs formed from more massive stars contain oxygen, neon, and sodium, and may contain atomic nuclei as massive as iron. Because white dwarfs consist of degenerate matter, the more massive a white dwarf, the smaller it is (as shown in Figure 14-11b). As a white dwarf gets older, its temperature and luminosity decline without a significant change in its size, for electron degeneracy prevents it from contracting further.

The Chandrasekhar Limit

Even though electron degeneracy supports the white dwarf against collapsing completely, there is a limit to the amount of pressure that degenerate electrons can withstand. In 1930, a 19-year-old student on his way from his native India to graduate school in England calculated this limit, showing it to be 1.4 solar masses. Subrahmanyan Chandrasekhar was awarded a share of the 1983 Nobel Prize in Physics for his discovery, and the limit is known as the *Chandrasekhar limit*.

Chandrasekhar's calculations showed that if a white dwarf becomes more massive than 1.4 solar masses, the pressure caused by gravity at its surface is greater than the maximum pressure a degenerate gas can support. This means that white dwarfs must have masses less than 1.4 times the Sun's mass. Main sequence stars with masses of up to about 4 solar masses (which we have classified as moderately low mass stars) can end up as white dwarfs only because they lose mass during the red giant and planetary nebula stages. Stars more massive than these stars retain cores whose mass exceeds the Chandrasekhar limit and cannot form white dwarfs. Such moderately massive and massive stars end their lives in a dramatically different way than do less massive stars. We discuss the more massive stars in the next chapter.

Characteristics of White Dwarfs

White dwarfs have been observed with surface temperatures from 4000 to 85,000 K, but computer models predict that it is possible for them to have even higher temperatures. The masses of white dwarfs range from perhaps 0.02 solar masses up to 1.4 solar masses. Because the typical white dwarf is comparable in size to the Earth, the density of these stars is very high, about 10^6 grams per cubic centimeter. A teaspoon (about 5 cm³) of white dwarf material would weigh 5 tons! **TABLE 14-3** lists the properties of a "typical" white dwarf.

When the Sun becomes a white dwarf, its mass will be about 0.6 of its present mass. The remainder of its material will have been puffed away during its red giant

Young people have made many major breakthroughs in science; Newton (age 23 in 1665) and Einstein (age 26 in 1905) are famous examples.

Chandrasekhar limit The limit to the mass of a white dwarf star, above which it cannot be supported by electron degeneracy and cannot exist as a white dwarf.

TABLE 14-3

A Typical White Dwarf

Absolute magnitude	+11
Mass	0.8 solar masses
Diameter	10,000 km (3/4 Earth diameter)
Density	10^6 g/cm^3
Surface temperature	15,000 K
Surface gravity	400,000 times Earth's

Earth

White dwarf

Surface of the Sun

FIGURE 14-26 When the Sun becomes a white dwarf, it will be slightly larger than today's Earth and therefore much smaller than the present Sun. Its mass, however, will be 0.6 of what it is now.

stage and blown away during its planetary nebula stage. It will be nearly as small as the Earth (FIGURE 14-26), with luminosity about a 10th of its current luminosity. As time passes, our Sun's luminosity will keep decreasing, and it will simply fade away.

To get to the white dwarf stage, Sun-like stars must go through the following stages: protostar, main sequence star, red giant, and planetary nebula. Protostars produce energy from gravitational contraction. Main sequence stars produce energy from nuclear fusion. Red giants produce energy from gravitational contraction of their cores (until the cores become degenerate) and from fusion within shells around the cores. White dwarfs, however, do not produce energy. They are hot because of leftover energy, and as they radiate this energy away, they get cooler. After billions of years, a white dwarf will have cooled enough that it no longer radiates in the visible region of the spectrum. It will appear on the H-R diagram at a position below and to the right of the bottom of the main sequence. As billions more years pass, it will cool further to become a ***black dwarf***, the burned-out cinder of a once-proud star. It is unlikely that the universe is old enough for many, if any, black dwarfs to have formed.

FIGURE 14-27 reviews the evolutionary steps taken by very low mass and moderately low mass stars. All begin as protostars and end up as black dwarfs. The end state of more massive stars—the moderately massive and very massive categories—is even more exotic, and we discuss it in the next chapter.

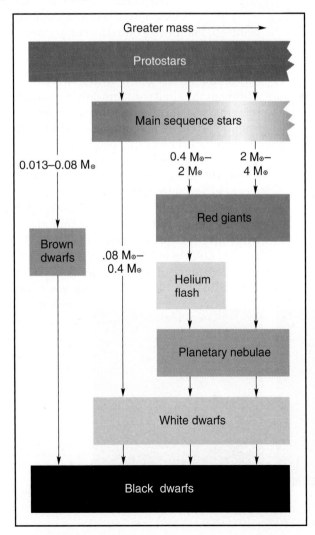

Greater mass ⟶

Protostars

Main sequence stars

0.013–0.08 M$_\odot$

0.4 M$_\odot$– 2 M$_\odot$

2 M$_\odot$– 4 M$_\odot$

Red giants

Brown dwarfs

.08 M$_\odot$– 0.4 M$_\odot$

Helium flash

Planetary nebulae

White dwarfs

Black dwarfs

FIGURE 14-27 This diagram shows the evolutionary steps taken by the stars discussed in this chapter. Unless we include planets in the category, it is probable that no black dwarfs have ever formed, and thus, their box could have been left off the chart. The boxes for the top two categories are open at the right to indicate that more massive stars also fall into these categories. Keep in mind that the limiting masses in each case are known only approximately.

black dwarf The theoretical final state of a star with a main sequence mass less than about 4 solar masses, in which all of its energy sources have been depleted so that it emits no radiation.

Novae

In 1054 AD, Chinese scholars recorded what they called a "guest star," a new star never seen before. In the next chapter we discuss this star, which was bright enough that it could be seen in the daytime.

Ancient astronomers believed that the sky never changed; however, in Chapter 12 we showed that stars move and that the constellations gradually change shape. Other changes also occur in the heavens. In 1572, Tycho Brahe observed a "new star." His excitement at the discovery is revealed in his words in a nearby Historical Note box. We know now that the phenomenon Tycho observed and similar phenomena observed by others since his time are not actually new stars, but are a phenomenon associated with white dwarfs.

Consider a binary star system in which one star is more massive than the other. The more massive star will end its main sequence life before its smaller companion. The massive star will then become a red giant, and if it is in our moderately low mass category, it will shed its outer portion and become a white dwarf. This will leave a white dwarf in orbit with a main sequence star, which then, in its turn, ends its fusion-burning life and begins to grow into a red giant.

At some point, the material of the outer portion of the new red giant is attracted to the white dwarf with more force than is exerted from its own core. This material is pulled away from the giant star. Although some might fall directly onto the white dwarf, analysis shows that most of the material pulled from the red giant will go into orbit around the white dwarf, forming an ***accretion disk*** (FIGURE 14-28).

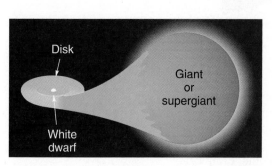

FIGURE 14-28 In a binary system composed of a white dwarf and a red giant, material from the growing giant will fall toward the dwarf and go into orbit around it.

In the accretion disk, matter swirling around the white dwarf is heated as it falls inward, another example of gravitational energy being changed into thermal energy. Collisions within the disk cause its material—mostly hydrogen from the outer portions of the red giant—to fall inward onto the surface of the white dwarf. The hydrogen builds up there, becoming denser and hotter. When the temperature reaches about 10 million kelvin, hydrogen ignites in an explosive fusion reaction. The explosion, which occurs *only* on the surface of the white dwarf, blows off the outer layers of the white dwarf. Although the shell contains only a relatively tiny amount of mass (perhaps 0.0001 solar masses), it can cause the white dwarf to become 10,000 to 100 million times brighter (10 to 20 magnitudes) within a few days.

accretion disk A rotating disk of gas orbiting a star, formed by material falling toward the star.

During Brahe's time, people thought such a newly brightened star was a new star and called it a ***nova***, the Latin word for new. In actuality, the star is not new, but is simply the sudden brightening of an old star. FIGURE 14-29 shows one of the brightest of recent novae, and TABLE 14-4 contains data for a typical nova.

nova (plural **novae**) A star that suddenly and temporarily brightens, thought to be due to new material being deposited on the surface of a white dwarf.

Because so little material is blown off during a nova, the explosion does not disrupt the binary system. The companion star soon resumes transferring matter to the white dwarf. Depending on how fast the hydrogen is transferred, fusion can be reignited as quickly as a few months later, or 10,000 to 100,000 years may be required for a recurrence of the nova. Binary systems including a white dwarf and (usually) a red dwarf star (like our Sun but less massive) are called *cataclysmic variables*. There are various types of cataclysmic variables, including *classical novae* (which undergo huge explosions) and *dwarf novae* (which erupt in smaller explosions), but these differences are not important here. They have orbital periods from 1 to 15 hours, and their sizes are

FIGURE 14-29 These photos of Nova Cygni 1975 show its dimming from magnitude 2 at maximum light to magnitude 15.

TABLE 14-4	
A Typical Nova	
Luminosity increase	10,000 times
Absolute magnitude	−8, or 10^5 Suns
Time to brighten	A few days
Time to dim	6 months to one year

HISTORICAL NOTE

Tycho Brahe's Nova

Tycho Brahe had been taught that the heavens were perfect and unchanging; therefore, when he saw a "new star"—a nova—he was very excited. (We know now that the "nova" observed by Tycho was actually a supernova.) His writings reveal his feelings:

In the evening, after sunset, when, according to my habit, I was contemplating the stars in a clear sky, I noticed that a new and unusual star, surpassing all the other stars in brilliancy, was shining almost directly above my head; and since I had, almost from boyhood, known all the stars of the heavens perfectly (there is no great difficulty in attaining

that knowledge), it was quite evident to me that there had never before been any star in that place in the sky, even the smallest, to say nothing of a star so conspicuously bright as this. I was so astonished at this sight that I was not ashamed to doubt the trustworthiness of my own eyes. But when I observed that others, too, on having the place pointed out to them, could see that there really was a star there, I had no further doubts. A miracle indeed, either the greatest of all that have occurred in the whole range of nature since the beginning of the world, or one certainly that is to be classed with those attested by the Holy Oracles.

about the Earth–Moon distance. It is estimated that there are about a million such variable stars in our Galaxy.

14-8 Type I Supernovae

White dwarfs consist mostly of degenerate carbon (but they probably contain heavier elements as well). Imagine a white dwarf in a binary system accreting material from its companion. When the accretion brings the mass of the white dwarf above the Chandrasekhar limit, electron degeneracy can no longer support the star, and it collapses. The collapse raises the core temperature enough that carbon fusion suddenly begins. This is somewhat similar to the helium flash during the red giant stage, except that now carbon rather than helium is the fuel. Runaway fusion reactions result in carbon fusing to elements as massive as iron. The fusion reactions increase the temperature in the interior, but the pressure remains the same, as the core matter is degenerate. As a result, the white dwarf cannot expand and cool. As the temperature increases, so does the rate of the fusion reactions, in a catastrophic fashion. At some point, the temperature becomes so high that the electrons are no longer degenerate; they start behaving like an ideal gas, resulting in an explosive expansion of the white dwarf. Whereas a red giant undergoing a helium flash has a surrounding envelope of gases to control its explosion, the white dwarf doesn't. The star explodes completely.

The destruction of a white dwarf in this manner is called a **supernova**. The name is unfortunate, for a supernova is not just a "super nova." A nova might reach an absolute magnitude of -8 (about 100,000 Suns), but a supernova attains a magnitude of -19 (10 *billion* Suns). When a supernova is observed in another galaxy, it may shine brighter than all the rest of the galaxy combined.

Astronomers classify supernovae into two categories, *Type I* and *Type II*, depending on their spectra. The spectrum of a Type II supernova contains prominent hydrogen lines, but the spectrum of a Type I supernova does not contain any hydrogen lines. Furthermore, Type I supernovae are divided into three subclasses: Ia, Ib, and Ic, again depending on their spectra. Astronomers think that *massive* stars that have lost different proportions of their outer layers before exploding cause Types Ib and Ic. These supernovae are found only near regions of recent star formation; however, Type Ia supernovae are found even in regions where there is no star formation. Because white dwarfs contain no hydrogen, they are thought to be responsible for Type Ia supernovae. Type II supernovae result from the explosion of a single star; we discuss them in the next chapter.

supernova The catastrophic explosion of a star, during which the star becomes billions of times brighter.

FIGURE 14-30 A Type Ia supernova, thought to be produced by the destructive explosion of a white dwarf. The light curves of brighter supernovae diminish slower that those of less bright supernovae.

A Type Ia supernova reaches maximum brightness after a few days. It fades quickly for about a month and then declines in brightness more gradually until it dissipates in about a year. **FIGURE 14-30** shows the light curve of a Type Ia supernova. Theoretical models indicate that its energy (after the initial explosion) comes from radioactive decay of nuclei produced in the explosion. The light curves and spectra of all Type Ia supernovae are very similar. This is surprising given the varied range of stars from which they start. It is likely that the slow process of accretion that brings these white dwarfs to the point of destruction erases most of the initial differences between the original stars. This similarity among the light curves of Type Ia supernovae is a powerful tool that astronomers use to trace the history of the expansion of the universe, as we discuss in Chapter 18.

A Type Ia supernova remnant is shown in **FIGURE 14-31**. The X-ray spectrum of the remnant DEM L71 shows a high concentration of iron atoms relative to oxygen and silicon. The mass of the ejected material was found to be comparable to the mass of the Sun. These observations show that we are looking at the remnants of an exploded white dwarf.

Even though astronomers agree on the basics of Type Ia explosions, there are still some very important details that are not well understood. We need to understand better the nature of the explosion and how symmetric it is. We also need to understand better the methods by which white dwarfs gain enough mass to exceed the Chandrasekhar limit. Direct spectroscopic evidence for the material surrounding a star before exploding into a Type Ia supernova (SN2006X) was found in 2007 using VLT, VLA and *HST* data; this supports the widely accepted model of a white dwarf orbiting, and feeding from a companion star. Also, the observation of a strong X-ray source before the explosion, and the lack of such a source after, would strongly support the model of a binary system of a white dwarf and companion star; after all, as material from the companion hits the surface of the white dwarf, it will heat the star and produce strong X-rays before the explosion, whereas after the star explodes, it will be undetectable in X-rays.

Extreme helium stars contain almost no hydrogen but are instead dominated by helium, with significant amounts of carbon, nitrogen, and oxygen.

However, in addition to accretion of mass from a companion giant star, merging white dwarfs could also produce supernovae. The mass of the merged object is only briefly above the Chandrasekhar limit, before the object explodes. In 2006 astronomers announced that spectroscopic observations of a rare group of stars, called "extreme helium stars," support theoretical predictions of the composition of a star formed by the merger of a helium-rich white dwarf and a more massive carbon–oxygen white dwarf. If the mass of the star is above the Chandrasekhar limit, the star will become a Type Ia supernova; if it is less, the new merged star will become an extreme helium supergiant star. SN2006gz (and possibly SN2003fg) is an example of a Type Ia supernova that resulted from the merging of two white dwarfs; it showed a very strong spectral signature of unburned carbon and evidence for compressed layers of silicon (which formed during the explosion), both supported by computer models of merging white dwarfs.

Finally, there is observational evidence for a new class of super-

FIGURE 14-31 The left panel shows X-ray data of the supernova remnant DEM L71 taken by the *Chandra Observatory*. A hot, 10 million K inner cloud of glowing silicon and iron is shown in aqua, surrounded by an outer blast wave. The right panel shows this blast wave at optical wavelengths. After a white dwarf explodes, the expanding material drives a shock wave in front of it and into the surrounding interstellar medium (the bright outer rim). The pressure behind this shock wave drives another shock wave inward that heats the expanding material (the cloud shown in aqua). The size and temperature of this remnant indicate that it is several thousand years old.

novae, called Prompt Type Ia. It includes a population of massive stars that evolve very quickly in a very dense environment. Accreting material from a companion star in such an environment at an early stage, the star will explode in only about 100 million years, much shorter than other Type Ia supernovae. Examples of such objects include Kepler's supernova in our galaxy (so named because Kepler observed it more than 400 years ago), DEM L238/L249 in the Large Magellanic Cloud, and others at greater distances. More data and better models are needed to understand Type Ia events, which play such an important role as yardsticks of cosmic evolution.

What happens to the remains of a supernova? They disperse into space. FIGURE 14-32 is a photograph of the Vela nebula,

FIGURE 14-32 The Vela nebula is a Type II supernova remnant. (Photos of other supernova remnants appear in Chapter 15.)

the remains of a Type II supernova that exploded some 11,000 years ago. To calculate its age, astronomers determined the Doppler shift of the part of the remnants that is moving toward us and calculated when the explosion had to have occurred to produce the present speed. In Chapter 15, we discuss Type II supernovae and describe examples of past and recent supernovae.

Conclusion

Mass is the single most important factor that determines a star's properties and how the star evolves. The least massive protostars never get hot and dense enough to join the main sequence and become hydrogen-fusing stars. These so-called brown dwarfs heat up from gravitational contraction during their protostar stage; however, after that they have no heat source and, thus, they cool to become dark, planet-size cinders. More massive protostars become stars on the main sequence, where they fuse hydrogen to helium (and, in more massive stars, to heavier elements). During their main sequence lives, stars become slightly more luminous and cooler, resulting in a small change in their position on the H-R diagram. The more massive a star is, the less time it takes to exhaust its fuel and end its main sequence life.

In stars massive enough to support fusion but with masses less than about 0.4 solar masses, their entire supply of hydrogen mixes as fusion takes place. Although the universe is not old enough for any of these stars to have had time to complete their main sequence lives, computer models show that when they run low on hydrogen, they will shrink and heat up until electron degeneracy sets a lower limit to their size. They will then live out their lives as white dwarfs until they, too, cool to become burned-out cinders.

Moderately low mass stars fuse hydrogen in their cores without any intermixing with the outer portions. When these stars run low on fuel, they become brighter, larger, and cooler; that is, they become red giants. Their electron-degenerate cores heat up until they become hot enough to begin helium fusion. When the Sun and other stars of similar mass reach this point, a helium flash occurs; the stars then consume their helium quickly, getting hotter and dimmer for a time.

During the red giant stage, stars lose great amounts of matter from their outer layers because of intense stellar winds. At the end of the red giant stage, Sun-like stars blow away their outer shells and become beautiful planetary nebulae. Left behind when the nebula has dispersed into space is the star's white-hot degenerate core—a white dwarf. White dwarfs are dim and hard to see, but a white dwarf that is part of a binary system will advertise its presence as a nova if its companion, as it swells to become a red giant, leaks material onto the hot surface of the white dwarf.

When the mass of a white dwarf that is accreting matter from a companion or merges with another white dwarf becomes greater than the Chandrasekhar limit, the star explodes in a brilliant supernova. This completely destroys the star, dispersing its radioactive remnants through space.

Stars with masses greater than about 4 solar masses end the red giant portion of their lives in a different way than stars of lower mass. In the next chapter we describe the behavior of these stars, including the supernovae that they produce.

STUDY GUIDE

1. The length of a star's main sequence lifetime is determined by the star's
   A. carbon content.
   B. distance from the center of its host galaxy.
   C. surface temperature.
   D. mass.
   E. spectral type.

2. Why do stars of greater mass live longer on the main sequence than stars of lesser mass?
   A. The massive stars have more hydrogen fuel.
   B. The massive stars use their fuel more slowly.
   C. The massive stars go through many stages of fusion.
   D. [More than one of the above.]
   E. [None of the above; the statement in the question is false.]

3. If the rate of hydrogen fusion within the Sun were somehow to increase, the core would
   A. collapse and the Sun would grow cool.
   B. collapse and heat up further.
   C. expand and therefore tend to slow the fusion.
   D. expand and, therefore, increase in temperature.
   E. stay the same size but become hotter.

4. Why does hydrogen fusion occur only in a star's center?
   A. Only near the center is there enough heat and pressure.
   B. Only near the center is there enough hydrogen that is not mixed with other elements.
   C. Only near the center is the speed of light favorable for the reaction to occur.
   D. Heat is transferred down to the center during the main sequence life of the star.
   E. [The statement is false; fusion occurs throughout the star's volume. This is what causes the surface to be bright.]

5. Why do massive stars run out of hydrogen in their cores faster than less massive stars?
   A. Their hydrogen fuses faster because of greater pressure.
   B. There is less hydrogen in their cores.
   C. The cores of less massive stars contain a greater percentage of helium, which slows hydrogen fusion.
   D. The cores of less massive stars contain a lesser percentage of helium, which slows hydrogen fusion.
   E. [The statement is false; more massive stars do not run out of hydrogen faster than stars of less mass.]

6. The Sun will at some time in the future become
   A. a red giant.
   B. a white dwarf.
   C. a black dwarf.
   D. [All of the above.]
   E. [None of the above.]

7. Which choice lists the stages in a star's life in correct order?
   A. Main sequence, protostar, white dwarf, red giant.
   B. Protostar, red giant, main sequence, white dwarf.
   C. Protostar, main sequence, white dwarf, red giant.
   D. White dwarf, protostar, main sequence, red giant.
   E. Protostar, main sequence, red giant, white dwarf.

8. Red giants are more luminous than white dwarfs because
   A. red giants are hotter.
   B. red giants are closer.
   C. red giants have greater radii.
   D. [All of the above.]
   E. [None of the above; the statement is not true.]

9. Why are all known white dwarfs relatively close to the Sun?
   A. White dwarfs are formed only in our neighborhood of the Galaxy.
   B. Light from distant white dwarfs has not yet reached the Earth.
   C. No white dwarfs are bright enough to be seen at great distances.
   D. Light from distant white dwarfs is too redshifted to be seen.
   E. [The statement is false; white dwarfs are seen at all distances from the Sun.]

10. What is the difference between the Sun and a one-solar-mass white dwarf?
    A. The Sun has a greater radius.
    B. The Sun has more hydrogen.
    C. They have different energy sources.
    D. [All of the above.]
    E. [None of the above.]

11. One of the causes for the phenomenon called a nova is
    A. the fusion of iron in the core of a massive star.
    B. the infall of material onto a neutron star from a white dwarf.
    C. the transfer of material onto a white dwarf in a double star system.
    D. the collapse of a protostar.
    E. the death of a massive star and the formation of a black hole.

12. The nuclear reactions in a star's core are kept under control so long as
    A. the star's luminosity depends on its mass.
    B. the pressure of the gas in the core depends on its temperature.
    C. the star's density depends on its mass.
    D. the star's mass depends on its temperature.

13. A planetary nebula is
    A. the vastly expanded shell of a dying star.
    B. a cloud of gas out of which stars form.
    C. a cloud of cold dust in space.
    D. the same as a white dwarf.
    E. a circular ring around a black hole.

14. Compared with a young star of the same mass, an older star contains
    A. more hydrogen.
    B. more elements heavier than hydrogen.
    C. about an equal amount of each element.
    D. more of every element.
    E. [No general statement can be made.]

15. The mass of a white dwarf is
    A. always greater than 4 solar masses.
    B. always less than 0.5 solar masses.
    C. less than the mass of its original main sequence star.
    D. greater than the mass of its original main sequence star.
    E. [Two of the above.]

16. A brown dwarf is
    A. the final fate of all stars.
    B. the final fate of stars like the Sun, but not of less massive stars.
    C. a stage of a star's life prior to the white dwarf stage.
    D. a stage of a star's life after the white dwarf stage.
    E. a warm starlike object that has too little mass to support fusion in its core.

17. When more material falls onto a white dwarf, its size
    A. increases.
    B. remains the same.
    C. decreases.
    D. [Any of the above, depending on the nature of the white dwarf.]

18. When the core of a star shrinks after hydrogen fusion stops,
    A. the core cools and the star expands.
    B. the core cools and the star contracts.
    C. the core heats and the star expands.
    D. the core heats and the star contracts.

19. The Chandrasekhar limit is a limit to a star's
    A. size.
    B. volume.
    C. density.
    D. mass.
    E. [Both A and B above.]

20. Some supernovae occur when the Chandrasekhar limit is exceeded in a white dwarf. In this case, the energy producing the explosion is
    A. chemical in nature.
    B. nuclear fusion.
    C. nuclear fission.

    D. degenerate electrons.
    E. gravity.

21. The primary source of energy that powers a main sequence star is
    A. gravity.
    B. chemical energy.
    C. nuclear fission.
    D. nuclear fusion.
    E. fossil fuel.

22. A star is considered to begin its main sequence life when
    A. it starts to collapse.
    B. nuclear reactions start.
    C. its protostar life begins.
    D. it begins to move off the main sequence.
    E. its planetary system has formed.

23. When a star "moves off" the main sequence to become a red giant,
    A. it moves across the sky toward regions where stars are hotter.
    B. it moves across the sky toward regions where stars are cooler.
    C. it stays in the same place in the sky, but becomes hotter.
    D. it stays in the same place in the sky, but becomes cooler.
    E. [Either A or B above, depending on the mass of the star]

24. When a star ends its protostar stage, what determines where it ends up on the main sequence?
    A. Its location in the sky.
    B. Its radial velocity.
    C. Its transverse velocity.
    D. Its mass.
    E. [Both B and C above.]

25. Which stars have longer lifetimes on the main sequence?
    A. The most massive stars.
    B. The least massive stars.
    C. Stars in binary systems.
    D. Stars in star clusters.

26. A planetary nebula occurs
    A. in a newly forming planetary system.
    B. in an old, dying planetary system.
    C. in a white dwarf near the end of its life.
    D. at the end of the life of a red giant.
    E. in the core of a white dwarf.

27. A white dwarf (compared to the Sun) has
    A. a very high average density and a high surface temperature.
    B. a very low average density and a high surface temperature.
    C. a very high average density and a low surface temperature.
    D. a very low average density and a low surface temperature.
    E. [No general statement can be made.]

28. What property of a star is most important in determining the stages of its evolution?

29. Why do stars of the lowest mass not become red giants?

30. What causes the core of a star to heat up after its hydrogen fusion ceases?

31. List the stages in the life of a one-solar-mass star.

32. What will happen to the Earth when the Sun becomes a red giant? How large will the Sun become?

33. Starting at the center and going outward, list the various layers of a red giant that contains a carbon core.

34. Describe two hypotheses designed to explain what causes a planetary nebula. Describe the appearance of a planetary nebula. What causes it to glow?

35. Describe a white dwarf with regard to size, mass, luminosity, and temperature.

36. What supports a white dwarf from further collapse?

37. What happens to the size of a main sequence star when mass is added to it? What happens to the size of a white dwarf when mass is added to it?

38. Why does a recurrent nova continue to flare up time after time?

1. What is a brown dwarf? What determines if a protostar becomes a brown dwarf or a main sequence star?

2. Gravity causes protostars to collapse. What stops the collapse?

3. Massive stars have much more hydrogen in their cores than do less massive stars. Why, then, do they run out of hydrogen faster than stars of low mass?

4. We see relatively few white dwarfs compared to main sequence stars, but astronomers are confident that white dwarfs are very common. Explain this discrepancy.

5. What determines whether the carbon cycle will occur in a particular star?

6. Based on how stars evolve during their main sequence lifetime, explain why the main sequence on an H-R diagram should not be a thin line, but should instead have a thickness.

7. What causes a star's radius to increase as it becomes a red giant? What causes its surface to cool?

8. Explain why a Sun-like star, after it becomes a red giant, undergoes a helium flash, but a star a few times more massive than the Sun begins helium fusion gently.

9. Explain what causes the pulsations of RR Lyrae and Cepheid variables.

10. Explain how star clusters provide evidence that supports our theories of what happens to stars after their main sequence life ends.

11. What do planetary nebulae have to do with planets? What are they and how did they get the name "planetary nebulae"?

12. Compare parts (a) and (b) in Figure 14-6. Although these are generally true to the actual data, they were not drawn carefully from the data. Look at the plotted stars and explain what tips you off that the diagrams do not actually fit real data.

13. Explain the meaning of the two graphs of Figure 14-11, and explain what happens to make the two types of stars act differently.

14. Why are novae and Type Ia supernovae not included in Figure 14-27, which shows the evolutionary steps of normal stars?

1. The Sun's life on the main sequence is expected to be 10 billion years. What is the life expectancy of a star with a mass half that of the Sun? What is the life expectancy of a star with a mass 10 times that of the Sun? (Hint: See the Tools of Astronomy box on page 396.)

2. Assume that you observe a circular nebula on the celestial sphere. Its angular size is 1.2 arcminutes, and it is located about 3000 light-years away. Material in the nebula is expanding at the rate of 20 km/s. How long ago did the central star lose its outer layers? (Hint: You will first need to use the small-angle formula to find the radius of the circular nebula.)

3. The star at the center of a planetary nebula has luminosity of 1000 times the Sun's and temperature of 100,000 K. What is the radius of the white dwarf in solar units? (Hint: Use the Stefan-Boltzmann law.)

4. We mentioned in the text that during a nova explosion, a white dwarf becomes 10,000 to 100 million times brighter. Show that this corresponds to a change in magnitude by 10 to 20.

5. The star Zeta Geminorum is a Cepheid variable with a period of about 10 days. Interferometric observations show that the star's angular diameter changes by about 4.7×10^{-8} of a degree during its cycle. Doppler measurements show that the change in the star's diameter is about 8.55 million kilometers. Show that the star is about 338 parsecs away.

1. "Planetary Nebulae," by N. Soker, in *Scientific American* (May, 1992).

2. "The Lives of Stars: From Birth to Death and Beyond," by I. Iben and A. V. Tutukov, in *Sky & Telescope* (December, 1997; January, 1998).

3. "Giants in the Sky: The Fate of the Sun," by J. Kaler, in *Mercury* (March/April, 1993).

4. "Stellar Metamorphosis," by S. Kwok, in *Sky & Telescope* (October, 1998).

5. "White Dwarfs: Fossil Stars," by S. Kawaler and D. Winget, in *Sky & Telescope* (August, 1987).

6. "The Mystery of Brown Dwarfs Origins," by M. Subhanjoy and R. Jayawardhana, in *Scientific American* (January 2006).

7. "How to Blow Up a Star," by W. Hillebrandt, H.-T. Janka, and E. Müller, in *Scientific American* (October 2006).

8. "Supersoft X-ray Stars," by P. Kahabka, E. P. J. van den Heuvel, and S. A. Rappaport, in *Scientific American* Special Edition (September 2004).

9. "The Extraordinary Deaths of Ordinary Stars," by B. Balick and A. Frank, in *Scientific American* (July 2004).

10. "The Discovery of Brown Dwarfs," by G. Basri, in *Scientific American* Special Edition (September 2004).

Quest Ahead to Starlinks
http://physicalscience.jbpub.com/starlinks

Starlinks is this book's online learning center. It features **eLearning**, which contains chapter quizzes and other tools designed to help you study for your class. You can also find **online exercises**, view numerous relevant **animations**, follow a guide to **useful astronomy sites** on the Internet, or even check the latest **astronomy news** updates.

EXPANDING THE QUEST

STARLINKS

15 The Deaths of Massive Stars

After and before (arrow) images of the region around the great supernova of 1987. SN1987A was discovered near the Tarantula nebula in the Large Magellanic Cloud, a companion galaxy to our Milky Way.

IT WAS WINDY AND THE ROOF WAS BROKEN THAT FEBRUARY night in 1987. Ian Shelton, resident astronomer at the Las Campanas Observatory in Chile, had to open the roof by hand in order to use the 10-inch telescope he had repaired. Ian was responsible for maintaining the larger 24-inch telescope, but seldom got to use it himself, because visiting astronomers kept it pretty busy. Shivering in the mountain air, he climbed a ladder and pushed the corrugated metal aside.

This night had started like most others. Winds up to 40 miles/hour pounded the cinderblock telescope shack, but once Ian had opened the roof, he was able to begin the work he liked: photographing the sky. This night he decided to photograph the Large Magellanic Cloud, which is not a cloud at all, but the nearest galaxy to the Milky Way. It and its companion, the Small Magellanic Cloud, are visible only from the Southern Hemisphere. To get a good bright photo, he decided to take a 3-hour time exposure. (Long exposures are the norm for astronomers.) His telescope, however, was not like more modern telescopes that use motors and computers to guide them so that they automatically follow the stars. Instead, he had to look through the eyepiece constantly and guide the telescope manually.

All cross references to chapters, sections, figures, and tables pertain to the main text, *In Quest of the Universe, Sixth Edition. In Quest of the Solar System* contains Chapters 1–11 and 19 of the main text. *In Quest of the Stars and Galaxies* contains Chapters 1–5 and 11–19 of the main text.

At 3 o'clock the sky suddenly went dark; the wind had blown the roof shut and jarred the telescope. What a night! Thinking that his photograph had been ruined, he considered going to bed, but then decided to develop the photographic plate and see what he had.

In the dim light of the darkroom, he examined the result. The Magellanic Cloud was apparent, but when things start going wrong, nothing stops the slide—there was a flaw on the plate. A bright blotch appeared near the edge of the galaxy's image. Of course, a bright star looks just like a blotch, but Ian knew the sky well enough to know that there is no bright star where the spot appeared. He had been using photographic plates of the same type for some time, however, and he knew that a flaw of this size would be extremely unusual. What was the alternative? A new star—a supernova? None bright enough to be seen with the naked eye had appeared since 1604. If this were a supernova, it certainly was a bright one.

The graduate school dropout argued with himself for 20 minutes before going outside to check the sky with his own eyes. There it was, the first naked-eye supernova since 1604, an object that would be studied by astronomers for years and one that has already caused us to change our theories about the death of stars. The unpromising night had yielded the astronomical event of the century, and Ian Shelton was the first to observe it.

Within hours, nearly all of the radio and optical telescopes in the Southern Hemisphere were focused on SN1987A, as it was named. The *International Ultraviolet Explorer* satellite was recording radiation from the supernova by the next day; the Japanese X-ray satellite *Ginga* was observing the area within weeks. The neutrino detection teams in Cleveland, Ohio and Kamioka, Japan ran to check their records of the past few days. High-altitude planes and balloons were launched to observe the region without interference from Earth's atmosphere. Said one astronomer, "It's so exciting. It's hard to sleep."

In Chapter 14 we described how stars with masses less than about four solar masses evolve from protostars to white dwarfs. In general, we might say that such stars end their lives in a fairly uneventful manner. Although all but the very low mass stars become red giants and some put on beautiful displays as planetary nebulae, all-in-all, low mass stars die not with a bang, but with a whimper; however, if a white dwarf happens to be part of a binary system, things may get explosive. The resulting novae and supernovae give a preview of what happens when massive stars die.

> You might say that the smallest stars don't die—they just fade away.

A massive star's death is truly a major event. Instead of gently puffing away their outer layers, some stars blow away their outer portions in cataclysmic supernova explosions, such as the one described in the chapter opening. Many end up as superdense neutron stars, sending out powerful lighthouse beacons across space. The most massive stars, however, end their lives as something even more exotic—as black holes.

15-1   Moderately Massive and Very Massive Stars (>4 M$_\odot$)

Although the final destinies of moderately massive stars (perhaps 4 to 8 solar masses) and very massive stars (greater than about 8 solar masses) are far different, they behave similarly during most of their lives and, thus, we consider them together for now. Recall from Figure 14-7 that the internal structure of main sequence stars depends on their mass. In a star of mass greater than about 4 solar masses, the core temperature and pressure are greater than in stars of low mass and so is the temperature difference between the core and outer layers. As a result, the energy created in the core by fusion reactions

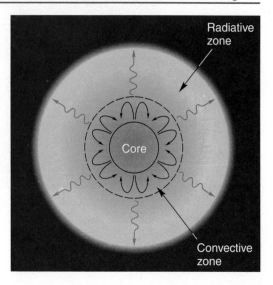

FIGURE 15-1 The internal structure of stars with mass greater than 4 solar masses. Energy transport from the core occurs by convection in the inner part of the star and by radiation in the outer part.

FIGURE 15-2 This *HST* image of Betelgeuse is the first direct image of a star (other than the Sun). It reveals a huge atmosphere with a mysterious hot spot on the star's surface. In the constellation Orion (see Figure 1-8), Betelgeuse is the bright star in the hunter's right shoulder.

FIGURE 15-2 This *HST* image of Betelgeuse is the first direct image of a star (other than the Sun). It reveals a huge atmosphere with a mysterious hot spot on the star's surface. In the constellation Orion (see Figure 1-8), Betelgeuse is the bright star in the hunter's right shoulder.

Size of Star

Size of Earth's Orbit

Size of Jupiter's Orbit

supergiant The evolutionary stage of a massive star after it leaves the main sequence.

is transported outward by convection, whereas the low density in the outer layers allows energy transport by radiation (**FIGURE 15-1**).

The stars that have the most mass live very short main sequence lives. A star 15 times as massive as the Sun takes only about 10 million years to burn up its hydrogen. Like a less massive star, it then expands to become a red giant. During its red giant stage, the 15-solar-mass star changes gradually from a hydrogen-fusing central core to one that fuses helium. Because of its greater mass and corresponding greater core temperature, it becomes brighter than the standard red giant, and we call it a **supergiant**. The most prominent supergiant is Betelgeuse, the bright star in Orion's right shoulder (**FIGURE 15-2**). A supergiant may be a million times brighter than the Sun and have an absolute magnitude of -10. Figure 12-17 shows the position of red supergiants on the H-R diagram, and **TABLE 15-1** lists some typical data for a supergiant.

As the core pressure and temperature increase inside a supergiant, the products of the previous cycle of fusion reactions become the fuel for the next cycle of nuclear reactions. Heavier elements are continuously produced, including neon, silicon, and even iron. As a result, successive cycles proceed faster. New shells of material are generated around the core, and new cycles of fusion reactions occur at the outer layers. The star continuously enters new red-giant phases and repeatedly moves back and forth on the H-R diagram (**FIGURE 15-3a**). The various reactions and their approximate longevity are shown in **TABLE 15-2** for a 15-solar-mass star. The core of the red supergiant now contains several layers, as illustrated in Figure 15-3b.

FIGURE 15-3 (a) This H-R diagram shows the evolution of two massive stars. Massive stars do not experience a helium flash; instead, when core helium fusion reactions start, the evolutionary track turns sharply downward in the red-giant region. (b) Most of the volume of a 15-solar-mass red giant is hydrogen, but the central part is multilayered. The hypothesized mass of each layer is shown.

(a)

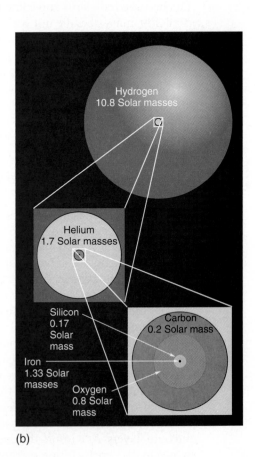

(b)

TABLE 15-1

A Typical Supergiant

Absolute magnitude	−5
Luminosity	10,000
Mass (solar units)	12
Diameter (solar units)	1200
Average density	10^{-8} g/cm³
(Sun's average density = 1.4 g/cm³)	
Surface temperature	3600 K

TABLE 15-2

The Evolution of a 15-Solar-Mass Star

Element Fused	Fusion Products	Time	Temperature
Hydrogen	Helium	10,000,000 years	4,000,000 K
Helium	Carbon	>1,000,000 years	100,000,000 K
Carbon	Oxygen, neon, magnesium	1000 years	600,000,000 K
Neon	Oxygen, magnesium	A few years	1,000,000,000 K
Oxygen	Silicon, sulfur	1 year	2,000,000,000 K
Silicon	Iron	A few days	3,000,000,000 K

15-2 Type II Supernovae

We classify supernovae into two types, based on their spectra. A Type I supernova has no hydrogen lines in its spectrum, and most supernovae of this type (Ia) are thought to be produced by white dwarfs in binary systems, as we described in Chapter 14. Type Ia supernovae are powered by nuclear energy released by runaway nuclear reactions as the white dwarf completely disintegrates. The spectra of Type II supernovae, on the other hand, reveal prominent hydrogen lines, indicating that these supernovae result from stars that still contain hydrogen in their outer layers. Type II supernovae (along with Ib and Ic) are powered by gravitational energy that is released as gravity continuously collapses the core. Differences between the two types of supernovae are outlined in **TABLE 15-3**; typical light curves are shown in **FIGURE 15-4**.

The process by which Type II supernovae occur is not well understood, but various models have been proposed. According to the leading model, after the core of a supergiant has reached the stage where silicon has formed and begins fusing to iron, things start to happen quickly. Computer modeling indicates that the silicon layer fuses to iron in only a few days. Considering that stellar lifetimes are measured in millions and billions of years, a few days is a remarkably short time. But after this, things change even faster!

Silicon fuses to iron in the center of the star. Previously, when a new central core (first of helium, then carbon, then oxygen, and finally silicon) was formed, the material of that core began to fuse to heavier elements when it got hot enough. Iron is different. All of the fusion reactions in Table 15-2 produce energy when they occur. When silicon nuclei fuse to form iron, for example, energy is produced; however, if iron were to fuse together to form even more massive nuclei, energy would be *absorbed* instead of released. In other words, if iron is to fuse, it must have a supply of energy; therefore, as the iron core shrinks and heats up, it does not fuse to something more massive. Instead, once its mass reaches the Chandrasekhar limit, the core collapses violently. In much less than a second, the tremendous pressure generated by gravity in the

TABLE 15-3

Typical Supernovae

	Type Ia	Type II
Spectrum	No hydrogen lines	Prominent hydrogen lines
Magnitude at peak	−19	−17
Light curve	Sharp peak	Broader peak
Expansion rate	10,000 km/s	5000 km/s
Mass ejected	0.5 solar masses	5 solar masses

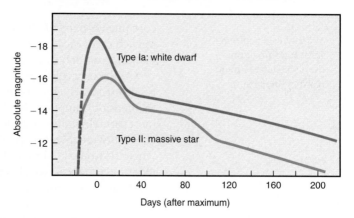

FIGURE 15-4 Typical light curves from the two types of supernovae are shown. Type Ia supernovae get brighter and have a sharper peak. The curve is dashed at the beginning, during the time that the luminosity of the star is usually not observed.

ADVANCING THE MODEL

Nucleosynthesis

Only hydrogen, helium, and lithium, the very lightest elements, were present in the very early universe. All of the other heavier elements that we now see around us (up to iron) were produced inside stars through nuclear fusion reactions; however, the fusion process cannot produce elements heavier than iron. Instead, these elements can be produced in a process where neutrons are added to the nuclei of atoms. This addition creates different, heavier isotopes and can take place because neutrons are neutral particles; thus, they do not feel any electrical repulsion from the charged nuclei.

There are two different stellar environments in which the process of neutron capture can happen. The first environment is inside very massive stars when they explode as supernovae. In such an event, the build-up proceeds via the "rapid-process." The explosion creates an enormous blast of neutrons that pulverizes atomic nuclei, which have no chance of decaying by emitting an electron and turning into a stable atom of the next element in the Periodic Table. As a result, nuclei that are extremely neutron-rich are formed, which finally decay very fast.

A second environment is inside normal stars during the end of their lives when they burn their helium. Here the addition of neutrons is done rather gently via the "slow-process." About half of all the elements heavier than iron are believed to be formed by this process, which takes place during a specific stage of stellar evolution, just before an old star expels its outer layers and dies as a white dwarf. During the slow-process, neutrons enter the nucleus of an atom, turning it into an isotope. This neutron capture continues until there are too many neutrons inside the nucleus for the isotope to remain stable. Then the isotope emits an electron and becomes a stable atom of the next element on the Periodic Table.

Computer-based stellar models predict that the slow-process is very efficient in stars whose metal content is low (metal-poor stars). Such stars were born at an early stage in our Galaxy and are therefore quite old. In these stars, the slow-process is expected to produce nuclei all the way up to the most heavy and stable ones, those with atomic numbers around 82 (the lead region). The discovery in late 2001 of metal-poor stars with high abundances of lead showed an excellent agreement between the predicted and observed abundances, reinforcing our current understanding of how the slow-process operates in the interiors of stars.

How does the slow-process operate? When a carbon-13 nucleus (which includes 6 protons and 7 neutrons) is hit by a helium-4 nucleus (which has 2 protons and 2 neutrons), they fuse to form oxygen-16 (which has 8 protons and 8 neutrons) while also releasing a neutron. A neutron is also released in a similar fusion reaction that involves a neon-22 nucleus and a magnesium-25 nucleus. It is these neutrons that become the building blocks for making the heavier elements. The carbon-13 isotope is in turn produced by fusion of a normal carbon nucleus (carbon-12) and a proton (a hydrogen nucleus). In order for this process to work, however, there must be a region in the star where sufficient amounts of carbon and hydrogen coexist. This is problematic because most hydrogen nuclei have already fused to heavier nuclei, including carbon. Current models of stellar interiors and the discovery of "lead" stars suggest that there must be a moderate mixing between the outer hydrogen-rich stellar layers and the inner carbon-rich regions. It is not yet clear how this mixing process works.

◆ We described neutrinos in Chapter 11, during the discussion of fusion reactions in the Sun.

◆ We know that a major fraction of the energy of a supernova appears in neutrinos. If this energy is included, Type II supernovae are by far more luminous than Type Ia.

core pushes pairs of electrons and protons together to form a neutron and a neutrino in each case. Most of these neutrinos escape from the core, carrying a large amount of energy, which causes the core to become cooler and therefore smaller and denser.

As the core collapses, its density increases and very quickly reaches the density found inside nuclei, which is about 4×10^{14} g/cm³. It is very difficult to compress the core beyond this density. Computer simulations indicate that when the core reaches this stage, its innermost part rebounds—it stops contracting and expands outward—sending a strong pressure wave outward. Meanwhile, the outer layers of the core are falling inward to fill the gap left when the iron core shrank. The rebounding surface collides violently with the infalling material and produces two effects: first, the collision is energetic enough to cause iron to fuse into heavier elements. (This requires an *input* of energy. The necessary energy comes from the collision.) Second, the collision sends shock waves outward that throw off the outer layers of the supergiant. Some astronomers question whether the shock wave is energetic enough to cause the star to explode. One theory holds that as the shock wave begins to lose its energy, it is heated by great numbers of neutrinos escaping the core. The heating action takes less than a second, and at the end of it, the newly energized shock wave has enough energy to blow away the outer portion of the star.

(a)

(b)

FIGURE 15-5 Supernova 1993J was discovered in a spiral arm of the galaxy M81 on March 28, 1993. (a) It is identified by an arrow in the left photo, taken March 30, when it had an apparent magnitude between 10 and 11. (b) Nothing appears at that spot in the right photo, which was taken earlier. The other dots in the images are stars in our Galaxy and are not associated with M81.

Some Type II supernovae are more luminous than others, but a typical one reaches a peak absolute magnitude of -17. This is nearly a billion times brighter than the Sun! FIGURE 15-5 shows a supernova that occurred in the galaxy M81 in March 1993. The other dots in the photograph are not part of M81, but are stars in our Galaxy. Except for the supernova, stars in M81 show up only as a haze.

Physicists have long recognized the special place that iron holds in the list of chemical elements. When lighter nuclei are fused to form heavier nuclei, energy is produced, but only so long as the newly formed nucleus is not more massive than iron. Elements heavier than iron cannot be produced without some source of energy and, thus, they are not formed spontaneously in nature. What, then, is the source of the heavy elements that we find here on Earth? Supernovae are a part of the answer. Supernova explosions in the distant past produced some of the heavy elements and blasted them away into space to become part of the interstellar material from which the Earth was formed. In the Advancing the Model box on "Nucleosynthesis," we describe in more detail the processes involved in nucleosynthesis, the building up of heavier elements from lighter ones.

Detecting Supernovae

Three supernovae in our Galaxy have been seen with the naked eye; they occurred in the years 1054, 1572, and 1604. The most spectacular on record occurred in the constellation Taurus on July 4, 1054, and was observed by Chinese astronomers, who reported that it was bright enough to be seen in daylight and to read by at night. It remained bright for a few weeks, and then gradually faded until it disappeared from view after about two years. Invention of the telescope was centuries away, of course, so the Chinese of the 11th century had no way to continue observing their "guest star" (as they called the object). In 1731, an amateur astronomer reported a small nebula in Taurus, and 200 years later Edwin Hubble discovered that the nebula consists of material expanding at a rate such that it must have begun its expansion at the time the Chinese reported the guest star. FIGURE 15-6 is a photograph of the supernova remnant,

Pulsar

FIGURE 15-6 The Crab nebula is the remnant of a supernova that was seen in the year 1054. The arrow indicates the position of the Crab pulsar.

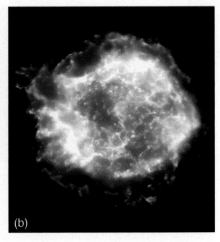

FIGURE 15-7 (a) The Veil nebula, shown here, is part of the Cygnus loop, a supernova remnant 2500 light-years away. (b) This *Chandra* X-ray image of Cassiopeia A shows the regions of greatest intensity in low-, medium-, and high-energy X-rays in red, green, and blue, respectively. The red material on the left outer edge is rich in iron. The bright greenish white region on the lower left is rich in silicon and sulphur. In the blue region on the right edge, low- and medium-energy X-rays have been filtered out by a cloud of dust and gas in the remnant.

Edwin Hubble (1889–1953), for whom the space telescope is named, was an important American astronomer whose name will appear often in the next two chapters.

TABLE 15-4

Some Supernova Remnants

Remnant	Distance (Light-Years)	Diameter (Light-Years)	Age (Years)
Cassiopeia A	10,000	15	330
Crab nebula	6000	4.4	955**
Cygnus loop	2500	100	20,000
Vela nebula	300*	2300	11,000
Tycho's supernova	9800	11	435
Kepler's supernova	20,000	14	405

*This is the distance to the nearest part of the nebula.

**Because the Crab nebula is 6000 light-years from us, the supernova actually occurred about 7000 years ago (6000 + about 955 years since 1054), but we speak of it as if it happened about 955 years ago.

called the Crab nebula because of its shape. Telescopic observations taken over the last half-century show its growth; they reveal that its outer portions are still expanding outward at about 1400 km/s and that it is now about 4.4 light-years in diameter.

We have also been able to find remnants of the supernova seen by Tycho Brahe in 1572 (which provided evidence to him that the heavens were not unchanging) and the one seen by Johannes Kepler in 1604. Kepler's supernova occurred 4 years before the invention of the telescope; since then there have been no supernovae in our Galaxy seen with the naked eye.

TABLE 15-4 lists some major supernova remnants. Images of two of these—the Cygnus loop and Cassiopeia A—appear in **FIGURE 15-7**.

15-3 SN1987A

When a new astronomical object is observed, a telephone call or telegram is sent to the International Astronomical Union's Central Bureau for Astronomical Telegrams, to establish priority of discovery. Telegram number 4316, received on February 24, 1987, read as follows:

> W. Kunkel and B. Madore, Las Campanas Observatory, report the discovery by Ian Shelton, University of Toronto, of a mag 5 object, ostensibly a supernova, in the Large Magellanic Cloud. . .

This supernova (shown in this chapter's opening image) is officially known as SN1987A ("A" because it was the first discovered that year). One of the first things

ADVANCING THE MODEL

Supernovae from Moderately Low Mass Stars?

A white dwarf accreting material from a binary companion continues to do so until its mass reaches the Chandrasekhar limit. It then collapses and suddenly initiates carbon fusion. A Type Ia supernova is the result. Some stellar models indicate that the same process might be responsible for Type II supernovae in red giants of close to 4 solar masses. Consider the point in its evolution when such a star is a red giant with a carbon core, surrounded by a shell of helium that is fusing together into carbon and dropping the carbon onto the core. If this model is correct, a 4-solar-mass star would form enough carbon that the mass of its core could reach the Chandrasekhar limit. When this occurs, the carbon core collapses, heats up, and undergoes violent carbon fusion.

According to this model, the sudden detonation of carbon is powerful enough to blast the remainder of the star away in a supernova explosion. Because the outer portions of the red giant are made up primarily of hydrogen, the spectrum of the hot expanding shell of gas will contain hydrogen lines and will have the characteristics of a Type II supernova.

The mass of the star discussed here is only about 4 solar masses, which puts the star in the category of moderately low mass stars, a group we described in the last chapter as evolving into planetary nebulae and then ending up as white dwarfs. If the model presented here is correct, some may die in a much more explosive way.

that astronomers did after the discovery of SN1987A was to examine recent photographs of the region where it occurred, to determine which star was its source. It is fortunate that the supernova occurred in a region of the Large Magellanic Cloud where new stars were known to be forming, for this meant that astronomers already had an interest in the region and many photographs of it could be found. Two very luminous blue stars were found very close together at the location where the supernova occurred. This caused confusion because it was thought that red giants, not blue stars, explode as supernovae. The explanation appeared when a shell of gas was detected (by the *International Ultraviolet Explorer* satellite) about a light-year from the central star. It appears that the shell consists of material that was shed from what was originally a 20-solar-mass red supergiant. The star ejected this material about 20,000 years ago, leaving behind its hotter, blue surface. Because 20,000 years is little more than an instant in a star's life, we can say that the red supergiant ejected its surface material shortly before it exploded as a supernova.

Supernova theory had predicted that a burst of neutrinos would be emitted by the explosion. As we discussed in Section 11-3, neutrinos are nuclear particles produced within stars and are the subject of research at various neutrino detectors around the world. Such devices make a record when they detect neutrinos. Our theory of supernovae was confirmed when neutrino researchers in the United States and Japan checked their records and reported that the number of neutrinos had increased a full three hours before the supernova was seen. The delay was due to the very low tendency of neutrinos to interact with matter. After they were formed in the core, most of these neutrinos traveled the remaining volume of the star and escaped into space; however, the shock produced when the rebounding core of the star collided with its infalling outer layers took about 3 hours to reach the star's surface. Only when this shock reaches the layers closest to the surface can we see the increase in the star's luminosity. By this time, the neutrinos were 3 hours ahead of the light and remained so for the rest of their travel between the star and Earth, a distance of about 169,000 light-years. Using the number of neutrinos detected and other factors (such as the sensitivity of the detector and the inverse square law of radiation discussed in Chapter 4, which applies to both light and neutrinos), astronomers were able to learn a great deal about this violent explosion. Over a period of about 10 seconds, SN1987A emitted a total of about 10^{58} neutrinos, which carried off an amount of energy equivalent to 100 times the energy that our Sun has emitted in its entire lifetime. As we mentioned earlier, if we take into account the energy carried off by neutrinos, Type II supernovae are by far more luminous than Type Ia.

Supernova theory is still young, and advances will have to be made before it can be considered well founded.

If neutrinos had no mass, they should have arrived at almost the same moment. The observed delay in the arrival times of the different neutrinos allowed astronomers to set an upper limit to the mass that they have.

FIGURE 15-8 (a) The light echo of SN1987A. Some light from the explosion was deflected by two dust sheets (about 470 and 1300 light-years from the supernova). Because it covers a longer path to reach us, it is seen after the star has faded away. This image was made by subtracting images taken before and after the explosion. (b) This *HST* image was taken in light emitted by nitrogen gas (658 nm) for the central part and using a visible filter (550 nm) for the debris. It shows the structure of the explosion debris of SN1987A, which is expanding at about 6 million miles per hour. The debris is resolved into two blobs moving in opposite directions along the short axis of the inner ring surrounding the supernova. The hourglass-shaped shell made by the three rings is probably the result of the interaction between slow/fast moving winds produced by the star before/after it became a blue supergiant. (c) The shock wave from the explosion hits the edge of the cavity that was carved by the high-speed wind from the star and produces a dramatic increase in X-ray radiation. This is shown in the *Chandra* image (on the left), revealing multimillion-degree gas at the location of the optical hot-spots seen in the *HST* image (on the right).

(a)

(b)

(c)

Besides its mass, other factors, such as the star's angular momentum, play a role in determining what the star leaves behind.

FIGURE 15-9 A composite *Chandra/HST* image of Eta Carinae. Dust and gas emission is shown in blue. X-ray emission produced as the stellar outflow rams into the interstellar medium is shown in orange and yellow.

We continue to observe and learn from SN1987A. FIGURE 15-8a shows its light echo, the deflection of light by two dust-sheets near the supernova. In Figure 15-8b we see the three-ring structure of SN1987A and its evolution between 1994 and 1996. Figure 15-8c shows the glowing gas ring around SN1987A, heated by the collision of a shock wave from the explosion. Observations of SN1987A and other supernovae provide valuable information about these self-destructing stars and the influence they have on their surroundings, but there are still many mysteries about supernovae.

Even in the case of SN1987A, a proposed competing theory for the origin of the nebula holds that the progenitor star was an unstable, massive blue supergiant; such stars, called *luminous blue variables*, eject material in volcano-type eruptions a few times before finally going supernova. A few examples similar to SN1987A have been observed, supporting this competing view that blue supergiants can explode even before becoming red supergiants. Probably the best known example of a luminous blue variable is Eta Carinae (FIGURE 15-9), a bright and massive star in our

Galaxy (between 100 and 150 solar masses) at only 7,500 light-years away; it is consuming its fuel at an incredible rate and it is very unstable. When it finally goes supernova, it will rival the Moon in brilliance.

Whatever their details, supernova explosions are singular in the lives of stars. In some cases, it appears that the entire star is blown apart, including the core, but in other cases, the core is left behind as a tiny remnant of the once-mighty star. The nature of this leftover core depends on whether the star was originally in our moderately massive or our very massive class. In either case, a unique, peculiar object is formed.

15-4 Neutron Stars

The neutron was discovered in 1932 by James Chadwick, although its existence had been suspected for some years before that. Only 2 years later, in 1934, the first suggestion was made that some stars might collapse into a strange object consisting of nothing but neutrons.

Theory: Collapse of a Massive Star

In the previous few chapters we have described much of the theory concerning the lives of stars, but have only occasionally cited evidence for it. (As we explained in Chapter 14, much of the evidence of premain and postmain sequence life comes from examining star clusters.) In addition, we have not detailed the many steps that accompanied the development of the theory. There is an interesting story, however, that illustrates a portion of the theory of stellar life cycles. It not only shows how the theory was confirmed, but also how the confirmation provided further knowledge—a common occurrence in science.

A hypothesis worked out in the 1930s predicted that after the mass of a star's core increases beyond the Chandrasekhar limit, the star will collapse further and its electrons and protons will combine to form neutrons, resulting in a *neutron star*. Just as electron degeneracy supports a white dwarf against collapsing under gravity, neutron degeneracy does the same for a neutron star. The hypothesis predicted that the remains of a moderately massive star's collapsed core would become a neutron star—a tremendously compressed star with a mass between 1.4 and about 3 solar masses. **TABLE 15-5** shows the properties of such a star. To try to imagine it, picture the entire mass of a star larger than the Sun compressed into a ball the size of a small city, about 20 kilometers across. The particles in a neutron star are packed so tightly together that a cubic centimeter (about the size of a sugar cube) of the star would have a mass of about a trillion kilograms; also, the gravitational force at the star's surface is so powerful that a marshmallow hitting the surface would release the energy of a Hiroshima-type bomb.

Astronomers had little hope of finding such a star because, despite its high temperature, its extremely small size results in it being very dim. The idea thus was put on astronomy's back burner as an interesting hypothesis but one that seemed beyond our ability to confirm or deny. In 1967, an accidental discovery changed this.

The diameter of a typical neutron star is only 0.2% of the diameter of a white dwarf, yet the neutron star is a billion times denser.

neutron star A star that has collapsed to the point at which it is supported by neutron degeneracy.

Observation: The Discovery of Pulsars

In 1967, Jocelyn Bell, a graduate student in astronomy at Cambridge University in England, was working with Antony Hewish and a group of researchers who were searching for quasars, energetic stellar sources that we discuss in Chapter 17. The radio telescope she was using for her research did not look at all like the giant radio telescope dishes normally associated with radio astronomy. Instead, it looked like a field of clotheslines covering a total of 4.5 acres (**FIGURE 15-10a**). It was designed to detect faint radio sources and to see quick changes

TABLE 15-5	
A Typical Neutron Star	
Mass	1.5 solar masses
Diameter	20 km (width of a small city)
Density	10^{15} g/cm^3
Temperature	10,000,000 K

FIGURE 15-10 (a) Part of the radio telescope that first detected a pulsar. (b) The chart of pulses from the Crab pulsar indicates their regularity. The difference between pulse duration and pulse period is illustrated. The pulsar's period is 33 milliseconds.

(a)

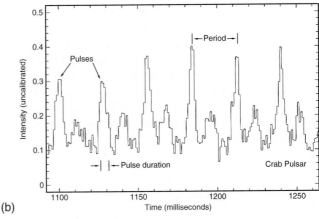

(b)

in their energy. In the course of research for her dissertation, Bell found a new, unexpected, and unexplained source of radio waves. The signal from it pulsed rapidly, about once every 1.3 seconds. This was a much more rapid pulsation than had ever been observed from a stellar energy source.

The researchers' first thought was that the received radio waves were of terrestrial rather than celestial origin. A check of local radio transmitters, however, failed to indicate a source. In addition, the signal was detected about 4 minutes earlier each night than the previous night. Recall that a given star sets four minutes earlier each night as a result of the Earth's moving around the Sun. The researchers concluded therefore that the source was in the sky and was not of human origin.

Their next thought was that a signal from an extraterrestrial race had been detected. In fact, the source was referred to for a short while as an LGM (the initials for "Little Green Men," a reference to science-fiction-type extraterrestrials). This speculation was abandoned for a couple of reasons. First, the pulsations continued in a very regular fashion, instead of changing as they would if they contained a message. More convincing, however, was the discovery by Jocelyn Bell of three more such sources in other directions in the sky, each with its own characteristic rate of pulsation. It was highly unlikely that several different civilizations were sending such signals toward us at the same time, and thus, the sources had to be natural ones. They were renamed *pulsars*.

The first pulsar detected had a period of 1.3373011 seconds. Such great precision is possible in measuring the rate of a regularly repeating phenomenon because we can measure over a great number of cycles and then divide by that number, obtaining the time for a single cycle. Figure 15-10b shows a record of pulses from the Crab pulsar, whose period is 33 milliseconds; although the pulses are extremely regular, they do vary in intensity.

All of the pulsars that were found had a pulse with a duration of about 0.001 seconds. This immediately revealed to the astronomers an upper limit to the size of the object emitting the signals. The objects could be no greater than about 0.001 light-seconds in diameter, which corresponds to 0.001 seconds × 300,000 kilometers/second = 300 kilometers. To see how astronomers could reach such a conclusion, even before the nature of the pulsation was known, consider what we would observe if the Sun were to brighten instantaneously. We would not see this instantaneous brightening as being instantaneous at all, for light from the part of the Sun closest to us would reach us about two seconds before light from its limb (FIGURE 15-11). Because the Sun is about 2 light-seconds in radius, we would see the intensity of light build up over 2 seconds. Likewise, if the Sun suddenly shut off, the dimming would appear to take 2 seconds, rather than appearing to happen all at once.

Six or eight weeks after starting the survey, I became aware that on occasion there was a bit of "scruff" on the records, which did not look exactly like a scintillating source, and yet did not look exactly like man-made interference either.

Jocelyn Bell, on first noticing a pulsar signal

pulsar A pulsating radio source with a regular period, between a millisecond and a few seconds, believed to be associated with a rapidly rotating neutron star.

FIGURE 15-11 The arrows indicate light that left the Sun at the same time. Because point X is about two light-seconds closer to Earth than points Y and Z, its light reaches us 2 seconds sooner. Thus, if the Sun were to increase in brightness instantaneously, we would see the light increase gradually over 2 seconds.

The smallest stars known in 1967 were the white dwarfs, but these are Earth-size objects, not small enough to emit pulsations that last only 0.001 seconds; at least, not if the pulsation is caused by a change in the light emitted from the entire object. The pulsar thus must be even smaller than a white dwarf. How could a star be so small? Enter the hypothetical neutron star.

15-5 The Lighthouse Model of Neutron Stars/Pulsars

Today, nearly 1800 pulsars have been detected in our Galaxy, most with pulses between 0.1 and 4 seconds. As with any scientific theory, a model that explains pulsars must work for all these various cases.

Theory: The Emission of Radiation Pulses

Let us consider how an object might emit pulses of radiation. One way would be for its surface to vibrate up and down. (Some kinds of variable stellar objects are known to do this, including Cepheid variables, as we discussed in Chapter 14.) Not only did the short duration of flashes from pulsars seem to indicate that they were not white dwarfs, but when astronomers considered the nature of the material of a white dwarf and the gravitational force on its surface, calculations showed that the surface of a white dwarf could not vibrate as quickly as once per second. Neutron stars are much denser than white dwarfs and have a much greater gravitational force on their surface and, thus, their surface could beat up and down more quickly. In fact, calculations showed that they should be unable to oscillate as *slowly* as once per second. That is, vibrations of white dwarfs were eliminated as a possibility because they have periods that are too long to explain the observed faster pulses, whereas vibrations of neutron stars were eliminated because they have periods that fall below the range of the slower observed pulses.

A second possible way for an object to emit radiation in pulses is by an eclipsing binary process, with a bright object orbiting a dark one; however, the radiation curve of pulsars is different in nature from one that can be explained by eclipses. In addition, Kepler's third law (as modified by Newton) for an eclipsing binary with a period of 1 second or less suggests that the average distance between the two stars must be less than a few thousand kilometers. This distance is even smaller than the diameter of a white dwarf. Now, neutron stars are small enough that two of them could orbit each other with a period in agreement with those observed for pulsars; however, this scenario actually leads to the neutron stars spiraling closer together (a result of Einstein's general theory of relativity, which we discuss later in this chapter). This would decrease the neutron stars' orbital period, which contradicts the observed increase in the pulsars' periods. Therefore, eclipsing binaries must be ruled out.

A final mechanism for producing pulses is by radiation that comes from a small part of the surface of a rotating object. This is the mechanism that causes sailors at sea to observe pulses of light from a lighthouse. On a foggy night, they might see the lighthouse beam sweeping through the fog, but on a clear night the sailors would see the light only when it shines directly at them. This makes it appear to blink on and off. Could a star rotate with a period as short as that observed for pulsars? A star the size of the Sun would be torn apart by such fast rotation, but white dwarfs or neutron stars would have two advantages in this regard: their smaller size would mean that less force would be needed to retain their surfaces under fast rotation, and their small size and great mass would result in a much greater gravitational force on their surfaces than is experienced on the surface of the Sun. Calculations showed that a white dwarf might be able to withstand the forces involved in rotating with a period of 1 second, and perhaps with a period of 0.25 seconds, but certainly no faster than that. A neutron star, on the other hand, would have no difficulty rotating with a period of a fraction of a second.

The observed stretching out of any sudden change in the Sun would not be due to our distance from it, but rather to its size. Be sure to understand this idea; it is a useful tool in astronomy that tells us the maximum size of some objects.

Compare Figure 15-10b to a light curve for an eclipsing binary— Figure 12-33, for example.

As we discussed in Section 7-6, the lack of a shorter rotation period for the Sun posed problems for astronomers in understanding the formation of the solar system from a nebula.

It is easy to see what would cause either a white dwarf or a neutron star to rotate so fast. As a spinning object decreases in size, its rotation rate increases. White dwarfs, and especially neutron stars, are so small that they would be expected to be spinning very fast.

Logic seemed to be pointing more and more to the neutron star as the explanation for pulsars. In analogy with a sailor's lighthouse, the model developed to explain how neutron stars create pulses is called the *lighthouse model*.

Recall from Chapter 11 that the Sun has a magnetic field. When the theory of the existence of neutron stars was developed back in the 1930s, it was suggested that such a star might have an extremely strong magnetic field, as the star is the compacted core of a main sequence star that presumably would have had a magnetic field. During its main sequence period, the star's magnetic field was spread out over its entire surface and was "frozen-into" the star's ionized gases. As the star evolved and collapsed into a neutron star, its surface area was reduced by many orders of magnitude, and thus, its magnetic field was concentrated on a much smaller area. As a result, the magnetic field of a neutron star is very strong. This strong magnetic field is a necessary part of the lighthouse model. Even though a neutron star is mostly made up of neutrons, the presence of a magnetic field requires the existence inside the star of protons and electrons. It is thought that inside a neutron star, neutrons flow without any friction and protons move around without any resistance. The solid crust of a neutron star is a few kilometers thick and consists of a lattice of atomic nuclei and electrons. The high electrical conductivity of the crust allows strong currents to flow in it and thus anchors the magnetic field.

Neutron stars with extremely strong magnetic fields (10^{14} to 10^{15} times that of Earth's) are called *magnetars*. Satellite observations confirm their existence and we now know of about a dozen such objects. The strong magnetic field of a magnetar stresses its solid crust to the point of triggering starquakes that snap the field lines; this produces violent and recurring X-ray bursts. We do not know the evolutionary relationship between magnetars (thought to be about 10,000 years old) and pulsars (thought to be much older). It is possible that magnetars do not constitute a rare class of pulsars and that at least some pulsars, during the early stages of their life cycles, go through a magnetar phase.

As we discussed when describing the solar system, it is common for the magnetic poles of a planet to be out of alignment with the axis of the planet's rotation. Refer back to Figure 6-23 to see the location of the Earth's magnetic pole in the Northern Hemisphere. Also, the magnetic field of the Earth traps charged particles, and these particles result in the auroras seen near the Earth's magnetic poles. In the case of a fast rotating neutron star, the rapidly changing strong magnetic field gives rise to an electric field that continuously rips charged particles from the star's surface. The charged particles are quickly accelerated near the neutron star's magnetic poles. These charged particles spiraling around magnetic fields produce a narrow cone of radiation in the forward direction. The overall picture is that of two oppositely directed beams of radiation emanating from the star. The energy associated with these beams is extremely intense, and each beam (of radio waves and other radiation) is emitted from each magnetic pole. If the star's magnetic poles were located off the rotation axis, these beams would sweep through space as the star spins (**FIGURE 15-12**). Then, if the Earth were located in the path of a beam, we would see a pulse of radio waves each time the beam sweeps by us. In other words, according to this model, the

lighthouse model The theory that explains pulsar behavior as being due to a spinning neutron star whose beam of radiation we see as it sweeps by.

FIGURE 15-12 A beam of radiation is emitted near each magnetic pole of the pulsar. As the star rotates, the beam sweeps through space.

observed pulses do not correspond to a "pulsing" source. Instead, energy is continuously being emitted by the pulsar, and we simply observe a pulse every time the star's beam sweeps by Earth.

The lighthouse model also predicts the existence of many pulsars we could not observe from Earth, for we would see only those whose lighthouse beam happens to sweep by us. Because the duration of every flash from a pulsar is very short compared with its period, we can conclude that the angular size of the beam is small (FIGURE 15-13). This means that from Earth we would see only a small percentage of the pulsars that exist. It also means that we may never see a pulsar in SN1987A, depending on how the leftover rotating neutron star aligns with respect to Earth.

In 1967, the lighthouse model seemed to be a logical explanation for the pulsar observations, but to test it, more pulsars would have to be found. Good evidence for the model would be finding a pulsar related to the remnants of a supernova, where neutron stars are theorized to be.

FIGURE 15-13 The angular width (A) of the beam from a pulsar determines how long we see its pulse. No pulsar has a long-duration signal, which indicates that pulsars' angular beam widths are narrow and therefore that we are seeing only a small fraction of the pulsars that exist. The sizes of the pulsar and Earth are not in scale.

Observation: The Crab Pulsar and Others

It was only a matter of months after the discovery of the first pulsar that one was found in the Crab nebula (shown in Figure 15-6). It might have been found sooner, but its rate of pulsation is much faster than was expected; it has a period of 0.033 seconds, so that it blinks 30 times per second. This short period finally ruled out completely the possibility of a spinning white dwarf as the source of pulses; a white dwarf would tear apart if it rotated 30 times per second.

Not only was the Crab pulsar flashing more frequently than others yet discovered, but it was emitting great amounts of energy in the radio region of the spectrum—the radio luminosity of the Crab's pulse is about 0.0025 of the total energy emitted by the Sun. Astronomers at the University of Arizona then observed that it also pulses in visible light, with the same pulse rate as it does in radio waves. Since that time, astronomers have found that the Crab pulsar emits radiation in all regions of the spectrum and that the total energy emitted from the Crab nebula is more than 100,000 times the energy from the Sun. FIGURE 15-14a is a *Chandra* X-ray image of the Crab pulsar and its neighborhood. We clearly see tilted rings of high-energy particles to a distance of a light-year from the pulsar, and jet-like features emanating from the pulsar. The *HST* image shown in Figure 15-14b indicates the presence of a knot on one side of the pulsar and a ring-like "halo" on the opposite side. The knot, pulsar, and center of the halo line up with the direction of a jet of X-ray emission.

Astronomers wondered what the source of the Crab pulsar's energy was. This question had been asked even before its pulsar had been discovered. Astronomers had long been puzzled by the luminosity of the nebula itself; it emits more energy than was thought possible. Both of these energy problems were solved when it was discovered that the Crab pulsar is slowing down; its pulses were found to be growing slightly less frequent, corresponding to an increase in its period by about 15 microseconds a year! It was hypothesized that the source of the energy that powers the nebula is the rotational energy of the pulsar. As the pulsar spins, its magnetic field propels electrons out into the nebula. These electrons are the cause of the nebula's great luminosity, but in being swept from the pulsar, the electrons, in turn, slow down the pulsar. If this hypothesis is correct, the amount of rotational energy lost as the object slows its spinning should correspond to the amount of energy emitted by the nebula. Calculations showed that the two amounts of energy did indeed correspond. The theory was confirmed quantitatively.

Direct observational evidence for the existence of a braking torque slowing down a pulsar was found in 2006. Observations of the pulsar PSR B1931+24 show that it periodically turns "off" (that is, there is no radio emission from the pulsar) for periods of 25 to 35 days and then turns "on" again for 5 to 10 days; during the "on" phases, its rotation slows down about twice as fast as during its "off" phases. This suggests

The pulse rate for a pulsar is sometimes observed to increase suddenly (this is called a *glitch*). This occurs because as the neutron star slows its spinning, forces on its surface change. It is possible that these changes cause "starquakes" and sudden changes in the pulsar's shape. It has also been suggested that perhaps the glitches result from the interaction between the pulsar's crust and the layer below it.

(a)

(b)

(c)

FIGURE 15-14 (a) This X-ray image clearly shows the Crab pulsar, the rings that surround it, and the jet-like structures. The X-rays from the Crab nebula are produced by fast-moving particles spiraling around magnetic fields in the nebula. The diameter of the inner ring is larger than 200 times the diameter of our solar system. (b) The Crab pulsar and other features seen in this *HST* image. The knot may be a "shock" in the jet, while the ring may be the boundary between the polar wind and jet and an equatorial wind that powers a larger torus of emission that surrounds the pulsar. (c) A time sequence for the Crab pulsar is shown in context against an image taken using an optical filter. The mosaic of 33 time slices is ordered from top to bottom and from left to right, with each slice representing about 1 millisecond in the period of the pulsar. The brighter, primary pulse is visible in the first column: the weaker, broader interpulse can be seen in the second column.

Three-dimensional simulations show that the spin of pulsars with periods in the range of 15 to 300 milliseconds is determined by the asymmetric shock wave created when the star's iron core collapses, and not by the spin of the original star.

that for this pulsar, about half of the slowing-down rate is due to the wind of fast-moving charged particles flowing out into space and the currents creating the pulsed radio emission; the other half is due to emission of radiation because of its rotating magnetic field.

The pulsar in the Crab nebula is spinning faster than most others because the supernova in which it had its start was so recent; it occurred only 955 years ago. As time passes, this pulsar will gradually slow down. As it loses its rotational energy, the intensity of its pulses will also decrease, and it will no longer emit X-rays. Finally, in tens of thousands of years, it will be just another radio pulsar with its nebula spread so far that it can no longer be seen. The final fate, however, of a pulsar depends on its neighborhood. Consider a pulsar in a binary system, with its companion being a low-mass star. As the pulsar slows down with time, while the companion star evolves and expands toward becoming a red giant, the pulsar might accrete material from the outer layers of the companion. As this material strikes the pulsar's surface at an angle and at high speed, it will cause the pulsar to spin faster. Astronomers believe that a small group of about 100 pulsars (with periods of 1 to 10 milliseconds) has been "spun up" by such transfer of matter. The companion in such a binary system might not survive the strong radiation of the pulsar and might eventually be destroyed. An example of such a millisecond pulsar system is shown in **FIGURE 15-15**. The observations show that the companion is not the expected white dwarf (the end stage of a low mass star), but a bloated red star. There is also a large amount of gas in the system, suggesting that we are seeing a millisecond pulsar just after it has been "spun up" by its companion star.

Neutron stars in binary systems give rise to two other exotic phenomena. As the neutron star captures material from the companion star, its strong magnetic field fun-nels this material onto the magnetic poles of the neutron star. The resulting high-speed impact creates extremely hot regions that emit large amounts of X-rays. As the neutron star rotates, the rotating beams of X-rays sweep the sky and may be observed as pulses of X-rays. On the other hand, if the magnetic field of the neutron star is not strong enough, the infalling material may be distributed more evenly over the surface of the neutron star. Because most of this material is hydrogen, the large pressures and temperatures in this layer result in fusion reactions that create a layer of helium under a layer of infalling hydrogen. When the conditions are such that helium fusion reactions begin, the surface of the neutron star gets very hot, and a sudden burst of X-rays is emitted that lasts for a few seconds. As a result of this emission, the star cools, but as new hydrogen

FIGURE 15-15 The millisecond pulsar system in the globular cluster NGC6397 in Ara (the Altar). In the *HST* image inset, the arrow marks the companion star. The artist's impression shows the pulsar (in blue with two radiation beams) and its bloated red companion star. After the pulsar has been spun up, it can no longer accrete gas from its companion.

flows onto the neutron star, this process repeats itself every few hours or days. This is an explosive thermonuclear process similar to a nova (where the degenerate star was a white dwarf, as we discussed in Chapter 14).

Normally, no nebula is found surrounding pulsars, for the nebula has long since dispersed. To confirm further that pulsars are indeed the neutron stars predicted to be left behind in supernovae, astronomers looked for more instances of pulsars associated with expanding nebulae. Since the discovery of the Crab pulsar, another has been found in the Vela nebula (Figure 14-32). The bizarre image of the Vela pulsar, shown in FIGURE 15-16a, suggests that after the star exploded, jets with unequal thrust along the neutron star's poles accelerated it like a rocket. Observed anisotropies in supernova explosions also lead to the resulting neutron stars moving at high speeds, up

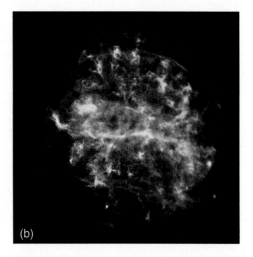

FIGURE 15-16 (a) A *Chandra* image of the compact nebula around the Vela pulsar. The two bows are thought to be the near edges of rings of X-ray emission from energetic particles produced by the pulsar at the center. The rings represent shock waves caused by matter moving away from the pulsar. The jets emanating from the pulsar are perpendicular to the bows and are along the direction of the pulsar's motion, as indicated by the arrow. (b) A *Chandra* image of G292.0+1.8, a young pulsar surrounded by a rapidly expanding shell of gas, 36 light-years across, that contains large amounts of oxygen, neon, magnesium, silicon, and sulfur. The estimated distance is about 20,000 light-years and the age about 1600 years.

ADVANCING THE MODEL

The Pulsar in SN1987A?

After the discovery of SN1987A in February 1987, astronomers began to look for a pulsar at its center. They were not particularly surprised that the pulsar had not been visible immediately because debris from the explosion would block our view of it.

On January 18, 1989, nearly 2 years after the supernova was discovered, an international team of astronomers observed the supernova from Cerro Tololo Inter-American Observatory in Chile for nearly 7 hours, using a detector that is sensitive to visible and near-infrared light. The signals contained pulses! To check their procedure and their instruments, the experimenters turned the telescope to another object that they knew did not pulse. Indeed, no pulses were detected, and measurements of that object's brightness corresponded to previous brightness measurements. They announced that the pulsar in SN1987A had been discovered!

Astronomers were excited about the new pulsar for at least three reasons: First, the discovery confirmed the theory that links pulsars and supernovae. Second, the pulsar was pulsing 1968.629 times per second, much faster than any other known pulsar. Although astronomers expected that a new pulsar would spin faster than an old one, this great rotation rate was difficult to explain, and it indicated that more theoretical work was necessary. Third, the pulses varied slightly in frequency over the 7-hour observation. This also could not be explained using present supernova theories.

Unfortunately, when the astronomers repeated their observations a week later in an attempt to confirm the discovery, they could find no pulses in the signal. Continued observation of the supernova through the remainder of 1989 failed to reveal pulsations. The only explanation seemed to be that, during the January 18 observation, light from the pulsar had reached Earth through a temporary gap in the debris cloud around the pulsar.

As 1989 passed, theoreticians worked to adapt pulsar models to the new findings, and experimental astronomers continued to look for the pulsar's reappearance, while concern was rising that perhaps the initial observation was flawed. The data and observational methods were examined over and over, but no flaw could be found. Then, at the February 1990 meeting of the American Association for the Advancement of Science, the solution to the problem was reported. An old video camera in the observatory was discovered; if the camera was left on during an observation, it sometimes caused an electronic pulse with a frequency of 1968.629 cycles per second—exactly that found for the pulsar. Apparently the camera had been on the night of the pulsar's "discovery," and conditions had been just right for its signals to join the signals received from the sky.

There are lessons to be learned from the would-be discovery of the SN1987A pulsar. Although skeptics might point to this as a failure of science, it is actually an example of a successful use of the scientific method, for it illustrates how science corrects itself. Although the team showed courage in reporting the mistake, their embarrassment would have been greater if someone else had found it. The supposed discovery prompted re-analysis of our theories of pulsars, and we should be better prepared for whatever we find when—and if—the pulsar of SN1987A is finally discovered.

to 1100 kilometers per second! These speeds are greater than those of ordinary stars in our Galaxy and, therefore, many neutron stars can escape its gravitational pull. Figure 15-16b is another spectacular image of a young, oxygen-rich supernova remnant with a pulsar at its center.

Astronomers are now confident that they have found the neutron stars that theory predicted 75 years ago; however, locating the pulsar associated with a given supernova remnant is not easy. When the star explodes, any asymmetry in the explosion might kick the resulting pulsar away from the site of the explosion. In other cases, the pulsar's beams might not sweep past the direction of the Earth and, thus, it is never seen. It is also possible, as is suspected for SN1987A, that the stellar core might collapse into a black hole. The Advancing the Model box on "The Pulsar in SN1987A?" in this section describes what was thought to be its discovery in 1989.

15-6 Moderately Massive Stars—Conclusion

FIGURE 15-17 reviews the steps a moderately massive star takes from protostar to pulsar/neutron star; however, only a small fraction of all stars are in this category, for two reasons. First, the lifetimes of such stars are short compared with the lifetimes of stars with lower mass. Even if they are being formed at the same rate, not as many thus will be in existence at any given time. Second, only stars in a small range of mass end up with a core too massive to be supported by electron degeneracy and of low enough mass to be supported by neutron degeneracy. We know that neutron stars are more massive than the Chandrasekhar limit of 1.4 solar masses, but we are not sure of the upper limit to their mass. (We certainly do not have any neutron-degenerate matter on Earth with which to experiment.) Theory indicates, however, that the limit falls somewhere around 3 solar masses. Only stars that end up with masses greater than—but not much greater than—1.4 solar masses thus can ever become neutron stars and send out their characteristic lighthouse beam of radiation. When a star collapses to form a neutron star, most of its metal-rich material from its interior is returned to its surrounding region.

15-7   General Relativity

FIGURE 15-17 These are the steps a moderately massive star takes from protostar to its final stages.

Albert Einstein stated that in his youth he wondered whether, if he were moving at the speed of light, he could see himself in a mirror. Such questions led him in 1905 to develop the *special theory of relativity*, which we discussed in Chapter 3. This theory makes the perception of electromagnetic waves independent of the motion of the observer. It allows us to answer Einstein's mirror question with a "yes," but it reveals a link between the nature of space and time that does not appear in our everyday perception of the universe. Special relativity has some interesting effects, but it is Einstein's expansion of the theory to the *general theory of relativity* (or *general relativity*) that must be used to describe the fate of massive stars.

In Section 3-8 we described how the general theory of relativity provided a different way of explaining what we normally call gravitation. We began the discussion with a "thought experiment" involving a woman in a spaceship far from Earth. We reached the conclusion that if the spaceship were accelerating upward with an acceleration equal to the acceleration due to gravity on Earth, the woman could not distinguish her situation in the accelerating spaceship from one in a stationary spaceship on Earth. That is, an object would seem to fall in the accelerating spaceship just as if the ship were in a gravitational field. General relativity is based on the *principle of equivalence*, which states that there is no way to distinguish between an accelerating reference frame in a location where there is no gravitational field and a nonaccelerating reference frame that is in a gravitational field.

Now we extend the thought experiment to include electromagnetic radiation. Suppose that the woman is in a spacecraft on the surface of the Earth, not accelerating. The spacecraft has a window on one side, and through the window a beam of light enters parallel to the floor. The principle of equivalence leads to a prediction that the beam will bend downward as it crosses the spacecraft. To see why this is so, imagine that the spacecraft is not on Earth but is in deep space, with an acceleration upward equal to the acceleration due to gravity. A quick burst of light enters the craft, as shown in FIGURE 15-18. As the craft accelerates upward, gaining speed all the time, the light takes the path shown in Figures 15.18b and c. From our point of view, in the unaccelerated frame of the page in the book, the light continues in a straight line. From the point of view of the woman in the accelerating craft, however, the light will have bent downward, as shown in FIGURE 15-19.

The principle of equivalence says that the same bending should happen when the spacecraft is stationary on the surface of the Earth. In this case, however, the bending will appear to be due to gravity.

special theory of relativity A theory developed by Einstein that predicts the observed behavior of matter due to its speed relative to the person who makes the observation.

general theory of relativity A theory developed by Einstein that expands special relativity and presents an alternative way of explaining the phenomenon of gravitation.

principle of equivalence The statement that effects of acceleration are indistinguishable from gravitational effects.

If gravity bends light, shouldn't we see it curve here on Earth?

FIGURE 15-18 A burst of
light entering the accelerating spaceship continues in a
straight line (a), but because
the spaceship is accelerating upward (b), the light is
getting closer to the floor (c).

FIGURE 15-18 A burst of light entering the accelerating spaceship continues in a straight line (a), but because the spaceship is accelerating upward (b), the light is getting closer to the floor (c).

FIGURE 15-19 As seen by a
person in the spacecraft (a),
the light beam bends downward (b) as if falling to the
floor (c). The acceleration
of the beam would be mea-
sured to be exactly equal to
the acceleration of the ship.

The drawings that show the bending of light exaggerate the amount of bending, of course, for in the time required for a beam of light to cross a room-sized spacecraft, its acceleration would not result in enough curvature of the light's path to make it measurable, but if the woman's craft were in an extremely strong gravitational field, where the acceleration caused by gravity is 10 billion times greater than on Earth, the bending would be appreciable.

If the principle of equivalence is valid, light should bend in the presence of a massive object. This prediction of the gravitational bending of light was confirmed by measurements taken during a solar eclipse in 1919, as we discussed in Section 3-9, and other eclipses since then. The general theory of relativity thus presents a different way of looking at the phenomenon we call gravitation. In Chapter 3 we described how the theory explains gravitation not as a force but as the result of the curvature of space. The particular result of interest to us here is that the theory predicts that electromagnetic radiation responds to this curvature in a way that makes it seem to be responding to the force of gravity. This discussion will continue to speak of the force of gravity in Newtonian terms, but we will accept the Einsteinian prediction that electromagnetic radiation, including visible light, appears to respond to this force.

General relativity has survived every test to which it has been put (some of which were described in Chapter 3), and it is a well-accepted theory—not a hypothesis, as is sometimes suggested by the media.

A Binary Pulsar

In 1974, Joe Taylor, a professor at the University of Massachusetts, and Russell Hulse, a graduate student working with him, were using the giant radio telescope at Arecibo to study pulsars. They discovered a very unusual pulsar, whose pulse period of about

59 milliseconds seemed to be changing in a regular way. Sometimes the pulses were received a bit later than expected, sometimes a bit earlier, and these variations repeated with a period of about 7.75 hours. After nearly a month studying the object, they deduced that the changes were due to the Doppler effect as this pulsar revolved around a companion in a binary system. The companion, however, could not be detected. As we explained in previous chapters, binary star systems are useful in determining the masses of stars, but when the spectrum of only one star is observed, the object's mass cannot be calculated; however, astronomers were very interested in determining the masses of the objects in this case, for it would provide the first measurement of the mass of a pulsar and thereby serve as a check on the neutron star/pulsar theory.

Fortunately, the short period of revolution of this binary system (about 7.75 hours) allowed Hulse and Taylor to observe many orbits over a few weeks. This permitted them to determine that the pulsar's orbit was precessing at the rate of about 4.2 degrees/year, a precession much greater than Mercury's because of the great mass of the pulsar and its nearby companion.

The amount of precession predicted by general relativity depends only on the masses of the two objects in orbit and their distance of separation. If the masses of the objects had been known, the binary pulsar would have served as one more experimental check on general relativity. On the other hand, if the applicability of the theory is assumed, general relativity can be used to calculate the masses of the two objects. By 1978, observational data suggested that both stars have masses very close to 1.4 solar masses (the Chandrasekhar limit), strengthening the conclusion that the companion star was also a neutron star. After 3 decades of observing the system, the orbits of the two objects are known very precisely, allowing a precise calculation of their masses. The pulsar has a mass of 1.441 solar masses and its companion's mass is 1.387 solar masses. The system has been perfect for studying the predictions of general relativity: It was the first instance of the use of general relativity to calculate a stellar property and the first precise determination of the mass of a neutron star.

What makes this binary system special, however, is that it indirectly confirms another of general relativity's predictions. As we discussed before, according to the general theory of relativity, matter tells space how to curve and space tells matter how to move. If the distribution of matter in a volume of space changes (for example, because of the motion of two stars in a binary system), the resulting changes ("ripples") in the curvature of the surrounding space may propagate outward as a ***gravitational wave***, carrying away energy and angular momentum. As a result, general relativity predicts that the two stars will spiral closer together. As of 2004, the observed decay rate of the period is in excellent agreement (at the 0.13% level) with the value of 75.8 microseconds per year predicted by the general theory of relativity. The separation of the two stars becomes smaller by about 3 millimeters/orbit, and the two stars will come together in about 300 million years. Even though we still have not directly observed gravitational waves, this binary system has made it very hard to doubt their existence.

15-8 The Fate of Very Massive Stars

Now that we have reviewed general relativity, let's return to the examination of the evolution and death of very massive stars. A very massive star proceeds through its life in basically the same manner as a moderately massive star, although each stage occurs more quickly. Very massive stars differ from moderately massive ones primarily in what happens to them when their core is compressed to a greater density than electron degeneracy can support. When this occurs in a moderately massive star, the resulting supernova leaves a neutron star at its center. In a very massive star, an even more spectacular event happens: The core becomes a black hole. The general theory of relativity plays a very important part in understanding black holes.

Joe Taylor and Russell Hulse won the 1993 Nobel Prize in Physics for this work.

We discussed the precession of Mercury's orbit in Section 3-9.

gravitational wave
Ripples in the curvature of space produced by changes in the distribution of matter.

The *Laser Interferometer Gravitational-wave Observatory* (LIGO) began full operations in 2005. It should be able to detect gravitational waves from collapsing cores of supernovae or colliding neutron stars up to 70 million light-years away.

TOOLS OF ASTRONOMY

The Distance/Dispersion Relationship

In Chapter 12 we described various methods to measure distances to stellar objects. Pulsars provide another method, which relies on two phenomena: each burst of radiation from a pulsar contains an entire spectrum of wavelengths, and different wavelengths of electromagnetic radiation travel through space at slightly different group speeds. For many purposes, it can be assumed that all wavelengths travel at exactly the same speed in space—the *speed of light* in vacuum—but in practice, because space is not a perfect vacuum, longer wavelengths travel at slightly lower group speeds than shorter wavelengths. Recall from Section 5-2 that this difference in speed—called *dispersion*—is the same property that causes chromatic aberration in lenses. The interstellar medium acts as tenuous plasma, and the number of charged particles along the line of sight between the pulsar and the observer affects the arrival times between the different wavelengths. Differences in the composition of the medium thus result in different dispersions.

When we stated in the text that the pulses from a pulsar are typically only 0.001 seconds in length, we were referring to pulses of a single wavelength. If we consider, for example, a pulsar that emits visible light as well as radio waves, we find that the visible-light portion of each pulse reaches us before the radio portion, although for any one wavelength of visible light, or any one wavelength of radio energy, the pulse length is the same—perhaps 0.001 seconds. The relative amount of dispersion might be stated as the time that

elapses between the detection of a given wavelength of visible light and the detection of a given wavelength of radio energy in the same pulse.

Two factors determine the amount of dispersion: the distance the pulse travels through the interstellar medium and the dispersion properties of that medium. We have here another triple connection (FIGURE B15-1). The amount of dispersion can be measured directly. To the degree that one of the other two quantities is known, the final one thus can be calculated. If the dispersion properties of the interstellar matter between us and a pulsar are known, the distance to the pulsar can be determined. On the other hand, if distances can be determined by another method, this provides a means of learning more about the interstellar material.

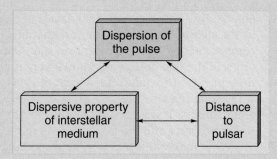

FIGURE B15-1 If any two of the three quantities are known, the third can be calculated.

Black Holes

Neutron degeneracy cannot support a neutron star whose mass is greater than about three solar masses. Such a star will collapse. How far it will collapse is still an open question, but there is no known force capable of keeping the force of gravity from collapsing a star to zero size. This is an unimaginable situation, for we cannot envision matter having no size whatsoever, especially an object several times more massive than the Sun. Fortunately, we do not have to answer the question of how far the star collapses to predict how it will appear from outside.

Shortly after Einstein introduced general relativity, Karl Schwarzschild calculated that when a star collapses to a dimension equal to or less than what is now called the **Schwarzschild radius**, light is unable to escape the object. As we discussed in Section 7-5, the escape velocity of a projectile at a distance r from the center of a star of mass M and radius R is given by

$$v_{esc} = \sqrt{\frac{2 \cdot G \cdot M}{r}},$$

Schwarzschild radius
The radius of the sphere around a black hole from within which no light can escape.

where G is the gravitational constant. For a projectile trying to escape from the star's surface, we have $r = R$ and, thus, the escape velocity increases as the star decreases in size. When the star's radius becomes so small that its escape velocity is greater than the velocity of light, the star has reached the Schwarzschild radius (R_s) (FIGURE 15-20a).

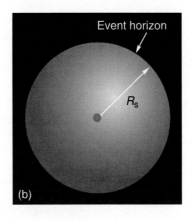

FIGURE 15-20 (a) The sphere at 1 R_S is the event horizon of a black hole. (b) The event horizon in (a) after a star has shrunk to inside the Schwarzschild radius; light can no longer escape its surface.

The size of the Schwarzschild radius depends on the mass of the star, for it is this mass that determines the force of gravity. The radius is given by

$$R_S = \frac{2 \cdot G \cdot M}{c^2} \text{ or (if } R_S \text{ is in km and } M \text{ in solar masses) } R_S \approx 3 \cdot M.$$

A star whose radius is less than the Schwarzschild radius is called a **black hole**; it is "black" because no light escapes from it, and "hole" because matter—or light—that falls into it can never be retrieved. A black hole exists if the star's radius is equal to or less than the Schwarzschild radius, but the radius of the black hole is considered to be the Schwarzschild radius.

The previous equation indicates that if matter falls into a black hole, its radius becomes larger. This is reasonable because as its mass increases it exerts more gravitational force and thus the escape velocity increases at any given distance. A star with a mass five times greater than the Sun's will have a Schwarzschild radius equal to about 15 kilometers. If we had the power to squeeze the mass of our Sun into a sphere of radius $R = 3$ kilometers, then it would become a black hole. This in no way would affect the Earth's orbit, because at 1 AU our planet is safely far away and Newtonian physics would still be all we need to describe its motion. The only problem, of course, would be the lack of sunlight and its negative effects on life on Earth, as we discuss in the Advancing the Model box on black holes.

A name given to the surface of the sphere formed at the Schwarzschild radius illustrates an important and interesting feature of black holes. The surface is called the **event horizon**. Just as we cannot see beyond the Earth's horizon, we cannot see inside the event horizon. Moreover, there is no way we can know about an event inside that sphere. Nothing that happens there is accessible to us and may just as well be in another universe, as we can have no experience of it. As far as we know, after a star collapses inside its event horizon, no force in the universe can stop the star from collapsing to a single point of infinite density. This point, at the center of the black hole, is called the **singularity**. Here the strength of gravity—and thus the curvature of space and time—is infinite. Time and space do not exist as separate entities at this point. Random things can happen here but do not affect the world outside the event horizon. It is the unpredictability of events and our lack of understanding as to what happens at a singularity that has forced astronomers to accept the proposition that singularities not surrounded (or shielded) by an event horizon cannot exist in nature. The structure of a black hole that is *not rotating* thus is easily described by the singularity and the event horizon.

Properties of Black Holes

Although the theory of black holes involves general relativity and therefore might be considered complicated, black holes themselves are very simple. A black hole can be described completely by only three numbers: one for its mass, one for its electric charge, and one for its angular momentum. A full description of any other object in

black hole An object whose escape velocity exceeds the speed of light.

Light can only exist at the speed of light in vacuum. The closer a light source is to a black hole, the more redshifted its light gets as it tries to escape.

event horizon A space-time boundary around a black hole from within which nothing can escape. Its radius is the Schwarzschild radius.

singularity The center of a black hole, where density, gravity, and the curvature of space and time are infinite.

Describing the structure of a *rotating* black hole requires the idea of an additional region surrounding the event horizon. In this region, the dragging of space and time is so severe that nothing can remain stationary; however, objects could travel through it without being sucked into the black hole.

In my talk, I argued that we should consider the possibility that the center of a [supernova remnant] is a gravitationally completely collapsed object. I remarked that one couldn't keep saying "gravitationally completely collapsed object" over and over. One needed a shorter descriptive phrase. 'How about black hole?' asked someone in the audience...Suddenly this name seemed exactly right. John Archibald Wheeler, usually credited with coining the term "black hole"

the universe would involve a long list of properties, including size, color, chemical composition, texture, and temperature (in addition to the three properties named above). For a black hole, these other properties have no meaning. For example, chemical composition is meaningless because it does not matter what original material condensed to form the black hole. The matter no longer exists as a chemical element in the black hole. Whatever the properties of the material that formed the black hole, that information is forever removed from the universe.

The mass of a black hole, in principle, is easy to measure. It would be measured the same way as the mass of any other celestial object. That is, we would observe an object that is in orbit around the black hole and apply Kepler's third law to calculate the total mass of the black hole and the object.

A black hole might have an electric charge, either positive or negative. In principle, this charge could be measured by detecting its effect on charged objects near the black hole. In reality, a black hole is not expected to have an electric charge because if it had a positive charge, for example, the black hole would draw in negative charges until it became neutral. For this reason, electric charge is not normally considered in discussing black holes.

The final property that a black hole may have is angular momentum. As an object shrinks in size, it increases its rotation rate and, therefore, a black hole would be expected to spin rapidly. Results of the theory of general relativity show that this rapid rotation would change space-time around the black hole. In effect, the spinning black hole would drag nearby space-time around with it. Because of this, light passing near a rotating black hole on one side behaves differently than light passing by the other side. On one side the light is moving along with space-time, and on the other side, it is moving against the motion of space-time. This, of course, is not easy to imagine, for motions of space-time are not part of our everyday experience. If instead of light we used two spaceships orbiting the black hole in opposite directions, they would have two different orbital periods. We thus could measure the black hole's angular momentum by comparing these orbital periods. In 2004, scientists announced that they observed variations in the orbits of satellites around the Earth consistent with the expected distortions of space-time due to the Earth's rotation.

Because a black hole can be described completely by just three properties, astronomers say that "a black hole has no hair." Any properties of objects that fall into it are forever gone from the universe. They leave behind only the properties of mass, electric charge, and angular momentum. A black hole is a simple, "hairless" thing.

Detecting Black Holes

Astronomers predicted the existence of black holes in the 1930s when they realized that a star's mass may cause it to collapse beyond neutron degeneracy. A prediction of something as unusual as a black hole certainly calls for observational verification.

There is, of course, no hope of seeing a black hole directly, for we cannot see something from which no light escapes. If, however, matter were falling into a black hole, we should expect some of that matter to orbit the black hole in a manner similar to the way matter falling onto a white dwarf orbits it (causing a nova in the process). Because the gravitational field near a black hole is so strong, the orbital speed of nearby matter would be extremely great. As collisions among particles turned the regular orbital motion to random thermal motion, the matter would reach temperatures of hundreds of millions of degrees. FIGURE 15-21 illustrates material being pulled into orbit around a black hole from a companion binary star. Such hot material would radiate great amounts of energy, and because it is not yet inside the event horizon, we should be able to detect it. We can predict the characteristics of the radiation, and we know that the object should appear as an X-ray source.

Numerous X-ray sources have been found in the heavens by orbiting X-ray observatories. Are all of these black holes? Probably not. Only if one of these sources is found to be associated with a particularly massive star can we hope that it is a black

Actually, Pierre Simon Laplace proposed in 1798 that a very massive star might have such a strong gravitational force that light could not escape it. This was 100 years before Einstein's theory linked gravitation with the travel of light!

hole. When we wish to know the mass of a star, we search for a binary system. Then if we find a binary system in which one of the stars is invisible with a mass greater than 4 or 5 solar masses, we can conclude that the star must be collapsed (or otherwise it would be visible). Finally, if the star emits X-rays characteristic of those predicted for a black hole, we would have good evidence for claiming to have found one.

In the 1960s, astronomers discovered Cygnus X-1, the first X-ray source in the constellation Cygnus. Emission from this source is highly variable and the time scale for the flickering can be as small as 0.01 seconds. Such a time scale sets an upper limit to the size of the object emitting the signals. In this case, the size of the emitting region cannot be larger than

FIGURE 15-21 If a black hole and red giant or supergiant form a binary system, material will be pulled from the giant (left) and will swirl around the black hole, causing X-rays to be released from the heated material in the disk.

0.01 light-seconds or about 3000 kilometers, which is smaller than the size of the Earth. Then, in 1971, they discovered that the location of Cygnus X-1 corresponds with a ninth-magnitude star named HDE226868, a blue supergiant of spectral type B0. A periodic Doppler shift of the spectrum of the supergiant indicates that it is part of a binary system with a period of 5.6 days, but its companion is invisible. A B0-type supergiant is expected to be a very massive star. Calculations reveal that if HDE226868 has the expected mass of about 30 solar masses, its companion must have a mass greater than 3 solar masses. If so, the companion is probably a black hole.

Cygnus X-1 was the first candidate for a black hole. Since its discovery, other black hole candidates have been found. A few are even part of eclipsing binary systems, thus providing us with further information about them.

In 1989, the star V404 Cygni, a G- or K-type star in our own Galaxy, called attention to itself by erupting with a powerful X-ray flare. In 1992, three European astronomers reported that Doppler shift analysis of V404 Cygni shows that it orbits an unseen companion with a period of 6.47 days (FIGURE 15-22). In this case, the mass of the visible star does not present a problem, for even if the calculation is based on its least possible mass, the dark companion must have a mass of at least 6.3 solar masses, and probably 8 to 12. V404 Cygni is now considered almost surely to be a black hole. It further convinces astronomers that black holes are a reality.

Another black-hole candidate is the flickering X-ray source A0620-00, which is also a member of a spectroscopic binary system. In this case, the visible companion (a K5 main sequence star) is relatively faint and orbits the X-ray source every 7.75 hours. Because we can observe the shifting spectral lines of both stars, the minimum mass of the X-ray source is about 3.6 solar masses and thus almost certainly a black hole. In Chapter 17 we discuss black hole candidates that astronomers are finding in the centers of some galaxies. The discovery of black holes not only confirms the theory of the death of the most

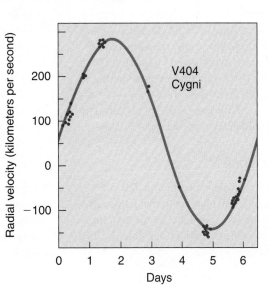

FIGURE 15-22 Applying Doppler shift analysis to the spectrum of V404 Cygni shows that its radial velocity changes with a period of 6.47 days. The dots indicate measured velocities (by the Doppler shift) at different times, and the curve is drawn to fit the data.

ADVANCING THE MODEL

Black Holes in Science, Science Fiction, and Nonsense

Black holes are fantastic objects and are fruitful subjects for science fiction as well as for a lot of nonsense. We will try to separate the science from the nonsense and the science fiction.

Nonsense

There is a common misconception that a black hole is a giant vacuum cleaner, sweeping up matter across wide portions of space. In fact, the gravitational force of a black hole is unusually great only near the black hole. To make this clear, suppose that the Sun could magically become a black hole without losing any mass. If it did so, the gravitational force it exerts on the Earth would not change. The force exerted on the Earth would remain the same, and the Earth would continue in its same orbit. The only difference to us on Earth would be that no radiation would arrive from the Sun. Newton's law of gravity states that the force of gravitational attraction between two objects depends only on the masses of the two objects and the distance between them. Although predictions from Einstein's theory differ from those of Newton's, these differences show up only where the forces are extremely great and, thus, Newton's theory can still be used to discuss Earth's orbit. The strength of Newton's gravitational force does not depend on the Sun's size, only its mass.

Where is the increased gravitational field, then? To understand this, note that with the Sun in its present state, the closest you can get to it (and still be outside) is its surface—some 700,000 kilometers from the center. If you could go down inside the Sun, the force of gravity on you would become *smaller*, for there would then be a gravitational force back toward the matter near the surface (**FIGURE B15-2a**). In fact, at the center of the Sun, you would be weightless, for you would be attracted equally in all directions.

The difference in the case of the solar-mass black hole is that now you can get closer to the center of the star while remaining outside its surface (Figure B15-2b). For such a black hole (only 6 kilometers across), you could get within a few kilometers of the center, and—as predicted by Newton's law of gravity—the force of gravity would be very great at these small distances. (Actually, Newton's law would not make accurate predictions this close to the black hole, but it correctly predicts that the force would be extremely large.)

Predictions from Science

Stephen Hawking made some interesting predictions concerning black holes. Based on calculations of the density of the universe at its beginning (discussed in Chapter 18), he predicted that it may be possible that *mini* black holes formed at the time. These might have been the size of a pinhead and

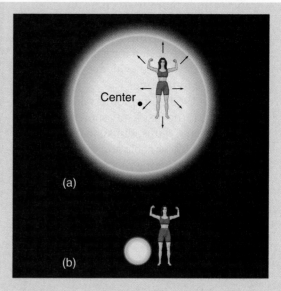

FIGURE B15-2 (a) If a person could exist inside the Sun, she would weigh less than she did on the surface, for gravitational forces would be exerted on her in all directions by parts of the Sun. (b) If the entire Sun could be shrunk to a small enough ball, a person could be the same distance from its center as in part (a) and still be outside its surface. She would then weigh much more than in part (a).

have had the mass of an asteroid. Alas, later theorizing by Hawking showed that if such mini black holes ever existed, they would have long since evaporated by radiation.

Unusual phenomena—by Earthly standards—occur as an object falls into a black hole. For one thing, as an object nears the black hole, it is pulled apart by tidal forces. Tidal forces result because of the difference between gravitational forces on one side of an object and the other. An object approaching a black hole would feel a much stronger gravitational force pulling on its side nearer the hole than on the other side. The force difference would pull the object apart. It would be impossible for a person to fall into a black hole and remain intact.

Even stranger would be the observation of something falling into a black hole. Forget for now the destruction caused by tidal forces. Einstein's theories of relativity tell us that if we could watch the object fall, we would never see it reach the event horizon. We would see it getting closer and closer to the event horizon and getting redder and redder (Doppler shift-like), but because of the distortion of time that is predicted by the theory of relativity, it would take forever—according to our observation—for the object to reach the event horizon. As time is reckoned on the object, however, it would fall into the hole very quickly.

ADVANCING THE MODEL

Black Holes in Science, Science Fiction, and Nonsense *(Cont'd)*

Science Fiction

Where does an object go when it falls into a black hole? Writers have speculated that it may appear at another place or another time. Such travel through "hyperspace" or through time has lent itself to numerous science fiction plots. If it indeed occurs, we should see "white holes" where matter and energy are appearing out of nowhere. (In the language used, the matter and energy enter a black hole, pass through a "worm hole," and emerge from a white hole.) No such phenomenon has been observed.

Even more speculative is the idea that the matter may come out in another universe—not in another galaxy, but in a parallel universe. Because by definition we have no contact with such a universe, we have no way of verifying such speculation. It thus is not in the realm of science at all. (A hypothesis must be verifiable to be classified as scientific.) While the hypothesis of white holes in our universe might perhaps qualify as a scientific hypothesis, the speculation of a parallel universe must remain pure science fiction.

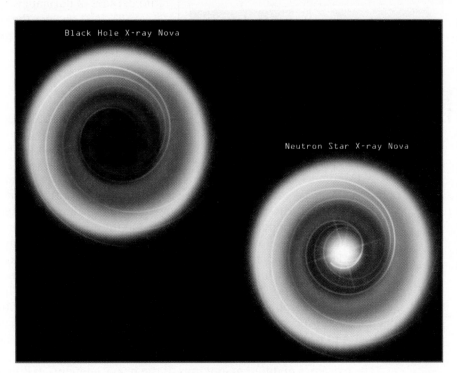

FIGURE 15-23 Gas from the companion star is drawn by gravity onto the compact object (black hole or neutron star) following a swirling pattern. As it nears the event horizon of the black hole (or the surface of the neutron star), a strong gravitational redshift makes the gas appear redder and dimmer. In the case of the black hole, when the gas finally crosses the event horizon, it disappears from view and the central region is black. In the case of the neutron star, when the gas strikes the star's solid surface, it glows brightly.

massive stars but also serves as another confirmation of the theory of general relativity. Although the general public may still think that black holes are on the fringes of science, these objects are in fact firmly entrenched in astronomical theory.

Black-hole candidates have been observed to have masses that span the entire spectrum, from just barely above the minimum 3 solar masses or so that separates the neutron stars from black holes to billions of solar masses at the cores of galaxies. Observations and numerical simulations show a direct path for forming massive black holes through successive mergers of smaller ones; this is especially true for the massive black holes at the centers of globular star clusters and the supermassive black holes at the cores of galaxies. Radiation from matter in the accretion disk around a black hole and jets of matter and energy emanating from such a system are but two of the many ways that black holes sculpt the region around them. Since the early 1990s, orbiting X-ray observatories have been providing important data that allow astronomers to distinguish between black hole candidates and neutron stars. When a neutron star accretes matter, energy is released when the infalling matter

FIGURE 15-24 The steps in the life of a very massive star.

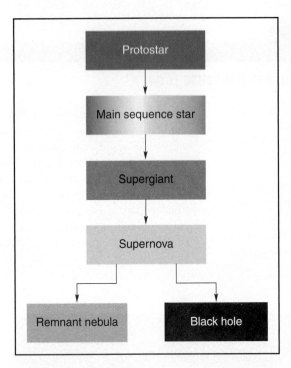

Black holes can also be formed by accreting white dwarfs and/or neutron stars if they accrete enough material. Two dead stars in a binary system coming together to form a single object may also give rise to a black hole.

hits the solid surface of the star; however, when a black hole accretes matter, there is no surface for the matter to hit. Instead, both the matter and the energy are lost after they cross the event horizon. A small amount of energy can escape just before the matter crosses the event horizon, but not as much as in the case of a neutron star. Observations made by X-ray satellites (*ROSAT*, *RXTE* and *Chandra*) support the idea of the event horizon around a black hole by showing that the X-ray emissions from neutron stars and black holes are different. FIGURE 15-23 illustrates these differences based on observations of X-ray novae, so named because they occasionally erupt as brilliant X-ray sources and then settle into decades of dormancy.

FIGURE 15-24 reviews the steps taken by very massive stars as they progress from protostars to black holes.

15-9 Our Relatives—The Stars

The idea that the stars are our relatives might be surprising, but in fact, astronomers can show that humans and stars are related—albeit distantly.

Astronomers divide stars into three classes, called *Population I* stars, *Population II* stars, and *Population III* stars. The three populations are distinguished by the amount of heavy elements they contain. The Population III class has been theorized to include the very first generation of stars formed in the cosmos. These stars formed using only hydrogen and helium, the only elements available in the early history of the universe. Population II stars contain very little material in their atmospheres other than hydrogen and helium. Heavier elements are produced in the cores of stars as fusion takes place and, thus, heavy elements do exist in their cores; however, little is seen in their atmospheres. The spectra of Population I stars, on the other hand, reveal that their atmospheres contain heavier elements. The separation of stars into these three groups is somewhat arbitrary, because a continuum actually exists in the chemical composition of stars, but the distinction is convenient.

The existence of different amounts of the heavy elements in different stars can be easily explained. Stars are formed from interstellar clouds of gas and dust, and most stars end their lives by blowing (or exploding) much of their mass back out into space; therefore, the material they expel into space contains some of the heavier elements produced within the star. Population II stars thus are those old stars that were formed from interstellar material long ago in the history of the universe, before the interstellar material became enriched in heavy elements. Population I stars, on the other hand, are young stars formed from material that contained the remains of previous generations of stars.

Theoretical calculations for Population III stars suggest that these stars lived for only about a million years before extinguishing themselves and showering the metals they had created in their cores into space. How then could we confirm their existence? We could be able to glimpse some signs of their existence by looking in the most distant realms of space. The proposed *James Webb Space Telescope*, the successor to the *HST*, could see these stars exploding as supernovae. *Integral*, a gamma-ray observatory currently in orbit around Earth, could also provide clues about these stars by observing some of the most violent events known in the universe: the gamma-ray

ADVANCING THE MODEL

Gamma-Ray Bursts (GRBs)

GRBs were discovered by accident in the late 1960s by satellites designed to observe clandestine nuclear detonations in space. By the mid-1980s, most astronomers thought that the bursts originated on nearby neutron stars in our Galaxy. This was based on spectroscopic observations that suggested the presence of intense magnetic fields. In 1991, observations by the *Compton Gamma Ray Observatory* showed that the GRBs were distributed isotropically, with roughly the same number of bursts in any direction in the sky.

A burst may last from a hundredth of a second to tens of minutes, and a few bursts are observed each day from somewhere in the universe. For a short time period, some bursts become the brightest objects in the gamma-ray sky (FIGURE B15-3). The distances to these energetic events were not known for over 20 years, until early 1997 when the Italian-Dutch satellite *Beppo-SAX* provided X-ray measurements that allowed astronomers to pinpoint the position of a burst to within a few arcminutes in the Orion constellation. This enabled them to take additional data using optical and other telescopes. These observations confirmed that gamma-ray bursts are very distant and, therefore, that extremely energetic explosions must cause them. Two years later, astronomers tracked the visible glow of another GRB while it was still emitting gamma rays. The intensity of the eruption was measured to be equal to that of millions of galaxies.

An analysis of thousands of bursts supports the idea that long bursts (those lasting more than 2 seconds) result from explosions of very massive stars (more than 30 solar masses); the star's core collapses to form a rapidly rotating black hole surrounded by a disk, while the star's outer layers are ejected to form a supernova. A short time later, the black hole-disk system produces energetic jets of high-speed particles that shoot out (FIGURE B15-4). The jets create a traffic jam close to the explosion, which quickly heats up and explodes. A shock wave is generated from this fireball and travels at a speed very close to the speed of light. If the jet and shock wave are aimed toward

FIGURE B15-4 An illustration that shows the connection between a GRB and a supernova explosion.

Earth, we observe the emitted gamma and X-rays as a burst. When the jet interacts with the expanding supernova shell, it produces an afterglow in X-rays and other frequencies, which can last for days or even months. Support for this scenario was provided by a 21-hour *Chandra* observation in August 2002 of the afterglow of GRB020813, which revealed the presence of elements characteristically ejected by the supernova explosion of a massive star. Since then, additional support has been provided by similar observations of other GRB afterglows. A competing explanation is gaining support from simultaneous multi-wavelength observations made by *Swift*; namely, the burst corresponds to the release of huge amounts of energy carried by the strong magnetic field in the jets.

A similar analysis supports the idea that short bursts (those lasting less than 2 seconds) result from mergers between a neutron star and a black hole, or a pair of neutron stars or black holes; the end product of such a merger is a black hole. Observations of short bursts, which are dimmer than long bursts, show that they originate from galaxies that contain very old stars and thus are different from the host galaxies of the long bursts. These observations are consistent with the idea of mergers between compact objects. The presence of flares and longer periods of activity following the initial burst distinguish mergers between black holes and neutron stars from mergers between neutron stars. A short burst (GRB050724) observed in 2005 provided the first evidence of a black hole's tidal effects stretching a neutron star into a crescent before swallowing it. Computer simulations of mergers between stars and black holes support such disruptions during the mergers of these compact objects. It is possible that some short GRBs are caused by soft gamma-ray repeaters and not by mergers; support for this was provided by LIGO, which could not measure any gravitational waves in the aftermath of a 2007 event (GRB070201).

FIGURE B15-3 An artist's impression of a GRB illustrating how it can flare dramatically over a short time period. There is no way to predict when or where a GRB will occur.

bursts, described in the previous Advancing the Model box. Some astronomers suspect that some of these bursts are created by the death of these first-generation stars.

In which population does our Sun belong? We can answer this question without knowing anything about the spectrum of the Sun. The solar system was formed from material that did not fall all the way into the Sun as the interstellar cloud collapsed; the planets were formed from the same material that made the Sun (see Section 7-6). The fact that Earth (and the other planets) contains heavy elements means that the cloud from which the planets formed contained those materials. The Sun is a Population I star (although it contains less heavy material than some other stars).

Fusion in the cores of stars continues to release energy as heavier and heavier elements are formed until iron is produced. In order for iron nuclei to fuse with other nuclei to form heavier elements, there must be an *input* of energy. The reaction that forms heavier elements from iron does not release energy; it absorbs it. Although most of the matter of which the Earth is made is less massive than iron, many elements are more massive than iron. Such matter could not have been formed by fusion within the core of a star. It was instead formed during a supernova explosion, when tremendous amounts of energy were available. Most of the energy of a supernova is used up in releasing radiation (especially neutrinos) and in blasting away the outer parts of the star, but a small fraction is absorbed by the material of the star, where light elements are fused into heavy elements.

In addition to carbon, nitrogen, oxygen, and other heavy elements that are necessary ingredients for life, dust is also produced by supernova explosions. This process takes less than 10 million years. (Dust can also be produced by old, sun-like stars at the end of their lives. This process takes billions of years. As the dying star expels its outer layers, the gas expands and cools, allowing some matter in it to condense into dust grains. Spectroscopic observations show the presence of silicate particles in the expelled layers of oxygen-rich giant stars and silicon carbide particles in the expelled layers of carbon-rich giant stars.)

Radioactive elements are also produced by supernova explosions. *Integral* has confirmed that radioactive aluminum (Al-26) and iron-60 (Fe-60) are produced in such events in star-forming regions throughout our Galaxy. The relatively short half-life of Al-26 (only 720,000 years) provides a direct proof that nucleosynthesis is currently occurring in young stars. The presence of decay traces of this element in meteorites connects the element's radioactivity to the early solar system; this suggests that the solar nebula could have been near an exploding star.

This discussion has implications for us humans. The material that makes up our bodies is from the Earth. Where was it before it was part of the Earth? In an interstellar cloud. And before that? In a star!

Harlow Shapley, former director of the Harvard College Observatory, whose work we discuss later, listed cosmic evolution as 1 of the 10 revelations that have most affected modern humans' life and thought. He said, "Nothing seems to be more important philosophically than the revelation that the evolutionary drive, which has in recent years swept over the whole field of biology, also includes in its sweep the evolution of galaxies, and stars, and comets, and atoms, and indeed all things material."*

The half-life of Fe-60 is 1.5 million years. The ratio of Fe-60 to Al-26 is about 15%, in good agreement with theoretical estimates.

*Harlow Shapley, *Beyond the Observatory*. New York: Scribner, 1967, pp. 15–16.

Conclusion

All stars get their starts when shock waves compress parts of cold interstellar dust clouds. Most differences between stars—from the various stages through which each star will progress as it lives and dies, to how long each of those stages lasts—result entirely from differences in mass. The universe itself has not existed long enough for the least massive stars to have ended their lives, but the most massive stars have short lives; at the end they become the most astonishing things in nature: black holes. FIGURE 15-25 summarizes the life cycles of all of the stars: very low mass, moderately low mass, moderately massive, and very massive stars.

We are star stuff.
Astronomer Carl Sagan

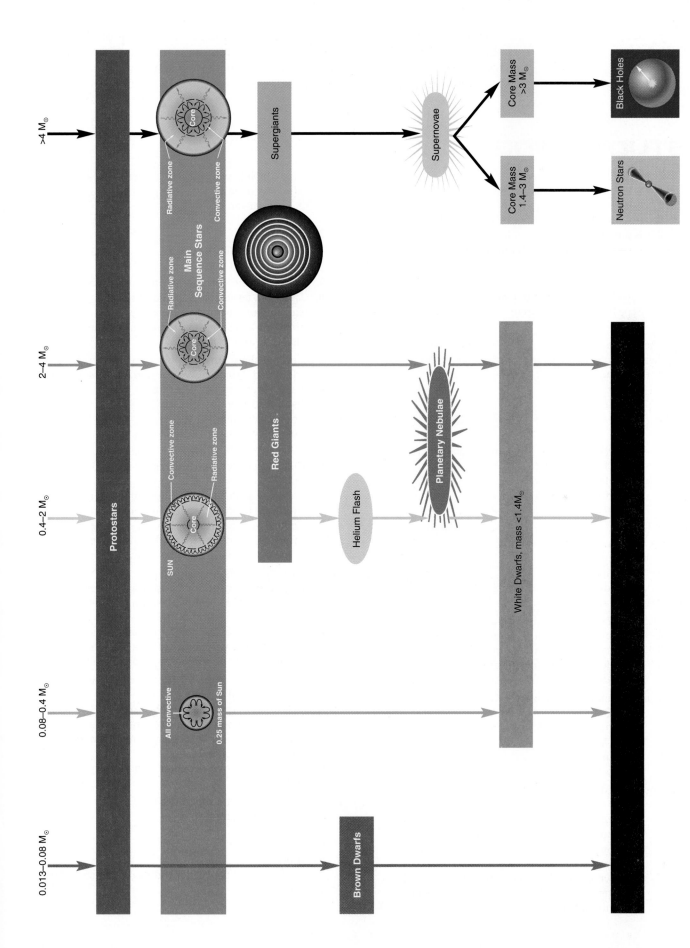

FIGURE 15-25 A summary of the steps in the life cycles of stars of various masses. The limits in mass are not well known.

With this chapter, we complete our examination of the stars. Just as our horizons expanded many times over when our focus changed from the solar system to the stars, they will expand again in the next chapter, where we begin to study the largest class of objects in the universe: the giant galaxies of stars.

STUDY GUIDE

1. The core of a mature supergiant
   A. is layered, with heavier elements in the center.
   B. is layered, with lighter elements in the center.
   C. is uniformly composed of hydrogen and helium.
   D. is uniformly composed of helium.
   E. is composed primarily of iron and carbon.

2. Which type of supernovae have hydrogen lines in their spectra?
   A. Type I (from binary systems).
   B. Type II (from single stars).
   C. [Neither type.]

3. The most massive element that can be formed by nuclear fusion with the liberation of energy is
   A. helium.
   B. carbon.
   C. oxygen.
   D. iron.
   E. lead.

4. The most recent naked-eye supernova was observed
   A. in 1054 by the Chinese.
   B. in the 1500s by Tycho Brahe.
   C. around 1600 by Kepler.
   D. in 1929 by Hertzsprung and Russell.
   E. in 1987 by Ian Shelton.

5. SN1987A was the explosion of a
   A. red giant.
   B. blue supergiant.
   C. white dwarf.
   D. pair of stars.

6. The pulse rate of pulsars is slowed because
   A. they convert rotational energy into radiation.
   B. they drag companion stars around.
   C. of friction with the interstellar medium.
   D. of the conservation of angular momentum.

7. The first candidate for a black hole was
   A. Cygnus X-1.
   B. Algol (the "Demon Star").
   C. Sigma Xi.
   D. Centaurus.
   E. Xi Ursa Majoris.

8. Theory predicts that a neutron star should spin fast because
   A. it was given increased speed by the supernova explosion.
   B. it was given increased speed by a companion star.
   C. it conserved mass as it collapsed.
   D. it conserved angular momentum as it collapsed.
   E. [The statement is false; neutron stars are not predicted to spin fast.]

9. Which of the following objects is a neutron star?
   A. The Crab nebula.
   B. A Cepheid variable.
   C. A dark nebula.
   D. A pulsar.
   E. [None of the above.]

10. Pulsars are
    A. larger and more massive than neutron stars.
    B. larger but less massive than neutron stars.
    C. smaller but more massive than neutron stars.
    D. smaller and less massive than neutron stars.
    E. the same as neutron stars.

11. Pulsars emit sharp bursts of pulses, each lasting for less than 1 second. From this we can conclude that pulsars
    A. have a great amount of energy.
    B. have little energy.
    C. are small in size.
    D. are moving rapidly away from us.
    E. are far away from Earth.

12. Which is the correct sequential order for the life cycle of a star?
    A. red giant, white dwarf, main sequence, protostar.
    B. protostar, main sequence, red giant, white dwarf.
    C. white dwarf, protostar, main sequence, red giant.
    D. protostar, main sequence, white dwarf, red giant.
    E. white dwarf, red giant, main sequence, protostar.

13. The first pulsar was discovered by
    A. a professional astronomer using a radio telescope.
    B. a professional astronomer using a visible-light telescope.
    C. a professional astronomer using an X-ray telescope.
    D. a professional astronomer using a CCD camera.
    E. a British graduate student using a radio telescope.

14. According to present theory, the pulses of radiation from a pulsar are due to
    A. pulsations of the surface of the star.
    B. pulsations from within the core of the star.
    C. eclipses of the star by a binary companion.
    D. rotation of the star.
    E. [Any of the above, depending upon the particular pulsar.]

15. What remains after a supernova?
    A. A main sequence star.
    B. A white dwarf.
    C. A neutron star.
    D. A black hole.
    E. [Either C or D above, depending on the mass of the star.]

16. Which of the following choices lists the stages in the life of *very massive stars* after they leave the main sequence?
    A. Supergiant, supernova, black hole.
    B. Supergiant, supernova, neutron star.
    C. Supergiant, white dwarf, black dwarf.
    D. Supergiant, planetary nebula, white dwarf.
    E. Planetary nebula, supergiant, black hole.

17. When more material falls into a black hole, the diameter of its event horizon
    A. increases.
    B. remains the same.
    C. decreases.
    D. [Any of the above, depending on the nature of the black hole.]

18. In which of the following categories are the objects the least dense?
    A. Main sequence stars.
    B. Nebulae.
    C. Pulsars.
    D. Red giants.
    E. White dwarfs.

19. Which objects have the greatest negative absolute magnitude when they are at their brightest?
    A. Black holes.
    B. Protostars.
    C. Pulsars.
    D. Supernovae.
    E. White dwarfs.

20. Which objects were first detected by Jocelyn Bell, a graduate student at Cambridge University in England?
    A. Black holes.
    B. Protostars.
    C. Pulsars.
    D. Supernovae.
    E. White dwarfs.

21. What do Cygnus X-1 and V404 Cygni have in common (other than that they are in the same constellation)?
    A. Both are neutron stars.
    B. Both are planetary nebulae.
    C. Both are white dwarfs.
    D. Both are probably black holes.
    E. Both are supergiants.

22. Which of the following statements is true?
    A. Black holes have been detected based on their gravitational effect on another star.
    B. Black holes have been detected based on radiation emitted from material falling into them.
    C. Black holes cannot be detected.
    D. [Both A and B above.]

23. The principal factor that determines the evolution of a star is
    A. its location in the sky.
    B. its radial velocity.
    C. its transverse velocity.
    D. its mass.
    E. [Both B and C above.]

(The following question is from an Advancing the Model box):

24. If the Sun could magically and suddenly become a black hole (of the same mass), the Earth would
    A. continue in its same orbit.
    B. be pulled closer, but not necessarily into the black hole.
    C. be pulled into the black hole.
    D. fly off into space.

25. Compare the luminosity of a supernova with that of a massive main sequence star.

26. What happens to the size of a main sequence star when mass is added to it? A white dwarf? A neutron star? A black hole?

27. Outline the stages in the lives of moderately massive and very massive stars. What causes them to end their lives differently?

28. What leads us to believe that the object seen by the Chinese in 1054 was a supernova?

29. Describe how pulsars were discovered. What led astronomers to conclude that they were neutron stars?

30. When astronomers were searching for the nature of pulsars, why, if one assumes that the pulses from a pulsar are caused by vibrations in their surfaces, did the observed rates of pulsation seem to rule out both white dwarfs and neutron stars?

31. Describe the lighthouse model of pulsars. What observation(s) led astronomers to select this model from among other suggested models?

32. What is a black hole? How can we expect to observe one?

33. Define *Schwarzschild radius* and *event horizon*.

34. What general statement can be made about the escape velocity from a black hole?

35. If the Sun (magically) became a black hole, what would be the effect on the Earth? Explain.

36. What is the observational evidence that black holes exist?

37. List in order the steps in the evolution of the most massive stars.

1. The fusion of lightweight nuclei is said to produce energy, yet fusion cannot occur until a high temperature is reached. Doesn't the high temperature indicate that energy is being supplied to the reaction rather than being produced by it? Explain.

2. Explain why, if a star could instantaneously change its luminosity, we would not see it as an instantaneous change. Explain how the time observed for the change allows us to calculate something about the star's size. Does this method yield the minimum or maximum size of the star?

QUESTIONS TO PONDER

3. When astronomers were looking for pulsars in super-nova remnants, they automatically searched the Crab nebula, for the result of a recent supernova. If the light-house model is correct, why was it unlikely that we would find a pulsar there (and therefore lucky that one was found)?

4. The Schwarzschild radius is not the radius of the matter that makes up the black hole. Of what is it the radius?

5. Explain why main sequence stars, white dwarfs, neu-tron stars, and black holes respond differently with regard to changes in their sizes when matter is added to them.

6. The two parts of Figure 15-5 were not taken with ex-actly the same orientation and are not printed with the same magnification. Match the stars in the two figures.

7. Explain why the observation that radiation from the first pulsar was appearing four minutes earlier each night led astronomers to conclude that the pulses were not of earthly origin (or, if they were, that astronomers had produced them).

8. The rotation of the Crab pulsar slowed due to the elec-trons sweeping away from it. Compare this with the problem of the rotational speed of the Sun that was dis-cussed in Section 7-6.

9. To calculate how fast a white dwarf (or neutron star) would pulse by vibrating its surface, we must know the strength of the gravitational field at its surface. What other property of the object must be known?

10. It is predicted that supernovae explode at the rate of one per second over the entire universe. Why don't we see more of them?

CALCULATIONS

1. What is the value of the Schwarzschild radius of a star of 7 solar masses?

2. If the mass of a black hole is doubled, how does the size of its event horizon change?

3. Betelgeuse is a red giant 428 light-years away. Tycho's supernova was 9800 light-years away. If Betelgeuse were to become a supernova, how many times brighter than Tycho's supernova would it appear?

4. In Section 15-5 we stated that Kepler's third law (as modified by Newton) for an eclipsing binary with a period of 1 second or less suggests that the average distance between the two stars must be less than a few thousand kilometers. Show that this is a correct state-ment. (Hint: What is the maximum mass that each star could possibly have?)

5. In Section 15-5 we stated that the strength of the magnetic field of a neutron star is orders of magnitude greater than that of its progenitor. Show that this state-ment is correct. (Hint: Would the radius of the progeni-tor star be greater than the radius of our Sun? How big is a neutron star? Compare the corresponding surface areas.)

6. Show how we obtain the relationship R_S (in km) = $3 \cdot M$ (in solar masses) from the expression of the Schwarzschild radius in Section 15-8.

EXPANDING THE QUEST

Information on the search for gravitational waves can be found at the following sites: http://www.ligo.caltech.edu (for the LIGO project), http://www.esa.int/science/lisa (for the LISA mission). Check also the American Museum of Natural History Project on Gravitational Waves.

Information on GRBs can be found at the site of the SWIFT mission: ttp://swift.gsfc.nasa.gov.

1. "The Great Supernova of 1987," by S. Woosley and T. Weaver, in *Scientific American* (August, 1989).

2. "Pulsars Today," by F. Graham-Smith, in *Sky & Telescope* (September, 1990).

3. "Do Black Holes Exist?" by J. McClintock, in *Sky & Telescope* (January, 1988).

4. "Wormholes and Time Machines," by P. Davies, in *Sky & Telescope* (January, 1992).

5. "Black Holes and the Information Paradox," by L. Susskind, in *Scientific American* Special Edition (May 2003).

6. "Eta Carinae's Year of Glory," by J. Roth, in *Sky & Telescope* (July 2003).

7. "Black Holes in the Middle," by S. Nadis, in *Astronomy* (March 2004).

8. "Catching Gamma-ray Bursts on the Wing," by G. Schilling, in *Sky & Telescope* (March 2004).

9. "Magnetars," by C. Kouveliotou, R. C. Duncan, and C. Thompson, in *Scientific American* Special Edition (September 2004).

10. "Binary Neutron Stars," by T. Piran, in *Scientific American* Special Edition (September 2004).

11. "The Weirdest Star in the Sky," by R. Villard, in *Astronomy* (March 2005).

12. "How to Blow Up a Star," by W. Hillebrandt, H.-T. Janka, and E. Müller, in *Scientific American* (October 2006).

13. "The Brightest Explosions in the Universe," by N. Gehrels, L. Piro, and P. J. T. Leonard, in *Scientific American* Special Edition (January 2007).

The Milky Way Galaxy

16

The *Cosmic Background Explorer (COBE)* satellite provided this false-color image (left) of the inner part of the Galaxy; the wide-angle view shows the nuclear bulge and the dense central plane near the bulge. The Milky Way is seen in radio wavelengths (right). Images of the Milky Way at different wavelengths were shown on page 96.

SERENDIPITY CAN BE DEFINED AS "MAKING A FORTUNATE and unexpected discovery by accident." An example occurred in 1933, when Karl Jansky of Bell Telephone Laboratories was using an antenna he had built to study radio static, hoping to improve radio telephone service to Europe. Jansky was studying the direction of arrival of static from thunderstorms. He detected radio waves he could not account for, and after much work, he determined that they were coming from the center of the Galaxy. Years later, in a letter to a colleague, Jansky wrote this.

> As is quite obvious, the actual discovery, that is, the first recording made of galactic radio noise, was purely accidental and no doubt would have been made sooner or later by others. If there is any credit due me, it is probably for a stubborn curiosity that demanded an explanation for the unknown interference and led me to the long series of recordings necessary for the determination of the actual direction of arrival.*

*Quoted by W. T. Sullivan III in *Serendipitous Discoveries in Radio Astronomy*, ed. K. Kellerman and B. Sheets. Green Bank, WV: National Radio Astronomy Observatory, 1983.

All cross references to chapters, sections, figures, and tables pertain to the main text, *In Quest of the Universe, Sixth Edition. In Quest of the Solar System* contains Chapters 1–11 and 19 of the main text. *In Quest of the Stars and Galaxies* contains Chapters 1–5 and 11–19 of the main text.

Serendipitous discoveries are fairly common in science, and analysis has shown that almost all of them have certain features in common. First, as Jansky wrote in his letter, the discoverer has a "stubborn curiosity that demand(s) an explanation for the unknown. . . ." The data that led to Jansky's discovery were only a series of tiny blips on a chart. Jansky could easily have put the chart aside and ascribed the unexpected blips to equipment problems or to any number of possible "unexplainable" sources. Instead, his stubborn curiosity led him to investigate.

A second feature common to serendipitous discoveries is that the discoverer is extremely knowledgeable about the subject that he or she is investigating. The fact that the discoveries are unexpected does not mean that just anyone can make them, for important discoveries are not made by the unprepared. Instead, they are made by competent observers engaged in serious scientific investigation.

Throughout this text we have seen how our perception of the universe has grown from a small universe centered on our immediate environment to a larger universe whose "center" was thought to be located farther and farther away. As we show in the next chapter, it now appears that the universe has no center. Hand in hand with this receding center has come a tremendous expansion of our realization of the universe's size. Galileo caused controversy not only because he placed Earth off-center, but also because the Earth played such a small part in his universe.

Yet Galileo did not realize that each of the stars he saw in the sky is another sun. When astronomers shift their focus from the solar system to the stars, their entire scale of thinking must expand. For example, as we have seen, the unit of measure used in the solar system, the astronomical unit (AU), is very inconvenient for stellar distances; therefore, astronomers use the light-year and parsec to describe such distances.

Another mental leap in our thinking about distances and sizes is required when we consider stars not as individual objects, but in galaxies. The leap is so great that it may be impossible to truly understand the distances involved. We'll see that our Galaxy contains about a trillion solar masses. Give some thought to what such a number means.

When we study objects at greater and greater distances from us, our knowledge of their nature and properties is more recent and less certain. In this chapter we discuss our Galaxy, of which the Sun is such an insignificant part, and describe how astronomers measure galactic properties. We then compare two different theories that attempt to explain the structure of galaxies like ours. Finally, we describe how our Galaxy formed and evolved to its present state. We'll see that in the case of galaxies, measurements are much less precise than we might be comfortable with.

> Galileo's contemporary, Giordano Bruno, did propose that the stars were suns, and he paid for his belief with his life; in 1600, he was burned at the stake for heresy.

16-1 Our Galaxy

FIGURE 16-1 shows part of the faint band of light that stretches around the sky, encircling the Earth at an angle of about 63° with respect to the celestial equator. The ancient Greeks named this hazy band *galaxies kuklos*, meaning "the milky circle." The Romans called it *via lactae*, "milky way." You are encouraged to find a good clear night sky away from city lights and look at the beautiful Milky Way, a sight many of us in the modern world never get a chance to experience. As shown on the star charts in your book, the Milky Way completely encircles the Earth, passing through the constellations Sagittarius, Aquila, Cygnus, Cassiopeia, and Auriga and between Gemini and Orion on the northern hemisphere of the celestial sphere. Then it passes through Monoceros, near Canis Major, and through Vela and Crux on the southern hemisphere.

We know today that the haze of the Milky Way results from the many stars in the disk of our Galaxy. The Sun is one of about 200 billion stars that make up what we call the **Milky Way Galaxy**, or simply the Galaxy. Most stars in the Galaxy are arranged in a wheel-shaped disk that circles around a bulging center (FIGURE 16-2). The diameter of the Galaxy is about 50,000 parsecs (160,000 light-years), and the Sun is

> Do some of the stars we see at night belong to other galaxies far, far away?

> **Milky Way Galaxy** The galaxy of which the Sun is a part. From Earth, it appears as a band of light around the sky.

FIGURE 16-1 This photo shows the Milky Way in Sagittarius. Compare it with Figure 16-3.

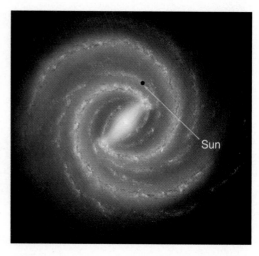

FIGURE 16-2 An artist's view of our Galaxy (seen face-on). The Sun is located about one third of the way out along the disk of the Galaxy. (See the Advancing the Model box "The Milky Way: A Barred Warped Galaxy.")

about a third of the way out from center (8000 parsecs or 26,000 light-years). The Galactic center is in the direction of Sagittarius (FIGURE 16-3) in our sky.

With only a few exceptions, every naked-eye object in our sky is part of the Galaxy. The Magellanic Clouds (see Figure 12-36) are exceptions that are visible from the Southern Hemisphere. These small galaxies are close to our Galaxy but are not part of it. An exception that those of us in the Northern Hemisphere can view in the fall sky is the Andromeda galaxy (FIGURE 16-4). It is the oval patch on the September sky chart at the end of this book.

The discovery that we live in a Galaxy of hundreds of billions of stars was made fairly recently. It began, though, 400 years ago when Galileo turned his telescope to the Milky Way and found that it is not made up of haze, but of stars far too numerous to count. The Milky Way appears misty because so many of the stars are so far away that the naked eye cannot distinguish individual stars and sees only the overall illumination from them. When Galileo looked through his telescope, he saw more haze behind the many stars his telescope revealed, and he concluded that it was caused by even more stars too faint to see individually.

William Herschel, discoverer of Uranus, wrote that through a telescope,

> We find [the stars] crowded beyond imagination along the extent of [the Milky Way]; . . . so that, in fact, its whole light is composed of nothing but stars of every magnitude from such as are visible to the naked eye down to the smallest points of light perceptible with the best telescope.

The telescopic view of the Milky Way led astronomers to conclude

In a spiral galaxy, are all the stars located in the spiral arms?

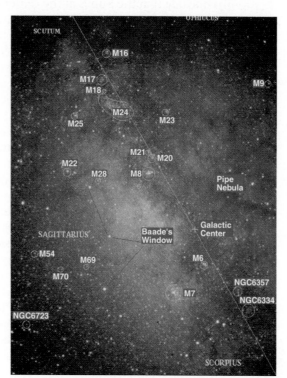

FIGURE 16-3 This image shows the region around the Galactic center near the border between Sagittarius and Scorpius. You can see the absorbing dust lanes that block the view of the Galactic center and some old bulge stars (yellow). The labels mark 17 Messier objects—including the nebulae Eagle (M16), Omega (M17), Lagoon (M8), and Trifid (M20)—globular clusters (M25, M22, M28, M54, M69, and NGC6723), open clusters (M6, M7, M23, M21, and M18), and the star cloud M24. Also marked are the dark Pipe nebula and Baade's Window (the region with the clearest view into the central bulge of our Galaxy).

FIGURE 16-4 The Andromeda galaxy (M31) is a spiral galaxy about 2.5 million light-years from our Galaxy. This galaxy can be seen with the naked eye as a fuzzy spot in the constellation Andromeda.

FIGURE 16-5 An edge-on view of our Galaxy. When we see the Milky Way in the sky, we are looking along the disk of the Galaxy. Otherwise, we are looking out of the disk.

FIGURE 16-6 The Herschels' counting of stars led them to conclude that the Galaxy is shaped like this. The Sun is located at the bright spot within the Galaxy.

Jacobus Kapteyn (1851–1922) held a position at the University of Groningen in The Netherlands from the age of 27 until he retired at 70.

Another analogy is this: if you are surrounded by dense fog, the fact that you can see the same distance in every direction is not evidence that you are in the center of the fog.

that we live in a disk of stars. When we view the Milky Way, we are looking along that disk (FIGURE 16-5), and when we are looking in other directions, we are looking out of the disk.

Based on naked eye observations and despite some local variations, the Milky Way seems to be about as bright in one direction as in another. This suggests that we may be at its center. In the 1780s, to determine where the Sun lies relative to the disk, William Herschel and his sister Caroline made star counts in nearly 700 selected regions distributed around the sky. They reasoned that if more stars were found in one direction than in another, that direction could be assumed to be toward the center of the disk. Their conclusions not only confirmed the disk-like shape of the Galaxy but also indicated that the Sun is indeed at the center, for they saw about the same number density of stars in all directions in the Milky Way. FIGURE 16-6 shows the shape they arrived at for the Galaxy. The Sun is nearly at its center.

In the early part of the 20th century, Jacobus C. Kapteyn sought to find the Sun's location by analyzing the density of stars in various directions from the Sun. He did this by measuring not only the number of stars in each direction but also their distances from us. He found that the density of stars decreases in every direction from the Sun and, like William and Caroline Herschel, it was logical for him to conclude that the Sun is at the center of the disk.

The conclusion that the Galaxy centers on the Sun was viewed with skepticism, as you might expect. After all, we once thought that the Earth was the center of the universe, only to find that it circles the Sun. Were we now discovering that the Sun is the center? The evidence from the Herschels and from Kapteyn pointed to an affirmative answer, but the finding seemed to be contrary to the trend that began before written history and continued through Copernicus and Galileo.

Today we know that the Sun is not at the center. To understand why the Herschels and Kapteyn obtained their erroneous results, imagine yourself standing in a large forest. Suppose you try to decide whether you are at the center of the forest by counting trees in all directions. Unless you are very near an edge, you will see the same number of trees in all directions even though you are nowhere near the center. The reason is that the trees themselves prevent you from seeing beyond a certain distance. If you cannot see to the edge of the forest, this method of determining your location is not valid.

The situation in the case of the stars is somewhat different, for the stars do not fill our view as do the trees in a forest. When we look out among the stars, however, interstellar dust and gas place a limit on how far we can see. The Herschels were unaware of the existence of this material. They assumed that they could see all the way to the edge of the group of stars within which our Sun lies. Because they could only see a limited distance and because the Sun is not near an edge, they concluded that it was at the center.

Likewise, interstellar dust kept Kapteyn from counting the stars correctly. The density of stars at greater and greater distances from the Sun appeared to decrease because when Kapteyn counted stars at great distances, the interstellar dust prohibited him from seeing them all. In Figure 16-1, the dark areas stretching along the Milky Way are dust and gas clouds.

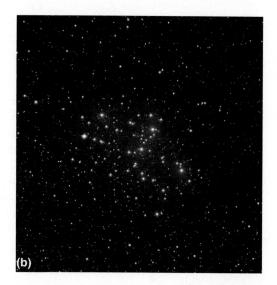

FIGURE 16-7 (a) The open cluster M7, about 1000 light-years away, in Scorpius; the Milky Way serves as the backdrop. The cluster, known to Ptolemy, includes about 80 stars. (b) The open cluster M6 (or Butterfly), in Scorpius.

These investigators reached erroneous conclusions simply because one of their assumptions—that there is nothing in space to block the view of distant stars—was wrong. Incorrect assumptions cause trouble not only in science but also in everyday life. Often we are not even aware of what our assumptions are, and this prevents us from even accepting the possibility that our conclusion may be in error.

Globular Clusters

As we discussed in Chapter 13, some stars begin their lives in galactic clusters. These clusters are called "galactic" because they are found within the disk of the Galaxy. The Pleiades (see Figure 13-7) is the most prominent example of this type of cluster, which may typically contain hundreds of stars. FIGURE 16-7 shows two other galactic or open clusters. FIGURE 16-8 shows two examples of a much larger

See also Figures 13-20 and 13-21 for more images of galactic and globular clusters.

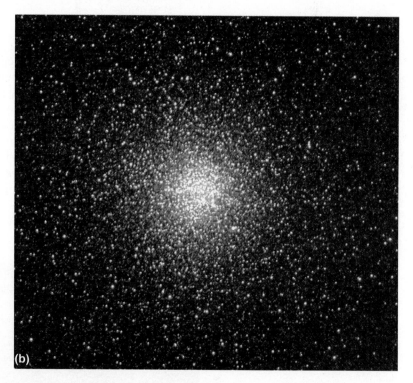

FIGURE 16-8 (a) An *HST* image of M15, the most tightly packed globular cluster in our Galaxy, 33,600 light-years away in the constellation Pegasus. Observations hint at the presence of a 4000-solar-mass black hole at its core. The horizontal scale is about 9 light-years. (b) A VLT image of 47 Tucanae, 16,000 light-years away in the constellation Tucana. It can be seen by the unaided eye from the Southern Hemisphere. Its mass is about 1 million solar-masses, and it is 120 light-years across; it appears on the sky as big as the full moon. It contains at least 20 millisecond pulsars.

globular cluster A spherical group of up to hundreds of thousands of stars, found primarily in the halo of the galaxy.

type of cluster, a ***globular cluster***. These beautiful, symmetrical clusters may look as though they have solid centers, but they are actually groups of hundreds of thousands of stars. The stars are so densely packed in the center of the cluster that we simply see a white area, not the individual stars. The average separation of stars near the center of a globular cluster is about 0.5 light-years. (In the Sun's region of space, stars are separated by an average distance of about 4 to 5 light-years.) Globular clusters are not confined to the disk of the Galaxy but are seen outside the disk.

While Kapteyn was seeking to determine the Sun's location in the Milky Way by studying star locations, Harlow Shapley was trying to do the same using globular clusters; however, he had a problem determining the distances to globular clusters, for they are much farther away than the stars Kapteyn was analyzing. Just a few years earlier, Henrietta Leavitt had discovered the relationship between the periods and the apparent magnitudes of Cepheid variables in the Magellanic Clouds. Shapley observed Population II Cepheids and RR Lyrae variable stars, which he considered to be like Cepheids but with shorter periods.

FIGURE 16-9 After Shapley had determined the relationship between the periods and absolute luminosities of RR Lyrae variable stars, he could use a sequence like the one shown here to determine the distance to any RR Lyrae variable.

THE PERIOD OF THE CEPHEID/ RR LYRAE STAR

Yields   (Via the period-luminosity relationship)

ITS ABSOLUTE LUMINOSITY   Combined with   ITS APPARENT LUMINOSITY

Yields

THE CEPHEID/ RR LYRAE'S DISTANCE

Population II Cepheids are about 1.5 magnitudes dimmer than the classical (Population I) Cepheids of the same period observed by Henrietta Leavitt (see Section 12-8) and thus are less luminous by a factor of 4. RR Lyrae variables are commonly found in globular clusters; their average luminosity is about 100 times that of the Sun, and their periods are less than 1 day. Because these stars are easily identified from their periodic changes in luminosity, it is relatively easy to find their distances using their period-luminosity relation and the distance modulus (**FIGURE 16-9**). The distances to these variable stars correspond to the globular cluster distances.

In 1917, Shapley published results of his survey of distances and directions to the then-known 93 globular clusters. He showed that they are not distributed evenly around the sky, but tend to be located more on one side, centered about the constellation Sagittarius. In fact, they seemed to be distributed in a sphere centered on a point about 50,000 light-years away from the Sun. **FIGURE 16-10** shows the approximate distribution of globular clusters compared with the Herschels' model of the Galaxy. Shapley assumed that the clusters revolve around the center of the Galaxy and therefore concluded that this center lies at the middle of the group of globular clusters. This meant that the Galaxy is much larger than indicated by the Herschels' model, and that it is not centered about the solar system.

In the 1920s, further evidence indicated that the Sun is not at a unique position in the Galaxy. Jan Oort (who proposed the comet cloud that bears his name) and Bertil Lindblad studied the motions of great numbers of stars near the Sun. They

I did not doubt that the center of the entire galactic system must coincide with that of the globular clusters, and that it must have a mass very much greater than that of the Kapteyn system in order to prevent the high-velocity stars and the clusters from escaping altogether.
Jan Oort

FIGURE 16-10 (a) The distribution of globular clusters as determined by Shapley is shown relative to the Sun and to the Herschels' model of the Galaxy. (b) The distribution of globular clusters and the nuclear bulge of the Galaxy shown through the interstellar dust. The lines mark the area blocked from view by the dust.

(a)

(b)

found that there is a pattern in their velocities, depending on their directions from the Sun. Kepler's third law, when applied to stars revolving around the center of the Galaxy, predicts that stars closer to the center should move faster and those farther from the center should move slower. This is the reason for the pattern of velocities shown in the Oort-Lindblad analysis. They concluded, as had Shapley, that the Galaxy's center was thousands of light-years away in the direction of Sagittarius.

It should be pointed out that Oort and Lindblad saw a pattern only after analyzing very great numbers of stars, for stars have random motions along with their pattern of motion around the Galactic center. This is similar to the way that cars on a multilane freeway have a pattern of motion in one direction, though at any given time certain cars may be changing lanes or otherwise deviating from the pattern. Oort and Lindblad ignored individual stellar motions and concentrated on patterns of average motions.

Finally, in 1930, the interstellar dust was discovered. This resolved the conflict between the conclusions of Herschel and Kapteyn on the one hand and of Shapley, Oort, and Lindblad on the other, for the interstellar dust had prevented Herschel and Kapteyn from seeing to the edge of the Galactic disk. It is interesting that interstellar extinction was the reason why both Kapteyn and Shapley were wrong. Because Kapteyn observed regions mostly in the Galactic disk (where extinction is strongest), he could not observe the far regions in our Galaxy, thus underestimating its size (to about 10,000 parsecs in diameter). A simple analogy is the case of a person standing in a dense fog, with limited visibility, trying to see the surrounding area. In Shapley's case, he observed globular clusters that are mostly above or below the plane of our Galaxy, in directions where extinction is not very strong; however, Shapley calibrated the period-luminosity relation by using variable stars near the Galactic plane, where extinction caused by dust in the disk dimmed the starlight, thus increasing the apparent magnitude of the stars. Shapley incorrectly concluded that the dimness of these stars implied large distances and thus calculated a diameter of about 100,000 parsecs. Although Shapley's original values for the size of the Galaxy had to be revised downward by a factor of about 2 when it was discovered that there are two types of Cepheid variables, his basic deductions were correct. He had shown that the Galaxy was much larger than previously thought. The boundaries of the universe were again pushed back.

Bertil Lindblad (1895–1965) was a Swedish astronomer who was president of the Royal Swedish Academy of Sciences for 22 years and was chair of the Nobel Foundation when he died in 1965.

Harlow Shapley (1885–1972) quit school after the fifth grade, returned to school at age 16, and earned a Ph.D. in astronomy from Princeton at age 27.

16-2 Components of the Galaxy

We can describe four components of the Galaxy: the disk (which contains the Sun), the nuclear bulge, the halo, and the Galactic corona (**FIGURE 16-11**). We describe each of these components here and then discuss some of them in more detail in later sections.

The *disk* is the large, flat part of the Galaxy that rotates in a plane around its center. The disk contains individual stars, clusters of stars—particularly open clusters—and almost all of the gas and dust found in the Galaxy. Most of the stars in the disk are young, metal-rich, Population I stars. The disk appears bluish because of the presence of the hot O and B main sequence stars, which indicates that there is active star formation in the

disk (of a galaxy) The flat, dense portion of a spiral galaxy that rotates in a plane around the nucleus.

FIGURE 16-11 The Galaxy consists of a nuclear bulge, a rotating disk, and a halo. The halo probably extends farther than indicated here.

Halo of globular clusters

Nucleus (core)

Disk

Nuclear bulge

Sun

Outer halo (corona)

HISTORICAL NOTE

The Shapley-Curtis Debate

In the late 1910s, there was considerable controversy about the size of the universe and the nature of the spiral nebulae. Several scientific papers were published on these topics, and the controversy attracted national attention. Harlow Shapley of Mount Wilson Observatories and Heber Curtis of Lick Observatory became the primary spokesmen for two opposing views. In April 1920, the National Academy of Sciences invited these two astronomers to present papers before a meeting of that group in Washington, D.C. and to engage in a public debate concerning their research and conclusions.

At that time, Shapley had calculated the diameter of the Galaxy to be about 300,000 light-years. The reason that his result was too large is that he did not know about the interstellar medium. Another error led him to calculate the distance to the Magellanic Clouds to be only 75,000 light-years—less than his calculated diameter of the Galaxy. He was using Cepheid variables to determine the distance to the clouds, but he did not know that there are two types of Cepheids and that he was seeing the unknown type in the Magellanic Clouds.

Adriaan van Maanen, a Dutch astronomer who was a friend of Shapley, had published results showing that he could observe rotation of the Andromeda nebula. In seeing the rotation, he was observing proper motion of parts of the nebula. Because we cannot observe proper motion within an object unless it is relatively close to us, this indicated that the nebula is nearby. (Van Maanen's observation was simply in error.) Because of his own observations and those of van Maanen, Shapley concluded that not only are the Magellanic Clouds and the Andromeda nebula part of our own system of stars, but also that other spiral nebulae are also part of that system.

Curtis held the opposite view. He believed that the group of stars that includes the Sun is much smaller than Shapley claimed and that the Andromeda nebula and other spiral nebulae are outside that group and are other "island universes." One bit of evidence he used to back his view was that Vesto Slipher of Lowell Observatory had investigated 15 spiral nebulae and found that 11 of them have significant redshifts. The redshifts indicated that they are moving away from us at great speeds, and this would make it unlikely that they are nearby. (These redshifts will be of major importance in Chapter 17.)

It is interesting that although Shapley thought that spiral nebulae are part of our Galaxy, he held that the universe is larger than Curtis envisioned. In his recollections of the debate, Shapley says that the subject assigned to the debaters was the size of the universe, but that Curtis turned the topic to the nature of the spiral nebulae.

Most of the 200 or 300 people present at the debate were members of the National Academy of Sciences, but the debate made headlines in the New York Times and excited public interest. When, just a few years later, Hubble discovered Cepheids in the Andromeda nebula and showed conclusively that it was indeed another "island universe" (as galaxies were called), it looked as though Shapley had been entirely wrong in the debate. In his own mind, however, Shapley felt that the score was even, for he had been more correct in predicting the overall size of the universe.

disk. The edges of the disk are not well defined and, therefore, its width and thickness cannot be stated exactly. As we noted earlier, its diameter is about 50,000 parsecs. Stars are most crowded near the plane of the Galaxy and become less crowded as we move from that plane. The disk is generally considered to be about 1000 parsecs thick, which makes its thickness about 2% of its diameter. It thus has the shape of about two compact disks stacked on one another.

Because star formation is more likely to occur where the interstellar material is most dense, stars are born with greatest frequency near the Galactic plane. Gradually, their motions result in them wandering away from the plane. Very massive stars have short lifetimes and, thus, we would expect to find few of them far from where they were formed. This is indeed the case, for almost all of the O-type stars lie within about 100 parsecs of the Galactic plane. Only less massive stars live long enough to move very far from the plane.

It is difficult to determine the structure of the Galactic disk from our position inside it because interstellar dust obstructs our view of distant locations. This dust is what limited early investigators' attempts to determine the Sun's position in the Galaxy. In Section 16-3 we describe how radio astronomy has provided evidence for the spiral arms, and in an Advancing the Model box, we outline new evidence that the Galaxy may not be a standard spiral galaxy after all.

The ***nuclear bulge*** of the Galaxy is about 2000 parsecs (6500 light-years) in diameter. If you imagine the disk to be a stack of two compact disks, you thus must add a peanut at their center to represent the bulge. This is necessary to represent the Galaxy correctly because the bulge is wider along the disk than it is perpendicular to the disk. Stars, dust, and gas are much more densely packed inside the nuclear bulge than they are anywhere else in the Galaxy. The bulge contains both young and old stars and appears reddish because of the presence of many red giants and supergiants. We discuss the bulge and its mysterious core in Section 16-5.

Figure 16-11 shows the Galactic ***halo***, which contains the globular clusters that caused Harlow Shapley to conclude that the Sun is not at the center of the Galaxy. A person viewing the globular clusters from the Sun's position would see many more in some directions than in others; and their distribution is centered at the nuclear bulge. Besides the globular clusters, which mostly consist of old, metal-poor Population II stars, the halo contains small amounts of gas and dust.

Globular clusters feel a gravitational force toward the center of the Galaxy and thus they orbit the Galactic nucleus, passing through the disk twice during each orbit. FIGURE 16-12 indicates their motion. About 150 globular clusters are known to be associated with the Milky Way, and the orbits of 75 of them have been calculated. Of these, 63 are in the halo, and 12 are confined to the disk.

In the next chapter we discuss an unresolved problem in galactic astronomy: the motions of galaxies indicate that much more gravitational force is exerted on galaxies than can be explained by the amount of mass that we can see. Astronomers conclude that there is more invisible mass in the universe than visible mass—by a factor of about 6. It is now thought that much of this mass exists in *extended halos* that surround galaxies. Therefore, an outer halo (or corona) was included in Figure 16-11. It is thought that the corona extends to perhaps two or three times the radius of the disk and halo. We do not know what the corona consists of—small black holes, cool dwarf stars, great numbers of neutrinos, or other exotic particles have been hypothesized. The first direct detection of such cool dwarf stars was announced in 2001. Thirty-eight previously unseen cool white dwarfs were observed within about 450 light-years of Earth. Observations suggest that, at most, 35% of the unseen matter in our Galaxy is made of normal matter, composed of neutrons, protons, and electrons.

TABLE 16-1 shows today's values for various Milky Way properties. Keep in mind, however, that the numbers are approximate, not only because every measurement is uncertain to some extent, but also because there are no specific boundaries for the various parts of the Galaxy. The total diameter of the halo is little more than a guess.

Galactic Motions

One method for determining the motion of the Sun around the Galactic center relies on the observation that the orbits of globular clusters seem to be randomly distributed around the center of the Galaxy. If we assume that the average velocity of all of the clusters, relative to the nucleus, is zero, we can measure their velocities relative to the Sun and attribute the average motion that is observed to the motion of the Sun. An analogy would be a person in a boat drifting on the ocean far from land and trying to measure the boat's speed. Suppose that the person is able to measure the speed of planes flying overhead and that equal numbers of planes are seen flying eastward and westward. Assuming that planes fly eastward at the same speed as planes fly westward, the person would know that the average speed of all the planes is zero. But if the measurements show that relative to the person the planes' average speed is 10 miles per hour toward the east, the person could conclude that the boat is moving 10 miles per hour toward the west.

nuclear bulge The central region of a spiral galaxy.

halo (around a galaxy) The outermost part of a spiral galaxy; fairly spherical in shape, it lies beyond the spiral component.

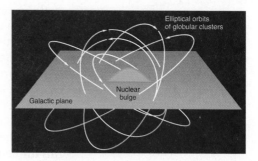

FIGURE 16-12 Globular clusters orbit the Galactic nucleus, passing through the disk twice during each orbit.

TABLE 16-1

Galactic Data

Radius of disk	80,000 light-years
Radius of nuclear bulge	3000 light-years
Total radius of halo	200,000 light-years
Sun's distance from center	26,000 light-years
Sun's orbital period	250,000,000 years
Thickness of disk	3000 light-years
Number of stars	200 to 400 billion

The Doppler effect is used to measure the radial speeds of the globular clusters.

In practice, wind speed would affect the speed of the planes, and the person's assumption would not be valid.

Saying that the Sun is moving toward Cygnus does not mean that it is getting closer to Cygnus; it means that the Sun is moving in that direction through space. Besides, each star of the constellation Cygnus has its own motion: some toward us and some away from us.

galactic rotation curve
A graph of the orbital speed of objects in the galactic disk as a function of their distance from the center.

Scientists always look for different methods to measure a quantity, and in this case, another method exists. Oort and Lindblad studied the motions of great numbers of stars relative to the Sun and applied statistical methods to determine the motion of stars in the Sun's neighborhood. Similar studies yield a value for the speed of the Sun. The best measurements show that the Sun is traveling in a nearly circular path around the Galactic center at a speed of about 220 kilometers/second (135 miles/second). It is now moving toward the constellation Cygnus. Knowing that the radius of the Sun's orbit is 8000 parsecs (26,000 light-years), we can calculate the circumference of the Sun's path and find that it takes about 230 million years to complete one revolution. Although this seems a tremendously long time, the Sun has completed some 20 orbits during its 5-billion-year lifetime.

If the Galaxy had almost all of its mass concentrated at its center, its parts would rotate according to Kepler's third law, just as the planets do in the solar system. The dashed line in **FIGURE 16-13a** shows the *galactic rotation curve* that would be expected in this case. If the mass were distributed so that most of it is fairly near the center, but not in the center, the curve would look more like the solid blue line. In fact, the Galactic rotation curve is somewhat like the solid red line in this figure. This indicates that the Galactic mass is unevenly distributed, and the fact that the speeds of objects located farther from the center than the Sun are not lower than the Sun's speed indicates that large amounts of mass lie beyond the Sun's distance. The amount of matter we "see" in our Galaxy because of the light it emits amounts to about 10% of the total mass necessary to give the observed rotation curve. The remaining 90% of the mass of the Galaxy is not visible. In the next chapter we discuss the possible nature of this unseen matter.

As we might expect, however, the orbits of stars are not perfectly circular. Along with the general orbiting motion of each portion of the Galaxy, each star has its own peculiar motion—perhaps having a component of motion from one side of the disk to the other or perhaps moving closer to the Galactic center at one time and moving farther away at another time as it follows an elliptical path. In general, however, the paths of stars seem to be nearly circular.

The Mass of the Galaxy

In Section 3-5 we showed that Isaac Newton revised Kepler's third law to read

$$\frac{a^3}{P^2} = (m_1 + m_2)/m_{Sun},$$

where a is the average radius of the orbit (in AU), P is the orbital period (in years), and m_1 and m_2 are the masses of the two objects. In Section 7-2 we showed that the

(a)   (b)

FIGURE 16-13 (a) If all the mass of the Galaxy were concentrated at its center, the Galactic rotation curve would be shown by the black dashed line in this graph. If the mass were distributed so that most of it is somewhat near, but not at the center, a rotation curve such as the one shown by the solid blue line would result. The observed rotation curve of the Galaxy is shown by the solid red line. It indicates that large amounts of mass orbit the center far beyond the Sun's orbit. The almost vertical segment of the rotation curve close to the center implies that matter in that region revolves as if it were a rigid body. (b) The mass enclosed in a sphere centered on the Galactic center increases with distance. As a result, the rotational speed stays approximately constant.

relationship holds not only for objects in orbit about the Sun, but also for satellites in orbit around the planets. Finally, in Section 12-6 we showed the law's application to binary star systems.

The discovery (in 1927) by Oort and Lindblad that the Galaxy in the Sun's neighborhood undergoes differential rotation meant that Kepler's third law might be applied to calculate the masses involved. In the case of a star revolving around the Galaxy's center, one of the masses in the equation is the mass of the star. The other mass is the mass of the *entire inner Galaxy*, including all objects in the Galaxy that are closer to the center than that star is. This may seem strange, as the inner portion of the Galaxy is made up of many objects rather than one, but it can be shown that this is the correct application of the equation.

The first step in using Kepler's third law to calculate the mass of the part of the Galaxy inside the Sun's orbit is to express the Sun's distance from the center (26,000 light-years) in AUs. Because 1 light-year is about 63,200 AU, the Sun is

$$26,000 \text{ ly} \times \frac{63,200 \text{ AU}}{1 \text{ ly}} \approx 1.6 \times 10^9 \text{ AU}$$

away from the Galactic center. Using this value in Kepler's third law, along with the Sun's period of 230,000,000 years, we find

$$m_1 + m_{Sun} = \frac{a^3}{P^2} \times m_{Sun} \approx \frac{(1.6 \times 10^9 \text{ AU})^3}{(2.3 \times 10^8 \text{ yr})^2} \times m_{Sun} \approx 10^{11} m_{Sun}.$$

The value obtained is the total of the mass of the Sun and the mass of the inner Galaxy. The mass of the Sun, of course, is negligible compared with this value and, thus, this answer is simply the mass of the part of the Galaxy that lies within the Sun's orbit. This value, 100 billion solar masses, must be taken as approximate. Recent analysis of the pattern of rotation in the outer parts of the Galaxy indicates that the total mass of the Galaxy is about 10^{12} (one trillion) solar masses, or about 10 times greater than we calculated above for the inner Galaxy. At present, the nature of this additional mass is unknown, for there are not enough stars to account for that much mass. We see later that a similar problem exists in the case of other galaxies.

Refer to the discussion of dark matter in Chapter 17 and again in Chapter 18.

16-3 The Spiral Arms

The *spiral* nature of the Galaxy is not obvious from observations in visible light because we can see only limited distances along the plane of the Galaxy. In 1951, however, astronomers at Yerkes Observatory discovered that as one looks either toward or away from the Galactic center, the distribution of O- and B-type stars is not uniform. They seem to be clustered at certain distances. FIGURE 16-14 illustrates the concentrations of this type. This was the first hint of the spiral nature of the Galaxy. Unfortunately, because such stars are best observed in visible light, interstellar extinction allows us to observe them only in the vicinity of the Sun. The same is true for the red emission nebulae found near many of these hot, luminous, blue main sequence stars; however, more evidence for the spiral nature of our Galaxy came with the discovery during that same year of a specific emission line of neutral hydrogen.

You might guess, correctly, that if we could map the distribution of hydrogen clouds in our Galaxy, we

spiral galaxy A disk-shaped galaxy with arms in a spiral pattern.

FIGURE 16-14 O- and B-type stars are found at greatest concentrations in the shaded areas.

should be able to infer its structure; however, most of the emission lines of hydrogen are at visible and ultraviolet wavelengths. Such radiation gets scattered or is absorbed easily by interstellar dust and this limits the range at which we could observe these clouds. Because the longer the wavelength, the easier it is for radiation to travel through interstellar dust without being scattered or absorbed, we need to look for radiation at infrared wavelengths. It turns out that cool hydrogen gas does emit such radiation in the radio portion of the spectrum (the ***21.1-centimeter radiation***).

The 21-cm emission photon results from a transition that a hydrogen atom makes from a higher energy level to a lower one (**FIGURE 16-15a**). To understand this transition, consider an approximate model in which the electron and proton of the hydrogen atom are small, charged spheres that spin around their axes. Because charges in motion create magnetic fields, we could visualize both the electron and proton as tiny magnets. When both magnets have their poles aligned in the same direction (as in the case of the electron and proton spinning in the same direction), they repel each other. When the two magnets are aligned in opposite directions (as in the case of the electron and proton spinning in opposite directions), they attract each other. The first configuration has a bit more energy than the second. When the transition occurs, a 21-cm photon thus is emitted. Of course, absorption can also occur that excites the hydrogen atom into aligning the spins of its electron and proton in the same direction.

Radio telescopes can use 21-cm radiation to detect high concentrations of cool hydrogen, such as exist in interstellar clouds. Because hydrogen is the main component of interstellar material—and the entire universe—this is an ideal method of detecting cool hydrogen clouds at great distances. Figure 16-15b is a false-color image of our Galaxy in 21-cm emission from interstellar hydrogen; this emission traces the "warm" interstellar medium, which on a large scale is organized into diffuse clouds of gas and dust that have sizes of up to hundreds of light-years.

As we have seen, new stars arise from gas and dust to which some of the material of a massive star returns at the end of the star's lifetime; therefore, hydrogen gas clouds detected by 21-cm radiation are located at the same places as newly forming stars. O and B stars are very massive and are therefore short lived. This means that they are found only where stars have recently formed and that we might expect to find hydrogen clouds at locations identified by astronomers as having high concentrations of O- and B-type stars.

It may seem that it would be impossible to determine the distance of a source of 21-cm radiation, for a radio telescope would seem to reveal only the direction of the source of the waves. In a sense this is true; however, the Doppler effect allows us to

21-centimeter radiation
Radiation from atomic hydrogen, with a wavelength of 21.1 centimeters.

(a)

(b)

FIGURE 16-15 (a) A 21-cm wavelength photon is emitted when the spins of the electron and proton in a hydrogen atom make the transition from being aligned in the same direction to being aligned in opposite directions. (b) Our Galaxy in 21-cm emission of hydrogen. Hydrogen gas is concentrated along the plane of our Galaxy (which extends horizontally across the image). The range of hydrogen density is shown from black/blue (lowest) to red/white (highest).

FIGURE 16-16 (a) The Sun and three hydrogen clouds (positions A, B, and C) are shown at different distances from the Galactic center. Assuming circular orbits and similar speeds, it seems that cloud A is stationary along the line of sight, while we seem to be approaching clouds B and C. (b) The 21-cm radiation observed along the line of sight shows peaks of blueshifted radiation; the peaks occur because the hydrogen is concentrated in spiral arms. (c) A smooth blueshifted 21-cm line would be observed if hydrogen were distributed uniformly in the Galaxy.

determine the *radial* motion of the hydrogen with respect to us. For example, suppose that a radio telescope is pointed in a direction across the Galaxy, as shown in FIGURE 16-16a. Let us also make the simplifying assumption that our solar system and the clouds at positions A, B, and C move on approximately circular orbits around the Galactic center and have about the same speed. Their instantaneous velocities are shown in red and are tangent to their orbits; the components of these velocities along the line of sight are shown in yellow. Then, from our point of view, cloud A seems stationary along the line of sight, while we seem to be approaching clouds B and C. As a result, the 21-cm radiation from clouds B and C will be blueshifted, as shown in part (b). If hydrogen gas were distributed uniformly in the Galactic disk, instead of being mostly concentrated in the Galaxy's spiral arms, the 21-cm radiation would show the fairly regular blueshift of part (c); however, what is observed is a graph similar to that in Figure 16-16b, providing us further evidence for the spiral structure of our Galaxy.

If another cloud were between the Sun and cloud A in Figure 16-16b, we would observe a *redshifted* 12-cm line from that cloud.

Mapping the Galaxy in 21-cm radiation contains plenty of room for error, but there is no doubt that ours is a spiral galaxy. As we show in the next chapter, a spiral appearance is common for galaxies. FIGURE 16-17 shows a spiral galaxy that may be similar to the Milky Way; recent work indicates that our Galaxy may have an elongated nucleus, as we discuss in the Advancing the Model box on page 467.

16-4 Spiral Arm Theories

It may seem at first glance that the spiral arms of a galaxy could be explained by the fact that stars near its center complete a circle in less time than those farther out. This would occur even if the stars do not orbit according to Kepler's third law, simply because stars near the center have less distance to cover to complete their orbits. Consider a group of stars that at a given time are in a straight line across the center of the galaxy, as shown in FIGURE 16-18a. As the stars move around the center (even if they all move at

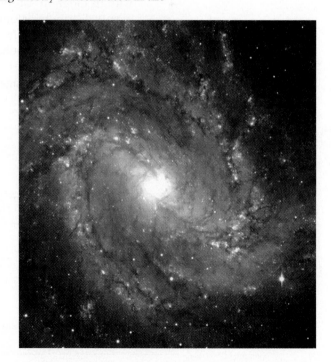

FIGURE 16-17 If we could get outside our Galaxy and view it face on, it would probably look like this galaxy, M83, in the southern constellation Hydra. The bright stars in the image are part of our Galaxy. Because these stars are much closer to us than M83, we see them as we see flies on a car windshield when we look through it. (Compare this to Figure 16-2.)

○ **FIGURE 16-18** Stars that start out in a straight line from the galaxy's center (a) would begin to show a spiral pattern (b and c), but after a few revolutions, the pattern would be lost (d).

the same speed), the line of stars will wind up into a spiral. The problem is that they would wind up so much that they would not be distinguishable as a line, as shown in Figure 16-18b, c, and d. The galaxy would appear as a fairly uniform disk. Yet we do perceive a spiral pattern in our Galaxy and in many other galaxies; therefore, this simple differential rotation hypothesis cannot be correct.

Currently, there are two competing theories to explain the spiral nature of galaxies: the density wave theory and the self-propagating star formation theory.

The Density Wave Theory

density wave theory A model for spiral galaxies that proposes that the arms are the result of density waves sweeping around the galaxy.

density wave A wave in which areas of high and low pressure move through the medium.

In a spiral galaxy, are all the stars located in the spiral arms?

The *density wave theory* was first proposed in 1940 by Bertil Lindblad and holds that what we see in a spiral arm of a distant galaxy is not a simple fixed line of stars but a line formed by the brightest stars and the glowing nebulae surrounding them. The theory holds that stars revolve around the galaxy independent of the spiral arms and that the arms are simply areas where the density of gas is greater than at other places. According to this theory, there are almost as many stars per unit volume between the arms as in the arms, but the arms contain more of the brightest stars and a higher density of gas and dust. The areas of denser gas move around the galaxy in *density waves*, causing the formation of new stars and glowing emission nebulae. This is best explained by an analogy, illustrated in **FIGURE 16-19**.

Suppose that cars are traveling on a long highway at a speed exceeding the speed limit. Also traveling along the road, at less than the speed limit, is a traffic patrol car with its radar on. Observing from a helicopter high in the sky, we see the cars fairly evenly distributed along the highway except around the police car. For a short distance behind and in front of the police vehicle, the cars are bunched up. As a given car approaches the police cruiser from behind, the car slows down, slowly passing the feared patrol car. Then when the driver believes that his or her car is safely in front of the police cruiser, it again speeds up. As a result, there is constantly a high density of

○ **FIGURE 16-19** An overhead view of a highway, seen as time passes. Car X is a police car, moving just slower than the speed limit. Bunched up around that car are other slow-moving cars that only gradually pass the police car. Thus, as time goes by, the cars near X are different, but a high density of cars remains there.

(a)

(b)

(c)

(d)

(e)

FIGURE 16-20 (a) The orbits of objects in the galaxy are very nearly circular. Because their orbital speed is greater than the speed of the density wave that forms the spiral pattern, they pass in and out of the spiral arms. (b) A cloud of dust and gas is about to enter a spiral arm. (c) The higher density of gas in the arm causes the cloud to compress, resulting in star formation. (d) As the cloud passes through the spiral arm, bright, massive stars make the arm itself appear brighter than the rest of the galaxy. (e) The bright stars burn out before they exit the spiral arm, as another cloud of dust and gas begins to enter the arm.

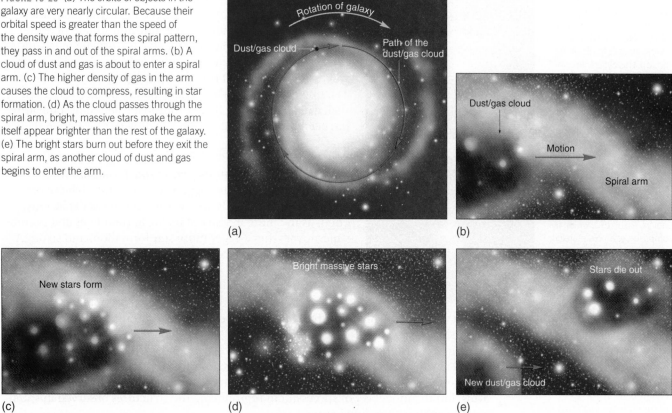

(a)

(b)

(c)

(d)

(e)

cars around the police car, even though the cars making up that group change all the time. The police car moves along, seeming to carry its high-density group along with it, in what we see from the helicopter to be a density wave.

Density waves are common here on Earth, for every sound wave is a density wave, with regions of high and low density making up the wave. In a galaxy, the density wave consists of a region of gas and dust that is denser than normal, perhaps by 10% to 20%. The major difference between sound waves and the density waves of a spiral galaxy is that in the atmosphere of Earth a sound wave travels faster than the particles of the gas itself; however, in the near-vacuum of a galaxy, the wave travels more slowly than the particles. The gas and dust particles—as well as stars—catch the wave from behind and pass through it in much the same way that cars in the analogy passed through the density pulse around the police car. FIGURE 16-20 illustrates the idea.

New stars are formed when an interstellar cloud of gas collapses. The density wave theory holds that the trigger for this collapse is the wave. As interstellar clouds approach the density wave from behind, they are compressed and stars are formed. Although stars of all masses are formed along the edge of the density wave, the brightest, most massive stars have ended their lives before they pass far from this edge. This means that when we look at a spiral galaxy, the spiral arms are obvious to us because they are the areas containing the bright stars.

One problem with the density wave theory is the question of how the density wave is sustained through the life of the galaxy. Computer simulations indicate that it would die out. In addition, infrared images of the center of the Whirlpool galaxy (FIGURE 16-21) indicate that spiral arms penetrate much farther into the nucleus of a galaxy than had previously been thought. The density wave theory had predicted that a galactic nucleus absorbs density waves, preventing the waves from extending into it. New information from the Whirlpool galaxy is causing a reexamination of the density wave theory.

It is possible that gravity is the driving mechanism behind the density wave. If the nucleus of a galaxy is not symmetrical (for example, if it is bar shaped, as it might be the case for our Galaxy), then the asymmetric gravitational field might

FIGURE 16-21 (a) A four-color composite in visible light of the Whirlpool galaxy (M51 or NGC5194); red corresponds to the H-alpha line. (b) This *Spitzer* image of M51 is a four-color composite; blue (3.6 μm), green (4.5 μm), orange (5.8 μm), and red (8.0 μm). The presence of the thin filaments between the arms is very puzzling. The star formation in M51 and its spiral structure are thought to be triggered by its on-going collision with its companion, NGC5195, which is composed of an older stellar population.

(a)

(b)

self-propagating star formation theory A model for spiral galaxies that explains the arms as resulting from a series of supernovae, each triggering the formation of new stars.

generate density waves by its interaction on stars and interstellar matter. Another possibility is that gravitational interactions between galaxies can generate and sustain density waves. Even if we resolve the issue of the driving mechanism, there is another problem. The spiral arms produced by density waves are well defined (for example, Figures 16-17 and 16-21); however, some galaxies have poorly defined arms. For such galaxies, another theory for the formation of spiral arms has been proposed: the self-propagating star formation theory.

The Self-Propagating Star Formation Theory

According to the ***self-propagating star formation theory*** of galactic spiral arms, the triggers that start the collapse of most interstellar clouds are nearby supernova explosions. Then, as the more massive stars finish their lives and become supernovae, they trigger more star formation, and so on. A simple analogy is a forest fire, with the flames jumping from one tree to the next. The formation of new stars thus is confined to areas where this process is taking place. Now differential rotation enters the picture. Computer analysis shows that at the rate at which massive stars would be formed, differential rotation would cause spiral arms to be formed and sustained.

The self-propagating star formation model is able to explain how a spiral arm would begin, as the process starts with a single supernova. Computer simulations based on this model can reproduce the spiral structure of galaxies with poorly defined arms, but the model is not successful in reproducing the structures observed in spiral galaxies with well-defined arms.

The two theories we presented for the formation of spiral arms are very different. In the density wave theory the spiral arms cause star formation, whereas the opposite is true in the self-propagating star formation theory. It is probable that we need a combination of these two theories to explain the observations.

16-5 The Galactic Nucleus

Observations by Shapley, Oort, and Lindblad in the early part of the 20th century revealed that the center of our Galaxy lies in the direction of Sagittarius. Because the presence of dust and gas in the Galactic plane dims visible light from the nucleus by about 28 magnitudes, astronomers had to await the development of nonoptical telescopes to learn more about that nucleus. To observe the Galactic nucleus, we use wavelengths in the infrared/radio part of the spectrum or in X-rays/gamma rays. Our observations helped us construct a picture of the nucleus of our Galaxy that includes a massive black hole and a history of violent events.

The *HST* image in FIGURE 16-22, taken in the infrared, shows a pair of the largest young star clusters, located less than 30 parsecs from the Galactic center. The ob-

FIGURE 16-22 These clusters are 10 times larger than typical young star clusters in our Galaxy; they will be destroyed in a few million years by the gravitational tidal forces in our Galaxy's core. The cluster on the left is so dense that 100,000 of its stars could fill the spherical volume between our Sun and its nearest neighbor star (about 4 light-years away). The cluster on the right is less dense; it has stars at the stage of becoming supernovae and is the home of the brightest star in our Galaxy (the Pistol star). The false colors in this *HST* image correspond to infrared wavelengths. Galactic center stars are white, red stars are located behind (or are surrounded by) dust, and blue stars are foreground stars (located between us and the Galactic center).

ADVANCING THE MODEL

The Milky Way: A Barred Warped Spiral Galaxy

In Chapter 17 we show that there are two types of spiral galaxies. About half are standard spiral galaxies, like the one shown in Figure 16-17. The other half have an elongated central bulge that appears as a bar across the center, like the one in FIGURE B16-1. Until recently, astronomers thought that the Milky Way is a standard spiral galaxy, but evidence is accumulating that our Galaxy is a barred spiral galaxy with an elongated nucleus that is probably shorter in proportion to the rest of the Galaxy than the one in Figure B16-1.

The new evidence comes primarily from data related to the 21-cm radiation from clouds of cool hydrogen gas near the nuclear bulge and observations using the *COBE* and *Spitzer* satellites. (The *Cosmic Background Explorer* was designed to measure short-wavelength radio waves from space, as we discuss in Chapter 18.)

FIGURE B16-2 Opposite sides of an elongated nucleus—a bar—do not appear the same when viewed from the Sun, because lines that make equal angles with the central line pass through different volumes of the bar. Data indicate that the nucleus of the Milky Way is slightly elongated with its long axis at 45° to the line between the Sun and the Galactic center.

FIGURE B16-1 The Milky Way may be a barred spiral galaxy similar to this one.

Suppose the central bulge is elongated with its long axis oriented at some oblique angle to the line of sight, as in FIGURE B16-2. The Sun (and Earth) is located at the point indicated in the figure. Line C extends to the center of the Galaxy, and lines L and R are drawn at equal angles on each side of line C. The line of sight on the near side of the nucleus (the left side here) passes through part of the nucleus, but the equivalent line of sight on the other side does not. If the nucleus is shaped like this and has this orientation, astronomers should detect an asymmetry in the radiation from near the nucleus. Data from *COBE*, as well as data from Japanese astronomers, correspond to what would be expected from such an elongated nucleus.

Further information comes from analyzing motions of the gas near the nucleus. The gas moves around the nucleus in a noncircular pattern, corresponding to what would be expected from a barred nucleus. Finally, using *Spitzer*, astronomers were able to see through interstellar dust clouds and survey more than 30 million stars around the Galactic center; the survey suggests the presence of a long bar of stars (about 27,000 light-years in length) at an angle of 45° to the line between the Sun and the Galactic center.

A map of Galactic atomic hydrogen gas emissions and the distribution of more than 100 million stars in the Galactic disk show that the disk is warped and that the warp extends across the entire diameter of the Galaxy. Computer simulations show that the warp is very dynamic and could be explained as the result of gravitational interactions between the Galaxy's dark matter and its prominent satellites, the Magellanic clouds.

served number density of stars is indeed increasing as we get closer to the Galactic center, down to about 2 parsecs from the center. For distances closer than 2 parsecs, observations of the velocities of stars suggest that there is a great deal of mass in a very small volume in the Galactic nucleus (less than 0.5 parsecs in radius). It seems that the Galactic nucleus harbors a massive black hole of mass about 3.7 million solar masses.

Radio observations show that a nuclear disk of neutral gas occupies a region between a few hundred parsecs to a thousand parsecs from the center. FIGURE 16-23a shows the region near the Galactic center, located at the edge of the bright object

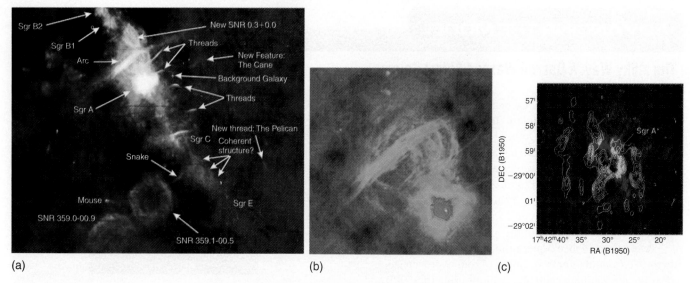

(a)   (b)   (c)

FIGURE 16-23 (a) This image was constructed from 1-meter radio data obtained by telescopes of the Very Large Array. It shows signs of a violent environment, including supernova remnants and filaments that may correspond to mass outflow from the Galactic center (located at the edge of the object Sgr A). (b) This image (in 20-cm) shows the inner region, about 60 parsecs across, of the Galactic nucleus. The nucleus is at the center of the strongest emission. The filament, running perpendicularly to the Galactic plane, may be associated with magnetic fields. (c) Ammonia emission (at 1.3 cm) in yellow contours in the region around the Galactic center; the resolution is as small as 0.13 light-years. The ring as seen at 3 mm is shown in the background. Streamers that possibly interact with the ring are numbered. The star labels the position of the massive black hole (Sgr A*).

labeled Sagittarius A (Sgr A). The Galactic plane runs diagonally across the image, which includes supernova remnants (SNRs), along with many elongated threads of ionized gas, almost perpendicular to the disk. One of the most intriguing features of this region is shown in Figure 16-23b. It is likely that this feature is the result of magnetic fields, with the radio emission being due to charged particles spiraling around the magnetic field lines. In the Sgr A region we find a large molecular ring, with an inner radius of 2 parsecs and outer radius of 8 parsecs, whose mass is at least 20,000 solar masses. The material in this ring is much warmer and denser than material in molecular clouds elsewhere in the Galaxy. The velocities of the ionized gas in this

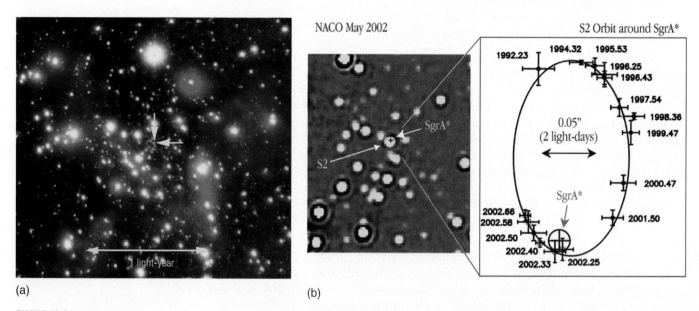

(a)   (b)

FIGURE 16-24 (a) The innermost area of our Galaxy, shown as a combination of three infrared images (wavelength between 1.6 and 3.5 μm). The compact objects are stars; blue denotes hot, and red denotes cool stars. There is also infrared emission from dust between the stars. The arrows mark the position of Sgr A*. (b) An infrared image of an area 60 × 60 light-days, centered on the position of Sgr A*. The inset shows the positions of a star, designated S2, during the period 1992–2002. The solid curve is the best-fitting elliptical orbit, with Sgr A* at one of the foci. As of 2009, astronomers have followed S2 making more than one complete orbit; using S2's orbital dynamics, they measured the distance between Earth and the Galactic center to be 7.94 ± 0.42 kpc, in good agreement with measurements by other methods.

region increase from about 100 km/s at the inner edge of the ring to 700 km/s at 0.1 parsecs from the Galactic center. These measurements, along with the presence of Sgr A*—a very small, unresolved (less than 20 AU in size) radio source inside the Sgr A region—suggest that at the center of our Galaxy we have a massive black hole of 3.7 million solar masses. This is consistent with the results obtained using stellar velocities in this region. Figure 16-23c shows the inner region of the Galactic nucleus. Narrow "streamers" can be seen connecting giant molecular clouds of gas and dust to the ring. The observed increase in velocity along a streamer suggests that gas/dust is being accreted from the molecular clouds and "fed" to the ring and then to the black hole as a result of its strong gravitational pull. Infrared observations of the innermost area of the Galactic nucleus, obtained in 2002 by ESO's VLT and shown in **FIGURE 16-24a**, show emission from interstellar dust between a great number of stars around the position of Sgr A*. In addition, years of observations allowed astronomers to trace the orbits of many stars around Sgr A*; one such orbit is shown in Figure 16-24b. The characteristics of these orbits leave little doubt that a supermassive black hole is present at the center of our Galaxy.

The case of a large black hole at the center of our Galaxy is also supported by observations of gamma rays emanating from a very small region in the Galactic nucleus. In addition, in late 2000, X-ray variability was observed from Sgr A* that lasted less than 10 minutes. As we discussed in Section 15-4, variability is a great indicator of the size of the radiating region because nothing can travel faster than light. This observation suggests that the hot, radiating gas could not occupy a region bigger than the distance between the Earth and the Sun. The most probable scenario is that the force that powers Sgr A* is a black hole, orbited nearby by a great number of stars. As matter falls into the black hole, collisions cause energy to be released. The release of energy here is similar to the energy released as matter falls into stellar black holes, which we discussed in Chapter 15. In the case of the Galactic nucleus, however, a *massive* black hole is at the center, and it is surrounded by a great amount of matter, causing enormous quantities of energy to be released. **FIGURE 16-25** shows the intensity of high-energy gamma-ray emission in our Galaxy.

An X-ray look at our Galaxy's central black hole has revealed numerous outbursts and some large explosions. **FIGURE 16-26a** shows large lobes of hot gas (20 million K) in the innermost region around Sgr A*. These lobes show that many enormous explosions have occurred during the past 10,000 years. A possible jet of particles,

FIGURE 16-25 This image was taken by the *Energetic Gamma-Ray Experiment Telescope (EGRET)* on board the *Compton Gamma-Ray Observatory*. Our Galaxy is a diffuse source of gamma-ray light. Superimposed on this image are several gamma-ray pulsars and some active nuclei of other galaxies.

Black holes are common in the Galaxy. A few isolated stellar-mass black holes have been detected indirectly by the way their gravity bends the light of a more distant star behind them. We discuss this phenomenon in Chapter 17. Stellar-mass black hole candidates have been observed both in the Galactic disk and halo by the effect they have on the motion of their normal companion star.

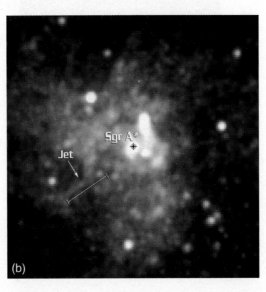

FIGURE 16-26 (a) A *Chandra* image that marks the position of the X-ray source associated with Sgr A*. Large lobes of gas (20 million K) are also shown. The image covers an area of 60 × 60 light-years. (b) A close-up Chandra image of the region around Sgr A*, showing a possible X-ray jet of length 1.5 light-years. The image covers an area of 9 × 9 light-years.

shown in Figure 16-26b, suggests that the observed X-ray flaring activity from the vicinity of the black hole has been occurring for many years.

Some other spiral galaxies also have tremendously powerful energy sources at their center, and we see signs of violent activity near those centers. The massive black hole hypothesis seems to be the best explanation for the energy source in our Galaxy and in similar galaxies. As we discuss in the next chapter, some galaxies produce even more energy in their nuclei. We are far from understanding the nucleus of our Galaxy, and further knowledge must come from observations of other galaxies as well as our own.

16-6   The Evolution of the Galaxy

The first step in developing a theory of the formation of the Galaxy is to consider the chemical content and the age of the Galaxy's components. After that is done, the pieces can be put together to give us a picture of how the Galaxy developed.

Age and Composition of the Galaxy

◆ Astronomers say that a star with a large abundance of heavy elements is *rich in metals*, or *metal rich*.

In Section 15-9 we discussed the division of stars into Population I, Population II, and Population III according to their percentage of heavy elements. Although in reality there is a continuum from the low percentage of heavy elements in extreme Population II to the greatest percentage in extreme Population I, the grouping is still convenient. On the average, Population II stars contain only about 1% of the heavy elements of Population I stars. An extreme case is the star HE0107-5240, 36,000 light-years in the southern constellation Phoenix, which has the lowest abundance of heavier elements ever observed, 1/200,000 that of the Sun.

◆ The abundance of heavy elements decreases by a factor of 0.8 for each thousand parsecs from the center of the disk.

Population I stars are stars that have formed from the remains of previous generations of stars, and most of them are found in the disk of the Galaxy. In fact, stars with the greatest percentage of heavy elements lie close to the nuclear bulge. The farther from the bulge, the lower the fraction of heavy elements. Most globular clusters, on the other hand, are made up of Population II stars. Of the known globular clusters in the Milky Way, about 70% have an average heavy-element content of about one twentieth of that of the Sun. The remaining 30% contain about one third the heavy-element content of the Sun.

◆ In Section 14-2 we discussed how we determine the age of a star cluster.

Star clusters provide a convenient method of measuring the age of stars. All stars in a cluster were formed at about the same time. Knowing this, astronomers can determine a cluster's age by analyzing its H-R diagram. FIGURE 16-27 is the H-R diagram of a cluster old enough that its heaviest stars have left the main sequence. The position of the main sequence turnoff point permits a calculation of the age of the cluster.

FIGURE 16-27 The H-R diagram of a galactic cluster shows a definite main sequence turn-off point. From the location of the turn-off point on the main sequence, astronomers can determine the age of the cluster.

The classification of stars in a specific portion of the Galaxy can provide a clue to the age of that portion. For example, there are no white dwarfs in the part of the Galactic disk near the Sun. Because white dwarfs do not form until after stars have gone through the main sequence and red giant stages, this sets an upper limit of about 10 billion years for the age of the Sun's portion of the disk.

Within the disk, O- and B-type stars are found primarily near the Galactic plane. Because these stars have short lifetimes, the fact that they are not found at great distances from the Galaxy's plane tells us that star formation does not occur to any great extent except along that plane.

Stars in the halo of the galaxy are older than those in the disk. While the oldest stars in the portion of the disk where the Sun is located are about 10 billion years old, the *youngest* stars in globular clusters are about 11 billion years old. Globular clusters thus formed before the disk portion of the Galaxy. The oldest globular clusters are about 13 billion years old, and because these are the oldest stars we find, we take this to be the minimum age of the Galaxy. Globular clusters were probably much more numerous in the early days of our Galaxy, but tidal interactions between a cluster and the Galaxy could tear the cluster apart. In 2002, astronomers announced the detection of a stream of stellar debris emanating from a globular cluster that is being torn apart by our Galaxy. Such streams provide a new way to determine how the mass of the dark matter halo of our Galaxy is distributed.

The age of stars in the nuclear bulge is difficult to determine because the bulge is obscured by dust. It can be studied only in the X-ray, infrared, and radio portions of the spectrum; however, observations through a few gaps in the dust have allowed astronomers to sample the outermost bulge population. We now know that the stars of the nuclear bulge are very rich in heavy elements, and they all appear to be red giants of types K and M. This tells us that the nuclear bulge must be very old, for two reasons: first, the stars themselves are old, for K- and M-type stars live long lives on the main sequence before becoming red giants. Second, they were formed from the remains of previous generations of stars.

The existence of a Galactic corona of hot gas has been confirmed based on data by NASA's *Far Ultraviolet Spectroscopic Explorer* (*FUSE*) satellite. Observations from *FUSE* show the presence in the corona of a specific species of highly ionized oxygen atom, which indicates the existence of coronal gas with temperatures close to a quarter million kelvin. The atoms observed by *FUSE* are believed to have been heated by supernova explosions to very high temperatures and pushed outward from the Galactic plane into the halo. The clouds of ionized oxygen appear in almost all directions and extend as much as 5 to 10 thousand light-years away from the Galactic plane.

FUSE operated between 1999 and 2007; it was designed to sample light (look at spectra) in the UV part of the spectrum. This light can only be observed above the Earth's atmosphere.

The Galaxy's History

Although astronomers disagree about the specifics, a general picture of the evolution of our Galaxy is emerging. The process is somewhat parallel to the way stars form. The Galaxy began as a tremendous cloud of gas and dust, bigger than the present Galactic halo (**FIGURE 16-28**). Mutual gravitation between the cloud's parts gradually pulled it together. The center portion was the first to become dense enough for stars to form, and it soon became a hotbed of star formation. Soon thereafter, stars began

FIGURE 16-28 (a) According to a leading theory of galactic evolution, the Galaxy began as a sphere of gas and dust about 13 billion years ago. (b) As the sphere collapsed toward the center, stars and clusters formed so that the Galaxy appeared like this some 12 to 13 billion years ago. (c) The Galaxy reached its present state after the remaining gas and dust formed into a disk and spiral arms developed.

forming in dense pockets, hundreds of light-years across, which were in orbit around the center. They formed what are now the globular clusters.

The initial giant cloud had some rotation, and as it contracted, it spun faster. Just as occurs during a star's protostar stage, the rotating matter formed into a disk. In the case of a star, almost all the orbiting material becomes caught in the disk, but in the Galaxy, the density of matter in the disk is low enough that globular clusters pass through it without being captured. Finally, density waves formed in the Galaxy's disk, creating the spiral arms where star formation continues today.

Even though this scenario is very sketchy, not all astronomers agree with all of it. For example, in some models, several separate clouds of gas merge to form the Galaxy rather than one. High-velocity atomic hydrogen clouds have been observed since 1963. They have the mass of a small galaxy and are about 15,000 parsecs across. Several hundred of these clouds have been mapped, and their orbits do not follow the approximately circular orbits of most objects in the Galaxy. If such clouds are indeed the building blocks of our Galaxy, then they represent the earliest structures that formed in the universe. They are also one of the few places where the material has not been heavily contaminated by later star formation. The theory that such clouds are the seeds of the Milky Way makes several predictions. First, because these clouds formed long ago, the abundance of heavy elements should be much lower than in our Galaxy. Second, the clouds should be large and of low pressure. Third, if these clouds are a part of the local group of about 30 galaxies (of which Andromeda and our Galaxy are members), they should show little of the fluorescence seen in the relatively nearby atomic hydrogen clouds. Fourth, if these clouds collide with the galaxies in the local group, there should be evidence of a large cloud of hot, ionized gas around our Galaxy and Andromeda.

Recent observations seem to support this theory of gradual formation of a galaxy through accretion of large hydrogen clouds. FIGURE 16-29 is a composite image showing a high-velocity cloud "raining" material into the Galaxy, supplying it with material to make new stars. Such evidence suggests that these clouds play a crucial role in the chemical evolution of our Galaxy; they supply it with metal-poor gas that counteracts the buildup of heavy elements in stars and in the interstellar medium of our Galaxy. This explains why most stars in the Galactic disk have similar concentrations of heavy elements, independent of their age. It also explains how our Galaxy can form about a new star every year without running out of its supply of gas after a tenth of its lifetime.

It is also possible that our Galaxy, like others, grew from smaller galaxies by collisions. This "hierarchical" picture seems to fit better with current theories that try to explain the present structure of the universe as it evolved through time. Data from the *Hipparcos* satellite support the idea of a dwarf galaxy colliding with the Milky Way some 10 billion years ago. As a result of the collision, and over a long period, the dwarf galaxy broke up into streams of stars that keep a common memory of their origin. Evidence for two such streams of stars was found in the *Hipparcos* data; they are among the oldest stars in our vicinity and spend most of their time in the Galactic halo. A map of stars in our Galaxy constructed in 2006 with data from the Sloan Digital Sky Survey (SDSS) revealed a number of giant streams of stars, suggesting that multiple merging events are currently occurring. Also, studying 20,000 stars observed by the SDSS, astronomers discovered that the Galaxy's halo is made of two components; the inner halo follows the motion of the Galactic disk, albeit at a slower rate, while the outer halo rotates in the opposite direction and it has a different chemical composition. In early 2003, astronomers announced the discovery of a ring of stars around our Galaxy, approximately 120,000 light-years in diameter (FIGURE 16-30). The presence of the ring is an indication that at least part of our Galaxy was formed by collisions of many smaller galaxies billions of years ago. If indeed our Galaxy has accreted small nearby satellite galaxies, then many of its stars have originated in dif-

As discussed earlier, the density wave theory is not the only possible explanation for the spiral arms.

Studies of globular clusters in other galaxies suggest that some of these clusters may be the remnant nuclei of dwarf galaxies that were consumed by the host galaxy. Observations have also identified a large number of globular clusters wandering freely in the intergalactic space as a result of gravitational interactions between galaxies.

FIGURE 16-29 An all-sky composite image. The false-color orange-yellow clouds contain neutral hydrogen and are observed in 21-cm radiation, while the rendition of our Galaxy is in visible light. The edge-on Galactic plane appears as a white horizontal strip. *HST*'s spectrograph measured the composition and velocity of the encircled cloud.

ferent places. More studies are needed of the distribution of the halo stars (some of the oldest in the Galaxy), their chemical composition, and their motion so that we can better understand when and how the halo formed.

Our knowledge of the Galaxy has only recently progressed to the point where we can formulate meaningful models of its formation. Today's models will have to be developed, and perhaps combined, before we can be confident of their validity. In the next chapter we expand on our discussion of the formation of galaxies.

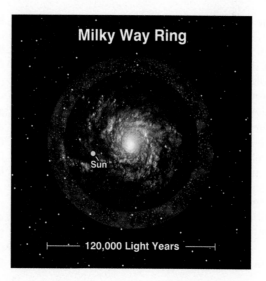

FIGURE 16-30 An artist's version of a ring of stars around our Galaxy was discovered by the Sloan Digital Sky Survey. The ring contains about half a billion stars, has a thickness of about 10,000 light-years, and encircles us like a giant doughnut.

Conclusion

Our Sun is one of some 200 billion stars in an enormous spiral galaxy that is itself just one of countless galaxies in the observable universe. The nature of our Galaxy was discovered only rather recently because our vision is obscured by gas and dust along the Galaxy's disk. Although measurements of the Galaxy's characteristics are necessarily imprecise, some of its properties can be measured using techniques dating from the time of Isaac Newton, such as the calculation of the Galaxy's mass using Kepler's third law. Detection and measurement of many other features of the Galaxy must rely on more modern methods and equipment, such as radio astronomy, which has opened many doors to understanding the Milky Way.

Analysis of 21-cm radiation leads us to conclude that our Galaxy is a spiral one, like many others we observe. Two principal theories have been proposed to explain the spiral arms of a galaxy: the density wave theory and the self-propagating star formation theory.

The nuclear bulge of our Galaxy contains a high density of stars. The tremendous energy that pours from the nucleus, as well as the rapid motions of objects near it, is consistent with the hypothesis that a massive black hole is at the center of the Galaxy.

Data that are accumulating about the Galaxy permit us to develop models of galactic formation, but these models, like many of astronomy's theories about the Milky Way, are very tentative and await further research by today's and tomorrow's scientists.

STUDY GUIDE

1. Our Sun is located
   A. at the very outer edge of the Galaxy.
   B. far from the center of the Galaxy, but not at the outer edge.
   C. near the center of the Galaxy, but not right at the center.
   D. at the center of the Galaxy.

2. Astronomers of the 18th and 19th centuries thought that the Sun was near the center of the Milky Way Galaxy because they counted the same number of stars in the disk of the Galaxy in every direction. The reason they were not correct is that the Galaxy
   A. is an irregular galaxy with a chaotic shape.
   B. contains dust that obscures its distant regions.
   C. has the shape of a tube with the Sun near one end.
   D. has two kinds of Cepheid variables, so that all distance measurements until recently were incorrect.
   E. has a giant black hole at its center.

3. The center of the Galaxy was first discovered by observing
   A. X-rays that it emits.
   B. radio waves that it emits.
   C. the intense light that comes from it.
   D. the bulge around it.
   E. its yellow glow.

4. When we look at the sky on a dark, clear night, sometimes we can see a faint band of light stretching across it. What we are observing is
   A. the plane of the Milky Way Galaxy.
   B. other galaxies.
   C. the stars of some other galaxy.
   D. the center of the Milky Way Galaxy.
   E. clusters of other galaxies that are drawn to the Milky Way.

5. The Sun is one of about how many stars in the Milky Way Galaxy?
   A. 100 to 200 million.
   B. One billion.
   C. 100 to 400 billion.
   D. One trillion.
   E. [We don't have any idea how many stars are in the Galaxy.]

6. Evidence for the spiral nature of the Galaxy comes primarily from
   A. Cepheid variable data.
   B. Doppler shift data of stars.
   C. 21-cm data.
   D. observations of globular clusters.
   E. [Both A and D above.]

7. We have learned that the Galaxy is a spiral galaxy by
   A. the reflection of light from nebulae.
   B. the Doppler shift of radio waves.
   C. observations of globular clusters.
   D. comparing ages of various clusters.
   E. plotting the stars of various clusters on an H-R diagram.

8. Why is observation of distant parts of the Galaxy limited in the visible region?
   A. Interstellar dust blocks visible light.
   B. The redshift of distant stars makes them difficult to detect.
   C. Opacity of our atmosphere blocks visible light.
   D. Relative motion of the spiral arms makes them difficult to detect.

9. Radio observations can provide information about the Galaxy that we cannot learn from observations in visible light because
   A. radio waves are able to pass through clouds of dust.
   B. stars emit a greater amount of energy in radio wavelengths than in visible wavelengths.
   C. the velocity of radio waves is greater than that of light.
   D. our Galaxy is spiral in nature.

10. William and Caroline Herschel counted stars in various directions in an attempt to determine the Sun's position in the Galaxy. Later, Jacobus Kapteyn tried to improve on their determination by taking into account
    A. the interstellar dust.

B. radio waves from stars.
C. bright nebulae between the stars.
D. redshift data on stars in various directions.
E. the density of stars at various distances.

11. Oort and Lindblad determined the motion of the Sun relative to other stars by analyzing
    A. the interstellar dust.
    B. radio waves from stars.
    C. bright nebulae between the stars.
    D. redshift data on stars in various directions.
    E. the density of stars at various distances.

12. A calculation of the mass of the inner Galaxy can be made based on
    A. Kepler's laws.
    B. observations of nebulae in spiral arms.
    C. star counts.
    D. distances to Cepheid variables.

13. According to the density wave theory of the spiral arms,
    A. the number of stars per volume is about the same between the spiral arms as in them.
    B. the number of stars per volume is much greater between the spiral arms than in them.
    C. the number of stars per volume is much less between the spiral arms than in them.
    D. [The theory predicts nothing about the number of stars per volume of space.]

14. How does the density wave theory of spiral arms explain why they are brighter than the regions between the arms?
    A. There are more stars per volume in the arms than between them.
    B. Brighter stars are in the spiral arms because they follow along with the arms as they move.
    C. Brighter stars are in the spiral arms because they are formed there and are short lived.

15. According to the self-propagating star formation theory of spiral galaxies' arms,
    A. stars revolve around the galactic center in perfect circles.
    B. stars obey Kepler's third law as they move around the galactic center.
    C. stars are about evenly spread around the galaxy.
    D. [Two of the above.]
    E. [None of the above.]

16. A black hole is thought to be at the center of the Galaxy because
    A. no light comes from that area of the Galaxy.
    B. large amounts of energy come from a small source there.
    C. motions of objects near the center indicate a large mass there.
    D. [Both A and C above.]
    E. [Both B and C above.]

17. Serendipity is the ability to
    A. detect small changes in data.
    B. make unexpected discoveries by accident.
    C. do mental calculations quickly and accurately.
    D. visualize situations in three dimensions.
    E. analyze data quickly and accurately.

18. The self-propagating star formation theory of spiral arms holds that
    A. nuclear reactions occur in cores of stars in chain reactions.
    B. the wave moves around the galaxy in chain reactions.
    C. new stars that form the arms are the result of shock waves from supernovae.

19. Use an analogy to explain the nature of a density wave.

20. Sketch the Galaxy both edge on and face on, showing its prominent features and the approximate location of the Sun.

21. Describe the Milky Way as seen from the Earth by the naked eye.

22. Distinguish between galactic clusters, globular clusters, and clusters of galaxies.

23. Name four principal components of the Galaxy and describe the location of each.

24. What two observations give evidence of spiral arms in the Galaxy?

25. What leads us to conclude that globular clusters are very old?

RECALL QUESTIONS

1. If stars revolve around the Galactic center independently of the spiral arms, it would seem that there should be as many stars per unit volume between the arms as inside them. Yet the text states that there is *almost* the same density of stars between the arms as inside them. Why would there be a difference at all?

2. Explain how Kepler's third law is used to calculate the mass of the Galaxy. Discuss the limitations of this method.

3. Explain why the hypothesized Galactic rotation curve of Figure 16-13a (solid blue line) extends down to very low speeds near the zero point on the bottom axis, whereas the dashed-line curve of Figure 16-13a does not.

4. If a radio telescope cannot reveal directly the distance to a source of 21-cm radiation, how can this radiation be used to reveal spiral arms in the Galaxy?

5. Write a report on various models of the formation of the Galaxy based on the article entitled, "How the Milky Way Formed," in *Scientific American*, January 1993, pp. 72–78.

6. What is the evidence that stars of the nuclear bulge formed before stars in other parts of the Galaxy?

7. The Milky Way looks more prominent in July than in December. Why?

8. How did William and Caroline Herschel seek to determine the Sun's position in the Galaxy? What measurements did Kapteyn make to answer the same question?

9. Explain why 21-cm radiation reveals the parts of the Galaxy in which O- and B-type stars are located.

10. We have never observed a globular cluster pass through the disk of the Galaxy. How do we know that they do? Approximately how long would it take for such a cluster to pass through the galactic disk?

11. Consider the H-R diagrams of two globular clusters (A and B), similar to the one shown in Figure 16-27. Assume that the turnoff point for cluster A is lower on the main sequence than that for cluster B. Which of the two clusters has a higher metallicity and why?

QUESTIONS TO PONDER

1. Show how you can calculate the period of the Sun's motion around the Galaxy, given that the Sun's distance to the center is 26,000 light-years and its speed is 220 kilometers/second.

2. Suppose that a portion of another galaxy is observed to move with a speed of 250 kilometers/second and to be at a distance of 40,000 light-years from the center of that galaxy. What is the period of revolution of that portion of the galaxy?

3. Use the data from Question 2 to calculate the mass of that galaxy that is inside the radius of the portion described.

4. Suppose we wish to construct a physical model of the Galaxy. If the Sun is represented by a small grain of sand 0.1 millimeters across, what will be the diameter of the model? (Hint: See the Activity below.)

CALCULATIONS

The Scale of the Galaxy

Suppose that you wish to construct a scale drawing of our region of the universe. The Sun has an actual diameter of about 1,500,000 kilometers, and you represent it by a dot the size of a period on this page, about 0.5 millimeters across. The average distance between stars in our region of the Galaxy is about 5 light-years; therefore, you must calculate what the corresponding distance would be on your drawing, given that one light-year is equal to 9.5×10^{12} kilometers.

First, set up the ratio of the distance on your scale to the actual distance:

$$\frac{\text{distance on scale}}{\text{actual distance}} = \frac{0.5 \text{ mm}}{1.5 \times 10^6 \text{ km}}.$$

Next, calculate the distance between stars in kilometers:

$$5 \text{ ly} \times \frac{9.5 \times 10^{12} \text{ km}}{1 \text{ ly}} = 4.8 \times 10^{13} \text{ km}.$$

ACTIVITIES

Now, use that value as the actual distance and solve for the distance in the drawing that represents the separation of stars:

$$\frac{\text{distance on scale}}{4.8\times10^{13}\ \text{km}}=\frac{0.5\ \text{mm}}{1.5\times10^{6}\ \text{km}};$$

$$\text{distance on scale}=1.6\times10^{7}\ \text{mm}.$$

Finally, change this to more appropriate units:

$$1.6\times10^{7}\ \text{mm}\times\frac{1\ \text{m}}{10^{3}\ \text{mm}}=1.6\times10^{4}\ \text{m}.$$

This is 16 kilometers! It means that on your drawing, stars (end-of-sentence periods) must be 16 kilometers, or 10 miles, apart.

The Galaxy is about 160,000 light-years in diameter, or 32,000 times the average distance between stars. This means that on your scale, the Galaxy would be 512,000 kilometers across, which is larger than the Earth–Moon distance! This is beyond imagining, and distances to other galaxies have not yet been calculated; therefore, you will have to try another scale.

Suppose you take the average distance between stars on your revised scale to be 5 centimeters. Although the stars would be too small to see on an actual drawing to this scale, you might cheat and make each star a very tiny speck.

On your drawing, 5 centimeters would correspond to 5 light-years. Now calculate the size of the Galaxy, the distance to the Andromeda galaxy (which is actually about 2 million light-years away) and the distance to the most distant objects we can see (which, as discussed in the next chapter, are about 13 billion light-years away).

1. "Meet the Milky Way," by V. Trimble and S. Parker, in *Sky & Telescope* (January, 1995).

2. "Searching for Dark Matter," by M. Mateo, in *Sky & Telescope* (January, 1994).

3. "Destination: Galactic Center," by R. Jayawardhana, in *Sky & Telescope* (June, 1995).

4. "How the Milky Way Formed," by S. van den Bergh and J. E. Hesser, in *Scientific American* (January, 1993).

5. "Our Growing, Breathing Galaxy," by B. P. Wakker and P. Richter, in *Scientific American* (January 2004).

6. "Redesigning the Milky Way," by W. H. Waller, in *Sky & Telescope* (September 2004).

7. "Tracing the Milky Way's History," by C. Chiappini, in *Sky & Telescope* (October 2004).

8. "Ripples in a Galactic Pond," by F. Combes, in *Scientific American* (October 2005).

9. "Messages from the Dark Side?" by G. Schilling, in *Sky & Telescope* (December 2006).

10. "The Ghosts of Galaxies Past," by R. Ibata and B. Gibson, in *Scientific American* (April 2007).

Quest Ahead to Starlinks
http://physicalscience.jbpub.com/starlinks

Starlinks is this book's online learning center. It features **eLearning**, which contains chapter quizzes and other tools designed to help you study for your class. You can also find **online exercises**, view numerous relevant **animations**, follow a guide to **useful astronomy sites** on the web, or even check the latest **astronomy news** updates.

A Diversity of Galaxies

17

Several hundred galaxies are visible in this *Hubble Space Telescope (HST)* photo. The image covers a speck of sky 1/30th the diameter of the full Moon.

SPIRAL NEBULAE WERE DISCOVERED IN THE LATE 1700s, but their nature remained a mystery for nearly 150 years. Early in the 20th century, Adriaan van Maanen, an astronomer at Mount Wilson Observatory, was convinced that they were clouds of gas rather than galaxies similar to the Milky Way. He determined to settle the question based on evidence, and between 1916 and 1923 he made careful measurements of pairs of photographs taken up to 12 years apart. He found that the nebulae rotated with periods of tens of thousands of years. Such a great rotation rate for a galaxy would mean that stars on its outer edge would have to be moving faster than the speed of light. His data thus proved that the nebulae were not galaxies.

Other astronomers obtained conflicting data, but van Maanen was using the largest telescope in existence, and he found a great rotation speed for each of the seven nebulae for which he had the necessary pairs of photographs.

In 1924, Edwin Hubble (also working at Mount Wilson Observatory) proved conclusively, by the use of Cepheid variables, that the nebulae were separate galaxies.

Why did van Maanen obtain incorrect results? In *Science and Objectivity* (Iowa State University Press, 1988), Norriss Hetherington argues that although van Maanen was attempting to be impartial, his preconceived ideas distorted his findings. Hetherington cites other examples of unintentional nonobjectivity in astronomy (including Lowell's

All cross references to chapters, sections, figures, and tables pertain to the main text, *In Quest of the Universe, Sixth Edition. In Quest of the Solar System* contains Chapters 1–11 and 19 of the main text. *In Quest of the Stars and Galaxies* contains Chapters 1–5 and 11–19 of the main text.

Martian canals) and warns that scientists must be constantly on guard against allowing their anticipated results to cloud the interpretation of their data.

Viewed with the naked eye in a good dark sky on a clear night, the Andromeda galaxy (see Figure 16-4) appears as a fuzzy little patch of light. After the invention of the telescope, many more such nebulous objects were found, but their nature remained a mystery. In 1924, Edwin Hubble found Cepheid variables in three of what had been called *spiral nebulae*, and he thereby showed that they were, in fact, spiral *galaxies*.

The importance of Hubble's discovery was tremendous, for it greatly expanded our appreciation of the size of the universe. Like the realization centuries earlier that our planet is just one of many planets, the realization that our Galaxy is just one of a multitude of galaxies was a giant leap in understanding our place in the universe. We know now that the Andromeda galaxy is a spiral galaxy much like our own and that it is about 2.5 million light-years (Mly) away. When you view the Andromeda galaxy, consider the fact that the light reaching your eye has been traveling through space for almost 3 million years.

In this chapter, we first describe how astronomers classify and measure properties of "normal" galaxies. Then we consider more unusual objects, including active galaxies and quasars.

17-1 The Hubble Classification

The serious study of galaxies began with their observation and classification. This is a common starting place in science. When we come on an assortment of objects about which we know little or nothing, we begin by grouping them into classes according to their observable properties.

Hubble provided the classification scheme that is the basis for the one still in use today. He divided galaxies into three types: **spiral**, **elliptical**, and **irregular**, with subdivisions within each category. More recently, astronomers have discovered objects in intergalactic space that fit none of Hubble's categories, not even irregular. In this chapter we first discuss each category in turn and then look at how properties of galaxies are measured. Then we examine the objects that are too peculiar to be called "irregular."

Spiral Galaxies

Hubble divided spiral galaxies into two groups: ordinary spiral galaxies (FIGURE 17-1) and spiral galaxies with bars—called **barred spirals** (FIGURE 17-2). Ordinary spirals are designated by the capital letter S and barred spirals by SB. Each type is then further subdivided into categories a, b, and c, depending on how tightly the spiral arms are wound around the nucleus. Galaxies with the most tightly wound arms (type a) also have the most prominent nuclear bulges. When a spiral galaxy is seen edge on, it often displays the lane of dust and gas clouds that we see in our own Galaxy. Up to two thirds of all spiral galaxies contain bars. The bar systems provide an efficient mechanism for fueling star births at the centers of SB galaxies. A few galaxies seem to have the nuclear bulge and disk of a spiral galaxy, but no arms. Hubble called these S0 (or *lenticular*) galaxies (FIGURE 17-3).

Differences between the three categories (a, b, and c) might be related to how much gas and dust they contain. Sc and SBc galaxies contain much more gas and dust than Sa and SBa galaxies, resulting in a larger proportion of their mass being involved in star formation. This may explain why Sc and SBc galaxies have larger disks and smaller bulges than Sa and SBa galaxies.

Most spiral galaxies are from 50,000 to 2,000,000 light-years across and contain from 10^9 to 10^{12} stars. (We see later how such measurements are made.) For comparison, recall that our Galaxy is about 160,000 light-years across and contains at least 2×10^{11} stars.

Back through the ages the Andromeda *nebula* must have been a great source of wonder to curious people.

elliptical galaxy One of a class of galaxies that have smooth spheroidal shapes.

irregular galaxy A galaxy of irregular shape that cannot be classified as spiral or elliptical.

barred spiral galaxy A spiral galaxy in which the spiral arms come from the ends of a bar through the nucleus, rather than from the nucleus itself.

Galaxies (and other objects) are named by their listings in the Messier catalog (prefix M) or in the New General Catalog (prefix NGC).

lenticular galaxy An S0 galaxy, having a flat disk like a spiral galaxy (with little spiral structure) and a large bulge like an elliptical galaxy.

FIGURE 17-1 (a) The Sombrero galaxy (M104, in Virgo) is a type Sa galaxy, so classified because of its large nuclear bulge. (b) M77 is a type Sb spiral galaxy in the constellation Cetus. (c) M51, the Whirlpool "nebula," comprises the large spiral galaxy NGC5194 (a type Sc galaxy) and its smaller, barred, and more amorphous companion NGC5195. The companion takes on a reddish tinge because it is behind the dust-filled arm connecting it to NGC5194.

Elliptical Galaxies

FIGURE 17-4 shows some elliptical galaxies and makes clear why they were given that name. Various elliptical galaxies show different eccentricities in their elliptical shape, depending in part on their orientation to Earth. (For example, a football appears round if viewed end on.) The actual eccentricity of an elliptical galaxy is difficult to determine because its orientation is unknown. Therefore, elliptical galaxies are classified based on how they appear, from round (E0) to very elongated (E7).

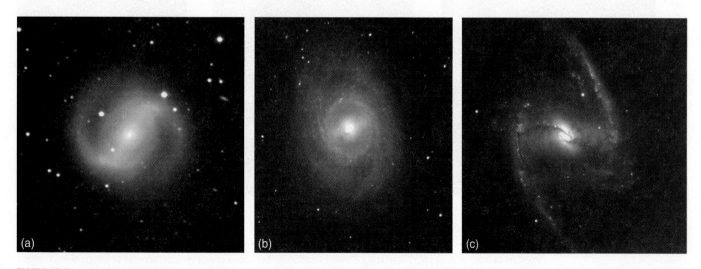

FIGURE 17-2 (a) The SBa barred spiral galaxy NGC4314 is in the constellation Coma Berenices. (b) M95 is an SBb barred spiral galaxy, possibly ringed, part of a cluster of galaxies at a distance of about 38 million light-years. (c) NGC1365 is a SBc barred spiral galaxy, part of a cluster of galaxies about 60 million light-years from our Galaxy.

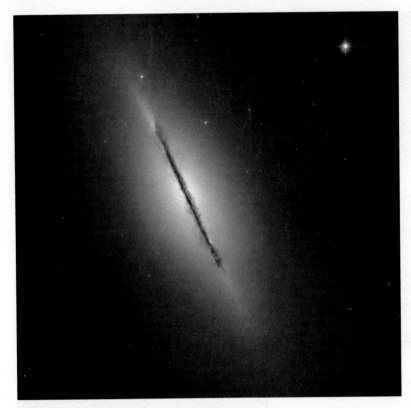

FIGURE 17-3 The S0 galaxy NGC5866, 13.5 Mpc away in the constellation Draco, is seen near edge on in this *HST* image. A warped dust lane, a reddish bulge surrounding the nucleus, a blue disk of stars along the dust lane, a transparent outer halo, and many globular clusters are shown.

Most of the galaxies in existence are ellipticals, but most galaxies listed in catalogs are spirals. The reason for this is that although a few giant elliptical galaxies are larger than any spiral galaxy (having 100 times more stars than our Galaxy), most are small and dim (with one millionth as many stars as our Galaxy). Dwarf elliptical galaxies are visible from Earth only if they are relatively nearby.

Irregular Galaxies

Hubble found that some galaxies did not fit into either of the above categories, nor did they exhibit other common characteristics. FIGURE 17-5 indicates why these were called "irregular" galaxies. Fewer than 20% of all galaxies fall in the category of irregulars, and they are all small, normally having fewer than 25% of the number of stars in our Galaxy.

The Magellanic Clouds are usually classified as irregular galaxies, although some astronomers think that the Large Magellanic Cloud is a barred spiral that has been disrupted by its proximity to the Milky Way and perhaps by a past collision with the Small Magellanic Cloud. Collisions between galaxies should not be unusual because on the average they are separated by distances only about 20 times their diameter. Stars within a galaxy, on the other hand, are separated by millions of times their diameter and therefore collide infrequently; however, as a result of their great distances from Earth, galaxies exhibit no proper motion (motion across our line of sight), and thus, we have to deduce past collisions from their present appearance. FIGURE 17-6a shows two galaxies, called "the Antennae," that are in the

(a)   (b)   (c)

FIGURE 17-4 (a) NGC5128 (or Centaurus A) is a type E0 peculiar elliptical galaxy. It is one of the most luminous and massive galaxies known. The dark band across the galactic disk is debris from a smaller dusty galaxy that is being absorbed by Centaurus A. (b) M32 is a type E2 dwarf elliptical galaxy and is one of the companions to the giant Andromeda Galaxy M31. (c) M59 is a type E5 elliptical galaxy in the constellation Virgo, one of the many members of the Virgo Cluster.

HISTORICAL NOTE

Edwin Hubble

Edwin Hubble (FIGURE B17-1) was born on November 20, 1889, in Marshfield, Missouri. In high school, he showed promise in both academics and athletics, and when he was 16, he entered the University of Chicago. After graduation he received a Rhodes scholarship and enrolled at the University of Oxford, where he studied law. By 1914, Hubble decided instead to do graduate work in astronomy at Yerkes Observatory in Wisconsin.

FIGURE B17-1 Edwin Hubble (1889–1953).

Early in his graduate career, Hubble attended a presentation by Vesto M. Slipher. A hot topic in astronomy at the time was whether spiral nebulae are part of our Galaxy or are galaxies in their own right. Slipher's presentation included observational data that supported the latter hypothesis, but not everyone was convinced. Possibly inspired by that talk, Hubble began photographing nebulae using the Yerkes' 24-inch reflecting telescope. His Ph.D. thesis, entitled "Photographic Investigations of Faint Nebulae," grew out of this earlier work. Although this work was not scientifically rigorous, it led Hubble closer to the conclusion that the nebulae were extragalactic objects.

Before Hubble could reach any final conclusions, the United States entered World War I. Three days after receiving his Ph.D., Hubble enlisted, but the Armistice was declared by the time his division reached Europe. Hubble returned to his study of the nature of "nongalactic nebulae," and began observing NGC6822 using the 100-inch reflector at Mount Wilson Observatory. By 1923, he had found 12 variable stars within it, as well as several smaller nebulae. In 1924, he began observing M31 (the Andromeda "nebula"), in which he distinctly resolved six variable stars. In the course of this work, Hubble observed several Cepheid variables in M31 and M33. By comparing each star's luminosity with his observations of the star's apparent brightness, Hubble was able to deduce that M31 and M33 are about 930,000 light-years distant. (Hubble's measurement was off by more than a factor of two because he did not know that there are two types of Cepheids.) This distance placed them far outside the known boundaries of the Milky Way and, thus, Hubble concluded that they are galaxies outside our own and that other spiral nebulae may be separate, distinct galaxies. Hubble also attempted to classify the galaxies that he observed, which led to his so-called *tuning fork diagram*, which is still widely used today.

In the mid-1920s, Hubble started investigating the expanding universe hypothesis. As he observed galaxies such as M31 and M33, his colleague Milton Humason measured their radial velocities. By combining these radial velocities with the measured distances to the observed galaxies, they deduced what is called the Hubble law of redshifts: $v = H_0 d$. The law was published in a 1929 paper on the expansion of the universe. It sent shock waves through the astronomical community. The Hubble law indicates that the universe is expanding because the velocities of galaxies increase at increasing distances from any chosen point. From 1931 to 1936, Hubble concentrated on extending this law to increasingly greater distances.

Hubble next began researching how the density of galaxies changes with distance, and writing books on astronomical subjects for the general public. In the last few years of his life, he pushed for the construction of a 200-inch reflecting telescope at Mount Palomar in California. During World War II, he joined the staff of the U.S. Army's Ballistics Research Laboratory, where he used his early astronomical training to lead a group calculating artillery-shell trajectories. After the war, he continued his work at the now-completed Palomar Observatory until he died in 1953. His memory lives on with the many researchers who have built on his earlier work, as well as the work of the space telescope named for him.

* Much of the material for this box comes from Osterbrock, Gwinn, and Brashear, "Edwin Hubble and the Expanding Universe," *Scientific American* (July, 1993).

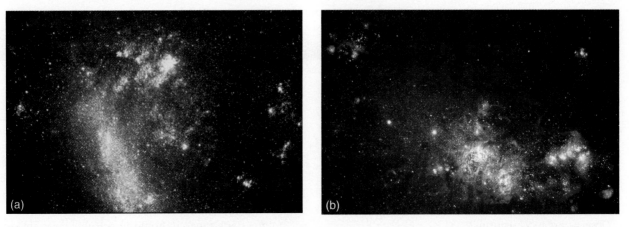

FIGURE 17-5 (a) The Large Magellanic Cloud, the nearest galaxy to the Milky Way at only 160,000 light-years away, is an irregular galaxy. (b) This is another irregular galaxy, NGC1313, which is visible from the Southern Hemisphere.

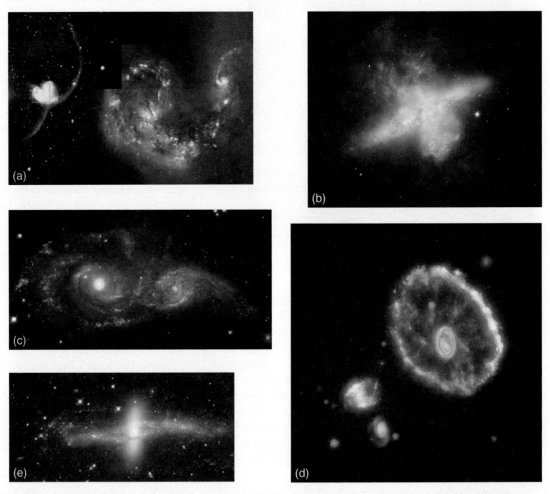

FIGURE 17-6 (a) NGC4038/4039 is known as "the Antennae." (Left) A ground-based view of the two galaxies. (Right) This *HST* image shows the orange cores of the galaxies, including filaments of dark dust. The collision has triggered star formation (bright blue star clusters along the spiral patterns). (b) M82 shows a "burst" of star formation (up to 50 times more than other galaxies). A composite image from *Chandra* (in blue), *Spitzer* (in red), and *HST* (hydrogen emission in orange, and the bluest visible light in yellow-green). The red dust clouds are believed to contain PAHs. (c) Tidal distortion as a result of a grazing encounter between two elliptical galaxies. This *HST* image (in the visible) reveals dust lanes in the spiral arms of NGC2207, silhouetted against IC2163. (d) A composite image of the Cartwheel galaxy from *GALEX* (far UV, in blue), *HST* (visible, in green), *Spitzer* (infrared, in red), and *Chandra* (X-ray, in purple). (e) The "polar-ring" galaxy (NGC4650A). The rotating inner disk of old red stars may be the remnant of one of the galaxies in the collision. The gas from the smaller galaxy probably got stripped off and captured by the larger galaxy, forming a new ring orbiting around the inner galaxy at right angles to the old disk.

process of colliding. Computer simulations show that gravitational forces between the galaxies produce such odd formations. When galaxies merge, especially in the case of a collision between a large and a small galaxy, the larger one swallows up the smaller, cannibalizing it. In the Antennae, observations by the *Infrared Space Observatory* have shown that shock waves generated by the collision excite the gas from which new stars will form. This process manifests itself in the infrared radiation emitted by molecular hydrogen. *Chandra* has also discovered rich deposits of neon, magnesium, and silicon, suggesting a high rate of supernova explosions caused by the collision.

Computer simulations also show that colliding galaxies actually pass through one another with few collisions between individual stars, as distances between stars are very large; however, the large sizes of the interstellar dust and gas clouds in the colliding galaxies make them more likely targets. The collisions between clouds of interstellar gas result in greater gas density and therefore increased star formation. Such "bursts" of star formation may even occur as a result of gravitational interactions among neighboring galaxies, as is the case for M82 (Figure 17-6b). In addition, gravitational forces drastically alter the shapes of the two colliding galaxies. Figure 17-6c shows a grazing encounter in which the strong tidal forces from the larger galaxy have distorted the shape of the smaller galaxy.

Figure 17-6d shows ripples of star formation that resulted when a smaller galaxy went through the heart of the Cartwheel galaxy about 100 million years ago. Figure 17-6e is an *HST* image of the "polar-ring" galaxy; the rings may be remnants of a collision between two galaxies at least a billion years ago.

Hubble's Tuning Fork Diagram

Edwin Hubble linked the three types of galaxies—ellipticals, ordinary spirals, and barred spirals—in what is called his ***tuning fork diagram*** (FIGURE 17-7). In his plan, S0 galaxies form the connecting link because they have characteristics of both elliptical galaxies and spiral galaxies. Astronomers once thought that the diagram represents an evolutionary sequence, with galaxies changing from one form to another; however, old stars are found in all three types, indicating that one type does not evolve to another, at least not as simply as indicated by the diagram. TABLE 17-1 summarizes the properties of the various galactic types.

tuning fork diagram A diagram developed by Edwin Hubble to relate the various types of galaxies.

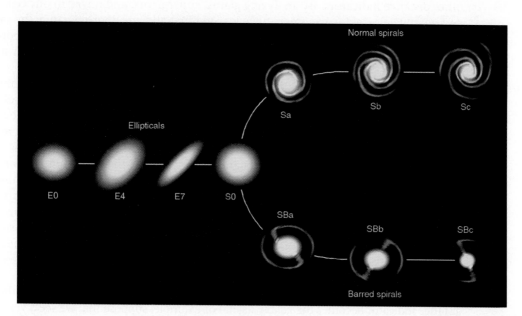

FIGURE 17-7 The tuning fork diagram developed by Edwin Hubble provides a convenient way to categorize galaxies; however, it does not represent an evolutionary sequence.

TABLE 17-1

Types of Galaxies

Type	Designation	Description
Elliptical	E0–E7	Galaxies that appear circular (E0) to very elongated (E7). Mostly Population II and old Population I stars.
Spiral	Sa, Sb, Sc	Disk-like galaxies with a nuclear bulge and spiral arms. Sa type have large nuclei and tightly wound arms. Sc type have small nuclei and open arms. Mostly young, Population I stars in the spiral arms, and a mix of Population II and old Population I stars in the disk and nucleus.
Barred Spiral	SBa, SBb, SBc	Spiral galaxies with elongated nuclei. Subtypes are determined as with spiral galaxies.
Lenticular	S0	Disk-like galaxies, but with no spiral structure.
Irregular	Irr	Galaxies that do not fit into any of the other types. Mostly Population I stars.

17-2 Measuring Galaxies

The most important properties of a galaxy we can measure are its distance, mass, and motion. As we have seen on several occasions, if we know the distance to an extended object, we can calculate its size and absolute luminosity from its angular size and apparent magnitude, respectively.

Distances Measured by Various Indicators

Distances to galaxies are measured using several different distance indicators. We have already discussed two of these, the Cepheid and RR Lyrae variables. The calculation of the distances to the Magellanic Clouds was the first use of Cepheid variables as distance indicators on an extragalactic (outside the Milky Way) object. Hubble also used two Cepheid variables in the Andromeda galaxy to show that the so-called spiral nebulae were indeed galaxies.

Although Cepheid variables are very bright stars, we can distinguish them only in relatively nearby galaxies, out to perhaps 200 million light-years. If we wish to measure the distance to a galaxy in which we are unable to see Cepheids, we must find other distance indicators. By analyzing giants, supergiants, and novae in our Galaxy and nearby galaxies, astronomers have learned that all have approximately the same range of luminosity. In addition, large globular clusters and supernovae are of consistent brightness from one galaxy to another. This allows us to use these bright stars and clusters as distance indicators in more distant galaxies.

The logic here is interesting. By determining the luminosities of nearby Cepheid variables, astronomers determined the period-luminosity relationship for Cepheids. Then they assumed that Cepheids in other galaxies are basically the same as the ones in our Galaxy and, thus, they used that same period-luminosity relationship in reverse to calculate the absolute luminosity and thereby the distances to Cepheids in the nearer galaxies. Knowing these distances, they learned that the brightest stars and globular clusters in galaxies of each type have approximately the same luminosity. That is, the brightest 50 stars in one spiral galaxy have approximately the same average luminosity as the brightest 50 in every other spiral galaxy. Likewise, this is also the case for globular clusters. Now astronomers can use these stars and clusters as distance indicators to learn the distances to galaxies in which they can see the individual objects. FIGURE 17-8 summarizes this chain, which allows us to determine distances as far as about 1000 million light-years.

At distances at which we can no longer see individual objects within a galaxy, the distance indicator becomes the galaxy itself. For example, suppose that we see a very distant spiral galaxy. Because we know the range of luminosities spiral galaxies have, we can make some judgment as to that galaxy's distance by assuming that it is an average spiral galaxy. If we assume that it is among the dimmest galaxies of its type, we find its

An object used to measure distance because its absolute magnitude is known is often called a *standard candle*.

Here again we assume—with successful results—that the same laws of science that apply here on Earth also apply in distant galaxies.

nearest probable distance. On the other hand, if we assume that it is among the brightest, we find its farthest probable distance. In this way, we find the range of distances within which we can be fairly certain the galaxy falls.

When applied to an individual galaxy, the whole-galaxy method of assessing distance is very imprecise. Fortunately, the method need not be restricted to individual galaxies. As we discuss later, galaxies exist in clusters, which contain from a few galaxies to thousands of galaxies per cluster. If we consider a cluster that contains a great number of spiral galaxies, we can logically assume that the brightest spiral galaxy in that cluster has about the same luminosity as the brightest spiral in another cluster. Thus, we use the brightest galaxies as a distance indicator to the cluster.

One measurement builds on another in a series of steps. As a result, if there is an error in a beginning step, the error will propagate up through the chain of steps. For example, if somehow there is an error in our understanding of the period-luminosity relationship for Cepheids, the stated distances to the farthest galaxies will have to be adjusted. This is the reason that astronomers constantly check their methods and assumptions as new data arrive; they also make cross-checks by comparing results obtained through different methods and tools and use statistical analysis wherever appropriate.

The previous analysis makes an important assumption: Galaxies in our neighborhood of the universe are basically the same as those farther away. This may seem reasonable, but remember that we are seeing distant galaxies not as they are today but as they were in the past. Light coming from a galaxy 100 million light-years away has been traveling 100 million years, and we cannot rule out the possibility that galaxies have changed in that time.

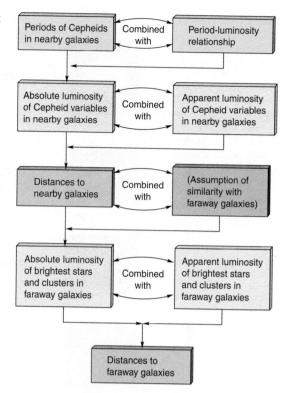

FIGURE 17-8 Starting with the period-luminosity relationship of Cepheids, astronomers are able to follow a chain of reasoning and observation that allows them to determine the distances to galaxies too far away for their Cepheids to be visible.

The Hubble Law

In 1912, Vesto M. Slipher, an astronomer working in Percival Lowell's observatory in Flagstaff, Arizona, was assigned the task of examining the spectrum of some of the spiral nebulae to learn about their chemical composition. A then-current hypothesis regarding the nature of these objects was that they were planetary systems in formation, and Lowell was seeking to discover life on other planets. Instead, Slipher found something else that had profound implications, namely a redshift in the spectra of most of the nebulae he examined. If the redshift were due to the Doppler effect, it meant that most of the other nebulae were moving away from us—as fast as 1800 km/s. There seemed to be no reasonable explanation for this strange finding.

William de Sitter, a Dutch astronomer, interpreted the redshifted spectra of the spiral "nebulae" as due to the Doppler effect and included this interpretation in his 1917 model of an expanding universe based on the general theory of relativity. In his 1920 debate with Shapley, Curtis used the relationship between redshifted spectra and spiral "nebulae" as evidence that they are extragalactic objects. In 1923, the German scientist Carl Wirtz suggested that there is evidence in Slipher's data that the recessional velocity of a spiral "nebula" is proportional to its distance.

In 1924, Edwin Hubble showed that the nebulae are, in fact, galaxies. Then he and Milton Humason used the 100-inch telescope on Mount Wilson to photograph the spectra of these objects. Their work not only confirmed Slipher's findings, but showed that there is a pattern in the speeds with which galaxies are receding from us. **FIGURE 17-9** is a diagram by Hubble and Humason on which they plot-

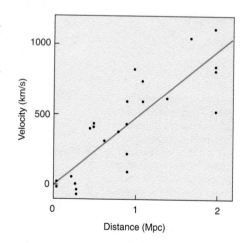

FIGURE 17-9 This graph, based on the data collected by Hubble and Humason in the 1920s, shows a relationship between the recessional velocities of galaxies and their distances.

FIGURE 17-10 The photos at the left in the figure are of galaxies in clusters at various distances from us. At the right, the spectrum of each galaxy is shown. (The spectrum is the white, horizontal streak between the reference lines.) Arrows indicate how far the two darkest absorption lines have shifted in each case. (λ = wavelength.)

CLUSTER GALAXY IN	DISTANCE IN LIGHT-YEARS	RECESSIONAL VELOCITIES
VIRGO	78,000,000	1,200 KM/SEC
URSA MAJOR	1,000,000,000	15,000 KM/SEC
CORONA BOREALIS	1,400,000,000	22,000 KM/SEC
BOOTES	2,500,000,000	39,000 KM/SEC
HYDRA	3,960,000,000	61,000 KM/SEC

Lowell's telescope on which Slipher worked had only a 24-inch aperture. The 100-inch telescope used by Hubble and Humason therefore had about $4^2 = 16$ times more light gathering power.

FIGURE 17-11 The data on Type Ia supernovae by Riess, Press, and Kirshner (1996) provide a dramatic confirmation of the relationship found by Hubble and Humason. Reevaluations of distances have caused the slope of the line to change.

cosmology The study of the nature and evolution of the universe as a whole.

ted the distances to a number of galaxies against the galaxies' recessional velocities. It indicates that the more distant a galaxy is, the faster it is moving away from us. An example of this relationship is shown in FIGURE 17-10, which includes photographs taken years after Hubble's work, of five galaxies and their spectra. The distances to the galaxies were determined by methods described earlier in this section. Compare the location of the two prominent absorption lines in each of the spectra, noting that the farther a galaxy is, the farther to the right (toward longer wavelengths) is the pair of lines; therefore, assuming that the redshift is due to the Doppler effect, the data show that the farther a galaxy is, the higher its redshift and thus the faster it moves away from us.

Hubble's data, shown in Figure 17-9, were taken in the 1920s and were based on distance indicators that relied on incorrect Cepheid variable values, so the data had to be adjusted when more was learned about Cepheids; however, as FIGURE 17-11 indicates, a better understanding of standard candles dramatically confirmed the relationship.

The implications of Hubble's findings for our understanding of the past and future of the universe are very important, for they imply that the universe is expanding. In fact, Hubble's work has become the foundation for today's theories of *cosmology*, which we study in Chapter 18. Even though the redshift that Humason observed is not really due to the Doppler effect, the difference is not important here; what is important is

HISTORICAL NOTE

Milton Humason, Mule Driver/Astronomer

Milton Humason (1891–1972) was born in Minnesota. He grew up in southern California, however, where he liked the mountain on which he lived, Mount Wilson, more than he liked school. When he finished the eighth grade, he dropped out of high school to wander the mountain. Later, when George Hale chose that mountain as the site of a large observatory with a 60-inch telescope, Humason was hired as a mule driver to transport equipment up the steep slopes.

Humason learned about the observatory by talking to the construction workers, and when it was completed, he was hired as its first janitor. Young and very curious, he constantly talked to the astronomers about their work, and eventually he was allowed to help them develop photographic plates in the darkroom, and even take photographs with the large telescope.

Humason was aware of the inadequacy of his education and persuaded Harlow Shapley and Seth Nicholson, astronomers at the observatory, to teach him math, including calculus. In a few years he was hired as a full-time night assistant and gave up his janitorial duties. Finally, in 1930, when he was 39 years old, he was appointed to the professional staff of

the observatory, which by then had built a 100-inch telescope. Humason worked closely with Edwin Hubble, using the 100-inch telescope on Mount Wilson, but because Hubble was the leader in their research, some astronomy books fail to even mention the former mule driver who worked with him.

When the 200-inch Hale telescope was completed in 1948 on nearby Mount Palomar, Humason used that instrument in his research. His contributions were so significant that he was awarded an honorary doctor's degree from the University of Lund, Sweden.

It is interesting that Milton Humason almost discovered Pluto. At the same time that Percival Lowell was attempting to find a planet beyond Neptune, W. H. Pickering was doing similar calculations in an attempt to predict its position. He asked Humason to take photographs of certain areas of the sky where he predicted the planet to be, but Humason was unable to locate the planet. Later examination of his plates showed that he had photographed Pluto twice, but in one case it was too close to a star to be visible, and in the other it happened to coincide with a flaw on the photographic plate.

that astronomers observe a regular relationship between redshift and distance, a pattern that is valuable to them in determining distances to faraway galaxies, as we will show. Because it is convenient (and common) to think of the redshift as being due to the Doppler effect, that practice will be followed here.

Whenever data can be represented by a straight line on a graph, there is a direct proportionality between the quantities on the two axes. Thus, the relationship between the two quantities, radial velocity, v, and distance, d, can be written as

$$v = H_0 d,$$

where H_0 is the constant of proportionality, called the **Hubble constant** in honor of the person who discovered this **Hubble law**. The value of the constant is simply the slope of the line on the graph, which is defined as the ratio of the change in the quantity plotted on the vertical (y) axis to the change in the quantity plotted on the horizontal (x) axis. In the following example we calculate the Hubble constant by determining the slope of a line that relates the recessional velocity and distance of galaxies.

Hubble constant The proportionality constant in the Hubble law; the ratio of recessional velocities of galaxies to their distances.

Hubble law The relationship that states that a galaxy's recessional velocity is directly proportional to its distance.

EXAMPLE

Calculate the Hubble constant based on the data for the five galaxies in Figure 17-10.

SOLUTION FIGURE 17-12 shows that the recessional velocities of the five galaxies are linearly related to their distances from us. Calculating the slope of the line requires a comparison of the changes in the two quantities represented on the graph. We thus must choose two points on this line. Observe what happens to cross the point where the velocity is 30,000 km/s and the distance is 2000 million light-years. This will

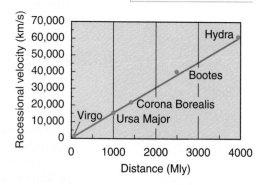

FIGURE 17-12

be one of the chosen points. The line also passes through the point where both quantities are zero; this will be the second point. Now calculate the slope as

$$\text{slope} = \frac{30{,}000 \text{ km/s} - 0}{2000 \text{ Mly} - 0} = 15 \text{ (km/s)/Mly}.$$

TRY ONE YOURSELF

Show that the slope of the line in the 1931 Hubble-Humason graph (Figure 17-9) corresponds to a value of the Hubble constant equal to 140 (km/s)/Mly, about seven times the modern value. This was due to their misunderstanding of the luminosity of Cepheids.

Astronomers usually use Mpc, megaparsecs (million parsecs), as their distance unit. One parsec is about 3.26 light-years; therefore, 15 (km/s)/Mly is about 50 (km/s)/Mpc.

According to the data represented in Figure 17-12, the Hubble constant thus is about 15 (km/s)/Mly (read as "kilometers per second per million light-years"). It is important to see what Hubble's constant means and what its units represent. This value means that for each million light-years a galaxy is farther from us, its speed is greater by 15 km/s. Refer again to the graph to check that a galaxy at a distance of 1000 million light-years has a speed of 15,000 km/s. In like manner, a galaxy 3000 million light-years away has a speed of 45,000 km/s.

The Hubble constant has been difficult to determine with accuracy. We can calculate the distance to galaxies in nearby clusters fairly accurately using established distance indicators, but the motion of a galaxy within a nearby cluster is significant compared with the motion of the cluster (so that the galaxy may even be approaching us). The velocity of a nearby galaxy thus is due in large part to random motions within its cluster. It therefore does not fit the Hubble law. A distant galaxy, on the other hand, is in a cluster whose motion away from us is much greater than the galaxy's individual random motion, so its redshift follows the Hubble law; however, for these galaxies, determination of the distance to the cluster is much less precise. In other words, in cases where we can measure the distance accurately, the value obtained for velocity is less meaningful, and where we can measure velocity accurately, the distance measurement is imprecise.

Through the years, the value of the Hubble constant obtained from observational data remained between 15 and 30 (km/s)/Mly, but this range has been decreasing as better data became increasingly available. The differences in the values were due to different methods and distance candles used and of course due to errors in the measurements. As we see in Chapter 18, we have entered the era of precision cosmology; the latest observations of the radiation left over from the hot big bang indicate that the value of the Hubble constant is about 21.5 ± 0.4 (km/s)/Mly or 70.1 ± 1.3 (km/s)/Mpc, in agreement with data from Type Ia supernovae, such as the ones shown in Figure 17-11. Note, however, that the Hubble constant does not remain constant as time goes on. As we see in Chapter 18, H_0 is the slope of the line in the graph of recessional velocity versus distance as measured during *this* period of time in the life of the universe. It is important to know the value of the Hubble constant because knowledge of the expansion rate of the universe is fundamental to our understanding of the universe as a whole. We discuss this idea again in the next chapter.

The Hubble Law Used to Measure Distance

As we've discussed, distances to nearby galaxies can be measured using Cepheid variables as distance indicators; however, as we progress to more distant galaxies, Cepheids can no longer be seen, and we must use globular clusters and the brightest stars as distance indicators. At even greater distances, these cannot be seen, and the brightest galaxies serve as distance indicators to clusters of galaxies. Finally, at the farthest distances, even this method cannot be used, and we turn to the Hubble law to indicate a galaxy's distance. We illustrate this idea with an example.

ADVANCING THE MODEL

Observations, Assumptions, and Conclusions

It is always important in science to separate observations from the conclusions that are based on the observations. Figure 17-10 serves as a good example of this rule. The figure shows simply that the dimmer a galaxy is, the greater the redshift of its spectrum. Although the figure only indicates this relationship for five galaxies, the relationship has been found to be true in innumerable cases and has been confirmed by a number of researchers. It is based directly on many *observations* and is considered indisputable.

The middle column of the figure shows the distance of each galaxy from Earth and allows us to conclude that the farther away a galaxy is, the greater its redshift. This conclusion, however, is *not* based directly on observations but on a conclusion about the distances to galaxies. Its validity depends on the accuracy of the distance determinations. One would suppose that the decreasing brightnesses of the galaxies in the figure are due to greater distance, but that is not *proven* by the figure. Actually, each of the galaxies in the figure is part of a cluster of galaxies, and the distance to the cluster has been measured using a variety of distance indicators. We are confident that the distances given are fairly reliable, although no one would pretend that they are exact.

Even though the distances to the galaxies are known with some accuracy, it is important to remember that the relationship between redshift and distance is a *conclusion*, not a direct observation. Now we take the next step: we assume that the redshift is caused by the Doppler effect and, therefore, that it is caused by the galaxies' motions relative to the Earth. The Hubble relationship between recessional velocity and distance depends on this *assumption*. Is there any other possible explanation for the redshift? In Chapter 18 we show that there is, although the explanation is similar to that of the Doppler effect and does not negate the Hubble law.

Scientists must be on guard to remember the difference between what is observed—the evidence—and the conclu-

sions that they reach based on those observations. Between an observation and a conclusion lies one or more assumptions, and the validity of the conclusion is based not only on the accuracy of the observations, but on the validity of the assumptions.

The Precision of Science

It is sometimes said that science is an exact study. If those who make such statements mean that the measurements of science are exact, they are wrong. It is obvious that measurements of distances to galaxies are not exact. What is not so obvious is that *every* measurement in science is to some degree an approximation. No measurement is absolutely exact. What scientists attempt to do is to be aware of how *inexact* their measurements are. For example, in calculating the distance to a galaxy, parallel calculations are made to determine the probable error in the measurement. Measurements may show that a galaxy is 200 million light-years away, with a likely error of 50 million light-years. This means that the galaxy is measured to be between 150 and 250 million light-years away. Calculating the likely error is a common practice in all natural sciences. Scientists thus attempt to be specific about their inexactness.

In addition, scientists must take into account assumptions that are consciously or unconsciously included in the measurements. For example, in the case of determining distances to faraway galaxies, astronomers assume that there is negligible intergalactic material that might diminish the light from those galaxies. Early measurements of the size of the Galaxy were in error because they did not take into account the interstellar dust and gas. A scientist tries to be aware of the assumptions involved in each measurement. There is no claim that a measurement is exact. In fact, there is little room in science for the word "exact."

EXAMPLE

Suppose a very faint source is observed to have a redshifted spectrum that indicates a recessional speed of 120,000 km/s. Assuming that the Hubble law applies to this object, calculate its distance.

SOLUTION   The most recent data suggest that the value of the Hubble constant is 21.5 ± 0.4 (km/s)/Mly or between 21.1 and 21.9 (km/s)/Mly. This gives us a range of distances within which we can be fairly confident the object lies. Using 21.1 (km/s)/Mly:

$$v = H_0 d,$$
$$120{,}000 \text{ km/s} = 21.1 \text{ (km/s)/Mly} \times d,$$
$$d = 5687.2 \text{ Mly}.$$

Now, using 21.9 (km/s)/Mly:

$$120,000 \text{ km/s} = 21.9 \text{ (km/s)/Mly} \times d,$$

$$d = 5479.5 \text{ Mly}.$$

The object thus is between about 5480 and 5690 million light-years away. This is 5.48 to 5.69 billion light-years!

You may be uncomfortable with the uncertainty of the answer, but remember that without the Hubble law and this calculation we would have no idea whatsoever of the distance to the object.

FIGURE 17-13 A more massive galaxy would be expected to be bright and to have a wide 21-cm spectral line. Similarly, a galaxy of low mass is dim and has a narrow line.

Tully-Fisher relation A relation that holds that the wider the 21-cm spectral line, the greater the absolute luminosity of a *spiral galaxy*.

Faber-Jackson relation A relation between the luminosity and central stellar velocity dispersion of an *elliptical galaxy*.

TRY ONE YOURSELF
Suppose an object is observed with a redshift that indicates a speed of 90,000 km/s. What is the range of distances within which we can feel reasonably sure that the object lies?

Other Relations

In 1977, astronomers Brent Tully of the University of Hawaii and J. Richard Fisher of the National Radio Astronomy Observatory discovered that *spiral galaxies* with wider 21-cm lines have greater absolute luminosities. The reason for the relationship is that a galaxy's spectral line is wide if the galaxy is rotating fast, because the Doppler effect causes a redshift from one side of the galaxy and a blueshift from the other side. The faster the rotation is, the wider the line. In addition, more massive galaxies would be expected to rotate faster and to be brighter. **FIGURE 17-13** shows the logic that indicates that a wide spectral line would be associated with a bright galaxy.

Using the ***Tully-Fisher relation***, astronomers can determine the absolute magnitude of a galaxy and use it as a distance indicator. This relationship is being used to check other methods of distance measurement and to improve our knowledge of distances to galaxies.

The ***Faber-Jackson relation***, noted in 1976 by Sandra Faber and Robert Jackson of the University of California at Santa Cruz, is a power-law relation between the absolute magnitude (or luminosity) of an *elliptical galaxy* and the central stellar velocity dispersion. Using spectroscopy, we can measure the Doppler shift of the light emitted by the stars and therefore the spread of their velocities. The relation then allows us to estimate the absolute magnitude of the elliptical galaxy; using the distance modulus and the observed apparent magnitude of the galaxy, we can estimate its distance.

Both the Tully-Fisher and Faber-Jackson relations relate the mass of a (spiral or elliptical) galaxy and the (rotational or random) speeds of its stars. In 2007 astronomers discovered a new relation between a galaxy's mass and a speed indicator that combines both rotational (ordered) and random (disordered) motion. As such, this relation applies to all galaxies, including irregulars. This new relation resulted from a study of about 500 galaxies at distances between 2 and 8 billion light-years. The study suggests that some galactic properties have changed very little over the last 8 billion years.

FIGURE 17-14 reviews the various methods used to measure distances in astronomy, from radar within the solar system to the Hubble law for the most distant objects.

10^{11} light-years	
10^{10}	
10^9	
10^8	
10^7	
10^6	
10^5	
10^4	
10^3	
10^2	
10	
1	
0.1	
0.01	
0.001	
0.0001	
0.00001 ly (about 1 AU)	

Hubble law
Brightest galaxies
Tully-Fisher
Brightest stars
Cepheid variables
Parallax
Radar

17-3 The Masses of Galaxies

A galaxy's mass can be determined in several ways, all of them limited in precision, primarily because of the tremendous distances involved. One method of measuring the mass of a galaxy is by observing the rotation periods of some parts of it. Naturally, we cannot wait for part of a galaxy to complete a revolution, for this takes millions of years. Instead, we use Doppler shift data to measure the velocity of part of a galaxy. Then, knowing the distance of that part from the center, we can determine the period of revolution of the stars located there. As in the case of our own Galaxy, Kepler's third law then allows us to calculate the mass of the material within the orbit of the part of the galaxy being studied.

FIGURE 17-14 A review of the various methods of measuring distance in astronomy. Approximate limits are indicated for each method.

Another method of measuring galactic masses is similar to that used to measure stellar masses. There are many cases of a pair of galaxies revolving around one another. Again, we cannot wait the long times necessary to measure the period of revolution, but we can use the Doppler shift to gauge the speeds of the galaxies. The problem with this method is that it is difficult to determine the angle of the plane of revolution to our line of sight (FIGURE 17-15), and knowledge of this angle is necessary for an accurate measurement; however, making measurements for great numbers of such binary galaxies allows us to determine an average mass for a given type of galaxy.

Clusters of Galaxies; Missing Mass

Most galaxies are part of clusters rather than lonely nomads drifting through space. FIGURE 17-16a shows a typical cluster of galaxies. Thousands of such clusters are known, and the largest clusters may contain as many as 10,000 galaxies. Figure 17-16b shows one of the most distant clusters known, about 8 billion light-years away. Thirteen of the galaxies in this cluster are remnants of recent collisions or pairs of colliding galaxies, the largest number of colliding galaxies found in a cluster so far. To determine whether a particular galaxy is part of a given cluster, astronomers must determine the galaxy's distance because a cluster of galaxies is not just a group of galaxies that are near each other on the celestial sphere (like a constellation), but a gravitationally linked assemblage.

Be careful with the terminology here. A *galactic cluster* is an open cluster of stars. It is not a *cluster of galaxies*.

All galaxies of a cluster have nearly the same redshift.

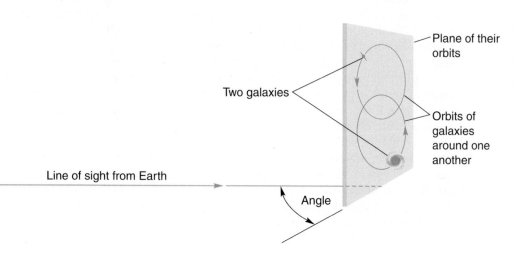

Plane of their orbits

Two galaxies

Orbits of galaxies around one another

Line of sight from Earth

Angle

FIGURE 17-15 To use the Doppler shift to measure the speeds of two galaxies that orbit one another, we would have to know the tilt of their plane of revolution to our line of sight.

(a)

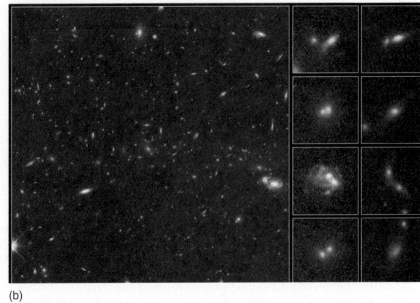

(b)

FIGURE 17-16 (a) Several galaxies are visible in this cluster located in the constellation Fornax in the Southern Hemisphere. (b) This *HST* image shows MS1054-03, a cluster of at least 81 galaxies. As a result of tidal interactions, streams of stars can be seen being pulled out of the galaxies (insets).

 Recent (2007) measurements of the three-dimensional velocities of the Magellanic Clouds show that they are greater than previously thought. This suggests that either our Galaxy's gravity is stronger or the Clouds are not gravitationally bound to our Galaxy.

local group (of galaxies)
The cluster of over 30 or so galaxies that includes the Milky Way Galaxy.

supercluster A group of clusters of galaxies.

Our Galaxy is part of a group of over 30 galaxies, including the Magellanic Clouds and the Andromeda galaxy, that form a cluster called the **local group**. The Andromeda galaxy and the Milky Way are by far the largest members of this cluster, which appears to contain only one other spiral galaxy. Our Galaxy is currently on a collision course with the Andromeda galaxy, closing the gap between the two at about 500,000 kilometers an hour. Within 5 billion years, the two galaxies will merge.

If stars are grouped into galaxies and galaxies are grouped into clusters, do clusters group into something bigger? Yes, we call them **superclusters**. Our local supercluster includes the local group and the Virgo cluster as well as other clusters. It has a diameter of perhaps 100 million light-years and contains some 10^{15} (a thousand trillion) solar masses. Between superclusters are great voids with no galaxies. Patterns of clusters, superclusters, and voids are clear in FIGURE 17-17, which shows the sky distribution of about 230,000 galaxies, with the Milky Way at the center. It seems that matter in the universe forms a cosmic web in which galaxies are formed along filaments of matter, and clusters are formed at the intersections of these filaments. This structure results in smooth "flows" of galaxies caused by the gravitational pull of great concentrations of galaxies. Observations show that our Galaxy is in a filament at the edge of a huge void, and that all galaxies within 15 million light-years in this filament are moving together. However, the asymmetric distribution of matter around us has the net effect of a push away from the void at a speed of about 270 km/s (170 mi/s). In addition, we have known for decades that our Galaxy is moving toward the Virgo Cluster (55 Mly away) and two huge concentrations of galaxies, one behind the other, at distances of about 200 and 600 Mly.

A third method of measuring the masses of galaxies takes advantage of their clustering. There is only one force that could hold a galaxy within its cluster: the gravitational force. If we observe a galaxy near the outside of a large cluster and assume that it is in a relatively circular orbit, we can use the Doppler effect to measure its speed and therefore its period. This allows us to calculate the total mass of the galaxies within its orbit. Calculating the mass of the cluster based on measurements for only one galaxy would not be meaningful because there would be too many uncertainties, but the same measurement, repeated for several galaxies on the outer portion of the cluster, gives a useful value for the mass of the cluster and therefore an average value for the masses of the galaxies within the cluster.

When measurements are made by the various methods, we find that clusters have much more mass than is accounted for by the visible stars within their galaxies.

Based on Doppler shifts in their spectra, galaxies in large clusters are observed to be moving at speeds greater than the escape speeds from the clusters as calculated from the luminous matter in them. The fact that these galaxies are part of their respective clusters suggests there is enough nonluminous mass in the clusters that keeps them gravitationally bound; this ***missing mass*** can be calculated from the observed speeds and cluster sizes, and it is several times greater than the mass measured by other independent methods.

Within our own Galaxy, the interstellar gas and dust account for at least 10% to 20% of the total mass, and the rotation curve of the Milky Way (Figure 16-13a) indicates that even considering the interstellar matter, we can account for as little as one tenth of the total mass of the Galaxy; recall that the rotation curve leads us to hypothesize a massive Galactic corona. The rotation curves of other spiral galaxies also suggest that there is a great amount of nonluminous mass at their outer reaches. Observations suggest that only 20% of the "ordinary" matter (such as electrons, protons, and neutrons) in the early universe converged to form the stars and galaxies we see today. There has been no accounting for the remaining 80% of this ordinary matter.

We know that intergalactic dust and gas exist between galaxies in a cluster, but this is also not nearly enough to account for the calculated mass. There are indications that the halo of our own Galaxy contains more material than previously thought, and perhaps galaxies' halos account for much or all of the matter that makes up the missing mass. For example, observations of 63 spiral and dwarf galaxies in the nearby Virgo cluster (chosen to be representative of the galactic population in the local universe) unveiled the presence of large amounts of very cold dust particles surrounding the galaxies. The data, taken by the *Infrared Space Observatory* and announced in 2002, also show that up to half the total energy output in normal galaxies has been converted from visible into infrared light. This implies that the total amount of emitted starlight is much greater than previously suspected. In addition, astronomers announced in 2003 that they discovered a warm fog in the local group of galaxies. The temperature of this diffuse fog is between 100,000 and 10 million K, causing it to shine faintly in X-rays. The data, taken by *Chandra* and the *FUSE* satellite, suggest that this warm fog contains as much as a trillion solar masses. This amount of matter is enough to gravitationally bind together the galaxies in the local group. The presence of hot gas around galaxies and in galactic clusters is shown in FIGURE 17-18. Although vast, this material is only a part of larger hot gas filaments that exist between all the galaxies in the universe; data taken by *Chandra* and *XMM-Newton* have provided evidence for such cosmic filaments.

Finally, when astronomers compare the total mass of a system with its total luminosity, the ratio is greater than 1. For stars in the solar neighborhood, the ratio is about 3. For clusters of galaxies, the ratio is about 300. For the universe, the ratio is about 1000 solar masses for every solar luminosity (assuming that the average mass and energy density of the universe is such that space has a flat geometry).

What does this nonluminous matter consist of? The search for the answer to this question is one of the most active areas of research in astronomy today. Several possibilities have been proposed, and the actual situation may be a combination of several kinds of matter.

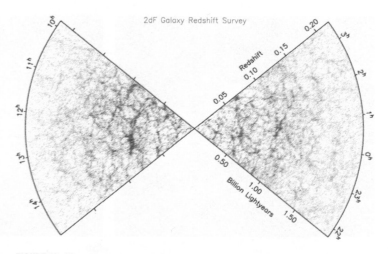

FIGURE 17-17 The cosmic web revealed by the Two Degree Field (2dF) Galaxy Redshift Survey. The universe contains long filamentary chains of galaxies, superclusters, and empty voids up to 200 million light-years across. The map contains about 230,000 galaxies, has a depth of 4 billion light-years, and covers 1/20th of the whole sky. The Milky Way is at the middle of this sky distribution.

missing mass The difference between the mass of clusters of galaxies as calculated from Keplerian motions and the amount of visible mass.

ESA's *Infrared Space Observatory* operated from 1995 until 1998.

Nature has played a trick on astronomers. We thought we were studying the universe; now we know we are studying only the small fraction that is luminous.
Astronomer Vera Rubin

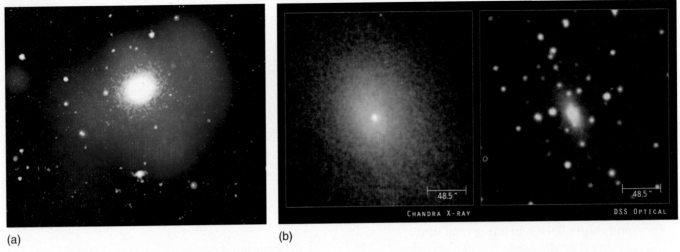

(a)   (b)

FIGURE 17-18 (a) A composite optical (in white/yellow) and X-ray (in blue) image of NGC4555, an isolated large elliptical galaxy embedded in a 10 million K hot gas. The gravity of the stars in the galaxy is too low to hold the cloud, requiring the presence of a massive halo of dark matter. The image's scale is 8 × 6.5 arcminutes. (b) A cloud of hot gas envelops the cluster Abell 2029, which is composed of thousands of galaxies. The presence of a massive (more than a hundred trillion Suns) dark matter halo is required to gravitationally hold the cloud.

Because particle physicists often use the term *baryons* to refer to massive particles such as protons and neutrons, ordinary "dark" matter is sometimes called "baryonic dark matter."

1. **Ordinary nonluminous matter**. In previous chapters, we discussed objects such as white dwarfs, which no longer generate their own energy and are no longer easily observable, and brown dwarfs, which have never generated enough energy to become easily observable. These are common examples of ordinary nonluminous matter, as are planets, meteors and comets, and the vast dust and cold molecular hydrogen clouds of interstellar space. All of this matter consists of particles with which we are familiar, primarily atoms containing protons, neutrons, and electrons.

2. **Hot dark matter**. As we discussed in Chapter 11, experiments indicate that neutrinos have a small amount of mass. There are so many neutrinos zipping around the universe that even a tiny mass could contribute to the mass of the universe; however, observations suggest that this contribution is not significant (otherwise the Cosmic Microwave Background radiation, which we discuss in Chapter 18, could not look as it does). Astronomers refer to this mass as "hot" dark matter because the particles are moving at high speeds, comparable to the speed of light. Other particles have also been proposed for this category, including particles that have been hypothesized in several theories of particle physics but that have not been detected.

3. **Black holes**. Astronomers speculate that a great number of black holes of all sizes could contribute to the dark matter.

4. **Cold dark matter**. This is an exotic form of matter that is not made up of the protons, neutrons, and electrons of ordinary matter. Particles that might be moving through space at relatively slow speeds make up "cold" dark matter. Such particles have been given various names, such as photinos, axions, or neutralinos, but have not been detected. We surmise their existence because estimates of ordinary nonluminous matter and hot dark matter do not make up the amounts of mass we can detect by gravitational effects but cannot see. In addition, various theories of particle physics and of galaxy formation in the early universe indicate that this kind of matter exists.

dark matter Matter that can be detected only by its gravitational interactions; it appears to be quite abundant throughout the universe.

Even though we do not yet know the composition of cold ***dark matter***, we do know that it can be detected by its gravitational interactions with ordinary matter, thus tracing its location through space. The evidence that dark matter is distributed in galaxies and clusters of galaxies in a way similar to visible matter comes from the

FIGURE 17-19 (a) A three-dimensional map of the dark matter distribution in the universe up to 6.5 billion light-years away. The *HST* survey covers an area of the sky nine times that of the Moon. The *HST* data were combined with multi-wavelength data from other telescopes such as the VLT, Subaru, VLA, and *XMM-Newton*. (b) An *HST* image of the cluster CL0024+17, 5 billion light-years away. The ring is 2.6 Mly across.

rotation curves of galaxies and from the way their gravity bends the light from an object farther away. FIGURE 17-19a is a three-dimensional map of the dark matter distribution in the universe. It is based on *HST* observations of the shapes of half a million galaxies at great distances from us, up to 6.5 billion light-years. The observed distortions of the shapes of the galaxies are the result of weak gravitational lensing due to the presence of dark matter between us and the galaxies. The map supports the idea that galaxies form along the densest concentrations of dark matter, in loose networks of filaments, which intersect at the locations of galactic clusters.

Several research teams are presently investigating the nature and amount of dark matter. One promising approach is to search the Galactic halo for stars that grow suddenly bright due to gravitational lensing as dark objects pass between them and the Earth. Such "microlensing" events have been observed, but the nature of the dark objects is not known for all events. Gravitational lensing has also been used to study the size and shape of dark matter halos surrounding galaxies; such halos appear flattened and extend more than five times further than the visible stars in a galaxy. The dark ring in the cluster CL0024+17, shown in Figure 17-19b, provides strong evidence that dark matter exists. Spectroscopic observations of the cluster's structure suggest that it is the result of a collision between two clusters about 1.5 billion light-years ago. Simulations on collisions between clusters support the idea that the ring is a ripple of dark matter that moved outward from the center of the combined cluster. This dense ripple, slowing down under the gravitational pull of the cluster's matter, causes changes in the observed shapes of the background galaxies, just as water ripples at the surface of a lake cause apparent changes in the shapes of stones at the bottom.

Other experiments assume that the particles of dark matter have a small probability of interacting with the ordinary matter of Earth, much like neutrinos do, and can be detected; however, the sensitivity required of the detectors is presently still beyond our capability. Modeling of faint shells that are observed around elliptical galaxies requires the presence of a massive halo composed of dark matter; these shells extend out a few times farther than most of the starlight in the galaxies. They appear to be remnants of mergers between the elliptical galaxies and smaller satellite galaxies, and their locations provide a measure of the gravitational field.

Some astronomers refer to "dark" matter in the Galactic halo (which might be brown dwarfs or stellar-mass black holes) as "massive compact halo objects," or MACHOs. Their name for the more exotic particles being looked for is "weakly interacting massive particles," or WIMPs. When you're looking for objects whose very existence has never been proven, it helps to have a sense of humor.

Chandra and *XMM-Newton* observations of hot gas clouds around galaxies and in clusters of galaxies (as shown in Figure 17-18) that cannot be held by the gravity of the stars in these systems suggest that massive halos of dark matter must be present. Advances over the next few years might enable us to begin setting limits as to the nature and amount of dark matter that interacts with the ordinary matter. A VLT study of tens of distant galaxies has found that over the past 6 billion years galaxies had the same amount of dark matter relative to that of their stars. This result, if confirmed by additional studies, suggests that there is a close interplay between normal and dark matter.

Different lines of evidence show that the universe is only about 4.6% ordinary matter, 23.3% dark matter, and 72.1% dark energy, which we discuss in Chapter 18; however, these numbers depend a bit on the specific cosmological model used. The quest for an understanding of the nature of dark matter and dark energy is a very active field in astronomy today because it is fundamentally important to cosmology.

17-4 The Origin of Galactic Types

Evidence for the lack of interstellar material in ellipticals comes from the *Infrared Space Observatory*, which detected very little infrared radiation from ellipticals. Interstellar material radiates in the infrared region of the spectrum.

Astronomers once thought that Hubble's tuning fork diagram might represent the evolutionary sequence of galaxies. Perhaps spirals evolve into ellipticals or vice versa. This hypothesis can be dismissed quickly. First, we know that ellipticals do not evolve into spirals because elliptical galaxies contain very little gas and dust, whereas spirals contain significant amounts. Ellipticals have already used up their gas and dust forming stars. What about evolution the other way? This proposal presents mechanical problems. After a disk has formed in a galaxy, there is no way that the galaxy, on its own, could disperse its disk and acquire a symmetric elliptical shape.

Another discarded theory held that the difference is caused simply by rotation: spiral galaxies evolved from dust clouds that were spinning fast and ellipticals came from slowly spinning clouds; however, this theory cannot account for the fact that elliptical galaxies have completed their star formation and have little interstellar material.

Today, there are two leading theories that explain why galaxies exist in various types. We discuss each in turn.

A puff of wind cannot pass through still air without carrying the still air along (and reducing the wind speed in the process).

1. **The Cloud Density Theory.** Early in the history of the universe, before galaxies, some gas/dust clouds must have been denser than others. One theory of galactic formation holds that elliptical galaxies are those that formed from the densest clouds. Because of the great density of these clouds, star formation would have proceeded quickly and would have used up all dust and gas before a disk had a chance to form. After stars have formed, they act as individual particles that orbit the center of the galaxy and have little interaction with one another. This is why galactic clusters are able to pass through the disk of our Galaxy without being captured. Thus, according to this theory, early star formation explains the lack of a disk in elliptical galaxies.

   Clouds that had a lower density of gas and dust would have formed stars less frequently when the cloud contracted, and the dust and gas would have collapsed into a disk before star formation used it all up. The reason that a rotating cloud of gas and dust forms into a disk is that gas acts like a fluid, where the particles interact a great deal. When two fluids collide, energy is dissipated and the fluids do not pass through one another. (In the case of star birth, a disk is a common occurrence.) Within a galactic disk, star formation proceeds slowly. Instabilities cause density waves that assist star formation, so that new stars are still being born in spiral galaxies today.

   Various hypotheses exist to explain why some spiral galaxies have bars and others do not. One idea is that faster spinning clouds form elongated nuclei, or bars. Another hypothesis notes that barred spiral galaxies generally do not have a halo of globular clusters. It proposes that the lack of a halo results in instabilities that cause a bar to form.

2. **The Merger Theory.** A more recent theory proposes that spiral galaxies formed before elliptical galaxies and that ellipticals result from mergers of spirals. The direction of spin of galaxies is random and, thus, merged galaxies would often have little or no overall rotation (which is what is observed for ellipticals). The small quantities of interstellar matter in ellipticals are explained by the fact that the merger would compress interstellar clouds and would cause strong density waves. During the merger, then, star formation would be frequent and interstellar matter would be used up.

The word *theory* is being used here for what we should probably call a *hypothesis*. There is no sharp dividing line between the terms.

This theory is supported by computer simulations and by the observation that ellipticals make up a greater percentage of the galaxies in large clusters, where galaxies are packed close together. In these clusters, mergers would have been frequent and would have produced numerous elliptical galaxies. In loosely packed clusters of galaxies, on the other hand, ellipticals are fairly rare.

You may have noticed that nothing has been said about irregular galaxies. Neither theory explains these oddballs well. Astronomers know that some galaxies that were once classified as irregulars are actually pairs of galaxies that are in the process of collision. Others are spiral galaxies with large, dense dust clouds that hide their spiral patterns. Perhaps all irregular galaxies can be explained like this. In any case, irregulars make up a small fraction of all galaxies.

It should be obvious that the question of why some galaxies are of one type and others are of another type is far from settled. This is just one of the unanswered questions that make extragalactic astronomy a lively source of research today.

Look-Back Time

As new observational techniques are developed, we are seeing objects farther and farther away. We have now detected objects that may be as far away as 13 billion light-years. If these objects are truly this far, the light we see left them 13 billion years ago. We are seeing far into the past. Astronomers speak of *look-back time*, a term that emphasizes this idea. An object 13 billion light-years away has a look-back time of 13 billion years.

look-back time The time light from a distant object has traveled to reach us.

One of the problems with using large galaxies as distance indicators relates to the idea of look-back time. When we see these galaxies, we are not seeing them as they are today but as they were in the past. There is some evidence that within large clusters of galaxies, some galaxies combine to form supergalaxies. That is, some galaxies are "cannibalized." If this occurs, the largest galaxies in nearby clusters are not the same size as the largest galaxies in distant clusters because we are seeing nearby clusters at a later stage of their life than we see distant ones. In the distant clusters, not enough time has passed for galaxies to have gobbled up one another. This would invalidate the assumption that distant clusters are similar to nearby clusters and would call into question the practice of using galaxies as distance indicators. Although this is a possible problem, the Hubble law seems to apply equally as well to faraway clusters, where galaxies are used as distance indicators, as it does to nearby galaxies, where other methods are used for determining distance. This indicates that the dilemma posed by look-back time is not a major obstacle in this case.

We are referring now to distant "objects" because, as we explain later, we cannot be sure that they are galaxies.

Among the objects with the greatest look-back times, we find a class of objects not yet discussed—active galaxies. These objects play a major part in helping us to determine the scale of the universe.

17-5   Active Galaxies

Until now we centered our discussion in this chapter on normal galaxies, those that fit the Hubble classification. Now we turn to objects that do not fit into those categories—objects that were discovered since the late 1940s by radio astronomy. Before then, our understanding of the distant universe was based on observations in the visible part of the spectrum. Radio observations opened new windows on our understanding of the cosmos by introducing us to several exotic objects and phenomena.

ADVANCING THE MODEL

Galaxy Formation and Evolution

A typical spiral galaxy is thought to have started as an enormous, slowly rotating cloud that lost energy (as its atoms and molecules collided and radiated energy) and collapsed under gravity; additional mergers with smaller clouds of hot gas and dark matter finally resulted in a faster spinning disk. As part of its formation process, a large spiral should be immersed in a leftover halo of hot gas. Indeed, *Chandra* observations show the presence of such a halo around the massive spiral galaxy NGC5746 (FIGURE B17-2); the galaxy shows no other activity that could possibly create such a halo.

The presence of gas in spiral galaxies dampens out the disruptive effects of mergers, allowing spirals to survive a violent collision. Over its lifetime, a spiral can make many transitions between being barred or unbarred; computer simulations show that a bar survives at least 2 billion years, redistributing mass and angular momentum in the galaxy, before dissolving as a result of its own gravitational effects on the orbits of passing stars.

VLT observations show the presence of massive elliptical galaxies at redshifts between 1.6 and 1.9, suggesting that they must have formed when the universe was only 2 billion years old. This implies that the buildup of elliptical galaxies from mergers of smaller galaxies started earlier and was much faster in the early universe than currently thought. This is supported by a study of very young galaxies using the deepest images taken by the *HST*.

As a result of mergers between galaxies, matter gets spun off and forms small dwarf galaxies. *Spitzer* data for these tidal dwarfs show strong emission lines from organic compounds such as polycyclic aromatic hydrocarbons (PAHs) and warm molecular hydrogen. Tidal dwarfs, together with dwarf galaxies that may be primordial remnants of the formation of the universe, are far more common than the more massive spiral or starburst galaxies.

Large surveys of galaxies suggest that, in addition to mergers, the rate of star formation also depends on the galaxy's mass. *Spitzer* data allowed astronomers to see through the dust obscuring star forming regions in distant galaxies; the data show that early in the universe's life, massive galaxies formed stars early and rapidly, whereas less massive galaxies formed stars over longer periods of time.

Results from a number of multi-wavelength surveys of thousands of galaxies up to 9 billion light-years away consistently show that star-forming activity has gradually decreased with time; they also show that a galaxy's mass (and therefore the supply of raw material) is the dominant factor in star formation, while mergers account for only 20% of the activity. This is consistent with the current leading theory of how galaxies have evolved. According to the theory, galactic properties (mass, shape, and size) develop through mergers of less massive proto-galaxies. During the first few (3 to 4) billion years, the landscape of the universe was dominated by mergers; as time went on, the immediate environment of a galaxy and its supply of raw materials gradually started to dominate the rate of star formation. A byproduct of merging is that collisions destroy the disks of spiral galaxies, send stars into more chaotic orbits, and therefore produce football-shaped (elliptical) galaxies. This scenario is supported by computer simulations.

While this is the accepted theory, there are observations of a few galaxies very early in the life of the universe that challenge the theory; observations of massive *disk* galaxies show a furious rate of star formation even though they very likely formed from a massive cloud that collapsed rapidly.

Strong winds resulting from massive stars and supernova explosions early in a galaxy's life, or from the activity of a black hole at its center, can blast significant amounts of the galaxy's material into intergalactic space. Such winds have been observed. Their presence explains why key elements for planetary formation and life (including carbon, oxygen, and iron) are widely distributed throughout the universe from its early stages. They also limit the size of a galaxy by preventing further star formation.

FIGURE B17-2   A large halo of hot gas (blue) surrounds the disk (white) of the massive spiral galaxy NGC5746.

All galaxies emit some radio waves; our Galaxy radiates them from its nucleus (see Figure 16-23); however, the radio waves from a normal galaxy constitute only about 1% of that galaxy's total luminosity. In the late 1940s, astronomers began observing strong extragalactic radio sources, and in 1951, it was discovered that a radio

FIGURE 17-20 (a) This false-color radio image of Cygnus A (a peculiar elliptical galaxy about 700 million light-years away) shows a jet extending from the source (an AGN) toward one of the radio lobes. Regions of brightest (fainter) radio emission are shown in red (blue). (b) This *Chandra* image shows X-ray emitting hot gas (bright orange region) that surrounds Cygnus A and within it a giant cavity (the yellow and light orange inner region) created by the two jets emitted from the galaxy's central black hole region. The low-density hot gas (tens of millions K) fills the space between the galaxies in the cluster containing Cygnus A and provides enough resistance to slow down the jets. The jets terminate in radio and X-ray emitting "hot spots" some 300,000 light-years from the center of the galaxy. The pressure of the particles and magnetic fields in the jets inflates the cavity. (c) An illustration of the Cygnus A system.

source in the constellation Cygnus is actually a double source associated with a galaxy (FIGURE 17-20). Cygnus A, as the source is called, emits about a million times more energy in radio waves than does the Milky Way.

Since the discovery of Cygnus A, many more such ***radio galaxies*** have been discovered, typically emitting millions of times more energy in radio waves than does a normal galaxy. FIGURE 17-21 shows Centaurus A. Observe that the visible galaxy in this case is an elliptical galaxy with a prominent lane of interstellar gas and dust, which is bisected at an angle by opposing jets of high-energy particles blasting away from the nucleus. The double-lobed radio image seen in Centaurus A is common in radio galaxies, and most of the galaxies associated with double-lobed radio sources are either giant ellipticals or spirals. The radio lobes are enormous, sometimes extending 15 million light-years from the visible galaxy. In general, radio lobes mark the positions where the outflows start interacting with the intergalactic medium.

Radio galaxies often appear unusual when viewed in visible light. FIGURE 17-22 shows a jet of hot gas being emitted from Virgo A (M87). This feature is seen in several cases. More recently, galaxies have been observed that have properties like those of radio galaxies, but have their primary emission at wavelengths other than the radio region of the spectrum. Astronomers therefore classify radio galaxies as one type of a group of high-energy galaxies called ***active galaxies***. Because the energy of an active galaxy comes from its nucleus, astronomers often refer to them as ***active galactic nuclei*** or ***AGNs***.

Jets of material, such as those shown in this section and in Section 17-6, seem to be a universal phenomenon. They are the natural byproducts of accretion onto a compact object, emanating at right angles to the disk that surrounds this compact

radio galaxy A galaxy having its greatest luminosity at radio wavelengths.

The Milky Way is about 160,000 ly, or 0.16 Mly, in diameter. From end to end, large double lobes are 150 times this size!

active galaxy (active galactic nucleus, AGN) A galaxy with an unusually luminous nucleus.

CHANDRA X-RAY   DSS OPTICAL   NRAO RADIO CONTINUUM   NRAO RADIO (21-CM)

(a)

(b)

FIGURE 17-21 (a) A composite image of Centaurus A (about 10 million light-years away) made with X-ray (blue), radio (pink and green), and optical (orange and yellow) data. The compact nucleus contains more than 200 million solar masses, suggesting the presence of a supermassive black hole. Two large arcs (part of a projected ring 25,000 light-years in diameter) of X-ray emitting, multimillion-degree hot gas exist in the outskirts of the galaxy on a plane perpendicular to the jets. The observations suggest that about 100 million years ago Centaurus A merged with a small spiral galaxy, shown as the parallelogram-shaped structure of dust in the *Spitzer* image in (b), which led to a burst of star formation in the galaxy's nucleus. About 10 million years ago a huge explosion occurred that produced the jets and a galaxy-sized shock wave that moved outward at about 450 km/s. Radio observations show that parts of the jet have speeds of about half the speed of light.

object. They occur not only in radio galaxies, but also in the entire range of objects from young stellar objects to extremely powerful galaxies. These "outflows" are mostly very well collimated (that is, they form straight beams, with very little spreading over their length) and can extend from a few to hundreds of thousands of light-years. They transfer energy, matter, momentum, and magnetic fields from the central region to the surrounding environment. The speeds of the observed outflows seem to remain constant or, in some cases, even increase along most of the length of the jets. Some outflows have speeds that are clearly close to the speed of light. Such speeds signify the presence of an acceleration mechanism that works along the entire length of the outflow. Magnetic fields in the disk and along the length of the jets, coupled with the rotation of the central object, offer a very likely mechanism for the formation, acceleration, and collimation of these outflows.

During the first decade of observing active galaxies, many types were discovered, and various hypotheses were put forward to explain them. Then, less than 10 years after the discovery of active galaxies, the mystery deepened with the discovery of what appeared to be an entirely new type of object.

Quasars

Before 1960, astronomers thought that intense radio waves like those from active galaxies necessarily come from large galaxy-sized objects. Individual stars are such weak sources of radio waves that before 1960 the Sun was the only star from which

FIGURE 17-22 (a) This visible-light photo shows Virgo A (M87), a giant E0 elliptical radio galaxy, 50 Mly away in the constellation Virgo. (b) A short-exposure infrared image by the *HST* shows a jet of material coming from the nucleus of the galaxy. The nucleus is the bright white spot toward the left. *HST* observations show a spiral-shaped disk of hot gas in the nucleus. The rapid rotation of the disk suggests the presence of a black hole of about 3 billion solar masses, concentrated in a space no longer than our solar system. (c) Very Large Baseline Array (VLBA) measurements show that the jet is formed within a few tenths of a light-year from the core of the galaxy. The jet's opening angle is initially large (about 60°), but a few light-years away it is reduced to only 6°. Material in the jet is seen to be moving at apparent speeds greater than that of light; however, this superluminal motion is a geometric illusion, as we describe later in this chapter.

radio waves had been detected. In that year, however, two radio sources were found that were so small that they appeared to be stars. Recall from Chapter 7 that planets' sizes can be measured when they occult a star. The same phenomenon can be used in reverse to measure the size of a distant object. In the case of one of these radio sources, 3C 273, its visual and radio images were observed as it was occulted by the Moon. By observing 3C 273 as its visible light and radio waves were blocked out by the Moon and again as they reappeared on the other side, details of the source could be determined (FIGURE 17-23). The object appeared to be very small—more like a star than a galaxy. In addition, it had a small jet protruding from it, like the jets that have been observed from some radio galaxies. The radio waves from 3C 273 seemed to have two sources: the jet and the main body of the object. We have seen in this section that double-lobed radio sources are common for active galaxies.

The spectra of both 3C 273 and 3C 48 (the other source mentioned previously here) were found to be extremely unusual. Although *emission* spectral lines were prominent, the lines could not be identified with any known chemical element. Were we seeing objects that had entirely different chemical elements than are known to us? Because of their unusual nature (their star-like appearance and strong radio emission), the objects were called ***quasi-stellar radio sources*** or ***quasars***.

In 1963, Maarten Schmidt of the California Institute of Technology found the solution to the puzzle of the unusual spectrum of 3C 273. He found that its prominent

3C 273 is so named because it is the 273rd object listed in the third Cambridge catalog.

quasar (quasi-stellar radio source) A small, intense celestial source of radiation with a very large redshift.

(a)   (b)

FIGURE 17-23 (a) The *HST* image at left shows the brilliant quasar 3C 273 (about 3 billion light-years in the direction of the constellation Virgo). The *HST* image at right is the clearest view yet in visible light of the quasar. After blocking the light from the central quasar, astronomers discovered the complexity of its host galaxy. A spiral plume wound around the quasar, a red dust lane, and a blue arc and clump in the jet's path are clearly seen. (b) The jet emanating from the core of quasar 3C 273, as seen, from left to right, in optical (*HST*), X-ray (*Chandra*), and radio (MERLIN). The scale is about 10′ from one end of the jet to the other. The source is beyond the top of the images.

The expression $z = \Delta\lambda/\lambda_0 = v/c$ relating redshift and speed should only be used for small speeds. After all, it implies that an object with redshift larger than 1 moves faster than the speed of light, which is not possible. The correct expression is

$$z = \frac{\Delta\lambda}{\lambda_0} = \sqrt{\frac{c+v}{c-v}} - 1,$$

which for speeds less than about $0.1c$ can be approximated by $z \approx v/c$.

spectral lines are simply hydrogen spectral lines that are very greatly redshifted. Each wavelength is redshifted to a value about 16% greater. (That is, the ratio of the change in wavelength to the nonshifted wavelength from a stationary source is 16%; $\Delta\lambda/\lambda_0 = 0.16$.) **FIGURE 17-24** illustrates the situation. Schmidt's colleague Jesse Greenstein examined the spectrum of 3C 48 and found that its spectral lines are shifted even farther—by about 37%.

If the redshifts of the two quasars are caused by the Doppler effect, then one quasar is moving at 15% of the speed of light and the other is moving at 30% of the speed of light. These were speeds far greater than any yet encountered for celestial objects (or for terrestrial objects, other than nuclear particles).

If these large redshifts follow the Hubble law, the closest of the two quasars must be as far away as the then-known farthest galaxies. Yet it is brighter than those galaxies, even though in size it is more like a star than a galaxy.

Since the early 1960s, more than about 23,000 quasars have been discovered. Unlike the first two, most (about 90%) are not sources of radio waves. Most quasars are bluish white objects and are X-ray emitters. In addition, almost all quasars show variability in their light output; some quasars quadruple in brightness in just a few hours, while the average is a change of 10% to 15% over a period of a year. This latter observation confirms their small size; they cannot be larger than a few light-months in diameter.

The first two quasars, seen with redshifts of 16% and 37%, have smaller redshifts than most. The smallest observed redshift is about 6%. The quasar SDSS J114815251, in the direction of the constellation Ursa Major, has the largest redshift observed to date ($z = 6.41$). It indicates that the quasar's speed is about 96% of the speed of light and that its distance, assuming that quasars' redshifts fit the Hubble law, is about 12.9 billion light-years away. We are seeing this quasar when the universe was very young, only about 800 million years after the big bang. The amount of dust observed in the quasar's region suggests that galaxies and stars formed earlier in the history of the universe and at a faster rate than previously thought. The black hole at this quasar's core has a mass of 3 billion solar masses (**FIGURE 17-25**).

(a)
410 nm   434 nm

476 nm   503 nm

(b)

FIGURE 17-24 (a) An "at rest" spectrum. The wavelengths of two lines are indicated. (b) The same spectrum shifted 16%. Observe that the pattern of lines is the same. The *average* redshift of a quasar is determined from measurements of a number of spectral lines.

Now consider what the luminosity of such an object must be for us to be able to detect it at that distance. We can calculate the luminosity by using the apparent brightness of the quasar and the inverse-square law of radiation. We find that a bright quasar is 1000 times more luminous than a galaxy like ours. Finally, remember that we are speaking about a small object—far smaller than a galaxy.

Competing Theories for the Quasar Redshift

When astronomers were faced with the prospect of an object being so small and yet so luminous, they were forced to reexamine their assumptions. As was pointed out earlier, strictly speaking, the Hubble law is not due to the Doppler effect, although the basis for the law is mathematically equivalent to that effect. In Chapter 18 we discuss the theorized cosmological reason for the validity of the Hubble relationship. Nevertheless, the Hubble law indicates that quasars are at tremendous distances from us. Is there any other possible explanation for the redshift?

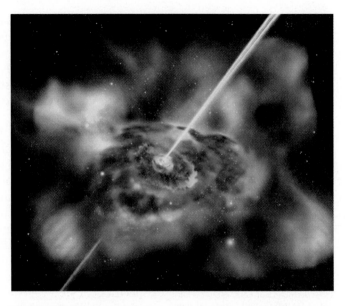

FIGURE 17-25 An artist's view of a quasar's core. The material in brown and yellow corresponds to the disk of dust and gas that hides the central black hole. The black hole's gravity pulls in this material, which swirls as it moves closer. The resulting friction heats the gas and makes it shine brightly.

Einstein's general theory of relativity predicts that light leaving a massive object is redshifted because of the mass of the object. Calculations show that to produce redshifts such as those seen in quasars, the gravitational field near the object must be far greater than that near the most massive neutron star, and well-grounded nuclear theory tells us that there is a limit to the mass of a neutron star. After a certain mass is reached, a neutron star cannot exist, and a black hole is formed instead. The theory of relativity simply cannot be used to explain the redshift.

Perhaps quasars are nearby objects with enough local motion that they do not fit the Hubble law. (Galaxies within the local group do not fit the Hubble law either.) FIGURE 17-26 shows fast-moving objects ejected from our Galaxy; some are moving at nearly the speed of light. If this is what quasars are, then they do not have such tremendous luminosities after all.

The problem with this *local hypothesis* is not only that we can imagine no source for such objects, but that we must also ask why we do not see similar objects from other galaxies. We cannot expect our Galaxy to be unique in this regard. Yet if other galaxies emit such fast-moving objects, we would see some of them with tremendous *blueshifts* as they move toward us. In fact, however, such blueshifted objects are not seen, and the local hypothesis is not considered a likely explanation.

Some quasars appear to be linked to nearby galaxies of different redshifts. Even though such links seem to suggest that the Hubble law may not be valid, they do not prove that the objects are *physically* connected and they can easily be explained as chance alignments. A few scientists who support non-standard cosmologies have suggested that the observed redshifts are the result of other physical effects unrelated to the expansion of the universe; however, these effects cannot reproduce the Hubble law on the observed scales.

Perhaps there is some other explanation that might require drastically different laws of

Because $v = H_0 d$, we get $d = \dfrac{c}{H_0} \cdot \dfrac{v}{c}$, where the ratio v/c can be calculated from the redshift.

The largest redshift observed today for a galaxy is $z = 7$. It implies a distance of 13 billion light-years, based on recent research indicating that the universe's age is 13.73 billion years.

local hypothesis A proposal stating that quasars are much nearer than a cosmological interpretation of their redshifts would indicate.

FIGURE 17-26 The local hypothesis holds that quasars are relatively nearby objects that have been ejected from the Galaxy at great speeds. If quasars are emitted by galaxies, however, some should be moving toward us from nearby galaxies, and these would show blueshifts. No observed quasar has a blueshift.

FIGURE 17-27 The core of the nearby active galaxy Circinus, which belongs in a class of mostly spiral galaxies called Seyferts. The galaxy is only 13 million light-years away, and most of the gas in its disk is concentrated in two rings (with diameters of 1300 and 260 light-years). At the center of the inner ring is a supermassive black hole that is accreting surrounding gas and dust.

Seyfert galaxy One of a class of spiral galaxies having active nuclei and spectra containing emission lines.

Seyferts and quasars are the same phenomenon, just with the rheostat turned up.
Astronomer Allan Sandage

gravitational lens The phenomenon in which the gravity caused by a massive body between a distant object and the viewer bends light from the distant object and causes it to be seen as two or more objects.

physics than those of today. We never can disregard such a possibility, but we must progress with what we know until it is definitely ruled out. The redshift *can* be explained by the Hubble law, even though that law leads us to conclude that quasars are at distances greater than we are accustomed to and are therefore much more energetic than we are accustomed to. Almost all astronomers now agree that quasars' redshifts do indeed fit the Hubble law.

Seyfert Galaxies

As we discussed previously in this section, one of the first two quasars seen (3C 48) has a double-lobed radio source and a jet from its center. In this regard, it resembles an active galaxy. As astronomers found more and more quasars, they discovered that most of the nearer ones are associated with clusters of galaxies and have essentially the same redshifts (and thus distances) as these galaxies. The quasars are more luminous than the galaxies, but the association causes us to look for more similarities.

One particular type of spiral galaxy, a **Seyfert galaxy** (FIGURE 17-27), has a very luminous nucleus that—although it is not as luminous as a quasar—in some cases varies in intensity in time periods even shorter than those of quasars. Similarities in the spectra of Seyfert galaxies and quasars point to a further link between galaxies and quasars, indicating that perhaps a quasar is a galactic nucleus.

Recent high-resolution photos of nearer quasars show a fuzz on the image near the quasar. Again, it appears that quasars are at the nuclei of some types of galaxies and that the fuzz is caused by the stars of the galaxies.

Quasars and Gravitational Lenses

Twin quasars were discovered in 1979 in Ursa Major. The two quasars are very close together, separated by only 6 arcseconds. They have the same luminosity, the same redshift ($z = \Delta\lambda/\lambda_0 = 1.4$), and identical spectra. The explanation for these identical twins lies with the theory of general relativity, which predicts the possibility of a large mass bending light from a more distant object so that two images of the distant object appear. The predicted phenomenon is called a **gravitational lens**, but until the discovery of the twin quasars, not much attention was paid to the prediction. Since the discovery of the twin quasars, the intervening galaxy has been found, and we are now confident that the twins are actually one quasar that has been made to appear double by the galaxy that lies between it and us (FIGURE 17-28). Many examples of gravitational lensing have been found since 1979. One interesting case is shown in FIGURE 17-29a. The two yellow-orange spots in the image are twin images of a single quasar behind a massive object that acts like a gravitational lens. The ring is caused by another object, behind whatever object causes the lensing effect, which is so well aligned that light passing on every side of the intervening massive object is bent toward Earth, making the distant quasar appear to be on all sides of it at once.

Arcs, such as in Figure 17-29a, are the most common type of lensing, although most cases are not as complete as that arc. Pairs of lensed objects are the next most common. Figure 17-29b shows a much rarer case, one with a quadruple pattern.

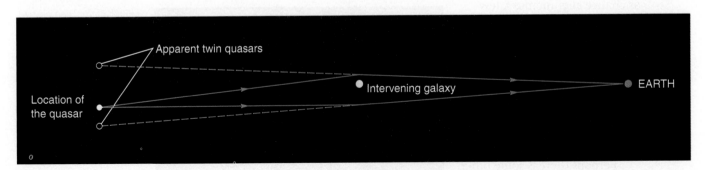

FIGURE 17-28 Light from the quasar at the left is bent as it passes by the intervening galaxy at the center. This causes the light to appear to come from twin quasars, one on either side of the galaxy.

(a)

(b)

(c)

(d)

FIGURE 17-29 (a) This false-color image of object MG 1131 + 0456 was made by radio interferometry with the Very Large Array. The ring is called an "Einstein Ring." This 1987 image is the first such ring ever observed. (b) In 1995 the *HST* was used to discover this case of quadruple gravitational lensing. (c) Abell 2218 is a rich galaxy cluster. The *HST* captured this arc-like pattern spreading across the image like a spider web, a great example of gravitational lensing. Abell 2218 has a total of seven multiple systems. (d) This *HST* image shows five images of the same galaxy, distorted from a normal spiral to an arc-shaped object. The lensing cluster is 5 billion light-years away, and the blue galaxy is two times farther away.

Figure 17-29c reveals numerous arcs, which are the distorted images of a galaxy population located 5–10 times farther than the cluster of galaxies doing the lensing. Figure 17-29d shows several blue, loop-shaped objects, which are multiple images of the same galaxy seen through the "lens" of the cluster of yellow, elliptical, and spiral galaxies near the center of the image.

The importance of the discovery of gravitational lenses is that they provide another confirmation of the general theory of relativity and they indicate that quasars are indeed very distant—that their redshift fits the Hubble law.

Suppose that we plot the number of known quasars versus their distances from our Galaxy. The graph would not be very instructive because as the distance from our Galaxy (or from any point) increases, the volume of space in a shell increases. This happens because the area of a large sphere is greater than the area of a small sphere (**FIGURE 17-30a**); therefore, even if quasars are evenly distributed throughout the universe, we would expect to see more of them at greater distances.

To truly illustrate the distribution of quasars, the graph should show the *density* of quasars—the number of quasars per unit of volume of space—versus their distance

(a)

Density of Quasars at Various Distances

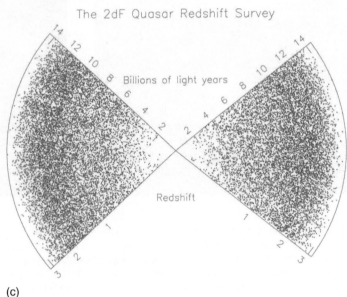

(b)

FIGURE 17-30 (a) If two equally thick shells are drawn at different distances from us, the more distant shell will contain more space. Even if quasars (dots in the figure) were equally spaced throughout the universe, more would be seen in the faraway shell. (b) The graph shows the relative abundance of quasars at various distances from the Milky Way. The distance scale is based on a Hubble constant of 23 (km/s)/Mly. (c) As seen in this two-degree field (2dF) survey of about 23,000 quasars, the quasars are clustered to the same extent as local, optically selected galaxies.

The 2dF Quasar Redshift Survey

(c)

from us. Figure 17-30b is such a graph. The distance shown on the horizontal axis depends on the value chosen for the Hubble constant, and other choices are possible. Nevertheless, even if a different value were chosen for the Hubble constant, the shape of the graph would remain the same. The graph leaves no doubt that quasars appear at a fairly specific distance from the Milky Way. Because distance is proportional to time, this indicates that quasars existed during a relatively short period in the distant past.

Quasars, Blazars, and Superluminal Motion

blazars (or BL Lac objects)
Especially luminous active galactic nuclei that vary in luminosity by a factor of up to 100 in just a few months.

In the early 1970s, astronomers discovered an important clue in their efforts to understand quasars. They found a new class of objects, called **blazars** or **BL Lac objects**. A blazar seems to be star-like and very luminous, just like a quasar. Its few faint emission lines show high redshifts, suggesting a very large distance, just like for a quasar. Blazars are unusual because they are highly variable—their luminosity can change by up to 30% in a day and by a factor of 100 in a few months. Radio observations showed that there is faint radio emission around a bright core, suggesting that a blazar is a double radio source oriented in such a way that one jet is coming straight (or

(a)

(b)

FIGURE 17-31 (a) This diagram shows how an object moving at a speed slower than the speed of light can appear to be moving at a speed faster than the speed of light because of projection effects. (b) The top panel shows the jet emanating from the galaxy's nucleus (at far left; see Figure 17-22). The box indicates the location of the observed superluminal motion. The bottom panel includes the sequence of *HST* images taken between 1994 and 1998. The slanted lines track the observed moving features in the jet, and the apparent speeds of these features are given in units of the speed of light.

FIGURE 17-31 (a) This diagram shows how an object moving at a speed slower than the speed of light can appear to be moving at a speed faster than the speed of light because of projection effects. (b) The top panel shows the jet emanating from the galaxy's nucleus (at far left; see Figure 17-22). The box indicates the location of the observed superluminal motion. The bottom panel includes the sequence of *HST* images taken between 1994 and 1998. The slanted lines track the observed moving features in the jet, and the apparent speeds of these features are given in units of the speed of light.

nearly so) at us. This was soon supported by observations of *superluminal motion*, which is also observed in some quasars.

FIGURE 17-31a shows a simple explanation for superluminal motion. Suppose that a source moves at 80% of the speed of light, along a line that makes an angle of 30° with the line of sight from Earth. At point *A*, it emits a photon toward us. After traveling for 5 days, it reaches point *B*, where it emits a second photon toward us. The real distance traveled by the source between points *A* and *B* is $5 \times 0.80 = 4$ light-days and, thus, the source has moved toward us along the line of sight by about 3.46 light-days. In the meantime, the first photon has traveled a distance of 5 light-days toward us; therefore, the first photon is ahead of the second by $5 - 3.46 = 1.54$ light-days. From our perspective, we see the source moving a horizontal distance on the sky (as a result of projection effects) equal to 2 light-days. Because this is the horizontal distance traveled by the source in the time period during which we receive the two photons, we conclude that the source is moving at a speed of $2/1.54 = 1.3$ times the speed of light! Figure 17-31b shows the observed superluminal motion in the M87 jet.

superluminal motion
Motion that appears to occur at speeds faster than the speed of light.

17-6   The Nature of Active Galactic Nuclei

The first question that has to be answered in trying to solve the puzzle of the nature of active galactic nuclei is this: "Why are these strange objects not found among nearby galaxies?" Here we use the term *active galactic nuclei* (AGNs) to mean the bright energy source at the centers of radio galaxies, Seyfert galaxies, quasars, and blazars. To answer this question, we invoke the idea of look-back time: AGNs are far away because they existed only in the distant past and are not part of today's universe; therefore, any theory about the nature of these mysterious objects must explain why they existed long ago but not today.

According to today's prevalent theories, the tremendous amount of energy that comes from an AGN is caused by an immense black hole at the nucleus of the galaxy. The black hole is surrounded by an accretion disk that is extremely hot because material falls into it with a very great speed. The temperature of the accretion disk explains the enormous energies emitted by the objects. What remains to be explained

Be aware of the tremendous scale of extragalactic astronomy; a few million light-years is a very small distance.

FIGURE 17-32 (a) Active galactic nuclei appear to be different because they are oriented at different angles to our line of sight. The leading model for AGNs holds that they are basically the same type of object, often involving a supermassive black hole. About 10% of quasars are BALs; they exhibit *broad absorption lines* and are likely surrounded by a thick cocoon of gas. (b) This photo of quasar PG 1012+008 (inset) could be explained by a supermassive black hole in one galaxy attracting matter from a nearby companion galaxy.

That period [1960–1966] was incredibly electric. Every time you went to the telescope and came down you had a major new discovery.
Astronomer Allan Sandage

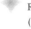

Recall from Chapter 13 (and from Figure 13-15) that jets of material have been observed coming from the poles of protostars. The galactic case is likely a similar phenomenon on a much larger scale.

is why some AGNs are so much more luminous than others, why some emit intense radio waves and others do not, why the luminosity of some of them changes so rapidly, and in general, why there appear to be so many different types of these peculiar objects.

Various theories have attempted to explain the many observations about AGNs, but none is completely satisfactory. The leading theory provides a link between the different types of objects. This "unification theory" holds that they are all basically the same and that they appear different depending on their orientation with respect to us. **FIGURE 17-32a** illustrates the hypothesized object, which is an active galactic nucleus. At its center is a supermassive black hole of many million (or even a few billion) solar masses. It is surrounded by an accretion disk, perhaps a few light-months across.

A much larger ring, shaped like a fat doughnut (a *torus*), surrounds the accretion disk in the same plane. The torus consists of relatively cool gas and dust. It may be several light-years across and is dense enough that light from the accretion disk cannot penetrate it. Light from the disk does reach the outside world, however, for it shines out of the "doughnut hole" in two directions, forming two cones of light. Radiation in all other portions of the electromagnetic spectrum, including high-energy wavelengths, pours out along with the light. A jet of material is ejected by some unexplained process along the axis of each of the cones. Finally, irregular clouds of gas and dust move in orbit around the center.

Now suppose that the active nucleus in the figure is oriented so that we see it edge on, so that the torus hides the accretion disk from our view. Telescopes would reveal infrared energy coming from the clouds, but would not show the high-energy radiation from the accretion disk. In some cases the jets cause emission of visible light, but in other cases they do not. If the active nucleus has energetic jets, astronomers would observe large radio-emitting areas at a great distance on either side of the galaxy. **FIGURE 17-33** (and 17-20a) shows the radio lobes and jets of some active galaxies.

When the torus is seen obliquely, radiation from the accretion disk reaches us, and the object appears as a very energetic source that emits radiation across the spectrum, including X-rays. These are the objects we call quasars. On the other hand,

Ground-Based Optical/Radio Image

HST Image of a Gas and Dust Disk

380 Arc Seconds
88,000 LIGHT-YEARS

17 Arc Seconds
400 LIGHT-YEARS

(c)

FIGURE 17-33 (a) A false-color image of the radio emission (red) is superimposed on a visible-light image (blue-white) of the radio galaxy NGC1316 (Fornax A). Each radio lobe is about 600,000 light-years across. The two faint pink extensions just visible in the center show the paths of the outflows (jets). (b) A false-color image of the jets in the radio galaxy NGC1265 (3C 83.1). The red circle denotes the galaxy's center. Red (blue) shows regions of intense (fainter) radio emission. The galaxy moves through the intergalactic medium at ~ 2000 km/s, resulting in the "U" shape of the jets. (c) (Left panel) A composite image of the giant elliptical galaxy NGC4261 in the Virgo Cluster. In visible light (white), the galaxy appears as a fuzzy disk of hundreds of billions of stars; the radio emission (orange) shows two jets emanating from the nucleus. (Right panel) A giant disk of gas and dust fuels a possible black hole at the core in this IR image.

A study by the Sloan Digital Sky Survey shows that clouds of gas and dust surround the central black hole of many of the most energetic quasars. More than half of the quasars in the relatively recent universe are hidden quasars. X-ray observations by *Swift* and *Suzaku* confirm this result.

One of the most powerful object in the local universe is quasar PDS-456. With a redshift of $z = 0.184$, it is only about 2.2 billion light-years away. It is powered by a black hole of about a billion solar masses.

suppose the jet is aimed directly toward us. Again it would appear as a small, energetic source, but in this case, it might vary quickly in intensity as clouds of dust move across our line of sight. These are the objects we call blazars.

How could we test this "unification theory"? The best test is by detecting radiation from AGNs that is not blocked by the dust in the torus and is not affected by how the torus is seen by the observer. These requirements are fulfilled by far-infrared radiation. Astronomers announced in early 2001 that observations made by the *Infrared Space Observatory* showed that very hot and luminous quasar cores are found even in weak radio galaxies at large distances. These and additional observations support the conclusion that all AGNs are similar objects that appear different depending on how they are oriented with respect to us.

How does this model explain the observation that active galaxies are not found in our neighborhood? There is a limited amount of material near the black hole in the galactic center, and after that material spirals into the black hole, the galaxy calms down to become a more standard galaxy. In today's universe, no galaxy remains with a nucleus that is still in the quasar stage. This means that previous quasars and active galaxies are the ancestors of today's galaxies.

FIGURE 17-34a provides further evidence that galaxies have progressed from having quasars or blazars at their centers, to Seyferts or radio galaxies, to normal spiral

FIGURE 17-34 (a) These three active galaxies are believed to contain supermassive black holes in their nuclei. One has a double nucleus. (b) Examples of different home sites of quasars. The images in the left column represent normal galaxies, in the center, colliding galaxies, and in the right, peculiar galaxies.

Once a supermassive black hole reaches a certain size, its activity (through radiation and outflows) affects the evolution of its host galaxy by dispersing raw material (gas and dust) for star formation from the area around the galactic core. A theoretical upper limit for the mass of a black hole is about 10 billion solar masses.

or elliptical galaxies. The three galaxies in the figure are classified as normal galaxies, but they all show characteristics of having black holes at their centers. A census of 27 nearby galaxies carried out by the *HST* and ground-based telescopes in Hawaii suggests that nearly all galaxies may harbor supermassive black holes that once powered quasars. It seems that supermassive black holes are so common that nearly every large galaxy has one. The *HST* images shown in Figure 17-34b give examples of quasars found in normal, colliding, and peculiar galaxies.

In addition, the black hole's mass is proportional to the mass of the host galaxy. This suggests that the growth of the black hole is linked to the formation of the galaxy in which it is located.

Finally, the number and masses of the black holes found are consistent with what would have been required to power the quasars. Observations in X-rays (using *Chandra*) show that black holes at the centers of AGNs grew more rapidly in distant (and therefore younger) galaxy clusters and were much more active in the past than at present, whereas infrared observations (using *ISO*) show hundreds of young active galaxies with high rates of star formation. The ancestors of today's galaxies were much more active than previously thought. By combining observations in ultraviolet and X-rays, astronomers can study the link between violent stellar activity and accretion by a supermassive black hole at the nucleus of an active galaxy (FIGURE 17-35).

Observations suggest that quasar variability is related to the mass of the central black hole and the efficiency of the quasar in converting gravitational potential energy into light energy; less efficient quasars are more massive and variable. A study by the Sloan Digital Sky Survey of more than 4000 bright quasars in the distant universe shows that they are clustered, with the clusters separated by huge voids. This is consistent with our current understanding of the evolution of our universe; quasars are powered by supermassive black holes at the center of massive halos within massive concentrations of dark matter. Perhaps a giant step has been taken in our understanding of the evolution of galaxies. Time will tell.

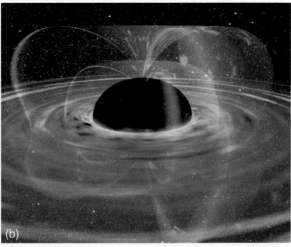

FIGURE 17-35 (a) The spiral galaxy M81 in UV (obtained by *XMM-Newton* in 2001). Strong ultraviolet emission is a feature of star formation, supernova explosions, and accretion by black holes. The emission from the galactic nucleus (the bright, point-like, white region) could support the idea of a miniquasar or intense and violent stellar activity at the center. Blue denotes regions where young, hot stars are formed. Red denotes cool regions (corresponding to older, less massive stars). The bright, red, point-like objects are foreground stars in our Galaxy. (b) An artist's impression of the central region of the spiral galaxy MCG-6-30-15. Its spectrum (obtained by *XMM-Newton* in 2000) shows that the number of measured photons and their energies far exceed the predictions of standard models for accretion disks around supermassive black holes. It is possible that strong magnetic fields exert a breaking effect on the black hole, extracting some of its rotational energy and heating the surrounding medium in the process.

Conclusion

In this chapter, we presented knowledge about which astronomers are fairly confident, as well as knowledge that is very tentative. Galaxies can be classified with confidence, and Hubble's classification is based simply on appearance. Although the tuning fork diagram may appear to indicate an evolutionary sequence, it does not. At least two competing theories are available to explain why galaxies exhibit such different appearances.

Not much can be known about a galaxy unless we first know its distance; thus, the study of galactic distances is important, and various distance indicators are in use today. To measure distances to the farthest galaxies, new tools, such as the Tully-Fisher and the Faber-Jackson relations, have been added to the Hubble law.

Astronomers can calculate the mass of a galaxy by applying gravitational theory to the measured motions of parts of the galaxy. They measure the mass of a cluster of galaxies in a similar manner. Both calculations show that we can account for only a small fraction of the mass that must exist, and the mystery of the missing mass has not been solved.

A busy area of research today is the study of active galactic nuclei. These distant, energetic objects that have been discovered by the methods of radio astronomy have brought about major changes in extragalactic astronomy. They seem to produce new questions almost as prodigiously as they produce energy.

With increasing distance our knowledge fades, and fades rapidly, until at the last dim horizon we search among ghostly errors of observations for landmarks that are scarcely more substantial. The search will continue. The urge is older than history. It is not satisfied and it will not be suppressed.
Edwin Hubble

STUDY GUIDE

1. Cepheid variables are important in calculating
   A. the distances to galaxies.
   B. the composition of stars.
   C. the composition of the interstellar medium.
   D. the ages of galaxies.
   E. the temperatures of stars.

2. About how many galaxies are within range of the largest telescopes?
   A. 20.
   B. 103.
   C. 1000 to 2000.
   D. 1 to 4 million.
   E. More than 100 billion.

3. The Magellanic Clouds are
   A. galaxies.
   B. extremely high atmospheric clouds.
   C. globular clusters.
   D. supernovae.
   E. of unknown nature.

4. The local group consists of
   A. about 100 nearby stars.
   B. about 30 nearby stars.
   C. about 100 nearby galaxies.
   D. about 30 nearby galaxies.
   E. the closest planetary nebulae.

5. Which of the following objects are used as a distance indicator to galaxies?
   A. Cepheid variables.
   B. Globular clusters.
   C. The brightest supernovae.
   D. [All of the above.]
   E. [None of the above.]

6. The masses of galaxies are determined by using the Doppler effect to measure the speeds
   A. of parts of individual galaxies.
   B. of individual galaxies in a cluster.
   C. of galaxies that are part of a binary pair.
   D. [All of the above.]
   E. [None of the above.]

7. Hubble found that the objects that were first called spiral *nebulae* are instead spiral *galaxies* by observing
   A. supernovae in them.
   B. Cepheid variables in them.
   C. radiation characteristic of black holes coming from them.
   D. black holes in their centers.
   E. that their spectra are characteristic of stellar spectra.

8. If galaxy X is four times more distant than galaxy Y, then according to the Hubble law, galaxy X is receding
   A. 16 times faster.
   B. 4 times faster.
   C. 2 times faster.
   D. 1.6 times faster.
   E. [No general statement can be made.]

9. Measurements of the total mass in galactic clusters indicate that they contain far more mass than we see. The "missing mass" is now known to be

A. tiny black holes.
B. cool gas and dust between the galaxies.
C. black dwarfs within the galaxies.
D. [None of the above; we don't know what it is.]

10. Which of the following objects has the greatest diameter?
    A. A galactic cluster.
    B. A cluster of galaxies.
    C. The Milky Way.
    D. The Large Magellanic Cloud.
    E. [Both A and B above; they are the same.]

11. The Tully-Fisher method of measuring distances to galaxies depends on the relationship between a galaxy's absolute magnitude and
    A. the galaxy's size.
    B. the galaxy's redshift.
    C. the galaxy's apparent color.
    D. the width of a line in the galaxy's spectrum.
    E. [Both A and C above.]

12. The Hubble law relates
    A. absolute magnitude and temperature.
    B. apparent magnitude and temperature.
    C. proper motion and radial velocity.
    D. proper motion and distance.
    E. distance and radial velocity.

13. The Hubble constant refers to
    A. the fact that the speed of light never changes.
    B. a number in a formula that will never change its value.
    C. the rate at which the universe is expanding now.
    D. the amount of mass in the universe.
    E. the amount of mass in galactic cores.

14. Suppose that we know that a galaxy 5 million light-years away is receding at 20 miles per second. What would be the Hubble constant based on this single galaxy?
    A. 4 (mi/sec)/Mly.
    B. 15 (mi/sec)/Mly.
    C. 25 (mi/sec)/Mly.
    D. 100 (mi/sec)/Mly.
    E. [None of the above.]

15. The look-back time of an object is
    A. how long light from the object takes to reach Earth.
    B. numerically equal to the object's distance in light-years.
    C. greater for more distant objects.
    D. [All of the above.]
    E. [None of the above.]

16. The Hubble law is based primarily on
    A. calculations of galactic masses.
    B. calculations of galactic rotational speeds.
    C. Doppler shift data.
    D. knowledge of galactic evolution.
    E. data concerning the number of stars in galaxies.

17. Which of the following statements is true about quasars?
    A. They seem to be extremely large compared to most galaxies.

RECALL QUESTIONS

B. They seem to be very small for the energy released.
C. If they are as far away as they seem, they are very energetic.
D. [Both A and C above.]
E. [Both B and C above.]

18. The evidence for small size of quasars comes from
A. the amount of energy they release.
B. their distance from us.
C. the rapidity of their luminosity changes.
D. comparison with Cepheid variables.
E. the magnitude of their blueshift.

19. We cannot judge quasars' distances by using their absolute luminosity as we do in the case of galaxies because
A. they have no absolute luminosity.
B. there are no nearby quasars with which to compare distant ones.
C. their luminosity is too great.
D. their recessional speeds are unknown.

20. The radio waves from a radio galaxy can come from an area many times bigger than the visible object.
A. True.
B. False.
C. No general statement can be made concerning this.

21. Which of the following statements is an observation rather than the result of theory?
A. Light from most galaxies is redshifted.
B. Most galaxies are receding from us.
C. The rate of expansion of the universe is slowing.
D. Galaxies farther away are moving away faster.
E. Quasars emit more energy than most galaxies.

22. If the local hypothesis for quasars were true, we would expect
A. that quasars would be less luminous.
B. that quasars would be more luminous.
C. to observe quasars with blueshifted spectra.

D. quasars to be emitted from other galaxies in addition to ours.
E. [Both C and D above.]

23. What is meant by a distance indicator and what serves as one for nearby galaxies? For more distant galaxies?

24. Describe three methods for measuring the mass of a galaxy other than the Milky Way.

25. What is the local group?

26. What is meant by *dark matter* in galactic astronomy?

27. The chapter stated that we know that elliptical galaxies do not evolve into spiral galaxies. The reason given was that we observe that spirals contain gas and dust while ellipticals do not. Explain why the observation proves the statement.

28. State the Hubble law. What is the currently accepted range of the Hubble constant? Include units in your answer.

29. Describe some difficulties encountered in determining the Hubble constant with accuracy.

30. Explain how the Hubble law can be used to determine the distance to a galaxy. Discuss the limitations of this method of determining distance.

31. What is meant by *look-back time*?

32. In what way are active galaxies "active"?

33. After the spectra of quasars were understood, why were the objects still so difficult to explain?

34. What do we mean when we say that a quasar has a redshift of 25%? Which quasar is moving away faster: one with a redshift of 25% or one with a redshift of 30%?

35. What is the present theory of the origin of the energy of quasars?

36. Why are there no nearby quasars?

QUESTIONS TO PONDER

1. Explain how we determine the distances to galaxies that are too far away to allow us to see Cepheids in them.

2. The difficulty in determining the orientation of the plane of revolution of binary galaxies limits the usefulness of Doppler shift measurements of velocity. Why does the same problem not exist in using Doppler shift data to determine the speed of part of an individual spiral galaxy?

3. Discuss the limitations on the accuracy of measurements of distances to galaxies. Doesn't the lack of precision in these measurements make galactic astronomy less a science than other sciences?

4. Compare the use of bright galaxies as distance indicators with grading a class "on the curve."

5. If the slope of the Hubble graph were greater (with distance plotted on the x axis), would the Hubble constant be larger or smaller? Explain.

6. What is a gravitational lens and what does the fact that they have been observed tell us about quasars?

7. Why is a spectral line of a galaxy broadened by the galaxy's rotation?

8. In describing what was called the *merger theory* of galaxy formation, no explanation was given for why some spiral galaxies have bars and others do not. Propose an explanation.

9. List similarities and differences between the collapse of an interstellar cloud to form a star and the formation of a galaxy.

1. Determine the slope of the graph shown in FIGURE 17-36. (The graph might represent the changing speed of a race car.) Be sure to include units in your answer.

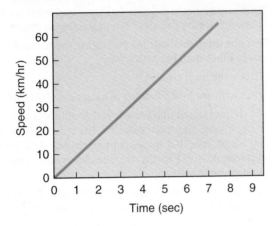

FIGURE 17-36 Graph for Calculation 1.

2. If the data for the Hubble expansion were as shown in Figure 17-9 or Figure 17-11, what would be the value of the Hubble constant for each graph?

3. Suppose that an object is seen with a redshift that indicates a speed of 100,000 km/s away from us. If this redshift fits the Hubble law, how far away is the object? (Assume some reasonable value for the Hubble constant.)

4. Suppose that Alex is moving away from you at a constant speed of 15 miles/hour and is 60 miles away at this moment. If he has maintained this speed since leaving you, how long ago were you together?

5. For the motion in question 4, calculate the "Alex constant" (analogous to the Hubble constant).

6. Figure 17-5a shows the Large Magellanic Cloud. It is 50 kpc from us, and has an angular size of 650' by 550'.

Use the small-angle formula (in Chapter 6) to calculate the dimensions of the Large Magellanic Cloud in kpc.

7. FIGURE 17-37 shows NGC4535. Its angular size is 6.8' by 5'. Assuming that its longest dimension is about 100,000 light-years, calculate its distance from us.

FIGURE 17-37 Galaxy NGC4535, Calculation 7.

8. The existence of supermassive black holes is actually less exotic than you might think. The average density of an object is given by the ratio of its mass to its volume. For a spherical object of radius R, density = $M/(4\pi R^3/3)$. Writing the radius in km and the mass in solar masses show that density = $4.8 \times 10^{20} \times (M/R^3)$ kg/m^3. The radius of a black hole (in km) is related to its mass (in solar masses) by the Schwarzschild expression: $R = 3M$. Now show that the density necessary to make a black hole of mass M (in solar masses) is $1.8 \times 10^{19}/M^2$ kg/m^3. What density is needed to make a black hole of a billion solar masses? A hundred million solar masses?

1. "Understanding the Hubble Sequence," by G. Lake, in *Sky & Telescope* (May, 1992).

2. "When Galaxies Collide," by J. Roth, in *Sky & Telescope* (March, 1998).

3. "Active Galactic Nuclei: Sorting Out the Mess," by A. Finkbeiner, in *Sky & Telescope* (August, 1992).

4. "Massive Black Holes in the Hearts of Galaxies," by H. Ford and Z. I. Tsvetanov, in *Sky & Telescope* (June, 1996).

5. "The Most Distant Radio Galaxies," by G. K. Miley and K. C. Chambers, in *Scientific American* (June, 1993).

6. "A New Look at Quasars," by M. Disney, in *Scientific American* (June, 1998).

7. "The Evolution of Galaxy Clusters," by J. P. Henry, U. G. Briel, and H. Böhringer, in *Scientific American* (December, 1998).

8. "Unmasking Black Holes," by J.-P. Lasota, in *Scientific American* (May, 1999).

9. "Another Look at Cosmic Distances," by T. A. Weil, in *Sky & Telescope* (August 2001).

10. "Quasars Explained," by W. Keel, in *Astronomy* (February 2003).

11. "The Midlife Crisis of the Cosmos," by A. J. Berger, in *Scientific American* (January 2005).

12. "A Quasar in Every Galaxy?" by R. Irion, in *Sky & Telescope* (July 2006).

13. "The Galactic Odd Couple," by K. Weaver, in *Scientific American* Special Edition (January 2007).

14. "Colossal Galactic Explosions," by S. Veilleux, G. Cecil, and J. Bland-Hawthorn, in *Scientific American* Special Edition (January 2007).

Cosmology: The Nature of the Universe

18

THROUGH THE CENTURIES, ASTRONOMERS HAVE STUDIED THE EARTH–MOON SYSTEM, the solar system, the stars, and the galaxies, recognizing the need for a new scale of size with each step. What is left to study? The universe itself is the subject of cosmology, and now we must come to terms with its nature. Yet even here, our understanding is based on observation and deduction, in the spirit of science and not of guesswork.

The scientific study of the universe is a fairly recent field; only since the 1940s have astronomers realized that we can make quantitative predictions about the nature and behavior of the universe and verify these predictions through observations. One of the first physicists to point out the connections between particle physics (whose subject is subatomic particles) and cosmology was Stephen Weinberg, who shared a Nobel Prize in 1979 for his work on the forces between elementary particles. He applied the theories of high-energy physics to the conditions of the entire universe at the time of its beginnings, describing the sequence of events in the "First Three Minutes" of the universe. He concludes his book as follows:

> The universe will certainly go on expanding for a while. As to its fate after that, the standard model gives an equivocal prophecy: It all depends on whether the cosmic density is

The cosmic microwave background (CMB) sky over Mt. Erebus in Antarctica. In this fanciful picture, the CMB sky, as seen by the *BOOMERANG* project, is shown behind the prelaunch preparations for the balloon that carried the equipment. The images of the early universe have been overlaid onto the sky to indicate what size the fluctuations would appear if a standard 35-mm camera were sensitive to microwave light. The color map has been changed to match the rest of the picture.

All cross references to chapters, sections, figures, and tables pertain to the main text, *In Quest of the Universe, Sixth Edition. In Quest of the Solar System* contains Chapters 1–11 and 19 of the main text. *In Quest of the Stars and Galaxies* contains Chapters 1–5 and 11–19 of the main text.

515

less or greater than a certain critical value. . . . [W]hichever cosmological model proves correct, there is not much of comfort in any of this. It is almost irresistible for humans to believe that we have some special relation to the universe, that human life is not just a more-or-less farcical outcome of a chain of accidents reaching back to the first three minutes, but that we were somehow built in from the beginning. . . . It is very hard to realize that [our world] is just a tiny part of an overwhelmingly hostile universe. It is even harder to realize that this present universe has evolved from an unspeakably unfamiliar early condition, and faces a future extinction of endless cold or intolerable heat. The more the universe seems comprehensible, the more it also seems pointless.

But if there is no solace in the fruits of our research, there is at least some consolation in the research itself. Men and women are not content to comfort themselves with tales of gods and giants, or to confine their thoughts to the daily affairs of life; they also build telescopes and satellites and accelerators, and sit at their desks for endless hours working out the meaning of the data they gather. The effort to understand the universe is one of the very few things that lifts human life a little above the level of farce, and gives it some of the grace of tragedy.*

*Steven Weinberg, *The First Three Minutes*, New York: Basic Book, 1988.

Weinberg has since expressed some regret over the somewhat pessimistic tone of these words, but he is certainly not alone in feeling the enormity of the universe around us. It is easy to feel lost in the vastness of space; however, an increasing understanding of how the universe works can give us a more uplifting sense of how we fit into existence. We can also turn to religion as a way of dealing with our place in the universe; we discuss this briefly in an Advancing the Model box on Science, Cosmology, and Faith. However you feel about the size of the universe, the very contemplation of it seems to be a uniquely human endeavor.

In this chapter, we ask three simple questions: What is the nature of the universe? What was its past? What will be its future? These questions are the subject of cosmology, which studies the universe as a whole rather than its individual parts. Many of the ideas from Chapter 17 will be useful for answering cosmology's questions, but the questions are not easy to answer, and today's answers must be regarded as tentative.

Nature has provided us with some clues in our quest to understand the universe. Analyzing these clues, astronomers have been able to reach very meaningful answers to our three questions—questions that must have been among the first asked by intelligent humans.

18-1   The Search for Centers and Edges

Throughout the first 17 chapters of this book, a story has unfolded about changes in our basic ideas of the nature and extent of the universe. These changes have produced different answers to the question of whether we are located at the center of the universe. FIGURE 18-1 shows the life spans of the scientists whose cosmological contributions we describe in this section. Ptolemy's geocentric model (Chapter 1) placed the Earth at the center, and the stars were believed to be on a sphere surrounding the Earth.

Copernicus (Chapter 2) moved the Earth from the center of the universe and replaced it with the Sun, but the stars remained on a sphere surrounding the solar system. This sphere was generally considered to lie just beyond the most distant planet, and this was the entire physical universe; however, some important observations did not fit Copernicus' heliocentric model. It could not explain why the spinning Earth did not leave behind objects thrown upward, nor could it explain the lack of stellar parallax as the Earth moved around the Sun. A half century later, Galileo (Chapter 3) introduced the concept of inertia to explain motion, and he argued that stellar parallax was not observed because the stars are simply too far away. For this to be true, the universe had to be much larger than people had suspected.

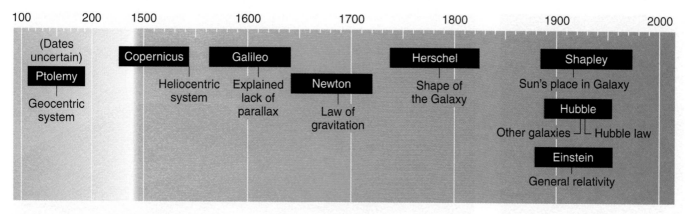

FIGURE 18-1 The life spans of the scientists whose cosmological contributions are described in this section.

Isaac Newton (Chapter 3) proposed that the universe is infinite in extent. He argued that if it were not, the force of gravity would cause the universe to collapse to its center. An infinite universe would not be in danger of collapse because each object in it would be pulled equally hard in all directions. Newton's idea did not catch on, however. Others claimed that the gravitational force has limited range and therefore cannot cause the universe to collapse. An infinite universe simply conflicted too strongly with "common sense."

During the 18th century, William Herschel's discoveries (Chapter 16) led to a better understanding of the Milky Way, again enlarging the boundaries of the known universe. Herschel's data, however, indicated that our solar system is at the center of the Galaxy, thereby returning the human race to center. Herschel proposed that the many fuzzy nebulae visible in telescopes are not part of the Milky Way, but are other galaxies like ours. Like Newton's idea of an infinite universe, Herschel's proposal was not accepted, and by the end of the 19th century, most astronomers were convinced that what we call the Milky Way Galaxy comprised the entire universe.

In 1917, Harlow Shapley (Chapter 16) used globular clusters to conclude that the Sun is not at the center of the Galaxy, and in the next decade other astronomers calculated the Sun's motion. This showed finally that the Sun is not "special," either in nature or in position.

In 1923, Edwin Hubble (Chapter 17) discovered Cepheid variables in the Andromeda "nebula." This pushed back the limits of the universe tremendously, for astronomers recognized that our Galaxy of hundreds of billions of stars is just one of numerous galaxies. People perceived the size of the universe to be on a vaster scale than ever before imagined, and humans were far removed from any central position.

At the time, galaxies were called *isolated universes*, a name suggested by German philosopher Immanuel Kant.

Einstein's Universe

While Hubble and others were using observations to advance our knowledge of the universe, several theoreticians were approaching the problem from a different perspective. Einstein's general theory of relativity (1915) substituted curved space for gravitational force. The theory holds that space itself is curved near a massive object and that the curvature causes the acceleration that previously had been attributed to the force of gravity. In Chapters 3 and 15 we described several observations that support Einstein's theory and show that it explains many phenomena better than does Newton's law of universal gravitation.

Newton knew that gravitational forces would cause a finite universe to collapse. The same situation appears in general relativity, but it is couched in different language. In the absence of any exotic forms of energy, if there is enough matter in the universe to eventually cause its collapse (because of the attractive nature of the gravitational force), space is curved enough that the universe is said to be *closed*. A closed universe has a positive curvature. Curvature of space is difficult to imagine because it involves a fourth dimension. The world of our direct experience is a three-dimensional one, and

closed universe The state of the universe if its total mass and energy density is greater than a specific value, called the critical density.

FIGURE 18-2 (a) A closed universe can be thought of as a two-dimensional plane curved into the third dimension so that it becomes a sphere. (b) Imagine that fleas on the surface of the sphere think that they live in only two dimensions. That is, the surface appears flat to them. Yet, if they travel far enough in one direction they will end up where they began.

Does a closed universe mean that nothing can get in our out?

open universe The state of the universe if its total mass and energy density is less than a specific value, called the critical density.

flat universe The state of the universe if its total mass and energy density is exactly equal to a specific value, called the critical density.

critical density The average mass and energy density of the universe at which space would be flat. It is equal to $3 \cdot H_0^2/(8 \cdot \pi \cdot G)$ and is equivalent to about 5.5 hydrogen atoms per cubic meter of space.

FIGURE 18-3 (a) An open universe can be represented as a plane curved into the shape of a saddle. The figure shows only a portion of the shape, for it extends forever in every direction. (b) A flat universe can be represented as a plane.

the best we can do to imagine a closed universe is to think of a two-dimensional plane being curved so that it forms a sphere (FIGURE 18-2a).

In Chapter 3 we compared our existence in a three-dimensional world that is curved into a fourth dimension with the situation of imaginary "flatfleas" on a two-dimensional surface that is curved (Figure 18-2b). If the creatures in the figure travel far enough in what they perceive as a straight line, they will return to their original positions. Likewise, in a closed universe, a beam of light sent in one direction will travel around the universe and return to its starting point (if the universe lasts long enough). Like the finite two-dimensional surface of a sphere, such a universe would have no boundaries, even though it would have a limited volume and a limited number of stars.

The alternative to a closed universe is an *open universe* that does not curve back onto itself. In the absence of any exotic forms of energy, the amount of matter in an open universe is not enough to slow down its expansion, and such a universe will continue expanding forever. An open universe has negative curvature; this can be visualized in a two-dimensional analogy as a saddle shape (FIGURE 18-3a). An open universe is infinite and continues on forever.

At the boundary between an open and a closed universe is the special case of a *flat universe*. In this case, the geometry that describes the universe is the well-known Euclidean geometry (Figure 18-3b). The universe is infinite and has just the "right" amount of matter and energy (the *critical density*) so that it shows no overall curvature; that is, it is flat.

Einstein believed that the universe is closed and finite. He would not accept the possibility that the universe was anything but static and unchanging (on a large scale). When he applied his equations of general relativity to the universe, he obtained a solution from which he concluded that such a universe would collapse on itself, just as Newton had concluded. (At the time, Einstein was unaware that his equations give rise to other solutions. One such solution, discovered by other scientists, corresponds to an expanding universe.) This seemed an unacceptable situation to Einstein, and he decided to adjust his theory to eliminate that conclusion. To do so, he inserted into the equations a *cosmological constant (Λ)*, a term that adds a cosmological repulsive force to support the universe against collapse. This force would tend to make the universe as a whole expand; however, this force would be very unusual, for instead of weakening with distance, it would become increasingly repulsive with distance. This explains why we do not experience the force at the small distances we normally deal with. The hypothetical cosmological repulsive force is significant only at large distances.

Einstein regretted having to adjust his theory in such an arbitrary, ad hoc manner. Adding the term violated the principle that a theory should be aesthetically simple. Nevertheless, he believed that the adjustment was necessary if his equations were to apply to a static universe. If he had rejected the cosmological constant, he probably would have concluded from his theoretical work that the universe is expanding. Instead, the expansion was discovered observationally.

Einstein abandoned the idea of a cosmological constant when evidence for the expansion of the universe and the big bang became almost completely accepted by the astronomical community; however, recent observations suggest the presence of an exotic form of energy, which results in a repulsive force helping the universe expand at an accelerating rate as time goes on. That is, the idea of a (positive) cosmological constant is supported by these observations. We do not really know yet the characteristics of this exotic form of energy.

> **cosmological constant**
> A term (denoted by the Greek capital letter "lambda," Λ) in the equations of general relativity that corresponds to a force throughout all space that helps the universe expand.

Something is said to be *ad hoc* if it is designed for one special purpose. An ad hoc committee, for example, is one that is created for a specific job.

18-2 The Expanding Universe

In 1929, Edwin Hubble announced that the pattern of redshifts of distant galaxies indicates that they are moving away from us and that the more distant the galaxy, the faster it is moving away. In Chapter 17, we explained how the resulting *Hubble law* has become a valuable tool to measure the distances to faraway galaxies. In addition, Hubble's law has tremendous implications concerning the nature of the universe.

First, if other galaxies are moving away from ours, does this not mean that our Galaxy must be at the center? Have we finally discovered that we are at a special location after all? Hubble published his findings in 1929, 12 years after Shapley's work with globular clusters had taken our Sun out of the central position within the Galaxy. By this time, it had become a working premise that our location within the cosmos is not central. To see why Hubble's discovery does not, in fact, conflict with this basic premise, consider the following analogy.

Imagine that you are a trainer in a flea circus and that you put a number of educated fleas on a balloon that your assistant is blowing up. You have instructed these fleas to hold their positions on the balloon. FIGURE 18-4 shows the balloon being blown up with the fleas in place.

Now imagine what a particularly intelligent flea sees when it looks out toward neighboring fleas. (Assume either that the flea can see around the curvature of the balloon or that the fleas are close enough together that the balloon seems flat to them.) The intelligent flea sees every other flea getting farther and farther away as the balloon is blown up. In addition, the more distant fleas are moving away at a greater speed than those nearby. The more distant a given flea is from the observer, the faster it is moving.

The important point is that the same result would be obtained no matter which flea is the observer. While the balloon is being blown up, every flea sees every other flea moving away with a velocity that depends on the flea's distance from the observer.

The analogy shows that if galaxies are part of an expanding universe, we would see exactly what Hubble and Humason observed: every galaxy is seen to be moving away from us at a speed that depends upon how far away

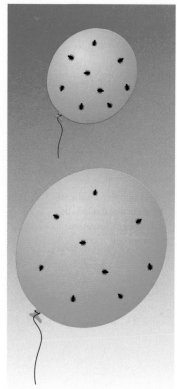

FIGURE 18-4 Fleas on a balloon get farther apart when the balloon is blown up.

it is. Many astronomers since Hubble have surveyed galaxies at greater and greater distances and have come to the same conclusion: the universe is expanding.

In Chapter 17 we included an Advancing the Model box concerning the differences between observations and conclusions. The distinction is important in this case. The pattern of redshifts is an *observation*. All spectral lines of distant (dim) galaxies show the redshift, not just the lines of the visible spectrum. The observations are 100% in agreement with what would be predicted for light from a receding object. We thus *conclude* that the galaxies are getting farther away from us. We do not, however, *observe* this.

What Is Expanding and What Is Not? The Cosmological Redshift

Saying that the universe is expanding certainly does not mean that the solar system is expanding, nor does it mean that stars within our Galaxy are getting farther apart. In fact, it does not even mean that all galaxies are getting farther apart.

The observed redshift leads us to conclude that other *clusters* of galaxies are moving away from ours. Some individual galaxies are actually moving toward us. This occurs in two ways. First, galaxies in our local group are moving randomly within the group as each responds to the overall gravitational force of the others. For example, the Andromeda galaxy and a half-dozen others in the local group are at this time moving toward our Galaxy.

Second, in nearby clusters, the same random motion of individual galaxies results in some of the galaxies moving toward us at the present time, even though the cluster in which each galaxy exists is moving away from the local group. A simple example can show how it is possible for an individual galaxy to show blueshifted lines even though it belongs to a cluster moving away from us. For a Hubble constant of, say, 70 (km/s)/Mpc, a cluster at a distance of 2 megaparsecs from us will be moving away from us at $70 \times 2 = 140$ km/s, due to the expansion of the universe; however, the random speeds of individual galaxies can easily exceed 140 km/s; therefore, if we were looking at an individual galaxy in this cluster with a random speed of 200 km/s, we could be seeing this galaxy moving at speeds between $140 + 200 = 340$ km/s and $140 - 200 = -60$ km/s. In the latter case, this galaxy will show blueshifted lines, even though its overall motion is away from us as a member of a cluster. No individual cluster—as far as we can tell—is expanding.

The argument presented here also explains why we do not use the Hubble law to find distances to nearby galaxies.

It is the clusters of galaxies that are moving farther apart. Although we often say that other galaxies are moving away from us, we thus should really say that other clusters are moving away from our cluster. Anything that is gravitationally bound is not expanding as a result of the expansion of the universe. This includes objects (like us) that are held together by forces stronger than the gravitational attraction between their individual components.

The Doppler shift is still the correct explanation of other observations in astronomy.

After the redshift of light from distant galaxies was discovered, astronomers assumed that the Doppler effect was the cause. Using the Doppler effect, they calculated the velocities of the galaxies. The Hubble law is a statement of the relationship between a galaxy's distance and its (Doppler effect) velocity, as we showed in Chapter 17; however, modern cosmology explains the redshift in an entirely different manner.

An expanding universe does not mean that clusters of galaxies are rushing *through* space. Instead, *space itself is expanding*. FIGURE 18-5 illustrates the difference, using the balloon analogy again. This time, tiny seeds have been glued to the balloon, each seed representing a cluster of galaxies. Part (a) shows the Doppler interpretation of the expansion of the universe. The balloon is expanding against a background grid that represents space, indicating that the galaxies move through space. Part (b) shows the modern cosmological interpretation of the expanding universe. The grid that represents space is part of the surface of the balloon here. As the balloon expands, space itself expands.

Why don't individual galaxies expand along with space? General relativity shows that objects that are held together by their own gravity, such as the Earth, the solar system, the Galaxy, and the local group, do not expand as space expands. The force

ADVANCING THE MODEL

Cosmological Redshift

Objects have been discovered that have a redshift (z) greater than 5. A redshift of 5 means that the ratio of the shift in a particular wavelength ($\Delta\lambda$) to the unshifted wavelength (λ_0) is equal to 5. In the standard application of the Doppler effect, this means that the velocity of the object (v) is equal to five times the velocity of light (c), because

$$z = \frac{\Delta\lambda}{\lambda_0} = \frac{v}{c}.$$

This cannot happen! An object cannot travel at a speed greater than the speed of light. The resolution to this problem lies in the fact that the standard expression for redshift ($z = v/c$) is valid only in the approximation of speeds much less than the speed of light. For objects moving at large speeds (v larger than about $0.1c$), astronomers must take into account special relativity. When the rules of special relativity are used, we get the following general expression for redshift:

$$z = \frac{\Delta\lambda}{\lambda_0} = \sqrt{\frac{c+v}{c-v}} - 1.$$

This expression is valid for all speeds. For small speeds, it gives us our familiar expression $z = v/c$, whereas for large speeds (and thus large redshifts), the calculated speed of a receding cluster of galaxies is always less than the speed of light.

The fallacy here is that special relativity is not applicable in a universe where general relativity is the controlling rule. Special relativity can be applied only where space can be considered to be exactly flat. In the case of distant clusters, the curvature of space must be taken into account, and thus special relativity cannot be used.

To review this relationship between laws, recall that Newton's law of gravitation should not be considered *wrong*. Rather, it is a law with limited applicability that must be replaced by general relativity in certain cases, but it is accurate enough for most everyday uses. Likewise, our standard concept of speed (where we do not worry about objects moving at speeds near the speed of light) works in everyday situations. But for accurate results, special relativity must be used for great speeds (especially for speeds greater than about $0.1c$). However, special relativity is also a law with limited applicability. It cannot be used when space curvature is a factor.

When we try to combine physical laws that are not consistent with one another, we violate the principle that a theory should be aesthetically pleasing. Consistency is important in applying scientific principles.

The Doppler effect thus cannot be used as the explanation for the cosmological redshift, as Doppler shifts are caused by an object's motion *through* space. The correct explanation lies in the idea of the expansion *of* space, as we discuss in the text.

of gravity (or, in terms of general relativity, the local curvature of space) holds them together just as each individual seed on the balloon holds itself together and does not expand with the balloon.

This interpretation of the expansion of the universe means that clusters of galaxies do not actually have a velocity through space and therefore that the Doppler effect does not explain the redshift in their spectra. A Doppler redshift is caused by the relative motion of an object that is emitting a wave. The ***cosmological redshift*** has a different cause. Long ago, when a distant galaxy emitted some electromagnetic waves, those waves were not redshifted, but as space expanded, the waves expanded—that is, they lengthened—along with space. The more time the radiation has traveled, the more its waves have stretched in wavelength. FIGURE 18-6 illustrates the difference between the two explanations.

When the Hubble law was written, astronomers assumed that the observed redshift was caused by the now-rejected Doppler explanation. The law is still valuable, however, if we think of the velocity in the Hubble equation as being caused by the expansion of space, rather than by velocity *through* space. Although astronomers sometimes use more modern ways of stating the redshift/expansion-rate relationship without using the concept of velocity, in this text, we continue to use the traditional Hubble relationship.

cosmological redshift
The shift toward longer wavelengths that is due to the expansion of the universe.

In equation form, the Hubble law is $v = H_0 d$, where v = the velocity of the object, d = the distance to the object, and H_0 is the Hubble constant.

Olbers' Paradox

Why is the sky dark at night? This appears to be a very simple question, but it actually has important cosmological implications. If stars (or galaxies or clusters of galaxies) are randomly distributed throughout space and if the universe were infinitely

FIGURE 18-5 Each tiny seed glued to the balloon represents a cluster of galaxies. (a) This is the old, incorrect interpretation of an expanding universe in which the universe expands through space. (b) This is the correct cosmological interpretation. Space expands, dragging the clusters of galaxies along with it.

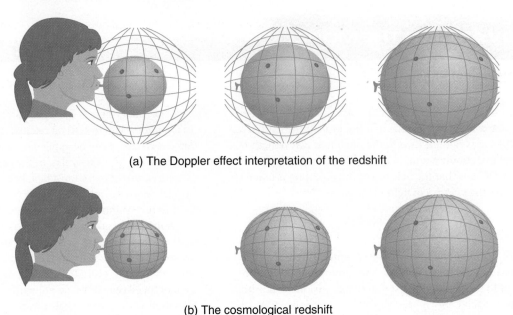

(a) The Doppler effect interpretation of the redshift

(b) The cosmological redshift

old, the sky should not be dark, because no matter in which direction you look, the line of sight should end on a star (**FIGURE 18-7a**). Light from any single star in the universe would have had infinite time to reach us. It is true that distant stars appear dimmer than nearby ones, but if we assume that stars are evenly distributed in our universe, then it is clear that there are more stars at great distances, and this eliminates the dimming effect. If you are deep within a forest, you see a tree no matter in which direction you look. Distant trees look smaller, but there are more of them (Figure 18-7b).

Perhaps the absorption of light by dust clouds prevents the sky from being bright, but dust clouds heat up as they absorb light. Because they absorb light from an infinite number of stars, they should get hot enough to glow. Dust clouds cannot be used to explain the dark sky.

FIGURE 18-6 (a) A Doppler redshift results from the *motion* of the source. The wave traveling toward the radio telescope is lengthened by the motion of the source. (b) When a wave is emitted by a *nonmoving* object, it has the same wavelength in all directions. As space expands, that wave lengthens. If the wave takes long enough to get from the source to the telescope, it will have lengthened significantly. This is the case for galaxies that exhibit the cosmological redshift.

FIGURE 18-7 (a) In an infinite, static universe, your line of sight would end at a star no matter in which direction you looked. (b) Deep in a forest, you see a tree in every direction.

The paradox between what is observed and the argument that the sky should not be dark was known long before it was popularized by Wilhelm Olbers in 1823. It is called **Olbers' paradox**.

The problem exists whether the universe is open or closed. An open universe extends without limit and, thus, the line of sight should extend through space until it hits a star. In a closed universe, the line of sight could possibly extend all the way around until the surface of a star is encountered.

The resolution of Olbers' paradox—the reason that the sky is dark—is based on two related ideas: one, that the universe has a finite age, and two, that it is expanding. First, a universe that has been expanding for billions of years, as suggested by observations, most likely had a beginning at one time in the past, emerging from a very dense state. This finite age for the universe (say about 14 billion years) implies that we cannot see any objects that are beyond a distance of 14 billion light-years from us. If we think of ourselves as being inside a sphere of radius 14 billion light-years, then our entire *observable* universe is located inside this sphere. Light from an object outside this sphere would have taken more than the age of the universe to reach us and thus we do not see it now. As a result, independently of whether the universe is finite or infinite, our line of sight does not always hit a star, which partially explains why the night sky is dark. Second, as a result of the expansion of the universe, light from distant galaxies is redshifted, and thus, it also loses energy. This occurs because the energy of a photon of light depends directly on the light's frequency, and thus, a photon of lower frequency and therefore greater wavelength (due to redshift) has less energy. This decrease in energy of the light we receive also helps explain (to a lesser degree) why the night sky is dark.

The resolution to the paradox depends on the fact that the universe is expanding and that it had a beginning. This latter point is at the heart of the major theory of modern cosmology, the *big bang theory*. Before discussing this theory, however, we need to describe the fundamental assumptions of modern cosmology.

Olbers' paradox An argument showing that the sky in a static universe could not be dark.

The resolution of Olbers' paradox due to the finite age of the universe was first pointed out in 1848 by the American writer Edgar Allan Poe.

We discussed photons in Section 4-6. The frequency of a photon is inversely proportional to its wavelength.

18-3 Cosmological Assumptions

The assumptions of cosmology cannot be proved, but evidence indicates that they are reasonable. The first assumption is that the universe is **homogeneous**. This means that no matter where an observer is positioned in the universe, the universe looks essentially the same. This does not mean, of course, that there is another Earth from which an observer can look to see another Mars in the sky. It does not even mean that there is another local group of galaxies similar to our local group. Rather, it means that on the largest scale, the universe has about the same density and composition of matter at one location as it has at another. As we have described, humans have come to learn that they are not in a favored place in the universe. In cosmology, this becomes an underlying assumption.

homogeneous Having uniform properties throughout.

FIGURE 18-8 Although the ocean surface is homogeneous, you see something different when you look in different directions because the surface is not isotropic.

isotropy (I-SOT-rah-pee) The property of being the same in all directions.

cosmological principle The basic assumption of cosmology that holds that on a large scale the universe is the same everywhere.

universality The property of obeying the same physical laws throughout the universe.

The second assumption is somewhat related to the first. The assumption of *isotropy* states that the universe looks the same in all directions. Although this sounds like homogeneity, it is actually a different quality. The ocean in **FIGURE 18-8** is homogeneous—for no matter where you are located on the surface of the ocean, the view is the same. You see, however, a different view when you look across the waves than when you look along the waves. This means that the ocean is not isotropic.

Like homogeneity, isotropy applies only on the largest scale. Recall from Chapter 16 that when we look out from Earth, we can see farther when we look out of the Galactic disk than if we look along the disk. The universe is not isotropic on this small scale. To apply the idea of isotropy, we must imagine being outside the Galaxy and even outside the local group of galaxies. In this case, the assumption is reasonable.

These two assumptions of cosmology are so much at the heart of the subject that they form what is called the *cosmological principle*. This principle formalizes the idea that we are not located at a special place in the universe. It brings to final completion the Copernican revolution that proposed that the Earth is not central. The cosmological principle not only states that the Earth is at no special place in the universe, but that there *is* no special place in the universe.

An additional cosmological assumption is *universality*. This means that the same physical laws apply everywhere in the universe. Although this may seem so obvious that it need not be stated, it was only fairly recently in human history that Newton found the first law of nature that could be shown to apply beyond the Earth. Now we have vastly more evidence for this assumption as we analyze radiation from the most distant objects, but we must remember that it is still an *assumption* that this principle holds throughout the universe.

These cosmological assumptions show our biases about the nature of the universe, but they are also necessary. Without them we would not be able to make any progress in understanding the universe. Unlike other disciplines, in cosmology we cannot control our subject, the universe, or make comparisons with another similar subject. There is only one observable universe. Based on these assumptions, our models have proven to be quite successful in describing the structure and evolution of the universe.

18-4   The Big Bang

big bang The theoretical initial explosion that began the expansion of the universe.

◆ It's interesting that progress in understanding how the universe itself began depends on understanding the forces that act between the tiniest particles we know of and how these forces affect the behavior of these particles.

The present motion of galaxies leads us to believe that at one time in the past, the matter in the universe must have been much closer together. If we run the "movie" of the expansion of the universe backward, there must have been a time when the density of matter was extremely high and some sort of "explosion" initiated the expansion of the universe. This explosion is called the *big bang*, an irreverently trivial name for the event that began the universe. In its most basic sense, the standard big bang model is simply the idea that every bit of the matter and energy in the universe was once compressed to an unimaginable density. In the big bang, the material exploded apart.

We must be careful not to think of the material of the big bang as existing at a certain place, at one point in the universe. It *was* the universe—the entire universe. It did not exist as part of the universe.

Understanding the details of what happened in the big bang requires an understanding of particle physics, sometimes called "high-energy physics" because elementary particles are used in high-speed collisions to help us better understand what they consist of. Certainly the big bang represents the highest concentration of energy ever reached in the history of the universe. We describe some of the events that immediately followed the big bang in the Advancing the Model box "The Early Universe" on page 528.

After the initial explosion, the steady decrease in the temperature of the universe allowed the nuclear particles to form into atoms of low mass (hydrogen and helium). These atoms then clustered under the force of gravity into stars, clusters of stars, galaxies, and clusters of galaxies. The clusters of galaxies are still moving apart. Again, we must be careful not to think of the universe as expanding *into* empty space around it, for space does not exist apart from the universe. The universe is all there is, and its parts are moving away from one another.

A common *misconception* is to consider the big bang as being similar to the situation shown in FIGURE 18-9. Suppose a large firecracker is placed at the center of a small stack of sand. Soon after the explosion of the firecracker, grains of sand are at various distances from their original position, and—here is the important point—grains that are farther from their respective starting points are moving faster. That is how they got farther from one another. No matter which grain one considers, all others are moving farther from it. Although this example is useful to illustrate that the fastest-moving galaxies would naturally be the farthest away, the example is misleading if you do not remember that in the case of cosmological expansion, galaxies do not move *through* space, as the grains of sand do. Because we have no experience with the expansion of space in our everyday lives, Earthly examples must involve motions through space.

FIGURE 18-9 An illustration of the misconception that the big bang is an explosion. (a) A firecracker about to explode inside a small pile of sand. (b, c) The sand shown later. The sand grains that are farthest from the initial explosion are moving fastest.

Evidence: Background Radiation

The idea of the big bang arose from the evidence for the expansion of the universe. We must ask, however, if there is other evidence to support the theory. The first evidence was found quite accidentally when a prediction made by the big bang theory was found to be correct. As scientists learned more about nuclear processes in the 1940s, they were able to make predictions about the character of the early universe shortly after the big bang. The material of the big bang was originally extremely hot, but it cooled as it expanded outward, in much the same way that a gas cools when it expands. The hot matter of the very early universe was opaque to radiation, but when it cooled to about 3000 K, it became transparent. This happened when the universe was about 376,000 years old, at a redshift of about $z = 1100$. At this point, the gas that made up the universe was emitting radiation that had the characteristics of radiation from an object at 3000 K, and this radiation existed over the entire universe.

The universe has remained transparent to radiation since that time and, thus, it was predicted that this radiation should still be in existence. Remember that as we look at objects at greater and greater distance, we are looking back in time. If we were to detect the radiation left over from the big bang, it would be coming from far back in time and therefore from a great distance. According to the Hubble law, then, it would be greatly redshifted. The original 3000-K radiation peaked in the infrared region of the spectrum, but calculations showed that it would by now have been redshifted to the microwave region, with wavelengths of a millimeter or so. Such radiation would not be characteristic of radiation from a 3000-K object, but it would appear the same as radiation from a very cold object—one at about 3 K ($-270°C$). It was predicted that this ***cosmic microwave background radiation (CMB)*** should be striking Earth from all directions but that it should be very faint.

In 1948, when the prediction of the CMB radiation was made, there was no way to detect such weak waves. The prediction was laid aside and forgotten. Then in the mid-1960s, a group of physicists at Princeton University was studying the big bang and again predicted the existence of the CMB radiation, not realizing that the prediction had been made some 15 years before. They were confident that they could build a radio receiver that would be able to detect the radiation, and they set about building one on the roof of the Princeton biology building. They were too late.

cosmic microwave background radiation (or ***CMB radiation***). Long-wavelength radiation observed from all directions; thought to be the remnant of radiation from the big bang.

ADVANCING THE MODEL

The Steady-State Theory

The cosmological principle holds that we are at no special place in space. It does, however, allow for us being at a special place in time. For at the present moment, the universe is less dense than it was in the past and more dense than it will be in the future because expansion reduces its density. In 1948, *a perfect cosmological principle* was proposed by astronomers Fred Hoyle, Hermann Bondi, and Thomas Gold. It states that our location in time is no more special than our location in space and that the universe of the past was the same as it is now and the same as it will be in the future. Because the overall universe does not change in this cosmology, it is called the *steady-state theory*.

Before looking at the implications of the perfect cosmological principle, consider why such an idea might be proposed. Remember that a theory should be aesthetically pleasing. The perfect cosmological principle is neater because it expands the nonspecialness to include time as well as space. The perfect cosmological principle carries the nonspecialness idea through both space and time.

It seems to be almost undeniable that the universe is expanding. How can this be squared with the steady-state theory? It seems that if clusters of galaxies are getting farther apart, the universe will necessarily be less dense in the future than it is now. Hoyle, Bondi, and Gold proposed that matter is created in the space between galaxies and that this new matter is sufficient for the universe to maintain its density (FIGURE B18-1). Such spontaneous creation of matter would violate a long-established principle of physics: the conservation of mass/energy, which holds that the total amount of mass and energy in the universe cannot change.

The principle of the conservation of mass/energy is dear to scientists, but it has changed in the past. Before this century, there were two such conservation principles: the conservation of mass and the conservation of energy. It was thought that neither matter nor energy could be created or destroyed. Then, in 1905, Einstein's theory proposed that mass could be changed into energy—a prediction that was dramatically demonstrated in the atomic bomb. Einstein combined the two principles into one, the conservation of mass/energy, which sees mass and energy as two forms of the same thing and holds that the total mass and energy in the universe remains the same.

The amount of mass that would have to be created to fill the gaps between galaxies as they move apart would be very small—only one new hydrogen atom in each cubic meter of space every 10 billion years or so. This means that if three new atoms were created every 10,000 years in the volume of Cowboys Stadium, the density of the universe would remain the same. The theory holds that as millions of years pass, newly formed atoms collect to form new stars and galaxies,

and that the expanded space is thereby refilled so that the universe is no different now than it was in the past and than it will be in the future.

The fact that the steady-state theory violates the principle of conservation of mass/energy should not be considered a strike against the theory. First, according to the predictions, the necessary creation events are so rare that they would be far below any possible detection limit and therefore far below the accuracy to which the principle has been verified. Second, the big bang theory may also involve a violation of the principle. In this case, it is a gigantic one-time violation, as all matter and energy are created in one big burst at the beginning.

One of the first predictions made by the steady-state theory involved the number of faint (very distant) radio sources. In this theory, the number density of such sources (that is, the number of radio sources per unit volume) remains constant, and so does the average energy radiated away by a radio source per unit time. This leads to a very specific relationship between the number density and the energy received per unit time per unit area; however, observations made in the 1950s implied a different relationship, suggesting that either the number density or the average energy increases with distance. This, of course, implies that the universe is evolving, in contradiction to the steady-state theory.

FIGURE B18-1 (a, b) If the universe does not decrease in density as galaxies move apart, matter must be created in the space between galaxies.

ADVANCING THE MODEL

The Steady-State Theory *(Cont'd)*

Another argument against this theory involves the amount of helium observed in the universe. This amount is much greater than what can be expected from stellar evolution; therefore, we will have to accept that either helium is also spontaneously created or that there was a special period in the universe's life during which a great amount of helium was created, along with other elements.

Finally, the discovery of the cosmic background radiation made it impossible to reconcile its existence with the steady state theory. Even if we assume an unknown mechanism that can produce such radiation in the steady-state theory, its temperature would have to be constant, independent of redshift; however, the measured temperature of this radiation depends linearly on redshift. That is, at redshift z, the measured temperature is greater by a factor $(1 + z)$. This implies that the universe is evolving.

Hoyle, Burbidge, and Narlikar proposed a quasi-steady-state theory in an effort to bring the theory closer to an agreement with the observations; however, none of the many versions of this theory has been successful so far. The historical development of both the big bang and steady-state theories provides another example in our discussion of how science is done. At the end, the theory that is accepted the most is the one that is simple and elegant, explains the current observations, makes predictions that can be tested, and allows itself to be shown wrong.

At the same time the predictions were being made at Princeton, only a few miles away two employees of Bell Telephone Laboratories, Arno Penzias and Robert Wilson (FIGURE 18-10), were doing applied research on microwave transmission in hopes of improving the transmission of messages. They were frustrated, however, by some low-intensity radio waves arriving at their receiver from all directions.

As you might suspect by now, the radiation they had found turned out to be the CMB radiation predicted by the physicists at Princeton and by astronomers years before—the prediction that was based on the big bang theory. Penzias and Wilson were awarded the Nobel Prize in 1978 for their discovery of a radiation for which they had not been searching and the cosmological implications of which they were unaware.

At the time of the big bang, the condensed material made up the entire universe. This is why the CMB radiation now comes to us from all directions. This radiation fills the universe just as it did at the beginning. Matter and energy comprise the entire universe, and no space is left over.

FIGURE 18-10 Arno Penzias (right) and Robert Wilson discovered the cosmic background radiation using Bell Laboratories' horn-shaped radio antenna, seen behind them.

Until the discovery of the CMB radiation, there was another popular cosmological theory (see the Advancing the Model box "The Steady-State Theory"), but this discovery established the big bang theory as the accepted explanation for the beginning of the universe.

In 1989, NASA launched the *Cosmic Background Explorer* (*COBE*, FIGURE 18-11). Its purpose was to measure the CMB radiation at various wavelengths and to map the sky in those wavelengths. *COBE*'s results provide an astounding corroboration of the accuracy of predictions concerning the CMB radiation. FIGURE 18-12 is an intensity-wavelength graph like those used to describe the temperature of stars in Chapters 12 through 15. The red line on the figure is the predicted intensity of radiation at each wavelength. The tiny black lines represent data points measured by *COBE*. Each data

FIGURE 18-11 The *Cosmic Background Explorer* (*COBE*), pronounced "KOH-bee," was launched in 1989 and for 4 years provided important data regarding the CMB radiation.

ADVANCING THE MODEL

The Early Universe

Stephen Weinberg's book, *The First Three Minutes*, was the first book written for the general public that describes the model cosmologists have developed to explain what happened at the beginning of the universe. Some of the events in this model have been refined over the past few decades as more data have accumulated from observations by satellites and balloon-borne instruments, but the sequence of events has become accepted enough to be called the "standard model of cosmology."

The model starts at about 10^{-43} seconds after the big bang itself. Why 10^{-43} seconds? Well, according to our present understanding of space and time, there is a limit to how closely you can look at tiny distances and still know what you're looking at. You know that if you look at a piece of paper, like a page of this book, through a microscope, it will no longer appear smooth, but will show a mixed-up jumble of wood fibers, along with filler that holds the fibers together. If you keep going in your imagination, you might think of the jumbled-up atoms that make up the page and the particles that make up the atoms, but if you keep going, eventually space itself becomes jumbled instead of smooth. Scientists have calculated the smallest distance that we can imagine before this jumbling occurs, coming up with a distance of about 4×10^{-35} meters. Light would take about 10^{-43} seconds to cross this distance, which makes this amount of time the smallest interval for which we can talk about the universe.

What was the universe like at this time? There were no atoms, and everything was scrunched up into a far smaller size than any particles we're familiar with. All we can say with any confidence is that the universe was hot, about 10^{32} K, and it was expanding. As it expanded, it cooled, very quickly. At about 10^{-35} seconds, a period of inflation may have occurred, lasting for only 10^{-32} seconds, but having tremendous implications for the history of the universe, as we discuss in Section 18-6.

By the time of one millionth of a second (10^{-6} s) after the big bang, the temperature had dropped to about 10^{13} K, which was cool enough (relatively speaking, of course!) for protons and neutrons to form. How do we know this? Because according to present theories, at temperatures higher than 10^{13} K, these particles break up into even smaller particles (called quarks; you may have heard about these littlest of all particles). After you get below this temperature, the quarks don't have enough energy to move away from each other and stay bound together in protons and neutrons.

To form nuclei more massive than hydrogen, the temperature of the background radiation must be low enough so that it does not break the nuclei apart. The first element more massive than hydrogen (whose nucleus is just a pro-

ton) is helium. Nuclei of helium consist of two protons and two neutrons or two protons and a single neutron. The easiest way of forming helium nuclei is by first forming deuterium nuclei, which consist of a single proton and a single neutron; however, for the first 10 seconds after the big bang, the temperature of the background radiation was too high (more than 5 billion K) for deuterium to form. As the universe cooled and deuterium nuclei formed, they led to the formation of helium nuclei. This continued for about 15 minutes, by which time the temperature had dropped to below about 1 billion K and no further nuclei were formed. Again, how do we know this? The evidence is in the proportions of hydrogen, helium, and deuterium we have observed in the universe. Other sequences of events in the early universe have been proposed, but they all predict formation of the light elements in different proportions than what we observe.

The formation of light elements (hydrogen, deuterium, helium, and lithium) in the early universe is called "Big Bang nucleosynthesis." Elements heavier than lithium were later formed in stars, as we described in an Advancing the Model box on "Nucleosynthesis" in Chapter 15.

FIGURE B18-2 shows how the predicted abundances of deuterium, helium, and lithium depend on the density of ordinary matter in the early universe. The circles correspond to the observed abundances. The predicted abundance for

FIGURE B18-2 The curves show the dependence of the predicted abundances of helium, deuterium, and lithium on the density of ordinary matter in the early universe.

ADVANCING THE MODEL

The Early Universe *(Cont'd)*

helium-4 is about 24% of the ordinary matter in the universe, which agrees very well with the observations. The abundance of deuterium in the interstellar gas in our Galaxy was measured by astronomers at Haystack Radio Observatory; their results, along with observations of abundances of the other light elements, imply that only 4% of the total mass/energy density is in the form of ordinary matter. This is consistent with the "standard model" of a universe with a flat geometry, as we discuss in Section 18-7.

What happened next? Nothing much. The universe, dominated by radiation, continued to expand and to cool; however, as the universe expanded, matter became increasingly dominant. About 10,000 years after the big bang, when the temperature dropped to about 20,000 K (at redshift of about $z = 6700$), the universe became matter dominated and became increasingly so ever since. The expansion and cooling of the universe continued for the next few hundred thousand years. Only then, when the temperature dropped below a few thousand degrees, did electrons slow down enough to be captured by nuclei and form atoms. At this point, about 376,000 years after the big bang, at redshift of about 1100, an amazing

thing happened: the universe became transparent. Before this time, the background photons were energetic enough that they would not allow electrons and protons to get together and form atoms. Instead, the photons were continuously and vigorously colliding with the charged particles, resulting in a very opaque universe. As the temperature of the background radiation dropped below about 3000 K (376,000 years after the big bang), the photons did not have enough energy to keep electrons and protons from forming hydrogen atoms. After hydrogen atoms formed, the photons could now move freely through space, resulting in a transparent universe. It is these photons that make up the cosmic microwave background we observe today.

How reliable is this picture of the early universe? Some of it is conjecture, some of it is debatable; certainly none of it is proven. There is no photograph or eyewitness account of the big bang, but the description given here, although somewhat simplified, fits all the data we have so far acquired about the early universe. As more data become available, we will continue to revisit and refine our ideas about what happened in the beginning.

point is depicted as a line, which takes into account possible errors in the measurement. The longer lines at the left indicate that the measurements at shorter wavelengths are less accurate. The data fit is extraordinary.

The *COBE* data show that the temperature of the background radiation is 2.725 K (with an uncertainty of 0.002 K). This matches the theory to within 0.03%, which is 1000 times better than the best data before *COBE*.

Additional Evidence for the Big Bang

The big bang theory is the best current model for the universe. Observational data support the theory but do not prove it, because scientific theories are not proven. We have already mentioned some of these observations: the darkness of the night sky, the Hubble law, homogeneity, and isotropy at large scales.

Another argument in favor of the big bang involves the time dilation of distant supernova light curves. This dilation is the result of the standard interpretation of redshift. A supernova that takes 20 days to decay will appear to take $20 \times (1 + z)$ days to decay when observed at redshift z. Such dilation has been observed, providing a very strong confirmation of the cosmological nature of redshift.

Some additional observations show the evolution of the universe and are consistent

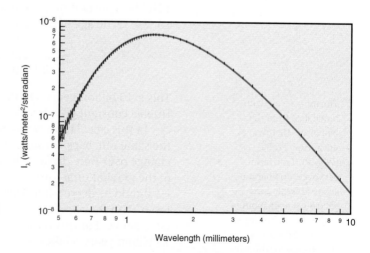

FIGURE 18-12 The theoretical intensity-wavelength graph for the cosmic microwave background radiation is shown in red. The tiny black lines represent data from *COBE*. The fit is remarkable!

with the big bang theory. For example, we mentioned in the Advancing the Model box on "The Steady-State Theory" that the observed relationship between the number density of distant radio sources and quasars and the energy received from them per unit time per unit area shows that the universe evolved. The existence of the CMB and the dependence of its temperature on redshift also show that the universe evolved from a hot and dense state.

Additional evidence that supports the big bang comes from the observed proportions of light chemical elements (such as deuterium, helium, and lithium). These proportions could not have formed in stars; however, they are consistent with a process of nuclear fusion in the first few minutes of a hot, young universe, as we described in the Advancing the Model box on "The Early Universe."

Finally, as we discuss later in this chapter, the observed anisotropies in the CMB radiation support a big bang model that includes an inflationary period and is dominated by dark matter and dark energy.

The Age of the Universe

If the big bang theory is correct, we can use the Hubble constant to determine how long ago the big bang occurred, for the constant tells us how fast galaxies are spreading apart. Here we make the simplifying assumption that the rate of expansion, given by the Hubble constant, has remained constant through time. Even though the assumption is not exactly correct, it allows us to find an approximate age for the universe. Instead of writing v for speed in the Hubble law, substitute it with the definition of average speed: the ratio of distance to time.

$$v = H_0 d, \quad \text{or} \quad \frac{d}{t} = H_0 d.$$

Now choose two widely separated galaxies and let d be the distance between them. Thus, t is the time taken to go that distance, or the age of the universe. Solving the equation for t gives

$$t = 1/H_0.$$

This indicates that the age of the universe is simply the reciprocal of the Hubble constant. This constant is normally expressed as (km/s)/Mly or (km/s)/Mpc. Before we can substitute numbers to calculate the age of the universe, both distances must be expressed in the same units, rather than one in kilometers and the other in millions of light-years. One million light-years is about 9.5×10^{18} kilometers, and thus, a Hubble constant of 20 (km/s)/Mly corresponds to 2.1×10^{-18} (km/s)/km or 2.1×10^{-18} s^{-1}. The age of the universe is the reciprocal of this, or

$$t = \frac{1}{2.1 \times 10^{-18} \text{s}^{-1}} = 4.8 \times 10^{17} \text{s} = 15 \times 10^9 \text{ yr.}$$

This is 15 billion years. On the other hand, using 25 (km/s)/Mly as the value of the Hubble constant gives an age for the universe of 12 billion years.

In this calculation we assumed that galaxies have continued to move apart at the same rate back through their history; that is, that the Hubble constant does not change over time. In fact, we would expect the speeds of galaxies to change. Because of the gravitational force they exert on each other, the recessional speeds of galaxies should be decreasing. This would mean that in the past, they were moving apart faster than they are now and that the age of the universe is therefore less than calculated above. For this reason and because the Hubble constant is not known precisely, 15 billion years is taken as the *upper limit* to the age of the universe. The universe is this age or younger.

The Hubble constant does *not* remain constant as time goes on. It is the slope of the line in the graph of recessional velocity versus distance (for example, see Figure 17-11) as measured during the *current* period of time in the life of the universe.

The most recent combined data from the Wilkinson Microwave Anisotropy Probe (WMAP), Type Ia supernovae, and baryon acoustic oscillations yield a value of about 70.1 ± 1.3 (km/s)/Mpc or about 21.5 ± 0.4 (km/s)/Mly for the Hubble constant. This puts the age of the universe at about 13.73 ± 0.12 billion years.

ADVANCING THE MODEL

Science, Cosmology, and Faith

Where did the matter and energy of the big bang originate? Science cannot answer that question at present. In fact, it seems possible—perhaps likely—that it will never be able to answer that question. For if matter existed in atomic form before the big bang, it did not carry information with it through the big bang. Matter itself thus can tell us nothing about its pre-big bang history. Actually, it is meaningless for us to talk about things "before" or "at the moment of" the big bang. Time did not exist until after the big bang. Because of the extreme conditions involved during the birth of our universe, the known laws of physics do not allow us to start describing its evolution until 10^{-43} seconds after the big bang. After this moment, we can consider the nature of space and time in the same way as we do today.

Does this then mean that science can say that there must be a creator and that science has, after all, found a need for God? An individual scientist may believe this, but science itself cannot use God as the explanation for the big bang or anything else. The reason that science avoids using God for explanations is basically that science has been successful in explaining the material world without reference to a God. Science, by intention, uses natural causes to explain natural effects.

We say that science is successful in its method because scientific explanations of the workings of the material world have led us to further understanding of that world. The fact that the success has come without reference to God indicates that the material universe seems to be describable by completely natural principles.

What about cases where science is unable to find an answer? If science, when it comes to something that it cannot explain at the time, were to explain it by reference to God, the search for an explanation would end. If Newton had used God as an explanation for why things fall to Earth, he would never have developed the theory of gravitation. If we use God as an explanation for the big bang, there would be no reason to look further for a natural explanation. Use of supernatural explanations would shut down science. History, however, tells us that it is profitable to look for natural explanations. Supernatural explanations cannot be used in natural science.

Testability

There is another reason that science cannot use God for an explanation, and this relates to the reason that traditional science does not accept creationism as a science: A theory of science must be able to be shown to be wrong. A theory must be testable. Every theory must be regarded as tentative, as being only the best theory we have at present. It must contain within itself its own possibility of destruction. The 1948 prediction concerning the cosmic microwave background radiation was such a case. If the background radiation had not been found, the big bang theory would have had to have been adjusted, or—if enough such contradictions appeared—the theory would have had to be dropped and replaced with another. This has happened many times in science. It happened to the steady-state theory and to other theories we presented in this text.

On the other hand, if science relied on a creator to explain the inexplicable, there would be nowhere to go, no way to prove that explanation wrong. The question would have already been settled. This is not to say that God might not be the explanation. Many people believe that a creator is the ultimate explanation of everything. Perhaps some questions, like the origin of the material for the big bang, simply cannot be answered without reference to a creator, but in that case, science simply cannot answer the question. The question is beyond the realm of science.

Science does not deny the existence of God. God is simply outside its realm.

As we noted in Chapter 17, the most distant quasar yet found has a redshift of 6.41. This indicates a look-back time of about 96% of the age of the universe. Although the age of the universe is not known exactly, Doppler shift data are accurate enough that we can be confident that the farthest quasar thus found has a look-back time of about 96% of whatever is the correct value for the age.

18-5 The Future: Will Expansion Stop?

What came before the big bang? As we discuss in the preceding Advancing the Model box, this question may not be a scientific one. However, to see how scientists might get a hint at what came before the big bang, we look into the *future*.

If galaxies are moving apart, they will obviously be farther apart in the future than they are now. Where does this stop? There *is* an agent to stop it: gravity.

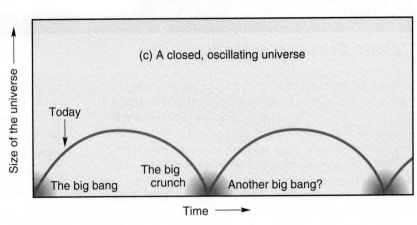

FIGURE 18-13 (a) An open universe would continue to grow in size indefinitely. (b) A closed universe would someday stop growing and begin to contract, assuming that there is no cosmological constant. (c) Could it be possible that a closed universe could oscillate, going through consecutive big bangs and big crunches?

The force of gravity must be slowing the expansion of the universe. The question is, will gravity slow the expansion enough to stop it and bring the galaxies back together?

First, suppose the expansion does not stop. This means, simply, that the clusters continue to get farther apart. **FIGURE 18-13a** illustrates a universe that continues to grow. In this universe, the stars use up the hydrogen fuel that powers them, the glowing stars become fewer, the glow fades, and the universe fizzles out.

On the other hand, suppose the expansion stops, as shown in Figure 18-13b. Gravity begins to pull the galaxies back toward one another. Intelligent beings living on some planet will be able to use the Doppler effect to observe that the galaxies are then getting closer together. The infall will continue until all matter in the universe is condensed into a tremendously dense ball—the "big crunch." What might happen then? Perhaps another big bang, another universe. If this is the future, perhaps it was the past. Perhaps this is what preceded the big bang: a previous universe containing the same matter and energy as ours. If so, then today's universe may be just one phase of a number of oscillations, each having its own big bang. Such a scenario is called an *oscillating universe* (Figure 18-13c). It is a much more exciting prospect than a fizzling-out universe.

A model for an oscillating universe with no beginning or end was first proposed in the 1930s. This model was abandoned because it could not be reconciled with the second law of thermodynamics; this law states that the entropy of a closed system (a measure of its disorder) can never decrease. As a result, if the universe were oscillating, it would actually become larger in every cycle, with each oscillation becoming longer; therefore, looking back, it would also have to have a beginning, a big bang.

New models for an oscillating universe have been proposed. Indeed, computer simulations using quantum modifications to Einstein's general theory of relativity show that in place of a classical big bang there is actually a quantum bounce, leading to a new expansion; however, more work needs to be done to understand better the nature of quantum gravity. In another model, dark energy drives the expansion of the universe to a stage where all matter disintegrates and the universe fragments into patches that are so far apart that they cannot be reconnected. At this point, just before the end of time, *each* patch starts collapsing; it contracts individually, and then bounces out again creating a new universe. In this model, each "causal patch" becomes an independent universe, initially almost empty of matter and entropy; as a result, the model avoids the difficulties encountered during the contraction phase. Future observations could give us enough data to determine the equation of state for dark energy and thus test such models.

◆ A closed universe will stop its expansion only in the absence of an exotic form of energy. An open universe won't stop at all.

oscillating universe model
A big bang theory that holds that the universe goes through repeating cycles of explosion, expansion, and contraction.

Evidence: Distant Galaxies and High-Redshift Type Ia Supernovae

As we described before, the borderline case between an open and a closed universe is called a flat universe. If the universe is flat and assuming no cosmological constant (that is, no influence that supports the universe against collapse), the universe will gradually slow its expansion, but will stop only after an infinite amount of time, never falling back inward. In order for the universe to be flat, however, it must meet an exact condition described by the value of the critical density. If the total mass and energy density of the universe is equal to the critical density, then the universe is flat. For simplicity, astronomers prefer to work with the ratio of the total mass and energy density of the universe to the critical density. This ratio is called the ***density parameter*** (Ω_0). If Ω_0 is equal to 1, the universe is flat and will expand forever, but only barely so. If it is greater than 1, the universe is closed, and it will eventually collapse. If it is less than 1, the universe is open and will expand forever.

In what we just described we assumed that there is no cosmological constant and that gravity is the main factor in determining the future of the universe. But do the observations support this assumption? To answer this question, astronomers study the relationship between distances and recessional velocities for distant galaxies and Type Ia supernovae. If the rate of expansion has decreased (because of gravity) or remained constant or increased (due to the effects of an unknown influence), any deviations from the Hubble law should become obvious at great distances.

FIGURE 18-14a shows the results of a project to measure H_0 based on a Cepheid calibration of a number of independent standard candles (such as Type Ia and Type II supernovae and the Tully-Fisher relation). The data show a linear relationship between recessional velocities and distances. This implies that the rate of expansion has not changed; however, the data go only as far as 400 Mpc, which corresponds to about 1.3 billion years into the past (only about 10% of the age of the universe). Even in the presence of gravity, the observations thus suggest that the rate of expansion has remained approximately constant over the past 1.3 billion light-years. The value of the Hubble constant obtained from the data is about 72 ± 8 (km/s)/Mpc. If we also take into account the current best estimates of the ages of globular clusters (about 12.5 billion years), these results favor a flat universe ($\Omega_0 = 1$) dominated by the existence of some form of exotic energy that supports the expansion of the universe. This

density parameter (Ω_0)
The ratio (denoted by the Greek letter "omega," Ω_0) of the total mass and energy density of the universe to the critical density.

The value of the Hubble constant changes with time. As a result, astronomers refer to times in the past in terms of redshift, not years. Since the time that light left an object at redshift z, the universe has expanded by a factor $1 + z$. At that time, distances between clusters of galaxies were $1/(1 + z)$ as great as they are now.

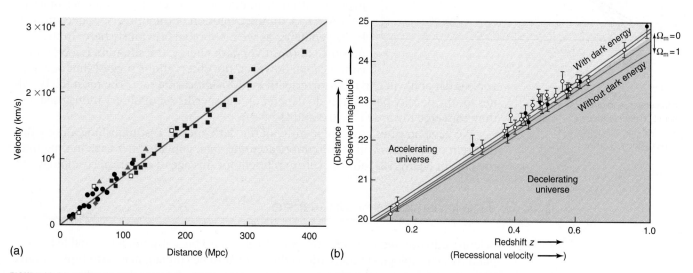

FIGURE 18-14 (a) The Hubble diagram for different standard candles calibrated by Cepheids. (The candles are shown by different symbols; filled squares correspond to Type Ia supernovae.) These are the final results of the HST Key Project (published in 2001). (b) The Hubble diagram for Type Ia supernovae. Supernovae at $z > 0.5$ appear dimmer (and thus farther away) than their redshifts would suggest if the universe were coasting or slowing down due to gravity. The data, published in 1998 by the Supernova Cosmology Project and the High-Z Supernova Search, suggest that the cosmic expansion has been accelerating since the universe was more than half its current age. The red curves correspond to models with $\Omega_\Lambda = 0$ (no dark energy) and range from an empty universe ($\Omega_m = 0$) to a universe of critical density ($\Omega_m = 1$). For a flat universe, the best fit is the blue line. It corresponds to a universe dominated by dark energy, with $\Omega_m = 0.3$ and $\Omega_\Lambda = 0.7$.

dark energy An exotic form of energy whose negative pressure currently accelerates the expansion of the universe.

energy, called ***dark energy***, cannot be detected by its gravitational effects and emits no radiation. It provides a strong negative pressure that, just like the cosmological constant, is currently accelerating the expansion of the universe.

The data shown in Figure 18-14b go as far as 10 billion years (about 75% of the age of the universe). This graph shows the observed magnitude versus redshift of a number of nearby and distant Type Ia supernovae. These objects have very similar absolute magnitudes and thus are great standard candles. Their slow march to a sudden explosive end seems to erase most of the differences among the original stars. Recall from Chapter 12 that the apparent magnitude of an object is related to its distance through the distance modulus. Also, recall that redshift is related to recessional speed. These relationships are not linear; however, the greater the redshift of a supernova, the greater is its recessional velocity; the greater the apparent magnitude of a supernova, the greater is its distance. Figure 18-14b, therefore, is also a graph of distance versus recessional velocity. The low-redshift points in the diagram ($z < 0.1$) are not shown, but they do imply a linear Hubble law consistent with Figure 18-14a as the data go only as far as 2.5 billion years in the past; however, the high-redshift data (up to $z = 1$) go as far as 10 billion years in the past. It is in this region that we see deviations from the linear Hubble law. The different curves correspond to different cosmological predictions, depending on what we assume for the density parameters for matter and dark energy. For a flat universe (as indicated by the latest measurements of the CMB radiation), the best fit is the blue line. This implies that the universe is dominated by dark energy.

Contributions to the density parameter come from three sources: matter (Ω_m), radiation (Ω_{rad}), and any possible form of exotic energy (Ω_Λ); however, as we discussed in the Advancing the Model box on "The Early Universe," the contribution of radiation is negligible to that of matter. We can, therefore, write $\Omega_0 = \Omega_m + \Omega_\Lambda$.

The observational data shown in Figure 18-14 (and in Section 18-7) show that the cosmic expansion is now accelerating and that the universe is dominated by dark energy. FIGURE 18-15 shows how the relative size of the universe (represented by the distance between two widely separated objects) evolves with time in different models. In the absence of dark energy ($\Omega_\Lambda = 0$), the evolution of the universe is determined by its geometry, as we mentioned previously here. In the presence of (positive) dark energy, the situation is a bit more complicated; however, the observations suggest that our universe is flat and will expand forever with an ever-increasing rate. The most likely values for the density parameters do depend on the specific set of observations used, but they converge toward $\Omega_m \approx 0.3$ and $\Omega_\Lambda \approx 0.7$.

We have no clues as to the identity of the dark energy. Distinguishing among the different possibilities will require more accurate data, going further back in time than the data in Figure 18-14b. The future is bright for this age of empirical cosmology.

Ω_0	Ω_m	Ω_Λ	Universe
1.0	0.3	0.7	Flat, open
0.0	0.0	0.0	Empty
0.3	0.3	0.0	Open
1.0	1.0	0.0	Flat
5.0	5.0	0.0	Closed

FIGURE 18-15 The evolution of the universe in different models. There is growing evidence that our universe is following the red curve.

18-6 The Inflationary Universe

Scientists do not like coincidences, and the standard big bang model is unable to explain two cosmological observations that appear to be coincidences. Attempts to solve these two problems, as well as others, led astronomers to propose a modification of the standard model.

The Flatness Problem

The universe seems to be either flat or very nearly flat. This would be an extreme coincidence because a flat universe is a special case. Of all the possible densities that the universe might have, why would it have a density that puts it exactly on the border between open and closed? The universe could be a little more dense or billions of times more dense, and in either case, it would be closed. (If it were much more dense than it is, it would be short lived so that planets—and life—would not have had time to form.) On the other hand, it could be slightly less dense or billions of times less dense, in which case it would be open. (If it were much less dense than it is, gravity would not have gathered the diffuse matter into stars and planets, so again life would not exist.) The *flatness problem* asks, "Of all the possible conditions of the universe, why is it so nearly flat?"

The flatness problem is even worse than just described, however, because if the universe's density had not been exactly equal to the critical density in the beginning, the curvature of the universe would have increased as time passed, and the curvature would be even greater now. Consider the ratio of the actual density of the universe to the critical density. If, immediately after the big bang, that ratio was equal to 1, then the ratio would still be equal to 1 today. If, however, the ratio at the big bang was less than 1, calculations show that it would be *much* less than 1 today. If the ratio just after the big bang had a value greater than 1, the ratio would have become even greater today. For today's ratio to be somewhere between 0.1 and 2, as suggested by our best calculations and observations, it must have been extremely close to 1 at the beginning. Could this be coincidence?

The *inflationary universe model* has an explanation for the flatness of the universe. The model provides details of the first fractions of a second after the big bang, and according to its predictions, during the short time interval between 10^{-35} seconds and 10^{-32} seconds after the big bang, the universe suddenly expanded at an extremely fast rate (FIGURE 18-16). In fact, it grew by a factor of 10^{50} during that time. To understand how this solves the flatness problem, consider the simple analogy of a large balloon. If you balance yourself on the balloon, you will feel the curvature beneath your feet; however, if we expand the balloon to the size of the Earth, what you feel is nothing but flat space. If we now blow up the balloon to a cosmic scale, you can imagine how inflation could vastly flatten the observable universe. The inflationary universe model holds that an "inflation" of the universe took place so quickly that any portion of it that had a great curvature before the inflation became flat as a result of the inflation.

Like any analogy, the balloon story does not work perfectly, for even a large balloon has some curvature. The inflationary model predicts that that curvature was completely removed during the quick expansion; therefore, the universe's flatness is not a coincidence, but a necessary consequence of the brief period of inflation very early in history. Recent measurements of the polarization of the CMB radiation, which we discuss in the next section, confirm some of the predictions of cosmic inflation theories. It is unclear at this stage whether dark energy has any relationship to the period of cosmic inflation.

The Horizon Problem

The CMB radiation is remarkably uniform, no matter in what direction one looks. *COBE* data reveal that, after correcting for the motion of the Earth, the radiation varies in temperature by less than one part in 100,000. This would indicate that the temperature of the universe was extremely uniform at the time that the CMB radiation was emitted. This does not seem possible in the standard model of the big bang because in that model the various portions of the universe could not have been in "communication" with one another when the radiation

flatness problem The inability of the *standard* big bang model to account for the apparent flatness of the universe.

Some scientists support the idea that our universe appears fine tuned so that it allows life as we know it to exist. This *anthropic principle*, in its many variations, has created a controversy. References on this topic are included at the end of this chapter.

If the diameter of a helium nucleus expanded by a factor of 10^{50}, the nucleus would be 40 billion billion light-years across!

inflationary universe model A modification of the big bang model that holds that the early universe experienced a brief period of extremely fast expansion.

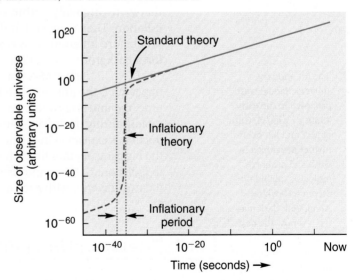

FIGURE 18-16 The solid line shows the size of the universe according to the *standard* big bang theory. The dashed line corresponds to the inflationary theory, according to which the universe's size was much smaller initially than in the standard theory. As a result, uniformity was established early before being stretched by inflation.

FIGURE 18-17 A summary of the big bang theory. The central image—the *WMAP* sky map—is a map of the CMB, the first light to break free in the infant universe. This light emerged about 380,000 years after the big bang. Its appearance is caused by minute temperature variations in the universe at the time the CMB was released. The observed patterns are the seeds for the development of the structures of galaxies we now see billions of years after the big bang.

horizon problem The inability of the *standard* big bang model to account for the directional uniformity of the background radiation.

◆ The inflationary universe model was proposed in the early 1980s by Alan H. Guth of MIT and has been further developed by Guth and other cosmologists, including Stephen Hawking. Along with dark matter, it is now the best explanation we have for the development of the universe.

was emitted. To see why this is so, return to the balloon analogy one more time. First, imagine a balloon that is not expanding, and suppose that thermal energy is added to one portion of the balloon. That energy will spread around the balloon over a time period that depends on how fast the energy travels. Nevertheless, the energy will eventually distribute uniformly around a non-expanding balloon.

Now suppose that the balloon is expanding when energy is added to one portion of it. If the balloon is expanding rapidly enough, the energy will not be able to reach distant portions of the balloon because those portions are moving away too fast. There is a "horizon" beyond which the change in energy cannot be transmitted. In this rapid-expansion case, any portion of the balloon that experiences a change will not communicate this change to the rest of the balloon, and therefore, the properties of the balloon will not be uniform.

In the case of the real universe, a change in one portion can be communicated to another portion with a maximum speed equal to the speed of light. The *standard* big bang model predicts that at the time that the CMB radiation was emitted, the universe was expanding at such a rate that the "horizon" distance was much less than the distance across the universe; therefore, any little change in one part of the universe could not be communicated to faraway parts. This means that there would be no reason for the entire universe to be at the same temperature and astronomers should not observe the same temperature in the background radiation in various directions—hence, the ***horizon problem***.

According to the inflationary universe model, before inflation occurred, the universe was smaller than the horizon distance; therefore, any change in one portion of the universe was transmitted everywhere, and it was possible for the entire universe to be at a uniform temperature. Then inflation occurred. Two parts of the universe that were originally within each other's horizons were outside those horizons after inflation. They were still at the same temperature, however, as a result of their condition before inflation. This is why all parts of today's observable universe show a uniform background radiation.

FIGURE 18-17 is a NASA drawing that summarizes the inflationary big bang theory. At upper left is the universe at the big bang and then just after the big bang. At the latter time, the universe contained extremely small irregularities. The universe then expanded rapidly during the inflationary period. The central image is from the *WMAP*, and its production is explained in the next section. It pictures the universe about 380,000 years after the big bang. By that time, the universe had cooled down enough to become transparent to radiation. Galaxies and stars began to form. The bottom right part of the image shows today's universe, with each dot representing a cluster of galaxies.

18-7 The Grand Scale Structure of the Universe

The success of the inflationary theory at first caused a problem in explaining the formation of galaxies, for in a completely uniform universe, there would be no irregularities around which matter could group into galaxies and clusters of galaxies. Not only did galaxies form, however, but the discovery of extremely old quasars indicates that matter clumped together relatively soon after the big bang.

Discoveries made during the 1980s added to the problem. As we accumulated data on the distribution of clusters of galaxies (FIGURE 18-18), we were able to construct three-dimensional drawings to show their locations. The drawings showed that clusters of galaxies are not distributed uniformly at all, but are arranged as if to form bubbles, with a void between the walls of the bubbles. (See also Figure 17-17.) To visualize this, think of soap bubbles in a sink. Galaxies make up the surfaces of the bubbles, and where the bubbles join, we find the largest clusters of galaxies.

How is the problem of the grand scale structure of the universe resolved? The inflationary model includes a random distribution of density irregularities (perturbations) during the earliest moments of the universe. The amplitudes of these perturbations were smoothed out by the sudden and fast expansion of the universe during inflation. This model explains why the original perturbations would have left such small-scale anisotropies in the CMB radiation.

To understand the observed features in the CMB radiation, consider the universe during its infancy. For the first 376,000 years, the density and tem-

FIGURE 18-18 Each dot on the diagram is a cluster of galaxies. The grey tone in each picture element is a measure of the count of galaxies in this patch of sky. The figure shows that clusters are clumped together in an irregular way.

perature of the universe were so great that it was opaque to electromagnetic radiation. The hydrogen and helium nuclei that were formed in the first few minutes of the universe's life, electrons, and radiation were all tightly coupled together through scattering and electromagnetic interactions. They behaved as a single fluid of **baryons** and photons with a single temperature. In this fluid, the baryons provided the inertia, the photons provided the pressure, and the density perturbations that remained after the big bang provided a mechanism for oscillations. The oscillations were caused by a competition between two factors: gravity and radiation pressure. As a region of excess mass would begin to collapse under its own gravity, becoming even denser, radiation pressure would become sufficient to stop the collapse and cause a rebound. As the universe aged, the horizon grew and oscillations of greater wavelength were included inside the horizon. These oscillations in the baryon-photon fluid sent out pressure waves that propagated at the local speed of sound.

About 376,000 years after the big bang, the universe became cool enough (about 3000 K) that protons were able to capture electrons and form neutral hydrogen. It is at this stage, at redshift of about $z = 1100$, that matter and radiation decoupled from each other. It is also at this stage that the radiation last interacted strongly with matter and the universe became transparent. This radiation is what we see today as the CMB. After decoupling, the interaction between the radiation and the now neutral matter was not significant. As a result, the temperature of the radiation evolved differently from that of matter. The photons were free to propagate in the universe carrying on them the signature of the density perturbations just before the decoupling. Meanwhile, with the release of their pressure support, the baryons started collecting under the influence of the gravity of the dark matter. Dark matter does not interact with radiation, and therefore, any dark matter formed early on would have been free to gravitationally collapse much earlier. It is these regions, where baryons collect under the influence of dark matter, which will grow into the structures we see today.

After decoupling, the wavelengths of the photons that last interacted strongly with matter have stretched so much due to the expansion of the universe that we see them as the CMB photons. These photons reach us from all directions and can tell us a great deal about the early universe. Photons that started their journey from very dense regions on this surface lost more energy escaping gravity than photons

baryons Subatomic particles, including the proton, the neutron, and a number of unstable, heavier particles. (The term *baryon* is derived from the Greek "barys," meaning "heavy.")

The transition from an opaque universe to a transparent one was not instantaneous. It lasted for a time interval that corresponds to a change in redshift of about 100.

FIGURE 18-19 The *COBE* map of the early universe. This false-color image shows tiny variations in the intensity of the CMB radiation. The features traced in this map stretch across the visible universe. The smallest feature in this map is larger than the largest features seen by optical telescopes.

◆ *BOOMERANG* stands for *Balloon Observations of Millimetric Extragalactic Radiation and Geophysics*. The project involved cosmologists from Canada, Italy, the United Kingdom, and the United States.

◆ The *BOOMERANG* telescope flew for 10.5 days (December 1998 to January 1999) around the Antarctic continent on a 800,000 m³ balloon at an altitude of 36 km, above 99% of our atmosphere. It was launched in early January 2003 for about 10 days.

from less dense regions. Because energy is related to temperature, this implies that a certain density perturbation on this surface gives rise to a certain temperature perturbation. As a result, the CMB radiation carries with it information about the early universe in the form of temperature anisotropies.

In 1992, the *COBE* team reported finding tiny irregularities (variations) in the CMB radiation that amounted to a deviation of only 0.00003 K! To detect these variations, thought to be due to tiny differences in the temperature of the early universe, the *COBE* team first had to subtract irregularities caused by known sources of radiation. These include the effect of the Sun's radiation, the effect caused by known radiators within the Milky Way, and a slight Doppler shift in the radiation that is caused by our motion through space. **FIGURE 18-19** represents the *COBE* map of the early universe. The blue and red spots represent temperature variations and thus correspond to regions of greater or lesser density in the early universe; they give us a sense as to how matter and energy were distributed before matter gave rise to the structures we see today. These tiny irregularities are the roots of the structures we see in today's universe. Without the anisotropy, there would be no galaxies, no stars, no Earth, no us.

The CMB radiation gives us a view of the early universe, and we can use it as a tool to probe the conditions prevalent at the time. When we look at the CMB radiation, we are looking back to a time before the first stars and galaxies formed, when the universe was only about 376,000 years old. The spectrum of the CMB radiation and its almost perfect uniformity in all directions can only have one source: a hot, uniform, dense early universe. Five years after *COBE*, which had an angular resolution of about 7°, the *BOOMERANG* project gave us a map of the early universe that was about 40 times more detailed.

The *BOOMERANG* images, like the one shown in the chapter-opening figure, bring the CMB into sharp focus. This sharp snapshot of the early universe offers us a powerful tool in distinguishing among competing theoretical models on the evolution of the universe. As we discussed earlier, after decoupling and as the universe expanded, the photons that last interacted strongly with matter cooled down to become the CMB radiation, while carrying with them the pattern of the "sound waves" at the moment the universe became transparent. We now use these waves as a cosmic ultrasound to image the conditions in the early universe. The tiny temperature variations we observe correspond to tiny density fluctuations in the primordial soup of particles. These density fluctuations are thought to grow by gravitational attraction into the structures we see today. The visible patterns in the *BOOMERANG* images confirm predictions of the patterns that would result from sound waves racing through the early universe.

The sizes of the hot and cold spots in the *BOOMERANG* data reflect directly on the geometry of space (its curvature) and thus its fate. FIGURE 18-20 includes a *BOOMERANG* image (top) and three computer-simulated images, differing only in whether the universe is closed, flat, or open (bottom). Computer simulations suggest that in a universe whose geometry is flat, the images of the CMB radiation should be dominated by hot and cold spots of about 1° in size (bottom center). In a universe in which geometry is not flat, the curvature of space will distort the images. Specifically, in a universe that is closed, the images will be magnified by the curvature and structures will appear larger than 1° on the sky (bottom left). In a universe that is open, the images will appear smaller (bottom right). FIGURE 18-21 shows how the geometry of space affects the size of the spots in the CMB radiation. In a flat universe, lines that are initially parallel remain parallel when extended. In a closed universe, parallel lines converge, whereas in an open universe, parallel lines diverge. The *BOOMERANG* images indicate that our universe is very nearly flat.

The *BOOMERANG* results were not only confirmed, but also extended to finer resolution by *MAXIMA*. This was another balloon-borne project, which was more

FIGURE 18-20 The *BOOMERANG* images allow us to determine the geometry of space. The image (top) is compared to images generated by computer simulations for a closed (bottom left), flat (bottom center) and open (bottom right) universe. The observations suggest that our universe is very nearly flat.

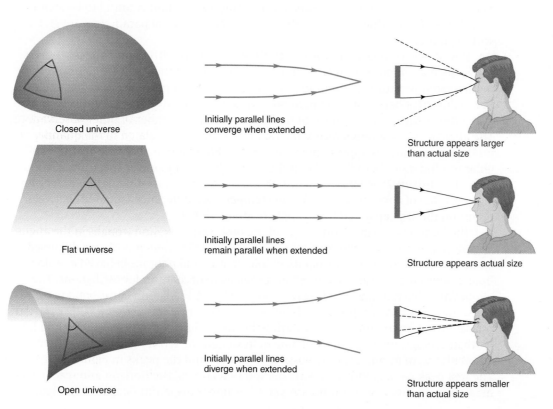

Closed universe

Initially parallel lines converge when extended

Structure appears larger than actual size

Flat universe

Initially parallel lines remain parallel when extended

Structure appears actual size

Open universe

Initially parallel lines diverge when extended

Structure appears smaller than actual size

FIGURE 18-21 The geometry of space affects the angular size of an object because the curvature of space determines the path followed by a light beam. If the universe is closed, a structure in the CMB will appear larger than actual size. If the universe is flat, the structure will appear actual size. If the universe is open, the structure will appear smaller than actual size.

FIGURE 18-22 *WMAP*'s image of the infant universe brings the *COBE* image into sharp focus. It shows temperature fluctuations, with red spots being the hottest and blue spots being coldest. Foreground radiation from our Galaxy, which *WMAP* distinguishes by observing at five microwave frequency bands, has been subtracted from the equatorial band. These fluctuations correspond to the seeds that grew to become galaxies. The new image provides strict limits to a number of cosmological parameters.

COBE

WMAP

MAXIMA stands for Millimeter *An*isotrophy *Ex*periment *Im*aging *A*rray. The project includes scientists from five countries. The balloon last flew in 1999. The project's sensitivity was from 4° to 10'.

WMAP observes the sky from an orbit about a semistable point on the line connecting the Earth and Sun (1.5 million km from Earth in the direction opposite the Sun). As the probe follows the Earth around the Sun, it observes the full sky every 6 months. *WMAP* is a partnership between Princeton and NASA.

sensitive than *BOOMERANG* but looked at a smaller area of the sky. The *WMAP*, launched in June 2001, has made an accurate map of the relative CMB temperature over the full sky with angular resolution of about 0.2° and sensitivity of about 20 μK. The probe measures temperature differences between points about 140° apart on the sky using five different frequency bands. The *WMAP* image of the CMB is much sharper than the image obtained by *COBE*, as shown in **FIGURE 18-22**.

What do the tiny temperature fluctuations tell us about the universe? As we discussed earlier, the observed temperature fluctuations imprinted on the CMB radiation reflect the conditions set in motion just after the big bang. That is, these fluctuations are like a fingerprint of the infant universe that we could use to compare with fingerprints predicted by various cosmic theories. The results from the projects observing the CMB all point to the same match. Our universe has about 4.6% normal matter (which makes us and the stars), about 23.3% dark matter (a mysterious, nonluminous form of matter that is indirectly detected by its gravity), and the remaining 72.1% is dark energy. (We discuss this exotic form of energy responsible for accelerating the expansion of the universe in the Advancing the Model box on page 541.) Also, the *WMAP* results suggest that the big bang occurred 13.73 ± 0.12 billion years ago and that the CMB is a snapshot of the universe when it was only about 376 ± 3 thousand years old. The Hubble constant is found to be about 70.1 ± 1.3 (km/s)/Mpc, and a number of other cosmological parameters are given with high precision.

How do we compare the various CMB observations with theory? **FIGURE 18-23** shows such a comparison. It is a graph of the strength of the CMB temperature fluctuations (temperature-fluctuation power) versus their angular size. The data points (including error bars) correspond to observations from four different projects. The curve shows the best theoretical fit to these data plus a number of other observations. The angular size of a temperature fluctuation on the sky is related to the quantity "ℓ" on the horizontal axis approximately as $180°/\ell$. For example, because *WMAP*'s angular resolution is about 0.2°, the probe cannot follow the power spectrum beyond about $\ell = 180°/0.2° = 900$. In Figure 18-23, the temperature-fluctuation power for a given value of ℓ measures the average temperature difference (squared) between points on the sky separated by an angle of about $180°/\ell$.

The locations, heights, and shapes of the observed peaks and troughs in the angular power spectrum serve to constrain the cosmological parameters. As we discussed earlier, before decoupling, normal (baryonic) matter and photons behaved as a single fluid. In this fluid, density perturbations provided a mechanism for oscillations. The temperature fluctuations we observe today in the CMB radiation correspond to the density and velocity components of the oscillations during this period (**FIGURE 18-24**). An oscillation at its maximum density during the decoupling will appear brighter and hotter than average, whereas an oscillation at its minimum density will appear colder.

With this in mind, it is now possible to understand the peaks in Figure 18-23. The first peak corresponds to a perturbation that crossed the horizon and reached its maximum density just when the universe became transparent (stage "b" in Figure

ADVANCING THE MODEL

Dark Energy

Observations of Type Ia supernovae and the CMB radiation suggest the existence of dark energy and so does the observed large scale structure of the universe. An imprint of dark energy on the CMB radiation was found in 2003 by correlating millions of galaxies in the Sloan Digital Sky Survey and CMB temperature maps from *WMAP*. This physical evidence for the existence of dark energy can be understood as follows. As a CMB photon passes through a gravitational well of either ordinary or dark matter, it gains energy as it falls into the well and loses energy as it comes out of the well; the overall effect should be zero in the absence of dark energy; however, observations show that the CMB temperature is a bit higher in regions with more matter, suggesting the presence of a repulsive force.

Observations of Type Ia supernovae suggest that dark energy began boosting the universe's expansion when it was about 5 billion years old; it overtook gravity and started accelerating the expansion when the universe was about 8 billion years old.

What is the nature of dark energy? A number of ideas have been suggested, and the following are the leading two forms. The first form is Einstein's cosmological constant, a constant energy density that fills space in a homogeneous way. The second form is a dynamic field, called *quintessence*, whose energy density changes as a function of time and space. Precision observations of the acceleration of the universe's expansion are needed to distinguish between the two forms.

In the form of the cosmological constant, dark energy can be considered as the intrinsic energy of a volume of space, and as such, it is sometimes called *"vacuum energy."* It is estimated by cosmologists to be about 10^{-29} g/cm^3.

(According to the special theory of relativity, energy is related to mass; as the universe expands, ordinary mass, and thus ordinary energy, gets diluted.) Even though most theories of particle physics predict that the quantum vacuum will have energy, its magnitude is 10^{120} times bigger than estimated by cosmologists!

In the form of quintessence, dark energy results in a slightly slower acceleration of the universe's expansion and it is very light so that it does not form structures like ordinary matter. Even though fields such as quintessence are predicted by the standard model of high-energy physics, such fields are supposed to have large masses. This is a similar problem to that of the cosmological constant. Support for a time-varying dark energy comes from observations of gamma-ray bursts. Even though their intrinsic energy varies greatly, their "wattage" can be determined fairly accurately; they are also brighter and more distant than Type Ia supernovae. A Hubble diagram similar to that of Figure 18-14b (covering GRBs up to a redshift of 6.30) shows a better fit for a time-varying dark energy.

The fate of the universe depends on the nature of dark energy. The expansion of the universe could continue forever, in which case we will slowly lose contact with the rest of the universe beyond our local supercluster. It is possible that the strength of dark energy decreases with time or that it even becomes attractive, in which case the influence of gravity could lead to a big crunch. If its strength increases with time, then it will overcome all other forces and lead to a big rip, tearing apart everything in the universe. It has also been suggested that the observed effects of dark energy are nothing but the effects of gravitational waves generated during the inflationary epoch of the universe.

18-24). The remaining odd peaks correspond to perturbations that underwent an additional integral number of oscillations by this time. The even peaks correspond to perturbations at their minimum density (for example, stage "d" in Figure 18-24); these perturbations give rise to power peaks of smaller heights because the rebound must fight against gravity. The troughs (for example, stage "c" in Figure 18-24) correspond to positions of maximum velocity. The amplitude of the fluctuations is reduced as ℓ increases (on the smallest scales) because the transition from an opaque universe to a transparent one was not instantaneous. The shape of the spectrum in Figure 18-23 depends then on the details of the oscillations, and it is a direct result of the conditions that existed at the time of decoupling; therefore, this spectrum serves to constrain the cosmological parameters. The curve in Figure 18-23 depends on the values of seven different cosmological parameters that were adjusted to fit the data.

The location of the first peak in Figure 18-23 is related to the geometry of the universe. That is so because the physical scale associated with the first peak is the horizon size at the time of decoupling. At this time, the universe became cool enough

FIGURE 18-23 The angular power spectrum of the CMB temperature fluctuations based on data obtained by four different projects. The curve shows the best theoretical fit to the observational data. The third overtone provides evidence for a neutrino background whose density is less than 0.65%. Courtesy of NASA and the WMAP Science Team. Modified from M.R. Nolta et. al., *ApJS* 180 (2009): 296–305. Reproduced by permission of the AAS.

(about 3000 K) that protons were able to capture electrons and form neutral hydrogen. This stage clearly occurs at about $z = 1100$, and the angle subtended by the physical scale at this redshift depends on the geometry of the universe. The first peak occurs at $\ell \approx 200$, which corresponds to an angular size for the temperature fluctuations of about $180°/\ell \approx 1°$. This is consistent with a flat universe, as predicted by the inflationary universe theory.

Astronomers have hailed the *WMAP* results as the beginning of precision cosmology. Observing temperature fluctuations at the 10^{-6} K scale is not easy. Imagine that a band is playing random tunes at a location far away from us. Between the band and us there are many sources that generate noise. Our job is to understand the nature of these sources, remove their contributions to the overall sound we receive, and interpret the final signal we get from the band. *WMAP*'s precision strongly confirms the standard inflationary big bang scenario.

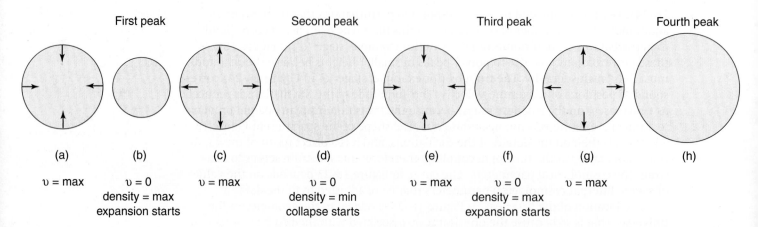

FIGURE 18-24 This illustration shows the relationship between the peaks and troughs in the angular power spectrum and the density and velocity components of the oscillations during the decoupling era.

In addition to the spectrum shown in Figure 18-23, *WMAP* mapped the intensity and direction of **linear polarization** everywhere on the CMB sky. Recall our discussion of light as an electromagnetic wave in Chapter 4. We say that light is linearly polarized when its electric field oscillates in a fixed plane, just like a length of rope that moves up and down in a vertical plane while the wave progresses horizontally. Natural light is a combination of random and rapidly changing fields that have a range of wavelengths. As a result, natural light is not polarized. A device that takes natural (unpolarized) light and transforms it into polarized light is a polarizer, as do certain sunglasses, for example; however, there are a number of natural processes that produce polarized light, one of which is scattering. The illustration in FIGURE 18-25 makes use of polarizing sunglasses to show how *WMAP* "sees" polarized light. The results of *WMAP*'s polarization measurements are shown in FIGURE 18-26, which correlates the temperature fluctuations and the polarization in the CMB radiation between points in the sky separated by an angle of about $180°/\ell$. The curve in Figure 18-26 is *not* a fit to the data; it is actually a *prediction* based on the observed temperature anisotropies in the CMB radiation. The overall shape of the cross-power spectrum contains a wealth of information about the conditions in the early universe. The rise in this curve at low ℓ values (large angles, about 90°) indicates that the first stars in the universe formed very quickly, about 430 million years after the era of decoupling.

Even though *WMAP* does not see the light of the first stars directly, the observed polarized light serves as the signature of the ultraviolet light released by the first stars. This ultraviolet light began the reionization of the neutral hydrogen that formed after decoupling. FIGURE 18-27 shows a sequence of events in the history of the universe, from the initial density perturbations to the formations of billions upon billions of stars and galaxies. FIGURE 18-28 is a more detailed illustration of important events in the early stages of the universe.

The *WMAP* results, along with results from other CMB projects and a range of different and independent observations (such as the galaxy and supernovae surveys), support the inflationary scenario. FIGURE 18-29 shows how the combination of data from different projects allows us to limit the range of values for the average density

Polarization: How It Works

how we see it...

how WMAP sees it...

FIGURE 18-25 This illustration demonstrates how *WMAP* sees polarized light. The polarization of the CMB radiation was produced by the scattering of the cosmic light when it last strongly interacted with matter.

linear polarization The situation when the electric field in an electromagnetic wave oscillates in a fixed plane.

FIGURE 18-26 The cross-power spectrum that correlates the temperature fluctuations and the polarization in the CMB radiation between points in the sky separated by an angle of about 180°/ℓ. The curve is a *prediction* based on the observed temperature anisotropies in the CMB radiation. The rise in the curve at low ℓ values indicates that the first stars in the universe formed very quickly. Courtesy of NASA and the WMAP Science Team. Modified from M.R. Nolta et. al., *ApJS* 180 (2009): 296–305. Reproduced by permission of the AAS.

◆ Polarization data from the Cosmic Background Imager (CBI) provide strong support for the standard model of the universe. CBI is a microwave telescope array located at a high plateau (5 km above sea level) in Chile.

FIGURE 18-27 A sequence of events in the life of the universe. The first frame shows temperature fluctuations (as color differences) in the CMB radiation observed by *WMAP*. These temperature fluctuations correspond to slight density perturbations. The second frame shows matter condensing to regions of higher and higher density as a result of gravitational attraction. The third frame shows the period of formation of the first stars, about 350 million years after the big bang. The fourth frame shows a greater number of stars and galaxies forming along the filaments first seen in frame two. The last frame shows the modern era, billions upon billions of stars and galaxies that grew from the seeds planted in the early universe.

of matter in space Ω_m (on the horizontal axis) and the density of dark energy in space Ω_Λ (on the vertical axis). The results from CMB projects support cosmological models whose parameters lie in the blue region. This region is concentrated near the diagonal red line, which corresponds to a flat universe. The results from the supernovae studies support cosmological models whose parameters lie in the yellow region. The results from surveys of galaxy clusters support cosmological models whose parameters lie in the orange region. If all measurements are correct, then only models whose parameters lie in the green overlap area are allowed. This region indicates that our universe has a flat geometry, started with a big bang, and will continue expanding.

Cosmic Evolution

Our efforts to look back in time and understand the conditions of the early universe are continuing through a number of space missions and other projects. We are slowly putting together a photo album of the universe's life. The CMB projects are giving us a snapshot of the universe during its infancy while observations with space and ground telescopes are providing us with pictures of its early adolescent years.

As we discussed earlier, after decoupling, the first neutral atoms of hydrogen and helium started forming. This transition plunged the universe into darkness because stars had not formed yet. When stars started forming these *dark ages* slowly gave way to a *cosmic renaissance*; the first stars were large in size and massive. They formed at a very fast rate and emitted huge amounts of ultraviolet light that ionized atoms in their surrounding region, slowly lifting the fog of the dark ages, starting at about 430 million years after the big bang. This *reionization* and heating of the universe slowed down further galaxy formation, making it harder for gravity to form small galaxies.

Time		Temperature
0	Big Bang	∞
10^{-32} sec	End of Inflation	10^{19} K
100 sec	Formation of Deuterium and Helium	10^9 K
1 month	CMB Spectrum Fixed	10^7 K
10,000 yrs	Radiation Energy = Matter Energy	20,000 K
376,000 yrs	CMB Last Scattering (Decoupling)	2970 K
	Dark Ages	
430 million yrs	Reionization	32 K
13.7 billion yrs	Present Universe	2.7 K

FIGURE 18-28 Important events in the early stages of the universe, including the formation of deuterium and helium 100 seconds after the big bang. During the era of decoupling (about 376,000 years after the big bang), radiation last interacted strongly with matter and the universe became transparent. This "surface of last scatter" for the CMB radiation is analogous to the light coming through the clouds to our eyes on a cloudy day.

Indeed, *Chandra* observations of distant quasars show that the universe at an age of a billion years was dominated by fewer, larger galaxies instead of more numerous, smaller galaxies. Infrared observations using ESO's VLT (in 2001) reveal that many rather large galaxies (some with spiral structure similar to that seen in nearby galaxies) existed at a time when the universe was less than 1 billion years old. These galaxies appear to have already formed most of their stars, and they probably account for at least half the total luminous mass of the universe at that time. Also, *HST* observations of some of the most distant quasars show the presence of iron and other heavier elements in their spectra; because such elements form during a supernova explosion and the life cycles of the progenitor stars are 500-800 million years, these observations support the idea that the first quasar engines started slightly before the universe was 1 billion years old. Even though stars continue to be formed today, the rate of star formation has been declining since the early years. Surveys of galaxies, using space telescopes and the tool of gravitational lensing, show that galaxies existed very early in the universe's life, when it was about 500 million years old. The surveys also show that the number of bright galaxies increases between 700 and 900 million years probably due to merging; this supports the hierarchical theory of galaxy formation described in Chapter 17.

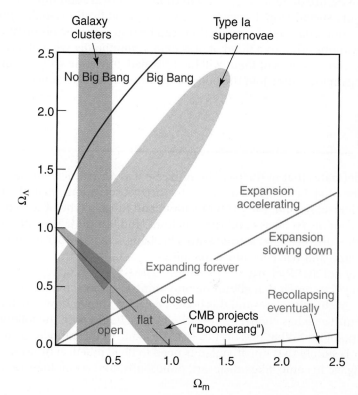

FIGURE 18-29 A comparison between results from CMB projects, surveys of galaxy clusters, and studies of Type Ia supernovae suggests that our universe is flat, started with a big bang, and will continue expanding. The horizontal axis shows Ω_m, the average density of matter in space compared with the critical density. Such matter (normal and dark) slows down the expansion of the universe. The vertical axis shows Ω_Λ, the density of the dark energy in the universe compared with the critical density. Such dark energy causes the expansion of the universe to accelerate. The latest results suggest that $\Omega_m = 0.279 \pm 0.015$, $\Omega_\Lambda = 0.721 \pm 0.015$, and $\Omega_0 = 1$ with an uncertainty of 1%. Courtesy of BOOMERANG Collaboration.

FIGURE 18-30 A computer model of the universe at an age of about 2 billion years. Gravity causes matter to arrange itself in thin filaments. Yellow, red, and blue correspond to high, medium, and low gas density, respectively. Stars will form in the yellow regions and slowly stream along the filaments. When the stars meet at the intersections of the filaments, they gradually form the galaxies we know today.

Three-dimensional maps of the large-scale structure of the universe, including hundreds of thousands of galaxies, show variations in galactic distribution on a scale of 450 million light-years; this directly reflects the temperature variations observed in the CMB radiation. Such maps also support the case for dark matter and dark energy by showing that the observed density fluctuations in the universe agree with theoretical predictions. They also support the idea that the universe has a spongy structure (**FIGURE 18-30**), with galaxies forming in nests of dark matter, clustering close to each other along filaments and having their rotation axes oriented along the direction of the filaments.

Studies of the dark ages will provide even more data to test the inflationary universe model. Astronomers have started studying the shadows that the first atoms imprinted on the CMB radiation. Between 20 and 100 million years after the big bang, the temperature of the universe was such that hydrogen atoms could absorb a 21-cm CMB photon. To observe such absorption during the early stages of the universe's expansion and because of this expansion, astronomers must study the CMB radiation at longer wavelengths, between 6 and 21 meters.

All of the recent observations confirm the generally accepted cosmological model that astronomers constructed over the past decade. **FIGURE 18-31** compares our current understanding of the make-up of the universe now and at its infancy. The model is, however, problematic. For example, because it is probable that ordinary matter and dark matter originate through different mechanisms, why is the abundance of ordinary matter similar (within an order of magnitude) to that of dark matter? Also, because the total abundance of matter is rapidly changing compared with that of dark energy as the universe expands, why are the two so similar (within an order of magnitude)? Finally, what is the nature of dark energy? Even though there are still uncertainties, the model is not pure speculation, for each of its various modifications makes predictions about today's universe, and the predictions can be tested against observations.

As new observations bring us a flood of new data, undoubtedly we will have to revise the models. Some aspects of them will be discarded, but some will live on to be tested again and again until they join the body of firmly established science.

Composition of the universe	Universe at 376,000 years	Universe now
Atoms	12%	4.6%
Dark Matter	63%	23%
Dark Energy	< 1%	72%
Neutrinos	10%	< 1%
Photons	15%	< 1%

FIGURE 18-31 The make-up of the universe now and at its infancy.

Science progresses best when observations force us to alter our preconceptions.
Astronomer Vera Rubin.

Conclusion

The big bang model states that in the past the universe was once much smaller, hotter, and denser. The model is supported mainly by three observations: first, the expansion of the universe; second, the CMB radiation; and third, by the observed proportions of light elements (such as deuterium, helium, and lithium). The latest results are consistent with a universe that started with a big bang, is about 13.7 billion years old, has flat geometry, and will continue expanding.

In *The Nature of Reality*,* Richard Morris writes, "The scientific conception of the universe has changed so much that about the only thing that has remained the same is the word itself." In this chapter—and this book—we have shown how much our perception of the universe has changed. Nevertheless, we might pose the following question to a cosmologist: "What practical use can be made of the study of cosmology?" The answer is simply that not all pursuits need to have practical or useful consequences. We engage in some, like music, art, philosophy, and cosmology, for the

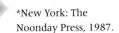

*New York: The Noonday Press, 1987.

sheer intellectual and artistic pleasure they provide. Curiosity is part of human nature, and questions like those raised in this chapter are among the most fundamental that can be asked—and perhaps answered—by science.

Our astronomical quest began 17 chapters ago in our home—the solar system. As you look back on the geocentric and heliocentric theories presented in the first few chapters, we hope that you see them as small, beginning steps in the development of today's view of the universe. After studying the solar system, we traveled outward to the stars and then much farther to galaxies. Finally, our study of cosmology considered the universe as a whole. We hope that this has given you a broader perspective on the natural world and a better appreciation of how the process of science helps us to understand the magnificent universe of which we are a part. We also hope that your quest for the universe will continue throughout your life.

Future data from space satellites should help astronomers choose among competing inflationary models. The European-based *Planck Surveyor*, launched in 2009, will map the CMB in unprecedented detail.

STUDY GUIDE

1. An open universe is one that
   A. will eventually collapse to form "a big crunch."
   B. will never stop expanding.
   C. [Either A or B above, depending on its density.]

2. Einstein's conviction that the universe is closed and finite
   A. resulted directly from his general theory of relativity.
   B. resulted directly from his special theory of relativity.
   C. was a belief that caused him to make a change in his general theory of relativity.
   D. was a belief that caused him to make a change in his special theory of relativity.

3. What *evidence* leads us to believe that the universe is expanding?
   A. The big bang theory.
   B. The inflationary universe theory.
   C. The expansion of the solar system.
   D. The redshift of most galaxies.
   E. [All of the above.]

4. The assumption of isotropy states that the universe looks the same
   A. at all times.
   B. in all locations.
   C. in all directions.
   D. [All of the above.]

5. The cosmological principle refers to
   A. a comparison of our location in the universe to other locations in the universe.
   B. the redshift used to determine distances.
   C. Cepheid variables used to determine magnitude and therefore distance.
   D. the Doppler effect used to determine velocities.
   E. [Both B and C above.]

6. The existence of the 3-K background radiation supports
   A. the big bang theory.
   B. the steady-state theory.
   C. the big bang theory and the steady-state theory about equally.

   D. neither the big bang theory nor the steady-state theory, for neither can explain it.

7. Big bang theories predict _____ speed for the most distant galaxies than do steady state theories.
   A. a lesser
   B. a greater
   C. the same

8. The Hubble law is a relationship between galaxies'
   A. redshifts and colors.
   B. distances and redshifts.
   C. redshifts and spectral types.
   D. colors and spectral types.

9. If present data are correct, the universe is
   A. closed, but not oscillating.
   B. closed and oscillating.
   C. flat.
   D. open.

10. A better knowledge of which quantity would most aid us in determining whether the universe is open or closed?
    A. The age of the Earth.
    B. The age of the solar system.
    C. The size of the Galaxy.
    D. The average density of the universe.
    E. [All of the above would help about equally.]

11. What *evidence* indicates that an explosion took place at the beginning of the universe?
    A. The density of matter in the universe.
    B. Low-intensity radiation from all directions.
    C. The big bang theory.
    D. The inflationary universe theory.
    E. The existence of supernovae.

12. If the average density of the universe is less than the critical density, the universe
    A. will expand forever.
    B. will eventually collapse.
    C. was produced in a big bang.
    D. is an inflationary universe.
    E. violates the laws of energy conservation.

13. Suppose that you read that astronomers calculate the maximum age of the universe to be 15 billion years. Their calculation is based on
    A. calculations of the density of matter in the universe.
    B. the Hubble constant.
    C. the age of rocks on Earth and Moon.
    D. the inflationary universe theory.
    E. [All of the above.]

14. The Hubble law is based on
    A. the big bang theory.
    B. the oscillating universe theory.
    C. redshift data.
    D. inflationary theories.
    E. [None of the above.]

15. Which of the following forces may halt the expansion of the universe?
    A. Nuclear forces.
    B. Electrical forces.
    C. Gravitational forces.

16. The cosmological redshift indicates that
    A. most stars in the Galaxy are moving away from the Sun.
    B. most planets are moving away from ours.
    C. stars at greater distances are hotter.
    D. space is expanding.
    E. [All of the above.]

17. The horizon problem and the flatness problem
    A. are solved by the standard big bang theory.
    B. are solved by the inflationary universe theory.
    C. have not yet been solved by modern cosmology.

18. Which of the following is/are *assumptions* of cosmology?
    A. The cosmological redshift.
    B. The homogeneity of the universe.
    C. Universality of physical laws.
    D. [Both B and C above.]
    E. [All of the above.]

19. The discovery of the cosmic background radiation was made by
    A. Jocelyn Bell, a British graduate student.
    B. cosmologists early in the twentieth century.
    C. two Bell Telephone employees.
    D. the *COBE* satellite.
    E. Edwin Hubble.

20. When we talk about the cosmological expansion of the universe, what is expanding?
    A. The planets are getting farther apart.
    B. The stars of the Galaxy are getting farther apart.
    C. All galaxies are getting farther apart from one another.
    D. Clusters of galaxies are getting farther apart from one another.
    E. [All of the above, for the entire universe is expanding.]

21. The *BOOMERANG* project
    A. had as its purpose a search for gravitational lensing.
    B. had as its purpose a search for the edge of the universe.
    C. examined the CBM before the *COBE* satellite was launched.
    D. examined the CBM after *COBE* data was all received.

22. It is said that the universe is expanding. Explain just what this means.

23. Explain how, if almost all galaxies are moving away from ours, we are not necessarily at or near the center.

24. Name and explain three basic assumptions of cosmology.

25. What is background radiation, and how does it enter the discussion of cosmological theories?

26. How is the age of the universe calculated?

27. Describe two methods of determining how quickly the expansion of the universe is slowing.

28. What is the oscillating universe?

1. Describe at least six steps in the historical progression of our ideas of the universe from Ptolemy's geocentric universe to Einstein's relativistic space curvature.

2. Quasars do not exist in our part of the universe. Why is this not a violation of the homogeneity principle?

3. Explain why a flat universe would be such a special case that it would seem to be an extremely unlikely state of the universe.

4. Why did Einstein add a term in his equation that predicted a repulsion force?

5. Popular science videos that illustrate the Big Bang commonly show an explosion as seen from outside. What would it mean to be "outside" the Big Bang? Comment on the noise that often accompanies such illustrations.

6. Discuss the observation of the CMB radiation as an example of the confirmation of a theory, comparing it with the prediction of stellar parallax in the 1600s.

7. The age of the universe calculated from the Hubble constant assumes a constant velocity of recession for galaxies. If, in fact, galaxies were moving faster at an earlier time, is the universe older or younger than calculated? Show your reasoning.

8. Where in the universe did the big bang occur? Explain.

9. It has been said—perhaps only half in jest—that when astronomers come on a problem they cannot solve, they use a black hole. Give two examples that may have led someone to say this.

10. Explain why the horizon problem exists in the standard big bang model.

11. The horizon problem results from difficulties explaining how the background radiation can be so uniform in all directions; however, Figure 18-19 shows that it is not perfectly uniform. Explain.

12. Explain how the *COBE* results of Figure 18-19 relate to the universe of today.

1. If the Hubble constant is 20 (km/s)/Mly, what is the maximum age of the universe? Repeat for a Hubble constant of 17 (km/s)/Mly.

2. Using Wien's law (Section 4-4), show that the blackbody curve for an object at temperature 3 K peaks in the microwave region of the electromagnetic spectrum.

At what part of the spectrum does the blackbody curve of a 3000-K object peak?

3. The observed redshift of a quasar is $z = 5$. Show that its speed due to the expansion of the universe is about 94.6% of the speed of light.

1. S. Weinberg, *The First Three Minutes* (New York: Basic Books, 1988).

2. S. Hawking, *A Brief History of Time* (New York: Bantam Books, 1988).

3. M. Rees, *Before the Beginning* (Reading, MA: Addison Wesley Longman, 1997).

4. M. Rowan-Robinson, *The Nine Numbers of the Cosmos* (New York: Oxford University Press, 1999).

5. D. Goldsmith, *The Runaway Universe* (New York: Perseus Books, 2000).

6. John D. Barrow and Frank J. Tipler, *The Anthropic Cosmological Principle* (New York: Oxford University Press, 1986).

7. Nick Bostrom's Web site devoted to the anthropic principle: http://www.anthropic-principle.com.

8. Gale E. Christianson, *Edwin Hubble, Mariner of the Nebulae* (Farrar, Straus, and Giroux, 1995).

9. "Inflation in a Low-Density Universe," by M. A. Buchner and D. N. Spergel, in *Scientific American* (January, 1999).

10. "Mapping the Universe," by S. D. Landy, in *Scientific American* (June, 1999).

11. "Cosmological Antigravity," by L. M. K. Krauss, in *Scientific American* Special Edition (December, 2002).

12. "Is Space Finite?" by J.-P. Luminet, G. D. Starkman, and J. R. Weeks, in *Scientific American* Special Edition (December, 2002).

13. "Surveying Spacetime with Supernovae," by C. J. Hogan, R. P. Kirshner, and N. B. Suntzeff, in *Scientific American* Special Edition (December, 2002).

14. "The Search for Dark Matter," by D. B. Cline, in *Scientific American* (March, 2003).

15. "Reading the Blueprints of Creation," by M. A. Strauss, in *Scientific American* (February, 2004).

16. "The Cosmic Symphony," by W. Hu and M. White, in *Scientific American* (February, 2004).

17. "From Slowdown to Speed-up," by A. G. Riess and M. S. Turner, in *Scientific American* (February, 2004).

18. "The Myth of the Beginning of Time," by G. Veneziano, in *Scientific American* (May, 2004).

19. "The First Stars in the Universe," by R. E. Larson and V. Bromm, in *Scientific American* Special Edition (September, 2004).

20. "The Midlife Crisis of the Cosmos," by A. J. Berger, in *Scientific American* (January, 2005).

21. "Does Dark Energy Really Exist?" by T. Clifton and P. G. Ferreira, in *Scientific American* (April, 2009).

Quest Ahead to Starlinks
http://physicalscience.jbpub.com/starlinks

Starlinks is this book's online learning center. It features **eLearning**, which contains chapter quizzes and other tools designed to help you study for your class. You can also find **online exercises**, view numerous relevant **animations**, follow a guide to **useful astronomy sites** on the web, or even check the latest **astronomy news** updates.

Life zone around galaxy

Life zone around star

19

The Quest for Extraterrestrial Intelligence

Life could exist only in certain regions of a galaxy, neither too close to the center nor too close to the edge. Similarly, planets that could support life could not be too close to a star nor too far away from it.

As far as the general public is concerned, probably the best-known astronomer in the last half of the 20th century was Carl Sagan (1934–1996). He appeared often on television, from late-night talk shows to educational programs about space flight, and hosted a 13-part series on astronomy, based in part on his own book, called *Cosmos*. His popularity was such that his reputation as a serious researcher suffered; critics assumed that anyone who spent so much time explaining fundamental astronomy to the public did not have much time for cutting-edge research. Yet Sagan published more than 600 scientific papers and nonscientific articles, including work on the environment of Venus, dust storms on Mars, the atmosphere of Jupiter, the origin of life on Earth, and the long-term environmental effects of nuclear war—the so-called "nuclear winter."

One of Sagan's strongest interests was in the *Search for Extraterrestrial Intelligence* (SETI). He played key roles in the *Viking* search for life on Mars and in designing the snapshots of life on Earth carried by the *Pioneer* and *Voyager* space probes. Here are some of his thoughts about the significance of SETI:

> Through all of our history we have pondered the stars and mused whether humanity is unique or if, somewhere else in the dark of the night sky, there are other beings who

All cross references to chapters, sections, figures, and tables pertain to the main text, *In Quest of the Universe, Sixth Edition. In Quest of the Solar System* contains Chapters 1–11 and 19 of the main text. *In Quest of the Stars and Galaxies* contains Chapters 1–5 and 11–19 of the main text.

contemplate and wonder as we do, fellow thinkers in the cosmos. Such beings might view themselves and the universe differently. Somewhere else there might be very exotic biologies and technologies and societies. In a cosmic setting vast and old beyond ordinary human understanding, we are a little lonely; and we ponder the ultimate significance, if any, of our tiny but exquisite blue planet. The search for extraterrestrial intelligence is the search for a generally acceptable cosmic context for the human species. In the deepest sense, the search for extraterrestrial intelligence is a search for ourselves.*

Carl Sagan, *Broca's Brain* (New York: Random House, 1979, p. 268).

Are we alone in the universe? Either answer to this question has immense consequences. If we are indeed alone, then our assumption that the universe is basically the same everywhere would be challenged. Earth once again will take a special place in the cosmos, a view that we have not subscribed to since the time of Copernicus. If other intelligent life forms exist, communicating with them will forever change the way we see ourselves as part of nature. Searching for extraterrestrial intelligence may not be a "scientific" activity. After all, the hypothesis that such intelligent species exist cannot be disproved; however, as Carl Sagan so eloquently put it, this is mostly "a search for ourselves."

19-1 Radio Searches and SETI

The presence of intelligent life on Earth, the huge number of stars in our Galaxy, and the enormous number of galaxies in the universe, coupled with the latest observations of planets around other stars, lead us to believe that, given sufficient time and the right conditions, life—maybe even intelligent life—can evolve elsewhere in the universe. An obvious way of searching for such life is by sending out unmanned spacecraft; however, with our current technology, even a trip to nearby stars would take thousands of years to complete. Instead, SETI is based on the detection of radio transmissions from other life forms. As we have emphasized in this text, radio waves can travel through gas and dust without significant degradation.

To search for signals from extraterrestrials, astronomers have had to decide not only where to look in the sky, but on what frequencies to expect the signals. In a sense, we must know what "channel" the extraterrestrials are broadcasting on. Taking into account the many natural sources of radio "noise," astronomers have selected certain ranges of frequencies as most likely. A primary consideration in making the decision is to select frequencies at which natural sources do not emit great amounts of energy. Strong natural signals would drown out intelligent signals over long distances. Early SETI receivers had to "listen" to one frequency at a time, but modern receivers are capable of tuning to tens of millions of different frequencies simultaneously. This makes the search much faster than was previously dreamed possible.

The best radio frequency range for communications is between 1000 and 10,000 MHz (megahertz). In this range, there is relatively little radio noise from other sources. At lower frequencies, we have strong emission from interstellar gas, whereas at higher frequencies, radio waves tend to be absorbed by our atmosphere. If an intelligent civilization chose to communicate with us, the frequency of choice could most likely be 1.4×10^3 MHz. This corresponds to a wavelength of $\lambda = c/f = (3 \times 10^{10}$ cm/s$)/ (1.4 \times 10^3$ MHz$) \approx 21$ cm, the same wavelength astronomers use to detect cool hydrogen clouds in our galaxy (as we discussed in Chapter 16). An intelligent civilization would very likely know that the 21-cm radiation is a useful probe for astronomers, and we could easily distinguish an ordered message from the random natural noise usually found at that wavelength.

Radio telescopes are designed and built to detect and measure radio waves coming from objects in space. If there are intelligent beings out there, these telescopes will also be useful both in detecting their presence and in communicating with them. Radio telescopes have been used on occasion to search the heavens for evidence of radio signals from intelligent beings. In 1960, American astronomer Frank Drake used a telescope of the National Radio Astronomy Observatory to search for signals from two nearby stars. The search, which Drake called Project Ozma, involved looking for unusual patterns in radio signals—patterns that were different from the signals emitted by inanimate objects such as stars and galaxies.

Since that time, several astronomers have conducted searches. For example, in an experiment conducted in the mid-1970s, more than 600 nearby stars were watched for about 30 minutes each. In 1971, a group of astronomers and engineers made plans for an elaborate array of radio telescopes to be devoted to a search. Their proposal, called Project Cyclops, would have cost billions of dollars to put into operation. Because of budget pressures, Congress canceled a search begun by NASA after $58 million had already been spent. This project was taken over by the SETI Institute, a private research group; Project Phoenix ran from 1995 to 2004, observed about 800 stars to a distance of about 240 light-years, and covered more than a billion frequency channels for each star. No extraterrestrial signals were detected. A number of new projects are underway, such as the Allen Telescope Array, a SETI-dedicated array of telescopes that will equal a 100-m radio telescope.

The Arecibo Radio Telescope in Puerto Rico receives more radio signals than we can search through for signals from extraterrestrial intelligence, even with the help of a large supercomputer. In May 1999, a project called SETI@home began using individual computers in people's homes and offices to examine the data. Over 5.5 million people worldwide have downloaded the necessary software and contributed computer time equal to 3 million years. The project is continuing using a different software platform that allows testing for more types of signals.

Plans have been made in case we detect a signal that we verify as coming from an extraterrestrial being. There is even a protocol for involving international bodies in decisions about possible replies.

◆ You can find the latest on SETI at http://www.seti.org/ and the latest on SETI@home at http://setiathome.berkeley.edu/.

19-2 Communication with Extraterrestrial Intelligence

◆ In Carl Sagan's science fiction novel *Contact* (later made into a movie), extraterrestrials first find out about civilization on Earth by detecting the TV broadcast of the 1936 Olympic games in Berlin, which was the first television transmission on Earth using significant power.

If our search for radio signals from a race of intelligent extraterrestrials is successful, it might succeed by detecting their stray, wasted radio signals. After all, we have been transmitting radio signals into space for decades now. If an extraterrestrial civilization exists nearby, say 20 light-years away, they have already received all the episodes of the "I Love Lucy" series, along with other radio and TV programming of the 50s and 60s. On the other hand, those beings may already be transmitting messages into space with the purpose of announcing their presence and telling others something about themselves. The same radio telescopes that are used to receive signals from space can be used to transmit radio signals. Considering the probable differences between beings in different parts of the Galaxy, what could one race of these beings communicate to another? The study of this question is called CETI, for *C*ommunication with *E*xtra*t*errestrial *I*ntelligence.

First, we must point out that if another intelligent race were found, the tremendous distances between stars would prohibit a dialogue. The nearest star is nearly 5 light-years away from us. It would require 5 years for our radio signals to reach a planet circling that star and another 5 years for the signal to return from beings on that planet, and the likelihood that life is so common that it exists around the nearest star is extremely remote. If extraterrestrial life exists, the closest life sites are likely to be much farther away, making it impossible to get a reply to our signal during the span of one generation on Earth.

At first glance, the language problems might seem insurmountable; however, we do have something in common with every other race of beings that might exist: the physical universe and its mathematical laws, which we believe to be the same everywhere. Every intelligent race knows that hydrogen is the most common element and that an atom of hydrogen is made up of one proton and one electron. The prime numbers—those numbers that cannot be divided evenly by any other numbers but one and themselves—are the same in every language. Those scientists studying the problem have concluded that an understandable message could indeed be sent if enough time were devoted to its transmission.

We Earthlings have already sent a very short message. In 1974, the reconditioned reflecting surface of the Arecibo telescope (FIGURE 19-1) was rededicated, and at the ceremony, the telescope was used to transmit a message toward a cluster of 300,000 stars in the constellation Hercules. This transmission lasted only about 10 minutes, and thus, the information that could be sent was very limited. The signal consisted of a series of Morse Code-type pulses containing 1679 data points. The number 1679 was chosen because, except for 1 and 1679, only one pair of numbers can be multiplied to obtain 1679: 23 and 73. If the data points are arranged into a rectangular array, there are only two ways to do it: either 23 across and 73 down or vice versa. One array produces no pattern, but the other array makes a pattern that includes crude pictures and numbers to tell the beings that intercept the signal a little about those who sent the message.

FIGURE 19-1 The Arecibo Radio Telescope has been used to send a message to anyone out there listening. It has also been used to search for messages from any other intelligent sources.

If extraterrestrial beings happen to detect our 10-minute message, will they be able to decipher it? Who knows? Although we cannot know how much of it they will be able to understand, we can be confident that they will know that it comes from an intelligent source rather than an inanimate object. If more time were available to transmit messages, a slower development of language could be used so that understanding would be much more likely, but with the time limitation that existed, scientists believed this message was the best that could be done.

When might we receive a reply? The cluster toward which the message was sent is 26,000 light-years away, and thus, we need only wait 52,000 years for an answer!

19-3 Letters to Extraterrestrials

In addition to our radio signals, we have sent "letters" into space in the form of a plaque and records.

The *Pioneer* Plaques

In late 1971, Carl Sagan learned that the trajectories of the *Pioneer 10* and *Pioneer 11* spacecraft would take them out of the solar system and that it might be possible to include on them a message to extraterrestrials. Sagan called NASA authorities and within 3 weeks got approval to put a plaque on both *Pioneer 10*, which was scheduled to be launched the following March, and *Pioneer 11*, which was to be launched a year later. Carl and his wife Linda, along with Frank Drake, designed the message, which was etched on a 6 × 9-inch gold-anodized aluminum plaque (FIGURE 19-2).

Some of the message on the plaque is easily recognizable (to humans, at least). The umbrella-shaped object behind the man and woman is an outline of the Pioneer spacecraft, drawn to scale with the people. The finder thus can determine the size of a human. (The man on this scale is 5 feet 9.5 inches tall.)

The two circles at the upper left represent hydrogen atoms emitting radiation of a particular wavelength. Binary numbers on the plaque (not visible in this small rendition) use this wavelength to show the size of the woman and of the solar system at the bottom, where the *Pioneer* spacecraft is shown leaving the third planet.

The spidery-looking feature at the left shows the directions from the solar system to pulsars, compact celestial objects that emit beams of radio waves that when

FIGURE 19-2 This plaque aboard *Pioneers 10* and *11* carried a message to extraterrestrials—and to Earthlings.

sweeping past the Earth are observed as radio pulses with regular periods (see Section 15-5). The binary numbers along the lines represent the periods of the pulses, expressed in terms of the period of the wave from hydrogen. By analyzing the directions and periods of the pulsars, the finders could tell where our solar system is located in the Milky Way. In addition, because pulsars slow down with time, they could tell when the craft was launched.

Could extraterrestrials interpret the message? Curiously enough, because observations of hydrogen atoms and pulsars are common to all creatures of the universe, it is thought that *they* would be more likely to interpret the pulsar sketch than the human figures, which *we* recognize immediately.

The *Voyager* Records

In 1977, *Voyager 1* and *Voyager 2* were launched into space to rendezvous with Jupiter and Saturn. Plans were later adjusted to allow *Voyager 2* to continue to Uranus and Neptune. Both *Voyager 1* and *2* are now headed for the outer boundary of the solar system, as we discussed in Chapter 7.

With more time available to plan a message, a group of people, including the three who prepared the *Pioneer* plaque, designed a much more complete message to go aboard *Voyager 1* and *2*. The messages on *Voyager* are contained on two copper phonograph records (FIGURE 19-3), designed to be played at 16-2/3 revolutions/minute. Instructions for playing the records are included in pictures on the cover. On the records are 90 minutes of music from around the world, 118 pictures, and greetings in nearly 60 languages (including one nonhuman message from a humpback whale).

The music on the *Voyager* includes parts of compositions from Bach (Brandenburg Concerto No. 2 and The Well-Tempered Clavier), Beethoven (Symphony No. 5, String Quartet No. 13 in B-flat), and Mozart (The Magic Flute). In addition, it includes Chuck Berry's "Johnny B. Goode," Australian Aborigine songs, a Peruvian wedding song, and numerous other selections from the cultures of our world.

The records contain pictures as well as sound. The pictures include many photographs of scenes of nature here on Earth, of the Earth from space, of the Earth as changed by humans, of people in various activities, and of the biology of humans.

FIGURE 19-3 The *Voyager* spacecraft carried these phonograph records beyond the solar system and into outer space.

Will the Message Be Found?

The messages were not put aboard the *Pioneer* and *Voyager* craft with high hopes of them ever being found. They were sent in much the same manner as someone might put a message in a bottle and throw it into the sea. In fact, the space messages have even less chance than the bottle of being found. Even if the Galaxy abounds in intelligent life, the emptiness of space and the slow speed of the spacecraft make the chances slim indeed. The soonest any of the craft will pass within 2 light-years of a star is 40,000 years!

The messages are really a symbol of hope, a shout that "we are here." As stated in the book *Murmurs of Earth*—which tells the story of the *Voyager* records—after the Earth has been reduced to a charred cinder by an expanded and brighter Sun, the messages will continue to travel through space, "preserving a murmur of an ancient civilization that once flourished—perhaps before moving on to greater deeds and other worlds—on the distant planet Earth."

This quotation is from the book Murmurs of Earth, *by Carl Sagan, F. Drake, A. Druyan, T. Ferris, J. Lomberg, and L. Sagan (New York: Ballantine Books, 1978).*

19-4 The Origin of Life

The search for extraterrestrial intelligence is interdisciplinary by nature. It involves physics, astronomy, geology, chemistry, and biology. Biology is an integral component of our search, as it concerns itself with the question of how life began. The answer to this question is important not just for biology, but for astronomy as well, as it helps us determine the probability of the existence of extraterrestrial life.

The theory of evolution, under development since the last half of the 19th century, explains how higher forms of life evolve from more primitive forms, but this still did not answer the question of the beginnings of life. Then, in the 1920s and early 1930s, J. B. S. Haldane, a Scottish biochemist, and A. P. Oparin, a Russian biochemist, proposed that soon after the Earth's formation, the necessary chemical elements were present for complex molecules to form—molecules that are needed for life. At the time, it was thought that the seas of the early Earth were composed primarily of water, methane, ammonia, and hydrogen. The two scientists hypothesized that these molecules would spontaneously collect into more complex, organic (carbon-based) molecules.

The Haldane/Oparin hypothesis remained an interesting conjecture until 1953, when Harold Urey (the Nobel Prize winner who discovered deuterium) suggested that his graduate student, Stanley Miller, test the hypothesis by simulating the conditions of the early Earth. Miller put a mixture of water, hydrogen, methane, and ammonia into a sealed container (FIGURE 19-4). He heated the liquid—the young Earth was hot—and used an electrical source to produce sparks in the gas above the liquid. The sparks simulated lightning, which must have been common in the Earth's early atmosphere.

After Miller's apparatus had heated and sparked for a week, the mixture had turned dark brown. Analysis showed that it now contained large amounts of four different amino acids (organic molecules that form the basis for proteins). He also found fatty acids and urea (a molecule that is necessary in many life processes).

The Miller-Urey experiment showed that given the right chemicals and a source of energy,

See the Tools of Astronomy box in Chapter 8 for a discussion of the search for life on Mars conducted by the Viking *landers.*

In the beginning, this world was nothing at all, Heaven was not, nor earth, nor space. Because it was not, it bethought itself; I will be. It emitted heat.
Ancient Egyptian text.

In the beginning God created the heaven and the earth. And the earth was without form, and void; and darkness was upon the face of the deep. And the Spirit of God moved upon the face of the waters. And God said, Let there be light: and there was light.
Genesis 1:1–3.

Electrical contacts

Water, hydrogen, methane, ammonia

Condenser (cools vapor to liquid)

Boiling water

Organic compounds trapped here

FIGURE 19-4 The Miller-Urey experiment showed that organic molecules necessary for life could form easily from the compounds and conditions of the young Earth.

chemical reactions could occur that produce the building blocks of life. Since then, researchers have learned that the early Earth's atmosphere was made up primarily of carbon dioxide, nitrogen, and water vapor, rather than the four compounds used in Miller's experiment. When these compounds are used in the sealed apparatus, even more complex organic molecules are produced. Furthermore, if instead of using electrical sparks for energy we use ultraviolet light (which strikes Earth from the Sun), we achieve the same results.

It must be emphasized that the Miller experiment did not produce life, only organic molecules. As yet, we have not been able to cross the gap between chemical evolution and biological evolution; however, the experiment confirmed the Haldane/Oparin hypothesis and showed that such molecules can form easily in a short time. The results of the experiment would indicate that the early Earth must have contained seas made up of organic goo.

As we have discussed in Sections 10-8 and 13-1, traces of amino acids have been found in some meteorites, and there is spectroscopic evidence that organic molecules exist in interstellar dust and gas clouds. The molecular building blocks of life thus seem to be common in the universe. How does life form from these blocks? We don't know, but it seems that nature's deck may be stacked in the direction of life.

19-5   The Drake Equation

So far we have not had any success in receiving a transmission from an extraterrestrial civilization. What are the chances that one day we may detect such transmissions? Astronomer Frank Drake proposed an equation for *estimating* the number (N) of technologically advanced civilizations in our galaxy whose signal we might be able to detect. The equation has been written in a variety of forms, including this one:

$$N = R_* \times f_p \times n_e \times f_l \times f_i \times f_c \times L,$$

where

R_* = the rate at which solar-type stars form in our Galaxy,
f_p = the fraction of these stars that have planetary systems,
n_e = the average number of planets per such system that are Earth-like enough to support life,
f_l = the fraction of those Earth-like planets on which life actually develops,
f_i = the fraction of those life-forms that evolve to intelligence,
f_c = the fraction of those intelligent species who are interested in interstellar communication and develop and use the necessary technology for it,
L = the average lifetime of such a technologically advanced civilization.

The factors in the equation, as you might surmise, are far from well known. Let's take a quick look at each factor.

Based on the average lifetime of stars and on the number of stars in the Galaxy, we have a pretty good idea of the rate of solar-type star formation; the first term on the right is known to be in the range of 1 to 10 solar-type stars per year. The emphasis on "solar-type" stars is necessary. We should probably exclude stars with masses larger than about 1.5 $M_\odot$ because their main-sequence lifetimes are shorter than the time it took for intelligent life to evolve on our planet. Stars less massive than the Sun have longer main-sequence lifetimes than our Sun, but they are also dimmer. This implies that only planets close enough to such stars would be suited for life, but short distances imply strong tidal interactions. It seems that the best candidates are stars with spectral types between F5 and M0. Other factors tend to limit the search for suitable stars to a range of distances from the center of a galaxy, sometimes called "Habitable Zones" or "Life Zones" (see the chapter-opening figure). Closer than the habitable zone, stars are too close together for stable planetary orbits and are bathed in X-rays and gamma rays from the Galactic center. Farther out than the habitable zone, stars don't have enough heavy elements to form solid Earth-like planets.

For those who are studying aspects of the origin of life, the question no longer seems to be whether life could have originated by chemical processes involving nonbiological components but, rather, what pathway might have been followed.
National Academy of Sciences

The hypothesis that life originated on Earth through moss-grown fragments from the ruins of another world may seem wild and visionary. All I maintain is that it is not unscientific.
Lord Kelvin

The more we learn about how planetary systems are formed, the better we can estimate what fraction of stars has planets orbiting around them. Better knowledge of the origin of our own system will help in this regard, and as we explained in Section 7-6, we are just beginning to understand the formation of our solar system. In addition, evidence is accumulating that planetary systems are common (see Section 7-7). It is then reasonable to assume that for solar-type stars, $f_p \approx 1$. We might suspect that if this is so, many systems probably have life-supporting planets. (After all, our solar system *almost* has three planets capable of supporting Earth-type life and a number of satellites where liquid water most likely exists.) A reasonable range for the value of n_e is, therefore, between 0.1 and 1. We see that we can make reasonably confident estimates of the values for the first three terms in the equation. Beyond this, things get fuzzier.

As we described earlier, the Miller-Urey experiment indicates that the most basic molecules from which life is made are formed easily and naturally under conditions expected to be prevalent on some young planets. Many biologists believe that, given the right conditions and enough time, life will develop from these components, but they have no way of testing this hypothesis. A reasonable estimate for f_l is about 1.

The last three terms are even less well known. Does life evolve easily to intelligence, and if so, is it common for intelligent species to be interested in communication with aliens? Finally, how long does the typical civilization last? How long will ours last? Even if we assume that evolution naturally leads to intelligence, which is far from certain, and that an intelligent species would naturally try to communicate with other intelligent species in our Galaxy, the last factor introduces the largest uncertainty in the estimated value of N. Since the invention of nuclear weapons, we have come very close to rendering ourselves extinct, and thus, a reasonable value for L might be only 100 years. On the other hand, it is certainly possible that L might have a value in the thousands or even millions of years.

Various astronomers have inserted their best guesses into the equation, and—depending on whether they are optimists or pessimists—have come up with answers anywhere from "only one" or "only a few" to "millions"; however, the value of the equation lies less in its mathematical answer than in showing us what we must learn to calculate an answer. It shows that we have a lot to learn.

Recall our discussion on the search for life on Mars and on the conditions on Jupiter's moons (especially Europa) and the similarities between Titan and young Earth.

Our obligation to survive is owed not just to ourselves but also to that Cosmos, ancient and vast, from which we spring.
Carl Sagan

19-6 Where Is Everybody?

The great size of our Galaxy and the tremendous number of stars in it suggest that the number of stars that could support a planet with intelligent life is very large. It is possible, therefore, that the value of N in the Drake equation is quite large.

There is an opposing point of view, however. The argument goes as follows: If the formation of life is common in the Milky Way, there should be a large number of civilizations like ours. We would expect many of the civilizations to be millions of years older than ours, because the Sun was formed fairly recently in the Galaxy's history. The older civilizations would be scientifically advanced enough to be able to travel to other stars. In fact, some would have been forced to leave their home planet when their star reached the end of its main sequence life and moved toward the red giant stage. These civilizations would have moved to hospitable planets near other stars and would have colonized space. (Aren't we likely to do so within the next million years, assuming our species lives that long?)

Therefore, if life begins and evolves as readily as some thinkers would have us believe, the Galaxy should be teeming with life. We should have encountered not only radio signals from extraterrestrial beings, but Earth should have been visited. The question is, "Where is everybody?" Although some people say that UFOs of extraterrestrial origin have visited Earth on many occasions, no report of UFOs controlled by extraterrestrial beings has been substantiated to the degree demanded for acceptance in science and, therefore, few astronomers consider the reports credible.

This question was first asked by the great physicist Enrico Fermi in 1950.

The argument presented here leads to either of two conclusions: (1) Earth has been (and continues to be) visited by extraterrestrials who for some reason do not want to reveal themselves, or (2) intelligent life is rare in the Galaxy. If we refuse to accept the first option, we are left with the second, and the money we spend searching is wasted. Or so the argument goes.

It is possible that conservative estimates for the parameters in the Drake equation are closer to reality; however, this would imply that we are somehow special, a view that would contradict the Copernican attitude that characterizes today's science. It is also possible that advanced civilizations outgrow technology and decide not to engage in interstellar communication. Maybe there is such a thing as "the prime directive," and other advanced civilizations are not interfering with our technological and biological evolution. The most likely answer to the question "Where is everybody?" is that the lifetime of a technological civilization is short. An order of magnitude calculation suggests that unless a technological civilization survives through some 10,000 to 10 million years of technology, we would not expect to find another such civilization still surviving in our Galaxy at the same time as we are.

There is another completely different argument against spending money on the SETI. A good theory in science must have within itself the seeds of its own destruction. The theory must be capable of being proved wrong. Some scientists point out that no matter how much we spend over the next decade in searching for extraterrestrial radio signals, it is very possible that we will find nothing. This would not prove that extraterrestrials are not broadcasting radio signals, however, but only that we have not found them. Will those in favor of the search continue to ask for more money? When do we stop? This line of thinking leads to the conclusion that SETI is bad science and is not worth the considerable amounts of money being proposed for it. What do you think?

Absence of evidence is not evidence of absence.
Frank Drake

Conclusion

Efforts to discover extrasolar planetary systems are intensifying. In the next few years we might be able to answer this question: "Are there Earth-like planets orbiting other stars?" If the results of these efforts turn out to be promising, searches for extraterrestrial intelligence will also intensify.

The potential benefits of knowledge and experience that would result from interstellar contact are immense. Beyond such benefits, SETI-type efforts will continue simply because we want to know what is out there, whether or not we are somehow unique. We want—and maybe need—to know where we came from and what it means to be human. Even if we never find the answers to these questions, it might still be worthwhile pursuing this quest. As in most cases, what is important at the end is the journey, not the destination.

STUDY GUIDE

RECALL QUESTIONS

1. Which of the following facts is the major factor that causes many astronomers to believe that extraterrestrial life is probable?
   A. UFOs that have been sighted on Earth.
   B. Laser signals that have been received from space.
   C. Radio signals that have been received from space.
   D. Signs of life that we have found on neighboring planets.
   E. The tremendous number of stars in the universe.

2. The most likely method of contact with extraterrestrial intelligence is likely to be
   A. radio waves.
   B. sound waves.
   C. light waves.
   D. actual visits.

3. The most likely wavelength at which to search for extraterrestrial intelligence is thought to be about
   A. 21 centimeters, the wavelength used to detect cool hydrogen clouds.
   B. 140 centimeters, the wavelength used to detect water.
   C. 1400 centimeters, the wavelength used to detect carbon.
   D. [Any of the above, for no wavelength is more likely than another.]

4. *SETI@home* is a project in which nonastronomers use
   A. dish antennae to search for extraterrestrial life.
   B. regular TV antennae to search for extraterrestrial life.
   C. radios to search for extraterrestrial life.
   D. antennae to send out signals to extraterrestrial life.
   E. computers to analyze data in a search for extraterrestrial life.

5. All of the following are projects that involve extraterrestrial life EXCEPT
   A. Project Phoenix.
   B. *COBE*.
   C. SETI.
   D. Project Ozma.
   E. *Voyager* records.

6. If intelligent life exists around a nearby star, it may be able to detect which of the following "signals" that we have sent?
   A. Sound waves emitted by loudspeakers at outdoor concerts.
   B. Radio and TV waves intended for communication on Earth.
   C. Radio waves sent from Arecibo intended to make contact.
   D. [All of the above.]
   E. [B and C above, but not A.]

7. Assuming that radio contact is established some day, which of the following do professionals in the field believe is true?
   A. Extraterrestrials will be able to figure out our message, but we will not be able to decipher theirs.
   B. We will be able to decipher their message, but extraterrestrials will not be able to understand ours.
   C. Neither we nor the extraterrestrials we contact will be able to understand the others' message.
   D. Communication will be monologues rather than dialogs because of the tremendous time lag.
   E. [Both C and D above.]

8. We have intentionally included messages to extraterrestrials on which of the following categories of spacecraft?
   A. The Space Shuttle.
   B. *Pioneer* and *Voyager*.
   C. *Magellan*.
   D. *Viking*.
   E. [All of the above.]

9. Assuming that extraterrestrial life is common, which of the following is true concerning the likelihood that one or more of our spacecraft will be picked up by extraterrestrials?
   A. It is so likely that it probably has already happened.
   B. It is likely to happen in the next few hundred years.
   C. It is likely to happen in the next few thousand years.
   D. It is unlikely to happen for many tens of thousands of years, if ever.

10. The *Voyager* record contains which of the following?
    A. Greetings in many languages.
    B. Music.
    C. Pictures of scenes on Earth.
    D. Pictures illustrating the biology of humans.
    E. [All of the above.]

11. The Miller-Urey experiment showed that if the chemical elements of the early Earth are put in a sealed container and energy is added,
    A. living matter in the form of viruses is formed.
    B. living matter in the form of bacteria is formed.
    C. some organic molecules are formed.
    D. [Two of the above.]
    E. [None of the above.]

12. The Drake equation shows us the factors that we need to know to calculate
    A. the rate at which stars form in the Galaxy.
    B. the number of planets in an average planetary system.
    C. the number of Earth-like planets in the Galaxy.
    D. the number of places in the Galaxy that contain the most basic life.
    E. the number of places in the Galaxy that contain technologically advanced civilizations sending out signals.

13. Which of the following factors in Drake's equation is *least* known?
    A. The rate at which solar-type stars form in our Galaxy.
    B. The fraction of solar-type stars that have planetary systems.
    C. The fraction of Earth-like planets on which life actually develops.
    D. The average lifetime of technologically advanced civilizations.
    E. [All of the above are about equally known.]

14. Most astronomers who hold the "Where is Everybody?" argument conclude that
    A. extraterrestrials must be hiding from us.
    B. extraterrestrial intelligence is rare or nonexistent.
    C. extraterrestrial communication is impossible because of technological constraints.
    D. there are not many Earth-like planets in the Galaxy.

15. What does "SETI" stand for? CETI?

16. Explain why the average lifetime of a technologically advanced civilization is a necessary factor in Drake's equation.

1. After years of listening at many frequencies, we have not picked up any artificial signals. Is this a proof that life has not evolved elsewhere? Is this a proof that technologically advanced life has not evolved elsewhere? Explain your answer.

2. What factors might limit the lifetime of a technologically advanced civilization? Explain your answer.

3. What would the consequences be if tomorrow we receive a radio signal from a civilization on a planet 10 light-years away, asking for a two-way communication? Explain your answer and consider both short- and long-term consequences.

4. Throughout our history, there have been many instances of devastation of certain cultures after contact with more "advanced" cultures. How does this historical fact affect your opinion on the searches for extraterrestrial intelligence?

1. Assume that there are 10,000 technologically advanced civilizations in a galaxy of 200 billion stars. How many stars would astronomers in this galaxy have to observe to have a reasonable chance of finding one such civilization?

2. Assume that in a galaxy that is about 10 billion years old, a thousand to a million technologically advanced civilizations have shown up at various times. On the average, for how long must a civilization last to communicate with another civilization?

3. Choose a reasonable value for each of the parameters in the Drake equation and estimate the value of N. Explain your reasoning behind your choices.

4. In the text, we mentioned that stars of mass greater than about $1.5 \, M_\odot$ have main-sequence lifetimes that are shorter than the time it took for intelligent life to evolve on our planet. Show that this is true.

The Web sites for the SETI Institute (http://www.seti.org) and SETI at the University of California, Berkeley (http://seti.ssl.berkeley.edu) offer the latest information on the search for extraterrestrial intelligence.

1. "The Search for Extraterrestrial Intelligence," by C. Sagan and F. Drake, in *Scientific American* (May, 1975).

2. *Murmurs of Earth*, by Carl Sagan, F. Drake, A. Druyan, T. Ferris, J. Lomberg, and L. Sagan (Ballantine Books, 1978).

3. "No Greater Discovery," by F. Drake and D. Sobel, and "Surfing The Cosmos," by A. K. Dewdney, in *Taking Sides*, 4th ed. (McGraw-Hill, 2000).

4. "The Evolution of Life on the Earth," by S. J. Gould, and "The Origin of Life on the Earth," by L. E. Orgel, in *Scientific American* (October, 1994).

5. *Extraterrestrials—Where Are They?* by B. Zuckerman and M. Hart, eds., 2nd ed. (Cambridge University Press, 1995).

6. *Rare Earth: Why Complex Life is Uncommon in the Universe*, by Peter Douglas Ward and Donald Brownlee (Copernicus Books, 1999).

7. *Here Be Dragons: The Scientific Quest for Extraterrestrial Life*, by Simon Levay and David W. Koerner (Oxford University Press, 2000).

8. Searching for Extraterrestrials: "Where Are They?" by I. Crawford; "Where They Could Hide," by A. J. LePage; and "Intergalactically Speaking," by G. W. Swenson, Jr., in *Scientific American* (July, 2000).

9. "Refuges for Life in a Hostile Universe," by G. Gonzalez, D. Brownlee, and P. D. Ward, in *Scientific American* (October, 2001).

10. "Did Life Come from Another World?" by D. Warmflash and B. Weiss, in *Scientific American* (November, 2005).

11. "Origin of Life on Earth," by A. Ricardon, and J. W. Szostak, in *Scientific American* (September, 2009).

Quest Ahead to Starlinks
http://physicalscience.jbpub.com/starlinks

Starlinks is this book's online learning center. It features **eLearning**, which contains chapter quizzes and other tools designed to help you study for your class. You can also find **online exercises**, view numerous relevant **animations**, follow a guide to **useful astronomy sites** on the Internet, or even check the latest **astronomy news** updates.

Appendices

Appendix A

Units and Constants

Metric Prefixes	
nano (n)	$= 10^{-9}$
micro (μ)	$= 10^{-6}$
milli (m)	$= 10^{-3}$
centi (c)	$= 10^{-2}$
kilo (k)	$= 10^{3}$
mega (M)	$= 10^{6}$

Temperature	Kelvin (K)	Celsius (°C)	Fahrenheit (°F)
Absolute zero	0	-273.15	-459.7
Freezing point of water	273.15	0	32
Boiling point of water	373.15	100	212
		$T_K = T_C + 273.15$	$T_F = 1.8 \times T_C + 32$

Units of Length	
1 astronomical unit (AU)	$= 1.495979 \times 10^{11}$ m
	$= 92.96 \times 10^{6}$ miles
1 light-year (ly)	$= 6.324 \times 10^{4}$ AU
	$= 9.461 \times 10^{15}$ m
	$= 5.879 \times 10^{12}$ miles
1 parsec (pc)	$= 206,264.81$ AU
	$= 3.086 \times 10^{16}$ m
	$= 3.262$ ly
1 nanometer (nm)	$= 10$ Angstroms (Å)
	$= 10^{-9}$ m

Constants	
Speed of light	$= 2.99792458 \times 10^{8}$ m/sec
Electron mass	$= 9.1094 \times 10^{-31}$ kg
Proton mass	$= 1.6726 \times 10^{-27}$ kg
Planck's constant	$= 6.6261 \times 10^{-34}$ J·s
Stefan-Boltzmann constant	$= 5.6705 \times 10^{-8}$ W·m^{-2}·K^{-4}

Metric–English Conversion	
1 kilometer (km)	$= 0.6214$ miles
1 meter (m)	$= 39.37$ inches
2.54 centimeters (cm)	$= 1$ inch
1 kilogram (kg)	$= 1000$ g (weighs 2.2 pounds)
1 gram (g)	$= 0.001$ kg (weighs 0.035 oz)

Appendix B

Solar Data

	Value	Compared with Earth
Diameter	1,392,000 km	109.2
Mass	1.9891×10^{30} kg	332,980
Average density	1.41 g/cm^3	0.255
Surface gravity	274 m/s^2	28.0
Escape speed	618 km/s	55.2
Effective temperature	5778 K	
Luminosity	3.846×10^{26} watts	
Absolute magnitude	4.83	
Tilt of equator to ecliptic	7.25°	
Sidereal rotation period		
Equator	25.05 days	
40° latitude	27.40 days	
80° latitude	33.83 days	

Appendix C

Planetary Data

Physical Data

Planet	Equatorial Diameter* (km)	(Earth = 1)	Oblateness	Mass** (Earth=1)	Density (g/cm³)	Surface Gravity*** (Earth =1)	Escape Speed (km/s)
Mercury	4,879	0.383	0	0.055	5.43	0.38	4.30
Venus	12,104	0.949	0	0.815	5.24	0.91	10.36
Earth	12,756	1	0.00335	1	5.52	1	11.19
Mars	6,794	0.533	0.0065	0.107	3.93	0.38	5.03
Jupiter	142,984†	11.2	0.065	317.83	1.33	2.36†	59.5
Saturn	120,536†	9.4	0.098	95.2	0.69	0.92†	35.5
Uranus	51,118†	4.0	0.023	14.5	1.27	0.89†	21.3
Neptune	49,528†	3.9	0.017	17.1	1.64	1.12†	23.5
Pluto§	2,390	0.2	0	0.002	1.75	0.06	1.1

* Equatorial diameter of Earth = 12,756 km.
** Mass of Earth = 5.9736 × 10²⁴ kg.
*** Surface gravity of Earth = 9.78 m/s².
† At 1 bar.
§ Dwarf planet

Orbital Data, Axis Tilt, and Rotation Period

Planet	Semimajor Axis (10⁶ km)	(AU)	Sidereal Orbital Period*	Mean Orbital Speed (km/s)	Orbital Eccentricity	Inclination to Ecliptic (degrees)	Equatorial Tilt to Orbital Plane (degrees)	Sidereal Rotation Period**
Mercury	57.9	0.387	87.97 d	47.9	0.2056	7.0	0.01	58.65 d
Venus	108.2	0.723	224.7 d	35.0	0.0067	3.39	177.36	−243.02 d
Earth	149.6	1	365.256 d	29.8	0.0167	0	23.45	23.9345 h
Mars	227.9	1.524	1.881 y	24.1	0.0935	1.85	25.19	24.623 h
Jupiter	778.6	5.204	11.86 y	13.1	0.0489	1.3	3.13	9.925 h
Saturn	1433.5	9.582	29.46 y	9.7	0.0565	2.49	26.73	10.66 h
Uranus	2872.5	19.20	84.01 y	6.8	0.0457	0.77	97.77	−17.24 h
Neptune	4495.1	30.05	164.79 y	5.4	0.0113	1.77	28.3	16.11 h
Pluto§	5869.7	39.24	247.7 y	4.7	0.2444	17.2	122.5	−6.39 d

* The symbols "h," "d," and "y" imply "hours," "days," and "years," respectively. One day is 24 hours; 1 year is 365.256 days.
** The "−" signs indicate retrograde rotation.
§ Dwarf planet

The Sun

Solar wind shapes the magnetic fields of all planets in the solar system, as Earth's field shown.

Interior

Sun Data

Sun	Value	Compared with Earth
Diameter	1,392,000 km	109.2
Mass	1.989×10^{30} kg	332,980
Density	1.41 g/cm^3	0.255
Surface Gravity	274 m/s^2	28.0
Escape speed	618 km/s	55.2
Effective temperature	5778 K	
Luminosity	3.85×10^{26} watts	
Tilt of equator to ecliptic	7.25°	
Sidereal rotation period		
Equator	25.05 days	
40° latitude	27.40 days	
80° latitude	33.83 days	

Overall Composition (by mass)

- 73% Hydrogen
- 25% Helium
- 2% other

QUICK FACTS

- Typical star, consisting mostly (98% by mass) of hydrogen and helium. Contains 99.85% of all mass in solar system. Gravitational contraction causes nuclear fusion in the core, where four hydrogen nuclei fuse into a helium nucleus (proton–proton chain). Resulting energy transported to surface of Sun by radiation and convection. Complex magnetic field causes eruptions of gas as spicules, flares, and prominences. Solar wind of high-energy particles affects magnetic fields of all planets in the solar system. Sunspot activity follows 11-year cycle of activity.

Mercury

Earth

Mercury

Mantle

Core
(nickel-iron)

Interior

Mercury Data

Mercury	Value	Compared with Earth
Equatorial diameter	4879 km	0.38
Oblateness	0	
Mass	3.302×10^{23} kg	0.055
Density	5.43 g/cm³	0.98
Surface gravity	3.7 m/s²	0.38
Escape speed	4.3 km/s	0.38
Sidereal rotation period	58.65 days	58.79
Solar day	176 days	176
Surface temperature	−150°C to +450°C	
Albedo	0.12	0.39
Tilt of equator to orbital plane	0.01°	
Orbit		
Semimajor axis	5.79×10^{7} km	0.387
Eccentricity	0.2056	12.3
Inclination to ecliptic	7.0°	
Sidereal period	87.97 days	0.24
Moons	0	

°C	K
450	723
0	273
−150	123
−273	0

Surface Temperature Extremes

QUICK FACTS

- Among the eight planets Mercury is the smallest; its diameter is one-third of Earth's, it is the closest planet to the Sun, and it has the most eccentric orbit. Greatest difference between maximum and minimum temperatures. Difficult to see from Earth. Almost no atmosphere. Surface cratered somewhat like Moon. Large iron core. Period of revolution 1.5 times period of rotation. Magnetic field not fully explained.

Venus

Earth   Venus

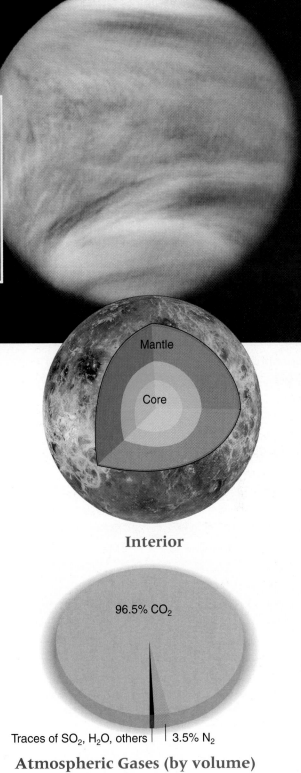

Venus Data

Venus	Value	Compared with Earth
Equatorial diameter	12,104 km	0.95
Oblateness	0	
Mass	4.869×10^{24} kg	0.82
Density	5.24 g/cm^3	0.95
Surface gravity	8.87 m/s^2	0.91
Escape speed	10.36 km/s	0.93
Sidereal rotation period	243 days	243.7
Solar day	117 days	117
Surface temperature	+464°C	
Albedo	0.75	2.5
Tilt of equator to orbital plane	177.4°	7.6
Orbit		
Semimajor axis	1.082×10^8 km	0.723
Eccentricity	0.0067	0.40
Inclination to ecliptic	3.39°	
Sidereal period	224.7 days	0.62
Moons	0	

Interior

Mantle

Core

96.5% CO_2

Traces of SO_2, H_2O, others   3.5% N_2

Atmospheric Gases (by volume)

QUICK FACTS

- Visible as morning and evening "star"; Earth's twin in size, mass, and density. Surface is hidden by cloud layer, mapped by radar. Slow retrograde rotation. Dry, hot surface. No large tectonic plates. Surface primarily solidified lava. Surface older than Earth's, younger than Moon's. Dense carbon dioxide atmosphere. Greenhouse effect causes high atmospheric temperature.

The Earth

Moon

Earth

Earth Data

Earth	Value
Equatorial diameter	12,756 km
Oblateness*	0.00335
Mass	5.97×10^{24} kg
Density	5.52 g/cm^3
Surface gravity	9.78 m/s^2
Escape speed	11.19 km/s
Sidereal rotation period	23.9345 hours
Solar day	24.0 hours
Surface Temperature	10°C to 20°C
Albedo**	0.306
Tilt of equator to orbital plane	23.45º
Orbit	
Semimajor axis	1.496×10^8 km
Eccentricity	0.0167
Sidereal period	365.26 days
Moons	1

*Recall that oblateness tells us how "flattened" an object is. The Earth's polar diameter is 12,714 km.

**The albedo of a solar system object is the fraction of incident sunlight that the object reflects without absorption.

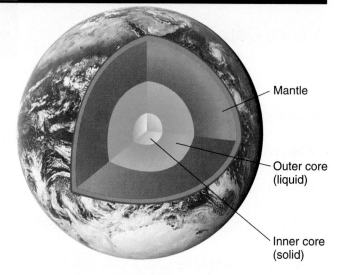

Mantle

Outer core (liquid)

Inner core (solid)

Interior

78% Nitrogen

21% Oxygen

1% Ar, H$_2$O, CO$_2$ and others

Atmospheric Gases (by volume)

QUICK FACTS

- Third planet from the Sun. Very circular orbit. Except for Pluto, has largest satellite compared with its size. Only planet with liquid water on surface. Active interior.

The Moon

Earth

Moon

Moon Data

Moon	Value	Compared with Earth
Equatorial diameter	3476 km	0.27
Oblateness	0.0012	0.36
Mass	7.35×10^{22} kg	0.0123
Density	3.35 g/cm³	0.61
Surface gravity	1.62 m/s²	0.166
Escape speed	2.4 km/s	0.21
Revolution period	27.322 days	
Sidereal rotation period	27.322 days	
Synodic period (phases)	29.531 days	
Surface temperature	−170° C to 130° C	
Albedo	0.11	0.36
Tilt of equator to orbital plane	6.68°	
Orbit		
Average distance from Earth	384,400 km (center-to-center)	
Closest distance	363,300 km	
Farthest distance	405,500 km	

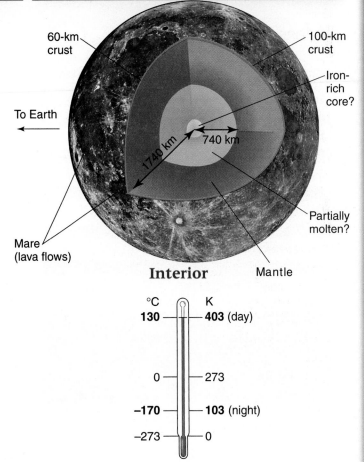

60-km crust

100-km crust

To Earth

Iron-rich core?

1740 km

740 km

Mare (lava flows)

Partially molten?

Mantle

Interior

°C	K
130	**403** (day)
0	273
−170	**103** (night)
−273	0

Surface Temperature Extremes

QUICK FACTS

- One fourth of Earth's diameter. Surface craters were caused by meteorite impacts. Maria were caused by lava flow. Extremely tenuous and transient atmosphere. Weak magnetic field. Likely to have formed as a result of a collision between Earth and a large object early in Earth's history.

Mars

Earth

Mars

Mars Data

Mars	Value	Compared with Earth
Equatorial diameter	6794 km	0.53
Oblateness	0.0065	1.93
Mass	6.419×10^{23} kg	0.11
Density	3.93 g/cm^3	0.71
Surface gravity	3.69 m/s^2	0.377
Escape speed	5.03 km/s	0.45
Sidereal rotation period	24.623 hours	1.03
Solar day	24.66 hours	1.03
Surface temperature	−140ºC to +20ºC	
Albedo	0.25	0.82
Tilt of equator to orbital plane	25.19º	1.07
Orbit		
Semimajor axis	2.28×10^8 km	1.524
Eccentricity	0.0935	5.6
Inclination to ecliptic	1.85º	
Sidereal period	1.881 years	1.881
Moons	2	

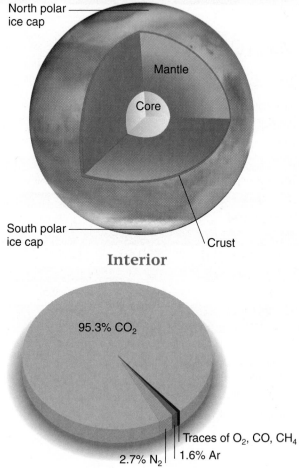

North polar ice cap

Mantle

Core

South polar ice cap

Crust

Interior

95.3% CO_2

2.7% N_2

1.6% Ar

Traces of O_2, CO, CH_4

Atmospheric Gases (by volume)

QUICK FACTS

- Known as the red planet. Half Earth's diameter. Least dense of terrestrial planets. Rotation rate and equatorial tilt very similar to Earth's. Has seasons. Water–carbon dioxide polar caps. Has largest mountain (Olympus Mons) and canyon (Valles Marineris) known. Low-pressure carbon dioxide atmosphere. Evidence of warmer, wetter past.

Jupiter

Earth   Jupiter

Jupiter Data

Jupiter	Value	Compared with Earth
Equatorial diameter*	142,984 km	11.2
Oblateness	0.065	19.36
Mass	1.899×10^{27} kg	317.8
Density	1.326 g/cm³	0.24
Surface gravity*	23.12 m/s²	2.36
Escape speed	59.5 km/s	5.32
Sidereal rotation period	9.925 hours	0.415
Albedo	0.34	1.12
Tilt of equator to orbital plane	3.13°	0.13
Orbit		
Semimajor axis	7.79×10^8 km	5.204
Eccentricity	0.0489	2.93
Inclination to ecliptic	1.3°	
Sidereal period	11.86 years	11.86
Moons	63	

* Measured where the pressure is one atmosphere, Earth's pressure at sea level.

Hydrogen/helium gas

Liquid hydrogen

Liquid metallic hydrogen

Heavy element core

Interior

89.8% Hydrogen

10.2% Helium

H_2O, NH_3, and CH_4

Atmospheric Gases (by volume)

QUICK FACTS

- The largest planet. Contains more than twice the mass of all other planets combined. Fast rotation. Atmosphere shows bands and the Great Red Spot and is mostly hydrogen and helium. Giant magnetic field because of liquid metallic hydrogen that makes up much of the planet. Emits more energy than it receives. Has a large family of moons and a faint ring system.

Saturn

Earth   Saturn

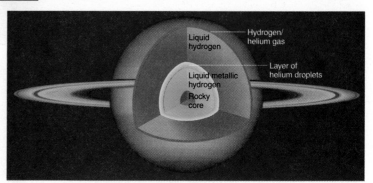

Interior

Saturn Data

Saturn	Value	Compared with Earth
Equatorial diameter*	120,536 km	9.45
Oblateness	0.098	29.24
Mass	5.685×10^{26} kg	95.16
Density	0.69 g/cm³	0.125
Surface gravity*	8.96 m/s²	0.916
Escape speed	35.5 km/s	3.2
Sidereal rotation period	10.656 hours	0.445
Albedo	0.34	1.12
Tilt of equator to orbital plane	26.73°	1.14
Orbit		
Semimajor axis	1.434×10^9 km	9.58
Eccentricity	0.0565	3.38
Inclination to ecliptic	2.49°	
Sidereal period	29.46 years	29.46
Moons	61	

* Measured where the pressure is one atmosphere, Earth's pressure at sea level.

Atmospheric Gases (by volume)

QUICK FACTS

- The ringed planet. Diameter is 84% of Jupiter's, but density is only half. Primarily hydrogen and helium, like Jupiter. Magnetic field 1/20 as strong as Jupiter's. Emits more energy than it receives—not fully explained. Large family of moons. Rings have detailed features and, seen from Earth, change greatly during its year.

Uranus

Earth

Uranus

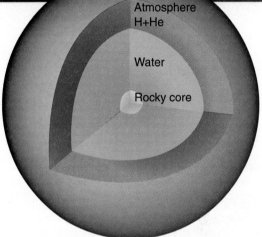

Atmosphere H+He

Water

Rocky core

Interior

Uranus Data

Uranus	Value	Compared with Earth
Equatorial diameter	51,118 km	4.0
Oblateness	0.023	6.84
Mass	8.683×10^{25} kg	14.5
Density	1.27 g/cm^3	0.23
Surface gravity*	8.69 m/s^2	0.89
Escape speed	21.3 km/s	1.9
Sidereal rotation period	−17.24 hours	0.72
Albedo	0.30	0.98
Tilt of equator to orbital plane	97.77°	4.17
Orbit		
Semimajor axis	2.872×10^9 km	19.20
Eccentricity	0.0457	2.7
Inclination to ecliptic	0.77°	
Sidereal period	84.01 years	84.01
Moons	27	

* Measured where the pressure is one atmosphere, Earth's pressure at sea level.

82.5% Hydrogen

15.2% Helium

H$_2$O, CH$_4$, and NH$_3$

Atmospheric Gases (by volume)

QUICK FACTS

- Four times Earth's diameter, but only one third of Jupiter's. Composition like other Jovian planets. Almost featureless atmosphere. Far greater tilt of axis than any other planet. Retrograde rotation. Uniform temperature. Many small moons, no large one.

Neptune

Earth

Neptune

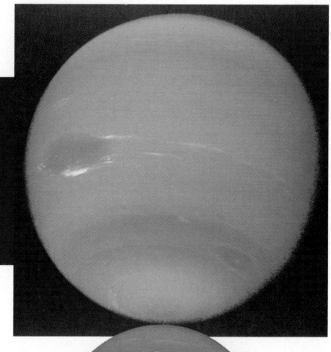

Neptune Data

Neptune	Value	Compared with Earth
Equatorial diameter	49,528 km	3.9
Oblateness	0.017	5.1
Mass	1.02×10^{26} kg	17.1
Density	1.64 g/cm³	0.30
Surface gravity*	11.0	1.12
Escape speed	23.5 km/s	2.1
Sidereal rotation period	16.11 hours	0.67
Albedo	0.29	0.95
Tilt of equator to orbital plane	28.3°	1.2
Orbit		
Semimajor axis	4.495×10^9 km	30.05
Eccentricity	0.0113	0.68
Inclination to ecliptic	1.77°	
Sidereal period	164.79 years	164.79
Moons	13	

* Measured where the pressure is one atmosphere, Earth's pressure at sea level.

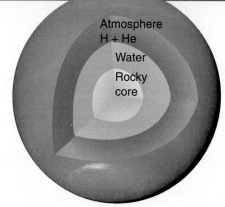

Atmosphere
H + He

Water

Rocky core

Interior

80% Hydrogen

19% Helium

H_2O and CH_4

Atmospheric Gases (by volume)

QUICK FACTS

- Blue surface because of methane. Jupiter-like atmospheric features, including Great Dark Spot. Composition is thought to be similar to other Jovian planets. Unexplained internal heat source. Extreme differential rotation. Largest moon, Triton, has retrograde revolution. The other major moon, Nereid, has the most eccentric orbit of any moon in the solar system. Lumpy rings.

Pluto

Earth

Pluto

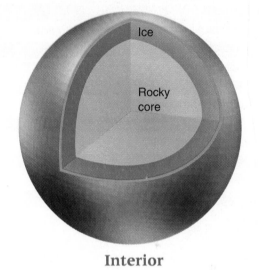

Interior

Pluto Data

Pluto	Value	Compared with Earth
Equatorial diameter	2300–2340 km	0.2
Mass	1.3×10^{22} kg	0.002
Density	2.00 g/cm³	0.32
Surface gravity	0.58 m/s²	0.06
Escape speed	1.1 km/s	0.1
Sidereal rotation period	–6.39 days	6.4
Surface temperature	–223°C	
Albedo	0.15	0.47
Tilt of equator to orbital plane	122.5°	
Orbit		
Semimajor axis	5.870×10^9 km	39.24
Eccentricity	0.244	14.6
Inclination to ecliptic	17.2°	
Sidereal period	247.7 years	247.7
Moons	3	

°C		K
–210		63
–235		38
–273		0

Surface Temperature Extremes

QUICK FACTS

- A dwarf planet; its eccentric orbit loops inside Neptune's orbit. Compared to the eight planets, Pluto's orbit has by far the greatest angle to the ecliptic. Receives 1/1600 the intensity of sunlight that Earth receives. Occultations by its moon Charon provided a method of determining its size and mass.

Appendix D

Planetary Satellites

The Moon	Value	Compared With Earth
Equatorial diameter	3476 km	0.27
Mass	7.35×10^{22} kg	0.0123
Density	3.35 g/cm^3	0.61
Surface gravity	1.62 m/s^2	0.166
Escape speed	2.4 km/s	
Revolution period	27.322 days	0.213
Sidereal rotation period	27.322 days	
Synodic period (phases)	29.531 days	
Surface temperature	−170°C to 130°C	
Albedo	0.11	0.36
Tilt of equator to orbital plane	6.68°	
Orbit		
Average distance from Earth	384,400 km	
Closest distance	363,000 km	
Farthest distance	405,500 km	
Eccentricity	0.055	

Satellite Data				
Planet Satellite	Average Distance (1000 km)	Sidereal (Orbital) Period (days)	Diameter (km)	Mass (10^{18} kg)
Earth				
Moon	384.4	27.322	3476	73,490
Mars				
Phobos	9.38	0.319	$27 \times 22 \times 18$	0.011
Deimos	23.46	1.262	$15 \times 12 \times 10$	0.002
Jupiter				
Metis	128.1	0.295	40	0.095
Adrastea	128.9	0.298	$26 \times 20 \times 16$	0.019
Amalthea	181.4	0.498	$262 \times 146 \times 134$	7.5
Thebe	221.9	0.675	110×90	0.78
Io	421.6	1.769	3643	89,320
Europa	670.9	3.551	3122	48,000

Satellite Data *(Continued)*

Planet Satellite	Average Distance (1000 km)	Sidereal (Orbital) Period (days)	Diameter (km)	Mass (10^{18} kg)
Jupiter *(continued)*				
Ganymede	1,070	7.155	5262	148,190
Callisto	1,883	16.689	4821	107,590
Leda	11,170	240.9	10	0.0057
Himalia	11,460	250.6	170	9.5
Lysithea	11,720	259.2	24	0.078
Elara	11,740	259.7	80	0.78
Ananke	21,280	629.8 R*	20	0.038
Carme	23,400	734.2 R	30	0.095
Pasiphae	23,620	743.6 R	36	0.30
Sinope	23,940	758.9 R	28	0.078
Saturn				
Pan	133.58	0.575	20	0.003
Atlas	137.67	0.602	$37 \times 34 \times 27$	0.01
Prometheus	139.35	0.613	$148 \times 100 \times 68$	0.33
Pandora	141.70	0.629	$110 \times 88 \times 62$	0.20
Epimetheus	151.42	0.694	$138 \times 110 \times 110$	0.54
Janus	151.47	0.695	$194 \times 190 \times 154$	1.9
Mimas	185.52	0.942	$418 \times 392 \times 382$	37.5
Enceladus	238.02	1.370	$512 \times 494 \times 490$	65
Tethys	294.66	1.888	$1072 \times 1056 \times 1052$	627
Telesto	294.66	1.888	$30 \times 25 \times 15$	0.007
Calypso	294.66	1.888	$30 \times 16 \times 16$	0.004
Dione	377.40	2.737	1120	1100
Helene	377.40	2.737	$36 \times 32 \times 30$	0.03
Rhea	527.04	4.518	1528	2310
Titan	1,221.83	15.945	5150	134,550
Hyperion	1,481.1	21.277	$370 \times 280 \times 226$	20
Iapetus	3,561.3	79.330	1436	1590
Phoebe	12,952	550.5 R	$230 \times 220 \times 210$	7.2
Uranus				
Cordelia	49.8	0.34	40	
Ophelia	53.8	0.38	42	
Bianca	59.2	0.43	54	
Cressida	61.8	0.46	80	
Desdemona	62.7	0.47	64	
Juliet	64.4	0.49	94	
Portia	66.1	0.51	136	
Rosalind	69.9	0.56	72	
Belinda	75.3	0.62	80	
Puck	86.0	0.76	162	

(Continued)

APPENDICES

Satellite Data *(Continued)*

Planet Satellite	Average Distance (1000 km)	Sidereal (Orbital) Period (days)	Diameter (km)	Mass (10^{18} kg)
Uranus *(continued)*				
Miranda	129.4	1.413	$480 \times 468 \times 466$	66
Ariel	191.0	2.520	$1162 \times 1156 \times 1155$	1350
Umbriel	266.3	4.144	1169	1170
Titania	435.9	8.706	1578	3520
Oberon	583.5	13.463	1523	3010
Caliban	7,230	579.5 R	96	
Stephano	8,002	676.5 R	20	
Trinculo	8,571	758 R	20	
Sycorax	12,179	1283 R	190	
Prospero	16,418	1993 R	30	
Setebos	17,459	2202 R	30	
Neptune				
Naiad	48.2	0.29	66	0.2
Thalassa	50.1	0.31	82	0.4
Despina	52.5	0.33	150	2
Galatea	62.0	0.43	176	4
Larissa	73.5	0.55	208×178	5
Proteus	117.6	1.12	$436 \times 416 \times 402$	50
Triton	354.8	5.877 R	2707	21,400
Nereid	5,513	360.1	340	30
Pluto[§]				
Charon	19.6	6.387	1186	1900
Nix	50	26.0	140	
Hydra	65	38.6	125	

* The symbol "R" indicates retrograde orbit.
[§] Dwarf planet

Appendix E

The Brightest Stars

Star	Popular Name	Apparent Magnitude	Apparent Brightness Compared*	Absolute Magnitude	Absolute Luminosity Compared**	Distance (ly)	Spectral Type
	Sun	−26.72	1.31×10^{10}	4.85	1	0.000015	G2
α CMa A	Sirius	−1.43	1	1.47	22.49	8.58	A1
α Car	Canopus	−0.62	0.474	−5.53	14,191	313	A9
α Boo	Arcturus	−0.05	0.281	−0.31	115.88	36.74	K2
α Cen A	Rigil Kentaurus	0.01	0.265	4.38	1.542	4.36	G2
α Lyr	Vega	0.03	0.261	0.58	51.05	25.32	A0
α Aur	Capella	0.08	0.249	−0.48	135.52	42.2	G5
β Ori A	Rigel	0.14	0.236	−6.62	38,726	733	B8
α CMi A	Procyon	0.38	0.189	2.66	7.516	11.42	F5
α Ori	Betelgeuse	0.45(v)†	0.177	−5.14 (v)	9,908	428	M2
α Eri	Achernar	0.45	0.177	−2.77	1,117	144	B3
β Cen	Hadar	0.61(v)	0.153	−5.42 (v)	12,823	525	B1
α Aql	Altair	0.77	0.132	2.21	11.38	16.79	A7
α Cru A	Acrux	0.77	0.132	−4.19	4,130	321	B1
α Tau A	Aldebaran	0.87(v)	0.120	−0.63 (v)	155.60	65.1	K5
α Vir	Spica	0.98(v)	0.109	−3.55 (v)	2,291	262	B1
α Sco A	Antares	1.06(v)	0.101	−5.28 (v)	11,272	604	M1
β Gem	Pollux	1.16	0.0920	1.09	31.92	33.74	K0
α Ps A	Fomalhaut	1.17	0.0912	1.74	17.54	25.09	A3
α Cyg	Deneb	1.23	0.0863	−7.23	67,920	1600	A2
β Cru	Becrux	1.25(v)	0.0847	−3.92 (v)	3,221	352	B0.5
α Cen B		1.34	0.0780	5.71	0.453	4.36	K0
α Leo A	Regulus	1.36	0.0765	−0.52	140.60	77.5	B7

* Compared with Sirius, the brightest star other than the Sun.
** Compared with the Sun.
† The symbol "(v)" indicates a variable star.

Appendix F

The Nearest Stars

Star	Apparent Magnitude	Apparent Brightness Compared*	Absolute Magnitude	Absolute Luminosity Compared**	Distance (ly)	Spectral Type
Sun	−26.72	1.31×10^{10}	4.85	1	0.000015	G2
Proxima Centauri	11.09	9.82×10^{-6}	15.53	5.3×10^{-5}	4.22	M5.5
α Centauri A	0.01	0.2655	4.38	1.542	4.36	G2
α Centauri B	1.34	0.0780	5.71	0.453	4.36	K0
Barnard's star	9.53	4.13×10^{-5}	13.22	4.5×10^{-4}	5.96	M4
Wolf 359	13.44	1.13×10^{-6}	16.55	2.1×10^{-5}	7.78	M6
Lalande 21185	7.47	2.75×10^{-4}	10.44	0.0058	8.29	M2
Sirius A	−1.43	1	1.47	22.49	8.58	A1
Sirius B	8.44	1.13×10^{-4}	11.34	0.00254	8.58	White dwarf
Gl 65 A***	12.54	2.58×10^{-6}	15.40	6.0×10^{-5}	8.72	M5.5
Gl 65 B (UV Ceti)	12.99	1.71×10^{-6}	15.85	4.0×10^{-5}	8.72	M6
Ross 154	10.43	1.80×10^{-5}	13.07	5.2×10^{-4}	9.68	M3.5
Ross 248	12.29	3.25×10^{-6}	14.79	1.1×10^{-4}	10.32	M5.5
ε Eridani	3.73	0.0086	6.19	0.291	10.52	K2
Lacaille 9352	7.34	3.10×10^{-4}	9.75	0.011	10.74	M1.5
Ross 128	11.13	9.46×10^{-6}	13.51	3.4×10^{-4}	10.91	M4
Gl 866 A (EZ Aquarii)	13.33	1.25×10^{-6}	15.64	4.8×10^{-5}	11.26	M5
Gl 866 B	13.27	1.32×10^{-6}	15.58	5.1×10^{-5}	11.26	
Gl 866 C	14.03	6.55×10^{-7}	16.34	2.5×10^{-5}	11.26	
Procyon A	0.38	0.1888	2.66	7.516	11.40	F5
Procyon B	10.70	1.41×10^{-5}	12.98	5.6×10^{-4}	11.40	White dwarf
61 Cygni A	5.21	0.0022	7.49	0.0879	11.40	K5
61 Cygni B	6.03	0.0010	8.31	0.0413	11.40	K7
Gl 725 A	8.90	7.4×10^{-5}	11.16	0.00299	11.52	M3
Gl 725 B	9.69	3.6×10^{-5}	11.95	0.00145	11.52	M3.5
Gl 15 A	8.08	1.6×10^{-4}	10.32	0.00649	11.62	M1.5
Gl 15 B	11.06	1.0×10^{-5}	13.30	4.2×10^{-4}	11.62	M3.5
ε Indi	4.69	0.0036	6.89	0.153	11.82	K5
DX Cancri	14.78	3.3×10^{-7}	16.98	1.4×10^{-5}	11.82	M6.5
τ Ceti	3.49	0.0108	5.68	0.466	11.88	G8

* Compared with Sirius, the brightest star other than the Sun.
** Compared with the Sun.
*** From Gliese and Jahreiss, *Catalog of Nearby Stars* (1991).

Appendix G

The Constellations

| Name | Genitive | Abbreviation | Approximate Position | | English Meaning |
			Right Ascension (hours)	Declination (degrees)	
Andromeda	Andromedae	And	01	+40	Andromeda*
Antlia	Antliae	Ant	10	−35	Air pump
Apus	Apodis	Aps	16	−75	Bird of paradise
Aquarius	Aquarii	Aqr	23	−15	Water bearer
Aquila	Aquilae	Aql	20	+05	Eagle
Ara	Arae	Ara	17	−55	Altar
Aries	Arietis	Ari	03	+20	Ram
Auriga	Aurigae	Aur	06	+40	Charioteer
Bootes	Bootis	Boo	15	+30	Herdsman
Caelum	Caeli	Cae	05	−40	Chisel
Camelopardus	Camelopardis	Cam	06	−70	Giraffe
Cancer	Cancri	Cnc	09	+20	Crab
Canes Venatici	Canum Venaticorum	CVn	13	+40	Hunting dogs
Canis Major	Canis Majoris	Cma	07	−20	Big dog
Canis Minor	Canis Minoris	Cmi	08	+05	Little dog
Capricornus	Capricorni	Cap	21	−20	Sea goat
Carina	Carinae	Car	09	−60	Keel of ship
Cassiopeia	Cassiopeiae	Cas	01	+60	Cassiopeia* (Queen of Ethiopia)
Centaurus	Centauri	Cen	13	−50	Centaur*
Cepheus	Cephei	Cep	22	+70	Cepheus* (King of Ethiopia)
Cetus	Ceti	Cet	02	−10	Whale
Chamaeleon	Chamaeleonis	Cha	11	−80	Chameleon
Circinis	Cirini	Cir	15	−60	Compass
Columba	Columbae	Col	06	−35	Dove
Coma Berenices	Comae Berenices	Com	13	+20	Berenice's hair*
Corona Australis	Coronae Australis	CrA	19	−40	Southern crown
Corona Borealis	Coronae Borealis	CrB	16	+30	Northern crown
Corvus	Corvi	Crv	12	−20	Crow
Crater	Crateris	Crt	11	−15	Cup
Crux	Crucis	Cru	12	−60	Southern cross
Cygnus	Cygni	Cyg	21	+40	Swan (or Northern cross)

(Continued)

APPENDICES

Name	Genitive	Abbreviation	Approximate Position		English Meaning
			Right Ascension (hours)	Declination (degrees)	
Delphinus	Delphini	Del	21	+10	Dolphin or Porpoise
Dorado	Doradus	Dor	05	−65	Swordfish
Draco	Draconis	Dra	17	+65	Dragon
Equuleus	Equulei	Equ	21	+10	Little horse
Eridanus	Eridani	Eri	03	−20	River Eridanus*
Fornax	Fornacis	For	03	−30	Furnace
Gemini	Geminorum	Gem	07	+20	Twins
Grus	Gruis	Gru	22	−45	Crane
Hercules	Herculis	Her	17	+30	Hercules*
Horologium	Horologii	Hor	03	−60	Clock
Hydra	Hydrae	Hya	10	−20	Hydra* (water monster)
Hydrus	Hydri	Hyi	02	−75	Sea serpent
Indus	Indi	Ind	21	−55	Indian
Lacerta	Lacertae	Lac	22	+45	Lizard
Leo	Leonis	Leo	11	+15	Lion
Leo Minor	Leonis Minoris	Lmi	10	+35	Little lion
Lepus	Leporis	Lep	06	−20	Hare
Libra	Librae	Lib	15	−15	Scales of justice
Lupus	Lupi	Lup	15	−45	Wolf
Lynx	Lincis	Lyn	08	+45	Lynx
Lyra	Lyrae	Lyr	19	+40	Harp or lyre
Mensa	Mensae	Men	05	−80	Table (or Mountain)
Microscopium	Microscopii	Mic	21	−35	Microscope
Monoceros	Monocerotis	Mon	07	−05	Unicorn
Musca	Muscae	Mus	12	−70	Fly
Norma	Normae	Nor	16	−50	Carpenter's level
Octans	Octantis	Oct	22	−85	Octant
Ophiuchus	Ophiuchi	Oph	17	00	Ophiuchus* (serpent bearer)
Orion	Orionis	Ori	05	+05	Orion* (hunter)
Pavo	Pavonis	Pav	20	−65	Peacock
Pegasus	Pegasi	Peg	22	+20	Pegasus* (winged horse)
Perseus	Persei	Per	03	+45	Perseus*
Phoenix	Phoenicis	Phe	01	−50	Phoenix
Pictor	Pictoris	Pic	06	−55	Easel

| Name | Genitive | Abbreviation | Approximate Position | | English Meaning |
			Right Ascension (hours)	Declination (degrees)	
Pisces	Piscium	Psc	01	+15	Fishes
Piscis Austrinus	Piscis Austrini	PsA	22	−30	Southern fish
Puppis	Puppis	Pup	08	−40	Stern of ship
Pyxis	Pyxidis	Pyx	09	−30	Compass of ship
Reticulum	Reticuli	Ret	04	−60	Net
Sagitta	Sagittae	Sge	20	+10	Arrow
Sagittarius	Sagittarii	Sgr	19	−25	Archer
Scorpius	Scorpii	Sco	17	−40	Scorpion
Sculptor	Sculptoris	Scl	00	−30	Sculptor
Scutum	Scuti	Sct	19	−10	Shield
Serpens	Serpentis	Ser	17	00	Serpent
Sextans	Sextantis	Sex	10	00	Sextant
Taurus	Tauri	Tau	04	+15	Bull
Telescopium	Telescopii	Tel	19	−50	Telescope
Triangulum	Trianguli	Tri	02	+30	Triangle
Triangulum Australe	Trianguli Australi	TrA	16	−65	Southern triangle
Tucana	Tucanae	Tuc	00	−65	Toucan
Ursa Major	Ursae Majoris	Uma	11	+50	Big bear
Ursa Minor	Ursae Minoris	Umi	15	+70	Little bear
Vela	Velorum	Vel	09	−50	Sails of ship
Virgo	Virginis	Vir	13	00	Virgin
Volans	Volantis	Vol	08	−70	Flying fish
Vulpecula	Vulpeculae	Vul	20	+25	Fox

* These are proper names.

Appendix H

Answers to Selected Questions, Calculations, and Try One Yourself Exercises

Chapter 1

Try One Yourself (Measuring the Positions of Celestial Objects)

4.5 arcseconds × (1 arcminute/60 arcseconds) = 0.075 arcminutes;

0.075 arcminutes × (1 degree/60 arcminutes) = 0.00125 degrees.

Recall Questions

2. D   **4.** A   **6.** C   **8.** B   **10.** D   **12.** E   **14.** B
16. C   **18.** D   **20.** D

22. Meteor, Moon, Sun, comet, planet, Milky Way (although it is a galaxy), galaxy, nebula.

24. A group of gravitationally bound stars, from billions to perhaps a thousand billion.

26. Stars near Polaris appear to move in circles around the north celestial pole.

28. Summer solstice occurs around June 21, and winter solstice occurs around December 22.

30. Normally, planets move eastward among the stars.

32. Mercury and Venus.

34. The elongation of a celestial object is the angle, viewed from Earth, from the Sun to the object.

36. Umbra is the portion of a shadow that receives no direct light from a light source, whereas penumbra is the portion of a shadow that receives direct light from only part of the light source.

38. The Moon darkens only slightly during penumbral eclipses.

Calculations

2. 1 light-year = (3 × 10⁸ meters/second) × (365 days/year) × (24 hours/day) × (3600 seconds/hour) = 9.46 × 10¹⁵ meters;

(9.46 × 10¹⁵ meters)/(1.5 × 10¹¹ meters/AU) = 6.3 × 10⁴ AU.

4. a) 109. b) No. The constellations are not actual objects. c) 733 years. We are seeing the star as it was 733 years ago, not as it is "now."

6. 15 arcseconds = 15 × (1/60) arcminutes = 0.25 arcminutes = 0.25 × (1/60) degrees = 0.0042 degrees.

8. 3 arcminutes = 3 × (1/60) degrees = 0.05 degrees.

10. The umbral shadow of the Moon barely reaches the Earth, and thus, the distance it reaches is about 380,000 km. The Earth's umbral shadow reaches a distance of about 1.4 million km. The ratio between the two is about 3.7, the same as the ratio between the diameters of Earth and Moon.

Chapter 2

Try One Yourself (Kepler's Third Law)

$a^3/P^2 = (1 \text{ AU})^3/(1 \text{ year})^2$;
$a^3/(0.615 \text{ years})^2 = 1 \text{ AU}^3/\text{year}^2$;
$a^3 = 0.615^2 \text{ AU}^3$;
$a = 0.723 \text{ AU}$.

Recall Questions

2. A   **4.** B   **6.** C   **8.** C   **10.** B   **12.** E
14. C   **16.** A   **18.** A   **20.** B   **22.** B   **24.** B

26. The 2nd century AD.

28. An epicycle is the circular orbit of a planet in the geocentric (Ptolemaic) model, the center of which revolves around the Earth in another circle. It was used in the model to explain retrograde motion. Copernicus' assumption that planets move at constant speeds around the Sun forced him to also use epicycles.

30. (a) The theory must fit the data. (b) The theory must make falsifiable predictions. (c) The theory must be aesthetically pleasing.

32. By comparing the directions of the Sun with respect to the vertical at two different cities at the summer solstice, he found that they were off by 7°. By assuming that the Sun was far from Earth, he correctly attributed the difference to the Earth's curvature. Thus, the ratio of 7° to 360° (for a full circle) corresponds to the ratio of the distance between the two cities to the Earth's circumference.

34. The theory held that the Earth rotates on its axis, causing the entire sky to appear to rotate around the Earth.

36. He used epicycles to improve accuracy. They were necessary because planets' motions are not the perfect circles that he assumed.

38. The farther a planet is from the Sun, the slower it moves.

40. Put two tacks in a board and put a loop of string loosely around them. Stretch the string taut with a pencil and sweep the pencil around, always keeping the string taut. To make it less eccentric, put the tacks closer together or use a longer string. Do the opposite for greater eccentricity.

42. Speeds from fastest to slowest: Mercury, Venus, Earth, Mars, Jupiter, Saturn. Distances from nearest to farthest: (the same).

Calculations

2. 4.2 AU and 6.2 AU.

4. 0.387 AU.

6. 3600 quarters.

8. Using the answer to Recall Question 32 we have $10°/360° = 500 \text{ km}/(2 \cdot \pi \cdot R)$. Solving for R we find $R = 36 \cdot 500/(2 \cdot \pi) = 2865 \text{ km}$.

10. Dividing both sides of the expression by 360° we get: $P_{syn}/P_E = P_{syn}/P_{sid} + 1$. Solving for P_{sid} we find: $P_{sid} = (P_{syn} \cdot P_E)/(P_{syn} - P_E)$. Because $P_E = 1$ year $= 365.256$ days, we have $P_{sid} = P_{syn}/(P_{syn} - 1)$. For Jupiter, $P_{syn} = 398.9$ days $= 1.092$ years, and thus, $P_{sid} = 1.092/(1.092 - 1) = 11.86$ years. The angle θ corresponds to the ratio between Jupiter's synodic and sidereal periods: $\theta = (1.092/11.86) \cdot 360° = 33°$.

Chapter 3

Try One Yourself (The Law of Universal Gravitation)

6400 kilometers + 300 kilometers = 6700 (to get distance from Earth-center).

When the astronaut moves above Earth, only the distance changes. The force of gravity depends inversely on distance squared, so

$(6400/6700)^2 \times 160$ pounds = 146 pounds.

When in orbit, an astronaut is "falling" around the Earth along with the Space Shuttle. (The "Travel to the Moon" box and the discussion of Figure B3-4 should help you understand why we can say the astronaut is "falling.")

Try One Yourself (Newton's Laws and Kepler's Laws)

$a^3_{(AU)}/P^2_{(yrs)} = (m_{Moon} + m_{satellite})/m_{Sun}$;
$(4 \times 10^{-5})^3/(1.3 \times 10^{-3})^2 = m_{Moon}/2 \times 10^{30}$ because the mass of the satellite is negligible. Thus,

$m_{Moon} = 7.6 \times 10^{22}$ kilograms.

Recall Questions

2. D   4. D   6. C   8. C   10. D   12. B
14. A   16. A   18. B   20. A   22. A

24. The phases of Venus.

26. The tendency of an object to retain its speed in a straight line. Countless examples are possible: a hammer resists stopping and thereby drives a nail; a car resists turning and slides sideways; a baseball is hit hard by a bat to change its motion.

28. See pages 75 and 77 for statements of the laws. Possible examples are:

Law 1) A ball rolling on a flat surface continues in a straight line unless a force changes its motion. 2) The more force that a bat exerts on a ball, the greater the acceleration of the ball. 3) An apple hanging from a tree exerts a downward force on the limb and the limb exerts an equal force upward on the apple.

30. The masses of the two objects and the distance between their centers of mass.

32. As a planet gets closer to the Sun, the distance between their centers of mass gets smaller, and thus (from Newton's law of gravity), the gravitational force from the Sun on the planet gets stronger. From Newton's law of motion, as the force acting on an object gets stronger, the object's acceleration increases.

34. The force of gravity from the Sun.

Calculations

2. 1/4 as much: about 63 pounds.

4. First: By Newton's revision of Kepler's third law: The star has two times the Sun's mass.

Second: B is at 6 AU. Using the same law we get 10.4 years.

6. The Moon's speed on its orbit is: $v = (2 \cdot \pi \cdot r)/\text{period} = (2 \cdot \pi \cdot 3.84 \cdot 10^8 \text{ m})/(27.32 \cdot 24 \cdot 60 \cdot 60 \text{ seconds}) = 1020$ m/s. The Moon's centripetal acceleration is: $v^2/r = 1020^2/(3.84 \cdot 10^8) = 0.0027$ m/s^2 = (9.8 m/s^2)/60^2.

Chapter 4

Try One Yourself (Characteristics of Wave Motion)

$v = \lambda \times f$;
344 m/s $= \lambda \times 4000$ cycles/s;
$\lambda = 0.086$ m.

(The resulting units are actually meters/cycle. This is appropriate, however, for one wave is one cycle.)

Try One Yourself (The Doppler Effect as a Measurement Technique)

The difference between the two wavelengths is 0.048 nanometers. Substitute the values into the Doppler equation:

$v = c \cdot (\Delta\lambda/\lambda_0) = (3.0 \times 10^8 \text{ m/s}) \cdot (0.048/656.285) = 2.2 \times 10^4$ m/s.

Because the shifted wavelength is shorter than the unshifted one, the star is moving toward the Sun.

Recall Questions

2. B   4. A   6. B   8. A   10. A   12. C
14. B   16. E   18. B   20. D   22. D   24. D

26. The 400-nanometer light. The shorter the wavelength, the higher the frequency.

28. Radio, infrared, visible, ultraviolet, X-rays, gamma rays.

30. The electron is the negatively charged object that orbits the nucleus. The nucleus is the central, massive core of the atom. A photon is the least possible amount of electromagnetic energy of a given wavelength.

32. The amount of energy of a photon is directly proportional to the frequency of the light. In equation form, $E = h \cdot f$, where E is the energy of the photon, h is a constant, and f is the frequency of the light.

34. A continuous spectrum is produced by a hot solid (or a very dense hot gas). An emission spectrum is produced by a hot gas with a density less than that which produces a continuous spectrum. An absorption spectrum is produced when light having a continuous spectrum passes through a gas at a low enough temperature.

36. The Doppler effect is the phenomenon whereby the wavelength (and therefore the frequency) of a wave changes because of relative motion between the wave's source and the observer. The Doppler effect has nothing to do with the intensity of the wave.

Calculations

2. 1.34 meters.

4. Receding at 9140 m/s.

6. X releases 81 times as much energy per unit area as Y.

8. –40 degrees.

10. Its Kelvin temperature is one third as much, and thus, it releases $(1/3)^4$, or 1/81 as much energy per given area. Because it has five times the area, it releases 5/81, or 0.062 as much energy as the Sun.

12. The bulb 30 feet away provides one ninth as much illumination as the one 10 feet away.

Chapter 5

Try One Yourself (Angular Size and Magnifying Power)

1.5 meters is 1500 millimeters;
$M = f_{obj}/f_{eye} = 1500$ mm/12 mm = 125.

Try One Yourself (Light-Gathering Power)

Light-gathering power depends on the square of the diameter of the objective lens, but first we must express both diameters in the same units. Let's use millimeters, and 10 centimeters = 100 millimeters.

$100^2/5^2 = 10,000/25 = 4000$.

Thus, the small telescope collects 4000 times as much light as the eye.

Try One Yourself (Resolving Power)

We will use the equation for resolving power, but first we must change 600 nanometers to meters, as the telescope diameter is expressed in meters.

600 nm = 600 nm $\times$ (10^{-9} m/nm) = 6.00×10^{-7} m;
$\theta = 2.5 \times 10^5 \times \lambda/D = 2.5 \times 10^5 \times (6 \times 10^{-7}/2.4)$
$= 0.0625$ arcseconds.

Recall Questions

2. A   4. D   6. C   8. A   10. B   12. C
14. E   16. B   18. A   20. C   22. A

24. An achromatic lens is actually composed of two lenses. The second lens recombines the colors that have been separated by the first lens. The defect, called chromatic aberration, is the separation of colors that occurs when only a single lens is used.

26. Light-gathering power is the measure of how much light is collected by a lens or mirror. The area of the lens or mirror determines its light-gathering power.

28. Figure 5-12b shows the Newtonian focal arrangement. (The objective mirror is also called the primary mirror.) The image formed by the objective is located where the two rays cross in the drawing.

30. A mirror reflects all wavelengths in the same direction, and thus, chromatic aberration does not occur.

32. Telescopes are placed on mountains so that they are above most of the atmosphere (and NOT so that they are closer to celestial objects).

34. Blurring effects of the atmosphere are eliminated.

Calculations

2. Two eyes collect 0.005 (or 1/200) as much light as the 10-centimeter telescope.

4. Each must have a diameter of 8 meters.

6. Using the 1.3-centimeter observations and the greatest distance, the best resolution is achieved. It is 1.5×10^{-4} arcseconds.

Chapter 6

Try One Yourself (The Small Angle Formula)

$D \approx (A''/206,265) \times d = (0.52 \times 3600/206,265) \times 384,000$ km = 3485 km.

The slight difference from the accepted answer is because the angle had been rounded to 0.52 rather than 0.518.

Recall Questions

2. E   4. A   6. D   8. C   10. C   12. C
14. They are approximately the same, at about 0.5°.

16. The effect depends on the mass of the planet and its distance from Mercury. Jupiter's mass is about 320 times that of Earth's, while Jupiter, even at its closest to Mercury, is only about 8 times farther from Mercury than Earth is. The dependence of the effect on mass and distance is such that Jupiter's contribution is about 1.7 times that of Earth's and 0.54 times that of Venus'.

18. A magnetic field is a region where magnetic forces can be perceived. A magnetic field can be detected by placing a magnet in the suspected location and determining whether there is a magnetic force on the magnet. The magnet used is commonly a small one that is free to turn, that is, a compass.

20. (a) Continental drift has been measured. (b) Rift zones, from which spreading is occurring, have been found. (c) Plate motion explains a number of earthquake zones, mountain ranges, and ocean trenches.

22. Craters were caused by impacts of meteorites. Material thrown out by the impact caused the rays that radiate from some craters.

24. There is a high tide on the area closer to the Moon because that area experiences a stronger gravitational pull from the Moon than the Earth's center. There is a high tide on the area farther from the Moon because that area experiences a weaker gravitational pull from the Moon than the Earth's center; it is as if the Earth's center is "pulled from under it."

Calculations

2. Use the small-angle formula to obtain $d = 1.65 \times 10^8$ km.

4. The expression for the force of gravity between the Sun (m_{Sun}) and the small mass m at point A is $F_A = G \cdot m_{Sun} \cdot m/(d_{ES} - R)^2$. Similarly, $F_B = G \cdot m_{Sun} \cdot m/d_{ES}^2$ and $F_C = G \cdot m_{Sun} \cdot m/(d_{ES} + R)^2$. Therefore, $F_A/F_B = d_{ES}^2/(d_{ES} - R)^2 = (1 + R/(d_{ES} - R))^2 \approx (1 + R/d_{ES})^2 \approx 1 + 2R/d_{ES}$. Similarly, $F_B/F_C = (d_{ES} + R)^2/d_{ES}^2 = (1 + R/d_{ES})^2 \approx 1 + 2 \cdot R / d_{ES}$. Since $2 \cdot R = 12,756$ km and $d_{ES} = 1.5 \cdot 10^8$ km we get $2 \cdot R/d_{ES} \approx 0.0001$.

6. For the case of Io and Jupiter, the diameter of Io is $2 \cdot R_{Io} = 3643$ km, and its distance from Jupiter is $d_{JI} = 421,600$ km. Therefore, $2 \cdot R_{Io}/d_{JI} \approx 0.009$. That's about 100 times stronger than for the case between Earth and Sun.

Chapter 7

Try One Yourself (Measuring Distances in the Solar System)

One half of 4.7 minutes is 141 seconds.

$d = v\,t = (3 \times 10^5 \text{ km/s}) \times 141 \text{ s} = 4.23 \times 10^7$ km;
$(4.23 \times 10^7 \text{ km}) \times (1 \text{ AU}/1.5 \times 10^8 \text{ km}) = 0.282$ AU.

Venus is 0.72 AU from the Sun, and $1 - 0.72 = 0.28$, in agreement with our answer.

Try One Yourself (Measuring Mass and Average Density)

$(a^3/P^2) = (G/4\pi^2)m_{\text{Earth}}$;
$(3.844 \times 10^8 \text{ m})^3/(2.36 \times 10^6 \text{ sec})^2 = 1.69 \times 10^{-12}\, m_{\text{Earth}}$;
$m_{\text{Earth}} = 6.03 \times 10^{24}$ kilograms.

This is close to the value in the appendix, 5.97×10^{24} kilograms. The difference is caused by our assumption that the Moon's mass is negligible. In fact, the value that we calculated is the total mass of the Earth and Moon.

Try One Yourself (Calculating Average Density)

Refer to the solution to the "Try One Yourself" in Chapter 6, where we calculated the diameter of the Moon to be 3485 kilometers.

Radius $= 1.74 \times 10^6$ meters.

Volume of Moon $= (4\pi/3)\, R^3 = (4\pi/3)\, (1.74 \times 10^6 \text{ m})^3 = 2.207 \times 10^{19} \text{ m}^3$.

Density = mass/volume $= (7.35 \times 10^{22} \text{ kg})/(2.207 \times 10^{19} \text{ m}^3)$

$= 3330 \text{ kg/m}^3$, in good agreement with the value 3350 kg/m³ in Appendix D.

Recall Questions

2. C   **4.** A   **6.** A   **8.** A   **10.** A   **12.** B
14. D   **16.** A   **18.** C   **20.** B   **22.** E   **24.** C

26. The total mass of the two objects.

28. Jupiter is the largest planet, with a diameter 11 times Earth's and a mass 318 times Earth's.

30. The masses of the planets that have moons were calculated using Kepler's third law. Mercury's and Venus' masses were calculated based on their gravitational effect on passing asteroids and comets, and later by their gravitational effects on spacecraft that passed near them.

32. All of the planets revolve around the Sun in the same direction. All except Venus, Uranus, and the dwarf planet Pluto rotate on their axes in the same direction as they revolve.

34. Compared with the Jovians, the terrestrials are nearer the Sun, smaller, less massive, more solid, slower rotating, more dense, and have thinner atmospheres and fewer moons. No terrestrial planet has a ring, whereas all Jovian planets have rings.

36. Earth is just slightly more dense than Mercury and Venus, somewhat more dense than Mars, and much more dense than the Jovian planets and Pluto.

38. The temperature of a gas is related to the speed of its molecules, and at the same temperature, the molecules of a more massive gas move more slowly.

40. Nonvolatile elements condensed in the inner solar system, but volatile elements were swept outward by the solar wind.

42. The asteroids are planetesimals that were prohibited from forming a planet by the effects of Jupiter's gravitational force. The Oort cloud is hypothesized to have resulted when small objects in the outer solar system were thrown outward by gravitational forces when Jupiter or Saturn passed near them.

Calculations

2. 77.2 AU.

4. 9.0×10^8 km, which is 6.0 AU.

6. Mass of Mars: 6.4×10^{23} kilograms. We assumed that the mass of Phobos is negligible compared with that of Mars. Density of Mars: 3.9×10^3 kg/m³, which is 3.9 g/cm³.

Chapter 8

Try One Yourself (Mercury via Mariner—Comparison with the Moon)

Time to cool is proportional to radius (and to diameter), and thus, because the diameter of Jupiter is 11.2 times that of Earth (from Appendix C), it takes Jupiter 11.2 times as long to cool as Earth does.

Recall Questions

2. B   **4.** B   **6.** D   **8.** C   **10.** E   **12.** D
14. C   **16.** B   **18.** D   **20.** B   **22.** D   **24.** A

26. Venus is most like Earth in size; Mars is most like Earth in rotation period.

28. Mercury's rotation period is exactly two thirds of its period of revolution. This has occurred because the mass of the planet is not evenly distributed through its volume. The planet has an eccentric orbit, and the gravitational forces toward the Sun have changed its rotation rate so that resonance occurs between its rotation and revolution.

30. There are two reasons for the extremes in temperature. First, day and night periods are very long (88 Earth days each), providing long periods of time for the surface to heat and cool. Second, there is no atmosphere to block sunlight during the day and to retain heat at night.

32. The greenhouse effect is the phenomenon of infrared radiation being prohibited from escaping through a planet's atmosphere, thereby causing a high temperature on the planet. In a florist's greenhouse an additional effect occurs: The hot air is trapped inside the greenhouse by the walls and roof.

34. The tilt of Mars' axis is very similar to that of Earth's. Mars' equator is tilted 25.2 degrees from its orbital plane, whereas Earth's is tilted 23.5 degrees. (Tables normally show equatorial tilt rather than axis tilt; they are numerically the same.)

36. The polar caps of Mars are made of frozen water and frozen carbon dioxide.

38. The temperature near the equator of Mars varies from $-135°C$ to $+30°C$—a much greater difference than ever experienced on Earth. The reason for the difference is that Mars' atmosphere is very thin and therefore does not shield sunlight during the day or provide a greenhouse effect to blanket the planet at night.

Calculations

2. Jupiter's volume is 11^3, or 1331, times Earth's volume.

4. The smallest feature that can be observed is about 750 km across. Caloris Basin is 1400 km in diameter, about twice the smallest feature that can be seen.

6. $a^3/P^2 = 1$ when units of AU and years are used.

   $1.524^3/a^2 = 1$;

   $a = 1.881$ years.

Chapter 9

Recall Questions

2.	B	4.	C	6.	A	8.	C	10.	D	12.	D
14.	B	16.	B	18.	C	20.	B

22. The band at Jupiter's equator has that rotation rate.

24. The outer atmosphere is primarily hydrogen and helium at a relatively low pressure. As we go deeper, pressure increases until the material would be judged a liquid. About 20,000 kilometers below the cloudtops, liquid metallic hydrogen is found, and it extends down to whatever heavy-element core exists.

26. Saturn's rings are aligned with its equator, which is tilted at about 27 degrees to the planet's orbital plane. Thus, as Saturn orbits the Sun, we on Earth (which is relatively near the Sun) sometimes see the southern side of Saturn and its rings and sometimes the northern side. Midway between these views, the rings are edge-on to our view and are nearly invisible.

28. 1) Knowing the distance to a planet and the planet's angular size, we can use the small-angle formula to calculate the diameter. 2) When a planet passes in front of a star, observation of the amount of time that the planet blocks the star's light, along with knowledge of the planet's speed, gives us another method to calculate the diameter.

30. Uranus' axis tilt (98 degrees) is such that each of its poles nearly points toward the Sun at one time during its revolution period.

32. When a moon changes its distance from its planet, the amount of tidal force exerted on the moon changes. This causes the moon to flex, and this produces heat. The more massive the planet, the greater the effect on its moon, and the closer the moon is to its planet, the greater the effect. Thus, the inner moons of Jupiter that have a noncircular orbit experience tidal heating the most. Io is the moon that shows the most prominent effect of tidal heating.

Calculations

2. Its density would be three fifths, or 0.6, of Earth's.

4. Period = 6 days and the circumference of the spot is about 60,000 km. Thus, the speed is 10,000 km/day, or 400 km/hour, or 0.1 km/s.

6. One percent of its mass is 8.9×10^{20} kilograms. At 1000 kilograms/second, it would take 8.9×10^{17} seconds, or about 28 billion years, much greater than the age of the solar system.

8. The energy per unit time emitted by the planet is $4\pi R^2 \cdot \sigma T^4$. The energy per unit time received by the planet (of cross-section πR^2) from the Sun is $4\pi R^2_{Sun} \cdot \sigma T^4_{Sun} \cdot (\pi R^2/4\pi d^2)$. The ratio then is $4 \cdot (T/T_{Sun})^4 \cdot (d/R_{Sun})^2$. For Jupiter this ratio is 1.3, but in reality the ratio is greater because Jupiter does not absorb all the Sun's light.

Chapter 10

Recall Questions

2.	E	4.	C	6.	D	8.	D	10.	D	12.	C
14.	B	16.	B	18.	C	20.	D	22.	B	24.	C

26. The most accurate values of Pluto's size come from observations of eclipses of its moon, Charon.

28. Before an asteroid is named, its orbit must have been determined accurately. The orbits of most observed asteroids have not been calculated.

30. Gravitational pull from Jupiter disrupts the orbits of asteroids so that the weaker gravitational forces between them cannot pull them together.

32. The nucleus of a comet is its solid core. Comet nuclei are irregular in shape and are typically a few kilometers across. The coma is made up of gas and dust surrounding the nucleus. It has a very low density and may be as large as 100,000 kilometers in diameter. A comet has two tails, one made up of ions and one of dust. Tails are typically from 10^7 to 10^8 kilometers long.

34. One tail is made up of ions swept away by the solar wind. It is straight because the ions move away from the coma at great speeds. The other tail consists of dust pushed away slowly by radiation pressure. The curvature results from the fact that the material moves away from the coma very slowly compared with the coma's speed.

36. First, the vast majority of long-period comets are in elongated elliptical orbits around the Sun. They must therefore spend most of their time far from the Sun. Second, comets are regularly being captured in the inner solar system. The existence of the cloud explains their origin.

38. A meteor shower results when the Earth encounters a swarm of meteoroids. As the Earth moves into the swarm, the resulting meteors seem to originate in the direction in which the Earth is moving.

Calculations

2. At 2×10^{-9} kilograms/meter² per day, it would take about 700,000 years.

4. The answer is simply the ratio of areas, 2.6×10^{-4}, which is about one chance in 4000.

6. Warning time = 10^6 seconds, which is less than 12 days. It would pass through the atmosphere in less than 10 seconds. (The asteroid will speed up as it approaches Earth.)

Chapter 11

Try One Yourself (Solar Energy)

Area of sphere = $4\pi R^2 = 4\pi (2.3 \times 10^{11} \text{ m})^2 = 6.64 \times 10^{23} \text{ m}^2$.

Energy/area = 3.9×10^{26} watts/$6.64 \times 10^{23} \text{ m}^2$ = 587 watts/m².

Recall Questions

2. C   4. D   6. C   8. A   10. E   12. B
14. B   16. A   18. A   20. D   22. A   24. C

26. The most convincing evidence is that if a chemical process were the source of the Sun's power, the Sun would burn out over a few centuries, and we know that it has released energy fairly uniformly for (at least) many millions of years.

28. The number of protons in nuclei distinguish one element from another.

30. Most of the Sun is made up of gas.

32. The pressure at any depth within the Sun is caused by the weight (and therefore by the mass) of gas above that layer. To calculate the mass of gas above a given point within the Sun, one needs to know the density at levels above that point. This density is calculated from knowledge of pressures and temperatures. (Because the pressures and densities at each layer depend on pressures and densities of layers above, the calculations are best done by a computer.)

34. Photons from the Sun's core are continuously absorbed and reemitted by material within the Sun. Because a photon is absorbed after traveling only about 1 cm and because photons are reemitted in random directions, the radiation travels a very great distance before arriving at the photosphere.

36. First, most of their radiation is in the X-ray portion of the spectrum. Second, they have a very low density, and therefore, there is not much material in them to emit light.

Calculations

2. Volume of Sun = $(4/3) \pi R^3 = (4/3) \pi (6.95 \times 10^8 \text{m})^3 = 1.4 \times 10^{27} \text{ m}^3$.

   Mass/Volume = $1.99 \times 10^{30} \text{ kg}/1.4 \times 10^{27} \text{ m}^3 = 1.4 \times 10^3 \text{ kg/m}^3$. The density of water is $1.0 \times 10^3 \text{ kg/m}^3$.

4. 500 nm. This is green (or yellowish green). It appears yellow because it has passed through the Earth's atmosphere, which scatters more light from the violet end of the spectrum than from the red end.

Chapter 12

Try One Yourself (Apparent Magnitude)

The difference in apparent magnitude between the two objects is 8. Referring to Table 12-1, we see that a difference of 5 corresponds to a ratio of 100, and a difference of 3 corresponds to a ratio of 16; therefore, we receive 1600 times more light from Mars than from Barnard's star.

Try One Yourself (Spectroscopic Parallax)

Using the H-R diagram in Figure 12-17 and the spectral type K1, we find that the absolute magnitude is between about +6.2 and +7.5. Because these numbers are greater than the star's apparent magnitude, we know that the star appears brighter than it actually is (because the greater the number, the dimmer the star). Thus, the star must be closer than 10 parsecs from us.

We can use the equation in the "Calculating Absolute Magnitude" box to get a better answer, as follows:

$m - M = 5 \times \log(d) - 5$ where m = apparent mag., M = absolute mag., and d = distance in parsecs.

Use 6.2 as the absolute magnitude:

$4.4 - 6.2 = 5 \log (d) - 5$;
$\log (d) = 0.64$;
$d = 4.4$ pc.

When we use the same method with the other limit of absolute magnitude, 7.5, we get

$d = 2.4$ pc.

Thus, we conclude that the star is between 2.4 parsecs and 4.4 parsecs from us.

(Actually, it is 3.2 parsecs away, close to the middle of our range.)

Try One Yourself (Luminosity and the Sizes of Stars)

Using solar units, luminosity = radius^2 × temperature^4.

$10,000 = r^2 \times (2/3)^4$;
$r^2 = 50,625$;
$r = 225$.

Therefore, the radius of this star is 225 times that of the Sun. (If a star's radius is 225 times the Sun's, its diameter is also 225 times the Sun's.)

Recall Questions

2. C   4. D   6. B   8. D   10. D   12. E
14. C   16. B   18. A   20. A   22. D   24. C

26. We must know the object's distance as well as its angular velocity.

28. Apparent magnitude is a scale of the amount of light received from an object, whereas absolute magnitude is a scale of the amount of light emitted by an object. Luminosity is closely related to absolute magnitude, whereas brightness relates more closely to apparent magnitude.

30. The Doppler effect is used to measure a star's radial velocity.

32. Figure 12-17 is such a sketch.

34. If white dwarfs were as large as most stars, they would be very luminous. Their small size results in their being dim.

36. (1) A visual binary is visible as two stars (normally only with the use of a telescope).

   (2) A spectroscopic binary is a binary that can be detected by periodic Doppler shifts of the two stars. If the spectra of both are visible, each spectral line periodically splits into two lines.

   (3) An eclipsing binary system changes brightness as one star eclipses the other.

   (4) An astrometric binary system is one in which only one star can be seen, and that star is observed to move in a periodic motion that indicates the presence of an orbiting companion.

(5) A composite spectrum binary can be detected because of great differences in the spectra of the two stars.

38. If the plane of revolution of a binary is along a line from Earth, the maximum speed of each component that is observed by the Doppler effect is actually the speed of the star. If the plane of revolution is not along a line from Earth, however, that observed speed is less than the star's actual speed, and unless the angle between the plane of revolution and the line from Earth is known, the actual speed of the star cannot be calculated.

40. From the period of a Cepheid's light variation, its absolute magnitude can be determined. Then, knowing its absolute magnitude and its apparent magnitude, its distance can be calculated.

Calculations

2. They differ in magnitude by 2.5, and thus, we receive between 6.3 (which corresponds to a difference of 2) and 16 (which corresponds to 3) times as much light from Antares than from τ Ceti. (The actual ratio is about 9.9, which we calculate by raising the number 2.5 to the power of the difference in magnitudes—which happens in this case to also be 2.5.)

4. Moving α Centauri to a distance of 10 parsecs would entail moving it more than seven times farther away than it is now, thereby making it much dimmer; therefore, its absolute magnitude must be greater than zero. (Its actual absolute magnitude is 4.4.)

6. It is closer than 10 parsecs. (Actual distance: 5.1 parsecs.)

8. Using Figure 12-34, we can see that it is more than 100 times as luminous as the Sun. Using the equation relating the mass and luminosity of a star on the main sequence we find that $4^{3.5} = 128$, and thus, it is actually 128 times as luminous as the Sun.

10. The time period between points B and C on the diagram is about 0.4 days; therefore, the diameter of the smaller star is (0.4 days) $\times$ (6.9×10^7 km/day) = 27.6 million km.

Chapter 13

Recall Questions

2. C **4.** A **6.** D **8.** D **10.** B **12.** C
14. A **16.** D

18. A protostar is a "star" in the process of formation; it is heated by gravitational energy as its material falls inward.

20. Less massive stars take longer because the lesser mass means that there is less gravitational force pulling each particle toward the center.

22. There is a lower limit because if a star does not have some critical amount of mass there will not be enough pressure at its center for nuclear fusion to be sustained.

More massive stars release more radiation as they join the main sequence, and stars above about 150 solar masses probably emit radiation so intense that no more material can fall onto them.

Calculations

2. Luminosity = radius^2 $\times$ temperature^4 when solar values are used for each quantity. (We could also use the Sun's diameter, as diameter is twice the radius.)

$1000 = r^2 \times (1/6)^4$;
$\quad r = 1140$.

Thus, the Sun at that time had a radius 1140 times greater than today's Sun.

This is 5.3 AU, which means the Sun would have extended to Jupiter's present position.

4. $\lambda = 2,900,000/T = 2,900,000/300 = 9700$ nm.

Visible light extends from about 400 to 700 nanometers, and 9700 nanometers is in the infrared region of the spectrum.

Chapter 14

Recall Questions

2. E **4.** A **6.** D **8.** C **10.** D **12.** B
14. B **16.** E **18.** C **20.** B **22.** B **24.** D
26. D

28. The star's mass.

30. After hydrogen fusion ceases, the core collapses and gravitational energy causes further heating.

32. The Earth will be absorbed in the outer part of the Sun. The Sun will expand so that its photosphere is somewhere between the present orbits of Earth and Mars.

34. (1) Pulsations in the core of a red giant increase in intensity until the outer layers of the star become unstable and are blown away.

(2) The stellar winds blow away the outer portions of the red giant, and two different stages of the wind overlap to cause the glowing shell.

36. Electron degeneracy.

38. Hydrogen is being deposited on a white dwarf from a binary companion. When enough pressure builds up, this hydrogen erupts in a fusion reaction. After it is fused to helium (and some of it is blown away) more hydrogen continues to build up again until fusion starts again.

Calculations

2. The small angle formula yields 1.05 light-years. At 20 km/s, this required 4.95×10^{11} s, or 15,700 years.

4. A magnitude change of 5 corresponds to a factor of 100 in brightness. Thus, a change of 10 corresponds to a factor of 100×100, or 10,000. A change of 20 corresponds to a factor of 100^4, or 100 million.

Chapter 15

Recall Questions

2. B **4.** E **6.** A **8.** D **10.** E **12.** B
14. D **16.** A **18.** B **20.** C **22.** D **24.** A

26. When mass is added to a main sequence star, the star becomes larger. White dwarfs and neutron stars become smaller when mass is added, however. If the size of a black hole is considered to extend to its event horizon, added mass makes a black hole larger.

28. The fact that the Chinese "guest star" was very bright and that today we see an expanding cloud of debris at its location leads us to conclude that it was a supernova.

30. Pulsars vibrate faster than the surface of a white dwarf could vibrate. On the other hand, they vibrate more slowly than neutron stars could vibrate.

32. A black hole is an object that is so dense that its gravitational force is great enough that light cannot escape. We might observe a black hole when material falls toward it, for that material would heat up as it falls and emit radiation. Another way to observe one is by observing the motion of another star (or stars) revolving around the black hole.

34. The escape velocity from inside the event horizon of a black hole is greater than the speed of light.

36. Radiation has been observed that has the characteristics predicted to occur when material falls toward the event horizon of a black hole. Other black holes have been detected by observing a star that is in orbit around an unseen companion, when calculations show that the companion is massive enough that if it were not a black hole it would be emitting light.

Calculations

2. The Schwarzschild radius is proportional to the mass. Thus, if the mass is doubled, the radius is doubled.

4. Section 15-6 indicates that the maximum mass of a neutron star is about 3 solar masses. Using 4 solar masses in Kepler's third law:

$a^3_{(AU)}/P^2_{(yrs)} = (m_1 + m_2)/m_{Sun} = 4\,m_{Sun}/m_{Sun} = 4$.
Using $P = 1$ second $= 3.2 \times 10^{-8}$ years, $a = 1.6 \times 10^{-5}$ AU = 2400 km.

6. $R_S = 2 \cdot G \cdot M/c^2$ and thus $R_S = 2 \cdot G \cdot (M/m_{Sun}) \cdot m_{Sun}/c^2 = 2 \cdot (6.67 \cdot 10^{-11}\ \text{N} \cdot \text{m}^2/\text{kg}^2) \cdot (2 \cdot 10^{30}\ \text{kg}) \cdot (M/m_{Sun})/(3 \cdot 10^8\ \text{m/s})^2 \approx 3000 \cdot (M/m_{Sun})$ meters $= 3 \cdot (M/m_{Sun})$ kilometers. Thus, R_S (in km) $= 3 \cdot M$ (in solar masses).

Chapter 16

Recall Questions

2. B	4. A	6. C	8. A	10. E	12. A
14. C	16. E	18. C			

20. Figure 16-2 or Figure 1-2a,b is what your drawing should look like. The exact location of the spiral arms is not important, however.

22. Galactic clusters are groups of up to a few dozen stars that share a common origin and are located relatively near one another. Most are found within the Galactic disk. Globular clusters are groups of up to hundreds of thousands of stars. They are found primarily in the halo of the Galaxy. Clusters of galaxies are groups of individual galaxies that are held near one another by gravitational force.

24. The brightest stars, O- and B-type stars, are clustered at certain distances from the Sun. Better evidence is provided by the 21-cm radiation, which indicates that cool hydrogen gas is located in spiral arms.

Calculations

2. 40,000 light-years $= 3.8 \times 10^{17}$ km. The circumference of the path is then 2.4×10^{18} km. Dividing this by 250 km/s, we obtain 9.6×10^{15} seconds, or 3×10^8 years.

4. Diameter of Galaxy $= 160,000$ light-years $= 1.5 \times 10^{18}$ km and the Sun's diameter is 1.5×10^6 km. Setting up a ratio, we find that the scale model would be 100,000 km across!

Chapter 17

Try One Yourself (The Hubble Law)

Figure 17-9 indicates that a distance of 1 million parsecs corresponds to a speed of 470 km/s.

slope $= (470\ \text{km/s} - 0)/1\ \text{Mpc} = 470\ \text{(km/s)/Mpc}$ or about 144 (km/s)/Mly.

Try One Yourself (The Hubble Law Used to Measure Distance)

Using a Hubble constant of 21.1 (km/s)/Mly:
$v = H_0 d$;
$90,000\ \text{km/s} = 21.1\ \text{(km/s)/Mly} \times d$;
$d = 4265$ Mly.

Using a Hubble constant of 21.9 (km/s)/Mly, we similarly get $d = 4110$ Mly. Therefore, the object is between about 4110 and 4265 Mly away.

Recall Questions

2. E	4. D	6. D	8. B	10. B	12. E
14. A	16. C	18. C	20. A	22. E	

24. (a) Using Kepler's third law with measured values of rotation rates of various parts of a galaxy. (b) Application of Kepler's third law to binary pairs of galaxies. (c) Calculations of the mass necessary to prevent a galaxy from leaving the cluster of galaxies in which it is observed.

26. Not enough mass is directly observed in clusters of galaxies to hold the clusters together. Because they do hold together, more mass must exist than we can observe. Because it is not observed, it must be dark matter.

28. The Hubble law states that the velocity of recession of a distant galaxy is proportional to the galaxy's distance. The Hubble constant seems to be between 21.1 and 21.9 (km/s)/Mly, which is between 68.8 and 71.4 (km/s)/Mpc.

30. To use the Hubble law to determine the distance to a galaxy, we measure the recessional velocity of the galaxy and then calculate its distance based on a value of the Hubble constant. Although recessional velocity can be accurately measured, some of that velocity may not be due to Hubble expansion. In addition, the Hubble constant is not known accurately.

32. An active galaxy emits more than normal amounts of radiation from its nucleus.

34. For a quasar with a redshift of 25%, the ratio of the amount of shift in wavelengths of its spectral lines to the unshifted wavelenghts is 0.25. The quasar with a redshift of 30% is moving away faster.

36. If they were nearby and moving at the speeds indicated by their redshifts, they would have had to have been produced recently. It is thought, instead, that quasars do not exist in the universe of today, and we see them only because they are very distant and therefore have a great look-back time.

Calculations

2. The slope for the data in Figure 17-9 is about 470 (km/s)/Mpc. The slope for the data in Figure 17-11 is about 65 (km/s)/Mpc.

4. 4 hours.

6. 8.0 kiloparsecs $\times$ 9.5 kiloparsecs.

8. Density $= d$. Also, m is mass in solar masses and r is the radius in kilometers; as such, both m and r are dimensionless numbers.

$$d = M/(4\pi R^3/3) = (m \times m_{Sun})/(4\pi r^3 \cdot 1000^3/3)$$
$$= 4.8 \times 10^{20} \, (m/r^3) \text{ kg/m}^3$$

For $r = 3 \cdot m$, we get $d = 1.8 \times 10^{19}/m^2$.
For $m = 10^9$, $d = 18$ kg/m^3.
For $m = 10^8$, $d = 1800$ kg/m^3. (The density of water is 1000 kg/m^3.)

Chapter 18

Recall Questions

2. C	**4.** C	**6.** A	**8.** B	**10.** D	**12.** A
14. C	**16.** D	**18.** E	**20.** D		

22. Clusters of galaxies are getting farther apart from one another. Theory tells us that space is expanding.

24. Homogeniety: The properties of the universe are the same throughout. On a sufficiently large scale, the universe looks the same everywhere. Isotropy: The universe is the same no matter in what direction we look.

Universality: The same physical laws apply throughout the universe.

26. The Hubble constant must first be determined. The maximum age of the universe is equal to the inverse of the Hubble constant, once million light-years (or million parsecs) have been converted to kilometers.

28. If the universe is an oscillating one, the present expansion will finally stop and compression begin. After compression leads to maximum density, the big bang will repeat, etc.

Calculations

2. $\lambda_{max} = 2{,}900{,}000/T$ where λ is in nm and T is in kelvin. Substituting 3 for the temperature, $\lambda_{max} = 9.7 \times 10^5$ nm. Figure 4-3 indicates that this is in the microwave region of the electromagnetic spectrum. 3000 K yields 970 nm, in the near infrared.

Chapter 19

Recall Questions

2. A	**4.** E	**6.** E	**8.** B	**10.** E	**12.** E	**14.** B

16. The longer the average civilization lasts, the more likely a civilization is to be in existence when we are observing. Analogy: Suppose that on the night of the Fourth of July, 1000 sparklers are lit on my street. If a sparkler stays lit only 5 seconds, a person in a low-flying plane may not have a chance to see one as he or she flies over, but if they stay lit 30 minutes, several will be lit at any particular time.

Calculations

2. If 1000 civilizations, $10^{10}/1000 = 10$ million years on the average. If there are a million advanced civilizations, this is 10,000 years.

4. From the Chapter 14 Tools of Astronomy Box "Lifetimes on the Main Sequence,"

$$t = t_{Sun}/M^{2.5} = 10^{10}/1.5^{2.5} = 3.6 \text{ billion years.}$$

Glossary

absolute magnitude   The apparent magnitude a star would have if it were at a distance of 10 parsecs.

absorption spectrum   A spectrum that is continuous except for certain discrete frequencies (or wavelengths).

accelerate   To change the speed and/or direction of motion of an object.

acceleration   A measure of how rapidly the speed and/or direction of motion of an object is changing.

accretion   The process by which an object gradually accumulates matter, usually due to the action of gravity.

accretion disk   A rotating disk of gas orbiting a star, formed by material falling toward the star.

achromatic lens (or **achromat**)   An optical element that has been corrected so that it is free of chromatic aberration.

active galaxy (active galactic nucleus, AGN)   A galaxy with an unusually luminous nucleus.

active optics   A technology that works by "actively" keeping a telescope's mirror at its optimal shape against environmental factors such as gravity and wind. It works on timescales of a second or more.

adaptive optics   A technique that improves image quality by reducing the effects of astronomical seeing. It relies on an active optics system and works on timescales of less than 0.01 seconds.

albedo   The fraction of incident sunlight that an object reflects.

altitude   The height of a celestial object measured as an angle above the horizon.

angular momentum   An intrinsic property of matter. A measure of the tendency of a rotating or revolving object to continue its motion.

angular separation   The angle between lines originating from the eye of the observer toward two objects.

angular size (of an object)   The angle between two lines drawn from the viewer to opposite sides of the object.

annular eclipse   An eclipse in which the Moon is too far from Earth for its disk to cover that of the Sun completely, and thus, the outer edge of the Sun is seen as a ring.

aphelion/perihelion   The point in its orbit around the Sun where a planet, or other object, is farthest from/closest to the Sun.

apogee/perigee   The point in the orbit of an Earth satellite where it is farthest from/closest to Earth.

Apollo asteroids   Asteroids that cross the Earth's orbit and have semimajor axes larger than Earth's.

apparent magnitude   A measure of the amount of light received from a celestial object.

asteroid   Any of the thousands of minor planets (small, mostly rocky objects) that orbit the Sun.

asteroid belt   The region between Mars and Jupiter where most asteroids orbit.

astrometric binary   An orbiting pair of stars in which the motion of one of the stars reveals the presence of the other.

astrometry   The branch of astronomy that deals with the measurement of the position and motion of celestial objects.

astronomical unit (AU)   A unit of distance equal to the average distance between the Earth and the Sun (about 150 million kilometers or 93 million miles).

astronomical seeing   The blurring and twinkling of the image of an astronomical light source caused by Earth's atmosphere.

astrophysics   Physics applied to extraterrestrial objects.

aurora   Light radiated in the upper atmosphere due to impacts from charged particles.

autumnal and vernal equinoxes   The points on the celestial sphere where the Sun crosses the celestial equator while moving south and north, respectively.

barred spiral galaxy   A spiral galaxy in which the spiral arms come from the ends of a bar through the nucleus, rather than from the nucleus itself.

baryons   Subatomic particles, including the proton, the neutron, and a number of unstable, heavier particles.

belts (and **zones**)   The dark-colored (and light-colored) bands that mark Jupiter's atmosphere.

big bang   The theoretical initial explosion that began the expansion of the universe.

binary star (system)   A pair of stars that are gravitationally bound so that they orbit one another.

binary system   A system of two objects orbiting each other due to their mutual gravitational attraction.

blackbody   A theoretical object that absorbs and emits all wavelengths of radiation, so that it is a perfect absorber and emitter of radiation. The radiation it emits is called **blackbody radiation.**

black dwarf   The theoretical final state of a star with a main sequence mass less than about 4 solar masses, in which all of its energy sources have been depleted so that it emits no radiation.

black hole   An object whose escape velocity exceeds the speed of light.

blazars (or BL Lac objects)   Especially luminous active galactic nuclei that vary in luminosity by a factor of up to 100 in just a few months.

blueshift   A change in wavelength toward shorter wavelengths.

Bohr atom   The model of the atom proposed by Niels Bohr; it describes electrons in orbit around a central nucleus and explains the absorption and emission of light.

brown dwarf   A star-like object that has insufficient mass to start nuclear reactions in its core and thus become self-luminous.

capture theory   A theory that holds that the Moon was originally solar system debris that was captured by Earth.

carbon (or CNO) cycle   A series of nuclear reactions that results in the fusion of hydrogen into helium, using carbon-12 in the process.

Cassegrain focus   The optical arrangement of a reflecting telescope in which a convex secondary mirror is mounted so as to intercept the light reflected from the objective mirror and reflect the light back through a hole in the center of the primary.

catastrophe theory   A theory of the formation of the solar system that involves an unusual incident, such as the collision of the Sun with another star.

celestial equator   A line on the celestial sphere directly above the Earth's equator.

celestial pole   The point on the celestial sphere directly above a geographic pole of the Earth.

celestial sphere   The imaginary sphere of heavenly objects that seems to center on the observer.

center of mass   The average location of the various masses in a system, weighted according to how far each is from that point.

centripetal force   The force directed toward the center of the curve along which the object is moving.

Cepheid variable   One of a particular class of pulsating stars.

Chandrasekhar limit   The limit to the mass of a white dwarf star, above which it cannot be supported by electron degeneracy and cannot exist as a white dwarf.

charge-coupled device (CCD)   A small semiconductor chip that serves as a light detector by emitting electrons when it is struck by light. A computer uses the pattern of electron emission to form images.

chemical differentiation   The sinking of denser materials toward the center of planets or other objects.

chromatic aberration   The defect of optical systems that results in light of different colors being focused at different places.

chromosphere   The region of the solar atmosphere between the photosphere and the corona.

closed universe   The state of the universe if its total mass and energy density is greater than a specific value, called the critical density.

cocoon nebula   The dust and gas that surround a protostar and block much of its radiation.

coma   The part of a comet's head made up of diffuse gas and dust.

comet   A small object, mostly ice and dust, in orbit around the Sun.

composite spectrum binary   A binary star system with stars having spectra different enough to distinguish them from one another.

conduction   The transfer of energy in a solid by collisions between atoms and/or molecules.

conservation of angular momentum   A law that states that the angular momentum of a system does not change unless there is a net external influence acting on the system, producing a twist around some axis.

constellation   An area of the sky containing a pattern of stars named for a particular object, animal, or person.

continental drift   The gradual motion of the continents relative to one another.

continuous spectrum   A spectrum containing an entire range of wavelengths, rather than separate, discrete wavelengths.

convection   The transfer of energy in a gas or liquid by means of the motion of the material.

core (of the Earth)   The central part of the Earth, consisting of a solid inner core surrounded by a liquid outer core.

corona   The outermost portion of the Sun's atmosphere.

coronal hole   A region in the Sun's corona that has very little luminous gas.

coronal mass ejection   An event in which hot coronal gas is suddenly ejected into space at speeds of hundreds of km/s.

correspondence principle   The idea that predictions of a new theory must agree with the theory it replaces in cases where the previous theory has been found to be correct.

cosmic microwave background radiation (or CMB radiation)   Long-wavelength radiation observed from all directions; thought to be the remnant of radiation from the big bang.

cosmic rays   Energetic charged particles that originate in outer space; they travel at nearly the speed of light and strike Earth from all directions.

cosmological constant   A term (denoted by the Greek capital letter "lambda," Λ) in the equations of general relativity that corresponds to a force throughout all space that helps the universe expand.

cosmological principle   The basic assumption of cosmology that holds that on a large scale the universe is the same everywhere.

cosmological redshift   The shift toward longer wavelengths that is due to the expansion of the universe.

cosmology   The study of the nature and evolution of the universe as a whole.

Coudé focus   The optical arrangement of a reflecting telescope in which two mirrors are used to reflect the light coming from the objective to a remote focal point.

crescent (phase)   The phase of a celestial object when less than half of its sunlit hemisphere is visible.

critical density   The average mass and energy density of the universe at which space would be flat. It is equal to $3H_0^2/(8\pi G)$ and is equivalent to about 5.5 hydrogen atoms per cubic meter of space.

crust (of the Earth)   The thin, outermost layer of the Earth.

dark energy   An exotic form of energy whose negative pressure currently accelerates the expansion of the universe.

dark matter   Matter that can be detected only by its gravitational interactions; it appears to be quite abundant throughout the universe.

dark nebula   An interstellar molecular cloud whose dust blocks light from stars on the other side of it.

declination   A star's angle north or south of the celestial equator.

density   The ratio of an object's mass to its volume.

density parameter   The ratio (denoted by the Greek letter "omega," Ω_0) of the total mass and energy density of the universe to the critical density.

density wave   A wave in which areas of high and low pressure move through the medium.

density wave theory   A model for spiral galaxies that proposes that the arms are the result of density waves sweeping around the galaxy.

deuterium   A hydrogen nucleus that contains one neutron and one proton.

differential rotation   Rotation of an object in which different parts have different periods of rotation.

diffraction   The spreading of light upon passing the edge of an object.

diffraction grating   A device that uses the wave properties of electromagnetic radiation to separate the radiation into its various wavelengths.

disk (of a galaxy)   The flat, dense portion of a spiral galaxy that rotates in a plane around the nucleus.

Doppler effect   The observed change in wavelength of waves from a source moving toward or away from an observer.

double planet (or co-creation) theory   A theory that holds that the Moon was formed at the same time as the Earth.

dynamo effect   The generation of magnetic fields due to circulating electric charges, such as in an electric generator.

dynamo model   The model that explains the Earth's (and other planets') magnetic fields as due to currents within a molten iron core.

eccentricity of an ellipse (*e*)   The result obtained by dividing the distance between the foci by the longest distance across an ellipse (the *major axis*).

eclipse season   A time of the year during which a solar or lunar eclipse is possible.

ecliptic   The apparent path of the Sun on the celestial sphere.

electromagnetic spectrum   The entire array of electromagnetic waves.

electron   A negatively charged particle that orbits the nucleus of an atom.

electron degeneracy   The state of a gas in which its electrons are packed as densely as nature permits.

ellipse   A geometrical shape of which every point is the same total distance from two fixed points (the foci).

elliptical galaxy   One of a class of galaxies that have smooth spheroidal shapes.

elongation   The angle in the sky from an object to the Sun.

emission nebula   Interstellar gas that fluoresces due to ultraviolet light from a star near or within the nebula.

emission spectrum   A spectrum made up of discrete frequencies (or wavelengths) rather than a continuous band of frequencies (or wavelengths).

epicycle   The circular orbit of a planet in the Ptolemaic model, the center of which revolves around the Earth in another circle.

escape velocity   The minimum velocity an object must have to escape the gravitational attraction of another object, such as a planet or star.

event horizon   A space-time boundary around a black hole from within which nothing can escape. Its radius is the Schwarzschild radius.

evolutionary track   The path on the H-R diagram taken by a star as its luminosity and color change.

eyepiece   The magnifying lens (or combination of lenses) used to view the image formed by the objective of a telescope.

Faber-Jackson relation   A relation between the luminosity and central stellar velocity dispersion of an *elliptical galaxy*.

fact   Generally a close agreement by competent observers of a series of observations of the same phenomenon.

field of view   The actual angular width of the scene viewed by an optical instrument.

fireball   An extremely bright meteor.

fission theory   A theory that holds that the Moon formed when material was spun off from the Earth.

flat universe   The state of the universe if its total mass and energy density is exactly equal to a specific value, called the critical density.

flatness problem   The inability of the *standard* big bang model to account for the apparent flatness of the universe.

fluorescence   The process of absorbing radiation of one frequency and re-emitting it at a lower frequency.

focal length   The distance from the center of a lens or a mirror to its focal point.

focal point (of a converging lens or mirror)   The point at which light from a very distant object converges after being refracted or reflected.

focus of an ellipse   One of the two fixed points that define an ellipse. (See the definition of *ellipse.*)

frequency   The number of repetitions per unit time.

full (phase)   The phase of a celestial object when the entire sunlit hemisphere is visible.

fusion (nuclear)   The combining of two nuclei to form a different nucleus.

galactic (or open) cluster   A group of stars that share a common origin and are located relatively close to one another.

galactic rotation curve   A graph of the orbital speed of objects in the galactic disk as a function of their distance from the center.

galaxy   A group of gravitationally bound stars, ranging from a billion to perhaps a thousand billion stars.

Galilean moons   The four natural satellites of Jupiter that were discovered by Galileo. Their names, starting closest to Jupiter, are Io, Europa, Callisto, and Ganymede.

general theory of relativity   A theory developed by Einstein that expands special relativity and presents an alternative way of explaining the phenomenon of gravitation.

geocentric model   A model of the universe with the Earth at its center.

giant star   A star of great luminosity and large size (10 to 100 times the Sun's diameter).

gibbous (phase)   The phase of a celestial object when between half and all of its sunlit hemisphere is visible.

globular cluster   A spherical group of up to hundreds of thousands of stars, found primarily in the halo of the galaxy.

granulation   Division of the Sun's surface into small convection cells.

gravitational lens   The phenomenon in which the gravity due to a massive body between a distant object and the viewer bends light from the distant object and causes it to be seen as two or more objects.

gravitational wave   Ripples in the curvature of space produced by changes in the distribution of matter.

greatest elongation   The configuration of an inferior planet at its greatest angular distance east or west of the Sun.

greenhouse effect   The effect by which infrared radiation is trapped within a planet's atmosphere through the action of particles, such as carbon dioxide molecules, within that atmosphere.

halo (around a galaxy)   The outermost part of a spiral galaxy; fairly spherical in shape, it lies beyond the spiral component.

heliocentric   Centered on the Sun.

helioseismology   The study of the propagation of pressure waves (similar to sound) in the Sun.

helium flash   The runaway helium fusion reactions that occur in the core during the evolution of a red giant.

hertz (abbreviated **Hz**)   The unit of frequency equal to one cycle per second.

Hertzsprung-Russell (H-R) diagram   A plot of absolute magnitude (or luminosity) versus temperature (or spectral type) for stars.

homogeneous   Having uniform properties throughout.

horizon problem   The inability of the *standard* big bang model to account for the directional uniformity of the background radiation.

Hubble constant   The proportionality constant in the Hubble law; the ratio of recessional velocities of galaxies to their distances.

Hubble law   The relationship that states that a galaxy's recessional velocity is directly proportional to its distance.

hydrostatic equilibrium   In a star or a planet, the balance between the downward pressure caused by the weight of material above a thin layer and the upward pressure exerted by material below.

hypothesis   An educated guess made in describing the results of an experiment or observation. A hypothesis can be wildly speculative but must be testable.

image   The visual counterpart of an object, formed by refraction or reflection of light from the object.

inclination (of a planet's orbit)   The angle between the plane of a planet's orbit and the ecliptic plane.

inertia   The tendency of an object to resist a change in its motion.

inferior planet   A planet that is closer to the Sun than the Earth is.

inflationary universe model   A modification of the big bang model that holds that the early universe experienced a brief period of extremely fast expansion.

instability strip   A region of the H-R diagram where pulsating stars are found.

interferometry   A procedure that allows several telescopes to be used as one by taking into account the time at which individual waves from an object strike each telescope.

interstellar cirrus   Faint, diffuse dust clouds found throughout interstellar space.

inverse square law   Any relationship in which some factor decreases as the square of the distance from its source.

ion   An electrically charged atom (or molecule), resulting from its loss or gain of at least one electron.

irregular galaxy   A galaxy of irregular shape that cannot be classified as spiral or elliptical.

isotope   One of two (or more) atoms whose nuclei have the same number of protons but different numbers of neutrons.

isotropy   The property of being the same in all directions.

Kelvin temperature scale   A temperature scale with its zero point at the lowest possible temperature ("absolute zero") and a degree that is the same size (same temperature difference) as the Celsius degree. ($T_K = T_C + 273$.)

kinetic energy   An object's energy due to its motion. For an object of mass m and speed v, its kinetic energy is equal to $(1/2)\,mv^2$.

Kuiper belt   A disk-shaped region beyond Neptune's orbit, 30–1000 AU from the Sun, closer to the solar system than the Oort cloud and presumed to be the source of short-period comets. The main Kuiper belt extends from 30 to 50 AU.

large impact theory   A theory that holds that the Moon formed as the result of an impact between a large object and the Earth.

law or **principle**   When a hypothesis has been repeatedly tested and has not been contradicted, it may become known as a law or principle.

lenticular galaxy   An S0 galaxy, having a flat disk like a spiral galaxy (with little spiral structure) and a large bulge like an elliptical galaxy.

light curve   A graph of the numerical measure of the light received from a star versus time.

light-gathering power   A measure of the amount of light collected by an optical instrument.

lighthouse model   The theory that explains pulsar behavior as being due to a spinning neutron star whose beam of radiation we see as it sweeps by.

light-year   The distance light travels in 1 year.

limb (of the Sun or Moon)   The apparent edge of the object as seen in the sky.

linear polarization   The situation when the electric field in an electromagnetic wave oscillates in a fixed plane.

local group (of galaxies)   The cluster of over 30 or so galaxies that includes the Milky Way Galaxy.

local hypothesis   A proposal stating that quasars are much nearer than a cosmological interpretation of their redshifts would indicate.

look-back time   The time light from a distant object has traveled to reach us.

luminosity   The rate at which electromagnetic energy is emitted.

luminosity class   One of several groups into which stars can be classified according to characteristics of their spectra.

lunar eclipse   An eclipse in which the Moon passes into the shadow of the Earth.

lunar month   The Moon's synodic period, or the time between successive similar phases.

lunar ray   A bright streak on the Moon caused by material ejected from a crater.

magnetic field   A magnetic field exists in a region of space if magnetic forces can be detected in that region.

magnetosphere   The volume of space in which the motion of charged particles is controlled by the magnetic field of the planet, rather than by the solar wind.

magnifying power, or magnification (of an instrument)   The ratio of the angular size of an object when it is seen through the instrument to its angular size when seen with the naked eye.

main sequence   The part of the H-R diagram containing the great majority of stars; it forms a diagonal line across the diagram.

mantle (of the Earth)   The thick, solid layer between the crust and the core of the Earth.

mare (plural maria)   Any of the lowlands of the Moon or Mars that resemble a sea when viewed from Earth.

mass   The quantifiable property of an object that is a measure of its inertia.

mass-luminosity diagram   A plot of the mass versus the luminosity of a number of stars.

meridian   An imaginary line that runs from north to south, passing through the observer's zenith.

meteor   The phenomenon of a streak in the sky caused not only by the burning of a rock or dust particle as it falls but also by the air molecules in the particle's path that, after being excited, then give off light as they de-excite.

meteor shower   The phenomenon of a large group of meteors seeming to come from a particular area of the celestial sphere.

meteorite   An interplanetary chunk of matter that has struck a planet or moon.

meteoroid   An interplanetary chunk of matter smaller than an asteroid.

microlensing   The effect of a temporary brightening of the light from a distant star orbited by an object such as a planet. Light rays from the star bend when they pass through the planet's gravity, which acts as a lens.

micrometeorite   A tiny meteorite.

Milky Way Galaxy   The galaxy of which the Sun is a part. From Earth, it appears as a band of light around the sky (**the Milky Way**).

minute of arc   One sixtieth of a degree of arc.

missing mass   The difference between the mass of clusters of galaxies as calculated from Keplerian motions and the amount of visible mass.

model (scientific)   An idea, a logical framework, that accounts for a set of observations and/or allows us to create explanations of how we think a part of nature works.

molecular cloud   A cold (10–50 K), dense (10^3–10^6 particles/cm^3), massive (from a few to a few million times the mass of the Sun) interstellar cloud; it consists mainly of molecular hydrogen, with traces of carbon monoxide and other molecules.

nanometer (abbreviated nm)   A unit of length equal to 10^{-9} meter.

neap tide   The least difference between high and low tide, occurring when the solar tide partly cancels the lunar tide.

nebula (plural nebulae)   An interstellar region of dust and/or gas.

neutrino   An elementary particle that has little rest mass and no charge but carries energy from a nuclear reaction.

neutron   The nuclear particle with no electric charge.

neutron star   A star that has collapsed to the point at which it is supported by neutron degeneracy.

Newtonian focus   The optical arrangement of a reflecting telescope in which a plane secondary mirror is mounted along the axis of the telescope in order to intercept the light reflected from the objective mirror and reflect it to the side.

nonvolatile element   An element that is gaseous only at a high temperature and condenses to liquid or solid when the temperature decreases.

nova (plural novae)   A star that suddenly and temporarily brightens, thought to be due to new material being deposited on the surface of a white dwarf.

nuclear bulge   The central region of a spiral galaxy.

nucleus (of atom)   The central, massive part of an atom.

nucleus (of comet)   The solid chunk of a comet, located in the head.

objective lens (or objective)   The main light-gathering element—lens or mirror—of a telescope. It is also called the primary lens.

oblate   Flattened at the poles.

oblateness   A measure of the "flatness" of a planet, calculated by dividing the difference between the largest (d_{large}) and smallest (d_{small}) diameter by the largest diameter: oblateness = $(d_{large} - d_{small})/d_{large}$.

Occam's razor   The principle that the best explanation is the one that requires the fewest unverifiable assumptions.

occultation   The passing of one astronomical object in front of another.

Olbers' paradox   An argument showing that the sky in a static universe could not be dark.

Oort cloud   The theorized spherical shell, lying between 10,000 and 100,000 AU from the Sun, containing billions of comet nuclei. The inner Oort cloud lies between 1000 and 10,000 AU.

open universe   The state of the universe if its total mass and energy density is less than a specific value, called the critical density.

opposition   The configuration of a planet when it is opposite the Sun in our sky. That is, the objects are aligned as Sun–Earth–planet.

optical double   Two stars that have small angular separation as seen from Earth but are not gravitationally bound.

oscillating universe model   A big bang theory that holds that the universe goes through repeating cycles of explosion, expansion, and contraction.

P waves   Seismic waves analogous to the waves produced by pushing a spring back and forth.

parallax   The apparent shifting of nearby objects with respect to distant ones as the position of the observer changes.

parallax angle   Half the maximum angle that a star appears to be displaced due to the Earth's motion around the Sun.

parsec   The distance from the Sun to an object that has a parallax angle of one arcsecond.

partial lunar eclipse   An eclipse of the Moon in which only part of the Moon passes through the umbra of the Earth's shadow.

partial solar eclipse   An eclipse in which only part of the Sun's disk is covered by the Moon.

particle density   The number of separate atomic and/or nuclear particles per unit of volume.

penumbra   The portion of a shadow that receives direct light from only part of the light source.

penumbral lunar eclipse   An eclipse of the Moon in which the Moon passes through the Earth's penumbra but not through its umbra.

perigee/apogee   The point in the orbit of an Earth satellite where it is closest to/farthest from Earth.

perihelion/aphelion   The point in its orbit around the Sun where a planet (or other object) is closest to/farthest from the Sun.

phases (of the Moon)   The changing appearance of the Moon during its revolution around the Earth, caused by the relative positions of the Earth, Moon, and Sun.

photometry   The measurement of light intensity from a source, either the total intensity or the intensity at each of various wavelengths.

photon   The smallest possible amount of electromagnetic energy of a particular wavelength.

photosphere   The visible "surface" of the Sun. The part of the solar atmosphere from which mostly visible radiation is emitted into space.

planet   Any of the eight large objects (Mercury to Neptune) that revolve around the Sun, or similar objects that revolve around other stars.

planetary nebula   The shell of gas that is expelled by a low mass red giant near the end of its life.

planetesimal   One of the small objects that formed from the original material of the solar system and from which a planet developed.

plate tectonics   The motion of sections of the Earth's crust (plates) across the underlying mantle.

positron   A positively charged electron emitted from the nucleus in some nuclear reactions.

power   The amount of energy exchanged per unit time.

precession   The conical shifting of the axis of a rotating object.

precession (of an elliptical orbit)   The change in orientation of the major axis of the elliptical path of an object.

pressure   The force per unit of area.

prime focus   The point in a telescope where the light from the objective is focused. This is the focal point of the objective.

principle or **law**   When a hypothesis has been repeatedly tested and has not been contradicted, it may become known as a law or principle.

principle of equivalence   The statement that effects of acceleration are indistinguishable from gravitational effects.

prominence   The eruption of solar material beyond the disk of the Sun.

proper motion   The angular velocity of a star as measured from the Sun.

proton   The positively charged particle in the nucleus of an atom.

proto-planetary nebula   An object in transition between the last stages of a red giant star's life and its planetary nebula phase.

proton–proton (p-p) chain   The series of nuclear reactions that begins with four protons and ends with a helium nucleus.

protostar   An object in the process of becoming a star, before it reaches the main sequence.

Ptolemaic model   The theory of the heavens devised by Claudius Ptolemy.

pulsar   A pulsating radio source with a regular period, between a millisecond and a few seconds, believed to be associated with a rapidly rotating neutron star.

quadrature   The position when a planet is 90° from the Sun in the sky as seen from Earth.

quarter (phase)   The phase of a celestial object when half of its sunlit hemisphere is visible.

quasar (quasi-stellar radio source)   A small, intense celestial source of radiation with a very large redshift.

radial velocity   Velocity along the line of sight, toward or away from the observer.

radiant (of a meteor shower)   The point in the sky from which the meteors of a shower appear to radiate.

radiation   The transfer of energy by electromagnetic waves.

radioactive dating   A procedure that examines the radioactivity of a substance to determine its age.

radio galaxy A galaxy having its greatest luminosity at radio wavelengths.

redshift A change in wavelength toward longer wavelengths.

reflection nebula Interstellar dust that is visible due to reflected light from a nearby star.

refraction The bending of light as it crosses the boundary between two materials in which it travels at different speeds.

resolving power (or resolution) The smallest angular separation detectable with an instrument. It thus is a measure of an instrument's ability to see detail.

retrograde motion The east-to-west motion of a planet against the background of stars.

revolution The orbiting of one object around another.

rift zone A place where tectonic plates are being pushed apart, normally by molten material being forced up out of the mantle.

right ascension A star's angle around the celestial equator measuring eastward from the vernal equinox.

Roche limit The minimum radius at which a satellite (held together by gravitational forces) may orbit without being broken apart by tidal forces.

rotation The spinning of an object about an axis that passes through it.

RR Lyrae variables Pulsating stars with periods shorter than a day.

S waves Seismic waves analogous to the waves produced by shaking a rope, attached to a wall, up and down.

scarp Transition zone from one series of sedimentary rocks to another of a different age and composition. They are found on Mercury, Earth, Mars, and the Moon.

Schwarzschild radius The radius of the sphere around a black hole from within which no light can escape.

scientific method A never-ending cycle of hypothesis, prediction, data gathering, and verification.

scientific model An idea, a logical framework, that accounts for a set of observations and/or allows us to create explanations of how we think a part of nature works.

second of arc One sixtieth of a minute of arc.

seeing The best possible angular resolution that can be achieved.

self-propagating star formation theory A model for spiral galaxies that explains the arms as resulting from a series of supernovae, each triggering the formation of new stars.

Seyfert galaxy One of a class of spiral galaxies having active nuclei and spectra containing emission lines.

sidereal day The amount of time that passes between successive passages of a given star across the meridian.

sidereal period The amount of time required for one revolution (or rotation) of a celestial object with respect to the distant stars.

singularity The center of a black hole, where density, gravity, and the curvature of space and time are infinite.

solar day The amount of time that elapses between successive passages of the Sun across the meridian.

solar eclipse (or eclipse of the Sun) An eclipse in which light from the Sun is blocked by the Moon.

solar flare An explosion near or at the Sun's surface, seen as an increase in activity such as prominences.

solar system The system that includes our Sun, planets and their satellites, asteroids, comets, and other objects that orbit our Sun.

solar wind The flow of charged particles from the Sun.

space velocity The velocity of a star relative to the Sun.

special theory of relativity A theory developed by Einstein that predicts the observed behavior of matter due to its speed relative to the person who makes the observation.

spectrometer An instrument that measures the wavelengths present in electromagnetic radiation. (A **spectrograph** is a spectrometer that produces a photograph of the spectrum.)

spectroscopic binary An orbiting pair of stars that can be distinguished as two due to the changing Doppler shifts in their spectra.

spectroscopic parallax The method of measuring the distance to a star by comparing its absolute magnitude with its apparent magnitude.

spectrum The order of colors or wavelengths produced when light is dispersed.

spicule A narrow jet of gas that is part of the chromosphere of the Sun and extends upward into the corona.

spiral galaxy A disk-shaped galaxy with arms in a spiral pattern.

spring tide The greatest difference between high and low tide, occurring about twice a month, when the lunar and solar tides correspond.

standard solar model Today's generally accepted theory of solar energy production.

star A self-luminous celestial object.

stellar parallax The apparent annual shifting of nearby stars with respect to background stars, measured as the angle of shift.

stellar wind The flow of particles from a star.

summer and winter solstices The points on the celestial sphere where the Sun reaches its northernmost and southernmost positions, respectively.

sunspot A region of the Sun's surface that is temporarily cool and dark compared with the surrounding regions.

supercluster A group of clusters of galaxies.

supergiant The evolutionary stage of a massive star after it leaves the main sequence; at this stage, the star has a very great luminosity and size (100 to more than 1000 times the Sun's diameter).

superior planet A planet that is more distant from the Sun than the Earth is.

superluminal motion Motion that appears to occur at speeds faster than the speed of light.

supernova The catastrophic explosion of a star, during which the star becomes billions of times brighter.

synodic period The time interval between two successive similar alignments between a celestial object and the Sun, as seen from Earth.

T Tauri stars A class of stars that show rapid and erratic changes in brightness.

tail (of comet)   The gas and/or dust swept away from a comet's head.

tangential velocity   Velocity perpendicular to the line of sight.

theory   A synthesis of a large body of information that encompasses well-tested (by repeatable experiments) and verified hypotheses about certain aspects of the natural world. No theory can be proved to be true, but data can prove a theory to be false.

thermal energy   Energy that is due to the random motions of molecules and atoms of a substance.

tidal force   A gravitational force that varies in strength and/or direction over an object causing it to deform.

tidal friction   Friction forces that result from tides on a rotating object caused by its gravitational interactions with another object.

total lunar eclipse   An eclipse of the Moon in which the Moon is completely in the umbra of the Earth's shadow.

total solar eclipse   An eclipse in which light from the normally visible portion of the Sun (the photosphere) is completely blocked by the Moon.

transit   The passage of a planet in front of its star.

triangulation   The use of parallax to determine the distance to an object.

troposphere   The lowest level of the Earth's (and some other planets') atmosphere.

Tully-Fisher relation   A relation that holds that the wider the 21-cm spectral line, the greater the absolute luminosity of a *spiral galaxy*.

tuning fork diagram   A diagram developed by Edwin Hubble to relate the various types of galaxies.

turnoff point   The point on an H-R diagram of a cluster of stars where the stars are just leaving the main sequence.

twenty-one-centimeter radiation   Radiation from atomic hydrogen, with a wavelength of 21.1 cm.

umbra   The portion of a shadow that receives no direct light from the light source.

universality   The property of obeying the same physical laws throughout the universe.

vernal and autumnal equinoxes   The points on the celestial sphere where the Sun crosses the celestial equator while moving north and south, respectively.

visual binary   An orbiting pair of stars that can be resolved (normally with a telescope) as two separate stars.

volatile (element)   A chemical element that can be vaporized at a relatively low temperature.

watt   A unit of power. It corresponds to a specific amount of energy each second.

wavelength   The distance from a point on a wave, such as the crest, to the next corresponding point, such as the next crest.

weight   The gravitational force between an object and the planetary/stellar body where the object is located.

white dwarf   The burnt-out relic of a low mass star. (Typical diameter is 0.01 that of the Sun—about the size of Earth.)

winter and summer solstices   The points on the celestial sphere where the Sun reaches its southernmost and northernmost positions, respectively.

zenith   The point in the sky located directly overhead.

zero-age main sequence   The main sequence of newly formed stars that just started hydrogen fusion in their cores.

zodiac   The band that lies 9° on either side of the ecliptic on the celestial sphere.

zones (and belts)   The light-colored (and dark-colored) bands that mark Jupiter's atmosphere.

INDEX

In Quest of the Universe (the main text) contains Chapters 1–19 (pages 1–560).
In Quest of the Solar System contains Chapters 1–11 (pages 1–337) and Chapter 19 (pages 550–560).
In Quest of the Stars and Galaxies contains Chapters 1–5 (pages 1–151) and Chapters 11–19 (pages 307–560).

PHOTO CREDITS

Courtesy of NASA/JPL-Caltech; **8-23a** Prepared for NASA by Stephen P. Meszaros; **8-24** Courtesy of IMP Team/JPL/NASA; **8-25** Courtesy of NASA/JPL-Caltech; **8-26** Courtesy of ESA/DLR/FU Berlin (G. Neukum); **8-27a** Courtesy of ESA/DLR/FU Berlin (G. Neukum); **8-27b** Courtesy of NASA/JPL/Arizona State University; **8-28** Courtesy of NASA/JPL-Caltech/University of Arizona/Texas A&M University; **B8-3** Courtesy of NASA/JPL/Cornell/USGS; **B8-4a-b** Courtesy of NASA/JPL/Malin Space Science Systems; **B8-5** Courtesy of NASA/JPL/Malin Space Science Systems/Philip Christensen; **B8-6** Courtesy of NASA/JPL/Malin Space Science Systems; **B8-7a-b** Courtesy of NASA/JPL-Caltech; **B8-8a-b** Courtesy of Goddard Space Flight Center Scientfic Visualization Studio/NASA; **B8-9** Courtesy of Goddard Space Flight Center Scientific Visualization Studio/NASA; **B8-10** Courtesy of Goddard Space Flight Center Scientific Visualization Studio/NASA; **B8-11a-b** Courtesy of NASA/JPL/Malin Space Science Systems; **8-30** Courtesy of D. Crisp, WFPC2 Team/NASA; **B8-12** Courtesy of ESA/DLR/FU Berlin (G. Neukum).

Chapter 9

Chapter Opener Courtesy of NASA/JPL/Space Science Institute; **9-1** Courtesy of California Institute of Technology; **9-2** Prepared for NASA by Stephen P. Meszaros; **9-3a** Courtesy of NASA/ESA/I. de Peter and M. Wong (University of California, Berkeley); **9-3b** Courtesy of Gemini Observatory/Association of Universities for Research in Astronomy; **9-4** Courtesy NASA/JPL; **9-5** Courtesy of NASA/JPL-Caltech; **9-7A** Courtesy of NASA/JPL/Johns Hopkins University Applied Physics Laboratory; **9-7b** Courtesy of NRAO/AUI; **9-8a** Courtesy of NASA, ESA & John T. Clarke (University of Michigan); **9-8b** Courtesy NASA/CXC/MSFC/R.Elsner et al.; **9-9** Courtesy of NASA/JPL-Caltech; **9-10** Courtesy of Galileo Project/JPL/NASA; **9-11** Courtesy of Galileo Project/JPL/NASA; **9-12** Courtesy of STScI; **9-13** Courtesy of Galileo Project/JPL/NASA; **9-14** Courtesy of Galileo Project/JPL/NASA; **9-15** Courtesy of Galileo Project/JPL/NASA; **9-16** Courtesy of Galileo Project/JPL/NASA; **9-17** Prepared for NASA by Stephen P. Meszaros; **9-18** Courtesy of NASA and the Hubble Heritage Team (STScI/AURA); Acknowledgment: R.G. French (Wellesley College), J. Cuzzi (NASA/Ames), L. Dones (SWRI), J. Lissauer (NASA/Ames); **9-21** Courtesy of J.T. Trauger (Jet Propulsion Laboratory) /NASA; **9-22a** Courtesy of Erich Karkoschka (University of Arizona)/NASA; **9-22B** Courtesy of NASA/JPL/University of Arizona; **9-23a-b** Courtesy of NASA/JPL/Space Science Institute; **9-24a-b** Courtesy of NASA/JPL/Space Science Institute; **9-25** Courtesy of NASA/JPL/Space Science Institute; **9-26** Courtesy of ESA/NASA/JPL/University of Arizona; **9-27a** Courtesy of ESA/NASA/University of Arizona; **9-27b** Courtesy of NASA/JPL/USGS; **9-28** Courtesy of NASA/JPL/Space Science Institute; **9-32** Courtesy of NASA and Erich Karkoschka, University of Arizona; **9-33** Courtesy of Erich Karkoschka (University of Arizona)/NASA; **9-34** Courtesy of NASA/JPL-Caltech; **9-38** Courtesy of NASA/JPL-Caltech; **B9-1** Courtesy of NASA/JPL-Caltech; **B9-2** Courtesy of NASA/JPL/Voyager; **B9-3** Courtesy of NASA/JPL-Caltech; **9-39** Courtesy of NASA/ESA/E. Karkoschka (University of Arizona), and H.B. Hammel (Space Science Institute, Boulder, Colorado); **9-40** Courtesy of NASA/JPL-Caltech; **9-42** Courtesy of NASA/JPL-Caltech; **9-43** Courtesy of NASA/JPL-Caltech.

Chapter 10

Chapter Opener Courtesy of NASA, ESA, and A. Feild (STScI); **10-1a-b** Courtesy of Lowell Observatory Photograph; **10-2a-c** Courtesy of NASA/JPL-Caltech; **10-4** Courtesy of Alan Stern (Southwest Research Institute), Marc Buie (Lowell Observatory), NASA and ESA; **10-5** Courtesy of NASA, ESA, H. Weaver (Johns Hopkins University/Applied Physics Lab), A. Stern (Southwest Research Institute), and the HST Pluto Companion Search Team; **10-6** Courtesy of Yerkes Observatory; **10-7a-b** Courtesy of Galileo Project/JPL/NASA; **10-7c** Courtesy of NASA/JPL-Caltech; **10-7e** Courtesy of the NEAR Project (JHU/APL)/NASA; **10-9** © Datacraft/age fotostock; **10-10** Courtesy of SOHO (ESA and NASA); **10-12a** Courtesy of J. A. DeYoung (USNO). 61-cm Telescope, Washington, DC; **10-12b** Courtesy of H.U. Keller/NASA/NSSDC; **10-15a** Courtesy of NASA/JPL-Caltech; **10-15b** Photo by Hope Ishii/Lawrence Livermore National Laboratory; **10-17** Courtesy of David Jewitt (University of California at Los Angeles) and Jane Luu (Lincoln Laboratories); **10-19** © Galaxy Picture Library/Alamy Images; **10-20** Courtesy of Kitt Peak National Observatory/AURA/NOAO/NSF; **10-23a** Courtesy of Theo Koupelis; **10-23b** Courtesy of NASA/JPL-Caltech; **10-23c** Courtesy of ANSMET/NASA; **10-24** © Ryan Tidwell, www.flickr.com/photos/ryantidwell; **B10-1** © AP Photos; **B10-2** © Stuart

Bayer, *Gannett Suburban*/AP Photos; **10-25** © Tonis Valing/ShutterStock, Inc.

Chapter 11

Chapter Opener Courtesy of SOHO–EIT Consortium/ESA/NASA; **11-1** © AbleStock; **11-3a** Courtesy of William P. Sterne, Jr.; **11-3b** Courtesy of Louis Strous, SOHO - MDI Consortium, ESA, NASA; **B11-1a** Courtesy of Brookhaven National Laboratory; **B11-1b** Courtesy of Kamioka Observatory, ICRR (Institute for Cosmic Ray Research), The University of Tokyo; **B11-1c** Courtesy of the Sudbury Neutrino Observatory; **11-14A** Courtesy of AURA/NOAO/NSF; **11-14b** Courtesy of NASA/JPL-Caltech; **11-14c** Courtesy of NASA/ESA; **11-15** Courtesy Marshall Spaceflight Center/NASA; **11-16a** Courtesy of NASA/JPL-Caltech; **11-18a** Courtesy of Dr. Göran Scharmer, The Institute for Solar Physics, Stockholm University; **11-19a** Courtesy of UCAR/NCAR/High Altitude Observatory/NASA; **11-19b** Courtesy of NASA/JPL-Caltech; **11-20** This image, taken at the Swedish 1-meter Solar Telescope (SST) on the island of La Palma, Spain, is courtesy of Dr. Bart De Pontieu of the Lockheed Martin Solar & Astrophysics Laboratory; **11-21** Courtesy of NASA/JPL-Caltech; **11-22** 2009 Copyright, University Corporation for Atmospheric Research, High Altitude Observatory; **11-23a** Courtesy of SOHO (ESA & NASA); **11-23b** Courtesy of CFA/TRACE Team/NASA; **11-23c** 2009 Copyright, University Corporation for Atmospheric Research, High Altitude Observatory; **11-24a** Courtesy of NASA/JPL-Caltech; **11-24b** Courtesy of Marshall Space Flight Center/NASA; **11-25A** Courtesy of NASA/NSSTC/Hathway 2009/04; **11-25b** Courtesy of NASA/NSSTC/Hathway 2006/07; **11-26** Courtesy of NASA/NSSTC/Hathway 2009/04; **11-28a-b** Courtesy of AURA/NOAO/NSF; **11-29** Courtesy of ESA/NASA/Office of Space Science/SOHO; **11-30a** Courtesy of Marshall Space Flight Center/NASA; **11-30b** Courtesy of SOHO/CDS, SOHO/EIT (ESA & NASA); TRACE (NASA); **11-31** Courtesy of SOHO–EIT Consortium/ESA/NASA; **11-32** The SOHO/LASCO data used here are produced by a consortium of the Naval Research Laboratory (USA), Max-Planck-Institut fuer Aeronomie (Germany), Laboratoire d'Astronomie (France), and the University of Birmingham (UK). SOHO is a project of international cooperation between ESA and NASA; **11-33a** Courtesy of Yohkoh/JAXA; **11-33b** Courtesy of SOHO (ESA & NASA); **11-34** Courtesy of SOHO/LASCO (ESA & NASA).

Chapter 12

Chapter Opener Courtesy of NOAO; **12-1** © Peresanz/Dreamstime.com; **12-8a-b** Courtesy of Yerkes Observatory Photograph; **12-12** Courtesy of Chad Trujillo; **12-13** Courtesy of Harvard College Observatory; **12-14** Courtesy of KPNO 0.9-m Telescope, AURA, NSF/NOAO; **12-24a** Courtesy of NASA/JPL-Caltech; **12-25** Courtesy of Sproul Observatory/Swarthmore College; **12-26** Image © UC Regents/Lick Observatory; **12-36** Courtesy of NOAO/AURA/NSF; **B12-2** Courtesy of Harvard College Observatory; **12-39** Courtesy of Dr. Wendy L. Freedman, Observatories of the Carnegie Institution of Washington and NASA.

Chapter 13

Chapter Opener Courtesy of Wolfgang Brandner (JPL/IPAC), Eva K. Grebel (Univ. Washington), You-Hua Chu (Univ. Illinois Urbana-Champaign), and NASA; **13-1a** Courtesy of T.A. Rector/University of Alaska Anchorage, H. Schweiker/WIYN and NOAO/AURA/NSF; **13-1b** Courtesy of ESO; **13-1c** Courtesy of NPS, Night Sky Program; **13-1d** Courtesy of ESO; **13-2a** Courtesy of Infrared Processing and Analysis Center, NASA/JPL-Caltech; **13-2b** Courtesy of NASA/JPL-Caltech; **13-5a** Courtesy of ESO; **13-5b** Courtesy of C.R. O'Dell, and S.K. Wong/Rice University/NASA; **13-5c** Courtesy of ESO; **13-7** Courtesy of NASA, ESA and AURA/Caltech; **13-8b** Courtesy of NASA/JPL-Caltech/J. Rho (SSC/Caltech); **13-9** Courtesy of Hubble Heritage Team (STScI) and NASA; **13-10a** Courtesy of Bill Shoening/AURA/NOAO/NSF; **13-10b** Courtesy of J.Hester and P. Scowen (Arizona State University), NASA; **13-10c** Courtesy of ESA & the ISOGAL team; **13-10d** Courtesy of ESO; **13-12a** Courtesy of ESO; **13-12b** Courtesy of NASA/JPL-Caltech/L. Allen (Harvard-Smithsonian CFA); **13-14a** Courtesy of NASA/JPL-Caltech/T. Megeath (University of Toledo) & M. Robberto (STScI); **13-14B** © Anglo-Australian Observatory/David Malin Images; **13-15a-c** Courtesy of J. Morse,AURA/STScI, NASA; **13-17a** Courtesy of Charles Robert O'Dell/Rice University; **13-17b** Courtesy of Charles Robert O'Dell/Rice University/NASA; **13-18a** Courtesy of NASA/JPL-Caltech/J. Bally (University of Colorado); **13-18b** Courtesy of NASA and the Hubble Heritage Team (STScI/AURA); **13-19** © Matthew Bate/Photo Researchers, Inc.; **13-20a** Courtesy of Don Figer/STScI/NASA; **13-20b** Courtesy of Andy Steere; **13-21** Courtesy of Hubble Heritage Team (AURA/STScI/NASA); **13-24a** Courtesy of NRAO/AUI; **13-24b**

Courtesy of 2MASS/UMass/IPAC-Caltech/NASA/NSF; **13-24c** Courtesy of Palomar Observatory, Caltech/DSS; **13-24d** Courtesy of NASA/CXC/PSU/L.Townsley et al.

Chapter 14
Chapter Opener Courtesy of NASA, ESA, HEIC, and the Hubble Heritage Team (STScI/AURA); **14-1b** Courtesy of S. Kulkarni (Caltech), D. Golimowski (JHU), NASA; **14-1c** Courtesy of Paranal Observatory, ESO; **14-16** © Anglo-Australian Observatory/David Malin Images; **14-17a** Courtesy of Hubble Heritage Team (AURA/STScI/NASA); **14-17b** Courtesy of NASA/ESA/JPL-Caltech/J. Hora (CfA) & C.R. O'Dell (Vanderbilt); **DP14-1a** Courtesy of Robert Rubin (NASA Research Center), Reginald Dufour and Matt Browning (Rice University), Patrick Harrington (University of Maryland), and NASA; **DP14-1b** Courtesy of A. Hajian (USNO) et. al., Hubble Heritage Team (STScI/AURA), NASA; **DP14-3a** Courtesy of B. Balick (U. Washington) et al., WFPC2, NASA, HST, NASA; **DP14-4a** Courtesy of B. Balick (.U. Washington), et.al, WFPC2, HST, NASA; **14-19a** Courtesy of ESO; **14-19b** Courtesy of H. Bond/STScI/NASA; **14-20a** Courtesy B. Balick (U. Washington) et al./WFPC2/HST/NASA; **14-20b** Courtesy of R. Sahai and J. Trauger (JPL), the WFPC2 Science Team, and NASA; **14-21a** Courtesy of NASA, ESA, Hans Van Winckel (Catholic University of Leuven, Belgium), and Martin Cohen (University of California, Berkeley); **14-21b** Courtesy of ESA & Valentin Bujarrabal (Observatorio Astronomico Nacional); **14-22** Courtesy of NASA, ESA & A. Zijlstra (UMIST, Manchester, UK); **14-23a** Courtesy of ESA/NASA; **14-23b** Courtesy of NASA, ESA and the Hubble Heritage Team (STScI/AURA); **14-25a** Image © UC Regents/Lick Observatory; **14-25b** Kitt Peak National Observatory 0.9-meter telescope, National Optical Astronomy Observatories; Courtesy M. Bolte (University of California, Santa Cruz) and Harvey Richer (University of British Columbia, Vancouver, Canada) and NASA; **14-29a-b** Image © UC Regents/Lick Observatory; **14-31** X-ray: NASA/CXC/Rutgers/J.Hughes et al.; Optical: Rutgers Fabry-Perot; **14-32** © Royal Observatory, Edinburgh/AATB/SPL/Photo Researchers, Inc.

Chapter 15
Chapter Opener © Anglo-Australian Observatory/David Malin Images; **15-2** Courtesy of A. Dupree (CfA), R. Gilliland (STScI), NASA; **15-5a-b** © Jack Newton, www.jacknewton.com; **15-6** Courtesy of ESO; **15-7a** Courtesy of T. Rector/University of Alaska Anchorage and WIYN/NOAO/AURA/NSF; **15-7b** Courtesy of NASA/CXC/SAO; **15-8a** © Anglo-Australian Observatory/David Malin Images; **15-8b** Courtesy of J. Pun (NASA/GSFC), R. Krishner (CFA), and NASA; **15-8c** X-ray: Courtesy of NASA/CXC/PSU/S.Park & D.Burrows.; Optical: Courtesy of NASA/STScI/CfA/P.Challis; **15-9** X-ray: Courtesy of NASA/CXC/GSFC/M.Corcoran et al.; Optical: Courtesy of NASA/STScI; **15-10a** Image courtesy of University of Cambridge, Mullard Radio Astronomy Observatory. With compliments of Professor Antony Hewish; **15-10b** Courtesy of ESO; **15-14a** Courtesy of NASA/CXC/SAO; **15-14b** Courtesy of NASA/CXC/HST/ASU/J. Hester et al); **15-14c** Courtesy of N.A. Sharp/NOAO/AURA/NSF; **15-15** Courtesy of ESA & Francesco Ferraro (Bologna Astronomical Observatory); **15-16a** Courtesy of NASA/PSU/G. Pavlov et al.; **15-16b** Courtesy of NASA/CXC/J. Hughes et al.; **15-21** © Stocktrek Images, Inc./Alamy Images; **15-23** Courtesy of NASA/CXC/M.Weiss; **B15-3** © ESA 2002.Illustration by Medialab; **B15-4** Courtesy of NASA/CXC/M.Weiss.

Chapter 16
Chapter Opener (right and left) Courtesy of NASA Goddard Space Flight Center; **16-1** © a. v. ley/ShutterStock, Inc.; **16-2** Courtesy of Robert Hurt (SSC/JPL/Caltech)/NASA; **16-3** Courtesy of Bill Keel, University of Alabama; **16-4** Courtesy of AURA/NOAO/NSF; **16-6** Courtesy of Yerkes Observatory Photograph; **16-7a** Courtesy of N.A.Sharp, REU program/NOAO/AURA/NSF; **16-7b** Courtesy of N.A.Sharp, Mark Hanna, REU program/NOAO/AURA/NSF; **16-8a** Courtesy of NASA and The Hubble Heritage Team (STScI/AURA); **16-8b** Courtesy of Rubina Kotak and Henri Boffin, ESO; **16-15b** Courtesy of NASA Goddard Space Flight Center; **16-17** Courtesy of FORS Team, 8.2-meter VLT, ESO; **16-21a** Courtesy of DSS/NASA/JPL-Caltech; **16-21b** Courtesy of NASA/JPL-Caltech/Robert C. Kennicutt, Jr. (Steward Observatory, Univ. of Arizona); **16-22** Courtesy of D. Figer (STScI) and NASA; **B16-1** Photo by Kim Zussman, Thousand Oaks, CA; **16-23a** Produced at the Naval Research Laboratory by Dr. N.E. Kassim and collaborators from data obtained with the National Radio Astronomy's Very Large Telescope, a facility of the National Science Foundation operated under cooperative agreement with Associated Universities, Inc. Basic research in radio astronomy at the Naval Research Laboratory is supported by the Office of Naval Research; **16-23b** Courtesy of NRAO; **16-23c** Reproduced by permission of the American Astronomical Society; 195th AAS Meeting, #05.01; *Bulletin of the American Astronomical Society*; McGary, R. S. and Ho, P. T. P.; Infalling Gas onto the Circumnuclear Disk; Vol. 31, p.1372. Photo courtesy of Doctor Paul. T. P. Ho; **16-24a-b** Courtesy of ESO; **16-25** EGRET All-Sky Gamma Ray Survey Avve 100 MeV; Courtesy of EGRET, NASA, GSFC; **16-26a** Courtesy of NASA/CXC/MIT/F.K. Baganoff et al.; **16-26b** Courtesy of CXC/MIT/F.K. Baganoff et al./NASA; **16-29** Image composite by Ingrid Kallick of Possible Designs, Madison Wisconsin. The background Milky Way image is a drawing made at Lund Observatory. High-velocity clouds are from the survey done at Dwingeloo Observatory (Hulsbosch & Wakker, 1988). Image courtesy of Dr. Bart Wakker; **16-30** Courtesy of Rensselaer Polytechnic Institute & the Sloan Digital Sky Survey (SDSS), www.sdss.org.

Chapter 17
Chapter Opener Courtesy of NASA, ESA, S. Beckwith (STScI) and the HUDF Team; **17-1a** Courtesy of ESO; **17-1b** Courtesy of NOAO/AURA/NSF; **17-1c** Courtesy of Todd Boroson/NOAO/AURA/NSF; **17-2a** Courtesy of G. Fritz Benedict, Andrew Howell, Inger Jorgensen, David Chapell (University of Texas), Jeffery Kenney (Yale University), and Beverly J. Smith (CASA, University of Colorado), and NASA; **17-2b** Courtesy of NOAO/AURA/NSF; **17-2c** Courtesy of ESO; **17-3** Courtesy of NASA, ESA, and The Hubble Heritage Team (STScI/AURA); **17-4a-c** Courtesy of NOAO/AURA/NSF; **B17-1** Courtesy of California Institute of Technology; **17-5a** Courtesy of AURA/NOAO/NSF; **17-5b** Courtesy of NASA and the Hubble Heritage Team (STScI); **17-6a** Courtesy of Brad Whitmore (STScI) and NASA; **17-6b** Courtesy of NASA/ESA/CXC/JPL-Caltech; **17-6c** Courtesy of NASA/ESA/and The Hubble Heritage Team (STScI); **17-6d** Courtesy of NASA/JPL-Caltech/P. N. Appleton (Spitzer Science Center/Caltech); **17-6e** Courtesy of Hubble Heritage Team (AURA/STScI/NASA); **17-10** Courtesy of California Institute of Technology; **17-16a** Courtesy of NASA, ESA, and the Hubble Heritage Team (STScI/AURA); **17-16b** Courtesy of P. van Dokkum (University of Groningen), ESA, and NASA; **17-17** Colless et al. (2001), *MNRAS*, 328, 1039. Image courtesy of the 2dF Galaxy Redshift Survey team and Professor Matthew Colless, Director of Anglo-Australian Observatory; **17-18a** Courtesy of NASA/CXC/E.O'Sullivan et al; Optical: Palomar DSS; **17-18b** X-ray courtesy of NASA/CXC/UCI/A.Lewis et al.; Optical courtesy of Pal.Obs. DSS; **17-19a** Courtesy of NASA, ESA, and R. Massey (California Institute of Technology); **17-19b** Courtesy of NASA, ESA, M. J. Jee and H. Ford et al. (Johns Hopkins Univ.); **B17-2** X-ray: Courtesy of NASA/CXC/U. Copenhagen/K.Pedersen et al; Optical: Courtesy of Palomar DSS; **17-20a** Courtesy of NRAO/AUI; **17-20b** Courtesy of NASA/UMD/A. Wilson et al.; **17-20c** Courtesy of NASA/CXC; **17-21a** X-ray (NASA/CXC/M. Karovska et al.); Radio 21-cm image (NRAO/VLA/J. Condon et al.); Optical (Digitized Sky Survey U.K. Schmidt Image/STScI); **17-21b** Courtesy of NASA/JPL-Caltech/J. Keene (SSC/Caltech); **17-22a** Courtesy of NOAO/AURA/NSF; **17-22b** Courtesy of NASA/Wide-Field Planetary Camera 2/Hubble Space Telescope/STScI; **17-22c** Courtesy of NASA, NRAO, and J. Biretta (STScI); **17-23a** WFPC2 image: NASA and J. Bahcall (IAS); ACS image: NASA, A. Martel (JHU), H. Ford (JHU), M. Clampin (STScI), G. Hartig (STScI), G. Illingworth (UCO/Lick Observatory), the ACS Science Team and ESA; **17-23b** Optical courtesy of NASA/STScI; X-ray: NASA/CXC; Radio courtesy MERLIN; **17-25** Courtesy of NASA Education and Public Outreach at Sonoma State University/Aurore Simonnet; **17-27** Courtesy of NASA, Andrew S. Wilson (University of Maryland), Patrick L. Shopbell (Caltech), Chris Simpson (Subaru Telescope), Thaisa Storchi-Bergmann and F.K.B. Barbosa (UFRGS, Brazil), and Martin J. Ward (University of Leicester, UK); **17-29a** Courtesy of NRAO/AUI; **17-29b** Courtesy of K. Ratnatunga (JHU), NASA; **17-29c** Courtesy of W.Couch (University of New South Wales), R. Ellis (Cambridge University), and NASA; **17-29d** Courtesy of W.N. Colley (Princeton University), E. Turner (Princeton University), J.A. Tyson (AT&T Bell Labs), and NASA; **17-30c** Reproduced from Smith R.J., Croom S.M., et al., *MNRAS*, 359 (2005), 57-72. Image courtesy of Dr. Robert Smith, Astrophysics Research Institute; **17-31b** Courtesy of John Biretta, STScI; **17-32b** Inset photo: John Bahcall, Institute for Advanced Study and NASA; **17-33a** Courtesy of NRAO/AUI; **17-33b** Courtesy of NRAO/AUI and C. O'Dea & F. Owen; **17-33c** Courtesy of Walter Jaffe/Leiden Observatory, Holland Ford/JHU/STScI, and NASA; **17-34a** Courtesy of Karl Gebhardt (University of Michigan), Tod Lauer (NOAO), and NASA; **17-34b** Courtesy of John Bahcall (Institute for Advanced Study, Princeton), Mike Disney (University of Wales) and NASA; **17-35a** Courtesy of ESA; **17-35b** Courtesy of Dana Berry/NASA; **17-37** Courtesy of Achut Reddy/Adam Block/NOAO/AURA/NSF.

Chapter 18
Chapter Opener Courtesy of BOOMERANG Collaboration; **18-7b** © Valenta/ShutterStock, Inc.; **18-8** © AbleStock; **18-10** Courtesy of AT&T Archives and History Center; **18-11** Courtesy of NASA/JPL-Caltech; **B18-2** Courtesy of NASA/WMAP; **18-17** Courtesy of NASA/WMAP; **18-18** Courtesy of Seldner, M., Siebers, B., Groth, E.J. and Peebles, P.J.E, 1977; **18-19** Courtesy of NASA Goddard Space Flight Center and the COBE Science Working Group; **18-20** Courtesy of NASA/NSBF; **18-22** Courtesy of NASA/WMAP; **18-23** Courtesy of NASA and the WMAP Science Team. Modified from M.R. Nolta et al., *ApJS* 180 (2009): 296-305. Reproduced by permission of the AAS; **18-25** Courtesy of NASA/WMAP; **18-26** Courtesy of NASA and the WMAP Science Team. Modified from M.R. Nolta et al., *ApJS* 180 (2009): 296-305. Reproduced by permission of the AAS; **18-27** Courtesy of NASA/WMAP; **18-29** Courtesy of BOOMERANG Collaboration; **18-30** Courtesy of ESO.

Chapter 19
Chapter Opener Courtesy of NASA; **19-1** The Arecibo Observatory is part of the National Astronomy and Ionosphere Center, which is operated by Cornell University under a cooperative agreement with the National Science Foundation; **19-2** Courtesy of Pioneer Project, ARC, and NASA; **19-3** Courtesy of Pioneer Project, ARC, and NASA.

Appendix Data Pages
Sun Courtesy of Skylab/NASA; **Mercury** Courtesy of NASA/JPL-Caltech; **Venus** Courtesy of NASA/JPL-Caltech; **Earth** Courtesy of NSSDC/NASA; **Moon** Courtesy of NASA/JPL-Caltech; **Mars** Courtesy of NASA/JPL-Caltech; **Jupiter** Courtesy of NASA/JPL-Caltech; **Saturn** Courtesy of STScI; **Uranus** Courtesy of NASA/JPL-Caltech; **Neptune** Courtesy of NASA/JPL-Caltech; **Pluto** Courtesy of Hubble Space Telescope/NASA

Unless otherwise indicated, all photographs and illustrations are under copyright of Jones and Bartlett Publishers, LLC, or have been provided by the author(s).